The Oxford Handbook of
Media Psychology

Helen Baker
Endowment

Presented to
Juniata College
Library
by Her Family

D1088403

OXFORD LIBRARY OF PSYCHOLOGY

EDITOR-IN-CHIEF

Peter E. Nathan

AREA EDITORS:

Clinical Psychology
David H. Barlow

Cognitive Neuroscience
Kevin N. Ochsner and Stephen M. Kosslyn

Cognitive Psychology
Daniel Reisberg

Counseling Psychology
Elizabeth M. Altmaier and Jo-Ida C. Hansen

Developmental Psychology
Philip David Zelazo

Health Psychology
Howard S. Friedman

History of Psychology
David B. Baker

Methods and Measurement
Todd D. Little

Neuropsychology
Kenneth M. Adams

Organizational Psychology
Steve W. J. Kozlowski

Personality and Social Psychology
Kay Deaux and Mark Snyder

OXFORD LIBRARY OF PSYCHOLOGY

Editor in Chief PETER E. NATHAN

The Oxford Handbook of Media Psychology

Edited by

Karen E. Dill

OXFORD
UNIVERSITY PRESS

Oxford University Press is a department of the University of Oxford.
It furthers the University's objective of excellence in research, scholarship,
and education by publishing worldwide.

Oxford   New York
Auckland   Cape Town   Dar es Salaam   Hong Kong   Karachi
Kuala Lumpur   Madrid   Melbourne   Mexico City   Nairobi
New Delhi   Shanghai   Taipei   Toronto

With offices in
Argentina   Austria   Brazil   Chile   Czech Republic   France   Greece
Guatemala   Hungary   Italy   Japan   Poland   Portugal   Singapore
South Korea   Switzerland   Thailand   Turkey   Ukraine   Vietnam

Oxford is a registered trade mark of Oxford University Press
in the UK and certain other countries.

Published in the United States of America by
Oxford University Press
198 Madison Avenue, New York, NY 10016

© Oxford University Press 2013

First issued as an Oxford University Press paperback, 2014.

All rights reserved. No part of this publication may be reproduced, stored in a retrieval system, or transmitted,
in any form or by any means, without the prior permission in writing of Oxford University Press, or as expressly
permitted by law, by license, or under terms agreed with the appropriate reproduction rights organization.
Inquiries concerning reproduction outside the scope of the above should be sent to the Rights Department,
Oxford University Press, at the address above.

You must not circulate this work in any other form
and you must impose this same condition on any acquirer.

Library of Congress Cataloging-in-Publication Data
The Oxford handbook of media psychology / edited by Karen E. Dill.
    p. cm.
    ISBN 978–0–19–539880–9 (hardcover); 978-0-19-939482-1 (paperback)
    1. Mass media—Psychological aspects.   I. Dill, Karen E.
P96.P75O94 2013
302.2301—dc23
2012023225

9 8 7 6 5 4 3 2 1

Printed in the United States of America
on acid-free paper

P
96
.P75
094
2014

To Russell G. Geen
Thanks for the memories.

SHORT CONTENTS

OXFORD LIBRARY OF PSYCHOLOGY

The *Oxford Library of Psychology*, a landmark series of handbooks, is published by Oxford University Press, one of the world's oldest and most highly respected publishers, with a tradition of publishing significant books in psychology. The ambitious goal of the *Oxford Library of Psychology* is nothing less than to span a vibrant, wide-ranging field and, in so doing, to fill a clear market need.

Encompassing a comprehensive set of handbooks, organized hierarchically, the *Library* incorporates volumes at different levels, each designed to meet a distinct need. At one level are a set of handbooks designed broadly to survey the major subfields of psychology; at another are numerous handbooks that cover important current focal research and scholarly areas of psychology in depth and detail. Planned as a reflection of the dynamism of psychology, the *Library* will grow and expand as psychology itself develops, thereby highlighting significant new research that will impact on the field. Adding to its accessibility and ease of use, the *Library* will be published in print and, later on, electronically.

The *Library* surveys psychology's principal subfields with a set of handbooks that capture the current status and future prospects of those major subdisciplines. This initial set includes handbooks of social and personality psychology, clinical psychology, counseling psychology, school psychology, educational psychology, industrial and organizational psychology, cognitive psychology, cognitive neuroscience, methods and measurements, history, neuropsychology, personality assessment, developmental psychology, and more. Each handbook undertakes to review one of psychology's major subdisciplines with breadth, comprehensiveness, and exemplary scholarship. In addition to these broadly conceived volumes, the *Library* also includes a large number of handbooks designed to explore in depth more specialized areas of scholarship and research, such as stress, health and coping, anxiety and related disorders, cognitive development, or child and adolescent assessment. In contrast with the broad coverage of the subfield handbooks, each of these latter volumes focuses on an especially productive, more highly focused line of scholarship and research. Whether at the broadest or most specific level, however, all of the *Library* handbooks offer synthetic coverage that reviews and evaluates the relevant past and present research and anticipates research in the future. Each handbook in the *Library* includes introductory and concluding chapters written by its editor to provide a roadmap to the handbook's table of contents and offer informed anticipations of significant future developments in that field.

An undertaking of this scope calls for handbook editors and chapter authors who are established scholars in the areas about which they write. Many of the nation's and world's most productive and best-respected psychologists have agreed to edit *Library* handbooks or write authoritative chapters in their areas of expertise.

For whom has the *Oxford Library of Psychology* been written? Because of its breadth, depth, and accessibility, the *Library* serves a diverse audience, including graduate students in psychology and their faculty mentors, scholars, researchers, and practitioners in psychology and related fields. Each will find in the *Library* the information they seek on the subfield or focal area of psychology in which they work or are interested.

Befitting its commitment to accessibility, each handbook includes a comprehensive index, as well as extensive references to help guide research. And because the *Library* was designed from its inception as an online as well as a print resource, its structure and contents will be readily and rationally searchable online. Further, once the *Library* is released online, the handbooks will be regularly and thoroughly updated.

In summary, the *Oxford Library of Psychology* will grow organically to provide a thoroughly informed perspective on the field of psychology, one that reflects both psychology's dynamism and its increasing interdisciplinarity. Once published electronically, the *Library* is also destined to become a uniquely valuable interactive tool, with extended search and browsing capabilities. As you begin to consult this handbook, we sincerely hope you will share our enthusiasm for the more than 500-year tradition of Oxford University Press for excellence, innovation, and quality, as exemplified by the *Oxford Library of Psychology*.

Peter E. Nathan
Editor-in-Chief
Oxford Library of Psychology

ABOUT THE EDITOR

Karen E. Dill

Karen E. Dill is on the faculty at Fielding Graduate University in Santa Barbara, CA where she teaches in the first Media Psychology doctoral program in the United States. She earned her Ph.D. social psychology while working with her mentor, Craig A. Anderson, studying media violence effects. Her dissertation on video game violence effects has been cited over 1000 times. She has testified twice before the U.S. Congress about media psychology issues and is the author of *How Fantasy Becomes Reality* (Oxford, 2009). She has namesake in the video game *Grand Theft Auto IV: the Karin Dillatante.*

CONTRIBUTORS

Debby E. Almonte
Division of Psychological & Educational
Services
Fordham University
New York, NY

Craig A. Anderson
Center for the Study of Violence
Department of Psychology
Iowa State University
Ames, IA

Jared S. Anthony
Division of Psychological & Educational
Services
Fordham University
New York, NY

Edward T. Arke
Department of Communication
Messiah College
Grantham, PA

Kira Bailey
Department of Psychology
Iowa State University
Ames, IA

Bruce D. Bartholow
Department of Psychological
Sciences
University of Missouri
Columbia, MO

Elizabeth Behm-Morawitz
Department of Communication
University of Missouri
Columbia, MO

Jim Blascovich
Research Center for Virtual Environments
and Behavior
University of California, Santa
Barbara
Santa Barbara, CA

Fran C. Blumberg
Division of Psychological & Educational
Services
Fordham University
New York, NY

Piotr Bobkowski
School of Journalism and Mass
Communications
University of Kansas
Lawrence, KS

Paul Bolls
Missouri School of Journalism
University of Missouri
Columbia, MO

Francesco Bricolo
Dipartimento delle Dipendenze
Verona, Italy

Jeanne Funk Brockmyer
Department of Psychology
University of Toledo
Toledo, OH

Jane D. Brown
School of Journalism and Mass
Communication
University of North Carolina-Chapel Hill
Chapel Hill, NC

Barbara Chamberlin
Learning Games Lab
New Mexico State University
Las Cruces, NM

Sarah M. Coyne
Department of Family Studies
Brigham Young University
Provo, UT

Janet de Merode
Department of International Psychology
The Chicago School of Professional
Psychology
Washington, D.C.

Ellen Baker Derwin
School of Arts and Sciences
Brandman University
Irvine, CA

Karen E. Dill
School of Psychology
Fielding Graduate University
Santa Barbara, CA

Ed Donnerstein
Department of Communication
University of Arizona
Tucson, AZ

Eric F. Dubow
Bowling Green State University
Bowling Green, OH
University of Michigan
Ann Arbor, MI

Douglas A. Gentile
Department of Psychology
Iowa State University
Ames, IA

Melanie C. Green
Department of Psychology
University of North Carolina-Chapel Hill
Chapel Hill, NC

Erik M. Gregory
Organizational and Leadership
Psychology
Massachusetts School of Professional
Psychology
Boston, MA

Naoko Hashimoto
Division of Psychological & Educational
Services
Fordham University
New York, NY

L. Rowell Huesmann
Research Center for Group Dynamics
Institute for Social Research
University of Michigan
Ann Arbor, MI

Jean-Pierre Isbouts
School of Psychology
Fielding Graduate University
Santa Barbara, CA

Elly A. Konijn
Center for Advanced Media Research
Amsterdam (CAMeRA)
Department of Communication Science
VU University Amsterdam
Amsterdam, The Netherlands

Barbara Krahé
Department of Psychology
University of Potsdam
Potsdam, Germany

Ann Maloney
Department of Psychiatry
University of Massachusetts Medical
School
Worcester, MA

Cade McCall
Department of Social Neuroscience
Max Planck Institute for Human Cognitive
and Brain Sciences
Leipzig, Germany

Jeff J. McIntyre
Washington, DC

Emily Moyer-Gusé
School of Communication
The Ohio State University
Columbus, OH

Robin L. Nabi
Department of Communication
University of California, Santa Barbara
Santa Barbara, CA

Michael R. Neal
School of Psychology
Fielding Graduate University
Santa Barbara, CA

Jason Ohler
School of Psychology
Fielding Graduate University
Santa Barbara, CA

Michelle Ortiz
School of Communication
The Ohio State University
Columbus, OH

Donald E. Polkinghorne
Fielding Graduate University
Santa Barbara, CA

W. James Potter
Department of Communication
University of California, Santa Barbara
Santa Barbara, CA

Sara Prot
Center for the Study of Violence
Department of Psychology
Iowa State University
Ames, IA

Pamela Brown Rutledge
Media Psychology Research Center
Boston, MA
Fielding Graduate University
Santa Barbara, CA

Akira Sakamoto
Department of Psychology
Ochanomizu University
Bunkyo, Tokyo, Japan

Erica L. Scharrer
Department of Communication
University of Massachusetts Amherst
Amherst, MA

Autumn Shafer
College of Media and
Communication
Texas Tech University
Lubbock, TX

Regina M. Tuma
Media Psychology Faculty
Fielding Graduate University
Santa Barbara, CA

Robert West
Department of Psychology
Iowa State University
Ames, IA

Grace Yang
Department of Communication
Studies
University of Michigan
Ann Arbor, MI

CONTENTS

PART 1

Introduction and Overview

Introduction

Karen E. Dill

Marshall McLuhan said that media are "extensions of man" and that media are "amplifiers" (Fiore & McLuhan, 1967; McLuhan, 1969). These fundamental ideas were true when he wrote about them in the 1960s, although they then referred to what we now call *legacy media* such as television and newspapers. What has changed since then is not the fundamentals, which are perhaps eerily unchanged, but the array of manifestations of extension and amplification available through new and emerging media.

Social Media and the Arab Spring

Now more than ever, there is a democratization of media use and production. The most poignant elaboration of these phenomena has been playing out recently in the form of the Arab Spring—a term for using social media as a populist tool for political uprising and revolution in the Arab world. Citizen revolutions in Tunisia, Egypt, and Libya succeeded in ousting autocratic governments aided by the power of social media tools such as Twitter, Facebook, and YouTube. At the time of this writing, discussion leading up to the awarding of this year's Nobel Peace Prize included a focus on the lead actors in the Arab Spring [http://www.alarabiya.net/articles/2011/10/05/170302.html].

The nature and capabilities of social media allowed citizen activists to organize, recruit, and communicate information that made these revolutions possible in ways never before seen. Social media shifted power to the people, and the world followed and even contributed to the stories of these revolutions. Social media extended the people's reach and amplified their messages in novel ways.

Using Media

Today media use is ubiquitous in the developed world. Television remains the bedrock of the media diet for many of us, although the way we access and choose programming has changed and continues to change. Web 2.0 or the read/write Internet has forever altered the flow chart of media communications and even made questionable the use of the term mass media (see Isbouts & Ohler and Potter, Chapters 2 and 24, this volume) as one-to-many communications are joined by multiple sources of many-to-many communications. Interactivity and media creation by ordinary people are hallmarks of current media use and production. Text messaging and the use of mobile applications are examples of media phenomena that were unheard of until recently, but have rapidly become so much a part of our everyday lives that we could scarcely imagine living without them now. In fact, smart phones and other mobile devices are considered so useful and addictive that we feel them most powerfully to be "extensions of man" (or, more properly, of all people)—perhaps more so than any previous media phenomena. In fact, in Japan they have a term for this; it is called *Keitai culture* (Ito, Okabe, & Matsuda, 2006; Matsuda, 2006; Sakamoto, Chapter 28, this volume).

It is a fact of no small importance that media use is by far the most common way human beings spend our free time in the modern world (Csikszentmihalyi, 2008; Dill, 2009). Bartholow and Bolls (Chapter 27, this volume) call modern media use the "Great American Pastime," noting that this massive level of media use really did not begin until the 20th century.

The ubiquity of media in our lives brings with it advantages and disadvantages. For example, the way we socialize has changed with the popularity of social media on the Internet and on mobile apps. People wonder whether using social media and smart phones will impair our social functioning or enhance it or both. Research is starting to address the changes and also the benefits and harms of our media-rich lives (Quitney-Anderson & Ranie, 2012). These types of changes are occurring much more rapidly than we have been accustomed to (see Isbouts & Ohler, Chapter 2, this volume, for an elaboration). It is in this context that this *Handbook* heralds the emergence of the field of media psychology. If indeed media have become so ubiquitous, so engaging, so useful, and attractive that they are experienced by so many as nearly constant extensions of ourselves, then understanding the psychology behind that relationship is no longer optional.

Media Psychology: Emerging Discipline or Hybrid?

This *Handbook* seeks to contribute to the definition of the emerging field of media psychology. In so doing, there are a number of issues, from the practical to the scholarly, that are addressed. Where did media psychology come from and where is it going? If media psychology is an interdisciplinary field, what are the challenges and opportunities scholars must navigate to strengthen and grow the field? These are some of the questions raised here.

Media psychology scholarship is informed by a variety of related fields. The two that are perhaps most prominent are psychology—especially social psychology—and communications—especially from the mass communication and media studies research traditions. Other related fields add depth and breadth to the field. These include sociology, visual studies, cultural studies, and a variety of humanities fields, including literature and theater and other humanities disciplines in which narrative and imagery play central roles. Business scholarship, including marketing and advertising, and technology approaches, including human factors, also inform the field.

I liken media psychology to other hybrid disciplines that use psychology as a basis for the study of a particular content area. Most notably, I think media psychology is similar in this way to health psychology and political psychology. Like media, health and politics are content areas with such broad applicability that they will continue to be studied in an interdisciplinary way. At the same time, the disciplines of health psychology, political psychology, and now media psychology each offer a unique and important perspective on the content they cover.

Historical Events in the Field of Media Psychology

When tracing the history of a discipline, there are benchmarks events that both build and confirm the existence of a unique discipline. These include the publication of books, journals, and even new media that name and define the field as well as the emergence of new university programs and professional organizations in the field. What follows is a brief version of the story of some of the history of media psychology. Brown Rutledge and Tuma (Chapters 3 and 4, this volume) also offer histories of media psychology.

In 1987, the American Psychological Association founded a media psychology division—Division 46. Originally, Div. 46 focused on psychologists appearing in the media as experts. Since then its focus has shifted to include an emphasis on media influence research. In 1998, Bernard Luskin and Lilly Friedland polled media psychology experts and identified 11 areas in which psychology is applied to the study of media as part of a Div. 46 report (Luskin & Friedland, 1998). In 2003, Luskin founded and began directing the first media psychology doctoral program in the United States, at Fielding Graduate University in Santa Barbara, CA (Williams, 2011). (For more on the program's history, see Brown Rutledge, Chapter 3, this volume.)

In 2003, David Giles published what, to my knowledge, was the first book titled *Media Psychology* (Giles, 2003). This book and its updated edition titled *Psychology of the Media* (Giles, 2010) offered a critical analysis of the dominant American media effects approach, but no discrete definition of media psychology. Its publication was a watershed event in the history of media psychology, and the book offers a valuable and interesting perspective. In 2008, Fielding media psychology doctoral student Jenny Whittemore Fremlin offered this analysis of the field in an article in the *APS Observer* titled *Understanding Media Psychology*:

> Media psychologists propose that although there may be negative impacts of media such as violence in video games and films, false interpretations of reality due to intense television viewing, and persuasion through advertising, there may also benefits, like the social bonds formed in virtual worlds, therapeutic uses of media, and certain psychological benefits of developing media skills. (Fremlin, 2008, para 3)

Fremlin cited Giles' book as one of her introductions to the field.

The journal *Media Psychology* (Taylor & Francis) was first published in 1999. As Derwin and de Merode (Chapter 5, this volume) report, the journal's stated purview was and is scholarly research at the intersection of psychology and mass communication. In 1996, Stuart Fischoff launched the *Journal of Media Psychology*, which went online in 1998.

Table 1.1. Survey of the Authors of the *Oxford Handbook of Media Psychology:* Definitions of Media Psychology

The following are some definitions of Media Psychology, with attributions. You may wish to refer to one or more of these definitions, or to parts of one or more of them, in your response to item 1.

1a. From APA's Division 46 (http://www.apa.org/divisions/div46/graduate.html, para. 1–2): "Media Psychology can be described as the merging of communication and human behavior. It is central to understanding behavior within many disciplines, including, in part, technology; public policy and government; telecommunications; software; education; health care; and entertainment."

1b. "Some of the roles Media Psychologists assume include: writing or being expert guests in various media; consulting with media personnel; researching ways to improve the media; making new technologies more effective and user friendly; using new technology to enhance clinical psychology; working in education or training; developing media standards; working in commercial fields; studying sociological and psychological media effects; developing material for challenged populations; working with deviant or criminal populations (Luskin & Friedland, 1998)."

2a. Fielding Graduate University's definition (http://www.fielding.edu/programs/psy/media/default.aspx, para). "We define media psychology broadly, as research and practice at the intersection of psychological theory and knowledge with the status and impacts of both legacy and emerging media, as these manifest themselves in a wide variety of individuals, groups, and cultures."

2b. "Media psychology thus addresses issues of how people of many backgrounds experience, develop, and respond to technology and mediated communication. We consider the study of media psychology as stretching across disciplines and extending beyond traditional media research paradigms."

3. From the editor of *The Oxford Handbook of Media Psychology,* Karen Dill: "Media psychology is the scientific study of human behavior, thoughts and feelings experienced in the context of media use and creation."

Fischoff also founded the first media psych-related master's degree in 2001 at California State University—Los Angeles (http://www.calstatela.edu/faculty/sfischo/vitarev.htm). Division 46 currently maintains a working list of graduate programs in media psychology (available at http://www.apa.org/divisions/div46/ graduate.html).

Defining Media Psychology

As media psychology programs, journals, books, and organizations formed, definitions of media psychology also appeared. These programs, publications, and organizations are some of the sources of early definitions of media psychology. As editor of this, the first *Handbook of Media Psychology*, I also conducted an informal survey of the authors as top experts in the field and asked them a few key questions. To begin, I provided them with three definitions of media psychology: the current definition from the Div. 46 website, the current definition used on Fielding Graduate University's media psychology doctoral program website, and my own working definition. (Table 1.1 shows the definitions of media psychology presented to the authors.) This is not a full-blown scientific investigation, but rather an opportunity to gather information from a number of experts in the field.

The *Handbook* authors were asked, "What is your definition of media psychology? If you wish, you may refer to the definitions listed above, in whole or in part." Next, they were asked, "If you were selecting from the definitions given above, or other definitions of which you are aware, which would you prefer?"

Survey Results: Handbook *Authors' Definitions*

Fifteen *Handbook* authors responded anonymously to the survey, which was hosted on SurveyMonkey.com. Survey Monkey provides analysis of textual responses. The top themes from the authors' definitions are found in Table 1.2. The complete text of the authors' definitions is available in Appendix A.

Table 1.2. The Nine Most Important Words and Phrases in the *Handbook:* Authors' Definitions of Media Psychology

Word/Phrase	Percent Using Word/Phrase
Individual	26%
Scientific Study	20%
Context	20%
Human Behavior	13%
Karen's Definition	13%
Impact of Media	13%
Theories	13%
Communication	13%
Influence Thoughts	13%

Next, the authors indicated which of the three definitions (APA Div. 46, Fielding Graduate University's doctoral program definition, *Oxford Handbook of Media Psychology,* editor definition) they preferred. Results indicated that 86.7%, or 13 of 15 authors, preferred my working definition of media psychology. My working definition of media psychology is as follows. *Media psychology is the scientific study of human behavior, thoughts, and feelings experienced in the context of media use and creation.*

Psychology And Communications

The *Handbook* authors also responded to the following:

Psychology and Communication are arguably the two fields that are most foundational to the emerging field of media psychology. What do you see as the most pressing issues as some of the scholars from each of these disciplines meet and potentially merge into a new discipline?

One scholar wrote:

[We] need to find ways to collaborate that demonstrate appreciation for theories in both fields as well as respect for methodologies and the expertise of professionals in both fields. It is also important for scholars to see the benefit of collaboration.

Another theme that was repeated was a need to agree on a definition of media. One scholar's response addressed a number of the aforementioned themes:

One issue is that the two fields sometimes draw on different bodies of literature even when discussing the same phenomenon (that is, psych people cite psychology theories and comm people cite comm theories—which is fine to an extent, but more cross-conversation would be helpful). There is also the usual interdisciplinary professional issue that publications outside one's own field sometimes 'don't count' for professional advancement. An issue somewhat unique to media psychology is that what constitutes 'media' is constantly and quickly changing (e.g., the rise of text messaging, Facebook, iPads, and whatever the next great thing is tomorrow)—so research done in one context may seem rather quickly outdated (thus the need for good, generalizable theories).

According to surveymonkey.com's automatic text analysis, the words "theories, definitions, methods and academic journals" were some of the most often used terms in these responses. Furthermore, the notions that scholars might believe one perspective

was "right" or might ignore journals in the other field were raised. Finally, one scholar noted:

I think it will take an enlightened and motivated set of academic administrators to establish either departments of media psychology or clear incentives for collaboration across departments. Europe seems to get this done.

I left an open item for additional comments. One scholar offered the following:

This discipline (and Div. 46) have a LONG way to go to start being respected. There is still a stigma about this type of research, as if it somehow not as 'serious' a subject of study as other psychological phenomena. This is baffling, given how insanely much time we spend with the media.

Derwin and de Merode (Chapter 5, this volume) offer a detailed analysis of the first 12 years of the journal *Media Psychology.* As part of their research, they interviewed journal editors, surveyed contributors, and analyzed important trends in the publication record of the journal. One area of particular interest was the relative contribution of psychology and communications scholars to the journal and the degree of collaborations. These data, which I will leave to them to present to you, add information to the survey data I report here. I think if you compare the two datasets, some clear themes emerge.

I agree with the other *Handbook* authors that the ubiquity and importance of media in our lives and the inherent connection with human psychology mean that ours is a field that is going to be vibrant and in demand for the foreseeable future. What form it takes is up to the scholars who, in fact, make up the field. I also agree that how psychologists and communications scholars collaborate and interact has important implications for the field. This is true at a number of levels, but it certainly includes how decisions are made at scholarly journals, what shared definitions we can generate, and how we move forward with important collaborations. Fortunately, as evidenced by the caliber of scholars represented in this *Handbook,* the excellence of our scholarly community and the breadth and depth of our scholarship suggest that the field shows the promise of a bright and fascinating future.

Overview of This *Handbook*
Contents By Section

I designed *The Oxford Handbook of Media Psychology* in six sections. The first and the last include my *Introduction* and *Overview* and *Media*

Psychology: Past, Present, and Future chapters. The final section includes a content analysis of this *Handbook* (Neal) that uses a semantic content analysis tool (Leximancer) to derive meaning from the text of the *Handbook* itself. The goal of this chapter is to provide a smart automation summary of the content areas of our field. Thus, in this chapter (Neal) we have an instantiation of a cutting-edge media psychology method and tool as well as an objective summary of the content of our field.

The four sections that remain are as follows: *History and Methods, Issues and Media Types, Interactive and Emerging Technologies,* and *Meta Issues in Media Psychology*.

In the *History and Methods* section, leading scholars tell the stories of some of the largest issues in the field, tracing their history. The issues addressed in this section include the history and importance of narrative (Isbouts & Ohler), an argument for Media Psychology as a distinct field (Brown Rutledge) and a history of Media Psychology with an emphasis on theory (Tuma). Derwin and Demerode tell the story of media psychology via an analysis of the first journal of the same name. Arke covers the history and future prospects of media literacy. Finally, there are two foundational research methods chapters in the *Handbook*, one focusing on quantitative (Prot & Anderson) and the other on qualitative (Polkinghorne) research.

In the *Issues and Media Types* section I invited scholars who could represent particularly important issues in the field as well as a sampling of important media psychology research content areas. Huesmann, Dubow, and Yang address the most often researched area in all of media psychology: media violence. Their approach here is to put that research in the controversial context in which the scholarship takes place, where scientists interface with business and political interests as well as public health interests. Additionally, content areas for media research represented here include a positive psychology approach to children's media use (Gregory), the role of emotion in media use and effects (Konijn), media violence and desensitization (Brockmyer), sexual content (Shafer, Bobkowsi, & Brown), portrayals of race (Behm-Morawitz & Ortiz) and gender (Scharrer) in the media, and media persuasion (Nabi & Moyer-Gusé).

The section on *Interactive and Emerging Technologies* includes coverage of social processes in virtual environments (Blascovich & McCall), games for health (Chamberlin & Maloney), serious games (Blumberg, Almonte, Anthony, & Hashimoto),

video game violence (Krahe), children and the Internet (Donnerstein), technology addictions (Gentile, Coyne, & Bricolo), and video games and attention (West & Bailey).

In creating a section on interactive and emerging technologies, one of my considerations was to not retread territory already addressed in the *Oxford Handbook of Internet Psychology* (Johnson, McKenna, Postmes, & Reips, 2009). This is especially true in that the *Oxford Library of Psychology* (of which both volumes are a part) was created with new media in mind more so than legacy media. This means that each volume in the *Oxford Library of Psychology* has much less rigid boundaries and chapters can be shared and linked among volumes. Given my expertise, and the desire to stay away from topics covered by the *Oxford Handbook of Internet Psychology*, this section is oriented more toward video games than it might have been with another editor. I argue that video games are one of the most popular forms of media and are the most ubiquitous form of interactive media with many educational and psychological ramifications. The coverage of video games in this *Handbook* is designed to avoid the wrongheaded approach of judging games to be all bad or all good. Such reductionist arguments fail to adequately represent the qualities of games (Anderson, Gentile, & Dill, 2011; see also my concluding chapter of this volume).

I agree with the converging opinion, evident in my *Handbook* author survey and in Potter's chapter (Chapter 24, this volume) arguing for a framework for media psychology research, that agreement on what the fundamental media psychology theories are is an important step in the development of the field. One focus of the section *Meta Issues in Media Psychology* is on theory and other meta issues in the field. For example, the chapters on the general framework (Potter), transportation theory (Green & Dill), and media psychophysiology (Bartholow & Bolls), among others, are relevant to our understanding of theory and current directions in the field. They also reflect some of the most exciting opportunities for current and future research in media psychology. This section also includes a chapter on the Japanese approach to media psychology (Sakamoto) and a chapter by a media psychology policy expert (McIntyre) on the political narrative of children's media research.

Handbook Features

When I envisioned the contents of this *Handbook*, I had a number of goals in mind. As a reader, I hope you will find it instructive to understand my vision for the *Handbook*. First and foremost, I was highly cognizant that the first-ever *Handbook of Media Psychology* should help define the field by documenting the content, methods, theories, and approaches that characterize our scholarship at this moment in history. I had other specific goals for the makeup of this *Handbook*. What follows is a nonexhaustive list of the perspectives I wanted to make sure were represented here:

1. Interdisciplinary perspectives, with particular emphasis on:

    a. Both psychology and communications scholars

    b. Collaborative interdisciplinary research

    c. Multiple areas of psychology, including social and developmental psychology and neuroscience

2. International scholarship, including:

    a. Coverage of non-American views of doing media psychology

    b. European and Asian perspectives in particular

3. Research showing positive as well as negative effects of media, including:

    a. A positive psychology approach to media psychology

    b. Emerging content areas in the positive effects of media such as serious games and games for health

4. Broad coverage that represents the most popular areas of research

5. An emphasis on a critical thinking approach to media psychology, which considers multiple perspectives on issues

6. Critical coverage of media psychology methods that has the potential to advance the field

7. Perspectives that capture the context in which the research takes place, such as:

    a. Scholarly debates

    b. The political context of media psychology research

As you might imagine, one of my goals for the *Handbook* in addition to selecting the content to cover was selecting and attracting the best minds in media psychology to be the voices of the field. That is one goal of the *Handbook* that I will be so bold as to declare an undeniable success. The authors of these chapters are no less than my scholarly heroes. I know that as each one tells the unique story of his or her expertise, what emerges is a vibrant map of this discipline.

Author Note

Karen E. Dill, School of Psychology, Fielding Graduate University.

Thanks to Elly Konijn, Pamela Kato, and Pamela Brown Rutledge for comments on an earlier draft of this chapter.

Appendix A

1. Media psychology uses the tools and theories of psychology to study and understand the complex interaction of human experience with media technologies, globally and individually.

2. Media psychology concerns applying psychological theories and research (including methods and measurements) to and integrating them with communication and media theories and research, in explaining individual differences and underlying mechanisms in media uses and effects on individual's cognitions, affect, and behavior. For example, explaining individual differences in susceptibility to specific media content.

3. I think about it as focused on the individual, so less concerned about context and other cultural factors.

4. I'm a fan of the Fielding definition. To me, media psychology is the intersection of psychology—with its focus on understanding the individual—and media studies—with its focus on understanding media-related issues and processes. So, to me, the field of media psychology investigates how and why individuals process media, how and why individuals are drawn to media, how and why individuals relate to and form opinions about media, and how and why individuals respond to (i.e., are affected by) media. Much emphasis is placed on individual differences as well as on additional variables that may play a part in these relationships (beyond those pertaining to the media and the individual, and including aspects of social and cultural context).

5. Study the ways we interact with media, and the ways in which those interactions (voluntary or involuntary) influence our thoughts, behavior, and communication.

6. Media psychology is a scientific study that addresses the intersection of and relationship between media and psychology.

7. Media psychology is the intersection of the study of human behavior and their experiences and reactions to media messages.

8. I like Karen's definition the best. It is the most direct and clear.

9. My definition has been until now very simplistic: "the impact of media on human behavior."

10. The scientific study of the effects of media exposure on cognition, emotion, and behavior.

11. The study of the impact of media of various forms on the mind and behavior.

12. I like Karen's definition!

13. What I think all of these miss is the effects side. They discuss the use of media, the creation of media, the being on the media, etc. but do not discuss the effects (on both individuals and groups). So my definition would be something like: Media Psych is the scientific study of how people use, experience, and are affected by media. This includes behavior, thoughts, and feelings on individual, group, and societal levels. It includes the study of media techniques and content, including how psychology and media mutually influence each other.

14. Media psychology is the study of individuals' behaviors and cognition in the context of diverse forms of media.

15. I prefer (3), which is the one used in the *Handbook*.

References

Anderson, C. A., Gentile, D. A., & Dill, K. E. (2011). Prosocial, antisocial, and other effects of recreational video games. In D. G. Singer & J. L. Singer (Eds.), *Handbook of Children and the Media* (pp. 249–272). Thousand Oaks, CA: Sage.

Csikszentmihalyi, M. (2008). *Finding Flow*. New York: Harper Perennial.

Derwin, E. B., & de Merode, J. (Chapter 5, this volume). Inside *Media Psychology*: The story of an emerging discipline as told by a leading journal. In K. E. Dill (Ed.), *Oxford Handbook of Media Psychology*. New York: Oxford University Press.

Dill, K. E. (2009). *How Fantasy Becomes Reality: Seeing Through Media Influence*. New York: Oxford University Press.

Fiore, Q., & McLuhan, M. (1967). *The Medium is the Massage*. New York: Bantam.

Fremlin, J. W. (2008). Understanding Media Psychology. [Student Notebook]. *The Association for Psychological Science Observer*, 21(1).

Giles, D. (2003). *Media Psychology*. New York: Palgrave Macmillan.

Giles, D. (2010). *Psychology of the Media*. New York: Palgrave Macmillan.

Green, M. C., & Dill, K. E. (Chapter 25, this volume). Engaging with stories and characters: Learning, persuasion and transportation into narrative worlds. In K. E. Dill (Ed.), *Oxford Handbook of Media Psychology*. New York: Oxford University Press.

Isbouts, J.-P., & Ohler, J. (Chapter 2, this volume). Storytelling and media: Narrative models from Aristotle to augmented reality. In K. E. Dill (Ed.), *The Oxford Handbook of Media Psychology*. New York: Oxford University Press.

Ito, M., Okabe, D., & Matsuda, M. (2006). *Personal, Portable, Pedestrian: Mobile Phones in Japanese Life*. Cambridge, MA: MIT Press.

Johnson, A., McKenna, K., Postmes, T., & Reips, U.-D. (Eds.). (2009). *Oxford Handbook of Internet Psychology*. New York: Oxford University Press.

Konijn, E. A. (Chapter 11, this volume). The role of emotion in media use and effects. In K. E. Dill (Ed.), *Oxford Handbook of Media Psychology*. New York: Oxford University Press.

Luskin, B. J., & Friedland, L. (1998). *Task Force Report: Media Psychology and New Technologies*. Washington, DC: Division 46 of the American Psychological Association.

Matsuda, M. (2006). Discourses of Keitai in Japan. In M. Ito, D. Okabe, & M. Matsuda (Eds.), *Personal, Portable, Pedestrian: Mobile Phones in Japanese Life*. Cambridge, MA: MIT Press.

McLuhan, M. (2000). Understanding Media: The Extensions of Men. The Correspondence of Masrshall McLuhan and Edward T. Hall. *Mass Communication and Society*, 3(1).

Potter, W. J. (Chapter 24, this volume). A general framework for media psychology scholarship. In K. E. Dill (Ed.), *Oxford Handbook of Media Psychology*. New York: Oxford University Press.

Quitney-Anderson, J., & Ranie, L. (2012). *Millennials Will Likely Suffer and Benefit Due to Their Hyperconnected Lives*. Washington, DC: Pew Research Center's Internet & American Life Project.

Sakamoto, A. (Chapter 28, this volume). Japanese Approach to Research on Psychological Effects of Use of Media. In K. E. Dill (Ed.), *The Oxford Handbook of Media Psychology*. New York: Oxford University Press.

Williams, S. (2011). Media Psychology Founder Honored by APA. Retrieved from http://news.fielding.edu/bid/72746/Media-Psychology-Founder-Honored-by-APA.

PART 2

History and Methods

Storytelling and Media: Narrative Models from Aristotle to Augmented Reality

Jean-Pierre Isbouts *and* Jason Ohler

Abstract

In the history of human experience, one of our most pervasive and enduring reference points is our need for story. Stories help us to understand ourselves in terms of who we are, what we need, and why we behave the way we do. The more those narratives stretch across cultures and throughout the ages, the more they become touchstones of the human experience. Indeed, the need for narratives to define ourselves has never been more apropos than today, when we find ourselves in the midst of the digital revolution. Part I of this chapter, written by Jean-Pierre Isbouts, traces the relationship between storytelling and media from ancient times to today, and argues why the last decades have forced us to radically redefine the traditional Aristotelian model of storytelling. Part II, written by Jason Ohler, investigates the future of storytelling, particularly with regard to online, participatory, and multidimensional media.

Key Words: digital media, multimedia, narrative, storytelling, television, Web 2.0

Part I. The Past and Present of Media Narrative from Aristotle to the Apple iPad

Introduction

Looking back over the mere span of a decade, the revolutionary impact of new media on society across the globe has been exponential. Few people could have imagined a mere decade ago that one day, videos of protests in totalitarian regimes such as China and Iran could boomerang around the world in a matter of minutes, or that 140-letter tweets could topple autocratic regimes from Tunisia to Egypt. The purpose of this chapter is to examine how these conditions came about and how they have molded one essential component of human communication—the ancient tradition of storytelling.

Storytelling, the art of framing a concept in the form of a plot involving both characters and events, is as old as the human condition itself. One of the oldest artifacts in the world—the depiction of herds in the caves of Lascaux, for example, which dates to

the 11th millennium b.c.e.[1]—is not what it seems. Our modern eyes, conditioned by more than a century of snapshot photography, see a static image of a group of animals. The prehistoric artists who created it, on the other hand, saw something else entirely: the action-packed story of a hunt, captured in a sequence of successive events, superimposed within the same pictorial frame. Masaccio, in his groundbreaking fresco *The Tribute Money* (1427) in the Brancacci Chapel in Florence, attempted to do exactly the same thing, as did Botticelli in his *Scenes from the Life of Moses* (1481–1482), painted for the Sistine Chapel in Rome. Unbound by the conventions of unity of space, time, and action that rule our modern, cinematic *mise-èn-scene,* these artists told a story in purely visual terms, driven not by linear sequential logic, but by the compositional possibilities of Renaissance illusionism (Baxandall, 1972) (Figure 2.1).

Stories, Aristotle famously declared in *Poetics,* are narrative patterns with a distinct beginning, middle,

Figure 2.1 Masaccio, *The Tribute Money* (1427). The Brancacci Chapel, Florence.
Unbound by our modern perception of visuals in unity of space, time and action, the Renaissance artist could tell his story chronologically, across the breadth of his canvas. The story depicted here is inspired by the gospel of Matthew (17:24–27). In the center, the publican asks Peter for the two-drachma temple tax, whereupon Jesus tells Peter to collect the coin from a fish. At the far left, Peter does find the coin in the mouth of a fish, after which he pays the same tax collector in the scene to the far right.
Copyright Pantheon Studios, Inc., reprinted with permission.

and end that appeal to both our emotional and intellectual faculties. Many of these patterns describe a hero character facing a sequence of challenges that he or she must overcome, and the hero is profoundly transformed in the process (Campbell, 1988). Over time, some of these stories found a particular resonance among a larger community—such as a clan, a village, or even a nation. They became myths—an expression of the way a community tries to make sense of itself and its place in the world. As Jerome Bruner puts it, good stories are the way in which we reinterpret and renegotiate our assumptions about our culture (Bruner, 1985).

Most scholars now accept that the Hebrew Scriptures (which Christians refer to as the Old Testament) owe much of their motifs to Mesopotamian myths, the oldest extant texts of which date to the Sumerian period of the third millennium b.c.e.[2] Genesis itself is in many ways the quintessential family saga, tracing the travels of a clan from Ur across the length and breadth of the Fertile Crescent, from Haran to Hebron, and from Egypt to Beersheba (Isbouts, 2011). Similarly, Homer's *Iliad* and *Odyssey,* equally grounded in oral traditions, perfectly express the moral aspirations of Greek civilization (and through Virgil, Roman civilization as well), just as the *Ramayana* serves as the foundational text for Hindu and Buddhist cultures, or the *Shâhnâma* forms the basis for Persia's cultural identity (Matini, 1990) (Figure 2.2).

Since the earliest times, then, elders have sat with their kin around a campfire at night and told stories, thus transmitting the ethical and cultural legacy of a family, clan, or tribe to the next generation. These elders may have understood that stories are arguably better containers of knowledge than any other form

Figure 2.2 In his *Poetics* (335 b.c.e.), Aristotle offered a definition of a story or "plot" (*mythos*) that remained valid until well into the 20th century.
Copyright Pantheon Studios, Inc., reprinted with permission.

of oral transmission. Narratives have the ability to activate human faculties—such as feeling, empathy, and affinity—that remain mostly dormant with intellectual rhetoric and learning. Stories can impart not only information, but also *meaning;* or in the words of Donald Polkinghorne, "narrative meaning functions to give form to the understanding of a purpose to life, and to join everyday actions and events into episodic units" (Polkinghorne, 1988). Stories, in sum, are quite simply the literary vehicle of our thoughts.

A key example is offered in the synoptic Gospels. When Jesus attempts to explain his sophisticated concept of a new social compact called "The Kingdom of God," he couches his ideas in the form of allegorical stories or *parables.* Each of these parables has a single but highly effective narrative arc, illuminating the concept in simple metaphorical terms, because a detailed intellectual exposition was well beyond the ability of his uneducated fishermen–disciples (Kistemaker, 2002).

It is not the purpose of this chapter to explore the full range of narrative theory, a subject that has seen an explosion of interest over the past few decades in a range of disciplines. Nor will it attempt to define *narrative,* which many authors have attempted to do, with varying results (Fulton, 2005). Rather, this chapter focuses on the rapidly changing relationship between storytelling and mediated platforms, capable of communicating stories in ways other than traditional oral means.

Orality and Literacy

Until the late 19th century all storytelling was overwhelmingly oral in nature. Only a very small percentage of the population in Asia and Europe was literate then, which is true for some regions of Africa and Asia today.[3] The gradual adoption of the printing press in Renaissance Europe multiplied the production of books, but did not necessarily boost literacy rates, at least not outside the circle of social elites. It was only with the invention of the rotary printing press in 1843, combined with steadily improving educational systems on both sides of the Continent, that newspapers, magazines, and books slowly began to supplant oral transmission as the conduit for narrative material (Graff, 1987) (Figure 2.3).

This transition from orality to literacy[4] culminated in the rise of the novel,[5] already a popular instance of *belles lettres* among the elites of the 18th century; it now emerged as the pre-eminent storytelling device for the rapidly growing literate mass market in the 19th century. A reader in early 18th century Britain, for example, could look forward to no more than 100 or so new novels per year.[6] This output multiplied exponentially in the 19th century, when numerous political movements stimulated public dissent and advocacy, finding a ready readership among the newly literate servant and worker classes. The novel became respectable, not only as a medium for entertainment, but also as a platform for couching politically controversial or

Figure 2.3 Printing Presses, mid-16th Century.
The Renaissance printing press multiplied the production of printed books but did not necessarily affect literacy rates, given the lack of educational opportunities for the vast majority of Europe's population.
Copyright Pantheon Studios, Inc., reprinted with permission.

even subversive ideas in fictional form—and thereby deftly circumventing the censor. Whether the 19th-century reader was aware that his or her views were being subtly challenged or manipulated under the guise of immersive fiction—an issue of urgent relevance with regard to modern media today—is not always clear. What is clear, however, is that the *roman* slowly changed from a *bagatelle* to a medium worthy of reflection and debate, aided by technology that could duplicate books more swiftly and cheaply than ever before. The rotary press has been mentioned, but the invention of the steel engraving process by which these mass-produced books could be illustrated (often in astonishing detail) was equally important. In the process, fictional narratives such as the novels of Zola, Flaubert, Proust, and Joyce became a stimulus for social change in a way no other narrative form had ever accomplished (Siskin, 1998). Novelists, a rather *louche* category in the 18th century, became a respectable class in the 19th century. Avidly sought by upper-class salons for the *frisson* of their bohemian lifestyles and dangerous ideas, they achieved what today we would term pop celebrity status (Figure 2.4).

In the United States, too, storytelling traditions underwent major change as millions of immigrants streamed into the country from Asia and Europe, each carrying the unique narrative legacy of his or her culture. Our Disneyesque fascination with fairy tales, for example, probably originated with the fables of the Brothers Grimm, brought to the United States by German immigrants in the early 19th century (Elliott, 1997). This growing dominance of European traditions came at a price: Many indigenous sagas related by Native Americans, especially those featuring heroic warrior women, or African-American storytelling traditions such as the tales of Uncle Remus, faded under the pressure of European archetypes, and were ultimately discarded (Sans Souci, 1993).

The Narrative Model

An axiom of storytelling since antiquity is the concept of unity of action. A proper story, or so the Aristotelian model holds, should focus on a single plot line, involving a consistent group of protagonists, without competing subplots, segues, or ancillary characters. Multiple and mutually competing storylines are to be eschewed. Stories must not only have a clear beginning, middle, and end; but their progression must also be motivated by a consistent and clearly articulated narrative thread—echoed by Joseph Campbell's *monomyth* concept (Campbell,

Figure 2.4 Gustave Doré, *Camelot,* an Illustration for *Idylls of the King* by Lord Tennyson, published Between 1856 and 1885. The steel engraving technique enabled 19th century publishers to illustrate mass market novels and nonfiction books. Copyright Pantheon Studios, Inc., reprinted with permission.

1988). Even today, a leading theorist such as Peter Brooks still insists that only closure can impart meaning and significance to the written narrative (Brooks, 1985). Obviously this principle, with its singular focus on plot, favored the type of structured, historical novels so popular in the mid- to late 19th century.

At the dawn of the 20th century, however, Aristotle's model faced challenges by the emergence of new storytelling platforms, the first of which was a medium called cinema. At first glance, cinema appeared to have the same qualities of live theater. Actors, scripted dialog, sets, costumes, lighting, and stage effects were all attendant ingredients of Greek and Roman plays, Renaissance masques, 18th century opera, or 19th century theater. The difference is that unlike live performances, film was the first medium capable of composing its story asynchronously, by shooting scenes over many days, dictated not by narrative chronology but by the availability of locations, lighting, actors, or props. For the first time, storytelling drama was relieved of the *diktat* of unity of space and time.

Inevitably, screenwriters seized on this freedom to attack the Aristotelian unity of plot, not only by changing the sequencing of time (through slow motion and flashbacks, first pioneered in the films of the early 1900s), but also by inviting secondary plots and characters. These not only helped to sustain dramatic tension, but also imbued the story's narrative structure with a complexity well beyond

the possibilities of the live stage. The development of the reverse angle and the close-up, of purposefully framing one character at the expense of another, robbed the audience of visual control but offered the filmmaker unprecedented opportunities to endow the story with subjective emphasis and emotional depth.[7] Soon, storytelling on film began to develop its own language, a vocabulary of cinematic semiotics, such as the dissolve, meant to communicate elapse of time. These semiotics were adopted by other filmmakers at home and abroad, and soon coalesced into a proper idiom of cinematic storytelling (Cook, 1990) (Figure 2.5).

Shortly after World War I, however, another storytelling medium emerged, which became known as *the wireless* in Britain and *radio* in the United States.[8] As in the case of many new technologies, it took a while for this medium to find its specific purpose and programmatic model. With no clear narrative precedent, early radio broadcasts defaulted to music, much to the chagrin of the commercial music industry. Sales of phonograph records, a technology first introduced in 1894, dropped from $75 million in 1929 to $28 million in 1938 as radio set ownership zoomed from two out of five homes in 1931 to four out of five homes in 1938 (Aitkin, 1985).

During the so-called Golden Age of radio, however, the medium began to experiment with a range of indigenous program formats, from farm reports and news broadcasts to quiz shows, variety shows, and what today we would called scripted drama.[9]

Figure 2.5 A Frame from *Fun in the Bakery Shop,* a 1902 Film by Edison.
Early films sought to mimic contemporary entertainment formats, such as live vaudeville on stage.
Copyright Pantheon Studios, Inc., reprinted with permission.

The result was an incredible variety of narrative programming, including genres such as adventure, classical drama, comedy, burlesque, mystery, thrillers, and romance—all firmly branded by whomever happened to be the sponsoring advertiser. Some of the finest shows from this era include drama classics such as Orson Welles' *Mercury Theater*, the *CBS Radio Workshop,* and *Theater Guild On the Air. Theater Guild* went as far as to stage Shakespeare plays, including a 90-minute Hamlet—thus introducing the Bard to vast new audiences in the United States (Figure 2.6).

Technically and structurally, however, radio storytelling was constrained by a number of factors, not the least of which was that all action had to be performed live, in real time, on stage in a radio studio. Unlike a live theater performance, however, characters could not be *seen;* they could only be *heard.* This placed a tremendous burden on what the industry today calls Foley artists—artists with the ability to evoke setting and action, purely through simulated sound effects. From a narrative point of view, therefore, early radio was the exact opposite of early cinema. Whereas a motion picture could be shot and edited over multiple weeks, but without the ability to reproduce an actor's voice, radio offered a rich palette of sounds, but only through live performances, without the ability to allow its characters to be seen.

Figure 2.6 Orson Welles (1915–1985) cofounded *The Mercury Theatre on Air* together with John Houseman in 1938, producing live radio dramas until 1940. The most infamous radio teleplay was *The War of the Worlds*, broadcast on October 30, 1938 as an adaptation of H. G. Wells' novel, which was presented as a newscast and briefly created panic among listeners nationwide. Copyright Pantheon Studios, Inc., reprinted with permission.

Many authors who lived through the Golden Age have commented that the "live" aspect of radio drama lent the listening experience a visceral intensity that was lost with the advent of recording technology and prerecorded shows. It gave audiences the intimate feeling of being witness to an art work in progress, an experience that today can only be found at the live theater or music stage.

With the advent of the 1930s, new technologies were introduced that had a profound effect on both radio and cinema. In 1932, the Radio Corporation of America (RCA) invented an instant audio recording process using aluminum discs coated with a layer of nitrate; by the mid-1930s, it was widely in use by radio stations across the country. These early 33⅓ RPM discs were capable of storing up to 15 minutes of programming on each side, enabling radio stations to prerecord programs of up to 30 minutes per disc.

Motion pictures, meanwhile, found their voice with synchronized sound, first pioneered in the motion picture *The Jazz Singer* and quickly adopted by Walt Disney to produce the first sound cartoon, *Steamboat Willie,* in 1929. Title cards that had previously sustained the development of narrative plot were now replaced with actual synchronized dialog. This development required an entirely new category of film talent. Whereas previously actors were expected to communicate action through dramatic gestures and expressions, they were now called on to act and behave in a persuasive and altogether far more realistic way.

While these rapid changes in radio and cinema were being absorbed, a third electronic medium made its appearance. RCA had initiated daily television broadcasts from New York City as early as 1929, but the Depression, the lack of television standards, and the subsequent outbreak of World War II postponed the commercial launch of American television until the late 1940s. In this instance, Europe beat America to the punch: Five German electronics manufacturers led by Telefunken began producing the first line of electronic cathode ray tube sets as early as 1934, followed by British and French firms in 1936 (Gulliland, 1939). Hitler and his Minister of Propaganda, Josef Goebbels, exploited both radio and television for their tremendous propaganda potential; the 1936 Olympic Games in Berlin were among the first events to be televised in Germany (Figure 2.7).

Early television found itself imitating early radio to an astonishing degree, largely because of the same technical limitations that had been imposed on radio

Figure 2.7 The Olympic Flame in Berlin, 1936.
The 1936 Olympic Games were the first major international event to be televised, as part of Goebbels' effort to project an image of Nazi Germany as a stable and peaceful society.
Copyright Pantheon Studios, Inc., reprinted with permission.

some 30 years earlier: the inability to record television shows for broadcast at a later date. As a result, variety shows ruled supreme, not only because these could be staged quickly and cheaply, but also because that is what viewers expected: For most people, television was simply radio with moving pictures.

Consequently, early television embraced live theater and drama as eagerly as early radio had done, marshaling a new generation of actors, producers, and playwrights for the production of both classic and original narrative programming. A number of memorable anthologies were the result, once again branded by their advertiser sponsors, such as *Kraft Television Theater, Playhouse 90,* and CBS' *Studio One* (Days, 2007). Early television thus offered starving young East Coast actors in the postwar era opportunities that would have been unthinkable outside the established domains of Hollywood and Broadway theater.

Charlton Heston was one of these actors. Reminiscing about those heady days in front of live television cameras, Heston told me in 1998, "I did Chekhov, Shaw, and Turgenev. You see, nobody really knew what television was supposed to be like. The networks who owned the technology didn't have

a clue as to how to program it. So more or less by default, this new medium was left in the hands of a bunch of unemployed 24-year-olds—including, fortunately, me."[10]

Of course, that happy condition could not last. Unlike in Europe, where radio and television were considered public utilities for the common good and thus the rightful preserve of government agency, the U.S. Congress readily turned these media over to the private sector. Thus, a small group of corporate entities—principally RCA/NBC, CBS, and ABC (NBC Blue)—took control of the nascent television medium in America and made it primarily a platform for advertising, rather than public enlightenment—a distinction that would continue well into the 21st century. What's more, the need for such a platform was obvious. World War II had long suppressed consumer demand; now, with America's industry once again churning out refrigerators and automobiles rather than Mustang fighters and B-24 bombers, television was an ideal medium to connect these products with America's recovering consumer markets.

But advertisers demanded a price. They readily grasped that the freewheeling and undisciplined approach to programming of early television left television audiences fragmented and difficult to quantify. What was needed was a broadcast schedule that consistently attracted specific demographic segments at particular times of the day. Only in this manner could the wide variety of products offered by corporate America be carefully matched with individual target audiences. The result was the concept of *serialization*—the idea of replicating a narrative episode with the same or similar plots and characters week after week, so as to build a loyal and committed audience segment that could be sold to the highest advertising bidder. Commercial serialization robbed the television medium of its creative innocence, but by the same token, it laid the foundation for the vast television industry we have today.

Serialization required that narrative content would not reach plot closure at the end of the program hour. Indeed, the opposite was required; by ending each episodic segment with a "cliffhanger," the network and its advertisers could confidently expect to reel in the same audience during the next broadcast.

Serials were not unique to television, of course. In 19th century Britain, publishers had developed penny dreadful serials, a series of fairly lurid episodic novels that cost a penny each, and were published over the course of several weeks (Louis, 1963). The silent movie era also had its episodic genre in the form of movie serials. These low-budget films were typically shown before the main feature and relied on a plot that unfolded over many weeks, invariably ending in a cliffhanger; a famous example is Edison's *What Happened to Mary?* (1912). During the sound era, these serials reached their apogee, boosted by higher budgets and better production values, which led to classics such as the renowned *Flash Gordon* series (Lahue, 1969). Radio, too, developed its version of serialization in the form of a genre known as the *soap opera,* so called because these shows, targeted to housewives, were often sponsored by soap and detergent companies such as Procter & Gamble and Colgate. One noted example is the soap opera the *Guiding Light,* which began on NBC radio in 1937, jumped to CBS television in 1952, and continued its run until September, 2009, for a total of more than 15,700 episodes. Soap opera storytelling pushed the episodic format to its very limits, because its narrative deliberately eschews both beginning and end. It simply meanders, dragging its characters along whether they like it or not, without any hope of resolution (Altman, 2008), and in the process, offers a perfect foil for continued exposure to advertised brands.

Television proved to be the most receptive platform for serialized programming by far. It embraced both the soap opera format, which features the same cast in a continuous plot, as well as the procedural drama format, which features the same cast but unique, individual plot lines per episode, each of which are resolved at the end of each show. The hypnotic repetition of television serialization gained such huge audiences that the soap opera eventually moved into prime time, the evening hours that typically command the largest audiences and thus the highest commercial advertising rates. Examples of prime-time, high-budget soap serials include *Peyton Place* in the 1960s, followed by *Dallas* and *Dynasty* in the late 1970s, and modern versions such as *Desperate Housewives.* Their success was not limited to North America; for example, *Dallas,* one of the most successful television shows in 20th century history, was broadcast in 90 countries (Olson, 1999).

Serials, however, require a radically different approach to the structure of the story and its narrative arc, mindful not only of an episode's individual structure (allowing for commercial breaks), but also of the need to encompass months and sometimes years of story development. In other words, screenwriters on serials face the challenge of stretching a basic framework of characters, relationships, and conflicts over many episodes in a manner that deftly avoids the prospect of resolution while, at the same time, offering sufficient dramatic development to motivate continued watching (Figure 2.8).

Why do these audiences continue to tune in, knowing full well that the plot line will advance by only marginal degrees? Clearly, the essential reward of this experience is not closure, as Peter Brooks would have it. A more plausible incentive may be what authors such as Richard Gerrig, Melanie Green, and Timothy Brock have described as *transportation.* As described elsewhere in this book (see Chapter 24), Transportation Theory argues that viewers can become so immersed in a fictional narrative that they feel literally "transported" to the story as a space they can inhabit, both emotionally and cognitively. Simply put, they become as involved with the characters as if these were actual human beings with whom they share a close relationship (Green & Brock, 2000). Hence, the principal appeal of these long-term serials is not so much the evolution of plot, but the viewer's imagined kinship with these characters, and the sharing of their emotions through the ups and downs of their scripted personal relationships.

For the network, however, such long-term serials pose a great risk, in that late entry into the series by

Figure 2.8 Filoli Mansion, located in Woodside, CA, was used as the exterior location for the 220-episode blockbuster serial *Dynasty*. *Dynasty* and *Dallas* were typical of 1980s-era television series that projected a heavily skewed image of American suburban wealth. Copyright Pantheon Studios, Inc., reprinted with permission.

new viewers is deterred. These viewers, who have never seen the show before, are invariably confused and frustrated when confronted with plots and characters that lack preparatory exposition. Consequently, these serials tend to develop a rather ossified base of hard-core viewers with very little demographic movement in or out of the show, once it is up and running.

As the 20th century progressed, television schedules became so reliant on serialized programming, whether news, children's, comedy, or drama, that the concept of a *season* emerged. Each "season" essentially consists of numerous streams of serialized shows, consistently pegged to their unique time slot, so as to encourage audiences to tune in at predictable times during the day. Until recently, each television "year" consisted of two seasons, providing 13 new episodes for all program categories, for 13 weeks. These "seasons," usually scheduled in spring and fall, then alternate with off-seasons in winter and summer, when viewership is typically lower because of holidays, and reruns of serials are programmed.

Serialization not only affects narrative development, but the consumption of narratives as well. The repetitive exposure to characters performing either heroically or poorly in predictable situations (e.g., crime dramas or situation comedies) fosters a familiarity with viewers to the extent that for many the line between reality and fiction is blurred (Dill, 2009). George Gerber, who studied this phenomenon in the 1970s, coined the term *cultivation,* arguing that the more episodes people watch, the more they believe the characters and plots they see represent reality, regardless of whether they emotionally identify with these characters or not (Gerbner et al., 1986). The actor Telly Savalas, the lead in the highly popular crime series *Kojak,* for example, was often stopped on the street by people praising or chiding him about his televised cases, as though he was a New York police detective in real life.

In 1968, Gerber conducted a survey among three types of television viewers: those with light viewing behavior (<2 hours a day), medium viewing (2–4 hours a day), and heavy viewing (>4 hours a day). Gerber found that particularly heavy viewers held beliefs and attitudes closely akin to those of the characters they watched on television. Gerber thereupon posited that repeat exposure to serialized programming fostered not only a familiarity with featured characters, but also the impression that their situations are preferable to the viewer's own reality. In that sense, serialized television could create symbolic belief systems akin to the moral or social values of a religion—placing a heavy responsibility on the show's screenwriters to avoid behaviors that could in any way be damaging or destructive to established social norms (Potter, 2002). Indeed, the ideas of Gerber as well as other sociologists and social psychologists, have stimulated an intense debate on the effects of television drama on psychologically vulnerable audiences, such as children, particularly with regard to content involving violence, sexual situations, or drug use.

Another unintended consequence of serialization is cultural homogenization, not only at home but particularly in foreign markets. In Olson's words, "the greater the exposure to the same media, the more the (native) culture will be homogenized" (Olson, 1999). Popular series such as *Dynasty* and *Desperate Housewives* present American culture as a normative lifestyle of property and wealth set in lavish and socially screened suburban communities, when in practice this lifestyle is not only limited to an ever-shrinking group of Americans but altogether unobtainable for most viewing audiences in foreign territories. This homogenization of American-made situational drama is further abetted by the acquisition and consolidation of American television channels by large, multinational corporations with little or no national or ethical accountability. The strategy of media giants such as Rupert Murdoch's News Corp is to ensure profitability by appealing to the largest possible consumer constituency at the lowest possible cost.

This trend has resulted in what is often decried as the "dumbing down" of Hollywood entertainment: the search for bland, "lowest common denominator" programming that can be broadcast and exploited globally without fear of riling local morals and ethics. As a consequence, indigenous cultural expression is inevitably ignored and left to wither on the vine. Over the last decade, Hollywood typically produced 70% of the world's television content and 80% of the world's theatrical features, often marginalizing indigenous television drama. By contrast, foreign films in the United States make up less than 1% of box office revenues (Ulff-Møller, 2003).

Cultivation and homogenization theories, however, assume that television audiences are essentially passive, that their only role in the transaction of television narratives is that of consumption, without any participation or influence in the development or performance of the story. This idea remained valid for much of the 20th century, until an entirely new class of media technology emerged, with far-reaching consequences for the relationship between medium and narrative. This new domain was called *interactive media*.

The Emergence of Interactive Media

In 1976, the electronics manufacturers of Japan decided to introduce a new consumer technology, the compact videocassette. Sony developed a format, widely believed to be superior, called Betamax; but its competitor, the Victor Company of Japan (JVC) came up with a system that, unlike Sony, it was prepared to license to its competitors at highly competitive rates (Owen, 2005). Thus, JVC's VHS system won the format battle, and Betamax was soon forced to exit the stage. For our purpose, VHS did little to affect the prevailing narrative formats on television. Most people used their VHS player to record their favorite programs for later viewing, a concept known as *time displacement*. Nevertheless, VHS remained a rather clumsy format, requiring the use of large videotape cassettes yielding a mediocre visual quality.

A group of physicists and engineers attached to the NatLab in Eindhoven, Holland, owned by Philips Electronics, believed they had a better solution.[11] Laser had recently become a commercially viable technology for a wide variety of industrial use. Assuming that a television signal could be recorded in tiny pits embedded on a reflective surface, in theory that signal could be reproduced by a laser beam in almost the same pristine quality with which it had been recorded. The resulting product was a 12-inch iridescent disc of startling beauty, called the laser videodisc (though the official product name at launch was *Laservision*). The laserdisc would only enjoy a tenuous 15-year existence, never penetrating more than 2 million households (Parker, 2009). But the laser videodisc concept—or the laserdisc as it became known in the United States—made two important contributions.

First, the idea of using a laser beam to decode pits from a reflective surface ultimately led to the development of the compact disc. Second, when recorded in constant angular velocity (CAV) mode, the laserdisc offered several unprecedented playback features, including instant chapter access, frame-accurate frame advance, and split audio channels. Although still rudimentary, the laserdisc thus became the first commercial platform for *interactive* storytelling.

For example, the *Van Gogh Revisited* laserdisc starring Leonard Nimoy, first introduced in 1981, offered viewers the ability to instantly jump to a particular program chapter; browse through a narrative sequence of paintings and captions, stored as a series of stills; or choose between two separate audio tracks. One track featured Leonard Nimoy as narrator; the other track featured Vincent van Gogh himself through excerpts from letters to his brother Theo, read by an actor (Isbouts, 1986). Many of these interactive story elements survived, 20 years later, in what is now ubiquitously known as bonus material on DVD releases of Hollywood motion pictures (Figure 2.9).

Interactivity, the ability for individuals to engage with narrative content, first emerged with the development of personal computers in the late 1970s.[12] To be true, these early "personal" computers (as distinct from the large mainframe computers in use at the time) already enabled an individual to create, edit, and store information, but this information was limited to ASCII text or very crude graphics. To do so, these computers used two binary digits (or "bits"), 0 and 1, to represent analog symbols in digital form.

As the personal computer market grew, the Eindhoven NatLab engineers wondered whether this binary code could also be used to encode and reproduce another form of analog information, namely music. One of Philip's subsidiary companies, the Polygram record company, had expressed an interest in a medium that could distribute music more cheaply and reliably than phonograph records, which essentially used 1890s technology (Knopper, 2009). The result was an encoding scheme called pulse code modulation (PCM), whereby music was encoded at 44 KHz at 16 bits and subsequently "written" in tiny

pits on a reflective surface, using the same technology developed for the laserdisc. Thus, in 1982, the compact disc was born—and with it, the first digital encoding standard for mediated entertainment (Schouhamer-Immink, 2007).[13]

The new technology, launched simultaneously by Philips and Sony, was not an immediate success, partly because Philips' home base was Europe, and Polygram's catalog was mostly limited to a classical repertoire. But after Sony began to market the CD format in the United States, the floodgates were opened. By 1984, 2 years after the introduction of the standard, the music CD had become a hit. The music industry reaped vast rewards, because consumers essentially found themselves buying albums they already owned—albeit in vinyl form (Knopper, 2009). This unprecedented situation repeated itself 10 years later with the launch of the DVD, when consumers once again doled out money to replace their aging VHS libraries (Figure 2.10).

For our purposes, however, the CD launched an even greater revolution, although this was not immediately apparent at the time. It dawned on the inventors of the CD that binary information, once stored on the disc, could also be read back in digital form—such as computer data. At first, this did not strike many people as an attractive proposition. Why would anyone wish to go through the laborious process of encoding and replicating data on a CD if such data could not be subsequently erased and revised, as one could with a floppy disc? At best, the CD was seen

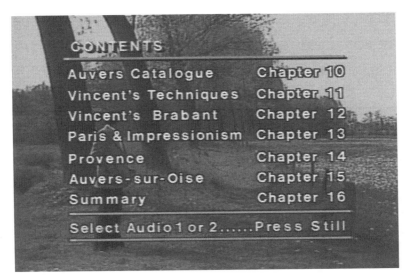

Figure 2.9 A Menu Frame from the Interactive Laserdisc "Van Gogh Revisited," Starring Leonard Nimoy and Published by North American Philips in 1982.
The laser videodisc was the first medium to offer viewers a modicum of control over the content they were watching.
Copyright Pantheon Studios, Inc.

Figure 2.10 The compact disc, introduced in 1982, is a landmark in media history by being the first format to offer a digital facsimile of analog programming content—music. Although the CD was a commercial success through much of the 20th century, the idea of digitization ultimately destroyed the music industry's business model and, in the process, launched the digital revolution.
Copyright Pantheon Studios, Inc.

as an archival medium for large databases, or what the industry termed read-only memory (ROM). The name stuck, and before long the first so-called CD-ROM players rolled off the assembly line.

CD-ROMs faced another limitation, however. In the early 1980s, the computer industry featured a number of incompatible operating systems, including SUN, DEC, IBM, and Apple. It seemed obvious that the CD-ROM, readable only on one of these proprietary operating systems, would never become a mass-market product. But then an event took place that is deservedly the stuff of legend. During one of the frequent computer conferences of the era, a group of engineers from different computer companies found themselves at the bar of the High Sierra Hotel and Casino in Lake Tahoe. Beer flowed copiously, as it tends to do when software engineers are in conclave, and the incompatibility of CD-ROMs was loudly bemoaned. When the meeting finally broke up, the engineers parted with the solemn promise that they would join hands to solve the problem—irrespective of the competitive concerns of their management. And they did. Within weeks, the first meeting of what informally became known as the High Sierra Working Group was held, and in time brokered a compromise file format, readable on most known computer platforms, which was eventually codified as ISO 9660.[14]

It is difficult to overstate the importance of this initiative for the subsequent evolution of digital media and associated narrative formats. For the first time a spontaneous, grassroots effort by industry professionals had overcome entrenched competitive rivalry to agree to a worldwide standard. This effort changed the CD-ROM from a mere CPU-specific storage device to a viable distribution medium. It made it possible for the first time for ISO-compatible CD-ROMs to be read on a Mac, PC, DEC, or SUN computer.[15]

This was serendipitous, because the decade of the 1980s was in need of exactly such a high volume data carrier. A new technology format with great promise for narrative material had emerged; namely, multimedia entertainment.

The Rise of Multimedia

Multimedia entertainment—a modality that combines text, graphics, audio, and video to provide multisensory *immersive* narratives in digital form—was the result of the convergence of three phenomena: the emerging standards for digital graphics, audio, and video; the development of multiprocessor chips capable of executing multiple tasks simultaneously; and the availability of a cheap, computer-readable distribution medium in the form of the CD-ROM. As a result, the personal computer was transformed from a *workstation* to an *entertainment platform*—a device, in short, that would become a premier medium for interactive programming.

One of the first published software programs to exploit the confluence of these three movements was a CD-ROM–based encyclopedia released by Grolier in 1992. It was unprecedented as an instance of multimedia publishing. In addition to searchable text culled from its printed original, this encyclopedic marvel also featured photos, digital audio, and its *pièce de resistance*: brief video clips, such as the one of President Kennedy announcing the race to the moon. Such was the revolutionary character of titles such as Grolier's that Microsoft launched a series of annual conferences dedicated solely to exploiting the potential of the CD-ROM medium (Miller, 1986).

The popularity of CD-ROM–based reference, education-, and entertainment-based programming spanned little more than a decade, until it was largely sidelined by the growing multimedia capabilities of the Web. In that time frame, however, the CD-ROM was embraced by another emerging narrative format, the computer-based videogame.

Videogames are as old as computers themselves, of course, but early games, such as the now-famous *Pong* created for Nolan Bushnell's Atari, offered little game-play beyond the movement of two-dimensional objects across the screen. Even during the so-called age of coin-operated arcades, a videogame like *Pac-Man* offered basic hand–eye coordination challenges with little or no narrative involvement. But this changed after the "crash" of the arcade industry in 1983, which forced game designers to look more closely at the personal computer as a platform for videogame delivery. Buoyed by the introduction of more powerful PC processors and new graphics standards such as VGA, game designers were able to conceive a new level of entertainment—one in which the user had control of not only the action but also the narrative, rendered in an environment that was both believable and lifelike (Donovan, 2010).

One prime example of this new genre was a videogame called *Myst*. *Myst* introduced the idea of a story that challenged the user to plot his or her way through an imaginary, multiended world, cued by puzzles and carefully cloaked hints, rendered in a beautiful and photo-real visual environment. In contrast to the visceral hand–eye coordination thrills offered by arcade games, this new class of videogames challenged the player on an entirely different level: the ability to chart a plausible path through a world of pure fantasy.

One unique aspect of *Myst* was that the story component was sustained almost entirely by nonverbal objects and musical cues. Although the narrative was pre-scripted in the form of puzzles and cues, the sequencing of these elements, and indeed the interpretation of the narrative's meaning, was left entirely up to the player. Thus, *Myst* (and games like it, such as *The 7th Guest*) introduced the concept of the nonlinear narrative: a plot offering multiple branches of development, providing the player with complete control over the sequential progression of the story. They offered, in Ryan's words, to "expand our mental horizon beyond the physical, actual world—toward the worlds of dreams and fantasy" (Ryan, 2004).

This idea strongly resonated with the gaming audience of its time. Some games went as far as to apply the nonlinear narrative concept to the literary domain, such as the games produced by Castle Rock Entertainment, now a division of Warner Studios. In Castle Rock's *Othello* (1997) and *Hamlet: A Murder Mystery* (1998) designers used elements from the studio's high-profile motion pictures (starring actors such as Laurence Fishburne, Julie Christie, and Kenneth Branagh) to create complex literary games in which players plotted through a combination of puzzles, clues, and swordplay in pursuit of different

Shakespearean branches, even to the point of changing the play's ending (Figure 2.11).

These high-end games, which spawned countless imitations, had many inherent limitations imposed by the slow speed of 1993-vintage CD-ROM drives as well as the processing power of 1990s-era personal computers.[16] A player could choose which environments to explore, but he could neither create nor manipulate them. In theory, however, it was possible to place the real-time rendering of realistic environments under control of the player, provided the system's processor was fast enough to convert user commands into movement and action while retaining the same standard of realism.

As every game designer will attest, rendering an object realistically in real time is a difficult and time-consuming task. This is why Walt Disney, when creating *Snow White,* carefully distinguished moving characters, drawn in two dimensions with primary colors, from fixed backgrounds, which could be painted in three dimensions with lush tones and hues. This idea remained an axiom of hand-drawn animation until the introduction of computer-based animation by Pixar and other animation studios. Certainly, the 1990s-era personal computer, primarily designed for word processing and spreadsheet computation, lacked the power to render objects and environments convincingly under immediate user control.

This changed with the introduction of a new generation of multiprocessing chips in the late 1990s. These multitask processors, such as the advanced 32-bit 68000 Motorola chip, were able to draw wireframe models in real time and simultaneously cover these with realistic "texture maps" to simulate elements such as skin, fabric, or other surfaces. These processors, in turn, led to the development of game platforms or *consoles,* essentially highly powerful multiprocessor computers solely devoted to delivering realistic, real-time rendering. Many of these platforms, such as 3DO, Atari, Jaguar, Amiga CD, and CD-i, are no longer with us, but others, including Sony's Playstation, Microsoft's Xbox, and Nintendo Entertainment System (later Nintendo Wii), persevered and form the backbone of the console-based videogame industry today.

With these new consoles, users were no longer given a choice of narrative development; they became, in a way, the authors of narrative sequences themselves. As Humphreys noted,

> Computer games are successful because they are more than repurposed "old" media; they are structurally different texts that exploit the multi-directional

Figure 2.11 *Hamlet: A Murder Mystery*, a videogame based on Kenneth Branagh's *Hamlet* and published by Castle Rock Entertainment and EMME in 1998, offers multiple levels of literary gameplay, even enabling players to change the ending of Shakespeare's tragedy. Copyright Pantheon Studios, Inc.

feedback loops offered by the medium. Computer games draw on their audiences' (players') inputs, require participation, and give feedback and rewards. (Humphreys, 2005)

Today, the videogame industry has annual sales of roughly $10 billion—triple the revenues of just a decade earlier (Meacham, 2010). A 2010 study by the Kaiser Family Foundation found that most boys and male adolescents spend at least 1 hour per day playing videogames, compared with an average of 25 minutes reading books.[17] Nor is video gaming the exclusive preserve of children and young adults. Surveys indicate that the average videogame player, whether using platform or online games, is 33 years old (ESA, 2008).

The Internet

The advent of the Internet once again profoundly changed the media landscape and its relationship to storytelling. Recent studies show that as early as 2007, people around the globe began to spend as much time using the Internet as they did watching television; in some territories, Internet usage exceeded time spent in front of the television display.[18] In the process, media use became not just a local or a national phenomenon, but a global one. Indeed, although the Internet was previously an English-language preserve, Anglophone sites now account for only 27.5% of all web sites worldwide. The second largest language group is Chinese (22.6%), followed by Spanish (7.8%) and Japanese (5.3%).

Once again, this development was not only the result of technological changes, but also of the growing consensus in the electronics industry for the need to establish joint standards—a vital aspect of the digital revolution that is often misunderstood or ignored in the literature. In 1986, for example, well before the Internet became a mass medium, Sony and Apple coauthored a standard for digital consumer cameras called mini-DV (digital video) with an attendant computer interface called FireWire. Grudgingly adopted by Microsoft for Windows-based computers, this revolutionary new product placed true-digital video in the hands of the consumer through the deceptively simple conceit of digitizing the signal *before* it was recorded to tape. Although few would realize it, with this invention Apple and Sony had created a cheap and easy way for consumers to produce digital video and subsequently upload their footage from camera to personal computers and onto web sites such as YouTube.

The second major factor was the standardization of a format in which such video would be disseminated over the Web, commonly referred to as *streaming video* (or podcast video, as distinct from downloadable video files, which are received and stored on the user's computer). One of the first streaming video standards, Real Video, proved a failure, partly because of the high licensing costs imposed by Real on client host computers. But by the early 21st century, as high-bandwidth transmission penetrated the majority of American homes, other standards such as those employed in cellular telephony (known as H.264) had become dominant. Today, few consumers who capture video with their cell phones and upload it to their Facebook page are aware of these standards, but without them the digital media revolution would not have been possible.

With Internet-based social media such as Facebook, YouTube, and scores of others, the engagement of narrative and medium has come full circle, as Part II of this chapter explores. Rather than a mere consumer of stories, as in the case of novels, or the manipulation of narrative, as in the case of videogames, individuals around the globe have become both author and publisher of stories themselves. Social media and the broad availability of digital acquisition devices enable us to create, shape, and interpret stories as we see fit.

The Apple iPad

In the latest and perhaps most important departure from the Aristotelian narrative model, the oldest narrative medium in the world—the bound book—is following the phonograph record and videocassette into the digital domain, to a format called the electronic book or e-book. First-generation e-book readers, such as Amazon's *Kindle,* were limited to the display of text. However, second-generation devices, most notably the Apple iPad, which was first introduced in 2010, incorporate all of the multimedia and Web-browsing features common in advanced laptop computers.[19] These advanced e-book devices are in the process of nurturing an entirely new form of literature that blends the hypertext capabilities of the Web with the multimedia

richness of embedded and streaming media—or what Roland Barthes once called *the ideal textuality.* These digital books, referred to in the publishing industry as "enhanced e-books," offer not only a plethora of hyperlinks to Web sources scattered throughout the text, but also numerous embedded multimedia modules that each offer a new dimension to the story. Like the multimedia entertainment titles of the 1990s, they aim to appeal to a whole range of senses beyond the imaginative resonance of mere words, enlisting the power of music, art, animation, and drama in the service of entertaining and educating the reader (Figure 2.12).

As a corollary, these *hypermedia* may begin to blur the sharply distinct roles of reader and writer in traditional literature, as Landow foresaw (Landow, 1997). In other words, the narrative construct of a fiction or nonfiction work is no longer the exclusive responsibility of the author: for the literary experience to be fully actualized, the intervention of the reader is equally essential. Significantly, that experience is unique for anyone "reading" the work—in Bolter's words, "the inevitable next step" toward a literary model without formal or structural limitations (Bolter, 1991). What's more, it is a literary form that, theoretically, can continuously renew itself by virtue of links to Web sources, unlike printed works that by definition refer to "factual or fictive events that have already taken place" (Blok, 2002). As such, books of infinite virtual textuality could liberate us from what Coover has coined literary *tyranny,* in which the "compulsory author-directed movement" of linear narratives leaves readers passive and unengaged (Coover, 1992).

Naturally, this form of digital literature is still in its infancy, precisely because the media tablets themselves are relatively new, and the literary world has yet to grasp the full potential of multimedia hypertext. And there are plenty of pitfalls. As several authors on the subject have argued, digital literature may ultimately produce narratives without beginning or end that, like the soap operas of an earlier age, can meander along for months or even years, carried along by the constant refreshing of Web media postings served by its hyperlinks. It would mean the final *coup de grâce* to the old Aristotelian model.

Would we want to read such books? Would we feel happier if liberated from the "tyranny" of linear narrative? Is there a readership for books in which the author merely indicates some broad parameters of the story, and meaning and continuity become the responsibility of the reader? Or in the words of Blok, "Must digital novels necessarily behave

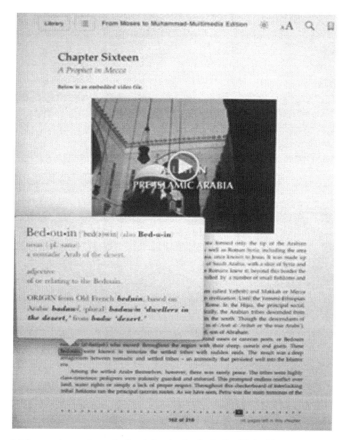

Figure 2.12 *From Moses to Muhammad,* an enhanced e-book for the Apple iPad published by Apple iBooks, offers color maps, hyperlinks, and video documentaries embedded in the text.

non-sequentially all the time and regardless of the outcome?" (Blok, 2002). In the end, will Aristotle triumph after all?

Part II. The Future of Media Narrative: Online, Participatory, and Multidimensional

Fish are unaware of the water.

Ancient proverb

Introduction

As shown in the foregoing, our current technological trajectory promises unfathomable, rollercoaster innovation with no braking system. Although the ride is exhilarating, it moves so quickly that we typically do not have time to think about the possible unintended consequences that might accompany it. The result is that we often find ourselves victims of the future, subject to the unforeseen repercussions of our own invention. Not knowing what tomorrow's Google newscast

will bring in terms of the next earth-shattering innovation that will change absolutely everything has become part of the Faustian bargain. We are allowed to have godlike power in the palms of our hands, so long as we are willing to accept that we won't know what form that power will take until it arrives. At that point, if you are a pessimist, it is too late. For optimists, it is the first day of the rest of our digital lives.

Although the future may not be what it used to be,[20] one thing hasn't changed—what Dertouzos (2001) calls "the ancient human" in each of us. That is, although we can think of wireless bits of someone else's digital narrative flying through the air and landing on someone else's screen half a world away as something entirely new, we can also view it simply as our latest effort to use the communication tools available to us to improve communication with others, a basic human desire that dates back to our earliest ancestors. Both perspectives are accurate and important in constructing a complete picture of the human condition in the digital age.

The tie that binds us to our ancestors is that both ancient and digital-age humans crave community and all the things that make community possible: survival, meaningful living, effective communication, cultural stability, purposeful education for our children, creative expression and, above all, narrative to tie it all together. Achieving community has always depended on developing a citizenship covenant, cemented through narrative, which provides the context that allows these elements of community to flourish. But life in the global village requires a covenant that covers a much broader area of social endeavor than ever before. It needs to embrace many cultures, time zones, and online communities. It needs to build on an expanded notion of behavior that transcends the physical and embraces the virtual, while somehow integrating both. And above all, the new covenant needs to assume that everyone has a story to tell and the right to tell it on the great stage of the Internet.

As we move forward into an uncertain future, we borrow a metaphor from Marshall McLuhan, whom I was fortunate to have as a teacher at the University of Toronto, to help us understand the road ahead of us: We steer our car going forward by looking into the rearview mirror to see where we have just been (McLuhan, 1967).[21] As we do so, we hang on to consistent cultural threads like lifelines. We have learned a great deal about those lifelines through our consistent response to the appearance of new media throughout centuries, namely: no matter what technology awaits us in the future, first and foremost we will find ways to tell stories with it.

Storytelling and Technology

Hopefully we will also find ways to tell stories *about* it. That is, our technology should not only facilitate our ongoing dance with narrative expression, it should also inspire us to ask questions about how it does so. If we want to understand our evolving narrative as an expression of our social evolution, then we must look to the nature of our communication tools for clues. Now more than ever we need to see the evolution of our new media narrative through at least two facets of the McLuhan lens (1967). First, as cliché as it may sound, the medium is still the message in that the nature of a communication medium itself shades, shapes and, in some cases, determines the nature of the content that it carries. The bottom line here is that technology is not neutral, and that "media is a filter while often pretending to be a clear window" (Goodman, year, page). Technology and media have built-in biases. A right-handed catcher's

mitt favors the right-handed. A cell phone that only supports English text excludes those who only read Spanish. Our artifacts encourage some behaviors while discouraging others. Understanding how this happens with our evolving narrative tools will tell us much about who we are, and who we are becoming (Figure 2.13).

Second, we need to understand the evolving narrative landscape in terms of McLuhan's "figure-ground" perspective (1989): Figure is what we notice, whereas ground is the environment in which figures appear. As with any environment, "ground" escapes our immediate notice, although it massages us totally. Thus we notice, and perhaps even reflect on, having a cell phone during the first days we own it. After that point, it becomes invisible—just another thread in the media tapestry that envelopes, comforts, and shapes us while we are not looking. If we are to understand the changing nature of media narrative so that we can ultimately understand how it changes us psychologically, sociologically, and psychically, then we must see it first. Once we do, we can begin to understand how our narrative changes because of it, and how ancient threads of narrative persist despite the ways in which technology recasts it in new dimensions using new voices.

Figure 2.13 Eric McLuhan in the Foreground, his Father Marshall Over His Shoulder, and James Joyce Behind Him in Glasses.

Joyce's work was critical to the McLuhans as they formed their theories of media.

Photo collage by Ken Steacy, illustration by Joan Steacy, photo by Michael McLuhan. Used with permission.

There is no better way to proceed with such an inquiry than by examining the evolution of narrative facilitated by the World Wide Web. After all, the Web is at once the new tool set, studio, stage and distribution hub for our narrative endeavors.

The Many Faces of the Web: From pre-Web to Web 3.0 and Beyond

As of 2011, it is hard to imagine a time without the Web at our fingertips, despite the fact that it had not become generally adopted until a mere 15 years ago. Once figure, in McLuhan's terms, the World Wide Web is now so firmly ground and so embedded in our psyche that we only notice it when it malfunctions. For the most part, normal life now consists of continually, and rather unconsciously, adapting to the ongoing narrative possibilities presented to us through the Web. Many of these come in the form of free, powerful social media and media development software tools that are used "in the cloud," that is, online without needing to download them. Our desktop has morphed into a Webtop. In terms of the other software that we purchase and use in more conventional ways, the Web has become our newspaper and trade magazine that tells us about it; storefront and product delivery system when we decide to purchase it; and support system when we need help understanding it. There is no escaping the Web.

One way to consider the evolving nature of Web-induced narrative is in terms of "web eras." When Tim O'Reilly announced that we had entered the Web's second major developmental stage, and dubbed it *Web 2.0* (2005), he suddenly made the "Web" *figure*. We were forced to see the Web again, if only briefly, and think about it in terms of its evolution as well as its permanence and unpredictably. If there was suddenly a Web 2.0, then there must have been a Web 1.0, and inevitably a Web 3.0, and so on. As we consider the nature of mediated narrative in terms of the Web's evolution, we will repeatedly discover that the meta-message of the digital age is simply this: Because of the variety of free, powerful multimedia tools that comprise the Web 2.0 narrative palette, a new reality has emerged; namely, that everyone gets to tell their own story in their own way, individually and collectively, on the great stage of the Internet.

This new reality began in pre-Web days.

The pre-Web Era

There are two aspects of pre-Web life to consider: (1) the world of personal computing, irrespective of connectivity; and (2) the online world before a publicly available Internet. Each is addressed in turn.

THE WORLD OF PERSONAL COMPUTING

The impact of personal computing on personal narrative capability is best exemplified by the *word processor,* one of the first tools to emerge as symptomatic of the shift from a world in which the vast majority of people consumed media created by a very few—often referred to as the world of *mass media*—to a new world in which everyone could both consume and produce media. The new world was facilitated by new narrative technology that allowed storytellers to do something that was unheard of during the era of the typewriter: erase. The ease with which text could be rearranged and reedited with impunity using a word processor turned a mass media audience into a society whose members could easily create and revise content themselves. Although global distribution of personalized content would require the Internet, still a few years in the offing, simply having one's own computer and printer was the first step in transforming a mass media landscape into a world of mass personalized media.

Although the word processor became "ground" to us many years ago, there was an historical moment in which it was figure for some of the leading computer scientists of world. It is captured dramatically in the book *Tools for Thought,* in which author Howard Rheingold (1985) chronicles the rise of personal computing by examining the efforts of some of its earliest pioneers. Among them was Douglas Engelbart, an electrical engineer from the Stanford Research Institute. A bit of an anomaly, Engelbart was trying to rescue computing from the throes of scientific abstraction by actually creating something that the general public could use. Toward that end, he staked his career on a presentation at the Fall Joint Computer Conference in San Francisco in 1968, which attracted an eclectic but highly influential group of computing enthusiasts who gathered to hear what he and others of his ilk had to say. His reputation preceded him, so when he took the stage it was before an appreciative audience. But when audience members watched him demonstrate, among other things, a new kind of software called a word processor that allowed him to effortlessly edit, copy, paste, and move text—and even combine it with images—they did something that no one could have expected from a group of computer scientists. They gave him a standing ovation.

Whether they realized it or not, they were also cheering for a public that had long been dissuaded from writing simply because of the sheer laboriousness of the rewriting process, whether using pen and paper or typewriter. In retrospect, the message implicit in Engelbart's demonstration was very clear: Writing—that cornerstone of literacy, narrative, and modern storytelling—was now within everyone's grasp. A world of readers was about to become a world of writers.

One of the first software applications that justified the microcomputer and rescued it from the domain of the hobbyist was in fact the word processor. Nearly 50 years later, the *word processor* is at the heart of one of the most enduring software constellations ever produced, Microsoft Office. Similarly, a word processor was Google's first foray into providing publically available tool software through its Google apps suite. As with all software applications included in the suite, the word processor is free, easy to use, and universally available. It is also compatible with its chief commercial competitor, Word, presenting a brazen challenge to Microsoft's dominance in the world of narrative development software. It is interesting to ponder the following historical possibility: How different would the microcomputer revolution have been had the first commercially available microcomputers, like the Apple IIe and IBM PC, booted up in a word processing program rather than the BASIC programming language?

The kind of empowerment represented by the word processor has been repeated throughout the advance of digital tools in all areas of media production. As of this writing, it is easy to find free, powerful software on the Web that allows anyone to create and edit a number of media in ways that were once reserved for the media elite, who had specialized skills and access to expensive, specialist software. Currently, free image editing software, audio development software, and even video editing software is abundant and ever evolving.

The contribution that such software makes to the expansion and democratization of modern, media-based storytelling cannot be underestimated. This author can report a revelation similar to that experienced by those watching Engelbart's presentation with regard to my first experience using free, user-friendly video editing software. Like many early adopters of microcomputers, I had been trying to share information between a video camera and a computer ever since it was possible to do so. This was a process that, in the early days of digital video editing, typically required a sledgehammer, a shaman, and more money than a university that was skeptical

of the future of computers was willing to commit. Digital video editing was immensely frustrating simply because of the many insidious, arcane technical challenges that made the process unenjoyable and rarely as successful as I would have liked.

Then in 2000 I was introduced to iMovie—a free video editing software package created for the Macintosh. The first time I plugged my video camera into my computer, iMovie prompted me with the question, "I see you have attached a video camera to your computer. Would you like to download its content?" I wept. Finally, those of us interested in developing digital narrative were free to focus on our stories rather than on resolving the many insidious, quirky technical issues that impeded the simplest of productions. Years later, the media production cycle would be fully democratized when YouTube provided everyone the ability to become video publishers. Doing so presented a serious counterthrust to the world of mass media by allowing anyone with an inexpensive video camera and home Internet connection to establish their own TV station.

In the egalitarian spread of narrative tools we see one of the first major dimensional shifts of McLuhan's maxim, "the medium is the message," which he later updated to "the medium is the massage" (1967). Although he meant both primarily as an observation about how the technical nature of a medium limited and massaged the content it carried, the democratization of media development meant that message and content would now be affected by the changing nature of those who actually created the content. Before publically available tools and distribution outlets, the very few professional *mediasts* (my term for those who create media) who had access to media tools tended to create media that focused on professional objectives. However, when everyone had access to media tools, the message became much more diverse, more populist, and much more of a challenge to the status quo.

pre-Web, Part II. The Online World Before the Internet

For many, the online world began with their first Internet experience. But the reality is that the online world was alive and evolving well before the Internet went public in the early 1990s. By the 1970s, mainframe e-mail communication was prevalent in academia, although typically limited only to those who were connected to the same mainframe. During the 1980s, mainframes used the phone system and ARPAnet (Advanced Research Projects Agency, the forerunner of the Internet) as distribution systems to connect to one another, linking universities and other professional organizations throughout the world. Services arose, such as USENET and BITNET, which took advantage of the communication channels established by e-mail and early file sharing systems to begin to allow users to organize in groups. Both services supported group-based narrative, USENET in the form of newsgroups, and BITNET in the form of listservs, both of which functioned more or less as e-mail–based mailing lists in which everyone could be both sender and receiver.[22] Both encouraged the democratization of public narrative by allowing millions of people to engage in public conversation once reserved, in a very limited sense, to the op-ed pages of a newspaper. Generally speaking, discussions were international in scope, open to anyone with access to them, and built around topics of interest, from sociology to Star Trek to sexual deviancy. Both survive in some form today. Both foretold the social media revolution we now take for granted.

Although it is not the intent of this chapter to delve deeply into the technical aspects of the developments presented here, it is at least metaphorically important to note that both USENET and BITNET used a *peer-to-peer* connection structure. That is, there was no centralized mainframe that sustained the system. Instead, control and administration were shared among all the computers that participated in the distribution network. This was a serious change to the top-down, mass media approach of controlling communication channels, and is the same approach used by the Internet today.

Both USENET and BITNET had as their informal charge the promotion of narrative created by users, rather than professional mediasts. As narrative began to shift from the few with broadcast licenses, to the many with distributed computers, commercial alternatives to university and corporate networks arose. Proprietary services like CompuServe and the Source,[23] both started during the 1980s, foretold the commercialization of the incipient social media revolution by providing e-mail, listservs, and bulletin boards on a subscription basis. Ultimately, the shift to media that depended on user-generated content and participatory narrative would be seen as one of the early steps that ultimately led to Facebook (Figure 2.14).

It is interesting to note that in addition to the development of more distributed approaches to media, the public had another response to a mediascape dominated by mass media: the development of an area of inquiry called media literacy. This area

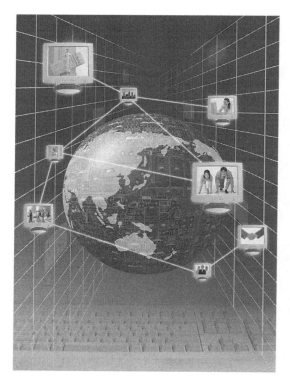

Figure 2.14 Global, participatory media is now the new reality and forms "the ground" of our daily experience.

was concerned almost entirely with making media "figure" by girding consumers with the critical thinking skills necessary to withstand the onslaught of someone else's narrative, much of which was aimed at selling a product or a perspective to the mass consuming public. The feeling was that consumers were lambs being led to psychological slaughter every time an advertisement aired, and that the public needed special skills to protect itself. Media literacy continues to be a staple of many educational curricula in the United Kingdom, Canada, Australia, and other countries. It is conspicuous by its absence in the United States (see also Chapter 6).

Although print was part of the mass media structure, it had not inspired the call to media literacy. Our collective suspicion was not aroused until radio and television arrived, and for good reason. Whereas you could stop reading a magazine or newspaper, and think about what you had just read, you could not do so with radio and television, which kept moving, compelling customers to commit to the moment, while simultaneously depriving them of reflection time. Thus, media literacy was dedicated to understanding the persuasive nature of electronic broadcast media. Doing so required consumers to be able to critically assess media, particularly in light of the fact that professional psychologists had been engaged to guide professional mediasts on how to sell to the mass audience. After all, it was the psychologists who understood how to penetrate the judgmental mind and head straight for the reptilian brain, where our fears, instincts, and buying potential lay.

The shift from mass media to participatory media eventually would lead to the ultimate realization of two more facets of McLuhan's world view.

First, to McLuhan, all technology, particularly media, was an extension of ourselves in some way; thus the subtitle of his most famous book, *Understanding Media: The Extensions of Man* (1964). For example, a car extended our feet through wheels, our ears through the radio, and our eyes through headlights. Electronics and media were an extension of our nervous system, both as input and output systems. Mass media gave us ears and eyes. Participatory social media gave us body and voice.

Second, interactive media gave us a glimpse of McLuhan's "global village" (1989), a perspective popularized throughout the 1970s and beyond. His vision of extending the backyard, over-the-fence neighborhood conversation on a global scale through electronic means was only partially realized in a world of radio and television, in which few talked and most listened. (Think in terms of a gabby neighbor who won't let you get a word in edgewise.) In a world of e-mail and interactive electronic communication, the feedback loop necessary to make a global village a reality was coming into view. Now that gabby neighbor would need to listen to you.

If participatory media had been a fad, then electronic communication might have stopped with e-mail and listservs; however, it didn't. Soon to follow were bulletin boards, which promoted a one-to-many communication structure in which anyone could assume the role of broadcaster. Soon thereafter came computer conferencing systems, which offered the first real glimpse of a community in virtual space because of the number of different kinds of public and private relationships and group activities it supported. Anthropologist Edward T. Hall (1966) appeared prophetic as his rules of proxemics, which articulated the ways in which human beings interact in physical space, played out in virtual space. Hall identified four kinds of human social space: public (one-to-many, such as a performance, lecture, or mass media broadcast), social (many-to-many; such as an open social gathering), personal (few-to-few, such as an invitation-only group function; or predefined social group, such as

a family or a class of students) and intimate (one-to-one). Each communication space encouraged a different kind of narrative. Collectively they form the communication backbone necessary to sustain any community. As people figured out how to craft narrative using computer conferencing systems and other emerging electronic tool sets, Hall's structures appeared in virtual space. Humans, bound and determined to organize themselves as well as share their stories, crafted the emerging mediascape in their own image.

Web 1.0

Eras are purposely hard to pinpoint. They are meant to embrace transitional periods that flow into one another, to emphasize the fluidity of history. The era of Web 1.0 is no different.

Recall that Web 1.0 did not exist until Web 2.0 was announced, creating Web 1.0 by implication. A reasonable approximation for the beginning of the Web 1.0 era is roughly 1992. Around this time, the U.S. government divested itself of its proprietary military and scientific network called ARPANet, dubbed much of it *the Internet,* and made it available to the public. A symbolic date for the ending of the Web 1.0 era is the year 2000. This is roughly the year that Blogger—to date the most popular, free blogging service created—was launched. As of Blogger, the era of modern social media, now referred to as the era of Web 2.0, began in earnest. Note that O'Reilly and his colleagues did not coin the phrase "Web 2.0" until 2005. Thus, it is in retrospect that we identify this crucial milepost in Web history.

In some ways Web 1.0 represented a slight setback on the road to public, participatory narrative. Whereas the pre-Web days began to flush out nascent digital communities, Web 1.0 temporarily returned power to the technicians. In the earliest days of Web 1.0, one had to learn the hyper text markup language (HTML) to produce Web material—that is, to make a Web page. Many were not up to the task. The age of blogs and free, easy-to-use Web page templates that allowed non-technicians to become Web developers was still a number of years in the future. Meanwhile, the social media tools developed during the previous decade, such as e-mail, listservs, and computer conferencing, were still in wide use, often running on proprietary systems. These systems remained fairly accessible and in many ways existed as a parallel universe as the Web evolved.

Two of the most notable advances of Web 1.0 that concern our discussion of digital narrative are hypertext and the ability to search the Web as a single community. Hypertext, which we know today simply as Web links, gave us our "click here, go there" narrative culture. Although "ground" to us now, links were figure in the early years of Web development as we wondered how best to use this new capability that was simultaneously confusing and empowering, and that forever changed the relationship between writer and reader. Media producers were forced to give up the linear format, and adapt to readers who quickly came to expect to be able to determine their own narrative flow when reading Web material.

Web 1.0's second advance, the ability to scan the entire Web in a single search, gave rise to what we now call the *digital community,* an abstract term used to describe the very real experience of being connected to others who are scattered throughout the world in places unknown to us, who may be total strangers whom we never meet in person or speak to in real time. Searching the world preceded our ability to draw from it to develop relationships, form groups, and find the information necessary to inform our efforts. Although this started in pre-Web days, it came to fruition during Web 1.0 as we began to harness HTML to create autobiographical presences in the form of Web pages. As we did so, we met others with whom we could share stories and create collective narratives.

Web 2.0

Recall our earlier discussion about the need for communities to produce covenants to sustain themselves, and that narrative was important to help produce the kind of shared meaning among community members that gave those covenants context and power. In the era of Web 2.0, the covenant that occurs through social media happens on an unfathomable scale and in a very different way than previously seen historically: Rather than a shared narrative and mythology, the sharing itself *is* the covenant. This was explained in more practical terms by Tim O'Reilly. When asked to define Web 2.0, he responded: "Web 2.0 is the understanding that the network is the platform…and that the cardinal rule is that users add value."[24] The new covenant, then, is that narrative is social almost to the point of codependence. Without each other, narrative is hollow, if not impossible. Notice that the topic around which we might gather to tell our stories is not relevant here; it is the gathering that is important. A clearer example of the medium being the message scarcely exists.

Although many might define Web 2.0 in terms of all the free narrative tools available to them, such as Blogger, Face-book, Ning, and Twitter, we gain a more thorough perspective by considering it in terms of the changes it has facilitated. What follows are just some of these changes that relate directly to the evolving nature of narrative.

First, we shift from the read-only Web to the read/write Web. Tools such as Blogger, Face-book, and other common Web 2.0 social media applications make the development of narrative and community relatively free, painless, and fun, even for non-technicians. One could consider this in the following way: The narrative model shifts from the library to impromptu poetry readings in the park. Libraries are populated with fixed texts, that consumers come to read, whereas poetry readings invite anyone to stand on a soapbox and hold forth. In the era of Web 2.0, everyone has the opportunity to be both poet and audience member.

Second, as Tim O'Reilly implied, Web participants go from being just value *seekers* to being also value *creators*. It used to be that only professional mediasts determined which stories would be presented to the public. Even though media developers may have conducted studies and run focus groups to determine what customers wanted, in the end there was a strict delineation between those who made media and those who consumed it. As customers we accepted their definition of value because we had little choice in the matter. In contrast, in the Web 2.0 world, customers and users add value. Imagine Face-book without users adding value—it falls apart immediately. Another way to consider this development is that everyone is a content provider and a customer, and the two are mutually supportive if not codependent.

Third, in the era of Web 2.0 we enjoy a narrative toolset that is historically unrivaled in terms of the kinds of narrative we can construct, both individually and collectively. Hall (1966) helped us understand the different kinds of social narrative spaces that we seek. Through his theory of multiple intelligences, educational psychologist Howard Gardner (2011) helped us understand that we all possess a number of intelligences, and we all learn and express ourselves differently, using a number of different tools, media, languages, and social contexts. In Web 2.0, Hall meets Gardner. New communities form in which its members can communicate in new ways, using tools that proliferate daily and keep pushing the outer edge of narrative possibility in multimedia format. From blogs, to wikis, to virtual worlds and sites that animate a picture of your favorite pet, there is certainly something for everyone.

Fourth, we enjoy access to an unprecedented cornucopia of content resources. Another way to consider this is that the mass media dynamic of one-to-many is still preserved, but in a very interesting way. Each of us can, in Hall's terminology, assume the helm of public space, broadcasting to the many. We might do this by posting a movie to YouTube, providing a podcast resource, or simply maintaining an interesting, informational web site that others want to visit. We also have the opportunity to be among "the many," as we hunt for and gather information in the overcrowded infosphere. In addition, we have all the narrative tools at our disposal to create all of Hall's spaces, a requirement for having a healthy community. We can post a video on YouTube video (public), invite public discussion about it (social), discuss it within the context of a university class (personal), and have a very private conversation about it with our confidants (intimate). The bottom line is that the members of the digital community have pursued mass customization on a scale that seems to defy the odds, largely because the desire and the tools to do so merged in the era of Web 2.0.

Lastly, Web 2.0 has enabled us to live in an era in which creativity cross-pollinates exponentially. A primary shift from Web 1.0 to Web 2.0 is a shift from the simple emergence of new narrative tools, to the creation of a global, entrepreneurial, narrative environment in which we use these tools. In earlier times, developers labored in isolation. Now, thanks to the vast, inclusive reach of the Internet, it is as though all the Web programmers and entrepreneurs of the world, as well as the less technical people who simply use Web 2.0 tools and services, occupy the same art studio. We look over each other's shoulders for inspiration and conversation about new ideas and possibilities. The result is that new tools, applications, and projects are being creating at a remarkable rate as everyone builds on everyone else's efforts.

There are specific developments often associated with Web 2.0 that merit special mention, because they contribute to the evolving nature of storytelling in ways that suggest a rich and unpredictable future. They include developments such as virtual environments, augmented reality, and robotics. These are addressed in the section, Web 4.0 and Beyond.

Web 3.0

Although the future is open to anyone to explore and name, the term *Web 3.0* seems to be already claimed, and has largely become synonymous with *the Semantic Web*. To understand the Semantic Web, we must see it as a response to a problem that is truly unique to the digital age: information overload (Ohler, 2008).

The informal mantra of the information age has been "the more information the better." But when a Google search for "global warming" yields well over 30 million hits in less than a second, as it currently does, we are compelled to ask, "What on earth do most people do with overwhelming search results like these?" If they are at all typical, they follow the first five to ten links, read a bit at each location and unconsciously cultivate the illusion of being informed.

This is much more dangerous than we think, especially given that Google's page rank algorithm ranks search results by popularity rather than source credibility. And although Google regularly adjusts its algorithm, largely to stay one step ahead of the search engine optimizers (SEOs), who try to outsmart Google's algorithm so as to give their clients preeminent placement in Google search results, Google has been very clear that a staple of their algorithm continues to be the popularity of a web site as a function of how many other sites link to it. In the meantime, we can only hope that popular web sites garner prominence because of the credibility of the information they provide.

The reality is we have gone from information underload to overload in about 25 years, and are left to wonder what kind of improvement this represents. After all, there simply isn't time to read a fraction of what's available via the Web, let alone reflect on it or determine whether it is fact, political spin or total baloney.

The Semantic Web to the rescue. It has the potential of bringing the Web much closer to Tim Berners-Lee's original conception of it as a universal network in which computers adapt to humans rather than the other way around (Miller, 2008). For this to happen, the Semantic Web must first make information much more understandable to machines. This is accomplished through a recoding of the Web so that the information it holds is identifiable on a word-by-word and datum-by-datum basis.

As ominous as recoding the Web sounds, there are three points to consider. First, the Web has already been recoded many times. The coding behind a web page created in 1992 is very different than the coding for the same web page today because it has been updated several times. Second, the work force that will undertake this project numbers in the millions. Everyone will recode his or her own small corner of the Internet. And third, new tools will emerge that can translate the old Web into the Semantic Web in real time, allowing a blend of Web 2.0 and Web 3.0. The point here is that the Semantic Web will most assuredly come to pass, and will arise must faster than many might expect.

Why should those interested in the evolution of media-based storytelling care? An example will help explain.

Today's search engine it is a blunt tool that returns very crude results. A typical Web search for "global warming" finds the presence of that phrase in a web page, and then tells the searcher where the web page is. The searcher is then left to do a good deal of grunt work as she or he digs through the results. In contrast, a search of the Semantic Web will "understand" the phrase "global warming" and link it to other concepts related to it, effectively second-guessing the kinds of context and connections the searcher was looking for at the outset. The result is that the search will produce something that reminds us of a report with chapters, headings, and summaries. The results will be imbued with much more intelligence than the results we generate today.

No doubt, this will inform the stories we tell. No doubt, new combinations of traditional and emerging media will emerge from the Semantic Web that will invite professionals and amateurs alike to create mashups and other digitalia that will expand our concept of narrative. But our primary concern with Web 3.0 and its impact on narrative should be simply this: The relationships that will drive the linkages that are established among the data will rewrite reality as we know it. For the most part, these relationships will be too far below the surface for us to see.

Consider this. It is quite possible for the semantic Web to link the phrase "global warming" with a number of scientific concepts, such as "greenhouse effect" and "ozone depletion." This is very handy, because it informs our search in ways that we either didn't think to ask or didn't have the tools to ask. But a semantic web programmer could also link "global warming" to "environmentalist," which another programmer has linked to "anti-prosperity" and "pro-big government." Alternately, it is also possible for programmers to link "global warming" to "preservationist," which itself is linked to "averting environmental catastrophe" and "ensuring that natural resources are left for our children."

Programmers will make choices like these. And the choices they make will be forwarded to other computers participating in the global Web of information, which will automatically begin replicating these choices in the development of semantic Web link associations. The result is that we will probably not see the relationships on which their choices are based. Instead, we will just see the search results. Will we be able to outsmart the systems, the way that search engine optimizers try to outsmart the Google algorithm today? Perhaps. But the semantic Web is much more integrated and suffused than today's Web. The cat-and-mouse game between semantic purveyors and semantic detectives defines a gray area that embraces the sum total of our knowledge.

Thus, we come to a startling conclusion: The efforts of programmers to address our need to navigate information overload will yield a kind of story all by itself. Our search, to again quote Goodman (2003), will "be a filter while pretending to be an open window." It will be a semiformed narrative that we will then use as though it were raw data. Hopefully there will be storytellers who tell stories about the Semantic Web, how it works, and what it is doing to our perception of reality. Hopefully there will be storytellers who treat the Semantic Web as figure, rather than ground.

Web 4.0 and Beyond

To McLuhan, artists comprise our most effective early warning system. More than anyone else, they have the ability to look into the future and tell stories about the unintended consequences of today's activities, perspectives, and inventions. Science fiction writers, filmmakers, and poets have been warning us about our future selves for centuries. And they do have somewhat of a track record. Television shows such as *Star Trek* and movies such as *2001: A Space Odyssey* seemed prescient when cell phones and space stations appeared.

Although it is not possible to provide a detailed analysis of how current technological trends may affect the evolution of media narrative, it is possible to summarize some of the impacts of some of the more generally accepted trends.

First, one of the next steps in Web evolution beyond the Semantic Web is the connection of things. That is, we go from connecting pages (Web 2.0), to connecting data (Web 3.0), to connecting all of our "stuff." Everything from shoes to cars will contain chips, often referred to as radio frequency identification (RFID) chips, which make them networkable, and thus part of the Web. We may question how a pair of shoes adds to our narrative until we realize that they can tell others where we are and where we are headed, as well as the location of others who like the same shoes and the location of stores that have those shoes on sale. In the end, these capabilities connect us to others who share our interests and might be interested in our stories.

Second, we will continue to develop alternate selves that tell alternate stories of our lives. Although this happens in a variety of ways, currently a very important method involves using a virtual environment, such as *Second Life*, which is available largely for free through any home Internet connection and currently has more than 15 million members. Although *Second Life* derives much from the gaming world, it is very different from the gaming world in that it has no inherent goal structure. One cannot "win" at *Second Life*. Instead, users enter the Second Life virtual environment as avatars (animated figures they use to represent themselves) and behave much as tourists do who are visiting a foreign country for the first time, stumbling about in a confused and excited manner as they traverse an immense learning curve.

However, *Second Life* (SL) offers users significant added value not often found in a typical tourist package. After they get their footing, SL users are free to change their appearances, often at no cost, by wearing any kind of clothing one might imagine, including new skins that appear to change their appearance at the biological level. Effectively, users "out" their inner desires.

Users can create homes using easy-to-learn 3D geometric tools. They can start businesses and make money that translates into real-life (RL) dollars. They can import images or movies they created in RL and share them in a number of ways, including through virtual art shows and public screenings. They can socialize by joining groups devoted to any number of interests, or by visiting one of the many meeting centers, beaches, bars, stores, impromptu electronic campfires, or hundreds of other kinds of venues that emerge in the SL landscape. They can also create relationships of a most intimate nature. And, they can fly. Although most communication in SL is in the form of texting, currently it supports a voice option. Given that users don't have to identify their RL identities in SL, they are free to reinvent themselves, and in so doing, reinvent whatever story they wish to project about themselves and their world.

Third, there is a convergence of a number of powerful technological developments that have led to a ubiquitous, continuous computer environment that is largely invisible to us but that follows us everywhere we go and enhances our narrative capabilities as it does so. At the epicenter of these developments is truly powerful mobile technology, which allows us to be continually plugged in, "always on, always on

you," as MIT professor Sherry Turkle (2008) refers says. Significant developments in artificial intelligence (AI) allow us to partner with our ubiquitous machines to make sense of our environment.

A particular application of AI is augmented reality (AR), which allows us to bathe ourselves in continuous data sources wherever we go so as to enlighten whatever we do. A basic description of AR follows.

In a typical AR application, two realities are blended on the screen of your cell phone: the one you point your phone at, and information about what is on your screen, which is supplied wirelessly. For example, you might point your AR-ready cell phone at a restaurant. Your phone would then "read" the restaurant sign, and download everything about the restaurant that was available about it, from operating hours to lunch specials. These two sources—the restaurant in front of you and the information it precipitated—literally blend together on your screen, thus *augmenting reality*. Often, you don't even need to point your phone, because your phone's GPS component knows where you are and can anticipate what you might want to know. Another example of AR is a clothing store mirror that allows you to blend your reflection with clothing available for purchase, allowing you to try on clothes without making a trip to the changing room. Medical applications of AR are under development, in which, for example, a patient's x-ray is supplemented by information from medical databases *as you are looking at the x-ray*. The possibilities for integrating the real and the augmented are endless, as are the possibilities for using AR in the development of narrative. One day we may be able to truly be beside ourselves with joy.

Living with ubiquitous computing is the new human condition, brought on by living in the tEcosystem, that secondary, technological ecosystem that we have created that consists of digital technology, connectivity, and the communication they facilitate (Ohler, 2007). This new condition allows us to create our stories on the go, wherever we are, with continuous access to secondary information sources to inform our activities. It also allows us to invite others, quickly if we like, should forming a smart mob[25] make sense at the moment. We are walking, talking, broadcasting media centers, with a good deal of audience participation.

Augmented reality and AI converge to add great value to our lives in the mediascape. A pair of shoes with a GPS chip not only links to a map, but also to secondary continuous data sources about the shoes and our location. Our shoes will be continually "on" because the act of walking generates enough electricity to keep them charged. In turn, they will charge our cell phone and whatever other digital devices enable us to be continuously connected to our data sources and the AI resources that help us understand our environment. We might connect to harmless factoids, like the fact that some of the raw materials used to make our shoes were mined nearby, or a report about inclement weather, suggesting we put on a different kind of shoes in the very near future.

But we might also connect to more important information, including who is nearby at the moment. Equally important is that fact that we will be someone else's factoid, as others determine we are nearby them. There are opportunities and dangers associated with this. The person nearby may be a friend, or perhaps an information savvy crook who has determined our socioeconomic status and made the educated guess that we may be carrying a lot of cash with us.

Fourth, nanotechnology and genetic engineering will allow us to reinvent ourselves at the biological level. We become a canvas as it were, on which we can recreate ourselves in whatever image we like. Ongoing discoveries in this arena have uncovered genetic links to everything from body type to athletic prowess. Our ability to manipulate our genes allows us to make manifest whatever hero we would like to become in our own life stories. Thus, life imitates art in that real life imitates Second life. It is important to note that these technologies will also allow us to generate new life forms, allowing us to forever alter the nature of our communities and our relationship with the natural world. The full extent of the kinds of stories we may tell, in which participants are completely of our own creation, defy current imagination.

Fifth, robotics continues to challenge our place in the scheme of things. In a sense robotics is the precursor to a world of new life forms—practice, as it were. Although we think of the future of robotics as being able to delegate mundane tasks to machines who are happy to oblige us, the reality is that robots will also be built that help our children at school and offer adults perspective about personal issues. We will find ourselves sharing stories not just with other people about the machines in our lives, but also with machines about the people in our lives. R2D2 and 3CPO, who appear in Star Wars as Campbellian hero assistants (Campbell, 2004) in the grand arc of the hero story, are robots. And they are highly effective, endearing robots, suggesting that in our next iteration of the future we may be *their* assistants.

Then we will listen to robots tell stories about us. In fact, they may routinely beat us at Jeopardy one day, following in the footsteps of IBM's Watson.[26]

Sixth, a desire for a multisensory experience will push narrative innovation in interesting directions, all of which are intended to do one thing: Restore some of the sensory input we have been missing in a world dominated by telecommunications. After all, for some time now we have been basically settling for a mediated environment that projects only two of the five senses (sight and sound), but that is changing.

For some time gamers have had rumble seats that allow them to feel movement implicit in the video game they are playing. The Wii, which has been with us for several years, allows gamers to project and sense body movement. As I write this, a story is circulating about a kissing machine that allows bussers to sense the tongue movements of others via the Internet.[27] Another machine in the news is the iPhone tickle app, which simulates a tickle for someone on the receiving end of your phone call.[28] One senses that all of this is just the tip of the sensory reemergence iceberg.

The desire for a more sensory rich narrative experience is nothing new. For example, Smellovision, which made its one and only appearance in movie theaters to accompany the movie *Scent of Mystery* in 1960, released odors during the film to enhance the sensory experience. Although it only lasted for one movie, the desire to add scent to the theatrical experience is beginning to resurface. Tom Hanks World War II movie, which currently plays only in the World War II Museum in New Orleans, fills the auditorium with the smell of gunpowder during battle scenes, and drops simulated snow on audience members to enhance their appreciation of travails of conducting warfare during the winter.

What is different now, and what commands our attention in this arena, is that narrative developers are getting more creative about adding richer sensory experiences to their work because of the existence of great bandwidth, processing speed, and powerful tools. As new narrative forms take shape that use more sensory stimuli, they will move us closer to a storytelling experience that approximates real life—whatever real life becomes in the future—while adding value to that experience in ways that defy current imagination.

Last, transmedia is the glue that will hold the new world of narrative together because of what transmedia guru Henry Jenkins (2006) calls *media convergence*. Because all media can work together, storytellers can tell stories across many channels. For example, Harry Potter is a franchise consisting of books, movies and the online world *Pottermore*. The TV show Heroes combines books, graphic novels, TV episodes and memorabilia, each of which tells a different part of an overall story. In the case of some media-based stories, alternative reality games and the use of GPS include RL events and locations as part of the narrative. Most importantly, in some cases fans can actually have a say in terms of the story through online portals. It is easy to think in terms of all the impacts discussed above coming together into an organic, yet organized transmedia platform. Developers have just scratched transmedia's surface.

If there is a bottom line here, it is simply this: The future of storytelling and technology lies at least partly in the fact that we can recreate ourselves, and use ourselves as characters and props in our real-life movies. It also lies in the fact that through our technology we project other versions of ourselves, not unlike the way drama throughout the ages has sought to uncover alternate versions of reality and put them on stage for our scrutiny.

Thus we go one step beyond telling stories. In partnership with our new technologies, we actually become stories, consciously crafted, deliberately scripted so as to be the hero of our life narrative. Alternatively, this also happens on an unconscious level, as we become so embedded in our tEcosystem (Ohler, 2010) that being part of our ongoing narrative in the mediascape becomes second nature. We may do so as new persona in a virtual community, or as biologically reconstituted humans who are desperate to tell a new story about ourselves, or as actors, directors, and producers of our own home movies, broadcast as we walk, and perhaps filmed using the ubiquitous cameras and satellites that watch us everywhere we go—a kind of personalized reality television show. Although we have always encouraged people to take charge of their lives and realize their full potential, we will probably find the new ways in which this can be a bit unsettling.

Conclusions

Let us rewind to the present, in which both authors of this chapter considered the tasks necessary to address the limitations and opportunities in a world in which new media narrative is plentiful and easy to produce. If we consider the impact of these developments on our communities, we are compelled to ask the question, "How do we teach children to thrive in a world in which narrative is changing rapidly because of the evolution of media?" More specifically, given that our children need to be able to not only "read" new media, but write it as well, we ask, "What does it mean to be literate in a world of new media?"

What follows are a few important points that emerge from these questions. First, we must help our educational systems shift some of our literacy focus away from text-centrism and toward the new media collage, a catchall term that describes the new kind of literacy represented by our web pages, movies, digital stories, mashups, and other kinds of multimedia narrative (Ohler, 2007). Text will always be important, particularly as a tool used in the development of new media, as we saw in the case of the iPad; but it is no longer the default form of expression. Therefore, our children need to understand how to think critically and creatively—"creatically," so to speak—about whatever issue is before them, and then select whatever media best suits their response.

Further, our children must be able to use their media tools professionally, with a sense of poise, purpose, and the skills to communicate with an audience. It is important to note that actually teaching our children how to use new media effectively represents a cultural schism with regard to literacy that is at once acute and persistent. Although most parents certainly hope that their children possess all the life skills represented by the digital economy on graduation, they rightfully worry that this is unlikely to happen if schools only test for the 3Rs.

Second, art must become the fourth "R" (Ohler, 2010). Until fairly recently, art has been seen largely as fluff within the context of a rigorous academic curriculum, desirable during good times, expendable when funding got tight. We cannot afford this perspective in a highly aesthetic world, in which the media collage is the new foundational literacy, and in which traditional and evolving narrative forms become part of the media collage. Art skills have practical value like never before. Thus, art needs to shift from being a content area to a foundational literacy along with reading, 'riting, and 'rithmetic. The world of new media narrative demands it.

Last, literacy needs to embrace understanding the effects of new media narrative and the tools used to create it. Currently, a term widely used to describe this concern is *digital citizenship*. It reflects our need to have students question their new tools—that is, see them as "figure"—rather than simply adopt them because they are available. The stories they tell must reflect literacy about the media, as well as a balanced understanding of media's opportunities and limitations.

We remind ourselves that although the future goes on for a very long time, technology evolves so rapidly that it is difficult to predict media evolution more than 5 years into the future. But we must also remind ourselves that Dertouzos's (year) ancient human will direct our efforts. We will always use our advancements in science, technology, and media to enable our communities, raise our children, and tell our stories. Whether we do so with authenticity, clarity, and humanity is up to us.

Future Directions

• What is the impact of the continuing corporate consolidation of the media industry on the increasing homogenization of global entertainment culture?

• Should foreign territories outside the United States adopt the far-reaching quota and subsidy systems that France has employed to protect and sustain its indigenous creative industry, even if such invites government control of public media?

• Would academic research benefit from an embrace by educational institutions of new media, rather than traditional rhetoric and written text, as valid platforms for student research and scholarly discussion?

• Will the ongoing digitization of media forms such as music, video, and text banish printed books forever in favor of electronic publications?

• Will advances in technology minimize or expand the role of individual storytellers in the development, execution, performance, and distribution of stories?

• To what extent will psychologists and social scientists consider the impacts of living in a media-saturated environment on the health and welfare of their clients and subjects?

Notes

1. This chapter uses the nondenominational form of b.c.e. (Before the Common Era) instead of the traditional b.c. (Before Christ); likewise, c.e. (Common Era) is used rather than a.d. (*Anno Domini,* or Year of the Lord) to identify dates.

2. A case in point is the Sumerian Creation Epic, which describes how the earth was first formed when the god Marduk was charged by all the other gods to defend their heavenly pantheon from the evil schemes of Tiamat, the ocean goddess. This story contains a description of the Creation of Earth in 7 days, with several attributes that would reappear in the biblical Creation account. Even though this saga has come to us in the form of Akkadian tablets dating from the first millennium b.c.e., it is likely that the epic is much older, dating to the Sumerian period itself. See Isbouts, *From Moses to Muhammad;* pp. 24–27.

3. In countries such as Togo, for example, current literacy rates are barely 60%, despite efforts to improve education.

4. Balling, Hans, From Muthos to Pathos; p. 13.

5. The term *novel* probably emerged in 16th century England, as evidenced by William Painters' *Palace of Pleasure well furnished with pleasant Histories and excellent Novelles* of 1566. In France, commercially printed and published novels were referred to as *petites histoires*.

6. Source: the *English Short Title Catalogue* or ESTC.

7. The first picture to use reverse angles was James Williamson's *Attack on a China Mission Station,* filmed in 1910. The close-up was pioneered in G. A. Smith's *The Little Doctors* of 1901.

8. Even though the first public radio broadcast in the United States originated from the Metropolitan Opera House in 1910, KDKA in Pittsburg is generally credited as the first station to receive a license to broadcast radio programming, starting in 1920; in Europe, the first country to witness radio broadcasts was the Netherlands.

9. The so-called Golden Age of radio, 1920 to 1949, was supplanted by the Golden Age of television, 1949 to 1961.

10. Isbouts, *Charlton Heston's Hollywood,* p. 26.

11. The impulse to search for a competitive system to VHS was in part motivated by the fact that Philips, too, had launched a home video cassette recorder called Video 2000, which never found market acceptance.

12. The first commercially available computer designed for consumers was the Sphere 1, created by Michael D. Wise as a kit in 1975, followed by the Apple I computer designed by Steve Jobs and Steve Wozniak in 1976 and the Commodore in 1977.

13. The first pop album to be released on a compact disc was Dire Straits in 1981, whereas the first classical album was a recording of Beethoven's Ninth Symphony by the Berlin Philharmonic conducted by Herbert von Karajan. There is a story, probably apocryphal, which suggests that the length of Beethoven's Ninth, encoded in PCM, determined the size and diameter of the original compact disc—650 megabytes.

14. Volume and file structure of CD-ROM for information interchange, available at http://www.pismotechnic.com/cfs/iso9660–1999.html.

15. The author was an observer at the High Sierra Group meetings, and later supervised several implementations of High Sierra–compatible CD-ROM applications while engaged by Philips and DuPont Optical, a leading CD-ROM manufacturer at the time.

16. *Myst* was designed by Robyn and Rand Miller and released by Brøderbund in 1993. For the next 10 years, it would remain the best-selling videogame of all time.

17. Daily Media Use Among Children and Teens Up Dramatically From Five Years Ago. Retrieved March 31, 2011 from http://www.kff.org/entmedia/entmedia012010nr.cfm.

18. *Internet World Stats*. Retrieved March 26, 2011 from http://www.internetworldstats.com/stats.htm.

19. The Apple iPad is generally considered the most successful electronic product in history, with sales of 15 million devices within just 1 year of its introduction

20. This often-used phrase is usually attributed to the French poet and philosopher, Paul Valery (1871–1945). One reference to this quotation can be found at: http://www.quotationspage.com/quotes/Paul_Valery/; retrieved August 23, 2010.

21. I (Jason Ohler) was fortunate to have Marshall McLuhan as a teacher during his heyday at the University of Toronto during the 1970s. His lectures were worth the price of admission, tuition in this case, and gave me enough to think about for a lifetime. Among his many ideas that have remained with me over the years is his visual metaphor of driving forward as looking in the rearview media. It captures the quintessence of living in an era of exponential change.

22. Much of this background comes from a joint history of the Internet written by its creators: *A Brief History of the Internet* (http://www.isoc.org/internet/history/brief.shtml).

23. "The Source was in operation from 1979 to 1989, when it was purchased by rival CompuServe and discontinued sometime thereafter." (http://en.wikipedia.org/wiki/The_Source_%28 online_service%29)

24. In this short impromptu interview, Tim O'Reilly, who is often credited with being one of the developers of the Web 2.0 concept, states succinctly what he thinks Web 2.0 is (http://www.youtube.com/watch?v=CQibri7gpLM).

25. *Smart Mob* is a term popularized by Howard Rheingold in his book *Smart Mobs: The Next Social Revolution.* It refers, among other things, to the facilitation of impromptu gatherings of people through the use of wireless, mobile technology. From Wikipedia: "A smart mob is a group that, contrary to the usual connotations of a mob, behaves intelligently or efficiently because of its exponentially increasing network links. This network enables people to connect to information and others, allowing a form of social coordination." (http://en.wikipedia.org/wiki/Smart_mob)

26. This is a reference to Watson, an artificial intelligence computer system developed by IBM. In 2011 it competed with two of *Jeopardy!*'s all-time, top contestants—and won.

27. "Japanese Researchers Invent 'French Kissing Machine'" PC Magazine, by Sara Yin, May 5, 2011 01:37pm EST (http://www.pcmag.com/article2/0,2817,2384958,00.asp).

28. "Tickle Me Apple: iPhone App Transmits Tingly Touches" May 25, 2011 (http://gajitz.com/tickle-me-apple-iph one-app-transmits-tingly-touches/).

References

Aitkin, H. G. J. (1985). *The Continuous Wave: Technology and the American Radio, 1900–1932.* Princeton, NJ: Princeton University Press.

Altman, R. (2008). *A Theory of Narrative.* New York: Columbia University Press.

Aristotle, Poetics, translated by Halliwell S. (1995). Cambridge, MA: The Loeb Classical Library.

Balling, H. (2002). From muthos to pathos. In Balling, H., & Madsen, A. K. (Eds.), *From Homer to Hypertext: Studies in Narrative, Literature and Media.* Odense, Denmark: University Press of Southern Denmark.

Baxandall, M. (1972). *Painting and Experience in Fifteenth Century Italy.* New York: Oxford University Press.

Blok, R. (2002). A sense of closure: The state of narrative in digital literature. In Balling, H., & Madsen, A. K. (Eds.), *From Homer to Hypertext: Studies in Narrative, Literature and Media.* Odense, Denmark: University Press of Southern Denmark.

Bolter, Jay David, *Writing Space: The Computer, Hypertext and the History of Writing.* Lawrence Erlbaum, 1991.

Brooks, P. (1985). *Reading for the Plot.* Visalia, CA: Vintage Press.

Bruner, J. (1985). *Actual Minds, Possible Worlds.* Cambridge, MA: Harvard University Press.

Campbell, J. (1988). *The Power of Myth.* New York: Doubleday.

Campbell, J. (2004). *The Hero with a Thousand Faces.* Princeton, NJ: Princeton Press.

Cook, D. A. (1990). *A History of Narrative Film,* 2nd ed. New York: W.W. Norton.

Coover, R. (1992, June 21). The end of books. *The New York Times Book Review,* p. 1.

Days, V. (2007). Here comes television: Remaking American life, 1948–1954. In Edgerton, G. R. (Ed.), *The Columbia History of American Television.* New York: Columbia University Press.

Dertouzos, M. (2001). *The Unfinished Revolution: Human-Centered Computers and What They Can Do dor Us.* New York: HarperCollins.

Dill, K. (2009). *How Fantasy Becomes Reality: Seeing Through Media Influence.* New York: Oxford University Press.

Donovan, T. (2010). *The History of Video Games.* Los Angeles: Yellow Ant Publishers.

Elliott, E., & Stallcup, J. (1997). American oral tradition. In Leeming, D. A. (Ed.), *Storytelling Encyclopedia: Historical, Cultural and Multiethnic Approaches to Oral Traditions Around the World.* Phoenix, AZ: Oryx Press.

ESA (2008). *Essential Facts about the Computer and Videogame Industry.* Entertainment Software Association.

Fulton, H., Huismans, R., Murphet, J., & Dunn, A. (2005). *Narrative and Media.* Cambridge, MA: Cambridge University Press.

Gardner, H. (2011). *New Horizons in Theory and Practice.* New York: Basic Books, 2011.

Gerbner, G., Gross, L., Morgan, M., & Signorielli, N. (1986). *Living with television: The dynamics of the cultivation process.* In Bryant, J., & Zillman, D. (Eds.), Perspectives on Media Effects. Hillsdale, NJ: Lawrence Erlbaum Associates, pp. 17–40.

Goodman, S. (2003). *Teaching Youth Media: A Critical Guide to Literacy, Video Production & Social Change.* New York: Teachers College Press.

Graff, H. J. (1987). *The Legacies of Literacy: Continuities and Contradictions in Western Culture and Society.* Tullamore, Ireland: Midland Books.

Green, M., & Brock, T. (2000). The role of transportation in the persuasiveness of public narrative. *Journal of Personality and Social Psychology, 79*(5), 701–721.

Gulliland, A. A. (1939). Television in Germany. *Television and Short-Wave World,* September, 1939.

Hall, E. T. (1966). *The Hidden Dimension.* New York: Anchor Books.

Humphreys, S. (2005). Productive players: Online computer games' challenge to conventional media forms. *Communication and Critical/Cultural Studies, 2*(1), 37–51.

Isbouts, J.-P. (1986). International videodisc design. Paper presented in Interactive Instruction Delivery Conference Proceedings, Society for Applied Learning Technology.

Isbouts, J.-P. (1997). *Charlton Heston's Hollywood.* Good Times Publishing (online).

Isbouts, J.-P. (2011). *From Moses to Muhammad: The Shared Origins of Judaism, Christianity and Islam.* New York: Pantheon Press.

Jenkins, H. (2006). *Convergence Culture.* New York: New York University Press.

Kistemaker, S. J. (2002). *The Parables: Understanding the Stories Jesus Told.* Grand Rapids, MI: Baker Books.

Knopper, S. (2009). *Appetite for Self-Destruction: The Rise and Fall of the Record Industry in the Digital Age.* New York: Simon & Schuster.

Lahue, K. C. (1969). *Continued Next Week: A History of the Moving Picture Serial.* Norman, OK: University of Oklahoma Press.

Landow, G. P. (1997). *Hypertext 2.0: The Convergence of Contemporary Critical Theory and Technology.* Baltimore: Johns Hopkins University Press.

Louis, J. (1963). *Fiction for the Working Man 1830–1850.* Harmondsworth, UK: Penguin Publishing.

Matini, J. (1990). Ferdowsi's role in protecting the national identity of UU Iranians. In *Kongress 1000 Jahre persisches Nationalepos: Ferdowsi's Schahnameh.* Mehr Verlag.

McLuhan, M. (1964). *Understanding Media: The Extensions of Man.* New York: McGraw-Hill.

McLuhan, M. (1967). *The medium Is the Massage.* Corte Madera, CA: Gingko Press.

McLuhan, M. Retrieved April 30, 2011 from *How to Study Media.* http://www.media-ecology.org/mcluhan/mc_38.txt.

McLuhan, M., & Fiore, Q. (1967). *The Medium Is the Massage: An Inventory of Effects.* New York: Bantam Books.

McLuhan, M. & Powers, B. (1989). *The Global Village: Transformations in world Life and Media in the 21st Century.* Oxford, UK: Oxford University Press.

Meacham, M. (2010). *The Effective Pursuit of Self-Interests in World of Warcraft.* Unpublished dissertation. Santa Barbara, CA: Fielding Graduate University.

Miller, D. C. (1986). Laser Discs at the Library Door: The Microsoft First International Conference on CD-ROM. *Library Hi Tech, 4*(2), 55–68.

Miller, P. *Sir Tim Berners-Lee: Semantic Web Is Open for Business.* Retrieved April 30, 2011 from *The Semantic Web,* http://blogs.zdnet.com/semantic-web/?p=105.

Ohler, J. (2008). The Semantic Web in Education. What happens when the read-write web gets smart enough to help us organize and evaluate the information it provides? *EDUCAUSE Quarterly, 31*(4), 7–9.

Ohler, J. (2010). *Digital Community, Digital Citizen.* Thousand Oaks, CA: Corwin Press.

Ohler, J. B. (2007). *Digital Storytelling in the Classroom: New Media Pathways to Literacy, Learning, and Creativity.* Thousand Oaks, CA: Corwin Press.

Olson, S. R. (1999). *Hollywood Planet: Global Media and the Competitive Advantage of Narrative Transparency.* Hillsdale, NJ: Lawrence Erlbaum Associates.

O' Reilly, T. (2005). Retrieved April 30, 2011 from *What Is Web 2.0?* http://www.oreillynet.com/pub/a/oreilly/tim/news/2005/09/30/what-is-web-20.html#mememap.

Owen, D. (2005). Retrieved March 31, 2011 from *The Betamax vs VHS Format War,* http://www.mediacollege.com/video/format/compare/betamax-vhs.html.

Parker, P. M. (2009). *Laserdisc: Webster's Timeline History, 1958–2004.* San Diego, CA: Icon Group International.

Polkinghorne, D. (1988). *Narrative Knowing and the Human Sciences.* New York: SUNY Press.

Potter, W. J. (2002). *The Eleven Myths of Media Violence.* Thousand Oaks, CA: Sage.

Rheingold, H. (1985). *Tools for Thought.* New York: Simon and Schuster/Prentice Hall.

Ryan, M.-L. (2004). *Narrative Across Media: The Languages of Storytelling.* Lincoln, NE: University of Nebraska.

Sans Souci, R. D. (1993). *Cut from the Same Cloth: American Women of Myth, Legend and Tall Tale.* New York: Philomel Books.

Schouhamer-Immink, K. A. (2007). Shannon, Beethoven, and the compact disc. *IEEE Information Theory Newsletter,* 42–46.

Siskin, C. (1998). *The Work of Writing: Literature and Social Change in Britain, 1700–1830.* Baltimore: Johns Hopkins University Press.

Turkle, S. (2008). Always-on/always-on-you: The tethered self. In Katz J. E. (Ed.), *Handbook of Mobile Communication Studies.* Cambridge, MA: MIT Press, pp. 121–138.

Ulff-Møller, J. (2003). *Hollywood's Film Wars with France: Film-trade Diplomacy and the Emergence of the French Film Quota Policy.* Rochester, NY: Rochester University Press.

Williams D. (2002). A structural analysis of market competition in the U.S. home video game industry. *International Journal on Media Management, 4*(1), 41–54.

Arguing for Media Psychology as a Distinct Field

Pamela Brown Rutledge

Abstract

The field of media psychology is a recent arrival to the academic world. In spite of apparent overlaps with other disciplines, such as media studies, communications, or sociology, media psychology serves a distinct and necessary role because it shifts the focus of inquiry from media-centric to human-centric. When the Internet replaced the one-to-many communication model of mass media with a many-to-many model, it created peer-to-peer connectivity and turned information distribution into a social system. Interconnectivity is blurring what we once perceived as distinct divisions among technologies. More profoundly, a networked society with real-time access has redefined the roles of media producer, consumer, and distributor, challenging many core beliefs about the world and our place in it. In this globally connected world, media technologies are inextricable from daily life. How individuals and society use these capabilities will be determined in large part by whether we, as a society, are preoccupied with the challenges or seek out the opportunities. Seeing potential demands a forward-looking science that can move beyond traditional models to embrace the complex social system of technology and human behavior. Media psychology bridges this gap. At its best, media psychology seeks to understand the intersection of human behavior and technology to connect the positive capabilities of technology with human needs and goals so that individuals and society can grow and flourish.

Key Words: convergence, media psychology, motivation, social change, technology

The question I pose is whether or not a separate field of media psychology adds critical value to the many existing fields, theoretical perspectives, applications, and topic areas in psychology. The short answer is "yes."

The proliferation of media, and particularly social technologies, has created growing interest across society in understanding how technologies fit into individual life and society as a whole. Media psychology uses the lens of psychology to study and understand the complex relationship between humans and the evolving digital environment. Media psychology is where the knowledge of human psychology meets the understanding of technology's attributes and affordances. The robust history of psychological theory, however, demands that media psychologists start their inquiries from the perspective of human experience and agency and look at technology not as a driver of behavior, but as part of the reciprocal interplay in an evolving psychosocial environment. Viewing media technologies as part of a complex environmental system positions media psychology as a multidisciplinary platform that can serve as an intellectual meeting ground for scholars and practitioners. Media psychology, much like a neural network, encourages collaborations across multiples fields to inspire new research and applications that benefit individuals and society. As an emerging field, it has the powerful advantage of flexibility and responsiveness in a continually developing media environment.

Defining Media Psychology

To explain the importance of media psychology, it would seem helpful to create a working definition. So far, however, consensus on a definition and differentiation of media psychology has proved illusive (however, see Chapter 1 for an exploration of this topic). There are overlaps with numerous fields, such as media studies, communication science, anthropology, education, and sociology, not to mention those within the discipline of psychology itself (e.g., Reeves & Anderson, 1991; Giles, 2003). Much of the research that would be considered media psychology has come from other fields, both academic and applied (Giles, 2010). In the 1920s, marketing, advertising, and public relations professionals, independent of academic institutions, began conducting research on consumer behavior and motivation for commercial applications (Bartels, 1976). The use of mass media during World War II created a surge of academic interest in mass media messaging and resulted in the creation of a new field, communication science (Lazarsfeld & Merton, 2000).

As late as the 1960s and 1970s, there was still no formally identified field of media psychology; however, psychologists took a more prominent research role in response to public concern over the widespread adoption of television and its impact on children and teens (Giles, 2003). The impact of media on children and teens continues to one of the dominant themes in media psychology research, subject to much debate in part resulting from the rapidly changing social and technological environment (Livingstone, 1996) and the often conflicting public, governmental, commercial, and academic agendas (Ferguson, 2009).

The official emergence of media psychology as a field is attributed to the 1986 formation of the Media Psychology Division 46 in the American Psychological Association with Stuart Fischoff as its inaugural president (Carll, 2003; Fischoff, 2005). The establishment of an official division was an important milestone, but it did not clarify or unify the goals and purpose of media psychology. Many early Division 46 members were clinicians (Giles, 2003). Their priorities at the time focused on using media to distribute psychological information, such as hosting programs and providing expert opinions, and the accurate representation of mental illness and psychological treatment in entertainment rather than on media impact and use (Luskin & Friedland, 1998). Although the Division's stated definition has broadened in the intervening years in response to members' more diverse interests and research, perceptions of the early focus persist.

Emerging Technologies and an Emerging Field

The field of media psychology is still neither well known nor understood (Rutledge, 2007). Two events, one large and one small, have helped energize the field since 2000. The first was the advent of society-wide Internet access that enabled social and mobile technologies. The resultant infiltration of technology into daily life triggered interest and concern, fueling an urgent need to understand the new technologies' psychological impact. The second event, a response to the first, was the 2003 establishment of the first doctoral program in the United States designated as media psychology, with the express purpose of applying psychological principles to understanding the impact and use of media technologies.

The Internet: Redefining Communication and Connection

Although the seeds of the Internet date back to the 1960s and years of collaboration among scientists and academics working with the U.S. Department of Defense Advanced Research Projects Agency (ARPA), it wasn't until the 1990s that the government released control and commercial service providers such as CompuServe, AOL, and Prodigy began to provide households with Internet access (Fang, 1997; McMichael, 2005). Although previous technologies such as the telegraph and telephone had provided glimpses of the way communication speeds compress time and space, the Internet delivered a suite of tools that is challenging society's understanding of media, communications, information, and individual participation.

Parallels between the Internet and Gutenberg's printing press are common because both shifted the balance of power in society, providing more democratic access to information and increasing the demand for and spread of literacy (e.g., Winston, 1998; Harris, 2004; P. H. Howard, 2004; Kellner & Share, 2007; Harp, Bachmann, Rosas-Moreno, & Loke, 2010; A. L. Howard, 2010). The impact of the Internet, however, has been much more profound psychologically. In less than 20 years, the Internet created a communication system that simultaneously allowed for autonomy and collaboration.

Like the printing press, the Internet transformed the model of communications. The printing press introduced the concept of mass media, in which for the first time many could receive the same information. The mass media model shifted communication from local participation to a unidirectional process in which information was controlled by a small number of distributors and delivered across large audiences (Ito, 2009). As mass media developed into television, radio, and film, audience members became increasingly seen as passive recipients of messaging, victims of persuasion and manipulation (Giles, 2003; see also Isbouts & Ohler, Chapter 2, this volume).

By contrast, the Internet has created a "many-to-many" world that is both mass in reach and participatory in experience, creating "networked publics" (Varnelis, 2009) and liberating Oldenburg's conception of the hang-out or "third place" from geographic tethers (Soukup, 2006). The Internet created a social web in which users can easily share information in all forms—text, video, image, and sound—across networks of people (Jenkins, 2008). Unlike the printing press, which was costly in time and resources, publishing on the Internet is free, instantaneous, and potentially far-reaching because networks distribute information like ripples in a pond, in all directions simultaneously rather than in linear paths (Barabasi, 2003). Of much greater importance, however, is that fact that information flows in both directions, creating the functional equivalent of a conversation; it is no longer only "pushed" by a few to a large audience. Even traditionally unidirectional mass media channels, such as television, have become "social." The rapidly emerging trend of Social TV integrates tools such as texting, Facebook, Twitter and web-based interaction into the program experience. The audience becomes a participant, voting for favorites, sharing opinions with other audience members, and simultaneously providing producers with invaluable real-time feedback (e.g., Nathan et al., 2008; Geerts & De Groof, 2009; Dumenco, 2011).

This new connectivity has many implications. As the sociologist Granovetter (1973) demonstrated in his seminal paper, *The Strength of Weak Ties,* how people are linked by social networks influences the new information they receive. Weak ties are the links between one network and another. The strength of weak ties is that they connect individuals with new opportunities outside of their normal access. Social technologies give individuals access to others who share similar interests, traits, or values and facilitate the development of subcultures that Fischer (1975) theorized was only possible with the physical density of urban life. From individuals with special interests like fan fiction (Black, 2009) to those who feel marginalized or stigmatized, online groups formed around common interests and needs provide a sense of belonging, positive identity, and connection (McKenna & Bargh, 1998).

Human Agency in Technology

Peer-to-peer, on-demand access and connectivity afforded by new technologies challenge core beliefs about many aspects of daily life, such as time, space, authorship, privacy, participation, community, and connection. The underlying psychological impact of technology use, however, is the promotion of human agency (Bandura, 2002). Information networks, from Wikipedia and Google Search to Facebook, shift the locus of control to the individual, who decides how, when, and what is sent or distributed and who also has the ability to create, personalize, and manipulate content (Russell, Ito, Richmond, & Tuters, 2009). Participatory media technologies are establishing a new baseline of expectations about individual and collective agency (e.g., Bandura, 2002) that is not just impacting texting urban teens. Because of less capital-intensive infrastructure requirements, mobile technologies are expanding rapidly in rural communities and across emerging economies like sub-Saharan Africa (Aker, 2008) and increasingly empowering underserved populations to make use of data and services beyond basic voice.

Networked technologies impact individuals and communities by providing opportunities to interact through multiple channels, such as education, social connection, and creative expression. A wide body of research shows that active participation as well as vicarious observation can influence the motivational mechanisms of self-regulation and affect perceptions of self-efficacy (e.g., Zimmerman, 2000; Bandura, 2004; Maddux, 2005; Pajares, 2006). Bandura (1977) defined self-efficacy as an individual's beliefs in his or her capabilities to act on the environment to achieve certain goals. Self-efficacy beliefs determine how people think, feel, and motivate themselves. Strong efficacy beliefs foster resilience and engagement. No matter what the proximal use of technology, from negotiating fair market prices for crops to posting LOLcats[1] on icanhascheezburger.com, networked technologies afford continual feedback and proof of one's ability to act on the environment. The result is validating and cumulative, creating an upward spiral of positive emotions (Fredrickson, 2004), engagement (Csikszentmihalyi, 1991), and resilience (Masten & Reed, 2005). The promotion of self-efficacy and human agency is an implicit result across all technology applications, from learning environments and civic participation to social support.

Learning Environments

Thanks to technology, distance education is a rapidly growing field offering the chance for educational and career advancement to people for whom cost, geography, or life commitments made traditional programs untenable. Once synonymous with low-quality "correspondence courses," online programs deliver a wide range of rigorous degree paths that are location-blind, and time-flexible because of both synchronous and asynchronous participation, and have significantly lower costs than traditional brick-and-mortar institutions. Consequently, online educational offerings and enrollments are skyrocketing. Two-thirds of all degree-granting institutions offer online degrees or online course choices. Online education added 1 million new students in the year 2010 with online enrollment up 21%, compared with 2% for traditional institutions (Allen & Seaman, 2007, 2010). Attitudes toward distance education are changing as mounting evidence suggests online learning can be as effective as face-to-face learning (e.g., Neuhauser, 2002). In one student survey, 75% believed their online courses to be as good or better than those they had face to face (Allen & Seaman, 2007, 2010).

Distance educational solutions are not limited to computer access. Mobile learning—or m-learning—the use of mobile or wireless devices such as smartphones and handheld computers—has attributes that provide positive pedagogical affordances and facilitate student engagement in a variety of course contexts (Cochrane & Bateman, 2010). Pea and Maldonado (2006) describe the features of handheld devices that take learning beyond the classroom:

> … portability, small screen size, computing power (immediate starting-up), diverse communication networks, a broad range of applications, data synchronization across computers, and stylus input device. (p. 428)

Mobile technologies also reach where there are no classrooms. An India-focused adult literacy program, TaraAkshar, combines technology with classroom learning, and has taught nearly 60,000 women to read and write in 3 years.[2] Mobile and Immersive Learning for Literacy in Emerging Economies (MILLEE)[3] has been testing mobile phones to create immersive, game-like experiences to make English-language learning resources available to underprivileged children in India and China. Text-messaging (short message service or SMS) literacy programs are broadcast to rural Bangladesh to create the skill base necessary for better jobs (Islam & Doyle, 2008).

Offline, there is a rising movement to transform education through the use of participatory technologies to create interactive and immersive environments that promote self-directed learning experiences (Gee, 2004; Prensky, 2007). The Quest-to-Learn school in New York uses an innovative game-based pedagogy to create a differentiated, rigorous challenge-based curriculum to bridge old and new literacies.[4]

Civic Participation

Social media allows unprecedented mobilization of citizen participation in the democratic process. President Barrack Obama's 2008 presidential campaign was the first to use new media connectivity through social networking sites such as Facebook and microblogging platforms such as Twitter to engage young voters and generate campaign funds (e.g., Kahn & Kellner, 2004; Qualman, 2009).

The same social media tools connect and amplify other opportunities for civic engagement, volunteerism, and donations through the use of mobile devices and social networking (Smith, 2010). After the 2010 earthquake in Haiti, the Red Cross credited Facebook and Twitter for the rapid distribution of news and information that resulted in $3 million in text message–based donations in the first 24 hours and $21 million in the first week (Gross, 2010).

Social technologies have also spurred the trend of micro-volunteerism, in which individuals can donate small amounts of their time to help nonprofits on specific projects, through organizations such as Sparks.com. The participatory environment has led to the emergence of crowdsourced funding for microloans, grassroots causes and entrepreneurial projects from around the world. Kiva.org, for example, allows individual lenders to read about, select, and fund all or part of microloans for individual borrowers whose stories and goals appeal to them. Kickstarter.com is one of a rising number of new crowdfunding platforms through which individuals donate the money necessary to launch new projects. In contrast to traditional funding mechanisms, such as venture capital, which have high minimum investment limits and aggressive equity stake requirements, organizations like Kickstarter enable small budget projects by connecting enthusiasts with projects they love in exchange for premium customer perks rather than equity participation. The success of Kickstarter and others like it has spawned a new crowdfunding industry that raised $1.5 billion in 2011 alone (Charman-Anderson, 2012).

Social Support

Online communities are developing around a myriad of special interests. From fan groups to health-related information and support, these connections result in significant positive impact and behavior change, with the potential to transform lives (Wellman, Haase, Witte, & Keith, 2001; Forster, 2004; Williams, Caplan, & Xiong, 2007).

Social media pundits predicted that older generations would never adopt social network technologies; however, the largest population growth on Facebook has come from seniors (Zichuhr, 2010), and classes on how to use Facebook are increasing in popularity in retirement homes and assisted-living facilities (Zafar, 2011). Research has suggested that using social networking and online sites reduces depression (Ford & Ford, 2009) and increases cognitive flexibility in seniors (Small, Moody, Siddarth, & Bookheimer, 2008). Social support from social networking sites such as Facebook also creates bridges for multigenerational communication to maintain relationships both near and far (e.g., Stroud, 2007).

Internet and social networking access have also improved both support and daily functioning for marginalized and minority members of society through emotional connection and social modeling in nonthreatening environments (Mehra, Merkel, & Bishop, 2004) as well as providing many safe avenues for identity development and exploration (Buckingham, 2008). Homeless adolescents use the Internet at public libraries and social services office to access health information and connect them with family and friends in ways that can reduce risk-taking behavior (Rice, Shepherd, Dutton, & Katz, 2007). Mobile networks also are used to provide real-time support and health information for young adults managing type 1 diabetes in the United Kingdom (Farmer et al., 2005).

Content Production

In 2009, 93% of teens were online, and nearly two-thirds were content producers, regularly uploading videos or photos or posting on forums or blogs (Moore, 2011). Teens aren't the only ones contributing content. Thanks to the easy-to-use features of smartphones with cameras and video capture, more than half of adult cell phone owners have used their device to share a photo or video (Pew Research Center, 2010). In 2011, 71% of all online Americans used videosharing sites such as YouTube and Vimeo, with online African Americans and Hispanics leading the way. Even news sites are highly social, used for commenting and sharing. The video sites serve a broad range of purposes, from learning how to do something and gathering the news to being entertained (Moore, 2011).

Information Environments

Access to information has significant economic, physical, and psychological impact by giving people control over different domains of their lives. Individuals now have on-demand access that provides solutions, like getting a word definition at Dictionary.com, finding medical symptoms and drug reactions at WebMD.com, or finding old product manuals using Google search (Lawson & Leck, 2006; Stevenson, 2008). Mobile devices with global positioning services (GPS) provide geographically relevant on-demand information, such as directions, maps, store hours, historical and tourist sites, or restaurant locations and reviews (Junglas & Watson, 2008). These acts and others all subtly reinforce individual agency.

Previously location-based services for posteducation advancement are now online. Professional connections and job-seeking sites, such as LinkedIn.com and Monster.com, allow for mentoring, networking, and feedback. Even dating has moved online, a welcome alternative to singles bars and chance encounters in the vegetable aisle of the local supermarket, with services such as Match.com and EHarmony.com.

Online services such as Meetup.com provide ways to connect in person to others with similar interests in local communities, from dog playdates and classic movies to business development. Instead of trolling through the coupon flyers, people can subscribe to sites such as Groupon.com, Amazon.com, and LivingSocial.com to find special offers that are self-selected, location-targeted services, and socially validated through reviews and voting systems.

In environments in which information has been severely limited, introducing technology can significantly improve economic and social well-being. The cell phone–based programs sponsored by the Manobi Development Foundation (2011) deliver current crop prices to rural Senegalese farmers and have raised the farmers' average monthly revenue by more than 500%, high enough to turn them into taxpayers. Paying taxes has led to increased civic participation, resulting in the development of village schools and increased legal rights through official documentation programs. The adoption of mobile technologies that allowed fisherman off the cost of northern Kerala, India, access to market prices of sardines reduced the price dispersion by 20%. Fishermen's profits rose by 8% and consumer prices dropped by 4%, through less waste and better management of resources like fuel (Jensen, 2007).

Multiple Tools, Fluid Uses

In the space of little more than 10 years, media technologies have transformed human experience from interpersonal communication and identity formation to global relations—and the changes will continue. People are mobile, untethered from desktops and geography. Mobile phone penetration in the United States, for example, went from 13% in 1995 to 96% in 2010 (CTIA, 2010). Even globally, the International Telecommunications Union (2010) estimates that 90% of the world's population has access to cell phones. Computers and mobile devices are equipped with user-friendly media production and distribution capabilities and on-demand connectivity. These technologies have created a networked society that has shaped and shifted social patterns and psychological, cultural, and economic trends (Benkler, 2006).

Just as individuals simultaneously assume roles of media consumer, producer, and distributor, the rapid innovation and time to market are continually redefining how technology is used, destroying the crisp functional delineation between each medium. Ask most 12-year-olds if they wear a wristwatch and they will look at you curiously and hold up their mobile device and say, "that's what *this* is for." The experience of using technology will unavoidably become fluid and interchangeable as users continually adjust to and adopt new products with new capabilities, making media in situ research more challenging and extrapolations of past research results to current understandings more tenuous.

Devices are increasingly used based on how they satisfy individual goals and needs rather than by their advertised purpose. Some people watch television programming on computers (Madden, 2009). Others use mobile phones to access the Internet (Smith, 2010), but use their computers to "call" one another around the world (e.g., www.skype.com). Online games such as Facebook's *FarmVille*[5] or *World of Warcraft,*[6] are a source of creative expression for some and social connectivity for others (Steinkuehler & Williams, 2006). By 2010, more than 70% of Americans were using their phones to take pictures and receive text messages (Smith, 2010) and more than 60% of Americans watched television and surfed the Internet simultaneously (Nielsen, 2010). In 2010, young people consumed an average of 7.5 hours of media a day, but they were not necessarily sitting around at home, as 20% of all media consumption occurs on mobile devices such as iPods (Rideout, Foehr, & Roberts, 2010).

The line between online and offline will continue to blur as people have the ability to overlay digital information onto the real world using mobile devices equipped with augmented reality applications (El Sayed, Zayed, & Sharawy, 2011). Augmented reality is mixed reality on the continuum between real and virtual. With augmented reality devices, users have a real-time view of their environment with multiple layers of computer-generated information superimposed on objects around them. The applications are endless, from medical training (e.g., Botden & Jakimowicz, 2009) and manufacturing design (e.g., Botden & Jakimowicz, 2009) to entertainment (e.g., Huang, Jiang, Liu, & Wang, 2011), and of course marketing. Frito-Lay's campaign for the snack food Cheez Doodles used augmented reality with an embedded contest to allow customers to build their own music video with an animated alternative band, the Cheez Dudes. Kia Motors created an augmented reality game for Facebook featuring animated hamsters giving players control over on-screen hamster action. The Tourist Bureau for the Italian region of Tuscany claims to have the first augmented reality tourist application with *Tuscany+*, which allows tourists to stand in a Tuscan village and, through their geographically linked camera phone, see information about local sites, transportation, or nearby restaurants and menus (translated into English for you).[7]

Augmented reality applications have tremendous potential for education by creating immersive learning environments in which learners can interact with and manipulate data and subject matter (e.g., Turner & Ayres, 2011). Squire and Jan (2007) argue that using place-based augmented reality in a game format helps school children to better learn and apply the process of scientific inquiry and argumentation to solve the presented problems by creating emotional engagement and effective scaffolding.

It's not just the technology that is more flexible. According to a Pew Research Center Report, consumer allegiance to a single news source or company is gone (Purcell, Rainie, Mitchell, Rosentiel, & Olmstead, 2010). Gathering information from multiple sources is no longer costly in time or money. Users have choice: They can compare multiple perspectives on the news or seek out specific information sources that confirm their beliefs (e.g., G. J. Jones, Quested, & Thomson, 2000). In 2011, 92% of U.S. Internet users actively multisourced their news, and the experience is becoming increasingly personalized, participatory, and social with increased sharing of information and stories (Purcell, 2011).

The result is a profound change in our relationship to information. Access is no longer difficult, in fact, just the opposite. Abundant information means the premium will be on high quality filters to determine data validity and relevance. It takes media and technologically literate critical thinkers to effectively navigating a media rich, participatory environment.

Media-Savvy Media Psychologists

It was in against this backdrop of rapid technological change that Bernard Luskin established the first doctoral program in media psychology at Fielding Graduate University (FGU) in 2003 (see Chapter 1 for a brief history). This was a pivotal turning point in the awareness of media psychology as a field. Graduates of the program have embraced the role of scholar–practitioners who integrate the study of psychological theory with media technologies (*Business Wire,* 2003). They are active promoters of media psychology in research, academia, and the public and private sectors, raising awareness of the importance of psychology as an anchor to how we develop and assess technologies across a wide range of industries and applications, from education, business, and health care to entertainment. Although the numbers are modest, the new generation of media psychologists has had a visible impact on awareness of media psychology as a dynamic area of study and practice. In an April 2011 search on Google Trends,

there were no measurable results for the term *media psychology* between the start of 2004 until 2008. The upsurge in 2008 is coincident with the graduation of FGU's first media psychology PhDs (Figure 3.1).

In April 2011, a Google search for the term *media psychology* returned 106,000 results of active articles, web sites, blog, programs, and scholars. Four months later, that number had nearly doubled to 198,000. Similar courses and programs have emerged, and the interest in understanding media psychology continues to grow as media technologies proliferate. As shown in Figure 3.2, the number of articles in peer-reviewed journals addressing the topic of media or technology use has increased by more than 4,000% since 1975.

The Playing Field

One of the challenges in raising awareness of media psychology as a field lies in the definition of *media*.[8] In popular discourse, the word *media* is often taken to mean the sum of mass communication media (e.g., radio, newspapers, television) or a means of communication conveyance, such as books, photographs, or film. This was appropriate to the time, but the definition no longer fits the permeable experience of technology use and applications. Although this adds to the confusion as to what constitutes *media,* this trend underscores the difference between media psychology and other media-related fields by illuminating the importance of psychology as an anchor.

Medium, at its root, means *something in the middle,* a more accurate description of the purview of media psychology. As the boundaries of media technologies shift and blur, the constant is not the tools, but mediated human experience—the psychological

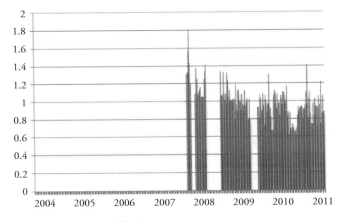

Figure 3.1 Google Trends Searches for "Media Psychology".
From Google Trends (www.google.com/trends).

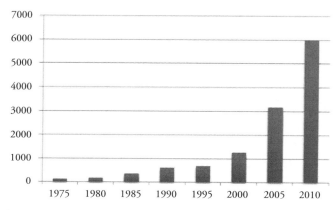

Figure 3.2 PsychInfo Search Peer-Reviewed Articles with Keywords "Media" or "Technology" and "Use" From www.psychinfo.com.

dimensions of perception and understanding. The overlap with other media-related fields emphasizes the point of communication. Arguably, any information exchange is, in fact, communication but that is not the heuristic understanding.

Each day is full of mediated events with psychological impact. Navigating single-player video games, setting voice preferences on a GPS navigation system, or finding documents on a computer desktop are all interactions with multiple levels of psychological experience—both conscious and unconscious (e.g., Sharritt, 2010; Yang, Han, & Park, 2010). A mediated experience by definition includes perception, attention, motivation, affect, engagement, and understanding, either instantaneous or scaffolded (e.g., Quintana, Krajcik, & Soloway, 2002; Jin, 2009). Media psychology is the only field that, by design, unites cognition, motivation, emotion, neuroscience, human development, and subjective understanding to evaluate mediated experience against the broader context of individual and group behaviors.

Overcoming Historical Assumptions to See the Future

If media psychology has a shortcoming in dealing with an increasingly complex environment, it is that psychological science has been primed by over a half-century of assumptions about the value of viewing the world in a reductionist way (Karlsson & Kamppinen, 1995; Day, 2007). Isolating elements is the basis of empirical research and has produced notable and valuable contributions. But in this model, social scientists are looking to achieve a yes/no solution and create answerable questions (Seligman & Csikszentmihalyi, 2000). Is it deviance or normal, sick or well, or significant or not significant? This implicitly encourages linear, binary

thinking, and deludes us into assuming that the world is causal and knowable. Although this makes scientific research more testable, it also plays into a innate human bias: The brain is a pattern and certainty-seeking organ (Wexler, 2006).

The reductionist tradition is evident in much of the research on the effects of mass media that employed experimental quantitative methods in an attempt to isolate and quantify the actual and potential impact of media exposure on individual and group behavior and norms. The inherent problem with this type of specificity is that it creates an artificial user environment and strips away the subjective experience and relational context that is a fundamental feature of media use. (See Chapters 7 and 8 for a discussion of the contributions of qualitative research methodologies to media psychology.) Responding to social and moral concerns rising from the rapid adoption of television, research often targets the negative consequences of media messaging, such as persuasive techniques in marketing, the exposure of young children to media use, and the impact of media content containing violence, sexuality, or social, racial, and gender stereotypes (Giles, 2003). The social and political climate cannot help but contribute to the framing and funding of research when society searches for answers to ease anxieties. Much of this body of work came to be known as "media effects" research and placed the methodological focus on the impact of media content over less easily isolatable variables, such as viewer choice, individual differences, and socioeconomic context.

The current media environment is even messier from a research perspective. Applying theoretical approaches used with mass media to emerging digital and Internet technologies is challenging at best and is forcing a redefinition of the "consumer" from a passive recipient to an active participant within a complex environment. The impact and use of new technologies is increasingly investigated using more complex and interactive constructs such as identity and self-efficacy (Bandura, 2007; Zheng, McAlack, Wilmes, Kohler-Evans, & Williamson, 2009). This has led to reexamining assumptions about media impact and agency, such as the role of audience beliefs on news sourcing, the role of audience feedback on mass media distributors' programming choices (e.g., Burke, 2008; Knobloch-Westerwick & Meng, 2008; Rutledge, 2008), and the meaning of community and friendship in the context of social networks (e.g., Hampton & Wellman, 2003; Subrahmanyam, Reich, Waechter, & Espinoza, 2008).

Research in disparate fields on the nonlinear dynamics of complex systems, such as cell development, ant colony structures, and infectious disease tracking, has given social scientists a better understanding of the properties that govern the behavior of information networks (Watts, 2003). The popularity of social networks, however, has made it impossible to ignore the psychological component. Networks are living systems with emergent properties and nonlinear behaviors, such the "viral" spread of videos or social unrest that are not visible by observing individual actors (Mitchell, 2009).

The heritage of media effects research does not lend itself to a systems model. However, increasing awareness of the phenomenon of emergent behaviors, such as flash mobs, crowd-sourcing, viral marketing, and other socially driven events that underscore the importance of understanding network properties, encourage researchers and theoreticians to reconceptualize the relationships between humans and technology and the attendant evolution of culture (Heylighen, 1999; Gilbert, Jager, Deffuant, & Adjali, 2007; Bampo, Ewing, Mather, Stewart, & Wallace, 2008).

The integration of systems thinking is a natural segue for media psychology because much of psychological theory is based on the understanding and analysis of relational systems, such as interactions within groups, families, and organizations, neural networks, or among human development, cognition, and the environment (Vygotsky, 1978; Bandura, 2002; Tooby, Cosmides, & Barrett, 2003; Kenrick, Li, & Butner, 2003; Kosslyn, 2006; Lin, 2007).

Systems theory not only improves the understanding of information flows, connections, and network behavior (Strogatz, 2003), but also provides a common language that allows insights from one discipline to influence others. The simple nomenclature of systems and network theory—such as nodes, links, attractors, power laws, and tipping points—are now part of everyday discourse (Mitchell, 2009). Media psychology can look at the system structure and overlay the psychological implications of network relationships and the qualitative experience of using new technologies.

In ecosystem of society and media technologies, the action of any agent influences the entire environment (e.g., Kauffman, 1995). This relationship is essential to understanding behavior in a participatory and media-rich environment. The implications are both powerful and intriguing: No part of the system, neither media conglomerate nor teenage consumer, functions in isolation and no part of the system wields all the power. With this shift in control toward the individual, comes the burden of both the opportunities and the responsibilities of access, agency, and action.

Media psychology by necessity is forward-looking. It is not possible for media psychology to be relevant without being technologically and theoretically current. Media psychology, however, is not focused on program content, tools, or hardware. It focuses on the "space between:" the space of interaction between humans and technology and the space of change between tools in the progression of technological innovation.

Ubiquitous Technology

It is clear that technology is here to stay. The growth of global Internet penetration alone has grown 480% from 2000 to 2011, as shown in Table 3.1 (Internet World Stats, 2011). In 2009, social networking users surpassed e-mail users (Meeker, 2010). Industry analysts predict that mobile use will be the primary Internet access path within 5 years, driven by adoption rate in emerging economies. For areas without existing information technology infrastructures, wireless networks are faster and less expensive to deploy and have greater adaptive capabilities for future bandwidth requirements (Gunasekaran & Harmantzis, 2007).

The trend has been for technology to recede. As it becomes smaller, mobile, and more personal, it better satisfies its primary functions—social connection and individual autonomy. Sales of mobile devices such as the iPhone and Android have skyrocketed, along with tablet computers such as the iPad and Google Chromebook, making mobile the fastest growing area in technology development (Pepitone, 2011). Apple's 2008 launch of the App Store unleashed a creative explosion of more than

Table 3.1. World Internet Usage[9]

World Regions	Population (2011 Est.)	Internet Users 12/31/2000	Internet Users Latest Data	Penetration (% Pop)	Growth 2000–2011	Users % of Total
Africa	1,038	5	119	11%	2,527%	6%
Asia	3,880	114	922	24%	707%	44%
Europe	816	105	476	58%	353%	23%
Middle East	216	3	69	32%	1,987%	3%
North America	347	108	272	78%	152%	13%
Latin America/Carib.	597	18	216	36%	1,037%	10%
Oceania/Australia	35	8	21	60%	179%	1%
WORLD TOTAL	**6,930**	**361**	**2,095**	**30%**	**480%**	**100%**

500,000 different apps,[10] with more than 15 billion downloaded—and that is Apple alone (Reisinger, 2011). More Americans are using mobile apps than full Web browsers (McMillian, 2011).

Smartphones are now an integral part of daily lives, providing an extension of desktop computers without the constraints. The smartphone experience is personal, sharable, and exchangeable. GPS-based applications have the ability not only to contact friends, but also to share, with mutual consent, other information such as location and status. Apps such as Friendlee and Foursquare deliver ambient awareness of social availability, facilitating communication (e.g., knowing when it's a good time to call or where to meet) and increasing face-to-face contact and friendship (Barkhuus et al., 2008; Ankolekar et al., 2009).

Communicating Across Multiple Platforms Simultaneously

The complexity of the media environment is evident in the convergence of media technologies. As technologies grow more sophisticated and Internet penetration spreads, there are fewer barriers to entry and less demarcation among the tools. Communication now happens "transmedia"—across multiple platforms (Jenkins, 2008). Messaging is no longer linear, isolated to a single channel, or unidirectional. The role of the consumer has also converged, as people move as fluidly through the functions of producer, distributor, and consumer as they do among technologies. The experience of technology use is increasingly social, participatory, and personalized (Rainie, Purcell, & Smith, 2011).

With the rapid adoption of social technologies among young adults, adolescents, and tweens,

many people express concerns over the substitution of virtual experience and contact for face-to-face social contact and engagement (e.g., Putnam, 1995; Turkle, 2011). Contrary to fears of isolation, researchers have found that mobile phones are used to enhance feelings of belonging and social identity and that social networking has a positive impact on social connectedness and traditional social behavior for most users (Valkenburg & Peter, 2009; Mathews, 2010).

Human Goals and Technology

Technology is designed by people to serve human goals. As often as humans anthropomorphize technology (Reeves & Nass, 1996), if a product, application, or interface does not satisfy fundamental human goals it does not succeed. Having technology mediate experience does not serve a fundamental goal unless it facilitates a connection not possible in any other way. This fact argues that innovation will work to diminish the "cost" of mediation in the service of the true goals of connection, creative expression, and information exchange. As technology evolves, it will become increasingly apparent that the psychology of interacting with technology—human goals and experience rather than high-tech bells and whistles—is the central and critical issues of technology in society.

Social Connection

Social connection is a primary human goal. Humans are biologically hardwired to connect; it is critical to our physical and emotional survival (Aronson, 2007). The staggering growth in social networks demonstrates the power of our social drives. The expanding media environment simplifies the development of multiple new social connections and access to knowledge. Information access is no longer a problem, but information filtering is (Q. Jones, Ravid, & Rafaeli, 2004; Klausegger, Sinkovics, & Zou, 2007). Digital connectivity demands new kinds of literacy to teach the tools and skills to manage relationships, screen information, and establish reliability and credibility.

Social relationships are the most important filtering device in a media and information-rich environment (Walter, Battison, & Schweitzer, 2007; Walther, Van Der Heide, Hamel, & Shulman, 2009). Search functions such as those offered by Google or Amazon.com are made up of complex algorithms to provide recommendations for users based on previous searches and other attributes. No matter how prescient they may seem, they are not as influential as the strength of personal connection or word of mouth (Brown & Reingen, 1987). In one of the first studies on word-of-mouth communication, Katz and Lazarsfeld (1955) showed that personal endorsements from known sources were the most important influence in purchasing behavior. Interpersonal trust relationships allow individuals to make judgments about people, behaviors, products, places, and organizations (Felfernig et al., 2008). Word of mouth is amplified and redefined on the social Web (Fogg & Eckles, 2007). Individuals continually make judgments balancing privacy against personal value and ease of access (Krause & Horvitz, 2008). For media psychologists, rich research areas exist in better understanding this impact, continuing to pursue questions such as: (1) how network ties and information patterns influence the conceptualization of privacy; (2) what factors in a mediated environment influence the constructs of persuasion and define the trustworthiness of a source; (3) how perceptions of self-relevance in computer-generated recommender systems compares with word of mouth; and (4) the tradeoff between personalization services for search efficiency and issues of privacy and unbiased information.

Psychology, Messaging, and Story

In a media-dense environment, the receiver battles with information overload, while the sender struggles to be heard. The challenge of rising above the noise plagues journalists, entertainers, businesses, politicians, advocacy groups, educators, and, of course, parents. Just as effective technology can be dissected to uncover the facilitation of human goals and motivations, identifying effective messaging trends in this

environment requires a similar return to fundamentals. A new appreciation of the psychological power of storytelling to communicate at multiple levels, or transmedia storytelling, has emerged in entertainment and marketing and is paving the way for a trend that will have broad impact across all industries and applications because it treats the audience as a valued collaborator and invites participation rather than demands attention. The enduring features of the transmedia storytelling approach are that it (1) recognizes the increasingly fluid use of media technologies; (2) employs the psychological features of emotions, metaphor, and sensory engagement wrapped around universal themes and a story arc; (3) invites and encourages audience exploration, participation, and contributions without diminishing autonomy; and (4) builds a coherent story using different media to supply additive contributions.

The media psychologist's interest, however, is in better understanding the holistic narrative experience in an interactive multidimensional space. The narrative is the essential core of a transmedia experience and functions as a powerful information filter by tapping into a fundamental form of human communication and connection. Narrative communication is multisensory and maps to universal themes that facilitate emotional engagement and understanding (Green & Brock, 2000; Ryan, 2002). Phenomenologically (Polkinghorne, 1988) and cognitively (Schleifer, David, & Mergler, 1992), stories are how people organize information and feelings so the world makes sense.

There are obvious links between game environments and transmedia stories in how they create avenues for discovery and self-directed engagement (Shaffer, Squire, Halverson, & Gee, 2004). Understanding how to sustain creative engagement has vast implications for education and civic participation. The trend toward transmedia communication also raises questions about both our ability to isolate a single medium in research and its relevance to the current and future media environments.

Resistance to Technology

For all the impressive predictions about the benefits of technology and the number showing the massive influx of technology penetration, there are still society-wide misgivings and resistance to new technologies. The cognitive shift from the pre-Internet world of information scarcity to a socially connected one of information surplus is enormous. Making this shift and adopting new tools and behaviors can conflict with individual core beliefs, identity, and assumptions, triggering negative emotions (Agarwal & Prasad, 1998).

Media psychology, because it is both academic and applied, is uniquely positioned to ease this transition and facilitate positive use and acceptance, and to advocate for access accompanied by training to overcome the digital divide. Awareness of technology—and even access—does not predestine adoption, yet using information technologies are increasingly essential to fully benefiting from and succeeding in today's society (Jenkins, Purushotma, Clinton, Weigel, & Robinson, 2006).

Technology adoption is hindered by many factors. Age is a primary determinant of ease of adoption. In the workforce, adoption among younger people was found to be most influenced by attitudes toward using technology, whereas older workers were more influenced by subjective understanding of social norms (Morris & Venkatesh, 2000). Until early adulthood, the brain is highly plastic and adaptive. The decrease in cognitive flexibility and adaptability that comes with age makes change such as accepting and adopting new technologies more difficult (Wexler, 2006). A mismatch between expectations and worldviews, such as social norms, results in the psychological discomfort of cognitive dissonance. The normal human reaction is to seek relief (Festinger & Carlsmith, 1959). Relief from restoring cognitive consonance can be achieved in two ways: by changing the worldview or adjusting the interpretation of incoming information to fit the existing beliefs (Beck, 1976).

A young brain is more able to adapt its structure and shape to fit the environment and can easily achieve relief by building new mental models, whether it's learning a new language, how to work an iPod, or how to decode the rules in a video game. Older brains do not lose their ability to learn new beliefs, but it requires intention and takes energy and motivation to do the hard work of cognitive restructuring (Wexler, 2006). It is a normal human response to ameliorate the cognitive dissonance of change by reshaping one's interpretation of the environment to fit the existing mental schemas (Seligman, 2002). With media technologies, this can manifest in suspicion, anxiety, or disparagement, such as refusing to use tools such as e-mail or Facebook, focusing on only the negative aspects, or denigrating the tools' usefulness or ease of access (Morris & Venkatesh, 2000; Porter & Donthu, 2006). As Abelson (1986) so aptly said, "Beliefs are like possessions" (p. 223). Beliefs are central to our sense of self and changes in the environment challenge an individual's sense of identity and control.

Because of the change in brain plasticity between youth and adulthood, successive generations can have significantly different internal structures (Wexler, 2006). This is the biological equivalent of what Prensky (2001) refers to as "digital natives" and "digital immigrants." The Net Generation growing up today does not remember a world without peer-to-peer connectivity. Their cognitive structures and core beliefs will differ from the generation before them, as will their impact on the environment (Tapscott, 2008).

Reasoned Responses and Moral Panics

Throughout history, the introduction of new technologies has challenged existing assumptions, triggering a wide range of responses from enthusiastic adoption to moral panics. Recorded examples of resistance to technological change include Socrates, who famously believed writing would cause "forgetfulness in the learners' souls, because they will not use their memories" (Plato, 360 b.c.e./2006, p. 64). In the early 16th century, the printing press led to concerns about the dangers of reading, especially for women; novels were feared to arouse dangerous emotions (Briggs & Burke, 2009). People also feared the impact of radio on children, as illustrated in a 1936 book review:

> For many hours each day the youngsters gather round the radio and listen with rapt attention to the thrilling adventures of their beloved comic strip heroes and heroines...So enthralled are they that they have developed the habit of dividing attention between the humdrum preparation of their school assignments and the compelling excitement of the loudspeaker...(Gramophone, 1936)

These are reminiscent of headlines today about the dangers of new technologies:

> *"Student 'addiction' to technology 'similar to drug cravings,' study finds"* (Hough, 2011)
> *"Social websites harm children's brains: Chilling warning to parents from top neuroscientist"* (Derbyshire, 2009).
> *"Twitter and Facebook could harm moral values, scientists warn"* (Science News, 2009)
> *"E-mails hurt IQ more than pot"* (CNN, 2005)

Whether researchers, practitioners, or the general public, the cognitive schema people hold implicitly inform the questions they ask, the concerns they have, and the answers they seek. The medical and disease model informed several decades of research in psychology and other social sciences (Linley & Joseph, 2004). That tradition, coupled with the concerns of rapid technological change, framed much of the early research on media technology. The demand for empiricism and public anxieties influence funding and push the social sciences to target negative impact. The fallout from moral panics can be long lasting; leaving society ill equipped to handle a changing world. Not only can they skew research and become embedded in public policy, but they also amplify the generational divide, as adults become more suspicious and hostile of the next generation's activities. They also divert scarce resources away from researching and addressing the real causes of social problems.

We cannot stop the spread of media technologies, nor should we want to. As an emerging and multidisciplinary field, however, media psychology can and should bring balance by understanding the fears, identifying problems, developing solutions, and ultimately highlighting and promoting potential.

Digital Citizenship

Media technologies are tools. Like all tools, they can be used with both positive and negative effect. The most powerful contribution of media psychology lies in applying the psychologies of human development, cognition, and culture to the prevention of the misuse and negative impact of technology by using it to develop strength.

A critical step to the positive adoption of media technologies across society is the development and implementation of media and technological literacy and digital citizenship (Jenkins et al., 2006; Ribble & Bailey, 2007).[11] Although digital citizenship is often equated with civic engagement (Bennett, 2008), it is inseparable from media and technological literacy in a world in which there is a blurring and blending of roles among consumers, producers, and distributors. No matter whether they are used for education or entertainment, media technologies are social spaces. They are public spaces and an active dynamic of society. Networked connectivity means that individual actions can reverberate across networks quickly and easily. This demands not only the ability to access, evaluate, and create messages across multiple media, but also an understanding of the technical and social rules of a digital public space (Livingstone, 2004).

The Role of Positive Psychology in Media Psychology

In 15 short years we have witnessed extraordinary technological change. The core of our communications backbone is now the Internet—an interconnected, peer-to-peer environment. Society has gone from marveling at what technology can do and what people can do with it, to taking much of it for granted. The capabilities are continually evolving, but there are several significant trends inherent in a network-based communication model with the availability of digital tools. The trends and influences are not tool-specific, but speak to the human goals and subjective experience.

The structure of the new environment is shifting core assumptions across society and creating a new global awareness. From the revolution that began at the end of 2010 with a violent individual statement of protest when a Tunisian fruit vendor set himself on fire, resulting in the toppling of the Egyptian government, to the global outpouring of donations and support in response to the devastating March 2011 earthquake in Japan, there is evidence of a fundamental change in human empathy that should be encouraged. To support the positive expression of freedom and empathy, media psychology must look to the potential, not the pathology.

Where positive psychology looks to amplify human strengths, media psychology uses the combined knowledge of psychology and technology to facilitate human growth and agency. Media psychology must begin to evaluate current and emerging technologies based on how well they are supporting our individual and collective goals. Media technologies have significant potential to improve lives and cultivate the development of well-being if we understand, acknowledge, and develop their affordances.

Media technologies are already having a profound effect on society. The act of engaging with technology promotes:

1. Voice. Social technologies allow people from all walks of life to share opinions, stories, complaints, jokes, and art without temporal or geographical constraints for either the sender or the receiver

2. Creativity. Greater connectivity and richer networks promote creative thought. With social technologies, people can create, collaborate, and share content—such as art, animation, photographs, texts, videos, playlists—in multiple permutations and combinations of expression with simple tools at relatively little cost.

3. Community. Digital connectivity creates new and strengthens old connections. It allows people to develop and maintain contact with friends and relatives, and preserve family cultures across distance. It opens the door to connections based on shared interests anywhere in the world.

4. Empathy. Through social technologies, people see other cultures. They can connect, learn about, and respond to those in need, locally and globally. No matter how narrow an individual's choices of media, it is impossible to avoid the ambient awareness of a larger world.

5. Self-Efficacy and Agency. Through technology, people can act on their environment and get immediate feedback. Getting and providing information on-demand, checking sources, demanding reliability, reaching out to others, and getting involved in the community or the country are all acts of agency that are self-reinforcing and build self-efficacy.

6. Collaboration. The social web is a collaborative environment for work and play, reinforcing an essential skill for the 21st century.

7. Social Capital. From strategy games and how-to videos to free university courses and mentors, people can access a multitude of opportunities to learn and develop new skills, careers, and connections.

8. Social Support. Social technologies provide unlimited opportunities to connect with people and develop meaningful relationships for social and emotional support, social validation, and feedback.

There is a new standard for behavior—participation and collaboration. Participation and collaboration imply trust, whether it's individuals, groups, or organizations. These capabilities have positive implications for individual beliefs about agency, self-efficacy, and validation, creating an upward spiral of empathy, engagement, and intrinsic motivation, as suggested in Fredrickson's (2004) Broaden and Build Theory of positive emotions.

Conclusion

Many of the most significant contributions to both scientific and public discourse come from challenging prevailing models. The rapid change in technologies and connectivity presents an opportunity to do just that. As a new field, media psychology has the potential to create an integrated approach, linking the potential of media technologies with the goal of promoting human strengths and optimal functioning (Linley & Joseph, 2004). Media psychology challenges prevailing models by recognizing the complex interaction of human experience and technology, and identifying the qualities that can be cultivated to support goal attainment and well-being.

The ubiquity of technology is driving home the point that human experience is not separable from technology and vice versa. Although emerging technologies and new models of communication add to the complexity of study, the integration of media into daily life highlights the importance of the human experience and systems of relationships as the focal point of study. It is here where media psychology brings a different perspective than other fields of study. It has the breadth of theory and tools to examine the behavior and interactions of individuals, groups, and organizations. It is not constrained by the type of technology, but understands the mediation that technology affords. Therefore, it can apply the lens of psychology to any form of human experience mediated by technology.

Interconnectivity and continuing innovations blur traditional boundaries and challenge many assumptions. A forward-looking science is necessary to anticipate and help people adapt to change and shift the view of technology away from the "evils of society" and toward the "tools of potential." Media psychology sits at the intersection of the dynamic system of technology and human experience. Moving beyond reductionist and medical models, media psychology, at its best, seeks to connect the positive capabilities of technology with human and group strengths that allow individuals and society to proactively engage and use technology to grow and flourish.

Future Directions and Challenges

Media psychology is a broad field by any measure. What distinguishes it from other areas of psychology and related social sciences is the knowledge of psychology combined with the knowledge of technology. The challenges for the field and its practitioners are threefold:

1. To stay abreast of technological innovations so as to anticipate substantive changes in how people, groups, and organizations are able to accomplish their goals.

2. To recognize that the psychological shifts linked with new technologies call into question the relevance of earlier research results. This is particularly important when we have built policy around them.

3. To be willing to continually monitor our own assumptions before we make judgments about another user's experience of technology.

Notes

1. LOLcats (text message shorthand for laugh out loud) are pictures of cats in funny poses with generally badly spelled

captions, hence the name of the site icanhascheezburger.com. There are many LOLcat (and other animals) sites in which people share their humor and creativity around pets. The original icanhascheezburger.com site was so popular that the original owners sold it for $2 million to a group of investors who went on to raise $30 million for a group of Internet sites credited with bringing Internet memes and tech culture mainstream, according to TechCrunch, January 17, 2011 http://techcrunch.com/tag/icanhascheezburger/.

2. TaraAkshar http://taraakshar.com/.

3. MILLEE is one of several organizations investigating the use of mobile devices for literacy, including Mobile Phones as a Literacy Platform in Niger, the m4Lit project in South Africa, Jokko in Senegal, and low-cost commercial projects, such as Nokia Life Tools in India and the BBC's Janala project in Bangladesh. Source: World Bank http://blogs.worldbank.org/edutech/mobile-phones-literacy.

4. Quest to Learn http://q2l.org/purpose.

5. *FarmVille* is a farming simulation social network game developed by Zynga in 2009. Game play involves farm management such as growing crops or managing livestock. Points are in the form of farm coins that are earned by working the farm or helping friends (http://www.farmville.com/).

6. World of Warcraft is a massively multiplayer online role-playing game (MMPORG) that was first introduced in 1994. Gameplay is subscription-based and users have customizable avatars that they use to explore the virtual landscape, tackle quests, and solve puzzles that often require collaboration to complete.

7. http://www.turismo.intoscana.it/allthingstuscany/aroundtuscany/tuscany-the-first-augmented-reality-tourism-application/

8. Isbouts & Ohler, in Chapter 2, tackle a definition of *mass media* in the context of this dilemma. My view of media and the importance of psychology encompasses the intersection of any technology and human experience, from device interfaces to social networks to traditional "mass" media. For the sake of clarity, when I use the term *mass,* I am referring to non-customizable, unidirectional media delivered to a mass audience.

9. Internet Usage and World Population Statistics are for March 31, 2011. Demographic (population) numbers are based on data from the US Census Bureau. (4) Internet usage information comes from data published by Nielsen Online, by the International Telecommunications Union, by GfK, local Regulators and other reliable sources. Compiled and published by www.internetworldstats.com.

10. Apps are applications made for mobile products (http://www.apple.com/iphone/built-in-apps/app-store.html).

11. For discussion on how digital citizenship fits into a more global approach to literacy, see Chapter 2.

References

Abelson, R. P. (1986). Beliefs are like possessions. *Journal for the Theory of Social Behavior, 16*(3), 223–250.

Agarwal, R., & Prasad, J. (1998). The antecedents and consequences of user perceptions in information technology adoption. *Decision Support Systems, 22*(1), 15–29.

Aker, J. (2008). *"Can You Hear Me Now?" How Cell Phones Are Transforming Markets in Sub-Saharan Africa.* Washington, DC: Center for Global Development.

Allen, I. E., & Seaman, J. (2007). *Online Nation: Five Years of Growth in Online Learning.* Needham, MA: Sloan Consortium/Babson Survey Research Group.

Allen, I. E., & Seaman, J. (2010). *Class Differences: Online Education in the United States, 2010.* Sloan Consortium/Babson Survey Research Group.

Ankolekar, A., Szabo, G., Luon, Y., Huberman, B., Wilkinson, D., & Wu, F. (2009). *Friendlee: A Mobile Application for Your Social Life.* Paper presented at the MobileHC109, Bonn, Germany.

Aronson, E. (2007). *The Social Animal,*10th ed. New York: Worth Publishers.

Bampo, M., Ewing, M. T., Mather, D. R., Stewart, D., & Wallace, M. (2008). The effects of the social structure of digital networks on viral marketing performance. *Information Systems Research, 19*(3), 273–290.

Bandura, A. (1977). Self-efficacy: Toward a unifying theory of behavior change. *Psychological Review, 84*(2), 191–215.

Bandura, A. (2002). Growing primacy of human agency in adaptation and change in the electronic era. *European Psychologist, 7*(1), 2–16. doi: 10.1027//1016–9040.7.1.2

Bandura, A. (2004). Health promotion by social cognitive means. *Health Education & Behavior, 31*(2), 143–164. doi: 10.1177/1090198104263660

Bandura, A. (2007). Reflections on an agentic theory of human behavior. *Tidsskrift for Norsk Psykologforening, 44*(8), 995–1004.

Barabasi, A.-L. (2003). *Linked: How Everything Is Connected to Everything Else and What it Means.* New York: Penguin Group.

Barkhuus, L., Brown, B., Bell, M., Sherwood, S., Hall, M., & Chalmers, M. (2008). *From awareness to repartee: sharing location within social groups.* Paper presented at the Proceeding of the 26th Annual SIGCHI Conference on Human Factors in Computing Systems, Florence, Italy.

Bartels, R. (1976). *History of Marketing Thought.* Columbus, OH: Grid, Inc.

Beck, A. T. (1976). *Cognitive Therapy and the Emotional Disorders.* New York: International Universities Press.

Benkler, Y. (2006). *The Wealth of Networks: How Social Production Transforms Markets and Freedoms.* New Haven, CT: Yale University Press.

Bennett, W. L. (2008). Changing citizenship in the digital age. In W. L. Bennett (Ed.), *Civic Life Online: Learning How Digital Media Can Engage Youth.* Cambridge, MA: MIT Press, pp. 1–24.

Black, R. W. (2009). Online fan fiction, global identities, and imagination. *Research in the Teaching of English, 43*(4), 397–425.

Botden, S. M. B. I., & Jakimowicz, J. J. (2009). What is going on in augmented reality simulation in laparoscopic surgery? *Surgical Endoscopy, 23*(8), 1693–1700.

Briggs, A., & Burke, P. (2009). *A Social History of the Media: From Gutenberg to the Internet,* 3rd ed. Cambridge, UK: Polity.

Brown, J. J., & Reingen, P. H. (1987). Social ties and world-of-mouth referral behavior. *Journal of Consumer Research, 14*(3), 350–362.

Buckingham, D. (Ed.). (2008). *Youth, Identity, and Digital Media.* Cambridge, MA: MIT Press.

Burke, J. (2008). Primetime spin: Media bias and belief confirming information. *Journal of Economics and Management Strategy, 17.*

Business Wire. (2003). First Ph.D. in media psychology starts at Fielding Graduate Institute. Retrieved August 8, 2011 from http://www.businesswire.com/news/home/20030926005482/en/Ph.D.-Media-Psychology-Starts-Fielding-Graduate-Institute.

Carll, E. K. (2003). Media psychology at the crossroads of information and communication technologies. *Media Psychology Amplifier, Fall/Winter*, 1–2. Retrieved August, 12, 2011 from http://www.apa.org/divisions/div46/images/ampfall03.pdf.

Charman-Anderson, S. (2012). Crowdfunding Raised $1.5bn in 2011, Set to Double in 2012. *Forbes.com* (May 11). Retrieved July 22, 2012 http://www.forbes.com/sites/suwcharmananderson/2012/05/11/crowdfunding-raised-1-5bn-in-2011-set-to-double-in-2012/

Cochrane, T., & Bateman, R. (2010). Smartphones give you wings: Pedagogical affordances of mobile Web 2.0. *Australasian Journal of Educational Technology & Society*(26), 1.

CNN.com (2005). E-Mails 'Hurt IQ More Than Pot'. *CNN.com International*, (April 22). Retrieved January 23, 2011 from http://articles.cnn.com/2005-04-22/world/text.iq_1_mails-iq-messages?_s=PM:WORLD

Csikszentmihalyi, M. (1991). *Flow: The Psychology of Optimal Experience*. New York: HarperCollins.

CTIA. (2010). Wireless Quick Facts. *2011*. Retrieved April 12, 2011 from http://www.ctia.org/advocacy/research/index.cfm/aid/10323.

Day, L. (2007). Healing environments and the limits of empirical evidence. *American Journal of Critical Care, 16*, 86–89.

Derbyshire, D. (2009). Social websites harm children's brains: Chilling warning to parents from top neuroscientist. *Daily Mail*. Retrieved January 12, 2011 from http://www.dailymail.co.uk/news/article-1153583/Social-websites-harm-childrens-brains-Chilling-warning-parents-neuroscientist.html.

Dumenco, S. (2011). How 'the X factor' vote-by-Tweet partnership with Twitter has affected its social-TV footprint. *AdAge MediaWorks*.

El Sayed, N. A. M., Zayed, H. H., & Sharawy, M. I. (2011). ARSC: Augmented Reality student card. An Augmented Reality solution for the education field. *Computers & Education, 56*(4), 1045–1061. doi: 10.1016/j.compedu.2010.10.019

Fang, I. (1997). *A History of Mass Communicaiton: Six Information Revolutions*. Boston: Focal Press.

Farmer, A., Gibson, O., Hayton, P., Bryden, K., Dudley, C., Andrew, N., & Tarassenko, L. (2005). A real-time, mobile phone-based telemedicine system to support young adults with type 1 diabetes. *Informatics in Primary Care, 13*(3), 171–178.

Felfernig, A., Gula, B., Leitner, G., Maier, M., Melcher, R., & Teppan, E. (2008). Persuasion in Knowledge-based Recommendation. *Persuasive Technology, 5033*, 71–82.

Ferguson, C. J. (2009). Violent video games: Dogma, fear, and pseudoscience. *Skeptical Inquirer, September/October*.

Festinger, L., & Carlsmith, J. (1959). Cognitive consequences of forced compliance. *Journal of Abnormal Psychology, 58*(2), 203–210.

Fischer, C. S. (1975). Toward a subcultural theory of urbanism. *American Journal of Sociology, 80*(6), 1319–1341.

Fischoff, S. (2005). Media psychology: A personal essay in definition and purview. *Journal of Media Psychology, 10*(1). Retrieved July 22, 2012 from www.apa.org/divisions/div46/images/MEDIADEF.pdf

Fogg, B. J., & Eckles, D. (Eds.). (2007). *Mobile Persuasion: 20 Perspective on the Future of Behavior Change*. Palo Alto, CA: Stanford University Press.

Ford, G. S., & Ford, S. G. (2009). *Internet Use and Depression Among the Elderly*, vol. 38. Phoenix, AZ: Phoenix Center Policy Paper.

Forster, P. M. (2004). Psychological sense of community in groups on the Internet. *Behaviour Change, 21*(2), 141–146.

Fredrickson, B. L. (2004). The broaden-and-build theory of positive emotions. *Philosophical Transactions of the Royal Society London, 359*, 1367–1377.

Gee, J. P. (2004). *What Video Games Have to Teach Us About Learning and Literacy*. New York: Palgrave Macmillan.

Geerts, D., & De Groof, D. (2009). *Supporting the Social Uses of Television: Sociability Heuristics for Social TV*. Paper presented at the CHI 2009 Conference: In the Living Room. Boston, MA.

Gilbert, N., Jager, W., Deffuant, G., & Adjali, I. (2007). Complexities in markets: Introduction to the special issue. *Journal of Business Research, 60*(8), 813–815. doi: 10.1016/j.jbusres.2007.01.016

Giles, D. C. (2003). *Media Psychology*. Hillsdale, NJ: Lawrence Erlbaum Associates.

Giles, D. C. (2010). *Psychology of the Media*. London: Palgrave Macmillan.

Gramophone. (1936). Film Review: Children and Radio Programmes. A Study of More than Three Thousand Children in the New York Metropolitan Area, by Azriel L. Eisenberg, 31–32.

Granovetter, M. (1973). The strength of weak ties. *American Journal of Sociology, 78*(6), 1360–1380.

Green, M. C., & Brock, T. C. (2000). The role of transportation in the persuasiveness of public narratives. *Journal of Personality and Social Psychology, 79*(5), 701–721.

Gross, D. (January 18, 2010). Red Cross text donations pass $21 million, *CNNTech*. Retrieved April 15, 2011 from http://articles.cnn.com/2010-01-18/tech/redcross.texts_1_red-cross-haiti-relief-facebook-and-twitter?_s=PM:TECH

Gunasekaran, V., & Harmantzis, F. (2007). Emerging wireless technologies for developing countries. *Technology in Society, 29*, 23–42.

Hampton, K., & Wellman, B. (2003). Neighboring in Netville: How the Internet supports community and social capital in a wired suburb. *City and Community, 2*(4), 277.

Harp, D., Bachmann, I., Rosas-Moreno, T. C., & Loke, J. (2010). Wave of hope: African American youth use media and engage more civically, politically than whites. *The Howard Journal of Communications, 21*(3), 224–246.

Harris, R. J. (2004). *A Cognitive Psychology of Mass Communication*, 4th ed. Hillsdale, NJ: Lawrence Erlbaum Associates.

Heylighen, F. (1999). *What Makes a Meme Successful? Selection Criteria for Cultural Evolution*. Paper presented at the 15th International Congress on Cybernetics, Brussels.

Hough, A. (2011). Student 'addiction' to technology 'similar to drug cravings,' study finds. *Telegraph*. Retrieved January 12, 2011 from http://www.telegraph.co.uk/technology/news/8436831/Student-addiction-to-technology-similar-to-drug-cravings-study-finds.html.

Howard, A. L. (2010). Engaging the City: Civic Participation and Teaching Urban History. *Journal of Urban History, 36*(1), 42–55.

Howard, P. H. (2004). *Society Online: The Internet in Context*. Thousand Oaks, CA: Sage Publications.

Huang, Y., Jiang, Z., Liu, Y., & Wang, Y. (2011). Augmented reality in exhibition and entertainment for the public. In Furht, B. (Ed.), *Handbook of Augmented Reality*, vol. 2. New York: Springer, pp. 707–720.

Internet World Stats. (2011). Internet Usage Statistic: The Internet Big Picture.

Islam, Y. M., & Doyle, K. O. (2008). Distance education via SMS technology in rural Bangladesh. *American Behavioral Scientist*, 52(1), 87–96.

Ito, M. (2009). Introduction. In K. Varnelis (Ed.), *Networked Publics*. Cambridge, MA: MIT Press, pp. 1–14.

ITU. (2010). ITU estimates two billion people online by end 2010: Access to mobile networks available to over 90% of world population 143 countries offer 3G services: International Telecommunications Union.

Jenkins, H. (2008). *Convergence Culture: Where Old and New Media Collide* (rev ed.). New York: New York University Press.

Jenkins, H., Purushotma, R., Clinton, K., Weigel, M., & Robinson, A. J. (2006). Confronting the Challenges of Participatory Culture: Media Education for the 21st Century. Retrieved September 12, 2009 from http://newmedialiteracies.org/.

Jensen, R. (2007). The digital provide: Information (technology), market performance, and welfare in the South Indian fisheries sector. [PowerPoint Presentation]. *Quarterly Journal of Economics*, 122(3), 879–924.

Jin, Y. (2009). The role of new media tools in young adults' engagement. *Journal of New Communications Research*, 4(1), 29–46.

Jones, G. J., Quested, D. J., & Thomson, K. E. (2000). Personalised delivery of news articles from multiple sources. *Research and Advanced Technology for Digital Libraries*, 1923, 340–343.

Jones, Q., Ravid, G., & Rafaeli, S. (2004). Information overload and the message dynamics of online interaction spaces: A theoretical model and empirical exploration. *Information Systems Research*, 15(2), 194–210. doi: 10.1287/isre.1040.0023

Junglas, I. A., & Watson, R. T. (2008). Location-based services. *Communications of the ACM—Urban Sensing: Out of the Woods*, 51(3), 65–69.

Kahn, R., & Kellner, D. (2004). New media and Internet activism: From the 'battle of Seattle' to blogging. *New Media & Society*, 6(1), 87–95.

Karlsson, H., & Kamppinen, M. (1995). Biological psychiatry and reductionism: Empirical findings and philosophy. *British Journal of Psychiatry*, 167, 434–438.

Katz, E., & Lazarsfeld, P. F. (1955). *Personal Influence: The Part Played by People in the Flow of Mass Communications*. New York: Free Press.

Kauffman, S. (1995). *At Home in the Universe*. New York: Oxford University Press.

Kellner, D., & Share, J. (2007). Critical media literacy, democracy, and the reconstruction of education. In Macedo, D., & Steinberg, S. R. (Eds.), *Media Literacy: A Reader*. New York: Peter Lang, pp. 3–23.

Kenrick, D. T., Li, N. P., & Butner, J. (2003). Dynamical evolutionary psychology: Individual decision rutles and emergent social norms. *Psychological Review*, 110(1), 3–28.

Klausegger, C., Sinkovics, R. R., & Zou, H. J. (2007). Information overload: A cross-national investigation of influence factors and effects. *Marketing Intelligence & Planning*, 25(7), 691–718. doi: 10.1108/02634500710834179

Knobloch-Westerwick, S., & Meng, J. (2008). Looking the other way: Selective exposure to attitude-consistent and counterattitudinal political information. *Conference Papers—International Communication Association*, 1–38.

Kosslyn, S. (2006). Mental images and the brain. *Cognitive Neuropsychology*, 22(333–347).

Krause, A., & Horvitz, E. (2008). *A utility-theoretic approach to privacy and personalization*. Paper presented at the 23rd AAAI Conference on Artificial Intelligence, Chicago, IL.

Lawson, H. M., & Leck, K. (2006). Dynamics of Internet dating. *Social Science Computer Review*, 24(2), 189–208.

Lazarsfeld, P. F., & Merton, R. K. (2000). Mass communication, popular taste and organized social action. In Marris, P., & Thornham, S. (Eds.), *Media Studies*, 2nd ed. New York: New York University Press, pp. 5–17.

Lin, C. A. (2007). An integrated communication technology and social change typology. *Communication Technology and Social Change: Theory and Implications*. Hillsdale, NJ: Lawrence Erlbaum Associates, pp. 283–307.

Linley, P. A., & Joseph, S. (2004). Applied positive psychology: A new perspective for professional practice. In Linley, P. A., & Joseph, S. (Eds.), *Positive Psychology in Practice*. Hoboken, NJ: John Wiley & Sons, pp. 3–13.

Livingstone, S. (1996). On the continuing problems of media effects research. In Curran, J., & Gurevitch, M. (Eds.), *Mass Media and Society*, 2nd ed. London: Edward Arnold, pp. 305–324.

Livingstone, S. (2004). Media literacy and the challenge of new information and communication technologies. *The Communication Review*, 1(7), 3–14.

Luskin, B. J., & Friedland, L. (1998). Task force report: Media psychology and new technologies. Washington, DC: Media Psychology Division 46 of the American Psychological Association.

Madden, M. (2009). The audience for online-video-sharing sites shoots up. *Pew Internet & American Life Project*. Retrieved December 3, 2010 from http://fe01.pewinternet.org/Reports/2009/13 – The-Audience-for-Online-VideoSharing-Sites-Shoots-Up.aspx.

Maddux, J. E. (2005). Self-efficacy: The power of believing you can. In Snyder, C. R., & Lopez, S. J. (Eds.), *Handbook of Positive Psychology*. Oxford, UK: Oxford University Press, pp. 257–276.

Manobi Development Foundation. (2011). Case studies: In Farming, from http://www.manobi.net/foundation/?M=2&SM=6.

Masten, A., & Reed, M. G. (2005). Resilience in development. In Snyder, C. R., & Lopez, S. J. (Eds.), *Handbook of Positive Psychology*. New York: Oxford University Press, pp. 74–88.

Mathews, R. (2010). The social and psychological implications of online social networking *2010 National Psychology Week*: Australian Psychological Association.

McKenna, K. Y. A., & Bargh, J. A. (1998). Coming out in the age of the Internet: Identity "demarginalization" through virtual group participation. *Journal of Personality and Social Psychology*, 75(3), 681–694. doi: 10.1037/0022–3514.75.3.681

McMichael, A. (2005). *History on the Web: Using and Evaluating the Internet*. Wheeling, IL: Harlan Davidson.

McMillian, G. (June 23, 2011). Study: Americans use mobile apps more than full web now. Retrieved October 10, 2011 from http://techland.time.com/2011/06/23/study-americans-use-mobile-apps-more-than-full-web-now/.

Meeker, M. (2010). Internet trends. *Morgan Stanley Reports*. Retrieved October 22, 2011 from http://www.morganstanley.com/institutional/techresearch/pdfs/Internet_Trends_041210.pdf

Mehra, B., Merkel, C., & Bishop, A. P. (2004). The Internet for empowerment of minority and marginalized users. *New Media & Society*, 6, 781–802.

Mitchell, M. (2009). *Complexity: A guided tour*. Oxford, UK: Oxford University Press.

Moore, K. (2011). 71% of online adults now use video-sharing sites: Pew Internet & American Life Project.

Morris, M. G., & Venkatesh, V. (2000). Age differences in technology adoption decisions: Implications for a changing work force. *Personnel Psychology, 53*, 375–403.

Nathan, M., Harrison, C., Yarosh, S., Terveen, L., Stead, L., & Amento, B. (2008). *CollaboraTV: Making Television Viewing Social Again*. Paper presented at the ACM 2009, Silicon Valley, CA.

Neuhauser, C. (2002). Learning style and effectiveness of online and face-to-face instruction. *The American Journal of Distance Education, 16*(2), 99–113.

Nielsen. (2010). Americans using TV and internet together 35% more than a year ago. *NielsenWire.com*. Retrieved April 2, 2011 from http://blog.nielsen.com/nielsenwire/online_mobile/three-screen-report-q409/.

Pajares, F. (2006). Self-efficacy during childhood and adolescence: Implications for teachers and parents. In Pajares, F., & Urdan, T. (Eds.), *Self-Efficacy Beliefs of Adolescents*. Greenwich, CT: Information Age Publishing, pp. 339–367.

Pea, R., & Maldonado, H. (2006). Wild for learning: Interacting through new computing devices anytime, anywhere. In R. K. Sawyer (Ed.), *The Cambridge Handbook of the Learning Sciences*. Cambridge: Cambridge University Press, pp. 427–441.

Pepitone, J. (April 19, 2011). Tablet sales may hit $75 billion by 2015. Retrieved April 27, 2011 from http://money.cnn.com/2011/04/19/technology/tablet_forecasts/index.htm.

Pew Research Center. (2010). Trend Data. Retrieved May 2, 2011 from http://www.pewinternet.org/Static-Pages/Trend-Data/Online-Activites-Total.aspx.

Plato. (360BC/2006). *Phaedrus* (Jowett, B., Trans.). Middlesex, UK: Echo Library.

Polkinghorne, D. E. (1988). *Narrative Knowing and the Human Sciences*. Albany, NY: State University of New York.

Porter, C. E., & Donthu, N. (2006). Using the technology acceptance model to explain how attitudes determine Internet usage: The role of perceived access barriers and demographics. *Journal of Business Research, 59*, 999–1007.

Prensky, M. (2001). Digital natives, digital immigrants: Do they really think differently? *On the Horizon, 9*(6). Retrieved September 15, 2007 from http://www.marcprensky.com/writing/Prensky—Digital Natives, Digital Immigrants—Part2.pdf.

Prensky, M. (2007). *Digital Game-Based Learning*. St. Paul, MN: Paragon House Publishers.

Purcell, K. (2011). *Information 2.0 and beyond: Where are we, where are we going?* Paper presented at the APLIC 44th Annual Conference, Washington, DC.

Purcell, K., Rainie, L., Mitchell, A., Rosentiel, T., & Olmstead, K. (2010). Understanding the participatory news consumer: How internet and cell phone users have turned news into a social experience *Project for Excellence in Journalism* (pp. 1–63). Washington, DC: Pew Research Center.

Putnam, R. D. (1995). Bowling alone. *Journal of Democracy*, 65–78.

Qualman, E. (2009). *Socialnomics: How Social Media Transforms the Way We Live and Do Business*. Hoboken, NJ: John Wiley & Sons.

Quintana, C., Krajcik, J., & Soloway, E. (2002). *A Case Study to Distill Structural Scaffolding Guidelines for Scaffolded Software Environments*. Paper presented at the SIGCHI Conference on Human Factors in Computing Systems, Minneapolis, MN.

Rainie, L., Purcell, K., & Smith, A. (2011). The social side of the Internet. *Pew Internet & American Life Project*. Retrieved February 15, 2011 from http://www.pewinternet.org/Reports/2011/The-Social-Side-of-the-Internet.aspx.

Reeves, B., & Anderson, D. R. (1991). Media studies and psychology. *Communication Research, 18*(5), 597–600.

Reeves, B., & Nass, C. (1996). *The Media Equation: How People Treat Computers, Television, and New Media Like Real People and Places*. Cambridge, MA: Stanford University Center for the Study of Language and Information and Cambridge University Press.

Reisinger, D. (July 7, 2011). Apple App Store hits 15 billion downloads. Retrieved August 12, 2011 from http://news.cnet.com/8301-13506_3-20077470-17/apple-app-store-hits-15-billion-downloads/.

Ribble, M., & Bailey, G. (2007). *Digital citizenship in schools*. Washington, DC: International Society for Technology in Education.

Rice, R. E., Shepherd, A., Dutton, W. H., & Katz, J. E. (2007). Social Interaction and the Internet: A comparative analysis of surveys in the US and Britain. In Joinson, A., McKenna, K. Y. A., Postmes, T., & Reips, U.-D. (Eds.), *The Oxford Handbook of Internet Psychology*. Oxford, UK: Oxford University Press, pp. 7–30.

Rideout, V. J., Foehr, U. G., & Roberts, D. F. (2010). Generation M2: Media in the lives of 8–18 year-olds *A Kaiser Family Foundation Survey*. Menlo Park, CA: Henry J. Kaiser Family Foundation.

Russell, A., Ito, M., Richmond, T., & Tuters, M. (2009). Culture: Media convergence and networked participation. In Varnelis, K. (Ed.), *Networked Publics*. Cambridge: MIT Press, pp. 43–76.

Rutledge, P. (2007). What is media psychology? A qualitative inquiry. *Media Psychology Review, September*(1). Retrieved May 2, 2009 from http://www.mprcenter.org/index.php?option=com_content&view=article&id=1&Itemid=64.

Rutledge, P. (2008). *The Influence of Media on Core Beliefs*. PhD dissertation. Santa Barbara, CA: Fielding Graduate University.

Ryan, M.-L. (2002). Beyond myth and metaphor: Narrative in digital media. *Poetics Today, 23*(4), 581–609. doi: 10.1215/03335372-23-4-581

Schleifer, R., David, R. C., & Mergler, N. (1992). *Culture and Cognition*. Ithaca, NY: Cornell University Press.

Science News. (2009). Twitter and Facebook could harm moral values, scientists warn. *The Telegraph*.

Seligman, M. E. P. (2002). *Authentic Happiness*. New York: The Free Press.

Seligman, M. E. P., & Csikszentmihalyi, M. (2000). Positive psychology: An introduction. *American Psychologist, 55*, 5–14.

Shaffer, D. W., Squire, K. R., Halverson, R., & Gee, J. P. (Eds.). (2004). *Video games and the future of learning*. Madison, WI: University of Wisconsin-Madison and Academic Advanced Distributed Learning Co-Laboratory.

Sharritt, M. (2010). Designing game affordances to promote learning and engagement. *International Journal of Cognitive Technology. Special Issue: Games for Good, 14*(2), 43–57.

Small, G., Moody, T., Siddarth, P., & Bookheimer, S. (2008). Your brain on Google: Patterns of cerebral activation during Internet searching. *American Journal of Geriatric Psychiatry, 17*(2), 116–127.

Smith, A. (2010). Mobile access 2010. *Pew Internet & American Life Project*. Retrieved January 12, 2011 from http://www.pewinternet.org/Reports/2010/Mobile-Access-2010.aspx.

Soukup, C. (2006). Computer-mediated communication as a virtual third place: Building Oldenburg's great good places on the world wide web. *New Media & Society, 8*(3), 421–440.

Squire, K. R., & Jan, M. (2007). Mad city mystery: Developing scientific argumentation skills with a place-based augmented reality game on handheld computers. *Journal of Science Education and Technology, 16*(1), 5–29.

Steinkuehler, C., & Williams, D. (2006). Where everybody knows your (screen) name: Online Games as "third places." *Journal of Computer Mediated Communication, 11*(4). Retrieved July 7, 2010 from: http://jcmc.indiana.edu/vol11/issue4/steinkuehler.html.

Stevenson, B. (2008). *The Internet and Job Search.* (NBER Working Paper No. 13886). Washington, DC: National Bureau of Economic Research

Strogatz, S. H. (2003). Sync: The emerging science of spontaneous order. New York: Hyperion.

Stroud, D. (2007). Social networking: An age-neutral commodity—Social networking becomes a mature web application. *Journal of Direct, Data and Digital Marketing Practice, 9*, 278–292.

Subrahmanyam, K., Reich, S. M., Waechter, N., & Espinoza, G. (2008). Online and offline social networks: Use of social networking sites by emerging adults. *Journal of Applied Developmental Psychology, 29*(6), 420–433.

Tapscott, D. (2008). *Growing Up Digital: How the Net Generation Is Changing Your World.* New York: McGraw-Hill.

Tooby, J., Cosmides, L., & Barrett, H. C. (2003). The second law of thermodynamics is the first law of psychology: evolutionary developmental psychology and the theory of tandem, coordinated inheritances: Comment on Lickliter and Honeycutt (2003). *Psychological Bulletin, 129*(6), 858–865.

Turkle, S. (2011). *Alone Together: Why We Expect More from Technology and Less from Each Other.* New York: Basic Books.

Turner, P., & Ayres, R. (Producer). (2011). Augmented Reality in a 4G World: Applications for Higher Education. *Educause.* [PowerPoint] Retrieved April 12, 2011 from http://www.educause.edu/Resources/AugmentedRealityina4GWorldAppl/224353.

Valkenburg, P. M., & Peter, J. (2009). Social consequences of the Internet for adolescents. *Current Directions in Psychological Science, 18*(1), 1–5. doi: 10.1111/j.1467–8721.2009.01595.x

Varnelis, K. (Ed.). (2009). *Networked Publics.* Cambridge, MA: MIT Press.

Vygotsky, L. S. (1978). *Mind in Society.* Cambridge, MA: Harvard University Press.

Walter, F. E., Battison, S., & Schweitzer, F. (2007). A model of trust-based recommendation system on a social network. *Journal of Autonomous Agents and Multi-Agent Systems, 16*(1), 57–74.

Walther, J. B., Van Der Heide, B., Hamel, L. M., & Shulman, H. C. (2009). Self-generated versus other-generated statements and impressions in computer-mediated communication: A test of warranting theory using Facebook. *Communication Research, 36*(2), 229–253.

Watts, D. J. (2003). *Six Degrees: The Science of a Connected Age.* New York: WW. Norton & Company.

Wellman, B., Haase, A. Q., Witte, J., & Keith, H. (2001). Does the Internet increase, decrease, or supplement social capital? Social networks, participation, and community commitment. *American Behavioral Scientist, 45*(3), 436–455. doi: 10.1177/00027640121957286

Wexler, B. E. (2006). *Brain and Culture: Neurobiology, Ideology, and Social Change.* Cambridge, MA: MIT Press.

Williams, D., Caplan, S., & Xiong, L. (2007). Can you hear me now? The impact of voice in an online gaming community. *Human Communication Research, 33*(4), 427–449. doi: 10.1111/j.1468–2958.2007.00306.x

Winston, B. (1998). *Media Technology and Society: A History: From the Telegraph to the Internet.* London: Routledge.

Yang, H., Han, S. H., & Park, J. (2010). User interface metaphors for a PDA operating system. *International Journal of Industrial Ergonomics, 40*(5), 517–529. doi: 10.1016/j.ergon.2010.04.002

Zafar, A. (2011). Facebook for centenarians: Senior citizens learn social media. *The Atlantic, August 31.*

Zheng, R., McAlack, M., Wilmes, B., Kohler-Evans, P., & Williamson, J. (2009). Effects of multimedia on cognitive load, self-efficacy, and multiple rule-based problem solving. *British Journal of Educational Technology, 40*(5), 790–803.

Zichuhr, K. (2010). Generations 2010. Washington, DC: Pew Internet & American Life Project.

Zimmerman, B. (2000). Self-efficacy: An essential motive to learn. *Contemporary Educational Psychology, 25*, 82–91.

Media Psychology and Its History

Regina M. Tuma

Abstract

Currently, media psychology appears to be a fragmented area of study, an appendage of sorts to many disciplines such as communication studies and even psychology. And yet, it is the case that this current state obscures a long history and tradition that leads to the development of media psychology within psychology as a discipline. The history of media psychology will be explored at two levels. First, it will be argued that the idea of media psychology emerges with the notion of mediation of reality by our senses in philosophy, the study of perception and cognition in early psychology. This tradition is then carried into a social psychology that is influenced by the study of perception and where the idea and role of media as instruments of culture, influence and cognition is further developed. The final section explores the status of media psychology within current research in psychology and social psychology.

Key Words: history, history of cognition, media psychology, psychology, social psychology

What is media psychology and what is its history? Such questions loom large as we consider the place of media psychology as a field of inquiry. Current views of media psychology place it as either a niche topic within the field of communication studies (Giles, 2003) or as a simple application of theories in psychology to the specialized topic of media (Pratkanis & Aronson, 2001). These approaches, however, ignore the broader history of the idea of media psychology, and do so to the peril of a discipline whose time has come. Indeed, given the importance of media in everyday life and the role of Internet culture and how individuals use media to shape society, I would say that if we didn't have media psychology, we would be poised and well advised to invent it.

In considering these questions it is important to distinguish, as Farr (1996) does, between the "long and short past of psychological disciplines." Following that tradition, this chapter explores the extended and noble past of media psychology. From the vantage point of this history, media psychology is not new. Indeed, its origins and roots can be traced back to the fundamental issues identified by philosophers and psychologists who grounded psychology in the study of the image and the mediation of reality through our senses.

The Roots of Media Psychology: Perception and the Mediation of Reality

Media act as instruments of perception and cognition, much like the eyes and ears, which act beyond the borders of our own senses. If we are looking to place media psychology, a good start would be to explore the history of psychology and its relationship to the psychology of perception. In fact, the argument can be made that the idea of media psychology begins with the study of perception and the mediation of reality.

The science writer Jonah Lehrer (2007) in his book, *Proust Was a Neuroscientist*, explores the work of various artists, who through their art anticipated some of the modern truths we know today about the brain. Lehrer's essay on Cezanne sheds light on the details of the perceptual process, which as he notes, begins with "atomic disturbance." On this, Lehrer writes: "Particles of light alter the molecular structure of the receptors in the retina…the photon's energy has become information" (p. 104). We do not, however, "see" the images on the retina, nor do we see the image that is further translated through the channels of angles and lights in the visual cortex. If we did, the world would look like a series of jagged edges and unresolved angles far removed from the reality we experience. Lehrer explains that "reality" at the level of the V1 neurons is "abstract" and "formless, nothing but a collage of chromatic blocks" (p. 107). The formless nature of the image, however, has nothing to do with the level of processing and should not be thought of as an image on its way toward resolving itself on its own. Lehrer reminds us that, "Ambiguity is an essential part of the seeing process," and this ambiguity remains even as the image is further processed and refined throughout other areas of the cortex. Yet our experience of the whole (to use a Gestalt psychology term) or the scene is organized and seamless, defined by the lyrical quality of its organization, which is the only reality we experience. It is for this reason, Arien Mack (1982) explains, that perception belongs not to "physiologists or biologists," but to psychologists (p. 951). Lehrer concurs that for reality to make sense, the "mind must intervene" (p. 107). He notes that modern neuroscience has confirmed what early psychologists had established, that "visual experience transcends visual sensations" (p. 117). At all levels of processing, perception demonstrates the will of the mind to make sense of the world. And it is in this sense the facts of perception and the story we tell about it is unchanging. As Mack observes, perception is "the end result of a complex, active process of organization, interpretation, and construction" (p. 962). It is this ability of the mind to organize experience in a manner that is not contained in the image, to go beyond that which is given to it, which led Kant to conclude that "imagination is a necessary ingredient of perception itself" (quoted in Lehrer, p. 116). Reality is mediated through the process of perception, and our experience of it is more than meets the eye.

The idea of mediation as a basic fact of perception becomes a cornerstone in the study of cognition beyond perception. As Leahey (2004) observed, Piaget's developmental psychology was "Kantian epistemology with a developmental twist" (p. 415). Similarly, Bruner's (Bruner et al, 1956) studies on thinking demonstrated the work of Kantian categories, not given in the external world, but the creation of an active intellect engaged in problem solving (Leahey, p. 418). That mediation should reverberate as such was not surprising given the foundational relation between perception

and cognition. "Perceiving," as Mack emphasizes, is the "single activity which serves as the basis for all psychological life" (p. 967). Even Fechner's (1876/1966) experiments in psychophysics demonstrated that "sensations cannot be totally divorced from their psychological environment" (Hearnshaw, (1989) p. 129). Later on, Bartlett's (1932/1995) studies on memory demonstrated memory as an active reconstruction, social in nature and mediated by the need of individuals to create meaning (Danziger, 2008, pp. 137–142).

The idea of mediation and perception, however, was not just important to early psychology. In fact, we see that artists and historians similarly make it a focus of their work and thus arrive at the psychology of perception from without. Again, Jonah Lehrer's essay on perception reminds us of how the paintings of Cezanne were intended as an artistic meditation on the nature and process of perception. Indeed, Cezanne objectified, through his paintings, the inner workings of perception with detail and accuracy long before neuroscientists were able to look inside the brain. His works engaged the viewer in a manner that the perceptual process and the work of the mind would reveal. Lehrer writes:

> But Cezanne was unfazed by his critics. He knew that his paintings were only literally blank. Their incompleteness was really a metaphor for the process of sight. In these unfinished canvases, Cezanne was trying to figure out what the brain would finish for him. As a result, his ambiguities are exceedingly deliberate, his vagueness predicated on precision. If Cezanne wanted us to fill his empty spaces, then he had to get his emptiness exactly right. (p. 114)

Similar interest in the relationship between art and perception can be found in Gombrich (1960) who argues that to understand "the central problems" of art history, "We have to get down to analyzing afresh, in psychological terms, what is actually involved in the process of perception" (p. 25).

Early Media Psychology: From the Perception of Form to the Aesthetics of Thought

The idea of mediation becomes prototypical of early psychology's relationship to media and it is here where we begin to see the kernel of the earliest forms of media psychology. The groundwork for this can be found in Gestalt theory and its analysis of forms. The laws of perceptual organization described by Wertheimer (1923/1938) pointed to how cognition contributes to our experience of forms and this analysis easily translated to our experience of art—shapes, forms, and depth on a two-dimensional canvas. Beyond forms, Wertheimer demonstrated the phi phenomenon, the familiar experience of being able to see motion in films when stationary images are flashed in rapid succession. As Leahey recounts this, Wertheimer considered the experience of motion in film as *real*, "real in consciousness," not an artifact of false inference, even though the experience "did not correspond to any physical stimulus" (p. 254).

Psychologists would soon begin to apply these ideas, along with the idea of mediation more generally, to the experience of media forms. An example of this can be seen in Munsterberg's (1916/2002) work on film or *photoplay*, which explored the aesthetics of film, as well as the relationship among art, film, and the nature of thought. As Munsterberg saw it, the purpose of film was art. What was unique about film, and what allowed it to realize its purpose, *art*, was the new medium's capacity to, as Carroll writes, "objectify the processes of the human mind" (p. 494). Munsterberg explains:

the photoplay tells us the human story by overcoming the forms of the outer world, namely space, time, and causality, and by adjusting the events to the forms of the inner world, namely attention, memory, imagination, and emotion. (italics original, p. 129)

For Munsterberg, "film operates like the human mind" (Langdale, 2002, p. 9) and like art, both film and the human mind *transform* and do not copy reality. It is important to note here that Munsterberg equates the nature of mind with the nature art. At a basic level, this means that thinking and the nature of mind themselves take on an aesthetic quality, if not dimension. Indeed, as the processes of mind are objectified through art, in film according to Munsterberg, and the perceptual process through Cezanne's style of art, the processes of mind themselves become media forms; while the psychology of thinking *itself* becomes a form of media psychology.

In writing about the nature of art, mind, and film, Munsterberg was borrowing from philosophical discourses of his time with a heavy dose of Kantian aesthetics informing his views (Carroll, 1988, p. 492). He was writing at a time when philosophy and psychology were neighboring disciplines with shared discourses, but there is a more specific psychology that emerges in *The Photoplay* as Munsterberg turns to the details of the relationship between film and mind. Film was an art form that was not the same as photography and different from live theater. Taking a cue from Wertheimer's phi phenomena, Munsterberg

(p. 73) begins with the experience of movement and depth—illusions in film—which he sees as "*super-additions* that the mind supplies to a series of flat surfaces of still photos" (Carroll, p. 491). He then explores the parallels between the techniques of film and processes of mind. In doing so, Munsterberg sets up the film/mind analogy that became standard in the study of film theory (p. 490) and influential to later psychologists (Arnheim, (2006). Whereas in live theater, attention is driven by gestures, in film a close-up not only imitates but becomes an objectified form of attention. Earlier scenes can provide clues to the past, but in film the flashback embodies the act of memory; imagination is similarly intimated in the flash forward as a cinematic technique (p. 491).

It is important to point out that there is an unresolved tension in Munsterberg's account of film and mind. His analogy rests on the similarity between film and cognition. Film, like the mind and art, move beyond and in effect transform reality—as art forms do. This view goes back to Kant's understanding of aesthetic judgment as belonging to the particular, that which is "not subsumable under a concept" (Carroll, p. 492). Although this is the case with the experience of depth and motion in film, which are added by the mind, it is not at all clear with the way film objectifies other processes of mind, namely attention and memory. Carroll has detailed the many issues with Munsterberg's psychological approach to film and among them he notes the contradiction of film controlling attention and memory. He observes:

For in the matter of film depth and motion, the psychologist tells us we add something to the visual array, where as with the close-up, the selecting is something that is done for us. That is, the mental process—attention—that Munsterberg discusses with the respect to the close-up is, roughly speaking, in the film, not in us. A similar shift in direction occurs in the rest of Munsterberg's account of cinematic articulations. (p. 491)

Langdale (2002) similarly observes a crucial difference between suggested thought in film and imagination, as the two were equated by Munsterberg. In film, Langdale writes, suggestion is a "stealth-thought" that originates from an "external" source meant to "instigate specific associations, taking their place like intruders alongside associations that really do spring from our own minds" (p. 19). For these reasons, Munsterberg's contribution to the psychology of film and media should be seen as behaviorist. Langdale quotes Hale (1980), the authority on Munsterberg's work, who noted that

"Munsterberg values film not because it allowed more creativity on the part of the audience, but because it permitted more control by the artist over aesthetic experience" (in Langdale, p. 16). Film and mind do mediate reality, but the mediation is controlled from the outside.

However, Munsterberg's psychology is based on the psychology of perception. The unresolved tension witnessed in Munsterberg's psychology of film is itself a leftover from the psychology of perception. "The practical human brain," returning to Lehrer's description of perception for a moment, "is not interested in a camera like truth; it just wants the scene to make sense" (p. 107). Top-down perception is open to suggestion, and influence is imposed from without, "Form is imposed...the outside world is forced to conform to expectations" (p. 108). So it is true that Cezanne objectifies the process of perception through his paintings. But in doing so he is guiding and directing the outcome of the viewer's perception, "Instead of giving us a scene of fully realized forms, Cezanne supplies us with layers of suggestive edges, out of which forms slowly unfurl" (p. 107).

Despite criticisms of Munsterberg's film/mind analogy outlined by Carroll and Langdale, it is the case that Munsterberg's psychology of film, based on aesthetics of thought and perception, should not be easily dismissed. In some sense, it proves prescient in that it sets the framework and issues that we will see as media psychology is further elaborated in social psychology.

Setting the Stage for Media Psychology: Social Psychology, Public Culture, and the Mediation of Appearance

The psychology of perception is then generalized to social psychology, in which the idea of media psychology is further elaborated and eventually nurtured. It is well known that Gestalt theories of perception had a direct influence on social psychology (Farr, 1996, p. 113). At this point, the turn to social psychology would appear to be a continuation of the psychology of perception now transposed to the social realm. But although the turn to media in social psychology is based on the psychology of perception, the psychology of perception becomes more complex as it now makes its way through the stage that is culture and society. Nonetheless, the shift is significant and one that nurtures the eventual turn to media, if not the idea of media psychology itself. To understand the confluence of media and social psychology, it is important to explore the relationship between the psychology of perception and the philosophy of appearance at the level of culture.

On Perception and Appearance

The philosopher Hannah Arendt (1958) long ago noted culture as a space of appearance. As the space of appearance, culture is the space where we become visible to each other and where the world becomes visible to us. This visibility confers reality. Arendt writes that "our feeling for reality depends utterly upon appearance in the public realm" (p. 51). She further explains: "For us, appearance—something that is being seen and heard by others, as well as ourselves—constitutes reality" (p. 50). There is a way in which Arendt's notion of appearance in public in part relies on the idea of perception. This makes sense if we consider that the relationship between perception and reality or "world" was the point of departure for earlier philosophical theories of perception. After all, we do have the image of Kant, observer of the French Revolution (Arendt would later use the term *spectator*) writing about perception and the nature of mind as he encountered ideas of enlightenment and democracy—all in seamless fluidity and without contradiction.[1] In some sense, the promise behind the study of perception is the idea that the world appears, or as Arien Mack (1982) aptly states, "We open our eyes and see." And it is the fact that we *see* and do so immediately that confers upon perception, as Mack notes, a "privileged epistemological status" (p. 950).

At the same time, it is important to observe that there are differences between perception and appearance. To be clear, Arendt's definition of the public implies more than visual perception—she does emphasize the importance of speech and discussion in making things real in public—but all of these work together in the service of the broader idea of appearance (Gottesegen, pp. 50–51). It is also true that Arendt's definition of appearance is not to be equated with perception of the image. Although appearance is or involves perception, it is perception of a different kind. Arendt follows Kant's definition of deductive thinking to differentiate between the two. Perception is a cognitive process that involves apprehending sensory data that allow identification of things, objects by means of established schemata. As Young-Bruehl (2006) explains, perception of the image, identification of the object or thing operates deductively, "starting from the generality and going to the particular" (p. 167), but as Gottsegen points out, there is a material reality (e.g., a two-dimensional, three-sided, and closed figure) behind the schema of triangle (p. 181). Appearance, on the other hand, is reserved for those intangible ideas around which societies coalesce—social reality for social psychologists—that can only take the dimensionality of reality when they are made to appear through debate and discussion in public culture.[2] And for these, Arendt re-works Kant's theory of aesthetic judgment—the kind of thinking involved in judging a work of art for Kant—and generalized it as a normative prototype for the kind of thinking that goes beyond the identification of shapes and objects. Aesthetic judgment in this Kantian-Arendtian sense, operates reflectively and "involves finding a relation between some form of particular and some form of generality" (Young-Bruehl, p. 167).[3]

Social Psychology at the Crossroads Between Perception and Appearance

It is the case that social psychology as a discipline is based on the psychology of perception, but it is also more than just perception. This can be seen early on in the debate over substantive differences between object perception and social perception and the applicability of the former in the social realm (Heider, 1958). And there is an aspect of social psychology that is concerned with public culture and appearance. This is what the French social psychologist Serge Moscovici (1988) has in mind when he declares social psychology to be a science of appearance and public life. Moscovici (1989) locates social psychology as existing within that space, neither social nor individual, thus "establishing the continuity between individual and collective phenomena" (p. 409), and that space that exists between the individual and society is culture (Moscovici and Markova, 1998, p. 385). Indeed, as Nederhof and Zwier (1983) point out, social psychology makes assumptions about the nature of culture and its theories and approaches are related to these assumptions.

What the psychology of perception and appearance in the cultural realm share, however, is the idea of mediation of reality and cultural reality. In other words, just like the image in perception is a mediated form, so too will forms that appear in cultural space be mediated. Arendt is clear that culture is a mediated space. The first source of mediation stems from the spectators or viewers themselves. Public culture is related to how we understand the world. As such, our positioning as individuals to the world will be mediated through the stories, traditions, folklore, and background knowledge that we pass to one another and successive generations. These cultural stories and knowledge do not so much determine choices as much as they help guide action (Gottsegen, p. 103). Arendt sees action as being rooted in novelty and capable of transcending the very "cultural conditioning" of forms (Gottsegen, p. 103). Although understanding is rooted in culture, it is not predetermined by it. Cultural indeterminacy is

to be found in the vastness and depth of the narratives and various stories, along with the creativity and transformation involved in the retelling of stories and its effects on memory and understanding.[4] Cultural indeterminacy works in favor of spectators being able to go beyond the cultural form given, in the same way that identification of an image in perception, although bound by the image, is open to interpretation. A further layer of mediation occurs through the positioning of individuals—Arendt's spectators—who bring their unique perspective as members of groups and communities, to bear on the world. As Arendt says, "Being seen and being heard by others derive their significance from the fact that everybody sees and hears from a different position" (Arendt, p. 57). And this difference guarantees the reality of appearance and perception so long as "everybody is always concerned with the same object" (p. 58) or referent in the common world.

At this level, Arendt presents a philosophical psychology of appearance based on aesthetics, not unlike Munsterberg's understanding of art and thought but without his equivocation. In her treatment of the spectator, which is modeled on the idea of aesthetic judgment, Arendt echoes that part of Munsterberg that sees both art and mind as capable of transforming reality. Following Kant, Arendt was convinced that only this kind of thinking (aesthetic thinking or judgment) could create the mental space for judging "without which no such objects would appear at all" (Young-Bruehl, p. 176). Although Arendt's work is about the power of spectators to reinterpret the reality that is given to them, Young-Bruehl emphasizes that Arendt also understood the conditions that could lead to the degradation of this process. Indeed, Arendt's early work focused on ideology and propaganda, which contrive and constrain the spectators' ability to see, understand and which ultimately degrades public culture. Arendt's later work emphasized the parallel dangers of "image making" through marketing, "public relations, the 'hidden persuasion' techniques of Madison avenue" (Young-Bruehl, p. 154) in directing attention to an image of reality, as opposed to reality itself (pp. 160–161). In effect, Arendt sets up yet another source of mediation that is at play in the spectators' attempt to understand reality, but one that is external to the spectator. Here culture is a mediated space because it is the space where images are created. Clearly, the media, in their capacity as instruments of culture and perception, can play a role in creating and crafting these images from without. What is at play in these cases is perception, not appearance, for although these images are projected onto the cultural realm, their aim is to provoke the kind of schematic, deductive thinking we see in perception and the identification of forms.

This differentiation between perception and appearance in Arendt provides a useful framework for understanding social psychology's approach to media. On the one hand, the turn to media in social psychology will be based on the psychology of perception, now applied in a social realm in which media images influence cognitive operations and constructions in a top-down process. On the other hand, the relationship between media and cognition will be explored through the eyes of spectators who look out and try to make sense of social reality. From this perspective, the filtering and mediation of reality, a basic fact of cognition, leaves open the possibility of the redefinition of media contents and images.

Early Social Psychology and Media: Walter Lippmann and the Psychology of Perception and Cognition

According to Cantril and Allport (1935), the idea of media comes late to social psychology. Pandora (1998) writes that Cantril and Allport's observations had to do with the landscape of social psychology at that time, which to their eyes, valued strict adherence to scientific rigor and detachment from the world (p. 8). Clearly, the study of media (radio, in their case) was a violation on both counts. But it is also true that social psychology has a built in level of complexity. Already mentioned, is social psychology's ties to the cultural realm. Social psychology is both part of yet separate from psychology, having origins in at least three disciplines (House, 1977), if not more (Moscovici, 1984). There are times in its history when there is a close relationship between its theories and the problems of society (Moscovici, 1972). And social psychologists have also had a history of injecting themselves in the problems of public culture and democracy—for better or worse (Herman, 1996; Pandora, 1997).

Nonetheless, Cantril and Allport's comments seem strange given that some 13 years earlier, Walter Lippmann (1997) had published *Public Opinion,* a classic work in media psychology that bridged social psychology and media. It is also a curious fact of history that Lippmann was a journalist, not a social psychologist. Therefore, the first important work in social psychology originates, not from within social psychology, but from without—external to the field. Lippmann the journalist turns to social psychology from a position of urgency. His consideration of issues bridging social psychology and media stemmed from his practical experience as a journalist who was all too familiar with the workings of media (newspapers), but

also from his role writing wartime propaganda during World War I. His biographer Ronald Steel (1997) writes in the foreword to *Public Opinion* that these experiences led Lippmann to conclude that reality was too easily distorted and public opinion too easily manipulated and this led Lippmann to consider processes of opinion formation. "What were the psychological forces that affected understanding? How did people interpret information, accurate or not? What emotional reactions did it trigger in them? How did their emotions affect their political judgment?" (p. xii). This realization of the dependency between cognition and media gave Lippmann his urgency, for what was at stake were the core assumptions inherent in democratic society: the ability of the "omnicompetent citizen" to make decisions without distortion and through rational deliberation (Lippmann, p. 173). The relationship between media and cognition is clearly seen by Lippmann as related to our overall competence to fulfill the broader deliberative needs of democratic society. In this way, Lippmann preserves the relationship between cognition and the world in a manner not unlike the early philosophers who studied perception and cognition as part of a broader social whole; and in a manner similar to Arendt who understood that what was at stake in how the world appears was the reality of the world itself.

The core of the relationship between media and cognition for Lippmann lies with the psychology of perception. He understood that the pictures we get from media were an important component driving cognition. "Each of us lives and works on a small part of the earth's surface," Lippmann writes. He continues, "Of any public event that has wide effects we see at best only a phase and an aspect" (p. 53). The media provide the first layer of mediation to reality.

"Our opinions," he writes, are "pieced together out of what others have reported and what we can imagine" (p. 53). But in this capacity, the media serve a functional role indistinguishable/similar to our senses. Following Munsterberg's monograph, *On the Witness Stand,* Lippmann writes about the impossibility of naïve observation. "A report is the joint product of the knower and known, in which the role of the observer is always selective and usually creative. The facts we see depend on where we are placed, and the habits of our eyes" (p. 54). This observation clearly applies to both media (the journalistic process) as well as the process of perception. But Lippmann does go on to provide an account of how the filtering of reality through media plays itself out in the case of journalism, at the various layers of the news-gathering process; beginning with characteristics of the journalist, to the role and power of editors, issues of censorship, and even pointing to the role of public officials and institutions in trying to influence how events are shaped for the public. Steel writes how throughout *Public Opinion* Lippmann often refers to Plato. Indeed, with Lippmann we are back in the shadows of Plato's cave, only now the parable has been updated to take into account how media contribute to the creation of the shadows cast on the wall.

However, Lippmann understood well that the shadows on the wall are also the product of human cognition and perception. And the very problem that Lippmann saw was the inability of mind to challenge or transform the media generated pictures of reality as a given. Lippmann's theory of cognition relies on the idea of the stereotype. Lippmann saw that "far from using rational or scientific criteria as a guide, people make judgments based on emotions, prejudices, or preconceptions" (Garcia, 2010, p. 6). But the idea of stereotype itself is based on a top-down theory of perception. Lippmann is clear on this when he writes, "For the most part, we do not first see, and then define, we define first and then see" (Lippmann, pp. 54–55). Cognition for Lippmann is driven through "preconceptions," and it was this collusion among mind, perception, and media that was toxic to the ideals of democracy. In Munsterberg's aesthetics of film and mind, there was tension between the freedom of mind to transform reality and media (film) as an external mediating source directing cognition. In Lippmann's view, the mind does mediate reality, but the mediation works in the direction of the reality that is pre-given to the mind. And that reality is itself a mediated reality created and shaped by media.

Cantril's Aesthetics of Radio and the Psychology of the Spectator

As has been mentioned, Arendt's philosophy of appearance and public culture "presupposes a viewer" (Gottsegen, 1994, p. 27). This psychology of the spectator as presented in philosophy and early psychology is carried into social psychology by way of Heider's work on attribution (1944) and interpersonal relations (1958). According to Farr (1996), Heider was the more "social" member of the Gestalt group, moving away from the individualizing perspective that specifically characterized Kurt Lewin's work (p. 114–115). Heider's work had long historical and philosophical roots—reaching back to "Goethe and Kant via Franz Brentano, Ernst Mach, Alexius von Meinong and Carl von Ehrenfels," in addition to Kurt Koffka, Wolfgang Kohler, Kurt Lewin, and Max Wertheimer (Jahoda, 2007, p. 216). Jahoda explains

that Heider's work on attribution and interpersonal relations were based on the psychology of perception, "dealing with social perception in general" (p. 217). Farr similarly sees Heider's roots in the psychology of perception and more specifically sees Heider's perceiver–observer distinction as an extension of figure–ground organization. "The distinction between figure and ground," writes Farr, "is sharp when the figure is another human" (p. 130). In this sense, and especially important for media psychology, is Heider and Simmel's (1944) work, which extends the psychology of perception to social perception. In what could be considered a proto study in a nascent field of media psychology, the researchers show participants a movie of animated geometric shapes and then explore the narratives formed in the face of what are really media stimuli. Heider and Simmel found the tendency to "anthropomorphize" as they formed complex narratives—"to attribute to them genders and also, more important, goals, intentions, and mental attitudes such as fear" (Noe, 2009, p. 27) that were not given or inherent in the stimuli. Although Noe sees this as an example of our having "evolved to see mind and consciousness in the world around us, even where none exists," it is also the case that we are seeing the mind and consciousness of these spectators at work as they go beyond the simplicity of the stimuli provided, bringing with them an active approach to media as demonstrated by their complex narratives.

It is precisely this perspective of the psychology of the spectator that emerges in the other classic work that defines social psychology's early approach to media, Hadley Cantril's (1940/2005), *The Invasion from Mars: A Study in the Psychology of Panic.* The Orson Welles radio dramatization of the H. G. Wells classic, *The War of the Worlds,* and the dramatic events of the broadcast and it s aftermath: "before the broadcast ended, people...praying, crying, fleeing" provided Cantril with an opportunity to explore the effects of radio on cognition (p. 47). What began as a familiar story of media influence soon turns into a parable of the spectator. Like Heider, Cantril's approach is based on the psychology of perception, and both were interested in the perceptual psychology and physiological optics of Adelbert Ames, Jr. (Behrens, 1999). Cantril's son, Albert Cantril, observes in the Introduction to *The Invasion from Mars* that his father was especially interested in Ames' work on signification—"how individuals *assign significance* to the images that appear on the retinas of their eyes" (original italics, p. xiii). As Albert explains, the collaboration between Ames and Cantril really aimed at explaining the "gap between the 'naïve experience' of viewing the demonstrations and a conceptual formulation that ascribes significance to what is 'seen'" (p. xiv).

It is important to note here that although Cantril's work is based on the psychology of perception, the foundation for this approach as applied to media was already visible in what Pandora regards as the "companion piece" that preceded *The Invasion from Mars,* namely, the book that Cantril cowrote with his former teacher and mentor, Gordon Allport, *The Psychology of Radio* (1935/1986). Like Lippmann, Cantril and Allport depart from the perspective of media as instruments of culture and perception that fulfill the broader sociopolitical needs of democracy. But unlike Lippmann, Cantril and Allport see the "natural properties of radio" as inherently democratic. Their description of radio is in keeping with the Kantian ideal of the enlarged mentality that Arendt was fond of quoting (Young-Bruehl, p. 165). In the case of radio, this enlarged mentality is created through radio's unrivaled quest for "internationalism" and "interpenetration of national cultures," potentially created an audience that is aware of the other (p. 22). They further observe that radio creates a common culture based on "common interests, common tastes, and common attitudes," but it does so while negotiating the differences of a "*heterogeneous* audience" (italics original, p. 20). Bringing this description within the context of Arendt's terminology and framework, it is clear that Cantril and Allport see a role for radio (the media of their day) in fostering appearance and awareness in public culture.

Furthermore, Cantril and Allport actually equate the psychology of radio with that of the listener so that radio becomes about the psychology of the listener. The listener is not just a listener but also a "citizen" (p. viii). Understanding radio as a medium of influence and its role in this way in the broader world becomes all important. Cantril and Allport, here again like Lippmann, understand the grasp that media have on cognition, "radio fills us with 'consciousness of kind' " (p. 18). They understand radio and its potential as a medium of and for propaganda, as used effectively by the likes of Hitler, Mussolini, and Huey Long in stoking or magnifying preexisting attitudes, on the one hand; and on the other, the effective use of radio to nurture new attitudes, as was the case with Father Coughlin—the Rush Limbaugh of his day (pp. 8–9; see also Pandora, 1998, p. 22). But Cantril and Allport go further than Lippmann in that they consider the role of free market economics in shaping attitudes through similar processes of censorship (p. 57) and propaganda (p. 60)—an omission for which Lippmann has been criticized (Schudson, 2008, p. 1040).

Most importantly from the perspective of perception and media is that in *The Psychology of Radio,* Cantril and Allport actually move away from audition as the dominant sensory frame for understanding radio and reframe radio as a medium that relies and augments visual perception. To begin with, they take a relational and comparative approach to radio (and media). Radio "relates the speaker and auditor in novel ways" in a manner unlike other existing media forms of their time (p. 19). The characteristics of radio are "more personal than the printed word" (p. 18). In comparison to movies, radio "appeals to more practical desires," not the "repressed desires" that characterize films (p. 16). But the transformational potential of radio can be seen in comparison to face-to-face interactions, which tend to be more constraining and confining for the listener. Cantril and Allport emphasize that radio releases listeners from the "social contract" that binds them as an audience in face-to-face events and performances. On radio, "the listener may respond in any way he pleases" (p. 10). There is "no compulsion to laugh at stale jokes, to applaud a bad actor, or to cheer the platitudes of a politician" (pp. 10–11). The listener is free to disagree without sanction and to "sing, dance, curse, or otherwise express emotions relevant or irrelevant" (p. 11). For Cantril and Allport the psychology of perception is built in to the specifics of radio as medium. Compared with face-to-face events, "a public meeting or lecture" (p. 9), it is the case that on radio "visual cues disappear"—we become "dependent exclusively upon audition" (p. 10). And yet, it is also true that the cognitive power of radio comes from the ability to visualize. As they say, "A great many people supply with their own imagery some kind of visual setting to supplement the bare auditory impression. They may see in their mind's eye the glamour of the stage, with its lights and costumes, as a suitable setting for a radio drama; they may create an imaginary appearance and set of mannerisms for the unknown speaker or announcer" (p. 10). Cantril and Allport conclude this important point by noting that radio may trigger a kind of hyper-perception in adults, a "keenness of imagery dulled since childhood" (p. 10).

The Martians and the Spectators

As Young Bruehl explains, "aesthetic judging begins when a particular phenomenon strikes you," the French term for this is *chose vue,* "having caught your attention, it sets you wondering and simultaneously makes you aware of yourself as someone who is trying to arrive at a judgment" (p. 168). It is the case that the radio broadcast that night caught people's attention. According to Cantril, 6 million people tuned in and at least 1 million were "frightened or disturbed" (p. 47). This means that a great many people, the majority of whom had tuned in late and missed the disclaimer at the beginning of the broadcast, were left *trying to arrive at judgment*. Trying to figure out fact from fiction provoked cognition. The cognitive psychologist Paul Bloom (2010) recently made the point that the necessity to know whether something is real or not is an important component to the pleasure we get from stories or art more generally. When we discover that what we think is real turns out to be a *trompe l'oeil*, "a switch is thrown... you have shifted to a different level of appreciation" (p. 179).

The point of departure for the study is the phenomenon of the radio broadcast and the presence or absence of critical ability for listeners here defined as "the capacity to evaluate the stimulus in such a way that were able to understand its inherent characteristics" and thus render an accurate judgment (pp. 111–112). Cantril found that generally speaking, higher levels of formal education do lead to attempts to check the veracity of the broadcast—either internally or externally (pp. 115–118). But as Cantril observes, sufficient "deviant" cases in the interview data demonstrating high levels of formal education did not guarantee critical ability—some listeners with high levels of formal education were not successful in finding the true nature of the broadcast, whereas some with less formal education were indeed able to render an accurate assessment of the drama (p. 120). He then explores the role of personality, not as a trait in the classic sense of personality assessment, but as a series of factors that secure a "general subjective relationship between the individual and his world" (p. 138). The idea of *world* here obviously extends to the world of the radio broadcast, its contents now part of that subjective relationship that Cantril observes develops between the individual and environment. This subjective relationship between individual and world (personality, as defined here), in turn becomes important in how individuals orient themselves to the contents of the broadcast. Based on the interviews, Cantril found several factors that when present together—insecurity, phobias, worries, lack of self-confidence, fatalism, religiosity, and frequency of church attendance—coalesced into a relationship in which the world is cognitively filtered through a sense of "personal inadequacy" (p. 138) that contributed to "susceptibility to suggestion" (p. 135). When individuals perceive themselves to be in situations in which their security and that of others is threatened, then critical ability is overwhelmed.

Beyond the listeners mediating the broadcast at the level of personality as subjective relationship to the world, Cantril also explored the listening situation as a second filter to the reality presented by the radio drama that also affects critical ability. He reminds us that the "listening situation like most other social stimuli, is a complex pattern which tends to be experienced as a unit and not as a series of discrete elements" (p. 139). And very clearly using the language of perception, he explains that the diversity of the listening situation would expose listeners to a "variety of stimulus configurations" (p. 140). Cantril's son, Albert, again reminds that from Ames' work, Cantril concluded that perceptions, attitudes, and prejudices are "significances for purposive behavior, significances which we ourselves have created in order to act effectively and which we are unlikely to alter unless and until our action is frustrated or our purposes change" (p. xiv). It is at this point where Cantril's study turns into a study of signification. What Cantril's study reveals is the thinking process involved when one is presented with the dilemma of whether to believe or not believe the broadcast. Regardless of whether people make an accurate or faulty assessment of the broadcast—both outcomes betray a certain amount of cognitive effort and perceptual sophistication (not necessarily given in the stimulus)—in this case, the radio broadcast. An event that started out as a seeming tale of overwhelming media influence turns into the parable of the spectator who does not just reproduce the pictures provided by Lippmann's media, but who in the process can rework, redefine, and augment the media created reality.

But how the listener responds is very much related to the configuration of the listening situation. For example, Cantril observes that people heard the news from others. They listened to the broadcast with others or talked with others in private or public spaces (friends, visitors, etc.). Therefore, the configuration of the listening situation was different for each individual. Some of the factors that he found made a difference include corroboration of fear by others; the disturbing effect of the fear behavior of others (p. 142); a person's status in the group to deny or confirm (p. 143); and immediacy of danger by geographical location and separation from family group (p. 143). Submissiveness in the group was "due to social context within which individual was placed" (p. 149). In paying attention to the listening situation, Cantril is introducing a very different model of media. Instead of the traditional transmission model (e.g., in Lippmann) that flows from medium to individual, Cantril is opening up the possibility of "otherness" as a mediating variable in relation to media. That is, the context that happens between people is as important as the relationship between the individual and the medium.[5]

But Cantril's view of the relationship between media and individuals (now plural) is in fact related to his view of the relationship between perception and environment. We experience media in the same way we perceive experience. Albert Cantril explains that for H. Cantril (and Ames), perception was a process in which "people 'transact' with the environment rather than 'interact' with it" (p. xiv). Albert continues, "The 'transactional' approach to perception conceives of the individual and environment as completely interdependent." This early view of perception is similar to a more recent point made by Noe (2009) who observes, "Seeing is an activity of exploring the world one that depends on the world and on the full character of our embodiment." He continues, "we find that we are at home in the world, that we are of it. Perceptual consciousness arises from our entanglement with it" (p. 146). One could speculate that entanglement with the world does not preclude *entanglement with others* and that in fact sociability of the kind described by Simmel (1910/1971) is indeed a requirement of it.

Although Cantril clearly develops the psychology of the spectator as applied to media (the radio broadcast), the study is by no means a full manifestation of the power of the spectator in the Arendtian sense. Cantril does point to otherness as a mediating factor that lies between the media stimulus and reactions to it. However, left out of the study is an exploration of the nature of the conversations and exchanges between people. It was this idea, which Dewey used to counter Lippmann's view of media, cognition, and democracy. And similarly, for Arendt what happens between people matters. Young-Bruehl explains how Arendt saw judgment as a distinct "mental ability," carried out "in relationship with others" and requiring a kind of mind travel "visiting others—physically or in your mind—consulting them, seeing things from their point of view, exchanging opinions with them, persuading them, wooing their consent (in Kant's lovely phrase)" (p. 165). In this way, judgment leads to the Kantian idea of "enlarged mentality," the kind of thinking that "allows a person to transcend the subjectivity and privacy of perceptions," leading to the formation of a Kantian "common sense"—a kind of critical appreciation of the world, rooted in the experiences of self, others, and broader community (p. 166). To be clear, Cantril stops short of this Arendtian ideal for rational mediation and consensus. This is so because Cantril explores the listening situation and the experience of otherness only in those cases in which listeners mistook the broadcast for reality (p. 145).[6] The only clue that the listening situation may contribute to a successful assessment of the broadcast emerges as an aside in this listener response that Cantril quotes:

> I don't think we would have gotten so excited *if those couples hadn't come rushin' in the way they did.* We are both very calm people, especially my husband, and if we had tuned in by ourselves I am sure we would have checked up on the program but *they led me to believe it was any station.* (italics original p. 141)

It stands to reason that the nature of the listening situation, the presentation of a calm demeanor as opposed to excitability, might provide a different context of otherness that can enhance and not dull critical ability. For an indication of this possibility one would have to turn to the results of the dissent condition in Asch's (1955) classic study on conformity. It is true that Asch's study is not related to media. Asch's intellectual origins were in Gestalt theories of perception, having worked closely with Max Wertheimer at The New School for Social Research (King & Wertheimer, 2006, p. 343). Fundamentally, Asch's classic study is one of the perception of visual lines because this experience is filtered and mediated by the kind of otherness that Cantril talks about. As Asch's results indicate, in conditions in which the group members presented dissent, accurate assessment of the lines increased and conformity was reduced.

Where Are We Today?

Where does this history leave media psychology today? For this, it is important to explore the legacies of Lippmann and Cantril and their approaches, respectively. Walter Lippmann today remains a peripheral figure in social psychology, credited with having introduced the notion of stereotype (Jahoda, 2007). His cognition by stereotype approach foreshadows the automaticity of cognition and its corresponding emphasis on unconscious processes that drives much of social psychology today (Banaji et al. 2003). However, this automaticity of cognition view was itself inherent in early discussions of perception and certainly present in Kant's discussion of schematic representations that guide thinking and perception (Young-Bruehl, p. 167). Lippmann's interest in the psychology of perception, however, was driven by a larger project of understanding the role of media and the possibility of rational deliberation essential to democracy. This broader project is all but ignored in psychology and social psychology. His theory of media and broader concern for democracy has been cut off from the corpus of his work on cognition and perception. What survives in psychology is the often-cited "pictures in our heads" quote (see, e.g., Pratkanis and Aronson, 2001) without reference to the role of media in filtering reality or the relationship among perception, media, and democracy. In effect, his theory of media is all but excised from psychology. The linguist Noam Chomsky, whose theories of language were instrumental in ushering theories of cognition in psychology, did pay attention to Lippmann's views on media (Herman and Chomsky, 1988), but Chomsky became important to media and cultural studies—with little to offer by way of psychology.

Cantril also presents a curious fate. His *War of the Worlds* study remains important enough to be included in introductory texts in communication and media (Campbell et al., 2012) in which Cantril is given credit for the shift away from big media effects to a more limited view of media effects on the audience. The *Psychology of Radio,* Cantril's book with Allport, remains a sleeper classic—all but neglected in psychology (Pandora, p. 9) and out of print until recently.[7] In psychology, Cantril is mostly known for his study, *They Saw a Game* (Hastorf and Cantril, 1954) on selective perception and social perception. Ignored is the fact that this study can be seen in context with Cantril's earlier work on media as an example of the social-cognitive mediation of media events—in this case the momentous game between two rival teams, Dartmouth and Princeton—by individuals. The media implications of this study, in which participants watch a film of the game, is not considered even in texts (Pratkanis and Aronson, 2001) about media and persuasion. A recent exception is Farhad Manjoo's (2008) book, *True Enough,* which explores the psychology of new media. Although Manjoo (like Lippmann a journalist, not a psychologist) sees the application of the study to media, he misses the more social and cultural components of Cantril's approach to media—norms of judgment, subjective relationship to the stimulus, listening situation; which similarly apply in the iconic *They Saw a Game* study as relevant to the cultural life of the two rival universities and interpretations and reactions to the game.

In fairness, the fate of Lippmann and Cantril's early work in media psychology—and hence the trajectory of the nascent field of media psychology—may have been caught up in the inevitable trends that would have effectively delegitimized those aspects of psychology and social psychology essential to the development of a media psychology. Moscovici (1972/2001) has written about the detachment of

theory in social psychology from the problems of society, a relationship that he identifies as vital in preserving the relevance and dynamism of a social psychology that is oriented toward exploring new social realities and social psychological landscapes. Both Lippmann and Cantril, however different their views, shared this concern for the problems of culture and democracy and role of media in this broader reality. Cantril and Allport make a similar point in their Preface to *The Psychology of Radio* when they note that "progress of social psychology" is tied to the "incisiveness and validity of its analysis of social problems" (p. vii). They clearly saw media and the "landscape of radio" as very much a part of such new and emerging social realities that in turn correspond to new social psychological spaces that needed to be explored.

Equally significant is Graumann's (1986) observation about the "individualization of the social"; that is, the tendency to redefine social processes as products of the individual mind. Cognition occurs in the "head" of the individual and "groupness" becomes a "projected attribute" of the individual (Gergen, 1989, p. 465).[8] The consequences of this are not trivial. As Moscovici (1982) commented, "whereas previously epistemological problems were conceived as social problems, social problems were now conceived as epistemological problems" (p. 119). This individualization of the social would certainly limit how social psychology subsequently viewed and approached media. It would certainly preclude the kind of analysis that Cantril provided in the *War of the Worlds*—an analysis that takes into account the broader relationship between individuals and media, in terms of the cultural positioning of radio as a media form at the time of the broadcast (pp. 68–69); the disorientation that results from economic uncertainty and how that can set the tone for how the interpretation of the broadcast (pp. 153–164); along with the configuration of the listening situation in providing a context for interpretation and mediation of the radio drama. It is interesting that similar trends can be seen in the more recent study of perception in psychology. Noe refers to this trend as the "grand illusion" thesis in perception, in which the world as reality is seen as "figment created 'for us' by our brains" (p. 130).

We can, however, pick up threads of this early history of media psychology as they exist today. Noe, for example, states the case for the relationship between perception and the broader world or reality—and the implication of this relationship for perceptual consciousness. As a cognitive philosopher, Noe understands the role of media and technology in creating consciousness and *presence.* "Technology increases the scope of our access, and so increases the extent of what is or can be present for us" (p. 83). Something of the aesthetic approach to thinking and perception found in Munsterberg is revived in Bloom's (2010) discussion of pleasure and cognition, and in particular his emphasis on the cognitive role of art and fiction, "technologies of the imagination" (p. 175) and our immersion in these fictional worlds and their relationship to reality.

Finally, the fullest expression of the psychology of the spectator, one that is partial to Arendt's take on the spectator, as well as Heider's psychology of commonsense, can be found in Moscovici's (1988) social representation theory. Social representation theory is anchored in the idea of the *thinking society*. Individuals seek each other out and cannot help but communicate, "in circles, clubs, cafes, political association, waiting rooms, on village benches and the rest" (Moscovici, 1998, p. 6).[9] Social representations are created through the art of conversation, for as Moscovici writes, "there can be no representation without communication and no communication without representation" (p. 2) and these in turn are sociocognitive forms that mediate our understanding of reality. From this perspective, the media serve to circulate and disseminate social representations as cultural forms, but these contents are reworked, transformed, and re-presented through the discursive exchanges of individuals and groups that have a need to create them. The nature of the *thinking society* is tied to the nature of conversations as mechanisms of communication and consensus that allow "communities to produce their facts" (Moscovici, 1988 p. 224). Moscovici presents a fuller understanding of the spectator in relation to media contents. The spectator—to borrow Arendt's term—is never passive in the face of media and cultural contents, for the creation of social representations always lead to the transformation of both "mental and social configurations" (Moscovici, 1988, p. 219). By taking into account the nature of conversations as mechanisms of consensus, Moscovici, unlike Cantril, sets up Arendt's condition for judgment that lead to transcendence of the limiting conditions of the stimulus and media contents.

As Sigmund Freud once commented in a different context, history rarely lies dormant. Eventually, the repressed *does* return, and it might even do so in a form that is more usable (Olick, 2007). Therein in lies the hope for the reappearance of media psychology, its future tied not to the illusion of its current fragmented form, but to the rediscovery of its rich history and the psychology that brought it to the precipice of its birth and relevance. New media landscapes and technologies are creating, as they always have in our technological past, new social spaces with corresponding psychological realities. We await the appearance of media psychology as a not so *new* form, framed by its history in psychology—and all that it implies.

Notes

1. Young-Bruehl recounts how Arendt pointed out the duality in Kant as moralist opposed to revolution, whereas Kant the spectator clearly was "enthusiastic about it" (p. 172).

2. What Arendt has in mind here values such as "justice, honor, virtue" (Gottsegen, p. 181) or value judgments of like and dislike (Young-Bruehl, p. 168).

3. A key difference between Kant and Arendt was that Arendt was more interested in the particularity of the examples that fit the universal ideal of, say "justice." Unlike Kant, who was more interested in universals, Arendt wanted to account for differences in meaning and understanding that characterize the understanding of universal ideals (Gottsegen, p. 182).

4. For the psychologist, cultural indeterminacy is something similar to the transformation of memory found in the retelling of stories in Bartlett's (1932/1995) experiments.

5. In fact, this was precisely Dewey's response to Lippmann. Namely, that democracy is to be found in the conversations between people. See Dewey, J. (1980). *The Public and Its Problems*. Chicago: Swallow Press (Original work published 1927).

6. See also Cantril's footnote 10 on p. 145.

7. *The Psychology of Radio* is now available as a Google e-book.

8. Similar critiques were made of social cognition in social psychology. See Forgas (1983). What is social about social cognition? *British Journal of Social Psychology, 22,* 129–144.

9. This 1998 reference is from a paper Moscovici delivered in New York at a conference on social representations. A modified version of this paper can be found in the edited book by K. Deaux and G. Philogene (2001), *Representations of the Social: Bridging Theoretical Traditions*. Malden, MA: Blackwell.

References

Arendt, H. (1958). *The Human Condition*. Chicago: University of Chicago Press.

Arnheim, R. (2006). *Film as Art*. Berkeley: University of California.(Original work published 1957)

Asch, S. (1955). Opinions and social pressure. Scientific American, 43, 713–720.

Banaji, M., Lemm, K., & Carpenter, S. (2003). The social unconscious. In Tesser, A., & Schwarz, N. (Eds.), *Blackwell Handbook of Social Psychology: Intra Individual Processes* (pp. 134–158). Malden, MA: Blackwell.

Bartlett, F. C. (1995). *Remembering: A Study in Experimental and Social Psychology*. Cambridge, UK: Cambridge University Press. (Original work published 1932)

Behrens, R. R. (1999). Adelbert Ames, Fritz Heider and the Ames chair demonstration. Retrieved April 7, 2011 from http://www.bobolinkbooks.com/Ames/ChairDemo.html.

Bloom, P. (2010). *How Pleasure Works: The New Science of Why We Like What We Like*. New York: W.W. Norton.

Bruner, J. S., Goodnow, J., & Austin, G. (1956). *A Study of Thinking*. New York: Wiley.

Campbell, R., Martin, C. R., & Fabos, B. (2012). *Media & Culture: An Introduction to Mass Communication*, 8th ed. Boston: Bedford/St. Martins.

Cantril, A. (2005). Transaction Introduction. In H. Cantril, *The Invasion from Mars: A Study in the Psychology of Panic.* New Brunswick, NJ: Transaction, pp. vii–xx.

Cantril, H. (2005). *The Invasion from Mars: A Study in the Psychology of Panic.* New Brunswick, NJ: Transaction. (Original work published 1940)

Cantril, H., & Allport, G. (1935). *The Psychology of Radio.* Retrieved from Google ebookstore.

Carroll, N. (1988). Film/mind analogies: The case of Hugo Munsterberg. The Journal of Aesthetics and Art Criticism, 489–499.

Danziger, K. (2008). *Marking the Mind.* Cambridge, UK: Cambridge University.

Farr, R. M. (1996). *The Roots of Modern Social Psychology.* Oxford, UK: Blackwell.

Fechner, G. T. (1966). *The Elements of Psychophysics.* New York: Holt, Rinehart & Winston. (Original work published 1876)

Garcia, C. (2010). Rethinking Walter Lippmann's legacy in the history of public relations. *PRism, 7,* 1–10. Retrieved March 23, 2011 from http://www.prismjournal.org.

Gergen, K. J. (1989). Social psychology and the wrong revolution. European Journal of Social Psychology, 19, 463–484.

Giles, D. (2003). *Media Psychology.* Hillsdale, NJ: Lawrence Erlbaum Associates.

Gombrich, E. H. (1960). *Art and Illusion.* Princeton, NJ: Princeton University Press.

Gottsegen, M. (1994). *The Political Thought of Hannah Arendt.* Albany: State University of New York.

Graumann, C. F. (1986). The individualization of the social and the desocialization of the individual: Floyd Allport's contribution to social psychology. In C. F. Graumann, & S. Moscovici (Eds.), *Changing Conceptions of Crowd Mind and Behavior.* New York: Springer, pp. 97–116.

Hastorf, A., & Cantril, H. (1954). They saw a game. Journal of Abnormal and Social Psychology, 49, 129–134.

Hearnshaw, L. S. (1989). *The Shaping of Modern Psychology.* London: Routledge.(Original work published 1987)

Heider, F. (1944). Social perception and phenomenal causality. Psychological Review, 51, 358–374.

Heider, F. (1958). *The Psychology of Interpersonal Relations.* New York: Wiley.

Heider, F., & Simmel, M. (1944). An experimental study of apparent behavior. American Journal of Psychology, 57, 243–259.

Herman, E. (1996). *The Romance of American Psychology: Political Culture in the Age of Experts.* Berkeley: University of California.

Herman, E., & Chomsky, N. (1988). *Manufacturing Consent: The Political Economy of the Mass Media.* New York: Pantheon.

House, J. (1977). The three faces of social psychology. Sociometry, 40(2), 161–177.

Jahoda, G. (2007). *A History of Social Psychology.* Cambridge, UK: Cambridge University Press.

King, D. B., & Wertheimer, M. (2006). *Max Wertheimer and Gestalt Theory.* New Brunswick, NJ: Transaction.

Langdale, A. (2002). S(t)imulation of mind: The film theory of Hugo Munsterberg. In H. Munsterberg, *Hugo Munsterberg on Film: The Photoplay—A Psychological Study.* New York: Routledge, pp. 1–41.

Leahey, T. H. (2004). *A History of Psychology: Main Currents in Psychological Thought,* 6th ed. Upper Saddle River, NJ: Pearson.

Lehrer, J. (2007). *Proust Was a Neuroscientist.* Boston: Houghton Mifflin,.

Lippmann, W. (1997). *Public Opinion.* New York: Free Press. (Original work published 1922)

Mack, A. (1982). Perceiving. Social Research, 49(4), 950–967.

Manjoo, F. (2008). *True Enough: Learning to Live in a Post-Fact Society.* Hoboken, NJ: Wiley.

Moscovici, S. (1982). The coming era of representations. In Codol, J., & Leyens, J. (Eds.), *Cognitive analysis of social behaviour* (pp. 115–150). The Hague: Nijhoff.

Moscovici, S. (1984). The myth of the lonely paradigm: A rejoinder. Social Research, 51(4), 939–967.

Moscovici, S. (1988). Notes towards a description of social representations. European Journal of Social Psychology, 18, 211–250.

Moscovici, S. (1989). Preconditions for explanation in social psychology. European Journal of Social Psychology, 19, 407–430.

Moscovici, S. (October, 1998). *Why a Theory of Social Representations?* Paper presented at the Conference on Social Representations: Introductions and Explorations, New York.

Moscovici, S. (2001). Society and theory in social psychology. In Duveen, G. (Ed.), *Social Representations: Explorations in Social Psychology.* New York: New York University, pp. 78–119. (Original work published 1972)

Moscovici, S., & Markova, I. (1998). Presenting social representations. A conversation. Culture and Psychology, 4(4), 371–410.

Munsterberg, H. (2002). *Hugo Munsterberg on Film: The Photoplay—A Psychological Study.* (Langdale, A., Ed.). New York: Routledge. (Original work published 1916)

Nederhof, A., & Zwier, A. G. (1983). The crisis in social psychology: An empirical approach. European Journal of Social Psychology, 13, 255–279.

Noe, A. (2009). *Out of Our Heads: Why You Are Not Your Brain, and Other Lessons from the Biology of Consciousness.* New York: Hill and Wang.

Olick, J. K. (2007). From usable pasts to the return of the repressed. The Hedgehog Review, 9, 19–31. Retrieved from http://www.iasc-culture.org/THR/archives/UsesPast/Olick.pdf

Pandora, K. (1997). *Rebels Within the Ranks.* Cambridge, UK: Cambridge University Press.

Pandora, K. (1998). "Mapping the new mental world created by radio": Media messages, cultural politics, and Cantril and Allport's The Psychology of Radio. Journal of Social Issues, 54(1), 7–27.

Pratkanis, A., & Aronson, E. (2001). *Age of Propaganda. The Everyday Use and Abuse of Persuasion,* rev. ed. New York: Freeman.

Schudson, M. (2008). The "Lippmann-Dewey Debate" and the invention of Walter Lippmann as an anti-democrat 1986–1996. International Journal of Communication, 2, 1031–1042. Retrieved from http://ijoc.org/ojs/index.php/ijoc/article/view/343/229.

Simmel, G. (1971). Sociability. In Levine, D. (Ed.), *Georg Simmel: On Individuality and Social Forms* (pp. 127–140). Chicago: University of Chicago. (Original work published 1910)

Steel, R. (1997). Foreword. In Lippmann, W., *Public Opinion.* New York: Free Press, pp. xi–xvi.

Wertheimer, M. (1938). Laws of organization in perceptual forms. In Ellis, W. D. (Ed.), *A Source Book of Gestalt Psychology* (pp. 71–88). London: Routledge & Kegan Paul. (Original work published in 1923 as Untersuchungen zur Lehre von der Gestalt II, in *Psychologische Forschung, 4,* 301–350)

Young-Bruehl, E. (2006). *Why Arendt Matters.* New Haven, CT: Yale University Press.

Inside *Media Psychology:* The Story of an Emerging Discipline as Told by a Leading Journal

Ellen Baker Derwin *and* Janet de Merode

Abstract

The journal *Media Psychology* debuted in 1999 as the first peer-reviewed academic publication in the United States dedicated to the intersection of psychology and communication research. Using abstracts ($N = 242$) and keywords ($N = 5,276$) we analyzed the focus of the first 12 years of publication. During this time, the journal was guided by the founding coeditors (1999–2005) and subsequent teams of editors in rotation (2006–2010). Output is traced overall and compared between the two editorship periods. Overall, television emerged as the focus of more articles than any other form of media, whereas technology, diversity, and political categories increased from the first to the second period. Young children received more attention than other age groups during all 12 years. Journal contributors indicated strong international scholarship. One particularly salient finding is that contributions from communication departments exceeded those from psychology departments. We recommend encouraging interdisciplinary work to reinforce the inaugural focus of *Media Psychology*.

Key Words: grounded theory, communication, content analysis, media, media psychology, psychology, SPSS

The *Journal of Media Psychology* (Routledge) represents a new and pioneering field attracting considerable interest. In their inaugural notes of the first issue in 1999, the cofounders and first editors described their mission as "theoretically oriented empirical research...at the intersection of psychology and media communication" (Bryant & Roskos-Ewoldsen, 1999).[1] Subsequent editors[2] who have guided the journal since 2006 have maintained this same focus. In our own survey of contributing authors, one respondent referred to this journal as the "gold standard" in the discipline, and others admired the clear focus of *Media Psychology* in both topics and opportunity to reach out to an appropriate audience for their work. An analysis of this influential journal's content and contributors serves several purposes.

First, a content analysis shows the distribution of research areas for the emerging field, thus identifying a baseline for establishing trends over time; this also may be used as a basis for comparison with other journals that publish articles in media psychology. In addition, it may help to identify areas of neglected research. Second, the identification of contributing authors reveals the researchers who are making the initial contributions and thus shaping the field. Third, the identification of institutions with which contributors are affiliated provides some indication of early research hubs in the field. Finally, the analysis compares journal output during two time periods to identify differences in focus: the early stage of the cofounder editors (1999–2006), and the subsequent stage of rotating teams of editors (2007–2010). We refer to these, respectively, as the first and second editorships. This analysis thus provides a baseline for observing longitudinal trends as the journal and the field both evolve. It addresses several specific questions:

- What topics have been emphasized in articles published in the journal since its inception in 1999 and how have these topics changed over time?
- What authors have been influential in the journal's early history, and what are their reflections on scholarship in the journal and in media psychology?
- What are the institutional affiliations of the contributing authors?
- What collaborations occurred, both across departments and between institutions, academic or otherwise?
- Do the contents of the journal support the intended focus described by the inaugural editors?
- Is there a convergence of themes that correspond to the evolution of this new discipline?

We look to answers to these questions as elements that help us tell the story of *Media Psychology* and the shape of the unique discipline it represents. Text-mining technology was employed in this analysis, perhaps particularly apt for this media-centric field. The use of a grounded theory approach in combination with this technology allowed for natural emergence of findings rather than the testing of hypotheses based on predetermined categories subject to rater agreement. The merits of this approach and how it differs from traditional content analysis is reviewed in the next section.

Literature Review

Academic journals provide a forum for researchers to share their findings with colleagues, thus promoting discussion of emerging thought, methodologies, and theories. They represent trends for a given community of scholars (Potter & Riddle, 2007). Content analyses of academic journals track key developments and evolution in a discipline. Several content analyses of education and psychology journals published between 1989 and 2010 reveal that trends, authors, and institutional affiliation are of interest across disciplines (Pelsma & Cesari, 1989; Williams & Buboltz, 1999; Cokley, Caldwell, Miller, & Muhammad, 2001; Lee, Driscoll, & Nelson, 2004; Loveland, Buboltz, Schwartz, & Gibson, 2006; Southern, 2006; Nolan, 2009; Blancher, Buboltz, & Soper, 2010). Other content analyses have focused on mass media effects and mass communication (Bryant & Miron, 2004; Potter & Riddle, 2007).

Bryant and Miron (2004) explored the evidence of theory present in mass communication articles from three journals. They determined that 59% of the references to theories were based in communication. Psychology theories were the next prominent at 12%, considerably lower. Potter and Riddle (2007) also addressed theory, but rather than breaking down the type of theory, they simply addressed whether or not the articles emphasized theory. In their study, 65% did not feature a theory at all. Potter and Riddle (2007) primarily focused on mass media effects and types of media in their review of 16 journals, which included *Media Psychology*. They discovered a fragmented representation of individual studies rather than a common theme uniting a discipline. This result does not seem unusual because contributors to communication and mass media journals often represent interdisciplinary interests. Elsewhere in this *Handbook,* Potter (2011) also suggests that a young field needs time to mature before settling on the clarity of a more established field. Blancher, Buboltz, and Soper (2010) focused on identifying the most published authors along with their institutions. They state that "authors who publish frequently in a journal not only investigate areas that are deemed important, but they also play a role in defining and verifying a discipline" (p. 139).

The current study concentrates on one emerging discipline that has grown out of the synergy in two fields: media and psychology. Yet this emerging discipline also draws on concepts in sociology, technology, and neurology—and an increasing integration with the principles of positive psychology—to understand the interaction of media and human behavior (Fremlin, 2008). When reviewing other content analyses of journals, Nolan's (2009) review of educational psychology journals drew special attention. Like media psychology, educational psychology does not have a shared discipline definition and has been viewed as either applying educational theories to psychology or relating psychological concepts to education. Along the same lines, how does the communication discipline based in media interact with psychology in this interdisciplinary field? Do authors contributing to a journal for such a combined discipline agree on what the focus of articles should be? Nolan (2009) found consistency of topics in educational psychology journals that pointed to an agreement among educational psychologist regarding their work and practice. What will we find in media psychology?

Method

We adopted a mixed methods approach, using grounded theory, content analysis, data analysis, and an online survey of leading authors. Thus, rather than seeking specific findings related to theories, effects, or other areas, we chose to analyze the article keywords, abstracts, authorship, and institutional affiliations without prior hypothesis, and see what patterns emerged.

Content Analysis

As a research method, content analysis may be in its prime. With roots reaching back to a fascination of Greek philosophers with their rhetoric and Renaissance scholars with their religious texts, a host of commercial and scholarly users in the last two decades has stretched the imagination of early applications. Neuendorf (2002) depicts content analysis as having a "motley history" (p. 27), but nevertheless accords it the status of "perhaps the fastest-growing technique in quantitative research" (p. 1). This is no small accolade for a now-mainstream technique supporting research not only in the fields of psychology and education, but in communication, marketing, business, anthropology, health, and sociology, among others.

Content analysis has moved a long way from its first association with the discernment of messages in text through systematic quantification. Perhaps it is best understood in Robert Weber's (1990) terms simply as a systematic methodology "applied to substantive problems at the intersection of culture, social structure and social interaction" (p. 11). His 1990 observation that "(t)here is no simple *right way* to do content analysis" (p. 13) seems prophetic. In particular, content analysis is criticized for reductionism (Thomas, 1994) and trivialization (Holsti, 1969, as cited in Riffe et al., 2005), a result of the methodological search for common denominators of messages, followed by combining these into categories of shared meaning for assessing message frequency and distribution. Thomas (1994) defends the disassembling and restacking involved in message quantification as a blow against researcher bias. "Counts are no minor contribution. When people write analyses of texts without systematic measurement, there is the possibility, if not the tendency, to build the desired case" (p. 694).

Grounded Theory

With persistent controversy about coding and intercoder reliability, the technique of foregoing predetermined categories of analysis in favor of what emerges from the text organically is growing in popularity. The availability of text mining technologies is one reason for this, but so is the contemporary trend in the social sciences of renewed interest in hermeneutics. Dick (2005) goes so far as to suggest that the traditional hypothesis-testing mindset might need to be unlearned to master the approach of allowing the theory to emerge freely from the data itself. Thus this qualitative approach, referred to as *grounded theory,* generally entails no prior assumptions about findings to come (Chapter 8). Instead, close screening of the data reveals groups of related ideas that are then assembled by the researcher into themes equivalent to findings. Different researchers indeed may find different themes from the same data. But this is not opposed to hypothesis-testing research, where it can be argued that the act of deriving categories before data analysis can be preemptive or neglectful of themes. Polkinghorne (Chapter 8) addresses grounded theory and other qualitative methods as they apply to media psychology.

Text-Mining Software

A formidable tool in content analysis is computer software designed to mine text and provide the counts that previously researchers spent long hours generating on their own. The hyperefficiency of the computer compared with the human in dealing with large quantities of data quickly is obvious, but two features are of particular interest in addressing semantic and syntactic validity for computer-assisted text analysis (CATA) research. A key-word-in-text (KWIC) or congruences capacity allows the researcher to verify word meanings in context, as opposed to word count only. Software with KWIC capacity systematically locates the mined terms within the text for review, and avoids double counts. Also, software permitting the researcher to develop a customized dictionary of terms and phrases allows accurate text mining for the specific topic of research, and in some cases, also provides an initial grouping of terms into categories of shared meaning. In this way, a lexicon may be built for the branches of knowledge specific to the research question.

Selecting appropriate software for CATA research can be complex. Neuendorf, in her *Content Analysis Handbook* (2002), includes a table summarizing 10 features of 20 software programs using four different operating systems (p. 226). In the near decade since publication of Neuendorf's book, the choice has become even more plentiful, including audio and visual applications such as Transana™ a computer-assisted, qualitative analysis software (CAQDAS) developed, hosted and maintained by researchers at the University of Wisconsin-Madison Center for Education Research. A particularly user-friendly feature of content analysis software, because of its uniquely visual data presentation, is *tag clouds* of differing font sizes representing weighted frequencies in a text.

Procedure

This section describes the analysis of keywords in the abstracts as a way of tracking topics, along with the procedure for determining lead authors and institutions. It also tabulates collaborations, both cross-departmentally and internationally. The data pertain to all articles ($N = 242$) in the 13 volumes of the first 12 years (1999–2010) of the journal *Media Psychology*, during which time it was under two separate editorships, the two original cofounding editors 1999–2005 (vols. 1–7); and teams of editors (in general serving 3 years, but operating on a rotation) 2006–2010 (vols. 8–13). Finally, we conducted an online opinion survey of leading authors.

Data Preparation and Analysis: Topics

We first created Microsoft® Excel spreadsheets that included a designator for each article with the volume, number, article number, year, and editorship. The spreadsheet also included each article's title, abstract, and keywords. Keywords were mined from the online database, Communication & Mass Media Complete Database, the repository for the articles accessed from the Fielding Graduate University Library. The database assigns keywords that researchers use in their search process. The keywords represent the main topics in each article.

In a content analysis of educational psychology, another interdisciplinary field, Nolan (2009) determined that keywords would be representative of article content and offered a model for organizing and analyzing data using SPSS Text Analysis for Survey Data (version 2.1) software.[3] We followed a similar model. To be confident that key terms would be representative of content, we first applied the software to the titles and to the abstracts separately, before focusing on the key terms. We found that a large number of extraneous terms were extracted from titles and abstracts, whereas the key term extractions provided the topic focus we were seeking. Once IBM® SPSS® Text Analytics for Surveys (version 4.0) extracts terms, the program automatically categorizes them based on its default library. Initially, 36 categories were created automatically. We could then refine, add, and delete categories to develop our own library of terms. For example, categories that were too broad, such as "psychology," were deleted. Categories that were discrete yet similar were combined. For example, "computer," "data processing," "Internet," and "technology" were combined into one category. We then reviewed uncategorized terms to determine the need for additional categories, and some new ones, such as "politics" were created. After refining, we consolidated terms to 23 categories. The categories and corresponding terms are detailed in Table 5.1.

Once categories were determined, the software counted the number of articles in which a term in a given category appeared. If one category included multiple terms from one article, the terms were counted only once. For example, if "computer graphics," "computer science," "computer systems," and "information resources," which were all grouped in one category, appeared in one article, the

Table 5.1 Consolidated Categories of Keyword Terms, *Media Psychology*, 1999–2010.

Categories (23)	Terms Within Categories
Advertising	Advertising, display advertising, persuasion, radio advertising, television advertising
Age	Child, teenager, youth, adolescence, age group, college students, school child, preschool child, toddlers, young adults
Arts	Art, artists, music, aesthetics, photographs
Attitude	Attitude
Behavior	Aggressiveness, assault, behavior, behavior modification, dominance, human behavior, health behavior, prosocial behavior, sexual behavior, sexual excitement, voyeurism, arousal, behavioral assessment, behavioralism, interbehavioral psychology, sex
Cognition	Attention, body image, cognition, cognitive processing, heuristic programming, memory, perception, risk, social cognition theory, autobiographical memory, cognitive analysis, decision making, sensation, visual perception

Table 5.1 *Continued*

Categories (23)	Terms Within Categories
Computer/data processing/ Internet/technology	Computer graphics, computer science, computer systems, information resources, operating systems, wireless communication, cell phones, text messages, data processing, area networks, computer networks, telecommunications, telephone systems, human information processing, human computer interaction, information storage, internet, internet publishing, Internet users, Web search portals, communication of technical information, telephone surveys, wired telecommunications carriers, wireless communications equipment manufacturing
Diversity	African Americans, Asians, Black, Black–White differences, comparative studies, cultural awareness, demographic characteristics, discrimination, Hispanic Americans, individual differences, minorities, prejudices, race relations, racism, social status, stereotypes, cross-cultural studies, ethnic groups, ethnocentrism
Education	Administration of education programs, education, educational psychology, elementary and secondary schools, experiential earning, learning, media literacy, tutoring, perceptual learning
Emotions	Anger, anxiety, doubt, emotional conditioning, emotions, facial expression, hostility, loneliness, mood, motivation, sadness, aggressiveness, depression
Ethics	Ethics, judgment, truthfulness
Gender	Gender, woman, masculinity, sex differences, machismo
Identity	Assimilation, group identity, identity, ingroups, online identities, outgroups, autobiography
Marketing	Marketing research, target marketing
Mass media/multimedia	Broadcast journalism, broadcasting, mass media, radio, video production, video tapes, magnetic resonance, periodicals, radio programs, video recording, digital media, interactive
Movies	Animated films, film, instructional films, motion pictures, horror films, motion picture actors
Narrative/reading	Narratives, reading, books, literacy, literature, narrative analysis, texts, detective
News	Attribution of news, news syndicates, newspaper reading, television broadcast of news, news, newspapers, press coverage
Physiological/health	Body, exercise, frontal lobes, heart, life science, physical fitness, pregnancy, psychophysiology, public health, reproductive health, well-being, anorexia, auditory adaptation, health, brainy, electroencephalography, galvanic skin response, neurophysiology, neurosciences, physiology
Politics	Campaign debates, environmental protection, legislators, political aspects, political participation, political attitudes, political psychology, politicians
Social	Civilization, interpersonal relations, peer communication, social aspects, social attitudes, social interaction, social participation, social perception, social skill, socialization, volunteerism, interpersonal relations, social, social advocacy, social aspects, social customs, social interaction, social psychology
Television	Reality television programs, television, television broadcasting, television programs, television viewers, television display systems, television series
Virtual reality/video games	Avatars, virtual environments, virtual reality, electronic games, video game characters, video games, video gamers, video production

Note: Consolidation was performed using IBM® SPSS® Text Analytics for Surveys (Version 4.0).

frequency count for that article was one. However, any given article may have included terms in multiple categories. Therefore, keyword counts, shown in Table 5.2, are not mutually exclusive. One article may have been counted in multiple categories.

We analyzed separately keywords in the first and second editorships so as to discern trends based on a common library of terms that we developed for the purpose. This is facilitated by the software, and aided in determining the comparative presence or

Table 5.2 Major Categories of Topics by Editorship, *Media Psychology,* 1999–2010.

Category	No. of Responses 1st Eds. 1999–2005	No. of Responses 2nd Eds. 2006–2010	% Change Responses 1st to 2nd Eds.	Topic Ranking 1st Eds. 1999–2005	Topic Ranking 2nd Eds. 2006–2010
Advertising	11	5	−55.55	8	9
Age	31	23	−25.81	3	4
Arts	5	6	+20.00	10	9
Attitude	6	9	+50.00	9	8
Behavior	22	24	+9.09	6	4
Cognition	29	31	+6.90	4	2
Computer/data Processing/Internet/ technology	18	31	+72.22	7	2
Diversity	5	21	+320.00	10	5
Education	9	11	+22.22	8	7
Ethics	5	0	−100.00	10	10
Emotions	21	27	+28.57	6	3
Gender	8	9	+12.50	9	8
Identity	4	10	+150.00	10	8
Marketing	1	3	+200.00	—	9
Mass media/multimedia	59	62	+5.08	1	1
Movies	10	15	+50.00	8	6
Narrative/reading	2	12	+500.00	10	7
News	9	6	−33.33	8	9
Physio/health	16	13	−18.75	7	7
Politics	3	10	+233.33	10	8
Social	26	29	+11.54	5	3
Television	47	31	−34.04	2	2
Uncategorized	1	3	+200.00	—	9
Virtual reality/video	6	18	+200.00	9	6
Total Responses	354	409			
in Total No. of Articles	129	113			

Note: For keywords included within categories, see Table 5.1. "Responses" infers an answer to the question "what topics are most frequently treated in the *Journal of Media Psychology?*"

Figure 5.1 Word Cloud of Top 50 Keywords, *Media Psychology*, 1999–2005.

Figure 5.2 Word Cloud of Top 50 Keywords, *Media Psychology*, 2006–2010.

absence of topics in the two time periods. To present a view of the raw data (Figures 5.1 and 5.2), we prepared word clouds of the top 50 keywords in each editorship, after following standard cleaning practice of removing common English words (e.g., "the," "and," prepositions); common denominator keywords such as "mass media," "psychology" and "communication"; and general phrases such as "aspects of" or "related to." We also extracted the top 10 keywords for comparison between the two periods (Figures 5.4 and 5.5).

FREQUENCIES OF RESEARCH METHODOLOGIES AND SAMPLE POPULATIONS

Using the abstracts as source, we manually tabulated for each article the type of research (e.g., theoretical, literature review, empirical) and recorded the N and demographic description of all empirical work as specified by the author in the abstract. Tables 5.3 and 5.4 show the consolidated findings.

LEAD AUTHORS

For authors, we operationalized "lead" as relative productivity in the journal. Commensurate with American Psychological Association (APA) guidelines, we assigned productivity weights using Howard, Cole, and Maxwell's (1987) methodology, resulting in the relative ranking of author productivity. Thus a sole author is credited with 1.0 point; for two authors, the first listed receives 0.6 and the second listed 0.4 points, respectively; three authors receive respectively 0.47, 0.32, and 0.21, and so forth according to the formula:

$$\text{Credit} = \left(1.5^{n-i}_{i-1}\right) \Big/ \left(\sum 1.5^{i-l}\right)$$

where n is the total number of authors and i is the ordinal position of each author (p. 976). An Excel spreadsheet was used to sort authors by total assigned points and provide counts for departments

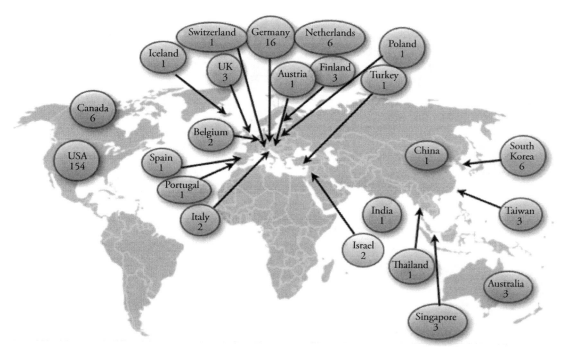

Figure 5.3 Author Institutions Represented by Country, *Media Psychology*, 1999–2010.

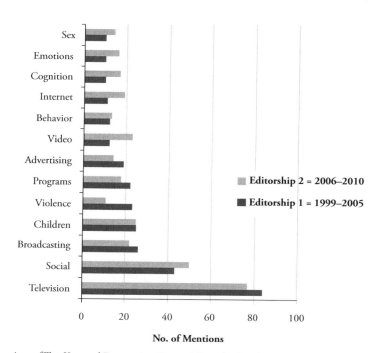

Figure 5.4 Comparison of Top Keyword Frequencies, First and Second Editorship Periods.

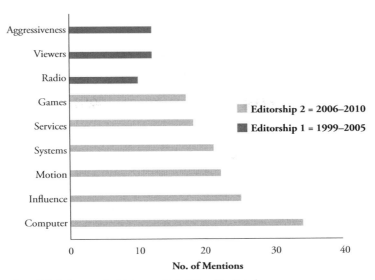

Figure 5.5 Top Keywords and Their Frequencies Unique to Each Editorship Period.

Table 5.3 Type of Methodology in Articles by Editorship, *Media Psychology,* **1999–2010.**

Type of Methodology	No. of Articles 1999–2005	Percent	No. of Articles 2006–2010	Percent
Empirical:				
$N < 100$	26		17	
$N = 101–500$	29		23	
$N = 501–1,000$	3		4	
$N > 1,000$	5		3	
Unspecified N in Abstract	0		62	
Total empirical	63	45	109	86
Theoretical	14	10	7	6
Literature review	8	6	2	2
Data analysis	8	6	3	2
Cross-cultural or ethnic	5	4	4	3
Meta-analysis	3	2	—	—
fMRI studies	3	2	1	.5
Research methods	1	—	—	—
Not specified in abstract	35	25	1	0.5
Total	140	100	127	100

Note: As described in the article abstract. Some articles appear in more than one category, for example, a functional magnetic resonance imaging (fMRI) empirical study with $N = 13$ adolescents would appear in three categories: $N < 100$; fMRI studies; and adolescents.

Table 5.4 Sample Populations in Empirical Research Articles by Editorship, *Media Psychology,* 1999–2010.

Sample Population	No. of Articles 1999–2005	Percent	No. of Articles 2006–2010	Percent
College students and young adults	17	32	9	21
Children <12 years	13	25	10	23
Adults	8	15	1	2
Mixed age groups*	6	11	1	2
Adolescents	5	9	13	30
Female gender	2	4	2	5
Male gender	2	4	—	—
Gender comparisons	—	—	7	16
Total Abstracts Describing Sample Population	53	100	43	100

Note: As described by the author(s) in the article abstract. Some articles appear in more than one category, for example, where more than one study was carried out. Some abstracts reported *N* but did not describe the demographic, and could not be included in this analysis.
*For example, "city residents," "soap viewers," "parents and teens."

of origin. An overall ranking for lead authors is shown in Table 5.5.

AFFILIATED INSTITUTIONS

A frequency ranking was performed using Excel, which established the list the institutions most represented in the journal by editorship and overall. Institutions were counted once in articles in which more than one author collaborated from the same institution. Simple counts were performed to derive percentages of institutions by type (academic, non-academic) and country. Tables 5.6 and 5.7 summarize the results, and a global map of institutions is shown in Figure 5.3.

COLLABORATIONS

Based on all articles, we computed percentages of sole author and various types of collaboration to track how authors of various disciplines combined to produce research in the first 12 years of the journal's history. This we believed would be a good reflection of early overall scholarship in media psychology, even beyond the journal. A summary is shown in Table 5.8.

Lead Author Reflections on the *Journal Of Media Psychology* and Scholarship in the Field

Finally, we conducted an online survey of the overall lead authors (see Table 5.5) to gather their ideas on the conduct of research in media psychology and the outlook for developments and collaborations in the field. Thirteen of the leading 15 authors ultimately were reached, and nine, or 70%, responded. The survey was hosted by PsychData.com, a site designed by researchers for secure surveys, and included 10 free response questions shown in Table 5.10.

Results and Discussion

TOPICS

The 23 consolidated categories of the content analysis appear as frequency rankings separately by editorship periods in Table 5.2. We use the term *responses* as the answer to the inferred question, "What topics are most frequently treated in the journal *Media Psychology?*" In determining increases and decreases in topics, we balanced the number of responses with percent change from one period to the next and the rankings in each period. Because the numbers of responses are relatively small because of total sample size, we determined that at least 25% change told a story.

Psychological themes dealing with attitude and emotions were readily apparent, and numbers of responses, percentage increases from one editorship to the next, as well as ranking indicate an increase in these themes, particularly in the area of emotions. Noticeable increases occurred in the computer/data processing/Internet/technology, virtual reality/video, identity, and narrative/reading, diversity, and politics categories. Fewer articles appeared to

Table 5.5 Top Contributing Authors to *Media Psychology*, 1999–2010.

Rank	Author	Institution	Department	No. of Articles	Total Points
1	Marina Krcmar	Wake Forest U./U. of Connecticut	Dept. of Communication/ Dept. of Communication Sciences	8	4.67
2	Annie Lang	Indiana U.	Institute for Communication Research	9	3.56
3	Eun-Ju Lee	U. of California, Davis	Dept. of Communication	3	3.00
4	Samuel D. Bradley	Texas Tech U./ Indiana U.	College of Mass Communications/Dept. of Telecommunications	4	2.86
5	Niklas Ravaja	Helsinki School of Economics	Center for Knowledge and Innovation Research	5	2.81
6	Silvia Knobloch-Westerwick	The Ohio State University	School of Communication	6	2.63
7	Dolf Zillmann	U. of Alabama	College of Communication and Information Sciences	4	2.41
8	Robert F. Potter	U. of Alabama	Telecommunication & Film	4	2.32
9	Rick W. Busselle	Washington State U.	Edward R. Murrow College of Communication	3	2.20
10	Patti M. Valkenburg	U. of Amsterdam	School of Communication Research	5	2.04
11	Chingching Chang	National Chengchi U.	Department of Advertising	2	2.00
	David K. Perry	U. of Alabama	College of Communication and Information Sciences	2	2.00
	Arthur A. Raney	Florida State U.	Department of Communication	2	2.00
	Erica Scharrer	U. of Massachusetts	Department of Communication	2	2.00
12	Marie-Louise Mares	U. of Wisconsin-Madison	Communication Arts	4	1.99

Note: Points calculated according to APA guidelines, using methodology outlined in Howard, Cole, & Maxwell (1987).

emphasize age and television when comparing the second time period with the first. The second editorship posted a large increase in articles addressing issues of diversity, such as stereotypes, various ethnicities, social status, and more. Several categories appeared to remain relatively constant, including gender, education, and social.

KEYWORDS

Because authors or database managers select keywords best representing the topics of the articles,

we considered word (or "tag") clouds a good way of quickly assessing the primary areas of research in the journal. Figures 5.1 and 5.2 present tag clouds of the top 50 prime words in each of the two periods of editorship. The size of the word font is relative to its weighted frequency. In both periods, *television* clearly dominates other topics, along with *broadcasting* and *social*. Comparing the two tag clouds then gives a quick measure of trends, and corroborates the keyword extractions. Some terms such as *computer* and *games* reflect technology advances and media

Table 5.6 Leading Institutions Contributing to *Media Psychology*, 1999–2010.

Institution	No. of Articles 1999–2005	No. of Articles 2006–2010	Change from 1st to 2nd Editorship	Total Articles 1999–2010
University of Wisconsin—Madison	18	4	−14	22
The Ohio State University	12	9	−3	21
Indiana University	13	6	−7	19
University of Alabama	10	7	−3	17
Stanford University	6	8	+2	14
University of North Carolina	1	9	+8	10
University of California—Santa Barbara	2	7	+5	9
University of Michigan	4	5	+1	9
Cornell University	3	5	+2	8
University of Massachusetts—Amherst	5	2	−3	7
Washington State University	5	2	−3	7
Wake Forest University	1	6	+5	7
University of Pennsylvania	1	6	+5	7
University of Amsterdam	2	6	+4	6
University of California—Davis	0	5	+5	5

Note: In the case of multiple authors from the same institution for a single article, institutions were counted once.

Table 5.7 Number of Institutional Contributions per Country Represented in *Media Psychology*, 1999–2010.

	Country	1st Editors 1999–2005	2nd Editors 2006–2010	Total 1999–2010
Countries represented in first editorship only				
1	Belgium	2	0	2
2	Iceland	1	0	1
3	India	1	0	1
4	Poland	1	0	1
5	Thailand	1	0	1
Countries represented in both editorships				
6	Australia	1	2	3
7	Canada	3	3	6
8	Finland	1	2	3

Table 5.7 (Continued)

	Country	1st Editors 1999–2005	2nd Editors 2006–2010	Total 1999–2010
9	Germany	6	10	16
10	Israel	1	1	2
11	The Netherlands	3	3	6
12	Singapore	2	1	3
13	South Korea	2	4	6
14	Taiwan	1	2	3
15	United Kingdom	2	1	3
16	United States	89	65	154
Countries represented in second editorship only				
17	Austria	0	1	1
18	China	0	1	1
19	Italy	0	2	2
20	Portugal	0	1	1
21	Spain	0	1	1
22	Switzerland	0	1	1
23	Turkey	0	1	1

Note: Each unique institution was counted once for its country, that is, a count of 2 for South Korea means that two institutions in South Korea were represented.

Table 5.8 Department of Lead Author Contributing Articles to *Media Psychology,* 1999–2010.

Department	No. of Lead Authors 1999–2005	% Share	No. of Lead Authors 2006–2010	% Share
Communication	73	57	62	55
Psychology	24	19	16	14
Communications psychology	1	<1	1	<1
Business management	4	3	3	3
Advertising/marketing	3	2	0	0
Other	10*	8	24†	21
Not stated	14	11	7‡	6
Total Articles	129	100%	113	100%

*"Other" includes departments of human ecology; neurology/medicine; engineering; child and poverty; journalism; health and social sciences; music and dance; knowledge and innovation; and languages.
†Includes public policy; arts; media and child health; knowledge and innovation; journalism and media; entertainment; language, translation and interpretation; media and visual arts; radiology.
‡In the publication, no departments were stated for 68 lead authors. An online search supplied information for all but seven authors.

Table 5.9 Departmental Collaborations Producing Articles in *Media Psychology*, 1999–2010.

Collaboration Type	No. of Articles 1999–2005	No. of Articles 2006–2010
Single department	76	83
Collaborations		
Psychology and communications departments	3	6
Communication department and other departments or corporation/ non-academic research institution/unknown	19	13
Psychology department and other departments or corporation/nonacademic research institution/unknown	13	9
Other collaborations	14	2
Total collaborations	49	30
Total Articles	125	113
Collaborations as Percent of Total Articles	39%	27%

Note: Other departments include telecommunications, engineering, business, management, journalism, public relations, advertising, health and social sciences, linguistics and languages, medical schools, among others. Other collaborations are those involving neither a communication nor a psychology department.

innovation. Others, such as the relative diminishment of *aggression* and increase in *sex* and *sexual,* may reflect shifting researcher interest according to public concerns. Similarly, the increase in *political* in the second period (2007–2010) undoubtedly derives from new applications of media to contemporary political campaigns and issues.

For another cross-check on these observations using the keywords, we looked at the top 10 keyword frequencies in the raw data for the two periods, and compared them. Figure 5.4 shows the key terms that were present in both editorships. The bar charts reinforce the dominant themes, particularly of *television* and *social* in both editorships. Additionally, it reflects the increase in *video* and *Internet* from the first to second time period as well as the decrease in *violence*. These findings continue to support the reflection of the overall trends in technology and possible decreased emphasis on violence and media in favor of recent concerns. Figure 5.5 shows the key terms that were unique to each editorship period. It reflects well the technological evolution over time, with terms such as *computer, systems,* and *games* present only in the second editorship. *Radio, viewers,* and *aggressiveness* were present in the first editorship but not the second, supporting a shift away from a focus on early media perhaps in tandem with the decrease in emphasis on violence mentioned earlier. It is important to note that the term *viewer* may reflect

the more passive television viewer more common to the earlier time period as opposed to the more current engaged creator who interacts with media.

FREQUENCIES OF RESEARCH METHODOLOGIES AND SAMPLE POPULATIONS

The abstracts did not uniformly provide information on the type of methodology or sample population. In the first period, 25% of the abstracts did not specify the research methodology. This absence of information did not occur in the second period. In the second period, however, information on the size of *N* for empirical research articles was not indicated in 57% of the abstracts. Despite these gaps, the information available is summarized in Table 5.3 and shows the range of methodologies employed and distribution of sample size in the empirical work. Even if all unspecified categories in the first period were attributed to empirical research, the second period shows a marked increase in the proportion of empirical articles, a total of 86%. In the future, it will be interesting to see if a shift toward larger samples will occur, made possible by online survey methodologies and other electronic methods such as implicit association tests.

For those abstracts describing the sample population, a tabulation of results is shown in Table 5.4 by time period. These data are limited by incomplete coverage, but it is interesting to note possible trends

Table 5.10 *Media Psychology* **Lead Author Survey Questions.**

No.	Lead Author Survey Questions
1.	Why did you submit your work to MPJ? Why was it the best fit for your work?
2.	What other journals did you consider or do you publish in now?
3.	What discipline or disciplines do you believe are most represented in MPJ?
4.	In what field do you see your work best fitting, and why?
5.	If you had collaborators for your articles, how were they selected?
6.	What has been your experience, if any, in collaborations between communication and psychology departments as they relate to media psychology?
7.	What challenges do you see for a field that relies on both communication and psychology disciplines?
8.	Describe any conflicts you see or might expect between psychology and communication departments as they relate to collaboration on media psychology; or state "none" if you do not see any impediments.
9.	Do you see media psychology emerging as an independent field, or do you think that by nature it requires collaboration of several disciplines?
10.	Kindly share any other thoughts you have about issues around scholarly work in media psychology.

Note: The survey was hosted by Psychdata.com and conducted electronically in April 2011.

away from college students and young adults and toward adolescents. Children appear to remain a constant across both time periods. In the 2007–2010 period, it appears that gender comparisons increased considerably. Note that this information about gender appears to contradict the earlier statement that gender appeared constant as a category topic. Keep in mind that as a category, gender includes specific terms, such as woman, machismo, and so on, as seen in Table 5.1. Gender comparisons were gleaned from the hand count of sample populations, which was not accessible through the keyword analysis.

AUTHORS

The 242 articles in the first 12 years were contributed by a total of 461 individual authors from 186 institutions, representing the academy, private sector, and nonprofit research organizations in the United States and 23 other countries.

Top ranked authors are shown in Table 5.5. Of these, 11 of 15 authors were academics based in communication(s) departments of their respective universities; two were housed in telecommunication(s) departments; one was based in an advertising department; and one was housed in a research center for knowledge and innovation. Three of the leading authors' home institutions were outside the United States, in Finland, the Netherlands, and Taiwan.

A tabulation of the departments of lead authors—in the sense of the sole or first listed author among several for each article—is shown in Table 5.8. Here, too, it is readily apparent that more than half the articles are contributed by communication researchers, from 57% in the first time period to 55% in the second. Psychology department researchers accounted for 19% and 14% of the total articles, respectively, over the same time periods. This finding is consistent with the journal's 2009 ISI ranking of 11/55 in Communication and 32/63 in Applied Psychology.[4] It appears that more communications than applied psychology journals reference articles in *Media Psychology*, an indicator of the relative influence of communications scholars contributing to this journal. A notable finding is that "other" departments grew substantially from 8% to 21% from the first to second period, representing a wide range of disciplines in the health, business, journalism, languages, and engineering fields, to name a few.

INSTITUTIONS

Leading institutions by time period are shown in Table 5.6, determined by the number of articles produced by authors based in the institution. The change between time periods is interesting to note. Although the University of Wisconsin-Madison is overall leader, 17 of the 22 articles produced were under the first editorship. The same is true of the next three leading institutions that show a similar decline under the second editorship period. But the reverse is also true; that is, universities of low activity under the first editorship show considerable gains in the more recent period. This raises the question of the extent to which editors influence article submission, either explicitly or by known profile of research interests. Or, does publication success by a single author influence submissions by her or his academic colleagues to the same journal? Our interest here was to find early research hubs in media psychology, but it appears that the map is yet very dynamic.

Overall since publication began, 154 of the 186 institutions represented, or 83%, were based in the United States. Nevertheless, 24 countries were represented, with Germany accounting for 16 articles, or 9% of the total contributions. This befits the country most historians associate with the origins of modern psychology, in the form of Wundt's innovative empirical research into mental processes and human behavior. Also, it reflects media psychology scholarship encouraged over the last two decades by the German journal *Zeitschrift für Medienpsychologie,* subsumed since 2008 under the *Journal of Media Psychology* (Hogrefe) with a global focus.[5] Table 5.7 shows all countries with contributing researchers or research institutions during the full period under review.

One of the interesting findings apparent in Table 5.7 is the way certain countries appeared only in the first or second periods of editorship. In some countries, and particularly in Asia, academics are evaluated by the publishing industry's ranking of journals in which they publish, leading them to wait until journals are well established before submitting articles. This factor apparently did not weigh heavily, given *Media Psychology*'s impressive ISI ratings and the presence of five Asian countries' authors in the first editorship alone. Again, as for the institutions, it is interesting to consider the source of how the journal became internationalized this early. Was it the editors' connections? Did international conferences play a role in disseminating research published in the journal? Did the publisher's Web presence and promotion of the journal encourage submissions globally?

The map in Figure 5.3 plots the information from Table 5.7 to visually demonstrate the reach of interest in the journal and its focus on media psychology. Considering the relatively short period since its inception, this degree of internationalization gives credence to the idea that media psychology is a topic that is culturally pervasive. The important exception to date—albeit judging only by this one journal—is the absence of scholarship from Latin and Central America, and Africa.

CROSS-DEPARTMENTAL COLLABORATIONS

We decided to look more closely at what types of collaborations had come together to produce articles in the journal, as the journal cofounders wrote in their inaugural statement that "in these harrowing times of streamlined academic budgets" they wanted to create a journal for interdisciplinary work, for "scholars from diverse disciplines who seek to understand and explain the roles, uses, processes, and effects of mediated communication in complex information societies" (Bryant & Roskos-Ewoldsen, 1999, p. 1). This analysis focused on collaborations between departments regardless of the disciplinary background and expertise of an author. For example, collaborations between an author from a psychology department and an author from a communications department were considered collaborations even if both authors' terminal degrees were in psychology. Certainly, institutions may hire communications researchers in psychology departments and psychologists in communications departments. After producing this analysis of contributions by institutional type and source, a wide variety is apparent. Table 5.9 presents these data by time period, also comparing the percentage of sole source academic articles (i.e., author[s] from a single department) with other configurations. Notably, collaborations actually declined in the more recent period, moving from 39% of 129 total articles produced during 1999–2005, to 27% of 113 articles during 2006–2010. The collaboration between communication and psychology departments remained low throughout the time period, with three articles in the first phase and six in the second.

OTHER COLLABORATIONS

Both nonprofit, for-profit, and government research institutions are represented in collaborations and indicate where funding outside of academic budgets is promoting media psychology. This explains in part how public agendas become research agendas, and perhaps also why, specifically, the journal includes persistent focus on television, broadcasting, and children. Examples of these institutions include the Children's Television Workshop, Nickelodeon, MediaKidz Research and Consulting, the Rand Corporation, the Audie L. Murphy Memorial Veterans Hospital, Memorial Sloan-Kettering Cancer Center, and the National Institutes of Health.

Lead Author Reflections on the JOURNAL OF MEDIA PSYCHOLOGY and Scholarship in the Field

We carried out an electronic survey of the leading authors in April 2011 to gain insight into several areas, such as why they wished to publish in *Media Psychology,* their perceptions of the journal content, their experiences with collaborating with authors from various disciplines, and their overall thoughts about the future of media psychology scholarship and the discipline itself (see survey questions, Table 5.10). Nine authors responded.

The first survey question addressed why authors chose to submit their work to *Media Psychology* and how they determined it was the best fit. Several respondents indicated that it is one of few journals that specifically focus on the intersection of the two disciplines, and they commented on its high status. They appreciated its value both for the opportunity to align their research with the appropriate vehicle, and to meet the needs of the readers. According to M. Krcmar, "*Media Psychology* is the best journal that focuses solely on media psychology." Silvia Knobloch-Westerwick noted that her coauthors, often graduate students, are attracted to the journal because it is consistent with the way they want to "market" themselves. This indicates a "proving ground" role of a seminal journal in an emerging field, one that launches and positions not only new ideas, but new scholars too.

In light of the minimal collaborations between communication and psychology departments discovered through this content analysis (see Table 5.9) we were particularly interested in exploring the lead authors' experiences with collaboration. One-third of the respondents expressed that psychology researchers tend to see communication as a discipline that is not as serious as their own or are simply not interested, thereby increasing tension in collaboration. Contributor and current *Media Psychology* editor A. Lang stated (April, 2011):

> When communication researchers do psychology they tend to primarily do social psychology which is fairly limiting. Psychologists, in general, find media to be too complex as stimuli, and thereby do not lend themselves to helping to learn about the mind/brain. Communication researchers often find the brain too complex and low level to contribute to theorizing about communication. The truth is somewhere in between in my opinion. When I have collaborated with psychologists, everyone has come away from the experience with a more complete view of both psychology and media.

As another indicator of this same tendency, one respondent also noted that although it is difficult for a graduate from a communication program to gain a faculty position in a psychology department, it is not as difficult for a graduate from a psychology program to gain a position in a communications department. It is useful to consider that although communications departments are represented more extensively than psychology departments, authors may be psychologists within communications departments.

Respondents mentioned institutional barriers because departments or colleges vary in culture and values. Another possible challenge is that perspectives of scholars from different disciplines may vary so much that it causes confusion and misunderstanding. Two disciplines often lack shared assumptions, thereby requiring additional time and effort to collaborate. Two respondents commented on challenges in methodologies of media psychology research overall, noting that it is difficult to develop longitudinal studies because of the constant changing nature of media, and external validity sometimes needs to be sacrificed because of the lack of control over media messages. It is possible that different preferences for methodology challenge collaborations between researchers in communication and psychology; communication researchers may embrace less traditional methodology than is practiced in psychology.

When asked about media psychology's current or potential place as an independent field, eight of the nine survey respondents believed that media psychology is necessarily cross-disciplinary, although only one believed media psychology has already emerged as its own independent field. Two respondents also felt that media psychology will continue to be better accepted and have a stronger fit in communication departments rather than psychology departments. In fact, S. Knobloch-Westerwick of The Ohio State University's School of Communication explained that her institution was unable to obtain formal approval for a course called "media psychology" because the psychology department did not want that school to use the word "psychology." Ultimately, the course was given a different name.

Conclusion

Working in a grounded theory approach, without the framing of preconceived hypotheses, the potential for findings is almost unlimited. We focused on the questions framed earlier in this chapter. We first looked at topic categories and changes over time. Two salient increases were in diversity and politics. Increased attention to diversity issues is encouraging, and, perhaps with its increased attention over time in psychology and other disciplines, its importance will be noticed early in the evolution of media psychology. The increased attention to politics was not unusual given the campaign activity for 2008 elections, and the dissemination of political information through various forms of media. The increase from the first period of editorship to the second involving computers, technology and the like was not surprising, given the rapid changes in technology. Similarly, the increase in virtual reality/ video gaming and identity (often associated with avatars) was not unusual. The trend toward adolescent populations and away from adults also seems to connect to the emphasis on new technology. These increases affirmed *Media Psychology*'s incorporation of current topics and supports the dynamic nature of the field as a whole.

A look at topic categories also showed large increases in two major psychological themes of attitudes and emotions. Behavior and cognition increased as well, but less dramatically. The psychological themes indicate the integration of psychology in this discipline, and may relate to growth of interest in the technology areas because investigations into the Internet, virtual reality, and other current media issues tend to include psychological influences and effects. Perhaps the most interesting aspect of these increases is that they occur concurrently with decreases in collaborations between psychology and communication departments, as well as the relatively high contribution of authors from communication departments as compared with those from psychology departments. This relationship between the category topics and the collaborations between disciplines begins to address our two initial questions: the first about what collaborations occurred and the second about whether the journal has maintained the focus proposed by the inaugural editors.

From within the academy, authors from communication departments contributed 57% of the articles, more than three times more research than authors from psychology departments. Among the top 15 most prolific authors, all but two were based in departments with "communication(s)" or "telecommunication(s)" somewhere in the title. Part of this is disciplinary: The scope of topics in communication tends to include issues related to psychology. Communication issues are generally broader in scope, whereas psychology has distinct subfields, such as personality, brain research, developmental, health, and many more that have their own academic research journals. Social psychologists are the most likely scholars to conduct research in media psychology, and these specialists may submit their work to journals in that field. Collaborations between faculty in communication and psychology departments produced in the journal only three of 129 articles under the first coeditors, and six of 113 articles under the second editorial period. As one of our survey respondents indicated, the lack of shared assumptions may discourage collaborations. However, producing articles that offer perspectives from two or more disciplines as well as shared perspectives could inform the discipline by showcasing similarities and differences. It may not be necessary to hold shared perspectives to produce research. Given the interdisciplinary nature of the field, it may be that we can learn as much from the acknowledgment of the differences in perspectives as we can learn from presenting the information from only one disciplinary perspective. More collaborations of this type could enhance research models, increasing the "ecological validity" called for by psychologist Ulric Neisser (1976). One option for this type of collaboration is an increase in articles submitted with coauthors from communications and psychology departments. Another, not tracked in this chapter, is collaboration between psychology and communications faculty regardless of the department in which they are housed. A third category of special interest is research conducted by academic and nonacademic professionals who consider themselves to be media psychologists. As the field grows, universities are developing media psychology programs, which will ultimately produce graduates and scholars in the field. Fielding Graduate University designed the first media psychology doctoral program in the United States, housed in its School of Psychology. Faculty include scholar–practitioners with backgrounds in communications and psychology disciplines, and the blend inspires an interdisciplinary balance. Additional programs are appearing globally, and more journals encouraging submissions in this interdisciplinary field have come on the scene to encourage and accommodate the growing research.

Overall, this points to a question of whether or not the journal supports its interdisciplinary intent. The lack of balance between communication and psychology departments indicates a strong presence of one discipline over another. In fact, all of the editors throughout the study period were housed in communication departments (including telecommunication, communication science, and communication research); none resided in a department of psychology. Nevertheless, the increase in participation of other departments under the second editorship is encouraging. Additionally, contributors from communications departments appear to embrace psychology, whereas psychology departments are more likely to demonstrate an overt or covert lack of interest in media. Finally, perhaps the 57% of communications contributors can be viewed as excellent progress. Journals with a more specific focus and no expressed purpose of encouraging interdisciplinary work may near 100% of contributions from one field. We may consider the 43% of contributions from other disciplines to be, after all, an achievement. Time and reviews of trends will better tell the continuing story.

Our initial questions also considered affiliations and background of authors. Answers to these questions pointed us to an interest in global involvement. The first editors' professional network and outlook clearly established an international perspective for the journal and indeed for the field. Including collaborations, one-fourth of the articles in the first time period were contributed at least in part by authors affiliated with non-US academic or research institutions. Once all 12 years were considered, 23 countries in addition to the United States have been represented. It seems unlikely this result would have occurred without the active efforts of the journal's editors.

Outside of the analysis of the departments represented, the listings of authors, institutions, and countries is interesting as a baseline for future comparisons to a similar analysis from the year 2011 forward or with a new form of editorship, or between more recently launched journals dedicated to media psychology. It appears that the high level of public interest and interdisciplinary nature of the field would seem to promote corporate–educational partnerships, as evidenced by a number of nonacademic sources of research in this very early stage of the field's development. This will be equally interesting to track over time. There appear to be more contributions from the eastern and midwestern sections of the United States than from the western portion of the country. A clear trend may emerge later. Globally, Europe is particularly well represented, most likely due to the existence of earlier journals in the field that predate *Media Psychology*, notably *Zeitschrift für Medien-psychologie,* a journal focusing on German and European scholarship in media research since the late 1980s. Asian-based authors published in *Media Psychology* emerged in six countries of that region, most actively in South Korea and Taiwan. Although Japanese researchers demonstrate a strong interest in media psychology, particularly in the areas of television, the Internet, video games, and mobile phones, Japan was not represented in *Media Psychology*. As Sakamoto (see Chapter 28)

notes, much Japanese media psychology scholarship is published in Japanese. Lack of English translations is a barrier to the influence of this scholarship. In considering other areas of the world, nothing has yet appeared from Latin or Central America, or from African scholars. At this point, we have addressed all of our initial questions with the exception of the final one which, perhaps, is all encompassing as it reminds us of the value of media psychology as a new discipline with an evolving story: Is there a convergence of themes that correspond to the evolution of this new discipline? The themes appear to be varied and current, supporting a discipline that addresses a broad number of issues and the interrelationship of these issues. In word clouds, we see that television, broadcasting, and social support are important themes that remain constant. Our recommendation is to continue to encourage contributors to add elements that tell the story. Do *Media Psychology* and more recently emerging journals in this discipline help shape the meaning of the discipline or reflect its changing nature? The answer is not one or the other; we hope that a somewhat parallel process is in place.

Future Directions

Understanding the reasons why media psychology research develops in certain institutions or is fostered in multidisciplinary collaborations may lead to ways to encourage this scholarship. Although *Media Psychology* included a clear, initial focus on multidisciplinary work, in practice, this focus waned as evidenced by the decrease in collaborations from the first period of editorship to the second. We encourage a renewed emphasis along with a strategy to demonstrate that emphasis. For example, the editors may explicitly seek cross-disciplinary collaborations by adjusting their review process to prioritize this type of work. In the end, it may come down to whether researchers are curious enough to cross their own borders and seek new perspectives and collaborations to define the field. As A. Lang stated (authors' online survey, April 2011):

> I think we need a better definition of the field. I don't think it's enough to cite some theory from psychology and then do a study and call it media psychology. Right now things are too fragmented. There is no agreement as to what the big questions media psychology should be asking are—so it is difficult to make progress. The field now is a mile wide and less than an inch deep and most people in it don't communicate with others.

It would be interesting to compare content analyses of appropriate communication and psychology academic journals to calibrate the presence of media-related topics. The relationship between psychology and a variety of media types, most especially computers, the Internet, and telephony is also still a frontier research topic, despite the rapid proliferation of applications in telehealth, social networks, and virtual reality, to name a few. Potter (Chapter 24) notes the wealth of topics with relatively few scholars focusing on the coverage, perhaps not an unusual phenomenon in a developing field. As the field grows, the fragmentation Potter and Lang each express may decrease. In addition to encouraging some scholarly unity on critical topics to research, it would be valuable to explore the relative degree of positive and negative representations of the media in research. This type of analysis may uncover funding interests and/or researcher bias that unduly influence scholarship in the field.

Finally, the *Journal of Media Psychology* is an excellent vehicle to encourage psychologists worldwide to conduct and publish more research about the influence of media, and embrace the notion that a media psychologist has much to contribute in understanding the impact of technology on human behavior. May the story continue to unfold.

Acknowledgments

The authors wish to thank E. A. Konijn for her review of this chapter and encouragement.

Correspondence concerning this chapter should be addressed to Ellen Baker Derwin at 16355 Laguna Canyon Road, Irvine, CA 92618; e-mail: derwin@brandman.edu.

Notes

1. Jennings Bryant and David Roskos-Ewoldsen were founders of the MPJ and coeditors from inception in 1999 through 2005, while faculty at the Institute for Communication Research of the University of Alabama.

2. From 2006, after the departure of Bryant and Roskos-Ewoldsen, the following served as editors, generally on a rotating basis within a 3-year term: Peter Vorderer, Annenberg School for Communication, University of Southern California; Mary Beth Oliver, College of Communications, Pennsylvania State University; Michael Shapiro, Department of Communication, Cornell University; Robin Nabi, Department of Communication, University of California, Santa Barbara; Ron Tamborini, Department of Communication, Michigan State University; Annie Lang, Department of Telecommunications, Indiana University, Bloomington; Cynthia Hoffner, Department of Communication, Georgia State University; and Elly A. Konijn, Department of Communication Science, VU University Amsterdam, Netherlands.

3. For additional information from the manufacturer of this software, see http://www.spss.com/software/statistics/text-analytics-for-surveys/.

4. For an explanation and review of ISI rating methodology, see originator Eugene Garfield's *Journal Impact Factor: A Brief Review* (1999), available at http://www.cmaj.ca/cgi/content/full/161/8/979.

5. More information about the *Journal of Media Psychology* may be found at http://www.hogrefe.com/periodicals/journal-of-media-psychology/about-the-journal-the-editor/.

References

Blancher, A. T., Buboltz, W. C., & Soper, B. (2010). Content analysis of the journal of counseling & development: Volumes 74 to 84. *Journal of Counseling & Development*, *88*, 139–145.

Bryant, J. & Miron, D. (2004). Theory and research in mass communication. *Journal of Communication*, *54*, 662–704.

Bryant, J., & Roskos-Ewoldsen, D. (1999). Inaugural notes: Raison d'etre. *Media Psychology*, *1*(1), 1–2.

Cokley, K., Caldwell, L., Miller, K., & Muhammad, G. (November, 2001). Content analysis of the Journal of Black Psychology (1985–1999). *Journal of Black Psychology*, *27*(4), 424–438.

Dick, B. (2005). Grounded theory: a thumbnail sketch. Retrieved March 2, 2008 from http://www.scu.edu.au/schools/gcm/ar/arp/grounded.html.

Fremlin, J. W. (2008, January). Understanding media psychology. *APS Observer*, *21*(1). Retrieved July 22, 2012 from http://www.psychologicalscience.org/observer/getArticle.cfm?id=2287.

Howard, G., Cole, D., & Maxwell, S. (1987). Research productivity in psychology based on publication in the journals of the American Psychological Association. *American Psychologist*, *42*(11), 975–986.

Lee, Y., Driscoll, M., & Nelson, D. (2004). The past, present, and future of research in distance education: Results of a content analysis. *The American Journal of Distance Education*, *18*(4), 225–241.

Loveland, J., Buboltz, W., Schwartz, J., & Gibson, G. (2006,). Content analysis of CDQ from 1994–2003: Implications and trends for practitioners and researchers from a decade of research. *The Career Development Quarterly*, *54*(3), 256–264.

Neisser, U. (1976). *Cognition and Reality*. San Francisco: Freeman.

Neuendorf, K. (2002). *The Content Analysis Guidebook*. Thousand Oaks, CA: Sage.

Nolan, A.L. (2009). The content of educational psychology: an analysis of top ranked journals from 2003 Through 2007. *Educational Psychology Review*. *21*, 279–289.

Pelsma, D., & Cesari, J. (1989,). Content analysis of the *Journal of Counseling and Development*: Volumes 48–66. *Journal of Counseling and Development*, *67*(5), 275–278.

Polkinghorne, D. (2012). Qualitative research and its application to media psychology. In Dill, K. E. (Ed.), *The Oxford Handbook of Media Psychology*. New York: Oxford University Press.

Potter, W. J. (2012). A general framework for media psychology scholarship. In Dill, K. E. (Ed.), *The Oxford Handbook of Media Psychology*. New York: Oxford University Press.

Potter, W. J. & Riddle, K. (2007). A content analysis of the media effects literature. *Journalism & Mass Communication Quarterly, 84*(1), 90–104.

Riffe, D., Lacy, S., & Fico, F. (2005). *Analyzing media messages: Using quantitative content analysis in research.* Hillsdale, NJ: Lawrence Erlbaum Associates.

Sakamoto, A. (2012). Japanese approach to research on psychological effects of use of media. In Dill, K. E. (Ed.), *The Oxford Handbook of Media Psychology.* New York: Oxford University Press.

Southern, S. (2006,). Themes in marriage and family counseling: A content analysis of *The Family Journal. The Family Journal: Counseling and Therapy for Couples and Families, 14*(2), 114–122.

Thomas, S. (December, 1994). Artifactual study in the analysis of culture: A defense of content analysis in a postmodern age. *Communication Research, 21*(6), 683–697.

Weber, R. (1990). *Basic Content Analysis. In Sage University Paper Series: Quantitative Applications in the Social Sciences (49).* Newbury Park, CA: Sage.

Williams, M., & Buboltz, W. (1999). Content analysis of the *Journal of Counseling & Development*: Volumes 67 to 74. *Journal of Counseling and Development, 77*(3), 344–349.

Media Literacy: History, Progress, and Future Hopes

Edward T. Arke

Abstract

This chapter aims to introduce the subdiscipline of media literacy through the examination of the genre's history, current challenges, and possible future directions. With roots dating back to the late 1920s, the idea of educating consumers about the content and production methods of media messages has been attempted in a number of ways and venues. With media consumption a large part of most people's leisure time, the need to get individuals to more critically engage the messages continues to be an important educational objective. The largest challenge, however, is the lack of government support for such an initiative coupled with an apparent lack of awareness on the part of most people. What needs to occur is a more organized and systematic approach for the inclusion of media literacy instruction in secondary and higher education.

Key Words: mass communication studies, media education, media history, media literacy, media literacy education, media messages, media studies

Introduction

The need for media literacy education and efforts to have it included in American curriculums might be one of the academy's best kept secrets. Although other English-speaking countries have recognized the importance of the subject area, the disjointed approach in the United States has had mixed results over the years. Evidence of its impact is scattered and the lack of a centralized, focused effort makes it difficult to forecast how and when more nations will follow the lead of countries such as Canada, the United Kingdom, and Australia.

The British Film Institute is generally credited with efforts to teach media consumers to be more analytical and critical beginning in the late 1920s and early 1930s. "As early as 1929, a British board of education urged teachers to elevate children's standards of taste and evaluation about motion pictures" through specific training as part of the general education process (Brown, 1991, pp. 56–57). Others have

written that media education has been a focal point for at least some scholars since newspapers became mass media in the 1850s (Anderson, 2008).

In the United States, The Wisconsin Association for Better Broadcasting was organized in the 1930s, this time by concerned educators rather than the government or industry sources (Cho & Heins, 2002). As evidenced by its growth into a national body known as the American Council for Better Broadcasts, cohesive, grassroots, educational efforts can gain traction. However, this early media literacy group would later see a less prominent public profile as the subsequent National Telemedia Council. Media literacy is a field that has had its fair share of highs and lows over the last 70 years in an effort to find its place in educational systems from the United Kingdom to the United States and from Israel to China.

Media education's first phase of development lasted from the early 1930s to the early 1960s and focused on protecting students from the evils of media by educating *against* the media (Masterman, 2001). The goal was to dismiss mass media in order to protect traditional forms of high culture in society. Film, advertising, to some extent radio, and even children's comics were targeted as potential threats to long-standing cultural standards.

The rapid yet sustained growth of television in the 1950s, which has continued through the present, has represented another era of media education with a focus on this dominant medium. Gerbner wrote that television particularly has penetrated our lives to such a degree that its consequences are felt around the world. He added that new delivery systems "signal even deeper penetration and integration of the dominant patterns of images and messages into everyday life" (Morgan, 2002, p. 193). With studies continually pointing to the amount of time consumed in people's lives with television viewing, this medium remains a focal point of media literacy studies.

As the Internet has developed into the newest and most complex form of mass communication to date, interest in educating students of all ages to become better informed media consumers has reemerged. Media literacy continues to be a vibrant field of study for educators, activists, and even community health care practitioners. It is also an educational discipline that struggles for inclusion in curriculums worldwide. Anderson (2008) feels the definition is not a question of what, but rather when. "The concepts and practices that form media literacy, in whatever its current configurations are a necessary cultural response to the force of media in society" (p. 397).

Past

Christ and Potter (1998) indicate that *media literacy* has been treated as a public policy issue, a critical cultural issue, or a scholarly inquiry from a physiological, cognitive, or anthropological tradition. They also indicate the term has been used synonymously with *media education* and can span across different kinds of media. Studies regarding the topic can be found in academic journals and other discipline-specific publications ranging from education to communication and including psychology and sociology. However, some common ground for researchers in the field was established in 1992.

The 1992 National Leadership Conference on Media Literacy resulted in a basic definition of the term that has helped to shape a more formalized field of study. "The ability to access, analyze, evaluate and communicate messages in a variety of forms" (Aufderheide, 1993; Christ & Potter, 1998) has provided a working definition for the field since the group met in Washington DC in December of that year. Among the scholars present were David Considine, Barry Duncan, Renee Hobbs, Elizabeth Thoman, and George Gerbner (http://www.medialit.org/reading_room/article582.html). To reach the point of consensus, a history of generally uncoordinated projects and efforts preceded the gathering.

One such project was the Media Action Research Center (MARC), which was originally formed in 1974. Three years later, the Center joined with the Church of the Brethren, American Lutheran Church, and the United Methodist Church to create Television Awareness Training (T-A-T), a program that included a 280-page *Viewer's Guide* and related workshops for parents and teachers (Brown, 1991). The program self-reported more than 400 trained "T-A-T leaders" in 44 states by 1985, with books, seminars, and workshops "estimated at hundreds of thousands" (Brown, 1991, p. 181). Although widely disseminated, T-A-T emphasized a values-based approach and media literacy as a faith-based endeavor rather than an educationally based curriculum.

A second curriculum project of MARC was *Growing with Television,* which consisted of 11 large booklets and audiovisual support material (Brown, 1991). Because of the religious origins of the program, the developers emphasized the relationship among life, television, and the values reflected in the Bible. The focus was on being a more discriminating user of television rather than instruction on what to and not to watch.

During the late 1970s through the mid-1980s, there were a number of systematic efforts to develop integrated curricula and long-term projects in media education, some of which were federally funded. The studies were conducted at a time when there was another wave of concerns being expressed over the impact of violent television programming on children.

An example is the work of Aimee Dorr, who was leading efforts to develop a curriculum hoping "to make children more critical evaluators of its (television's) content" (Dorr et al., 1980, p. 71). The teaching of the curriculum and subsequent assessment reflected much of the inoculation philosophy that tended to motivate early media literacy efforts. The authors opened their report on *Television Literacy for Young Children* by stating, "much of what children watch on television...has not been produced with their welfare or that of their parents' values in mind"

(p. 71). However, although the authors appeared to be stressing the protection of young minds, their approach also stressed the critical analysis of television content, which would become a fundamental component of subsequent media literacy efforts.

The researchers concluded that children can learn about television, evaluate it, and apply their knowledge in discussing program content. However, interviews with the study's participants showed some evidence of selectivity and reasoned judgment, but not a noticeable change in the young children's social attitudes regarding race. They also acknowledged logistical and financial costs could be stumbling blocks to the creation of effective television curricula.

The late 1970s and early 1980s were a fertile time for media literacy studies because there was federal funding available. During the Carter Administration, in 1978, the U.S. Office of Education and the Library of Congress called for funding proposals for curricular projects that would instruct students in critical viewing skills (Heins & Cho, 2002). The industry was also funding research. Yale University received a grant from the American Broadcasting Company (ABC) to support a study targeting third, fourth, and fifth grade students.

Two of the principal researchers of the Yale-based study, Dorothy and Jerome Singer, have looked at ways to teach media literacy over the last four decades. One of their early studies looked to integrate media literacy education into the existing curriculum as a means of interesting students in reading, writing and other language arts skills through a better understanding of television. Their study "suggests that children can be taught about the medium in the regular school curriculum by tying their natural interest in TV with exercises in reading, writing and critical thinking" (Singer, D. et al., 1980, p. 93).

The Singer study also identified two potential obstacles to a much wider acceptance of media literacy in the overall school curriculum. First, there was a reluctance of parents to have their children participate in the study because they did not appear very concerned about the impact of television on their children's development. And second, the more broadly identified belief that media impacts others far more than one's self or immediate family members.

Known as the "third-person effect," researchers have documented evidence that people generally believe they will be less influenced by the mass media than others and, are in their own minds, above manipulation by media messages (Comstock &

Scharrer, 2005). These remain among the obstacles and challenges facing media literacy educators today.

When major funding in the United States ceased, the largest structured experiments disappeared (Brown, 1991). There became a widespread belief that education should be focused on preparing students to compete in the global marketplace. "Back to the basics" pushed media education and other related literacies, such as computer literacy, to the sidelines (Tyner, 1991). This type of political response to educational policy has resulted "in a long history of disjointed funding and confused teaching practices in the United States" (Tyner, 1991, para. 5).

Although things may have stalled in the United States in the early and mid-1980s, some global developments helped continue to move the field ahead. In January of 1982, the United Nations Educational, Scientific and Cultural Organization (UNESCO) gathered representatives of 19 nations at their International Symposium on Media Education in Grunwald, Germany. Their formal declaration, which received unanimous approval, called for among other things: comprehensive media education programs from preschool to university level, and stimulation of research and development of media education from domains such as psychology, sociology, and communication science. Some nations have certainly heeded the call more closely than others.

Whether it was a direct result of the UNESCO symposium or not, Canada's leadership in media education started to rise to a new level in 1984 when the Jesuit Communication Project formed. Later, working closely with the Association for Media Literacy, the Project ensured that media education would become a mandated part of the language arts curriculum in Ontario. The groups' Ontario Media Literacy Resource Guide has been translated into French, Italian, Spanish, and Japanese (Pungente, 2009, p. 3). Father John Pungente has been with the project since its origins. He also became known across Canada as the host of a media literacy–oriented television show, *Beyond the Screen,* on Canada's national arts channel.

As the decade of the 1980s neared a close, more organizations were beginning to emerge in the United States. For example, the Center for Media Literacy (CML) in Los Angeles was established as an expansion of *Media & Values* magazine. Although the periodical, first published in 1977, is no longer being printed, the Center continues to provide professional development and educational resources in media literacy education. Center for Media Literacy was a founding organizational member of the Alliance for a Media Literate America (AMLA), which originated the National Media Education Conferences gathering media literacy professionals every 2 years.

The 1990s began with more inclusion of media literacy language in state education competencies. For example, the Minnesota Department of Education created a list of desired educational outcomes in the area of educational media and technology that were completely compatible with media literacy (Considine, 2002). Today, the Minnesota Educational Media Organization gives leadership and support to school media and information technology personnel in the schools.

Media literacy education seemed to find a home in the English classrooms of middle and high schools. The Media Commission of the National Council of Teachers of English (NCTE) met in Seattle in November 1991 to discuss the future of media education in the United States. Among the recommendations was to encourage NCTE teacher accreditation standards to require teachers to be knowledgeable in critical analysis of media and that the requirement be addressed seriously through workshops, training, materials, and guidelines for media education (www.medialit.org). A 1993 journal article published by the National Council of Teachers of English encouraged English teachers to consider comprehension of media texts an important part of teaching reading in general (Goodwyn, 1993).

In the first year of the Clinton Administration, three cabinet members, Attorney General Janet Reno, Education Secretary Richard Riley, and Health and Human Services Secretary Donna Shalala convened *Safeguarding Our Youth: Violence Prevention for Our Nation's Children.* The gathering included a working group on media who considered "issues related to mass media and our growing culture of violence" (Thoman, 1993, p. 1). The group concluded, among other things, that there are at least four social effects of mediated violence that need to be considered: an increase in aggression and meanness, an increase in fear and concern for self-protection (the *victim effect*), an increased callousness and insensitivity (the *bystander effect*), and an increased appetite for violence needed to keep people watching (Thoman, 1993). The group also noted that the media are so much a part of daily life that few people are aware of their impact, whether positive or negative.

The group of media practitioners, professional educators and two student representatives,

concluded that media violence is the first phase of a major cultural debate about life in the 21st century and that "violence does attract an audience" (Thoman, 1993, p. 4). The final report's fourth and final recommendation was: "Broad-based media literacy education needs to be a priority in the U.S. and implemented in an interagency, interdisciplinary approach" (Thoman, 1993, p. 4). The Media Working Group said on the federal level the Departments of Education and Health and Human Services, the FCC, FTC, and others should specifically target media literacy programs.

In a series of Common Core State Standards released in 2010, skills related to media analysis and production were integrated throughout. The National Governors Association and Chief State School Officers were responsible for the state-led education standards draft. As of July, 2012, 45 states had voiced support for a nationwide effort to adopt the standards. Only Alaska, Nebraska, Minnesota, Texas and Virginia had not yet provided approval (www.corestandards.org) Institutions of higher education also took a more active and higher-profile role in promoting the discussion of media education. The Harvard Graduate School of Education sponsored the Institute on Media Education in 1993. The program continued for a second year, but funding cuts then discontinued the program. Other institutions would later adopt and adapt the Harvard model of summer teaching institutes (Duncan, 1993).

North Carolina's Appalachian State University cohosted the first national media literacy conference in September 1995 (Considine, 2002). In July 2000 the university opened the first institutionalized graduate program in media literacy (Considine, 2002). The program acknowledges "its unique American context as well as media literacy's roots in Canada, Australia and the United Kingdom" (Considine, 2002, p. 8). The graduate program continues to offer a 36-hour degree and an 18-hour certificate and is part of the university's interdisciplinary approach to media education.

Also in 1995, the Carnegie Council on Adolescent Development, based on research by Renee Hobbs, argued media literacy "may help protect young adolescents against strong advertising pressures to smoke, drink, have sex or eat unhealthy foods" (p. 118). The panel also suggested that schools would make a positive contribution in the information age by introducing instruction and activities that contribute to media literacy. The think tank emphasized the potential of media to be used more constructively in the lives of adolescents rather than perpetuating the ongoing emphasis on violence and sexuality.

The National Communication Association has tried to capture and convey competency standards in their *K-12 Speaking, Listening and Media Literacy* statements. Among the original 23 standards: "The effective media participant can demonstrate knowledge and understanding of the effects of the various types of electronic audio and visual media, including television, radio, the telephone, the Internet, computers, electronic conferencing, and film on media consumers" (National Communication Association, 1996). As a result of the NCA standards, many school districts began including or reviewing communication skills education in their programs (Berko et al., 1998).

In 1998, the NCA copyrighted an updated list of *K-12 Speaking, Listening, and Media Literacy Standards and Competency Statements* (www.natcom.org). Of the 20 standards published, the final five standards cover competencies for media literate communicators. The organization also states, "Media literacy is recognized as a fundamental competency for literate citizens" (National Communication Association, 1998, p. 1).

The NCA's efforts were designed to respond to and implement national educational reforms based on the Goals 2000: Educate America Act. Among those goals and objectives was: "Goal 5: By the year 2000, every adult American will be literate and will possess the knowledge and skill necessary to compete in a global economy and exercise the rights and responsibilities of citizenship…Objective 5: The proportion of college graduates who demonstrate an advanced ability to think critically, communicate effectively, and solve problems will increase substantially" (National Education Goals Panel, 1992, p. 16). Although not much has been written about the success or failure of the Goals 2000 initiative, it does point to a desire to have Americans become more literate about the media options they consume in an era in which the media's role in society continues to grow.

Present

Media literacy education has become a more organized field of study and gained momentum over the last four decades. To try and assess the current state of affairs is a somewhat daunting task, for several reasons. First, the number of other academic areas of which media literacy might be considered a subdiscipline. As outlined, media education can be located in the subjects of English, Psychology, Sociology, Education, Health Education, Communication,

and even the sciences. Because of the wide breadth of research perspectives, there is not a centralized clearinghouse of research data, agreed-on methodologies, or theoretical foundations to which to point.

Although there is a great variety of differences of opinion or philosophy regarding media literacy education, not only in the United States but worldwide, some common principles are shared by a majority of individuals studying and practicing media literacy education. The National Association for Media Literacy Education (NAMLE) developed a set of Core Principles of Media Literacy Education that were adopted by the organization's board in 2007. Among the concepts embedded in the statement are active critical thinking, expansion of the concept of literacy beyond reading and writing, media literacy as an important skill for the preservation of democracy, media as a part of culture and an agent of socialization, and the fact that an individual's beliefs and experiences contributes to his or her own meanings of media messages (www.namle.net). All or at least some of these principles are normally found as general characteristics in media literacy education today. Even broader is agreement on the need for knowledge and understanding of the areas of media industries, media messages media audiences, and media effects (Potter, 2004; Martens, 2010).

Second, in the United States, there is no well-defined set of media literacy objectives or federal government mandates to provide direction for an agreed-on curriculum to be developed and studied. Although Kubey (2003) notes that as of the year 2000 all 50 states have elements of media education in their core curricular frameworks, those elements vary in number, appropriate grade levels for their achievement, and emphasis from state to state. As federal programs and guidelines continue to evolve and change, the amount of actual teaching time devoted to nonemphasized or nonevaluated skill sets is difficult to measure and accurately report. Historically there has always been a focus on core literacies such as reading, writing, and arithmetic. New competencies or subject areas rarely are considered for addition to an already crowded school day.

Because there are so many ways to define media literacy, an air of confusion surrounds the discipline. In discussing this lack of name recognition, Silverblatt (2010) states, "Although media literacy is included in the educational standards of all fifty states in the U.S., many of these states do not include the term 'media literacy' in their statements" (www.gmlpstl.org, para. 1). Because there are so many ways to define the subject and so many concepts and objectives covered by the term, it is easy for someone to arrive at the conclusion that all of the states require some form of media literacy instruction. However, without an agreed-on, clearly articulated set of outcomes available, it is nearly impossible to research whether or not this type of instruction is occurring and whether or not success is truly being achieved.

For example, "The National Governors Association (NGA) and the Council of Chief State School Officers (CCSSO) has included media literacy in the Common Core Standards for what American school children should learn" (Perry, 2010, para. 5). However, the paragraph cited to make this claim does not use the exact phrase *media literacy*. In addition, the direct quote from the source news release states, "…research and media skills and understandings are embedded throughout the Standards rather than treated in a separate section" (Perry, 2010, para 6). Although this might seem as an encouragement or evidence of growing inclusion of media literacy in educational standards, the ongoing challenges of measurement and guaranteed inclusion in the school day remain.

In addition, other challenges have emerged as "growing pains." For example, there is a lack of teacher education opportunities associated with media literacy. Because various states mandate different criteria for licensed teachers, a lack of consistency exists regarding media literacy preservice knowledge and exposure. "Most active media educators in the United States are self-taught" (Kubey, 2003). Not only are there few student teaching or in-service opportunities available, but also formal media education training of any sort is relatively limited nationwide.

Another area of discussion or difference of opinion is how best to deliver media literacy education. Some scholars and activists argue for a media studies or analytical approach, whereas others tout immersing students in media message production as the best means of teaching them how to become more media literate. The latter is the result of ongoing differences of opinion that stem from most pedagogical discussions across the curriculum.

Once a delivery method is determined, how to go about researching the outcome(s) is another challenge for an educator and researcher to navigate. Fox (2005) argues that qualitative forms of research make the most sense in relation to media literacy studies. However, he points out that it is often difficult to obtain grants or other funding "unless they employ scientifically based research" (p. 255), meaning quantitative methodology. There is still a

segment of the academy, and for that matter federal and state agencies, which insists quantitative measures provide the only evidence worth considering.

The lack of research instruments available to measure media learning outcomes makes quantitative studies difficult. Trying to empirically represent the interactions among classroom instruction, individual information processing, and social differences is difficult (Martens, 2010). Without a valid, reliable, and recognized method of gathering and reporting the data, any numbers posted in a quantitative study run the risk of gaining little or no attention or recognition by those outside of the individual study's researchers.

Scharrer (2002) concurs. "It is necessary to move beyond implicit assumptions about the benefits such efforts can achieve and toward their explicit definition and measurement" (p. 354). Because there is no universally established and recognized organization providing well-distributed assessment and outcome standards, there are no national standards in the United States regarding how and what to measure or how to define success. Various small-scale studies have reported successful outcomes primarily based on qualitative measures and standards determined on a case-by-case basis.

Although there is agreement that a measurement standard needs to be developed, there are factors that are difficult to control. The volume of media messages that individuals are exposed to daily, personality traits, and other susceptibility factors can affect the success of any curricular efforts designed to increase media literacy. Because media do not affect all audiences in a consistent fashion, it cannot be presumed that media literacy and the measurement of an individual's media literacy will be consistent or stable from day to day. Therefore, the limitations of measurement tools need to be acknowledged, as they are with any standardized educational methodology.

In recent years there have been additional efforts to develop more valid and reliable research instruments geared toward measuring media learning outcomes. Martens (2010) notes, "Primack, Sidani, Carroll and Fine (2009), Arke and Primack (2009), and Duran, Yousman, Walsh and Longshore (2008) provide good starting points" (p. 15). Again, it might be helpful to have researchers collaborate or cooperate under the guidance of an oversight organization.

More recently, China has faced similar challenges as the United States as interested parties try to develop a comprehensive media education program. With a history of media literacy that is 10 to 15 years old, advocates are working to raise awareness and understanding of media literacy and the need for education in that area. Liao's (2008) assessment of progress marking the tenth anniversary of media literacy education efforts in that country notes the lack of noticeable public support. "Facing with the severe pressure of entering the next higher schools, media literacy education generally is limited to the academic field, without wide recognition and public attention" (p. 52). Although most successful efforts at true education reform begin at the grassroots level, there does not seem to be the level of awareness necessary to create a ground swell of innovation or support for change in either China or the United States at this point.

To create interest and support for media literacy education in the schools, awareness and enthusiasm has to be cultivated among today's parents and school administrators. Adults need to understand the need for and benefits of this type of instruction and how the media affect all of us, not just school-aged members of society. This need for adult education needs to influence college curriculums, particularly in education departments. Teachers need to be trained, parents need to understand, and society as a whole has to realize the implication of the media and their effects. Quin and McMahon (2001) advise that parental involvement in media education needs to be informed, and that neither the energy and investment necessary nor the rewards it will bring should be underestimated.

Kubey (2003) writes, "media education advocates generally recommend to teachers that media education be integrated by existing curricula" (p. 359). There are multiple reasons for the suggestion. First, teachers and curricular specialists are dealing with an overcrowded and ever-growing environment. Coursework and instruction dealing with significant current public issues are continually added on top of the basic, mandated skills. In addition, funding to cover the expense of formal media education training and resources so as to make the topic come alive in the classroom are rarely provided by local school districts. The latter is in contrast to successful media literacy efforts in other nations such as the United Kingdom. "The funding typically comes from the local education authority, and according to the teachers, it has been among the most crucial steps in media education development in those locales" (Kubey, 2003, p. 358).

One area in which integration could occur is areas of "information literacy," which is often taught by librarians and information scientists. With the Internet and the World Wide Web providing such a multitude of information, from sometimes very difficult to identify sources, educators interested in developing critical thinkers in a democratic society should look at developing curricula that help students evaluate the information they are gathering and are being exposed to online (Kubey, 2003).

Growing numbers of students are being asked to conduct at least some research for school using the Internet. Researchers have found that reading for understanding online requires not only basic literacy skills, but also additional critical-thinking skills that "reflect the open-ended, continually changing online context" (David, 2009, p. 85). Without instruction on the media literacy aspects of how to access, analyze, and evaluate reliable and accurate information sources through the Internet, current students and future generations run the risk of being ill-equipped to fully use the information-laden, technology-based medium. Major curricular additions and the academic research to support them often lag behind the advances of media-related technology. Therefore, it is important to begin discussions immediately on the inclusion of new literacy skills.

In the United States, a few lawmakers have recognized the need to help fund such instruction. The 21st Century Skills Incentive Fund Act proposed matching federal funds to states offering curriculum options that include information and media literacy (Hobbs, 2010). Unfortunately, for a second straight legislative session, the bill proposed by West Virginia Senator Jay Rockefeller died in legislative committee and failed to be considered by federal lawmakers. Another bill, the Healthy Media for Youth Act, which would authorize $40 million in support of media literacy programs for children and youth, also failed in a U.S. House committee.

At present, it seems that although a number of significant positive ideas are circulating, even within pockets of the federal government, there is an inability to draw financial support to actually carry out these proposals on a large-scale basis. School administrators lack the incentives, financial or legislative, to implement new programs in this area. Because many United States school districts as well as state governments face budget shortfalls, it is unlikely the money needed to carry out additional meaningful media literacy programs will become available in the near future.

Future

As a future direction for media literacy efforts is contemplated, at least one thread of research needs to be considered and discussed. So-called boomerang effects have been identified as a response to strategic messages that are intended to generate prosocial responses. Most recently, Byrne, Linz, and Potter (2010) researched possible explanations for a boomerang effect in response to media literacy messages aimed at curbing negative behavior as a result of exposure to media violence. They concluded violent media clips used as examples during media literacy lessons can activate aggression as a result of priming. Specifically, the researchers found that groups that viewed violent clips "with or without the media literacy intervention, were more willing to use aggression than children exposed to lessons without clips" (p. 239). The study also found that students are more likely to focus on the clips rather than the teacher's message that accompanies the examples.

Byrne et al. (2010) conclude their study confirms that boomerang effects should be a concern for media literacy practitioners who employ media examples as part of the intervention. They cite other studies; for example, one found that antismoking campaigns cause adolescents to have more positive attitudes toward smoking (Wakefield et al., 2006); and messages attempting to prevent drug use do not always achieve the desired results (Fishbein, Hall-Jamison, Zimmer, von Haeften, & Nabi, 2002). As efforts to develop a more formalized and widely administered media literacy curriculum evolve, strategies to minimize or prevent boomerang effects must be considered.

As we move forward, media literacy education needs to take place on a number of fronts, for a variety of demographics, and beyond public health intervention strategies. For example, Hobbs indicates that the topic of media economics is an area lacking instruction. She cites a 1993 study she conducted that showed almost 40% of adults could not articulate that consumers indirectly pay for television through their purchase of the goods and services that actually fund television advertising (Hobbs, 1994). Consumers are unaware of how they pay for "free" television, in addition to what they pay their cable or satellite provider, and they also do not take the time to determine how advertisers are passing those costs along to them.

Another potential problem overlooked as a result of the lack of information and education surrounding media economics is ownership consolidation. Because the somewhat tight knit corporate circle of media owners shares little with the public, and people fail to recognize that multiple options of television and radio programming represent a limited number of voices, fewer and fewer interests actually hold an ownership stake in electronic media. Cable companies along with radio and television stations are merging as U.S. government officials look to weaken ownership limits even further.

Hobbs (1994) has also written about the American need to move beyond the model of media literacy generated in the United States in the 1970s and to look toward better integration of intellectual traditions from abroad. The Canadians, British, and Australians in particular have developed scholarship and practices that could serve as important worldwide models for this type of education. However, training American teachers to master and pass along those traditions to future generations of students at the elementary and secondary levels is an even bigger challenge. Including a requirement for media literacy education for new generations of teachers would be helpful, but seems to be overlooked in the constant reform efforts that occur within the American educational system.

One area of debate that would need to be reconciled among media educators in North America, Europe, and Australia is over the merits of text analysis and reading versus those associated with hands-on experience. "Although U.S. media educators could learn much from our international colleagues, Americans have typically exhibited a xenophobia about incorporating educational ideas from outside the country" (Tyner, 1991, para. 25). Media arts programs in American schools have operated for decades, often designed to motivate underachieving students. Those programs are often focused on mastery of technical skills of production as with any vocational program, rather than the thoughtful analysis and evaluation of the messages produced. Because many American school districts are working through financial difficulties, the upkeep and upgrade of such facilities is in jeopardy. In addition, the structure of the school day with emphasis on core subjects such as traditional reading, science, and arithmetic, provides a barrier to the incorporation of such an applied integration of media literacy–related production skills.

Writing in 1991, Kathleen Tyner noted how media and computer literacy were placed on the educational sidelines as the "back to the basics" movement in education gained importance in the early 1980s. As noted earlier, federal government funding for media literacy education programs dried up in the early 1980s as a result of an economic recession and "a widespread belief that students should be trained to compete in the global marketplace" (Tyner, 1991, para. 4). Governmental funding and attention have yet to return. As Tyner notes, "this type of kneejerk political response to educational reform has resulted in a long history of disjointed funding and confused teaching practices in the United States" (para. 5). Until media literacy education returns to the funding spotlight in the nation's and states' capitals, the necessary emphasis on teacher training, formalized curriculum, equipment acquisition, and modernization, along with other support materials and personnel, will continue to lag behind other disciplines and areas of study.

On a broader, more global scale, writing in the *Canadian Journal of Educational Communication,* Australian scholars Quin and McMahon (1993) note, "the aims of media education need to be clearer to students and parents" (p. 24). The goal is to create competent and critically analytical consumers of media messages, a process that can be started in the classroom, but needs to continue and be reinforced at home. Like any successful educational reform or effort, strategies to encourage students and parents to work together to link the coursework to the "real world" need to be established.

In areas in which media literacy has earned a place in the classroom, a complacent approach to teaching cannot be tolerated. Educators and administrators must continue to work to discover new and more effective ways to accomplish their goals. This requires continuing education and an up-to-date awareness of technology, programming trends, and other developments in the various forms of media available. Again, like in other educational areas, progress needs to be measured and future paths marked so as to fully educate and prepare students to engage critically with media messages.

The Carnegie Council on Adolescent Development (1995) once recommended making media literacy programs a part of school curricula as well as a focus of youth and community organizations, and of family life. The suggestion was based on the inability of adolescents to analyze and evaluate the large number of media messages they absorb every day. Their report, "Preparing Adolescents for a New Century" stated media literacy training "should cover the whole spectrum of contemporary media—including newspapers, magazines, radio, television, videos, music, computer programs, and electronic games" (p. 122). Although some forms of media listed continue to see their popularity decline, other forms such as the Internet need to be added. Although the mediums might change and evolve over time, the central goal of promoting analysis and evaluation can remain constant.

The Council finished their report with the statement, "Widespread public education about the positive potential and the negative consequences of leading-edge communications technologies must be a high priority" (p. 123). Today, questions remain concerning who is going to be responsible and where the funding is going to originate to provide for the widespread educational efforts that are necessary.

As we stand poised to consider the next phase of development for media literacy, few government agencies or elected officials seem eager or even prepared to speak about making room for media literacy education in an already packed curriculum of traditional subjects. In fact, the British government attempted to delete media literacy requirements from the national curriculum of England and Wales in 1992 and 1993, only 2 years after inserting it (Bazalgette, 2001). Bazalgette writes that the next phase of media literacy education should be a time when "media literacy comes to be regarded as a universal right, not merely a privilege or a randomly available opportunity for a few" (2001, p. 72). To move in the direction of evolution from privilege to right, a number of obstacles have to be cleared.

One of the largest hurdles is getting supporters and enthusiasts on the same page because the term *media literacy* means so many different things to different people. There are multiple organizations and agencies advocating for inclusion of this form of education, sometimes even within a nation. What forms of media should it include? Should the instruction be purely theoretical and analytical, or should there be hands-on application? Where does media education fit in the overall curriculum, and what are its goals and objectives? These rather broad but fundamental questions still need to be answered.

To help facilitate the discussion and arrival at solutions for these questions, a central clearinghouse needs to be established, especially for academically based research and evaluation. In the last few years, the National Association for Media Literacy Education (NAMLE) established the online *Journal of Media Literacy Education* (JMLE). The publication is described as "an online interdisciplinary journal that supports the development of research, scholarship and the pedagogy of media literacy education" (NAMLE, 2011, para. 1). The peer-reviewed publication features academic research and essays submitted from practitioners in the field. The journal also embarked on a joint project with the Italian journal, *Media Education. Studi, Ricerche, Buone Pratiche,* following the 5th World Summit on Media for Children and Youth, held in Karlstad, Sweden in June 2010. International collaboration such as this can foster a more unified vision and assessment of the state of media literacy worldwide as well as within a nation's boundaries.

There is also the issue of formal higher education, particularly teacher education, which still looms. The Appalachian State University in North Carolina started the "first institutionalized graduate program in media literacy" in July 2000 (Considine, 2002, p. 7). Since then, Webster University in St. Louis has added a master's program in communication specialization that features media literacy content. A number of other schools offer certificate programs and/or coursework at the graduate and undergraduate level dealing with media literacy education. But even with the formalization of graduate education in the discipline, the vast majority of new teachers are receiving undergraduate degrees and teaching certifications without any formalized instruction in media literacy. The absence of such instruction not only inhibits the development of the subject area in schools, but also it does little to further promote the concept among teachers, educational administrators, and even parents.

In the subsequent decade, little progress seemed to be made. Hobbs (2010) assessed that many K–12 educators were still unfamiliar with instructional practices of digital and media literacy education. The lack of awareness has led to a leadership gap in schools and a parallel gap between disciplines at most colleges and universities. She attributes the intra-institutional gap to a lack of interaction between education and communication faculties. Without an abundance of formal certificate and degree programs at colleges and universities, the likelihood is severely limited that school districts can and will hire teachers with a specific set of knowledge and skills in this area.

The shortfall of formal teacher education program then leads to the lack of formal media literacy programs and curricula in schools. Scharrer (2002) notes that the identification and assessment of outcomes associated with media literacy is a crucial step in arguing for the widespread adoption of such curricula, in not only schools, but also after-school programs and programs for adults in community-based organizations. Abstract benefits or gains are not sufficient to promote the adoption of media literacy in school curriculums. Rather, explicit definition and measurement has to be established (Scharrer, 2002). The National Communication Association (NCA) has adopted guidelines that include explicit media literacy skills, although the NCA does not accredit programs or have a major influence on national educational policy.

UNESCO held a seminar on media education in Paris in 2007. The international expert group assembled deliberated over specifics for a recommendation to introduce media education through the basic training of teachers. In answering the question about why to focus on teacher training, the session's report cited previous and current failings as a main motivation. "In general, digital literacy initiatives have failed due to a lack of specific training, leading to a culture of reluctance and resistance to the technological innovations and new media. The experiences were similar when introducing methods of dealing with the mass media into curricula" (Tornero, 2008, p. 16). The report went on to conclude that without adequate teacher training, media literacy will not be seriously considered in schools. What will occur then is the separation of school and media culture development leading to an ever-widening gap between what takes place in schools and what young people do with the media once they leave the building (Tornero, 2008). UNESCO's observation on an international level amplifies the situation in the United States, where not only is there disconnect between school districts and states, but also a lack of recognition of this gap on a national level.

Once educators commit to programs in media literacy, measures of learning and educational progression need to be developed. Taking advantage of ever-evolving technology, an online test dedicated to digital and media literacy could be created. Hobbs (2010) suggests, based on recommendations by the Knight Commission on the Information Needs of Communities in a Democracy, that such a test could measure students' abilities to use digital tools, analyze and evaluate author's purpose and point of view, identify ethical issues in message production and reception, evaluate information sources, and compose messages using language, image, and sound. Evaluation and assessment based on the quantitative results from a large sample of elementary and even high school–age students could put media literacy in a position to be seriously considered for inclusion as a "must-learn" subject area for educated citizens of our global community.

Final Thoughts and Conclusions

With the advent of media that are available 24 hours a day, there has never been a better time or a more urgent need for more comprehensive instruction in how to consume and process media messages. This type of instruction needs to be particularly targeted at school-aged children, who not only spend more than 7½ hours a day using entertainment media, but also have found a way to cram more than 10½ hours of content into that time frame through media multitasking (Kaiser Family Foundation, 2010). Somehow, this should become at least a partially productive time because it exceeds the number of hours most 8 to 18 year olds sleep.

Although most people recognize the vast amount of time spent with media, regardless of age, there is still an unwillingness to spend time considering the possible effects of such an investment of time. This unwillingness is the primary reason media literacy education has not become a mandatory and prominent part of compulsory education in the United States. Media studies scholars have long recognized that people believe media influence others more than themselves, and that media consumers are too smart to be manipulated by media messages. Comstock and Scharrer (2005) provided the formal label *third-person* effect and published documented evidence of this obstacle to proponents of media literacy education. Because few individuals prioritize such instruction, particularly lawmakers and other government officials who control funding sources, the idea of media literacy education becoming more widely available seems unlikely.

Despite this major challenge, advocates cannot give up efforts to try to provide experiences in the classroom that foster a sense of critical analysis of media messages. At a time when state and federal governments are struggling to balance budgets and are actually cutting education spending, creativity is necessary to better prepare individuals to more actively engage the media they consume. Perhaps meeting this goal falls to organizations outside of the formal educational system. Churches such as those that partnered to create the Media Action Research Center in 1974, or the Catholic Church, whose supportive position for critical evaluation of mass media in the 1990s was expressed by Pope John Paul II (www.medialit.org), could be avenues for formal media literacy education efforts.

The United Nations Educational, Scientific and Cultural Organization (UNESCO) continues to provide global leadership in the area of media and information literacy. Recently, their efforts have been focused on Namibia, Swaziland, and Malaysia, not a major media exporter like the United States. Having the United States take a more active and supportive role of the initiatives being developed and implemented across the globe would be in line with UNESCO's stated mission of encouraging "the development of national information and media literacy policies, including in education" (portal. unesco.org). The lack of government endorsement of any national media literacy policy needs to change for media education programs to become established as a common experience for school-age children in the United States.

The Common Core State Standards released in 2010 made progress toward trying to unify some inclusion of media analysis and production, but not all 50 states have agreed to sign on to the guidelines and objectives. Once again, evidence of a lack of unified vision for inclusion of media literacy education has been presented. Not only for media education advocates, but for the benefit of the country's educational system as a whole, there needs to be at least some centralized direction provided to guide what is being taught in classrooms across the country. More education for future classroom educators would enhance the discussion of how to better educate school age children and their parents about the potential influence of media messages.

The discipline also needs to agree on unified ways of measuring the success of media literacy instruction methods. Anecdotal evidence can be found throughout the literature in the publications and refereed journals of a number of different academic disciplines. What is still lacking is an agreed-on quantitative means of measuring the media literacy level of an individual. Although we know that audience members can fall anywhere along a continuum in terms of media literacy savvy, there has not been a recognized means of placing someone along that line. Standardized tests have legitimate detractors, but a media literacy standard would help practitioners in the field, and perhaps more importantly, government officials, speak the language of educational administrators.

Finally, further advocacy for the field of media literacy needs to occur. Although there have been a number of accomplishments over the years, some of which are documented in this chapter, there is also a growing body of literature that reiterates hopes and goals for the field. Some of the desired outcomes and dreams have been reiterated for decades. More needs to be done to educate the general public about the impact such educational opportunities can provide. It seems that as media consolidation occurs, mentions of media literacy in mainstream media are infrequent. Divisions among advocates, academics, educators, and others promoting media literacy must be closed so that the available energies and resources can be spent to bring about more substantial and long-lasting positive accomplishments in the field.

References

Anderson, J. A. (2008). Media literacy, the first 100 years: A cultural analysis. In Asamen, J. K., Ellis, M. L., & Berry, G. L. (Eds.), *The SAGE Handbook of Child Development, Multiculturalism, and Media*. Thousand Oaks, CA: Sage, pp. 381–409.

Arke, E. T., & Primack, B. A. (2009). Quantifying media literacy: development, reliability, and validity of a new measure. *Educational Media International*, 46(1), 53–65.

Aufderheide, P. (1993). *Media Literacy: A Report of the National Leadership Conference on Media Literacy*. Aspen, CO: Aspen Institute.

Bazalgette, C. (2001). An agenda for the second phase of media literacy development. In Kubey, R. (Ed.), *Media Literacy in the Information Age: Current Perspectives*, 2nd ed. New Brunswick, NJ: Transaction, pp. 69–78.

Berko, R, Morreale, S., Cooper, P., & Perry, C. (1998). Communication standards and competencies for kindergarten through grade 12: The role of the national communication association. *Communication Education*, 47(2), 174–182.

Brown, J. (1991). *Education: Major Media Literacy Projects in the United States and Selected Countries*. Hillsdale, NJ: Lawrence Erlbaum Associates.

Byrne, S., Linz, D., & Potter, W. J. (2010). A test of competing cognitive explanations for the boomerang effect in response to the deliberate disruption of media-induced aggression. *Media Psychology*, 11(7), 227–248.

Carnegie Council on Adolescent Development. (1995). *Great Transitions: Preparing Adolescents for a New Century*. New York: Carnegie Corporation of New York.

Center for Media Literacy. (2002). *Aspen Institute Report of the National Leadership Conference on Media Literacy*. Retrieved August 2010 from http://www.medialit.org/reading_room/article582.html.

Cho, C., & Heins, M. (2002). *Media Literacy: An Alternative To Censorship*, 2nd ed. New York: Free Expression Policy Project.

Christ, W., & Potter, W. J. (1998). Media literacy, media education and the academy. *Journal of Communication*, 48(1), 5–13.

Common Core State Standards Initiative. (2010). *Common core state standards initiative*. Retrieved January 10, 2011 from www.corestandards.org.

Comstock, G., & Scharrer, E. (2005). *The Psychology of Media and Politics*. San Diego: Elsevier/Academic Press.

Considine, D. (2002). Media literacy: National developments and international origins. *Journal of Popular Film and Television*, 30(1), 7–15.

David, J. (2009). Teaching media literacy. *Educational Leadership*, 66(6), 84–86.

Dorr, A., Graves, S. B., & Phelps, E. (1980). Critical TV viewing television literacy for young children. *Journal of Communication*, doi:608476461.

Duncan, B. (1993). *Harvard University Hosts first U.S. Media Literacy Teaching Institute*. Retrieved April 25 2011 from http://www.medialit.org/reading-room/harvard-university-hosts-first-us-media-literacy-teaching-institute.

Duran, R. L., Yousman, B., Walsh, K. M., & Longshore, M. A. (2008). Holistic media education: An assessment of the effectiveness of a college course in media literacy. *Communication Quarterly*, 56(1), 49–68.

Fishbein, M., Hall-Jamison, K., Zimmer, E., vonHaeften, I., & Nabi, R. (2002). Avoiding the boomerang: Testing the relative effectiveness of antidrug public service announcements before a national campaign. *American Journal of Public Health*, 92, 238–245.

Fox, R. F. (2005). Researching media literacy: Pitfalls and possibilities. In Schwarz, G., & Brown, P. (Eds.), *Media Literacy: Transforming Curriculum and Teaching*. Malden, MA: Blackwell, pp. 251–259.

Goodwyn, A. (1993). News from nowhere: Reading the media. *English Journal, September*, 60–65.

Hobbs, R. (1994). Pedagogical issues in U.S. media education. *Communication Yearbook*, 17, 453.

Hobbs, R. (2010). *Digital and Media Literacy: A Plan of Action*. (A white paper on the Digital and Media Literacy Recommendations of the Knight Commission on the Information Needs of Communities in a Democracy. Washington, DC: The Aspen Institute.

Kaiser Family Foundation. (2010). *Generation M2: Media in the Lives of 8 to 18 Year Olds*. Retrieved April 26 2011 from http://www.kff.org/entmedia/mh012010pkg.cfm.

Kubey, R. (2003). Why U.S. media education lags behind the rest of the English-speaking world. *Television & New Media*, 4(4), 351–370. doi:1527476403255808.

Liao, F. (2008). Achievements and difficulties-review ten years of media literacy education in china. *Canadian Social Science*, 4(6), 50–58.

Martens, H. (2010). Evaluating media literacy education: Concepts, theories and future directions. *Journal of Media Literacy Education*, 2(1), 1–22.

Masterman, L. (2001). A rationale for media education. In Kubey, R. (Ed.), *Media Literacy in the Information Age: Current Perspectives*, 2nd ed. New Brunswick, NJ: Transaction, pp. 15–68.

Morgan, M. (2002). *The Selected Works of George Gerbner*. New York: Peter Lang.

NAMLE . (2011). *Journal of media literacy education*. Retrieved March 16, 2011 from http://jmle.org/index.php/JMLE.

National Association for Media Literacy Education. (2011). Retrieved April 26, 2011 from www.namle.net.

National Communication Association. (1996). *Speaking, Listening and Media Literacy: Standards for K-12 Education*. Annandale, VA: National Communication Association.

National Communication Association. (1998). *K-12 Speaking, Listening and Media Literacy Standards and Competency Statements*. Annandale, VA: National Communication Association.

National Education Goals Panel. (1992). *Executive Summary: The National Education Goals Report. Building a Nation of Learners*. Washington, DC: Author.

Perry, K. A. (2010). Media literacy in the digital age. Retrieved from http://reboot.fcc.gov/futureofmedia/blog?entryId=549398, August 6, 2010.

Potter, W. J. (2004). Argument for the need for a cognititve theory of media literacy. *American Behavioral Scientist*, 48(2), 266–272.

Primack, B. A., Sidani, J., Carroll, M. V., & Fine, M. J. (2009). Associations between smoking and media literacy in college students. *Journal of Health Communication*, 14(6), 541–555.

Pungente, J. (2009). *The Jesuit Communication Project Celebrates 25 Years*. Retrieved August 9, 2010 from http://jcp.proscenia.net/publications/articles/JCP_25.pdf

Quin, R., & McMahon, B. (1993). Evaluating standards in media education. *Canadian Journal of Educational Communication*, *22*(1), 15.

Quin, R. & McMahon, B. (2001). Living with the tiger: Media curriculum issues for the future. In Kubey, R. (Ed.), *Media Literacy in the Information Age: Current Perspectives*. New Brunswick, NJ: Transaction, pp. 307–321.

Scharrer, E. (2002). Making a case for media literacy in the curriculum: Outcomes and assessment. *Journal of Adolescent and Adult Literacy*, *46*(4), 354–358.

Silverblatt, A. (2010). A comprehensive definition of media literacy. Retrieved August 6, 2010 from http://www.gmlpstl.org/a-comprehensive-definition-of-media-literacy/2010/.

Singer, D. G., Zuckerman, D. M., & Singer, J. L. (1980). Helping elementary school children learn about TV. *Journal of Communication*, *30*(3), 84–93.

Thoman, E. (1993). *Safeguarding Our Youth: Violence Prevention for Our Nation's Children*. Washington, DC: U.S. Department of Education.

Tornero, J. M. P. (2008). *Teacher Training Curricula for Media and Information Literacy: Background Strategy Paper International Expert Group Meeting*. Strategy paper, Paris: United Nations Educational, Scientific and Cultural Organization (UNESCO).

Tyner, K. (1991). *The Media Education Elephant*. Retrieved June 15, 2010 from www.medialit.org/reading_room/article429.html.

Wakefield, M., Terry-McElrath, Y., Emery, S., Saffer, H., Chaloupka, F., Sczcypka, G., et al. (2006). The effect of televised, tobacco company-funded smoking prevention advertising on youth smoking-related beliefs, intentions and behavior. *American Journal of Public Health*, *96*, 2154–2160.

Research Methods, Design, and Statistics in Media Psychology

Sara Prot *and* Craig A. Anderson

Abstract

This chapter provides an overview of contemporary research methods used in the field of media psychology. Basic scientific principles are discussed. Commonly used research designs are described. Some methodological pitfalls in media psychology research are explained and suggestions are given on how to avoid them. Finally, guidelines are given on how to convey scientific methodology and findings to the general public (see Chapter 26). We hope that this chapter will aid readers from other fields in becoming informed consumers of media psychology research and aid media psychology researchers in continuing the trend toward better methodological quality in the field.

Key Words: media psychology, research designs, research methods

The 20th century witnessed a mass media explosion after the invention of television, digital computers, and the Internet. This rapid technological development was followed by rapid growth in the field of media psychology.

Researchers have gone from asking relatively simple, basic questions such as, "Does observing filmed aggression increase aggressive behavior?" (Bandura, Ross, & Ross, 1963a) to asking complex and highly specific questions, such as, "Through which cognitive and affective mechanisms do violent media exert their influence on aggression?" (Anderson et al., 2003), "How robust and consistent are media violence effects on different outcomes?" (Anderson & Bushman, 2001; Anderson et al., 2010) and "What are the long-term consequences of habitual media violence exposure?" (Huesmann et al., 2003; Bartholow, Bushman, & Sestir, 2005).

This chapter offers a broad review of contemporary methodology used in the field of media psychology

in studying *the effects of exposure to media violence on the consumer of such media*. Although the basic principles and ideas described here apply more broadly to other domains of media-related research, such as motivations underlying media choices and preferences (e.g., Ryan, Rigby, & Przybylski, 2006), we focus on the *effects of exposure* domain—and within this domain, we focus on *media violence* effects.

We discuss basic scientific principles that are at the foundation of all psychological research. An overview of widely used research designs is given. Common methodological pitfalls in media psychology are described as well as some suggestions on how to avoid them. Finally, guidelines are given on how to convey scientific methodology and findings to the general public. We hope that this chapter will aid media psychology researchers in continuing the trend toward better methodological quality in the field, aid journal editors and reviewers in doing a better job of screening out weak and promoting strong research, and aid readers from other fields in becoming informed consumers of media psychology research.

Science, Causality, and Media Psychology
Empirical Research and Theory Development
TEST/REVISE/TEST/REVISE CYCLE

Research in the field of media psychology can generally be divided into two approaches: quantitative and qualitative. Qualitative methods (e.g., content analyses, ethnographic studies and phenomenological studies) generate descriptive findings and are usually conducted without forming a priori hypotheses (for a discussion of qualitative methods see Chapters 8 and 23). The majority of media effects research, however, is quantitative and follows a different pattern, progressing through a cyclic interaction between theory and empirical research. Researchers identify a question of interest (e.g., What effects does media violence have on viewers?). One or more hypotheses are generated (e.g., Observing media violence will increase the likelihood of later aggression. Exposure to media violence will decrease helping.) and tested using multiple research methods. Empirical results lead to revisions and refinement of the original hypotheses. Over time, a set of related hypotheses and empirical findings is developed, a set that can be integrated into a larger conceptual model or theory. The theory can then be used to develop novel hypotheses that can be tested further through empirical research. The cycle is repeated, leading to further refinement of the theory. This extensive test/revise/test/revise process leads to the development of theoretical models based on sound principles which are unlikely to be invalidated by future research. For example, the general aggression model (GAM) (Anderson & Bushman, 2002b; Anderson & Huesmann, 2003; DeWall & Anderson, 2011) and the general learning model (GLM) (Buckley & Anderson, 2006; Barlett, Anderson, & Swing, 2009; Gentile et al., 2009) integrate a number of earlier models and are based on more than 100 years of psychological research on learning, emotion, cognition, and behavior. Well-tested models such as these provide a solid foundation for interpreting findings, making new predictions, and developing interventions. Nonetheless, specific interpretations can always be changed as a result of new discoveries. It is for this reason that scientists are reluctant to use the words *fact,* or *proven,* or *truth,* even when speaking with audiences and individuals who do not understand

this perpetual cycle of theory and data. Thus, the general public may view the "theory" of evolution as a mere guess or hypothesis, whereas the scientific community knows that the basic tenants of the theory are as well established and as factual and basic as the law of gravity. This differential understanding of the meaning of "theory" and other common words leads to much unnecessary miscommunication among scientists and nonscientists, a topic that is addressed in a later section of this chapter.

TRANSLATIONS FROM CONCEPTUAL TO EMPIRICAL

One frequently overlooked (or underevaluated) aspect of scientific theory development and testing concerns the multiple translations that take place between the conceptual/theoretical level and the specific procedures used to conduct empirical tests. That is, one must translate the conceptual hypothesis into specific empirical realizations of the independent and dependent variables (Carlsmith, Ellsworth, & Aronson, 1976; Anderson & Anderson, 1996). Figure 7.1 illustrates some of the multiple levels and translations that underlie an experimental manipulation of violent versus nonviolent violent game exposure. As can be seen, there are lots of levels between the most basic (and therefore the conceptually broadest) theoretical level and the specific manipulation that a researcher creates in an empirical study. Keep in mind that a similar set of translations are needed to get from the conceptual dependent variable (e.g., aggression) to its empirical realization. Thus, there are lots of ways one can test the same conceptual hypothesis. Furthermore, although theory provides many constraints on what should be considered reasonable tests of any given conceptual hypothesis, there is no such thing as a perfect empirical realization of that hypothesis. For this reason, multiple studies using multiple methods give a better overall picture of the validity of any conceptual hypothesis than any single method or study can give. Further discussion of this appears in the next section.

Causality

The majority of scientific theories and models in nomothetic scientific disciplines (those that seek to uncover general laws that underlie phenomena, such as natural sciences and psychology; Münsterberg, 1899) are causal. Widely used theories in media effects psychology such as social learning theory and social cognitive theory (Bandura, 1973, 1983), general aggression model (Anderson & Bushman, 2002b; Anderson & Huesmann, 2003), cultivation

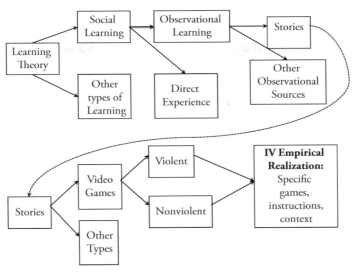

Figure 7.1 Illustration of Multiple Translation Levels from Learning Theory to Empirical Realization of the Independent Variable: Experimental Manipulation of Video Game Violence.

theory (Comstock & Scharrer, 2007), and social information processing theory (Crick & Dodge, 1994) all imply causal relationships among variables. The central characteristics of any good theory, the ability to predict and control outcomes, require causal models. Of course, establishing causality is often a difficult task, one that is seldom understood by public policy makers or the general public, and too often is misunderstood even by members of the scientific community. What follows is a partial listing of the most common difficulties.

SCIENTIFIC CAUSALITY IS PROBABILISTIC

The old Logic 101 principles of establishing causality do not apply to most modern science (Anderson & Bushman, 2002a). Scientific causality is probabilistic, instead of "necessary and sufficient." Stating that X causes Y means that variable X causes an increase in the likelihood of outcome Y (Anderson, 2004). For example, saying that smoking causes lung cancer means that smoking increases the likelihood of developing lung cancer. This does not mean that all smokers get lung cancer; many do not (a violation of the principle of "sufficient" causality). Furthermore, some nonsmokers do get lung cancer (a violation of the principle of "necessary" causality). Correspondingly, saying that violent video games cause aggression does not mean that every person who plays violent video games will necessarily become aggressive, or that all aggressive behavior is a result of violent video game play. It means that exposure to violent video games increases the likelihood of future aggression.

Probabilistic causality is a result of the fact that most (if not all) biological outcomes, disease processes, and human behaviors are multicausal (Gentile & Sesma, 2003). Complex behaviors of interest, such as prosocial behavior and aggression, are influenced by a large number of factors (e.g., genetic predispositions, parental practices, cultural influences) (Anderson & Huesmann, 2003; DeWall, Anderson, & Bushman, 2012). Media use is just one of many relevant factors that influence the likelihood of these behaviors. In most cases, it is neither a necessary nor a sufficient cause. Nonetheless, media effects are not negligible and have important practical consequences in many domains, including aggression (Anderson & Dill, 2000; Gentile et al., 2004; Anderson et al., 2010), helping (Greitemeyer, 2009; Greitemeyer & Osswald, 2010), risk taking (Fischer et al., 2011), and school performance (Sharif & Sargent, 2006; Anderson, Gentile, & Buckley, 2007; Rideout, Foehr, & Roberts, 2010), among others.

A methodological difficulty in the field of media psychology stems from the fact that many media effects are subtle, cumulative, and unintentional. For example, advertisements can have a subtle influence on viewers without their awareness (Gentile & Sesma, 2003). Although such short-term influences may be small, over time they can produce large cumulative effects. To use the cigarette smoking analogy, although short-term effects of smoking are relatively harmless and transient, long-term cumulative effects of this risk factor are lasting and severe. Likewise, although effects of watching a single violent TV show dissipate fairly quickly, habitual exposure to violent media has long-lasting effects on desensitization to violence (Bartholow, Bushman, & Sestir, 2005), hostile attribution biases (Anderson, Gentile, & Buckley, 2007), development of an aggressive personality (Bartholow, Sestir, & Davis, 2005), and aggressive behavior (Huesmann, Moise-Titus, Podolski, & Eron, 2003; Anderson, Sakamoto, Gentile, Ihori, Shibuya, Yukawa, Naito, & Kobayashi, 2008; Möller & Krahé, 2009).

An interesting solution to the methodological difficulty of studying cumulative effects of media exposure is proposed by Potter (see Chapter 23). The author suggests that, instead of measuring group differences in effects of media exposure, as is done in the majority of media effects studies, attention should be shifted to patterns of effect score changes for individuals over time. This approach would allow researchers to directly examine the course of long-term changes produced by media influences, identifying how mass media influences gradually change a person's baseline. Indeed, this is essentially what longitudinal studies of media violence do (e.g., Huesmann, Moise-Titus, Podolski, & Eron, 2003; Anderson, Sakamoto, et al., 2008).

ROLE OF PLAUSIBLE ALTERNATIVE EXPLANATIONS

Testing scientific theories largely involves creating alternative explanations for a given phenomenon and then empirically testing whether the originally hypothesized relations among variables fits the data better than the alternative explanation. In essence, establishing causality involves testing and ruling out *plausible* alternative explanations. We emphasize "plausible" because the total number of alternative explanations—plausible + implausible—approaches infinity. Furthermore, only alternative explanations that are empirically testable (at least in principle) qualify as plausible. Alternative explanations that cannot be empirically tested (e.g., god did it) usually fall outside the realm of science. Of course, technological advances often create opportunities to test alternative hypotheses that previously had been untestable, which is why the "in principle" aspect of plausible alternative explanations is important. For example, recent advances in genetics and in neuroimaging have allowed tests of numerous new hypotheses about aggression and violence (DeWall, Anderson, & Bushman, 2011, 2012).

Relevant empirical results can cast doubt on alternative explanations and lend support to the target theory. Or, such tests can support an alternative

explanation, thereby pointing to parts of the theory that need further revision. As the number of plausible alternative explanations is reduced, the strength of the remaining theoretical explanation increases.

TRIANGULATION AND ALTERNATIVE EXPLANATIONS

No single test of a theory-based hypothesis is definitive, irrespective of whether it confirms or disconfirms the prediction (Anderson & Anderson, 1996). One reason for this is because theoretical models involve abstract conceptual variables, whereas empirical tests involve concrete operationalizations of those variables (Carlsmith, Ellsworth, & Aronson, 1976). In other words (and as noted earlier), there are multiple levels of interpretation and specification between the theoretical model and empirical tests of the implications of that model (see Anderson & Anderson, 1996, for an example concerning the heat/aggression hypothesis). Operationalization of a conceptual hypothesis involves making several assumptions concerning the empirical methods being used (e.g., reliability and validity of the measures, adequacy of the sample of variables and participants). Because of this, null results are often less informative than confirming results, especially when new measures or procedures are used. Findings that are in line with theory-based predictions give support not only to the target conceptual hypothesis, but also to various implicit assumptions made in the study. If, on the other hand, the study fails to support the hypothesis, a common reaction of researchers is to acknowledge that there are many possible reasons for those findings. The unexpected results possibly reflect the fact that the original hypothesis is wrong, but also might be a product of methodological weaknesses of the specific study. Typically, for null results to be informative and result in a major change in theory they have to be replicated many times, shown to be not the result of mere poor methods or small samples, and have to lead to a more comprehensive theory that accounts not only for the null results but also accounts for the many results explained by the original theory (Kuhn, 1962). Unfortunately, occasional unreplicated null results based on small samples or poor methods, are frequently misinterpreted in the media violence domain as evidence of a lack of effects overall. Nonsignificant findings from specific studies have been regularly used by media industry apologists to question the validity of studies showing significant harmful media effects, a criticism media violence scholars have faced many times (Huesmann & Taylor, 2003; Bushman, Rothstein,

& Anderson, 2010). For example, one of the methodologically poorest media violence studies ever published (Williams & Skoric, 2005) is frequently promoted by the video game industry and gamers as proof that violent games don't increase aggression. They conveniently ignore that fact that that study didn't measure aggression, had severe dropout rate problems, had differential dropout rates in the two conditions, and failed to show that the "violent" and "nonviolent" game conditions actually differed on the amount of exposure to violent games.[1]

Far greater support for a conceptual hypothesis is given if conceptual relations are repeatedly tested and confirmed using different methodologies in different contexts. This is the logic of multiple operationalism or triangulation (Campbell & Fiske, 1959; Anderson, 1987, 1989; Anderson, Gentile, & Buckley, 2007). Different types of research designs make different methodological assumptions, so if a conceptual relationship is confirmed time after time in studies using different designs, it is extremely unlikely that the results are just a byproduct of methodological flaws. Similarly, conceptual relationships that yield similar results using different (but theoretically compatible) measures or manipulations greatly strengthen one's confidence in the basic conceptual model. When weaknesses of a particular type of study do not apply to other types, this enables researchers to triangulate or home in on a true causal factor (Anderson, 1989). When a hypothesis survives many potential falsifications using varied methods, a robust effect is established. For example, Bandura's initial findings concerning the effect of televised violence on modeling of aggressive behavior may have been falsified by several possible alternative explanations (Bandura, Ross, & Ross, 1961, 1963a). However, today researchers have no doubt that televised violence increases aggression because this effect has been repeatedly shown using correlational studies (Eron, Huesmann, Lefkowitz, & Walder, 1972; McLeod, Atkin, & Chaffee, 1972), experimental studies (Bjorkqvist, 1985; Josephson, 1987), and longitudinal studies (Huesmann, Moise-Titus, Podolski, & Eron, 2003). The interpretation of Bandura's early studies has changed slightly as a result of changes in definitions of aggression. But our main point in this example is that when studies using various research designs and measures, done in a number of different contexts and with samples from diverse populations all converge on the same answer, we can be much more confident that this answer is indeed true. In the words of Richard Cardinal Cushing when asked about the propriety of calling Fidel Castro a communist, "When I see a bird that walks like a duck and swims like a duck and quacks like a duck, I call that bird a duck" (*The New York Times,* 1964).

Although this chapter is focused almost exclusively on quantitative research methods, it is important to emphasize that qualitative methods also play a significant role in the field of media effects, providing rich knowledge on the content of media messages and people's individual experiences that cannot be obtained through experimentation or other forms of quantitative research (see Chapter 8). Also note that the line between qualitative and quantitative research is sometimes quite blurry.

Outcome Measures, Research Designs, and Review Types
Outcome Measures

Choice of outcome measure is crucial to any study, both because it influences the likelihood that the study will yield useful results and because of theoretical relevance. A measure of aggressive behavior that is appropriate in one research context may well be inappropriate in another. For example, a count of how often each child trips, pushes, or bites another child in a daycare setting can be a useful measure of physical aggression in that research context (i.e., young children at daycare), but would not be a valid measure of physical aggression for college students in a laboratory setting. A less obvious but equally important example frequently arises in the study of violent video game effects. Because violent video games involve a lot of physical aggression and almost no indirect or relational aggression, the dominant theoretical models of social learning and development all predict that playing such games is most likely to influence physical aggression. Measures of verbal and indirect aggression are unlikely to provide sensitive tests of the main hypothesis that exposure to violent video games increases the likelihood of aggressive behavior. Similarly, the measure of physical aggression has to match the age of the participants and the research context. For example, a measure of trait physical aggression in which the participant reports the frequency of aggressive acts over the past year is inappropriate as the main outcome measure in a short-term experimental study in which participants have just played a randomly assigned violent or nonviolent video game. The recent game play cannot change the frequency of aggressive acts that the person committed in the year before the game play, unless of course time travel is involved. Of course, such a trait physical aggression measure might be influenced by the content (violent versus nonviolent) of a recently played game, but in such a case it would represent some type of memory or reporting bias, not a true measure of the video game effect on physical aggression (Anderson & Bushman, 2001). Yet, several short-term experimental studies have used traitlike measures of aggression as the main dependent variable.

It is impossible to succinctly describe all of the measures that have been used or could be used in the study of the effects that media have on consumers. We focus here on a few of the measures related to antisocial effects (e.g., aggressive behavior, cognition, and affect) and to prosocial behaviors, cognitions, and affect.

AGGRESSIVE BEHAVIOR MEASURES

Because definitions of conceptual variables such as "aggression" and "violence" differ somewhat between disciplines and even over time, clarity of definition is critical in theory development and in translating conceptual variables into empirical realizations (e.g., Carlsmith et al., 1976). Social psychologists have come to rely on a specific definition that is much narrower than what is used by the general public and in some other areas of psychology. Specifically, human aggression is "...any behavior directed toward another individual that is carried out with the *proximate* (immediate) intent to cause harm. In addition, the perpetrator must believe that the behavior will harm the target, and that the target is motivated to avoid the behavior" (Anderson & Bushman, 2002b, p. 28; see also Berkowitz, 1993; Baron & Richardson, 1994; Geen, 2001). *Aggression* and *aggressive behavior* are used interchangeably throughout this chapter. It is important to note that aggression is always a behavior; it is not an emotion, thought, or desire. Also note that it is not the outcome of a behavior that defines it as aggressive or not, but the intent of the behavior, that is, the intent to harm. Thus, shooting an arrow at another person with the intent to harm them is an act of aggression, regardless of whether the arrow strikes or missed the target person. A shortcoming of many media effects studies arises from failure to use this definition.

Physical Aggression in a Lab Setting

Numerous methods have been developed that allow direct observation and measurement of aggressive behavior in laboratory settings. A common procedure used to measure physical aggression is the *teacher/learner paradigm*, sometimes known as the *Buss aggression machine* paradigm (Buss, 1961; Geen

& O'Neal, 1969; Milgram, 1974; Donnerstein & Berkowitz, 1981). In this procedure, participants are told that purpose of the study is to explore effects of punishment on learning. They are paired with a supposed second participant (actually a confederate). The real participant is selected to be the "teacher" and the confederate is selected to be the "learner." The participant presents stimuli to the confederate who seemingly tries to learn them. When the "learner" gives an incorrect response, the participant is supposed to punish him or her with an electric shock. Aggression is measured by the intensity and/or the duration of the shock the participant chooses to give the confederate. For example, Donnerstein and Berkowitz (1981) used this procedure to measure effects of combining violent and sexual content on aggression of males toward a female target. Participants who had viewed a violent, sexual film delivered shocks of a higher intensity to a female "learner" than did those who viewed films containing only violent or sexual content. There have been many variations of this task, including use of different types of punishments (e.g., hand in ice water instead of electric shock) (Ballard & Lineberger, 1999) and different rationales for why the participant is delivering punishments (Baron & Richardson, 1994, pp. 69–75).

Another common method of measuring physical aggression in the laboratory is the *competitive reaction time task* (Taylor, 1967; Bushman, 1995; Giancola & Parrott, 2008). Participants in this task compete against a supposed opponent on a reaction time task in which the winner delivers aversive stimulation (an electric shock or a noise blast) to the loser. In actuality, the pattern of wins and losses is predetermined by the experimenter. Provocation can be manipulated by increasing the intensity of shocks set by the "opponent." Aggression can be measured as the intensity, duration, or number of high-intensity blasts given. For example, Anderson and Carnagey (2009) used this paradigm to test the effects of violent and nonviolent sports video games on aggression. They found that playing violent sports games increased aggressive behavior, even after controlling for competitiveness. In other words, competitive reaction time task measures aggression, not competitiveness (Gaebelein & Taylor, 1971; Bernstein, Richardson, & Hammock, 1987). Like the teacher/learner paradigm described earlier, the competitive reaction time task has been used in various modified forms in hundreds of studies, and is one of the most extensively validated measures of physical aggression.

Another commonly employed method to study direct physical aggression is to place the participant and the confederate in a situation that requires the confederate to evaluate the participant and *later* requires the participant to evaluate the confederate. In the *evaluation paradigm* (Berkowitz, 1962), for example, participants are led to believe that they will be evaluating another student's performance on an assigned task. Solutions are evaluated using anywhere from one to ten electric shocks, in which one shock indicates a very favorable evaluation and ten shocks indicates a very unfavorable evaluation. In some studies, the confederate evaluates the participant's solution. Generally, half of the participants receive a positive evaluation from the confederate (e.g., one shock), whereas the other half receive a negative evaluation (e.g., seven shocks). After exposure to some treatment (e.g., a violent or nonviolent film), the participant then evaluates the confederate's solution. The measure of aggression is the number of shocks the participant gives the confederate.

Barlett, Branch, Rodeheffer, and Harris (2009) used a more recently developed laboratory measure of physical aggression, the *hot sauce paradigm* (developed by Lieberman, Solomon, Greenberg, & McGregor, 1999) to measure how long the effects of brief exposure to violent video games persist. In this procedure, participants decide how much hot sauce another person (known to dislike spicy food) must consume. Alternatively, one can have the participant determine the degree of hotness of the sauce that the other person must consume. Aggression is measured as the amount of hot sauce given to the target and/or the degree of hotness of the sauce selected.

Indirect, Verbal, and Other Laboratory Aggression Measures

Some laboratory based studies use *verbal aggression* measures. For example, in some studies the participant is given the opportunity to provide a potentially harmful written or verbal evaluation of another person (e.g., another participant, a confederate, or the experimenter), and does so knowing that the evaluation could hurt the other person. Sometimes the verbal aggression is *direct,* meaning that the participants believe that the target of their harmful evaluations will see or hear it. For example, Wheeler and Caggiula (1966) had participants listen and later evaluate another person's (actually, a confederate's) extreme and socially undesirable statements. The participants believed that the other person would hear their evaluations, so anything negative in the evaluations would presumably cause

some harm. These evaluations were recorded and later coded for the degree of hostility.

Sometimes the evaluation is in the form of ratings that the target will not see, but that the participant believes will harm the target *indirectly.* For example, Berkowitz (1970) randomly assigned some female undergraduates to an anger induction condition (in which they listened to a job applicant's insulting statements about university women) or a control condition. Half in each condition then listened to either a hostile or a nonhostile comedian. All participants then rated the job applicant on several measures, with the knowledge that their ratings could affect the applicant's chances of getting the job. Interestingly, the women who had heard the hostile humor gave the applicant worse ratings than those who had heard the neutral humor. Other similar indirect verbal aggression measures have ranged from ratings of competence, to liking, job performance, and grades (Obuchi, Kameda, & Agarie, 1989; Dill & Anderson, 1995).

Perhaps the most recent addition to the list of laboratory aggression tasks is the *tangram task* (Gentile et al., 2009). In one study Gentile et al. randomly assigned participants to play a violent video game, a prosocial video game, or a game that was neither violent nor prosocial. Later, participants assigned an anonymous partner a set of 11 easy, moderately complex, or difficult tangram puzzles to attempt to solve within 10 minutes. Participants were led to believe that the partner would win a prize if they completed a sufficient number of puzzles in 10 minutes. The number of hard puzzles chosen constituted a measure of aggression, whereas the number of easy puzzles measured helping behavior. As expected, the violent video games increased aggressive choices, whereas the prosocial games increased helpful choices. Because this measurement task is the newest, it has received less empirical attention that the older measures described earlier, and thus does not yet have an extensive network of validation studies.

Aggression Measures Outside the Lab

The variety of ways that one can measure aggressive behavior outside of controlled laboratory settings is huge, limited only by the combination of the conceptual definition and the creativity of researchers. Generally, they can be categorized as self-reports, other reports, and archival.

Self-reports may be very specific, such as reporting how many physical fights one has been in during the past school year. Or, they may be broad trait-like measures of habitual aggressiveness. They may include any type of aggression (e.g., verbal, physical) at any severity level (e.g., said mean things about a classmate, attacked a peer with a knife or gun). Common self-report measures of trait aggression in the media effects domain include the physical and verbal aggression subscales of the Buss and Perry (1992) Aggression Questionnaire and the physical violence subscale from the National Youth Survey (Elliot, Huizinga, & Ageton, 1985; Anderson & Dill, 2000). Other commonly used self-report trait aggression scales that include relatively more items that are not strictly aggressive behaviors are the Caprara Irritability scale (Caprara et al., 1985) and the Cook-Medley Hostility Inventory (Cook & Medley, 1954). Of course, there are many self-report measures, and researchers create new ones as the empirical and theoretical need arises.

Others' reports of aggression include a wide range of measures, usually subcategorized into peer reports, teacher/supervisor reports, parent reports, and direct observation. Peer reports are frequently used in pre–high school settings. Often these involve asking each student in a classroom to rate each of their classmates on specific behaviors, or to nominate classmates who do certain aggressive behaviors. For example, it is common to ask, "Who pushes, shoves, or hits other kids to get what they want?" Teacher and supervisor reports ask similar questions about those under their care or supervision. Parent reports often ask about the frequency with which their child has done specific aggressive behaviors; other parent reports are vaguer, asking for ratings of "how aggressive" is your child. Direct observation studies often involve the recording of behavior in some naturalistic setting, followed by standardized coding of the recorded behavior. Sometimes, however, trained observers watch and code behaviors directly in the setting, such as while watching children on a playground.

Archival measures are derived from written records, such as crime reports and school incident records. Frequently archival measures are combined with other types of aggression measures.

AGGRESSIVE COGNITION MEASURES

Exposure to violent media has a host of cognitive consequences, which in turn can lead to aggressive behavior. A number of outcome measures have been used to assess influences of violent media on cognition in both short- and long-term contexts.

Aggressive Cognition in Lab Settings

Laboratory experiments measure short-term influences of exposure to violent media on cognitive processing. Such short-term effects mainly occur through priming of aggressive knowledge structures, making them more accessible (Anderson & Huesmann, 2003). Various methods have been successfully used in laboratory settings to measure these increases in aggressive thinking.

A number of studies have shown an increased frequency of aggressive thought content during or immediately after media violence exposure. For example, Calvert and Tan (1994) used a *thought-listing* questionnaire to measure differences in aggressive thoughts while observing or playing a violent game in virtual reality. In a study by Bushman (1998), participants made *free associations to nonaggressive words and to homonyms* with one meaning more aggressive than the other (e.g., cuff, mug). More aggressive associations were made to both types of words by participants who had just watched a violent video.

Several studies have used a *word completion task* to measure accessibility of aggressive thoughts (Anderson, Carnagey, & Eubanks, 2003; Anderson, Carnagey, Flanagan, Benjamin, Eubanks, & Valentine, 2004; Barlett et al., 2008). In this kind of task, participants are given a list of word fragments and are asked to fill in the missing letters to form the word. Some of the fragments can be completed to form either an aggressive word or a nonaggressive word (e.g., "h_t" can become *hit* or *hat*). Aggressive thought accessibility can be calculated as the proportion of word completions that were aggressive. Similar tasks have been commonly used to measure implicit memory (e.g., Roediger, Weldon, Stadler, & Riegler, 1992), and have been used to assess accessibility of prosocial thoughts as well (e.g., Greitemeyer, 2011).

A number of studies have used *reading reaction times* to aggressive and nonaggressive words as a measure of accessibility of aggressive cognitions (also called the *word pronunciation task*) (e.g., Bushman, 1998; Anderson & Dill, 2000; Anderson, Carnagey, & Eubanks, 2003). In the reading reaction time task (e.g. (Anderson et al., 1996; Anderson, 1997; Anderson, Benjamin, & Bartholow, 1998), participants are timed as they read aggressive and nonaggressive words. Average reaction times to aggressive and nonaggressive words can be compared to assess relative accessibility of aggressive thoughts. An advantage of this task is that suspicion or hypothesis-related demand characteristics are unlikely to influence responses because participants are taxed with trying to read all words as quickly as possible (Anderson, 1997). Furthermore, attempts by suspicious participants to bias the results in either direction can be detected by examining the distribution of reaction times, because such biasing attempts typically yield unusually long reaction times.

In a somewhat different approach, Uhlmann and Swanson (2004) measured the effects of violent video game play on automatic aggressive thoughts using the implicit association test. This study showed that media violence exposure can teach a person to automatically associate the self with aggressive traits and actions. More recently, Saleem and Anderson (in press) have used another version of this task to assess anti-Arab bias.

Interesting methods have been used to assess cognitive biases that result from media violence exposure. For example, to assess hostile expectation bias Bushman and Anderson (2002) had participants read ambiguous story stems about potential interpersonal conflicts. Participants were then asked to list what the main character will think, feel, say, and do next and their responses were coded for aggressive content. Several media effect studies (Kirsh, 1998; Anderson, Gentile, & Buckley, 2007; Möller & Krahé, 2009) have also used ambiguous provocation stories to assess hostile attribution bias. In each story, an actor causes a negative event to happen, but the intent of the actor is unclear. After each story, participants are asked a series of questions concerning the provocateur's intent. It has been shown that exposure to media violence leads to the development of a hostile attribution bias, a tendency to interpret ambiguous behaviors of others as malevolent (Kirsh, 1998).

Yet another method of assessing accessibility of aggressive cognitions is the word pair similarity rating task. This task was originally developed by Bushman (1996) to assess individual differences in aggressive cognitive-associative networks. But a minor revision to the task has been used to examine the effects of short-term experimental manipulations of variables, including pain (K. Anderson, Anderson, Dill, & Deuser, 1998), cooperative versus competitive video game instructions (Anderson & Morrow, 1995), and violent versus nonviolent music lyrics (Anderson, Carnagey, & Eubanks, 2003). This task consists of rating the degree of meaning similarity of each paired combinations of 20 words. Ten of these words have both aggressive and nonaggressive connotations (e.g., bottle, night, stick). These words are referred to as ambiguous words. The remaining ten words are more obviously related to aggression (e.g., butcher, choke, hatchet). Ratings of each word pair are made on a 1 to 7 scale of how "similar, associated, or related" they are. Each participant gets three

scores, the average similarity rating of all ambiguous/aggressive word pairs, ambiguous/ambiguous pairs, and aggressive/aggressive word pairs. Anderson, Carnagey, and Eubanks (2003) found that participants who had just listened to songs with violent lyrics gave higher similarity ratings to ambiguous/aggressive word pairs than did participants who had just listened to nonviolent songs. In other words, the violent lyrics increased the accessibility of the aggressive meaning of the ambiguous words.

Aggressive Cognition Outside the Lab

Correlational studies and longitudinal studies provide an opportunity to explore long-term influences of violent media on cognition. Repeated exposure to media violence strengthens aggression-related knowledge structures and can make them chronically accessible. Additionally, long-term exposure reinforces normative beliefs that violence is common and appropriate (Carnagey & Anderson, 2003; Bushman & Huesmann, 2006). Dependent variables in correlational and longitudinal studies of aggressive cognition often include normative beliefs about violence (Gerbner, Gross, Jackson-Beeck, Jeffries-Fox, & Signorelli, 1978; Gerbner, Gross, Morgan, & Signorelli, 1980; Bryant, Carveth, & Brown, 1981), positive attitudes toward violence (Funk et al., 2004; Anderson, Gentile, & Buckley, 2007) and hostile attribution bias (Anderson, Gentile, & Buckley, 2007). These long-term consequences can be assessed using self-report measures, such as the Normative Aggressive Beliefs Scale (Anderson, 2004; Anderson, Gentile, & Buckley, 2007), Huesmann's NOBAGS scales (Huesmann et al., 1992), Funk's Attitudes toward Violence Scales (Funk, Elliott, Urman, Flores, & Mock, 1999), and the Revised Attitudes toward Violence Scale (Anderson, Benjamin, Wood, & Bonacci, 2006). Some studies also use trait measures of aggressive cognition, such as the hostility subscale of the Buss-Perry Aggression Questionnaire (Anderson, Carnagey, Flanagan, Benjamin, Eubanks, & Valentine, 2004; Shibuya, Sakamoto, Ihori, & Yukawa, 2004; Bartholow, Sestir, & Davis, 2005).

AGGRESSIVE AFFECT MEASURES

Another route through which violent media can increase aggression is by producing feelings of anger and hostility (Anderson et al., 2003; Swing & Anderson, 2010). Brief exposure to media violence has been shown to lead to temporary increases in aggressive affect (Barlett et al., 2009), whereas chronic exposure leads to the development of a hostile personality (Bartholow, Sestir, & Davis, 2005; Bushman & Huesmann, 2006).

Aggressive Affect in Lab Settings

Experimental studies in laboratory settings measure effects of media violence exposure on short-term affective states. Short-term affective consequences are most often assessed using self-report scales such as the State Hostility Scale (SHS) (Anderson, Deuser, & DeNeve, 1995), the Multiple Affect Adjective Checklist (Zuckerman, 1960; Zuckerman, Lubin, Vogel, & Valerius, 1964), or the State Anger subscale of the State-Trait Anger Expression Inventory (STAXI) (Spielberger, 1988). Many other studies have used the Positive and Negative Affect Schedule (PANAS) (Watson, Clark, & Tellegen, 1988). This widely used self-report scale has the advantage of assessing both positive and negative affect, as well as several more specific subtypes of affect. However, it is a less sensitive measure of hostility/anger, most likely because of fewer items for this more specific affective state (Anderson, Deuser, & DeNeve, 1995; Anderson, Anderson, & Deuser, 1996; Anderson, Anderson, Dorr, DeNeve, & Flanagan, 2000).

Such self-report measures can be complemented with physiological indicators such as heart rate, blood pressure, or skin conductance (Ballard, Hamby, Panee, & Nivens, 2006; Carnagey, Anderson, & Bushman, 2007). Additionally, researchers have started examining neural bases of short- and long-term media effects on emotional processing by using techniques such as magnetic resonance imaging (Weber, Ritterfeld, & Mathiak, 2006) and event-related brain potentials (Bartholow, Bushman, & Sestir, 2005; Bailey, West, & Anderson, 2011a).

Aggressive Affect Outside the Lab

Long-term changes in affective processing as a result of habitual media violence exposure can be assessed outside the laboratory using trait measures such as the Caprara Irritability Scale (CIS) (Caprara et al., 1985), the Cook-Medley Hostility Inventory (Cook & Medley, 1954), and the anger subscale of the Buss-Perry Aggression Questionnaire (Buss & Perry, 1992). Once again, more general trait-affect scales may be appropriate in some research contexts, but researchers need to be aware that general measures of positive and negative affect usually are less sensitive measures of any give specific affect type.

PHYSIOLOGICAL AROUSAL MEASURES

For most people, exposure to media violence tends to produce physiological arousal (Anderson

et al., 2003; Swing, Gentile, & Anderson, 2008). Arousal can be measured in experimental studies using indicators such as heart rate, blood pressure, or skin conductance (Ballard & Wiest, 1996; Fleming & Rickwood, 2001; Anderson et al., 2004; Barlett et al., 2008).

How lasting are these effects? Barlett et al. (2009) showed that heightened arousal immediately after playing a violent video game lasts between 4 and 9 minutes. However, these short-term changes can start aggression promoting processes that last much longer than 4 to 9 minutes, such as long-term desensitization to violence. Even within a short-term context, exposure to violent media may increase arousal (and hostile affect) for longer periods of time if the violent media episode increases processes that typically last long and that increase anger arousal, such as rumination on a perceived unjust harm.

A popular belief in our culture is that playing violent video games or watching violent television and films allows people to "vent" their aggression, decreasing arousal and reducing subsequent aggressive behavior (Anderson, Gentile, & Buckley, 2007). According to the catharsis hypothesis, engaging in real or imagined aggression helps relieve angry feelings, leaving us emotionally calmed (Dollard et al., 1939; Campbell, 1993). However, the bulk of research evidence opposes the catharsis hypothesis (Mallick & McCandless, 1966; Geen, Stonner & Shope, 1975; Geen & Quanty, 1977; Bushman, Baumeister, & Stack, 1999; Geen & Quanty, 1977Bushman, 2002). Although physiological arousal can decrease after the initial aggressive act, later aggressive behavior does not (Geen & Quanty, 1977). Instead, studies show that viewing, thinking about or performing aggressive acts increases the likelihood of aggressive behavior (Dill & Dill, 1998; Geen, 2001).

DESENSITIZATION/EMPATHY MEASURES

Repeated exposure to violence can lead to desensitization, best defined as a reduction in emotional and physiological reactivity to violence (Carnagey, Anderson, & Bushman, 2007). Empathy can be defined as the degree to which a person identifies and commiserates with a victim and feels emotional distress (Anderson et al., 2010). A small number of high-quality studies exist in this domain (Anderson et al., 2010). However, media violence has been clearly linked to both short-term desensitization as a result of brief exposure (Carnagey, Anderson & Bushman, 2007), and chronic desensitization and decreased empathy as a result of habitual, long-term exposure (Mullin & Linz, 1995; Funk et al., 2003; Bartholow, Bushman, & Sestir, 2006).

Short-Term Effects on Desensitization/Empathy

Desensitization to violence after brief periods of exposure is typically explored in experimental studies using physiological indicators such as heart rate, blood pressure, and galvanic skin response (Thomas, Horton, Lippincott, & Drabman, 1977; Linz, Donnerstein, & Adams, 1989; Carnagey, Anderson & Bushman, 2007). For example, participants in the Carnagey et al. (2007) experiment played a violent or nonviolent video game, and then watched film clips of real violent behavior, including shootings, stabbings, and fights. Heart rate and skin conductance were recorded before and during video game play, and during observation of the violent film clips. Both physiological indicators of emotional arousal increased in both game conditions while playing the assigned video games, but only those who had played a violent game showed decreases in arousal while watching the violent film clips.

Long-Term Effects on Desensitization/Empathy

Neurological evidence of chronic desensitization to violence through playing video games also exists. Bartholow, Bushman, and Sestir (2005) found that habitual violent game players have reduced amplitudes of the P300 component of the event-related brain potential while viewing violent images. Other laboratory studies have found similar effects (Kronenberger et al., 2005; Bailey et al., 2011a). Outside the laboratory, long-term effects on desensitization and empathy can be measured using self-report scales such as the Basic Empathy Scale (Jolliffe & Farrington, 2006), the Interpersonal Reactivity Index (Davis, 1980), the Index of Empathy for Children and Adolescents (Bryant, 1982) or Children's Empathic Attitudes Questionnaire (Funk et al., 2008). Indeed, longitudinal studies have yielded evidence of long-term changes in desensitization/empathy as a result of media violence exposure (see Anderson et al., 2010, for the video game case).

PROSOCIAL BEHAVIOR/HELPING MEASURES

Prosocial behavior involves helping or rewarding others, especially when this behavior brings no benefit to the helper (Barlett, Anderson, & Swing, 2009). Effects of violent media on prosocial behavior have been less frequently explored than effects on aggression. In spite of this, several measures have been developed that make it possible to perform reliable and valid measurement of prosocial behavior and helping.

Prosocial Behavior in Lab Settings

Several procedures have been used in media violence research that allow direct observation and measurement of prosocial behavior in the laboratory. For example, Chambers and Ascione (1987) showed that children who had played a violent game donated less to charity. Ballard and Lineberger (1999) employed a variation of the teacher/learner paradigm in which participants could award jelly beans to their partner. The number of jelly beans awarded served as a measure of helping and it was shown that participants who had just played a violent game tended to award a smaller number of jelly beans.

Bushman and Anderson (2009) simulated a fight in a laboratory experiment and found that participants who had played a violent video game were less likely to help and took more time to help the "victim." These participants perceived the fight as less serious and were less likely to notice the fight than the participants who played a nonviolent game.

Sheese and Graziano (2005) used a prisoner's dilemma game in which participants were given a choice to cooperate with their partner for mutual gain, exploit their partner for their own benefit or withdraw. Participants in the violent condition were significantly more likely to choose to exploit their partner.

Gentile et al. (2009) developed a new task to measure helping—the previously mentioned *tangram task*. In this task, participants are asked to assign easy, moderately complex or difficult tangram puzzles to an anonymous partner. Participants are told that the partner will win a prize if they complete a sufficient number of puzzles in 10 minutes. The number of easy puzzles represents a measure of helping behavior. Participants who had just played a prosocial video game assigned the most easy tangrams, where as those who had just played a violent game assigned the fewest.

Prosocial Behavior Outside the Lab

The most common type of measure chosen outside laboratory settings are self-report questionnaires such as the Prosocial Orientation Questionnaire (Cheung, Ma, & Shek, 1998). For example, a correlational study by Gentile et al. (2009) assessed video game habits of a large sample of children, along with several prosocial measures. Playing violent video games was negatively related to helping behavior, whereas prosocial gaming was positively associated with helping.

A longitudinal study by Anderson, Gentile, and Buckley (2007) measured children's media violence exposure and prosocial behaviors twice during a school year and showed that video game violence at time 1 significantly predicted a relative decrease in prosocial behavior over time. In this study, prosocial behavior was measured using teacher ratings and peer ratings.

Another less common measurement procedure is naturalistic observation. In an unusual field experiment by Bushman and Anderson (2009), violent and nonviolent movie attendees saw a young woman with an injured leg struggle to pick up her crutches. Participants who had just watched a violent movie took longer to help than those who had just watched a nonviolent movie. Violent and nonviolent moviegoers did not differ in their helpfulness before seeing the movie.

It is important to emphasize that prosocial and antisocial behaviors are not simply opposite sides of the same coin. Measures of aggressive and prosocial behavior tend to be negatively correlated, but not strongly so. One can be high both in helpful and in hurtful behaviors—for example, hostile toward enemies and kind toward friends (Gentile et al., 2009).

Research Designs

Researchers generally use three broad types of research designs: experimental studies, cross-sectional correlational studies, and longitudinal studies (Anderson & Bushman, 2001; Swing & Anderson, 2010). Each design has its own advantages and disadvantages and is appropriate for certain kinds of research problems. Findings from different kinds of studies complement each other and help researchers form a complete picture of media effects.

EXPERIMENTAL STUDIES
Advantages

In experimental studies, researchers manipulate exposure to media content and measure brief, short-term effects. Participants are randomly assigned to treatment and control groups; for example, playing a violent or nonviolent video game (Anderson & Dill, 2000). With all other factors controlled, a difference between two groups, for example, in aggression, establishes a causal link between violent media and subsequent aggression. Random assignment ensures that there are no preexisting differences between the two comparison groups (within certain statistical limits) and allows researchers to rule out a host of alternative explanations. If a difference in aggressive behavior of the two groups is found, it is very

likely that this difference was caused by experimental manipulation (exposure to video game violence). It is very improbable (although not impossible) that highly aggressive individuals just happened to be randomly assigned to the experimental group and nonaggressive individuals were assigned to the control group. The larger the sample size, the less likely it is that a disproportionate percentage of highly aggressive people were randomly assigned to any one condition, just as tossing a coin 100 times is less likely to yield 80% "heads" than tossing it only ten times.

If the researcher has additional information about the research participants before they are assigned to condition, information that may be relevant to the dependent variables of interest such as gender or trait aggressiveness, they may decide to "block" on these other variables in the random assignment procedure. For example, they may separately randomize males and females to the different experimental conditions to ensure that each gender is represented equally across the conditions; but the logic and power of true experiments does not require this.

Methodologically sound experimental studies in the field of media psychology share several characteristics—they are designed so that they control for many possible alternative explanations (i.e., high internal validity), have adequate sample sizes, employ effective experimental manipulations, and use a reliable and valid measure of the dependent variable.

High-quality laboratory experiments use well-validated paradigms to test relevant hypotheses. For example, Anderson and Dill (2000) conducted a laboratory experiment to test short-term effects of playing a violent video game on aggressive thoughts and behavior. In this study, a large sample of 227 college students participated. Participants were randomly assigned to play a violent or a nonviolent game. Games used in the study were carefully pretested and matched on several relevant dimensions (e.g., difficulty, frustration, and the physiological arousal levels they produce). Aggressive behavior was measured using a modified version of the Competitive Reaction Time Task (Taylor, 1967), a widely used measure of aggressive behavior that has well-established internal and external validity (Carlson, Marcus-Newhall, & Miller, 1989; Anderson & Bushman, 1997; Giancola & Chermack, 1998; Anderson, Lindsay, & Bushman, 1999). Aggressive cognition was measured with a reading reaction time task that had been successfully used in previous aggression studies (Anderson, 1997; Anderson, Benjamin, & Bartholow, 1998) as well as in many studies in cognitive psychology. Violent video game play led to significant increases in aggressive cognition and aggressive behavior. This study made an important contribution to the violent video game effects literature because previous experimental studies in this area had methodological weaknesses that put their results into question. A number of early experiments testing for violent video game effects (Cooper & Mackie, 1986; Silvern & Williamson, 1987; Schutte, Malouff, Post-Gorden, & Rodasta, 1988; Irwin & Gross, 1995) did not match violent and nonviolent games on important dimensions and thus could not rule out the possibility that other variables such as arousal, difficulty, or frustration caused the observed difference in aggressive behavior.

High-quality field experiments use measures of real-life behavior in natural settings. For example, as mentioned earlier, Bushman and Anderson (2009) tested effects of media violence on helping behavior by staging a minor emergency outside movie theaters that were showing either a violent or a nonviolent movie. Moviegoers saw a young woman with a wrapped ankle "accidentally" drop her crutches outside the theater and struggle to pick them up. The emergency was staged either before the movie (to control for helpfulness of people who choose to view violent versus nonviolent movies) or after the movie (to test for the effect of viewing media violence on helping). In this case, the randomization was whether the measure of helpfulness occurred before or after viewing the movie. Before watching a movie, no differences in helping were found between those going to a violent versus nonviolent movie. However, after the movie, participants who had just viewed a violent movie took significantly longer to help the confederate than those who had viewed a nonviolent movie.

Disadvantages

The main advantage of experimental studies is that they enable strong causal inferences. A potential disadvantage concerns the ability to generalize results to real-life conditions. Field experiments don't suffer this concern. But, because most experiments are conducted in the laboratory, the generalizability of findings from such studies to real-world settings is sometimes questioned. However, such doubts have been challenged and refuted both by rational arguments (e.g., Mook, 1983) and empirical studies of external validity of laboratory experiments (e.g., Anderson & Bushman, 1997).

The main purpose of most laboratory studies is to explore conceptual relationships between variables and thus test and develop theories. The goal is to be able to generalize these underlying theoretical principles, not specific features of the sample, manipulation, or measure (Berkowitz & Donnerstein, 1982; Henshel, 1980; Mook, 1983; Banaji & Crowder, 1989; Anderson & Bushman, 1997). Conceptual relationships between variables generalize, even if specific operationalizations do not.

The external validity of laboratory experiments is also supported by empirical findings from several studies. For example, in the aggression domain it has been shown that laboratory measures of aggression are positively associated with each other, and that variables that influence aggression and violence in the real world have the same kind of effects on laboratory measures of aggression (Carlson, Marcus-Newhall, & Miller, 1989; Anderson & Bushman, 1997; Bushman & Anderson, 1998). Similarly, Anderson, Lindsay, and Bushman (1999) explored the consistency between findings obtained in laboratory and field settings across several domains in psychology (e.g., aggression, helping, leadership style, social loafing, self-efficacy, depression, and memory). This study found considerable correspondence between lab- and field-based effect sizes, suggesting that laboratory experiments have high external validity.

Laboratory settings also enable researchers to explore relationships between variables that may never be sufficiently isolated in real life to enable precise testing (Mook, 1983). If increasing the similarity of the laboratory situation to real-world conditions interferes with the internal validity of the study, external dissimilarity (to achieve high internal validity) is strongly favored (Anderson & Bushman, 1997).

There are two additional potential disadvantages of experimental designs in media effects studies. Both involve ethical considerations. First, one cannot ethically conduct an experiment in which one of the experimental treatments is expected to increase a seriously harmful behavior, such as aggravated assault or homicide. One can't randomly assign a group of 10 year olds to play either a violent or nonviolent video game, then give each a handgun, and turn them loose on the playground to see which group does the most killing during recess. For this reason, alternative measures of aggressive behavior have been developed and used. Field experiments typically measure milder forms of physical aggression, such as hitting, pushing, shoving, and biting. Laboratory experiments use a variety of measures of aggression, including measures of physical and verbal aggression. And as noted earlier, these measures have been well validated, showing high levels of external validity.

The second potential disadvantage of experimental designs in this domain concerns duration of the manipulation. It is not ethical to intentionally expose a group of participants to a long-term high media violence diet to see whether this randomly assigned group becomes more aggressive than a randomly assigned control group. One can't randomly assign a group of 4 year olds to grow up in either a high or low media violence household, and then measure their level of aggressiveness in school or criminal records at age 18. One can, however, use a long-term experimental design to see if an intervention designed to reduce exposure to media violence has any effect on aggression. A few such experimental intervention studies have been done (e.g., Huesmann, Eron, Klein, Brice, & Fischer, 1983; Robinson, Wilde, Navracruz, Haydel, & Varady, 2001), and have found that such interventions can reduce aggression.

CROSS-SECTIONAL CORRELATIONAL STUDIES
Advantages

Cross-sectional correlational studies explore the direction and magnitude of associations among relevant variables. The independent variable is measured instead of manipulated, and both the independent and dependent variable are measured once, usually at the same point in time. Strengths of correlational studies include the ability to measure real-world outcomes, test different alternative explanations, and suggest new hypotheses about causal relationship.

Disadvantages

The main weakness of correlational research is difficulty in establishing causality. Results of a single correlational study in which variables are measured at the same single point in time cannot ascertain cause-and-effect relationships. In other words, correlational studies generally have lower internal validity than experimental studies (Anderson & Bushman, 1997). Of course, some correlational studies are more informative about causality than others. For example, some of the early violent video game effect studies had serious methodological difficulties (Dominick, 1984; Lin & Lepper, 1987; Fling et al., 1992). These studies showed significant associations between playing video games and aggression, but did not distinguish between playing violent versus nonviolent games. In contrast, Anderson, Gentile, and Buckley (2007) tested the strength of the association between aggression and violent video game play, while controlling for several key competitor

variables (total screen time, normative aggression beliefs, positive orientation toward violence and sex). This example leads us to the important concept of destructive testing.

Destructive Testing

Because of the critical role played by testing plausible alternative explanations in theory development, even cross-sectional correlational studies can play an important part in testing causal hypotheses. They can provide an opportunity for falsification of the causal hypothesis as well as for testing and ruling out alternative hypotheses. Well-designed correlational studies can measure many theoretically relevant variables along with the target independent variable and the target dependent variable, and then statistically control for effects of those other variables. For example, Anderson and Dill (2000, Study 1) used the *destructive testing approach* (Anderson & Anderson, 1996) to assess the strength of the relationship between violent video game exposure and aggression. In this approach, a predicted relationship between variables is first established. Then one attempts to break the relationship by adding competitor variables. The key question is not whether the relationship can be broken—even strong truly causal links can eventually be rendered nonsignificant in a correlational study by adding more correlated predictors into the model. Instead, the focus of destructive testing is on how difficult it is to break the relation, considering the theoretical and empirical strength of the competitor variables used to test it. If the inclusion of several relevant competitor variables fails to break the relationship, this gives strong support to the validity of the target link. For example, in the study by Anderson and Dill (2000), the effect of violent video game play on aggression remained significant even with the inclusion of variables such as time spent playing any kind of video game and sex. Statistically controlling for these covariates invalidated several possible alternative explanations of the video game violence effect, thereby strongly supporting the authors' prediction that playing violent games will increase aggression. When using destructive testing, relevant covariates may include confounds (e.g., sex), potential competitors (e.g., total time spent playing), and potential mediators (e.g., aggressive personality). Occasionally, researchers also have mistakenly included as covariates variables that are better conceived as additional outcome (dependent) variables.

If the target link is broken by a single competitor variable or a single confounded variable, this puts the validity of the original causal hypothesis into question. However, mediating variables and secondary outcome variables have a very different theoretical status in correlational studies. Mediating variables are those that theoretically link the predictor variable to the outcome variable. In essence, they are another outcome variable of the same independent variable. For example, repeated exposure to violent video games (the predictor or independent variable) may increase aggressive behavior (outcome or dependent variable) because such exposure increases trait aggressiveness (the mediator variable). Thus, a proposed mediator variable should significantly weaken or even break the link between the predictor and outcome variables, even when that link is causal. When this happens, it lends support for the predicted theoretical model. Unfortunately, some gamers/media researchers (e.g., Ferguson et al. 2010) either don't understand this principle or they choose to ignore it when promoting their position. They have incorrectly concluded that when mediator variables such as trait aggressiveness weaken the correlation between habitual exposure to violent video games and aggressive behavior, this weakening of the key link contradicts the main theoretical hypothesis; in reality, such a result supports the causal model.

Figure 7.2A displays this issue with a Venn diagram. The three circles represent the variance of three variables, media violence, trait aggression, and bullying behavior. The area represented by sections A + B represents the correlation (or overlap) between media violence and trait aggression. C + B represents the correlation between media violence and bullying. B + D is the correlation between trait aggression and bullying behavior. Significance tests of the various relations can be thought of tests of whether overlapping areas are significantly greater than zero. If media violence truly causes an increase in the likelihood of bullying behavior, and it does so at least in part because it increases trait aggression as a mediating variable, then the theoretically most appropriate test of whether media violence is significantly related to bullying is the B + C area. But when trait aggression is treated as a nuisance variable that is statistically controlled, then the test of the hypothesis includes only area C, an unrealistically conservative test. By adding more restrictions on what gets counted as media violence/bullying variance, such as by adding additional covariates that themselves are theoretical outcomes of high media violence exposure, one can further inappropriately reduce the "unique" overlap between media violence and bullying.

A related problem occurs when two conceptually related predictors are used in the same regression model. For example, one study included both television violence and video game violence as separate predictors of aggression (Ferguson, San Miguel, & Hartley, 2009). This also removes considerable predictive variance inappropriately because television violence and video game violence are highly correlated (in that sample: r (602) = .47, p < .001) yet both contribute to the same theoretical explanation (i.e., media violence increases aggression). Figure 7.2B displays this problem. Testing the video game effect on aggression after controlling for the television violence effect, that is, testing area B, is overly

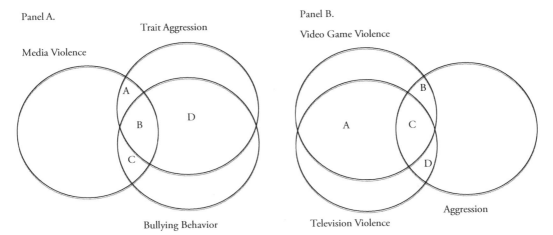

Figure 7.2 Inappropriate Uses of Covariates in Regression Analyses. A. When a mediator variable is added as a covariate, it can significantly weaken or even break the link between the predictor and outcome variables, even when that link is causal. B. When two conceptually related predictors are used in the same regression model, considerable predictive variance is removed which results in an overly conservative significance test.

conservative. It may be appropriate to include two conceptually and empirically overlapping predictors in a model if one wants specifically to compare the unique contributions of these two predictors (as in Anderson et al., 2007 tests of the relative strength of old versus new media), but otherwise the hypothesis that media violence increases aggression is better tested by including these two variables in separate regression models or by statistically combining them into a single "media violence" predictor. Thus, models that test the hypothesis of media violence effects on aggression with more than one distinct media violence predictor are unnecessarily biased against this hypothesis, losing a substantial portion of the effect(s) of interest to a covariate that is not an alternative explanation at all.

A third version of this problem concerns cases in which a control variable (e.g., sex of participant) is correlated with both the main independent variable (e.g., video game violence) and the main dependent variable (e.g., physical aggression). Males spend more time playing violent video games than females, and also are more likely to use physical aggression in many contexts. If playing violent video games is truly a causal risk factor for later physical aggression, then at least part of the confounded variance predicting physical aggression truly belongs to the violent video game effect. Controlling for the sex effect in essence overcorrects for the confound between sex and exposure to violent video games. Thus, correlational studies that control for sex likely underestimate the true effect size of violent video games on physical aggression (Anderson et al., 2010).

This problem is not unique to the media violence domain; indeed, this is pretty basic to research design, statistics, and methodology. This diagram also illustrates another point. Although the media violence critics are quick to note that "correlation is not causation," they seem to miss the necessary counterpoint that "lack of correlation is not lack of causation." That is, the same third variable problems that make it risky to conclude on the basis of one or several cross-sectional studies showing significant overlap between X and Y that "X causes Y," also make it risky to conclude that "X is not a cause of Y" based on studies showing that X and Y do not significantly overlap, especially if theoretically inappropriate covariates are first controlled for the overlap tests.

LONGITUDINAL STUDIES
Advantages
In longitudinal studies, independent and dependent variables are measured at two or more points in time. Such studies provide an opportunity to assess real-life consequences of long-term media exposure. Causality is easier to establish in longitudinal studies than in cross-sectional correlational studies because temporal relations among variables make it possible to rule out a host of alternative explanations. For example, media habits and school performance can be assessed both early and late in a school year (as was done in a study by Anderson, Gentile, & Buckley, 2007). Results can be analyzed to see if the amount of habitual entertainment screen time (television, film, video games…) at measurement Time 1 predicts school performance at Time 2 after statistically controlling for Time 1 school performance. The finding that total habitual screen time measured at Time 1 is a significant negative predictor of grades at Time 2 provides much stronger support for the hypothesis that time spent on television and video games has a negative effect on school performance than results from cross-sectional correlational studies showing a significant association at a single point in time (Anderson & Dill, 2000; Gentile et al., 2004; Sharif & Sargent, 2006).

In cases in which experimentally manipulating a particular independent variable would be difficult or unethical, longitudinal studies represent an excellent way for making sound causal inferences. For example, in a study by Hopf, Huber, and Weiß (2008), cumulative long-term influences of media violence exposure on adolescents' violence and delinquency were investigated—two behaviors that cannot be ethically investigated in an experimental study. The frequency of adolescents' exposure to media violence was measured over a 2-year period as well as exposure to eight other risk factors. Exposure to media violence at age 12 was a significant predictor of violence ($b = .28$) and delinquency ($b = .39$) at age 14, even after controlling for earlier levels of violence and delinquency and several other relevant variables.

Disadvantages
The main disadvantages of longitudinal designs are that they are time consuming and expensive. Repeated measurement requires researchers to keep track of participants and pay them to stay in the study. Large samples need to be taken to compensate for dropout rates. Another potential concern is nonrandom attrition. For example, in a 3-year study of television violence effects commissioned by the NBC television company (Milavsky, Kessler, Stipp, & Rubens, 1982), data from a large portion of the most aggressive participants in the sample were deleted because they allegedly had not

given accurate reports of their television viewing. Although the original authors concluded that there was little evidence of a television violence effect, closer examination of this study reveals different conclusions (Kenny, 1984; Anderson et al., 2003; Huesmann & Taylor, 2003).

MIXED DESIGNS

Many high-quality media effects studies combine multiple design features. Adding a correlational component in experimental designs can have several advantages. Including measures of relevant covariates makes it possible to perform additional tests of key hypotheses and explore effects of possible mediating and moderating variables. Including individual difference variables can also decrease error variance and increase the precision or power of statistical analyses, maximizing the likelihood that true effects will be detected. For example, an experimental study by Konijn, Bijvank, and Bushman (2007) elucidated the role of wishful identification as a possible moderator/mediator of violent video game effects. In this study, exposure to video game violence was experimentally manipulated. In addition to the dependent variable (aggressive behavior), several relevant covariates were measured (e.g., trait aggressiveness, general exposure to video games, immersion, and wishful identification). It was shown that playing a violent video game had the strongest effect on aggression for participants who wished they were like a violent character in the game. Furthermore, identification was associated with realism of the game and with immersion.

Some experimental studies also include a longitudinal component. For example, Huesmann, Eron, Klein, Brice, and Fischer (1983) conducted a 2-year intervention study that aimed to mitigate effects of television violence on aggressive behavior of school-aged children. Children selected because of their high exposure to violent television were randomly assigned either to a control group or an experimental group that received treatments designed to decrease effects of television violence (lessons about the unreality of television violence and an attitude change treatment). After the intervention, children in the experimental group were rated as significantly less aggressive by peers and showed a lower association between viewing violence and aggression.

A potential methodological difficulty in long-term experiments concerns the effective manipulation of the independent variable and control and measurement of possible confounds over a period of time. For example, an experimental study by

Williams and Skoric (2005) attempted to measure effects of violence in a massively multiplayer online role-playing game (MMORPG, a type of online game in which a large number of players interact and play the roles of different characters) on aggression after 1 month of game play. However, exposure to other violent games was not controlled or measured during this 1-month period so no evidence existed that participants in the violent game condition actually spent more time playing violent video games than participants in the control condition. Furthermore, the MMORPG used in this study was not very popular, which apparently resulted in players being unable to do much fighting in the game because of a lack of opponents. The participants in this study were recruited from online gaming sites. Furthermore, the overall dropout rate was huge, especially in the control condition, thus ruining the main advantage of experimental studies. Therefore, it is possible that during the study period participants in the control condition were exposed to as much (or even more) violent video game play than those in the violent game condition.

Scientific Literature Reviews

Each research design plays an important role in the study of media effects. Sound causal conclusions are based on consistent results across each of these designs (Abelson, 1995; Swing & Anderson, 2010). When a sufficient number of studies have been done on a specific topic, the results can be combined in a literature review. Such a review can answer additional questions, support or refute theoretical models, and point toward areas that are in need of further research. Reviews enable researchers to draw more advanced conclusions than would be possible on the basis of results from any single study. Two types of reviews can be performed—narrative and meta – analytic reviews.

NARRATIVE REVIEWS

In traditional narrative literature reviews findings from relevant published empirical studies are described, categorized, and summarized. Possible goals of narrative reviews include providing an overview and integration of an area, theory evaluation and development, identification of weaknesses or contradictions in a specific field of investigation, and generating new problems and hypotheses (Baumeister & Leary, 1997). By searching for connections among a large number of empirical findings, narrative reviews can address much wider questions than any single empirical study. The major strength of narrative literature reviews is their focus on conceptual relationships between key variables that can lead to rich theoretical and methodological insights (Anderson, Gentile, & Buckley, 2007).

However, different studies necessarily yield somewhat different findings. Even if a study was replicated perfectly using the exact same methods, the results would be different because of effects of random factors. How should these differing results be interpreted and what conclusions should be drawn? A weakness of narrative literature reviews is that many critical decisions that are made while selecting and interpreting studies are subjective. This opens the door for reviewer biases that can result in drastically different interpretations of the empirical findings by different reviewers. People generally have a tendency to disregard evidence that contradicts their beliefs (Lord, Ross, & Lepper, 1979; Kunda, 1990; Koehler 1993), and reviewers are not exempt from such biases. Differing theoretical and empirical orientations can lead reviewers to form different inclusion criteria and organizational schemes, leading to different conclusions (Dill & Dill, 1998; Griffiths, 1999). Because of this, it's important that reviewers pay attention to counterexamples and allow themselves to be led by evidence rather than rigidly imposing a priori beliefs and expectations (Baumeister & Leary, 1997).

META-ANALYTIC REVIEWS

Meta-analytic reviews use statistical techniques to combine the results of a number of empirical studies that tested the same hypothesis. Meta-analyses describe the typical strength of an effect, its variability, its statistical significance, and variables that moderate it (Rosenthal, 1995). When a sufficiently large number of studies are available that tested the same hypothesis and a meta-analysis is usable, it is generally the preferred review method (Baumeister & Leary, 1997). By combining results from multiple studies, meta-analytic reviews can resolve inconsistencies caused by small sample sizes. The main strength of meta-analytic reviews is objectivity (Anderson, Gentile & Buckley, 2007). Unlike narrative reviews, meta-analyses done to answer a particular research question tend to give similar answers irrespective of different perspectives held by different reviewers. However, the meta-analytic reviewer still has to make important decisions concerning what studies to include and what studies to exclude from the sample. Thus, poorly conducted meta-analyses, those that do not include all relevant studies (Ferguson et al., 2010), can be just as

misleading as a biased narrative review. The major weakness of meta-analyses is that the focus on statistical aspects sometimes leads the researchers to ignore important conceptual aspects.

In well-conducted meta-analyses, researchers attempt to find all available published and unpublished studies that might be eligible for inclusion in the sample, construct a clear and explicit set of inclusion criteria, and conduct publication bias analyses. For example, the most recent and comprehensive meta-analysis in the violent video game effects domain was conducted by Anderson et al. (2010). This meta-analysis combined a total of 136 research papers with 381 effect size estimates involving more than 130,000 participants from Eastern and Western countries. Six outcome variables were included in the meta-analysis: aggressive behavior, aggressive cognition, aggressive affect, physiological arousal, desensitization/low empathy, and prosocial (helping) behavior. Newer studies of higher methodological quality made it possible to use more stringent inclusion criteria in this meta-analytic review than in prior reviews, and allowed tests of the effects of a number of relevant moderators (e.g., sex, culture, player's point of view). Both the best practices sample and the full sample yielded the same results: Violent video games had significant effects on all six outcome variables, showing that video game violence is indeed a causal risk factor for increased aggression and decreased prosocial behavior.

Methodological Pitfalls in the Field of Media Psychology
Conducting Studies in a "Theoretical Vacuum"

When attempting to understand underlying processes of media effects, it's important to keep in mind general knowledge in the field of psychology concerning mechanisms of memory, learning, social cognition, and development. Media effects research is informed by extensively replicated findings and well-validated theoretical models from several disciplines, including, among others, cognitive psychology, developmental psychology, personality psychology, social psychology, and neuroscience. Well-tested and generally accepted theories such as schema theory (Alba & Hasher, 1983; Schmidt & Sherman, 1984), social learning theory and social cognitive theory (Bandura, 1973, 1983), script theory (Huesmann, 1986, 1988, 1998), and risk and resilience models (Glantz & Johnson, 1999; Gentile & Sesma, 2003) provide a solid foundation for predicting and explaining findings in the field of media psychology. As Kurt Lewin (1951) put it, "There is nothing so practical as a good theory." However, even though there are well-developed and well-validated theoretical models behind media violence effects (Anderson et al., 2003), some other research domains involving media effects suffer from a lack of theoretical focus (see Chapter 23).

A dangerous error sometimes made by media effects researchers is planning studies and interpreting results as if they are completely disconnected from the field's general knowledge of psychological functioning. For example, researchers who deny the existence of media violence effects on aggression are ignoring reliable and extensively replicated findings regarding priming (Bargh, 1982; Bargh & Pietromonaco, 1982), observational learning and imitation (Bandura, Ross, & Ross, 1961, 1963a,b; Meltzoff & Moore, 1977), excitation transfer (Zillmann, 1971, 1983) and desensitization (Wolpe, 1982). Given this extensive literature concerning ways that aggressive and nonaggressive social behaviors are learned and induced, it would indeed be very surprising if media violence did not affect us.

Using Inadequate Sample Sizes

Because most effects found in media psychology are small or medium in size, adequately large samples are needed to detect media effects. If the average effect size is about $r = .20$ (Anderson & Bushman, 2001), a sample of at least 200 participants should be taken to have .80 power. If sample sizes being used are too small, this will lead to results that are unstable and seemingly inconsistent. More reliable estimates can be obtained through combining such studies using meta-analytic techniques, of course, but researchers need to use adequate sample sizes in every study.

Using Inappropriate Experimental Manipulations

Any experimental manipulation represents an attempt by the researcher to construct a valid empirical realization of the conceptual independent variable (Carlsmith et al., 1976). Ideally, the various experimental manipulations: (1) differ from each other on the conceptual independent variables that they are supposed to represent, and (2) do not differ on other aspects that might (theoretically) influence responses on the dependent variable. For example, an experimental study to test the theoretical hypothesis that violent video game content increases the likelihood or amount of physical aggression minimally requires two conditions that differ in the amount of violent content (one should have a lot, the other should have none). Some early experiments (which shall remain nameless) did not successfully do this, in part because the researcher used an inappropriate definition of "violent content." That is some experiments used violent video games in the nonviolent control condition, because the researcher defined violent content as content that contained blood and gore, rather than the now-accepted definition of violent content as content in which player–characters try to harm other game characters. Also, recall our earlier comments on the failure of the Williams and Skoric (2005) "experiment" to appropriately manipulate exposure to violent video games.

The second requirement of the ideal case, that the relevant comparison conditions do not differ in aspects that might influence the dependent variable, also requires careful attention. We know, for example, that variables such as excitement, arousal, and frustration can sometimes increase aggressive behavior in some circumstances. Therefore, such extraneous factors (extraneous to the violent content/physical aggression hypothesis) need to be controlled.

There are two basic strategies for controlling such extraneous factors. One is to pretest several possible empirical realizations of the independent variable on the extraneous factors (using the same participant population as will be used in the main experiment), and then choose those that meet the theoretical and empirical requirements for use in the main experiment. For example, in a pilot study one could use several violent and several nonviolent video games, measure excitement, arousal, and frustration, and then select games that differ in violent content but that do not differ in induced excitement, arousal, and frustration for use in the main experiment (e.g., Anderson et al., 2004).

The second strategy is to measure the extraneous factors in the main experiment on the main participants, and then statistically control for those factors in analyses of the violent content manipulation on aggressive behavior. If it turns out that an extraneous factor (e.g., excitement) doesn't contribute significantly to aggressive behavior, then one doesn't need to control for it. However, if it does relate to aggressive behavior, then one can use the measure of excitement as a covariate in the statistical analysis. And of course, both of these strategies can be used in the same program of research as has been done in many of the methodologically strongest studies (e.g., Anderson & Dill, 2000, Study 2; Anderson et al., 2004).

It is important to keep in mind that the comparison conditions still will likely differ in other ways. This is especially likely in media psychology studies and any domain in which the stimuli tend to be selected rather than created. Although beyond the scope of this article, one solution to this issue is to use multiple stimuli (e.g., games) of each type (violent and nonviolent) such as in Anderson and Carnagey's (2009) study of violent and nonviolent competitive games. In addition, if one uses many examples of each game type, one could use random effects statistical models rather than the more common fixed-effect models.

Yet another approach to equating experimental conditions on extraneous factors is to use the same stimuli with changes only to the violent content. For example, Carnagey and Anderson (2005) reprogrammed the violent video game *Carmageddon* (a driving game in which one gets points for running over pedestrians) so that in the nonviolent condition there were no pedestrians to kill. Similarly, Anderson et al. (2004, Experiment 3) modified the violent video game *Marathon 2*. However, even this approach does not guarantee that the comparison games will be "equal" on relevant extraneous factors. So, it is useful to control such factors by pretests, measuring and statistically controlling for them in the main study, or both.

Finally, combining the effects of well-designed experiments in a meta-analysis also helps eliminate alternative explanations based on potential extraneous factors coinciding with the experimental variable of interest. Because different researchers have used a wide range of violent and nonviolent video games in their experiments, the likelihood that some extraneous factor existing in all or most of them is quite remote. Indeed, if one comes up with a plausible alternative explanation that might account for some of the results, one can test that alternative in a meta-analysis. For example, some gamer/scholars have proposed that the violent video game effect in experimental studies only works with the competitive reaction time task. Anderson et al. (2010) tested this alternative hypothesis, and found that the average effect size of such CRT studies is actually slightly smaller than the average effect found in the other experimental studies of violent video games, thus disproving that alternative explanation.

It is important to keep in mind that this type of reasoning, development, and assessment of experimental manipulations, and theory testing can and should be done in other media psychology domains, once sufficient numbers of studies are available. We use the media violence domain as an example because it is large, has had many excellently designed and executed studies published, has had a number of poorly executed studies published, and also because we are most familiar with this domain.

Using Poor or Inappropriate Measures

Differences in the direction of findings and in effect sizes can sometimes be a result of different measures of the independent, the dependent, or the control variables in particular studies. To detect effects and accurately assess their magnitude, reliable and valid measures need to be used. For example, the meta-analysis by Anderson et al. (2010) showed that the way one measures violent video game exposure in nonexperimental studies significantly influences the magnitude of effects found. Using specific measures of the length of exposure and violence levels in particular games (Anderson & Dill, 2000) yielded larger effect sizes than did other methods of assessing exposure to violent games.

Another potential pitfall involves using dependent measures that don't fit the research context. This can happen in multiple ways. For example, some short-term experimental studies of violent media effects have used traitlike measures as the dependent variable. Such traitlike measures essentially assess how frequently one has behaved aggressively in recent years. How can a 15-minute experimental manipulation today (violent versus nonviolent video game) influence how often one has behaved aggressively before today? Another version of this problem concerns what is an appropriate measure of aggression. Is having an argument with a friend or spouse a measure of aggression, as claimed by Williams and Skoric? Is the proximal intent of such an argument to harm the friend or spouse? In most cases, the answer is probably "no," so this is a very poor measure of the conceptual variable "aggression." It is even more inappropriate in a study designed to test the effects of violent video games on the kinds of aggression most frequently modeled in violent games, physical aggression. And it is even more inappropriate when most of the participants don't have a spouse with which to argue (Williams & Skoric, 2005). Certainly, there is evidence that school children arguing with teachers and other authority figures is one valid aspect of antisocial tendencies, but that is very different from using arguments with friends/spouses as a measure of video game–induced aggression in adult participants.

Often, the most important findings are acquired by using multiple measures. For example, in a longitudinal study of media violence effects, Anderson, Gentile, and Buckley (2007) obtained multiple measures of children's aggressive behavior through self-report, peer nominations, and teacher nominations. Sometimes such measures can be usefully combined into an overall index of aggression (Study 3).

An interesting recent direction in the media psychology field concerns examining neurocognitive bases of media effects through techniques such as event-related brain potentials (ERPs) and functional magnetic resonance imaging (fMRI). For example, Bartholow, Bushman, and Sestir (2005) showed that habitual violent video game players have reduced amplitudes of the P300 component of the event-related brain potential while viewing violent images and that this reduced response predicts more aggressive behavior. Research by Kronenberger et al. (2005) has shown similar fMRI and Stroop attention differences in conduct disordered and high violent gaming adolescents (Mathews et al., 2005; Weber et al., 2006). Similarly, Bailey, West, and Anderson (2010, 2011a,b) have used ERPs, Stroop tasks, and photo rating tasks to compare high and low action gamers on their attention control and emotional reactions to violence. Relative to low gamers, high gamers show deficits in proactive control, other more general attention deficits, and brain activation patterns suggesting desensitization to violent images. Overall, these various findings, each using multiple ways to measure theoretically related processes, provide converging support on desensitizion and decreased empathy as results of media violence exposure (Mullin & Linz, 1995; Dexter, Penrod, Linz, & Saunders 1997).

However, obtaining multiple measures sometimes comes at a cost. A potential pitfall stems from the fact that measurement of one variable of interest may influence the values of other related variables. Similar to the Heisenberg uncertainty principle in physics, the *psychological uncertainty principle* states that that measurement of one variable may change the psychological processes at work and thus change the values of downstream variables (Lindsay & Anderson, 2000). For example, measuring attitudes toward aggression after watching a violent movie may reveal the purpose of the study to participants and influence their later behavior. The possibility of such an influence can be controlled by experimentally varying the order in which variables are assessed and then testing for order effects. If significant order effects are found, this shows that the psychological uncertainty principle is at work. To test for mediation effects in such cases, multiple experiments need to be conducted, each of which assesses one of the key variables (Lindsay & Anderson, 2000).

Significance Testing

A problematic statistical practice employed in many media violence studies consists of using null-hypothesis significance testing without reporting effect sizes and confidence intervals. This widely used approach (in psychology as well as other social sciences) has been the subject of much criticism (Rozeboom, 1960; Cohen, 1994; Kirk, 1996; Thompson, 1998; Bonett & Wright, 2007). Unfortunately, null hypothesis tests are often misinterpreted (Nickerson, 2000). Failing to reject the null hypothesis is frequently viewed as proof that the null hypothesis is true, whereas rejection of a null hypothesis is taken as evidence of a practically and theoretically relevant finding (Bonett & Wright, 2007).

In the media violence domain, in which effect sizes are in a small to medium range (Anderson & Bushman, 2001; Anderson et al., 2010), interesting findings may be overlooked because of Type II errors (failure to reject the null hypothesis when it is true) and may go unpublished. The absence of significant differences found in particular studies are sometimes misinterpreted as evidence that there indeed are no effects, without taking into account other possible reasons for the nonsignificant result (e.g., inadequate control of extraneous variables, inappropriate overcontrol of mediating outcome variables, unreliable measurement techniques, and small sample sizes). A wide confidence interval immediately indicates to the reader that the sample estimate may not be reliable and may be quite different from the true effect in the population. Meta-analytic technique can then be used to combine such studies and enable researchers to draw firmer conclusions.

The American Psychological Association (APA) Task Force on Statistical Inference advocated for an improvement of statistical practices by including effect size estimates along with confidence intervals more than 10 years ago (Wilkinson & the Task Force on Statistical Inference, 1999). However, these changes have not yet been widely implemented in psychology journals (Finch et al., 2004; Cumming & Finch, 2005; Cumming et al., 2007). As the APA *Publication Manual* now strongly encourages authors to include confidence intervals (APA, 2011), it is our hope that this change in reporting styles will reduce miscommunication and misunderstanding in the media violence literature.

Effect Size Interpretation

Media effects research has sometimes been criticized on the grounds that effect sizes found in most studies are small and are thus unimportant

(Ferguson & Kilburn, 2010). However, it is dangerous to assume that just because most studies find small effect sizes, media do not have important practical consequences.

The effect sizes found in most media effects studies conform to the range of effect sizes usually found in social psychology studies in general (Richard, Bond, & Stokes-Zoota, 2003). Because complex behaviors are determined by a multitude of personal and situational factors, no one causal factor by itself can explain more than a small proportion of the variance in a particular behavior. Because of this, some authors suggest that effect size conventions should be revised so that $r = .1$ is small, $r = .2$ is medium, and $r = .3$ is large (Hemphill, 2003).

Some of the effects found in media psychology are, in fact, considerably larger than effect sizes found in medical research that are seen as extremely important (Bushman & Huesmann, 2001). For example, the effect of violent video games on aggression outweighs effects of substance use, abusive parents, and poverty (U.S. Department of Health and Human Services, 2001) and is larger than the effects of passive smoking on lung cancer and the effect of calcium intake on bone mass (Anderson, 2004). Furthermore, because a large proportion of the population is exposed to violent mass media, even small statistical effects can have important societal consequences (Abelson, 1985; Rosenthal, 1986; Prentice & Miller, 1992; Anderson et al., 2003).

Communicating Research Findings and Methodology to the General Public

An important role for many scientists involves disseminating knowledge gained from their research not only among the scientific community, but also among the general public. Indeed, several American Psychological Association presidents have urged its members to "give psychology away" to the public. One of the goals of media psychology as an applied field is to benefit society with its insights, a goal that requires effective communication between media researchers and the media, public policy makers, parents, teachers, and so on. Unfortunately, the scientific community has not always been successful in communicating research findings to the general public. For example, a content analysis of research papers and newspaper articles conducted by Bushman and Anderson (2001) revealed a large disparity between news reports and the actual state of scientific knowledge concerning media violence effects.

Researchers often do not see themselves as public educators. Differences in terminology and basic assumptions between scientists and nonscientists can impede effective communication and contribute to misinterpretation of scientific findings in the general public. Additionally, public involvement comes with costs (e.g., time, effort, money, and personal costs)—a price that researchers frequently are unwilling to pay. The costs are especially large when the research suggests that certain products are harmful (e.g., lead, tobacco, violent media), and when there is a large and committed group of product users and industry leaders who are highly threatened (e.g., by threats to self-image, profits) by the research findings. There is a long history of industries in the United States spending large sums of money attacking research findings that they don't like, attacking the integrity or scientific reputations of researchers whose work discovered the harmful effects. There is such a history in the television and film violence domain. For example, both Albert Bandura and Leonard Berkowitz were excluded from key governmental review panels on media violence because of pressure brought by the entertainment media industry. Similar attacks are widespread in the video game violence domain, and with the rise of the Internet, the personal attacks on and outright fabrications about key researchers has taken on a new dimension. One need only Google the names of the leading video game violence researchers to find such fabrications about them and their research.

However, it is our belief that the benefit of effective communication between scientists and the general public outweighs such costs. Therefore, a final task of successful researchers in the field of media psychology is to be able to clearly and effectively inform general audiences concerning their findings and methods used to obtain them.

Notes

1. We find it ironic that the lead author of that study, Dmitri Williams, in 2005 criticized the experimental study reported in Anderson and Dill (2000) for selecting a violent and a nonviolent game based on pilot testing of several games that included self-reported ratings on a variety of dimensions and physiological measures of arousal. Williams apparently didn't like the two games chosen because they didn't fit his intuitions about excitement levels induced by the games. What he fails to note is that: (1) Anderson and Dill reported that there were differences in self-reported excitement; (2) there were not differences in heart rate or blood pressure; (3) excitement was statistically controlled in the main experiment; (4) the excitement did not influence the results of the main experiment. Furthermore, in science when intuition conflicts with empirical data, it is intuition that has to yield. In fact, the Anderson and Dill studies set the methodological standard for

later video game studies (both experimental and correlational), and their basic findings have been replicated numerous times by numerous research teams from many countries around the world. We are not saying that this early experimental study was perfect; no single study is perfect. In fact, several more recent studies from our and other labs are, in our view, stronger methodologically; they built on the insights and knowledge gained from the earlier study.

References

Abelson, R. P. (1985). A variance explanation paradox: When a little is a lot. *Psychological Bulletin, 97*, 129–133.

Abelson, R. P. (1995). *Statistics as Principled Argument*. Hillsdale, NJ: Lawrence Erlbaum Associates.

Alba, J., & Hasher, L. (1983). Is memory schematic? *Psychological Bulletin, 93*, 203–231.

American Psychological Association (2011). *Publication Manual of the American Psychological Association*, 6th ed. Washington, DC: Author.

Anderson, C. A. (1987). Temperature and aggression: Effects on quarterly, yearly, and city rates of violent and nonviolent crime. *Journal of Personality and Social Psychology, 52*, 1161–1173.

Anderson, C. A. (1989). Temperature and aggression: Ubiquitous effects of heat on occurrence of human violence. *Psychological Bulletin, 106*, 74–96.

Anderson, C. A. (1997). Effects of violent movies and trait hostility on hostile feelings and aggressive thoughts. *Aggressive Behavior, 23*, 161–178.

Anderson, C. A. (2004). Violence in the media: Its effects on children. An edited transcript of a seminar presented on September 11, 2003, in Melbourne, Australia. Published by Young Media Australia (Glenelg, South Australia) and the Victorian Parenting Centre (Melbourne, Victoria).

Anderson, C. A., & Anderson, K. B. (1996). Violent crime rate studies in philosophical context: A destructive testing approach to heat and southern culture of violence effects. *Journal of Personality and Social Psychology, 70*, 740–756.

Anderson, C. A., Anderson, K. B., & Deuser, W. E. (1996). Examining an affective aggression framework: Weapon and temperature effects on aggressive thoughts, affect, and attitudes. *Personality and Social Psychology Bulletin, 22*, 366–376.

Anderson, C. A., Anderson, K. B., Dorr, N., DeNeve, K. M., & Flanagan, M. (2000). Temperature and aggression. *Chapter in Advances in Experimental Social Psychology, 32*, 63–133.

Anderson, C. A., Benjamin, A. J., & Bartholow, B. D. (1998). Does the gun pull the trigger? Automatic priming effects of weapon pictures and weapon names. *Psychological Science, 9*, 308–314.

Anderson, C. A., Benjamin, A. J., Wood, P. K., & Bonacci, A. M. (2006). Development and testing of the Velicer Attitudes Toward Violence Scale: Evidence for a four-factor model. *Aggressive Behavior, 32*, 122–136.

Anderson, C. A., Berkowitz, L., Donnerstein, E., Huesmann, R. L., Johnson, J., Linz, D., Malamuth, N., & Wartella, E. (2003). The influence of media violence on youth. *Psychological Science in the Public Interest, 4*, 81–110.

Anderson, C. A., & Bushman, B. J. (1997). External validity of "trivial" experiments: The case of laboratory aggression. *Review of General Psychology, 1*, 19–41.

Anderson, C. A., & Bushman, B. J. (2001). Effects of violent video games on aggressive behavior, aggressive cognition, aggressive affect, physiological arousal, and prosocial behavior: A meta-analytic review of the scientific literature. *Psychological Science, 12*, 353–359.

Anderson, C. A., & Bushman, B. J. (2002a). Media violence and the American public revisited. *American Psychologist, 57*, 448–450.

Anderson, C. A., & Bushman, B. J. (2002b). Human aggression. *Annual Review of Psychology, 53*, 27–51.

Anderson, C. A., & Carnagey, N. L. (2009). Causal effects of violent sports video games on aggression: Is it competitiveness or violent content? *Journal of Experimental Social Psychology, 45*, 731–739.

Anderson, C. A., Carnagey, N. L., & Eubanks, J. (2003). Exposure to violent media: The effects of songs with violent lyrics on aggressive thoughts and feelings. *Journal of Personality and Social Psychology, 84*, 960–971.

Anderson, C. A., Carnagey, N. L., Flanagan, M., Benjamin, A. J., Eubanks, J., & Valentine, J. C. (2004). Violent video games: Specific effects of violent content on aggressive thoughts and behavior. *Advances in Experimental Social Psychology, 36*, 199–249.

Anderson, C. A, Deuser, W. E., DeNeve, K. (1995). Hot temperatures, hostile affect, hostile cognition, and arousal: Tests of a general model of affective aggression. *Personality and Social Psychology Bulletin, 21*, 434–448.

Anderson, C. A., & Dill, K. E. (2000). Video games and aggressive thoughts, feelings, and behavior in the laboratory and in life. *Journal of Personality and Social Psychology, 78*, 772–790.

Anderson, C. A., Gentile, D. A., & Buckley, K. E. (2007). *Violent Video Game Effects on Children and Adolescents: Theory, Research, and Public Policy*. New York: Oxford University Press.

Anderson, C. A., & Huesmann, L. R. (2003). Human aggression: A social-cognitive view. In Hogg, M. A., & Cooper, J. (Eds.), *Handbook of Social Psychology*. London: Sage, pp. 296–323.

Anderson, C. A., Lindsay, J. J., & Bushman, B. J. (1999). Research in the psychological laboratory: Truth or triviality? *Current Directions in Psychological Science, 8*, 3–9.

Anderson, C. A., & Morrow, M. (1995). Competitive aggression without interaction: Effects of competitive versus cooperative instructions on aggressive behavior in video games. *Personality and Social Psychology Bulletin, 21*, 1020–1030.

Anderson, C. A., Sakamoto, A., Gentile, D. A., Ihori, N., & Shibuya, A., Yukawa, S., Naito, M., & Kobayashi, K. (2008). Longitudinal effects of violent video games aggression in Japan and the United States. *Pediatrics, 122*, e1067–e1072.

Anderson, C. A., Shibuya, A., Ihori, N., Swing, E. L., Bushman, B. J., Sakamoto, A., Rothstein, H. R., & Saleem, M. (2010). Violent video game effects on aggression, empathy, and prosocial behavior in Eastern and Western countries. *Psychological Bulletin, 136*, 151–173.

Anderson, K. B., Anderson, C. A., Dill, K. E., & Deuser, W. E. (1998). The interactive relations between trait hostility, pain, and aggressive thoughts. *Aggressive Behavior, 24*, 161–171.

Bailey, K., West, R., & Anderson, C. A. (2010). A negative association between video game experience and proactive cognitive control. *Psychophysiology, 47*, 34–42.

Bailey, K., West, R., & Anderson, C. A. (2011a). The association between chronic exposure to video game violence and affective picture processing: An ERP study. *Cognitive, Affective, and Behavioral Neuroscience, 11*, 259–276.

Bailey, K., West. R., & Anderson, C. A. (2011b). The influence of video games on social, cognitive, and affective information processing. In Decety, J., & Cacioppo, J. (Eds.), *Handbook of Social Neuroscience*. New York: Oxford University Press, pp. 1001–1011.

Ballard, M. E., Hamby, R. H., Panee, C. D., & Nivens, E. E. (2006). Repeated exposure to video game play results in decreased blood pressure responding. *Media Psychology, 8,* 323–341.

Ballard, M. E., & Lineberger, R. (1999). Video game violence and confederate gender: Effects on reward and punishment given by college males. *Sex Roles, 41,* 541–558.

Ballard, M. E., & Wiest, J. R. (1996). Mortal Kombat (tm): The effects of violent videogame play on males' hostility and cardiovascular responding. *Journal of Applied Social Psychology, 26,* 717–730.

Banaji, M. R., & Crowder, R. G. (1989). The bankruptcy of everyday memory. *American Psychologist, 44*(9), 1185–1193.

Bandura, A. (1973). *Aggression: A Social Learning Analysis.* Englewood Cliffs, NJ: Prentice-Hall.

Bandura, A. (1983). Psychological mechanisms of aggression. In Geen, R. G., & Donnerstein, E. (Eds.), *Aggression: Theoretical and Empirical Reviews.* New York: Academic Press, pp. 1–40.

Bandura, A., Ross, D., & Ross, S. A. (1961). Transmission of aggressions through imitation of aggressive models. *Journal of Abnormal and Social Psychology, 63,* 575–582.

Bandura, A., Ross, D., & Ross, S. A. (1963a). Imitation of film-mediated aggressive models. *Journal of Abnormal Social Psychology, 66,* 3–11.

Bandura, A., Ross, D., & Ross, S. A. (1963b). Vicarious reinforcement and imitative learning. *Journal of Abnormal Social Psychology, 67,* 601–607.

Bargh, J. A. (1982). Attention and automaticity in the processing of self-relevant information. *Journal of Personality and Social Psychology, 43,* 425–436.

Bargh, J. A., & Pietromonaco, P. (1982). Automatic information processing and social perception: The influence of trait information presented outside of conscious awareness on impression formation. *Journal of Personality and Social Psychology, 43,* 437–449.

Barlett, C. P., Anderson, C. A., & Swing, E. L. (2009). Video game effects confirmed, suspected and speculative: A review of the evidence. *Simulation & Gaming, 40,* 377–403.

Barlett, C. P., Branch, O. L., Rodeheffer, C. D., & Harris, R. H. (2009). How long do the short-term violent video game effects last? *Aggressive Behavior, 35,* 225–236.

Barlett, C. P., Rodeheffer, C. D., Baldassaro, R. M., Hinkin, M., & Harris, R. J. (2008). The effect of advances in video game technology and content on aggressive cognitions, hostility, and heart rate. *Media Psychology, 11,* 540–565.

Baron, R. A., & Richardson, D. R. (1994). *Human Aggression,* 2nd ed. New York: Plenum Press.

Bartholow, B. D., Bushman, B. J., & Sestir, M. A. (2006). Chronic violent video game exposure and desensitization to violence: Behavioral and event-related brain potential data. *Journal of Experimental Social Psychology, 42*(2), 283–290.

Bartholow, B. D., Sestir, M. A., & Davis, E. (2005). Correlates and consequences of exposure to video game violence: Hostile personality, empathy, and aggressive behavior. *Personality and Social Psychology Bulletin, 31,* 1573–1586.

Baumeister, R. F., & Leary, M. R. (1997). Writing narrative literature reviews. *Review of General Psychology, 1*(3), 311–320.

Berkowitz, L. (1962). *Aggression: A social psychological analysis.* New York: McGraw-Hill.

Berkowitz, L. (1970). Aggressive humor as a stimulus to aggressive responses. *Journal of Personality & Social Psychology, 4,* 710–717.

Berkowitz, L. (1993). *Aggression: Its Causes, Consequences, and Control.* New York: McGraw-Hill.

Berkowitz, L., & Donnerstein, E. (1982). External validity is more than skin deep: Some answers to criticism of laboratory experiments. *American Psychologist, 37,* 245–257.

Bernstein, L. S., Richardson, D., & Hammock, G. (1987). Convergent and discriminant validity of the Taylor and Buss measures of physical aggression. *Aggressive Behavior, 13,* 15–24.

Bjorkqvist, K. (1985). *Violent Films, Anxiety, and Aggression.* Helsinki: Finnish Society of Sciences and Letters.

Bonett, D. G., & Wright, T. A. (2007), Comments and recommendations regarding the hypothesis testing controversy. *Journal of Organizational Behavior, 28,* 647–659.

Bryant, B. K. (1982). An index of empathy for children and adolescents. *Child Development, 53,* 413–425.

Bryant, J., Carveth, R. A., & Brown, D. (1981). Television viewing and anxiety: An experimental examination. *Journal of Communication, 31,* 106–119.

Buckley, K. E., & Anderson, C. A. (2006). A theoretical model of the effects and consequences of playing video games. In Vorderer, P., & Bryant, J. (Eds.), *Playing Video Games—Motives, Responses, and Consequences.* Hillsdale, NJ: Lawrence Erlbaum Associates, pp. 363–378.

Bushman, B. J. (1995). Moderating role of trait aggressiveness in the effects of violent media on aggression. *Journal of Personality & Social Psychology, 69,* 950–960.

Bushman, B. J. (1996). Individual differences in the extent and development of aggressive cognitive-associative networks. *Personality and Social Psychology Bulletin, 22,* 811–819.

Bushman, B. J. (1998). Priming effects of violent media on the accessibility of aggressive constructs in memory. *Personality and Social Psychology Bulletin, 24,* 537–545.

Bushman, B. J. (2002). Does venting anguish feed or extinguish the flame? Catharsis, rumination, distraction, anger, and aggressive responding. *Personality and Social Psychology Bulletin, 28,* 724–731.

Bushman, B. J., & Anderson, C. A. (1998). Methodology in the study of aggression: Integrating experimental and nonexperimental findings. in Geen, R., & Donnerstein, E. (Eds.), *Human Aggression: Theories, Research and Implications for Policy.* San Diego: Academic Press, pp. 23–48.

Bushman, B. J., & Anderson, C. A. (2001). Media violence and the American public: Scientific facts versus media misinformation. *American Psychologist, 56,* 477–489.

Bushman, B. J., & Anderson, C. A. (2002). Violent video games and hostile expectations: A test of the general aggression model. *Personality and Social Psychology Bulletin, 28,* 1679–1686.

Bushman, B. J., & Anderson, C. A. (2009). Comfortably numb: Desensitizing effects of violent media on helping others. *Psychological Science, 20,* 273–277.

Bushman, B. J., Baumeister, R. F., & Stack, A. D. (1999). Catharsis, aggression, and persuasive influence: Self-fulfilling or self-defeating prophecies? *Journal of Personality and Social Psychology, 76,* 367–376.

Bushman, B. J., & Huesmann, L. R. (2001). Effects of televised violence on aggression. In D. Singer & J. Singer (Eds.),

Handbook of children and the media (pp. 223–254). Thousand Oaks, CA: Sage Publications.

Bushman, B. J., & Huesmann, L. R. (2006). Short-term and long-term effects of violent media on aggression in children and adults. *Archives of Pediatrics & Adolescent Medicine, 160,* 348–352.

Bushman, B. J., Rothstein, H. R., & Anderson, C. A. (2010). Much ado about something: Violent video game effects and a school of red herring: Reply to Ferguson and Kilburn. *Psychological Bulletin, 136,* 182–187.

Buss, A. H. (1961). *The Psychology of Aggression.* New York: Wiley.

Buss, A. H., & Perry, M. (1992). The Aggression Questionnaire. *Journal of Personality & Social Psychology, 63,* 452–459.

Calvert, S. L., & Tan, S. (1994). Impact of virtual reality on young adults' physiological arousal and aggressive thoughts: Interaction versus observation. *Journal of Applied Developmental Psychology, 15,* 125–139.

Campbell, A. (1993). *Men, Women and Aggression.* New York: Basic Books.

Campbell, D. T., & Fiske, D. W. (1959). Convergent and discriminant validation by the multitrait-multimethod matrix. *Psychological Bulletin, 56,* 81–105.

Caprara, G. V., Cinanni, V., D' Imperio, G., Passerini, S., Renzi, P., & Travablia, G. (1985). Indicators of impulsive aggression: Present status of research on irritability and emotional susceptibility scales. *Personality & Individual Differences, 6,* 665–674.

Carlsmith, J. M., Ellsworth, P. C., & Aronson, E. (1976). *Methods of Research in Social Psychology.* Reading, MA: Addison-Wesley.

Carlson, M., Marcus-Newhall, A., & Miller, N. (1989). Evidence for a general construct of aggression. *Personality and Social Psychology Bulletin, 15,* 377–389.

Carnagey, N. L., & Anderson, C. A. (2003). Theory in the study of media violence: The General Aggression Model. In Gentile, D. (Ed.), *Media Violence and Children.* Westport, CT: Praeger, pp. 87–106.

Carnagey, N. L., & Anderson, C. A. (2005). The effects of reward and punishment in violent video games on aggressive affect, cognition, and behavior. *Psychological Science, 16,* 882–889.

Carnagey, N. L., & Anderson, C.A., & Bushman, B. J. (2007). The effect of video game violence on physiological desensitization to real-life violence. *Journal of Experimental Social Psychology, 43,* 489–496.

Chambers, J. H., & Ascione, F. R. (1987). The effects of prosocial and aggressive video games on children's donating and helping. *Journal of Genetic Psychology, 148,* 499–505.

Cheung, P. C., Ma, H. K., & Shek, T. L. D. (1998). Conceptions of success: their correlates with prosocial orientation and behavior in Chinese adolescents. *Journal of Adolescence, 21,* 31–42.

Cohen, J. (1994). The earth is round (p < .05). *American Psychologist, 49*(12), 997–1003.

Comstock, G., & Scharrer, E. (2007). *Media and the American Child.* San Diego: Academic Press.

Cook, W. W., & Medley, D. M. (1954). Proposed hostility and pharisaic virtue scales for the MMPI. *Journal of Applied Psychology, 38,* 414–418.

Cooper, J., & Mackie, D. (1986). Video games and aggression in children. *Journal of Applied Social Psychology, 16,* 726–744.

Crick, N. R., & Dodge, K. A. (1994). A review and reformulation of social information processing mechanisms in children's adjustment. *Psychological Bulletin, 115,* 74–101.

Cumming, G., Fidler, F., Leonard, M., Kalinowski, P., Christiansen, A., Kleinig, A., et al. (2007). Statistical reform in psychology: Is anything changing? *Psychological Science, 18,* 230–232.

Cumming, G., & Finch, S. (2005). Inference by eye: Confidence intervals and how to read pictures of data. *American Psychologist, 60*(2), 170–180.

Davis, M. H. (1980). Measuring individual differences in empathy: Evidence for a multidimensional approach. *Journal of Personality and Social Psychology, 44,* 113–126.

DeWall, C. N., & Anderson, C. A. (2011). The General Aggression Model. In Shaver, P., & Mikulincer, M. (Eds.), *Human Aggression and Violence: Causes, Manifestations, and Consequences.* Washington, DC: American Psychological Association, pp. 15–33.

DeWall, C. N., Anderson, C. A., & Bushman, B. J. (2012). Aggression. Suls, J. (Ed.), *Handbook of Psychology.* New York: Wiley.

DeWall, C. N., Anderson, C. A., & Bushman, B. J. (2011). The general aggression model: Theoretical extensions to violence. *Psychology of Violence, 1*(13), 245–258.

Dexter, H.R., Penrod, S. D., Linz, D., & Saunders, D. (1997). Attributing responsibility to female victims after exposure to sexually violent films. *Journal of Applied Social Psychology, 27,* 2149.

Dill, J., & Anderson, C. A. (1995). Effects of justified and unjustified frustration on aggression. *Aggressive Behavior, 21,* 359–369.

Dill, K. E., & Dill, J. (1998). Video game violence: A review of the empirical literature. *Aggression and Violent Behavior, 3,* 407–428.

Dollard, J., Doob, L., Miller, N., Mowrer, O., & Sears, R. (1939). *Frustration and Aggression.* New Haven, CT: Yale University Press.

Dominick, J. R. (1984). Videogames, television violence, and aggression in teenagers. *Journal of Communication, 34,* 136–147.

Donnerstein, E., & Berkowitz, L. (1981). Victim reactions in aggressive erotic films as a factor in violence against women. *Journal of Personality and Social Psychology, 41,* 710–724.

Elliot, D. S., Huizinga, D., & Ageton, S. S. (1985). *Explaining delinquency and drug use.* Beverly Hills, CA: Sage.

Eron, L. D., Huesmann, L. R., Lefkowitz, M. M., & Walder, L. O. (1972). Does television violence cause aggression? *American Psychologist, 27,* 253–263.

Ferguson, C. J., & Kilburn, J. (2010). Much ado about nothing: The misestimation and overinterpretation of violent video game effects in Eastern and Western nations: Comment on Anderson et al. (2010). *Psychological Bulletin, 136.*

Ferguson, C. J., Olson, C. K., Kutner, L. A., & Warner, D. E. (2010). Violent video games, catharsis-seeking, bullying and delinquency: A multivariate analysis of effects. *Crime and Delinquency.*

Ferguson, C. J., San Miguel, C., & Hartley, R. D. (2009). A multivariate analysis of youth violence and aggression: The influence of family, peers, depression and media violence. *Journal of Pediatrics, 155*(6), 904–908.

Finch, S., Cumming, G., Williams, J., Palmer, L., Griffith, E., Alders, C., et al. (2004). Reform of statistical inference in psychology: The case of Memory & Cognition. *Behavior Research Methods, Instruments, & Computers, 36,* 312–324.

Fischer, P., Greitemeyer, T., Kastenmüller, A., Vogrincic, C., & Sauer, A. (2011). The effects of risk-glorifying media exposure on risk-positive cognitions, emotions, and behaviors: A meta-analytic review. *Psychological Bulletin.* Advance online publication.

Fleming, M. J., & Rickwood, D. J. (2001). Effects of violent versus nonviolent video games on children's arousal, aggressive mood and positive mood. *Journal of Applied Social Psychology, 31,* 2047–2071.

Fling, S., Smith, L., Rodriguez, T., Thornton, D., Atkins, E., & Nixon, K. (1992). Videogames, aggression, and self-esteem: A survey. *Social Behavior and Personality, 20,* 39–46.

Funk, J. B., Baldacci, H. B., Pasold, T., & Baumgardner, J. (2004). Violence exposure in real-life, video games, television, movies, and the Internet: is there desensitization? *Journal of Adolescence, 27*(1), 23–39.

Funk, J. B., Buchman D. D., Jenks, J., & Bechtoldt, H. (2003) Playing violent video games, desensitization, and moral evaluation in children. *Applied Developmental Psychology, 24,* 413–436.

Funk, J. B., Elliott, R., Urman, M. L., Flores, G. T. & Mock, R. M. (1999). The Attitudes Towards Violence scale: A measure for adolescents. *Journal of Interpersonal Violence, 14,* 1123–1136.

Funk, J. B., Fox, C. M., Chan, M., & Curtiss, K. (2008). The development of the Children's Empathic Attitudes Scale using classical and Rasch analyses. *Journal of Applied Developmental Psychology, 29,* 187–198.

Gaebelein, J. W., & Taylor, S. P. (1971). The effects of competition and attack on physical aggression. *Psychonomic Science, 24,* 65–67.

Geen, R. G. (2001). *Human Aggression,* 2nd ed. Philadelphia: Open University Press.

Geen, R. G., & O'Neal, E. C. (1969). Activation of cue-elicited aggression by general arousal. *Journal of Personality and Social Psychology, 11,* 289–292.

Geen, R. G., & Quanty, M. B. (1977). The catharsis of aggression: An evaluation of a hypothesis. In Berkowitz, L. (Ed.), *Advances in Experimental Social Psychology.* New York: Academic Press, pp. 1–37.

Geen, R. G., Stonner, D., & Shope, G. L. (1975). The facilitation of aggression by aggression: Evidence against the catharsis hypothesis. *Journal of Personality and Social Psychology, 31,* 721–726.

Gentile, D. A., Anderson, C. A., Yukawa, N., Saleem, M., Lim, K. M., Shibuya, A., Liau, A. K., Khoo, A., Bushman, B. J., Huesmann, L. R., & Sakamoto, A. (2009). The effects of prosocial video games on prosocial behaviors: International evidence from correlational, longitudinal, and experimental studies. *Personality and Social Psychology Bulletin, 35,* 752–763.

Gentile, D. A., Lynch, P. J., Linder, J. R., & Walsh, D. A. (2004). The effects of violent video game habits on adolescent aggressive attitudes and behaviors. *Journal of Adolescence, 27,* 5–22.

Gentile, D. A., & Sesma, A. (2003). Developmental approaches to understanding media effects on individuals. In D. A. Gentile (Ed.), *Media violence and children.* Westport, CT: Greenwood Publishing.

Gerbner, G., Gross, L., Jackson-Beeck, M., Jeffries-Fox, S., & Signorielli, N. (1978). Cultural indicators: Violence profile no. 9. *Journal of Communication, 28,* 176–207.

Gerbner, G., Gross, L., Morgan, M., & Signorielli, N. (1980). The "mainstreaming" of America: Violence profile no. 11. *Journal of Communication, 30,* 10–29.

Giancola, P. R., & Chermack, S. T. (1998). Construct validity of laboratory aggression paradigms: A response to Tedeschi and Quigley (1996). *Aggression and Violent Behavior, 3,* 237–253.

Giancola, P. R., & Parrott, D. J. (2008). Further evidence for the validity of the Taylor aggression paradigm. *Aggressive Behavior, 34,* 214–229.

Glantz, M. D., & Johnson, J. L. (Eds.) (1999). *Resilience and Development: Positive Life Adaptations.* New York: Kluwer.

Greitemeyer, T. (2009). Effects of songs with prosocial lyrics on prosocial behavior: further evidence and a mediating mechanism. *Personality and Social Psychology Bulletin, 35,* 1500–1511.

Greitemeyer, T. (2011). Exposure to music with prosocial lyrics reduces aggression: First evidence and test of the underlying mechanism. *Journal of Experimental Social Psychology, 47,* 28–36.

Greitemeyer, T., & Osswald, S. (2010): Effects of Prosocial video games on prosocial behavior. *Journal of Personality and Social Psychology, 98*(2), 211–221.

Griffiths, M. (1999). Violent video games and aggression: A review of the literature. *Aggression and Violent Behavior, 4,* 203–212.

Hemphill, J. F. (2003). Interpreting the magnitudes of correlation coefficients. *American Psychologist, 58,* 78–79.

Henshel, R. L. (1980). The purpose of laboratory experimentation and the virtues of deliberate artificiality. *Journal of Experimental Social Psychology, 16,* 466–478.

Hopf, W. H., Huber, G. L., & Weiß, R. H. (2008). Media violence and youth violence: A 2-year longitudinal study. *Journal of Media Psychology: Theories, Methods, and Applications, 20*(3), 79–96.

Huesmann, L. R. (1986). Psychological processes promoting the relation between exposure to media violence and aggressive behavior by the viewer. *Journal of Social Issues, 42,* 125–139.

Huesmann, L. R. (1988). An information processing model for the development of aggression. *Aggressive Behavior, 14,* 13–24.

Huesmann, L. R. (1998). The role of social information processing and cognitive schema in the acquisition and maintenance of habitual aggressive behavior. In Geen, R., & Donnerstein, E. (Eds.) *Human Aggression: Theories, Research, and Implications for Policy* . New York: Academic Press, pp. 73–109.

Huesmann, L. R., Eron, L. D., Klein, R., Brice, P., & Fischer, P. (1983). Mitigating the imitation of aggressive behaviors by changing children's attitudes about media violence. *Journal of Personality and Social Psychology, 44,* 899–910.

Huesmann, L. R., Guerra, N. G., Miller, L., & Zelli, A. (1992). The role of social norms in the development of aggression. In Zumkley, H., & Fraczek, A. (Eds.), *Socialization and Aggression* . New York: Springer, pp. 139–151.

Huesmann, L. R., Moise-Titus, J., Podolski, C. L., & Eron, L. (2003). Longitudinal relations between children's exposure to TV violence and their aggressive and violent behavior in young adulthood: 1977–1992. *Developmental Psychology, 39,* 201–221.

Huesmann, L. R., & Taylor, L. D. (2003). The case against the case against media violence. In Gentile, D. (Ed.) *Media Violence and Children.* Westport, CT: Greenwood Press, pp. 107–130.

Irwin, A. R., & Gross, A. M. (1995). Cognitive tempo, violent video games, and aggressive behavior in young boys. *Journal of Family Violence, 10,* 337–350.

Jolliffe, D., & Farrington, D. P. (2006). Development and validation of the Basic Empathy Scale. *Journal of Adolescence, 29,* 589–611.

Josephson, W. L. (1987). Television violence and children's aggression: Testing the priming, social script, and disinhibition predictions. *Journal of Personality and Social Psychology, 53,* 882–890.

Kenny, D. A. (1984). The NBC study and television violence: A review. *Journal of Communication, 34,* 176–188.

Kirk, R. (1996). Practical significance: A concept whose time has come. *Educational and Psychological Measurement, 56,* 746–759.

Kirsh, S. J. (1998). Seeing the world through Mortal Kombat-colored glasses: Violent video games and the development of a short-term hostile attribution bias. *Childhood, 5,* 177–184.

Koehler, J. J. (1993). The influence of prior beliefs on scientific judgments of evidence quality. *Organizational Behavior and Human Decision Processes, 56,* 28–55.

Konijn, E. A., Bijvank, N. M., & Bushman, B. J. (2007). I wish I were a warrior: The role of wishful identification in effects of violent video games on aggression in adolescent boys. *Developmental Psychology, 43,* 1038–1044.

Kronenberger, W. G., Matthews, V. P., Dunn, D. W., Wang, Y., Wood, E. A., Giauque, A. L., et al. (2005). Media violence exposure and executive functioning in aggressive and control adolescents. *Journal of Clinical Psychology, 61,* 725–737.

Kuhn, T. S. (1962). *The Structure of Scientific Revolutions.* Chicago: University of Chicago Press.

Kunda, Z. (1990). The case for motivated reasoning. *Psychological Bulletin, 108,* 480–498.

Lewin, K. (1951). Problems of research in social psychology. In Cartwright, D. (Ed.), *Field Theory in Social Science* (pp. 155–169). New York: Harper & Row.

Lieberman, J. D., Solomon, S., Greenberg, J., & McGregor, H. A. (1999), A hot new way to measure aggression: Hot sauce allocation. *Aggressive Behavior, 25,* 331–348.

Lin, S., & Lepper, M. R. (1987). Correlates of children's usage of video games and computers. *Journal of Applied Social Psychology, 17,* 72–93.

Lindsay, J. J., & Anderson, C. A. (2000). From antecedent conditions to violent actions: A general affective aggression model. *Personality and Social Psychology Bulletin, 26,* 533–547.

Linz, D., Donnerstein, E., & Adams, S. M. (1989). Physiological desensitization and judgments about female victims of violence. *Human Communication Research, 15,* 509–522.

Lord, C. G., Ross, L., & Lepper, M. R. (1979). Biased assimilation and attitude polarization: The effects of prior theories on subsequently considered evidence. *Journal of Personality and Social Psychology, 37,* 2098–2109.

Mallick, S. K., & McCandless, B. R. (1966). A study of catharsis of aggression. *Journal of Personality and Social Psychology, 4,* 591–596.

Mathews, V. P., Kronenberger, W. G., Wang, Y., Lurito, J. T., Lowe, M. J., & Dunn, D. W. (2005). Media violence exposure and frontal lobe activation measured by functional magnetic resonance imaging in aggressive and nonaggressive adolescents. *Journal of Computer Assisted Tomography, 29,* 287–292.

McLeod, J. M., Atkin, C. K., & Chaffee, S. H. (1972). Adolescents, parents, and television use: Adolescent self-report measures from Maryland and Wisconsin samples. In Comstock, G. A., & Rubinstein, E. A. (Eds.), *Television and Social Behavior: A Technical Report to the Surgeon General's Scientific Advisory Committee on Television and Social Behavior: Vol. 3. Television and Adolescent Aggressiveness* (DHEW Publication No. HSM 72–9058, pp. 173–238). Washington, DC: U.S. Government Printing Office.

Meltzoff, A. N., & Moore, K. M. (1977). Imitation of facial and manual gestures by human neonates. *Science, 109,* 77–78.

Milgram, S. (1974). *Obedience to Authority.* New York: Harper & Row.

Milavsky, J. R., Kessler, R. C., Stipp, H. H., & Rubens, W. S. (1982). *Television and aggression: A panel study.* New York: Academic Press.

Möller, I., & Krahé, B. (2009). Exposure to violent video games and aggression in German adolescents: A longitudinal analysis. *Aggressive Behavior, 35,* 75–89.

Mook, D. G. (1983). In defense of external invalidity. *American Psychologist, 38,* 379–387.

Mullin, C. R., & Linz, D. (1995). Desensitization and resensitization to violence against women: Effects of exposure to sexually violent films on judgments of domestic violence victims. *Journal of Personality and Social Psychology, 69,* 449–459.

Münsterberg, H. (1899). Psychology and history. *Psychological Review, 6,* 1–31.

Nickerson, R. S. (2000). Null hypothesis significance testing: A review of an old and continuing controversy. *Psychological Methods, 5*(2), 241–301.

Ohbuchi, K.-I., Kameda, M., & Agarie, N. (1989). Apology as aggression control: Its role in mediating appraisal of and response to harm. *Journal of Personality and Social Psychology, 56*(2), 219–227.

Prentice, D. A., & Miller, D. T. (1992). When small effects are impressive. *Psychological Bulletin, 112,* 160–164.

Richard, F. D., Bond, C. F., Jr., & Stokes-Zoota, J. J. (2003). One hundred years of social psychology quantitatively described. *Review of General Psychology, 7,* 331–363.

Rideout, V. J., Foehr, U. G., & Roberts, D. F. (2010). *Generation M2—Media in the Lives of 8- to 18-Year Olds.* Menlo Park, CA: Kaiser Family Foundation.

Robinson, T. N., Wilde, M. L., Navracruz, L. C., Haydel, K. F., & Varady, A. (2001). Effects of reducing children's television and video game use on aggressive behavior: A randomized controlled trial. *Archives of Pediatric Adolescent Medicine, 155,* 17–23.

Roediger, H. L., Weldon, M. S., Stadler, M. L., & Riegler, G. L. (1992). Direct comparison of two implicit memory tests: Word fragment and word stem completion. *Journal of Experimental Psychology: Learning, Memory, and Cognition, 18,* 1251–1269.

Rosenthal, R. (1986). Media violence, antisocial behavior, and the social consequences of small effects. *Journal of Social Issues, 42,* 141–154.

Rosenthal, R. (1995). Writing meta-analytic reviews. *Psychological Bulletin, 118*(2), 183–192.

Rozeboom, W. W. (1960). The fallacy of the null hypothesis significance test. *Psychological Bulletin, 57,* 416–428.

Ryan, R., Rigby, C. S., & Przybylski, A. (2006). The motivational pull of video games: A self-determination theory approach. *Motivation and Emotion, 30,* 344–360.

Saleem, M., & Anderson, C. A. (in press). Arabs as terrorists: Effects of stereotypes within violent contexts on attitudes, perceptions and affect. *Psychology of Violence.*

Schmidt, D. F., & Sherman, R. C. (1984). Memory for persuasive messages: A Test of a Schema-Copy-Plus-Tag Model. *Journal of Personality and Social Psychology, 47,* 17–25.

Schutte, N. S., Malouff, J. M., Post-Gorden, J. C., & Rodasta, A. L. (1988). Effects of playing video games on children's aggressive and other behaviors. *Journal of Applied Social Psychology, 18,* 454–460.

Sharif, I., & Sargent, J. D. (2006). Association between television, movie, and video game exposure and school performance. *Pediatrics, 118*(4), 1061–1070.

Sheese, B. E., & Graziano, W. G. (2005). Deciding to defect. The effects of video-game violence on cooperative behavior. *Psychological Science, 16,* 354–357.

Shibuya, A., Sakamoto, A., Ihori, N., & Yukawa, S. (2004). Media bouryoku heno sesshoku, sesshoku kankyo ga kougekisei ni oyobosu choukiteki eikyou: Shougakusei heno paneru chosa [The long-term effects of media violence and its situational variables on aggression: A panel study to elementary school children]. *Proceeding of the 45th convention of the Japanese Society of Social Psychology,* pp. 248–249.

Silvern, S. B., & Williamson, P. A. (1987). The effects of video game play on young children's aggression, fantasy and pro-social behavior. *Journal of Applied Developmental Psychology, 8,* 453–462.

Spielberger, C. D. (1988). *State-Trait Anger Expression Inventory.* Odessa, FL: Psychological Assessment Resources.

Swing, E. L., & Anderson, C. A. (2010). Media violence and the development of aggressive behavior. In DeLisi, M., & Beaver, K. M. (Eds.), *Criminological Theory: A Life-Course Approach.* Sudbury, MA: Jones & Bartlett, pp. 87–108.

Swing, E. L., Gentile, D. A., & Anderson, C. A. (2008). Violent video games: Learning processes and outcomes. In R. E. Ferdig (Ed.), *Handbook of research on effective electronic gaming in education* (pp. 876–892). Hershey, PA: Information Science Reference.

Taylor, S. (1967). Aggressive behavior and physiological arousal as a function of provocation and the tendency to inhibit aggression. *Journal of Personality, 35,* 297–310.

Thomas, M. H., Horton, R. W., Lippincott, E. C., & Drabman, R. S. (1977). Desensitization to portrayals of real life aggression as a function of television violence. *Journal of Personality and Social Psychology, 35,* 450–458.

Thompson, B. (1998). In praise of brilliance: Where that praise really belongs. *American Psychologist, 53,* 799–800.

Uhlmann, E., & Swanson, J. (2004). Exposure to violent video games increases automatic aggressiveness. *Journal of Adolescence, 27,* 41–52.

U.S. Department of Health and Human Services (2001). *Youth violence: A report of the Surgeon General* Rockville, MD: U.S. Department of Health and Human Services, Centers for Disease Control and Prevention. National Center for Injury Prevention and Control; Substance Abuse and Mental Health Services Administration, Center for Mental Health Services; and National institutes of Health, National Institute of Mental Health. Retrieved April 2, 2010 from http://www.ncbi.nlm.nih.gov/books/NBK44293/.

Watson, D., Clark, L. A., & Tellegen, A. (1988). Development and validation of brief measures of positive and negative affect: The PANAS scales. *Journal of Personality and Social Psychology, 54,* 1063–1070.

Weber, R., Ritterfeld, U., & Mathiak, K. (2006). Does playing violent video games induce aggression? Empirical evidence of a functional magnetic resonance imaging study. *Media Psychology, 8,* 39–60.

Wheeler, L., & Caggiula, A. R. (1966). The contagion of aggression. *Journal of Experimental Social Psychology, 2,* 1–10.

Wilkinson, L., & the Task Force on Statistical Inference. (1999). Statistical methods in psychology journals: Guidelines and explanations. *American Psychologist, 54,* 594–604.

Williams, D., & Skoric, M. (2005). Internet fantasy violence: A test of aggression in an online game. *Communication Monographs, 72,* 217–233.

Wolpe, J. (1982). *The Practice of Behavior Therapy,* 3rd ed. New York: Pergamon Press.

Zillmann, D. (1971). Excitation transfer in communication-mediated aggressive behavior. *Journal of Experimental Social Psychology, 7,* 419–434.

Zillmann, D. (1983). Arousal and aggression. In Geen, R., & Donnerstein, E. (Eds.), *Aggression: Theoretical and Empirical Reviews,* vol.1. New York: Academic Press, pp. 75–102.

Zuckerman, M. (1960). The development of an affect adjective checklist for the measurement of anxiety. *Journal of Consulting Psychology, 24,* 457–462.

Zuckerman, M., Lubin, B., Vogel, L., & Valerius, E. (1964). Measurement of experimentally induced affects. *Journal of Consulting Psychology, 28,* 418–425.

Qualitative Research and Media Psychology

Donald E. Polkinghorne

Abstract

Qualitative research is a family of approaches designed to study people's experiences. In media psychology it is used to study the experiences of receiving and creating media messages and for analyzing media messages. Qualitative research principles also can be used in content analysis to study message meanings. Ethnographers, grounded theory researchers, and phenomenological researchers developed techniques and procedures employed in contemporary qualitative research. Qualitative researchers produce descriptive findings by analyzing gathered and generated information. This analysis leads to a description of the structures that produce meaning and understanding of media-communicated events. The analyzed information is generated through interviews and focus groups and gathered from media presentations and documents.

Key Words: concepts, ethnography, grounded theory, interviews, media psychology, qualitative research

Introduction

Media psychology is a specialty within the general discipline of psychology. Psychology has different types of specialties: those dealing with particular aspects of human life (cognition, social realm, and life development); those related to psychological practice (clinical, educational, and industrial/organizational); and those that study specific areas of human activity (political, cultural, and media) (Giles, 2003). Media psychology applies the theories and research designs from cognitive, social, and development psychology to the study of media in people's lives. Media psychology research contributes to the knowledge base of these specialty areas and to psychology's general understanding of human beings.

Psychological research is composed of two approaches to knowledge development—extensive or nomothetic and intensive or idiographic. Extensive knowledge is about what is so in general about relations among or within groups of people. Intensive knowledge is about what is so in particular about a person or a local group of people. Extensive knowledge is based on statistical testing to determine if what was found in a sample probably holds true for the sample's population. Intensive knowledge is based on qualitative analysis of information gathered from and about the person or group that was the object of the study. Intensive research aims to produce integrative descriptions of the network of historical, situational, and personal contexts operating in the unit of study.

Although both extensive and intensive research approaches are presented in most of the major research design textbooks in psychology (Kazdin, 2003; Goodwin, 2008), by and large most research in psychology has been aimed at producing extensive knowledge. Media psychology has retained this emphasis on extensive knowledge in its research. Pre-posttest experimental studies have been primarily used in media effects studies. Regression analysis of survey data has been used in cultivation and uses and gratification research. Potter's (2009) recent volume has noted the limits of this research by its isolation of participants from their personal histories with media. Within media studies some have called for greater interest in studying people's interpretative understanding of media messages. Lindlof (1987) edited an early volume on the use of qualitative research for studying the meanings various media messages hold for viewers. Mann and Stewart (2000) have authored a book on the use of qualitative research for studies of computer-mediated communication.

Qualitative research approaches have and can be used to advance the knowledge base of media psychology by intensive studies of the role media has in the life of individuals, the experiences of receiving and producing messages through media (both public and private messages), the experience of community through media exchanges, the role of media in a person's social life, the use of knowledge gained through media, and other aspects of life lived in a time of media saturation. The purpose of this chapter is to describe the qualitative approach to research. The approach has its roots in anthropology and sociology and has been adopted by disciplines such as nursing and education. It provides media psychology with an additional research approach for intensive study of media products and their audiences.

The term *qualitative research* has been used in a broad sense to refer to any research that does not use statistics or uses words instead of numbers as data. In this chapter, qualitative research is used in a more limited sense to refer to a family of research approaches that have been developed to study the understandings people have of the situations and circumstances in which they carry out their lives. These qualitative approaches are specifically intended for the study of people and the understandings or meanings they attribute to events in their social and physical environments. This research assumes that people's actions flow from their understandings of events rather than from the events themselves. Understanding is a mental process and is not directly observable to an outside observer; thus, qualitative findings are derived from what people express about their understandings and inferences based on their actions. Understanding is produced by fitting sensory information into concepts so as to classify its appearance as a kind of something; for example, as *fearful, approachable, useful,* or *unworthy.*[1] There are other classifying sciences, such as botany and qualitative chemistry. Qualitative research differs from these in that its focus is on the classifying processes people use to understand themselves and their social worlds. Because human experience is the subject matter for which qualitative research is designed, this research is not suitable for studies of objects as they are in themselves, independent of how they appear in people's awareness.

Although researchers across the social sciences employ qualitative research approaches, these approaches are particularly important for media psychology research. Media messages are forms of human communication. Thus people need to arrange and classify them into concepts and themes to understand them. The analysis of recipients' experiences of media messages needs to attend to the fund of organizing concepts that recipients employ in understanding messages. Qualitative research has developed a repertoire of processes to identify conceptual structures and describe their role in producing understanding.

The chapter begins with a theoretical discussion of the realm of interest for qualitative studies, the realm of concepts and their qualities. Following this is a brief history of qualitative research and the origins of its different approaches. The next section is about conducting a qualitative study in media psychology. This is the major section and describes the various processes and how they are used in generating qualitative data, analyzing qualitative data, and communicating a study's findings. The concluding section emphasizes the importance of qualitative studies in advancing the field of media psychology.

Qualities and Qualitative Research

Qualitative research studies concepts and their attributes or qualities to develop knowledge about how individuals and groups understand themselves, others, and the world.

(The word *quality* also has the meaning "a standard of excellence" to which products and actions are compared; in qualitative research the word refers to conceptual attributes.) Qualitative research is based on the view that human actions are generated from the *understanding*[2] people have of events and are not simple responses to external stimuli. Between the reception of sense information[3] and one's experience is mental activity that classifies the sense information as representing a kind of something. Understanding something involves experiencing it *as* something; that is, as an instance of a class or concept. Thus, what appears in awareness is a mental production that has already attached meaning to an object[4] by classifying it (Eco, Santambrogio, & Violi, 1988). Classification connects the presently experienced object through memory to previous similar experiences. Because memory includes what have been successful and unsuccessful responses in the past to similar objects, people can anticipate and act on what will be successful in the present situation. Understanding something means knowing to which class it belongs.

Concepts and Understanding

Classifying, also referred to as conceptualizing or categorizing, is the process in which attributes of sensed and felt objects are matched with the attributes that define a class or concept. For example, the attributes of the concept *ball* include an object with a spherical shape. When sense information presents a spherical object, it is classed as a *ball*. Understanding that the object is a *ball* allows that it also has the other attributes attached to this concept, such as usefulness for throwing. The attributes that define a class or concept are also referred to as qualities, traits, characteristics, properties, or features. Concepts, or what was termed *ideas,* have been of interest since classical Greece. Plato held that ideas existed in a special spiritual realm that was independent of the human realm. The actual physical objects people experienced were only shadowy copies of the ideas. Medieval Christianity believed that ideas were unchanging and existed in God's mind. Worldly objects were physical expressions of God's ideas. In general, qualitative research approaches ideas or concepts as human constructions used to organize experiences into kinds. These constructions are embedded in a culture and are passed on through its language to succeeding generations. A culture's stock of concepts is dynamic; some concepts drop out of use and new ones are added. Media messages are made up of images and words that draw on a stockpile of shared concepts to produce entertainment, information, and other kinds of experiences. Although individuals share enough conceptual background to understand media communications, they also maintain their own interpretations of these common concepts and develop their own additional conceptual background.

Individuals accumulate a repertoire of concepts with their attributes through learning. Cultures present a large set of common concepts to their new members through parents, friends, schooling, media, and other social institutions. When a person encounters a new object that cannot be assimilated into an existing concept, he or she develops a new concept to accommodate it (Piaget, 1936/1952). Newly learned concepts occur within the context of previously learned concepts. The nuances of meaning[5] they hold for individuals depend on their connections with other concepts and on where they are placed within the person's conceptual network. People also have different interests and build up special sets of concepts related to these interests. For example, a physicist has many more concepts related to physics in his or her conceptual repertoire than does a nonphysicist. Thus, members within a community group differ somewhat in what concepts they possess and what attributes they attach to these concepts. Because of these differences among the members of a community, individuals can understand the meaning of the same media message differently. Qualitative research is especially useful in studies about how individuals vary in their interpretation of a certain media message.

Concepts are present in the mind in several different forms (Murphy, 2002). Two of these forms are the classical or containment view and the prototype or typicality view. The classical view holds that a concept is represented as lists of necessary properties that an object must have to be classified as an instance of its kind. In this form, a concept has hard and precise boundaries and an object either has the necessary properties or it does not count as a token of the concept type. Mathematical and syllogistic logic require classical concepts. To know how many cats are in a room, it is essential to know what attributes are necessary to classify an object as a *cat*. In comparison, the prototype or typicality view holds that an exemplar or typical member of the category represents a concept. Determining whether or not an object is an instance of a particular kind involves comparing the item to a typical representative image or narrative of the concept. In the prototype view, the borders of a concept are fuzzy. For example, if one's exemplar of the concept *bird* is a robin, a wren would appear to be a *bird,* but there is ambivalence in whether or not an ostrich belongs to the category.

In addition to the distinction between the forms in which concepts are held, there are differences in the ways concepts are organized. Concepts are organized both vertically and horizontally. Vertically, they are related in hierarchical patterns in which less general concepts are placed under more general ones. Mid-range in the hierarchy are concepts about everyday experiences, such as *dogs* and *cats*. Above the mid-range concepts are more abstract, superordinate levels, and below them are more precise, subordinate levels (Rosch, 2000). For example, above the mid-range concept *dog* is the superordinate concept *animal* and below it is the subordinate concept *spaniel*. Horizontally, concepts are cross-linked to one another. The concept *sweet food* might be linked to the concept *overweight*. One of the tasks of research is to demonstrate these relations; for example, the concept *moon* is related to the concept *tides*. Most concepts have multiple branching links to other concepts, and these concepts in turn have multiple links to others. These links lead to complex networks of interconnected concepts.

Language is closely related to concepts. Words are signs that refer to concepts. When someone asks, "What does this word mean?" he is using a shorthand method of asking, "What concept does this word represent?" In this sense, words do not *have* meanings; they *point to* meanings. Most concepts are represented by a word or phrase, but not all (Jackendoff, Bloom, & Wynn, 2002). The meaning of a word or phrase is the concept to which it refers. In general, the sound pattern or alphabetical letters denoting the sound pattern of a word is arbitrarily associated with the concept to which the word points (Saussure, 1907–1911/1966; Danesi, 2007). There is no intrinsic or imitative relationship between a word and the concept it represents. (Onomatopoeic words, such as imitations of animal sounds like *bow-wow* and *meow*, are exceptions.) Acquiring a language involves knowing which concept is culturally attached to a particular sound pattern. Dictionaries are repositories of a language's words with the concepts that a community has attached to them. Not all concepts held by people are represented by a word, and some words are used to represent more than one concept (as is the case with the word *quality*). And, as Foucault's (1969/1973) archeology of words has shown, the words can change the concepts to which they point over time. Communication about concepts occurs through the words that stand for them, but words themselves are not concepts. They are signs that stand for concepts and serve as somewhat invisible vehicles to communicate about concepts and the relations among them. Media are vehicles through which spoken and written words are communicated.

In speaking and writing, concepts are joined together to relay more specific meaning than isolated individual words. A phrase such as *tall person* joins together the concepts *tall* and *person* to communicate a more precise understanding than each separate concept alone. In addition to phrases, languages allow for the sequencing of words into sentences.

Combining worded concepts into sentences produces meaning beyond that contained in the individual words. Grammatical and syntactic rules about word order provide indicators of the relationships that hold among the concepts that make up the sentence. For example, "Straw shelters leak when it rains" communicates a relationship between things that are instances of the concepts *straw shelters, leak,* and *rain*. Sentences are combined into still larger units as paragraphs and then, as in the present case, sometimes into chapters and books, in which the sentences' meanings are linked to produce the overall meaning of the written product. Understanding of the whole product builds up from the individual words through their connections within the sentences and through the connections among sentences. Thus, understanding is the result of a to-and-fro process from the elements to the whole. In qualitative research, developing the understanding of a message by circling back and forth from its parts to its whole is called the *hermeneutic circle* process. This qualitative research process is used for an intense analysis of a single media message, while quantitative content analysis is used for an analysis of a large collection of texts.

Concepts are represented by images as well as words. For example, an octagonal shape can represent the concept *stop,* and the color red can represent *danger*. Peirce (1931, 1936/1958) proposed that representations of concepts occur in three modes—indexicals, icons, and symbols. Indexicals are signs that are physically or causally connected to what they represent, for example, smoke with *fire* and physical symptoms with a disease. Icons are signs in which the image imitates an instance of a concept, such as sound effects in a radio drama and scale models. Symbols are signs arbitrarily connected with concepts. The most important symbols used to indicate concepts are words. Other symbols include color, such as the color yellow in a stoplight connecting with *caution*. All three modes are present in the objects investigated by media psychologists. Motion pictures and television provide a mixture of visual and auditory signs, and understanding their messages involve integrating the conceptual indicators from both modes. Web pages often include trademarks in which visual forms, as well as words, communicate meaning.

Qualitative research studies the meanings people intend in the communications they produce and in the understandings of communications they receive. People communicate meaning through speaking and writing and through productions of motion pictures, videos, email, Twitter, web sites, etc. The various vehicles through which communications occur add their own additional levels of meaning to the message. Media psychology uses qualitative research to uncover the shades of meaning that the authors of messages intend. Meanings and understandings are mental or subjective events that are not directly observable. Qualitative research seeks to study these subjective events in an objective way through a close analysis of the statements and productions that represent them.

Qualitative and Quantitative Research

Qualitative research is frequently distinguished from quantitative research. One of the differentiating features is that, in general, quantitative research works with classically defined concepts and qualitative research works with prototypes of typical exemplar-defined concepts. Quantitative research transforms concepts into classical definitions by specifying and operationalizing them into lists of required properties. For example, the *Diagnostic and Statistical Manual of Mental Disorders* (American Psychiatric Association, 2000) has converted prototype concepts, such as *anxiety* and *depression* into classical ones by specifying the attributes required for being included in the particular diagnostic category. When required attributes of a concept are commonly accepted within a discipline, objects can be consistently categorized across the discipline. For example, different psychologists had assigned varied attributes to the concept *schizophrenia* until the *DSM* established the current set of necessary attributes.

Classical definitions make concepts available for counts and statistical operations. By having precise borders, counts of how many people have an instance of a concept are possible. This modality has some value in analyzing media events, although it does not provide the same depth as qualitative research. For example, to count how many in a group watching a television program display *aggression* requires knowing what is included inside its boundary and what is excluded. Classically defined concepts appear in quantitative research as "variables." When the interest is simply noting whether or not a subject is an instance of a category, the variable is termed a *categorical, nominal,* or *qualitative* variable. Examples of a "qualitative" variable or concept used in quantitative research are *Protestant, Catholic,* and *Jewish,* which fall under the superordinate concept *religion.*

In addition, classical definitions allow some concepts to be scaled. These concepts are divided into subordinate concepts of, for example, *high aggression,* *mid-range aggression,* and *low aggression.* Scaled subordinate concepts can use numbers to represent the extent or amount of the concept. Once scaled subordinate concepts are represented by numbers, mathematical and statistical procedures can be used to test a relationship among subordinate scores on a concept with subordinate scores on other concepts. Such calculations can also produce a probability statement about how likely the relationships determined to hold among concepts in an examined group are likely to hold among the members of the population as a whole.

In the early decades of the 20th century, psychology followed the physical science model in which only publically observable data were acceptable for scientific inquiry. Only stimuli and responses were observable and, thus, mental operations (in the black box of the mind) could not be investigated. With the "cognitive turn" in psychology beginning in the 1970s, quantitative as well as qualitative research began to attend to mental operations. However, proponents differed in the approaches they used to study mental phenomena. Quantitative research translated mental phenomena, such as *desire, motivation, fear,* and *depression,* into classical definitions termed *constructs.* The conceptual constructs were linked to sets of certain behavioral observations or to a set of answers to an instrument designed to recognize the presence and extent of the mental phenomena. Valid instruments were held to reflect the meaning of the original, usually prototypic concept. In contrast, qualitative researchers approach mental concepts in their prototypic form.

Another property that distinguishes quantitative research from qualitative research is its focus is on the relationships among concepts as they hold for groups of people rather than on how they hold for individuals. Subordinate scores are collected from groups (see Chapter 23) and the mean and distribution of those scores are compared with those of other groups or those within the same group. The scores are abstracted from the current context of the individual group members. The nuanced and special meaning a concept has in a particular situation for each person is unexamined, as is the relationship of that concept to others in a particular context. Quantitative research used to assume that the conceptual relations were universal (the same for all people). In recent decades, it has refined theory to notice that the same concepts may have different personal meanings and relationships depending on certain characteristics of the person, such as gender, ethnicity, education, culture, and income.

Qualitative research focuses on the way concepts give meaning to individuals in particular social interactions; it is also widely used in analyzing individuals' interactions with films, videogames (see Chapter 7) and other media experiences.

Qualitative research focuses on historically and socially situated conditions and how the individuals within a setting conceptually interpret them. Qualitative research is interested in the *qualities* people assign to their concepts. The qualities that individuals assign to a conceptual definition overlap enough to allow for a common understanding, but they also contain personal differences. Most often qualitative researchers attend, not to concepts classifying physical objects, but to concepts for understanding oneself and others, such as values, social roles, aims, emotions, and cares. Concepts of this kind resist transformation into classical definitions. They retain fuzzy boundaries and ambiguity and are best known through examples. Qualitative researchers examine complex personal situations and media messages in which experiences are generated through the interactions of multiple concepts. Some studies seek to draw out the operating concepts or themes by illustrating their presence with examples from personal or media texts. Other studies seek to develop new, unnamed concepts and their attributes that are operating to produce situated understandings. Later sections of the chapter describe the processes used by qualitative researchers to fill in the meanings associated with a person's social and personal concepts and generate prototypical descriptions of new concepts.

The Development of Qualitative Research

Before the 1970s, qualitative research approaches were primarily limited to the disciplines of anthropology and parts of sociology. In the other social science disciplines, including psychology, research employed an adapted physical science model to study behavioral responses to controlled stimuli. Under the influences of the social movements of the 1960s and 1970s (Schwandt, 2000), the model was criticized for its neglect of the uniquely human aspects of people, including their thoughts, feelings, and desires (Polkinghorne, 1983). In response to this critique, the social-science disciplines developed two responses. One was the development of cognitive psychology (Neisser, 1966) in which constructs of aspects of the cognitive realm were developed and linked to publically observable behaviors. This response allowed the disciplines to continue to use the research techniques that produced data

in numeric form and analyze data statistically. The other response was qualitative research. It held that the meanings people assign to their experienced events are integrated and contextualized and are better grasped through natural language than through counts. It proposed that isolating meanings from their appearances within persons and tabulating these isolations across persons missed how they functioned within a particular person in a particular context.

In the 1970s qualitative research was taken up in most of the social-science disciplines. It was a minority movement in the disciplines and remains so today. It passed through a period in the 1980s of what was termed the "paradigm wars" in which discipline members who were strongly committed to the quantitative approach strongly resisted qualitative research. These members were concerned that qualitative studies lacked the precision provided by numeric data, were not protected from biases by methods of design, and did not provide statistically based tests of generalization. Today qualitative research is generally accepted in the disciplines as an alternative research approach, although a secondary one those students can learn after they have mastered the quantitative approach.

The expansion of qualitative research was aided by the introduction into the United States of European existential philosophy (Heidegger, 1927/1962; Sartre, 1943/1965), whose focus was on human experience. Another contributing field was English ordinary language philosophy, which recognized that the words used to talk about people differ from those used to talk about physical objects (Austin, 1975). These philosophical contributions provided a theoretical rationale for studies aimed at describing the ways in which people experience themselves, others, and their social environment.

In expanding the use of qualitative research by the social science disciplines, sources for how to conduct this type of research were consulted. Prior qualitative studies were examined for models. Works of Piaget, Kohlberg, and Maslow and others (see Wertz 2011) provided useful examples. Of most importance were the disciplines that were already using qualitative approaches, such as anthropology and the Chicago School of sociology. Although some nascent psychological research (e.g., Wundt's *Folk-Psychology* and phenomenological studies by students of Brentano) used introspection and a type of qualitative research, they were not consulted in the early development of contemporary qualitative approaches (Polkinghorne, 2004).

Ethnography

Qualitative research in anthropology is termed *ethnography* research. In its beginnings in the early 20th century, its purpose was to understand the customs and organizations of foreign cultures. Researchers spent time in the culture under study (field study) and gathered data through observation and informant interviews; these methods of data gathering are still used in qualitative research. The template through which the data were analyzed was composed of Western categories. In the 1970s Geertz (1973) proposed that ethnography should change its perspective from presenting an outsider's or *-etic* view of a culture to presenting the view of the culture from the perspective of the people living in the culture, that is, an *-emic* view. He noted that such a view would require *thick descriptions* from inhabitants themselves and called this insider's knowledge *local knowledge.*

Current ethnography has expanded its interests to include studies of a diverse range of local cultures and communities, including classrooms, business organizations, and other groups. It is also producing life histories, which study the effect of a culture's values and beliefs on the life of a member or group in that culture. For example, such a history might show how American culture's beliefs impinge on the life of a member who has a disability (Frank, 2000). Ethnography is one of the major current qualitative research approaches and is now used by researchers in most of the social science disciplines. Altheide (1996), in his *Qualitative Media Analysis,* recommended the use of ethnography as the primary approach to use in analysis of visual/oral presentations and textual documents. Ethnographers can spend time with a family to observe the interactions that take place regarding television viewing or serve as a participant– observer in a Facebook topic, such as the communications about a campus shooting. Lemish and Tidhar (2001) interviewed 44 Israeli mothers and experts about how a program designed for global children's audiences, *Teletubbies,* was given a local interpretation in Israel.

Grounded Theory

Researchers associated with the Chicago School of Sociology used qualitative methods to investigate urban phenomena, such as political meetings, halfway houses, and youth sports. It was concerned with the effects of social structures on the lives of the people who were involved in them. A theoretical base was provided by Mead's (1934) symbolic interactionism. Symbolic interactionism holds that people learn what the symbols and words used by members of their culture mean or stand for through communicating with others. Human actions are based on these meanings rather than on the uninterpreted events themselves. One of the most important figures in the spread of qualitative research was Strauss, who was a student of Mead.

Strauss was a professor in the nursing department in the medical school at the University of California (San Francisco). Strauss and his colleague Glaser conducted a qualitative study (B. Glaser & Strauss, 1965) of nurses' interpreted responses to the death of a patient on their ward. They were interested in the meanings the patient's death had for them, and in the emotional and behavioral responses that followed based on these meanings. The study departed from the usual approach in the department in which a theory about social behavior was reduced to a testable hypothesis and data were collected through surveys to determine whether or not they supported the hypothesis.

The rise of qualitative research in sociology in the 1970s can be traced to the work of Strauss (B. G. Glaser & Strauss, 1967). The Glaser and Strauss study began without a theory. They began by gathering data through observations and interviews about the meaning of the patient's death for the nurses on the ward. From a careful and close examination of these data, they inferred a conceptual description of the examined nurses' response to the death event. They termed their research approach *grounded theory* because rather than test the fit of a prior understanding of how the nurses would respond, their theory followed from and was derived from or grounded in the nurses' descriptions.

Despite the deviation of Glaser and Strauss from mainstream sociological research, their study was well received by the academic community. Requests were made for them to describe how they produced their results. In response, Glaser and Strauss published *Discovery of Grounded Theory* (1967). This book included techniques such as theoretical sampling, constant comparative analysis of data, and conceptual coding. It noted that the purpose of grounded theory research was not to test preexisting theory, but to generate new theory. The book has served as an important source for techniques used by qualitative researchers. The term *grounded theory* has come to refer to two different things—one, a theory that is derived from data rather than one based on prior assumptions; and two, the set techniques used by Glaser and Strauss in their research. A study that simply employs the techniques, but is not aimed at producing a data-derived theory, falls short of the intentions of grounded theory research. In 1990, Strauss coauthored with Corbin *Basics of Qualitative Research* (Strauss & Corbin, 1990) describing how to use the techniques developed for grounded theory research. The book was revised in 1998 and in 2008 (after Strauss died in 1996). It has been widely used as a qualitative research textbook across the social science disciplines. Grounded theory was used to study themes in the press coverage of the emergence of Twitter usage (Arceneaux & Weiss, 2010). They found ambivalence in the coverage that paralleled the earlier press reception of the introduction of new forms of electronic communication.

Glaser, Strauss's coauthor of the *Discovery of Grounded Theory* book, objected to what he held to be the mechanization of the grounded theory approach in the *Basics of Qualitative Research* book. In 1992 he published his own book, *The Basics of Grounded Theory Analysis* (B. G. Glaser, 1992). In his book, he argued that deriving theory from data did not depend on following a set of rules, but on the sensitivity and creativity of the researcher. Glaser has continued to publish and speak about his approach and a second wing of grounded theory representing his ideas has formed, which is called *Glaserian Ground Theory*.

In the last decade practitioners of grounded theory research have proposed that the early grounded theory researchers had neglected to give attention to how the beliefs, needs, and situatedness of researchers contributed to their findings. These early practitioners assumed the theories they produced were objective descriptions of the experiences of the situations they studied. Recent practitioners (Charmaz, 2000, 2006) have advanced the position that the researchers' personal and cultural assumptions contribute to their findings. The data generated and the order and organization they find in the data occur through a lens that reflects their personal backgrounds. Researchers' findings do not describe situations as they are, independent of the researchers' own viewpoints; rather, findings are what appears from the researchers' particular perspectives. This position is called *constructionism* and proposes that in writing up findings, qualitative researchers should include a reflexive section in which they describe characteristics of their background that could have influenced their findings. Researchers need to be sensitive to how cultural backgrounds affect their own and others' interpretation of media messages. The Internet allows circulation of messages to audiences whose cultural assumptions vary

from the sender of the messages. Researchers using grounded theory are challenged by the knowledge that their participants may understand and respond to the same message differently than the researcher does. Grounded theorists attend to and describe the voice of the participants rather than assuming that participants' experiences match their own.

Another recent development in grounded theory research emphasizes the effect of situational forces on the interpretations people give to events. In situational analysis (Clark, 2005), maps of the surrounding environment (from international, national, state, city, to local events) are used to describe how outside influences contribute to the understandings and actions of the participants who are the focus of the study.

Phenomenology

There are two types of qualitative phenomenological research; one is labeled *empirical phenomenological research* and the other is labeled *existential* or *interpretive phenomenological research*. Both draw heavily on European philosophers—empirical phenomenology on Husserl and interpretive phenomenology on Heidegger. Empirical phenomenology was introduced in the 1970s and contributed to the general expansion in the use of qualitative approaches. Interpretative phenomenology was introduced in the 1990s, but it appears that its use by qualitative researchers has surpassed the empirical approach.

Although qualitative research approaches were advancing in most social science disciplines, psychology remained less accepting of them. However, the introduction of phenomenological research approaches came to the social sciences through a psychologist. Phenomenology is the study of phenomena; that is, what appears in awareness. The early 20th century philosopher, Husserl, proposed that what is experienced is not raw sense data; instead, what is experienced has already been identified as a kind of something. That is, the mind identifies an object as an instance of a category before it presents it to awareness. For example, what is experienced is a ball rather than uncategorized spherically outlined raw data. Husserl's early work focused on what he held were innate categories shared by all humans, such as mathematical categories; for example, what appears is a three-party group, not three independent objects (1913/1973). His later work focused on culturally learned categories that vary among people (1937/1970). Husserl developed several techniques for studying the categorizing activity of the mind. He held that the researcher's concern about whether or not what appeared in awareness represented something that existed outside awareness had to be held in abeyance (reduction). He further described the technique of imaginative variation, in which one holds a mental image representing a category, for example a *chair,* and imaginatively removes parts and changes color to determine the necessary properties one holds for an object to be classified as a chair. Imaginative variation can be used in media research as a technique to clarify a viewer's understanding of a media message. For example, determining if a viewer understood that a character in a motion picture received proper punishment for his deeds, the researcher could ask the viewer to imagine that the character's race was different, if the character was of the other gender, if he or she gave back the stolen property, and so on. Through the imaginative variation, a clearer understanding was gained of the viewer's idea of "just punishment."

Giorgi (1970), a psychologist who taught at Duquesne University, introduced a qualitative research approach to phenomenological inquiry in 1970. His approach was adapted from Husserl's philosophy and included several techniques used in Husserl's studies. Like Husserl, the aim of Giorgi's phenomenological research was to carefully describe the structures or definitions of the categories or concepts that the mind employed so as to show the received sense information as kinds of things. Giorgi (1985) conducted an exemplar study on the category *learning.* His purpose was to determine what it means for an activity to be classified as learning; that is, what are the essential properties an experience needs to have to be interpreted as a learning activity? Although Husserl's studies were based on his reflective observations of his own mental classifying activity, Giorgi used interviews of others in which he asked for reports of examples of life activities that participants experienced as learning activities. He analyzed the transcribed texts of the interviews by dividing them into meaning-units. He first examined the texts from each participant interviewed to note the common properties used by each individual to identify an activity as learning (individual or situated structural analysis). Then he compared the results across the collection of descriptions given by the individual participants to produce a general description (general structural analysis) of the essential features or essence of the concept *learning* (Polkinghorne, 1989). Giorgi established the *Journal of Phenomenological Psychology,* in which articles using his phenomenological approach are published. He has remained as an active participant in the development of qualitative research and graduates of his program are teaching and directing phenomenological dissertations at a number of universities across America.

The second type of phenomenological research, interpretive phenomenology, was developed in the 1990s. The development of interpretive phenomenological research is closely associated with the discipline of nursing and the writings of Benner (1994). Although it was first used to study *caring,* it is now used across the social science disciplines to study a variety of experiences. Interpretive phenomenology traces its roots to the ideas in the 1927 book *Being and Time* by Heidegger, an existentialist philosopher. Heidegger, who was Husserl's student, instead of looking at general classification schemes shared across people, focused on the uniqueness of individuals. He held that people's personal histories and interpersonal interactions led to differences in the way individuals interpret or give meaning to the same objects and events. Interpretive phenomenology conducts intense studies of the way individuals understand and respond to important life events, such as the birth of a child or the occurrence of a debilitating injury. When more than one person is examined in a study, the emphasis is on the different ways they interpret similar life events. The techniques used are similar to those developed to produce a grounded theory—interviews, coding processes, and identification of themes—but they serve a different purpose, which is the production of an integrated description of an individual's understanding and response to critical events in his or her life. As applied to media psychology, one can rightly say that when a movie is shown to a theater full of people, every person sees a different movie. A phenomenological researcher would interview different members of the audience to discern what each person understood from the film and show how that unique understanding is linked to the individual's unique life experiences.

Integration of Approaches

In the decades since the use of qualitative research approaches has expanded across the social science disciplines, new approaches have been added to the three initial ones, including narrative research, Foucauldian analysis, conversational analysis, and memory work (Willig, 2001). The initial approaches have been revised and amended, as in constructionism and situational approaches in grounded theory and life histories in ethnography. Ethnography and grounded theory are now used throughout the social sciences. For example, in media psychology, ethnography has been used to study viral messages about political figures on blogs (Healey, 2010), grounded theory to study a blog content (Sanderson, 2008), and phenomenological research to study responses to playing a computer game (Whitty, Young, & Goodings, 2011).

The attachment of specific techniques and procedures to specific qualitative approaches has loosened. Coding and purposive sampling from grounded theory have been used by some researchers who identify their studies as phenomenological or ethnographic. Qualitative researchers have begun to use techniques and cognitive tools from across the approaches in solving problems specific to their studies. The various techniques have been gathered in books using the generic title *Qualitative Research* (Denzin & Lincoln, 2008). Because the use of processes has spread beyond their original approach, the names of the approaches have come more to signify the type of question addressed by the research than by the techniques used. For example, an ethnographic study is one that addresses questions related to a community's cultural environment as experienced by its members. A grounded theory is one directed at producing insights about the way social processes influence participants. A phenomenological study seeks to answer how individuals organize their experiences (Patton, 2002).

Qualitative research is guided by a set of principles rather than a set of detailed instructions about how a study must be conducted. The principles include, among others, paying attention to the participants' understanding, focusing on the total context that frames the understanding, looking for the conceptual themes and their dimensions that underlay the understanding, and clearly describing and communicating the understanding to readers. How a researcher implements these principles will vary depending on the research question under investigation, the resources available to the researcher, and the researcher's skills. Almost all qualitative research includes three tasks—generating and gathering information, analyzing this information, and communicating findings. However, the manner in which each of these is carried out varies in different studies. The tradition provides examples of how researchers have accomplished the tasks; nevertheless, the researcher must judge which example is appropriate for a particular study. Each qualitative study is a journey from a question to an answer. Because the questions asked are special to each study, the paths to those answers are different.

A study is analogous to a hiker walking to a destination. Along the way rocks, brush, and hills block the way and the hiker has to find ways around them to reach the destination. The hiker has studied how previous hikers solved these kinds of problems and he or she can try out these solutions, but they may not solve his specific problem; the hiker might have to develop a new solution. Because the hiker is headed to a different destination that takes him over different terrain, he cannot simply retrace the steps of previous hikers.

Qualitative researchers lay out a plan for going from question to answer, but problems often arise on the way. Access to selected respondents is closed; the interviews are not producing rich data; the analysis does not coalesce; and time and resources run out. The plan has to be adjusted to achieve an answer. As this is an answer-driven enterprise rather than a method-driven one, what counts is the value of the arrived-at answer. In this regard, conducting a qualitative study has some resemblance to producing a worthy painting. What is important is the value of the final product rather than the steps used to produce it. Studying and mastering the techniques and processes used by those who have produced valued works is crucial to being able to produce one's own product of worth. But simply imitating what one's predecessors have done is likely to produce a second-rate product. The following sections of this chapter offer descriptions of the various techniques and processes used by previous qualitative researchers in producing answers to their research questions.

Doing Qualitative Research

Qualitative research studies human experience, an area that has unique characteristics that differ from the characteristics of biology and physics. Human experience is not publically observable and access to it is only directly available to the individual whose experience it is. Thus, qualitative researchers gather information about participants' experience through their subjective descriptions of their experiences and through interpreting observations of their behavior. Researchers draw on their capacity to assume the perspective of another person and on their assumption that others' experiences are similar to their own and are composed of such things as beliefs, emotions, and motives (the theory-of-mind) (Wellman, Cross, & Watson, 2001). Although both quantitative and qualitative researchers aim to develop knowledge, qualitative studies are based on different principles because of the special properties of their area of study.

Many terms used in qualitative research have been borrowed from quantitative research, but the meanings attached to them have been changed. Just as quantitative research uses the word *significance* to represent the idea *likely generalizable to a population* rather than *important,* qualitative research employs terms such as *data, sample,* and *theory* to mean something different than they do in quantitative research. In qualitative research, *data* refers to information in textual or visual form gathered for a study rather than numeric scores. *Sample* refers to the purposely selected participants rather than a representative subset of a population. *Theory* refers to a general description of what participants in the studied situation are experiencing rather than an abstract speculation of what holds across situations from which hypotheses can be derived and tested as confirmation or refutation of the theory. The use of these homonyms could blur the differences in research principles that guide qualitative and quantitative approaches.

Qualitative research is a descriptive rather than a predictive science. Its goal is to produce revealing textual portraits that display the complexity of participants' experiences. Changing the meta-phor, one can say that the aim is to describe the threads that run through experiences and the experiential tapestry woven with the threads. Effective descriptions give their readers insight into the way a situation appeared to the participants; they allow readers to assume the participants' place and view through their eyes. One of the interests of media psychology is in understanding the experiences of the receivers of media messages. Producing such understanding is one the primary purposes of qualitative research.

The development of a description does not proceed through a series of steps in which one task, such as data or information gathering, is completed before moving on to the next step. Although in quantitative research all the data need to be collected before they can be submitted to statistical analysis, in qualitative studies researchers circle through information gathering, analysis, and findings. The circling stops when the description has become sufficiently formed that its parts have coalesced into an integrated whole.

The following subsections present descriptions of various techniques and processes that have been used by qualitative researchers. Often these presentations are temporally ordered according what is done first, then second, and so on. Such an organization begins with data gathering, then moves to data analysis, and concludes with writing up findings. But because developing an answer to the research question and the form the answer will take (organizing themes, narratives, etc.) guide how the analytic work will be conducted as well as from whom and how information is gathered, the presentation begins with findings, then addresses analysis, and finally describes information gathering.

Findings

Qualitative research findings are reported as textual descriptions of participants' experiences related to an event or activity. They are not simple summaries of the gathered information, but presentations that depict the conceptual patterns and structures that give organization to the information. A finding is an answer to a specific research question. Questions imply the kind of answer sought. For example, a media psychologist might ask a question of an 8-year-old boy playing the computer game *Darksiders.* The research might differentiate between the questions asked of the young boy and questions asked of an older boy playing the game, or he or she might ask both participants the same questions and highlight their different experiences. Questions asking about changes in experience over time have findings that take the form of descriptions about process; that is, stages and steps through which individuals and groups move, or stories that connect earlier experiences to later ones. For example, the findings of Kübler-Ross' qualitative study *On Death and Dying* (1969) identified stages of experiencing grief. Questions asking about the outline or frame of an experience will likely be answered by thematic portrayals tied together into a local theory. A recent study by Lehti (2011) of political blogs proposed that they could be organized into five types, including diary, scrapbook, notice-board, essay, and polemic. The form of the anticipated description indicates what information will be gathered and the analytical process that will be used.

Findings need to do more than report the conceptual themes or temporal patterns; they need to describe the attributes or qualities that compose them. They need to supply contextual information about the situation studied. They also need to support their organizing concepts with examples from the collected information or data. Unlike reports of quantitative findings, an extensive portion of a qualitative report is taken up with description of findings. What was done, and the analytic trials, as well as the final conclusions, are integrated into the text rather than separated into "methods" and "analysis" sections. Reports of qualitative studies have traditionally been written in narrative style and are monograph length.

Journal editors often require authors of contemporary publication of qualitative studies to squeeze the reports into the American Psychological Association (APA) format (Introduction, Method, Results, and Conclusion sections) and limit the length to around eight printed pages. The APA format was designed for reporting quantitative findings (Bazerman, 1987) and assumed peer reviewers would have a prior understanding of quantitative designs and statistical procedures. This assumed understanding allowed for the reports to short-cut descriptions of the researcher's various excursions on the way to developing findings. The case differs with qualitative research. Without the narrative about the movement from research question to research findings, the reader is not taken along on the process that led to the finding. Because of this disconnect between the nature of qualitative analysis and the structure of the preestablished format, findings reported in APA format often appear as having no evidential backing and questionable validity.

Research reports take the form of arguments. A knowledge claim is offered and supporting evidence for the claim is given. The author considers evidence against the claim and shows why it does not defeat the claim. In quantitative research the author begins with an answer or claim (a hypothesis) and then evidence is collected to test if the claim can be supported. The finding is a statement that the hypothesis is or is not supported by the collected evidence.

Qualitative research proceeds differently. It begins with a question, but not an answer, or claim, or hypothesis to be tested. It gathers information related to the question, and analyzes and reanalyzes the information; on the way, it produces an answer. Its reports tell the reader about the progression of moves by the researcher and how it led to the development of an answer. It moves through a series of information-gathering and trial answers. More information is gathered to check on the adequacy of the provisional answer. The information serves to correct or expand the dimensions of the provisional findings. Thus, instead of proposing a claim (hypothesis) and testing it with data, qualitative research gathers information from which an answer is proposed and then gathers more information to test this answer. There is a spiraling movement toward the proposed answer: gathering information to test the answer, making adjustments to the answer as a result of the new information, and returning to gather more information. The goal of the movement is to achieve an answer to the research question that best fits the gathered information.

Qualitative findings are local in character. They are descriptions of participants' experiences in a particular situation, such as watching a film, attending a play, or working in an office. Their knowledge claims reflect the information gathered for the study. The claims are not about people or situations that were not specifically part of the study. Thus, qualitative research is only able to provide answers to questions that ask about explicit events and settings. For example, instead of asking, "How do executives experience producing a motion picture?" the question needs to ask, "How did executive John Jones or the three Paramount executives experience producing the motion picture *Space Men Invade Los Angeles*?" Qualitative research produces a high level of detail and in-depth answers. These bring attention to the distinctiveness of the social and physical environments, the effect of a setting's history, and the weight of the participants' personalities.

Quantitative findings are most often intended to be general. Their knowledge claims are about relationships among variables (concepts) that embrace populations. They test statements such as, "Executives have higher IQ scores on average than nonexecutive employees." It is not enough to demonstrate that the average IQ scores of the 50 executives, whose scores were available, have on average a higher IQ score than the 50 tested nonexecutives. This information is only descriptive. Inferential statistics must support the claim that the population of executives is higher on average. The study assumes that the executives and nonexecutives examined were representative of their populations and that the IQ scores of the populations of executives and those of the nonexecutives are close to being distributed normally. Statistical calculations can then establish a probability that the difference that was found in the examined executive and nonexecutive participants would hold across their populations. The power of the calculations to produce a high enough probability (95%) to be considered support for the claim of differences in the populations depends on the size of the population and the likely size of the difference in IQs in the two groups. Claims tested in quantitative research relate to differences in the average scores from the members of a group or population. But the scores of individuals in these groups are distributed around the average. Individual scores other than the average are termed *noise* or *errors*. In contrast, it is the individuals that are of interest in qualitative studies.

Qualitative research works with small numbers of participants so that it can attend to the complexities and combinations of concepts operating in a setting.

These participants are specially selected as sources of needed information, not randomly chosen as representatives of a population. Qualitative researchers work directly with prototypic concepts rather than with operationalized conversions into scaled classical concepts. Thus, their processes are not intended to lead to statistical generalizations. Instead of lifting concepts out of individual lives and comparing their extent across aggregated groups, qualitative research seeks to understand individuals and operating groups in specific, historical situations; that is, to build local knowledge. Because the purposes of qualitative and quantitative studies differ in the kind of knowledge they pursue, it is inappropriate to critique one for not being enough like the other.

Local or intensive knowledge is an integrated understanding of how a particular situation appeared to its participants. It is not a claim that participants in a similar situation will experience it in the same way as those in the studied event. Rather, it is a declaration that, from the position of the researcher, this is the way those particular participants experienced the event. Reports of local knowledge provide readers with a vicarious understanding of what it was like for the participants to be in a situation. Such understandings add to readers' background of memories through which they attend to other situations. Local knowledge serves as a lens that draws into focus various areas of interest about how people are experiencing other similar events. It allows for recognition of the differences and similarities of experiences between the event described in a research report and the present one. Aspects of participants' experience of the present event that would not have been noticed before reading the research report are now perceived. Reports can serve to shed light on conceptual areas at work that had been hidden from the viewer in the past. Local knowledge descriptions do not inform about what will be found, but it sharpens the vision to see more deeply what is there.

Analysis

Analysis is the in-depth inspection of items to identify their parts and structures. What is termed *qualitative analysis* consists of both separating something into its constituent elements (analysis) and reorganizing these (synthesis) into an integrated whole. Altheide writes that "analysis consists of extensive reading, sorting, and searching through your materials; comparing within categories, coding, and adding key words and concepts; and then writing minisummaries of categories" (1996). Qualitative analysis is not mechanical and

is contrasted to statistical analysis in which computers can test relationships within numerical data. In qualitative studies, the researcher uses his or her mental effort to build concepts that give order to the information's surface and hidden meanings. Doing qualitative analysis is similar to analysis conducted by historians and literary critics. From their studied collections of documents they identify historical patterns of development or literary arrangements of topics that order the content of the documents. The purpose of the analysis is to produce an answer to the research question.

Qualitative research in media psychology is used to study both the content of media messages (delivered through a large variety of formats) and peoples' experiences of receiving and those of producing media messages. In both cases, analysis requires intensive engagement with the information in the messages or the information from the person based on observations or dialog. To review and re-review this information, it needs to be placed into a form that allows the researcher to move back and forth through the information so as to gather together similar elements. Most often this is done through translating the information into text. Interviews are transcribed and visual/oral presentations are broken down into stills with transcriptions of the accompanying dialog. The text can include images as well as words. The text, which is the collection of all the gathered and generated information, becomes the object to be analyzed. The text that is analyzed can be scrutinized by others to determine if it supports the researcher's final analysis. A grounded theory final analysis of a writers' meeting of a weekly television show would give an integrated description of:

- The external pressures of time, financing, and diminished viewership
- The personal values and needs of those at the meeting and the roles taken in the group by each member
- The process steps through which the task of the group was accomplished (or not accomplished)
- An account of the conflicting agendas of the members
- A report of the themes that gave organization to the discussions

A qualitative analysis of an episode or several episodes of a television show such as *Two and a Half Men* would involve a description of the main characters and their relationships to one another, the internal dynamics and tensions within the characters (if any), the cultural assumptions on which the comedy is based, the cultural types the characters represent, the flow from the beginning of the episode to its ending, and so on.

The information to be analyzed consists of a collection of examples of the experience being investigated. The task of the analytic process is to locate the conceptual organization that gives structure to the examples. In other terms, the job is to distinguish the abstract *types* or concepts from their *tokens,* which are specific textual instances of the type. This kind of analysis employs an inductive thinking process in which a number of instances are brought together under a concept or idea. Snyder, a historian of science, paraphrases Whewell's (1794–1866) description of induction. "We use our ideas and concepts as the 'thread' on which we string the facts about the world, the pearls" (Snyder, 2011, p. 252). The "facts about the world" in qualitative research are the observations and interview information gathered by the researcher. The ideas and concepts come from the researcher's mental processes. The most difficult aspect of analyzing qualitative information is creating or finding ideas that give order to the qualitative facts. Whewell noted that, "In many cases finding the correct concept to use in colligating the facts is the most difficult and most crucial part of discovering a new theory" (Snyder, 2011, p. 253).

Inductive reasoning as been critiqued by Popper (1959), among others for not producing certain knowledge about membership in classically represented concepts. For example, observing a number of white swans does not prove the statement, "All swans are white." At some future time, one might observe a black swan and falsify the original claim. Quantitative research accepted Popper's critique and adopted the hypothetical/deductive format in which research studies are designed to falsify a hypothesized statement. Qualitative research, which describes what is observed, does not generate statements about universals. It might state, "I observed 12 birds on the lake behind my house last evening; four were swans, five were geese, and three were ducks." The ordering of the observations by concepts is an inductive process in which the birds that shared similar attributes were compared with and distinguished from those that did not share the attributes. "A qualitative document analysis seeks to illustrate relevant categories" (Altheide, 1996, p. 22).

Conducting an analysis of qualitative information requires advance preparation. Preparation involves a mastery of the general field, in this case media psychology, and an additional mastery of previous research (both qualitative and quantitative) that has addressed questions similar to the specific research question asked in a study. Such mastery helps researchers understand the subtleties and depth that can be found in a text; that is, researchers develop a *theoretical sensitivity* (B. G. Glaser, 1978) to the intricacies the information holds. Qualitative researchers approach the analysis without preconceived notions about what they will find.

This preparation differs from the literature reviews done in quantitative research. There, the purpose is to develop a statement (hypothesis) to be tested and match the definition of the statement's classically defined terms with the definitions established in the discipline. In qualitative research, the literature review increases the acuity to recognize similarities and differences among collected instances. Preparation also involves mastery of the special skills used for conducting a qualitative study. Successful information production, such as making and recording observations, in-depth interviewing, and managing focus groups, is the result of learned skills; it improves with practice. If software is used to manage a study's information, researchers should have experience with its functions before beginning a research project. A well-conducted analysis requires high cognitive levels of pattern recognition, which is a skill that can be developed through training and practice on exercise texts (Polkinghorne, 2010).

Different strategies have been proposed for analyzing qualitative information (Gibbs, 2007; Bernard & Ryan, 2010); that is, moving from a collection of examples to descriptions of their ordering categories. All the strategies include first reading through the whole collected text before returning to its parts (the hermeneutic circle) and focusing on categories that relate to the research question. After grasping the entire text, an often-used strategy involves breaking down the text into its phrases, sentences, or paragraphs (termed *meaning* units by Giorgi) and identifying these units as instances of a concept relevant to answering the research question. This process is termed *coding* the units. The name *coding* was used in earlier sociological research and came into qualitative research through Glaser and Strauss in their *Discovery of Grounded Theory* book (Fieldling & Lee, 1998; see also Chapter 2). The process is compared to indexing a book in which items mentioned in the book are gathered together as instances of concepts listed in the index. After initially breaking down the text into first-level conceptual units (open coding), these units are examined to determine if they can be organized under higher-level concepts (axial coding). Axial coding is repeated to see if they can be fit into still higher-level concepts. Axial coding leads to the identification of a few major concepts that give an overall organization of the textual examples into types or kinds. The concepts are defined by giving the attributes associated with them; their meaning is illustrated with examples from the text. For example, in the television program *How I Met Your Mother,* the major concepts discovered might include the tension between the restraints and happiness that come from making commitments and the isolation and indulgence of making no commitments. The final step is the production of a theory about the whole textual content by description of the relationships among the final concepts.

Coding is a technique that can help in analyzing qualitative data, although it does not do the analysis itself (Saldaña, 2009). The decisions about what categories and subcategories are assigned to textual instances depend on the skill and creativity of the researcher. There are other approaches to analysis besides Glaser and Strauss' coding system. Some qualitative researchers give the text multiple readings during which they note possible overarching categories. They return to the textual detail to check and refine their categories. They begin the hermeneutic circular process from the perspective of the whole and then focus on the parts. This differs from the coding technique, which begins by focusing on the parts and building up to an understanding of the whole. Another approach to analysis begins with a prior set of concepts and uses the text to illustrate the operation of these concepts. Studies that interpret text through psychoanalytic, Marxist, or sociological concepts (Berger, 2005) are examples. In these cases, conceptual organization is not derived from the text, but is already decided before analysis is undertaken. Traditional qualitative research does not approach a study with predetermined categories. Instead it develops categories that reflect the organization that exists in the information analyzed. However, once developed, qualitative researchers need to provide quotes and other evidence from the information that lend support to the operation of the categories in the text.

In many qualitative studies, analysis takes place in phases. Some information is gathered and then it is analyzed. From the initial analysis, organizing categories are identified and then used in selecting sources for additional information that can expand as well as challenge the initial categories. This is termed an *iterative* process and is often used in interview studies. After one or two interviews have been conducted, the audio or visual tapes are transcribed and analyzed. The analysis produces questions about the categorical organization of the interviews. Further interviews with the same interviewees are conducted to clarify and explore further their understandings of the situation being investigated. Other people, whose experiences are expected to differ from those first interviewed, are also selected for interviews. In this approach the evolving analysis informs what additional information is needed to move the analysis forward to a conclusion.

Media psychology studies are often interested in the analysis of messages as well as people's responses to messages. Messages can be intended for a personal or public audience. Personal messages, such as those delivered in conversations (in person and telephone), letters, and e-mails, can be analyzed for their structures and strategies. Conversational or discourse analyses are qualitative approaches developed for mining the categories that inform the sequencing and meanings in personal messages (Wiggens & Potter, 2008; J. Potter, 2011). Public messages, such as blogs, magazines, newspapers, television programs, and motion pictures have been the primary concern of media studies. The different kinds of media through which public messages are delivered have greatly expanded in the last decade; for example, people now communicate through Twitter, Facebook, computer games, and iPhones.

Analysis of public messages is generally termed *content analysis*. Content analysis can be conducted using qualitative analysis or quantitative analysis, although in current usage, the term *content* analysis usually refers to statistically based studies (Neuendorf, 2002; Krippendorf, 2004). The overall meaning of a public message can also be investigated using qualitative analysis. Public messages can be complexly organized and make use of multiple sensory inputs. Motion pictures, for example, communicate with moving visual images and multiple sounds—oral dialog, music, and miscellaneous sounds (e.g., gunshots, door openings). All of these message outputs as well as their location in the temporal unfolding of the message are considered as parts of the whole in a qualitative analysis. The finding is a description of the meaning of the total message. The meaning of the message parts is established by their contribution to this total. Qualitative content analysis is most useful when the unit of study is a particular message, for example, one of the public service nonsmoking advertisements.

Quantitative content analysis often extracts parts from the total message and examines how often they occur and their relation to the number of occurrences of another part. For example, one might count how many violent incidents occurred or, more complexly, how often antisocial acts were unpunished. Counting the occurrences of a part or concept in a message requires that one use classical definitions of the attributes necessary for including the occurrence as an instance of the part. Classical definitions are required whether counts are conducted by human raters or computers. Raters are trained to recognize the same part of the message as an instance of the studied part. For example, if the task is to count the number of times "violence" occurs in the message, the ambiguity and fuzziness of the prototypical understanding has to be removed and replaced by the exactness of observable necessary qualities. If a computer is used for counts, a classical dictionary has to be written so that the computer will only count message instances that match the definition. For example, if researchers are interested in how many times a domestic setting appears in a message, they might program the computer to count the appearances of spaces around the letters *dwelling, residence, abode,* and *home.* However, *home* is not to be counted if the word *plate* immediately follows it. When the extracted parts are scaled, classical definitions for each unit of the scale are needed. For example, if counts of the concepts *slight violence, routine violence,* and *excessive violence* are asked for, a classical definition for each needs to be developed. Quantitative studies often seek to produce general findings that state the probability that the appearance and/or extent of certain concepts in a message will produce a certain effect on the receiver of the message. For example, is there a relationship between the number of violent acts in a television program and changes in the propensity to violence by selected viewers of the program? By extracting incidents of a concept from its context and noting how the viewer responds, the researcher can make rational assumptions about the relationship between the message occurrences and the average viewer response. Qualitative studies gain an understanding of how a whole message is understood by a particular viewer, but they lack the capacity to state that this understanding would be so for other viewers. The knowledge produced by qualitative research is about the particular participants or media message studied. Its depth of understanding of specific instances is offset by its lack of extending its findings to those not directly studied. Media psychology is also interested in what is so in general about a population; for example, how, on average, the public responded to a message. When the research question asks about a population's response, statistical methods that test for the probability that the findings from a representative sample hold for the sample's population.

Qualitative researchers frequently use software programs to assist them in their analytic work. Unlike statistical software, such as IBM SPSS, qualitative software programs do not conduct the analysis; rather, they manage the text and keep track of the concepts used in its organization (Lewins & Silver, 2007). When the entire text for a qualitative study has been gathered, it normally consists of hundreds of pages. The software programs allow for lifting out portions of the text that are instances of an organizing concept and placing them in a separate file. Current versions of programs, such as ATLAS.ti, NVivo, and Transana provide for the display of visual images (stills from motion pictures and videos) alongside the accompanying textual dialog. A limitation of theses packages is that they assume the researcher is using a parts-to-whole coding approach associated with grounded theory–based studies. These software programs contain other tools that may be of aid for qualitative researchers, such as finding specific words in the text and for word counts. These programs simply record and organize the researcher's judgments about themes and patterns; they do not make these judgments. Qualitative textual analysis is usually limited to the analysis of a single text or small number of texts. The intent is an intense analysis of *a* text (e.g., a speech, a motion picture, a television program, a newscast) in which the interaction of characters, situation, genre, and plot are brought together.

When the task is an analysis of a large body of texts, quantitative content analysis is more appropriate. For example, a study of all the articles in *The New York Times* in the year 2007 that mention *Obama* in the title or the analysis of a large number of open-ended survey responses would aim at a summation of themes across the articles and responses rather than an intensive description of each article or response. A set of software programs that differ from qualitative research software is available for the summary analysis of large bodies of text; for example, IBM SPSS Text Analytics for Surveys and CATPAC. Skalski (2002) lists 19 such programs. These programs produce frequency lists of words, concordances (keyword in context list), and conceptual lists under which the parts of the text are organized. They are becoming more sophisticated and are using neural network theory to identity word meaning in relation to the other words in the text. Operating the programs requires a dictionary that directs their performance. Some programs have built-in general dictionaries, but allow for the substitution of custom dictionaries. The usefulness of the programs for a particular research question depends on whether or not the program's dictionary can draw out the words and phrases that relate to the research question.

Gathering and Generating Information

Findings in a qualitative study are produced from analyzing a text that is gathered and generated to answer the research question. Contents of the text need not include only written materials, but can contain other genres as well. The kind of materials needed for the text is determined by the research question. A research question that asks about the conceptual organization, structures, and themes that are used in the video game *Grand Theft Auto* to communicate its meaning would include a copy of the game. A research question that asks about the experiences of a person who plays the game would need written observational descriptions of the player's behavior and transcriptions of interviews with the player. The final text for analysis is a compilation of all the information needed to answer the research question. Information for the text may be gathered from existing sources or newly generated through interviews, focus groups, and written participant responses to questions. Studies about the content of e-mails, speeches, video games, television programs, and so on gather existing copies of these materials. Studies about persons' experience usually require newly generated information from them.

The selection of what information to include in a text is determined by the purpose of qualitative research—to provide a detailed and in-depth understanding of an event. Researchers need information from sources that can contribute to understanding the event. Because qualitative research questions are not about what is universally so, or so for all members of classification (e.g., all members of an ethnic group), a text's included information is not a representative sample. Information is gathered and generated that is critical to understanding the studied episode. The text may consist of information from multiple sources; for example, it might include a copy of a television program and interviews with the show's writers. In deciding what to include in a text, researchers also need to consider what not to include. Extraneous information can detract from the analytical work's focus.

Participants must describe their experiences to generate new information. Descriptions are frequently generated through in-depth interviews. Effective qualitative interviewing is a skill developed through practice (Kvale & Brinkmann, 2009). It allows the participant to share vivid and nuanced descriptions of his or her experience. The interviewer is required to develop an interpersonal environment in which the interviewee is open to describing his or her feelings and understandings. The interviewer needs to guide the interaction by using probing and follow-up questions to solicit information relevant to the research question. A single 1-hour interview is often not sufficient to produce rich and full descriptions, and interviewers may have several sessions with the interviewee (Gubrium & Holstein, 2002; Rubin & Rubin, 2005; Seidman, 2006). Transcripts can be supplemented in the research text with notes about facial expressions, sitting positions, and so on. Descriptions of experiences can also be generated in focus groups. These groups consist of six to ten participants along with the researcher (and usually an assistant). The interaction among the participants engenders a flow of descriptive information as one participant's description stimulates the others' responses. Morgan and Krueger (1997) outlined the organizational requirements and suggested techniques for leading focus groups. Survey instruments can present participants with open-ended questions. However, information recorded as answers to these questions is usually not sufficient in depth of description to be included in text to be analyzed. They more often serve to produce information about the answerer's general opinions.

Excellence of a qualitative research finding is judged by how well it gives the reader an understanding of the event or message it investigated. A finding is the product of careful analysis of a wisely assembled text. When the text includes information generated from participants, it needs to include intensive descriptions filled with detailed examples and descriptions. If the text is thin, containing superficial descriptions, the analysis cannot access deeper organizational structures and meaning-giving concepts. Although excellence in findings depends on the researcher's skill to call out the deeper layers of the text through which its meaning is constructed, this skill cannot produce worthwhile findings without a text of abundant richness and thickness (Geertz, 1973).

Conclusion

Qualitative research aims at developing knowledge of those cognitive processes that individuals use to transform information received through the senses into meaning. Although there is an overlap of these processes in the individuals who make up a culture, there are also divergences. A person's meaning-making processes develop from his or her particular social interactions and varying interests. In addition to the differences among individuals, the processes change over lifetimes as individuals accumulate new concepts. Connecting an event to a meaning concept is not a mechanical operation; rather, the connection is sensitive to the historical and social setting in which the event occurs. The connection also relates to the past experiences and future aims of the person. Thus, the meaning produced by cognitive processes happens with consideration of the total context of the event. This relates to media psychology in the sense that every qualitative analysis of a media event is a snapshot in time of the way that event affected specific individuals in a specific time and place. For example, showing the movie *Schindler's List* to a group of Holocaust survivors in 1949 (if the film had existed then) would have yielded substantially different results from showing the film to a group of high-school students in 2011.

Qualitative research is a science specially developed to study human meaning making in individuals. Its knowledge has some similarities of the knowledge people have of friends, parents, and others they know well. It differs in aims and techniques from the physical sciences and their adaptation in mainstream psychology. Qualitative knowledge claims are descriptions of people's experiences. They do not presume that all people or people of a group will have the same experience of the same event. The claims are about local, not generalized, knowledge. Knowing in detail how one person has constructed an understanding of a situation can help one appreciate how another person might be similar and different. Local knowledge provides a lens through which to view possibilities of understanding. However, knowledge of others' understandings of a situation requires a qualitative study of those others.

The knowledge produced by qualitative research provides a balance to generalized knowledge produced by quantitative studies. Generalized knowledge compares the average response of a group of people to the average response to another group. The individual responses that contribute to the average are not the focus. They appear only as noise or error in the research (Oliver & Krakowiak, 2009). Qualitative studies focus on knowledge about the individual participants—the outlier, the typical person, the one-standard-deviation-below-the-mean

person, and so on. Both kinds of knowledge contribute to a discipline whose object of study is people.

Qualitative findings are the product of researcher choices as they move from asking research questions to writing up findings. It is an iterative process of circling through information generating, analysis, and write-up. Often during the write-up, it becomes apparent that information is missing and the researcher needs to return to information gathering and generating. The new information may lead to a revision of the analysis and findings. Each of these activities is informed by the researcher's judgment about the fullness of the description developed so far. There is no single correct way of conducting a study that assures a worthwhile finding. Techniques and procedures have been developed by the qualitative traditions that have proved useful in other studies. They are available for use in new studies, but new studies may themselves develop other techniques.

Potter (2009), in his *Arguing for a General Framework for Mass Media Scholarship,* notes that "the number of qualitative content studies published is much smaller than the number of quantitative content studies" (p. 232). A review of media psychology publications shows a similar result for studies of producers of the messages and the audience members of the messages. Potter argues for greater use of qualitative studies (what he terms *humanistic scholarship*) throughout media studies when the interest is in what happens when people are constructing meaning of messages (p. 238). Knowledge about individuals' understandings in their production or reception of messages is the purview of qualitative research.

Future Directions

1. If the discipline of psychology is to obtain a greater balance in the kinds of knowledge it produces, more attention will need to be given to training qualitative researchers. In most psychology doctoral programs, qualitative research is seen as a possible add-on after mastering the statistical approach to research. Mastery of qualitative research is rarely required as part of doctoral curricula. Consequently, students who produce doctoral dissertations using a qualitative approach are often not well prepared. A question to be addressed is how courses in qualitative research can become part of an already crowded doctoral curriculum.

2. Qualitative approaches require specific skills in gathering and generating worthwhile information and in analyzing this information.

Methods for teaching these skills need further development. Successful techniques and processes need to be accumulated and shared. This is a different issue from learning what to do; rather, it is developing the skills needed for doing it.

3. Research publications, including those that publish qualitative research, require that articles be submitted in the APA format. Write-ups of qualitative research processes and findings do not fit well into the APA format. They are more adequately reported as narratives and require greater length. Including reports of qualitative studies in psychology's body of knowledge will require acceptance of different publication formats.

4. For psychology to develop a balanced body of knowledge consisting of generalized and local findings, funding for both kinds of research must be balanced. Federal funding guidelines favor research designed to produce generalized findings about what works across individuals and situations. The importance of studies producing local knowledge needs to be argued for and recognized by funding sources.

Notes

1. A convention to differentiate between concepts and the words that represent them is to underline when referring to a concept and italicize when referring to a word.

2. Although the term *perception* is sometimes used as the equivalent of *understanding*, I limit the use of *perception* to the reception of information through the senses before its conceptual interpretation. *Understanding* is used to refer to the meaning the perceived sensual information has for the person. People respond to themselves, others, and the world from their understanding of the meaning perceptions have for them.

3. Sense information from both external bodily receptors (eyes, ears, skin, etc.) and internal receptors (body movement, feelings, etc.) is understood by conceptualizing or categorizing it as an instance of something; for example, a threat, pain, or helpful.

4. The word *object* is used in its broad sense to refer to any sensed occurrence, including feelings and thoughts as well as physical objects.

5. *Meaning* and *understanding* are used interchangeably. *Meaning* is used to refer to the significance or sense of something has, such as the meaning of a word or sense experience. It is not used in the sense of "meaning of life." Both *understanding* and *meaning* of something is known when it is classified as an instance of a concept.

References

Altheide, D. L. (1996). *Qualitative Media Analysis*. Thousand Oaks, CA: Sage.

American Psychiatric Association. (2000). *Diagnostic and Statistical Manual of Mental Disorders*, 4th, text revision ed. Washington, DC: American Psychiatric Association.

Arceneaux, N., & Weiss, A. S. (2010). Seems stupid until you try it: Press coverage Twitter, 2006–9. *New Media Society*, *12*(8), 1262–1279.

Austin, J. L. (1975). *How to Do Things with Words*. Cambridge, MA: Harvard University Press.

Bazerman, C. (1987). Codifying the social scientific style: The APA Publication Manual as a behaviorist rhetoric. In Nelson, J. S., Megill, A., & McCloskey, D. N. (Eds.), *The Rhetoric of the Human Sciences: Language and Argument in Scholarship and Public Affairs*. Madison, WI: University of Wisconsin Press, pp. 125–144.

Benner, P. (1994). Introduction. In Benner, P. (Ed.), *Interpretative Phenomenology: Embodiment, Caring, and Ethics in Health and Illness*. Thousand Oaks, CA: Sage, pp. xiii–xxv.

Berger, A. A. (2005). *Media Analysis Techniques*, 3rd ed. Thousand Oaks, CA: Sage.

Bernard, H. R., & Ryan, G. W. (2010). *Analyzing Qualtitative Data: Systematic Approaches*. Los Angeles: Sage.

Charmaz, K. (2000). Grounded theory: Objectivist and constructivist methods. In Denzin, N. K., & Lincoln, Y. S. (Eds.), *Handbook of Qualitative Research*, 2nd ed. Thousand Oaks, CA: Sage, pp. 509–535.

Charmaz, K. (2006). *Constructing Grounded Theory: A Practical Guide Through Qualitative Analysis*. Thousand Oaks, CA: Sage.

Clark, A. (2005). *Situational Analysis: Grounded Theory After the Postmodern Turn*. Thousand Oaks: CA: Sage.

Danesi, M. (2007). *The Quest for Meaning: A Guide to Semiotic Theory and Practice*. Toronto: University of Toronto Press.

Denzin, N. K., & Lincoln, Y. S. (Eds.). (2008). *Handbook of Qualitative Research*, 3rd ed. Thousand Oaks, CA: Sage.

Eco, U., Santambrogio, M., & Violi, P. (Eds.). (1988). *Meaning and Mental Representation*. Bloomington, IN: Indiana University Press.

Fieldling, N. G., & Lee, R. M. (1998). *Computer Analysis and Qualitative Research*. Thousand Oaks, CA: Sage.

Foucault, M. (1969/1973). *The Archaeology of Knowledge* (Smith, A. M. S., Trans.). New York: Vintage Books.

Frank, G. (2000). *Venus On Wheels: Two Decades of Dialogue on Disability, Biography, and Being Female in America*. Berkeley, CA: University of California Press.

Geertz, C. (1973). *Interpretation of Cultures*. New York: Basic Books.

Gibbs, G. (2007). *Analyzing Qualitative Data*. Thousand Oaks, CA: Sage.

Giles, D. (2003). *Media Psychology*. Hillsdale, NJ: Lawrence Erlbaum Associates.

Giorgi, A. (1970). Toward a phenomenologically based research in psychology. *Journal of Phenomenological Psychology*, *1*(1), 75–98.

Giorgi, A. (1985). A phenomenological approach to the problem of meaning and serial learning. In Giorgi, A. (Ed.), *Phenomenology and Psychological Research*. Pittsburgh, PA: Duquesne University Press, pp. 23–85.

Glaser, B., & Strauss, A. (1965). *Awareness of Dying*. Chicago: Aldine.

Glaser, B. G. (1978). *Theoretical Sensitivity: Advances in the Methodology of Grounded Theory*. Mill Valley, CA: Sociology Press.

Glaser, B. G. (1992). *The Basics of Grounded Theory Analysis*. Mill Valley, CA: Sociology Press.

Glaser, B. G., & Strauss, A. L. (1967). *The Discovery of Grounded Theory: Strategies for Qualitative Research*. New York: Aldine de Gruyter.

Goodwin, C. J. (2008). *Research in Psychology: Methods and Design*, 5th ed. Hoboken, NJ: John Wiley & Sons.

Gubrium, J. F., & Holstein, J. A. (Eds.). (2002). *Handbook of Interview Research: Context and Method*. Thousand Oaks, CA: Sage.

Healey, K. (2010). The pastor in the basement: Discourses of authenticity in the networked public sphere. *Symbolic Interaction*, *33*(4), 526–551.

Heidegger, M. (1927/1962). *Being and Time* (Robinson, J. M. E., Translator). New York: Harper & Brothers.

Husserl, E. (1937/1970). *The Crisis of European Sciences and Transcendental Psychology* (Carr, D., Translator). Evanston, IL: Northwestern University Press.

Jackendoff, R., Bloom, P., & Wynn, K. (Eds.). (2002). *Language, Logic, and Concepts*. Cambridge, MA: The MIT Press.

Kazdin, A. E. (2003). *Research Design in Clinical Psychology*, 4th ed. Boston: Allyn & Bacon.

Krippendorf, K. (2004). *Content Analysis: An Introduction to Its Methodology*, 2nd ed. Thousand Oaks, CA: Sage.

Kübler-Ross, E. (1969). *On Death and Dying*. New York: Routledge.

Kvale, S., & Brinkmann, S. (2009). *InterViews: Learning the Craft of Qualitative Interviewing*, 2nd ed. Thousand Oaks, CA: Sage.

Lehti, L. (2011). Blogging politics in various ways: A typology of French politicians' blogs. *Journal of Pragmatics*, *43*(6), 1610–1627.

Lemish, D., & Tidhar, C. E. (2001). Howglobal does it get? The *teletubbies* in Israel. *Journal of Broadcasting & Electronic Media*, *45*(4), 558–574.

Lewins, A., & Silver, C. (2007). *Using Software in Qualitative Research: A Step-by-Step Guide*. Thousand Oaks, CA: Sage.

Lindlof, T. R. (Ed.). (1987). *Natural Audiences: Qualitative Research of Media Uses and Effects*. Norwood, NJ: Ablex.

Mann, C., & Stewart, F. (2000). *Internet Communication and Qualitative Research: A Handbook for Researching On Line*. London: Sage.

Mead, G. H. (1934). *Mind, Self, and Society*. Chicago: University of Chicago Press.

Morgan, D. L., & Krueger, R. A. (1997). *Focus Group Kit*, vol. 1–6. Newbury Park, CA: Sage.

Murphy, G. L. (2002). *The Big Book of Concepts*. Cambridge, MA: MIT Press.

Neisser, U. (1966). *Cognitive Psychology*. New York: Appleton-Century-Crofts.

Neuendorf, K. A. (2002). *The Content Analysis Guidebook*. Thousand Oaks, CA: Sage.

Oliver, M. B., & Krakowiak, K. M. (2009). Individual differences in media effects. In Bryant, J., & Oliver, M. B. (Eds.), *Media Effects: Advances in Theory and Research* . New York: Routledge, pp. 517–531.

Patton, M. Q. (2002). *Qualitative Research and Evaluation Methods*, 3rd ed. Newbury Park, CA: Sage.

Peirce, C. S. (1931, 1936/1958). *Collected Papers of Charles Sanders Peirce*, vols. 1–6. Cambridge, MA: Harvard University Press.

Piaget, J. (1936/1952). *The Origins of Intelligence in Children*. New York: International Universities Press.

Polkinghorne, D. E. (1983). *Methodology for the Human Sciences: Systems of Inquiry*. Albany: State University of New York Press.

Polkinghorne, D. E. (1989). Phenomenological research methods. In Valle, R. S., & Halling, S. (Eds.), *Existential-Phenomenological Perspectives in Psychology*. New York: Plenum Press, pp. 41–60.

Polkinghorne, D. E. (2004). Franz Brentano's *Psychology from an Empirical Standpoint* In Sternberg, R. J. (Ed.), *The Anatomy of Impact: What Makes the Great Works of Psychology Great?* (pp. 43–70). Washington, DC: American Psychological Association.

Polkinghorne, D. E. (2010). Qualitative research. In Thomas, J. C., & Hersen, M. (Eds.), *Handbook of Clinical Psychology Competencies* . New York: Springer, pp. 425–456.

Popper, K. R. (1959). *The Logic of Scientific Discovery*. New York: Basic Books.

Potter, J. (2011). Discourse analysis as a way of analyzing naturally occuring talk. In Silverman, D. (Ed.), *Qualitative Research: Theory, Method and Practice*, 3rd ed. London: Sage, pp. 187–207.

Potter, W. J. (2009). *Arguing for a General Framework for Mass Media Scholarship*. Los Angeles: Sage.

Rosch, E. (2000). Principles of categorization. In Margolis, E., & Laurence, S. (Eds.), *Concepts: Core Readings* . Cambridge, MA: The MIT Press, pp. 189–206.

Rubin, H. J., & Rubin, I. S. (2005). *Qualitative Interviewing: The Art of Hearing Data*, 2nd ed. Thousand Oaks, CA: Sage.

Saldaña, J. (2009). *The Coding Manual for Qualitative Research*. Thousand Oaks, CA: Sage.

Sanderson, J. (2008). Spreading the word: Emphatic interaction displays on Blog Maverick.com. *Journal of Media Psychology*, *20*(4), 156–167.

Sartre, J.-P. (1943/1965). *Being and Nothingness: An Essay in Pheomenological Ontology*. (Barnes, H. E., Translator, special abridged edition). New York: Citadel.

Saussure, F. D. (1907–1911/1966). *Course in General Linguistics* (Baskin, W., Translator). New York: McGraw-Hill.

Schwandt, T. A. (2000). Three epistemological stances for qualitative inquiry: Interpretation, hermeneutics, and social construction. In Denzin, N. K., & Lincoln, Y. S. (Eds.), *Handbook of Qualitative Research*, 2nd ed. Thousand Oaks, CA: Sage, pp. 189–213.

Seidman, I. (2006). *Interviewing as Qualitative Research*, 3rd ed. New York: Teachers College Press.

Skalski, P. D. (2002). Computer content analysis software. In Neuendorf, K. A. (Ed.), *The Content Analysis Guidebook*. Thousand Oaks: Sage, pp. 225–239.

Snyder, L. J. (2011). *The Philosophical Breakfast Club*. New York: Broadway Books.

Strauss, A., & Corbin, J. (1990). *Basics of Qualitative Research*. Newbury park, CA: Sage.

Wellman, H. M., Cross, D., & Watson, J. (2001). Meta-anaysis of theory-of-mind development: The truth about false belief. *Child Development*, *72*, 655–684.

Wertz, F. J., Charmaz, K., McMullen, L. M., Josselson, R., Anderson, R., & McSpadden, E. (2011). *Five Ways of Doing Qualitative Anaysis: Phenomenological Psychology, Grounded Theory, Discourse Analysis, Narrative Research, and Intuitive Inquiry*. New York: Guilford.

Whitty, M. T., Young, G., & Goodings, L. (2011). What I won't do in pexels: Examining the limits of taboo violation in MMORPGs. *Computers in Huan Behavior*, *27*(1), 268–275.

Wiggens, S., & Potter, J. (2008). Discursive psychology. In Willig, C., & Hollway, W. (Eds.), *The Sage Handbook of Qualitative Reseach in Psychology* . London: Sage, pp. 72–89.

Willig, C. (2001). *Introducing Qualitative Research in Psychology: Adventures in Theory and Method*. Philadelphia: Open University Press.

PART 3

Issues and Media Types

Why It Is Hard To Believe That Media Violence Causes Aggression

L. Rowell Huesmann, Eric F. Dubow, *and* Grace Yang

Abstract

Research studies on how media violence influences aggressive and violent behaviors face unusual hurdles in having an impact on the public, journalists, and even other scientists. Despite the existence of compelling empirical evidence that media violence causes increased aggression in the observer or game player, intelligent people still doubt the effects. A fundamental reason is that the outcomes of such research have implications not only for public policy, but also for how one views oneself. Through several well-understood psychological processes, this leads to many people denying the results of the scientific research. There are four psychological processes that together can account for most denials of media violence effects: (1) the need for cognitive consistency; (2) reactance; (3) the "third-person effect"; and (4) desensitization. This chapter illustrates how these processes lead to disbelief. Finally, it offers conclusions and ideas for future directions of how research may contribute to public opinion and public policy.

Key Words: media violence; psychological processes; public perceptions of research; violent video games

Long before the introduction of video games into the everyday lives of children, the question of whether exposure to violence in the mass media makes the viewer more violent was being widely debated. It was debated with regard to oral and written communications even in antiquity; it was debated with regard to movies when they were introduced; and it became a major topic of research and debate with the emergence of television as a fundamental part of every child's development by the end of the 1950s. Both the research and the debate have accelerated, however, as modern electronic recording and communication media make movie and television portrayals of violence available to everyone everywhere, and as the modern electronic video game has become a central part of every child's life. We now have reached the point at which not only are all children being socialized as much by electronic media as by parents and peers, but

also today's researchers, policy makers, and debaters have mostly now been raised in these environments themselves.

To the current authors, the research of the last 50 or so years is compelling in demonstrating at least two cause–effect relations about media socialization: (1) short exposures of almost anyone to violent scenes or playing violent games cause an increase in the likelihood of behaving aggressively immediately afterward; and (2) habitual exposure to violent scenes or playing violent games changes children's developing brain structures to cause an increase in the likelihood of behaving more aggressively even many years later. These statements are true of violence observed in the family, neighborhood, or school or true of violent games played with peers, and they are true of violence in the mass media or electronic games. There is a clear consensus of opinion among most scholars who actually do research on the topic of the truth of these statements. Surveys have shown that more than 80% of those doing research on the topic have long ago concluded from the evidence that media violence is causing aggression (Murray, 1984). Most major health professional groups and governmental organizations have issued statements citing exposure to media violence as one cause of youth violence (Eron, Gentry, & Schlegel, 1994; Joint Statement of Congress, 2000; Anderson et al., 2003; American Academy of Pediatrics, 2009). Two Surgeon Generals of the United States (in 1972 and 2001) have warned the public that media violence is a risk factor for aggression. For example, in March 1972, then Surgeon General Jesse Steinfeld told Congress:

> ... it is clear to me that the causal relationship between [exposure to] televised violence and antisocial behavior is sufficient to warrant appropriate and immediate remedial action ... *there comes a time when the data are sufficient to justify action. That time has come.* (Steinfeld, 1972)

Yet, despite this conclusion supported by prestigious individuals and most scientific organizations, and despite the sizable body of empirical evidence accumulated over several decades confirming the negative effects of the consumption of media violence, a relatively small number of critics continue to challenge this conclusion, disregarding the weight of empirical data, and further disregarding the theoretical explanations underlying the effects. Many dissenters obviously believe passionately in what they have concluded and write prolifically and compellingly about it. The quantity of such writing, in which the flaws are often difficult for nonexperts to discern, eventually may influence informed public opinion and give even those policy-making organizations that have opposed media violence second thoughts about their positions. For example, we note that recently, the American Psychological Association, which had previously issued statements opposing media violence, decided against submitting an amicus brief on the research evidence to the Supreme Court, which was hearing a challenge to a California law requiring parental approval for sales of violent video games to minors (Azar, 2010). They explained their decision as follows:

> APA was invited to submit a brief, but after a review of the literature, the association concluded it was premature to advise the court on research-based links between violent video games and problematic behavior in the context of a First Amendment

challenge. Breckler (APA's Executive Director for Science) explained that although *most of the research in this area supports a connection between violent games and aggression*, there is also some credible research to the contrary, and APA concluded that there was not a basis to weigh in with the Supreme Court given the nature of the relevant research and the legal issues at question. (Azar, 2010, p. 38)

To the authors of this chapter this explanation represents an admission that APA, despite believing that media violence is harmful, is caving in to pressure not to take a position because of potential legal consequences from either first amendment advocates or those with economic interests in violent media.

The goal of this chapter is to present an explanation of why, when the evidence that media violence and violent video games causes aggression is as compelling as the evidence supporting many other public health threats, many people who are intelligent and well informed don't accept that there are significant effects on aggression for media violence. It is not our goal to review extensively the empirical literature in this area. A plethora of extensive reviews have appeared in print in the past decade (e.g., Anderson et al., 2003, 2010; Huesmann & Kirwil, 2007; Bushman & Huesmann, 2011). Nevertheless, we must begin with a very brief summary of the empirical evidence to set the stage for our major argument.

Meta-analyses Demonstrating That Media Violence Stimulates Aggression

When the body of research in an area becomes very large, single studies in the body may be expected to show contradictory results; so a meta-analysis becomes the best way to get an overall grasp of what the empirical evidence shows. Meta-analyses combine effect sizes from large numbers of studies to reach a "best" estimate of the true population effect size. In 1994, Paik and Comstock conducted the first large comprehensive meta-analysis of the relation between observing media violence and aggressive or antisocial behavior. They analyzed 217 studies conducted from 1957 to 1990. The studies included laboratory and field experiments, surveys, and time series designs. The authors found that the average effect size for experiments testing causal effects was $r = .40$ and for field studies (cross-sectional or longitudinal) was $r = .19$. These effects sizes, although moderate to small in absolute terms, were highly significant. The effect sizes were significant for college-age students

($r = .39$), preschoolers ($r = .49$), 6- to 11-year-olds ($r = .32$), and 12- to 17-year-olds ($r = .23$). The overall effect sizes were also somewhat stronger for males ($r = .37$) than females ($r = .26$).

The Paik and Comstock review did not include many studies of video games, but 7 years later Anderson and Bushman (2001, 2002) published meta-analyses that include the effects of *violent video games*. Using 280 studies conducted before 2001 across multiple media types (television, movies, video games, comic books, and music), the authors found effect sizes somewhat smaller than those reported earlier by Paik and Comstock (1994), but highly significant. Effect sizes across study designs (laboratory and field experiments, cross-sectional and longitudinal studies) ranged from $r = .17$ to $r = .23$. Most recently, Anderson et al. (2010) conducted a meta-analysis of the results from 136 high-quality studies (yielding 381 effect size estimates) published through 2008 on the relation between *playing violent video games* and aggressive behavior, aggressive cognitions, aggressive affect, physiological arousal, empathy/desensitization, and prosocial behavior. This meta-analysis yielded a pattern of effect sizes consistent with their prior meta-analysis showing that playing violent video games causes increases in aggression in the short run and playing violent video games is a risk factor for increased aggression in the long run.

To be fair, not all experiments have shown causal effects of exposure to media violence on aggression and not all field studies have shown positive longitudinal effects of exposure to media violence on aggression. Although many such studies have glaring flaws, some seem to be very well done; for example, a longitudinal study by von Salisch, Vogelgesang, Kristen, and Oppl (2001) that indicated that the relation between aggression and violent video game play in third and fourth graders is more caused by aggressive children liking violent games than children who play violent games becoming more aggressive. From a theoretical standpoint, it is quite plausible that there would be effects in both directions (Huesmann et al., 2003; Slater, Henry, Swaim, & Anderson, 2003); however, it is unusual in this body of research not to have a longitudinal effect from prior exposure to media violence to subsequent aggression. How threatening should be the effect of any one such study to the overall conclusion that media violence stimulates aggressive behavior in the short run and in the long run? This is why the meta-analyses are so important. Meta-analyses serve the important function of statistically aggregating the results of many diverse studies—some with positive effects, some with negative effects, some with no effects—to reach an overall conclusion. And the conclusion shown by the vast majority of such meta-analyses is that media violence causes increases in aggression. The few dissenting meta-analyses (e.g., Ferguson, 2007a,b), Ferguson & Kilburn, 2009) have been conducted by the dissenters we discuss in the following pages, and have flaws described in detail elsewhere (Anderson et al., 2010).

Theoretical Explanations for Media Violence Effects

Empirical evidence by itself, however consistent and powerful, should not be enough to convince scientists or the public that a particular environmental substance is dangerous. One needs a process-model explanation of how it exerts its dangerous effect. For more than four decades, scientists have been building a consistent psychological process model of why exposure to violence stimulates aggression both in the short run and in the long run (Eron et al., 1972; Bandura, 1977; Huesmann, 1988, 1998; Bushman & Huesmann, 2001; Huesmann et al., 2003; Huesmann & Kirwil, 2007). We now know why and how it happens. In the short term, priming, mimicry, and excitation transfer account for the effects. In the long term, observational learning of aggressive scripts, schemas, and beliefs and emotional desensitization account for the effects.

Short-Term Processes

Priming explains relatively short-term underlying processes by which exposure to media violence can incite aggression. The logic of priming is based on cognitive and neurological perspectives that consider human memory as an associative network of scripts or ideas representing semantically related thoughts, feelings, and behavioral tendencies (Fiske & Taylor, 1984; Berkowitz, 1989, 1993). Priming from observing violence refers to the neurological fact that related violent thoughts, emotions, and concepts residing in memory are automatically activated when violence is observed. These primed or activated thoughts and emotions bias the processing and interpretation of subsequently encountered situations, even without one's perception of this influence (Bargh & Pietromonaco, 1982). Empirical studies reveal that violent media content activates aggressive scripts in one's memory, and these aggressive scripts in turn increase the likelihood of subsequent hostile responses to certain situations, especially those involving interpersonal conflicts or frustration (Bargh & Pietromonaco, 1982). In addition, the mere presence of objects associated with violence, such as weapons, primes aggressive responses (Berkowitz & LePage, 1967; Anderson, Benjamin, & Bartholow, 1998; Payne, 2001).

Activation and processing of aggressive scripts occurs even without one's conscious awareness, and, when repeated, eventually makes aggressive scripts chronically accessible (Huesmann & Kirwil, 2007, p. 549). This increase in chronic accessibility is owing to a "lowered threshold of activation," which makes the construct more easily activated by other stimuli for at least a short period (Bushman, 1995, p. 538). Thus, although the priming effect is considered relatively fleeting compared with enduring social learning effects (described in the following pages), because aggression-activated thoughts become chronically accessible through repeated priming, violent media consumption can have a considerable cumulative impact on increasing the likelihood of aggressive behavior through the priming process.

Another short-term process is mimicry, which explains why exposure to violent media immediately precipitates aggressive behavior, especially among young children. Neurophysiological research on automatic imitation has revealed that humans have an innate tendency to mimic any behavior they observe (Meltzoff & Moore, 2000; Hurley & Chatter, 2004; Rizzolatti, 2005). Applied to the violent media, aggressive actions performed by media heroes can be immediately mimicked by young children, especially if children perceive the observed model to be similar to themselves and if the model's behavior is reinforced (Bandura, 1977). Short-term imitation can occur after a single observation of an action without elaborate cognitive processing (Huesmann, 1998; Bushman & Huesmann, 2006). The observation and imitation of a specific aggressive behavior can lead to acquisition of more coordinated aggressive scripts for future behavior (Huesmann, 1988, 1998).

The third short-term psychological process accounting for why exposure to media violence can temporarily increase aggression relates to arousal and excitation transfer. Excitation transfer is the idea that physiological arousal dissipates slowly and if two arousing events are separated by a short amount of time, some of the arousal caused by the first event may pass on to the second event (Zillmann, 1983, 1988). In general, observing violent media creates a sense of excitement in most people. As Bandura (1983) explained, this emotional arousal can increase the likelihood of aggressive action, particularly if the person conceives his or her aroused experience as negative, such as frustration or anger. Other types of arousal such as sexual or physiological arousal (by exercise) are thought to facilitate aggressive reaction during the subsequent event. A number of experimental studies have reported that emotionally or physiologically aroused individuals are especially prone to be aggressively stimulated by violent scenes (e.g., Bryant & Zillmann, 1979; Zillmann, Bryant, Comisky, & Medoff, 1981).

Long-Term Processes

Unlike priming, mimicry, and arousal, whose effects are relatively short lived, observational learning of aggressive scripts and schemas for behavior includes specific mechanisms through which viewing violent media increases aggression in the long run. According to Huesmann, "a script serves as a guide for behavior by laying out the sequence of events that one believes are likely to happen and the behaviors that one believes are possible or appropriate for a particular situation" (1998, p. 80). Huesmann (1988, 1998) developed a cognitive processing model to account for one's own and others' actions during social situations and how exposure to violence might influence behavior. Huesmann's model provides a detailed explanation of how an individual develops aggressive problem-solving behavior through a four-step sequential process. The four steps involve perception and interpretation of environmental cues, activation of retrieved scripts, evaluation of scripts against normative beliefs, and interpretation of environmental responses (Huesmann, 1998).

To begin with aggressive children have a larger repertoire of aggressive scripts than nonaggressive children and thus are more likely to call on these scripts in social conflict situations. Aggressive scripts are acquired initially mainly though observational learning of others behaving aggressively in the child's environment including the mass media. They are then cemented in place through reinforcement of the use of aggressive scripts that achieve desired outcomes. Aggressive children will seek out environments that are consistent with their aggressive scripts (e.g., violent media, aggressive peers, opportunities to use aggression), and aggressive children can create their own aggressive environments. Thus, a downward spiral of increasing aggression can occur (Slater et al., 2003). The maintenance of an aggressive script also depends on how frequently and competently the child rehearses it (Huesmann, 1988); rehearsal of observed information enhances its connectedness in memory, thereby making it more accessible (Klatzky, 1980). Thus, frequent enactment of aggressive scripts (even through fantasizing) should make their retrieval more likely (Huesmann, 1998). Huesmann also contends that once in place, aggressive scripts are relatively resistant to change, and therefore chronically influence aggressive behavior throughout development. However, an activated script may remain unused if it is evaluated as negative or inappropriate given the situation. Huesmann posits that whether children act out an aggressive script depends on the self-perception that the script is doable, that enacting the script will lead to desired consequences and that the script is socially acceptable.

Two cognitive schemas that affect whether aggressive scripts will be selected and employed include the child's "normative belief about aggression" and "world views" (Huesmann & Guerra, 1997; Anderson & Huesmann, 2003; Huesmann & Kirwil, 2007). Through inferences drawn from observational learning, children develop normative beliefs about what aggressive behaviors are socially appropriate and develop schemas about how violent they perceive the world to be in general (world schemas). Like aggressive scripts, normative beliefs and world schemas are learned through observation of parents, peers, and media characters (Huesmann, Lagerspetz, & Eron, 1984; Miller, 1991; Henry et al., 2000). A child who is repeatedly exposed to violence in real life or the mass media (including video games) will perceive the world to be a more violent place (i.e., "have hostile attributional biases" or "perceive a mean world ") (Signorielli, 1990; Gerbner, Gross, Morgan, & Signorielli, 1994), and also may think that it is socially acceptable to resolve any encountered conflict with violence. Consequently, the child is more likely to enact aggressive scripts in response to perceived provocation.

Thus, through such observational learning and enactment of aggressive schemas, scripts, and beliefs, children not only learn specific aggressive behaviors, but also internalize the values, beliefs, and attitudes that are associated with the process and context of their learning (Huesmann, 1998). Accordingly, as Huesmann and Kirwil (2007) describe, this process can result in "habitual modes of [aggressive] behavior," which last a long time (p. 552). Consistent with this theoretical model, Huesmann et al. (Eron, Huesmann, Lefkowitz, & Walder, 1972; Huesmann, Moise-Titus, Podolski, & Eron, 2003) found that higher levels of childhood exposure to television violence significantly predicted higher levels of aggressive behavior in adulthood (e.g., crime records, traffic tickets, spouse abuse, child hitting), even when other relevant individual and social factors (e.g., education, early parenting, parent aggression, socioeconomic status) were statistically controlled.

Emotional desensitization is another psychological process with long-term implications for aggressive behavior. Desensitization to media violence refers to "emotional habituation" or the gradual increase in emotional tolerance for violence and the reduction of the unpleasant physiological responses to violence that occur with repeated exposures to violence (Carnagey, Anderson & Bushman, 2007; Krahe et al., 2011). Thus, by repeatedly viewing violence over an extended period of time, a person becomes less affected by the unpleasantness associated with violence, both emotionally and physiologically, and as a result, he or she may be less inhibited about behaving aggressively. According to researchers, then, the risk of consuming extensive amounts of violent media is that the likelihood of having aggressive thoughts and acting aggressively increases when depictions of violence no longer cause emotional distress (Huesmann et al., 2003). It should be noted that, like precipitating effects of priming and excitation transfer, this desensitization also is experienced as a "natural" and "unconscious" process, and the enduring effects on aggressive attitudes and behaviors also develop outside of one's conscious awareness.

Disputing Media Violence Effects

Given the compelling amount of empirical data summarized in the preceding and the consistent theoretical explanations for the effects reviewed there, one must wonder how an informed layman, much less an informed social scientist, can dispute the conclusion that media violence causes aggression. Why do "disbelievers" continue to adamantly hold their views in the light of the evidence? Of course, it is amazing to most of us what many people do and don't believe. Large portions of the American population still believe that President Obama was not born in the United States (although a significant portion of people who say "not in the USA," when asked where he was born, then say "in Hawaii"). Many people also believe that all sorts of dietary substances improve or worsen their health when there is absolutely no evidence that the effects exist. But there should be a difference between what the general public may accept about influences on behavior and health and what well-read "public intellectuals" and especially those trained in science and health should accept. Highly educated people, especially those with training in social science research, should be able to evaluate the quality of media violence research and understand what conclusions follow from the preponderance of the evidence. If they are not doing so in a way that represents the conclusions that can be drawn from this body of evidence, it may be that other psychological factors within them, perhaps unconsciously, are influencing their beliefs.

The remainder of this chapter describes some underlying psychological processes that may motivate (consciously or unconsciously) the disbelievers to reject the evidence drawn from the vast research relating media violence and aggression. We offer theory-driven explanations of the critics' denials. Then we offer conclusions and ideas for future directions of how research may contribute to public opinion and public policy.

Some Flawed Arguments Used to Discredit Media Violence Research

First, however, before we describe the psychological processes that lead to disbelief, we need to briefly address the surface arguments presented by disbelievers as reasons for their disbelief. One common argument is that the evidence accumulated to date has provided little or no indication of a *causal* effect of media violence on viewers' aggressive behavior (e.g., Ferguson, 2009b). Typically, when making this argument, disbelievers ignore experiments and focus on one-shot field studies that, indeed, do not provide evidence of causation. However, other critics (or the same critics at other times) focus only on experiments and argue that the results of such studies are unimportant because they are done in an artificial laboratory setting using measures that do not represent real-world aggression. (Typically, when making this argument, disbelievers ignore one-shot and longitudinal field studies.) Perhaps the most frequent methodological criticism is that experimental studies are contaminated by the artificiality of the viewing situations and laboratory settings (Howitt & Cumberbatch, 1975), and thus the findings are not generalizable to the "real world." This lack of generalizability, however, is not critical if the primary goal of the experiment is to test a causal hypothesis, which requires demonstrating only that manipulating the independent variable can cause the changes in dependent variable. Crano and Brewer (2002) referred to this goal as "psychological realism," which represents the extent to which "the psychological processes that occur in an experiment are the same as psychological processes that occur in everyday life"

(p. 110). As the authors argue, although an experimental setting may bear little resemblance to real-life experiences, or what they call "mundane realism," the experimental operations still may capture important underlying processes that are highly representative of those that reflect events in the real world. For this reason, establishing experimental realism would be more imperative for validity of true experimental results. To achieve this, the researcher must ensure the internal validity of his or her research by controlling for the effects of confounding variables that might contaminate the findings.

Of course, the good scientist should combine evidence from well-controlled internally valid experiments with more externally valid field studies in which the criterion measures assess severe forms of actual physical aggression and violence such as fighting, hitting, and bullying at school (McLeod, Atkin, & Chaffee, 1972; Buchanan, Gentile, Nelson, Walsh, & Hansel, 2002; Huesmann et al., 2003; Lee & Kim, 2004). The best way to do this is not to "cherry-pick" selected studies that fit your preconceived ideas, but to conduct a meta-analysis that combines the effects of all studies. When this is done, as described, the comprehensive meta-analyses show positive and very significant effect sizes.

A second approach used by those who want to argue against positive effects has been to combine small truths and minor accurate criticisms with the "big lie" that there are no effects. For example, Freedman (2002) found a number of studies on exposure to media violence in which he could correctly point out specific flaws (e.g., experimenter demands, confounding factors, poor aggression measures). As with any other large body of research in the social sciences, there are studies with methodological flaws—some minor, some major. After reviewing only this subset of studies, Freedman concluded that studies finding positive effects are flawed, and therefore the conclusion that media violence promotes aggressive behavior is not justified. However, as Cantor (2003) stated in her review of Freedman's book, although Freedman raised valid questions on certain issues (e.g., the exaggerated number of published articles on violent media and aggression), he failed to differentiate between "the lack of a statistically significant difference" and "a finding of no effect" (p. 468). Moreover, Huesmann and Taylor (2003) pointed out that Freedman's study-by-study analysis was based on a theoretical vacuum, giving no reference to "a psychological theory that has been advanced to explain why observation of violence engenders aggressive behavior" (p. 119). The authors also argued that Freedman's criteria for evaluation were not consistent across studies, leading to biased and inaccurate readings of the findings of extant literature (see reviews by Cantor, 2003; Crooks, 2003; Huesmann & Taylor, 2003).

A third approach to arguing against the conclusion that viewing media violence causes increased aggression has been to argue that viewing media violence reduces aggression. For example, Fowles (1999) and Jones (2002) have contended that watching violent television serves as an outlet for natural violent impulses and therefore decreases aggression in the viewer. This "catharsis" view, perhaps because it draws on Freudian thinking, is often accepted by mass media and pop psychologists who then encourage angry people to vent their feelings through various aggressive and violent activities (e.g., hitting a pillow or punching bag). Despite its popularity, the catharsis hypothesis has no significant empirical support (Geen & Quanty, 1977; Bushman, Baumeister, & Phillips, 2001). For example, one study showed that people who hit the punching bag after reading a procathartic message subsequently became *more* aggressive than people who read an anticathartic message (Bushman, Baumeister, & Stack, 1999).

A fourth argument frequently offered by disbelievers is that media violence researchers have failed to consider alterative causes of aggression such as personality traits, evolution, or domestic violence (Freedman, 2002; Olson, 2004; Savage, 2004). However, no reputable media violence researcher has ever argued that aggressive behavior is caused only by media violence. In fact, it has been shown in several longitudinal studies that the effects of frequent viewing of violent television shows on later aggression are significant even after statistically controlling for other significant causes of aggression such as the child's prior level of aggression, the child's intelligence or academic achievement, and family of origin socioeconomic status (e.g., Huesmann & Eron, 1986; Huesmann et al., 2003).

Still another badly flawed argument by the disbelievers has been that one should not believe that media violence has an effect because as violent video game sales and violent movie sales have increased in the country in recent years, homicides have decreased. This argument would only make sense if one believed that the only cause of homicides was media violence. It makes as little sense as the counterargument that because homicides increased in the 1960s and 1970s, exactly 15 years after most people got televisions, homicides must be caused by television violence.

A remaining common criticism offered by disbelievers, however, has been that the agreed-on effect sizes (around .15 to .20 for field studies and .30 to .35 for experiments) are too small to be "socially significant" even if they are statistically significant. However, a number of scholars (e.g., Abelson, 1985; Rosenthal, 1986; Anderson et al., 2003) have argued that these effect sizes really are socially significant. These researchers pointed out that although correlations around .20 may seem to explain only small proportions of variance, the squared correlation is the wrong metric with which to evaluate the social significance of a public health threat. Effect sizes of $r = .20$ are very socially meaningful because a very large population is exposed to the risk factor, the effects are likely to accumulate with repeated exposure, and no other explanatory factors have much larger effect sizes. Furthermore, a correlation of .20 amounts to a shift in odds from 50/50 to 60/40 for a dichotomous outcome that is binomially distributed. Such a shift in odds for violence is certainly socially significant. Additionally, Bushman and Huesmann (2001) have shown that such effect sizes are as large as or larger than public health threats such as the link between passive exposure to cigarette smoke and lung cancer, condom use and HIV risk, and calcium intake and bone mass. Recently, Ferguson (2009a) has tried to argue that these kinds of comparisons are inappropriate because medical effect sizes are really usually underestimates of true effect sizes. He argues that most effect sizes for therapeutic drugs are computed by examining samples of both well and sick people and therefore underestimate the true effect sizes because, of course, the drug won't do anything for people who are not sick. However, he misses the fact that his argument is irrelevant to the computation of effect sizes for public health threats like smoking and asbestos, which do not just affect ill people.

Psychological Processes Driving the Denial of Media Violence Effects

Given the existing empirical data, existing theoretical explanations for it, and weakness of the counterarguments reviewed in the preceding that the disbelievers have offered, one has to remain puzzled about why the disbelievers disbelieve. In 2003, Huesmann and Taylor first addressed this issue and offered several psychological explanations for why the disbelievers are so adamant in their disbelief. Here, we present and expand on those explanations.

The Need for Cognitive Consistency

First, we argue that a strong drive toward cognitive consistency is behind several reasons for denying the effects of media violence. Cognitive consistency is a remarkably powerful psychological force that affects behaviors and beliefs (Abelson et al., 1968); it requires that new discrepant beliefs be denied or existing beliefs or behaviors be changed when beliefs or beliefs and behaviors are perceived as dissonant. For example, individuals involved in the production or marketing of media violence will find it difficult to believe that viewing violence could be damaging to audiences because that belief would be *cognitively inconsistent* with their existing behavior of producing or marketing violence. The economic fact is that violence in entertainment attracts audiences and makes large amounts of money for its purveyors (Hamilton, 1998). Many of the most vociferous disbelievers represent companies or organizations with vested interests in the money being made by media violence, and a few have been paid by such organizations for what they write (e.g., Friedman, 2002). Recognizing that media violence has negative effects would be discrepant with accepting financial benefits that producing violence engenders or arguing against it produces.

Perhaps equally important, accepting that media violence has negative effects would be discrepant with the purveyors' images of themselves as doing something valuable for society by producing artistic entertainment. This same type of reasoning would apply to those social science consultants to media industries who are paid for their work. Is it possible to be unaffected when one's identity becomes connected to a group with a view? Furthermore, if the purveyors of violence accepted that violence has serious effects on children, they would have to categorize themselves with other purveyors of products that threaten health (e.g., tobacco), which would produce even more dissonance. Years ago the senior author of this chapter was verbally berated in front of a meeting of the director's guild in Hollywood by director Rob Reiner who was incensed that producers of violent films could be compared with purveyors of tobacco. Perhaps his need for cognitive consistency as a director of violent films required him to deny negative effects of media violence, which made it seem cognitively inconsistent and outrageous to him that he could be compared to the tobacco sellers who clearly distribute harmful substances.

This need to maintain a positive self-image also affects the beliefs and behaviors of younger social scientists who have no financial interest in media violence but have grown up using media violence. The generation that graduated from college in the 1960s and began to influence social thinking in the 1970s was the first generation for which television was a major socializer. The generation that graduated from college in the 1990s and began to influence social thinking in the 2000s, however, was the first generation for which video games was a major socializer. We argue that if one grows up developing a self-image that includes "violent television viewer" or "violent video game player" as a major part of one's self-image, the cognitive consistency process will make it very difficult for one to accept that violent television programs or violent video games could cause problems.

In fact, some of the most regular and vocal dissenters in the social science literature have reported having intense and long-lasting involvement with violent media of one kind or another. They do not hide this information; in fact, the information about their spending years of playing multiplayer violent games, or being "glued" to video game consoles, or playing strategy and war games, or playing violent games like "The Borgias" or "Grand Theft Auto," or watching lots of violent television and movies, or even information about their writing violent prose is readily available on their web sites. We are not suggesting that these experiences make the dissenters *consciously* biased. In fact, a number are scientists who strive to be unbiased and value unbiased evaluations. The problem is that cognitive consistency exerts its effect at an unconscious level. Anyone, academic or not, who has an identity associated both with behaving nonviolently and playing violent video games or viewing media violence faces a cognitive inconsistency if he or she accepts the view that those activities make people more violent. This cognitive dissonance creates an unconscious bias against believing that media violence could cause violence that is hard for even them to see.

In addition to affecting those who have grown up using violent media, the cognitive consistency process can lead to a denial of effects for those who believe strongly in the free expression in the mass media. Many individuals with strong liberal beliefs about free expression in the mass media also have strong beliefs about society having a duty to protect children. If they accepted the fact that media violence harms children, they might have to rethink their beliefs about balancing freedom of expression with protecting children. It is easier for them to reduce this cognitive dissonance by denying that media violence has effects than it would be for them to resolve the dissonance by having to alter their beliefs about free expression.

Reactance to Control

Another psychological concept that can account for denial of media violence effects, *reactance,* is most relevant to the artistic community, including authors, movie makes, and game producers. Most humans at a young age develop an aversion to being controlled and respond to such attempts with *reactance,* or attempts to regain or increase their own control (Brehm & Brehm, 1981). We suggest that artists, writers, and producers are particularly susceptible to displaying such reactance when attempts are made to control their creative products, in which their egos are heavily involved. Artists often view statements that their programs or films harm viewers as threats over control. Suppose a researcher tells an artist that a program of his or hers, which is a financial and critical success, is bad because it stimulates violence in the children watching it. The artist, rightly or wrongly, consciously or unconsciously, may well interpret this statement as a threat over control. Therefore, a plausible response by the artist who detests control according to reactance theory would be to attack the researcher's thesis that the program has negative effects on the viewer.

The Third Person Effect

A third psychological phenomenon that is relevant to denial of media violence effects is the *third person effect* in communication research (Davison, 1983). This is the tendency of people to believe that the mass media may be affecting *other* people, but it is not affecting *them* or *their* children—specifically, in this case, the opinion is that "media violence may affect some 'susceptible' people, but it will not affect 'me' or 'my children' because we are impervious to such influences." The third person effect is really not a separate psychological process, but probably a consequence of the two processes described in the preceding (cognitive consistency and reactance). First, with regard to reactance, what viewer wants to admit that he or she is being influenced by messages in the media? To admit this, the viewer would have to admit to being "controlled" to some extent by the media. Reactance would demand some action, then. But if one denies that one is being controlled by the media, one does not need to act, according to reactance theory. Second, with regard to cognitive consistency, if one believes that violence is bad and media violence is causing his or her own aggression or his or her child's aggression, one is in a state of

dissonance. The inconsistency could be resolved, for example, by turning the child away from media violence, but it could also be resolved by simply denying that media violence plays any role in causing one's child's aggressive behavior. Similarly, if one's own self-identity is heavily invested in video games and behaving nonaggressively, it is inconsistent with the individual's self-image to play violent video games if they cause *you* to be aggressive. However, it would be fine if you believe that *you* are impervious to the influence, even if *others* are not.

Desensitization

A fourth psychological process that might account for denial of media violence effects is *desensitization.* As reviewed, researchers have shown that repeated exposure to violence both reduces the negative emotional impact that violence has on an observer and generates a cognitive desensitization in the sense that violence is perceived as more normative (Krahe et al., 2011). We are now at a point in history when the emerging generation of policy makers and researchers has mostly grown up playing violent video games as well as observing violent television and movies. The public today, on average, has been exposed to more scenes of violence than any recent generation. Beatings, mutilations, rapes, and murders are all common in violent video games, movies, and television. Although the total level of violence may not have increased substantially on television and in movies in recent years, the explicitness of the violence and blood and gore has increased. Inevitably, this must desensitize the public more to violence. Consequently, the public is less likely to "see" violent video games or violent movies as violent. Thus, it becomes harder for the public to be concerned about the general issue of media violence.

Desensitization to media violence might also account for the argument that a focus on media violence effects takes attention away from what some researchers and policy makers believe to be "more important" causes of aggression (e.g., observing or being victimized by violence in the family, school, and peer group). Indeed, researchers and policy makers themselves are not immune to desensitization. Dedicated individuals opposed to violence may not "see" the violence in video games, movies, or television as particularly upsetting because they have been raised on a diet of that violence. Consequently, they may focus more on exposure to violence in the real world because they have not been exposed to it themselves. If one is not aware of the theory about why observation of violence stimulates violence, one can easily imagine that observation of real-world violence might have a much more potent effect.

Exposure to "Unbalanced" News Coverage of the Research Findings

Finally, in addition to these four psychological processes that might account for denial of media violence effects, it also is important to note the potentially important influence of news media reports on the topic. Bushman and Anderson (2001) showed that from 1975 to 2000, effect sizes based on scientific studies of the effects of media violence on aggression have actually increased. However, the strongest statements in news reports (the authors found 636 newspaper and magazine articles) about negative effects of media violence peaked in the 1970s and early 1980s, and then weakened through 2000. Specifically, the authors had judges rate news reports on a 21-point scale with −10 assigned to reports stating that violence viewing causes a *decrease* in aggression, −5 assigned to reports saying or implying that parents should *encourage* their children to watch violence, 0 assigned to reports stating there was *no association* between media violence and aggression, +5 assigned to reports saying or implying that parents should *discourage* their children from watching violence, and +10 assigned to reports stating that media violence *causes* aggression. Between 1975 and 1985, the average article was judged at 5.09, but from 1990 to 2000 it was judged as 4.06. This led the authors to speculate on why, as scientific evidence for media violence effects became *stronger,* news articles reported *weaker* effects. The authors speculated that: (1) the news industry might have a vested economic interest in denying the effect; (2) scientists have failed to explain the effect; and (3) the news media may operate according to a "fairness doctrine," that is, in an attempt to present both sides of any argument, they give equal weight to the opinions of both sides. Thus, news reports give "balanced" coverage to both sides of the debate, *despite the fact that the weight of the scientific evidence supports the link between media violence and aggression.* Thus, we argue that the news media may represent a powerful source of influence that shapes public attitudes about media violence effects.

Our view is that the psychological processes we have described along with unbalanced news coverage about any topic, not just media violence, would be likely to lead to intellectually flawed critical thinking by many people about information that is new and in conflict with those individuals' already established beliefs. Scriven and Paul (1987) defined critical thinking thus:

> intellectually disciplined process of actively and skillfully conceptualizing, applying, analyzing, synthesizing, and/or evaluating information gathered from, or generated by, observation, experience, reflection, reasoning, or communication, as a guide to belief and action. In its exemplary form, it is based on universal intellectual values that transcend subject matter divisions: clarity, accuracy, precision, consistency, relevance, sound evidence, good reasons, depth, breadth, and fairness.

They go on to say:

> Critical thinking varies according to the motivation underlying it. When grounded in selfish motives, it is often manifested in the skillful manipulation of ideas in service of one's own, or one's groups,' vested interest. As such it is typically intellectually flawed, however pragmatically successful it might be. When grounded in fairmindedness and intellectual integrity, it is typically of a higher order intellectually, though subject to the charge of 'idealism' by those habituated to its selfish use.

Future Directions

Bushman and Anderson (2001) described some steps that social scientists themselves could take to present their findings and educate the public about the link between exposure to media violence and aggressive behavior. One step is simply to recognize that different types of communication styles are required for the "conservative scientist role" (e.g., presenting research with appropriate caution at scientific conferences) versus the "public educator role" (e.g., offering opinions, without technical language, based on one's general knowledge of the empirical findings). Second, Bushman and Anderson suggested that regarding the public educator role, researchers may communicate to the public how the findings have led to their own personal choices regarding use of violent media. For example, have the research findings affected whether they restrict their own children's violent media use?

Third, the authors argued that researchers need to "realize that the role of disseminating insights gained from their research *is* a part of their job..." (p. 487). In this vein, it is instructive to note that media violence researchers did indeed contribute to the recently highly publicized court case involving a California law requiring parent approval for sales of violent video games to minors. Thirteen scientific experts (all of whom had published original empirical research on media violence effects in peer-reviewed journals) authored a "Statement on Video Game Violence" to accompany a court brief (the Gruel Brief) in support of the media violence–aggression relation; that report was cosigned by 115 additional experts. An opposing brief (the Millett Brief), filed in support of the video game merchants, was signed by 82 individuals, including researchers, medical scientists, and video game industry executives. Two lower courts, followed by the Supreme Court in June 2011, struck down the law based on an infringement of the First Amendment's freedom of speech guarantee. Gentile and Anderson (2011) noted, "Yet, we can imagine that many parents may misunderstand this ruling as suggesting that there is no evidence that video games can have effects on children. It is important to recognize that this ruling is based on constitutional grounds and is only peripherally related to scientific evidence." Interestingly, Sacks et al. (2011) analyzed the scientific credibility of the "experts" who filed the opposing briefs. Sacks et al. found that Gruel Brief authors and signatories were much more likely to have published peer-reviewed journal articles in the field of aggression/violence, and in particular, media violence effects (including in top-tier journals), compared with Millett Brief signatories. For example, 100% of the 13 Gruel Brief authors and 37% of the 115 Gruel signatories had published at least one peer-reviewed article on media violence, compared with 13% of the 82 Millett Brief signatories. Sacks et al. suggested that the courts need to have at their disposal a way to judge the degree to which briefs' "experts" are truly qualified to make judgments to support their arguments.

Gentile and Anderson (2011) anticipated the Supreme Court's decision to overturn the California law. They wrote, "…we understood that many other factors are relevant to this case beyond research, such as legal precedent, constitutional issues, and political factors." Those authors concluded that perhaps the most effective roles for media violence researchers are to continue to collaborate with industry representatives to improve media ratings systems and educate parents to understand and use these systems. Although we agree with this approach, we also think that, as with other socially relevant effects in the past that the public and courts had trouble accepting (e.g., smoking causes cancer, segregating schools causes poor education for minorities), eventually truth will triumph and dissonance between beliefs and behaviors will be reduced more easily by changing behaviors rather than by denying that effects exist.

References

Abelson, R. P. (1985). A variance explanation paradox: When a little is a lot. *Psychological Bulletin, 97*, 129–133.

Abelson, R. P., Aronson, E., McGuire, W. J., Newcomb, T. M., Rosenberg, M. J., & Tannenbaum, R. H. (Eds.) (1968). *Theories of Cognitive Consistency: A Sourcebook*. Chicago: Rand McNally.

American Academy of Pediatrics. (2009). Media violence. *Pediatrics, 124*, 1495–1503.

Anderson, C. A., Benjamin, A. J., & Bartholow, B. D. (1998). Does the gun pull the trigger? Automatic priming effects of weapon pictures and weapon names. *Psychological Science, 9*(4), 308–314.

Anderson, C.A., Berkowitz, L., Donnerstein, E., Huesmann, L.R., Johnson, J., Linz, D., Malamuth, N., & Wartella, E. (2003). The influence of media violence on youth. *Psychological Science in the Public Interest, 4*(3), 81–110.

Anderson, C. A., & Bushman, B. J. (2001). Effects of violent video games on aggressive behavior, aggressive cognition, aggressive affect, physiological arousal, and prosocial behavior: A meta-analytic review of the scientific literature. *Psychological Science, 12*, 353–359.

Anderson, C. A., & Bushman, B. J. (2002). Media violence and the American public revisited. *American Psychologist, June/July 2002*, 448–450.

Anderson, C. A., & Huesmann, L. R. (2003). Human aggression: A social–cognitive view. In Hogg, M. A., & Cooper, J. (Eds.), *Handbook of Social Psychology* . London: Sage, pp. 296–323.

Anderson, C. A., Shibuya, A., Ihori, N., Swing, E. L., Bushman, B. J., Sakamoto, A., Rothstein, H. R., & Saleem, M. (2010). Violent video game effects on aggression, empathy, and prosocial behavior in Eastern and Western countries. *Psychological Bulletin, 136*, 151–173.

Azar, B. (2010). Virtual violence. *Monitor on Psychology, 41*(11), 38.

Bandura, A. (1977). *Social Learning Theory*. New York: General Learning Press.

Bandura, A. (1983). Psychological mechanisms of aggression. In Geen, R., & Donnerstein, E. (Eds.), *Aggression: Theoretical and Empirical Reviews*, vol. 1, pp. 1–40. New York: Academic Press.

Bargh, J. A., & Pietromonaco, P. (1982). Automatic information processing and social perception: The influence of trait information presented outside of conscious awareness on impression formation. *Journal of Personality and Social Psychology, 43*, 437–449.

Berkowitz, L. (1989). Frustration-aggression hypothesis: Examination and reformulation. *Psychological Bulletin, 106*, 59–73.

Berkowitz, L. (1993). *Aggression: Its Causes, Consequences, and Control*. Boston, MA: McGraw Hill.

Berkowitz, L., & LePage, A. (1967). Weapons as aggression-eliciting stimuli. *Journal of Personality and Social Psychology, 7*, 202–207.

Brehm, J. W., & Brehm, S. S. (1981). *Psychological Reactance: A Theory of Freedom and Control*. San Diego: Academic Press.

Bryant, J., & Zillmann, D. (1979). Effect of intensification of annoyance through unrelated residual excitation on substantially delayed hostile behavior. *Journal of Experimental Social Psychology, 15*, 470–480.

Buchanan, A. M., Gentile, D. A., Nelson, D. A., Walsh, D. A., & Hensel, J. (August, 2002). *What goes in must come out:*

Children's media violence consumption at home and aggressive behaviors at school. Paper presented to the International Society for the Study of Behavioral Development Conference, Ottawa, Ontario, Canada.

Bushman, B. J. (1995). Moderating role of trait aggressiveness in the effects of violent media on aggression. *Journal of Personality and Social Psychology, 69*, 950–960.

Bushman, B. J., & Anderson, C. A. (2001). Media violence and the American public: Scientific facts versus media misinformation. *American Psychologist, 56*, 477–489.

Bushman, B. J., Baumeister, R. F., & Phillips, C. M. (2001). Do people aggress to improve their mood? Catharsis beliefs, affect regulation opportunity, and aggressive responding. *Journal of Personality and Social Psychology, 81*(1), 17–32.

Bushman, B. J., Baumeister, R. F., & Stack, A. D. (1999). Catharsis, aggression, and persuasive influence: Self-defeating prophecies? *Journal of Personality and Social Psychology, 76*(3), 367–376.

Bushman, B. J., & Huesmann, L. R. (2001). Effects of televised violence on aggression. In Singer, D., & Singer, J. (Eds.), *Handbook of Children and the Media* . Thousand Oaks, CA: Sage, pp. 223–254.

Bushman, B. J., Huesmann, L. R. (2006). Short-term and long-term effects of violent media on aggression in children and adults. *Archives of Pediatrics & Adolescent Medicine, 160*, 348–352.

Bushman, B. J., & Huesmann, L. R. (2011). Effects of violent media on aggression. In Singer, D. G., & Singer, J. L. (Eds.), *Handbook of Children and the Media*, 2nd ed. . Thousand Oaks, CA: Sage, pp. 231–248.

Cantor, J. (2003). Review of Jonathan L. Freedman's *Media Violence and Its Effect on Aggression. Journalism and Mass Communication Quarterly, 80* (Summer), 468.

Carnagey, N. L., Anderson, C. A., & Bushman, B. J. (2007). The effect of video game violence on physiological desensitization to real-life violence. *Journal of Experimental Social Psychology, 43*, 489–496.

Crano, W. D., & Brewer, M. B. (2002). *Principles and Methods of Social Research*, 2nd ed. Hillsdale, NJ: Lawrence Erlbaum Associates.

Crooks, C. V. (2003). *Media Violence and Its Effect on Aggression: Assessing the Scientific Evidence—A book review. Canadian Psychology, 44*, 179–180.

Davison, W. P. (1983). The third-person effect in communication. *Public Opinion Quarterly, 47*, 1–15.

Eron, L. D., Gentry, J. H., & Schlegel, P. (Eds.). (1994). *Reason to Hope: A Psychosocial Perspective on Violence and Youth*. Washington, DC: American Psychological Association.

Eron, L. D., Huesmann, L. R., Lefkowitz, M. M., & Walder, L. O. (1972). Does television violence cause aggression? *American Psychologist, 27*(4), 253–263.

Ferguson, C. J. (2007a). Evidence for publication bias in video game violence effects literature: A meta-analytic review. *Aggression and Violent Behavior, 12*, 470–482.

Ferguson, C. J. (2007b). The good, the bad and the ugly: A meta-analytic review of positive and negative effects of violent video games. *Psychiatric Quarterly, 78*, 309–316.

Ferguson, C. J. (2009a). Is psychological research really as good as medical research? Effect size comparisons between psychology and medicine. *Review of General Psychology, 13*, 130–136.

Ferguson, C. J. (2009b). Media violence effects: Confirmed truth or just another x-file? *Journal of Forensic Psychology Practice, 9*(2), 103–126.

Ferguson, C. J., & Kilburn, J. (2009). The public health risks of media violence: A meta-analytic review. *Journal of Pediatrics, 154*, 759–763.

Fiske, S. T., & Taylor, S. E. (1984). *Social Cognition*. Reading, MA: Addison-Wesley.

Fowles, J. (1999). *The Case for Television Violence*. Thousand Oaks, CA: Sage.

Freedman, J. (2002). *Media Violence and Its Effect on Aggression*. Toronto: University of Toronto Press.

Geen, R. G., & Quanty, M. B. (1977). The catharsis of aggression: An evaluation of a hypothesis. In Berkowitz, L. (Ed.), *Advances in Experimental Social Psychology*, vol. 10. New York: Academic Press, pp. 1–37.

Gentile, D., & Anderson, C. A. (2011). Don't read more into the Supreme Court's ruling on the California video game law. Iowa State University. Retrieved on September 17, 2011 from http://www.psychology.iastate.edu/faculty/caa/ Multimedia/VGV-SC-OpEdDDAGCAA.pdf .

Gerbner, G., Gross, L., Morgan, M., & Signorielli, N. (1994). Growing up with television: The cultivation perspective. In Bryant, J., & Zillmann, D. (Eds.), *Media Effects* . Hillsdale, NJ: Lawrence Erlbaum Associates, pp. 17–41.

Hamilton, J. T. (1998). *Channeling Violence: The Economic Market for Violent Television Programming*. Princeton, NJ: Princeton University Press.

Henry D. B., Guerra, N. G., Huesmann, L. R., Tolan, P. H., VanAcker, R., & Eron, L. D. (2000). Normative influences on aggression in urban elementary school classrooms. *American Journal of Community Psychology, 28*, 59–81.

Howitt, D., & Cumberbatch, G. (1975). *Mass Media Violence and Society*. New York: John Wiley.

Huesmann, L. R. (1988). An information processing model for the development of aggression. *Aggressive Behavior, 14*, 13–24.

Huesmann, L. R. (1998). The role of social information processing and cognitive schema in the acquisition and maintenance of habitual aggressive behavior. In Geen, R. G., & Donnerstein, E. (Eds.), *Human Aggression: Theories, Research, and Implications for Social Policy* . New York: Academic Press, pp. 73–109.

Huesmann, L. R., & Eron, L. D. (Eds.). (1986). *Television and the Aggressive Child: A Cross-National Comparison*. Hillsdale, NJ: Lawrence Erlbaum Associates.

Huesmann, L. R., & Guerra, N. (1997). Children's normative beliefs about aggression and aggressive behavior. *Journal of Personality and Social Psychology, 72*(2), 408–419.

Huesmann, L. R., & Kirwil, L. (2007). Why observing violence increases the risk of violent behavior in the observer. In Flannery, D. J., Vazsonyi, A. T., & Waldman, I. D. (Eds.), *The Cambridge Handbook of Violent Behavior and Aggression* . Cambridge, UK: Cambridge University Press, pp. 545–570.

Huesmann, L. R., Lagerspetz, K., & Eron, L. D. (1984). Intervening variables in the TV-violence-aggression relation: Evidence from two countries. *Developmental Psychology, 20*, 746–775.

Huesmann, L. R., Moise-Titus, J., Podolski, C., & Eron, L. (2003). Longitudinal relations between children's exposure to TV violence and their aggressive and violent behavior in young adulthood: 1977–1992. *Developmental Psychology, 39*(2), 201–221.

Huesmann, L. R., & Taylor, L. D. (2003). The case against the case against media violence. In Gentile, D. (Ed.), *Media violence and children*. Westport: CT: Greenwood Press, pp. 107–130.

Hurley, S., & Chatter, N. (2004). *Perspectives on Imitation: From Cognitive Neuroscience to Social Science*. Cambridge, MA: MIT Press.

Joint Statement of Congress. (2000). *Joint statement on the impact of entertainment violence on children*. Retrieved December 2, 2003, from http://www2.aap.org/advocacy/releases/jstmtevc.htm.

Jones, G. (2002). *Killing Monsters: Why Children Need Fantasy, Super Heroes, and Make-Believe Violence*. New York: Basic Books.

Klatzky, R. L. (1980). *Human Memory: Structures and Processes*. New York: Freeman.

Krahe, B., Moeller, I., Huesmann, L. R., Kirwil, L., Felber, J., & Berger, A. (2011). Desensitization to media violence: Antecedents, consequences, and content specificity. *Journal of Personality and Social Psychology*, *100*(4), 630–646.

Lee, E., & Kim, M. (2004). Exposure to media violence and bullying at school: Mediating influences of anger and contact with delinquent friends. *Psychological Reports*, *95*(2), 659–672.

McLeod, J, M., Atkin, C. K., & Chaffee, S. H. (1972). Adolescents, parents, and television use: Adolescent self-report measures from Maryland and Wisconsin samples. In Comstock, G. A., & Rubinstein, E. A. (Eds.). *Television and Social Behavior*, vol. 3. Washington, DC: Government Printing Office, pp. 239–313.

Meltzoff, A. N., & Moore, M. K. (2000). Imitation of facial and manual gestures by human neonates: Resolving the debate about early imitation. In Muir, D., & Slater, A. (Eds.), *Infant Development: The Essential Readings* . Malden, MA: Blackwell, pp. 167–181.

Miller, A. H. (1991). Where is the schema? Critiques. *American Journal of Political Science*, *85*, 1369–1380.

Murray, J. P. (1984). Results of an informal poll of knowledgeable persons concerning the impact of television violence. *Newsletter of the American Psychological Association Division of Child, Youth, and Family Services*, *7*(1), 2.

Olson, C. (2004). Media violence research and youth violence data: Why do they conflict? *Academic Psychiatry*, *28*, 144–150.

Paik, H., & Comstock, G. (1994). The effects of television violence on antisocial behavior: A meta-analysis. *Communication Research*, *21*, 516–546.

Payne, B. K. (2001). Prejudice and perception: The role of automatic and controlled processes in misperceiving a weapon. *Journal of Personality and Social Psychology*, *21*, 181–192.

Rizzolatti, G. (2005). The mirror neuron system and its function in humans. *Anatomy and Embryology*, *210*, 419–421.

Rosenthal, R. (1986). Media violence, antisocial behavior, and the social consequences of small effects. *Journal of Social Issues*, *42*, 141–154.

Sacks, D. P., Bushman, B. J., & Anderson, C. A., (2011). Do violent video games harm children? Comparing the scientific amicus curiae "experts" in Brown v. Entertainment Merchants Association. *Northwestern University Law Review: Colloquy.*

Savage, J. (2004). Does viewing violent media really cause criminal violence? A methodological review. *Aggression and Violent Behavior*, *10*, 99–128.

Scriven, M. & Paul, R. (1987). *A statement on critical thinking*. Presented at the 8th International Conference on Critical Thinking and Education Reform,

Signorielli, N. (1990). Television's mean and dangerous world: A continuation of the cultural indicators perspective. In Signorielli, N., & Morgan, M. (Eds.), *Cultivation Analysis: New Directions in Media Effects Research* . Newbury Park, CA: Sage, pp. 85–107.

Slater, M. D., Henry, K. L., Swaim, R. C., & Anderson, L. R. (2003). Violent media content and aggressiveness in adolescents: A downward spiral model. *Communication Research*, *30*, 713–736.

Steinfeld, J. (1972). *Statement in hearings before Subcommittee on Communications of Committee on Commerce* (United States Senate, Serial #92–52, pp. 25–27). Washington, DC: United States Government.

von Salisch, M., Vogelgesang, J., Kristen, A., & Oppl, C. (2001). Preference for violent electronic games and aggressive behavior among children: The beginning of the downward spiral? *Media Psychology*, *14*, 233–258.

Zillmann, D. (1983). Arousal and aggression. In Geen, R., & Donnerstein, E. (Eds.), *Aggression: Theoretical and Empirical Reviews*, vol. 1. New York: Academic Press, pp. 75–102.

Zillmann, D. (1988). Mood management through communication choices. *American Behavioral Scientist*, *31*, 327–340.

Zillmann, D., Bryant, J., Comisky, P. W., & Medoff, N. J. (1981). Excitation and hedonic valence in the effect of erotica on motivated intermale aggression. *European Journal of Social Psychology*, *11*, 233–252.

Children's Media Use: A Positive Psychology Approach

Erik M. Gregory

Abstract

The sky isn't falling when it comes to children's media use. The time is ripe to use media strategically, drawing from the field of positive psychology that promotes socially constructive outcomes that educate, inform, and entertain children for the 21st century. Although much of the academic literature on children's media use has focused on the negative impact media have on children (especially television violence), less has been written on the ability of media to provide greater and more equal access to information for children around the world, or enrich and broaden the learning and understanding of children regardless of geographic location. Certainly, the great opportunities that the information age has brought with it have included risks for children. Parents, educators, and health care professionals are naturally concerned about the negative consequences to children who are interacting more with television and new media (such as the Internet, mobile phone texting, and MP3 players) than they often are with each other. This chapter presents arguments on the prosocial opportunities of children's media use as informed by positive psychology's rise in the past 10 years. Given that the proliferation of media and its globalization are shaping children today, it is important to use this powerful tool for constructive outcomes of engagement.

Key Words: Children and media, children's media, educational media, educational television, impact of media, media and children, media effects, positive psychology, prosocial effects of media

Introduction: A New World of Children's Media

It was the fourth week of my work with Roger, as he liked to be called, and he was still silent. In 2002, I worked as a clinical psychology intern at the well-known Tavistock Psychoanalytic Institute in London treating refugee children and their families who had fled war-torn countries and had made a home in London. These children experienced unspeakable harm as a result of civil war horrors. Roger was an 8-year-old boy from Somalia who was not communicating with his peers, and faced many adjustment issues.

My attempts to engage Roger in discussion were met with no response week after week. I was eager to work with him but became increasingly frustrated. Nonetheless, I held steady. The fifth week passed in silence. During the sixth week, as Roger carefully cut paper into small pieces over a trash bin, he said to me "You are an American." Roger had a passion for American television and films and noticed that I spoke with the same accent. This remark opened the door to my being able to connect with Roger and support him in living a healthier life. As human beings we are storytelling creatures, and capturing story tells one a great deal about individuals, groups, and communities (see Chapter 2). When I returned to the United States, I established the Media Psychology Research Center for Social Change aimed at using the theory and practice of positive psychology to create socially constructive media.

Forty years earlier, when Gerald Lesser, Joan Cooney Ganz, and their colleagues established *Sesame Street,* they were in the company of the only other existing educational television program, *Mr. Rogers' Neighborhood.* The Sesame Workshop, then known as the Children's Television Network, was established to provide educational scaffolding for underserved children. Today there are more than 80 programs considered educational television for children spread across commercial networks and cable television, many with accompanying web sites that add an extra level of interaction for the viewer.

Sesame Street found an audience that was much broader than its original target audience. Sesame Street, and its sibling for older children, The Electric Company, has pioneered a model of creating educational content and then developing compelling stories and characters around that content. Today, there are more than 30 coproductions of Sesame Street around the world designed specifically for the needs and cultures in which the program is aired.

Much has changed since the inception of *Sesame Street.* The world of media has shifted tremendously in terms of technology, access to information, and models of "edutainment." The BBC, for example, funded by a surcharge for television use in the United Kingdom, pioneered programming for children two and younger with The Teletubbies. BBC Children long since departed from the *Sesame Street* model and instead embraced, as commercial producers of educational television do, by first creating compelling characters and story lines with which children will engage followed by the creation of the educational content. It may seem to be a subtle difference, but it has been a successful strategy, giving the Sesame Workshop's model a formidable challenge. In response, *Sesame Street* has changed its well-known introduction and has created a greater number of segments of shorter length, quick cuts, and fast changes to keep today's viewers engaged.

My colleagues and I at the Media Psychology Center for Social Change in Boston worked collaboratively on the program *Sid the Science Kid* in conjunction with KCET Los Angeles, Henson Studios, and Fablevision. *Sid the Science Kid,* originally titled *What's the Big Idea,* was underwritten by a grant from Boeing. The leaders at Boeing wanted to increase an interest in science for children and help adults model how to respond to the natural inquisitiveness of children. The character of Sid was designed to be a lively ethnically ambiguous boy who asked questions about the world around him. He carries a microphone with him as if he is both the interviewer and interviewee, addressing questions about the physical world around him. Sid is meant to be a compelling and likeable character within an environment that children ages 3 to 6 could typically identify with, including a family life, a younger sibling, a loving older adult (his grandmother), a school setting, including a classroom and playground, and friends with unique characteristics that make a well-rounded person when put together.

We emphasized a science/practice model rooted in positive psychology to test the story lines and characters as they were developed so as to provide immediate feedback to the practitioners/creators. Researchers across five sites within urban and suburban communities and all socioeconomic classes led focus groups of children age 3 to 6 using a semistructured interview format. The parents signed waivers to have their children's responses to the story, graphic stills, and television clips recorded. The information was coded and sent to the lab for aggregation. The children provided consistent feedback about the program, characters, and educational content despite their varying backgrounds. Children had particular responses to the colors presented in the programming, including the color of the schoolhouse or the colors of the characters' hair. They engaged with appropriately humorous or fantastical story lines and diverted their attention to storylines that were strongly educational in content. With the accompanying web site activities in which children could practice the scientific experiments they saw on the program, they found similarly certain activities entertaining and engaging, and others that led them to other forms of engagement (such as hand-held gaming systems or other electronic games).

As a result, practitioners were able to refine, discard, or improve their approach with a minimal cost to the producers. This formative research approach provides a model for children's television production, viewer engagement, and a product that can be constructively presented to children.

What Is Positive Psychology?

Historically, American psychology has been predominated by research of that which is unhealthy or pathological. The study of popular media has followed a similar path. Certainly the declining markers of mental health warrant such research. Markers of depression, suicide, anxiety, and divorce are high. Although as a nation we are materially wealthy in comparison with other countries, we seem to be less healthy.

It should not come as a surprise that Americans have embraced positive psychology, with its emphasis on self-betterment, and made the pursuit of happiness an industry unto itself. Book publishers in the United States have seen an increase of 12% growth annually in these sales (Carpenter, 2008). Happiness is so part of the very fabric of this country that it is written as a right in the Declaration of Independence, which emphasizes the pursuit of "life, liberty, and happiness." Much of this pursuit of happiness is fueled in the form of consumerism created by industries that promote the consumption of goods (Gilbert, 2007).

Today, the question of well-being continues to play a central role in our personal lives and the life of modern science. Researchers have a wealth of data regarding individual physical and material well-being, yet despite all of this data they are just beginnings to understand why some people seem to experience more well-being than others.

Daniel Meyers' (1992) *The Pursuit of Happiness* captures the dilemma our society faces today in trying to understand well-being. He wrote:

> For never has a century known such abundance, or such massive genocide and environmental devastation.
> Never has a culture experienced such comfort and opportunity, or such widespread depression.
> Never has a technology given us so many conveniences, or such terrible instruments of degradation and destruction.
> Never have we been so self-reliant, or so lonely.
> Never have we seemed so free, or our prisons so overstuffed.
> Never have we had so much education, or such high rates of teen delinquency, despair, and suicide.
> Never have we been so sophisticated about pleasure, or so likely to suffer broken or miserable marriages.
> (Myers, 1992)

In a meta-analysis of studies examining well-being, David Meyers found a number of popular notions about what it takes to be happy dispelled. These *myths* include the ideas that:

- Few people are genuinely happy.
- Wealth buys well-being.
- Tragedies or traumatic events destroy happiness.
- Happiness springs from memories of intense, if rare, positive experiences.
- Teens and the elderly are the unhappiest populations.
- One gender is happier than the other.

In the past 20 years since Meyers wrote this, there has been a great deal of research on what makes us happy and healthy. Positive psychologists have led the way in asking questions about positive traits, fostering excellence, subjective well-being, resiliency, life satisfaction—and have done so with the use of the scientific method so as to understand the complexity of human behavior (Seligman & Csikszentmihalyi, 2000). Seligman and Csikszentmihalyi (2000) wrote "psychology is not just the study of pathology, weakness, and damage; it is also the study of strength and virtue . . . treatment is not just fixing what is broken; it is nurturing what is best" (p. 7).

Positive psychologists study the building blocks of characteristics such as courage, forgiveness, optimism, hope, and joy, so that there can be a greater understanding of how to promote that which is healthy in human beings. Media may be one of the greatest means of providing a model for how to implement tools of well-being.

This provides an entirely different framework in which to understand the potential impact of children's media use. By providing frameworks for learning, problem solving, collaborative and prosocial behaviors, and an understanding of self and others, children's media can go beyond passive consumption for entertainment purposes only, and act as a scaffolding for learning and understanding in addition to entertainment.

Applying Positive Psychology

One's lived experience may vary greatly depending on age, culture, gender, geographic upbringing, and socioeconomic status. There is a large component of life that is biologically determined: body type, physical characteristics, and a predisposition to certain ailments, for example. In contrast, there is also an aspect of living that is determined by how one thinks and feels about life. Today, media have become central to the 21st century individual's experience from the moment one wakes up to the time one goes to bed with media interaction including television, Internet, smartphones, billboards, radio, and newspapers.

Much of positive psychology research in the past decade has focused on happiness. It is a slippery term that can be defined in many ways and it joins other interests of positive psychology, including morality, resiliency, courage, and hope.

There have been several approaches to understanding happiness, and many of these studies have found that most of all, an individual's personal qualities such as intelligence, health, attractiveness, income, and education are the most important individual difference variables to happiness (Campbell, 1981). These variables influence an individual's social competence, which in turn improves the individual's ability to develop relationships, which is central to well-being. An early study on happiness by Andrews (1976) found that only 10% of the variance in happiness is a result of demographic factors such as age, gender, and socioeconomic status. Diener (1984) estimated that demographic factors accounted for 15% of the variance in happiness and that more than 75% of the determinants of happiness are related to environmental and social qualities. More recently, Lykken and Tellegen (1996) argued that demographic factors (defined by socioeconomic status, educational attainment, family income, marital status, and religious commitment) accounted for only 3% of the variance in well-being and added genetic traits as contributing from 44% to 52% of the variation in well-being. Today, we are often influenced by what the media has to tell us we need to have, look, or be like so as to be happy. Some programming can uplift us, provide diversion and entertainment, but a lot of programming makes us feel less good about ourselves. Furthermore, commercials compel individuals to want and purchase items they may not need.

Regardless of the 3% or 15% figure, overall an individual's temperament (whether from nature or nurture), cognitive abilities, goals, culture, and coping skills have a far greater mediating influence of life events and their effects on an individual's sense of well-being. This is not to say that nothing can change an individual's sense of well-being or that one is or isn't genetically born predisposed to subjective well-being. What is known is that a happy person in today's Western society has a profile of a positive temperament, a resilient ability to look on the positive more than the negative, does not focus on bad circumstances, lives in an economically developed society in which food and shelter are not the focus of one's primary efforts, has friends, and is able to make progress toward reaching his or her goals (Diener et al., 1999). Children's television writers, producers, and developers are now embracing this research in the crafting of characters and prosocial learning objectives.

Measuring Well-Being

Research has largely focused on subjective well-being (SWB) has focused on the ultimate rating of well-being—the individual's self-assessment (Diener, 1984). Those individuals who report a high degree of SWB tend to have more positive thoughts and feelings about their lives. More specifically, such individuals speak of satisfaction with life in a number of domains, including relationship and occupation. Affectively, individuals with a high degree of SWB have a positive appraisal of events around them. Individuals with a lower SWB tend to feel that their lives contain a number of undesirable qualities and affectively feel more anxious and depressed.

However, the knowledge of how *well* an individual feels overall does not provide information about how the individual feels poorly overall (Bradburn & Caplovitz, 1965; Myers & Diener, 1995). Although the frequencies of good and bad feelings may be inversely related, individuals who experience intense high moods may also experience intense low moods. Therefore, subjective well-being cannot be considered simply the absence of bad feelings.

There are a number of common beliefs about happiness that have been verified and refuted by research. For example, happiness is not related to age. There is no time in life in which individuals are markedly happier than other years. In a 1980s survey of 169,776 people across 16 nations, knowing an individual's age did not give insight into an individual's sense of well-being (Myers & Diener, 1995). Emphasis on what was important to the individual did vary with age, however.

The most concrete contributor to happiness is adaptation. Although many individuals equate subjective well-being with health, age, or income, there is a minimal long-term effect because of the variability of these factors. Rather, predictors of higher subjective well-being include having goals, having the freedom to pursue those goals, and making progress toward goals. Diener et al. (1993) found that money, social skills, and intelligence were predictive of subjective well-being only if they were relevant to how a person structured his or her life and personal goals. In the case of media use, happiness increases not from passive media consumption, but rather from involvement in media and other valued activities that engage one and provide progress toward one's goals (Diener et al., 1993).

There is evidence that individuals who cultivate experiences of positive emotions do indeed experience greater psychological well-being and possibly also physical health (Fredrickson, 2001). Media have been a major factor in shaping emotional states. Folkman et al. (1997) found that experiences of positive emotions during periods of stress helped individuals cope with the event (Folkman, 1997). This has led to research on positive emotions and resiliency. Individuals who are resilient are considered to be able to recover more quickly and efficiently from stressful experiences. A study by Fredrickson (2001) found that individuals who experienced more positive emotions became more resilient over time to adversity. Educational programming and sitcoms have demonstrated an ability to increase affective states. This upward spiral, as the authors refer to it, enhanced coping skills over time. This finding suggests that positive emotions, although often temporary, may have a cumulative effect and positive long-term consequences for the well-being of an individual.

Optimism and Pessimism: What We Watch, Read, or Surf Influences How We Think and Feel

In his research on learned helplessness and learned optimism, Martin Seligman (1991) argues that how an individual approaches the world through thoughts, feelings, and actions markedly influences the way in which the individual both experiences and explains the world. Seligman in particular has spent the past 30 years looking at how optimistic thoughts can influence the well-being of an individual and how pessimistic thoughts can lead to depression (Seligman, 1991). An optimist may explain the experiences of the world in terms that are more self-efficacious, which in turn influences his or her thoughts, feelings, or action. These thoughts, feelings, and actions in turn influence the experience of the individual. This looping mechanism can function at higher and lower levels depending on the spectrum of an individual's explanatory style.

Seligman (1991) defines a pessimist as an individual who tends to "believe bad events will last a long time, will undermine everything they do, and [bad events] are their own fault;" whereas he defines an optimist as an individual who "believes defeat is a temporary setback . . . that defeat is not their fault: circumstances, bad luck, or other people brought [the circumstances] about" (Seligman, 1991 p. 45).

Researchers have found that optimists have different coping skills than pessimists when confronting challenging situations (Scheier, Carver, & Bridges, 2001). Optimists use more problem-focused coping strategies, acceptance, use of humor, and positive reframing when confronted with challenges. Pessimists tend to cope through denial, and disengaging from the situation at hand. Scheier et al. (2001) found the following coping tendencies for optimists and pessimists—characteristics that can be modeled via media.

The coping tendencies of optimists include:

- Information seeking
- Active coping and planning
- Positive reframing
- Seeking benefit
- Use of humor
- Acceptance

The coping tendencies of pessimists include:

- Suppression of thoughts
- Giving up
- Self-distraction
- Cognitive avoidance
- Focus on distress
- Overt denial

The media have the ability to model constructive coping strategies that include adaptive changes to life's challenges, for example, through the documented lives of others via film, television, or print.

In today's world, Seligman sees that the pursuit of happiness in industrial societies such as the United States has led to an emphasis of the "I," which again is largely reflected in media narratives with an emphasis on individualism and the promotion of an egocentric perspective. He argues that more individuals today experience depression because of modern society's emphasis on personal control and autonomy over commitment to duty and common enterprise (Seligman, 1991). This creates a heightened expectation of individual power with the view that achievement is one's own success and failure is one's own downfall. Without social supports such as family, church, or friends, the failure or fall of an individual is often in isolation. Such buffers existed earlier, Seligman argues, when a greater "we" existed in the form of extended family, faith, and community. Without such buffers, individuals are more prone to depression.

Such different approaches to the world or "explanatory styles," have a great impact on an individual's thoughts, feelings, and actions (Seligman, 1991). At the center of understanding the influence of optimism and pessimism on an individual's life is the notion of helplessness—a feeling that nothing an individual does influences the outcomes of his or her actions. An optimist's explanatory style will stop the experience of helplessness, whereas a pessimist's explanatory style spreads the experience of helplessness.

Seligman argues a pessimist's belief that his or her actions are "futile" is at the center of depressed functioning. He has labeled this *learned helplessness*.

Learned helplessness affects the individual's quality of life (as measured through thoughts, feelings, and actions in this study) (Seligman, 1991):

- Depressed mood
- Loss of interest in activities
- Decreased energy and psychomotor retardation
  - Inattentiveness and inability to think clearly

Most individuals who experience some sort of failure will feel a sense of helplessness. For optimists this experience is short-lived and creates a positive resiliency allowing the individual to continue with life in other domains. For pessimists, the explanatory style tends to maintain helplessness for longer periods of time and casts a shadow on current events.

Human beings are meaning making creatures and we search for explanations for events and experiences in our lives. We differ in the way we explain events and is referred to as an individual's "explanatory style." The habit of explaining events influences individual achievements, quality of life, and physical and mental health (Seligman, 1991).

Media and Flow

Flow is defined as activities in which there is a match between high challenge and high skills (Csikszentmihalyi, 2008). The outcome of Flow is that the ego, or self-consciousness, disappears. After the experience of Flow, people report feeling stronger and more vital (Csikszentmihalyi, 2008). Research participants of Flow report feeling best when skills and challenges are both high, and tend to be negative, regardless of the activity, if challenges and skills are low (Csikszentmihalyi, 2008). Flow experiences may emerge from media consumption, including interactive video gaming, and challenging and engaging narratives. In fact, much of the appeal of video games is that it does provide flow states for the user in which the skills the user develops are placed against an equal challenge. Once the individual has developed the skill set to complete a game level, the challenge increases to a higher level of sophistication.

An opportunity for action that is in balance with the ability to act (the match of skills and challenges) can produce a Flow experience. If one considers any sort of game or art form, there is a match of skill to a challenge (in sports, for example, one wants to play an equal opponent so as to be challenged and not to be bored). The experience of such engagement, ecstasy, or Flow creates a condition in which people feel a sense of peace and a decrease in anxiety and depression. Csikszentmihalyi argues that worries disappear because the individual does not have the information processing capacity to simultaneously focus on the task at hand *and* to worry. This results from the concentration, skills are in balance, goals are clear, and feedback is present. Flow researchers have found that the worst moments in an individual's day-to-day life are when he or she is self-conscious (Csikszentmihalyi & Figurski, 1982). Today's gaming consoles that interact with the user in the form of motion control devices (Nintendo Wii Controller, Sony Move, Xbox Kinect) are using this principle to engage and move players.

When challenge and skills are out of balance, life can feel unsatisfying and overwhelming (the challenges of life exceed the individual's time or skills), which results in anxiety and stress. Those who feel "underwhelmed" (the challenges of life do not engage an individual's time or skills) become bored and anxious. The findings from positive psychology are that individuals need to find creative means of including flow experiences in their lives so as to feel greater engagement in daily life.

Tuning in to Today's Concerns

In the daily life of today's children, there is access to a large number of media choices, including satellite and cable television, Internet, radio, MP3 players, computers, video games, mobile phones, and texting, as well as magazines designed for them. Across the globe, children are also exposed to much of the similar media in the form of television programs such as *The Simpsons* and *Sesame Street,* and video game titles that have similar large followings in the United Kingdom, the United States, France, Germany, and Israel. In addition, the proliferation of Twitter, Facebook, and e-mail messaging has created social networks that allow information to be sent at the click of a button.

The United Nations Convention on the Rights of the Child (CRC) adopted in 1989 foresaw the impact media would continue to have on children globally. This convention defines the rights of children reflected in four points that are designed to guide political decision making and the well-being of children.

1. The child's best interests are primary in all decision making.
2. The opinions of children should be included in decision making.
3. The ability of a child to thrive, not only survive, is critical.
4. Children should enjoy rights without discrimination.

The CRC recognizes the importance of media in the context of the information age. We recognize media's potential to provide access to information and material from a diversity of national and international realms that promote "social, spiritual and moral well-being and physical and mental health" (UNICEF, 2004).

The CRC recommends that countries that ratify it should:

- Encourage the mass media to disseminate information and material of social and cultural benefit to the child.
- Encourage international cooperation in the production, exchange, and dissemination of such information and material from a diversity of cultural, national, and international sources.
- Encourage the production and dissemination of children's books.
- Encourage the mass media to have regard to linguistic needs of children who belong to minority groups or who are indigenous.
- Encourage the development of appropriate guidelines for the protection of the child from information and materials injurious to his or her well-being

In particular, Article 17 of the CRC addresses the role of children's use of media and its impact. Media is seen primarily as a tool to disseminate information that promotes the well-being of the child. Central to Article 17 is that media contribute to the healthy development of children while also nurturing the possibility of well-informed citizens. Thus, children are accorded the right to both participate and benefit from today's media as both a moral and ethical mandate.

Television Consumption

Television continues to be the predominant source of media consumption for children around the world. According to the January 2010 research report from the Kaiser Family Foundation, the average child in the United States consumed on average 8 hours of media per day, with 5 of those hours dedicated to television viewing. In other words, media consumption is now equal to the average amount children sleep. This is a 1½-hour average increase from media consumption 5 years ago (Kaiser Family Foundation, 2010). It is a trend that is taking place around the world. If most of today's children (especially in industrialized countries) spend so much time with media, then it is critical to develop content that reflects constructive social outcomes.

From the 1980s to the 1990s the number of television channels, household television sets, and hours spent watching television doubled across all three domains (UNICEF, 2004). In the late 1990s, 50 cable channels were launched specifically targeted at children, with many having great success (Nickelodeon, Cartoon Network, Disney Channel, ABC Family, TV Land). The consolidation of commercial media has led to programming that is owned by a few media producers who provide programming for much of the world. This business model has reduced local productions and challenged public broadcasters, who have traditionally created high-quality, educational programming, with far fewer resources. For example, today, nearly 90% of children's programming in Latin America is imported. This is problematic in that the content often includes characters or situations that do not reflect the local culture. On the other hand, the gaps between children and varying cultures is increasingly bridged, and has created a shared worldview—as well as a global love of Bart Simpson (now translated into more than 100 languages) (Kaiser, 2010).

Radio Consumption

Although radio listening has been eclipsed by Internet usage in the United States, internationally this is the second most popular use of media for children (UNICEF, 2004). With an increase in quality programming across countries in Africa and in Russia, there has been a boom in radio listening. Most children and youth listen to the radio for music or entertainment. In the former Yugoslavia, the ANEM network, for example, has created a large following by providing information and entertainment for social connections (UNICEF, 2004).

Internet Consumption

The fastest rise in media consumption has been in Internet usage, especially among boys. There are differences in access to computers and the Internet between developed and developing countries, but this gap is quickly closing as governments invest in computer purchasing programs, and consumers tap into and seek locally provided Internet access (such as cafés or libraries). Users of the Internet are utilizing this medium for entertainment, gaming, education, consumerism, communication, and socializing.

Print Media Consumption

Although the use of television, radio, and the Internet increase, print media continues to suffer declines in readership. Many newspapers and magazines that are adapting to vehicles of new media are producing their content specifically for the Internet or electronic readers. The availability of news content online immediately and at the touch of a button has made reading print newspapers outdated to most children and youth. On the other hand, print media that caters to specialized interests such as comic books, and magazines that focus on fashion, sports, science, or music continue to find a market for children and youth (Kaiser, 2010).

Turning Off Antisocial Programming

Research on media effects often examines the impact that violence has on children. Indeed, we consume a great deal of media in the United States (which is exported abroad) that depicts murder and mayhem. Researchers estimate that by the time a child reaches the age of 18 in the United States, he or she will have seen 200,000 acts of violence on television (Robinson, 2001). These reports reflect that such consumed violence produces aggressive attitudes and behaviors, desensitizes one to violence, and promotes a worldview of fear and danger. The conclusions to these studies argue that reducing the amount of television and video games that children consume will also reduce aggressive behavior in elementary-age school children (see Chapter 9). We are living in a digital age in which media surrounds us and is being consumed more than less (Kaiser, 2010). Although I agree that media use should be regulated for children, I believe that the content consumed is a more critical question for the 21st century.

Niche Audiences

The producers of entertainment media are looking for niche audiences as the consumption of media becomes more fragmented. Today it is no longer the case that millions of people gather around the television at the same time and day to watch such milestones as they did for the finale of *M*A*S*H* (with 106 million viewers) (*Los Angeles Times*, 2010), or *I Love Lucy*'s "Lucy Goes to the Hospital" (with 72% of all television viewers tuned in) (Bianco, 2004). Some notable sports events are the exception to this rule. Viewers today watch programming when and where they want, with the ability to record or stream programming to tablets, phones, and gaming devices.

The Teletubbies ushered in programming targeted at a new market for children age 2 and younger. The success of this program brought a number of competitors into this niche market, including the Baby Einstein videos (later bought by Disney) that promised that viewing would increase language acquisition and help with developmental steps for toddlers. The videos were later recalled when evidence did not support the claims made by the manufacturer (Noah, 2009). In fact, a recent study confirmed that babies who watch television 60 minutes or more daily had developmental scores one-third lower at 14 months than babies who were not exposed (Schute, 2010). Even if television viewing includes educational programming, children at this early stage in life need to interact, play, and engage with their world for basic developmental and learning needs. Later, educational programming can act as a scaffolding to further inquiry and curiosity.

Age-Inappropriate Content

Inappropriate viewing (content constructed for audiences that have the skills to suspend belief) of media content does have long-lasting effects on children that may induce fear and anxiety. In a survey of 2,000 elementary and middle school children, reported anxiety or depression from watching television that frightened them and 90% could recollect the disturbing image in detail (Wilson, 2008).

The fear factor induced by watching age-inappropriate content goes beyond children. Clearly, viewers across the age spectrum of development are affected by television content. In particular, catastrophic news coverage psychologically draws us to listening and watching. With 24-hour cable news programming that needs to be filled, individuals are exposed to graphic violence that induces a lack of safety that is not in proportion to reality. Children are particularly vulnerable to such exposure.

It is no wonder that 70% of Americans report that they are worried about popular culture and moral standards (Wilson, 2008). The Public Broadcasting Network (PBS)'s programming contains 18% violent content compared with the 84% of violent content on premium cable shows. Perhaps public objections to violent entertainment are different from what a majority of the public consumes in the privacy of the home. Some psychologists argue that a mixture of culture (American individualistic frontier culture) combined with a sense of powerlessness in our daily 21st century lives shapes the media we consume, and thus often reflects feelings of disempowerment.

Media Literacy

As a society, we have let consumerism run amok, and we do not protect our children from wisely crafted and expensive commercials designed to elicit a desire and purchase response (see Chapter 6). Children do not have the cognitive savvy to reject seductive advertising (in fact, neither do most adults). The average child sees more than 20,000 commercials per year, of which more than 60% promote high sugar and fat foods and toys (Canadian Pediatric Society, 2003).

The Benefits of Prosocial Media

It is a fact of 21st century life that many children today are socialized through media. Children develop their emotional and social life through an interactive process with the world. This includes absorbing rules, norms, and values of the culture in which they live so as to create individual and group connections. Typically, children have found models of behavior through emotional interaction with parents, teachers, and friends. Yet today, television, Internet, radio, and other types of media also interact with children and reflect back models of emotional and social behavior.

The media's influence depends on choice and content. Certainly exposure to media affects children's well-being and development, and links have been found between increased consumption of media and obesity rates. On the other hand, researchers have found that children can learn about sympathy and empathy from watching the emotions of their favorite characters on television (Wilson, 2008). There is additional evidence that children who engage in educational programming and situational comedies that are age appropriate experience prosocial outcomes including altruism, cooperation, and tolerance.

Children become attached to their television characters and often reflect the affective states of these characters. *Sesame Street* has included the role of emotions and coping with emotional situations into its educational content. This increases some children's sense of empathy and tolerance for others (Wilson, 2008).

Many child advocacy groups have rallied against the morals and values represented in popular media from graphic language, suggestion of sexual situations, acts of violence, theft, and other antisocial behaviors. Yet researchers continue to point out the prosocial impact and its potential in media to shape moral development. Kremar and Curtis (2003) found that just as exposure to media violence led to judgments that violence is morally acceptable, exposure to media that provided a model of socially constructive outcomes led viewers to discount violence as a choice for social interaction and problem solving.

Rather than model antisocial behaviors in media, we need to examine how media can also model and teach prosocial behaviors—behaviors that benefit another person through altruism, sharing, friendliness, cooperation, and acceptance.

Smith et al. (2006) sampled hundreds of entertainment programs over a 1-week period and found that 73% of the programs had at least one act of altruism. Children who were exposed to such programming exhibited more prosocial behavior than children who were not. This is not a short-term situation. Children who were exposed to programs that demonstrated helping, donating, or sharing were more likely to enact such behavior 2 to 3 days later as compared with a control group. As social creatures, we model our behaviors on what we observe in our environment, and this is reflected in the viewers' behavior. Reinforcement of these messages enhances the impact of prosocial media.

Similarly, children exposed to programming that included a diversity of ethnic characters interacting collaboratively, expressed greater positive attitudes toward different groups, including respect and tolerance (Smith, 2006). This model has been used by the Sesame Workshop for a series in which the characters live on Israel Street who are friends with characters on Palestine Street. One study compared the social attitudes of Israeli and Palestinian preschoolers before the series aired in 1998 and 4 months later (Anderson et al, 2007). Before the debut of the programs, most of the children 4 and older held negative stereotypes about the other culture. Four months after the program aired, the Israeli children showed more positive attitudes toward Arabs. Palestinian children's attitudes became more negative, but later studies revealed that fewer Palestinian children had access to the program.

Educational software programs have been associated with increased academic skills as well, including improved reading and writing ability (Strommen & Revelle, 1990). Certain types of video gaming have improved physical and cognitive abilities for those who are able to master the games (see Chapter 18).

Switching Channels: The Prosocial Opportunities of Television and Media

In a meta-analysis of 1,043 studies on the effects of television on social behavior, Hearold (1986) found that effect sizes for prosocial "behavior treatments and behavior were consistently greater than for antisocial treatments of behavior." Therefore, according to this study, viewers of television who watched violent programs that included "antisocial treatments" would reflect an increase of antiso-cial behavior such as aggression (moving from the 50th percentile to the 62nd percentile of antisocial behavior), and if viewers watched "pro-social treatments" they would move from the 50th percentile of prosocial behavior to the 74th percentile which was typically reflected in altruistic behavior. In fact, 27 acts of altruistic behavior were identified in 26.5 hours of prime time programming, which reflects more than one act per hour of such behavior.

The potential for media to increase tolerance, cooperation, and altruism is reflected in the existing studies on media effects, although far fewer in number (in a similar way to anxiety and depression studies far outweighing studies in resiliency and health). Wilson (2008) in particular has led the pack in this research and has found that susceptibility to media, both positively and negatively, depends a great deal on the child's age, gender, and the extent to which he or she identifies with characters on the screen.

After 40 years on television with countless learning outcome studies, *Sesame Street* has demonstrated that it can help children ages 3 to 6 learn not only about preschool academic content, but also about emotions. In fact, *Sesame Street* has incorporated storylines about Hurricane Katrina (with Big Bird's nest destroyed) and the 9/11 terrorists attacks through Mr. Hooper's store being engulfed in fire.

Central to the healthy development of children is their ability to acquire emotional empathy. Children who are emotionally empathic tend toward more socially desirable group behavior. Empathy is of course the ability to recognize the emotions of someone else and put oneself in another's situation. Children's characters that are viewed as realistic, empathic, and reflect the gender of the young viewer provide a model to emulate. In fact, the most beloved children's characters are those with a sense of depth, in semirealistic situations, and act as models for prosocial behavior.

In a sample of 2,000 programs on television, a recent study showed that 73% included some form of altruism (defined by the researchers as supporting, helping, giving, or sharing) (Wilson, 2008). Examples of such programming for children beyond *Sesame Street* included *Dora the Explorer, Dragon Tales, Arthur, The Suite Life of Zach and Cody,* and *Drake and Josh*. These shows, *Dora the Explorer* in particular, provide children a world that may be different from their own with characters from various ethnic backgrounds and cultures that have adventures around the world.

Long-Term Impact

It remains debatable how much media influences children over the lifespan of development. What is known from the research literature is that social trends exist that include media as a factor (across culture and geographic regions) (American Institute of Research, 2004):

- Entertainment media continue to be a growing influence on children's identity development and style choices.
- There is a decreasing role of traditional sources of influence, including family, school, community, and faith.
- Popular media glorifies individualism and minimizes collective problem solving.
- Popular media emphasizes celebrity and glamour.
- Media may perpetuate stereotypes.
- A distortion of reality and increased expectation of what is needed in life is found in higher consumers of media.

Some of these effects are troublesome, especially given the exponential consumption of all types of media by children regardless of content, yet the negative outcome of these attributes only speaks to the missed opportunities of the positive impact media can have on children, individuals, groups, and communities. Children's world outlook can be opened, while stereotypes are destroyed, ideas are ignited, critical thinking is nurtured, and social and political engagement is increased through media. Human beings are natural born storytellers, and we learn about the opportunities and constraints in life and how to react to them from stories. Media are our modern-day storytellers that have the proven ability to inform, educate, and entertain. The opportunity to create socially constructive positive psychology-based programming that is authentic, enriching, challenging, and engaging, and allows children to understand and interact with the world around them is tremendous. It is time to examine the healthy, optimistic, coping, meaningful, resilient, hopeful, kind, compassionate, and courageous content that can be modeled through creative and quality media programming.

Children engage with entertainment-oriented media that provide intriguing and interesting characters, and fun style and language within a colorfully packaged presentation. They, like all media consumers, are drawn to particular areas that interest them with messages that are often uplifting or engage the skill set they have developed. Beyond entertainment, children look for models of how to negotiate life and make sense of the world from the simple to the sophisticated. This includes themes such as identity development and social group formation. Children need to be reflected in the media they consume; and within that reflection, there need to be healthy messages that better incorporate prosocial content, such as curiosity, tolerance, collaboration, and service.

Recommendations

Media can be used to inform, entertain, and educate. The academic literature on children's media use focuses mainly on the negative impact of media consumption, and in particular television violence, and misses the socially constructive possibilities of media. Children's media designed from a positive psychology framework reflected in programming such as *Dora the Explorer* or *Sid the Science Kid* are useful for not only educating children, but also for providing models of courage, hope, and optimism.

Television continues to be a primary source of media consumption for children, although other types of media are vying for attention. Most content is built around the television screen and then has a life in other content forms. Although the amount of media consumption is startling and imbalanced, it is the content consumed by children that is the central issue.

Children have mediated experiences daily that shape their understanding and experience of the world. Many parents, teachers, and educators naturally worry about exposure to media and its harmful outcomes, there is research evidence that exposure to television that includes strong academic and positive social content can be useful as well (Wilson, 2008). A child who watches the characters from *Bob the Builder* work with friends to fix a challenge receives a very different message than the use of aggression and violence to solve a problem in other cartoons or adult entertainment.

It stands to reason that anything taken to the extreme is unhealthy. Children's media use is ultimately about the quality and quantity consumed. Most of us reading this probably grew up on a healthy diet of formulaic sitcoms and police dramas. In retrospect, I would have preferred to be a proactive consumer of media than a passive one, but I have arrived at that point today and encourage us to help future generations navigate this digital era as such as well.

Children will consume media whether we like it or not. The good news is that adults can influence how children use media. The key is to work toward helping children choose time for physical activity wisely and to shape children's exposure to media that emphasizes prosocial learning, whether it is entertainment or video gaming. It is ideal to watch with your child and be there to answer questions.

Media literacy is important to help children consume media in a healthy manner through guidance, making choices, and making time in front of any screen useful, enjoyable, and entertaining without detracting from the many other important aspects of playing, growing, and learning. The key is to tap into the positive rich potential of media. As parents, educators, or health care workers, we can help by being media literate ourselves so as to be better consumers of the increasing media content and technological access to media.

Storytelling has shifted locations, from around the medieval community hearth listening to stories crafted largely for adults, to the Victorian nursery where many children first engaged in listening to stories, to the screens of today where stories are many and varied. We love our stories; and we need to make sure we choose the healthiest ones for our children.

In particular, suggestions for healthier media use include (Adapted from the American Institute for Research, 2004 and Gentile, 2004):

• Helping children to consume media in a healthier manner by differentiating between entertainment and reality. In addition, adults can help children become more media literate by deconstructing commercials and watching programming critically.

• Sharing television viewing. Young children should not have a television or Internet access in their private room.

• Choosing not only wisely, but also in proportion to other activities. Limiting viewing is OK.

• Looking at media as a wonderful resource of information to understand the world. It provides quick and inexpensive communication with friends and family around the world.

Well-constructed media can provide children with a way of developing their personal strengths and using resources for further discovery and growth. Media that includes the following aspects can actually provide a model for resiliency that helps individuals negotiate the future challenges of life. These include:

- Creative problem solving skills
- Learning to get along with others
- Seeing oneself reflected in a positive manner in television programming
- A model of humor and optimism as *Bob the Builder* exclaims "Can we fix it, Yes we can"
- An exposure of the application of talents or assets or interests to spark interest in a child
- Examples of altruism and nurturance
- Exposure to models of self-efficacy
- Establishing healthy prosocial models
- Modeling positive behavior
- Create new stories about the self and the world
- Concepts of positive functioning
- Self-acceptance
- Personal growth
- Purpose in life
- Environmental mastery
- Autonomy
- Positive relations

Learned optimism emerges from one's environment (Seligman, 1995). Modeling optimism for children often enables them to be more resilient and feel better about themselves. Although Seligman attributes high television watching to pessimism, he points out that viewing television violence leads to this explanatory style but does not expand on constructive television viewing and its opportunity for modeling optimistic explanatory styles.

Optimism is believed to be shaped by early childhood experiences that include trust and secure attachments with the primary caregiver (Bowlby, 1990).

Synder et al. (1994) believes that hope is independent of heredity and is a learned component that is influenced by caregivers. Again, Snyder looks at the importance of attachment the child has with a caregiver and that strong attachment is critical for acquiring a sense of hope as an adult.

The same foundations applied to positive schooling, which consists of promoting care, trust, and respect for diversity and to help students attain learning goals, is seen in media and can be promoted with media developed for children. The goals are translated into greater hope with an ultimate outcome of that child eventually making a social contribution.

Media consumption is very much part of the 21st century's digital lifestyle. Positive psychology, its approaches, and goals are the antidote to creating media content that educates, informs, and entertains. In the words of my beloved mentor and cocreator of *Sesame Street,* Gerald Lesser, television's appeal can be focused with educational value that is "engaging, intelligent, informative, and fun."

Questions

- Will media research continue to focus on that which is bad rather than media that are constructive?
- Does children's media have cross-cultural/ universal appeal. Should it?
- Do we seek violence in our entertainment media?
- Can media consumption act as scaffolding to creating prosocial behaviors and healthier communities?
- Is a reorientation to media consumption through a positive psychology approach sustainable?
- Can children learn positive coping strategies, approaches to forgiveness, means of cooperation through media as a model?

Textbox Interview with Adrian Mills, Chief Adviser BBC Children's and BBC Learning

1. How have children's media changed since your start in the field?

The most significant change I've witnessed since the mid-1980s has been the development of children's media from relatively diverse national and international provision, into a powerful billion dollar global industry, brand-driven, addicted to specific genres, striving for a substantial return on investment, and highly skilled in competing for children's attention. Concomitant with that has been the growth of children's commercial influence, as their significant spending power has transformed them into valuable global consumers.

Children's relationship with media has also changed significantly, as they have transitioned from passive viewers of linear content to highly demanding and critical consumers of and participants in cross-platform media experiences, with a relish for, a sophisticated understanding of, and an intimate relationship with the technologies that enable them. This relationship with the technology as well as the content defines a new generation.

More recently, these changes combined with the global economic downturn have presented major challenges for the children's media industry, with high-quality, culturally relevant children's content increasingly difficult to fund, children's attention ever more difficult to hold, and profit progressively difficult to achieve. An industry once confident of its commercial prowess and performance seems to be in decline and now more reliant on the public sector— through public broadcasters and cultural/industrial subsidies—for its sustainability and survival.

2. Do children's media have cross-cultural/universal appeal? Should they?

Narrative sits at the heart of children's media, regardless of country of origin, source of funding, genre of production, or mode of delivery. High quality children's media providers, particularly public broadcasters, have always assumed a responsibility for creating content which both reflects children's own cultures, and introduces them to cultures of others, and as stories have for centuries, children's media can and do have recognizable and accessible universal/cross-cultural appeal. However, a global market has less tolerance for this, and the current challenge is to find mechanisms and economies which support local storytelling, and to encourage an industry which looks at the world through a global lens, and a risk-averse marketing filter, to appreciate that narrative derived from the local experience can have universal appeal.

3. How do you see media consumption as scaffolding to creating prosocial behaviors and healthier communities if at all?

The power of media to scaffold and create prosocial behaviors and build healthier communities is enhanced when consumption of linear content is complemented by and extended through interaction with content and with others. For example, narrative through linear drama is often seen as the primary medium/genre through which such progress is achieved, via character role-models, and plots which explore behaviors and reflect particular values. However, while linear content is effective at raising issues, and inspiring change through a shared experience, I remain unconvinced of its ability to engage the viewer or listener in complexity, or to engender a sustained change in behaviors. Using new technologies, a powerful drama or stimulating factual programme can be enhanced with opportunities to engage in dialog which supports and challenges, and which enables young people to explore issues with their peers and others. This combination of technologies and opportunity can lead to a deeper level of engagement with content and can have a greater, more sustainable impact on understanding and behavior. As an industry, I think we are in the early stages of understanding what this means and how we might harness the power of the different technologies available to us and our audiences.

4. What trends do you see emerging in children's media use currently?

There are a number of trends that I see emerging in children's use of media: an obvious trend of spending more and more time with media, multitasking while using media, an increase in the use of social networking, and an increase in children's passion for and consumption of programming designed primarily for adults.

Significantly, I see an increase in the amount of content being created and manipulated by young people themselves, for their own amusement/edification, as well as others, familiar and unknown. Perhaps this intense desire to publish is symptomatic of a wider issue facing children and demonstrates their desire for a voice in an increasingly complex and fragmented society.

Another trend relates to transience and children's progressive consumption and exploitation of technology as they devour a technology/application, before abandoning it and moving on to a new one. We frequently hear of children as technological locusts. This will have a big future impact on the industry, both in terms of what it makes and how it makes it.

5. How do you respond to teachers, educators, or parents that children's media are harmful?

The primary imperative is to listen to and consider the concerns and respond to them openly and honestly, with a clear sense of the complexity of issues involved.

The media can be very good at claiming responsibility for positive impact it can have on individuals and society, but rather defensive when it comes to responding to charges of its negative impact. For me, it isn't possible to have one without the other. While I remain convinced of the media's power for good, I am concerned that on the surface at least, there is more evidence of and interest in research which focuses on its harmful effects. Much of this research is simplistic, ill informed, and sensationalist and I would like to see more objective, rigorous, and robust research undertaken in this field.

References

American Institutes for Research (2004). *Navigating the Children's Media Landscape: A Parent's and Caregiver's Guide*. Washington, DC. Available from www.pta.org.

Anderson, C et al. (2007). *Violent Video Games Effects on Children and Adolescents*. Oxford University Press, New York.

Andrews, F. M., & Withey, S. B. (1976). *Social Indicators of Well-Being: Americans' Perceptions of Life Quality.* New York: Plenum.

Bianco, Robert (2004). 10 turning points for television. *USA Today.* Retrieved January 13, 2008 from a February 24, 2004 article.

Bowlby, J (1990). *A Secure Base: Parent-Child Attachment and Healthy Human Development.* New York: Basic Books.

Bradburn, N. M., & Caplovitz, D. (1965). *Reports on happiness: A pilot study of behavior related to mental health.* Chicago, IL: Aldine Publishing Co.

Canadian Pediatric Society (2003). Impact of media use on children and youth. *Pediatric Child Health,* 8(5) (301–306).

Csikszentmihalyi, M. (2008). *Flow: The psychology of optimal experience.* New York: Harper Perennial Modern Classics.

Csikszentmihalyi, M., & Figurski, T. J. (1982). Self-awareness and aversive experience in everyday life. *Journal of Personality,* 50, 15–28.

Diener, E., Sandvik, E., Seidlitz, L., & Diener, M. (1993). The Relationship Between Income and Subjective Well-Being: Relative or Absolute? *Social Indicators Research,* 28, 195–223.

Diener E., Suh, E., Lucas, R. E., & Smith, H. L. (1999). Subjective well-being: three decades of progress. *Psychological Bulletin,* 125(2), 276–302.

Folkman, S. (1997). Positive psychological states and coping with severe stress. *Social Science Medicine,* 45, 1207–1221.

Fredrickson, B. L. (2001). The Role of Positive Emotions in Positive Psychology. *American Psychologist,* 56(3), 218-226.

Gentile, D. A., et al. (2004). well-child visits in the video age: pediatricians and the American academy of pediatrics' guidelines for children's media use. *Pediatrics,* 114 (1235–1241).

Gilbert, D. T. (2007). *Stumbling on Happiness.* New York: Vintage Press.

Hearold, S. (1986). A synthesis of 1043 effects of television on social behavior. In Comstock, G. A. (Ed.), *Public Communication and Behavior* (pp. 65–133), vol. 1. San Diego: Academic Press

Kaiser Family Foundation (2010). *Daily Media Use Among Children and Teens Up Dramatically from Five Years ago.* Retrieved July 19, 2012 from www.kff.org.

Kaiser Family Foundation (2010). *Generation M2: Media in the Lives of 8 to 18 Year Olds.* Retrieved July 19, 2012 from www.kff.org.

Lykken, D. (1999). *Happiness.* New York: Golden Books.

Myers, D. G. (1992). *The Pursuit of Happiness.* New York: Avon Books.

Scheier, M. F., Carver, C. S., & Bridges, M. W. (1994). Distinguishing optimism from neuroticism (and trait anxiety, self-mastery, and self-esteem): A reevaluation of the Life Orientation Test. *Journal of Personality and Social Psychology,* 67(1063–1078).

Scheier, M. F., Carver, C. S., & Bridges, M. W. (2001). Optimism, pessimism, and psychological well-being. In Chang, E. C. (Ed.), *Optimism and Pessimism: Implications for Theory, Research and Practice.* Washington, DC: American Psychological Association.

Seligman, M. E. P. (1991). *Learned Optimism: How to Change Your Mind and Your Life.* New York: Knopf.

Seligman, M. E. P. (1995). *The Optimistic Child.* New York: Houghton Mifflin.

Seligman, M. E. P., & Csikszentmihalyi, M. (2000). Positive psychology: An introduction. *American Psychologist,* 55(1), 5–14.

Shute, N. (2010). 3 Ways electronic media harm kids' health and 3 ways they can help. *US News and World Report,* March 1, 2010.

Shute, N. (2010). TV watching is bad for babies' brains. *US News and World Report.* December 9, 2010.

Smith, S. (2006). Altruism on American television: Examining the amount of, and content surrounding acts of helping and sharing. *Journal of Communications 4* (707–727).

Snyder, C. R., & Lopez, S. J. (Eds.) (2007). *Positive Psychology: The Scientific and Practical Explorations of Human Strengths.* Thousand Oaks, CA: Sage.

Snyder, C. R., Sympson, S. C., Michael, S. T., & Cheavens, J. (2001). Optimism and hope constructs: Variants on a positive expectancy theme. In E. C. Chang (Ed.), *Optimism and pessimism: Implications for theory, research, and practice.* Washington DC: American Psychological Association.

Strommen, E. F., & Revelle, G. L. (1990). Research in interactive technologies at the Children's Television Workshop. *Educational Technology and Research and Development,* 38(4) (65–80).

UNICEF (2004). *Children, Youth and Media Around the World: An Overview of Trends and Issues.* 4th World Summit on Media for Children and Adolescents as presented in Rio De Janeiro, Brazil, April 2004.

Wellner, A. S., & Adox, D. (2000). Happy days. *Psychology Today,* 32(3), 32–37.

Wells, A. (1988). Self esteem and optimal experience. In Csikszentmihalyi, I. S., & Csikszentmihalyi, M. (Eds.), *Optimal Experience.* New York: Cambridge University Press, pp. 327–341.

Wilson, B. J. (2008). Media and children's aggression, fear, and altruism. *Future of Children,* 18(1), 87–118.

11

The Role of Emotion in Media Use and Effects

Elly A. Konijn

Abstract

This chapter provides a summary of the existing media psychology literature regarding the role of emotions in media use and effects. Traditionally, emotions as an object of study from a media psychological perspective have largely been understood within the context of media entertainment research. General involvement mechanisms and affective dispositions of media users toward characters are addressed, as well as the effects of more specific displays of media violence, and frightening and otherwise disturbing materials. However, other branches of media-related emotion research can also be found, such as those related to persuasion and news effects. Most recently, emotions have become a hot topic, and an increased emphasis can be found on emotions as a mechanism underlying media use and effects. Likewise, studies in emotions have become omnipresent in online and computer-based communication, most notably including virtual humans expressing and detecting emotions. The newest trends in applying psychological emotion theories in modeling emotions in virtual humans are discussed. Although a review, this chapter goes beyond the boundaries of the extant knowledge base by raising new questions and providing innovative views on future research in media psychology.

Key Words: emotions/affect/mood, information processing, media effects, media entertainment, virtual humans

Introduction

Overlooking the field that has become known as media psychology over the recent decades, some interesting observations can be made. First of all, several initiatives marked the field including the publication of the book entitled *Media Psychology* (Giles, 2003), establishing an APA-division *Media Psychology* in 1980s (Rutledge, 2008; http://www.apa.org/divisions/div46/), the journal *Media Psychology* (founders Bryant & Roskos-Ewoldsen, 1999; for an analysis of journal content, see Chapter 5), while in 1988 the German-language *Zeitschrift für Medienpsychologie* was established (founders Mangold, Viehoff, & Vorderer), which has been published as the English-language *Journal of Media*

Psychology since 2008. Clearly, media psychological research has a *user*-centered perspective on media effects, in studying how, why, by whom, and when media are used; underlying mechanisms in processing media messages; and under which circumstances certain effects may be expected to occur. A second observation is that the journal-focused initiatives seemed to be biased toward media entertainment as their main subject, whereas the APA division clearly emphasizes a developmental perspective rooted more strongly in "traditional" psychology. Third, the rise of media psychology shows a strong interest in the role of emotions in media use and effects. A growing number of media studies demonstrate how important the role of emotions is in message processing (e.g., Konijn & Hoorn, 2005; Konijn et al., 2009; Krämer et al., 2005; Lang, 2000; Nabi, 2009; Nabi, So, & Prestin, 2010; Zillmann, 2003). For example, the study of affective processing of media characters dominated the field from an entertainment perspective (see the pioneering work of Dolf Zillmann), whereas Lang et al. made a strong case for motivated processing of media messages (e.g., limited capacity theory) (Lang, 2000). Likewise, a long-standing tradition in studying aggression from media violence and fearful responses to media fare in children is clearly acknowledged in media psychological studies (Cantor, 2010; Strasburger, Jordan, & Donnerstein, 2010; see also Chapter 9). Finally, studies in media psychology are empirically based by and large (see Chapter 7), often applying experimental designs and research methods in the tradition of mainstream psychology.

Media psychology has long been associated with studies in media entertainment, with a special focus on children's television use (see Chapters 1 and 6). With the introduction of television in the 1950s, concerns about the unconscious (e.g., subliminal) influences of advertising attracted the attention and interest of communication scholars and psychologists (Hovland, Janis, & Kelley, 1953; Byrne, 1959; see also Chapter 16). However, then, news broadcasts and political campaigns were not really seen as objects of study in media psychology. Given today's broader understanding of what media psychology entails (see Chapters 1 3, and 5), there is no reason not to include such studies as long as they embrace media psychological theorizing: even more so because they often belong to the same discipline as media entertainment studies and can be found in Communication Studies departments. Likewise, recent developments in user-centered computer-based studies, such as digital games, online communication, social media, and human–computer interaction studies, are increasingly embraced in media psychology (see Chapters 19 and 20). Again, such studies often focus on emotions; for example, emotional expressions of avatars or emotion regulation (see later section). In brief, from its start and increasingly in recent developments, media psychological research shows a marked interest in how emotions and affects play a key role in media use and effects.

The present chapter sketches how the field has developed in regard to studying media-related emotions while gradually evolving into future directions for media research. First, it describes how the study of cognitive effects has been analyzed as separate from affective responses to media content. Then, the various threads of media psychological research related to media entertainment are reviewed, illustrating how most early studies applied a more dimensional view to emotional involvement mechanisms, whereas more recent studies also include discrete or specific emotions. Important lines of research have recently been developed in how emotions affect attention, memory, and information processing of media content, which are discussed next. The chapter draws particularly on recent insights from the neurosciences to increase our understanding of media's impact. Finally, recent trends in media psychological theorizing and research relating to virtual media environments, in which virtual humans, which express and "understand" emotions play a central role, including so-called emotion modeling, are reviewed. In closing, some future perspectives for media psychological research into affects and emotions are sketched.

Cognition and Emotion in Early Media Research

When it comes to studying the role of emotion in media-based research,[1] separate strands of scholarship have evolved. On the one hand, research originated in the dominant tradition of mass communication with a rather heavy focus on cognitions or cognitive effects, often rooted in political, persuasive, or sociological theoretical frameworks. Such research mainly focused on analyzing the content of informative messages and their impact on the public at large. Informative messages, such as the news, political campaigns, and educational media were worth studying in their effort to offer the public serious messages about the world's state of affairs. Thus, such messages should appropriately inform the public by presenting genuine content and portrayals—arousing emotion, affect, or mood, certainly was not considered part of that (Zillmann, 2003). However, although studying the news was usually not related to emotions, this academic practice obviously overlooked the fact that much of daily news reports do portray emotions or incite emotions in their viewers. Interestingly, scholars studying children and media acknowledged this fact early on when focusing on frightful images for (young) children (e.g., Walma van der Molen, 2004; Cantor, 2010; see also Chapter 6). Recently, more general studies can be found on the role of emotions in processing the news, in particular highlighting the impact of emotional exemplars (e.g., Aust, 2003; Brosius, 2003; Sundar, 2003; Hendriks Vettehen, Nuijten, &

Peeters, 2008; Bucy, 2010). Thus, mass media had to serve public welfare in providing authentic images of and reliable information about the surrounding world, thereby emphasizing the cognitive aspects of information (e.g., recall), ironically often through disclosing threats and dangers of direct concern to the public. Until recently, the news was not thought of as inciting emotions or creating agreeable moods in the public (Zillmann, 2003). To play the emotional cords of the media user clearly was considered the mission of entertainment.

It is not a surprise, on the other hand, that the entertainment industry in the early 20th century raised both public and scholarly attention and concerns. With their argument against "escapism," Katz and Foulkes (1962) expressed their concern for the public fleeing in "superficial entertainment just for pleasure" while turning away from duties, social responsibilities, and political connectedness. They saw mass media as simply providing an entertaining, dreamlike world to which people escape and get narcotized (Katz & Foulkes, 1962). Probably such concerns were fed by the increasing use of media for purposes of propaganda in view of World War II. From here, media and entertainment studies expanded and the role of affect and emotions entered the field of mass communication, propagating a hedonistic media user's perspective. Thus, early media scholars such as Katz wondered how media could serve the public if they would just bring pleasure, enjoyment, oblivion, and escapism. In their view, the media turned away from their information function to serve the public in their daily societal duties.

Looking at these worries and early theorizing on media effects within their historical background, one gets a strong sense of theorizing on emotions and media effects as captivated in old Cartesian thinking in which cognitions and emotions were seen as separate entities (Damasio, 1994; Konijn & Van Vugt, 2008). Likewise, in psychology, behaviorism and stimulus–response models prevailed, ignoring "black boxes" like inner feelings, whereas only in the late 1980s and 1990s did emotion research start to flourish, and the old battle between cognitions and emotions melted down in cognitive appraisal theories on emotions (Arnold, 1960; Frijda, 1986; Lazarus, 1991, 1993). In cognitive appraisal theories, emotions are seen as *functional* responses of the organism to a demanding environment that offers threats, challenges, and opportunities for overcoming negative feelings, keeping up positive ones, or improving affective states in general. Emotions signal what is relevant and point the human being at threats, dangers, and opportunities to serve one's well-being in general. Emotions *include* some cognitive processing of information for an emotion to occur, even if subconscious. For example, an initial, primary fearful response to a swiping twig on the floor that resembles a snake, immediately dissolves once one realizes the "snake" is a piece of wood (Damasio, 1994; LeDoux, 1996). Therefore, in contemporary emotion research, we see a less strict dichotomization of cognition versus emotion (Rolls, 2003; Lewis, Haviland-Jones, & Barrett, 2008). Clearly, media-based emotion research is following this pattern, be it more slowly and much later, only starting to increase attention among media scholars over the last decade (Nabi & Wirth, 2008). In contemporary research in media psychology and communication science in general, we see a merging of theoretical thinking in line with cognitive appraisal theories of emotion. The following zooms in a little closer on the nature of emotions studied in media psychology.

Emotional Response to Entertainment Fare

A strong line of research evolved around the 1980s to 1990s in answering the question, "How do people respond emotionally to entertainment fare and develop strong emotional bonds with fictional characters?" Much of such theorizing reflected on Aristotelian conceptions of catharsis (after his influential *Poetics*; cf., Feshbach, 1956; Oatley, 1994), Freudian concepts of identification (Freud, 1942/1904), or Coleridge's "willing suspension of disbelief" (1960) in further stretching these concepts to more modern media fare (Zillmann, 2010). In reversed order, these conceptualizations may even be seen as conditional to each other, in that a willing suspension of disbelief eases identifying with a character, which may eventually lead to a (belief in) purification of one's anger, sadness, or otherwise unpleasant feelings (i.e., catharsis, also called the ventilation hypothesis) (Kennedy-Moore, & Watson, 1999). Today, each of the concepts regularly returns the stage, for example, as applied to new forms of media entertainment such as interactive storytelling (Cohen, 2009) or catharsis from playing video games (e.g., Bushman & Whitaker, 2010).

In this line of theorizing, the concept of identification has been devoted quite some attention while it also received serious criticism. In particular, the definition of identification as covering emotional connectedness with media characters seems problematic and has often been mixed up with the liking of a character (Tannenbaum & Gaer, 1965; Zillmann et al.,

1980; Mayne, 1993; Oatley, 1994; Zillmann, 1994; Smith, 1995; Konijn, 1999; Hoffner & Buchanan, 2005; Konijn & Hoorn, 2005). Furthermore, identification falls short of explaining the complexity and intrinsic affectivity that is inherent in media exposure. Sometimes the behavior and affective experiences of media users seem to reflect those of the hero, sometimes only vaguely, and at other times not at all. Moreover, they might well experience the reverse: antipathy, aversion, or ambiguity, whereas intense negative affect toward a character can promote enduring involvement (Hoffner & Cantor, 1985; Konijn & Hoorn, 2005). Another drawback is the way identification has been measured. According to its definition, measurements of identification should be largely based on similarity with the media figure; sharing of several important features between respondent and character (e.g., including similarity in emotions). However, if the observer does *not* share important features with the character but *wishes* to be like the character, the concept of wishful identification is more appropriate (Von Feilitzen & Linné, 1975; Konijn et al., 2007). Furthermore, if the observer does *not* share important features with the character and does not wish to be like the character, yet feels compassion, understanding, or sympathy for the character, then empathy seems a more appropriate construct. Empathy in media users has been conceptualized as resulting from being a witness to emotions in others (Zillmann, 1991; Nathanson, 2003). Close inspection reveals that many identification measures include a variety of related concepts. Finally, empirical support for identification in the sense of similarity-identification with media characters has rarely been found (Zillmann, 1994; Konijn, 1999).

A plethora of concepts related to identification or emotional involvement in general have been coined ever since, ranging from parasocial relationships (Horton & Wohl, 1956; Cohen, 2004), connectedness (Russell, Norman, & Heckler, 2004), to transportation (Green & Brock, 2000; also Chapter 25), immersion (Schubert, 2003), and presence (Biocca, 2002). Certainly, each concept in itself brings interesting perspectives to the understanding of viewer, character, and story relationships. However, a concept-forest seems to be blurring a clear sight on how individuals establish emotional connectedness, involvement with fictional characters, or media figures more generally. Clearly, a key mechanism underlying the various concepts mentioned in the preceding is some measure of emotional involvement or connectedness with the character, story, or narrative. Although the definitions do not always draw clearly on emotional involvement or emotional responsiveness to the media content, the measurements of the various constructs are contaminated with a measurement of emotional responsiveness and often also include a measure of "liking" the character or narrative. Therefore, emotional involvement has been coined (Konijn & Hoorn, 2005; Wirth, 2006) as a more generic concept covering the various forms of emotional bonding with a character, story, or narrative. Involvement has been conceptualized as engagement with the narration and its character (Slater & Rouner, 2002). It would be an important contribution to the field of media psychology to review all of these concepts and clearly chart how constructs overlap and to delineate their differences. Likewise, it would bring the field a big step forward to compare the various measurement devices in detail, particularly as many scales are newly devised independently from others.

A drawback of such identification or involvement-based theories is illustrated by their lack of explaining the liking for antiheroes, bad characters, or villains in movies and video games. The same problem holds for influential affective disposition theories (Zillmann, 1994, 2003; Raney, 2004, 2010). Affective disposition theory states that individuals are predisposed to empathize with the sufferings of others whom we like. Therefore, we fear for the fate of the sympathetic protagonist (and enjoy his or her victory), and experience relief at the devastation of his or her rivals (and fear their triumph). The problem here is that most such theorizing presupposes that more involvement or more character-liking means more media enjoyment, which implies that if you do not like the character you do not like the program. However, this is obviously not true, because numerous programs and stories have unlikable—even abhorrent—characters, who are nevertheless very involving. In the movie *Silence of the Lambs,* for example, the serial killer Hannibal Lecter is an essential, intriguing, and also empathy-evoking character. Currently, research into the experience of negative affects through media use and liking villains and abject characters is falling short. After all, entertainment does not always display or evoke emotions that we would normally consider entertaining, with such films as *Funny Games, A Nightmare on Elm Street,* or games such as *Manhunt,* offering emotional roller-coaster rides that certainly leave us affected and may even cause nightmares. Yet such intense "unpleasant" experiences (filled with fear, suspense, anger, or sadness) seem to add to our liking or appreciation of the movie, game, or experience in general, although we feel very distant from the bad characters.

A broad range of affective states related to media entertainment, character or story involvement, and appreciation of certain media content has thus been overlooked in media research until recently. As illustrated, distant or detached feelings were neglected (yet acknowledged in Konijn & Hoorn, 2005; Bilandzic, 2006). Furthermore, emotional responses to media content can emerge from so-called task emotions (e.g., admiration for the actor) (Konijn, 1999) or relate to aesthetic appraisals or "the artifact" (Tan, 1996), as well as emotionally moving sensations in response to technically sophisticated media products such as the 3D movie *Avatar*. Recently, scholars have pointed at the notion of mixed or multileveled emotions and parallel processing of positive *and* negative affects. Appreciating, liking, or enjoying a character may then be defined as a tradeoff between involvement (e.g., empathy) and detachment (e.g., disgust) (Konijn & Hoorn, 2005; Konijn & Ten Holt, 2010). Thus, we may burst into tears when Jack drowns in the *Titanic,* feeling with Rose and simultaneously appreciating the film of pulling the heart strings so skillfully. As said, traditional theories saw negative affects or emotions as opposed to positive ones. However, progressing insights from emotion psychology (e.g., Cacioppo, Gardner, & Berntson, 1999) enables media psychologists to gain a better understanding of how we may like the often negative feelings that are stirred by the mass media.

Finally, most emotional responsiveness considered thus far merely reflects affective states or moods, not what is understood as discrete, basic, or specific emotions. Eventually, identification and emotional involvement may be considered mechanisms through which discrete emotions may result as media effect.

Emotional Involvement, Moods, and Discrete Emotions

As has become clear, most theories dealing with emotions and media thus far related to general understandings of getting emotionally involved with media fare as opposed to dealing with discrete or more specific emotions. Likewise, most theories are based on hedonistic principles, stating that media fulfill a function in improving negative moods (and sustaining positive ones), with mood management theory (MMT) (Zillmann, 1988; reviewed in Oliver, 2003) as the most prominent one. A modification of this theory is found in the mood adjustment theory, allowing for counter-hedonic media selection in

using "negative" media fare to adjust for a subsequent task (Knobloch, 2003a), or for example, an imagined future encounter in which one may retaliate one's anger (Knobloch-Westerwick & Alter, 2006). Although mood management theories have received empirical support in various studies (Oliver, 2003), scholars have pointed out that such theorizing seems limited in addressing more complex experiences in encountering contemporary media offerings. Mood management–based theorizing is criticized for (1) overlooking nonhedonistic views on media use, and (2) demonstrating an unspecific, dimensional view on emotions. Although these theories explain *why* people are motivated to select specific media fare, the same criticisms hold for the involvement-based theories while individuals are encountered with media (i.e., after selection). This brings us to briefly define mood, affect, and emotions.

A crucial difference between affects and emotions is that *emotions* have an object, relate to meaningful events, and are clearly defined by a specific event with a beginning and an end, whereas affect is rather free-floating and objectless (Russell & Barrett, 1999). An emotion is the awareness of situational demands and personal concerns, often including physiological change along with hedonic quality, comprising the felt need to act or not to act, to serve one's needs, goals, or concerns (Frijda, 1986; Ortony, Clore, & Collins, 1988). Likewise, emotions are characterized by vital implications of threats and rewards for the human system (Rolls, 1999). Hence, emotions indicate that personal concerns are touched by an event (including imagined events). In contrast, *affect* is usually reflected in varying degrees of pleasure–displeasure, or positive–negative, as well as (de)arousal or (de)activation. Affect usually covers various concepts such as moods, feelings, and emotions. *Mood* is often applied to an enduring affective state, characterized by being global and not clearly elicited by an external event. Moods are not felt as motivated by inner drives related to situational demands. Moods may also simply have a biochemical source (e.g., epinephrine) or may be experimentally induced, as in some media exposure studies (Lang, 2000).

At this point it is important to note that media-related studies in emotion and affect may refer to quite different aspects of emotions (Konijn, 2008). That is, emotions or affect may be used to indicate subjective experiences (i.e., feelings) in media users, but may also indicate the behavioral expression (e.g., facial expressions, verbal and nonverbal behavior) of emotion as (visible) in a media portrayal. Obviously, experiencing (felt) emotions in users should be clearly differentiated from the depiction of emotions in media offerings. For example, sadness expressed in a media message (e.g., tears) does not necessarily imply sadness in the observer. Likewise, emotions may pertain to different stages of a media encounter such as motivation processes (or input for media selection), an underlying mechanism, or an outcome. For example, "Because I feel sad, I want to watch a comedy" is in line with mood management motivations. Sadness as an underlying mechanism is illustrated in, "Because I felt sad while watching, I gained greater understanding of the important values in life, which makes me feel good." Sadness as an outcome or media effect is illustrated by, "I now feel sad because I empathized with the poor character."

Clearly, the concepts of emotion, mood, and affect are not often used in the strict senses as defined, but rather are used interchangeably. However, given the definitions, we must conclude that most studies in media psychology thus far dealt with general affects or mood (i.e., a dimensional or aspecific view on emotions), whereas studies in discrete or specific emotions are relatively sparse. Exceptions are studies into fear and aggression, which have been studied abundantly (see the following). Notably, these studies were inspired by portrayals of fearful and violent events in media fare out of concerns for their detrimental impact. Studies thus far hardly addressed emotional experiences in the media users as a starting point. The following briefly addresses several studies of discrete emotions related to media.

Most studied clearly is *aggression* from media violence, with Bandura et al.'s (1961) bobo-doll study as a well-known marker. An important criticism of that study long plagued media violence research—the question of whether experimental manipulations could be considered representative for real-life occurrences of aggression and whether the measurements really indicated aggression (Anderson & Bushman, 1997; Anderson & Dill, 2000; Ferguson & Kilburn, 2010; see Chapter 9). In 1998, Dill and Dill reported an important review of the empirical literature showing a consistent effect of media violence on increased aggressiveness. With the introduction of video games, research in media violence effects received a new impetus, with violent games being among the best selling. Highly realistic graphics, lifelike virtual environments, interactivity, and games' highly immersive potential attracted increased concern of parents, pediatricians, and policy makers (e.g., see Chapter 20). Although still debated (e.g., Ferguson & Kilburn, 2010; also see Chapter 9), a

recent high quality meta-analysis covering a broad range of (inter)national studies confirmed the earlier conclusions of Dill and Dill (Anderson et al., 2010). A number of studies address intervention strategies to reduce children's aggressive responses to media exposure, mostly including parental and media literacy interventions (Cantor & Wilson, 2003; also see Chapter 6). Meanwhile, a number of related studies focused on the underlying mechanisms to sort out who is vulnerable under which circumstances (e.g., boys with lower educational ability, perceiving relatively high levels of realism in the games, wishing to be like the aggressive heroes; see the risk factors approach in Anderson, Gentile, & Buckley, 2007; Konijn et al., 2007; Nije Bijvank et al., 2011). However, important questions remain; for example, in establishing appropriate risk profiles and clarifying underlying mechanisms (see Chapters 9 and 20). Obviously, games sorting detrimental effects can likewise be used to sort beneficial effects, such as with serious games (Anderson, Gentile & Dill, 2012; Konijn & Nije Bijvank, 2009; Ritterfeld, Cody, & Vorderer, 2009; Belman & Flanagan, 2010; see also Chapter 19).

Another large number of studies can be found devoting attention to *fear,* both in addressing children's fear in response to scaring and fearful movies and television (including media violence), and fear as a persuasion technique in so-called fear appeals (often used in prevention campaigns, such as showing rotten lungs to reduce smoking). Children's fright responses to motion pictures were reported by Blumer as early as 1933. In the 1970s, public attention for such fright responses increased when *Jaws* and *The Exorcist* aroused intense emotional reactions, but by the mid-1980s researchers were focusing sustained attention on the media and children's fears (Cantor, 2009, 2010). An important focus of research efforts in this area include developmental differences in the coping potential of what frightens children, including longer-term effects, and the lessons learned from them (Hoffner & Cantor, 1985). Sometimes, intensely frightening images on television or a movie (e.g., *Jaws, Poltergeist*) endure well beyond the time of viewing, even in students and adults (Cantor, 2004, 2010). Studies show that such television exposure not only incites anxieties in children (Singer et al., 1998), but also nightmares and sleep disturbances (Owens et al., 1999; Van den Bulck, 2004; Paavonen et al., 2006). Retrospective studies show that having been frightened by a television show or movie could last into adults' memories (e.g., through unwanted recurring thoughts, or disturbances in eating and sleeping) and indicate the severity and duration of media-induced fear (Harrison & Cantor, 1999). Cantor (2010) summarizes what researchers have uncovered about viewers' fear reactions to the mass media.

Interestingly, however, harmful effects of media violence and fear-arousing images on children have mainly focused on entertainment media, whereas real-life violence depicted in television news has largely been ignored. For example, large-scale content analyses of media violence all excluded broadcast news programs (Walma van der Molen, 2004).

Finally, fear has been studied intensively within the context of persuasion, ads, and commercials, starting with the early work of Hovland et al. (1953) and extending into a large body of studies in *fear appeals* (Witte & Allen, 2000). The results of such affect-laden exposures are mixed; for example, either because people consider the relevance of the related risks as rather limited to themselves, or consumers may remember the affect-arousing image (e.g., the rotten lungs) but not the message (Obermiller et al., 2005). Other reasons for the mixed results are that the affect-laden images may not match the advertised product (e.g., women and trucks), the affective appeal may not arouse the intended affect (e.g., laughter among adolescents instead of fear), or it may not be relevant to the consumer (e.g., considering oneself not susceptible). Likewise, attaching *humor* and *sexual affect* to commercial content have been widely studied based on the idea that a positive attitude toward a product, service, or brand would result from creating an association of positive affect, thereby increasing purchase behavior (Weinberger & Gulas, 1992). Over the past decade, including and studying emotions within persuasive contexts have become highly popular because "emotions sell"—even negative affect seems more effective than no affect (Williams & Aaker, 2002). The role of emotions and affect in persuasive communication is further discussed in Chapter 16.

Related to studying fear, yet clearly focused on (young) adults in response to media entertainment, is research into the enjoyment of *horror* and *suspense*. Exposure to horror has been explained by clear gender socialization effects: Young males enjoy horror even more when accompanying females are afraid (Zillmann, Weaver, Mundorf, & Aust, 1986; Zillmann & Weaver, 1996; Mundorf & Mundorf, 2003). Some claim that horror is enjoyed just for reasons of sensory delight (Sparks & Sparks, 2000), although many puzzles still remain unsolved in

this respect (Tamborini, 2003). Knobloch (2003b) reviews the various theoretical approaches to the enjoyment of suspense and mystery in entertainment media. Suspense has been studied within the contexts of affective disposition theory through empathy with the character and fearing bad outcomes, as well as in the context of excitation transfer (Zillmann, 1971). According to excitation transfer, distress and related arousal-based emotional states develop along with exposure to the plot, whereas residual excitation of one episode transfers onto the next. The intensity of build-up suspense and its ultimate resolution in the film's ending predicts the viewer's final relief and enjoyment.

Research into *sexually arousing* and pornographic media content has engendered huge commercial interests (Brown, 2009; see Chapters 13, 16) and has given rise to a highly concerned public. Research shows that roughly 65% of television programs contain some sexual material and more than half of adolescents cite television as an important source of information about birth control, contraception, and pregnancy prevention (Kunkel, Farrar, Eyal, Biely, Donnerstein, & Rideout, 2007). Studies show that first exposure to pornographic materials is occurring at younger ages than in previous generations, whereas the exposure rate is higher among (young) males than females (Bryant & Zillmann, 2001). Effects found from a sexually oriented media diet include more permissive sexual attitudes (Bryant & Rockwell, 1994; Brown, 2003; Taylor, 2005), desensitization, and habituation to pornography (Zillmann & Bryant, 1986), early sexual initiation among adolescents (Collins et al., 2004), endorsement of sexual stereotypes (Donnerstein, 1984; Ward & Friedman, 2006), and early teen pregnancy (Chandra et al., 2008). A recent study in a European context assessed causality in the relationship between adolescents' risky sexual online behavior in a two-wave longitudinal study, in which peer involvement, perceived vulnerability, and perceived risks were all significant predictors of risky sexual online behavior 6 months later (Baumgartner, Valkenburg, & Peter, 2010). The importance of studying the underlying processes (e.g., perceived realism) in the effects of adolescents' use of sexually explicit Internet material is discussed in Peter and Valkenburg (2010).

Sadness has triggered many researchers' attempt to understand how people may enjoy tragedy, tearjerkers, sad movies, and tragically ending media fare. The puzzle has been termed the *sad movie paradox* (Oliver, 1993). It has been found that enjoyment of sadness depended on how people appraised their sad response (Oliver, Weaver, & Sargent, 2000). Another explanation has been found in downward comparison; through comparison with another's bad fortune, people may feel uplifted (Suls & Wheeler, 2000) or be self-satisfied in having the capacity to empathize with suffering others (Mills, 1993). Vicariously going through sad experiences as portrayed in media fare may also serve valuable learning experiences in preparing for possible real tragedy in one's own live (Goldenberg, Pyszczynski, & Johnson, 1999). Most recently, the concept of *eudaemonia* has been coined to explain the paradox (Oliver, 2008; Oliver & Woolley, 2010). In search of greater meaning in life and an increase in one's psychological well-being, people are motivated to expose themselves to distressing media content. A eudaemonic explanation coincides with the content of sad media in which interpersonal relationships, love, overcoming life's obstacles, and human's strengths and weaknesses are often highlighted (de Wied, Zillmann, & Ordman, 1994).

A few studies can be found exploring the role of *Schadenfreude* or *malicious pleasure* in media use, "taking delight in the suffering of another" (Adorno, 1996). Research shows that malicious pleasure was increased by threats of Dutch inferiority regarding a German loss in soccer (Leach, Spears, Branscombe, & Doosje, 2003). Likewise, enjoying "suffering others" in *Idols* occurred in particular in viewers who were low in self-esteem (Van Dijk, Ouwerkerk, Goslinga, & Nieweg, 2005). Malicious pleasure is explained by social comparison theory (Suls & Wheeler, 2000) suggesting that the suffering of others might actually make us feel good in comparison, because it makes our own lives appear better and helps individuals gain a sense of mastery over threats through ego-enhancing experiences. Thus, the function of such media-related emotions can be identified as restoring self-esteem or resources generally, while engaging in the suffering of others.

Feelings of *guilt* have only recently been studied as a discrete emotion in the context of *moral emotions* and moral disengagement while playing violent video games (Bandura, 1990, 2002; Hartmann, Toz, & Brandon, 2011). *Moral disengagement* is understood as disconnecting one's inner moral standards from doing harm in game-play (Bandura, 1990). Movies, games, and related violent media fare ease such disengagement by providing cues for "justifying" the violence (e.g., fighting for a higher goal, such as saving the world, dehumanization, and fighting nonhuman creatures such as aliens). As such, players may enjoy the violence without moral concerns

or guilt (Raney, 2004, 2010; Dill, Gentile, Richter, & Dill, 2005). Empathetic players showed increased levels of guilt when confronted with unjustified virtual violence (Hartmann et al., 2011).

The role of *regret* in selecting and perceiving regret-related media content has been studied by Nabi, Finnerty, Domschke, and Hull (2006). Their findings show that participants who had been cheating on their partner more strongly preferred regret-related storylines over those who had not cheated. In addition, in a subsequent experimental design, participants were presented with two different story endings; one expressing self-blame and regret, and the other rationalizing the cheating behavior. The regretful cheaters enjoyed the rationalization ending more than the self-blame ending. Moreover, regret after watching was reduced, although this was not dependent on the story ending. The authors conclude that entertainment programming can help viewers to cope with regret, perhaps through reframing the experience.

Effects of *anger* in media use and effects have been studied by several scholars. One study showed that anger resulted in lower risk perceptions than fear while judging risks of terrorist attacks after 9/11 (Lerner & Keltner, 2000). Likewise, another study found that anger frames the interpretation of news reports differently than fear leading to differences in policy preferences (Nabi, 2003). An older study (O'Neal & Taylor, 1989) found that angry participants selected violent or hostile materials over mood-improving comedies if they were led to believe the characters would get a chance for revenge (see also Knobloch-Westerwick & Alter, 2006). A recent study revealed that anger played a major role in moral judgment of antisocial media content (Plaisier & Konijn, in press). Adolescents who were rejected by their peers and experienced anger as a result showed a tolerant moral judgment of and a preference for watching antisocial media content in YouTube clips.

As mentioned, studies differ in their focus on particular stages of the process of encountering media. Most of the described studies reported on discrete emotional responses (as effects) to specific emotion-rich media content. However, several of the latter studies (e.g., regarding regret and anger) did not study discrete emotions in response to emotion-evoking media displays, but rather the impact of users' emotions before encountering emotion-rich media fare. Because these studies highlight an important role of emotions in the way media information is processed, they are discussed further in an information processing perspective later in this chapter, particularly the role emotions play in attention and recall from media exposure and how processes of learning from fiction and entertainment media may evolve.

Emotions Direct Attention and Memory

An important reason to study emotions related to media exposure is that emotions and affect play a significant role in processing the information provided through media exposure (Lang, Newhagen, & Reeves, 1996). Affective processing of media fare may modify the way in which the presented information is perceived, stored, retrieved, and valued, and how it becomes integrated into our real-life knowledge structures, whether fictitious (entertainment) or factual (news) media. Given the hybrid status of many contemporary media messages, studies on the role of affect are becoming increasingly important because they give us information about the underlying processes of the media's power to influence people. Media formats such as reality television, virtual worlds, and today's highly sophisticated graphics and 3D presentations in games and movies may add to ambiguity regarding the reality status of its content, at least for our primary perceptual system or lower path of processing in the brain (Konijn & Ten Holt, 2010).

Moreover, in our current "mediated society," we not only develop intimate relationships online, but also acquire real-world knowledge in large part through mediated exposure in which affects and emotions play a vital role to get messages across. It is generally understood that emotions serve an attention-grabbing function and motivate people to focus their attention on distinctive information or objects. Emotions are thus helpful to selectively direct attention to parts of a media message (e.g., tears on a victim's face) because people are limited in their capacity to process information (Lang, 2000). Therefore, selective attention refers to the process of prioritizing particular objects or events while ignoring others (Theeuwes, 1993). A relatively limited number of studies thus far have studied the extent to which emotions (media generated or otherwise) affect the way a message is perceived and recalled.

Most studied is the influence of emotionally laden content on memory. However, the results seem mixed and may depend on differences in arousal level (or intensity) and the valence of emotions (or direction of affect; positive or negative), whereas even specific emotions with a similar valence may sort different effects (e.g., anger versus sadness). Selective attention

related to media exposure was evidenced in a study showing emotional pictures in television news. This led participants to narrow attention to certain parts of the message, subsequently provoking recall errors (Brosius, 1993). In general, studies showed that emotionally arousing media messages increased recall of information related to the emotion-arousing content (David, 1996; Lang et al., 1996; Zillmann, Knobloch, & Hong-sik, 2001). However, information processing was impaired when presented after the emotionally arousing material (Mundorff, Drew, Zillmann, & Weaver, 1990; Christianson & Loftus, 1991; Grabe, Yegiyan, & Kamhawi, 2008).

Studies in which participants were explicitly shown negative images exhibited enhanced memories of events that immediately followed those images, and led to a generally poorer recall of narrative information in the long run (Reeves, Newhagen, Maibach, Basil, & Kurz, 1991; Newhagen & Reeves, 1992). Likewise, specific or discrete emotions with a negative valence; that is, disgust and surprise, resulted in better recall of the central topics of advertisements just presented, whereas happiness, fear, and guilt weakened such recall (Englis, 1990). However, differences for similarly valenced emotions were also found. Images that evoked fear and anger enhanced visual recall, whereas images that evoked disgust reduced visual recall (Newhagen, 1998). Such effects were also found for the memories of children. Sad children were more suggestible than those in either happy or angry moods (Levine, Burgess, & Laney, 2008). In contrast, other studies showed that positive messages may be remembered better than negative ones (Mathur & Chattopadhyay, 1991; Lang, Dhillon, & Dong, 1995; Lang et al., 1995; Bolls, Lang & Potter, 2001). One's emotional state also determines what aspect of a message one focuses on: People in a negative emotional state are more likely to focus on threats, and those in a positive emotional state being more likely to focus on rewards (Tamir & Robinson, 2007).

Differences in attention and recall for positive and negative emotions should be further studied in terms of mood congruency (cf., affect infusion model) (Forgas, 1995; Gendolla, 2000) such that negative emotions may enhance recall for (subsequent) negative information, whereas positive emotions may enhance recall for (subsequent) positive information. This also connects to an older study demonstrating that memories are organized by affect; that is, the mood we were in when we stored information is stored together with the information and is thus more accessible when we are in a similar affective state (Isen, Shalker, Clark, & Karp, 1978).

Furthermore, recent insights from positive psychology (Seligman & Csikszentmihalyi, 2000) and the "broaden and build" effect of positive emotions (Fredrickson, 1998) indicate that although negative emotions narrow attention down to one specific problem, positive emotions broaden our attention to take in more of the world around us (for empirical evidence, see Isen, 2008; for media and positive psychology, see Chapter 10).

In all, media producers may not just focus on what they are trying to tell, but also on what emotions they evoke while spreading a message; the emotional waters a message sinks in, so to speak. Emotional waters can easily spread a message as moral panic (e.g., the Columbine school shootings) or a hoax (e.g., the anthrax letters) through today's fast and global online communications and highly popular social media.

Emotions Affect Information Processing

In addition to differences in recall of media information from similarly valenced emotions, a few studies investigated differences in perception of media messages because of different yet similarly valenced *discrete* emotions. Fear and anger (both negatively valenced) differently influenced people's risk perception after news reports about 9/11 such that participants perceived higher levels of risk when fearful than when angry (Lerner & Keltner, 2000). Another study showed the differential framing effects of fear and anger on the processing of media messages. Students induced with fear decided to a more protection oriented approach in determining what kind of action should be taken against an undesirable activity as presented in a news report, whereas in the case of anger a more retributive approach was taken (Nabi, 2003). Likewise, participants in bad moods were better at detecting lies in news reports than individuals who were in neutral or positive moods (Forgas & East, 2008). Furthermore, people who were uncertain processed information more systematically than those who were more certain (processing the information more heuristically) (Tiedens & Linton, 2001). Similarly, sad people engaged in local and item-level processing, whereas happy people engaged in more global and category-level processing (Gasper, 2004). This is in line with the affect infusion model, arguing that people in negative moods use more detailed and systematic schemas and process persuasive messages more systematically (Forgas, 2007). Isen (2008) then added the important condition that this is only in terms of how relevant the information is to the person doing the processing.

Two studies in particular applied an emotion processing perspective in demonstrating the relevance of the presented information to reveal important new insights in media use and effects.

Based on functional regret theory, Nabi, Finnerty, Domschke, and Hull (2006) predicted that entertainment programming may be selected to cope with a regretted experience. Their findings showed clear differences between participants who regretted a cheating experience and those without regret. The regretful participants showed higher preferences for regret-related storylines and story endings rationalizing the cheating behavior, whereas regret after watching was reduced. Thus, the study illuminates the importance of a close connection between the emotion experienced in the user and relevant information in the media message to explain counter-hedonic media preferences and outcomes.

In an experimental design, causal effects were shown for adolescents who were angry to show a preference for antisocial and amoral media content compared with either adolescents who were not angry or young adults (Plaisier & Konijn, in press). Note that anger induced by peer rejection influenced the perceptions of the participants in loosening their moral judgment of antisocial media content, subsequently increasing their preference for such media content compared with neutral and pro-social media content. Thus, anger played a significant role in explaining how the information from media was perceived and processed.

Another line of research examined how emotions influence the believability, source credibility, or perceived realism of media content. Especially in view of the hybrid nature of many contemporary media offerings, it is increasingly important to understand how people interpret the level of realism in media content (Shapiro & Lang, 1991; Brosius, 1993; Lea & Spears, 1995). Likewise, the "laws of fiction" (e.g., emotional close-ups, perspective-taking, and dramatic storylines) are increasingly applied in contemporary media fare (including reality-based programming and broadcast news) to enhance a program's emotion potential (Bragg, 2000; Konijn & Hoorn, 2004; Walma van der Molen & Konijn, 2007). Ambiguously real media require people to make ever more sophisticated judgments to determine what is factual. Several studies found that stories labeled fiction lead to attitude change equal to—and sometimes even greater than—those labeled nonfiction (Slater, 1990; Murphy, 1998; Strange & Leung, 1999; Green & Brock, 2000). Mares (1996) reported source confusion; that is, erroneous attributions of news-to-fiction as well as fiction-to-news among respondents who saw news reports and a movie trailer on the same subject. However, these studies did not take the role of emotions into account.

Research suggests that the more emotional people are when processing media, the more likely that they will believe it. Individuals experiencing higher levels of negative emotions (i.e., annoyance in Study 1 and empathetic sadness in Study 2) while presented with audiovisual materials taken from a television documentary, attributed higher levels of perceived realism and information value to the contents than those who were less emotionally moved, especially when the materials were framed as fictional (in contrast to "reality-based" material) (Konijn, Van der Molen, & Van Nes, 2009). The authors reasoned that the underlying mechanisms are in line with emotion psychology such that "emotions point to the presence of some concern" (Frijda, 1988, p. 351). Because emotions signal what is relevant to us, such as a threat or a reward, emotions may as well serve as a signal for the program's reality status. "If I feel, it must be real." In line with emotion psychology, emotional experiences signal to individuals that something is real, psychologically real, or of real importance. Thus, processing media messages in an emotional state (whether preexposure or in response to) may alert the viewer that something real, psychologically real, or of real importance is occurring (i.e., relevant in challenging their well-being) (Konijn et al., 2009). This may explain why even fictional media can affect one's real-world perceptions.

Such emotional responding to what is in fact fictional (and most often we know we are just watching a movie or playing a game) can be further explained by how the brain responds to mediated images. So-called "mirror neurons" (Rizzolatti & Craighero, 2004) contribute to such an understanding. Mirror neurons "mirror" the behavior of another individual without conducting the behavior itself. They are active both when people perform an action and when they watch it being performed. Such mirror neurons are assumed to also be incorporated in empathy or emotional contagion—a kinesthetic response through which we may "feel with" the observed other. Mirror neurons may explain why we feel the sufferings of "just" a movie character, for example, when we watch a Nazi war criminal "dentist" torturing Dustin Hoffman's character in *Marathon Man* (1976) by drilling his teeth without anesthesia.

Research using functional magnetic resonance imaging (fMRI) among other techniques, has shown that certain brain regions comparable with the mirror neurons are active when a person experiences an emotion (e.g., disgust, happiness, pain) and when he or she sees another person experiencing an emotion (Gallese, 2001; Jabbia, Swarta, & Keysers, 2007). Likewise, brain activation differed in responding to sad films as compared with amusing films (Goldin, Hutcherson, & Ochsner, et al., 2005). Empathy involves not only the firing of mirror neurons representing a form of simulation of the observed states, but the sensed states are also attributed to the other individual, distinguishing them from the observer's own emotions.

Research in neuroscience, with fMRI scans and electroencephalography recordings provide us a glimpse of the human brain in action. An important finding in view of processing media messages is that we have a higher and lower pathway that processes information from the outside world (Damasio, 1994; LeDoux, 1996). The lower pathway runs to the amygdala, which is part of the limbic system and is involved in the processing of emotions, including fear and pleasure. The higher pathway leads to our higher brain faculties and ultimately conscious awareness. The lower pathway is markedly faster than the higher pathway, allowing us to react before we have fully cognitively processed the information (Damasio, 1994; LeDoux, 1996, 2000; Panksepp, 1998; Rolls, 2003). This means that we can react to a threat before we are consciously aware of it, offering important evolutionary advantages in enabling us to respond immediately to conditioned and evolutionarily determined dangers (for a review, see LeDoux & Phelps, 2008).

However, the lower pathway is often triggered by "false-positives," or things that only roughly match the fear-evoking response—such as a stick that resembles a snake triggering a fear reaction. Moreover, the immediate response of the amygdala is not the whole response. Instead, the higher path moderates our behavior and guides us down rehearsed or automatized danger-avoidance paths. In this way, the initial response can largely be controlled when necessary; for instance, when we realize the "snake" has twigs and leaves. Thus, media images that only roughly match a real-world event may trigger the amygdala to respond. As emotion theory predicts, touching relevant concerns seems a prerequisite (as discussed). For example, virtual displays of human physiology while performing surgery at a distance represent artery and muscles in various nonnatural colors depending on its meaning and relevance for the surgery at hand (Hoorn et al., 2003; Yee, Bailenson, & Rickertsen, 2007; Hoorn, 2012).

The amygdala thus responds to simple perceptual cues, especially the face and eyes (Adolphs et al., 2005) and is involved in detecting significant threats or potential rewards (Barrett & Wager, 2006). Therefore, it may be hard for the lower pathway to distinguish between imagined and perceived images when using graphically rich media, having trouble distinguishing between the fictional and factual (Zillmann, 2003, 2010). Indeed, positron emission tomography studies demonstrated that two-thirds of the activated brain substrates used to process imagined versus perceived images are the same (Kosslyn, Thompson, & Alpert, 1997). Likewise, neuropsychological research showed that the brain responds in similar ways to emotion-rich media events as to real-life events (Murray, 2008). Especially when ambiguous audiovisual stimuli are involved, or in case of doubt, people may then err on the side of safety (Shapiro & Lang, 1991) or take the "low road" and err on the side of caution (LeDoux, 1996) when emotions signal a threat—either factual or fictional.

Specifically in the case of danger, threats, or fear; that is, when negatively valenced emotions arise, emotions may incite the viewer to process a media message at least partly as a real event, and leave traces in memory that may later be remembered as if the event had really happened (cf. source confusion in Mares, 1996). Perhaps, this explains the sleeper effect (Hovland & Weiss, 1951; Kumkale & Albarracín, 2004), in which messages from sources with low credibility show opinion change, not directly, but over time. Thus, emotions may blur perceptions of the factual and fictional directly as well as over time. The emotional impact of a message may last and add to its credibility, supported by the affective storage of information (Isen et al., 1978).

In conclusion, mass media may sort its effects in much more implicit and less understood ways than we may have assumed thus far. Until recently, the "fictionality" of many messages has been rather obvious. However, new technologies and contemporary media fare make it increasingly difficult for the human brain to detect or experience the difference between real and virtual worlds, at least in its primary response of mirror neurons and the lower pathway, even if we might consciously realize they are fictional or virtual. Research as discussed shows that emotions play a key role here. The fabric of our emotional system seems to help contemporary media exert even more influence than any of us would admit.

Emotions in Virtual Media Environments

The salient role of emotions in processing information is clearly understood in how new computer technologies emerge. Given the all-pervading use of computers and sophisticated technological innovations that allow computers to incorporate preexisting media devices, it is not surprising that computers are the top-rated topic in content analyses of *Media Psychology* (see Chapter 5). Increasingly, emotions are implemented in software applications that look and act like people—virtual humans. Positive results of implementing "emotions" in virtual humans are obtained in line with the generally positive effects of human functions of emotions in the context of decision making (LeDoux, 1996), memory storage and retrieval (Rolls, 1999), learning (Bower, 1991), social reasoning (Forgas, 2007), and their social and communicative functions (Manstead et al., 1999). Users may feel emotionally attached to virtual humans that portray emotions, and interacting with such "emotional" embodied computer systems positively influences their perceptions of humanness, trustworthiness, and believability. Affective computing is a research domain that studies such virtual humans to enrich them with emotional capabilities (Picard, 1997; Picard & Daily 2005; Konijn & Van Vugt, 2008), thereby drawing on knowledge from emotion psychology.

Research shows that even experienced computer users are inclined to treat their computers as largely social and interact in affective ways with them (Reeves & Nass, 1996; Brave, Nass, & Hutchinson, 2005). For example, people can feel pleased by the flattery of a computer, even though the flatterer is a piece of software. When confronted with a virtual human, people responded more politely and tended to make more socially desirable choices than without (Krämer, Iurgel, & Bente, 2005), and responded more empathically (Paiva, Dias, & Aylett, 2005). Positive effects of mirroring the interlocutor's emotional state have likewise been confirmed with virtual humans (Bailenson & Yee, 2005). Furthermore, the success of the *Cyberball* game (Williams, Cheung, & Choi, 2000) demonstrates that a simple piece of software is capable of inducing strong feelings of anger, frustration, and exclusion in participants. In addition, very elementary, simple forms of behavior representing emotional behavior in the emotionally expressive robot Kismet triggered sympathetic responses (Breazeal, 2003). Therefore, the rapid developments in this area of affective computing seem quite promising for the future.

Virtual humans (also called robots, avatars, or embodied agents) (Konijn & Van Vugt, 2008) that exhibit emotional behavior are used effectively in a range of applications, especially those in which human–human relationships are crucial, such as health care, psychotherapy, and education. For example, Bickmore, Gruber, and Picard (2005) incorporated the virtual human Laura into a health care system to motivate people to do their daily physical exercises. The patient's desire to continue working with Laura was highest when she showed relational, emotional behavior. The emotional and relational communication behaviors of patients were considered analogous to responses to real-life health providers. Therefore, emotional virtual humans may improve patient satisfaction and outcomes of health systems.

Increasingly, virtual humans are used in applications ranging from e-learning environments, online banking sites, psychotherapy applications, to games and virtual reality worlds (Bates, 1994; Breazeal, 2003; Mateas & Stern, 2006; Pontier & Siddiqui, 2008; Gratch, 2010; Krämer, 2010). Its success may be a result of the human system being hard-wired to respond to such emotional displays—most find it difficult to suppress responding to emotional displays (Fridlund, 1997; De Waal, 2003). Emotional displays are strong vehicles to communicate personal information and guide interpersonal behavior (Smith & Scott, 1997; Manstead et al., 1999). A random sample of effective applications of virtual humans that make use of emotions is illustrated in the following.

A virtual human psychotherapy application has been developed based on cognitive appraisal models of human emotion (Marsella, Johnson, & LaBore, 2003). The application aimed at improving the social problem solving skills of parents of children with chronic diseases (e.g., cancer). The user is positioned to make decisions on behalf of the mother of the sick child to learn about the consequences of various decisions. Another application in the health domain is a serious game developed for children suffering from cancer to increase their self-efficacy and insight in the disease (Kato, Cole, Bradlyn, & Pollock, 2008).

In an educational context, the FearNot! system was developed to teach children to cope with bullying behavior in schools (Aylett, Vala, Sequeira, & Paiva, 2007). The system lets the user play-act in various bullying situations to which the child is asked to respond, for example, by avoiding the bully, talking to the bully, fighting back, telling a friend or teacher, and so forth. For adults, the interactive system "Façade" (Mateas & Stern, 2003) has been developed to provide insights in

marital problems through engagement with the virtual couple Grace and Trip. The user plays the character of a longtime friend who is unaware of these problems. His or her responses define the course of the conversation and even the course of Grace and Trip's lives.

Interesting parallels with media entertainment crop up, in particular the emphasis on emotional involvement with a character, narrative, and fictional world. Role-playing games are an intriguing mixture of traditional media and technological innovation, allowing one to present oneself as a "fictional" character in virtual worlds and create one's own narrative. This principle is increasingly used in serious games (Ritterfeld et al., 2009; Kato, 2010; see also Chapter 19). The interactive nature enforces high levels of emotional involvement. "What if" scenarios force changes in perspective taking, which are probably among the main carriers of serious games' educational effectiveness (Gee, 2007). *America's Army* is one of the first online digital games that can be named a serious game. It was developed by the United States Army and is in fact a recruitment tool. It has been criticized for serving as a propaganda device (United States Army, 2002; Konijn & Nije Bijvank, 2009). Another example is *Peacemaker,* in which the player is forced to take the perspective of the Israeli prime minister as well as the Palestinian authority (http://www.peacemakergame.com/game.php).

Virtual leaders may also have disastrous consequences; however, as is illustrated by *Pro Ana* (http://www.msnbc.msn.com/id/8045047/). "Ana" exists only in a virtual world and promotes anorexia and self-starvation. *Pro Ana* appeared to be a very real presence in the lives of many adolescent girls, who felt encouraged in extreme dieting behavior by Ana's words of "thinspiration" and "pain is temporary, but thin is forever." In 2005, experts estimated that Ana influenced several million girls. Many examples of virtual leaders and the influential role of opinion makers can be found in today's highly popular social media (Mitchell & Ybarra, 2009).

The impact and options of creating virtual characters empowered with emotional expressiveness as well as emotional responsiveness to users and the capability of emotionally binding users seem endless and very promising for future applications. However, to create virtual humans that respond appropriately in various situations, sophisticated software is required that asks for a deep understanding of the user's situation and characteristics. Therefore, a number of research efforts are taking place and various techniques are currently under study to design virtual humans that exhibit emotions and may detect emotions in the users.

Designing Virtual Humans and Emotion Modeling

Obviously, because human emotions are complex, they are also difficult to appropriately design in virtual humans and computer applications. Not only the face and body contribute in conveying emotional states, but also their co-occurrences. For example, many observers judging a facial expression are also strongly influenced by emotional body language (Meeren, Van Heijnsbergen, & De Gelder, 2005). Therefore, ideally, virtual humans exhibit emotions using both face and body. For example, sadness can be specified in terms of depressed corners of the mouth and weeping, and in addition, in terms of hanging shoulders and head hanging down. Many scripting languages and tools exist to enable virtual humans to express affect and emotion. The Affective Presentation Markup Language, for example, enriched the virtual human GRETA with multimodal emotional expressions using both face and gestures (De Rosis, Pelachaud, & Poggi, 2003). To ease the interpretation of an emotional state exhibited by a virtual human, it may be helpful to amplify significant features and signify only the necessary or most relevant for emotional expressions to be recognized, as is the custom in theater, art, and movies (Hoorn et al., 2003; Yee, Bailenson, & Rickertsen, 2007).

In addition to techniques to have virtual humans express emotions, various systems, and devices are developed that can somehow *detect* or predict the emotional state of the user in several ways. Just to name but a few are self-report systems that ask the user to indicate its emotional state to the computer (Picard & Daily, 2005) or emotion recognizers based on haptic data that originate from touching devices such as keyboards, mice, and touchpads (Bailenson, Yee, Brave, Merget, & Koslow, 2006). For example, button pressure as a measure of a game player's arousal, which was related to game difficulty (Sykes & Brown, 2003) or indicated user's frustration, stress, or anger (Mentis & Gay, 2002). Sensors and physiological indicators such as skin conductance and muscle activity have been used in preparing for a job interview (The Emphatic Companion) (Prendinger & Ishizuka, 2005).

Because haptic and physiological methods for emotion detection are error prone and quite demanding on their users, which reduces their reliability, techniques are used to *automatically* "detect" a user's emotional state without the need of self-reports or sensors. To that end, recordings of facial expressions of computer users are analyzed to assess underlying feelings and emotions. However, although facial expressions are fundamental in human emotion communication, facial expressions are not always clear indicators of emotion (Fridlund, 1997; Manstead, Fischer, & Jacobs, 1999; Konijn & Van Vugt, 2008). Nevertheless, facial expression analysis has become an active research area in the field of affective computing (Zhao, Chellappa, Phillips, & Rosenfeld, 2003; Ahn, Bailenson, Fox, & Jabon, 2010). Likewise, complex pattern recognition algorithms are needed for the recognition of gestures; for example, glove- and vision-based gesture recognition systems have been developed to recognize gestures (Wu & Huang, 2001; Karpouzis, Raouzaiou, Drosopoulos, Ioannou, et al., 2004). Eye-tracking technology is another important research tool in the area of affective computing, because gaze is also important in face-to-face interpersonal communication, for example, to regulate the flow of conversation (Vertegaal, Slagter, Van der Veer, & Nijholt, 2001; Partalaa, & Surakkaa, 2003; Drewes, Atterer, & Schmidt, 2007). Despite the difficulties, however, such automatic detection of assumed emotions in users can be useful in virtual environments to improve the communication between virtual human and user.

Finally, various approaches aim at recognizing emotions based on conversational content. A number of analytical tools have been developed to automatically analyze huge databases with emotion-tagged speech signals (e.g., specific words or other utterances), such as the Affective Reasoner (Elliott, 1992) and recent emotion recognition technology (Matsumoto & Ren, 2011). Other systems may apply a statistical approach based on the idea that certain word combinations are more probable for the expression of certain emotions than others (Polzin & Waibel, 2000). However, emotional cues are mostly implicitly hidden because users most often do not explicitly verbalize their emotional state; automatically detecting emotions in media content is not easy. In the last decade a number of developments have taken place to improve emotion recognizers, for example based on speech characteristics (e.g., pitch, prosody, durations of silence, speaking rate) (Van den Broek, 2004), real-world knowledge to evaluate the affective qualities of the underlying semantic content of text (Liu, Liberman, & Selker, 2003), or semantic analyses (Van Atteveldt, Kleinnijenhuis, Ruigrok, & Schlobach, 2008). However, such methods do not allow for *real-time* and *continuous* determination of a (changing) user's emotional state while speaking, although they can provide useful information after the fact.

In sum, verbal and nonverbal behaviors allow the researcher to unobtrusively detect the user's emotion through a computer in ways parallel to face-to-face communication. Because of the ambiguity in interpreting individual cues of emotion expression, *multimodal automatic emotion recognition* (based on multiple cues) seems the most promising approach because it reduces the uncertainty associated with using a single mode (Picard & Daily, 2005); for example, combining signals from facial features, prosody, and content in speech to recognize emotions (Fragopanagos & Taylor, 2005). Nevertheless, environmental contexts and specific task demands further influence the way verbal and nonverbal behaviors should be interpreted. Therefore, Gratch and Marsella (2005; Gratch, 2010) propose complex emotion modeling mainly based on appraisal and coping theories of emotion. Such modeling allows for appropriately functioning virtual humans that may resemble common interpersonal communication or at least act similarly powerful.

Psychological emotion theory is at the basis of many research efforts to improve the development of virtual human applications. For example, the virtual human should show *consistent* emotional behavior for users to get engaged in human–computer communications and to understand what is going on (Nass, Brave, & Takayama, 2006). Psychological appraisal theories have been implemented (i.e., translated into computer software) to design emotionally consistent systems that are able to operate in interactive environments (i.e., emotion modeling) (Gratch, 2010). This allows the computer to predict or determine the emotional state of the user and his or her potential to cope with the particular situation, subsequently adjusting the system's response. The output of such an emotion model is an emotional representation to be displayed by the virtual human. The thus selected emotion pattern (output from the emotion model, for example, sadness) is converted into appropriate behavioral components, such as facial expressions, head nods, gestures, eye gaze, body movements, and/or speech qualities such as utterances and prosody.

Psychological emotion models in combination with affective character models have served as input for developing the add-on software Silicon Coppélia (Pontier & Siddiqui, 2008; Hoorn, Pontier, & Siddiqui, 2012). This software can build up and

regulate the affective behavior of virtual humans in response to the behavior of users. For example, a game character that is armed and dangerous may start shooting when approached by an aggressive user or hold its fire when approached with empathy. Thus, users can influence the behavior of the virtual human through their own behavior, yet the system is too complex to predict which behavior. Such emotion modeling software has a number of promising applications for the future. In combining this software with packages to create state-of-the-art gamelike situations and characters, methodologically sound experiments can be created to study, for example, up-to-date gaming experiences (Konijn, Walma van der Molen, & Hoorn, 2011). Apart from visible interventions with characters, features, and contexts, unobtrusive manipulations can be investigated that are directed at the cognitive function level of task performance and response execution (e.g., variations in time lag, lighting, expected position on the screen, warnings) without spoiling the excitement of playing a video game. Such emotion modeling software thus has promising applications not only for experimental emotion psychology, but also for training programs, learning and development, serious games, and e-health applications (Ritterfeld et al., 2009; Kato, 2010; see Chapter 19).

In conclusion, observers will ascribe emotions to virtual humans, even if they are construed solely by technical means, because of their habit of deriving emotions from outer appearances (Reeves & Nass, 1996). Future research will explore what type of virtual humans and what type of emotional displays, including in response to user's emotions, fits best with what type of applications. Just as in real life, different emotional responsiveness is expected from teachers, bankers, and psychotherapists. Developments in emotion modeling and programming languages continue to have virtual humans "reason" about emotions and respond with emotional displays in ways as expected from humans given a particular context. Clearly, designing emotionally competent virtual humans poses computer scientists, communication scholars, and emotion psychologists alike for interesting and collaborative research challenges.

Conclusions and Future Directions

This chapter described how early media psychological research has developed from emphasizing cognitions, attitudes, and recall from media exposure, to a steady increase in studying emotions, both in terms of emotional displays in media content and as an emotional state in users. Media research that focuses on emotions now include not only entertainment and persuasion media, but also the role of emotions in processing the news, online communication, and virtual worlds. The impact of emotional exemplars in the news and media generally seems significant because they are more accessible and influential than non-arousing exemplars, although their impact requires more detailed research in how emotional exemplars in the media may affect real-world knowledge structures. Special attention is needed in this respect for the influence of emotional portrayals in fiction and entertainment media, how they may eventually cultivate various beliefs, such as stereotypical ideas about unfamiliar issues, or in answering questions such as, "How do emotional exemplars facilitate stimulus generation?" After all, the extant literature suggests that we tend to respond to media images as we do to real images (at least at the lower path of processing), and media images are processed such that they may affect one's perceptions of social reality.

Quite some research in the tradition of media psychology has been devoted to emotional responses to entertainment fare. However, such research efforts seem to have boundaries that constrain their findings to uplifting media fare, and less so to the intriguing phenomenon of enjoying sad, violent, or gory media. Progress needs to be made in understanding the appreciation of villains, abject and bad characters, and antiheroes, particularly because they are common in contemporary movies and video games. Experiencing intense unpleasant emotions and affects seems to add to media users' enjoyment and appreciation of the movie, game, or experience in general, although we may feel very distant from the "bad characters". Exploring one's emotional borders is especially salient for the developmental stage of adolescence, for which media lend themselves perfectly. One may also think of the role of emotion-rich media in acquiring emotional competence; that is, to learn to understand emotions in others and oneself, develop one's emotion regulation skills, and learn how to cope with and behave in emotionally taxing situations. In a similar vein, it may well be that amoral or antisocial media fulfill an important function of adolescent development in exploring one's borders. After all, it is inherent in this developmental stage that growing individuals develop their own identity, such as sexual maturation, emotional growth, and developing one's moral standards (Subramanyam & Šmahel, 2011). This coincides with an overrepresentation of sexual and emotion-rich portrayals, including high levels of (a)

moral and ethical considerations. As such, the positive role of even negative or antisocial media content also should be taken into account.

Clearly, media may fulfill a wider array of functions than has generally been considered from hedonistic perspectives. Media may not only fulfill a function in improving our bad moods, but counter-hedonic media selections may help us to adjust for a subsequent task, fulfill coping needs (e.g., overcoming guilt or regret), or eudaemonic functions. For example, most recent research showed how the enjoyment of sadness depended on how people appraised their sad response. When appraised as adding meaning in life, sad media increased viewers' psychological well-being (Oliver & Woolley, 2010). Likewise, processes of social comparison clarify how sufferings of others, in particular others that we most likely will not meet in person, may increase our self-esteem, weaken our own disappointments, or make our life seem better in comparison. However, social comparison may also result in less comfortable feelings; for example, body dissatisfaction, when the object of comparison represents an unattainable ideal (Knobloch-Westerwick & Romero, 2011; Veldhuis et al., 2012). What is the role of emotion (both in media depictions as in users' responses) in predicting which (part) of the observed behaviors are most likely to be compared, imitated, or learned— emotions deriving from the wish to be like an idealized image, beliefs in achieving self-ideals, one's hope of actualizing self-ideal images? As argued herein, people may be motivated to expose themselves to distressing or upsetting media content in serving coping needs and the social sharing of emotions (Nabi et al., 2010). Finally, sad or bad media may serve valuable learning experiences in preparing for possible real misfortunes in one's own life.

Because emotions are defined as the awareness of situational demands and personal concerns, interesting research challenges lie ahead in discovering how situational demands and personal concerns are specified in media-related emotional responsiveness. Likewise, additional specific research applying emotional psychological frameworks is needed to more fully and specifically understand which needs, goals, and concerns are served by using media, particularly emotion-evoking media. Likewise, because emotions are characterized by vital implications of threats and rewards for the human system, which ones relate to media use? After all, emotions signal what is relevant and point the human being at threats, dangers, and opportunities to serve one's well-being in general. From an emotion psychological perspective, in which emotions are seen as functional responses of the organism to a demanding environment, a relevant question is, "What functions are served, under which circumstances and to what ends, in using media?" More specifically, "What threats, challenges, and opportunities for overcoming negative feelings, keeping up positive ones, or improving affective states are offered by media use that either display or evoke unpleasant emotions in its users?" Another unexplored question is, "What is the extent to which media play a role in satisfying needs for experiencing emotions as such, just for the sake of being moved?" Future research may further substantiate such questions and discover other important and specific functions of supposedly "negative" media offerings.

Further theorizing and research are needed into parallel processing of positive *and* negative affects, or the occurrence of multileveled emotions. Contemporary emotion psychology acknowledges that positive and negative emotions are not bipolar, but rather occur in parallel. Similarly, appreciating or enjoying media fare that evokes emotions with a negative valence can be explained as such. However, research into specific emotions is needed to further understand how such parallel processing may occur, under which circumstances, and with what effects.

Studies differ in their focus on particular stages of the process of encountering media, although the extant literature is not always clear in this respect. Most of the described studies reported on emotional responses (as effects) to specific emotion-rich media content. That is, emotions as outcome of media portraying gory, fearful, or graphic displays of emotion-evoking content. However, subjective experiences (i.e., feelings) in media users may also serve as a starting point. Only a few studies, thus far, examined discrete emotions in users *before* encountering emotion-rich media fare, and how these emotions affected preferences and processing of specific media content. The results highlight an important role of emotions in the way media information is selected and processed. Thus, emotional frameworks may be applied to various stages of a media encounter, to motivation processes (or input for media selection), an underlying mechanism, or an outcome.

Many studies have focused on general involvement processes. Certainly, developing strong emotional bonds with fictional characters, and portrayed events and narratives is important in appreciating entertainment media. However, important progress can be made in reviewing the various concepts that have evolved (e.g., transportation, immersion,

presence, parasocial interaction), how constructs overlap, and how to delineate their differences as well as compare the various measurement devices in detail. Furthermore, emotional involvement may be considered a mechanism through which discrete emotions may result as media effect.

A number of studies have been described in this chapter that showed how affective processing of media fare modifies how the presented information is perceived, stored, retrieved, and valued, and how it becomes integrated into our real-life knowledge structures. The results of the influence of emotions in relation to media content on memory are mixed and depend on differences in arousal level and the valence of emotions, whereas discrete emotions with a similar valence also sorted differences in attention and recall. Effects of positive and negative emotions could be further studied in terms of (dis)congruency between users' emotional states and the emotional portrayals in media images. For example, negative emotional states may enhance attention for and recall of negative information in the media. Likewise, moods while storing information seem to be more readily accessible when we are in a similar affective state while recalling that information, because memories seem to be organized by affect. However, this has hardly been studied in media-related contexts thus far. Undoubtedly, emotions play an important role and often seem contagious when mediated events are still remembered years later, in media messages that create hoaxes, social unrest, or moral panic, or in specific media fare that go viral (e.g., a YouTube clip). Thus, it is important to study in much greater detail than has been done thus far how, when, and under what circumstances specific media messages pull the heart strings in excessive ways.

In addition, emotions and affect have been shown to influence information processing. Findings showed that different emotions differently influenced people's risk perceptions, policy preferences, and reality perceptions. Various theories have been discussed that explain parts of the puzzle. On the one hand, theories argue that people in negative moods process media-related information in a more detailed and systematic way than people in positive moods (Forgas, 2007), whereas others argue that this is only in terms of how relevant the information is to the person doing the processing (Isen, 2008). Some recent studies confirmed that a close connection between the emotion experienced in the user (e.g., regret, anger) and information in the media message relevant to that emotion explained counter-hedonic media preferences as well as outcomes in accordance with a functional view of emotions. Much more research is needed, however, in studying correspondence between specific emotional states and emotion-relevant media, especially how emotions serve emotion regulation and coping needs and direct information processing of media content.

Many studies in recall and information processing of media pertained to factual (news) media; however, future research should examine how emotional processing of information occurs with fictitious (entertainment) fare or ambiguous materials such as today's popular formats as reality television, infotainment, sophisticated graphics, and virtual worlds. Moreover, intimate relationships develop online, and much of our real-world knowledge is acquired through media exposure. The hybrid status of such media messages and blurring of mediated and real worlds demand further study in the role of affect and the underlying processes of the (entertainment) media's power to influence people implicitly, subconsciously, or in the long run. Research results thus far suggest that the more emotional people are when processing media, the more likely it is that they will believe it. More work needs to be done here.

Sophisticated research methodology such as used in neuroscience may be helpful in this respect. Although media-related research using functional magnetic resonance imaging scans, electroencephalograph recordings, positron emission tomography scans, and the mirror neurons is still scarce, they all provide a glimpse of the human brain in action when processing media content. One of the important findings is that we have two pathways along which we process such information, a higher and lower pathway (Damasio, 1994; LeDoux, 1996). However, the lower, faster pathway is often triggered by false-positives because it scans the environment for possible threats and dangers and prepares the human system for possible (immediate) action. Therefore, it may be hard for our lower path to process ambiguously real or graphically real media and discern between the real and the not-so-real, or fictitious (Murray, 2008). Both such insights and the technological developments in graphically realistic media fare may thus require people to make ever more sophisticated judgments to distinguish between fictional and factual events (Konijn & Ten Holt, 2010; Zillmann, 2010). As a consequence, future findings may show that such media leave traces in memory that may later be remembered as if the media event had actually happened (cf. source confusion in Mares, 1996) or explain "sleeper effects"

(Kumkale & Albarracín, 2004). Thus, the emotional system may get blurred in distorting perceptions of the factual and fictional, directly as well as over time. Moreover, important questions arise as to what extent ambiguously real and emotion-evoking media may extend to real-life events; for example, in terms of desensitization effects or distorted reality perceptions. Thus, to what extent do media-evoked emotions intensify media's impact or transfer to real-life situations and make (heavy) users of particular media less responsive to daily life occurrences of related events?

In a similar vein, not much is known about how positive emotions may direct information processing from media. When applying recent insights from positive psychology and the "broaden and build" effects of positive emotions (Fredrickson, 1998; Seligman & Csikszentmihalyi, 2000), positive emotions as derived from media use may fulfill important functions of restoring energy and resources. Although not yet in media-related contexts, research showed that positive emotions broaden our attention to take in more of the world around us, whereas negative emotions narrow attention down to one specific problem (Isen, 2008). Thus, it might well be that people in positive emotional states realize an ambiguous or virtual state of media content more clearly than those in negative emotional states that prohibit the broader picture in zooming in on the details. Also, people may use specific media fare displaying (or evoking) positive emotions to bounce back from negative emotional experiences during the day (cf. Tugade & Fredrickson, 2004). Future research may more closely connect insights from positive psychology to specific media use in serving such a need for positive emotions to build up.

Finally, this chapter discussed emotions as related to virtual media environments. New technologies regarding computer usage emerge rapidly, and a large number of media applications show virtual humans or avatars that express emotions, detect emotions in users, and respond in an emotionally appropriate way. Increasingly, emotions are implemented in software applications, especially in virtual humans that look and act like people, with positive results. Developments in this area of affective computing seem quite promising for future applications, especially those in which human–human relationships are crucial, such as in health care, psychotherapy, and education. Not only insights from emotion psychology are used, but insights from media entertainment and art perception are also included. For example, the importance of emotionally binding the user to a virtual human, and some narrative or storyline in the virtual world, can easily be recognized.

However, in line with the complexity of human emotions, it is also complex to appropriately design virtual humans in computer applications. For example, in humans expressing emotions, the various body parts co-act consistently in appropriately conveying emotional states, and possible human deception usually goes unnoticed. In having virtual humans express emotions, various systems and devices have been developed that cannot only express emotions fairly well, but that are also able to somehow "know" the emotional state of the user. To that end, multi-modal automatic emotion recognition systems seem a promising way to go (Picard & Daily, 2005). In addition, over the last decade sophisticated efforts have been undertaken to model human emotion processing in virtual humans, called emotion modeling (Pontier & Siddiqui, 2008; Gratch, 2010). Most such efforts thus far are based on appraisal and coping theories of emotion, allowing virtual humans to more or less resemble common interpersonal communication and function appropriately in a given context. The output of such emotion modeling is "emotional behavior" displayed by a virtual human. Promising applications of such emotion modeling software are awaited. Obviously, various types of applications and training goals need different types of virtual humans, emotional displays, and emotional responsiveness. In online shopping worlds, for example, quite different emotional responsiveness is expected than from teachers and psychotherapists, or virtual coaches that take over repetitive monitoring behavior in health care.

Especially promising are the developments relating to serious games for learning and development (Ritterfeld et al., 2009; see also Chapter 19), sophisticated training programs, and a variety of health applications (Kato, 2010). The options of creating virtual characters empowered with emotional expressiveness as well as emotional responsiveness to users, including the ability of emotionally binding users, seem endless and very promising. Smart mixtures of traditional entertainment media tools and technological innovations allow the user in role-playing games to explore various perspectives of oneself in confronting a diversity of possible events. The interactive nature and vicariously experiencing possible actions enforce high levels of emotional involvement and provide rich learning experiences. In designing emotionally competent virtual humans, computer scientists, emotion psychologists, and media psychologists are needed to challenge each other in collaborative research endeavors.

Although the field of media psychology has devoted much research attention to the possible detrimental effects of questionable media content, the time is ripe to also focus on how media functions to serve human well-being. In particular, in view of contemporary developments in media technology and use, more in-depth theorizing and research are warranted. Media's potential to emotionally connect to users and create emotionally rich virtual worlds may serve important functions for both general life satisfaction and the relative balance of positive and negative affects in daily life. Thus, relating human well-being to media-based research seems a worthy pursuit for future media psychology.

Notes

1. Most often such media-based research is done in departments named Communication, Communication Studies, or Communication Science. Sometimes, and increasingly, media-based research can be found in departments of psychology, often in pedagogy or developmental psychology.

References

Adorno Th. (1996 [lived 1870–1941]). *Aesthetic Theory*. Minneapolis: University of Minnesota Press.

Adolphs, R., Gosselin, F., Buchanan, T. W., Tranel, D., Schyns, P., & Damasio, A. R. (2005). A mechanism for impaired fear recognition after amygdala damage. *Nature, 433*, 68–72.

Ahn, S. J., Bailenson, J., Fox, J., & Jabon, M. (2010). Using automated facial expression analysis for emotion and behavior prediction. In Döveling, K., Von Scheve, Chr., & Konijn, E. A. (Eds.), *The Routledge Handbook of Emotions and Mass Media*. New York: Routledge, pp. 349–369.

Anderson, C. A., & Bushman, B. J. (1997). External validity of "trivial" experiments: The case of laboratory aggression. *Review of General Psychology, 1*, 19–41.

Anderson, C. A., & Dill, K. E. (2000). Video games and aggressive thoughts, feelings, and behavior in the laboratory and in life. *Journal of Personality and Social Psychology, 78*, 772–790.

Anderson, C. A., Gentile, D. A., & Buckley, K. E. (2007). *Violent Video Game Effects on Children and Adolescents: Theory, Research, and Public Policy*. Oxford, UK: Oxford University Press.

Anderson, C. A., Gentile, D. A., & Dill, K. E. (2012). Prosocial, antisocial, and other effects of recreational video games. In Singer, D. G. & Singer, J. L. (Eds.) *Handbook of Children and the Media* (2nd edn, pp. 249–272), Thousand Oaks, CA: Sage.

Anderson, C. A., Shibuya, A., Ihori, N., Swing, E. L., Bushman, B. J., Sakamoto, A., et al. (2010). Violent video game effects on aggression, empathy, and prosocial behavior in Eastern and Western countries: A meta-analytic review. *Psychological Bulletin, 136*(2), 151–173.

Arnold, M. (1960). *Emotion and Personality*. New York: Columbia University Press.

Aust, C.F. (2003). Factors in the appeal of news. In: Bryant, J., Roskos-Ewoldsen, D., & Cantor, J. (Eds.), *Communication and emotion: Essays in honor of Dolf Zillmann*. Hillsdale, NJ: Lawrence Erlbaum Associates, pp. 511–530.

Aylett, R., Vala, M., Sequeira, P., & Paiva, A. (2007). FearNot!—An emergent narrative approach to virtual dramas for anti-bullying education. *Lecture Notes in Computer Science, 4871*, 202–205.

Bandura, A. (1990). Mechanisms of moral disengagement. In Reich, W. (Ed.), *Origins of Terrorism: Psychologies, Ideologies, Theologies, States of Mind.* Cambridge, UK: Cambridge University Press, pp. 161–191.

Bandura, A. (2002). Selective moral disengagement in the exercise of moral agency. *Journal of Moral Education, 31*(2), 101–119.

Bandura, A., Ross, D., & Ross, S. A. (1961). Transmission of aggressions through imitation of aggressive models. *Journal of Abnormal and Social Psychology, 63*, 575–582.

Bailenson, J. N., & Yee, N. (2005). Digital chameleons: Automatic assimilation of nonverbal gestures in immersive virtual environments. *Psychological Science, 16*, 814–819.

Bailenson, J. N., Yee, N., Brave, S., Merget, D., & Koslow, D. (2006). Virtual interpersonal touch: Expressing and recognizing emotions through haptic devices. *Human-Computer Interaction, 22*, 325–353.

Barrett, L. F., & Wager, T. (2006). The structure of emotion: Evidence from the neuroimaging of emotion. *Current Directions in Psychological Science, 15*, 79–85.

Bates, J. (1994). The role of emotions in believable agents. *Communications of the ACM, 17*(7), 122–125.

Baumgartner, S. E., Valkenburg, P. M., & Peter, J. (2010). Assessing causality in the relationship between adolescents' risky sexual online behavior and their perceptions of this behavior. *Journal of Youth and Adolescence, 39*, 1226–1239.

Belman, J., & Flanagan, M. (2010). Designing games to foster empathy. *Cognitive Technology, 14*(2), 5–15.

Bickmore, T., Gruber, A., & Picard, R. (2005). Establishing the computer–patient working alliance in automated health behavior change interventions. *Patient Educational Counseling, 59*(1), 21–30.

Bilandzic, H. (2006). The perception of distance in the cultivation process: A theoretical consideration of the relationship between television content, processing experience, and perceived distance, *Communication Theory, 16*, 333–355.

Biocca, F. (2002). The evolution of interactive media: Toward "Being there" In nonlinear narrative worlds. In Green, M. C., Strange, J. J., & Brock, T. C. (Eds.), *Narrative Impact: Social and Cognitive Foundations.* Hillsdale, NJ: Lawrence Erlbaum Associates, pp. 97–129.

Blumer, H. (1933). Emotional possession: Fear and terror. In Blumer, H. (Ed.), *Movies and Conduct.* New York: Macmillan, pp. 74–94.

Bolls, P. D., Lang, A., & Potter, R. F. (2001). The effects of message valence and listener arousal on attention, memory, and facial muscular responses to radio advertisements. *Communication Research, 18*, 627–651.

Bower, G. H. (1991). Emotional mood and memory. *American Psychologist, 31*, 129–148.

Bragg, R. (2000). Weaving story telling into breaking news. *Nieman Reports, 54*(3), 29–30.

Brave, S., Nass, C., & Hutchinson, K. (2005). Computers that care. *International Journal of Human—Computer Studies, 62*(2), 161–178.

Breazeal, C. (2003). Emotion and sociable humanoid robots. *International Journal of Human-Computer Studies, 59*(1–2), 119–155.

Brosius, H. (1993). The effects of emotional pictures in television news. *Communication Research, 20*, 105–124.

Brosius, H. (2003). Exemplars in the news: A theory of the effects of political communication. In Bryant, J., Roskos-Ewoldsen, D., & Cantor, J. (Eds.), *Communication and Emotion: Essays in Honor of Dolf Zillmann.* Hillsdale, NJ: Lawrence Erlbaum Associates, pp. 179–194. Brown, D. (2003). Pornography and erotica. In J. Bryant, D. Roskos-Ewoldsen, & J Cantor (Eds.), *Communication and emotion: Essays in honor of Dolf Zillmann.* Hillsdale, NJ: Erlbaum, pp. 221–253.

Brown, J. D. (2009). Media and sexuality. In Nabi, R., & Oliver, M. B. (Eds.) *Handbook of Media Processes and Effects.* Thousand Oaks, CA: Sage, pp. 409–422.

Bryant J., & Rockwell, S. C. (1994). Effects of massive exposure to sexually oriented prime-time television programming on adolescents' moral judgment. In Zillman, D., Bryant, J., & Huston, A. C. (Eds.), *Media, Children and the Family: Social Scientific, Psychodynamic, and Clinical Perspectives.* Hillsdale, NJ: Lawrence Erlbaum Associates, pp. 183–195.

Bryant, J., & Zillmann, D. (2001). Pornography: Models of effects on sexual deviancy. In Bryant, C. D. (Ed.), *Encyclopedia of Criminology and Deviant Behavior.* Philadelphia: Brunner-Routledge, pp. 241–244.

Bucy, E. (2010). Nonverbal communication, emotion, and political evaluation. In Döveling, K., Von Scheve, Chr ., & Konijn, E. A. (Eds.), *The Routledge Handbook of Emotions and Mass Media.* New York: Routledge, pp. 195–220.

Bushman, B. J., & Whitaker, J. L. (2010). Like a magnet: Catharsis beliefs attract angry people to violent video games. *Psychological Science, 21*(6), 790–792.

Byrne, D. (1959). The effect of a subliminal food stimulus on verbal responses. *Journal of Applied Psychology, 43*(4), 249–252.

Cantor, J. (1998). *'Mommy, I'm Scared': How TV and Movies Frighten Children and What We Can Do to Protect Them.* San Diego, CA: Harvest/Harcourt.

Cantor, J. (2004). *Teddy's TV Troubles.* Madison, WI: Goblin Fern Press.

Cantor, J. (2006). Why horror doesn't die: The enduring and paradoxical effects of frightening entertainment. In Bryant, J., & Vorderer, P. (Eds.), *Psychology of Entertainment.* Hillsdale, NJ: Lawrence Erlbaum Associates, pp. 315–327.

Cantor, J. (2009). Fright reactions to mass media. In Bryant, J., & Oliver, M. B. (Eds.), *Media Effects: Advances in Theory and Research*, 3rd ed. New York: Routledge, pp. 287–303.

Cantor, J. (2010). Fear reactions and the mass media. In: Döveling, K., Von Scheve, Chr ., & Konijn, E. A. (Eds.), *The Routledge Handbook of Emotions and Mass Media.* New York: Routledge, pp. 148–165.

Cantor, J., & Wilson, B. J. (2003). Media and violence: Intervention strategies for reducing aggression. *Media Psychology, 5*, 363–406.

Cacioppo, J. T., Gardner, W. L., & Berntson, G. G. (1999). The affect system has parallel and integrative processing components: Form follows function. *Journal of Personality and Social Psychology, 76*, 839–855.

Chandra, A., Martino, S. C., Collins, R. L., Elliott, M. N., Berry, S. H., Kanouse, D. E., et al. (2008). Does watching sex on television predict teen pregnancy? Findings from a national longitudinal survey of youth. *Pediatrics, 122*, 1047–1054.

Christianson, S. A., & Loftus, E. F. (1991). Remembering emotional events: The fate of detailed information. *Cognition and Emotion, 5*, 81–108.

Cohen, J. (2004). Parasocial break-up from favorite television characters: The role of attachment styles and relationship intensity. *Journal of Social and Personal Relationships, 21*(2), 187–202.

Cohen, J. (2009). Mediated relationships and media effects: Parasocial interaction and identification. In: Nabi, R., & Oliver, M. B. (Eds.), *Handbook of Media Processes and Effects*. Thousand Oaks, CA: Sage, pp. 223–236.

Coleridge, S. T. (1960; original work published in 1817). *Biographia Literaria or Biographical Sketches of My Literary Life and Opinions*. London: Dent and Sons.

Collins, R. L., Elliott, M. N., Berry, S. H., Kanouse, D. E., Kunkel, D., Hunter, S. B., et al. (2004). Watching sex on television predicts adolescent initiation of sexual behavior. *Pediatrics*, 114, e280–e289.

Damasio, A. R. (1994). *Descartes' Error: Emotion, Reason, and the Human Brain*. New York: Putnam.

De Rosis, F., Pelachaud, C., & Poggi, I. (2003). From Greta's mind to her face: modeling the dynamics of affective states in a conversational embodied agent. *International Journal of Human-Computer Studies*, 59(1–2), 81–118.

Dill, K. E., & Dill, J. C. (1998). Video game violence: A review of the empirical literature. *Aggression and Violent Behavior: A Review Journal*, 3, 407–428.

Dill, K. E., Gentile, D. A., Richter, W. A., & Dill, J. C. (2005). Violence, sex, race, and age in popular video games: A content analysis. In Cole, E., & Henderson, D. J. (Eds.), *Featuring Females: Feminist Analyses of the Media*. Washington, DC: American Psychological Association, pp. 115–130.

Donnerstein, E. (1984). Pornography: Its effect on violence against women. In Malamuth, N. M., & Donnerstein, E. (Eds.), *Pornography and Sexual Aggression*. Orlando: Academic Press, pp. 53–81.

Drewes, H., Atterer, R., & Schmidt, A. (2007). Detailed monitoring of user's gaze and interaction to improve future e-learning. *Proceedings of the 12th International Conference on Human-Computer Interaction HCII 2007, Springer. Lecture Notes in Computer Science*, 4555, 802–811.

Elliott, C. D. (1992). *The Affective Reasoner: A Process Model of Emotions in a Multi-Agent System*. PhD thesis, Northwestern University, Illinois.

Englis, B. G. (1990). Consumer emotional reactions to television advertising and their effects on message recall. In Agres, S., Edell, J., & Dubitsky, T. (Eds.), *Emotion in Advertising: Theoretical and Practical Explorations*, New York: Quorum Books.

Ferguson, C. J., & Kilburn, J. (2010). Much ado about nothing: The misestimation and overinterpretation of violent video game effects in Eastern and Western nations: Comment on Anderson et al. (2010). *Psychological Bulletin*, 136(2), 174–178.

Feshbach, S. (1956). The catharsis hypothesis and some consequences of interaction with aggressive and neutral play objects, *Journal of Personality*, 24, 449–462.

Forgas, J. P. (1995). Mood and judgment: The affect infusion model (AIM). *Psychological Bulletin*, 66, 56–68.

Forgas, J. P. (2007). When sad is better than happy: negative affect and improve the quality and effectiveness of persuasive messages and social influence strategies. *Journal of Experimental Social Psychology*, 43, 513–528.

Forgas, J. P., & East, R. (2008). On being happy and gullible: mood effects on skepticism and the detection of deception, *Journal of Experimental Psychology*, 44, 1362–1367.

Fragopanagos, N., & Taylor, J. G. (2005). Emotion recognition in human-computer interaction. *Neural Networks*, 18(4), 389–405.

Fredrickson, B. L. (1998) "What good are positive emotions?" *Review of General Psychology*, 2, 300–319.

Freud, S. (1942). Psychopathic characters on the stage. *Psychoanalytic Quarterly*, 11, 459–464. (original work published in 1904).

Fridlund, A. J. (1997). The new ethology of human facial expressions. In Russell, J. A., & Fernández- Dols, J. M. (Eds.), *The Psychology of Facial Expression*. Cambridge, MA: Cambridge University Press, pp. 103–129.

Frijda, N. H. (1986). *The Emotions*. New York: Cambridge University Press.

Frijda, N. H. (1988). The laws of emotion. *American Psychologist*, 43(5), 349–358.

Gallese, V. (2001). The "Shared Manifold" hypothesis: from mirror neurons to empathy. *Journal of Consciousness Studies*, 8, 33–50.

Gasper, K. (2004). Do you see what I see? Affect and visual information processing. *Cognition & Emotion*, 18(3), 405–421.

Gee, J. P. (2007). *Good Video Games and Good Learning: Collected Essays on Video Games, Learning and Literacy*. New York: Peter Lang.

Gendolla, G. H. E. (2000). On the impact of mood on behavior. An integrative theory and a review. *Review of General Psychology*, 4, 378–408.

Giles, D. (2003). *Media Psychology*. Hillsdale, NJ: Lawrence Erlbaum Associates.

Goldenberg, J. L., Pyszczynski, T., & Johnson, K. D. (1999). The appeal of tragedy: A terror management perspective. *Media Psychology*, 1, 313–329.

Goldin, P. R., Hutcherson, C. A. C., Ochsner, K. N., Glover, G. H., Gabrieli, J. D. E., & Gross, J.J. (2005). The neural bases of amusement and sadness: A comparison of block contrast and subject-specific emotion intensity regression approaches. *Neuroimage*, 27(1), 26–36.

Grabe, M. E., Yegiyan, N., & Kamhawi, R. (2008). Experimental evidence of the knowledge gap: Message arousal, motivation, and time delay. *Human Communication Research*, 34, 550–571.

Gratch, J. (2010). Emotionally-resonant media: Advances in sensing, understanding and influencing human emotion through interactive media. In: Döveling, K., Von Scheve, Chr ., & Konijn, E. A., (Eds.), *The Routledge Handbook of Emotions and Mass Media*. New York: Routledge, pp. 370–387.

Gratch, J., & Marsella, S. (2005). Some lessons from emotion psychology for the design of lifelike characters. *Journal of Applied Artificial Intelligence*, 19(3–4), 215–233.

Green, M. C., & Brock, T. C. (2000). The role of transportation in the persuasiveness of public narratives. *Journal of Personality and Social Psychology*, 79(5), 701–721.

Harrison, K., & Cantor, J. (1999). Tales from the screen: Enduring fright reactions to scary media. *Media Psychology*, 1, 97–116.

Hartmann, T., Toz, E., & Brandon, M. (2011). Just a game? Unjustified virtual violence produces guilt in empathetic players. *Media Psychology*, 13(4), 339–363.

Hendriks Vettehen, P., Nuijten, K., & Peeters, A. (2008). Explaining effects of sensationalism on liking of television news stories: The role of emotional arousal. *Communication Research*, 35(3), 319–338.

Hoffner, C., & Buchanan, M. (2005). Young adult's wishful identification with television characters: The role of perceived similarity and character attributes. *Media Psychology*, 7, 325–351.

Hoffner, C., & Cantor, J. (1985). Developmental differences in responses to a television character's appearance and behavior. *Developmental Psychology*, 21, 1065–1074.

Hoorn, J. F. (2012). *Epistemics of the Virtual*. Philadelphia: John Benjamins.

Hoorn, J. F., Konijn, E. A., & Van der Veer, G. (2003). Virtual reality: Do not augment realism, augment relevance. *Upgrade: Human-Computer Interaction*, IV(1), 18–26.

Hoorn, J. F., Pontier, M. A., & Siddiqui, G. F. (2012). Coppélius' concoction: Similarity and complementarity among three affect-related agent models. *Journal of Cognitive Systems Research*, 33, 49.

Horton, D., & Wohl R. R. (1956). Mass communication and para-social interaction: Observations on intimacy at a distance, *Psychiatry*, 19, 215–229.

Hovland, C., Janis, I., & Kelley, H. (1953). *Communication and Persuasion*. New Haven, CT: Yale University Press.

Hovland, C. I., & Weiss, W. (1951). The influence of source credibility on communication effectiveness, *Public Opinion Quarterly*, 15, 635–650.

Isen, A. M. (2008). Some ways in which positive affect influences decision making and problem solving. In Lewis, M., Haviland-Jones, J. M., & Barrett, L. F. (Eds.), *Handbook of Emotions*, 3rd ed. New York: Guilford Press, pp. 548–573.

Isen, A. M., Shalker, T., Clark, M. S., & Karp, L. (1978). Affect, accessibility of material and behaviour: a cognitive loop? *Journal of Personality and Social Psychology*, 36, 1–12.

Jabbia, M., Swarta, M., & Keysers, C. (2007). Empathy for positive and negative emotions in the gustatory cortex. *NeuroImage*, 34, 1744–1753.

Karpouzis, K., Raouzaiou, A. Drosopoulos, A., Ioannou, S., Balomenos, T., Tsapatsoulis, N., et al. (2004). Facial expression and gesture analysis for emotionally-rich man-machine interaction. In: Sarris, N., & Strintzis, M. (Eds.), *3D Modeling and Animation: Synthesis and Analysis Techniques*. Hershey, PA: Idea Group Publishing, pp. 175–200.

Kato, P. M. (2010). Video games in health care: Closing the gap. *Review of General Psychology*, 14(2), 113–121.

Kato, P. M., Cole, S. W., Bradlyn, A. S., & Pollock, B. (2008). A video game improves behavioral outcomes in adolescents and young adults with cancer: A randomized trial. *Pediatrics*, 122, e305–e317.

Katz, E., & Foulkes, D. (1962). On the use of the mass media as "escape": Clarification of a concept. *The Public Opinion Quarterly*, 26(3), 377–388.

Kennedy-Moore, E., & Watson, J. (1999). *Expressing Emotion*. New York: Guilford Press.

Knobloch, S. (2003a). Mood adjustment via mass communication. *Journal of Communication*, 53(2), 233–250.

Knobloch, S. (2003b). Suspense and mystery. In Bryant, J., Roskos-Ewoldsen, D., & Cantor, J. (Eds.), *Communication and Emotion: Essays in Honor of Dolf Zillmann*. Hillsdale, NJ: Lawrence Erlbaum Associates, pp. 379–396.

Knobloch-Westerwick, S., & Alter, S. (2006). Mood adjustment to social situations through mass media use: How men ruminate and women dissipate angry moods. *Human Communication Research*, 32, 58–73.

Knobloch-Westerwick, S., & Romero, J. P. (2011). Body ideals in the media: Perceived attainability and social comparison choices. *Media Psychology*, 14(1), 27–48

Konijn, E. A. (1999). Spotlight on spectators; emotions in the theater. *Discourse Processes*, 28, 169–194.

Konijn, E. A. (2008). Affect and media exposure. In Donsbach, W. (Ed.), *The International Encyclopedia of Communication*. Oxford, UK: Blackwell, pp. 123–129.

Konijn, E. A., & Hoorn, J. F. (2004). Reality-based genre preferences do not direct personal involvement. *Discourse Processes*, 38, 219–245.

Konijn, E. A., & Hoorn, J. F. (2005). Some like it bad. *Media Psychology*, 7(2), 107–144.

Konijn, E. A., & Nije Bijvank, M. (2009). Doors to another me. Identity construction through video game play. In Ritterfeld, U., Cody, M. J., & Vorderer, P. (Eds.), *Serious Games: Mechanisms and Effects*. New York: Routledge, pp. 177–201.

Konijn, E. A., Nije Bijvank, M., & Bushman, B. J. (2007). I wish I were a warrior: The role of wishful identification in the effects of violent video games on aggression in adolescent boys. *Developmental Psychology*, 43, 1038–1044.

Konijn, E. A., & Van Vugt, H. C. (2008). Emotions in mediated interpersonal communication: Toward modeling emotion in virtual humans. In: Konijn, E. A., Utz, S., Tanis, M., & Barnes, S. (Eds.), *Mediated Interpersonal Communication*. New York: Routledge, pp. 100–130.

Konijn, E. A., & Ten Holt, J. (2010). From noise to nucleus: Emotion as key construct in processing media messages. In: Döveling, K., Von Scheve, Chr., & Konijn, E. A. (Eds.), *The Routledge Handbook of Emotions and Mass Media*. New York: Routledge, pp. 37–60.

Konijn, E. A., Walma van der Molen, J. & Hoorn, J. F. (2011). Character identification, empathy and digital game play. In: Poels, K. & Malliet, S. (Eds.) *Digital Game Play and Moral Issues* (pp. 151–176). Leuven, Belgium: ACCO Academic.

Konijn, E. A., Walma van der Molen, J. H., & Van Nes, S. (2009). Emotions bias perceptions of realism in audiovisual media. Why we may take fiction for real. *Discourse Processes*, 46, 309–340.

Kosslyn, S. M., Thompson, W. L., & Alpert, N. M. (1997). Neural systems shared by visual imagery and visual perception: A positron emission tomography study. *NeuroImage*, 6(4), 320–334.

Krämer, N. C. (2010). Psychological research on embodied conversational agents: The case of pedagogical agents. *Journal of Media Psychology*, 22(2), p. 47–51.

Krämer, N. C., Iurgel, I. A., & Bente, G. (2005). Emotion and motivation in embodied conversational agents. In: Canamero, L. (Ed.), *Proceedings of the Symposium "Agents That Want and Like," Artificial Intelligence and the Simulation of Behavior (AISB) 2005* Hatfield: SSAISB, pp. 55–61.

Kumkale, G. T., & Albarracín, D. (2004). The sleeper effect in persuasion: A meta-analytic review. *Psychological Bulletin*, 130, 143–172.

Kunkel, D., Farrar, K. M., Eyal, K., Biely, E., Donnerstein, E., & Rideout, V. (2007). Sexual socialization messages in entertainment television: Comparing content trends 1997–2002. *Media Psychology*, 9, 595–622.

Lang, A. (2000). The limited capacity model of mediated message processing. *Journal of Communication*, 50, 46–70.

Lang, A., Dhillon, K., & Dong, Q. (1995). The effects of emotional arousal and valence on television viewers' cognitive capacity and memory. *Journal of Broadcasting and Electronic Media*, 39, 313–327.

Lang, A., Newhagen, J., & Reeves, B. (1996). Negative video as structure: Emotion, attention, capacity and memory. *Journal of Broadcasting and Electronic Media*, 40, 460–477.

Lazarus, R. S. (1991). *Emotion and Adaptation*. New York: Oxford University Press.

Lazarus, R. S. (1993). Coping theory and research: past, present, and future. *Psychosomatic Medicine, 55*, 234–247.

Lea, M., & Spears, R. (1995). Love at first byte? Building personal relationships over computer networks. In Wood, J. T., & Duck, S. (Eds.), *Under-Studied Relationships: Off the Beaten Track*. Thousand Oaks, CA: Sage, pp. 197–233.

Leach, C. W., Spears, R., Branscombe, N. R., & Doosje, B. (2003). Malicious pleasure: schadenfreude at the suffering of another group. *Journal of Personality and Social Psychology, 84*(5), 932–943.

LeDoux, J. E. (1996). *The Emotional Brain*. New York: Simon & Schuster.

LeDoux, J. E. (2000). Emotion circuits in the brain. *Annual Review of Neuroscience, 23*, 155–184.

LeDoux, J. E., & Phelps, E. A. (2008). Emotional networks in the brain. In Lewis, M., Haviland-Jones, J. M., & Barrett, L. F. (Eds) *Handbook of Emotions*, 3rd ed. New York: Guilford Press, pp. 159–179.

Lerner, J. S., & Keltner, D. (2000). Beyond valence: Toward a model of emotion-specific influences on judgement and choice. *Cognition & Emotion, 14*(4), 473–493.

Levine, L. J., Burgess, S. L., & Laney, C. (2008). Effects of discrete emotions on young children's suggestibility. *Developmental Psychology, 44*, 681–694.

Lewis, M., Haviland-Jones, J. M., & Barrett, L. F. (Eds.) (2008). *Handbook of Emotions*, 3rd ed. New York: Guilford Press.

Liu, H., Lieberman, H., & Selker, T. (2003). A model of textual affect sensing using real-world knowledge. In *Proceedings of IUI 2003*. Miami.

Manstead, A. S. R., Fischer, A., & Jacobs, E. B. (1999). The social and emotional functions of facial displays. In Phillipot, P., Feldman, R. S., & Coats, E. J. (Eds.), *The Social Context of Nonverbal Behavior*. Cambridge, UK: Cambridge University Press, pp. 287–316.

Mares, M. L. (1996). The role of source confusions in television's cultivation of social reality judgments. *Human Communication Research, 23*(2), 278–297.

Marsella, S. C., Johnson, W. L., & LaBore, C. M. (2003). Interactive pedagogical drama for health interventions. In Hoppe, U., et al. (Eds.), *Artificial Intelligence in Education: Shaping the Future of Learning through Intelligent Technologies*. Amsterdam: IOS Press, pp. 341–348.

Mateas, M., & Stern, A. (2003). Façade: an experiment in building a fully-realized interactive drama. In *Game Developer's Conference: Game Design Track*, March 2003, San Jose, CA. Retrieved from http://interactivestory.net/.

Mathur, M., & Chattopadhyay, A. (1991). The impact of moods generated by television programs on responses to advertising. *Psychology and Marketing, 8*, 58–78.

Matsumoto, K., & Ren, F. (2011). Estimation of word emotions based on part of speech and positional information. *Computers in Human Behavior, 27*(5), 1553–1564.

Mayne, J. (1993). *Cinema Spectatorship*. New York: Routledge.

Meeren, H. K., Van Heijnsbergen, C. C., & De Gelder, B. (2005). Rapid perceptual integration of facial expression and emotional body language. *Proceedings of the National Academy of Science, U S A 102*(45), 16518–16523.

Mentis, H. M., & Gay, G. (2002). Using TouchPad Pressure to Detect Negative Affect. *ICMI 2002*, 406–410.

Mills, J. (1993). The appeal of tragedy: An attitude interpretation. *Basic and Applied Social Psychology, 14*(3), 255–271.

Mitchell, K. J., & Ybarra, M. (2009). Social networking sites. Finding a balance between their risks and benefits. *Archives of Pediatrics & Adolescent Medicine, 163*(1), 87–93.

Mundorf, N., & Mundorf, J. (2003). Gender socialization of horror. In Bryant, J., Roskos-Ewoldsen, D., & Cantor, J. (Eds.), *Communication and Emotion: Essays in Honor of Dolf Zillmann*. Hillsdale, NJ: Lawrence Erlbaum Associates, pp. 155–178.

Mundorff, N., Drew, D., Zillmann, D., & Weaver, J. (1990). Effects of disturbing news on recall of subsequently presented news. *Communication Research, 17*, 601–615.

Murphy, S. T. (1998). The impact of factual versus fictional portrayals on cultural stereotypes. *Annals of the American Academy of Political and Social Science, 560*, 165–179.

Murray, J. P. (2008). Media violence: the effects are both real and strong. *American Behavioral Scientist, 51*, 1212–1230.

Nabi, R. L. (2003). Exploring the framing effects of emotion: Do discrete emotions differentially influence information accessibility, information seeking, and policy preference? *Communication Research, 30*(2), 224.

Nabi, R. L. (2009). Emotion and media effects. In Nabi, R. L., & Oliver, M. B. (Eds.), *The SAGE Handbook of Media Processes and Effects*. Newbury Park, CA: Sage, pp. 205–221.

Nabi, R. L., Finnerty, K., Domschke, T., & Hull, S. (2006). Does misery love company? Exploring the therapeutic effects of TV viewing on regretted experiences. *Journal of Communication, 56*(3), 689–706.

Nabi, R. L., So, J., & Prestin, A. (2010). Media-based emotional coping: Examining the emotional benefits and pitfalls of media consumption. In Döveling, K., Von Scheve, Chr ., & Konijn, E. A. (Eds.), *The Routledge Handbook of Emotions and Mass Media*. New York: Routledge, pp. 116–133.

Nabi, R. L., & Wirth, W. (2008). Exploring the role of emotion in media effects: An introduction to the special issue. *Media Psychology, 11*, 1–6.

Nass, C., Brave, S., & Takayama, L. (2006). Socializing consistency: From technical homogeneity to human epitome. In Zhang, P., & Galletta, D. (Eds.), *Human-Computer Interaction in Management Information Systems: Foundations*. Armonk, NY: Sharpe, pp. 373–391.

Nathanson, A. I. (2003). Rethinking empathy. In Bryant, J., Roskos-Ewoldsen, D., & Cantor, J. (Eds.), *Communication and Emotion: Essays in Honor of Dolf Zillmann*. Hillsdale, NJ: Lawrence Erlbaum Associates, pp. 107–130.

Newhagen, K. E. (1998). Approach-avoidance and memory for images of anger, fear, and disgust on television news, *Journal of Broadcast and Electronic Media, 42*, 265–276.

Newhagen, J. E., & Reeves, R. (1992). The evening's bad news: Effects of compelling negative television news images on memory. *Journal of Communication, 42*(2), 25–40.

Nije Bijvank, M., Konijn, E. A., Bushman, B. J. (2011). "We don't need no education": Video game preferences, video game motivations, and aggressiveness among adolescent boys of different educational ability levels. *Journal of Adolescence, 4*(1), 49–58. doi: 10.1016/j.adolescence.2011.04.001.

Nije Bijvank, M., Konijn, E. A., Bushman, B. J., & Roelofsma, P. H. M. P. (2009). Age and content labels make video games forbidden fruit for youth. *Pediatrics, 123*, 870–876.

Oatley, K. (1994). A taxonomy of the emotions of literary response and a theory of identification in fictional narrative. *Poetics, 23*, 53–74.

Obermiller, C., Spangenberg, E., & MacLachlan, D. (2005). Ad skepticism: The consequences of disbelief. *Journal of Advertising, 34*, 7–17.

Oliver, M. B. (1993). Exploring the paradox of the enjoyment of sad films. *Human Communication Research, 19*, 315–342.

Oliver, M. B. (2003). Mood management and selective exposure. In Bryant, J., & Roskos-Ewoldsen, D. (Eds.), *Communication and Emotion*. Hillsdale, NJ: Lawrence Erlbaum Associates, pp. 85–106.

Oliver, M. B. (2008). Tender affective states as predictors of entertainment preference. *Journal of Communication, 58*, 40–61.

Oliver, M. B., Weaver, J. B., & Sargent, S. L. (2000). An examination of factors related to sex differences in enjoyment of sad films. *Journal of Broadcasting and Electronic Media, 44*(2), 282–300.

Oliver, M. B., & Woolley, J. (2010). Tragic and poignant entertainment: The gratifications of meaningfulness as emotional response. In Döveling, K., Von Scheve, Chr ., & Konijn, E. A. (Eds.), *The Routledge Handbook of Emotions and Mass Media*. New York: Routledge, pp. 134–147.

O'Neal, E. C., & Taylor, S. L. (1989). Status of the provoker, opportunity to retaliate, and interest in video violence. *Aggressive Behavior, 15*, 171–180.

Ortony, A., Clore, G. L., & Collins, A. (1988). *The Cognitive Structure of Emotions*. New York: Cambridge University Press.

Owens, J., Maxim, R., McGuinn, M., Nobile, C., Msall, M., & Alario, A. (1999). Television-viewing habits and sleep disturbance in school children. *Pediatrics, 104*, 27, p. e27-.

Paavonen, E. J., Pennonen, M., Roine, M., Valkonen, S., & Lahikainen, A. R. (2006). TV exposure associated with sleep disturbances in 5- to 6-year-olds. *Journal of Sleep Research, 15*, 154–161.

Paiva, A., Dias, J., & Aylett, R. S. (2005). Learning by feeling: evoking empathy with synthetic characters. *Applied Artificial Intelligence, 19*(3–4), 235–266.

Panksepp, J. (1998). *Affective Neuroscience: The Foundations of Human and Animal Emotions*. Oxford, UK: Oxford University Press.

Partalaa, T., & Surakkaa, V. (2003). Pupil size variation as an indication of affective processing. *International Journal of Human-Computer Studies, 59*, 185–198.

Peter, J., & Valkenburg, P. M. (2010). Processes underlying the effects of adolescents' use of sexually explicit internet material: The role of perceived realism. *Communication Research, 37*, 375–399.

Picard, R. W. (1997). *Affective Computing*. Cambridge, MA: MIT Press.

Picard, R. W., & Daily, S. B. (2005). *Evaluating affective interactions: Alternatives to asking what users feel*. Paper presented at the CHI Workshop on Evaluating Affective Interfaces: Innovative Approaches, Portland, OR.

Plaisier, X. S., & Konijn, E. A. (in press). Rejected by peers— Attracted to antisocial media content: Rejection-based anger impairs moral judgment in adolescents, *Developmental Psychology*.

Polzin, T. S., & Waibel, A. (2000). Emotion-sensitive human-computer interfaces. *Proceedings of the ISCA Workshop on Speech and Emotion*, Belfast 2000.

Pontier, M. A., & Siddiqui, G. F. (2008). A virtual therapist that responds empathically to your answers. In Prendinger, H., Lester, J., & Ishizuka, M. (Eds.), *Proceedings of the 8th International Conference on Intelligent Virtual Agents, IVA'08*, pp. 417–425.

Prendinger, H., & Ishizuka, M. (2010). Virtual interface agents that adapt to user emotion and interest. In Döveling, K., Von Scheve, Chr., & Konijn, E. A. (Eds.), *The Routledge Handbook of Emotions and Mass Media*. New York: Routledge, pp. 388–405.

Raney, A. A. (2004). Expanding disposition theory: Reconsidering character liking, moral evaluations, and enjoyment. *Communication Theory, 14*(4), 348–369.

Raney, A. A. (2010). Media enjoyment as a function of affective dispositions toward and moral judgment of characters. In Döveling, K., Von Scheve, Chr ., & Konijn, E. A. (Eds.), *The Routledge Handbook of Emotions and Mass Media*. New York: Routledge, pp. 166–177.

Reeves, B., & Nass, C. (1996). *The Media Equation: How People Treat Computers, Television, and New Media Like Real People and Places*. Cambridge, UK: Cambridge University Press.

Reeves, B., Newhagen, J. E., Maibach, E., Basil, M., & Kurz, K. (1991). Negative and positive television messages: Effects of message type and context on attention and memory. *American Behavioral Scientist, 34*(6), 679–694.

Ritterfeld, U., Cody, M. J., & Vorderer, P. (2009). (Eds.), *Serious Games: Mechanisms and Effects*. New York: Routledge.

Rizzolatti, G., & Craighero, L. (2004). The mirror-neuron system. *Annual Review of Neuroscience, 27*, 169–192.

Rolls, E. T. (1999). *The Brain and Emotion*. Oxford, UK: Oxford University Press.

Rolls, E. T. (2003). A theory of emotion, its functions, and its adaptive value. In Trappl, R., Petta, S., & Pyar, P. (Eds.), *Emotions in Humans and Artifacts*. Cambridge, MA: MIT Press, pp. 11–34.

Russell, J. A., & Barrett, L. F. (1999). Core affect, prototypical emotional episodes, and other things called emotion: Dissecting the elephant. *Journal of Personality and Social Psychology, 76*, 805–819.

Russell, C. A., Norman, A. T., & Heckler, S. E. (2004). The consumption of television programming: Development and validation of the connectedness scale. *Journal of Consumer Research, 31*(1), pp. 150–161.

Rutledge, P. (2008). What is media psychology? A qualitative inquiry. *Media Psychology Review, 1*, 1.

Schubert, T. W. (2003). The sense of presence in virtual environments: A three-component scale measuring spatial presence, involvement, and realness. *Zeitschrift für Medienpsychologie, 15*, 69–71.

Seligman, M. E. P., & Csikszentmihalyi, M. (2000). Positive psychology: An introduction. *American Psychologist, 55*(1), 5–14.

Shapiro, M. A., & Lang, A. (1991). Making television reality. *Communication Research, 18*, 685–706.

Singer, M. I., Slovak, K., Frierson, T., & York, P. (1998), Viewing preferences, symptoms of psychological trauma, and violent behaviors among children who watch television. *Journal of the American Academy of Child and Adolescent Psychiatry, 37*, 1041–1048.

Slater, M. D. (1990). Processing social information in messages: Social group familiarity, fiction versus nonfiction, and subsequent beliefs. *Communication Research, 17*(3), 327.

Slater, M. D., & Rouner, D. (2002). Entertainment-education and elaboration likelihood: Understanding the processing of narrative persuasion. *Communication Theory, 12*(2), 173–191.

Smith, C. A., & Scott, H. S. (1997). A componential approach to the meaning of facial expressions. In Russell, J. A., & Fernandez-Dolls, J. M. (Eds.), *The Psychology of Facial Expression*. Cambridge, UK: Cambridge University Press, pp. 229–254.

Smith, M. (1995). *Engaging Characters. Fiction, Emotion, and the Cinema*. Oxford, UK: Clarendon.

Sparks, G. G., & Sparks, C. W. (2000). Violence, mayhem, and horror. In Zillmann, D., & Vorderer, P. (Eds.), *Media Entertainment: The Psychology of Its Appeal*. Hillsdale, NJ: Lawrence Erlbaum Associates, pp. 73–92.

Strange, J. J., & Leung, C. C. (1999). How anecdotal accounts in news and in fiction can influence judgments of a social problem's urgency, causes, and cures. *Personality and Social Psychology Bulletin*, 25(4), 436.

Strasburger, V. C., Jordan, A. B., & Donnerstein, E. (2010). Health effects of media on children and adolescents. *Pediatrics*, 125, 756–767.

Subramanyam, K., & Šmahel, D. (2011). *Digital Youth: The Role of Media in Development*. New York: Springer.

Suls, J., & Wheeler, L. (eds.) (2000). *Handbook of Social Comparison Theory and Research*. New York: Springer.

Sundar, S. S. (2003). News features and learning. In Bryant, J., Roskos-Ewoldsen, D., & Cantor, J. (Eds.), *Communication and Emotion: Essays in Honor of Dolf Zillmann*. Hillsdale, NJ: Lawrence Erlbaum Associates, pp. 275–296.

Sykes, J., & Brown, S. (2003). Affective gaming: Measuring emotion through the gamepad. In *CHI '03 Extended Abstracts on Human Factors in Computing Systems*. New York: ACM Press, pp. 732–733.

Tamborini, R. (2003). Enjoyment and social functions of horror. In Bryant, J., Roskos-Ewoldsen, D., & Cantor, J. (Eds.), *Communication and Emotion: Essays in Honor of Dolf Zillmann*. Hillsdale, NJ: Lawrence Erlbaum Associates, pp. 417–444.

Tamir, M., & Robinson, M. D. (2007). The happy spotlight: positive mood and selective attention to rewarding information. *Personality and Social Psychology Bulletin*, 33, 1124–1136.

Tan, E. S. (1996). *Emotion and the Structure of Narrative Film: Film as an Emotion Machine*. Hillsdale, NJ: Lawrence Erlbaum Associates.

Tannenbaum, P. H., & Gaer, E. P. (1965). Mood change as a function of stress of protagonist and degree of identification in a film-viewing situation. *Journal of Personality and Social Psychology*, 2, 612–616.

Taylor, L. D. (2005). Effects of visual and verbal sexual television content and perceived realism on attitudes and beliefs. *The Journal of Sex Research*, 42, 130–137.

Theeuwes, J. (1993). Visual selective attention: a theoretical analysis. *Acta Psychologica*, 83, 93–154.

Tiedens, L. Z., & Linton, S. (2001), Judgment under emotional certainty and uncertainty: the effect of specific emotions on information processing. *Journal of Personality and Social Psychology*, 81, 973–988.

Tugade, M. M., & Fredrickson, B. L. (2004). Resilient individuals use positive emotions to bounce back from negative emotional experiences. *Journal of Personality and Social Psychology*, 86, 320–333.

United States Army. (2002). *America's Army—Operations*. Digital game: http://www.americasarmy.com/., Retrieved August, 2011.

Van Atteveldt, W., Kleinnijenhuis, J., Ruigrok, N., & Schlobach, S. (2008). Good news or bad news? Conducting sentiment analysis on Dutch text to distinguish between positive and negative relations. In Cardie, C., & Wilkerson, J. (Eds.), *Special Issue of the Journal of Information Technology and Politics on "Text Annotation for Political Science,"* 5(1), 73–94.

Van den Broek, E. L. (2004). Emotional Prosody Measurement (EPM): A voice-based evaluation method for psychological therapy effectiveness. *Medical and Care Compunetics*, 1, 118–125.

Van den Bulck, J. (2004). Media use and dreaming: The relationship among television viewing, computer game play, and nightmares or pleasant dreams. *Dreaming*, 14, 43–49.

Van Dijk, W. W., Ouwerkerk, J. W., Goslinga, S., & Nieweg, M. (2005). Schadenfreude and deservingness. *Cognition and Emotion*, 19, 933–939.

Veldhuis, J., Konijn, E. A., & Seidell, J. C. (2012). Weight information labels on media models reduce body dissatisfaction in adolescent girls. *Journal of Adolescent Health*, 15(4), 451–477.

Vertegaal, R. P. H., Slagter, R., van der Veer, G. C., & Nijholt, A. (2001). Eye gaze patterns in conversations: There is more to conversational agents than meets the eyes. In J. Jacko, A. Sears, M. Beaudouin-Lafon, & R. J. K. Jacob (Eds.), *Proceedings ACM SIGCHI Conference CHI 2001: Anyone. Anywhere*, New York: ACM Press, pp. 301–308.

Von Feilitzen, C., & Linné, O. (1975). Identifying with television characters. *Journal of Communication*, 25, 51–55.

de Waal, F. B. M. (2003). Darwin's legacy and the study of primate visual communication. In Ekman, P., Campos, J. J., Davidson, R. J., & de Waal, F. B. M. (Eds.), *Emotions Inside Out: 130 Years After Darwin's The Expression of the Emotions in Man and Animals*. New York: New York Academy of Sciences, pp. 7–31.

Walma van der Molen, J. H. (2004). Violence and suffering in television news: Toward a broader conception of harmful television content for children. *Pediatrics*, 113, 1771–1775.

Walma van der Molen, J. H., & Konijn, E. A. (2007). Dutch children's emotional reactions to news about the second Gulf war: Influence of media exposure, identification, and empathy. In Lemish, D., & Götz, M. (Eds.), *Children, Media, and War: The Case of the Iraq War*. Cresskill, NJ: Hampton Press, pp. 75–99.

Ward, L. M., & Friedman, K. (2006). Using TV as a guide: Associations between television viewing and adolescents' sexual attitudes and behavior. *Journal of Research on Adolescence*, 16, 133–156.

Weinberger, M. G., & Gulas, C. S. (1992). The impact of humor in advertising: A review. *Journal of Advertising*, 21, 35–59.

de Wied, M., Zillmann, D., & Ordman, V. (1994). The role of empathic distress in the enjoyment of cinematic tragedy. *Poetics*, 23, 91–106.

Witte, K., & Allen, M. (2000). A meta-analysis of fear appeals: implications for effective public health campaigns. *Health Education and Behavior*, 27, 591–615.

Williams, K. D., Cheung, C. K. T., & Choi, W. (2000). CyberOstracism: Effects of being ignored over the Internet. *Journal of Personality and Social Psychology*, 79, 748–762.

Williams, P., & Aaker, J. L. (2002). Can mixed emotions peacefully coexist? *Journal of Consumer Research*, 28, 636–649.

Wirth, W. (2006). Involvement. In Bryant, J., & Vorderer, P. (Eds.), *Psychology of Entertainment*. Hillsdale, NJ: Lawrence Erlbaum Associates, pp. 199–213.

Wu, Y., & Huang, T. S. (2001). Hand modeling, analysis, and recognition for vision-based human computer interaction. *IEEE Signal Processing Magazine*, 18(3), 51–60.

Yee, N., Bailenson, J. N., & Rickertsen, K. (2007). A meta-analysis of the impact of the inclusion and realism of human-like faces on user experiences in interfaces. *CHI 2007 Proceedings*, 1–10.

Zhao, W., Chellappa, R., Phillips, P. J., & Rosenfeld, A. (2003). Face recognition: A literature survey. *ACM Computer Survey, 35*(4), 399–458. doi: http://doi.acm.org/10.1145/954339.954342.

Zillmann, D. (1971). Excitation transfer in communication-mediated aggressive behavior. *Journal of Experimental Social Psychology, 7*, 419–434.

Zillmann, D. (1988). Mood management through communication choices. *American Behavioral Scientist, 31*(3), 327–340.

Zillmann, D. (1991). Empathy: Affect from bearing witness to the emotions of others. In Bryant, J., & Zillmann, D. (Eds.), *Responding to the Screen: Reception and Reaction Processes.* Hillsdale, NJ: Lawrence Erlbaum Associates, pp. 135–167.

Zillmann, D. (1994). Mechanisms of emotional involvement with drama. *Poetics, 23*, 33–51.

Zillmann, D. (2003). Theory of affective dynamics: Emotions and moods. In Bryant, J., Roskos-Ewoldsen, D., & Cantor, J. (Eds.), *Communication and Emotion.* Hillsdale, NJ: Lawrence Erlbaum Associates, pp. 533–567.

Zillmann, D. (2010). Mechanisms of emotional reactivity to media entertainments. In Döveling, K., Von Scheve, Chr., & Konijn, E. A. (Eds.), *The Routledge Handbook of Emotions and Mass Media.* New York: Routledge, pp. 101–115.

Zillmann, D., & Bryant, J. (1986). Shifting preferences in pornography consumption. *Communication Research, 13*, 560–578.

Zillmann, D., Hezel, R. T., & Medoff, N. J. (1980). The effect of affective states on selective exposure to televised entertainment fare. *Journal of Applied Psychology, 10*, 323–339.

Zillmann, D., Knobloch, S., & Hong-sik, Y. (2001). Effects of photographs on the selective reading of news reports. *Media Psychology, 3*, 301–324.

Zillmann, D., & Weaver, J. B. (1996). Gender-socialization theory of reactions to horror. In Weaver, J., & Tamborini, R. (Eds.), *Horror Film: Current Research on Audience Preferences.* Hillsdale, NJ: Lawrence Erlbaum Associates, pp. 81–101.

Zillmann, D., Weaver, J. B., Mundorf, N., & Aust, C. F. (1986). Effects of an opposite-gender companion's affect to horror on distress, delight, and attraction. *Journal of Personality and Social Psychology, 51*, 586–594.

Media Violence, Desensitization, and Psychological Engagement

Jeanne Funk Brockmyer

Abstract

This chapter presents a framework for understanding desensitization to violence as an outcome of exposure to media violence. The term *desensitization* is defined, and behavioral and psychophysiological research documenting this phenomenon are presented. Aspects of moral evaluation, including empathy and attitudes toward violence, are discussed as proxy measures of desensitization. An individual's propensity to become deeply involved in media experiences is proposed as one factor that increases the relative risk of desensitization. The term *psychological engagement* is recommended as an umbrella term for all levels of media involvement. Terms describing the progression of intensity of engagement, including *immersion, presence, flow,* and *psychological absorption* are discussed. Future research must be built on definitional consensus in this area. Psychophysiological and behavioral research will be complementary in elucidating the neural and psychological processes that underlie the desensitization process. The role of desensitization in increasing aggression and decreasing helping behavior requires additional study.

Key Words: absorption, desensitization, empathy, media violence, moral evaluation, presence, psychological engagement

Media Violence, Desensitization, and Psychological Engagement

Imagine a world in which violence is considered to be fun and there are no realistic consequences; in which the suffering of victims of violence does not matter. This would represent the ultimate desensitization to violence and is an accurate description of the landscape of many violent video games. This chapter describes what is known about desensitization to violence as it occurs following exposure to media violence.

Media researchers have just begun to aggressively investigate desensitization to violence as an outcome of exposure to media violence (Funk, 2005; Huesmann & Kirwil, 2007; Krahe et al., 2010). One logical next step is to determine what factors might lead one person to become desensitized to violence and another to remain unaffected. It is proposed that the capacity to become psychologically engaged is a key characteristic that influences the impact of exposure to media violence, and one that can be measured and studied. This chapter takes note of the large body of research on media violence effects, defines the constructs of desensitization and psychological engagement, summarizes research on desensitization to media violence, and suggests directions for future research on psychological engagement in violent media as one route to desensitization.

Media Violence Research

Violence in the media is pervasive, particularly in entertainment media. Consider a typical episode of an action movie or television show. Often the hero must use violence to serve the common good. Therefore, violence is portrayed as being justified ("Might makes right"). In most but not all cases in movies and television, the hero prevails, reinforcing the notion that violence in the right hands and for the right cause is justifiable (Huesmann, Moise-Titus, Podolski, & Eron, 2003). By the time he or she is a senior in high school, the average American youth has viewed 20,000 hours of television and movie content (Rideout, Foehr, & Roberts, 2010), and much of this contains violence. For movies and television, the viewer is a passive content recipient (although theoretically free to change the channel or leave the movie theater). Video gaming adds an interactive component that theoretically could increase content impact, whether nonviolent or violent (Funk & Buchman, 1996; Gentile & Gentile, 2008). In video games, the player takes part in developing the game scenario, and in violent games is routinely rewarded for identifying and selecting the violent strategies that are built in by the game designer (Funk & Buchman, 1996). With the advent of multiple platforms for gaming, it is difficult to obtain accurate estimates of typical gaming time; however, researchers believe that children and adolescents play for about an hour and a quarter per day on average (Rideout et al., 2010). The content of games played is varied; however, most surveys suggest that many children have a preference for violent video games (Buchman & Funk, 1996). In one recent survey, more than half of 8- to 18-year-olds reported having played a game from the violent Grand Theft Auto series, and almost half reported playing Halo, another violent game (Rideout et al., 2010). Both games are rated for mature audiences.

Much has been written about media violence effects. This work is described in several other chapters in this Handbook (see, for example, Chapter 9). The majority of researchers conclude that media violence does have negative effects in a number of ways (Anderson et al., 2003). In a recent meta-analysis of research on violent video games, Anderson et al. (2010) examined 136 "best practice" research reports. The researchers concluded that exposure to violent video games was positively associated with aggressive outcomes in behavior, cognition, and affect. As with many controversial issues, some have questioned the research approach and conclusions. Two of the current proponents of the "no impact" position (Ferguson & Kilburn, 2010) argued that the methodology of the 2010 Anderson et al. meta-analysis was flawed, the sample biased, and the findings overinterpreted. These concerns were subsequently addressed by three of the paper's authors (Bushman, Rothstein, & Anderson, 2010) who noted, "We rely on well-established methodological and statistical theory and on empirical data to show that claims of bias and misinterpretation on our part are simply wrong" (p. 182). The reader will find that the Bushman et al. response is well reasoned and conclusive, and their meta-analysis definitive.

Working from the large body of research on the effects of violent media, the present chapter is built on the premise that exposure to media violence can and does have negative impact in some situations for some individuals. This impact includes not only aggressive outcomes, but also desensitization to violence. Although desensitization research is relatively limited, this may be one of the most important unintended consequences of exposure to media violence. Many social interactions could be affected by desensitization to violence, not only the propensity for aggression, but also a person's willingness to respond to others in need (Bushman & Anderson, 2009).

Desensitization Defined

Desensitization can be broadly defined as the reduction or eradication of cognitive, emotional, physiological, and ultimately behavioral responses to a stimulus (Funk, 2005). Desensitization to a negative stimulus can be a protective, normal process (Funk, 2005). Consider your initial response to a major tragedy, perhaps the 9/11 terrorist attacks or the 2011 earthquake in Japan and subsequent tsunami. It was common to have a significant cognitive (This is horrible!) and affective (I feel terrible for those people!) reaction to both events. However, over time both reactions have dissipated for most. As noted, this is a normal and protective progression. As humans, we are simply not capable of prolonged arousal to other people's tragedies. There is typically an initial helping response, which then dissipates as the crisis is mitigated, even if some degree of suffering continues. Unless the individual is directly affected, attention shifts back to the demands of everyday life. This type of desensitization is an automatic, adaptive response to a negative event.

However, automatic desensitization can also be maladaptive, particularly in the case of desensitization to violence. In the real world, researchers have found that many children who are exposed to high levels of community violence view violence as an ordinary part of life (Guerra, Huesmann, & Spindler, 2003). Guerra et al. suggest that this perspective could desensitize children to the true consequences of violence and possibly result in an increased propensity for aggressive and violent behavior.

Desensitization can also be intentional. For example, desensitization is a well-studied treatment approach in clinical psychology. In general, the goal is to reduce or eliminate undesirable responses such as fear and avoidance through graded and supervised exposure to stimuli that are initially anxiety provoking. Helping a patient become desensitized to subconscious cognitive and emotional reactions is one of the key goals of trauma-focused therapies (Rubin & Springer, 2009).

Media Violence and Desensitization

Research suggests that exposure to unreal, and specifically media violence can also be desensitizing (Anderson et al., 2003). In entertainment media, violence is often portrayed as being not only justified, but fun (Funk, 1992; Funk & Buchman, 1996). In this type of violence, the antisocial behavior demonstrated and required to win rarely generates realistic consequences, and the true impact of violent actions is disguised (NTSV, 1996–1997). Anderson et al.'s General Aggression Model (GAM) provides a relevant theoretical framework for understanding these effects (Anderson & Bushman, 2002; Anderson & Huesmann, 2003). The GAM integrates several theoretical perspectives, including social learning, social cognition, affective aggression, and excitation transfer (Anderson, Gentile, & Buckley, 2007). The GAM suggests that repeated exposure to media violence can lead to the development of aggressive beliefs and attitudes, aggressive behavioral scripts, and desensitization to violence. This model organizes relevant variables into short- and long-term influences. Regarding desensitization to violence, long-term processes may be most important (Huesmann & Kirwil, 2007). In early childhood, media violence is first encountered through cartoon characters, with violent actions presented as entertaining and fun. This leads to positive emotional reactions that are incompatible with any negative reaction to violence and may reflect what has been termed *sensitization* (Krahe et al., 2010). Older children and adults are exposed to more realistic violence with more obvious negative features, but the increases are gradual and violence often continues to be presented as fun, with the addition of justification. As noted by Carnagey, Anderson, et al. (2007), this developmental progression of exposure to media violence is a very effective form of systematic violence desensitization.

Measuring Desensitization to Violence

The measurement of desensitization to violence is somewhat complicated by differing views on what should be measured (Carnagey, Anderson, & Bushman, 2007; Krahe et al., 2010), and the fact that it is, by definition, the absence of an expected response (Funk, Buchman, Jenks, & Bechtoldt, 2003). In research on real-world phenomena such as media effects, it is important to have a convergence of evidence from a variety of research approaches (Anderson et al., 2007). Studies of desensitization to media violence have examined both short- and long-term effects in the domains of attitudes, affect, behavior, and physiological responding.

Short-Term Desensitization Effects

Several researchers have examined how attitudes and affect may be affected by short-term exposure to media violence. For example, Mullin and Linz (1995) described a short-term desensitization effect on male adults' self-reported sympathy for female victims of domestic violence following exposure to sexually violent films. The researchers also reported that enjoyment of the films increased with increased exposure, possibly supporting the sensitization hypothesis. However, there was a rebound "resensitization" effect 5 days after the last viewing. Mullin and Linz suggest that frequent exposure to media violence could cause more rapid desensitization with future exposures, perhaps resulting in lower overall sensitivity (desensitization) in the long run. Along these lines, changes in affective response to violent film scenes were demonstrated by Fanti, Vanman, Henrich, and Avraamides (2009). In their research with male and female college students, an initial decline in enjoyment of violent film scenes was followed by a later increase in enjoyment. Overall, enjoyment of violent scenes increased from the beginning to the end of the presentation. In addition, with repeated exposure to violent film scenes, sympathy for victims of violence decreased. Both results suggest a desensitization effect. In research with interactive media, college students played either a more violent or less violent video game and then assigned prison sentences to hypothetical violent criminals (Deselms & Altman, 2003). Men who had played the more violent game endorsed lower sanctions, which the researchers concluded was an indication of desensitization.

Affective desensitization to media violence has also been examined through classic laboratory paradigms such as the competitive reaction time task. In recent work with German undergraduates, Krahe et al. (2010) found that following exposure to a violent film clip, unprovoked aggression during the reaction time task was predicted by lower anxious arousal to the violent scenes. In addition, self-reported anxious arousal to the violent film clips was generally lower in those with higher long-term exposure to media violence, and pleasant arousal was greater. These last findings also suggest longer-term desensitization.

Other researchers have focused on how actual helping responses are affected by exposure to media violence. In a classic study by Drabman and Thomas (1974), children who viewed an aggressive film later took significantly longer to seek adult assistance to stop what they thought was a fight between younger children, compared with those who did not see the film. In a subsequent replication, Molitor and Hirsch (1994) confirmed the original findings: Viewing violence increases tolerance for violent behavior in children. In similar work with adults, Bushman and Anderson (2009) found that individuals were less likely to aid someone in need after either playing a violent video game or viewing a violent movie. These results are all consistent with desensitization to violence.

PHYSIOLOGICAL MEASURES

Several physiological measures of desensitization have been used in combination with self-report and/or behavioral measures (Ravaja, 2004). Averill, Malmstrom, Koriat, and Lazarus (1972) assessed changes in skin conductance, self-reported distress, and heart rate after male students viewed clips of industrial accidents. There was habituation (less reactivity) for all three responses, but only to the same scene when viewed in the context of the entire film. Staude-Müller, Bliesener, and Luthman (2008) examined reactions to high versus low violence video game play, collecting physiological measures of arousal and self-reports of emotional responses to unpleasant and aggressive images. Participants in the high-violence condition showed significantly weaker physiological reactions to aversive stimuli indicating desensitization. In a similar paradigm, participants who played a violent game had lower physiological reactivity to scenes of real-life violence than those playing a nonviolent game (Carnagey, Anderson, & Bushman, 2007).

Using more sophisticated approaches to measure neural indicators of desensitization to violence is becoming increasingly popular as the technology to examine such effects is developing (Carnagey, Anderson, & Bartholow, 2007; Cacioppo, Berntson, & Nusbaum, 2008). Admittedly, this literature is young (Haslam, Illner, & Chuang, 2003; Heinzl & Northoff, 2009; Sterzer & Stadler, 2009) and an in-depth discussion is beyond the scope of the present chapter. However, the importance of existing work, as well as its future promise, merits some consideration. Using facial myography, skin conductance, and cardiac measures, Ravaja, Saari, Salminen, Laarni and Kallinen (2006) found that both positive and negative video game events elicited positive emotional arousal. They concluded that consistently pairing violent actions with positive emotional responses could lead to desensitization to violent behavior. Kelly, Grinband, & Hirsch (2007) performed functional magnetic resonance imaging (fMRI) while adult volunteers watched a series of film clips that demonstrated physical violence, fearful facial expressions, and neutral physical interactions such as dance or sports. Exposure to the violent clips resulted in a decreased response in a neural network that is considered important for the control of reactive aggression. The researchers concluded that this diminished responsiveness indicated desensitization. In research with adolescents, Strenziok, Krueger, Deshpande, et al. (2010) reported that their fMRI results indicated that repeated exposure to aggressive media affects an emotion–attention network that may reduce emotional responses through diminished attention if there is repeated viewing of aggressive media. The researchers speculated that this may restrict the linking of the consequences of aggression with an emotional response, eventually resulting in desensitization.

Englehart, Bartholow, Kerr, and Bushman (2011) combined electroencephalogram and behavioral measures to examine the short-term impact of playing a violent or nonviolent video game. The primary physiological measure of interest was the P3 amplitude, which is a component of event-related brain potential that has been shown to be responsive to stimuli that activate the aversive motivational system (Delplanque, Silvert, Hot, Rigoulot, & Sequeira, 2006). A smaller P3 response to violent images indicates weaker activation of aversive motivation, in this case to the use of aggression. After game-playing, participants viewed violent and nonviolent pictures while their brain activity was measured, and then they completed a competitive reaction time task. Participants with high prior exposure to violent video games had small P3 amplitudes to violent images regardless of game played. Those with low prior exposure who played a violent game had smaller P3 amplitudes than low exposure participants who played a nonviolent game. For low exposure participants, this difference in brain response mediated the effect of video game content on (more) aggressive behavior during the reaction time task. The authors concluded that their results demonstrate short-term desensitization after playing a violent video game and, more importantly, that this desensitization accounts for increased aggression (Englehart et al., 2011).

Desensitization Over the Long Term

PHYSIOLOGICAL MEASURES

A variety of physiological measures have also been used to examine long-term desensitization to violence. Bartholow, Bushman, and Sestir (2006) also used the P3 response to evaluate adult male college students' responses to violent, neutral, and negative but nonviolent stimuli. The researchers reported that more long-term exposure to violent video games was associated with reduced in P3 amplitude while viewing violent images. In addition, this reduced brain response predicted increased aggressive behavior in a subsequent competitive reaction time task. The researchers concluded that this demonstrates long-term desensitization. In related work, Strenziok, Krueger, Pulaski, et al. (2010) reported that in 37 male adolescents, higher self-reported media violence exposure was associated with lower left lateral orbitofrontal cortex density. The researchers noted that the direction of this relationship could not be determined with their research design. However, they expressed concern that such lower density could be associated with inaccurate interpretation of environmental cues. This could disrupt an individual's ability to make an appropriate response to ambiguous environmental cues, which could be interpreted as desensitization.

Matthews et al. (2005) used fMRI to examine relationships between media violence exposure and brain activation in typical adolescents and those diagnosed with disruptive behavior disorder. Typical adolescents with high media violence exposure, and those with the disruptive behavior diagnosis demonstrated reduced frontal lobe activation while performing a counting Stroop task. The researchers concluded that over the long term media violence exposure may be associated with alterations in brain functioning that could indicate desensitization. Using a similar paradigm, Kalnin et al. (2011) found that adolescents with a disruptive behavior diagnosis and high media violence exposure had decreased activation in frontolimbic areas, which could also be consistent with desensitization.

Only one published work was found that did not support some type of activation pattern that was interpreted as being consistent with possible desensitization. Regenbogen, Herrmann, and Fehr (2010) presented video game–based and real scenes of violence to young men with and without a history of long-term violent video game play. Most relevant to the present discussion, the researchers reported that their fMRI results did not indicate a differential neural network response to real versus virtual violence in the gamers that they believe would be consistent with desensitization.

It is clear that the majority of the small body of published research using a psychophysiological approach finds patterns of activation consistent with desensitization in response to media violence exposure. In many cases it appears that alterations in frontal lobe functioning occur, suggesting that processes such as executive functioning, emotion regulation, and memory storage and retrieval could be affected.

As yet there is very little research of this type with child populations, who are potentially most vulnerable to long-term effects (Funk, 2005; Carnagey, Anderson, & Bartholow, 2007). As noted by Perry and Pollard (1998), experience alters the organized brain of adults, but in children experience organizes the developing brain. However, the potential neurophysiological and neuropsychological consequences of heavy exposure to media violence on the developing brain have yet to be examined. There is literature to suggest that some deleterious psychophysiological effects of early experience are long lasting if not permanent (Cichetti, 2010). It is also possible that children with neurological deviations, such as those that occur in attention deficit hyperactivity disorder or autism spectrum disorders, may be especially vulnerable to long-term negative impact from media violence exposure.

MORAL EVALUATION

Aspects of moral evaluation including normative beliefs, empathy, and helping behavior have also been used to examine the phenomenon of desensitization to violence. Moral evaluation is an automatic process that is triggered when the individual encounters a situation in which ethical issues must be considered. For situations related to violence, the choice may be to take or not take a violent action, or to assist or not assist a victim of violence. The individual must selectively attend to and then interpret the relevant cues using internalized moral evaluation mechanisms. The process of moral evaluation is disrupted by desensitization to violence because the desensitized individual does not either perceive or respond to the cues that typically would initiate evaluative processes. Consequently, negative actions may be taken without consideration of their moral implications, or a needed prosocial action may not be taken (Funk, 2005). In violent subcultures in the real world, desensitization through dehumanizing victims is a commonly used technique for minimizing the activation of moral reasoning (Guerra, Nucci, & Huesmann, 1994). In violent media, similar processes are often seen (Johnson, Bushman, & Dovidio, 2008; Dill, 2009). The moral evaluation process is influenced by the individual's normative beliefs about and attitudes toward violence, and by their affective repertoire, particularly the capacity for empathic response.

Normative beliefs are cognitions that are used by the individual to determine the appropriateness of certain behaviors. Normative beliefs about aggression include thoughts about what is typical and what is appropriate in terms of aggressive behavior. Research suggests that aggression-related normative beliefs and attitudes toward violence are influenced by exposure to media violence. For example, Moller and Krahe (2009) studied normative beliefs about aggression in German adolescents as related to their exposure to violent video games over a 30-month period. Their results suggest that exposure to violent video games increased the acceptance of physical aggression to solve conflicts. In other words, exposure to violent video games strengthened the normative belief that aggression is an acceptable behavioral response.

Attitudes develop as a result of complex and selective evaluation processes, based on an individual's experience with, associated cognitions about, and affective reactions to a situation or object (Fazio & Olson, 2003). Attitudes may be formed automatically and unconsciously (consider the effects of advertising), or through a deliberate and goal-oriented process, for example, in jury deliberations (Olson & Fazio, 2001). Established attitudes influence how judgments are made in new situations, and can exert a direct impact on behavior. The development of attitudes toward violence is influenced by many factors, including exposure to family and community violence, as well as exposure to violence in the media. When the normative belief is that aggressive behavior is appropriate, then the attitude may develop that aggression and violence are acceptable, and the process of desensitization to violence has begun. Proviolence attitudes play an important role in the translation of negative cognitions and affect into behavior (Velicer, Huckel, & Hansen, 1989).

Empathic responding is another critical element in the moral reasoning process. Contemporary definitions of empathy include both cognitive (perspective-taking) and affective (experiencing the emotional state of another) elements. The relative importance of each element varies with the level of distress either perceived or experienced (Funk, Fox, Chan, & Curtiss, 2008). Although there is some inborn propensity for empathy, the development of mature empathy requires certain experiences. These include opportunities to view empathic models, interact with others in certain kinds of stressful situations, and experience feedback about the behavioral choices made during these interactions. Hoffman (2000) emphasized the role of inductive discipline in the development of empathy. Inductive discipline requires children to imagine how they would feel in a victim's situation, and encourages the development of moral scripts based on empathy. Theoretically, when confronted with a victim, empathic scripts will automatically be triggered and guide behavioral choice. There is considerable experimental evidence that empathy inhibits aggressive behavior, with lower empathy being a factor in increased aggression (see, for example, Stams et al., 2006; van Baardewijk, Stegge, Bushman, & Vermeiren, 2009).

Considering attitudes toward violence and empathy as proxy measures of desensitization, researchers have examined relationships between exposure to violent media on these characteristics. In a meta-analysis examining the reasons viewers enjoyed violent content, individuals lower in empathy, and those higher in aggressiveness reported more enjoyment of fright and violence (Hoffner & Levine, 2005). Funk, Buchman, Jenks, and Bechtoldt (2003) reported results of a study with children age 5 through 12 who responded to vignettes about everyday occurrences following playing either a violent or nonviolent video game. Long-term exposure to violent video games contributed to lower empathy vignette scores, which could be consistent with desensitization.

In research reported by Funk, Bechtoldt-Baldacci, Pasold, and Baumgardner (2004), fourth and fifth graders completed measures of a variety of forms of real-life and media violence exposure, empathy, and attitudes toward violence. Only exposure to video game violence was associated with (lower) empathy. Both video game and movie violence exposure were associated with stronger proviolence attitudes. In a survey of Chinese adolescents, Wei (2007) found that a higher level of exposure to violent video games online was associated with lower empathy. Based on findings from surveys and experimental work with adults, Bartholow, Sestir, and Davis (2005) suggested that exposure to video game violence can lead to lower empathy, a hostile perceptual bias, and increased aggressive behavior. Krahe and Moller surveyed a large sample of seventh and eighth graders in Germany (2010) twice over a 12-month period. Self-reports of habitual violent media usage were related to self-reports of lower empathy and higher physical aggression at Time 2. Analyses suggested that higher aggressive and lower prosocial behavior resulted from the acceptance of aggression as normative following exposure to media violence, which could indicate desensitization (Krahe & Moller, 2010). Behavioral research seems consistent in identifying associations between exposure to media violence and lower empathy, as well as some support for stronger proviolence attitudes.

No psychophysiological research specifically examining links between moral development and desensitization were found. However, brain imaging studies suggest that specific regions and pathways responsible for emotions and moral reasoning can be identified (see, for example, Decety & Jackson, 2006; Schulte-Ruther, Markowitsch, Fink, & Piefke, 2007). Studies that combine behavioral measures with neural indices such as fMRI have particular promise for examining the link between media violence exposure and desensitization to violence (Bartholow, Bushman, & Sestir, 2006; Heinzl & Northoff, 2009).

Psychological Engagement

Exposure to media violence will not desensitize every individual. A relative risk model is useful in understanding this caveat (Funk et al., 2002; Gentile & Bushman, in press). With few risk factors for desensitization, and some protective factors such as optimal parenting and economic security, exposure to media violence may have no obvious negative effects on a particular individual. With some risk factors such as a difficult childhood or poverty, the negative effects may be subtle, such as having lower empathy for victims, or more positive attitudes about the use of violence, reflecting the onset of desensitization to violence. As risk factors accumulate, and in the absence of protective factors, desensitization may become pervasive, resulting in either active aggression or failure to intervene to assist a victim.

Individual difference variables may either increase or decrease the relative risk of desensitization to violence as a result of exposure to media violence. An individual's propensity to become deeply involved (psychologically engaged) in his or her media experience has been proposed to be one variable that is worth studying, assuming that deeper involvement could increase the impact of media violence exposure (Funk et al., 2004; Brockmyer et al., 2009). Brockmyer et al. (2009) proposed *psychological engagement* as an umbrella term to describe the experience of involvement in media.

The Importance of Psychological Engagement

Being engaged in media appears to be a critical component of the experience, and one that motivates the user to continue participation. Wood, Griffiths, Chappell, and Davies (2004) used an online survey of 14- to 50-year-olds to examine the characteristics of video games that enticed players to begin and then to continue playing. Among other factors, the researchers noted that what they termed *rapid absorption* ("how long it takes to get into the game") in game-playing was considered important by more than three-fourths of the sample. Schneider, Lang, Shin, and Bradley (2004) examined the impact of story on the sense of engagement in a violent video game. The researchers found that, compared with games with little or no story line, the presence of a story was associated with more engagement and more enjoyment.

Funk, Chan, Brouwer, and Curtiss (2006) conducted focus groups with children and adults to discuss the experience of playing video games. Most participants spontaneously reported that becoming deeply engaged in the game was a powerful incentive for continued play that also encouraged imitation of game actions. Interestingly, for children, deep involvement could also be a negative experience: Some children reported being frightened by deep engagement in violent video games. Participants of all ages reported time distortions consistent with an altered state of consciousness during periods of deep engagement in game-playing. Chapter 24 describes the process by which deep engagement develops, termed *transportation,* as well as its neural underpinnings and implications.

Measuring Psychological Engagement

The terms *immersion, presence, flow,* and *absorption* have each been used to describe aspects and degrees of media involvement. Brockmyer et al. (2009) suggested that these terms be conceptualized as representing different and deepening levels of engagement, although one may move back and forth between levels.

Immersion is the first level of psychological engagement in the media experience. This term is often used to describe the experience of becoming partially engaged (Banos et al., 2004). Awareness of one's surroundings, a key marker for level of engagement, is maintained. The term *presence* represents the next phase of deeper engagement in media. Most simply defined, presence is the sense that one is actually within a mediated environment, with no awareness of mediation and little sense of one's actual surroundings, suggesting at least a partial alteration of the normal state of consciousness (Ravaja, 2004). Tamborini and Skalski (2006) noted that interest in understanding the experience of presence has grown with the development of virtual environments. Much of this research has focused on using technology to increase the sense of presence so as to gain a specific outcome. Desired outcomes include not only entertainment, but also diverse therapeutic effects such as the treatment of anger (Miyahira, Folen, Stetz, Rizzo, & Kawasaki, 2010) and pain (Guitierrez-Maldonado, Guitierrez-Martinez, Loreto, Pealoza, & Nieto, 2010).

Flow, now a concept adopted by positive psychology, can be conceptualized as the next deeper level of media engagement. The term *flow* describes the positive feelings experienced when a perfect balance between skill and challenge occurs while one is fully engaged in performing an intrinsically rewarding activity (Csikszentmihalyi & Csikszentmihalyi, 1988). Flow represents an altered state of consciousness in which there is a nearly complete lack of awareness of one's surroundings and time distortions occur. The term *psychological absorption* represents the deepest level of media involvement and is used to describe total engagement in an experience (Roche & McConkey, 1990; Irwin, 1999). The real world is irrelevant when one is psychologically absorbed. Although both flow and absorption are states of significantly altered consciousness, they can be distinguished by the accompanying emotional experience. Flow, by definition, involves positive affect, but psychological absorption can also include frustration and anxiety (Funk et al., 2006). Motivation also distinguishes these two states. Flow is intrinsically motivated and rewarding, whereas the motivation for media involvement may be extrinsic. For example, video game players often cite competition as a primary motivation for play (Funk et al., 2006).

In the altered states that occur when one is deeply involved in media, possibly beginning with presence, normally integrated processes such as thinking, feeling, and experiencing are separated. Rational thought, including moral evaluation, may be suspended. Combined with exposure to media violence, deep engagement could allow the development of scripts for violence that could later be activated, again without moral evaluation. The deeply engaged individual could experience desensitization to the consequences of violence completely out of conscious awareness.

To research specific levels of psychological engagement, some researchers have created study-specific questionnaires with little assessment of the instrument's psychometric properties. However, this approach complicates evaluation and interpretation of findings. Brockmyer et al. (2009) combined classical and Rasch analysis to create the Game Experience Questionnaire (GEQ). The GEQ is a conceptually sound, psychometrically strong measure of levels of engagement in playing video games that could serve as a model for the development of measures of engagement with other media. Although initial research is promising, additional work is needed to substantiate the progression from lower to higher engagement (immersion, presence, flow, and absorption) identified in the GEQ's measure development phase. Researchers should also continue to work toward definitional consensus on the descriptors of levels of media involvement.

Conclusion

This chapter has described the etiology and possible outcomes of desensitization to violence as a result of exposure to media violence. Emerging research identifies evidence of desensitization, as measured in psychophysiological and strictly behavioral research, over both the short and long term. An individual's degree of psychological engagement in media may be one factor that increases the relative risk of negative effects. In addition to behavioral investigations, researchers should continue to use newer imaging technologies to study the impact of media violence on specific neural structures, particularly those involved in processes such as empathic responding, that are theoretically related to both short- and long-term desensitization to violence.

Future Directions

Both short- and long-term studies are needed to (1) gain consensus on indicators of desensitization to violence; (2) substantiate the role of exposure to violent media in causing an increase in the relative risk for desensitization; (3) identify individual-level characteristics that contribute to desensitization to violence, including psychological engagement; (4) develop consensus on definitions of degrees of media involvement; and (5) confirm the hypothesized outcomes of desensitization to violence such as increased aggression and decreased prosocial behavior.

References

Anderson, C. A., Berkowitz, L., Donnerstein, E., Huesmann, L. R., Johnson, J., Linz, D., & Wartella, E. (2003). The influence of media violence on youth. *Psychological Science in the Public Interest, 4,* 81–110.

Anderson, C. A., & Bushman, B. J. (2002). Human aggression. *Annual Review of Psychology, 53,* 27–51.

Anderson, C. A., Gentile, D. A., & Buckley, K. E. (2007). *Violent video game effects on children and adolescents: Theory, research, and public policy.* New York: Oxford University Press.

Anderson, C. A., & Huesmann, L. R. (2003). Human aggression: A social cognitive view. In Hogg, M. A., & Cooper, J. (Eds.), *Handbook of Social Psychology.* London: Sage, pp. 296–323.

Anderson, C. A., Shibuya, A., Ihori, N., Swing, E. L., Bushman, B. J., Sakamoto, A., & Saleem, M. (2010). Violent video game effects on aggression, empathy, and prosocial behavior in Eastern and Western countries: A meta-analytic review. *Psychological Bulletin, 136,* 151–173. doi:10.1037/a0018251

Averill, J. R., Malmstrom, E. J., Koriat, A., & Lazarus, R. S. (1972). Habituation to complex emotional stimuli. *Journal of Abnormal Psychology, 80,* 20–28.

Banos, R. M., Botella, C., Alcaniz, M., Liano, V., Guerrero, B., & Rey, B. (2004). Immersion and emotion: Their impact on sense of presence. *CyberPsychology and Behavior, 7,* 734–741.

Bartholow, B. D., Bushman, B. J., & Sestir, M. A. (2006). Chronic violent video game exposure and desensitization to violence: Behavioral and event-related brain potential data. *Journal of Experimental Social Psychology, 42,* 532–539.

Bartholow, B. D., Sestir, M. A., & Davis, E. B. (2005). Correlates and consequences of exposure to video game violence: Hostile personality, empathy, and aggressive behavior. *Personality and Social Psychology Bulletin, 31,* 1573–1586.

Brockmyer, J. B., Fox, C., McBroom E., Curtiss, K., Burkhart, K., & Pidruzny, J. (2009). The development of the Game Experience Questionnaire: A measure of levels of engagement in video game-playing. *Journal of Experimental Social Psychology, 49,* 624–634.

Buchman, D., & Funk, J. B. (1996). Video and computer games in the '90s: Children report time commitment and game preference. *Children Today, 31,* 12–15.

Bushman, B. J., & Anderson, C. A. (2009). Comfortably numb: Desensitizing effects of violent media on helping others. *Psychological Science, 20,* 273–277.

Bushman, B. J., Rothstein, H. R., & Anderson, C. A. (2010). Much ado about something: Violent video game effects and a school of red herring: Reply to Ferguson and Kilburn (2010). *Psychological Bulletin, 136,* 182–187. doi:10.1037/a0018718

Cacioppo, J. T., Berntson, G. G., & Nusbaum, H. C. (2008). Neuroimaging as a new tool in the toolbox of psychological science. *Current Directions in Psychological Science, 17,* 62–67.

Carnagey, N. L., Anderson, C. A., & Bartholow, B. D. (2007). Media violence and social neuroscience: New questions and new opportunities. *Current Directions in Psychological Science, 16,* 178–182.

Carnagey, N. L., Anderson, C. A., & Bushman, B. J. (2007). The effect of video game violence on physiological desensitization to real-life violence. *Journal of Experimental Social Psychology, 43,* 489–496. doi:10.1016/j.jesp.2006.05.003.

Cichetti, D. (2010). Resilience under conditions of extreme stress: A multilevel perspective. *World Psychiatry, 9,* 145–154.

Csikszentmihalyi, M., & Csikszentmihalyi, I. S. (1988). *Optimal experience. Psychological Studies of Flow in Consciousness.* Cambridge, UK: Cambridge University Press.

Decety, J., & Jackson, P. L. (2006). A social-neuroscience perspective on empathy. *Current Directions in Psychological Science, 15,* 54–58.

Delplanque, S., Silvert, L., Hot, P., Rigoulot, S., & Sequeira, H. (2006). Arousal and valence effects on event-related P3a and P3b during emotional categorization. *International Journal of Psychophysiology, 60,* 315–322.

Deselms, J. L., & Altman, J. D. (2003). Immediate and prolonged effects of videogame violence. *Journal of Applied Social Psychology, 33,* 1553–1563.

Dill, K. E. (2009). *How Fantasy Becomes Reality: Seeing Through Media Influence.* New York: Oxford.

Drabman, R. S., & Thomas, M. H. (1974). Does media violence increase children's tolerance of real-life aggression? *Developmental Psychology, 10,* 418–421.

Englehart, C. R., Bartholow, B. D., Kerr, G. T., & Bushman, B. J. (2011). This is your brain on violent video games: Neural desensitization to violence predicts increased aggression following violent video game exposure. *Journal of Experimental Social Psychology, 47,* 1033–1036. doi: 10.1016/j.jesp.2011.03.027.

Fanti, K. H., Vanman, E., Henrich, C. C., & Avraamides, M. N. (2009). Desensitization to media violence over a short period of time. *Aggressive Behavior, 35,* 179–187. doi:10.1002/ab.20295

Fazio, R. H., & Olson, M. A. (2003). Attitudes: Foundations, functions, and consequences. In Hogg, M. A., & Cooper, J. (Eds.), *The Sage Handbook of Social Psychology.* London: Sage, pp. 139–160.

Ferguson, C. J., & Kilburn, J. (2010). Much ado about nothing: The misestimation and overinterpretation of violent video game effects in Eastern and Western Nations: Comment on Anderson et al. (2010). *Psychological Bulletin, 136,* 174–178. doi:10.1037/a0018566.

Funk, J. B. (1992). Video games: Benign or malignant? *Journal of Developmental and Behavioral Pediatrics, 13,* 53–54.

Funk, J. B. (2005). Children's exposure to violent video games and desensitization to violence. *Child and Adolescent Psychiatry Clinics of North America, 14,* 387–404.

Funk, J. B., Bechtoldt-Baldacci, H., Pasold, T., & Baumgardner, J. (2004). Violence exposure in real-life, video games, television, movies, and the Internet: Is there desensitization? *Journal of Adolescence, 27,* 23–39.

Funk, J. B., & Buchman, D. (1996). Playing violent video and computer games and adolescent self-perception. *Journal of Communication, 46,* 19–32.

Funk, J. B., Buchman, D. D., Jenks, J., & Bechtoldt, H. (2003). Playing violent video games, desensitization, and moral evaluation in children. *Journal of Applied Developmental Psychology, 24,* 413–436.

Funk, J. B., Chan, M., Brouwer, J., & Curtiss, K. (2006). A biopsychosocial analysis of the video game playing experience of children and adults in the United States. *Studies in Media Literacy and Information Education (SIMILE).*

Accessed July 13, 2012 at http://utpjournals.metapress.com/content/h2g0732025831q89/fulltext.pdf

Funk, J. B., Fox, C., Chan, M., & Curtiss, K. (2008). The development of the Children's Empathic Attitudes Questionnaire using classical and Rasch analyses. *Journal of Applied Developmental Psychology, 29*, 187–196.

Funk, J. B., Hagan, J., Schimming, J., Bullock, W. A., Buchman, D. D., & Myers, M. (2002). Aggression and psychopathology in adolescents with a preference for violent electronic games. *Aggressive Behavior, 28*, 134–144.

Gentile, D. A., & Bushman, B. J. (in press). Reassessing media violence effects using a risk and resilience approach to understanding aggression. *Psychology of Popular Media Culture.*

Gentile, D. A., & Gentile, J. R. (2008). Violent video games as exemplary teachers: A conceptual analysis. *Journal of Youth and Adolescence, 9*, 127–141.

Guerra, N. G., Huesmann, L. R., & Spindler, A. (2003). Community violence exposure, social cognition, and aggression among urban elementary school children. *Child Development, 75*, 1561–1576.

Guerra, N., Nucci, L., & Huesmann, L. R. (1994). Moral cognition and childhood aggression. In L. R. Huesmann (Ed.), *Aggressive behavior: Current perspectives* (pp. 13–33). New York: Plenum Press.

Guitierrez-Maldonado, J., Guitierrez-Martinez, O., Loreto, D., Pealoza, C., & Nieto, R. (2010). Presence, involvement and efficacy of a virtual reality intervention on pain. *Annual Review of CyberTherapy and Telemedicine, 8*, 78–81.

Haslam, R. H. A., Illner, A., & Chuang, S. (2003). Functional brain imaging: Evaluation of the effects of violent media exposure. *Paediatrics & Child Health, 8*, 283–284.

Heinzl, A., & Northoff, G. (2009). Emotional feeling and the orbitomedial prefrontal cortex: Theoretical and empirical considerations. *Philosophical Psychology, 22*, 443–464.

Hoffman, M. L. (2000). *Empathy and Moral Development: Implications for Caring and Justice.* New York: Cambridge University Press.

Hoffner, C. A., & Levine, K. L. (2007). Enjoyment of mediated fright and violence: A meta-analysis. *Media Psychology, 7*, 207–237.

Huesmann, L. R., & Kirwil, L. (2007). Why observing violence increases the risk of violent behavior by the observer. In Flannery, D. J., Vazsonyi, A. T., & Waldman, I. (Eds.), *The Cambridge Handbook of Violent Behavior and Aggression.* Cambridge, UK: Cambridge University Press, pp. 545–570.

Huesmann, L. R., Moise-Titus, J., Podolski, C. L., & Eron, L. D. (2003). Longitudinal relations between children's exposure to TV violence and their aggressive and violent behavior in young adulthood: 1977–1992. *Developmental Psychology, 39*, 201–221.

Irwin, H. J. (1999). Pathological and nonpathological dissociation: The relevance of childhood trauma. *The Journal of Psychology, 133*, 157–164.

Johnson, J. D., Bushman, B. J. & Dovidio, J. F. (2008). Support for harmful treatment and reduction of empathy toward Blacks: "Remnants" of stereotype activation involving Hurricane Katrina and "Lil' Kim." *Journal of Experimental Social Psychology, 44*, 1506–1513.

Kalnin, A. J., Edwards, C. R., Wang, Y., Kronenberger, W. G., Tummer, T. A., Mosier, K. M., Dunn, D. W., Mathews, V. P. (2011). The interacting role of media violence exposure and aggressive-disruptive behavior in adolescent brain activation during an emotional Stroop task. *Psychiatry Research.* Advance online publication.

Kelly, C. R., Grinband, J., & Hirsch, J. (2007). Repeated exposure to media violence is associated with diminished response in an inhibitory frontolimbic network. *PLoS ONE 2*(12), e1268. doi:10.1371/journal.pone.0001268.

Krahe, B., & Moller, I. (2010). Longitudinal effects of media violence on aggression and empathy among German adolescents. *Journal of Applied Developmental Psychology, 31*, 401–409.

Krahe, B., Moller, I., Huesmann, L. R., Kirwil, L., Felber, J., & Berger, A. (2010). Desensitization to media violence: Links with habitual media violence exposure, aggressive cognitions, and aggressive behavior. *Journal of Personality and Social Psychology, 100*(4), 630–646.

Matthews, V. P., Kronenberger, W. G., Wang, Y., Lurito, J. T., Lowe, M. J., & Dunn, D. W. (2005). Media violence exposure and frontal lobe activation measured by functional magnetic resonance imaging in aggressive and nonaggressive adolescents. *Journal of Computer Assisted Tomography, 29*, 287–292

Miyahira, S. D., Folen, R. A., Stetz, M., Rizzo, A., & Kawasaki, M. M. (2010). Use of immersive virtual reality for treating anger. *Annual Review of CyberTherapy and Telemedicine, 8*, 65–68.

Molitor, F., & Hirsch, K. W. (1994). Children's toleration of real-life aggression after exposure to media violence: A replication of the Drabman and Thomas studies. *Child Study Journal, 24*, 191–208.

Moller, I., & Krahe, B. (2009). Exposure to violent video games and aggression in German adolescents: A longitudinal analysis. *Aggressive Behavior, 35*, 75–89.

Mullin, C. R., & Linz, D. (1995). Desensitization and resensitization to violence against women: Effects of exposure to sexually violent films on judgments of domestic violence victims. *Journal of Personality and Social Psychology, 69*, 449–459. doi:10.1037/0022–3514.69.3.449.

NTSV. (1996–1997). National Television Violence Study Year Three: 1996–97; Summary of Recommendations. *Report of the University of California, Santa Barbara The Center for Communication and Social Policy web site.* Available at http://www.kff.org/entmedia/upload/key-facts-tv-violence.pdf.

Olson, M. A., & Fazio, R. H. (2001). Implicit attitude formation through classical conditioning. *Psychological Science, 12*, 413–417.

Perry B. D., & Pollard, R. (1998). Homeostasis, stress, trauma, and adaptation: A neurodevelopmental view of childhood trauma. *Child and Adolescent Psychiatric Clinics of North America, 7*, 33–51.

Ravaja, N. (2004). Contributions of psychophysiology to media research: Review and recommendations. *Media Psychology, 6*, 193–235. doi: 10.1207/s1532785xmep0602_4.

Ravaja, N., Saari, T., Salminen, M. Laarni, J., & Kallinen, K. (2006). Phasic emotional reactions to video game events: A psychophysiological investigation. *Media Psychology, 8*, 343–367. doi: 10.1207/s1532785xmep0804_2

Regenbogen, C., Herrmann, M., & Fehr, T. (2010). The neural processing of voluntary completed, real and virtual violent and nonviolent computer game scenarios displaying predefined actions in gamers and nongamers. *Social Neuroscience, 5*, 221–240.

Rideout, V. J., Foehr, U. G., & Roberts, D. F. (2010). *GENERATION M2: Media in the Lives of 8- to 18-Year-Olds:*

A Kaiser Family Foundation Study. Menlo Park, CA: Henry J. Kaiser Foundation.

Roche, S. M., & McConkey, K. M. (1990). Absorption: Nature, assessment, and correlates. *Journal of Personality and Social Psychology, 59*, 91–101.

Rubin, A., & Springer, D. W. (Eds.). (2009). *Treatment of Traumatized Adults and Children: Clinician's Guide to Evidence-Based Practice*. Hoboken, NJ: Wiley.

Schneider, E. F., Lang, A., Shin, M., & Bradley, S. D. (2004). Death with a story: How story impacts emotional, motivational, and physiological responses to first-person shooter video games. *Human Communication Research, 30*, 361–375.

Schulte-Ruther, M., Markowitsch, H. J., Fink, G. R., & Piefke, M. (2007) Mirror neuron and theory of mind mechanisms involved in face-to-face interactions: A functional magnetic resonance imaging approach to empathy. *Journal of Cognitive Neuroscience, 19*, 1354–1372.

Stams, G. J., Brugman, D., Dekovic, M., van Rosmalen, L., van der Laan, P., & Gibbs, J. C. (2006). The moral judgment of juvenile delinquents: A metaanalysis. *Journal of Abnormal Child Psychology, 34*, 697–713.

Staude-Müller, F., Bliesener, T., & Luthman, S. (2008). Hostile and hardened? An experimental study on (de-)sensitization to violence and suffering through playing video games. *Swiss Journal of Psychology, 67*, 41–50.

Sterzer, P., & Stadler, C. (2009). Neuroimaging of aggressive and violent behavior in children and adolescents. *Frontiers in Behavioral Neuroscience, 3*, 35. doi: 3389/neuro.08.035.2009.

Strenziok, M., Krueger, F., Deshpande, G., Lenroot, K., van der Meer, E., & Grafman, J. (2010). Fronto-parietal regulation of media violence exposure in adolescents: A multi-method study. *Social Cognitive and Affective Neuroscience, 6*(5):537–547.

Strenziok, M., Krueger, F., Pulaski, S. J., Openshaw, A. E., Giovanna Zamboni, G., van der Meer, E., & Grafman, J. (2010). Lower lateral orbitofrontal cortex density associated with more frequent exposure to television and movie violence in male adolescents. *Journal of Adolescent Health, 46*, 607–609. doi:1016/j.jadohealth.2009.11.196.

Tamborini, R., & Skalski, P. (2006). The role of presence in the experience of electronic games. In Vorderer, P., & Bryant, J. (Eds.), *Playing Video Games: Motives, Responses and Consequences*. Hillsdale, NJ: Lawrence Erlbaum Associates, pp. 225–240.

van Baardewijk, Y., Stegge, H., Bushman, B. J., & Vermeiren, R. (2009). Psychopathic traits, victim distress and aggression in children. *Journal of Child Psychology and Psychiatry, 50*, 718–725.

Velicer, W. F., Huckel, L. H., & Hansen, C. E. (1989). A measurement model for measuring attitudes toward violence. *Personality and Social Psychology Bulletin, 15*, 349–364.

Wei, R. (2007). Effects of playing violent videogames on Chinese adolescents' pro-violence attitudes, attitudes toward others, and aggressive behavior. *CyberPsychology and Behavior, 10*, 371–380.

Wood, R. T. A., Griffiths, M. D., Chappell, D., & Davies, M. N. O. (2004). The structural characteristics of video games: A psycho-structural analysis. *CyberPsychology and Behavior, 7*, 1–10.

Sexual Media Practice: How Adolescents Select, Engage with, and Are Affected by Sexual Media

Autumn Shafer, Piotr Bobkowski, *and* Jane D. Brown

Abstract

This chapter focuses on the role media play in the sexual socialization of adolescents and emerging adults in modern societies. The review of relevant research and theory is organized around the Sexual Media Practice Model's core components of identity, selection, engagement, and application, which are based on the following assumptions: (1) media consumers are active participants and sometimes content producers; (2) selection and use of sexual media are motivated by the adolescent's identity or sexual self-concept; (3) sexual media effects are a cyclical process, such that sexual content may be sought that reinforces existing tendencies that leads to further use of relevant content and further effects; and (4) friends and peers are important throughout the process in generating, sharing, and interpreting media. The discussion includes suggestions for further research and an examination of potential media-related solutions to enhance healthy adolescent sexuality.

Key Words: adolescent sexuality, adolescents, emerging adults, media practice model, sexual media effects, sexual socialization

Introduction

Sex is an important part of most people's lives. Some aspects come pretty naturally, but many aspects of sexual behavior are culturally determined. Standards of sexual attractiveness, courtship rituals, and expectations of who does what sexually to whom and under what circumstances are stipulated by the culture in which a person lives. The prevailing sexual norms and standards must be learned by young people as they mature. In traditional societies, elders, parents, and religion were the primary sexual socialization agents (Katchadourian, 1990). In modern societies, however, media (television, movies, music, magazines, Internet, video games), and peers have also become important purveyors of sexual models and norms. The more interactive media technologies, such as texting and social networking (e.g., Facebook) also provide easy access to friends who may introduce, reinforce or participate in sexual behavior.

Just a quick look at songs popular with teens in 2011 such as "Tonight I'm Fu__ing You" (Enrique Eglasias), and "S+M Sado Masochism," in which Rihanna sings "sticks and stones may break my bones, but chains and whips excite me" while Britney Spears sings about a ménage a trois in "3," illustrates how important sexual topics are in the media that young people consume. Online monikers with which adolescents identify themselves as "SexKittenPrr" or "Playa1" suggest sexual self-expression is also important in the media youth create.

Although a number of socialization agents, such as parents, teachers, and religious leaders also play important roles, this chapter focuses on the role media play in the sexual socialization of adolescents and emerging adults in modern societies. We think of media as important sources of cultural norms that young people interact with as they "learn to express affection, love and intimacy in ways consistent with their own values…and general social expectations and scripts about adolescent sexuality" (Pinquart, 2010, p. 440). Because media and the ability of youth to be creators and distributors of media have changed so dramatically in the past decade, it is important to look closely at the ways in which adolescents select, engage with, and incorporate what they see and hear in the media about sex into their own sexual lives.

In most of the developed world, adolescence (12–18 years old) is an important period for sexual exploration, development of sexual identities and orientation, formation of romantic relationships, and establishment of patterns of sexual behavior. In early adolescence (12–13 years old) the focus typically is on the sexually maturing body and how to get it to conform to prevailing standards of sexual attractiveness. In middle adolescence (14–16 years old), romantic relationships are formed that may include sexual touching and for some, sexual intercourse. By late adolescence (17–18 years old), from one-half to two-thirds of adolescents in the United States (and in most European countries) have been in a romantic relationship and many have had sexual intercourse (Hubert, Bajos, & Sanfort, 1998). In emerging adulthood (18–24 years old), romantic and physical sexual exploration and development continue. Emerging adults tend to try out long-term relationships, and some enter committed relationships and become parents. Approximately 10% of emerging adults experience some same-sex attraction, and approximately 3% engage in same-sex sexual behavior (Savin-Williams & Ream, 2007).

In the process of developing a sense of who they are sexually, young people seek information and guidance about what is appropriate, inappropriate, expected, and condoned or not condoned. In some countries, such as the Netherlands, France, and Germany, young people are expected to be sexually responsible and are provided age-appropriate sex education throughout their school years. They also have access to health care and contraceptives, so their rates of sexually transmitted infections (STIs), and unplanned pregnancies are much lower than in countries such as the United States that do not consistently provide medically accurate sex education in schools or confidential health services (Alford & Hauser, 2011). Thus, we might expect that the media will be more influential in young people's sexual development when other socialization agents and institutions that might support sexually healthy behavior are reticent or absent.

This chapter uses the Media Practice Model (MPM) (Steele & Brown, 1995; Steele, 1999; Brown, 2000) to organize the growing body of studies addressing the media's effects on the sexual development of adolescents. The MPM was introduced in the late 1990s in an attempt to move toward a less linear way of thinking about media effects, especially for adolescents. The model built on the thinking of European scholars (Hall, 1980; Bourdieu, 1990; Valsiner, 1993), who were asserting that more attention should be paid to the receiver of media messages. This "active audience" conceptualization is even more appropriate now as the media become more under the control of consumers, whenever and wherever they are.

Although the model is probably appropriate for describing other domains of media use, it was originally conceived to describe adolescents' sexual media use, so we will discuss it with that focus in mind.[1] The main assumptions of the MPM as applied to adolescent sexuality (Figure 13.1) are: (1) media consumers are active participants and sometimes even producers themselves (e.g., "sexting"— sending revealing pictures of themselves to others), thus becoming what futurist Alvin Toffler (1980) presciently called "prosumers;" (2) selection and use of sexual media is motivated by the adolescent's identity or sexual self concept; (3) sexual media effects are a cyclical process, such that sexual content may be sought that reinforces existing tendencies that leads to further use of relevant content and further effects; and (4) friends and peers are important throughout the process in generating, sharing, and interpreting media.

The model depicts three main "moments," Selection, Engagement, and Application, in adolescents' encounters with sexual media. Given the ubiquity and variety of media choices available, media consumers must choose which medium and content to which they will attend. At least initially, those choices depend on whom the consumers are, both socially and individually. Given that adolescence is an especially important period in identity development, at least some of the selection of media content is probably driven by adolescents' current and future conceptions of themselves.

The MPM model suggests that if sex and sexuality are an important part of an adolescent's identity, then he or she will be more interested in and may even seek out sexual content in the media. Once selected, the adolescent may or may not engage with the content. A number of factors, such as identification with characters, perceived realism of the

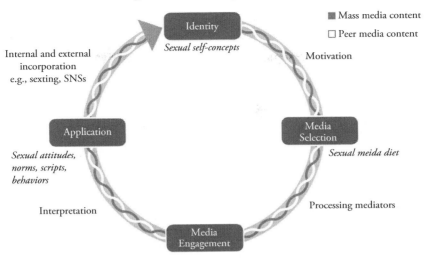

Identity
Sexual self-concepts

■ Mass media content
□ Peer media content

Internal and external
incorporation
e.g., sexting, SNSs

Motivation

Application

Media
Selection

*Sexual attitudes,
norms, scripts,
behaviors*

Sexual meida diet

Interpretation

Processing mediators

Media
Engagement

Figure 13.1 Sexual Media Practice Model.

depicted behaviors, and the extent of involvement or transportation into a narrative will affect to what extent that engagement occurs. Media users who are distracted (e.g., multitasking) may be less engaged than those who are paying full attention; some may be physically and/or emotionally aroused by what they see. Engagement may shift prebehavioral sexual outcomes, such as perceived sexual norms, attitudes, beliefs, outcome expectancies, and sexual scripts (typical sequences of behavior) that may in turn affect adolescents' sexual behaviors (e.g., seeking sexual partners, sexual touching, initiation of sexual intercourse). Because the production and dissemination of media content is easier today than ever before, engaged and motivated media consumers may also use their cell phones, video cameras, and laptops to become producers and distributors of sexual media content.

In the two decades since the MPM was introduced, evidence has continued to accumulate that media effects on behavior are not simply a linear process with the media as the independent variable and sexual behaviors as the dependent variables. In the violence domain, Slater and colleagues (Slater, Henry, Swaim, & Anderson, 2003; Slater, Henry, Swaim, & Cardador, 2004; Slater, 2007) have shown with longitudinal panel surveys that exposure to violent content (in action films, video games, and websites) does affect aggressive behavior, but primarily for adolescents who are socially isolated, victimized, or who have aggressive tendencies. Slater's analysis painted a picture of a "downward spiral" of selection

of violent content reinforcing aggressive tendencies or suggesting that violence is a way to solve frustrations. Ultimately, the adolescents who used more violent media content behaved more aggressively (Slater et al., 2003).

A similar cyclical pattern has been suggested in research on the effects of the media on body image and eating disorders. The evidence points to a pattern of some adolescent girls both learning from and seeking media content that reinforces their ideals of feminine beauty. Internalization of the thin beauty ideals they see in women's magazines, on television shows and websites, may lead to body dissatisfaction, weight concerns, excessive dieting and disordered eating behaviors, as well as further consumption of the thin-ideal media with which they compare their bodies (Harrison & Hefner, 2008; López-Guimerà, Levine, Sánchez-Carracedo, & Fauquet, 2010).

Although the body of evidence is not yet as robust for sexual outcomes, at least two three-wave longitudinal analyses suggest a similar pattern for early adolescents—as adolescents enter puberty, sexual content in the media is more relevant, is paid more attention, maybe even sought out (Kim, Collins, Kanouse, Elliott, Berry, Hunter, Miu, & Kunkel, 2006; Bleakley, Hennessy, Fishbein, & Jordan, 2008). The sexual media content these adolescents see or listen to increases the saliency of this content and influences the adolescents' sexual scripts or ideas about how sexual encounters unfold. Some of what they see may shift perceptions of norms such that heavier users may begin to think that early and unprotected sexual intercourse is typical for young people. The lack of discussion or depiction of negative consequences in the media content may increase the adolescent media users' positive perceptions of sexual behavior and may stimulate earlier sexual behavior than would have occurred otherwise (Wright, 2011).

We turn now to look more closely at each moment in the MPM to see what is currently known about adolescents' sexual media practice and then to discuss briefly what solutions have been posited to minimize negative media effects and enhance adolescents' healthy sexual development. We close with some intriguing research questions and a few comments about the challenges of conducting research on sexuality with young people.

Media Are the Air Adolescents Breathe

On an average day, an adolescent (8–18 years old) in the United States spends 7.5 hours of her leisure time attending to various media, which is more time than she spends in school or interacting with her parents (Rideout, Foehr, & Roberts, 2010). Many teens use two or more media simultaneously, for example, listening to music while surfing the Web or watching television while chatting with friends online. Accounting for such media multitasking, an average adolescent spends more than 10 hours per day using media. This chapter refers to the amount and type of media content an adolescent consumes as an adolescent's media diet.

The amount of time adolescents spend with media varies by gender, ethnicity, and age. Boys in the United States use media about 1 hour more per day (11.25) than girls (10.25). Hispanic and black youth use media about 13 hours per day, whereas white teens average 8.5 hours per day. Media use increases between early and middle adolescence and then declines somewhat in late adolescence. Tweens (8–10 years old) average just shy of 8 hours of media per day, early teens (11–14 years old) nearly 12 hours per day, and late teens (15–18 years old) less than 11.5 hours per day (Rideout et al., 2010).

In 2009, adolescents in the United States used media about an hour more per day than they did 10 years earlier (Rideout et al., 2010), to a large extent because different forms of media have become more portable. With the advent of MP3 players, laptop computers, and cell phones, the time adolescents spent listening to music increased by nearly 50 minutes per day, and the time they spent watching television, using computers, and playing video games, each increased by half an hour per day. Adolescents'

use of print media (e.g., magazines, books) decreased by about 5 minutes per day.

Considering only "new" media devices, adolescents spent 1½ hours texting on their cell phones daily, and more than 45 minutes listening to music, playing games, and watching television programs. They spent 1½ hours using a computer outside of school (using social networking websites, playing games, watching videos, etc.), and close to another hour playing video games on either a console or a hand-held device.

Selection of Sexual Media Content

A number of personal and contextual factors, including timing of pubertal development, sexual identities, and prior sexual experience, as well as access to media, influence the extent to which adolescents see and/or hear sexual content. Some adolescents choose heavier sexual media diets in entertainment media than others; some look for sexual health information, often online (Ackard & Neumark-Sztainer, 2001).

Teens' exposure to sexual media may also have a biological basis: Teens who are predisposed to be more sexual than their peers may be more likely to select sexual media content. Biologically, hormone levels are associated with adolescents' sexual motivations and behaviors. For example, in a study of 12- to 16-year-old white males, fewer than one in five (16%) of those with the lowest testosterone levels had had sexual intercourse, whereas more than two-thirds (69%) of those with the highest testosterone levels had (Udry, 1990).

Social factors can also either delay or accelerate adolescents' sexual development. In a follow-up study, the adolescent boys' testosterone levels appeared to interact with their religious involvement in predicting sexual debut (Halpern, Udry, Campbell, & Suchindran, 1994). Boys with high testosterone levels but infrequent religious attendance were the most likely to initiate sex over a 3-year period between study waves; those with low testosterone and frequent religious attendance were the least likely to have sex. Adolescents' sexual development may also be affected by social status aspirations, the progression of a romantic (or nonromantic) relationship, or other emotional needs (Diamond & Savin-Williams, 2009).

Such interactions between biological predispositions, socialization, and experience result in diverse sexual self-evaluations among adolescents. One Australian study showed that adolescents vary in sexual self-esteem, sexual self-efficacy, and sexual self-image (Buzwell & Rosenthal, 1996). The study measured adolescents' levels of sexual interest, arousal, confidence, anxiety, as well as sexual risk behaviors, and categorized individuals into five "sexual styles," which ranged from the "sexually naïve" to the "sexually driven." The "sexually naïve" teens were not confident with respect to their sexual and physical characteristics, had low sexual self-efficacy, arousal, and exploration, and reported high sexual anxiety, but the ability to say "no" to sex. The "sexually driven," in contrast, were characterized as sexually aroused and curious, confident adolescents who were uninterested in commitment and who found it difficult to decline sexual activity.

We may easily imagine "sexually driven" teens being more avid consumers of sexual media, perhaps using these media to both inform and reinforce their sexual identities. The "sexually naïve" teens, however, may also consume sexual media, looking to build up their sexual self-efficacy and confidence by learning from sexual media role models or situations. Such teens may also shield themselves from sexual content that might conflict with their sexual values. In a national survey, for example, US teens who were more religious and who had less permissive attitudes about premarital sex, reported liking less mature (including less sexual) television programs than their peers who were not as religious (Bobkowski, 2009). In contrast, in another study, girls who entered puberty earlier than their age mates expressed more interest in sexually oriented media than girls who matured later (Brown, Halpern, & L'Engle, 2005).

A longitudinal study of a US national sample found that black, female, younger, and more highly viewer-involved teens (12–17 years old) watched significantly more sexually oriented television than did other groups. Teens who had had more precoital sexual experiences and those who believed that their friends approved of sex also were more likely to be viewing more sexual content on television a year later. Media access also plays a role in sexual media diets. In that same study, teens who had a television in their bedroom and teens who spent more unsupervised time at home watched more sexual content (Kim et al., 2006).

The Internet also gives young people access to a wide range of sexual information that may be too embarrassing or personal to discuss with parents, teachers, health care providers, or even with friends (Buhi, Daley, Fuhrmann, & Smith, 2009). Three-fourths of online adolescents say they have used the Internet to look up health information

(Rideout, 2001); sexual health is one of the most frequently sought health topics (Lenhart, Purcell, Smith, & Zickuhr, 2010). Teens search for information on sexual issues such as puberty, menstruation, sexual abuse, contraception, pregnancy, and STIs (Ackard & Neumark-Sztainer, 2001).

As posited in the MPM, a young person's identity may also affect what kinds of media are selected and engaged with. Similar to the Australian study described in the preceding, a cluster analysis of early adolescents in the United States (12–14 years old) identified four sexual self-concept clusters that included both boys and girls and blacks and whites. Each cluster (*Virgin Valedictorians, Curious Conservatives, Silent Susceptibles,* and *Sexual Sophisticates*) was named to reflect the different patterns of sexual behavior as well as media use (L'Engle, Brown, Romocki, & Kenneavy, 2007).

Virgin Valedictorians were the least likely to have had sexual intercourse. These boys and girls were focused on doing well in school, books were their preferred medium, and they paid the least attention to and were the most critical of the rare popular media they did use. *Curious Conservatives,* in contrast, were heavy users of media and strongly identified with the teens in popular music and magazines, such as *Seventeen.* Adolescents in this cluster had low intentions to have sex, but were interested in sexual content and were knowledgeable about sexual health (e.g., knew that condoms were effective in preventing STIs).

Silent Susceptibles were interested in engaging in sexual behavior but had little sexual health knowledge; they were on the Internet frequently and were the most avid videogame players. *Sexual Sophisticates* used different kinds of media frequently. They were the most likely to identify with and wish they were like media characters, and were the most likely to have had sexual intercourse. Thus, it appears that sexual self-concepts may affect which kinds of media and which kinds of sexual media content adolescents prefer.

Sexual Media Content

Content analyses have shown that all media and genres are not the same in frequency or kind of sexual portrayals, so adolescents may choose media that have more or less and different kinds of sexual content. Sexual behavior is more frequent and explicit in movies than on prime time television (Gunasekera, Chapman, & Campbell, 2005; Pardun, L'Engle, & Brown, 2005). Music videos and soap operas and some premium channels, notably HBO, contain the most sexual content of different television genres (Fisher, Hill, Grube, & Gruber, 2004). Popular music, especially rap and hip hop, contains more sexual references than most television genres (Pardun, L'Engle, & Brown, 2005). Blacks are more likely to listen to music with sexually degrading lyrics than whites; female adolescents, regardless of race, are more likely to listen to sexual music that does not contain degrading lyrics than males (Martino, Collins, Elliott, Strachman, Kanouse, & Berry, 2006).

One estimate has suggested that more than one-third (37%) of all websites are dedicated to sexually explicit content or pornography (Optenet, 2010). Given such volume, it is relatively easy for adolescents to stumble on sexually explicit Internet content. Indeed, more than one-fourth (28%) of 10- to 17-year-olds in the United States reported experiencing unwanted exposure to online pornography in the previous year (Wolak, Mitchell, & Finkelhor, 2007). In a study of adolescents in North Carolina, by the time they were 14 years old, two-thirds of males and more than one-third of females had seen at least one form of sexually explicit media (magazines, videos, or on the Internet) in the previous year (Brown & L'Engle, 2009). Some adolescents look for online pornography—8% to 11% of American adolescents reported seeking out Internet pornography or intentionally going to X-rated websites in the previous year (Ybarra & Mitchell, 2005; Ybarra, Mitchell, Hamburger, Diener-West, & Leaf, 2011).

In the most comprehensive series of analyses of a range of US television content (more than 1,000 television shows on 10 channels), Kunkel et al. found that more than two-thirds of all programs included talk about sex, and more than one-third included sexual behavior (Kunkel, Eyal, Finnerty, Biely, & Donnerstein, 2005). About 90% of television programs with teenage characters include sexual content (Aubrey, 2004).

Compared with music, movies, magazines, and the Internet that adolescents use, television also contains the least amount of healthy sexual content (Pardun et al., 2005). Few television programs include talk about or portrayals of negative physical consequences (e.g., unplanned pregnancy, sexually transmitted infections) or the emotional and social risks or responsibilities of sex (Cope-Farrar & Kunkel, 2002; Aubrey, 2004). Kunkel et al. (2005) found that fewer than one in ten of the programs with sexual content most watched by teens discussed some kind of sexual risk; only about one in four of the programs that talked about or depicted sexual intercourse included some mention or depiction of risks and responsibilities.

An analysis of four media (music, movies, television, and magazines) used most frequently by early adolescents concluded that less than 1% of the content included any mention of three Cs of sexual health: Commitment, Contraceptives, or Consequences (Pardun et al., 2005). A qualitative analysis of the rare sexual health messages in the same dataset concluded that messages about responsibility for sexual health were gender stereotypical, such that "boys will be boys and girls better be prepared" (Hust, Brown, & L'Engle, 2008).

Social cognitive theory (SCT) (Bandura, 2009), which argues that people learn through observation and imitation of behavior that is rewarded and/or not punished, suggests that the lack of negative consequences in media sexual portrayals will increase the likelihood that adolescents will think they, too, will not suffer if they engage in sexual behavior. Sexual scripting theory (Gagnon & Simon, 1973) similarly predicts that if contraceptives are rarely shown as a normal part of a sexual script, adolescents who are learning about the typical steps in a sexual encounter by watching television or movies will be less likely to include the use of contraceptives in their own sexual relationships.

The social and immersive nature of digital media content also has important implications for what adolescents might learn from sexual content. First, the sexual media content that young people consume is often endorsed, and sometimes even produced by, their peers. To an extent, peers have always acted as one of the sources of adolescents' sexual media diets, with information about sexy movies to watch or magazines to read being circulated in peer networks. Digital media have made this process more immediate. With a click of a button, an adolescent can "like" a sexy song or movie on Facebook and instantaneously inform his or her friend network of this preference. Just as quickly, the adolescent can snap a suggestive photo of himself or herself and circulate it among friends.

Social cognitive theory also suggests that sexy media content endorsed or produced by a close friend may be more compelling than media content not similarly sanctioned. Research has documented that adolescents who identify with media characters are more likely to have the same sexual attitudes as their media models than those adolescents who do not find the characters as compelling (e.g., Ward & Friedman, 2006). Youth may be more open to learning new sexual identities or behaviors from more immediate models such as close peers and the media models they endorse than from more distant media models.

Video games, increasingly popular among both young men and women (Rideout et al., 2010), also regularly portray sexualized characters and situations (Scharrer, 2004; Ivory, 2006). For example, a player's sole objective in some video games, such as RapeLay and Stockholm: An Exploration of True Love, is the perpetuation of sexual violence against women. Scholars have argued that the immersive and interactive qualities of video games increase the potential for detrimental effects (Carnagey, Anderson, & Bartholow, 2008). Video games that allow players to take on sexualized personas and engage in sexualized behaviors may affect players' sexual self-perceptions and norms.

Getting Sexually Attractive

From a developmental perspective, one of the earliest indicators of a young person's interest in sexuality is a desire to be attractive—to have an appealing body and the right "look." Although body standards have shifted over time, media typically present a narrow range of possibilities—in the last two decades, the ideal male has been strong and fit with a v-tapered, muscular body (Kolbe & Albanese, 1996); the ideal female is curvaceously thin ("large breasts on a skinny body") (Harrison & Hefner, 2008, p. 387). Although adolescents and adults in the developed world are increasingly overweight and obese (Popkin, 2009), fatness in media is rare and often treated with disdain. On television, overweight female characters are more likely insulted by male characters than thin women (Fouts & Burggraf, 2000). Online sites designed to reinforce eating disorders such as anorexia, promote the idea that thin is beautiful and fat is ugly (Norris, Boydell, Pinhas, & Katzman, 2006).

Thin-ideal media depictions have been shown to affect body dissatisfaction among adolescent girls and women (see meta-analysis by Grabe, Hyde, & Ward, 2008), and muscle dissatisfaction among older boys and young men (see meta-analysis by Barlett, Vowels, & Saucier, 2008). Such patterns apparently are exacerbated when adolescents internalize the sexualized standards of media models and begin to monitor their own bodies as objects that should conform to the ideals.

Self-objectification (Fredrickson & Roberts, 1997), or viewing oneself from an outsider's perspective, and subsequent body dissatisfaction, have been linked to a number of adverse psychological and physical outcomes including depression (Mond, van den Berg, Boutelle, Hannan, & Neumark-Sztainer, 2011), concern about weight and eating disorders (López-Guimerà et al., 2010), as well as sexual risk-taking. Impett, Schooler, and Tolman (2006) found that among a group of adolescent girls, self-objectification predicted nonuse of a condom at first sexual intercourse. Sexual self-efficacy, or the belief that one can abstain from sex, or convince a partner to engage in safe sexual practices (e.g., condom use), mediated[2] the relationship (Rosenthal, Moore, & Flynn, 1991). Thus, it may be that the media's sexual objectification of women (and increasingly of men) affects adolescents' developing sense of what their bodies should look like to be sexually alluring, and if their bodies do not compare favorably, may reduce their ability to engage in healthy sexual behavior because they do not consider themselves worthy of the attention.

As the MPM suggests, however, all adolescents will not be affected similarly by media content. A recent experiment examining reactions to body ideals in media illustrates that both selective exposure and attention can reduce possible negative effects. Knobloch-Westerwick and Romero (2011) found that body-dissatisfied college students who were not forced to view a set of advertisements paid less attention to advertisements that featured ideal bodies than those who were satisfied with their bodies. Analyses of the sexual scripts and counterscripts presented in media also suggest that adolescents must do some work to sort through various conceptualizations of the meaning and sequence of sexual behavior, and find scripts and portrayals that fit with their developing sexual identities.

Sexual Scripts in Media

The sexual scripts in the media typically are different for males and females, and are focused on heterosexual romantic and sexual relationships, enforcing what Rich (1980) called "compulsory heterosexuality." Homosexual relationships, although more frequent in US media than previously, are rarely depicted as overtly sexual (Fisher, Hill, Grube, & Gruber, 2007) and even those relationships are presented as adhering to gendered stereotypes of a strong dominant "male" partner and a more submissive "female" partner (Ivory, Gibson, & Ivory, 2009). Blacks and other minority youth may also have difficulty finding models and scripts that support their cultural norms (Milbrath, Ohlson, & Eyre, 2009).

The traditional heterosexual script on prime time television (Kim, Sorsoli, Collins, Zylbergold, Schooler, & Tolman, 2007), reality dating shows (Ferris, Smith, Greenberg, & Smith, 2007), teen dramas (Aubrey, 2004; Kelly 2010), and popular music and music videos (Dukes, Bisel, Borega, Lobato, & Owens, 2003; Primack, Gold, Schwarz, & Dalton, 2008) depicts males as actively and aggressively pursuing sex and female characters willingly objectifying themselves and being judged by their sexual conduct. Teen girl magazines, such as *Seventeen*, have been described as teaching young women how to "transform themselves from girls into proper women" (Carpenter, 1998, p. 160). Young men's or "lad" magazines, such as *Maxim* and *FHM*, and women's magazines, such as *Cleo* and *Cosmo*, suggest that sex for men is primarily for recreation and sexual pleasure rather than a part of long-term relationships, and that men should have a variety of sexual partners (Taylor, 2005; Farvid & Braun, 2006).

Expectations about love, romance, and marriage may also be affected by media depictions as soap operas, reality dating shows, and romantic comedies provide scripts about desirable characteristics of partners, long-term relationships, and when sex should occur (Segrin & Nabi, 2002; Ferris et al., 2007; Johnson & Holmes, 2009). In an analysis of storylines about loss of virginity in teen television dramas, for example, Kelly (2010) identified three dominant scripts: (1) *Abstinence*: virginity is a gift that can be pleasurable, and sex is dangerous; (2) *Management*: virginity loss is a rite of passage to adulthood, but should be done in an appropriate way (e.g., after 15 years old, in an established monogamous romantic relationship, with contraceptives); and (3) *Urgency*: virginity is a kind of stigma that might even be lied about to maintain traditional masculinity. We should expect that adolescents with different sexual self-concepts would find the various scripts more or less compelling, depending on their interest in sexual behavior, and on the solidity and quality of their own attitudes and beliefs about romantic and sexual relationships.

Sexual and racial minority adolescents may be turning to entirely different media fare to find models and scripts that speak more directly to them. Studies have shown, for example, that black adolescents are more likely than their white counterparts to watch television shows that feature black characters (Brown & Pardun, 2004). It is likely that such differential patterns of selection are replicated for other media and on the Internet. One analysis of Internet home pages constructed by 14- to 17-year-old black girls found that many of their sexual self-representations as *Virgins, Freaks, Down-Ass Chicks/Bitches,* and *Pimpettes* mirrored the sexual scripts portrayed in hip hop music culture that typically features black men and women. A few of the girls resisted the dominant scripts, however, creating "counter-discourses" and more independent self-definitions (Stokes, 2007). Anthropologists have found that black and Mexican-American youth have different cultural models of romantic relationships than European-Americans (Milbrath et al., 2009), but we know little about the role media play in supporting or changing those culturally grounded ideas about courtship, love, and fidelity. More work on the ways in which marginalized young people select, engage with, and resist the dominant sexual scripts presented in the media is needed.

Engagement with Sexual Media Content

Once media content has been selected, the ways in which adolescents engage with the content will determine the effects of that exposure. In the MPM we use the term *Engagement* to encompass the psychological, interpretative, and physical interactions adolescents can have with sexual media content. Some types of engagement occur automatically and perhaps outside of conscious awareness. Counterarguing against sexual messages that do not match personal values may be less likely; for example, when an adolescent is multitasking (e.g., surfing the Internet and watching television at the same time) because cognitive resources are overtaxed. Engagement can also be physically active, for instance, when an adolescent wants to get pumped up before a party and starts dancing and singing along with a song's lyrics. Not all media are consumed in the same way, and how an adolescent engages with media content in the moment of consumption can influence the effect of that content on sexual attitudes, beliefs, and behaviors.

Processing Mediators

Studies of how people process messages have identified a host of psychological and physical factors that mediate the relationship between message exposure and message engagement. Some of the "processing mediators" that have been studied in relation to sexual content include interest, and the level of attention an adolescent chooses to or is capable of allotting, arousal (both sexual and general physiological excitement), character evaluations, narrative transportation, and resistance to persuasion. These processing mediators may suppress or enhance the effects of exposure to sexual content.

For example, two teenagers watching the same music video featuring men saying sexually degrading things about women, one watching attentively and the other multitasking by surfing the Internet simultaneously, are likely to be affected differently by the sexual content. The multitasker may be more likely to adopt program-consistent behaviors (Collins, 2008) because he has fewer cognitive resources to devote to counterarguing or critical evaluation. In this example the teenagers' attention, cognitive load, and resistance to persuasion are processing mediators that influence the effects of exposure to sexual content. Here we'll look at some of the main processing mediators in turn.

ATTENTION

Attention has long been studied as a factor in message processing and message effects (e.g., Chaffee & Schleuder, 1986). Some level of attention is necessary to process any message. Researchers have shown that we have a finite amount of cognitive resources that we can allocate to the processing of messages (Lang, 2000). The sum of cognitive demands is the cognitive load. High cognitive load should result in less careful scrutiny of the factual and realistic nature of a message (Gilbert, 1991). The importance of attention as a processing mediator between sexual media exposure and effects is probably most relevant to adolescents in the context of multitasking.

Adolescents are estimated to multitask between half and three-fourths of the time they are engaged with media (Jeong & Fishbein, 2007). Although Collins (2008) found that watching television while surfing the Internet increased the sexual effects of media, another study (Jeong, Hwang, & Fishbein, 2010) found no significant relationship between television/Internet multitasking and sexual effects. Jeong et al. (2010) found, however, that exposure to sexual media had significantly less effect on subsequent sexual behavior for heavy media/nonmedia multitaskers (e.g., watching television while doing homework, listening to the radio while driving) compared with light media/nonmedia multitaskers. The conflicting findings suggest that more research is needed to distinguish the effects of media as the primary versus secondary task and any cumulative effects of media/media multitasking.

INVOLVEMENT

In contrast to multitasking, which might inhibit elaboration, a highly involved viewer/reader/listener will be paying close attention to the media he or she is engaged with and be motivated to process it (Ward & Rivadeneyra, 1999; Peter & Valkenburg, 2010). In one correlational study, young adult female television viewers who reported high involvement in television shows with sexual content held more recreational attitudes toward sex and higher expectations of the sexual activity of peers, in keeping with the content they were watching (Ward & Rivadeneyra, 1999). A study of the effects of reality dating television shows on viewers' attitudes about sex and dating found that the positive correlation between watching the shows and having sexual beliefs similar to those portrayed in the shows (e.g., dating is adversarial, physical appearance is important in dating, men are motivated by sex) was fully mediated through viewer involvement (Zurbriggen & Morgan, 2006). Thus, the shows had more effect on viewers who were immersed in their viewing.

It is thought that greater involvement may make a media experience feel more like a real or personal experience, which may be especially likely for adolescents who have less personal sexual experience from which to draw. Peter and Valkenburg (2010), for example, found that adolescents who watched sexually explicit content on the Internet reported greater feelings of sexual uncertainty (unstable sexual beliefs and values) than adolescents who watched little or no sexually explicit content. The pattern was mediated by involvement and was stronger for females, suggesting that girls who are involved in their viewing of Internet pornography may be more susceptible to changing their existing sexual beliefs and values than those who look at the content in a more detached way. In another study, involvement was more predictive of expectations about sexual outcomes than amount of television viewed, suggesting that how television is consumed matters more than the volume of consumption (Ward & Rivadeneyra, 1999). More research is needed to explore the gender differences found in some studies and also to better understand why some adolescents become more involved while engaging with media than others. Nevertheless, the level of involvement with which an adolescent consumes sexual media content appears to be an important determinant of the magnitude of effects.

AROUSAL

Physical and emotional arousal may also help explain the effects of exposure to sexual media content. When adolescents engage with sexual content in media they may become aroused sexually or in a more general physiological way (e.g., excitement, anticipation) (Hansen & Krygowski, 1994). Arousal is believed to operate as a processing mediator by both focusing the individual on the arousing content and strengthening the memory and retrieval functions of the brain related to the content. Peter and Valkenburg (2008) found that the relationship between viewing sexually explicit content online and sexual preoccupancy ("a strong cognitive engagement in sexual issues, sometimes at the exclusion of other thoughts," [p. 208]) was mediated by arousal. So if a teen was aroused when watching pornographic content online, then he was more likely to think a lot about sexual activities than the teen who was less aroused when watching. Arousal may also serve as a processing mediator for less explicit sexual content in the media, such as music videos, but little research has investigated this possibility.

PERCEPTIONS AND ATTACHMENTS

Perceptions of and attachment with characters and stories may also serve as processing mediators. Perceived similarity to and identification with media characters, as well as the perceived realism and desirability of characters' actions can affect the extent to which content will be believed and incorporated into the media consumer's life. The Message Interpretation Process (MIP) model incorporates a number of character and story elements to describe how adolescents process media messages (Austin & Meili, 1994; Austin & Knaus, 2000; Pinkleton, Austin, Cohen, Miller, & Fitzgerald, 2007). The MIP model posits that perceived realism of media portrayals (the authenticity of the character and storyline) influences adolescents' perceptions of similarity to and identification with the characters. Alternatively, adolescents may focus on the desirability of the media portrayals (believing the characters are happy and have a good life), which can also influence identification with the characters. The route through perceived realism is considered to be primarily logical, whereas the desirability route is more affective. Identification is predicted to influence outcome expectations about the behaviors

within the storyline, and ultimately the viewer's own decision making.

For example, a teen may feel that a character on a popular television show is similar in some way and may think that the character's life is desirable. Portrayals of that character engaging in risky sexual relations (e.g., inebriated sex) with positive outcomes (e.g., the character is proud about the experience) may lead the viewing teen to expect that having sex after a night of excessive drinking is normal and likely to result in positive outcomes. Who identifies with which characters may depend on the viewer's existing sexual self concept. *Sexual Sophisticates,* for instance, may be quicker to identify with sexually expressive characters. *Virgin Valedictorians,* on the other hand, would be expected to find little in common with such characters.

The MIP model defines identification as wanting to be like the characters and to have a life like the storyline (Pinkleton et al., 2007). Other theorists have suggested that identification with characters is more about taking the perspective of a character by feeling as if you are experiencing the media situation as the character would (Cohen, 2001). Both identification and involvement speak to the importance of having the media experience feel real in the sense that a reader/viewer/listener experiences real emotions, imagines that the events are happening to them, and creates vivid images of the narrative (Green & Dill, 2013). Ward and Friedman (2006), for example, found in a correlational study that high school students who had higher levels of identification with popular television characters featured in shows with sexual content also reported more sexual experience (e.g., had a romantic relationship, had oral sex, had sexual intercourse). It may be that sexually experienced teens are emotionally attracted to characters who validate or share life experiences similar to their own, or, as predicted by the MIP model, that identification with sexual characters increases the likelihood that teens will adopt the behaviors of the characters.

Experimental evidence for the power of identification has been mixed. In one study with college students, intentions to practice safe sex measured immediately following exposure to a television show promoting safe sex were not associated with identification with the show's characters (Moyer-Gusé & Nabi, 2010). A long-term effect, however, was found such that identification emerged as a significant mediating variable in a 2-week delayed posttest. Youth who identified more with the characters practicing safe sex were more likely to express intentions to practice safe sex in their own lives 2 weeks after the original exposure. This sleeper effect for identification may be the result of initial discounting of the show as unrealistic or fictional and over time forgetting the lack of realism but remembering the behavior.

TRANSPORTATION

Much of the media content adolescents consume follows a narrative (story) structure. Growing scholarly attention has focused on the idea that powerful narratives can "transport" the reader or viewer into the story world (e.g., Green & Dill, 2013). Transportation occurs when readers are immersed in a narrative, so much so that it feels like they are experiencing that narrative world (they have been transported to it) (Green & Brock, 2000). Transportation is similar to involvement because both concepts entail being absorbed in media content. Unlike involvement, however, transportation does not necessarily lead to more elaboration about the people or issues in the media portrayal, but instead leads to a loss of the sense of or connection to the nonmedia world. Transported readers and viewers are less likely to notice others around them or to be thinking of contradictions in the narrative (Green & Brock, 2002).

Research has shown that greater transportation leads to greater persuasion or story-consistent beliefs (Green & Brock, 2000). There are three primary ways that transportation is thought to lead to greater persuasion: (1) making the narrative feel like a real experience, (2) suppressing counterarguing, and (3) promoting attachment to the characters within a narrative (Green, Garst, & Brock, 2004).

Thus far, little research has examined transportation in the context of sexual media content. In one study, however, participants read a story about a gay man witnessing homophobic behaviors during his college reunion and the more transported readers held more story-consistent beliefs about homosexuality after reading the story (Green, 2004). The quality of the story is believed to be crucial as to whether viewers/readers will be transported (Slater & Rouner, 2002); thus, we should expect that more engaging sexual stories will have more effect on sexual beliefs and behaviors.

Transportation may also promote interpersonal communication and health information seeking. In a three-wave survey study about a cancer subplot in the television show *Desperate Housewives,* viewers who reported being more transported over the course of the series were more likely to talk to other people about lymphoma and to seek out information about lymphoma compared with viewers who were less transported (Murphy, Frank, Moran, & Woodley, 2011). Thus, the extent of transportation into a media story may be an important predictor of when exposure to sexual media will stimulate adolescents to seek supplemental information on their own or by talking with others. By teaching the audience and cuing information seeking, media programs may act as health educators.

RESISTANCE TO PERSUASION

Resistance to persuasion is a reaction, either automatic or conscious, against a message in response to some perceived pressure for change in belief, attitude, or behavior (Knowles & Linn, 2004). Resistance to persuasion has rarely been examined as a processing mediator in sexual media effects research, perhaps because sexual content in media (e.g., a romantic date scene on a teen television show or explicit lyrics in a popular teen song) is rarely seen as designed to be persuasive.

Classic forms of resistance to persuasion include reactance and counterarguing. A media consumer is said to experience reactance and is predicted to reject the message when she feels a message threatens one of her freedoms (i.e., freedom of choice) (Brehm & Brehm, 1981). Reactance is triggered by an awareness of persuasive intent (Dillard & Shen, 2005; Moyer-Gusé, 2008). In the context of sexual media effects, reactance could occur, for example, when an adolescent posts a sexually degrading song on a friend's Facebook page, suggesting that the song's lyrics will help him deal with his girlfriend's "drama." The recipient of the song may react negatively, feeling like his friend is trying to limit his freedom. His girlfriend may see the post and react against it as well. Reactance could also occur when storylines on television become overtly persuasive or are seen as "educational" rather than simply entertaining.

Counterarguing occurs when a person generates thoughts that rebut or refute a persuasive statement or position within the narrative (Busselle, Bilandzic, & Zhou, 2009; Moyer-Gusé & Nabi, 2010). Cacioppo (1979) operationalized counterarguments as "statements directed against the advocated position that mentioned specific unfavorable consequences, statements of alternative methods, challenges to the validity of arguments in the message, and statements of affect opposing the advocated position" (p. 494). Counterarguing may occur if a teen notices something that seems unrealistic or counter to his or her experiences. For instance, a character in a television show may say something like, "My mom would be happy if I were a teen parent." This statement is likely counter to the existing beliefs of many teens and may elicit a counterargument in which the viewer says aloud or to himself or herself, "That's not the way my mom would react. This show is dumb."

Moyer-Gusé and Nabi (2010) found that after viewing a television scene in which the characters positively discussed using condoms, participants who reported stronger reactance against the safe sex portrayal were the least likely to report intentions to practice safe sex themselves. Unexpectedly, however, counterarguing did not have a significant effect on safe sex intentions. Clearly more research is needed to sort out these different forms of reaction to messages youth may see as trying to persuade them to engage in healthy or unhealthy sexual behavior.

Interpretation

Most of the processing mediators discussed thus far are automatic or even nonconscious, but media can also evoke conscious processing and interpretation of the messages and values depicted in the content. Interpretation is the meaning-making process through which adolescent consumers form attitudes, beliefs, norms, scripts, and intentions related to sexual behavior. The mostly qualitative research that has focused on the ways in which youth understand sexual messages in the media has shown that interpretations are often quite varied. Typically interpretations fall into three main categories identified originally by British cultural studies scholars (e.g., Hall, 1980) as "preferred," "oppositional," or "negotiated" from the point of view of the intentions of the media producer.

Some media texts and genres are more open to interpretation than others, and sometimes it is not clear what the producer intended. A study of pop star Madonna's early music video "Papa Don't Preach" illustrates both points. In that song, Madonna sings, "Papa don't preach, I'm in trouble deep, I'm going to keep my baby." Whereas white female college students interpreted the lyrics and images to mean the teen girl in the video was pregnant and intended to keep the child, black males thought the "baby" she was singing about was her boyfriend. In this case, and as often is the case with media produced primarily for entertainment, Madonna refused to say what her intended meaning was when health advocates criticized the video as a "commercial for teen pregnancy" (Brown & Schulze, 1990). Clearly, however,

the different interpretations would be related to different kinds of effects—young female viewers focused on the pregnancy might be persuaded that keeping the child would be the best option, whereas young male viewers might not be thinking about pregnancy at all, but rather about how to navigate romantic relationships.

Too few studies have taken into account the varied interpretations possible as teens come to content from different backgrounds, with different motivations, beliefs, and expectations. As the MPM posits, such variations are likely and will affect subsequent outcomes, both behavioral and prebehavioral.

Prebehavioral Outcomes

A number of theories have been used to explain sexual media effects, such as Social Cognitive Theory, Cultivation Theory, Uses and Gratifications, and Priming. These theories support the idea that prebehavioral outcomes such as attitudes, social norms, outcome expectations (or scripts), self-efficacy, beliefs, and intentions may be affected by media exposure and ultimately contribute to sexual behavior.

Social cognitive theory helps explain how adolescents interpret the sexual content in media message and may come to imitate that behavior (Bandura, 1986). According to the SCT, characters in the media act as models that help adolescents predict likely consequences of sexual beliefs, attitudes, and behaviors. When a media character is rewarded for his or her behavior, an adolescent viewer may be motivated to imitate that behavior; the adolescent's desire to imitate will be suppressed if the modeled behavior is punished or not rewarded. Perceived similarity of the characters will moderate the relationship between exposure and effects, such that similar characters should have stronger effects.

According to Bandura (2004), media influence behavior directly and through social mediation. In the direct pathway, media content affects behavior by informing, modeling, motivating, and guiding imitation. In the socially mediated pathway, media serve to link individuals to social networks (e.g., Facebook, YouTube) and community settings, which provide the guidance, incentives, and social supports that reinforce behavior. Social cognitive theory suggests that outcome expectations associated with a sexual behavior are likely to be a crucial mechanism that helps explain how exposure to sexual content in the media results in behavioral effects. Self-efficacy, an individual's belief that she can do the action to produce the desired result, is also an important motivator in SCT (Bandura, 1997). In their three-wave survey of adolescents, Bleakley, Hennessy, Fishbein, and Jordan (2009) found that self-efficacy for having sex was greater among youth who used friends and media as sexual information sources.

The basic idea of Cultivation Theory is that over time and repeated exposure to similar television content, viewers will begin to adopt views of the real world consistent with those portrayed on television (Gerbner & Gross, 1976). Most research on cultivation has focused on the extent to which television presents a distorted portrait of life. The cultivation effect may occur as some ideas (e.g., boys are preoccupied with sex) are frequently portrayed, and thus become salient and accessible (Shrum, 1996). Adolescents may form beliefs about expected sexual behavior and norms based on the distorted view of reality presented within the television shows they attend to most frequently. More research is needed to understand what, if any, relevance this theory may have for exposure to social media and other platforms increasingly popular with adolescents.

Uses and Gratification Theory posits that the motivations with which consumers come to the media will affect what they take away (Rubin, 1984). In one study, for example, college males who said they used sexual television to learn had stronger expectations about the variety of sexual behaviors that should occur within a romantic relationship than their counterparts who were not watching to learn anything (Aubrey, Harrison, Kramer, & Yellin, 2003). Ward (2002) similarly found that women who used television as a learning tool and for entertainment were more likely than those with different motives to believe in traditional gender roles and have stereotypical attitudes about sex and dating.

Priming Theory, in the context of sexual media effects, involves the activation of sexual scripts by relevant media content (Huesmann, 1988). To illustrate how this might work, in one study, college students either listened to sexually provocative lyrics or innocuous music immediately before viewing and evaluating online dating profiles of potential partners. Those who had been primed by the sexual lyrics were more likely to focus on the sexual characteristics of the potential partner than those who listened to the less provocative music (Dillman-Carpenter, Knobloch-Westerwick, & Blumhoff, 2007). Although priming effects are believed to last for only minutes, research suggests that some scripts are activated through primes so frequently that

they become more accessible (Roskos-Ewoldsen, Roskos-Ewoldsen, & Dillman-Carpenter, 2009). Because much of the media draw on dominant sexual scripts, these frequently primed scripts may have a greater influence on beliefs and behavior over time than scripts that appear less frequently. Such a pattern would help explain the effect hypothesized in the Cultivation Theory.

ATTITUDES

In a comprehensive review of the research on television's effects on sexual behavior, Ward (2003) concluded that attitudes formed by television viewing were an important precursor to sexual behavior. Some studies have found, for example, that teens who watch more prime time television shows with sexual content are more likely than teens who view less frequently to think sex is primarily recreational rather than part of a relationship or for procreation (Ward & Friedman, 2006). We would reasonably think that such attitudes would be related to subsequently different patterns of sexual behavior.

A number of studies have found that exposure to some kinds of sexual content can affect sexual attitudes. Greeson and Williams (1986), for example, found that watching sexy music videos resulted in more positive attitudes about premarital sex. MacKay and Covell (1997) conducted an experiment in which emerging adults either viewed advertisements with sexual themes or advertisements that depicted females in progressive roles. Participants who saw the sexual advertisements reported more sexually aggressive attitudes (e.g., rape myth acceptance and adversarial sexual beliefs) and less supportive attitudes toward feminism.

NORMS

One concern about the frequency with which young media characters engage in sexual behavior is that adolescent viewers will think that most adolescents are having sex and maybe they should be too. In an early correlational study, Davis and Mares (1998) found that frequent television viewers overestimated how many youth were sexually active and/or pregnant. One longitudinal study has found that feelings of pressure to have sex are stronger for teens with heavier sexual media diets (Bleakley et al., 2008). Another longitudinal study (Martino, Collins, Kanouse, Elliott, & Berry, 2005) also found that heavier sexual media diets were marginally predictive ($p > .05$ and $< .10$) of less healthy normative beliefs about sex (e.g., those with heavier sexual media diets believed more of their friends were having sex), which in turn predicted sexual initiation.

Two correlational studies of college males suggest that media portrayals can influence perceptions of peers' sexual activity and that those normative perceptions influence casual sexual behavior (Chia & Gunther, 2006). Ward, Epstein, Caruthers, and Merriwether (2011) found that reading men's magazines (e.g., *Maxim*) and watching movies was positively associated with higher estimates of peers' sexual risk taking and more permissive attitudes about sexual behavior. Both attitudes and perceptions of peers' behavior were positively associated with earlier sexual debut.

OUTCOME EXPECTATIONS

A great deal of survey and experimental research has documented an association between sexual media exposure and sexual outcome expectations and scripts. Aubrey et al. (2003), for example, found that females who watched television frequently expected that sex would occur earlier in a romantic relationship than females who watched less television. In an experimental test of the effects of reward versus punishment in portrayals of sexual intercourse, Eyal and Kunkel (2008) found that outcome expectations aligned with the media portrayals participants viewed.

Two longitudinal studies have found support for outcome expectations as an underlying mechanism between exposure to sexualized media content and behavior (Martino et al., 2005; Fisher, Hill, Grube, Bersamin, Walker, & Gruber, 2009). In the Fisher et al. study, teens with heavy sexual media diets were more likely to believe that sex would lead to positive outcomes such as feeling more grown up and preventing a relationship from ending. Martino et al. found that teens with heavy sexual television media diets were also less likely than teens with lighter sexual media diets to have negative outcome expectancies—such as that sex will result in a bad reputation or pregnancy. Lower negative outcome expectancies were marginally significant predictors for sexual initiation.

SELF-EFFICACY

In a survey, adolescents who reported movies, Internet, or magazines as their primary source of information about sex were more likely to have greater self-efficacy that they could have sex even if they encountered obstacles such as upset parents or intoxication, than adolescents who did not report any form of media as a primary sexual information source (Bleakley et al., 2009). Given the rarity of portrayals about practicing safe sex, a longitudinal study surprisingly found that the teens with heavy sexual media diets had greater self-efficacy for practicing safe sex than teens with lighter sexual television media diets. Further analysis revealed that teens with greater safe sex self-efficacy were more likely than teens with lower self-efficacy to practice safe sex (Martino et al., 2005).

In sum, existing research supports the notion that exposure to sexual media content will not result in uniform effects across the adolescent population. How youth engage with sexual media at the moment of exposure is likely to influence the effects of that exposure. The extent of attention, involvement, arousal, perceptions of and attachment with characters, transportation, and resistance to persuasion can mediate the relationship between exposure and effect, creating differential effects. We have also discussed that adolescents must also make sense of what they are seeing and hearing as they sort through the multiple, and sometimes mixed, messages about sexuality available in media.

The media provide sexual information and models that adolescents use to form and refine their sexual attitudes, norms, outcome expectations (or scripts), and sense of sexual self-efficacy. A number of studies, correlational, longitudinal, and experimental, provide empirical evidence that such prebehavioral sexual outcomes are affected by sexual content in the media. Some outcomes and processing mediators, such as sexual attitudes and involvement, have been studied more thoroughly than others. Other mediators and outcomes such as transportation and resistance to persuasion deserve more attention. As youth become creators and distributors of media (e.g., YouTube, sexting), more research is needed to better understand the role of engagement and interpretation in the new media landscape. How adolescents engage with and interpret media messages to form sexual attitudes, beliefs, norms, scripts, and behavioral intentions likely mediate the relationship between sexual media exposure and sexual behavior, thus resulting in various sexual media effects. Although the focus of this chapter is on media effects, it is important to note that many other factors, such as opportunity to act and parental monitoring, are likely to influence adolescent sexual behaviors.

Application

The process of adolescents moving from engagement with sexualized media to incorporation of these messages in their lives is called application in the MPM. It is in the application stage that adolescents will try out various behaviors to see what they feel like, if outcomes align with their expectations, and how their peers react. We define sexual behavior broadly to include not only sexual intercourse, but also other precoital behaviors such as treatment of romantic partners, sexual talk, sexual touching, and use (or not) of contraception.

Two excellent scholarly reviews generally support the assertion that exposure to sexual content in media affects adolescents' sexual behavior (American Academy of Pediatrics, 2010; Wright, 2011). Wright (p. 360), for example, concluded that "all five longitudinal studies and all three national studies found a main or moderated effect" between sexual media exposure and virginity status. Exposure to sexual media content has also consistently been linked to earlier initiation of sexual intercourse, even after controlling for dozens of likely covariates.

The Teen Media project, for example, a two-year longitudinal study, found that 12- to 14-year-old white adolescents who had heavier sexual media diets (television, music, movies, and magazines) were 2.2 times more likely to have had sexual intercourse by the time they were 16 years old, than white teens with lighter sexual media diets (Brown, L'Engle, Pardun, Guo, Kenneavy, & Jackson, 2006). In a national longitudinal study that assessed exposure to sexual content only on television, Collins, Elliott, Berry, Kanouse, Kunkel, Hunter, and Miu (2004) similarly found that adolescents who were exposed to high levels of sexual content (90th percentile of exposure) were twice as likely as adolescents who watched little sexual content on television (10th percentile) to initiate sex within a year of the baseline survey.

Four studies also have examined the influence of sexual media diet on precoital behaviors (e.g., touching, oral sex) and found support for the effect of media on these behaviors, as well (Wright, 2011). At least four studies have also examined whether sexual media diet has an effect on the number of sexual partners. Wright (2011) concluded that there was "suggestive evidence" but noted that the evidence was not as compelling as the research on precoital and coital sexual initiation (p. 366).

Use of birth control, pregnancy, and STIs as well as other sexual behaviors have also been studied as possible sexual media effects. With a national sample of teens, a three-wave longitudinal study found that teens in the 90th percentile of sexual television exposure were twice as likely to have experienced a teen pregnancy than teens in the 10th percentile of exposure (Chandra, Martino, Collins, Elliot, Berry, Kanouse, & Miu, 2008). Other studies have found associations between watching professional wrestling and lower rates of birth control use (DuRant, Neiberg, Champion, Rhodes, & Wolfson, 2008), and exposure to rap music among black teen girls and testing positive for an STI (Wingood, DiClemente, Bernhardt, Harrington, Davies, Robillard, & Hook, 2003). Longitudinal studies of adolescents also have found that exposure to more sexually explicit content predicted perpetration of sexual harassment among males and earlier oral sex and sexual intercourse among male and female adolescents (Brown & L'Engle, 2009), uncommitted sexual exploration (i.e., one-night stands, hooking up) (Peter & Valkenburg, 2010), as well as sexual violence (Ybarra et al., 2011).

A few longitudinal studies suggest that the relationship between exposure to sexualized media and sexual behavior may best be characterized as one of reciprocal causation. One three-wave study of adolescents found that those adolescents who were sexually active (pre-coital or coital) at baseline were more likely to have heavier sexual media diets (television, music, magazines, and video games) in subsequent waves of the survey. Such consumption of sexualized media subsequently increased the probability that adolescents progressed in their level of sexual activity within the following year (Bleakley et al., 2008).

Distribution/Creation as a Sexual Behavior

In the 20th century we were primarily concerned about young audiences' interaction with sexual content in professionally produced mass media: music, television programs, films, and magazines. Today, these young audiences also play an active role in producing and circulating sexual content. This has been facilitated by increasingly easy access to inexpensive production hardware (e.g., digital cameras, smartphones), editing software, and dissemination platforms (e.g., social media). Young people today are "prosumers" (Toffler, 1980), both producers and consumers, of sexual media content.

We understand youth-produced sexual media broadly, as any sexual content that youth transmit to audiences via communication technologies. This may include a self-description in a Facebook profile that characterizes the profile owner as a "boob girl"; a Facebook photograph that depicts the profile owner suggestively licking a lollipop; a text message with a nude photograph of the sender; a link to a sexual music video posted on Facebook or

Twitter; or a video created from photos of scantily clad celebrities posted on YouTube.

The production and dissemination of such sexual content fits best on the "Application" arch of the MPM. These acts may also be characterized as sexual self-presentations or sexual self-disclosures. We thus address two broad issues: Who are the young people who engage in mediated sexual self-disclosure? and What are the implications of sexual self-disclosure for these youth?

WHO PRODUCES SEXUAL MEDIA CONTENT?

The way individuals present themselves and what they disclose about themselves is shaped through an interplay of their personal attributes, the characteristics of their audience, and the context of their disclosure (Leary, 1995; Schlenker, 2005). Among personal characteristics, an adolescent's sexual self-concept may be one of the most salient predictors of sexual self-disclosure. Those items that are more vital, more centrally located within the self-concept, have a greater likelihood of being readily displayed (Schlenker, 2005). Youth for whom sexual identity is a more salient component of the self-concept likely engage in more sexual self-disclosures, whereas youth for whom sexuality is not an important characteristic are more likely to refrain from disclosing sexually.

Research has supported this association. Sexually active emerging adults and those with a history of casual sex presented more sexual self-disclosures in their MySpace profiles than their peers who have not had sex or who engaged in less risky sex (Bobkowski, Brown, & Neffa, 2010). In an experiment, girls who had suffered sexual abuse as children were more likely to select sexier characters (i.e., avatars) to represent them in an online game than matched girls without a history of abuse (Noll, Shenk, Barnes, & Putnam, 2009). Thus, youth for whom sex figures more prominently as a component of their identities, as measured by a history of sexual behavior, are more likely to be sexual content producers.

Certain personal dispositions may curb sexual self-disclosure among some young people and promote it among others. Self-monitoring (Fuglestad & Snyder, 2009) is one individual characteristic closely associated with self-disclosure. Self-monitors tend to be concerned about situationally appropriate self-presentations more than self-presentations that accurately reflect their self-attributes. Bloggers who are high self-monitors, for instance, updated their blogs more frequently and were more concerned about managing what they share with their audiences and what they keep private than bloggers who are low self-monitors (Child & Agyeman-Budu, 2010).

Youth who are high self-monitors may be less likely to self-disclose sexually if they perceive that some in their audience may consider such disclosure as inappropriate. Other attributes such as self-consciousness, social anxiety, and inhibition, have been associated with overall lower online self-disclosure among adolescents (Schouten, Valkenburg, & Peter, 2008).

Young people with good offline social skills, meanwhile, have been shown to use the Internet to enhance their offline relationships (Peter, Valkenburg, & Schouten, 2005; Schouten et al., 2008; Valkenburg & Peter, 2009).

In general, research suggests that online sexual content may be produced by those youth who are also more likely to engage in sexual self-disclosure in offline contexts. More research is needed to understand the extent to which online platforms might promote sexual self-disclosure among youth who are not predisposed to this behavior offline.

It is also important to consider the audience-related goals that motivate a young person to portray herself sexually in a digitally mediated context. The primary audiences for disclosures made in social networking websites, for instance, are friends and other individuals whom a user knows offline (Manago, Graham, Greenfield, & Salimkhan, 2008; Subrahmanyam, Reich, Waechter, & Espinoza, 2008). The way a youth relates to these offline friends and his or her goals for these relationships will thus determine how the adolescent presents himself or herself online, and whether it is done in a sexual way. Friendship group norms also inform the way that a young people digitally present themselves. In what an adolescent communicates about his or her sexual self, a youth is likely to conform to what his or her friends find appropriate and the way they present themselves online (Liu, 2007). An analysis of online religious self-disclosure showed that, holding their religiosities constant, MySpace users whose friends were religious were three times as likely to identify religiously in their profiles as users who had no religious friends (Bobkowski & Pearce, 2011). As with other behaviors, both problematic and prosocial, friends influence how young people present themselves in new media.

Because online communication often takes place asynchronously, individuals have more time online than they do in face-to-face interactions to construct their self-presentations. Online users also have fewer identity cues to control than individuals communicating in person. Internet users thus harness these unique characteristics of online communication to selectively and favorably present themselves to their audiences (Walther, 1996, 2007). Young people's digital sexual self-disclosures may deviate from the ways in which they present themselves offline. The Theory of Symbolic Self-Completion (Wicklund & Gollwitzer, 1982), for instance, suggests that individuals who are committed to a specific identity but feel that they have not fully lived out this self-definition, will use symbols to approximate their desired self. Thus, in one study, undergraduate MySpace users said that online profiles allow them and their peers to present not only their actual selves, but also the selves they aspire to become (Manago et al., 2008). Youth who perceive themselves as sexy or who want to be seen as such, may use online sexual self-disclosures to symbolically communicate a sexual identity to their audiences and themselves. Conversely, however, some youth may use online technologies to tone down their offline sexual portrayals or reputation.

Because offline friends are the primary audiences on social networking sites, the extent to which young people are able to embellish their offline identities in online spaces may be limited. In instances in which individuals who do not know each other offline connect online, the new visitor to a profile may look for difficult-to-change data such as friends' posts and photos to corroborate the accuracy of online self-claims (Walther, Van Der Heide, Hamel, & Shulman, 2009; Gibbs, Ellison, & Lai, 2011). Online users' preference for confirmatory information that cannot be manipulated by the presenter is known as the warranting principle (Walther & Parks, 2002). A youth who uses the Internet to meet a potential friend or mate will ask, "Is what she is saying about herself online warranted by what her friends are saying about her and by what she looks like in pictures?"

WHAT ARE THE EFFECTS OF PRODUCING SEXUAL MEDIA CONTENT?

Understanding the characteristics of youth who produce and distribute sexual media content is important in light of the potential effects of such production. Sexual self-disclosure online puts youth at greater risk for offline sexual encounters. Young people who communicate with strangers via the Internet about sex are more likely to receive aggressive sexual solicitations than young people who do not engage in such behaviors (Wolak, Finkelhor,

Mitchell, & Ybarra, 2008). In an experiment, girls who chose sexualized avatars in a virtual environment were more likely to be approached in sexual ways by other characters, and were also more likely to have met someone offline (Noll et al., 2009).

Beyond this increased risk of victimization, a young person's digital, sexual self-disclosure may reinforce the centrality or salience of sexual self-concepts within his or her broader identity. Studies have shown that affirming a particular position or enacting a behavior results in the internalization of that position or behavior within one's self-concept, especially when the position or behavior is performed publicly for an audience (e.g., Fazio, Effrein, & Falender, 1981; Kelly & Rodriguez, 2006). This "identity shift" dynamic has been shown to operate in online environments. For instance, participants whose interview responses were published in a public blog and who answered the interview questions as extroverts scored higher on a subsequent extroversion scale than those who answered the questions as introverts (Gonzales & Hancock, 2008). Participants in the introverted and extroverted conditions who answered questions in a text document that was not going to become public did not differ in their extroversion scores. Research conducted in virtual environments has also shown that participants take on attributes of the virtual characters (i.e., avatars) to whom they are assigned. Thus, participants assigned to "be" more attractive avatars were more extroverted than participants assigned to be represented by less attractive avatars, and those assigned to taller avatars acted more aggressively than those with shorter avatars (Yee & Bailenson, 2007).

Researchers have suggested two mechanisms that may account for this internalization of outward characteristics. Drawing on Self-Perception Theory (Bem, 1972), some have argued that individuals look to their self-presentations and self-disclosures to inform their self-concepts (e.g., Yee, Bailenson, & Duchenaut, 2009). Others have argued that the public nature of a self-presentation commits the presenter to be and act consistently with what is publicly disclosed (Kelly & Rodriguez, 2006; Gonzales & Hancock, 2008). According to the "public commitment" perspective, individuals thus strive for their self-concepts to match their self-presentations.

The exact means by which internalization occurs deserves further attention and the two mechanisms mentioned here may not be mutually exclusive. The literature does suggest that when young people portray themselves sexually in social media or send sexual text messages, they position their sexual attributes more centrally within their self-concepts. When repeated, such sexual self-presentations may lead to an ingraining of the sexual attributes, a reordering of self-understandings to prioritize the sexual aspects of the self over other characteristics. Although research has tested only the short-term effects of internalizing online disclosures (e.g., Gonzales & Hancock, 2008), studies on virtual environments have suggested that these effects may linger beyond the duration of an experimental manipulation. In one study, participants playing a card game against avatars who appeared shorter than themselves played more aggressively even after they were taken out of the virtual environment than those playing against avatars who appeared taller (Yee et al., 2009). In another experiment, participants who observed avatars who looked like them and who exercised on a treadmill, reported engaging in more exercise in the 24 hours following the experiment than participants who observed avatars who looked like them but who did not exercise (Fox & Bailenson, 2009). Such empirical evidence supports the notion that engaging in public sexual self-disclosures may lead to a sexualization of the self-concept.

Audience feedback is an essential component of the interactive digital media world. Each sexy photo that a youth posts on Facebook, for instance, is likely to generate comments from her Facebook friends. Research has shown that the identity shift is magnified when an online self-presentation is followed by a feedback message affirming the presented self-attributes (Walther, Liang, DeAndrea, Tong, Carr, Spottswood, et al., 2011). For example, study participants who answered interview questions as extroverts and who received a message affirming their extroversion, scored higher on a subsequent extroversion scale than those who did not receive a feedback message. Participants in the introverted condition who received a message affirming their introversion scored lower on the extroversion scale than those who did not get feedback.

From the perspective of public commitment, feedback may communicate to the presenter the level of commitment to which he or she has obligated himself or herself through the self-presentation. Although research has thus far examined only the effect of positive feedback, it is possible that a young person who receives little feedback or whose friends' comments are tepid or negative will not internalize the sexual elements disclosed digitally to the extent that a youth who receives positive, lavish, and enthusiastic friends' comments will. Negative feedback, however, may also have negative consequences, especially for youth who already have less self-esteem than their peers (e.g., Brockner, Derr, & Laing, 1987). In some cases, negative feedback may even rise to the level of cyber bullying, particularly when it is repeated, hostile, and meant to inflict harm or discomfort (Tokunaga, 2010). Feedback to sexual self-disclosures may also take the form of unwanted sexual solicitation, which is more likely when youth communicate with strangers about sex (Wolak et al., 2008). Whether negative or positive, feedback is a key characteristic of new media environments and must be considered when examining the ways in which young people perceive and communicate their sexual selves.

Researchers have only begun to examine the function of sexual self-disclosure within the digital media environment and much work remains to be done. For one, the effects of the mediated self-disclosure that we have discussed here (e.g., internalization, feedback) have not been tested within the context of sexual self-disclosure. The hypotheses presented here need careful scrutiny using innovative, ethically conducted study designs. Second, although in this discussion we have not distinguished between different types of sexual self-disclosure, all sexual self-disclosures are not the same and their effects are also likely to be disparate. Even within the same communication venue such as Facebook, content disclosed via different communication modes will likely generate unique effects. Posting one's sexy photos in a Facebook photo album is different from sending a private message with a sexy photo attached, and different still from posting a Facebook status update about the sexual appeal of a celebrity. The intensity of the content, the intended goals of the disclosure, and the audience response to the disclosure all contribute to the differential effects that each of these disclosures may stimulate.

Finally, we have emphasized the potentially negative effects of sexual self-disclosure rather than the potentially constructive ways in which new media may facilitate composing and communicating the sexual self. The Internet offers unprecedented opportunities for connecting with remote like-minded individuals and for exploring and affirming identities, especially for those who are otherwise stigmatized (McKenna & Bargh, 1998). Gay and lesbian youth, for instance, may find positive peers and mentors in online communities, and these relationships may facilitate the rehearsal of disclosing their sexual orientations, same-sex friendships, attractions, and sexual expressions (Hillier & Harrison, 2007). More research is needed to understand the ways in which digital media help young people engage in positive sexual development. These and other potentially constructive outcomes of sexual disclosure via new media underscore the need for new media literacy initiatives that educate youth about both the risks and opportunities of sexual self-disclosure in online contexts.

Conclusion
"Protecting" Youth from Harmful Effects

As evidence has accumulated that media play an important role in adolescents' sexual socialization, different strategies have been proposed to address potentially harmful effects and increase the possibility of sexually healthy outcomes. Health organizations, such as the American Academy of Pediatrics and the American Medical Association, have issued policy statements calling on parents, medical professionals, and the entertainment media to limit children's exposure to unhealthy media messages about sex, and increase access to information about contraceptives and healthy sexuality (American Academy of Pediatrics, 2010). The courts have forbidden sexually explicit content that features children (child pornography), but have been reluctant to restrict the distribution of other kinds of sexually explicit material because such regulations could infringe on adults' free speech rights (Iannotta, 2008). Ratings systems for movies, television, and video games that specify the amount and sometimes kind of sexual content have been developed but often are inconsistently applied, not understood or used by parents, and may actually stimulate some adolescents to taste the forbidden fruit (Gentile, 2008).

Media literacy education (MLE) is another strategy that holds some promise and speaks more to the idea of young people as active media consumers and producers. Media literacy education programs have been designed to teach young people about the production process of media and critically evaluate media content; many include media production skills training, as well (Chakroff & Nathanson, 2008). Although few systematic field tests of MLE curriculum have been conducted, a few have been shown to be effective in changing attitudes about substance use in early adolescence (Austin & Johnson, 1997; Pinkleton et al., 2007; Kupersmidt, Scull, & Austin, 2010) and body image issues and eating disorders in late adolescence (Irving & Berel, 2001; Watson & Vaughn, 2006).

A meta-analysis of 27 large randomized control trials of university-based health promotion programs found that the MLE programs were more successful at changing body image outcomes than knowledge-based and cognitive behavioral interventions (Yager & O'Dea, 2008).

Although more research and theorizing about how media literacy education works is needed (Chakroff & Nathanson, 2008), successful MLE interventions apparently alter media-related cognitions, such as reducing the perceived realism of and similarity to media portrayals by engaging youth in message deconstruction exercises. Such skill development is expected to change adolescents' cognitions and attitudes about the unhealthy behavior and beliefs about the normativeness of the behavior (Pinkleton, Austin, Cohen, Chen, & Fitzgerald, 2008). Production exercises help young people see that material has to be cut and constructed, and learn first-hand persuasion techniques. Media literacy education typically includes training in the persuasive techniques used by media creators, which can enhance skepticism in media messages and also help make adolescents aware of persuasive intentions, which in turn may promote greater resistance to persuasion. Changes in attitudes and beliefs, in turn, are predicted to result in decreased intentions to enact the unhealthy behaviors.

Only a few curricula have applied MLE to sexual health. One, "Take it Seriously: Abstinence and the Media," developed and evaluated in Washington state, is a five-lesson peer-led MLE program aimed at early adolescents. The evaluation field experiment showed that students who participated in the lessons had more accurate normative beliefs regarding teen sexual activity, perceived sexual portrayals in the media as less realistic, were more likely to believe that media messages influence adolescents' sexual behaviors, had lower positive expectations about what would happen if they had sex, and more positive attitudes about abstaining from sex (Pinkleton et al., 2008).

Other such curricula are needed for older adolescents that focus not only on abstinence, but also on contraception and other aspects of sexual relationships. Young people also need guidance on how to use the Internet and interactive media in sexually healthy ways. Buhi et al. (2009) concluded from their study of college students' use of the Internet for sexual health information that even older adolescents and young adults need training in how to find and distinguish accurate information online.

Using Media for Sexual Health

Media have also been used to promote healthier sexual behavior. Effective mass and new media campaigns promoting abstinence, teen pregnancy prevention, condom use, and HIV testing have been run in countries around the world, as well as in the United States. Some have taken a social marketing approach, including public service announcements as well as other media strategies. Some have included entertainment-education, in which educational messages are embedded in entertaining content. Other interventions are making use of newer media, such as interactive websites and cell phones to attract and engage youth in healthy sexual practices (for reviews, see Brown, 2008; Collins, Martino, & Shaw, 2011).

SEXUAL HEALTH MASS COMMUNICATION CAMPAIGNS

Mass communication campaigns are defined as organized sets of communication activities, intended to generate specific effects in a relatively large number of individuals, and usually within a specified period of time (Rogers & Storey, 1987). The Two-City Safer Sex campaign run in Kentucky in 2003 is one of the best examples of the successful use of mass media for sexual health in the United States. Designed to promote condom use among older adolescents and young adults (18–23 years old), messages were tailored to appeal to high sensation seekers and impulsive decision makers who were most likely to engage in sexual risk taking. Ten safer sex PSAs were aired for 4 months during programs known to be popular with the target audience. A 21-month controlled time-series evaluation beginning before the campaign and continuing for 10 months afterward documented high exposure to the ads, and increased condom use self-efficacy and use for 3 months after the campaign (Zimmerman, Palmgreen, Noar, Lustria, Hung-Yi, & Horosewski, 2007).

Meta-analyses of the effectiveness of media campaigns have found that such campaigns can be effective (Snyder & Hamilton, 2002). Media campaigns are an attractive strategy even though the proportion of people who change their behavior typically is modest because a campaign can reach much larger segments of the population than individual or group-based interventions. A review of international and US campaigns designed to improve sexual health among adolescents and a 10-year (1998–2007) systematic review of HIV/AIDS mass communication campaigns focused on sexual behavior, HIV testing, or both concluded that successful campaigns draw from behavior-change theories, have clear target audiences, use multiple media channels, and strive for long-term exposure and sustainability (Brown, 2008; Noar, Palmgreen, Chabot, Dobransky, & Zimmerman, 2009). Media campaigns conducted as part of community-based programs supported by behavior change policies and available services, such as school-based health clinics and comprehensive sex education, are most likely to be effective (Wakefield, Loken, & Hornik, 2010).

ENTERTAINMENT-EDUCATION

Entertainment-Education (E-E) is the intentional placement of education content in entertainment messages (Singhal & Rogers, 2002). Entertainment-Education is a versatile approach because media characters in different kinds of media and genres can be used to model behavior, teach skills, provide behavioral cues, and simulate consequences of behaviors over time in a compelling way (Green, Strange, & Brock, 2002). Used effectively for many years around the world to promote sexual health practices such as condom use and HIV testing, E-E also has been used in the United States by organizations such as the Centers for Disease Control and Prevention, and the National Campaign to Prevent Teen and Unplanned Pregnancy.

The National Campaign, for example, consulted with MTV producers as they developed the *16 and Pregnant* reality television series that featured 16-year-old girls dealing with the challenges of teen pregnancy. The Campaign developed discussion guides for each show that MTV then distributed with a DVD of the first season's six episodes to the more than 4,000 Boys & Girls Clubs of America. Evaluations showed that club teens who saw and discussed the shows were more likely than those who did not see or discuss the shows to talk with a parent or friend about teen pregnancy (The National Campaign to Prevent Teen and Unplanned Pregnancy, 2010).

Previously, the Kaiser Family Foundation (2004) had partnered with MTV's parent company Viacom to sponsor the KNOW HIV/AIDS campaign that included PSAs and print and outdoor advertising worth more than $120 million. Viacom also directed the producers of its television programs to include storylines that would raise awareness about AIDS and encourage prevention, counseling, and testing. Surveys showed that the campaign was especially effective in increasing awareness and intentions to practice safe sex among adolescent blacks who had seen Black Entertainment Television (BET)'s campaign component called "Rap It Up."

In other countries, whole programs and long story lines have focused on characters who serve as positive or negative models of sexual behavior for viewers. *Soul City*, a long-running E-E campaign in South Africa, was a prime-time television drama series that addressed various health-related topics each year, including HIV prevention and control. Using pre- and posttest panel surveys, evaluations showed that the broadcast was associated with increases in knowledge of HIV transmission and prevention, positive attitudes toward condom use, and increases in prevention behaviors (Singhal & Rogers, 2001).

Systematic evaluations of E-E messages on attitudes toward safer sex are rare in the United States, but generally positive. In one study, female participants who read an excerpt from a romance novel that mentioned condom use reported more positive attitudes and stronger intentions to use condoms than participants who read a similar excerpt that did not mention condom use (Diekman, McDonald, & Gardner, 2000). In another experiment (Farrar, 2006), college students who watched a prime time dramatic program featuring sexual intercourse and a safe sex message had more positive attitudes toward condoms than students who saw similar depictions without mention of condoms.

Although more theoretical work to understand the mechanisms by which narrative persuasion works is needed (Moyer-Gusé & Nabi, 2010), preliminary theorizing suggests that because the narrative's message is directed at the character, the reader/viewer may not see the message as manipulative, and persuasive defenses such as selective exposure and attention are circumvented. Some theorists also suggest that highly engaged (transported) viewers are devoting all of their cognitive energy to constructing a mental model of the story, making critical thinking less likely and emotional attachments more likely (Busselle et al., 2009).

DIGITAL MEDIA INTERVENTIONS FOR SEXUAL HEALTH

Novel interventions using interactive and portable media such as websites and text messaging services have been developed to communicate with youth about sexual health. Such interventions may be especially effective among youth because these are the media they use frequently, and the benefits of interpersonal communication can be combined with the advantages of mass communication by tailoring messages based on feedback while reaching more people than one-on-one or group counseling.

Interventions using digital media have included text messaging services for information about sex (e.g., "What if the condom breaks?") (Levine, McCright, Dobkin, Woodruff, & Klausner, 2008) and to get STI test results and counseling referrals. A soap opera depicting safer sex scripts that could be played on a hand-held computer was successful in persuading young black women to be more assertive in using condoms (Jones, 2008). The pediatrician "Dr. Meg," successfully encouraged young MySpace users to reduce their risky sexual disclosures on their personal profiles and to implement privacy controls (Moreno, VanderStoep, Parks, Zimmerman, Kurth, & Christakis, 2009). Multiple-lesson curricula to delay sexual behavior among middle school students, and increase HIV prevention behaviors among high school students have been delivered effectively on computers (Lightfoot, Comulada, & Stover, 2007; Tortolero, Markham, & Peskin, et al., 2010). (For a comprehensive review of evaluated digital media interventions for adolescents' sexual health, see Collins, Martino, & Shaw, 2011.)

A meta-analysis of 20 computer-mediated interventions for safer sex practices for youth and adults found that interventions significantly improved HIV/AIDS knowledge, perceived susceptibility, sexual/condom attitudes, and communication about condoms as well as self-efficacy and intentions to use condoms (Noar, Pierce, & Black, 2010). The analysis suggested that programs were especially appealing to youth, and were more successful if they were tailored for individual participants and included more sessions.

As more such programs using varieties and combinations of digital media are developed for sexual health, it will be important to consider questions of confidentiality and informed consent, especially when targeting youth on their cell phones. Although social networking sites seem like an ideal venue for such interventions, privacy settings may limit the extent to which researchers can gain access and/or evaluate impact. Online curricula and interactive sexual heath websites are also difficult to evaluate because users may skip modules so it will be hard to know which parts are most effective. Despite these concerns, the possibility of using digital media to reach teens where they are, when they have questions, is exciting and worthy of much more attention.

Future Directions

We have used the MPM to organize our discussion of the role of the media in sexual socialization because it is clear from existing research that adolescents and emerging adults do learn from the media and that who they are, what they are looking for, and how they process and react to what they see, read, and hear matters. The research shows that young people do come to media to learn more about their sexual feelings and interests and that although a heterosexual script of love, sex, and relationships prevails, what media provide is often open to interpretation, depending on what the adolescent already knows and believes. A host of processing mediators, or factors that influence how the content will be attended to and retained, also affect whether media scripts and messages will be incorporated into the adolescent's sexual self-concept and will affect subsequent sexual beliefs and behavior. Throughout the process, the digital media provide the means for friends to play a bigger role than ever before in supporting or refuting what the commercial media provide. We have also seen that the media can be positive players in helping young people develop healthier sexual lives, as campaigns have effectively taught adolescents about safer sex practices in compelling ways.

This overview of what we currently know about media and adolescent sexual socialization also points to a number of topics that still should be addressed. First, we must find ways to look at the array of media adolescents are using rather than only one medium at a time. Although adolescents still do spend more time with television than any other medium, even television is now being watched in very different ways—on laptop computers, tablets, and cell phones. We currently know very little about whether these different ways of viewing affect what is learned. These new ways of viewing also make it much easier to pass on favorite bits, comment on shows while they are being watched, and go to other kinds of media, such as online magazines, songs, music videos, and even interviews with the actors that are stimulated by the viewing. That kind of involvement could lead to very different outcomes.

Measurement of those kinds of patterns will be difficult in population studies, but one approach may be to construct measures that focus on the outcome of interest, such as Ward et al. (2011) did in their study of masculinity among college men. The measure of media exposure combined self-reports of use of four media, men's magazines, music videos, movies, and prime time television programs that are known from previous content analyses to contain high proportions of content about male gender roles. More innovative measurement techniques, such as experience sampling (Hektner, Schmidt, &

Csikszentmihalyi, 2007) that would allow simultaneous assessment of content, context, and level of involvement could be valuable.

The results of the small body of work on the effects of adolescents' use of online pornography are troubling and worthy of further study. The program of research in the Netherlands (e.g., Peter & Valkenburg, 2010) and the few studies elsewhere suggest a pattern in which initial curiosity may lead to more negative outcomes, including preoccupation with sex, feelings of sexual inadequacy, and even sexual violence (Ybarra et al., 2011). Given youths' unprecedented access to sexually explicit content, much more work is needed to answer the question, How does early exposure to the bodies and scripts of pornography affect adolescents' developing sense of their own sexuality?

Given that current and future generations of adolescents will be growing up in a 24-7 media world in which they can be producers as well as consumers, we must learn more about the effects of audience-generated and distributed content such as sexting and viral sexually explicit videos. A developmental approach will be especially relevant in this domain because research suggests that peers are most influential at transitional moments in an adolescent's life. The need for identity validation and support from popular teens is most needed as adolescents move from middle school to high school and then to college (IOM & NRC, 2011), so focus on those moments in adolescents' lives may be most fruitful.

More longitudinal and experimental studies that will provide better evidence of the sequence of causality are needed. Only a few studies have included both good measures of media exposure and sexual outcomes at more than one time. Cross-sectional surveys can establish that a relationship between exposure and sexual beliefs and behaviors exist, but they cannot be sure about time-order. The few surveys that have included more than two waves of data support the MPM's assumption that, in fact, the process is reciprocal—early adolescents do seek sexual content in the media and that exposure then is related to their sexual behavior. Those studies have not found consistent results across racial groups, however, and may have begun too late to detect the patterns of media use for adolescents who are coming to sexual maturation earlier or for those who are using sexual content in late childhood.

The interplay of gender, race, and class as contexts in which young people come to the media with different expectations and life possibilities has also not been taken into consideration sufficiently. Similarly, we know very little about how non-heterosexual youth find relevant and supportive media fare or how they cope with dominant scripts in mainstream media. Qualitative research may be particularly important to study how individuals incorporate sexual media in their lives by helping us to better understand the meaning-making processes adolescents engage in when experiencing sexual media (Polkinghorne, 2013).

Broader definitions of what we mean by sex and sexuality will also be helpful. Further studies of the extent to which adolescents learn standards of sexual attractiveness, masculinity/femininity, romantic relationship and breakup scripts, norms of fidelity, and expectations about pregnancy, motherhood, and fatherhood, from the media are needed.

A word here about the challenges of enrolling preteens and teens in research about sexuality may be worthwhile. Especially in the United States, but also in other countries in which sexual topics are rarely discussed openly, it is often difficult to obtain permission to talk with young people about sex. Given that sexual media content is increasingly available to children and preteens, it is important that we find ways to start earlier with good longitudinal studies. One possibility is to recruit samples from schools for the media-related questions and administer the more sensitive sexual behavior–related questions in the child's home so parents may see what is being asked. This was the strategy used successfully in the Teen Media longitudinal study conducted in North Carolina with middle-school students (L'Engle, Pardun, & Brown, 2004). Institutional review boards also need to be educated about the importance of being able to enroll children and preteens in age-appropriate studies of the role of the media in sexual socialization.

Finally, the media can be helpful in guiding young people to lifelong healthy sexuality (Halpern, 2010). Media literacy education may help young people make healthier choices about which media to use and to approach content with a more critical eye. Campaigns to promote safer sex practices may help fill in the gap in the current media script that rarely includes patience or protection. The potential of digital media to reach teens where they are, when they are receptive to messages about sexual health is exciting. As Robinson, Patrick, Eng, and Gustafson (1998) have suggested, we will learn more about media effects as we evaluate interventions. We should proceed on both fronts with the ultimate goal of helping young people develop healthy sexual lives.

Notes

1. We have updated the figure of the original model (Steele & Brown, 1995 Steele, 1999; Brown, 2000) to depict the changing media environment: (1) added a second layer on the pathway to depict the importance of peers; (2) changed "Interpretation" to "Engagement" and included lists of "processing mediators" and "prebehavioral outcomes" that are the components of the work a media consumer does when consuming media; and (3) added "media production/circulation" to signify that media consumers can also create and distribute their own media.

2. In statistical models, mediation occurs when the relationship between the independent variable (X) and dependent variable (Y) is explained by the presence of a third intermediary variable, the mediator. The independent variable influences the mediator variable, which in turn influences the dependent variable. This effect can be complete, meaning the mediator explains the entire effect of X on Y or partial, meaning that the mediator explains some of the relationship between X and Y (MacKinnon, 2008).

References

Ackard D. M., & Neumark-Sztainer D. (2001). Health care information sources for adolescents: age and gender differences on use, concerns, and needs. *Journal of Adolescent Health, 29*, 170–176.

Alford, S., & Hauser, D. (2011). *Adolescent sexual health in Europe and the US.* Advocates for Youth. Retrieved May 24, 2011 from http://www.advocatesforyouth.org/publications/publications-a-z/419-adolescent-sexual-health-in-europe-and-the-us.

American Academy of Pediatrics (2010). Policy statement: Sexuality, contraception, and the media. *Pediatrics, 126*(3), 576–582.

Aubrey, J. S. (2004). Sex and punishment: An examination of sexual consequences and the sexual double standard in teen programming. *Sex Roles, 50*(7), 505–514.

Aubrey, J. S., Harrison, K., Kramer, L., & Yellin, J. (2003). Variety versus timing. Gender differences in college students' expectations as predicted by exposure to sexually oriented television. *Communication Research, 30*, 432–460.

Austin, E. W., & Johnson, K. K. (1997). Effects of general and alcohol-specific media literacy training on children's affinity for alcohol. *Journal of Health Communication, 2*, 17–42.

Austin, E. W., & Knaus, C. S. (2000). Predicting the potential for risky behavior among those too young to drink, as the result of appealing advertising. *Journal of Health Communication, 5*, 13–27.

Austin, E. W., & Meili, H. K. (1994). Effects of interpretations of televised alcohol portrayals on children's alcohol beliefs. *Journal of Broadcasting & Electronic Media, 38*, 417–435.

Bandura, A. (1986). *Social Foundations of Thought and Action: A Social Cognitive Theory.* Englewood Cliffs, NJ: Prentice-Hall.

Bandura, A. (1997). *Self-Efficacy: The Exercise of Control.* New York: Freeman.

Bandura, A. (2004). Social cognitive theory for personal and social change by enabling media. In Singhal, A., Cody, M. J., Rogers, E. M., & Sabido, M. (Eds.), *Entertainment-Education and Social Change: History, Research, and Practice.* Hillsdale, NJ: Lawrence Erlbaum Associates, pp. 75–96.

Bandura, A. (2009). Social cognitive theory of mass communication. In Bryant, J., & Oliver, M. B. (Eds.), *Media*

Effects: Advances in Theory and Research, 3rd ed. New York: Routledge, pp. 94–124.

Barlett, C. P., Vowels, C. L., & Saucier, D. A. (2008) Meta-analyses of the effects of media images on men's body-image concerns. *Journal of Social and Clinical Psychology*, *27*(3), 279–310.

Bem, D. J. (1972). Self-perception theory. *Advances in Experimental Social Psychology*, *6*, 1–62.

Bleakley, A., Hennessy, M., Fishbein, M., & Jordan, A. (2008). It works both ways: The relationship between exposure to sexual content in the media and adolescent sexual behavior. *Media Psychology*, *11*(4), 443–461.

Bleakley, A., Hennessy, M., Fishbein, M., & Jordan, A. (2009). How sources of sexual information relate to adolescents' beliefs about sex. *American Journal of Health Behavior*, *33*(1), 37–48.

Bobkowski, P. S. (2009). Adolescent religiosity and selective exposure to television. *Journal of Media and Religion*, *8*, 55–70.

Bobkowski, P. S., Brown, J. D., & Neffa, D. R. (March, 2010). *"Hit me up and we can get down:" Youth sexual histories and sexual self-disclosure in online social networking profiles.* Paper presented to the Society for Research on Adolescence, Philadelphia.

Bobkowski, P. S., & Pearce, L. D. (2011). Baring their souls in online profiles or not: Religious self-disclosure in social media. *Journal for the Scientific Study of Religion*, *50*(4), 744–762.

Bourdieu, P. (1990). *The Logic of Practice.* Stanford, CA: Stanford University Press.

Brehm, S. S., & Brehm, J. W. (1981). *Psychological Reactance: A Theory of Freedom and Control.* San Diego: Academic Press.

Brockner, J., Derr, W. R., & Laing, W. N. (1987). Self-esteem and reactions to negative feedback: Toward greater generalizability. *Journal of Research in Personality*, *21*, 318–333.

Brown, J. D. (2000). Adolescents' sexual media diets. *Journal of Adolescent Health*, *27*(2), 35–40.

Brown, J. D. (Ed). (2008). *Managing the media monster: The influence of media (from television to text messages) on teen sexual behavior and attitudes.* Washington, DC: National Campaign to Prevent Teen and Unplanned Pregnancy.

Brown, J. D., Halpern, C. T., & L' Engle, K. L. (2005). Mass media as a sexual super peer for early maturing girls. *Journal of Adolescent Health*, *36*(5), 420–427.

Brown, J. D., & L' Engle, K. L. (2009). X-rated: Sexual attitudes and behaviors associated with U.S. early adolescents' exposure to sexually explicit media. *Communication Research*, *36*, 129–151.

Brown, J. D., L'Engle, K. L., Pardun, C. J., Guo, G., Kenneavy, K., & Jackson, C. (2006). Sexy media matter: Exposure to sexual content in music, movies, television, and magazines predicts black and white adolescents' sexual behavior. *Pediatrics*, *117*(4), 1018–1027.

Brown, J. D., & Pardun, C. J. (2004). Little in common: Racial and gender differences in adolescents' television diets. *Journal of Broadcasting & Electronic Media*, *48*(2), 266–278.

Brown, J. D., & Schulze, L. (1990). The effects of race, gender, and fandom on audience interpretations of Madonna's music videos. *Journal of Communication*, *40*(2), 88–102.

Buhi, E. R., Daley, E. M., Fuhrmann, H. J., & Smith, S. A. (2009). An observational study of how young people search for online sexual health information. *Journal of American College Health*, *58*(2), 101–111.

Busselle, R., Bilandzic, H., & Zhou, Y. (May, 2009). *The Influence of Television Fiction on Real World Victim Sympathy: The Roles of Narrative Engagement and Counterarguing.* Presented at the International Communication Association.

Buzwell, S., & Rosenthal, D. (1996). Constructing a sexual self: Adolescents' sexual self-perceptions and sexual risk-taking. *Journal of Research on Adolescence*, *6*, 489–513.

Cacioppo, J. T. (1979). Effects of exogenous changes in heart rate on facilitation of thoughts and resistance to persuasion. *Journal of Personality and Social Psychology*, *37*(4), 489–498.

Carnagey, N. L., Anderson, C. A., & Bartholow, B. D. (2008). Media violence and social neuroscience: New questions and new opportunities. *Current Directions in Psychological Science*, *16*, 178–182.

Carpenter, L. M. (1998). From girls into women: Scripts for sexuality and romance in Seventeen magazine, 1974–1994. *Journal of Sex Research*, *35*, 158–168.

Chaffee, S. R., & Schleuder, J. D. (1986). Measurement and effects of attention to media news. *Human Communication Research*, *13*, 76–107.

Chakroff, J. L., & Nathanson, A. I. (2008). Parent and school interventions: Mediation and media literacy. In Calvert, S. L., & Wilson, B. J. (Eds.), *The Blackwell Handbook of Children, Media, and Development.* Boston: Blackwell, pp. 552–576.

Chandra, A., Martino, S. C., Collins, R. L., Elliot, M. N., Berry, S. H., Kanouse, D. E., & Miu, A. (2008). Does watching sex on television predict teen pregnancy? Findings from a national longitudinal survey of youth. *Pediatrics*, *122*, 1047–1054.

Chia, S. C., & Gunther, A. C. (2006). How media contribute to misperceptions of social norms about sex. *Mass Communication & Society*, *9*(3), 301–320.

Child, J. T., & Agyeman-Budu, E. A. (2010). Blogging privacy management rule development: The impact of self-monitoring skills, concern for appropriateness, and blogging frequency. *Computers in Human Behavior*, *26*, 957–963.

Cohen, J. (2001). Defining identification: A theoretical look at the identification of audiences with media characters. *Mass Communication & Society*, *4*(3), 245–264.

Collins, R. L. (2008). Media multitasking: Issues posed in measuring the effects of television sexual content exposure. *Communication Methods and Measures*, *2*, 65–79.

Collins R. L., Elliott M. N., Berry S. H., Kanouse, D. E., Kunkel, D., Hunter, S. B., & Miu, A. (2004). Watching sex on television predicts adolescent initiation of sexual behavior. *Pediatrics*, *114*(3), 280–289.

Collins, R. L., Martino, S., & Shaw, R. (2011). *Influence of New Media on Adolescent Sexual Health: Evidence and Opportunities*, RAND Corporation. Retrieved May 24, 2011 from http://www.rand.org/pubs/working_papers/WR761.html.

Cope-Farrar, K. M., & Kunkel, D. (2002). Sex in teen programming. In Brown, J., Steele, J., & Walsh-Childers, K. (Eds.), *Sexual Teens, Sexual Media.* Hillsdale, NJ: Lawrence Erlbaum Associates, pp. 59–78.

Davis, S., & Mares, M.-L. (1998). Effects of talk show viewing on adolescents. *Journal of Communication*, *48*, 69–86.

Diamond, L. M., & Savin-Williams, R. C. (2009). Adolescent sexuality. In Lerner, R. M., & Steinberg, L. (Eds.), *Handbook of adolescent psychology*, vol. 1. *Individual bases of adolescent development,* 3rd ed. Hoboken, NJ: Wiley, pp. 479–523.

Diekman, A. B., McDonald, M., & Gardner, W. L. (2000). Love means never having to be careful: The relationship between reading romance novels and safe sex behavior. *Psychology of Women Quarterly, 24,* 179–188.

Dillard, J. P., & Shen, L. (2005). On the nature of reactance and its role in persuasive health communication. *Communication Monographs, 72,* 144–168.

Dillman-Carpentier, F., Knobloch-Westerwick, S., & Blumhoff, A. (2007). Naughty versus nice: Suggestive pop music influences on perceptions of potential romantic partners. *Media Psychology, 9*(1), 1–17.

Dukes, R. L., Bisel, T. M., Borega, K. N., Lobato, E. A., & Owens, M. D. (2003). Expressions of love, sex, and hurt in popular songs: a content analysis of all-time greatest hits. *Social Science Journal, 40,* 643–650.

DuRant, R. H., Neiberg, R., Champion, H., Rhodes, S., & Wolfson, M. (2008). Viewing professional wrestling on television and engaging in violent and other health risk behaviors by a national sample of adolescents. *Southern Medical Journal, 101,* 129–137.

Eyal, K., & Kunkel, D. (2008). The effects of sex in television drama shows on emerging adults' sexual attitudes and moral judgments. *Journal of Broadcasting & Electronic Media, 52,* 161–181.

Farrar, K. M. (2006). Sexual intercourse on television: Do safe sex messages matter? *Journal of Broadcasting and Electronic Media, 50*(4), 635–650.

Farvid, P., & Braun, V. (2006). 'Most of us guys are raring to go anytime, anyplace, anywhere': Male and female sexuality in *Cleo* and *Cosmo*. *Sex Roles, 55,* 295–310.

Fazio, R. H., Effrein, E. A., & Falender, V. J. (1981). Self-perceptions following social interaction. *Journal of Personality and Social Psychology, 41,* 232–242.

Ferris, A. L., Smith, S. W., Greenberg, B. S., & Smith, S. L. (2007). The content of reality dating shows and viewer perceptions of dating. *Journal of Communication, 57,* 490–510.

Fisher, D. A., Hill, D. L., Grube, J. W., Bersamin, M. M., Walker, S., & Gruber, E. L. (2009). Televised sexual content and parental mediation: Influences on adolescent sexuality. *Media Psychology, 12,* 121–147.

Fisher, D. A., Hill, D. L., Grube, J. W., & Gruber, E. L. (2004). Sex on American television: An analysis across program genres and network types. *Journal of Broadcasting & Electronic Media, 48*(4), 529–553.

Fisher, D. A., Hill, D. L., Grube, J. W., & Gruber, E. L. (2007). Gay, lesbian, and bisexual content on television: A quantitative analysis across two seasons. *Journal of Homosexuality, 52*(3), 167–188.

Fouts, G., & Burggraf, K. (2000). Television situation comedies: Female weight, male negative comments, and audience reactions. *Sex Roles, 42*(9–10), 925–932.

Fox, J., & Bailenson, J. N. (2009). Virtual self-modeling: The effects of vicarious reinforcement and identification on exercise behaviors. *Media Psychology, 12,* 1–25.

Fredrickson, B. L., & Roberts, T. (1997). Objectification Theory: Toward understanding women's lived experiences and mental health risks. *Psychology of Women Quarterly, 21,* 173–206.

Fuglestad, P. T., & Snyder, M. (2009). Self-monitoring. In Leary, M. R., & Hoyle, R. H. (Eds.), *Handbook of Individual Differences in Social Behavior.* New York: Guilford Press, pp. 574–591.

Gagnon, J. H., & Simon, W. (1973). *Sexual Conduct: The Social Sources of Human Sexuality.* Chicago: Aldine.

Gentile, D. A. (2008). The rating systems for media products. In Calvert, S. & Wilson, B. (Eds.), *Handbook of Children, Media, and Development.* Oxford, UK: Blackwell, pp. 527–551.

Gerbner, G., & Gross, L. (1976). Living with television: The violence profile. *Journal of Communication, 26*(2), 172–199.

Gibbs, J. L., Ellison, N. B., & Lai, C. (2011). First comes love, then comes Google: An investigation of uncertainty reduction strategies and self-disclosure in online dating. *Communication Research, 31,* 70–100.

Gilbert, D. T. (1991). How mental systems believe. *American Psychologist, 46,* 107–119.

Gonzales, A. L., & Hancock, J. T. (2008). Identity shift in computer-mediated environments. *Media Psychology, 11,* 167–185.

Grabe, S., Hyde, J., & Ward, L. (2008). The role of the media in body image concerns among women: A meta-analysis of experimental and correlational studies. *Psychological Bulletin, 134*(3), 460–476.

Green, M. C. (2004). Transportation into narrative worlds: The role of prior knowledge and perceived realism. *Discourse Processes, 38*(2), 247–266.

Green, M. C., & Brock, T. C. (2000). The role of transportation in the persuasiveness of public narratives. *Journal of Personality and Social Psychology, 79*(5), 701–721.

Green, M. C., & Brock, T. C. (2002). In the mind's eye: Imagery and transportation into narrative worlds. In Green, M. C., Strange, J. J., & Brock, T. C. (Eds.), *Narrative Impact: Social and Cognitive Foundations.* Hillsdale, NJ: Lawrence Erlbaum Associates, pp. 315–341.

Green, M. C., & Dill, K. (2013). Why conscious differentiation between fantasy and reality does not prevent media influence: Unconscious mechanisms of persuasion via fiction. In Dill, K. (Ed.), *The Oxford Handbook of Media Psychology.* New York: Oxford University Press.

Green, M. C., Garst, J., & Brock, T. (2004). The power of fiction: Determinants and boundaries. In Shrum, L. J. (Ed.). *The Psychology of Entertainment Media: Blurring the Lines Between Entertainment and Persuasion.* Hillsdale, NJ: Lawrence Erlbaum Associates, pp. 161–176.

Greeson, L. E., & Williams, R. A. (1986). Social implications of music videos for youth: An analysis of the content and effects of MTV. *Youth and Society, 18,* 177–189.

Gunasekera, H., Chapman, S., & Campbell, S. (2005). Sex and drugs in popular movies: An analysis of the top 200 films. *Journal of the Royal Society of Medicine, 9,* 464–470.

Hall, S. (1980) 'Encoding/decoding'. In Hall, S., Hobson, D., Lowe, A., & Willis, P. (Eds.), *Culture, Media, Language.* London: Hutchinson, pp. 128–138.

Halpern, C. (2010). Reframing research on adolescent sexuality: Healthy sexual development as part of the life course. *Perspectives on Sexual & Reproductive Health, 42*(1), 6–7.

Halpern, C., Udry, J., Campbell, B., & Suchindran, C. (1994). Testosterone and religiosity as predictors of sexual attitudes and activity among adolescent males: A biosocial model. *Journal of Biosocial Science, 26,* 217–234.

Hansen, C. H., & Krygowski, W. (1994). Arousal-augmented priming effects: Rock music videos and sex object schemas. *Communication Research, 21,* 24–47.

Harrison, K., Hefner, V. (2008) Media, body image, and eating disorders. In Calvert, S. L., & Wilson, B. J. (Eds.), *The*

Handbook of Children, Media, and Development. Malden, MA: Blackwell, pp. 381–406.

Hektner, J. M., Schmidt, J. A., & Csikszentmihalyi, M. (Eds.) (2007). *Experience Sampling Method: Measuring the Quality of Everyday Life.* Thousand Oaks, CA: Sage.

Hillier, L., & Harrison, L. (2007). Building realities less limited than their own: Young people practicing same-sex attraction on the Internet. *Sexualities, 10*, 82–100.

Hubert, M., Bajos, N., & Sanfort, T. (Eds.) (1998). *Sexual Behavior and AIDS in Europe.* London: UCL Press.

Huesmann, L. R. (1988). An information processing model for the development of aggression. *Aggressive Behavior, 14,* 13–24.

Hust, S. J. T., Brown, J. D., & L' Engle, K. L. (2008). Boys will be boys and girls better be prepared: An analysis of the rare sexual health messages in young adolescents' media. *Mass Communication & Society, 11*(1), 1–21.

Iannotta, J. G. (2008). Regulating the media: Sexually explicit content. In Calvert, S. L., & Wilson, B. J. (Eds.), *The Handbook of Children, Media, and Development.* Malden, MA: Blackwell, pp. 479–502.

Impett, E. A., Schooler, D., & Tolman, D. L. (2006). To be seen and not heard: femininity ideology and adolescent girls' sexual health. *Archives of Sexual Behavior, 35*(2), 129–142.

IOM (Institute of Medicine), & NRC (National Research Council) 2011. *The Science of Adolescent Risk-Taking: Workshop Report.* Committee on the Science of Adolescence. Washington, DC: The National Academies Press.

Irving, L. M., & Berel, S. R. (2001). Comparison of media-literacy programs to strengthen college women's resistance to media images. *Psychology of Women Quarterly, 25*(2), 103–111.

Ivory, H. A., Gibson, R., & Ivory, J. D. (2009). Gendered relationships on television: portrayals of same-sex and heterosexual couples. *Mass Communication & Society, 12*(2), 170–192.

Ivory, J. D. (2006). Still a man's game: Gender representation in online reviews of video games. *Mass Communication & Society, 9*, 103–114.

Jeong, S. H., & Fishbein, M. (2007). Predictors of multitasking with media: Media factors and audience factors. *Media Psychology, 10*(3), 364–384.

Jeong, S. H., Hwang, Y., & Fishbein, M. (2010). Effects of exposure to sexual content in the media on adolescent sexual behaviors: The moderating role of multitasking with media. *Media Psychology, 13*(3), 222–242.

Johnson, K. R., & Holmes, B. M. (2009). Contradictory messages: A content analysis of Hollywood-produced romantic comedy feature films. *Communication Quarterly, 57*(3), 352–373.

Jones, R. (2008). Soap opera video on handheld computers to reduce young urban women's HIV sex risk. *AIDS and Behavior, 12*(6):876–884.

Kaiser Family Foundation (2004). *About Viacom: KNOW HIV/ AIDS.* Retrieved May 24, 2011 from http://www.kff.org/ entpartnerships/viacom/index.cfm.

Katchadourian, H. (1990). Sexuality. In Feldman, S. S., & Elliott, G. R. (Eds.), *At the Threshold: The Developing Adolescent.* Cambridge, MA: Harvard University Press, pp. 330–351.

Kelly, A. E., & Rodriguez, R. R. (2006). Publicly committing oneself to an identity. *Basic and Applied Social Psychology, 28,* 185–191.

Kelly, M. (2010). Virginity loss narratives in "teen drama" television programs. *Journal of Sex Research, 47*(5), 479–489.

Kim, J. L., Collins, R. L., Kanouse, D. E., Elliott, M. N., Berry, S. H., Hunter, S. B., Miu, A., & Kunkel, D. (2006). Sexual readiness, household policies, and other predictors of adolescents' exposure to sexual content in mainstream entertainment television. *Media Psychology, 8*(4), 449–471.

Kim, J. L., Sorsoli, C. L., Collins, K., Zylbergold, B. A., Schooler, D., & Tolman, D. L. (2007). From sex to sexuality: Exposing the heterosexual script on primetime network television. *Journal of Sex Research, 44*(2), 145–157.

Knobloch-Westerwick, S., & Romero, J. P. (2011). Body ideals in the media: Perceived attainability and social comparison choices. *Media Psychology, 14*(1), 27–48.

Knowles, E. S., & Linn, J. A. (2004). The importance of resistance to persuasion. In Knowles, E. S., & Linn, J. A. (Eds.), *Resistance and persuasion.* Hillsdale, NJ: Lawrence Erlbaum Associates, pp. 3–11.

Kolbe, R. H., & Albanese, P. J. (1996). Man to man: A content analysis of sole-male images in male-audience magazines. *Journal of Advertising, 25*(4), 1–20.

Kunkel, D., Eyal., K., Finnerty, K., Biely, & Donnerstein, D. (2005). *Sex on TV 4: A biennial report to the Kaiser Family Foundation.* Menlo Park, CA: Kaiser Family Foundation.

Kupersmidt, J. B., Scull, T. M., & Austin, E. W. (2010). Media literacy education for elementary school substance use prevention: Study of media detective. *Pediatrics, 126*(3), 525–531.

Lang, A. (2000). The limited capacity model of mediated message processing. *Journal of Communication, 50*, 46–70.

Leary, M. R. (1995). *Self-Presentation: Impression Management and Interpersonal Behavior.* Madison, WI: Brown & Benchmark.

L' Engle, K., Brown, J., Romocki, L., & Kenneavy, K. (May, 2007). *Adolescents' Sexual Self-Concepts and Media Use Patterns: Implications for Sexual Health Communication.* Presented at the International Communication Association Conference.

L'Engle, K. L., Pardun, C. J., & Brown, J. D. (2004). Accessing adolescents: A school-recruited home-based approach to conducting media and health research. *Journal of Early Adolescence, 24*(2), 144–158.

Lenhart, A., Purcell, K., Smith, A., & Zickuhr, K. (2010). *Social Media and Mobile Internet Use Among Teens and Young Adults.* Washington, DC: Pew Internet and American Life Project.

Levine, D., McCright, J., Dobkin, L., Woodruff, A. J., & Klausner, J. D. (2008). SEXINFO: A sexual health text messaging service for San Francisco youth. *American Journal of Public Health, 98*(3), 393–395.

Lightfoot, M., Comulada, W. S., & Stover, G. (2007). Computerized HIV preventive intervention for adolescents: Indications of efficacy. *American Journal of Public Health, 97*(6), 1027–1030.

Liu, H. (2007). Social network profiles as taste performances. *Journal of Computer-Mediated Communication, 13,* 252–275.

López-Guimerà, G., Levine, M. P., Sánchez-Carracedo, D., & Fauquet, J. (2010). Influence of mass media on body image and eating disordered attitudes and behaviors in females: a review of effects and processes. *Media Psychology, 13,* 387–416.

MacKay, N. J., & Covell, K. (1997). The impact of women in advertisements on attitudes toward women. *Sex Roles, 36*(9–10), 573–583.

MacKinnon, D. P. (2008). *Introduction to Statistical Mediation Analysis.* Hillsdale, NJ: Lawrence Erlbaum Associates.

Manago, A. M., Graham, M. B., Greenfield, P. M., & Salimkhan, G. (2008). Self-presentation and gender on MySpace. *Journal of Applied Developmental Psychology, 29*, 446–458.

Martino, S., Collins, R., Elliot, M., Strachman, A., Kanouse, D., & Berry, S. (2006). Exposure to degrading versus non-degrading music lyrics and sexual behavior among youth. *Pediatrics, 118*, 430–444.

Martino, S., Collins, R., Kanouse, D., Elliott, M., & Berry, S. (2005). Social cognitive processes mediating the relationship between exposure to television's sexual content and adolescents' sexual behavior. *Journal of Personality & Social Psychology, 89*(6), 914–924.

McKenna, K. Y. A., & Bargh, J. A. (1998). Coming out in the age of the Internet: Identity "demarginalization" through virtual group participation. *Journal of Personality and Social Psychology, 75*, 681–694.

Milbrath, C., Ohlson, B., & Eyre, S. L. (2009). Analyzing cultural models in adolescent accounts of romantic relationships. *Journal of Research on Adolescence, 19*(2), 313–351.

Mond, J., van den Berg, P., Boutelle, K., Hannan, P., & Neumark-Sztainer, D. (2011). Obesity, body dissatisfaction, and emotional well-being in early and late adolescence: findings from the project EAT study. *Journal of Adolescent Health, 48*(4), 373–378.

Moreno, M. A., VanderStoep, A., Parks, M. R., Zimmerman, F. J., Kurth, A., & Christakis, A. (2009). Reducing at-risk adolescents' display of risk behavior on a social networking web site: A randomized controlled pilot intervention trial. *Archives of Pediatrics & Adolescent Medicine, 163*(1):35–41.

Moyer-Gusé, E. (2008). Toward a theory of entertainment persuasion: Explaining the persuasive effects of entertainment-education messages. *Communication Theory, 18*(3), 407–425.

Moyer-Gusé, E., & Nabi, R. (2010). Explaining the effects of narrative in an entertainment television program: Overcoming resistance to persuasion. *Human Communication Research, 36*(1), 26–52.

Murphy, S. T., Frank, L. B., Moran, M. B., & Woodley, P. (2001). Involved, Transported, or Emotional? Exploring the Determinants of Change in Knowledge, Attitudes, and Behavior in Entertainment Education. *Journal of Communication, 61*, 407–431.

National Campaign to Prevent Teen and Unplanned Pregnancy (2010). Evaluating the impact of MTV's 16 and pregnant on teen viewers' attitudes about teen pregnancy. *Science Says, 45*, 1–5.

Noar, S. M., Palmgreen, P., Chabot, M., Dobransky, N., & Zimmerman, R. S. (2009). A 10-year systematic review of HIV/AIDS mass communication campaigns: Have we made progress? *Journal of Health Communication, 14*(1), 15–42.

Noar, S. M., Pierce, L. B., & Black, H. G. (2010). Can computer-mediated interventions change theoretical mediators of safer sex? A meta-analysis. *Human Communication Research, 36*(3), 261–297.

Noll, J. G., Shenk, C. E., Barnes, J. E., & Putnam, F. W. (2009). Childhood abuse, avatar choices, and other risk factors associated with Internet-initiated victimization of adolescent girls. *Pediatrics, 123*, 1078–1083.

Norris, M. L., Boydell, K. M. Pinhas, L., & Katzman, D. K. (2006). Ana and the Internet: A review of pro-anorexia websites. *International Journal of Eating Disorders, 39*(6), 443–447.

Optenet (2010). *More than one third of web pages are pornographic*. Retrieved May 24, 2011 from http://www.optenet.com/en-us/new.asp?id=270.

Pardun, C. J., L'Engle, K. L., & Brown, J. D. (2005). Linking exposure to outcomes: early adolescents' consumption of sexual content in six media. *Mass Communication and Society, 8*(2), 75–91.

Peter, J., & Valkenburg, P. M. (2008). Adolescents' exposure to sexually explicit internet material and sexual preoccupancy: A three-wave panel study. *Media Psychology, 11*(2), 207–234.

Peter, J., & Valkenburg, P. M. (2010). Adolescents' use of sexually explicit internet material and sexual uncertainty: The role of involvement and gender. *Communication Monographs, 77*(3), 357–375.

Peter, J., Valkenburg, P. M., & Schouten, A. P. (2005). Developing a model of adolescent friendship formation on the Internet. *CyberPsychology & Behavior, 8*, 423–430.

Pinkleton, B. E., Austin, E. W., Cohen, M., Chen, Y., & Fitzgerald, E. (2008). Effects of a peer-led media literacy curriculum on adolescents' knowledge and attitudes toward sexual behavior and media portrayals of sex. *Health Communication, 23*(5), 462–472.

Pinkleton, B. E., Austin, E. W., Cohen, M., Miller, A., & Fitzgerald, E. (2007). A statewide evaluation of the effectiveness of media literacy training to prevent tobacco use among adolescents. *Health Communication, 21*(1), 23–34.

Pinquart, M. (2010). Ambivalence in adolescents' decisions about having their first sexual intercourse. *Journal of Sex Research, 47*(5), 440–450.

Polkinghorne, D. E. (2013). Qualitative research and media psychology. In Dill, K. (Ed.), *The Oxford Handbook of Media Psychology*. New York: Oxford University Press.

Popkin, B. (2009). *The world is fat: The fads, trends, policies, and products that are fattening the human race*. New York: Avery/Penguin Group USA.

Primack, B. A., Gold, M. A., Schwarz, E. B., & Dalton, M. A. (2008). Degrading and non-degrading sex in popular music: A content analysis. *Public Health Reports, 123*(5), 593–600.

Rich, A. (1980). Compulsory heterosexuality and lesbian existence. *Journal of Women in Culture and Society, 5*, 631–660.

Rideout, V. (2001). *Generation Rx.com: How young people use the internet for health information*. Menlo Park, CA: The Henry J. Kaiser Family Foundation.

Rideout, V., Foehr, U. G., & Roberts, D. F. (2010). *Generation M2: Media in the lives of 8–18 year-olds*. Menlo Park, CA: The Henry J. Kaiser Family Foundation.

Robinson, T. N., Patrick, K., Eng, T. R., Gustafson, D. (1998). An evidence-based approach to interactive health communication: A challenge to medicine in the Information Age. *Journal of American Medical Association, 280*, 1264–1269

Rogers, E. M. & Storey, J. D. (1987). Communication campaigns. In Berger, C., & Chaffee, S. (Eds.), *Handbook of Communication Science*. Newbury Park, CA: Sage, pp. 817–846.

Rosenthal, D., Moore, S., & Flynn, I. (1991). Adolescent self-efficacy, self-esteem and sexual risk-taking. *Journal of Community and Applied Social Psychology, 1*, 77–88.

Roskos-Ewoldsen, D. R., Roskos-Ewoldsen, B., & Dillman-Carpentier, F. R. (2009). Media priming. An updated synthesis. In Bryant, J., & Oliver, M. B. (Eds.), *Media Effects: Advances in Theory and Research*. New York: Psychology Press, pp. 74–93.

Rubin, A. (1984). Ritualized and instrumental television viewing. *Journal of Communication, 34*(3), 67–77.

Savin-Williams, R. C., & Ream, G. L. (2007). Prevalence and stability of sexual orientation components during adolescence and young adulthood. *Archives of Sexual Behavior, 36,* 385–394.

Scharrer, E. (2004). Virtual violence: Gender and aggression in video game advertisements. *Mass Communication & Society, 7,* 393–412.

Schlenker, B. R. (2005). Self-presentation. In Leary, M. R., & Tangney, J. P. (Eds.), *Handbook of Self and Identity.* New York: Guilford Press, pp. 492–518.

Schouten, A. P., Valkenburg, P. M., & Peter, J. (2008). Precursors and underlying processes of adolescents' online self-disclosure: Developing and testing an "Internet-attribute-perception" model. *Media Psychology, 10,* 292–315.

Segrin, C., & Nabi, R. (2002). Does television viewing cultivate unrealistic expectations about marriage? *Journal of Communication, 52,* 247–263.

Shrum, L. J. (1996). Psychological processes underlying cultivation effects further tests of construct accessibility. *Human Communication Research, 22,* 482–509.

Singhal, A., & Rogers, E. M. (2001). The Entertainment-Education strategy in communication campaigns. In Rice, R. E., & Atkins, C. (Eds.), *Public Communication Campaigns,* 3rd ed. Thousand Oaks, CA: Sage.

Singhal, A., & Rogers, E. M. (2002). A theoretical agenda for entertainment education. *Communication Theory, 12*(2), 117–135.

Slater, M. D. (2007). Reinforcing spirals: The mutual influence of media selectivity and media effects and their impact on individual behavior and social identity. *Communication Theory, 17,* 281–303.

Slater, M. D., Henry, K. L., Swaim, R., & Anderson, L. (2003). Violent media content and aggression in adolescents: A downward-spiral model. *Communication Research, 30,* 713–736.

Slater, M. D., Henry, K. L., Swaim, R. C., & Cardador, J. M. (2004). Vulnerable teens, vulnerable times: How sensation seeking, alienation, and victimization moderate the violent media content-aggressiveness relation. *Communication Research, 31,* 642–668.

Slater, M., & Rouner, D. (2002). Entertainment-education and elaboration likelihood: Understanding the processing of narrative persuasion. *Communication Theory, 12*(2), 173–191.

Snyder, L. B. & Hamilton, M. A. (2002). Meta-analysis of U.S. health campaign effects on behavior: Emphasize enforcement, exposure, and new information, and beware the secular trend. In Hornik, R. (Ed.), *Public Health Communication: Evidence for Behavior Change.* Hillsdale, NJ: Lawrence Erlbaum Associates, pp. 357–383.

Steele, J. (1999). Teenage sexuality and media practice: Factoring in the influences of family, friends and school. *Journal of Sex Research, 36,* 331–341.

Steele, J. R., & Brown, J. D. (1995). Adolescent room culture: Studying media in the context of everyday life. *Journal of Youth & Adolescence, 24*(5), 551–576.

Stokes, C. E. (2007). Representin' in cyberspace: Sexual scripts, self-definition, and hip hop culture in Black American adolescent girls' home pages. *Culture, Health & Sexuality, 9*(2), 169–184.

Subrahmanyam, K., Reich, S. M., Waechter, N., & Espinoza, G. (2008). Online and offline social networks: Use of social networking sites by emerging adults. *Journal of Applied Developmental Psychology, 29,* 420–433.

Taylor, L. D. (2005). Effects of visual and verbal sexual television content and perceived realism on attitudes and beliefs. *Journal of Sex Research, 42,* 130–137.

Toffler, A. (1980). *The Third Wave.* New York: William Morrow and Company.

Tokunaga, R. S. (2010). Following you home from school: A critical review and synthesis of research on cyberbullying victimization. *Computers in Human Behavior, 26,* 277–287.

Tortolero, S. R., Markham, C. M., Peskin, M. F., Shegog, R., Addy, R. C., Escobar- Chaves, S., & Baumler, E. R. (2010). It's your game: Keep it real: Delaying sexual behavior with an effective middle school program. *Journal of Adolescent Health, 46*(2), 169–179.

Udry, J. (1990). Hormonal and social determinants of adolescent sexual initiation. In Bancroft, J., & Reinisch, J. (Eds.), *Adolescence and Puberty.* New York: Oxford University Press, pp. 70–87.

Valkenburg, P. M., & Peter, J. (2009). Social consequences of the Internet for adolescents: A decade of research. *Current Directions in Psychological Science, 18,* 1–5.

Valsiner, J. (1993). Bi-directional cultural transmission and constructive sociogenesis. In Maier, R., & de Graaf, W. (Eds.), *Mechanisms of Sociogenesis.* Springer, New York, pp. 47–70.

Wakefield, M. A., Loken, B., & Hornik, R. C. (2010). Use of mass media campaigns to change health behaviour. *The Lancet, 376*(9748), 1261–1271.

Walther, J. B. (1996). Computer-mediated communication: Impersonal, interpersonal, and hyperpersonal interaction. *Communication Research, 23,* 3–43.

Walther, J. B. (2007). Selective self-presentation in computer-mediated communication: Hyperpersonal dimensions of technology, language, and cognition. *Computers in Human Behavior, 23,* 2538–2557.

Walther, J. B., Liang, Y. J., DeAndrea, D. C., Tong, S. T., Carr, C. T., Spottswood, E. L., et al. (2011). The effect of feedback on identity shift in computer-mediated communication. *Media Psychology, 14,* 1–26.

Walther, J. B., & Parks, M. R. (2002). Cues filtered out, cues filtered in. In Knapp, M. L., & Daly, J. A. (Eds.), *Handbook of Interpersonal Communication.* Thousand Oaks, CA: Sage, pp. 529–563.

Walther, J. B., Van Der Heide, B., Hamel, L., & Shulman, H. C. (2009). Self-generated versus other-generated statements and impressions in computer-mediated communication: A test of warranting theory using Facebook. *Communication Research, 36,* 229–253.

Ward, L. M. (2002). Does television exposure affect emerging adults' attitudes and assumptions about sexual relationships? Correlational and experimental confirmation. *Journal of Youth and Adolescence, 31,* 1–15.

Ward, L. M. (2003). Understanding the role of entertainment media in the sexual socialization of American youth: A review of empirical research. *Developmental Review, 23,* 347–388.

Ward, L. M., Epstein, M., Caruthers, A., & Merriwether, A. (2011). Men's media use, sexual cognitions, and sexual risk behavior: Testing a mediational model. *Developmental Psychology, 47*(2), 592–602.

Ward, L. M., & Friedman, K. (2006). Using TV as a guide: Associations between television viewing and adolescents' sexual attitudes and behavior. *Journal of Research on Adolescence, 16,* 133–156.

Ward, L. M., & Rivadeneyra, R. (1999). Contributions of entertainment television to adolescents' sexual attitudes and expectations: The role of viewing amount versus viewer involvement. *Journal of Sex Research, 36*, 237–249.

Watson, R., & Vaughn, L. M. (2006). Limiting the effects of the media on body image: Does the length of a media literacy intervention make a difference? *Eating Disorders, 14*(5), 385–400.

Wicklund, R. A., & Gollwitzer, P. M. (1982). *Symbolic Self-Completion.* Hillsdale, NJ: Lawrence Erlbaum Associates.

Wingood, G. M., DiClemente, R. J., Bernhardt, J. M., Harrington, K., Davies, S. L., Robillard, A., & Hook, E. W. (2003). A prospective study of exposure to rap music videos and African American female adolescents' health. *American Journal of Public Health, 93*, 437–439.

Wolak, J., Finkelhor, D., Mitchell, K. J., & Ybarra, M. L. (2008). Online "predators" and their victims: Myths, realities, and implications for prevention and treatment. *American Psychologist, 63*, 111–128.

Wolak, J., Mitchell, K. J., & Finkelhor D. (2007). Does online harassment constitute bullying? An exploration of online harassment by known peers and online-only contacts. *Journal of Adolescent Health, 41*, 51–58.

Wright, P. (2011). Mass media effects on youth sexual behavior: Assessing the claim for causality. In Salmon, C. T. (Ed.), *Communication Yearbook.* New York: Routledge Press, pp. 343–386.

Yager, Z., & O'Dea, J. A. (2008). Prevention programs for body image and eating disorders on University campuses: A review of large, controlled interventions. *Health Promotion International, 23*(2), 173–189.

Ybarra, M. L., & Mitchell, K. J. (2005). Exposure to Internet pornography among children and adolescents: A national survey. *CyberPsychology & Behavior, 8*, 437–486.

Ybarra, M. L., Mitchell, K. J., Hamburger, M., Diener-West, M., & Leaf, P. J. (2011). X-rated material and perpetration of sexually aggressive behavior among children and adolescents: Is there a link? *Aggressive Behavior, 37*, 1–18.

Yee, N., & Bailenson, J. (2007). The Proteus Effect: The effect of transformed self-representation on behavior. *Human Communication Research, 33*, 271–290.

Yee, N., Bailenson, J. N., & Duchenaut, N. (2009). The Proteus Effect: Implications of transformed digital self-representation on online and offline behavior. *Communication Research, 36*, 285–312.

Zimmerman, R. S., Palmgreen, P. M., Noar, S. M., Lustria, M. A., Hung-Yi, H., & Horosewski, M. (2007). Effects of a televised two-city safer sex mass media campaign targeting high-sensation-seeking and impulsive-decision-making young adults. *Health Education & Behavior, 34*(5), 810–826.

Zurbriggen, E. L., & Morgan, E. M. (2006). Who wants to marry a millionaire? Reality dating television programs, attitudes toward sex, and sexual behaviors. *Sex Roles, 54*, 1–17.

Race, Ethnicity, and the Media

Elizabeth Behm-Morawitz *and* Michelle Ortiz

Abstract

This chapter charts the historical development as well as key findings of media psychology research examining the representations of racial/ethnic minorities in the media and the subsequent effects of exposure to these portrayals. A special effort is made by the authors to document the perspectives used to date to understand such effects, as well as to draw on psychology research that has yet to be applied in this domain. Additionally, suggestions are made for advancing this research both theoretically and methodologically and in light of the new media environment.

Key Words: race, ethnicity, media effects, intergroup, stereotyping

Introduction

Portrayals of racial/ethnic minority groups in US media have been shown to influence viewers' cognitions of these groups. Historically represented in stereotypical ways, portrayals of racial/ethnic minority groups have relatively recently come to the attention of scholars. The present chapter summarizes the findings of the effects that these portrayals have on viewers' beliefs about, and behaviors toward, members of these groups. Discussion of the effects of portrayals is grounded in empirical findings as well as theoretical frameworks from psychology, communication, and sociology. In addition, theories and concepts that have yet to be extended to this line of research but nonetheless offer unique insight into the portrayals' likely effects on viewers are discussed. Before discussion of the effects, the chapter presents a summary of the representation of racial/ethnic minority groups in US media.

Media Representations of Race/Ethnicity

Intergroup research suggests that people engage in social categorization and often use stereotypes to negatively judge others who do not share similar social group memberships (e.g., race/ethnicity) to reinforce the status quo and/or preserve a positive identity (Tajfel & Turner, 1979, 1986). Racial/ethnic stereotypes may be applied to justify existing social hierarchies and rules (Crandall & Eshleman, 2003). Mass media, as cultural storytellers, serve as widely available and shared sources of stereotype information. Historically, minorities have been underrepresented, stereotyped, and sometimes completely erased from US media. These portrayals have shifted over time, alongside the sociocultural environment; however, inequities and negative characterizations continue to plague racial/ethnic minorities in the United States. Even as some minority groups gain wider representation in entertainment television, they are still criminalized in news and largely absent from newer media representations, such as video games. Traditionally, analysis of racial/ethnic representation in the media has been made using comparisons of minority groups to the dominant racial group (whites). Additionally, most work analyzes groups in isolation, rather than examining the social interaction between members of different racial and ethnic groups in the media.

Black Representations

Arguably, the bulk of the content analytic research examining representations of race/ethnicity in US media has focused on television. This research has investigated such representations in three contexts: entertainment programming, news, and advertising. The most studied minority group appearing with the most frequency on television is blacks. Blacks constitute approximately 13% of the real-world population (US Census 2010) and 14% to 17% of the characters in the prime time television population (Mastro & Greenberg, 2000; Children Now, 2001, 2004; Mastro & Behm-Morawitz, 2005). Overall, blacks are the only racial/ethnic minority group that is proportionally represented, and in some cases "overrepresented," on US prime time television in relation to real-world population statistics.

Despite achieving parity in frequency of representation in entertainment media relative to US Census figures, it is important to note that blacks have historically been underrepresented and subject to problematic portrayals in the media. Television, film, and radio alike have a history of representing blacks in roles that serve to perpetuate and perhaps increase negative stereotyping of this cultural group (Cummings, 1988). Indeed, entertainment television, films, and radio programs similarly depicted blacks rather unfavorably and in subordinate roles to white characters. When examining the intersection of gender with portrayals of blackness, different images emerge for black women and men in these entertainment media. Notable historic media characterizations of black women include the "Black Mammy," a friendly, faithful, self-sacrificing, and asexual servant to white characters, the "Jezebel," a lighter complexioned, highly sexualized, and sexually aggressive competitor for white male attention, and the "Sapphire," the typification of the stereotype of the angry black female (Jewell, 1993). Black males, on the other hand, have traditionally been depicted as servants, buffoons, and criminals (Greenberg, Mastro, & Brand, 2002).

In the present day, entertainment media representations of blacks have arguably improved and departed from these historical roles. On prime time television, for example, black women are likely to inhabit professional roles and be represented as intelligent, motivated, and as having equal status with white women (Mastro & Behm-Morawitz, 2005). Black men, too, most often appear in moderate to high status roles on prime time television, and are depicted as being hard-working and intelligent. Representations of black men on entertainment television have moved away from the stereotype of the criminal, a deviant, aggressive, and dangerous individual (Mastro & Behm-Morawitz, 2005). This shift in representations of blacks in US entertainment media, particularly television, demonstrates a turn to promotion of a more "embraceable" (Page, 1997) and authoritative image of the black American.

This image of blacks in entertainment television, however, strongly contrasts with patterns of representation in television news. Generally, in local news broadcasts blacks are overrepresented as criminals and underrepresented as victims of crime in comparison with real-world crime statistics (Dixon & Linz, 2002; Dixon, Azocar, & Casas, 2003). Additionally, black suspects are more likely to have their picture shown in accompaniment of the coverage of a crime than are white suspects (Entman, 1992). So, although entertainment programming is no longer as reliant on the image of the black (male) criminal, news representations may continue to promote the stereotype of the black criminal by providing undue focus on black suspects in comparison with white suspects. Moreover, there are potentially problematic outcomes of the contrast between the image of the successful black American in entertainment programming and this image of the low class, criminal black American in local news programming. It is argued that the bifurcation of the image of blacks in the media (Shanahan & Morgan, 1999) may promote the sentiment that black Americans have every possibility of success today, and failure to achieve such success is attributable to internal flaws of the members of the cultural group who do not "make it" in America.

Additionally, scholars have examined black representation in sports and advertising. Analysis of sports commentators' mediated discourse about black versus white athletes reveals that commentators use different adjectives to describe athletes based on the race of the athlete and sometimes express assumptions that differences in athletic performance are a result of inherent racial differences (Davis, 1990; Rada, 1997; Rada & Wulfemeyer, 2005). In terms of television advertising, blacks have recently been depicted in numbers that approximate or exceed their real-world US population numbers and in a wide variety of roles (Mastro & Stern, 2003); however, they are not as likely to be shown as spokespeople or active leaders in comparison with whites (Li-Vollmer, 2002).

Last, a small number of studies have examined the representation of blacks in video games. Generally, blacks are not depicted as frequently or favorably in video games as they are in television and film. Indeed, blacks make up only about 7% to 10% of characters represented in popular video games and video game magazines (Behm-Morawitz, 2008; Williams, Martins, Consalvo, & Ivory, 2009; Burgess et al., 2011), in comparison with 14% to 17% of prime time television characters. Additionally, research suggests that representations of black males in video games adhere more closely to historic representations of the black male criminal and the athlete, whereas black females are nearly absent altogether (Glaubke, Miller, Parker, & Espejo, 2001; Burgess et al., 2011).

Latino Representations

Latinos are the largest and fastest growing minority group in the United States, yet remain the most underrepresented minority group on prime time television. Latinos make up approximately 16% of the US population (US Census Data, 2010) but only 2% to 5% of the prime time television population (Mastro & Greenberg, 2000; Mastro & Behm-Morawitz, 2005). Overall, research indicates that the portrayals of Latinos on prime time television are less favorable than their white and black counterparts (Greenberg et al., 2002; Mastro & Behm-Morawitz, 2005). Further, unlike blacks, Latinos continue to be stereotypically presented. Historically, Latinos have been presented as: the "Latin Lover" (male) and "Harlot," who are sexualized, fiery, and sexually aggressive characters; the (male) criminal, who is deviant, slovenly, and dangerous; and the buffoon, who is unintelligent, disrespected, and lazy (Ramirez Berg, 1990; Greenberg et al., 2002). Current entertainment television representations adhere to the stereotype of the Latin Lover/Harlot and buffoon but the image of the young Latino criminal has diminished in the 21st century (Mastro & Behm-Morawitz, 2005).

In the news media, Latinos are likely to appear as criminals; however, unlike blacks, not at a rate that is disproportionate to real-world crime figures (Dixon & Linz, 2000; Mastro & Greenberg, 2000). What is problematic is the paucity of other roles for Latinos in the news to balance this portrayal. Additionally, heightened US political attention to the issue of illegal immigration has resulted in what is likely an increase in portrayal of Latinos (as a group) as poor, dangerous, and criminal in the news (Streitmatter, 1999; Ono & Sloop, 2002; Stewart, Pitts, & Osborne, 2011). Research suggests that this news coverage constructs them as dissimilar to other Americans and a threat to the American way of life (Stewart, Pitts, & Osborne, 2011).

When examining Latinos in video games, they appear very infrequently, in only 1% to 3% of video games and advertisements (Behm-Morawitz, 2008; Williams et al., 2009). Because Latinos appear in such small numbers in video games, it has not been possible to meaningfully quantitatively analyze these portrayals in terms of embodied roles and characteristics.

Asian Representations

Asians are the third largest US minority group, making up 4.8% of the population (US Census, 2010); however, Asians account for only 1% to 3% of television characters (Children Now, 2001, 2004; Mastro & Behm-Morawitz, 2005). Further, Asian characters that do appear are sometimes played by white rather than Asian actors (Iiyama & Kitano, 1982; Aucion, 2010). Recent examples of this are non-Asian actors being cast to play primary Asian characters in the films *Avatar: The Last Airbender* (2010) and *The Weapon* (2012).

Given the infrequency with which Asians appear in the media, little content analytical work has examined media imagery of this minority group. Instead, what we do know about Asian representations in US media has largely taken a critical approach. This research suggests Asians have historically been portrayed as villains in US films, particularly so at times of heightened political tension between the US and Asian countries (Harris, 2004). The stereotype of the villain is characterized by a devious nature, intelligence, and martial arts skills. The Asian male villain is typically asexual and not depicted as desirable; however, the Asian female villain (the "Dragon Lady") is exoticized and presented as a sexually desirable but dangerous being (Sheridan, 2005; Park, Gabbadon, & Chernin, 2006). Additionally, Asian women are more likely to appear as passive, emotional, and irrational than Asian men and their white and black counterparts in the media (Harris, 2004).

For Asians, roles in video games appear to mirror those in film and television. Specifically, research suggests that the stereotype of the Asian villain (in the form of the ninja) is present in video game imagery (Behm-Morawitz, 2008; Burgess, Dill, Stermer, Burgess, & Brown, 2011). Additionally, likely because of the strong Asian influence in the global video gaming industry, Asians appear in greater numbers than they do on television. Asians make up approximately 5% to 7% of video game characters appearing in popular games and advertisements in the United States (Behm-Morawitz, 2008; Williams et al., 2009).

Last, in television advertising, Asians are most often shown in professional settings and dressed in conservative attire (Mastro & Stern, 2003). They are also more likely than their white, black, and Latino counterparts to appear in technology advertisements (Mastro & Stern, 2003). In magazine advertising, research (e.g., Lee & Joo, 2005; Knobloch-Westerwick & Coates, 2006) suggests that Asian Americans are depicted as models in approximately 3% to 8% of ads in popular magazines, appearing most often in ads for tech-related products and are typically featured in business settings. These representations may be deemed to be consistent with the "model minority" stereotype of Asian Americans, which is characterized by intelligence, academic and professional success, and a reserved and more passive demeanor. Although this is arguably a more positive representation than that of the criminal or buffoon, for example, it may still be problematic. Namely, the model minority stereotype is thought to put undue pressure on Asian Americans to succeed and may perpetuate the idea that Asian Americans do not face problems such as employment, health, and housing in the United States (NAAPIMHA, 2010).

Native American Representations

Little research has examined Native American representation because of the infrequency with which they appear in the media. This group, however, is not underrepresented in the media. Native Americans make up less than 1% of the US population (US Census, 2010) and less than 1% of US television (Mastro & Behm-Morawitz, 2005) and video game (Behm-Morawitz, 2008; Williams et al., 2009) characters. Most of what we do know about the representation of Native Americans in US media comes from the few but memorable portrayals in cartoons and films. Largely, these few representations in entertainment media have not been very favorable. Rarely do we see contemporary representations of Native Americans—instead, most portrayals are historical representations (Bird, 1996, 1999; Merskin, 1998). Two contrasting images of the Native American dominate entertainment media. First, the stereotype of the savage is common, depicting Native Americans as animalistic, aggressive, and uncivilized (Bird, 1999; Harris, 2004). Second, Native Americans are constructed as being wise, connected to nature, and kind (Bird,

1996, 1999). What is common across these two stereotypes, however, is the presentation of Native Americans as being historic peoples and dissimilar from other Americans.

Middle Eastern Representations

A relatively new area of examination is the analysis of Middle Easterners in US media. Mostly, this research has noted the portrayal of Middle Eastern men as terrorists in the news and entertainment media. Again, because of US politics and world events, there has been a heightened focus on Middle Easterners as terrorists, particularly in news media (Wilkins, 1995; Steet, 2000; McConnell, 2003). Cho et al. (2003) content analyzed television and newspaper news about terrorist attacks and found that television had significantly higher narrative emotionality in comparison with newspaper reporting. Similarly, Gadarian (2010) suggests that since 9/11, US news media—television news, in particular—have increased the practice of presenting "threatening information and evocative imagery" (p. 469) to cover issues related to foreign policy involving Middle Easterners. Threat and fear are thus strongly linked to representations of Middle Easterners in contemporary US news media. In entertainment, Hollywood films have historically relied on images of Middle Eastern persons for depiction of terrorists (Shaheen, 2001), and recently the tie between the image of Middle Eastern people and terrorism has become further cemented through representations in post-9/11 films (Dodds, 2008). Similar images appear in action-oriented (e.g., first-person shooter) video games, with Arabs and Muslims depicted as dangerous and violent enemies (Šisler, 2008).

Effects of Media Representations of Race/Ethnicity

Research has shown that there is a significant relationship between exposure to racial/ethnic portrayals in the media and audience evaluations of race/ethnicity in terms of social roles (Atkin, Greenberg, & McDermont, 1983), pro-minority policies (Ramasubramanian, 2010), and stereotype consistent race-related attitudes and beliefs (Ford, 1997; Mastro, 2003; Oliver, Jackson, Moses, & Dangerfield, 2004; Dixon & Maddox, 2005; Mastro, Tamborini, & Hullett, 2005; Dixon, 2006a, 2006b; Mastro, Behm-Morawitz, & Ortiz, 2007). This scholarship examines the potential for the media to affect prejudicial attitudes and beliefs. Additionally, some research suggests media representations of race/ethnicity may be influential on individuals' behaviors and self-concept. Most of this research has focused on the influence of media representations of blacks, to the exclusion of other minority groups. Additionally, this body of literature most often examines the impact of this media imagery on whites (the dominant group), rather than on minority group members.

Effects on Prejudicial Attitudes and Beliefs

First, research suggests that exposure to media stereotypes of racial/ethnic minorities may increase individuals' propensity for making prejudicial real-world judgments of these groups. Most of the scholarship within this relatively young and small body of literature examines the short-term effects of exposure to media stereotypes on individuals' race-based attitudes and beliefs. From the media priming perspective, the racial/ethnic stereotypes that one has stored in memory are activated on exposure to media stereotypes, and these cognitions are then made more available for use in making judgments about those groups.

An early study taking this approach is Ford's (1997) examination of the effect of viewing stereotypic portrayals of blacks in television comedy skits on subsequent judgments of a black suspect's guilt. Individuals who viewed the stereotypical skit reported higher guilt ratings of the black suspect in comparison with those that viewed a neutral media stimulus. Such research demonstrates the potential for media primes to activate racial/ethnic stereotypes, such as that of the black male criminal, and suggests that racial/ethnic media representations impact our judgments of others. This research predominantly examines the impact of minority portrayals in the media on white audiences, based on the assumption that media depictions of minorities may be more impactful on those who are not a member of the group. Additionally, it is argued that examination of the influence of racial/ethnic media stereotypes on whites is particularly important in the US context given than whites remain the dominant group and are, therefore, more likely to be afforded the opportunity to serve in high status roles that affect the well-being of minority members of society. Thus, scholars have focused research on understanding how media imagery may affect whites' attitudes and beliefs about minority groups, at the expense of examining the effects of media on minorities' perceptions of selves and others.

Similar results to the Ford (1997) study have been found in the context of television news, indicating that the presentation of blacks as criminals in local news may, under some conditions, produce less egalitarian judgments of blacks and harsher sentencing for black defendants by white individuals (Peffley, Shields, & Williams, 1996; Dixon & Maddox, 2005; Mastro, Lapinski, Kopacz, & Behm-Morawitz, 2009). Research suggests that the skin tone of the suspect depicted in the news (Dixon & Maddox, 2005) as well as the race of the viewer (Gilliam & Iyengar, 2000; Tamborini, Huang, Mastro, & Nabashi-Nakahara, 2007) impacts the effect of such representations on individuals' cognitions. More recently, a relationship between exposure to images of Middle Easterners in US news media and less favorable real-world attitudes and beliefs about this group has been established. This relationship may be explained by the fear-evoking, emotionally charged nature of news reporting that uses images of foreigners such as Middle Easterners (Das et al., 2009; Gadarian, 2010). For example, Das et al. (2009) observed that exposure to terrorism news stories heightened prejudice toward Arabs, with increased death-related thoughts serving as the explanatory link between news exposure and real-world attitudes.

Preliminary work suggests that similar effects may also occur from exposure to racial/ethnic stereotypes in video games. Like studies using television and film clips as stimuli, Burgess et al. (2011) found that exposure to recordings of video game content consistent with the stereotype of the black criminal resulted in increased racial stereotyping. When examining the effects of game play, Behm-Morawitz and Chen (unpublished) experimentally demonstrated that playing a black criminal character in a gang-based, action video game predicted an increase in white college students' negative evaluations of blacks. Thus, taking on the role of the stereotyped character did not mitigate negative effects; identification with the video game character had no bearing on subsequent race-based attitudes. These studies suggest that video games may have effects on racial/ethnic attitudes and beliefs that are analogous to the effects other media such as television and film.

Further, exposure to stereotypes of minorities in the media may result in negative real-world judgments that deviate from the media stereotype but are representative of other minority stereotypes (Givens & Monahan, 2005; Mastro et al., 2009). This occurs through the process of spreading activation (Collins & Loftus, 1975). For example, exposure to the media stereotype of the "Lazy Latino" may make salient additional Latino stereotypes (e.g., the Latin Lover) that are distinct from, but cognitively linked to, this stereotype. As a result, additional negative judgments may be made about a representative of this group following exposure to a single media stereotype.

Beyond a priming approach that assumes that prejudicial responses result from media portrayals activating *preexisting* racial/ethnic stereotypes, other theoretical approaches suggest that the media play a role not only in triggering stereotypes, but in creating them. From a mental models perspective (e.g., Shrum, 1996; Mastro, Behm-Morawitz, & Ortiz, 2007), exposure to media stereotypes may create and shape the cognitive structures one has about a racial/ethnic group. Unlike priming, this framework acknowledges that media messages can generate new cognitions as well as change and activate existing stereotypes. This may be a more appropriate psychological explanation for the impact of media portrayals on race-related attitudes and beliefs when trying to understand how media produce as well as modify stereotypes, rather than simply activate them (Mastro et al., 2007). Although not often cited in media effects research, psychology research on prototypes and exemplars may help to explain the role of media in the process of stereotype activation and creation.

Prototypes are abstract models of memory, or more specifically, "a set of features commonly associated with members of a category (hence, abstracted from experience)" (Cohen & Basu, 1987, p. 458). In the case of cognitive processing of racial/ethnic groups, a prototype would provide individuals with a generalization consisting of de-individuating information that could be applied when making judgments about a person who is determined to be a member of that group. A related but distinct concept is that of the exemplar. Exemplars are specific examples of a categorical group that are used as a basis for comparison when making judgments about a member of the group; assessments may be made in terms of how closely the member fits with the individual exemplars stored in memory (Cohen & Basu, 1987). Application of these models of memory to understanding media creation and activation of stereotypes would provide more specificity in how media representations are used to make judgments of others.

Additionally, individual differences in real-world contact with racial/ethnic groups should be considered in this research. The influence of media stereotypes of racial/ethnic groups on individuals' attitudes and beliefs is thought to be more impactful the less real-world contact one has with a minority group. Based on intergroup contact theory (Allport, 1954; Pettigrew, 1997, 1998), greater interpersonal experience with members of a minority group, and the more positive that contact, the less influence negative media stereotypes will have on one's judgments. Conversely, little and/or poor relations with a minority group may heighten the reliance on media stereotypes as a source of information for making real-world race-related judgments (Mastro et al., 2007; Ortiz & Harwood, 2007).

In addition to these lines of research, the psychology literature on stereotyping offers up other potential explanations for the effects of media representations on attitudes and beliefs about racial/ethnic minority groups. Namely, heuristic processing and the illusory correlation are relevant to the present topic. First, heuristic processing may aid in explaining the observed priming effects discussed in the preceding. Media stereotypes may be used as heuristics for making quick judgments about minorities, particularly in situations in which information load is high and individuals may be less able and/or less motivated to carefully process race-related information (Tamborini et al., 2007; Mastro, 2009). Second, although the portrayal of most racial/ethnic minority groups in US media is infrequent, research on the illusory correlation suggests that the mere scarcity of minority media representations may increase stereotyping of these groups (Chapman, 1967; Sanbonmatsu, Smittipatana, Shavitt, & Posavac, 1999). In cases in which an individual is exposed to few portrayals of a group (i.e., the minority group) in comparison to another group (i.e., the majority group), one may overestimate the negative characteristics of the minority group even when the presentation of those groups in the media are characteristically similar other than the frequency of portrayal.

This phenomenon, called *illusory correlation* (Chapman, 1967), suggests that the underrepresentation of minority groups in US media would increase stereotyping, even regardless of the equity of the portrayals in terms of roles, characteristics, and so on. The illusory correlation, then, might be particularly applicable when examining racial/ethnic groups that have seen improvement in the diversity but not necessarily frequency of media representation. Most notably, the effects of exposure to portrayals of blacks in US entertainment television programming may be interesting to examine from this lens. For example, although blacks no longer seem to be overrepresented as criminals on television in comparison with whites, the diminished number of black characters in comparison with white characters may result in viewers' incorrectly associating the minority group (blacks) with criminal behavior (a memorable and less common behavior in comparison with other more mundane occurrences). Because we infrequently see minority characters, in comparison with their white counterparts, we may incorrectly assume a relationship between this relatively unique group and behavior when, in fact, a significant relationship does not actually exist. The illusory correlation phenomenon suggests that in addition to achieving more favorable representations in the media, it may be important to continue to simply increase minority media presence. Therefore, frequency of minority portrayal in the media becomes important to combating real-world prejudice.

Research on vividness lends additional explanation for the impact of infrequent but memorable media content, such as racial/ethnic minority representations. Vivid information is thought to often garner more attention, be more readily accessible for decision making, and generally be more influential on individuals' attitudes and beliefs (Nisbett & Ross, 1980; Taylor & Thompson, 1982). Thus, vividness of media messages may contribute to stereotyping (O'Neill, 2000). Media images of minorities may be particularly vivid, resulting in greater attention to and cognitive storage of these representations, which makes them impactful on attitudes and beliefs despite their infrequency of appearance in the media (Nisbett & Ross, 1980; Mastro et al., 2007).

In addition to producing short-term effects, racial/ethnic media representations are thought to have long-term effects on how people view others. Most often, long-term media effects on attitudes and beliefs are studied through the lens of cultivation theory (Gerbner et al., 2002). For example, Armstrong, Neuendorf, and Brentar (1992) found that heavy television news consumption was associated with negative judgments of blacks among young white viewers.

Taken together, this literature demonstrates that racial/ethnic media stereotypes negatively influence the judgments of guilt and punishment for black defendants (Dixon & Maddox, 2005; Dixon, 2006b; Mastro et al., 2009), policy beliefs (Dixon, 2006a; Mastro & Kopacz, 2006), and stereotyping (Oliver, Jackson, Moses, & Dangerfield, 2004; Dixon 2006a; Mastro et al., 2009).

PROSOCIAL EFFECTS

In addition to this demonstration of the influence of race/ethnicity media representations on negative evaluations of minority groups, there is some limited support for the idea that exposure to counter-stereotypes, or positive portrayals of these groups, may positively impact race-related judgments.

For example, Bodenhausen, Schwarz, Bless, and Wanke (1995) and Ramasubramanian (2010) found that exposure to positive exemplars of black celebrities produced increased sympathy for pro-minority policy. However, positive exemplars that do not coalesce with racial/ethnic stereotypes may decrease the likelihood that individuals will readily categorize those exemplars as being members of the minority group (Richeson & Trawalter, 2005). A process called *subtyping* may occur, in which persons who violate the stereotype are grouped into a sub-category, and the original stereotype persists (Taylor, 1981; Hewstone, 1994; Maurer, Park, & Rothbart, 1995). Thus, cognitive distancing of these counter-stereotypical exemplars from the mental constructions of the minority group may diminish the potential for media to positively impact race-related attitudes and beliefs. However, it is not unreasonable to assume that, over time, repeated exposure to such positive representations may alter one's mental model of a racial/ethnic group such that it is adapted to account for these positive portrayals.

Effects on Prejudicial Behaviors

Research on the effects of mediated portrayals on behaviors, although rare, has shown that portrayals of racial/ethnic groups have the potential to influence behavior. These studies have examined the effects of exposure to group portrayals at the aggregate level as well as the effects of exposure to specific portrayals. One line of research has focused on viewers' evaluations of portrayals of Latinos and blacks in relation to white portrayals (Mastro & Kopacz, 2006; Ramasubramanian, 2010). According to this research, portrayals of racial/ethnic groups become incorporated into viewers' intergroup cognitions of these groups in the real-world. Specifically, the more discrepant normative outgroup portrayals are seen from white normative portrayals (i.e., less prototypical of the ingroup), the more likely white viewers are to endorse crime- and laziness-related stereotypes for these groups in the real world. Tests of these models have shown that perceptions of black (Tan, Fujioka, & Tan, 2000) and Latino (Mastro & Kopacz, 2006) portrayals not only predict real-world stereotypes of these groups, but ultimately predict opposition to affirmative action policies. Related specifically to behaviors, Ramasubramanian (2010) also found that the discrepancy between portrayals of these groups with portrayals of whites predicted a decreased likelihood of performing certain behaviors related to support of affirmative action. Specifically, the more criminal and lazy black and Latino characters are evaluated in relation to white characters, the less likely people are to "vote for a petition to increase government spending to assist racial minorities," "sign a petition in favor of requiring companies who have historically discriminated against racial minorities to give racial minorities preferences in hiring," and "vote for a petition to increase admission of racial minorities in state universities" (p. 111).

Another framework that predicts behaviors from stereotypes is the BIAS map (Cuddy, Fiske, & Glick, 2007). Dill and Burgess (in press) developed a theory of media imagery and social learning (MISL) that extends and applies the BIAS map to mediated group portrayals. Growing from the stereotype content model (Fiske, Cuddy, Glick, & Xu, 2002), the BIAS map posits that stereotypes held for different groups vary in terms of warmth and competence dimensions. The warmth dimension is influenced by the target group's potential to harm (low warmth) or benefit the group (high warmth), whereas the competence dimension is influenced by whether or not the target group is perceived as capable of enacting its goals. The content of a stereotype along the warmth and competence dimensions subsequently affects the emotion elicited by the stereotyped group. According to the BIAS map, these emotions predict behaviors that are either meant to passively or actively help or harm the stereotyped group. Stereotypes that are high in competence and warmth lead to feelings of admiration, which predicts passive and active facilitation behaviors (e.g., helping). Stereotypes that are high in competence but low in warmth lead to envy, which predicts behaviors associated with passive facilitation (e.g., cooperating with an outgroup member out of convenience) or active harm (e.g., verbal harassment). Stereotypes that are low in competence but high in warmth lead to pity, which predicts active facilitation and passive harm (e.g., neglecting). Finally, stereotypes that are low in both competence and warmth lead to contempt, which predicts harming behaviors.

Applying the predictions of the BIAS map to racial/ethnic group stereotypes, we may predict general behaviors likely to emerge from exposure to the stereotypes. For example, media stereotypes commonly associated with blacks and Latinos are those of aggressiveness or criminality, unintelligence, and laziness. These stereotypes are low in both warmth and competence, which evoke contempt and are related to behaviors that are aimed at harming the group. According to the model, exposure to these stereotypes in the media has the potential to lead viewers to enact such behaviors as demeaning, excluding, or attacking blacks or Latinos. In line with the BIAS map and looking at helping behavior in a virtual environment, Eastwick and Gardner (2009) found that participants were more likely to decline requests (i.e., passive harm behavior) employing the door-in-the-face compliance-gaining strategy when performed by a black avatar than when performed by a white avatar.

In contrast, the model minority stereotype, which is commonly associated with Asian Americans, is seen as low in warmth but high in competence, thus leading to envy and behaviors associated with active harm and passive facilitation (Cuddy et al., 2007). Therefore, the model predicts that exposure to this stereotype in the media may potentially lead viewers to discriminate against Asian Americans while at the same time cooperating with them.

The priming literature also lends insight into likely behavioral effects of exposure to a racial/ethnic group stereotype. Specifically, stereotype activation may not only lead to automatic processing of information, but may also lead to automatic behavioral manifestations (Bargh, Chen, & Burrows, 1996). Indeed, on activating a stereotype, individuals may engage in behaviors that are either consistent or in direct contrast with the primed social category (Spears, Gordijn, Dijksterhuis, & Stapel, 2004; Cesario, Plaks, & Higgins, 2006). An automatic behavioral effect that is congruent with the primed stereotype is considered an assimilation effect, whereas a behavior that is the opposite of those commonly associated with the primed stereotype is considered a contrast effect (Dijksterhuis & Van Knippenberg, 1998). According to Spears et al. (2004), when individuals do not engage in the social comparison process, they assimilate the behavior of the primed stereotype. However, when intergroup comparison is salient, priming the outgroup stereotype leads to contrasted behavior. This process can be explained by the tenets of social identity theory—when social comparison is salient and there is some sense of antagonism between the groups, individuals will want to distance themselves from the outgroup by contrasting their behaviors from those of the outgroup.

According to this line of research, when the criminality stereotype is primed yet viewers do not engage in the social comparison process, their behavior will assimilate to the primed stereotype. In support of this contention, Bargh et al. (1996) subliminally primed participants with a picture of a young black male for a small fraction of a second. Those who were primed with the black picture displayed more hostile behaviors than those who were not primed with the picture of a black. The authors interpreted these findings as the picture automatically activating the stereotype of black hostility among participants, who in turn assimilated their behavior in line with the primed stereotype.

Additionally, this process may result in prejudicial behavioral responses by dominant group members toward outgroup members. For example, Unkelbach, Forgas, and Denson (2008) experimentally tested the influence of turban-clad versus bare-headed non-white characters in a computer-based shooter video game on college students' likelihood to shoot the character. College students were more likely to shoot at the turban-wearing characters, suggesting that this imagery primes a negative stereotype that resulted in the behavioral shooting response.

Although media effects research has rarely examined behavioral priming effects from exposure to media stereotypes, it is likely that exposure to a stereotype involving a minority group may lead viewers to engage in behaviors that are in line (if race or ethnicity is not salient for the viewer) or in contrast to the primed stereotype (if race or ethnicity is salient for the viewer).

PROSOCIAL EFFECTS

Recently, communication scholars have begun to examine the positive effects that exposure to outgroup portrayals has on viewers. Specifically, mediated intergroup interactions are seen as providing viewers with examples of successful intergroup relationships that they may learn from and perhaps mimic in their own life (e.g., Ortiz & Harwood, 2007). Seen through a social cognitive theory perspective (Bandura, 2002), viewers can learn from media models ways of interacting with members of different groups. Observing successful intergroup interactions allows viewers to learn about such interactions while avoiding the anxiety that often accompanies intergroup interactions in the real world. This type of vicarious intergroup contact has been shown to lead to positive effects through increased self-efficacy beliefs among viewers, who on observing mediated intergroup contact, feel that they are capable of engaging in that type of contact themselves (Mazziotta, Mummendey, & Wright, 2011).

Additionally, likeable outgroup characters facilitate viewers' likelihood of developing parasocial relationships with them. Parasocial relationships resemble face-to-face interpersonal relationships, with the exception that viewers develop these relationships with media models (Horton & Wohl, 1956). Parasocial interactions that are developed with outgroup characters have been shown to improve attitudes toward the outgroup (Schiappa, Gregg, & Hewes, 2005). Although this line of research does not focus on the effects of exposure to stereotypes, it does point to the importance of presenting well-developed outgroup characters with which viewers may develop parasocial relationships.

Effects on Self-Image

Ethnic minority adolescents face a challenge in attending to media for self-definition because portrayals of their group are either limited in number or in quality. During this stage of the lifespan, adolescents turn to media to aid in their process of self-definition and learn how society views them (Ward, 2004). However, media exposure has been found to be negatively associated with self-esteem among ethnic and racial minority youth. Specifically, among African-American adolescents, increased consumption of sports programming and music videos is associated with lower self-esteem (Ward, 2004). Additionally, identification with popular white male characters is associated with lower self-esteem among African-American youth, but identification with popular African-American male characters is associated with higher self-esteem (Ward, 2004). Among Latino adolescents, higher levels of prime time programming, soap opera, and movie exposure are associated with less confidence in one's social skills (Rivadeneyra, Ward, & Gordon, 2007). Among Native American adolescents, mere exposure to a stereotyped image of their group (e.g., Pocahontas) leads to lower self-esteem and less community worth (Fryberg, Markus, Oyserman, & Stone, 2008). Media images have also been linked with how racial/ethnic minority adolescents feel about their body. Specifically, magazine reading as well as prime time and soap opera viewing are associated with body dissatisfaction among Latino adolescents (Rivadeneyra et al., 2007), whereas believing that rap music videos portray African-American women in sexually stereotyped ways is associated with a negative body image among female African-American adolescents (Peterson, Wingood, DiClemente, Harrington, & Davies, 2007). Among Latinos, a negative body image also is associated with the degree to which they actively think about the media messages they consume, particularly among female adolescents (Rivadeneyra et al., 2007).

The pervasiveness of negative stereotypes of racial/ethnic minority groups in the media also serves as a constant reminder for members of the stereotyped group of the way society views them. Frequent media exposure may result in a negative stereotype becoming chronically accessible among viewers (Dixon & Maddox, 2005), and for members of the stereotyped group, it may increase their likelihood of recalling the stereotype when in the domain for which the stereotype applies. African-American and Latino viewers, in particular, are exposed to a stereotype regarding their group's diminished intellectual ability. According to Steele and Aronson (1995), a negative stereotype regarding intellectual ability may lead to impaired performance on tests of intellectual ability. Known as *stereotype threat*, this results from the fear experienced by members of the stereotyped group of confirming the negative stereotype. The diminished performance occurs when the social identity for which the negative stereotype applies is salient. Research on stereotype threat among African-Americans and Latinos has primarily been examined in the intellectual domain (e.g., Major, Spencer, Schmader, Wolfe, & Crocker, 1998; Gonzales, Blanton, & Williams, 2002), which is related to the media's stereotypes of the two groups.

Exposure to English-language media has not only been linked to how a minority group member feels about himself or herself (as discussed), but also influences perceptions of his or her racial/ethnic group's status in society. Specifically, Abrams and Giles (2007) found that African Americans who identify strongly with their racial group are likely to avoid watching television because they believe that the messages presented in the medium undermine their racial group. These individuals believe that television presents African Americans in stereotypical ways and fails to provide them with models with whom they can identify. This behavior, termed *ethnic identity gratifications avoidance,* is related to beliefs that their racial group holds lower status in society. Among Latinos, negative evaluations of entertainment media's representation of their ethnic group leads individuals to believe that others view their group as having lower status in society (Fujioka, 2005). However, exposure to, and evaluations of the news media's images of their group does not seem to influence Latinos' perceptions of the group's status (Fujioka, 2005) or treatment (Sizemore & Milner, 2004) in society.

Conclusion

The analysis of racial/ethnic representations in US media suggests that most minority groups are underrepresented in comparison to the real-world US population. Further, although overt racism in the media has dramatically decreased over the past 30 years, media stereotyping of racial/ethnic minorities remains problematic. To get an accurate picture of such media imagery, it is necessary to consider not only changes over time and differences across racial/ethnic groups, but notable variations also seem to exist in minority media representation based on the medium (e.g., television versus video games) and type of content (e.g., news versus entertainment).

In terms of effects of media depictions of race/ethnicity, both short- and long-term effects have been demonstrated on individuals' attitudes, beliefs, behaviors, and self-image. This body of research is still relatively small; however, the literature suggests that both the frequency and nature of portrayal of minorities affects prejudicial responses. Last, an even smaller group of studies has examined the potential for counter-stereotypical images of minorities to increase favorable responses to members of those groups.

Although the discipline of psychology as well as media effects has much to offer in terms of theoretical explanations for the cognitive processing of media representations of race/ethnicity, to date, much of this literature has yet to be applied to the present topic.

Future Directions

Research on the effects of racial/ethnic group portrayals has revealed that these mediated messages become incorporated into viewers' social identity process and are interpreted along stereotypical lines or in ingroup-serving ways. Following past recommendations (e.g., Harwood & Roy, 2005), we believe that media effects research would benefit from extending theories of intergroup processes to this realm. Media consumers may learn from the media their group's relative status in society through the numerical representation afforded to their group as well as through the way in which their group is represented. Moreover, consumers integrate media portrayals into their perceptions of other groups, ultimately influencing their attitudes toward these groups as well as their policy preferences on issues that are associated with racial/ethnic groups (Mastro & Kopacz, 2006; Ramasubramanian, 2010). The nature of the media portrayal influences the type of effect, positive or negative, such that exposure to stereotypical images of minorities is indeed linked to prejudicial attitudes and beliefs. However, the media's role in leading to *negative* effects should not be overstated given that positive minority representations may produce prosocial outcomes. Thus, the media also have the ability to improve race relations. As research extending intergroup contact theory (Allport, 1954; Brown & Hewstone, 2005) to mediated intergroup portrayals has shown, outgroup portrayals may also lead to improved attitudes toward the outgroup (Schiappa et al., 2005; Ortiz & Harwood, 2007). From an intergroup contact perspective, media portrayals serve at least two functions: (1) they provide viewers with outgroup models with whom to develop intergroup relationships, and (2) they provide viewers with exemplars of successful intergroup relationships from which to learn ways of engaging in similar behaviors in their lives. Media scholars are uniquely suited to examine the effects of mediated intergroup contact because they have the theoretical background on media effects that is required to extend this line of research.

Embedded in the preceding recommendation is a call for researchers to examine not just the effects of exposure to a single representative of the outgroup, but to focus on the effects of exposure to intergroup and intragroup interactions. Traditionally, media scholars have looked at the role that a minority character plays within a story (e.g., criminal, villain, hired help) and examined the effects of such representation on viewers. However, these minority characters are involved in different relationships with different characters within the story. Relational and interpersonal variations involving minority group characters may lead to different effects among viewers. Even though a single outgroup character may have the effect of perpetuating stereotypes about a group, when observed interacting with ingroup characters, that same character may lead to improved attitudes toward the outgroup. Similarly, an outgroup character may be evaluated differently by viewers depending on the race/ethnicity of the characters with whom he or she most closely associates. We believe that examining the effects of the type of relationship (i.e., intergroup versus intragroup) combined with the nature and quality of the relationship (e.g., good friends, disliked coworkers, criminal partners) is an area ripe for theoretical development.

Collectively, media effects research on minority group portrayals has focused on how these messages are interpreted by white viewers. Future research should focus on the equally important effects that these messages have on viewers belonging to the stereotyped group. The research that has been employed using non-white samples has shown that racial/ethnic minority group members are aware of the negative ways in which mainstream media portrays their group and therefore opt to avoid these messages (Abrams & Giles, 2007). Perceptions of how society views their group may not only influence how they feel about their group's placement in society, but may influence their attitudes toward the majority group as well. This may lead to a lessened desire to interact with members of the majority group, which may ultimately lead to stereotypes remaining intact among members of the majority group. Future research should examine this potential effect.

Insight into the effects of minority group portrayals in the media would be strengthened by invoking mixed-method approaches and broadening this investigation to other media environments. Mediated portrayals of some groups, such as those of Asian and Native Americans, are so few that they are often necessarily excluded from statistical analyses in content analytic research. Despite their small number, these portrayals may influence viewers' perceptions of the groups. Examination of these portrayals through qualitative methods would shed light on the nature of these portrayals in a way that quantitative research does not. Further, as Polkinghorne (see Chapter 8) argues, a qualitative approach is useful for increasing understanding of how one experiences and makes sense of racial/ethnic media representations. Although not generalizable, such observations provide in-depth information about a person's relationship to a media text and understanding of racial/ethnic representations.

Finally, the rise in popularity of new media technologies provides researchers with new platforms in which to investigate the effects of outgroup representations. In particular, virtual environments offer individuals the ability to select avatars that are either ingroup or outgroup members. If the selected avatar is, or resembles an outgroup member, it may affect how one subsequently feels about the outgroup. Here, there may be different cognitive processes at play as video games and virtual worlds offer an arguably more interactive media experience, in which the user takes an active role in creating and controlling the mediated representations. Some research (e.g., Yee, Bailenson, & Ducheneaut, 2009) has demonstrated that one's virtual representation may affect perceptions of self as well as communicative behaviors both online and offline.

Additionally, computer-mediated communication (CMC) research (e.g., Yee et al., 2007) suggests that social norms adhered to offline transfer to online environments, and racial/ethnic stereotypes may plague virtual interactions (e.g., Nakamura, 2009). Thus, racial/ethnic stereotyping that is known to occur in offline situations may also be exhibited in virtual worlds and social networking sites, affecting users' real-world attitudes, beliefs, behaviors, and self-concept. Future research should probe further into the processes through which this occurs as well as the prevalence of racial/ethnic stereotyping in virtual environments. Scholars should also expand on work (e.g., Tynes, 2007; Loya & Cuevas, 2010) that examines the potential for virtual environments and online communication to decrease racism and improve race relations.

Overall, researchers have made some great strides in uncovering the effects of exposure to portrayals of racial and/or ethnic minority groups. However, the adoption of additional theoretical and methodological approaches and the examination of race/ethnicity in an online context will provide a more sophisticated understanding of the cognitive and behavioral effects of racial/ethnic media representation in a new media environment, in which both traditional (e.g., television) and new (e.g., video games) media technologies must be studied.

References

Abrams, J. R., & Giles, H. (2007). Ethnic identity gratifications selection and avoidance by African Americans: A group vitality and social identity gratifications perspective. *Media Psychology, 9*, 115–134.

Allport, G. W. (1954). *The Nature of Prejudice*. New York: Addison-Wesley.

Armstrong, G. B., Neuendorf, K. A., & Brentar, J. E. (1992). TV entertainment, news, and racial perceptions of college students. *Journal of Communication, 42*, 153–176.

Atkin, C. K., Greenberg, B. S., & McDermott, S. (1983). Television and race role socialization. *Journalism Quarterly, 60*, 407–414.

Aucoin, D. (2010, July 4). 'Airbender' reopens race debate. Retrieved from http://www.boston.com/ae/movies/articles/2010/07/04/last_airbender_opens_debate_on_race/

Bandura, A. (2002). Social cognitive theory of mass communication. In Bryant, J., & Zillmann, D. (Eds.), *Media Effects: Advances in Theory and Research*, 2nd ed. Hillsdale, NJ: Lawrence Erlbaum Associates, pp. 121–153.

Bargh, J. A., Chen, M., & Burrows, L. (1996). Automaticity of social behavior: Direct effects of trait construct and stereotype activation on action. *Journal of Personality and Social Psychology, 71*, 230–244.

Behm-Morawitz, E. (2008). *Representations of race, gender, and crime in video game advertisements*. Paper presented at the National Communication Association Annual Convention, San Diego, CA.

Behm-Morawitz, E., & Chen, S-W. Priming prejudice: *The effects of playing a racially stereotyped video game character on White players' race-based attitudes and beliefs*. Unpublished manuscript. Columbia, MO: University of Missouri.

Bird, S. E. (Ed.). (1996). *Dressing in feathers: The construction of the Indian in popular culture*. Boulder, CO: Westview Press.

Bird, S. E. (1999). Gendered construction of the American Indian in popular media. *Journal of Communication, 49*, 61–83. doi:10.1111/j.1460-2466.1999.tb02805.x

Bodenhausen, G., Schwarz, N., Bless, H., & Wanke, M. (1995). Effects of atypical exemplars on racial beliefs: Enlightened racism or generalized appraisals? *Journal of Experimental Social Psychology, 31*, 48–63.

Brown, R., & Hewstone, M. (2005). An integrative theory of intergroup contact. *Advances in Experimental Social Psychology, 37*, 255–343.

Burgess, M. C. R., Dill, K. E., Stermer, S. P., Burgess, S. R., & Brown, B. P. (2011). Playing with prejudice: The prevalence and consequences of racial stereotypes in video games. *Media Psychology, 14*, 289–311.

Cesario, J., Plaks, J. E., & Higgins, E. T. (2006). Automatic social behavior as motivated preparation to interact. *Journal of Personality and Social Psychology, 90*, 893–910.

Chapman, L. J. (1967). Illusory correlation in observational report. *Journal of Verbal Learning and Verbal Behavior, 6*, 151–155.

Children Now. (2001). *Fall colors, 2000–2001: Prime time diversity report*. Oakland, CA: Children Now.

Children Now. (2004). *Fall colors, 2003–2004: Prime time diversity report*. Oakland, CA: Children Now.

Cho, J., Boyle, M. P., Keum, H., Shevy, M. D., Mcleod, D. M., Shah, D. V., & Pan, Z. (2003). Media, terrorism, and emotionality: Emotional differences in media context and public reactions to the September 11th terrorist attacks. *Journal of Broadcasting & Electronic Media, 47*, 309–327.

Cohen, J. B., & Basu, K. (1987), Alternative models of categorization: Toward a contingent processing framework. *Journal of Consumer Research, 13*, 455–472.

Collins, A. M., & Loftus, E. F. (1975). A spreading activation theory of semantic processing. *Psychological Review, 82*, 407–428.

Crandall, C. S., & Eshleman, A. (2003). A justification-suppression model of the expression and experience of prejudice. *Psychological Bulletin, 129*, 414–446.

Cuddy, A. J. C., Fiske, S. T., & Glick, P. (2007). The BIAS map: Behaviors from intergroup affect and stereotypes. *Journal of Personality and Social Psychology, 92*, 631–648.

Cummings, M. S. (1988). The changing image of the Black family on television. *Journal of Popular Culture, 22*, 75–85.

Das, E., Bushman, B., Bezemer, M., Kerkhof, P., & Vermeulen, I. (2009). How terrorism news reports increase prejudice against outgroups: A terror management account. *Journal of Experimental Social Psychology, 45*, 453–459.

Davis, L. R. (1990). The articulation of difference: White preoccupation with the question of racially linked genetic differences among athletes. *Sociology of Sport Journal, 7*, 179–187.

Dijksterhuis, A., & Van Knippenberg, A. (1998). The relation between perception and behavior or how to win a game of Trivial Pursuit. *Journal of Personality and Social Psychology, 74*, 865–877.

Dill, K. E., & Burgess, M. C. R. (in press). Seeing is believing: Towards a theory of media imagery and social learning (MISL). In Shrum, L. J. (Ed.), *The psychology of entertainment media: Blurring the lines between entertainment and persuasion, 2nd ed. New York: Routledge.

Dixon, T. L. (2006a). Psychological reactions to crime news portrayals of Black criminals: Understanding the moderating roles of prior news viewing and stereotype endorsement. *Communication Monographs*, 73(2), 162–187.

Dixon, T. L. (2006b). Schemas as average conceptions: Skin tone, television news exposure, and culpability judgments. *Journalism & Mass Communication Quarterly*, 83(1), 131–149.

Dixon, T. L., Azocar, C. L., & Casas, M. (2003). The portrayal of race and crime on television network news. *Journal of Broadcasting & Electronic Media*, 47(4), 498–523.

Dixon, T. L., & Linz, D. (2000). Overrepresentation and underrepresentation of African Americans and Latinos as lawbreakers on television news. *Journal of Communication, 50*, 131–154. doi:10.1111/j.1460–2466.2000.tb02845.x.

Dixon, T. L., & Linz, D. (2002). Television news, prejudicial pretrial publicity, and the depiction of race. *Journal of Broadcasting & Electronic Media, 46*, 112–136. doi:10.1207/s15506878jobem4601_7.

Dixon, T. L., & Maddox, K. (2005). Skin tone, crime news, and social reality judgments: Priming the stereotype of the dark and dangerous Black criminal. *Journal of Applied Social Psychology, 35*, 1555–1570.

Dodds, K. (2008). Screening terror: Hollywood, the United States and the construction of terror. *Critical Studies on Terrorism, 1*, 227–243.

Eastwick, P. W., & Gardner, W. L. (2009). Is it a game? Evidence for social influence in the virtual world. *Social Influence, 4*, 18–32.

Entman, R. (1992). Blacks in the news: Television, modern racism, and cultural change. *Journalism Quarterly, 69*, 341–361.

Fiske, S. T., Cuddy, A. J. C., Glick, P. S., & Xu, J. (2002). A model of (often mixed) stereotype content: Competence and warmth respectively follow from perceived status and competition. *Journal of Personality and Social Psychology, 82*, 878–902.

Ford, T. (1997). Effects of stereotypical television portrayals of African-Americans on person perception. *Social Psychology Quarterly, 11*, 155–169.

Fryberg, S. A., Markus, H. R., Oyserman, D., & Stone, J. M. (2008). Of warrior chiefs and Indian princesses: The psychological consequences of American Indian mascots. *Basic and Applied Social Psychology, 30*, 208–218.

Fujioka, Y. (2005). Black media images as perceived threat to African American ethnic identity: Coping responses, perceived public perception, and attitudes towards affirmative action. *Journal of Broadcasting and Electronic Media, 49*, 450–467.

Gadarian, S. (2010). The politics of threat: How terrorism news shapes foreign policy attitudes. *Journal of Politics, 72*, 469–483.

Gerbner, G., Morgan, M., Gross, L., Signorielli, N., & Shanahan, J. (2002). Growing up with television: Cultivation processes. In Bryant, J., & Zillmann, D. (Eds.). *Media Effects: Advances in Theory and Research*, 2nd ed. Hillsdale, NJ: Lawrence Erlbaum, pp. 43–68.

Gilliam F. D. Jr, & Iyengar, S. (2000). Prime suspects: The influence of local television news on the viewing public. *American Journal of Political Science, 44*, 560–573.

Givens, S. M. B., & Monahan, J. L. (2005). Priming mammies, jezebels, and other controlling images: An examination of the influence of mediated stereotypes on perceptions of an African American woman. *Media Psychology, 7*, 87–106.

Glaubke, C. R., Miller, P., Parker, M. A. & Espejo, E. (2001). *Fair Play? Violence, Race, and Gender in Video Games.* Children NOW.

Gonzales, P. M., Blanton, H., & Williams, K. J. (2002). The effects of stereotype threat and double-minority status on the test performance of Latino women. *Personality and Social Psychology Bulletin, 28*, 659–670.

Greenberg, B. S., Mastro, D., & Brand, J. E. (2002). Minorities and the mass media: Television into the 21st century. In Bryant, J., & Zillmann, D. (Eds.), *Media Effects: Advances in Theory and Research*, 2nd ed. Hillsdale, NJ: Lawrence Erlbaum Associates, pp. 333–351.

Harris, R. J. (2004). *A cognitive psychology of mass communication* 4th ed. Mahwah, NJ: Lawrence Erlbaum Associates.

Harwood, J., & Roy, A. (2005). Social identity theory and mass communication research. In Harwood, J., & Giles, H. (Eds.), *Intergroup Communication: Multiple Perspectives*. New York: Peter Lang, pp. 189–212.

Hewstone, M. (1994). Revision and change of stereotypic beliefs: In search of the elusive subtyping model. In Stroebe, W., & Hewstone, M. (Eds.), *European Review of Social Psychology*. Chichester, UK: Wiley, pp. 69–109.

Horton, D., & Wohl, R. R. (1956). Mass communication and para-social interaction. *Psychiatry, 19*, 215–229.

Iiyama, P., & Kitano, H. H. L. (1982). Asian-Americans and the media. In Berry, G. L., & Kitchell-Kernas, C. (Eds.), *Television and the Socialization of the Minority Child*. New York: Academic Press, pp. 151–186.

Jewell, S. K. (1993). *From Mammy to Miss America and Beyond: Cultural Images and the Shaping of US Social Policy*. London: Routledge.

Knobloch-Westerwick, S., & Coates, B. (2006). Minority models in advertisements in magazines popular with minorities. *Journalism & Mass Communication Quarterly, 83*, 596–614.

Lee, K-Y, & Joo, S-H (2005). The portrayal of Asian Americans in mainstream magazine ads: An update. *Journalism & Mass Communication Quarterly, 82*, 654–671.

Li-Vollmer, M. (2002). Race representation in child-targeted television commercials. *Mass Communication and Society, 5*, 207–228.

Loya, M., & Cuevas, M. (2010). Teaching racism: Using experiential learning to challenge the status quo. *Journal of Teaching in Social Work, 30*, 288–299. doi:10.1080/08841233.2010.497130.

Major, B., Spencer, S., Schmader, T., Wolfe, C., & Crocker, J. (1998). Coping with negative stereotypes about intellectual performance: The role of psychological disengagement. *Personality and Social Psychology Bulletin, 24*, 34–50.

Mastro, D. (2003). A social identity approach to understanding the impact of television messages. *Communication Monographs, 70*, 98–113.

Mastro, D. (2009). Effects of racial and ethnic stereotyping. In Bryant, J., & Oliver, M. B. (Eds.), *Media Effects: Advances in Theory and Research*, 3rd ed. New York: Routledge, pp. 325–341.

Mastro, D., & Behm-Morawitz, E. (2005). Latino representation on primetime television. *Journalism & Mass Communication Quarterly, 70*, 98–113.

Mastro, D., Behm-Morawitz, E., & Ortiz, M. (2007). The cultivation of social perceptions of Of Latinos: A mental models approach. *Media Psychology, 9*, 1–19.

Mastro, D., & Greenberg, B. (2000). The portrayal of racial minorities on prime time television. *Journal of Broadcasting & Electronic Media*, *44*, 690–703. doi:10.1207/s15506878 jobem4404_10.

Mastro, D. E., & Kopacz, M. A. (2006). Media representations of race, prototypicality, and policy reasoning: An application of self-categorization theory. *Journal of Broadcasting & Electronic Media*, *50*, 305–322.

Mastro, D., Lapinski, M. K., Kopacz, M. A., & Behm-Morawitz, E. (2009). The influence of exposure to depictions of race and crime in TV news on viewer's social judgments. *Journal of Broadcasting & Electronic Media*, *53*(4), 615–635. doi:10.1080/08838150903310534.

Mastro, D., & Stern, S. (2003). Representations of race in television commercials: A content analysis of prime-time advertising. *Journal of Broadcasting & Electronic Media*, *47*, 638–647.

Mastro, D., Tamborini, R., & Hullett, C. (2005). Linking media to prototype activation and subsequent celebrity attraction: An application of self-categorization theory. *Communication Research*, *32*, 323–348.

Maurer, K. L., Park, B., & Rothbart, M. (1995). Subtyping versus subgrouping processes in stereotype representation. *Journal of Personality and Social Psychology*, *69*, 812–824.

Mazziotta, A., Mummendey, A., & Wright, S. C. (2011). Vicarious intergroup contact effects: Applying social-cognitive theory to intergroup contact research. *Group Processes & Intergroup Relations*, *14*, 255–274.

McConnell, H. A. (2003). *The terror: Examination of the emerging discourse on terrorism and its media representations.* Toronto, Ontario: University of Toronto Press.

Merskin, D. (1998). Sending up signals: A survey of Native American media use and representation in the mass media. *Howard Journal of Communication*, *9*, 333–345. doi:10.1080/106461798246943.

Nakamura, L. (2009). Don't hate the player, hate the game: The racialization of labor in World of Warcraft. *Critical Studies in Media Communication*, *26*, 128–144. doi:10.1080/15295030902860252.

National Asian American Pacific Islander Mental Health Association. (2012). *Fact Sheet.* Retrieved July 17, 2012 from http://www.healthcare.gov/news/factsheets/2012/05/asian-americans05012012a.html.

Nisbett, R. E., & Ross, L. (1980). *Human Inference: Strategies and Shortcomings of Social Judgment.* Englewood Cliffs, NJ: Prentice-Hall.

Oliver, M. B., Jackson II, R., Moses, N., & Dangerfield, C. (2004). The face of crime: Viewers' memory of race-related facial features of individuals pictured in the news. *Journal of Communication*, *54*, 88–104.

O'Neill, P. (2000). Cognition in social context: Contributions to community psychology. In Rappaport, J., and Seidman, E. (Eds.), *Handbook of Community Psychology.* New York: Plenum, pp. 115–132.

Ono, K. A., & Sloop, J. M. (2002). *Shifting Borders: Rhetoric, Immigration, and California's Proposition 187.* Philadelphia: Temple University Press.

Ortiz, M., & Harwood, J. (2007). A social cognitive theory approach to the effects of mediated intergroup contact on intergroup attitudes. *Journal of Broadcasting & Electronic Media*, *51*, 615–631.

Page, H. (1997). "Black male" imagery and media containment of African American men. *American Anthropologist*, *99*, 99–111.

Park, J. H., Gabbadon, N. G., & Chernin, A. R. (2006). Naturalizing racial differences through comedy: Asian, black, and white views on racial stereotypes in *Rush Hour 2*. *Journal of Communication*, *56*, 157–177. doi:10.1111/j.1460–2466.2006.00008.x.

Peffley, M., Shields, T., & Williams, B. (1996). The intersection of race and crime in television news stories: An experimental study. *Political Communication*, *13*, 309–327.

Peterson, S. H., Wingood, G. M., DiClemente, R. J., Harrington, K., & Davies, S. (2007). Images of sexual stereotypes in rap videos and the health of African American female adolescents. *Journal of Women's Health*, *16*, 1157–1164.

Pettigrew T. F. (1997). Generalized intergroup contact effects on prejudice. *Personality and Social Psychology Bulletin*, *23*, 173–185.

Pettigrew, T. F. (1998). Intergroup contact theory. *Annual Review of Psychology*, *49*, 65–85.

Rada, J. (1997). Color blind-sided: Racial bias in network television's coverage of professional football games. In Biagi, S., & Kern-Foxworth, M. (Eds.) *Facing Difference: Race, Gender, and Mass Media.* Thousand Oaks, CA: Pine Forge Press, pp. 23–28.

Rada, J., & Wulfemeyer, K. T. (2005). Color coded: Racial descriptors in television coverage of intercollegiate sports. *Journal of Broadcasting and Electronic Media*, *49*, 65–85.

Ramasubramanian, S. (2010). Television viewing, racial attitudes, and policy preferences: Exploring the role of social identity and intergroup emotions in influencing support for affirmative action. *Communication Monographs*, *77*, 102–120. doi:10.1080/03637750903514300.

Ramirez Berg, C. (1990). Stereotyping in films in general and of the Hispanic in particular. *Howard Journal of Communication*, *2*, 286–300.

Richeson, J. A., & Trawalter, S. (2005). On the categorization of admired and disliked exemplars of admired and disliked racial groups. *Journal of Personality and Social Psychology*, *89*, 517–530.

Rivadeneyra, R., Ward, L. M., & Gordon, M. (2007). Distorted reflections: Media exposure and Latino adolescents' conceptions of self. *Media Psychology*, *9*, 261–290.

Sanbonmatsu, D. M., Smittipatana, S., Shavitt, S., & Posavac, S. S. (1999). Broadening the conditions for illusory correlation formation: Implications for judging minority groups. *Basic & Applied Social Psychology*, *21*, 263–279.

Schiappa, E., Gregg, P. B., & Hewes, D. E. (2005). The parasocial contact hypothesis. *Communication Monographs*, *72*, 92–115.

Shaheen, J. G. (2001). *Reel Bad Arabs: How Hollywood Vilifies a People.* New York: Olive Branch Press.

Shanahan, J., & Morgan, M. (1999). *Television and Its Viewers: Cultivation Theory and Research.* New York: Cambridge University Press.

Sheridan, P. (2005). *The Asian mystique : Dragon ladies, geisha girls, & our fantasies of the exotic Orient.* New York: Public Affairs.

Shrum, L. J. (1996). Psychological processes underlying cultivation effects: Further tests of construct accessibility. *Human Communication Research*, *22*, 482–509.

Šisler, V. (2008). Digital Arabs. *European Journal of Cultural Studies*, *11*, 203–219.

Sizemore, D. S., & Milner, W. T. (2004). Hispanic media use and perceptions of discrimination: Reconsidering ethnicity, politics, and socioeconomics. *The Sociological Quarterly*, *45*, 765–784.

Spears, R., Gordijn, E., Dijksterhuis, A., & Stapel, D. A. (2004). Reaction in action: Intergroup contrast in automatic behavior. *Personality and Social Psychology Bulletin, 30*, 605–616.

Steele, C. M., & Aronson, J. (1995). Stereotype threat and the intellectual test performance of African Americans. *Journal of Personality and Social Psychology, 69*, 797–811.

Steet, L. (2000). *Veils and daggers: A century of National Geographic's representation of the Arab world*. Philadelphia, PA: Temple University Press.

Stewart, C. O., Pitts, M. J., & Osborne, H. (2011). Mediated intergroup conflict: The discursive construction of "illegal immigrants" in a regional U.S. newspaper. *Journal of Language & Social Psychology, 30*, 8–27.

Streitmatter, R. (1999). The nativist press: Demonizing the American immigrant. *Journalism & Mass Communication Quarterly, 76*, 673–683.

Tajfel, H., & Turner, J. C. (1979). An integrative theory of intergroup conflict. In Austin, W. G., & Worchel, S. (Eds.), *Social Psychology of Intergroup Relations*. Monterey, CA: Brooks/Cole Publishing, pp. 33–47.

Tajfel, H., & Turner, J. C. (1986). The social identity theory of intergroup behaviour. In Worchel, S., & Austin, W. G. (Eds.), *Psychology of Intergroup Relations*. Chicago: Nelson-Hall, pp. 7–24.

Tamborini, R., Huang, R. H., Mastro, D., & Nabashi-Nakahara, R. (2007). The influence of race, heuristics, and information load on judgments of guilt and innocence. *Communication Studies, 58*, 341–358.

Tan, A., Fujioka, Y., & Tan, G. (2000). Television use, stereotypes of African Americans and opinions on affirmative action: An affective model of policy reasoning. *Communication Monographs, 67*, 362–371.

Taylor, S. E. (1981). A categorization approach to stereotyping. In Hamilton, D. L. (Ed.), *Cognitive Processes in Stereotyping and Intergroup Behavior*. Hillsdale, NJ: Lawrence Erlbaum Associates, pp. 83–114.

Taylor, S. E., & Thompson, S. C. (1982). Stalking the elusive "vividness" effect. *Psychological Review, 89*, 155–181.

Tynes, B. M. (2007). Role taking in online "classrooms": What adolescents are learning about race and ethnicity. *Developmental Psychology, 43*, 1312–1320. doi: 10.1037/0012–1649.43.6.1312

Unkelbach, C., Forgas, J. P., & Denson, T. F. (2008). The turban effect: The influence of Muslim headgear and induced affect on aggressive responses in the shooter bias paradigm. *Journal of Experimental Social Psychology, 44*, 1409–1413. doi:10.1016/j.jesp.2008.04.003.

US Census (2010). The Black Population: 2010. Retrieved July 17, 2012 from, http://www.census.gov/prod/cen2010/briefs/c2010br-06.pdf

Ward, L. M. (2004). Wading through the stereotypes: Positive and negative associations between media use and Black adolescents' conceptions of self. *Developmental Psychology, 40*, 284–294.

Wilkins, K. G. (1995). Middle Eastern women in Western eyes. In Y. R. Kamalipour (Ed.), *The U.S. media and the Middle East: Image and perception*. Westport, CT: Praeger, pp. 50–61.

Williams, D., Martins, N., Consalvo, M., & Ivory, J. D. (2009). The virtual census: representations of gender, race and age in video games. *New Media & Society, 11*, 815–834.

Yee, N., Bailenson, J. N., & Ducheneaut, N. (2009). The Proteus Effect: Implications of transformed digital self-representation on online and offline behavior. *Communication Research, 36*, 285–312.

Yee, N., Bailenson, J. N., Urbanek, M., Chang, F., & Merget, D. (2007). The unbearable likeness of being digital: The persistence of nonverbal social norms in online virtual environments. *CyberPsychology & Behavior, 10*, 115–121. doi:10.1089/cpb.2006.9984.

Representations of Gender in the Media

Erica L. Scharrer

Abstract

Individuals young and old can learn a great deal from the ways in which men and women and boys and girls are depicted in the media. Alongside other socializing influences such as family and peers, the media help form perceptions of gender roles, and can shape the behaviors that stem from those perceptions. This chapter first reviews the evidence from content analysis research to determine the most prevalent patterns in gender representations in the media, with particular emphasis on television, video games, advertising, and magazine content. It then connects the themes that emerged in the content analysis literature—underrepresentation of women, depictions of physical appearance, domestic roles, and professional roles—to studies measuring the influence of such media depictions. In doing so, the topics of gender role socialization and body image disturbance are discussed, and the social implications of such media effects are identified.

Key words: Body image, content analysis, gender, men's roles, representation, socialization, women's roles

Introduction

The media are among the most important socializing agents of the modern era, informing audiences directly and indirectly of cultural norms, beliefs, and expectations. With both adults and children spending vast and increasing amounts of time with various media forms, the media join the ranks of parents, other family members, friends, and others in shaping individuals' perceptions of the world around them and their position within. Audience members learn a great deal about what is valued and accepted in the culture (and what is less so) from the media, and identities can form and reform from what is gleaned from the characters and other individuals who populate the programs on television and the advertisements between and within them, the pages of magazines, web sites and social media, and video and computer games.

Chief among the various messages communicated to audiences through media are messages about gender. Witnessing the men and women and boys and girls who appear on television and in other media forms, including what they say, what they do, what they look like, and how they interact, can help form audience members' views of gender roles and their corresponding conceptions of themselves and others. The media can thus shape perceptions of masculinity and femininity, attitudes regarding gender roles (including what is deemed acceptable for girls and women or for boys and men) and behaviors that derive from these conceptions.

The socialization of gender roles is an especially important topic of scholarly inquiry. Very young children begin to develop a sense of themselves and others based on biological sex and socially constructed gender. These conceptions are likely to shift and reshape as children mature, primarily in adolescence as identity is in flux. Yet, adults too are guided by their own perceptions of gender roles. From division of household chores to beliefs about occupations, and from views of one's own attractiveness to ideas about romantic or familial roles, gender role conceptions can govern the daily lives of individuals young and old.

This chapter examines social science research on media representations of gender and the consequences of attending to these representations for the ideas, beliefs, and behavior of audiences. It begins by reviewing the most recent content analyses documenting patterns in gender portrayals, primarily on television, magazines, advertising, and video games, because the bulk of the research investigates these media types. Next, it synthesizes the body of research regarding media effects on gender role–related outcomes, including the experiments that show causal connections and the surveys that demonstrate correlations. In doing so, the chapter provides important insights into social norms for gender as reflected and shaped through media.

Content Analysis Research

What types of information might viewers receive from monitoring the media regarding what it means to be a boy or a girl, a man or a woman, in our society? The body of evidence from decades of content analysis research, a body that traces long-term, stable patterns as well as provides many important updates, answers that critical question. Content analysis research allows for systematic estimations of aggregate patterns in media content, thereby illuminating the most common themes. An overarching conclusion from media content research is that although one can point to some progress in wider and more encompassing gender roles, stereotypical portrayals persist.

Numbers of Characters

Women continue to be underrepresented on television and in other media forms compared with men on television and the actual population. The very first content analyses of television programming documented this pattern (Head, 1954) and the situation persisted through the 1970s, when there were approximately three male characters for every one female character on network television (Signorielli, 1985). There was some progress toward greater parity in the 1980s and through the 1990s, but even then the distribution of characters by gender was 60% in favor of males, and 40%

females (Signorielli & Bacue, 1999). More recently, Greenberg and Worrell (2007) determined that female characters comprised on average just 39% of the new characters introduced each fall season by the networks between 1993 and 2004. Signorielli's (2013) analysis of an extensive database consisting of prime time broadcast network programming over time finds a 58% male, 42% female split that has characterized the last 10 years.

Although underrepresentation of women on television is the consistent conclusion from this research, studies show some variation according to genre as well as additional evidence of male dominance in other media types. The underrepresentation of female characters is particularly profound in drama and action-adventure programming and somewhat less so in situation comedies (Lauzen & Dozier, 1999; Signorielli & Bacue, 1999; Signorielli, 2013). A recent analysis of music videos from multiple music television networks found three times as many males as females (Turner, 2011). Within film rather than television, Smith, Pieper, Granados, and Choueiti (2010) conducted a content analysis of popular G-rated titles and found a 2.57:1 ratio in favor of males.

Among cartoons, a perennially popular aspect of children's programming, the tendency either mirrors or further distorts the favoring of male characters. The number of males outdistanced the number of females 58% to 42% among major characters in the sample of programs that had been labeled as satisfying the social/emotional aspect of the Children's Television Act analyzed by Barner (1999). Leaper, Breed, Hoffman, and Perlman (2002) discovered that male characters outnumbered female characters four to one in traditional adventure cartoons (e.g., *Spiderman),* two to one in comedy cartoons (e.g., *Animaniacs*), and 1.5 to one in educational/family cartoons (e.g., *Where in the World Is Carmen Sandiego, The Magic School Bus*). Most recently, Baker and Raney (2007) found an unequal distribution of superheroes in preference of males and Signorielli (2008) determined that the lopsided male-to-female ratio pervaded all Saturday morning cartoon types. In television as well as in film, therefore, implicit messages about who is privileged with a larger presence on the screen are sent to very young viewers and continue throughout general audience programming, as well.

The numbers are often even more uneven within the increasingly popular medium of video games. In an analysis of more than 1,000 ads appearing in video game fan magazines, Scharrer (2004) found males outnumbered females by 3 to 1. In the games themselves, Beasley and Collins Standley (2002) found 71.5% of all characters appearing in the first 20 minutes of game play were males and only 14% were females (the rest were gender indeterminate). Williams, Martins, Consalvo, and Ivory (2009) examined thousands of human characters in video games, and found males comprised 85.23% of all characters, 89.55% of primary characters, and 85.47% of secondary characters (after weighting by sales figures of the games so as to emphasize those most widely circulating). Downs and Smith (2010) studied top-grossing games for the most popular consoles and found males appeared more frequently within the games than females at a rate of approximately 7 to 1.

The overall tendency to overrepresent men compared with women is also consistent across race. A recent analysis found, for example, women comprised 45% of all prime time television characters of color, whereas men made up the remaining 55% (Signorielli, 2009a). Both black/African-American female characters and Latino female characters tend to populate situation comedies more frequently than their male counterparts, who enjoy a wider array of roles across other program types (Signorielli, 2009a). Thus, underrepresentation is both the overall condition for female characters and is exacerbated in particular genres for female characters of color. (See Chapter 13 for more research on race and ethnicity.)

Physical Appearance

The media present a narrow definition of attractiveness, emphasizing thinness as an essential component, particularly for females. On television, in the programs that are broadcast and the commercials between them, thinness and a narrow definition of attractiveness are presented as the overwhelming ideal. As evident in this section, content analysis research consistently finds that media characters are thinner than individuals in the actual population, thin characters tend to be portrayed more positively than less thin characters, and the emphasis on attractiveness and physical appearance—particularly for women but also for men—is profound.

Fouts and Burggraf (2002a) found, for instance, characters on sitcoms underrepresent above-average weight individuals compared with population statistics, and overrepresent female underweight individuals. In a study of more than 1,000 primary characters on prime time television, Greenberg, Eastin, Hofschire, Lachlan, & Brownell (2003)

found that overweight characters were also coded as less attractive, and they were less likely than their thinner counterparts to be shown dating, interacting with romantic partners, or engaging in sexual behavior. In an analysis of programming on Fox, the WB, and UPN (the latter two now merged but then separate networks), Glascock (2003) also determined that female characters were dressed more provocatively than male characters, calling attention to their attractiveness and sexuality. Thinness and sexuality appear to co-occur in televised depictions, therefore, and heavier characters are not typically shown as objects of romantic or sexual interest.

These emphases occur within particular television genres as well. Females were coded as more attractive than males in a study of Spanish-language prime time programming, for instance, and their appearance was emphasized to a greater degree in the narrative (Glascock & Ruggiero, 2004). A recent study of rap music videos by Zhang, Dixon, and Conrad (2010) found 51% of the female characters appearing were coded as thin, a percentage that was consistent across race. Thinness was associated with sexuality in the study, and because the US Centers for Disease Control estimates that just 24% of women in the actual population meet the clinical definition of "thin," the finding points to a decided overrepresentation. In another study of music videos representing multiple musical genres, Turner (2011) found women were more likely than men and black characters more likely than white to be dressed provocatively.

In advertising, males outnumber females in commercials for all product types except health- and beauty-related and household products (Bartsch, Burnett, Diller, & Rankin-Williams, 2000; Ganahl, Prinsen, & Netzley, 2003), thereby establishing the association of femininity with beauty (as well as domestic roles). Female characters are typically younger than male characters and older women are the least visible group that appears in advertising (Ganahl et al., 2003). Stern and Mastro (2004) found further that young adult females were the most attractive as well as the thinnest group of characters appearing in television advertising, whereas older females were shown to be less attractive and heavier. In children's programming on Nickelodeon and Disney, Northrup and Liebler (2010) discovered a strong emphasis on a slender white body as the standard for beauty. Indeed, the tendency of media forms from advertising to video games and from magazines to music videos to present young women and girls in a sexualized manner that emphasizes not only thinness, but also presents them as objects for others' sexual stimulation prompted the American Psychological Association to issue both a report on the topic and a call for more research into the phenomenon (APA, 2011).

The physical appearance of characters belonging to varying racial and gender groups has been compared in a number of content analyses of magazine advertising content, as well. Baker (2005) studied characters in ads appearing in magazines targeted primarily toward white women (e.g., *Cosmopolitan*), white men (e.g., *GQ*), black women (e.g., *Essence*), and black men (e.g., *Black Men*), and found white characters were more often shown as objectified (defined by a strong emphasis on their bodies and physical attributes and a de-emphasis on their faces) than black women across most magazine types. Yet, black female characters across magazine types largely conformed to a white norm for attractiveness, with medium complexions, straight hair, and curvy figures. And when black female characters appeared in the magazines targeted toward primarily white audiences, they were more likely to have lighter skin, straighter hair, and thinner bodies. Many of these themes were echoed in a more recent analysis of gender and race in ads appearing in *Essence* and *Jet* magazines (geared toward black women and black men and women, respectively) conducted by Hazell and Clarke (2008). They found black women characters were often shown as dominant—with faces presented as a focal point or "head shots" used rather than visuals emphasizing body parts—but also with light to medium complexions, straight and long hair, and increasingly thin figures, thereby reflecting the dominant white standard for beauty.

Television content analysis research has not only tracked the relative attractiveness and body size and shape of characters, but has also analyzed comments made about appearance, as well. Northrup and Liebler (2010), for instance, found evidence of the reinforcement of the importance of attractiveness and low body weight in characters' verbal interactions. Lauzen and Dozier (2002), in a sample of prime time characters, found that although males and females were equally likely to make appearance-related comments, females were twice as likely to receive them. Somewhat similarly, Fouts and Burggraf (2002a) found that those female characters who were below average in weight received more positive comments about their appearance from other characters than those female characters who were average or above in weight. Female characters who were portrayed as dieting admonished themselves for their weight and

body shape, adding further force to a drive toward thinness (Fouts & Burggraf, 2002a). In a parallel study, Fouts and Burggraf (2002b) found that heavy male characters frequently made negative verbal comments about their own weight, often played to the audience for laughs.

Once again, video game content stands out as among the most problematic of media types in the sexualization of female characters and the strong emphasis on their attractiveness. Dietz (1998), in a content analysis of top-selling and top-renting titles, found female video game characters to frequently have clothing that exposed their bodies and to have exaggerated sexual features. Beasley and Collins Standley (2002) found female characters in video games were more likely than males to wear fewer items of clothing and show more skin, and 41% of all female characters were coded as having "voluptuous" breasts. Downs and Smith (2010) found approximately 40% of the female characters who appeared in the popular games in their sample wore clothing that emphasized curves or other body parts and another approximately 40% were partially or fully nude. The body proportions of many of the female characters were skewed toward large breasts and curvaceous hips accompanied by a very thin waist. In magazine ads for video games, Scharrer (2004) found the female characters appearing in the ads were more likely to be coded as attractive, wore more revealing clothing, and were more likely to be presented with an emphasis on sexuality than the male characters.

Although the topic has received comparatively less research attention, the depiction of male media characters' attractiveness and physical appearance has been examined, as well. Across these studies, the body type that pervades and is presented as the most ideal for men is muscular and lean. For example, Lin (1998) studied more than 500 commercials appearing on ABC, CBS, and NBC and determined that a common body type for male characters was muscular (30%), with only very few male characters coded as either "skinny" (4%) or "chunky" (9%). Within magazine content, an increasingly muscular male body has been identified as the norm (Leit, Pope, & Gray, 2000; Hatoum & Belle, 2004; Frederick, Fessler, & Haselton, 2005). Morrison and Halton (2009) studied a random selection of top-grossing action films from 1980 to 2006 and found the body fat among the male characters decreased over time and their muscularity increased. The muscular male characters in the films were more likely than their less muscular counterparts to interact with others both romantically and sexually and were also more likely to be physically aggressive. Just as we saw for female characters, male characters that meet an increasingly narrow definition of physical attractiveness are more often presented as objects of desire in media compared with those who fail to measure up against such standards.

Domestic Roles

Another realm in which gender roles can be communicated via media is within the household, through domestic roles and responsibilities. From sitcoms that feature families and depict mothers and fathers in particular ways to advertisements for cleaning products and other household goods, the media can be a source of information regarding the division of labor and duties within and around the home. Such depictions can suggest to audience members that males or females are somehow "naturally" better at particular tasks and roles, or "naturally" worse.

Televised female characters' marital status is more likely to be readily identified compared with male characters (Signorielli & Kahlenberg, 2001), thereby suggesting to the audience the relative importance of marriage to and for women. Female characters in telenovelas and serial dramas on Spanish-language television were responsible for more childcare than were male characters and they also had lower status occupations outside the home (Glascock & Ruggiero, 2004). An analysis of 124 programs on the broadcast networks aired during the 2005 to 2006 television season found female characters are more often depicted in roles and scenarios having to do with interpersonal relationships—including those familial, between friends, and with romantic partners—than males (Lauzen, Dozier, & Horan, 2008). Although there have been greater depictions of women working outside the home (as we will see in the following section of this chapter), the relative tendency to associate female characters with domestic spaces and tasks and with relationships (children, romantic partners, and friends) more so than male characters persists.

Within televised families, studies have also found some pointed differences in how mothers and fathers are represented. The general trend has been toward emancipation for women and mothers over time, with recent roles reflecting more independence and fewer domestic duties (Reep & Dambrot, 1994). However, on close scrutiny stereotypes and narrow depictions remain within media depictions of motherhood. Both Keller (1994) and Douglas and Michaels (2004) found within the content of women's magazines that the traditional roles of motherhood (including being in charge of care and upkeep of the home as well as of childcare) persist in articles and ads across the decades examined. Also within content in women's magazines, Smith (2001) found an increasing tendency to feature negative articles about working mothers and daycare between 1987 and 1997, thereby indirectly reinforcing the importance of women's roles within rather than outside the home. Johnston and Swanson (2003) studied 1998 and 1999 issues of women's and parenting magazines and found employed mothers were present in just 12% of all mother-related text units (i.e., an article, ad, letter, column) compared with 88% for at-home mothers. Mothers of color were underrepresented, with 89% of working mothers and 95% of at-home mothers being white. The working mothers were more likely than the at-home mothers to be presented as happy, busy, and proud, whereas the at-home mothers were more likely to be shown as confused and overwhelmed. Within depictions of motherhood, therefore, contradictions prevail, which seem to simultaneously deliver the message that work and family do not mix and that a maternal role for women is paramount, especially for white women.

In a rare quantitative study investigating masculine roles within the home, Scharrer (2001a) studied 136 episodes of 29 domestic sitcoms airing from the 1950s through the 1990s. She found the father figure increasingly portrayed in a foolish manner, serving as the butt of 60% of all jokes involving the father in the 1990s sitcoms compared to approximately 30% in the 1950s, 1960s, and 1970s. Indeed, if joke telling can be considered a manifestation of power between the sexes, women increasingly showed that they had the upper hand. Fathers told jokes at the expense of mothers an average of two to three times per episode in the more recent sitcoms, whereas mothers told jokes at the expense of fathers three to five times. Although in some ways these data suggest progress for the depiction of gender because women have an increasing amount of power, the bumbling role of the sitcom father can suggest to audiences that women are somehow "naturally" more adept at childcare.

Callister and Robinson (2010) looked at expressions of physical affection among characters populating children's programs in the United States, and found some evidence of gender equality, yet additional data pointing toward gender biases. There were no differences, for instance, in whether male or female characters initiated affection (including hugging and kissing and other forms of affection-ate touching) more often. Yet, males received more affection than females and sons were on the receiving end of affection from parents more than daughters, especially from mothers. In this study, therefore, we see that masculinity in this genre can include expressions of warmth and fondness, but interestingly, children's television characters appear to perceive males as more appropriate recipients of such expressions compared with females.

Perhaps in no other television genre do gender stereotypes regarding the domestic sphere pervade than in advertising on television (Browne, 1998; Coltrane & Messineo, 2000; Scharrer, Kim, Lin, & Liu, 2006). Not only are household responsibilities distributed stereotypically, with women, for instance, doing the majority of the cleaning and cooking and men the majority of the outdoor chores and household repairs in commercials (Kaufman, 1999; Scharrer et al., 2006), but in the few instances in which males do take on chores that run counter to gender expectations, their efforts are often presented as humorously inept. Kaufman (1999) coded more than 900 characters appearing in more than 1,000 commercials broadcast on the major networks and found that 72% of the time cooking was done by female characters, and females did more cleaning, shopping, and other indoor chores than males. Scharrer et al. (2006) coded 477 characters in prime time television commercials and found 64% of all domestic chores were performed by women, whereas only 3% of all stereotypically masculine domestic chores (like taking out the trash) were carried out by women. Tellingly, 50% of all chores taken on by men were met with a humorous response compared with just 9% of all chores done by women. When the father figure burns the dinner because the wife who usually cooks is working late, for instance, the subtle message is that one should not transgress traditional gender boundaries.

Women were found to be portrayed as home-makers and mothers and otherwise appearing in the domestic sphere in a recent sample of Spanish television commercials (Royo-Vela, Aldas-Manzano, Kuster, & Vila, 2008) and in the United Kingdom (Lewin-Jones & Mitra, 2009). A relatively recent study of television commercials in Australia by Milmer and Higgs (2004) shows that compared with past analyses, there is more evidence of stereotypical gender roles rather than less. Thus, the assignment of women to a domestic space, increasingly out-of-step with the realities of many women in the actual population, is the tendency in other cultural contexts outside the United States, as well.

In commercials within children's television programming, just 12% of commercials featuring boy characters only had an in-home setting compared with 39% of those featuring only girls (Larson, 2001). The girls-only commercials were overwhelmingly more likely than the boys-only to show cooperative interactions with others, whereas the boys-only were more likely to feature competition with others. This study joins prior research in determining that within the advertisements that appear during children's programming on television, girls are much more likely to be shown in a domestic setting and boys in an outdoor setting (Bretl & Cantor, 1988; Smith, 1994). Furthermore, girls in commercials during children's television have also been found to be significantly more nurturing, dependent, and deferential, whereas boys have been determined to be more aggressive and active (Barner, 1999). Thus, the placement of girls in roles within the home can coincide with their engagement in quieter, more calming pursuits (playing with baby dolls or kitchen sets, for instance), whereas the placement of boys outdoors can translate into more active and physically demanding activities (like running with trucks, planes, or other toy vehicles).

Occupational Roles

Another key area in which gender roles can be analyzed and understood is within the world of work. What jobs and occupations are held by male and female media characters, respectively? A number of content analysis studies identify the occupational status of media characters (whether they are depicted working outside the home or not), the jobs at which they are employed, and the relative prestige of those jobs. Within these analyses, once again we see some evidence of improving gender equality over time as well as additional indication of lingering limits and stereotypes.

Importantly, male characters are more likely to be explicitly presented as having a job outside the home than female characters on television. Signorielli and Kahlenberg (2001) found approximately 60% of female characters were identified as having an occupation compared with an estimated three-fourths of male characters. That disparity lingers in the most recent analysis of prime time television programs, as well (Signorielli, 2013). Just as women are associated with a home setting more than men, men are connected to the working world more than women on television.

Additional analyses have determined the sorts of occupations that are taken on by male and female characters on television, defining "traditionally male" occupations such as doctors, lawyers, and politicians and "traditionally female" occupations such as teachers and those in the service sector, as well as "gender neutral" occupations. Here we see some progress as well as remaining obstacles standing in the way of wider roles. In terms of progress, women are just as likely as men on television to be found in white collar or professional occupations (Signorielli & Kahlenberg, 2001; Signorielli, 2013). Furthermore, only about 20% of female characters are currently in "traditionally female" occupations, with an estimated one-third crossing traditional gender boundaries by occupying "traditionally male" jobs (Signorielli, 2013). Limiting circumstances persist for male characters, however, in that an estimated one-half has "traditionally male" jobs and careers, and just 5% are depicted in "traditionally female" occupational roles (Signorielli, 2013). Thus, the roles of male characters are more restricted within the professional realm than those of female characters in the contemporary television scene.

Important differences arise for gender and race when examining television programs that mostly feature characters from a single racial or ethnic group compared with those that feature characters that span multiple racial and ethnic groups. Signorielli (2009b) found only 40% of black women in mostly minority programs were depicted working outside the home. Of those black women in mostly minority programs who did hold out-of-the-home occupations, they tended to be classified in non-professional jobs. Likewise, white women in programs with all or mostly white casts were also less likely to have high-prestige occupations. No such pattern was found for the occupations of male characters in the study. Their occupational status and prestige was not related to the overall racial and ethnic composition of the cast.

A limited number of studies examine the messages audiences receive through magazines regarding occupations. Massoni (2004) compared data from the National Center for Education Statistics to study career aspirations of teens of color and white teens and depictions of occupations in the highly popular *Seventeen* magazine in the same year. The analysis yielded more than 1,000 references to jobs and occupations in the editorial copy of the magazines to which gender could be ascribed. Men were depicted as having an occupation three times more often than women were in the magazine, and men

held about three-fourths of the white collar, highly skilled occupations. Women held the majority of white collar, low-skilled occupations, but that was mostly explained by the predominance of females employed as models highlighted in the magazine. A total of 40 discrete jobs were depicted, and of those, 24 were male-dominated, 10 female-dominated, and 6 gender-neutral. Somewhat similarly, Peirce (1997) generated a random selection of fiction stories published in five women's magazines from 1990 to 1995 and found men were more likely to be shown as having an occupation and occupations were gender stereotyped, with common roles for men including doctors, lawyers, and business people, and common roles for women including secretaries, nurses, and housekeepers.

Finally, a subset of the existing content analyses depicting occupational activities examines the use of computers and information communication technologies (ICTs) by gender. Studies have found males outnumber females in magazine ads for computers, and differences exist in how males and females interact with computers as well, with males more often portrayed in executive or managerial roles and women as sales clerks and clerical employees (Ware & Stuck, 1985; Marshall & Bannon, 1988). Knupfer (1998) studied gender in banner ads appearing on the Web and found females were presented as lower in technological skills and in more subordinate roles compared with men. White and Kinnick (2000) examined 351 commercials during prime time television and determined that although female characters were shown as computer users nearly as often as male characters, their occupations were lower in status (e.g., secretaries or telemarketers) compared with males (who were, for instance, business professionals). Raphael, Bachen, Lynn, Baldwin-Philippi, and McKee (2006) studied 35 Web sites that expressed a mission to increase the involvement of girls and women in ICTs and found these sites show just the opposite trend, with girls and women depicted in elite and high-powered professional occupations.

Effects Research

One of the primary reasons why content analysis research is conducted is as a necessary first step to understanding media effects (Neuendorf, 2002). To determine whether and how and under what circumstances individuals are influenced by media, it is crucial to know what messages prevail in media texts. There is not always a direct correspondence between media content and media effects, however. The media effects research tradition has made great strides in recent years in showing that individuals are not always affected by media in uniform ways, but rather that individual differences and situational variables shape media effects. Therefore, the same media content can have differential effects on audiences. At the same time, content analysis research can identify the themes and patterns in media messages that ultimately may be called on by individuals—again, perhaps in differing ways—as they make sense of social norms and their relative position within those norms.

Like most media effects topic areas, the potential influence of media representations of gender is often studied through the use of surveys and experiments. The former lends external validity and generalizability but often falls short of asserting causal claims (unless, of course, it is conducted longitudinally). The latter is often rather artificial but allows for declarations of cause-and-effect relationships among variables. Studies using survey methodology are effective at measuring long-term, cumulative associations between media use patterns and gender-role related variables. Studies using experimental methodology capture the short-term, direct impact of media exposure. Both techniques have been used extensively to determine the ways in which media can shape conceptions about gender roles, attitudes toward those roles, and corresponding behavior.

The organization of this latter section of the chapter parallels the organization of the first section, with the subtopics identified in the content analysis research informing the review of effects research. Therefore, the surveys and experiments conducted to understand the impact of media depictions of physical appearance, roles within the home, and roles at work are synthesized and summarized here. However, one exception to this parallel structure surfaces. The content analysis section of the chapter provides evidence for the systematic underrepresentation of women in many media forms. This is a topic that has not been taken up directly in effects research to date, and therefore there is no corresponding subsection in the latter part of the chapter exploring the ramifications of underrepresentation. What are the consequences of an inequitable representation by gender on television, in video games, and in other media forms—where males consistently outnumber females—for audience members? Collins (2011) identifies this question as a critical gap in the media and gender literature. She suggests that the closest parallel in the existing research is the very small number of studies that show audiences of color gain increases in self-esteem when they see

fellow people of color in the media (e.g., McDermott & Greenberg, 1984). Perhaps women in the audience, too, would experience a boost in self-esteem if they saw more women in primary roles in the media. Yet, clearly this phenomenon is not well understood and this chapter author joins Collins in calling for future research attention devoted to this important question.

Influence on Overall Gender-Role Attitudes

Before a more specialized review of the subtopics considered in this chapter (physical appearance, domestic roles, and occupational roles) is conducted, it is also necessary to consider the evidence for the influence of the media on attitudes and views about gender, in general. In other words, before discussing the evidence for effects of gendered portrayals of physical appearance, domestic roles, and professional roles, we first turn to the studies that explore the role of media in fostering overall conceptions of gender norms. For this task, meta-analysis is a useful approach. With the technique of meta-analysis, a number of studies on a shared topic are examined in the aggregate to arrive on overall conclusions that span the individual studies that comprise the analysis. Thus, meta-analysis identifies the overall size and strength of statistical relationships across numerous studies on a shared topic that encompass multiple methodologies and samples of various size and characteristics.

A small number of meta-analyses exist on the topic of media's effect on gender-related attitudes and behavior. Herrett-Skjellum and Allen (1996) integrated 30 existing studies and found an average effect size of .10 between television use and gender role stereotypes. The relationship held across age of subjects, and among the strongest associations was that between television exposure and views of occupational roles (a topic taken up in more detail in the following). An average effect size of .10 was also found by Morgan and Shanahan (1997), whose meta-analysis consisted of 14 studies of overall television use and gender roles that used cultivation analysis as a theoretical frame. Most recently, Oppliger (2007) conducted a meta-analysis of 31 studies and found a statistical relationship between television exposure and gender-role outcomes among experimental studies of $r = .24$ and among surveys of $r = .12$. Across each of the meta-analyses that exist on the topic; therefore, the effect size is small to moderate but in a consistently positive direction, suggesting television contributes modestly yet significantly to relatively more stereotypical and traditional gender-related outlooks.

Individual studies have also shown links between television exposure and overall conceptions of gender. For instance, Signorielli (1989) used the General Social Survey (GSS) from 1975 to 1986 to examine the association between amount of television viewing and gender-stereotypical attitudes. Although overall, views became less gender-stereotyped over time, a statistical association between television viewing and holding more traditional views of the role of women in society held across the time period examined. Jennings, Geis, & Brown (1980) used experimental methodology to expose college-aged women to either a gender-stereotyped commercial or a counter-stereotypical commercial and found the assertiveness of those in the counter-stereotypical group outscored those in the gender-stereotypical group in both a conformity and a public speaking task that took place after exposure. Garst and Bodenhausen (1997) exposed male college students to magazine advertisements that varied according to how androgynous or traditionally masculine they were. Those in the traditionally masculine condition, and in particular those who had scored as more "nontraditional" before exposure, displayed more traditional views of gender when reporting gender-related attitudes later, in a task that was ostensibly unrelated to their exposure. Hurtz and Durkin (2004) asked 72 adult residents of an Australian city to listen to radio ads that varied in terms of gender stereotyping (e.g., promoting soccer among males or sewing machines among females) presented alongside music programming. Those exposed to the set of stereotypical radio commercials processed gender-related trait words more efficiently following exposure compared to those exposed to neutral commercials. From this brief review, therefore, we see that radio, magazine advertising, television commercials, and television programming each has the potential to exert an influence on the overall view of gender held by individuals and the behaviors that emerge from those views.

Other studies have examined these processes among particular subgroups of the population or particular genres of television programming. For example, Ward, Hansbrough, and Walker (2005) found that black high school students who viewed both more music videos and more sports had more gender-typed attitudes than those who watched less of those program types. In their study, viewing of other genres including situation comedies, dramas, and movies, was not related to gender-related attitudes. Rivadeneyra and Ward (2005) surveyed a sample of Latino high school students, measuring gender-related attitudes through such items as

"the husband should make all the important decisions in the marriage" and "a wife should do whatever her husband wants" (p. 462). They found girls who watched more television, especially talk shows and situation comedies, were more likely to endorse gender-role stereotypes than girls who watched less. For both the males and the females in the sample, exposure to Spanish-language programs was also associated with traditional gender-role attitudes. Importantly, television use was more strongly correlated with these attitudes when participants had higher levels of perceived realism and viewer involvement.

A number of studies also examine television's contribution to gender role attitudes outside the United States. In one such study, Saito (2007) surveyed 417 adult Tokyo residents and determined that amount of television viewing was significantly associated with more stereotypical responses to the Scale of Egalitarian Sex Role Attitudes (Suzuki, 1991) and remained marginally significant ($\beta = -.094$, $p = .07$) when controlling for age, education, occupational status, and political orientation in hierarchical regression analysis. Follow-up analyses revealed stronger or weaker results depending on subgroup. For instance, politically conservative respondents who were heavy television viewers had *less* stereotyped responses to the scale than heavier viewing liberal respondents. These analyses support the notion of mainstreaming, a concept within cultivation theory that shows the ability of television to reduce differences in individuals' viewpoints that would typically be found based on demographics (Morgan, Shanahan, & Signorielli, 2009). Thus, in some individuals and under some circumstances, television use can associate with less rather than more stereotypical attitudes regarding gender.

In fact, additional analyses have supported the ability of television to contribute to gender role attitudes that run counter to gender stereotypes in other cultural contexts. In Kuwait, Abdulrahim, Al-Kandari, and Hasanen (2009) found that amount of viewing of American television programming was associated with more open, nontraditional views of gender, measured using items including, "Women should have the same rights as men in every way" and "Men and women should get equal pay when they are in the same jobs" (p. 64). Exposure to US television remained a significant predictor of less gender-stereotypical views even when accounting for demographic variables and perceptions of television's ability to provide transcultural knowledge. The direction of television's correlation can change, therefore, depending on its message in comparison with other cultural and social forces.

Physical Appearance

The research record is quite clear that there are negative repercussions of the media's depiction of the thin ideal, particularly for women. Groesz, Levine, and Murnen (2002) performed a meta-analysis on 25 experiments examining the effect of thinness-depicting media on women's body image. They found an overall effects size of −.31, showing lower body satisfaction among women who saw media depictions of the thin ideal compared with those in control groups (most of whom saw more realistic images of women). The effects were stronger when research participants were less than 19 years old. A meta-analysis conducted by Grabe, Ward, and Hyde (2008) consisting of 77 studies found effects sizes of women's media exposure with their dissatisfaction with their bodies of −.28, with their internalization of a thin ideal of −.39, and with their eating behavior and beliefs (which included restricting one's eating, bingeing and purging, and excessively exercising) of −.30. Holstrom (2004) meta-analyzed 34 studies for which an effects size could be determined between exposure to media and judgments about one's own physical appearance, particularly regarding body size and shape. When weighting effects sizes by number of participants in each study, Holstrom arrived on smaller but still significant results: a mean effects size of .08 for the experimental studies and .07 for correlational. We can confidently conclude from these meta-analyses that media exert a small to moderate sized effect on body image–related outcomes.

Some of the existing research uses survey methodology to examine the relationship between overall amount of television exposure and feeling dissatisfied with the appearance of one's body. For example, Harrison and Cantor (1997) and Tiggemann (2003) have each found overall amount of television exposure predicts body dissatisfaction. Zhang and Lien (2010) determined from a sample of 301 Taiwanese adolescent girls that among those with low self-esteem and heavier body weight, television viewing associated with body dissatisfaction. Other surveys have examined exposure to particular genres or types of television programming (such as programs that are particularly "thinness depicting") rather than (or sometimes in addition to) overall amount of television viewing, and have found associations with body image disturbances (Harrison, 2003; Bissell & Zhou, 2004; Stice, Schupak-Neuberg, Shaw, & Stein, 1994; Park, 2005; Tiggemann, 2003, 2005).

Similar results have been found to stem from exposure to fashion and beauty-centered magazines, as well (Harrison, 2000a).

An important new trend in the literature is to examine these relationships between media and body image as they develop over time. For example, Moriarty and Harrison (2008) conducted a longitudinal study of 315 second, third, and fourth graders, gathering data at two points in time 1 year apart and measuring disordered eating, a phenomenon that includes having a negative body image, binge eating, restricting one's diet, abusing laxatives, pills, and other substances in an attempt to control weight, and over-exercising. They found television exposure significantly predicted eating disorder symptomology among both the white and the black girls in the sample, but not among boys of either race, after controlling for a number of variables, including disordered eating at baseline.

Indeed, one particularly disturbing subtopic within the literature examines the age at which media-influenced body image disturbances begin. Harrison and Hefner (2006) studied a sample of prepubescent girls over time, some as young as 6 years old, and found television viewing predicted later disordered eating as well as a thinner view of the ideal adult body type. Dohnt and Tiggemann (2006) surveyed girls age 5 through 8 and found significant associations between viewing "appearance-focused television" and the girls' satisfaction with their own appearance. Boys are not immune from such influence. Harrison (2000b) studied boys and girls age 6 to 8 and found that television exposure predicted disordered eating for both.

Another recent direction in research on this topic is to examine the impact of playing video games that feature sexualized portrayals of female characters that emphasize their body and their beauty on individuals' attitudes toward sexual harassment and sexual aggression. Yao, Mahood, and Linz (2010), for example, randomly assigned 74 male college students to play either a sexually explicit game with objectified female characters (*Leisure Suit Larry: Magna Cum Laude*) or one of two control games. Posttest measures included a lexical task to measure the priming of sex-related thoughts and a scale measuring likelihood to sexually harass. Yao et al. found those in the sexually objectifying condition responded faster to both sexual words and to sexually objectifying descriptions of women, thereby indicating priming had occurred, and scored higher on the likelihood to sexually harass scale than those in the control conditions. Dill, Brown, and Collins

(2008) also found a link between playing video games featuring appearance-related gender stereotypes and greater tolerance for sexual harassment (but not rape myth acceptance) in a prior experiment (see Chapter 12 for other effects of sexually explicit media).

For males, there is evidence that boys are driven not necessarily toward thinness but rather toward muscularity as a body ideal (Cohane & Pope, 2001; Moriarty & Harrison, 2008). Barlett, Vowels, and Saucier (2008) have used meta-analysis to summarize and synthesize the existing studies on the topic of media and the body image disturbances of males. They examined 25 studies comprising 93 different effects sizes between media exposure and males' body satisfaction (how one thinks about one's body), body esteem (how one feels about one's body) and self-esteem. Within the correlational studies, the overall effects size was –.19 and within the experimental studies, the overall effects size was –.22, thereby determining that, like females, males are negatively affected by media depictions of thinness and muscularity among male media characters.

The vast majority of studies examining media influence on body image–related variables examine the role of television and magazines and the advertisements contained within (Holstrom, 2004; Grabe et al., 2008). Yet, recently the phenomenon has been extended into video games, as well, with Barlett and Harris (2008) finding that playing a game that featured either an exceptionally thin or an exceptionally muscular character for 15 minutes led to decreases in self-esteem among male and female research participants. Furthermore, two recent studies have examined the consequences of viewing television programs that focus explicitly on appearance-related makeovers. Nabi (2009) studied exposure to reality-based programs specifically about cosmetic surgery makeovers, such as *The Swan, Extreme Makeover,* and *I Want a Famous Face.* Exposure to the cosmetic surgery makeover programs was positively linked to self-reported likelihood to engage in "appearance-enhancing procedures" if cost were no object, including those procedures minimally as well as more invasive. Somewhat similarly, Kubic and Chory (2007) found amount of viewing of makeover programs to be negatively related to self-esteem and positively related to dissatisfaction with one's body and a drive toward "perfectionism."

Although the occasional study fails to find a significant link between negative body image and either overall amount of television exposure (e.g., Botta, 1999; Tiggemann, 2005) or viewing of specific genres (e.g., Botta, 1999; Stice, Spangler, & Agras, 2001), the majority of the evidence suggests conclusively that media exert a small- to moderate-sized influence on body image. For individuals young and old, for males as well as females, and for individuals who vary by race, the profound emphasis in the media on beauty, thinness, and physical attractiveness does have negative consequences for the ways in which they perceive themselves and others. Such consequences can span the range from momentary lapses in self-esteem to longer lasting and more troubling forms of eating disorder symptomology.

Domestic and Relational Roles

Television and other media forms have also been examined for their potential contribution to gender roles regarding responsibilities in and around the home. One of the primary questions under this heading is whether the consistently gender-stereotyped information audiences receive from advertising and other media sources regarding housework responsibilities (as we have seen in the first section of this chapter) sways perceptions among individuals in the audience regarding whether males or females should do particular chores. Although the existing research is rather dated, the available evidence suggests television use is related to children and adolescents holding traditional attitudes about who should be or is suited for particular roles and responsibilities, such as females cooking and cleaning and males fixing things and taking out the trash (Morgan, 1987; Signorielli & Lears, 1992). In an interesting split between attitudes and behavior, the role of television does not seem to extend to the issue of who actually does these domestic tasks. Rather, the distribution of housework and chore behavior (although often shown to be quite gendered) is not typically related to amount of television use. For example, in Morgan's (1987) longitudinal data from 287 adolescents, television viewing predicted changes in adolescents' views of whether males or females should perform certain chores toward those more traditional in nature. Yet, television viewing was not related to the adolescents' own household chore responsibilities. In a sample of fourth and fifth graders, Signorielli and Lears (1992) also found significant associations between television use and gender-typed attitudes toward housework but no such link between viewing and actually doing particular chores in and around the house.

Another research question regarding domestic roles is whether media can play a part in forming individuals' perceptions of what mothers or fathers should be like, as well as how men and women form and behave within romantic relationships in general. One study on the topic took place in the Netherlands and featured the survey responses of 166 female adolescents and young women age 15 to 22 (Ex, Janssens, & Korzilius, 2002). Ex et al. found the amount of exposure to sitcoms and soap operas that feature more conventional gender-role depictions, but not the overall amount of television viewing, was associated with the young women anticipating a more traditional approach to their own future roles within motherhood, one in which family and children were emphasized over work. From this study, it seems specific television genres can shape the notions that girls and young women hold regarding potential roles for themselves as mothers.

Additional analyses have studied perceptions of dating and intimate relationships, and have generally supported the hypothesis that specific forms of television viewing can promote gender-related stereotypes. In a sample of 259 undergraduate students, Ward (2002) found amount of exposure to prime time comedies, prime time dramas, soap operas, and music videos were each associated with support for such stereotypical conceptions, including women being viewed as sex objects and men being seen as driven by sex as well as being unlikely to maintain a monogamous relationship. Ferris, Smith, Greenberg, and Smith (2007) found male heavy viewers of reality-based television dating programs endorsed the same sorts of stereotypes that surfaced in the Ward (2002) study (women as sex objects, men as sex driven) compared with their lighter viewer counterparts. Bryant (2008) determined that greater exposure to rap videos was related to black adolescents endorsing adversarial attitudes about romantic relationships, including economic equality and roles taken up within relationships. The more the young people watched rap videos, the more accepting they were of the ways in which both males and females were depicted in the videos. In an experiment conducted by Ward, Hansbrough, and Walker (2005), it was determined that black high school students who saw clips of music videos with stereotypical portrayals of men and women expressed more traditional views about sexual relationships and gender than those assigned to a different experimental condition.

We can safely conclude, therefore, that exposure to particularly gender-stereotyped content on television—whether it is found in music videos or soap operas, reality-based programs or prime time sitcoms or dramas—can contribute to audience members' stereotypical views of gender in sexual and romantic relationships. The effects research in this topic area has also shown that amount of television viewed by children and adolescents can shape their views of whether males or females should be responsible for particular household chores, although such exposure has not been shown to extend to the domestic responsibilities actually enacted by children and adolescents. There appears to be few if any recent scholarly inquiries into the possible effects of media depictions of household tasks and roles, however, and therefore the ways in which media might or might not influence the contemporary audience in this regard remain largely unknown.

Occupational Roles

Television has been found to affect perceptions of the careers that are deemed open to and suitable for males and females, as well as those that are deemed less so. These effects have the ability to limit one's view of career aspirations if they uphold gender stereotypical norms. On the other hand, the research evidence is also quite clear that when television and other media forms portray a counter-stereotypical set of occupations, exposure can translate into a more encompassing view of "acceptable" occupations.

Research conducted in the 1970s and 1980s points to television's ability to foster traditional notions of gender and occupation. Beuf (1974) found amount of television viewing to predict stereotypical views of careers among 3- to 6-year-old children. A longitudinal study of sixth to eighth graders conducted by Morgan (1982) found among girls that television viewing predicted stereotypical responses over time to an index that included such measures as "women are happiest at home raising children" and "men are born with more ambition than women," even after controlling for a number of additional variables. Jeffries-Fox and Jeffries-Fox (1981) surveyed 200 seventh to ninth graders and found that television exposure made a small but significant contribution to their conceptions of gender roles regarding occupations and work-related capacities. In early research conducted on the topic, therefore, television was associated with support for traditional occupational assignments, such as men as doctors and women as nurses, men as lawyers and women as secretaries, and so on.

Other studies examined audience members' perceptions of the ways in which television depicts gender and occupations. Within a sample of more than 1,200 Israeli adults, Zemach and Cohen (1986) found heavy television viewing to be associated with a smaller gap between perceptions of the ways in which television depicts gender and occupations and actual population statistics regarding gender and occupations. In other words, those who watched more television perceived the "real world" to more closely approximate the television world in terms of whether and how men and women were employed. Wroblewski and Huston (1987) found fifth and sixth grade girls who were frequent viewers of television programs with traditional gender depictions and infrequent viewers of programs with counter-stereotypical gender depictions expressed stronger aspirations toward more traditionally feminine occupations such as those featured on the screen. Both boys and girls in the study had negative attitudes about male characters participating in traditionally female-associated occupations on television.

Among the first studies to consider whether reverse stereotypical depictions can have a liberating effect on conceptions of gender roles was the experiment conducted by Atkins and Miller (1975). In their study, young research participants in the treatment group watched commercials that featured female characters in traditionally male-dominated careers. Following exposure, treatment group members were more likely than control group members to endorse male-dominated occupations as being acceptable for women, too. In an analysis of the prominent "Freestyle" television series featuring counter-stereotypical occupations (e.g., females as car mechanics and males as nurses), Johnston and Ettema (1982) found exposure to be associated with less stereotypical views of gender, especially with accompanied by an in-school curriculum. Geis, Brown, Walstedt, & Porter (1984) exposed research participants to either gender-stereotypical commercials or counter-stereotypical commercials and then asked them to write about what they imagined their lives would be like in 10 years. The women in the stereotypical commercial condition brought up aspects of domesticity more so than professional achievements compared with both the men and the women who were in the counter-stereotypical condition. In a much more recent study, Nathanson, Wilson, McGee, and Sebastian (2002) also determined that parental mediation can shape children's responses to stereotypes on television, with those in a mediation condition less likely to have favorable views of stereotyped characters and, among the younger children in the sample, more likely to score lower on a scale measuring stereotypical attitudes.

It is clear that children perceive television's depiction of occupations as stereotypical rather early on in childhood (Wroblewski & Huston, 1987; Wright et al., 1995). In fact, in Wright and colleagues' (1995) study of second and fifth graders, the children were more likely to aspire to a career seen on television if that career was not seen as gender stereotypical. Nonetheless, despite the skepticism that awareness of gender stereotyping would suggest, there is at least tentative evidence of television's effects in the existing research. The topic does not appear to have been taken up in more recent research, yet the (admittedly aging) research record does suggest that depending on the nature of the depiction—whether it upholds or runs counter to gender stereotypes—television use can contribute to views of gender and occupations. More recent explorations of what audiences may be learning from television and other media depictions of work are curiously absent in the literature.

Conclusions

The body of evidence accrued through content analysis regarding gender representations in media has pointed decidedly to progress in the opening up of gender roles on television, particularly those for women, both within and outside the home. Yet, a careful review of the content patterns suggests there still exists room for improvement, with some gendered depictions proving more stubborn to overturn, including within roles for men, within the close association of marital status to women and occupational status to men, and perhaps most egregiously, within the strict assignment of individuals to specific housework, parenting, and domestic care practices, particularly in advertising. Furthermore, all of these depictions and others occur within a scenario in which women continue to be underrepresented in media compared with men and their presence in the actual population. Such lack of visibility has the potential to send a message that women are undervalued in society.

Content analysis research also establishes conclusively that the men and women who populate media increasingly bear little resemblance to the men and women in the audience. Female characters in media are thin yet curvaceous. Many are clothed, photographed, or filmed in such a manner as to draw particular attention to their bodies. Male characters are lean and muscular. Both male and female characters who meet these increasingly strict definitions of beauty are more likely than their less fortunate (and less visible) counterparts to receive positive comments about how they look and to be presented in romantic as well as sexual contexts.

The effects research has shown that these media depictions of gender do, indeed, matter in that audiences young and old are absorbing these messages about gender and using them to shape their attitudes, intentions, and behavior. First, we have seen through both meta-analysis and through individual studies that myriad media forms—from overall amount of television to exposure to particular program types or genres, from video games to magazines, and increasingly ubiquitous ads—contribute to overall attitudes held by individuals regarding gender roles. The direction of this relationship is typically positive: Increased exposure relates to increased stereotypical or traditional views. However, we have also seen evidence that when television is among the more liberal or progressive messages an individual receives from the culture, the direction of the relationship can change. Television use can associate in these contexts with more open and wider views of gender roles.

The implications of the underrepresentation of women in terms of effects on the audience are unknown at this time. Yet, the implications of the other content patterns identified in this chapter have been explored in media effects research, some more thoroughly and some more recently than others. It is clear, for instance, that the profound emphasis on physical beauty and thin and lean bodies has negative consequences for media audiences. Media impact on body image disturbances begins as a disturbingly young age and has the potential to impact across gender and race. We can also confidently conclude that individuals are responding to the ways in which romantic and sexual relationships, often occurring within domestic settings, are portrayed in the media according to gender. The views of young audience members regarding how and why men and women form romantic relationships take shape, at least in part, from the media messages they receive, which include males being loathe to make commitments and women being viewed as objects of sexual attention. Early research established that television could also shape young people's views of housework and division of labor by gender, although this topic is in need of updating in future research. Finally, once again, early research showed the ability of television to contribute to conceptions about jobs, careers, and related skills and roles within. The conclusion from that body of research, that the television influence can either promote or refute stereotypes, should also be revisited in future research and should be extended into other popular media forms.

Future Directions

The body of knowledge on media and gender, as we have seen, is extensive and robust. Yet, key unanswered questions remain. First, it is essential to update the effects research in this area, as much of the existing research record on a number of subtopics relies on studies conducted in the 1970s or 1980s. The effects research has not kept pace with the content analysis research, and future researchers should use the most recent content findings to guide explorations of the ways in which audiences are receiving and responding to those depictions. Do modern media audience members draw from media in forming their notions of gender roles related to domestic and professional realms? With real-world statistics showing more equity in housework and child care roles within the home and more participation of women in the out-of-home workforce, how do media portrayals potentially resonate with or challenge individuals' day-to-day experiences?

Second, it is also quite evident from this review that men's roles and the depiction of masculinity have received much less attention than women's roles and the depiction of femininity, in both content analysis and effects research (Scharrer, 2012). One exception not yet discussed in this chapter is the existing research linking masculinity with aggression and violence in media portrayals. The longitudinal analyses of prime time television content conducted by Gerbner and, most recently, by Signorielli, for instance, establish conclusively that males are both the most frequent perpetrators and the most frequent victims of violence (Signorielli & Gerbner, 1995; Signorielli, 2003). Scharrer (2001b, 2012) has expanded these analyses to examine not just physical aggression but other indicators of "hypermasculinity"—including having a calloused attitude toward sex, a sensation-seeking tendency, and a tight control over emotions—in police and detective shows on television over time. The consequences of hypermasculinity for the aggressive responses of viewers to violent television has also been explored (Scharrer, 2001c, 2005). Yet, with this exception aside, the relative failure to explore masculinity and media from a quantitative, media effects perspective is a considerable gap in the literature that should be addressed in future research. Increasingly, scholars from sociology, psychology, cultural studies, and other fields are recognizing that the study of masculinity is important as a means of examining social and cultural norms, dominance and power in society, and implications for everyday interactions between and within people of varying genders. With some content analysis evidence that men's roles, too, are often restricted and constrained in media depictions (once again, as we have begun to see in this chapter), it is likely that media could contribute to conceptualizations of male roles. How do views of masculinity form in our media-saturated culture? New research in this area would make an important contribution to the body of knowledge regarding gender and media.

Another area that needs greater attention in future research is the issue of gender and the online media environment. A meta-analysis of 132 articles pertaining to gender and the Internet published between 1995 and 2003 in 28 publications found just two content analysis studies of gender roles in Internet content (Royal, 2005). The vast majority of articles in Royal's analysis were about women's access to Internet technology and women's uses of the Internet, thereby demonstrating the need not just for additional content analyses in this area, but also more effects research. Of course, the challenge of Internet research is the vast and ever-changing landscape that is represented in the millions of pages and sites. Nonetheless, with audiences young and old spending more time using social media (e.g., Facebook) and visiting other web sites, future research must overcome these obstacles. What are the ways that Internet use might contribute to gender-related perceptions, norms, and other outcomes among individuals young and old? This, too, is largely unanswered in the existing research, most of which focuses on television. Although television continues to dominate other media forms in how most individuals devote their time to media, exploring the Internet and other media forms more fully is necessary, nonetheless.

Finally, as the field of media psychology continues to embrace and attempt to capture the complexity of individuals' responses to media, future research in this area should reserve a central role for the study of individual differences. How does one's own degree of gender conformity, lived experiences with distribution of labor within the family or within the home, and professional status and roles shape one's response to media representations of gender? Close attention to these questions in future research in this area would make important contributions to the ever-important topic of media and gender.

References

Abdulrahim, M. A., Al-Kandari, A. A. J., & Hasanen, M. (2009). The influence of American television programs on university students in Kuwait. *European Journal of American Culture*, *28*(1), 57–74.

American Psychological Association (APA). (2011). *Sexualization of Girls: Executive Summary*. Retrieved July 8, 2011 from http://www.apa.org/pi/women/programs/girls/report.aspx.

Atkins, C., & Miller, M. (1975). *The Effects of Television Advertising in Children: Experimental Evidence*. Paper presented at the annual meeting of the International Communication Association, Chicago, IL.

Baker, C. N. (2005). Images of women's sexuality in advertisements: A content analysis of Black- and White-oriented women's magazines. *Sex Roles, 52*, 13–27.

Baker, K., & Raney, A. A. (2007). Equally super?: Gender-role stereotyping of superheroes in children's animated programs. *Mass Communication & Society, 10*(1), 25–41.

Barlett, C., & Harris, R. (2008). The impact of body emphasizing video games on body image concerns in men and women. *Sex Roles, 59*(7/8), 586–601.

Barlett, C. P., Vowels, C. L., & Saucier, D. A. (2008). Meta-analyses of the effects of media images on men's body image concerns. *Journal of Social and Clinical Psychology, 27*(3), 279–310.

Barner, M. R. (1999). Sex-role stereotyping in FCC-mandated children's educational television. *Journal of Broadcasting & Electronic Media, 43*(4), 551–564.

Bartsch, R. A., Burnett, T., Diller, T. R., & Rankin-Williams, E. (2000). Gender representation in television commercials: Updating an update. *Sex Roles, 43*(9/10), 735–743.

Beasley, B., & Collins Standley, T. (2002). Shirts vs. skins: Clothing as indicator of gender role stereotypes in video games. *Mass Communication & Society, 5*, 279–293.

Beuf, A. (1974). Doctor, lawyer, household drudge. *Journal of Communication, 24*(2), 142–154.

Bissell, K. L., & Zhou, P. (2004). Must-see-TV or ESPN: Entertainment and sports media exposure and body-image distortion in college women. *Journal of Communication, 54*, 5–21.

Botta, R. (1999). Televised images and adolescent girls' body image disturbance. *Journal of Communication, 49*, 22–41.

Bretl, D. J., & Cantor, J. (1988). The portrayal of men and women in U.S. television commercials: A recent content analysis and trends over 15 years. *Sex Roles, 18*, 595–609.

Bryant, Y. (2008). Relationships between exposure to rap music videos and attitudes toward relationships among African American youth. *Journal of Black Psychology, 34*(3), 356–380.

Browne, B. A. (1998). Gender stereotypes in advertising on children's television in the 1990s: A cross-national analysis. *Journal of Advertising, 27*(1), 83–96.

Callister, M. A., & Robinson, T. (2010). Content analysis of physical affection within television families during the 2006–2007 season of U.S. children's programming. *Journal of Children & Media, 4*(2), 155–173.

Cohane, G. H., & Pope, H. G. (2001). Body image in boys: A review of the literature. *International Journal of Eating Disorders, 29*, 373–379.

Collins, R. (2011). Content analysis of gender roles in media: Where are we now and where should we go? *Sex Roles, 64*, 290–298.

Coltrane, S., & Messineo, M. (2000). The perpetuation of subtle prejudice: Race and gender imagery in 1990s television advertising. *Sex Roles, 42*(5/6), 363–389.

Dietz, T. (1998). An examination of violence and gender role depictions in video games: Implications of gender role socialization and aggressive behavior. *Sex Roles, 38*, 425–441.

Dill, K. E., Brown, B. P., & Collins, M. A. (2008). Effects of exposure to sex-stereotyped video game characters on tolerance of sexual harassment. *Journal of Experimental Social Psychology*, *44*(5), 1402–1408.

Dohnt, H., & Tiggemann, M. (2006). The contribution of peer and media influence to the development of body satisfaction and self-esteem in young girls: A prospective study. *Developmental Psychology*, *42*, 929–936.

Douglas, S. J., & Michaels, M. (2004). *The Mommy Myth: The Idealization of Motherhood and How It Has Undermined Women*. New York: Free Press.

Downs, E., & Smith, S. L. (2010). Keeping abreast of hypersexuality: A video game character content analysis. *Sex Roles*, *62*, 721–733.

Ex, C. T. G. M., Janssens, J. M. A. M., & Korzilius, H. P. L. M. (2002). Young females' images of motherhood in relation to television viewing. *Journal of Communication*, *52*(4), 955–971.

Ferris, A. L., Smith, S., Greenberg, B. S., & Smith, S. L. (2007). The content of reality dating shows and viewer perceptions of dating. *Journal of Communication*, *57*(3), 490–510.

Fouts, G., & Burggraf, K. (2002a). Television situation comedies: Female body images and verbal reinforcements. *Women and Language*, *25*(2), 473–481.

Fouts, G., & Burggraf, K. (June, 2002b). Television situation comedies: Male weight, negative references, and audience reactions. *Sex Roles: A Journal of Research*, 439–443.

Frederick, D. A., Fessler, D. M., & Haselton, M. G. (2005). Do representations of male muscularity differ in men and women's magazines? *Body Image*, *2*, 81–86.

Ganahl, D. J., Prinsen, T. J., & Netzley, S. B. (2003). A content analysis of prime time commercials: A contextual framework of gender representation. *Sex Roles*, *49*(9/10), 546–551.

Garst, J., & Bodenhausen, G. V. (1997). Advertising's effects on men's gender-role attitudes. *Sex Roles*, *36*, 551–572.

Geis, F. L., Brown, V., Walstedt, J. J., & Porter, N. (1984). TV commercials as achievement scripts for women. *Sex Roles*, *10*(7/8), 513–525.

Glascock, J. (2003). Gender, race, and aggression in newer TV network's primetime programming. *Communication Quarterly*, *51*(1), 90–100.

Glascock, J., & Ruggiero, T. E. (2004). Representations of class and gender on primetime Spanish language television in the United States. *Communication Quarterly*, *52*(4), 390–402.

Grabe, S., Ward, L. M., & Hyde, J. S. (2008). The role of the media in body image concerns among women: A meta-analysis of experimental and correlational studies. *Psychological Bulletin*, *134*(3), 460–477.

Greenberg, B. S., Eastin, M., Hofschire, L., Lachlan, K., & Brownell, K. D. (2003). Portrayals of overweight and obese individuals on commercial television. *American Journal of Public Health*, *93*, 1342–1348.

Greenberg, B. S., & Worrell, T. R. (2007). New faces on television: A 12-season replication. *The Howard Journal of Communications*, *18*, 277–290.

Groesz, L. M., Levine, M. P., & Murnen, S. K. (2002). The effect of experimental presentation of thin media images on body satisfaction: A meta-analytic review. *International Journal of Eating Disorders*, *31*, 1–16.

Harrison, K. (2000a). The body electric: Thin-ideal media and eating disorders in adolescents. *Journal of Communication*, *50*, 119–143.

Harrison, K. (2000b). Television viewing, fat stereotyping, body shape standards, and eating disorder symptomatology in grade school children. *Communication Research*, *27*, 617–640.

Harrison, K. (2003). Television viewers' ideal body proportions: The case of the curvaceously thin woman. *Sex Roles*, *48*, 255–264.

Harrison, K., & Cantor, J. (1997). The relationship between media consumption and eating disorders. *Journal of Communication*, *47*, 40–66.

Harrison, K., & Hefner, V. (2006). Media exposure, current and future body ideals, and disordered eating among preadolescent girls: A longitudinal panel study. *Journal of Youth and Adolescence*, *35*, 153–163.

Hatoum, I. J., & Belle, D. (2004). Mags and abs: Media consumption and bodily concern in men. *Sex Roles*, *51*, 397–407.

Hazell, V., & Clarke, J. (2008). Race and gender in the media: A content analysis of advertisements in two mainstream Black magazines. *Journal of Black Studies*, *39*(5), 5–21.

Head, S. (1954). Content analysis of television drama programs. *Quarterly Journal of Film, Radio, and Television*, *9*, 175–194.

Herrett-Skjellum, J., & Allen, M. (1996). Television programming and sex stereotyping: A meta-analysis. In Burleson, B. R. (Ed.), *Communication Yearbook 19*. Thousand Oaks, CA: Sage, pp. 157–185.

Holstrom, A. J. (2004). The effects of the media on body image: A meta analysis. *Journal of Broadcasting & Electronic Media*, *48*(2), 196–218.

Hurtz, W., & Durkin, K. (2004). The effects of gender-stereotyped radio commercials. *Journal of Applied Social Psychology*, *34*(9), 1974–1993.

Jeffries-Fox, S., & Jeffries-Fox, B. (1981). Gender differences in socialization through television to occupational roles: An exploratory approach. *The Journal of Early Adolescence*, *1*(3), 293–302.

Jennings, J., Geis, F. L., & Brown, V. (1980). Influence of television commercials on women's self-confidence and independent judgment. *Journal of Personality and Social Psychology*, *38*, 203–210.

Johnston, D. D., & Swanson, D. H. (2003). Invisible mothers: A content analysis of motherhood ideologies and myths in magazines. *Sex Roles*, *49*(1/2), 21–34.

Johnston, J., & Ettema, J. S. (1982). *Positive Images: Breaking Stereotypes with Children's Television*. Beverly Hills, CA: Sage.

Kaufman, G. (1999). The portrayal of men's family roles in television commercials. *Sex Roles: A Journal of Research*, *41*, 439–458.

Keller, K. (1994). *Mothers and Work in Popular American Magazines*. Westport, CT: Greenwood.

Knupfer, N. N. (1998).Gender divisions across technology advertisements and the WWW: Implications for educational equity. *Theory into Practice*, *37*(1), 54–64.

Kubic, K. N., & Chory, R. M. (2007). Exposure to television makeover programs and perceptions of self. *Communication Research Reports*, *24*(4), 283–291.

Larson, M. S. (2001). Interactions, activities, and gender in children's television commercials. *Journal of Broadcasting & Electronic Media*, *45*(1), 41–56.

Lauzen, M. M., & Dozier, D. M. (1999). Making a difference in prime time: Women on screen and behind the scenes in the 1995–1996 television season. *Journal of Broadcasting & Electronic Media*, *43*, 1–43.

Lauzen, M. M., & Dozier, D. M. (2002). You look mahvelous: An examination of gender and appearance comments in the 1999–2000 primetime season. *Sex Roles, 46*(11/12), 429–437.

Lauzen, M. M., Dozier, D. M., & Horan, N. (2008). Constructing gender stereotypes through social roles in primetime television. *Journal of Broadcasting & Electronic Media, 52*(2), 200–214.

Leaper, C., Breed, L., Hoffman, L., & Perlman, C. A. (2002). Variations in the gender-stereotyped content of children's television cartoons across genres. *Journal of Applied Social Psychology, 32*(8), 1653–1662.

Leit, R. A., Pope, H. G. Jr., & Gray, J. J. (2000). Cultural expectations of muscularity in men: The evolution of *Playgirl* centrefolds. *International Journal of Eating Disorders, 29*, 90–93.

Lewin-Jones, J., & Mitra, B. (2009). Gender roles in television commercials and primary school children in the UK. *Journal of Children and Media, 3*(1), 35–50.

Lin, C. A. (1998). Uses of sex appeals in prime-time television commercials. *Sex Roles, 38*, 461–475.

Marshall, J. C., & Bannon, S. (1988). Race and sex equity in computer advertising. *Journal of Research on Computing in Education, 21*(1), 15–27.

Massoni, K. (2004). Modeling work: Occupational messages in *Seventeen* magazine. *Gender and Society, 18*(1), 47–66.

McDermott, S. T., & Greenberg, B. S. (1984). Parents, peers, and television as determinants of Black children's esteem. In Bostrom, R. (Ed.), *Communication Yearbook 8*. Beverly Hills: Sage, pp. 164–177.

Milmer, L. M., & Higgs, B. (2004). Gender sex-role portrayals in international television advertising over time: The Australian experience. *Journal of Current Issues and Research in Advertising, 26*(2), 81–95.

Morgan, M. (1982). Television and adolescents' sex-role stereotypes: A longitudinal study. *Journal of Personality and Social Psychology, 43*, 947–955.

Morgan, M. (1987). Television, sex-role attitudes, and sex-role behavior. *The Journal of Early Adolescence, 7*(3), 269–282.

Morgan, M., & Shanahan, J. (1997). Two decades of cultivation research: An appraisal and meta analysis. In Burleson, B. R. (ed.), *Communication Yearbook, 20*. Thousand Oaks, CA: Sage pp. 1–46.

Morgan, M., Shanahan, J., & Signorielli, N. (2009). Growing up with television: Cultivation processes. In Bryant, J., & Oliver, M. (Eds.), *Media Effects: Advances in Theory and Research*, 3rd ed. New York: Routledge, pp. 34–49.

Moriarty, C. M., & Harrison, K. (2008). Television exposure and disordered eating among children: A longitudinal panel study. *Journal of Communication, 58*(2), 361–381.

Morrison, T. G., & Halton, M. (2009). Buff, tough, and rough: Representations of muscularity in action motion pictures. *The Journal of Men's Studies, 17*(1), 57–75.

Nabi, R. (2009). Cosmetic surgery makeover programs and intentions to undergo cosmetic enhancements: A consideration of three models of media effects. *Human Communication Research, 35*(1), 1–27.

Nathanson, A., Wilson, B. J., McGee, I., & Sebastian, M. (2002). Counteracting the effects of female stereotypes in television via active mediation. *Journal of Communication, 52*(4), 922–937.

Neuendorf, K. A. (2002). *The Content Analysis Guidebook*. Thousand Oaks, CA: Sage.

Northrup, T., & Liebler, C. M. (2010). The good, the bad, and the beautiful. *Journal of Children & Media, 4*(3), 265–282.

Oppliger, P. A. (2007). Effects of gender stereotyping on socialization. In Press, R. W., Gayle, B. M., Burrell, N., Allen, M., & Bryant, J. (eds.), *Mass Media Effects Research: Advances Through Meta-analysis*. Hillsdale, NJ: Lawrence Erlbaum Associates, pp. 199–214.

Park, S. (2005). The influence of presumed media influence on women's desire to be thin. *Communication Research, 32*, 594–614.

Peirce, K. (1997). Women's magazine fiction: A content analysis of the roles, attributes, and occupations of main characters. *Sex Roles, 37*(7/8), 581–593.

Raphael, C., Bachen, C., Lynn, K. M., Baldwin-Philippi, J., & McKee, K. A. (2006). Portrayals of information and communication technology on World Wide Web sites for girls. *Journal of Computer-Mediated Communication, 11*(3), 771–801.

Reep, D. C., & Dambrot, F. H. (1994). TV parents: Fathers (and now mothers) know best. *Journal of Popular Culture, 28*(2), 13–23.

Rivadeneyra, R., & Ward, L. M. (2005). From Ally McBeal to Sabado Gigante: Contributions of television viewing to the gender role attitudes of Latino adolescents. *Journal of Adolescent Research, 20*, 453–475.

Royal, C. (2005). A meta-analysis of journal articles intersecting issues of internet and gender. *Journal of Technical Writing and Communication, 35*(4), 403–430.

Royo-Vela, M., Aldas-Manzano, J., Kuster, I., & Vila, N. (2008). Adaptation of marketing activities to cultural and social context: Gender role portrayals and sexism in Spanish commercials. *Sex Roles, 58*(5/6), 379–390.

Saito, S. (2007). Television and the cultivation of gender-role attitudes in Japan: Does television contribute to the maintenance of the status quo? *Journal of Communication, 57*(3), 511–531.

Scharrer, E. (2001a). From wise to foolish: The portrayal of the sitcom father, 1950s to 1990s. *Journal of Broadcasting & Electronic Media, 45*(1), 23–41.

Scharrer, E. (2001b). Tough guys: The portrayal of aggression and hypermasculinity in televised police dramas. *Journal of Broadcasting & Electronic Media, 45*(4), 615–634.

Scharrer, E. (2001c). Men, muscles, and machismo: The relationship between television violence and aggression in the presence of hypermasculinity. *Media Psychology, 3*(2), 159–188.

Scharrer, E. (2004). Virtual violence: Gender and aggression in video game advertisements. *Mass Communication & Society, 7*(4), 393–412.

Scharrer, E. (2005). Hypermasculinity, aggression, and television violence: An experiment. *Media Psychology, 7*(4), 353–376.

Scharrer, E. (2012). More than "just the facts?" Portrayals of masculinity in police and detective dramas over time. *Howard Journal of Communications, 23*, 1–21.

Scharrer, E., Kim, D. D., Lin, K., & Liu, Z. (2006). Working hard or hardly working? Gender, humor, and the performance of domestic chores in television commercials. *Mass Communication & Society, 9*(2), 215–238.

Signorielli, N. (1985). *Role Portrayal on Television: An Annotated Bibliography of Studies Relating to Women, Minorities, Aging, Sexual Behavior, Health, and Handicaps*. Westport, CT: Greenwood Press.

Signorielli, N. (1989). Television and conceptions about sex-roles: Maintaining conventionality and the status quo. *Sex Roles, 21*(5/6), 341–360.

Signorielli, N. (2003). Prime-time violence 1993–2001: Has the picture really changed? *Journal of Broadcasting & Electronic Media, 47*(1), 36–58.

Signorielli, N. (2008). *Children' Programs 2007: Basic Demography and Violence*. Paper presented at the annual conference of the National Communication Association. San Diego, CA.

Signorielli, N. (2009a). Minorities representation in prime time: 2000 to 2008. *Communication Research Reports, 26*(4), 323–336.

Signorielli, N. (2009b). Race and sex in prime time: A look at occupations and occupational prestige. *Mass Communication and Society, 12*(3), 332–352.

Signorielli, N. (2013). Gender role socialization in the 21st century. In Scharrer, E. (Vol. Ed.), *Media Effects/Media Psychology* and A. Valdivia (Gen. Ed.) *The International Encyclopedia of Media Studies*. Boston: Wiley Blackwell.

Signorielli, N., & Bacue, A. (1999). Recognition and respect: A content analysis of prime-time television characters across three decades. *Sex Roles, 40*(7/8), 527–544.

Signorielli, N., & Gerbner, G. (1995). Violence on television: The Cultural Indicators Project. *Journal of Broadcasting & Electronic Media, 39*(2), 278–284.

Signorielli, N., & Kahlenberg, S. (2001). Television's world of work in the nineties. *Journal of Broadcasting & Electronic Media, 45*(1), 1–19.

Signorielli, N., & Lears, M. (1992). Children, television and conceptions about chores: Attitudes and behaviors. *Sex Roles, 27*, 157–170.

Smith, A. M. (2001). Mass-market magazine portrayals of working mothers and related issues, 1987 and 1997. *Journal of Children and Poverty, 7*, 101–119.

Smith, L. (1994). A content analysis of gender differences in children's advertising. *Journal of Broadcasting & Electronic Media, 38*(3), 323–337.

Smith, S. L., Pieper, K. M., Granados, A., & Choueiti, M. (2010). Assessing gender-related portrayals in top-grossing G-rated films. *Sex Roles, 62*, 774–786.

Stern, S. R., & Mastro, D. E. (2004). Gender portrayals across the life span: A content analytic look at broadcast commercials. *Mass Communication & Society, 7*(2), 215–236.

Stice, E., Schupak-Neuberg, E., Shaw, H. E., & Stein, R. I. (1994). Relation of media exposure to eating disorder symptomatology: An examination of mediating mechanisms. *Journal of Abnormal Psychology, 103*, 836–840.

Stice, E., Spangler, D. L., & Agras, W. S. (2001). Exposure to media-portrayed thin-ideal images adversely affects vulnerable girls: A longitudinal experiment. *Journal of Social and Clinical Psychology, 20*, 271–289.

Suzuki, A. (1991). Egalitarian sex role attitudes: Scale development and comparison of American and Japanese women. *Sex Roles, 24*, 245–259.

Tiggemann, M. (2003). Media exposure, body dissatisfaction, and disordered eating: Television and magazines are not the same! *European Eating Disorders Review, 11*, 418–430.

Tiggemann, M. (2005). Television and adolescent body image: The role of program content and viewing motivation. *Journal of Social & Clinical Psychology, 24*, 361–381.

Turner, J. S. (2011). Sex and the spectacle of music videos: An examination of the portrayal of race and sexuality in music videos. *Sex Roles, 64*(3/4), 173–191.

Ward, L. M. (2002). Does television exposure affect emerging adults' attitudes and assumptions about sexual relationships? Correlational and experimental confirmation. *Journal of Youth and Adolescence, 31*(1), 1–15.

Ward, L. M., Hansbrough, E., & Walker, E. (2005). Contributions of music video exposure to Black adolescents' gender and sexual schemas. *Journal of Adolescent Research, 20*(2), 143–166.

Ware, M. C., & Stuck, M. F. (1985). Sex-role messages vis-a-vis microcomputer use: A look at the pictures. *Sex Roles, 13*(3/4), 205–214.

White, C., & Kinnick, K. N. (2000). One click forward and two clicks back: Portrayal of women using computers in television commercials. *Women's Studies in Communication, 23*, 392–413.

Williams, D., Martins, N., Consalvo, M., & Ivory, J. (2009). The virtual census: Representations of gender, race, and age in video games. *New Media & Society, 11*(5), 815–834.

Wright, J. C., Huston, A. C., Truglio, R., Fitch, M., Smith, E., & Piemyat, S. (1995). Occupational portrayals on television: Children's role schemata, career aspirations, and perceptions of reality. *Child Development, 66*(6), 1706–1718.

Wroblewski, R., & Huston, A. (1987). Televised occupational stereotypes and their effects on early adolescents: Are they changing? *The Journal of Early Adolescence, 7*(3), 283–297.

Yao, M. Z., Mahood, C., & Linz, D. (2010). Sexual priming, gender stereotyping, and likelihood to sexually harass: Examining the cognitive effects of playing a sexually explicit video game. *Sex Roles, 62*(1/2), 77–88.

Zemach, T., & Cohen, A. A. (1986). Perception of gender equality on TV and in social reality. *Journal of Broadcasting & Electronic Media, 30*(4), 427–444.

Zhang, Y., Dixon, T. L., & Conrad, K. (2010). Female body image as a function of themes in rap music videos: A content analysis. *Sex Roles, 62*, 787–797.

Zhang, Y. B., & Lien, S. C. (2010). Television viewing and Taiwanese adolescent girls' perceptions of body image. *China Media Report Overseas, 6*(4), 15–24.

The Psychology Underlying Media-Based Persuasion

Robin L. Nabi *and* Emily Moyer-Gusé

Abstract

Attempts at persuasion are as ubiquitous as the media often used to disseminate them. However, to explore persuasion in the context of media, we must first consider the psychological processes and mechanisms that underlie persuasive effects generally, and then assess how those strategies might apply in both traditional as well as more innovative media. This chapter overviews three dominant frameworks of persuasion (cognitive response models, expectancy value theories, and emotional appeals), along with three more subtle forms of influence (framing, narrative, and product placement) to explore how psychological theory and media effects research intersect to shed light on media-based persuasive influence.

Key Words: Cognitive response, emotion, expectancy value theories, framing, media effects, narrative, persuasion, product placement

Introduction

Attempts at persuasion are as ubiquitous as the media often used to disseminate them. Given that decades of persuasion research has documented just how challenging it can be to alter the beliefs, attitudes, and especially the behaviors of others, it is unsurprising that media strategies have evolved in response to emerging technologies to help overcome barriers to persuasion, thus yielding the modern persuasive forms of, for example, infomercials, product placement, and viral videos. But ultimately the psychological theories of how people process such messages are relatively indifferent to the messages' particular forms. That is, despite the rapid changes in media forms and modes of transmission, the theories used to understand their effects remain largely unchanged. Thus, to explore persuasion in the context of media, we must first consider the psychological processes and mechanisms that underlie persuasive effects generally, and then assess how those strategies might apply to both traditional as

well as more innovative media, with an eye toward useful avenues for theoretical advancement. Given the vastness of the topic of persuasion has been well-addressed in volumes previously (e.g., Eagly & Chaiken, 1993; Dillard & Pfau, 2002; Perloff, 2010), we will not attempt to offer a comprehensive review of the extant psychological research on persuasion here. Rather, we focus on the theoretical frameworks most directly linked to current research in media effects, how these theories have been applied in media contexts, and issues that might prove fruitful for future examination.

Although many definitions of persuasion exist, they tend to share several common elements. Persuasion is typically understood as a process whereby a message sender intends to influence an (uncoerced) message receiver's evaluative judgments regarding a particular object. Given media effects research tends to emphasize the unintended and often negative influence of media content on receivers, we wish to be clear that this chapter focuses exclusively on intentional effects at persuasion rather than the incidental social influence that might occur as a result of mass media exposure.

There are a number of classes of persuasion theories that focus on a range of psychological mechanisms driving influence that might be applied to the study of media effects. However, there are three theoretical orientations that have received substantial attention from media effects scholars interested in more direct and obvious attempts at persuasion, such as advertisements or public service announcements: cognitive response models, expectancy-value theories, and emotional appeals. Further, there are three additional frameworks that have been given particular attention in the context of more subtle, although arguably more powerful, forms of media-based persuasive influence: framing, narrative, and product placement. This chapter reviews the literature in each of these areas, with particular attention to how such research might evolve in response to the ever-changing media environment.

Theory Underlying Mediated Persuasive Appeals

As noted, a plethora of theories and models have been applied in media contexts, but three stand out as guiding the discussion of media influence: cognitive response models, expectancy-value theories, and fear appeals. We address each one in turn.

Cognitive Response Models of Persuasion

Cognitive response models of persuasion assume that the thoughts people have during message exposure drive their subsequent attitudes. As such, message recipients are viewed as active participants whose cognitive reactions mediate the influence of a persuasive attempt. Most notable among these models is Petty and Cacioppo's (1986) elaboration likelihood model (ELM) of persuasion, which suggests two possible routes to persuasion—central and peripheral. If sufficient processing motivation and ability are present, central processing is expected to occur during which the receiver will give thoughtful consideration to the arguments and information presented. The ratio of favorable to unfavorable cognitive responses generated about the message is then expected to predict persuasive outcome. If either processing motivation or ability is impaired, the receiver is expected to engage in peripheral processing during which simple, though not necessarily relevant, cues present in the persuasive setting will influence attitudinal response.

Petty and Cacioppo (1986) note that because greater message elaboration is expected to generate more thoughts that are then incorporated into cognitive schema, attitude change based on central processing is expected to be more stable, enduring, and predictive of behavior than attitude change based on peripheral processing. The nature and valence of the cognitive responses generated during central processing may be guided by a range of factors, including initial attitude, prior knowledge, personality factors, and mood. Moreover, they acknowledge that biased processing may occur to the extent various factors, particularly initial attitude, influence motivation or ability to process the message, resulting in more or less favorable thoughts about the object than might have been expected otherwise.

The ELM has been tested in numerous lab studies, the results of which tend to support its predictions (Eagly & Chaiken, 1993). However, several important theoretical and empirical criticisms have been launched against it, including the dichotomy between central and peripheral processing, the tautological definition of argument strength, and the inability to specify a priori whether particular message features will be processed centrally or peripherally (Stiff, 1986; Stiff & Boster, 1987; and responses by Petty, Cacioppo, Kasmer, & Haugtvedt, 1987 and Petty, Kasmer, Haugtvedt, & Cacioppo, 1987; also, see Eagly & Chaiken, 1993). The ELM has not been appreciably modified in light of these criticisms; however, the notion of thought confidence influencing outcomes was introduced in the early 2000s, suggesting that confidence in one's thoughts about the message intensifies their effect (i.e., confidence in favorable thoughts enhances persuasion and confidence in unfavorable ones detracts) (Petty, Brinol, & Tormala, 2002). However, this element of the model has seen little additional attention in the extant research since its introduction.

Chaiken's heuristic-systematic model (HSM) of persuasion offers a similar, although more clearly specified dual-processing approach. The HSM suggests that accuracy-motivated people may assess message validity through two types of message processing—heuristic and systematic—which may operate concurrently depending on the receiver's judgmental confidence threshold for a particular issue (Chaiken, 1980, 1987; Chaiken, Liberman, & Eagly, 1989; Eagly & Chaiken, 1993). As cognitive misers, individuals are expected to base decisions on heuristics if they can be sufficiently confident in the accuracy of those decisions. If sufficient confidence cannot be reached using simple decision rules, individuals are expected to then also engage in the more effortful systematic processing. Although the

HSM's systematic processing and the ELM's central processing are essentially the same, heuristic and peripheral processing differ in that the former is conceptualized as only cognitive and rational, whereas the latter is believed to encompass any cognitive or affective processes other than close message scrutiny. Research testing the unique aspects of the HSM has offered some evidence consistent with the model's propositions, particularly that of concurrent processing and the attenuation of heuristic effects by systematic processing (Eagly & Chaiken, 1993). Further, the model has been elaborated by identifying multiple motives for message processing (i.e., accuracy, defensive, and impression motivations). However, research has not directly targeted the sufficiency threshold construct, thus limiting insights into the factors that might move the threshold higher or lower, which would have implications for the information needs of the audience.

Given that media effects scholars have generally adopted the view of audiences as active consumers of messages rather than mere passive information recipients, it is understandable why cognitive response models have been readily embraced by media effects scholars. Indeed, the ELM and HSM have been applied in numerous traditional advertising contexts, including those related to health (e.g., Wilson, 2007; Smith, Lindsey, Kopfman, Yoo, & Morrison, 2008), politics (e.g., Holbert, Garrett, & Gleason, 2010), and of course commercial products (e.g., Whittler & Spira, 2002). Generally speaking, such research tends to apply these theories to understand how various features of the audience (e.g., motivation) and features of the messages (e.g., arguments and cues) interact to lead to changes in attitudes, behavioral intentions, and behaviors.

There is a wealth of evidence supporting the tenets of cognitive-response models in advertising contexts. However, perhaps because they were developed with a focus on psychological mechanisms rather than message design, they are not particularly responsive to the complexities with which modern media messages may be presented. For example, whereas the majority of ELM-based studies are based on text-only messages, an overwhelming proportion of mediated persuasive messages contain visuals. According to Petty and Cacioppo's (1986) arguments, the persuasive impact of visuals would depend on whether the receiver is motivated and/or able to process the message. If motivated and able, the visuals will be taken as arguments. Otherwise, they will be used as cues and have ephemeral effects on attitudes. However, given visuals (unlike text) can

be processed quickly with minimal cognitive effort, one might have low motivation and ability and yet still be greatly impacted by a particularly gripping image that can be processed nearly automatically and, in turn, result in long-lasting attitude change. Thus, the ELM, in its current form, seems somewhat insensitive to more modern persuasive contexts.

As the design of persuasive media messages evolves, some research will certainly continue to work within the typical framework of dual-processing cognitive response models, examining, for example, how innovative message features, like interactive social agents (e.g., Skalski & Tamborini, 2007) and online reviews (Lin, Lee, & Horng, 2011), influence processing motivation or serve as peripheral cues. However, given the ELM and HSM were developed largely in the context of more text-based, expository messages—a less typical form of media presentation in recent years—some fundamental assumptions about the nature of message processing as captured by these theories, may be challenged by newer media formats. For example, Cho (1999) articulated a modified elaboration likelihood model to address the processing of Web advertising, arguing for the roles of both voluntary and involuntary ad exposure as well as the mediating effects of repeated exposure, attitude toward the site, and attitude toward Web advertising, beyond the roles of processing motivation and ability as articulated by the ELM. San Jose-Cabezudo, Gutierrez-Arranz, and Gutierrez-Cillan (2009) also argue that how Web pages are presented influences the nature of the information processing that ensues.

In sum, cognitive response models have provided a very useful framework for understanding how media messages may lead to persuasive effects, and will surely continue to guide examination of unique media features in the coming years. However, newer media forms may bring to light limits of these theories developed in an era of less complex message design and thus ideally generate theoretical innovations sensitive to these technological changes.

Expectancy Value Theories

A second class of persuasion theories—expectancy value theories—also focuses on cognition, but these theories assume audiences are rational decision makers who weigh the pros and cons of their options. More specifically, they assume people have expectancies regarding whether an object has a certain attribute, and they ascribe a particular value to that attribute. In combining these assessments, one's attitude is formed. Indeed, it was the endeavor to understand the conditions under which stable attitude–behavior relationships could be found that resulted in the development of the most well-known expectancy-value theory—the theory of reasoned action (TRA) (Fishbein & Ajzen, 1975), one of the more influential theories of social influence in the last 50 years.

According to the TRA, the best predictor of volitional behavior is behavioral intention (Fishbein & Ajzen, 1975). Behavioral intentions, in turn, are based on two types of cognitive antecedents: (1) attitudes toward performing a particular behavior, and (2) the subjective norm surrounding that behavior. Attitudes are comprised of groups of salient beliefs regarding behavioral outcomes and evaluations of those outcomes. Comparably, the subjective norm is comprised of perceptions of important others' attitudes regarding one performing the behavior and motivation to comply with their opinions. Under this conceptualization, other variables, like demographics, personality traits, and related attitudes, affect behavior only insofar as they affect the individual's beliefs, evaluations, or motivations to comply. A meta-analysis of TRA-based research supports the model's propositions that attitudes and subjective norms can accurately predict behavioral intentions and, in turn, behaviors (Sheppard, Hartwick, & Warshaw, 1988). In addition, a meta-analysis of 138 attitude–behavior correlations further supports the TRA's position that attitudes can have strong associations with behaviors across a range of topics (Kim & Hunter, 1993).

Despite the wealth of evidence supporting the TRA, its critics argue that its utility and predictive ability are limited by its intended applicability to: (1) volitional behaviors only, (2) stable attitudes and behavioral intentions, and (3) corresponding attitude and behavior measures in terms of target, context, time, and action (see Eagly & Chaiken, 1993 for a critical review). In fact, several individual and situational barriers have been identified as having a significant impact on the translation of attitudes and/or intentions into behaviors, including time, money, the cooperation of other people, and personal self-efficacy (Triandis, 1977; Ajzen, 1985; Ajzen & Madden, 1986; Madden, Ellen, & Ajzen, 1992). Indeed, the theory of planned behavior was developed to help address these limitations (Ajzen, 1985), and recently Fishbein and Ajzen (2010) have elaborated on the critical elements of the reasoned action perspective, including the origins of beliefs, the role of injunctive versus descriptive norms, and the determinants of perceived behavioral control. Still, within its self-identified boundaries, TRA-based research has generated evidence to demonstrate that under the appropriate circumstances, attitudes can reliably predict behavioral intentions and behaviors.

Applied to media-based persuasion, the TRA is most helpful in suggesting what message content, rather than message design features, might best produce persuasive effects. To the extent a behavior is more heavily influenced by attitudes, one might attempt to change already-held outcome–belief expectancies or the valuations ascribed to those outcomes. Or one might look to add new belief clusters to the attitude equation. If the subjective norm is more dominant in predicting behavioral intentions and behaviors, then producing messages that speak to perceptions of what others think, motivation to comply, or adding new important others to the equation may be effective. Moreover, one might also attempt to alter the weighting of the attitude relative to the subjective norm to affect shifts in behavioral intentions and behaviors. Although this framework is extremely useful in guiding conceptually what one might hope to achieve with a persuasive message, the TRA is silent on how one might actually implement those ideas in message design. Further, the TRA is very limited in its consideration of factors beyond "rational" beliefs. Most notably, the role of emotion is not incorporated into the model in any direct or meaningful way. Given emotion (as described in a later section) is a primary motivational force underlying behavior, this is a very notable limitation of the TRA.

As media message platforms shift such that persuasive messages may be easily avoided (e.g., fast forwarding through commercials or blocking pop-up ads on web sites) or alternatively hard to avoid (e.g., embedded in web sites of interest), it has become increasingly important to take into consideration how belief-based information is presented to capture attention. Yet, it is this very presentation that may shift audiences away from more rational and deliberative decision making (see discussions of emotion and framing that follow). Although Fishbein and Ajzen (2010) would likely argue that such message features (e.g., emotional presentations) act merely as background variables influencing behaviors only indirectly through the beliefs formed, the action tendencies associated with emotions generated from media presentations may actually serve to intensify the likelihood of action *without* full mediation through beliefs. Thus, important directions for future research will be to consider not just how various message features may influence the construction of attitudes and subjective norms via information salience, but also how the process of influence through to behavior is influenced by the psychological state the audience may be in because of those attention-getting contextual features.

Emotion and Persuasion

A third dominant framework for media-based persuasion research focuses on affective states. Most of the research here has centered around fear arousal and its effects on both message processing and persuasion-related outcomes (e.g., attitudes, behavioral intentions, and behaviors), although the persuasive influence of other emotional states is receiving increasing attention.

FEAR APPEAL RESEARCH

The fear appeal literature has cycled through several theoretical perspectives over the past 50 years (see Nabi, 2007 for more detailed discussion), including: (1) the drive model, which conceptualized fear as resembling a drive state, motivating people to adopt recommendations expected to alleviate the unpleasant state (e.g., Hovland, Janis, & Kelley, 1953); (2) the parallel processing model (PPM) (Leventhal, 1970), which separated the motivational from the cognitive aspects involved in processing fear appeals, suggesting that those who respond to fear appeals by focusing on the threat (cognition) would engage in adaptive responses, whereas those responding with fear (emotion) would engage in maladaptive responses; (3) the expectancy value–based protection motivation theory (Rogers, 1975, 1983), which ultimately focused on four categories of thought generated in response to fear appeals—judgments of threat severity, threat susceptibility, and response and self-efficacy—and how they might combine to predict message acceptance; and (4) the extended parallel process model (EPPM) (Witte, 1992), which integrated the PPM and PMT, predicting that if perceived efficacy outweighs perceived threat, danger control and adaptive change will ensue. If, however, perceived threat outweighs perceived efficacy, then fear control and maladaptive behaviors are expected.

Although meta-analyses of fear research essentially suggest that the cognitions identified in the PMT, and later the EPPM, are important to fear appeal effectiveness, no model of fear appeals has been endorsed as accurately capturing the process of fear's effects on decision making and action (see Mongeau, 1998; Witte & Allen, 2000). Regardless, evidence does support a positive linear relationship between fear and attitude, behavioral intention, and behavior change. Thus, to the extent message features evoke perceptions of susceptibility and severity, as well as response and self-efficacy, fear may moderate persuasive outcome, although there are still important questions about the interrelationships among these constructs that remain unanswered. Further, questions about whether severity and susceptibility information should always be included in fear appeals or whether "implicit" fear appeals might be more effective have also been raised (Nabi, Roskos-Ewoldsen, & Dillman Carpentier, 2007). Thus, there is still much work to be done in linking the theory of fear appeals to appropriate message design.

BEYOND FEAR APPEALS

There is growing interest, as well, in understanding the effects of emotions other than fear in the processing of persuasive messages (see Nabi, 2007 for a more extensive discussion), and emerging models attempt to examine those processes. For example, the cognitive functional model (CFM) (Nabi, 1999) attempts to explain how message-relevant negative emotions (e.g., fear, anger, sadness, guilt, disgust) affect the direction and stability of persuasive outcome based on three constructs—emotion-driven motivated attention, motivated processing, and expectation of message reassurance. An initial test of the model (Nabi, 2002) offered support for some, although not all, of the model's propositions, but as it awaits future tests, the CFM offers insight into the process through which a range of discrete emotions, not just fear, influences message processing, and outcomes.

In a similar vein, Nabi (2003, 2007) posits an emotions-as-frames model to explain the effects of more general media exposure on attitudinal and behavioral outcomes. In this model, emotions are conceptualized as frames, or perspectives, through which incoming stimuli are interpreted. The model first notes the message features likely to evoke various discrete emotions. These emotional experiences, moderated by individual differences (e.g., schema development, coping style), are predicted to influence both information accessibility and information seeking that ultimately generate emotion-consistent decisions and action. Nabi argues that through this perspective we may develop a better understanding of the central role emotions may play in understanding how frames in a range of media messages, including those designed to persuade, might impact attitudes and behaviors.

Notably missing from this discussion thus far, however, is research on the persuasive effect of positive emotional states. There has been a fair amount of attention to humor; however, reviews of the humor literature have concluded that though humor may enhance message attention and source liking, it is generally no more persuasive than nonhumorous messages (see Weinberger & Gulas, 1992 for a more nuanced discussion). With the increasing popularity of political satire programs, such as the *Daily Show* and the *Colbert Report,* there has been an upswing in interest in examining the process through which humor may have persuasive influence. For example, Nabi, Moyer-Gusé, and Byrne (2007) argue that humor may not have immediate persuasive effect because although audiences attend closely to the message, they discount it as a joke that is not intended to persuade, thus minimizing the message content's effects on their attitudes. However, they also posit that this type of processing may lead to a "sleeper effect" such that the persuasive effect of humor may emerge after some time has passed (see also Young, 2008). Clearly, future research would benefit from closer examination of the persuasive effect of positive emotions like hope and pride and the processes through which such effects might emerge.

Beyond the types of emotions investigated, future research would also benefit from greater attention to issues such as the role of emotion in overcoming barriers posed by selective attention. In the cluttered media environment, garnering attention to one's persuasive message is increasingly challenging and yet a necessary (although not sufficient) step in the persuasion process. Emotional appeals may be particularly well-suited to this task. Of course, once attention is gained, it is critical that the rest of the message be structured appropriately for the target audience. Risk of boomerang effects due to psychological reactance (message resistance stemming from perceiving an unjust restriction on one's freedom to choose) (Brehm, 1966), denial, problem minimization, and the like persist. Understanding the delicate balance between gaining attention and harnessing it to intended effect has been an elusive challenge in the area of emotional appeals and persuasion, and future research would be well served by tackling this difficult message design issue.

Further, understanding in greater detail how the specifics of message content may relate to an audience's emotional state is a surprisingly understudied issue. For example, the assumption in fear appeal research is that people are scared by threats to their physical body, most especially thoughts of death. Yet fears of disability (e.g., paralysis, blindness) or disfigurement may prove equally, and sometimes more, frightening than death. Further, not all fears are rooted in physical well-being. Evidence suggests that younger audiences' assessments of their likelihood of experiencing a range of health problems are characterized by the optimism bias, and compared with adults, teenagers minimize the perceived risk associated with the occasional involvement in health-threatening acts (Cohn, Macfarlane, Yañez, & Imai, 1995). However, given that teenagers and young adults are still forming their identities, threats to social acceptance may be far more salient and thus more frightening to such audiences than threats to physical well-being. Thus, *social harm–based* fear appeals may be more effective for young audiences than physical harm–based fear appeals. Future research would be well served by considering not simply a greater range of emotional responses, but also the matching of message content and features to the intended emotional arousal for particular target audiences and by continuing to explore the impact of discrete emotional arousal states on information processing and decision making.

Subtler Forms of Persuasion

In addition to the three dominant frameworks of persuasion that have been examined in media contexts, there are three other, subtler forms of persuasion that warrant close attention: framing, narrative, and product placement.

Framing

Framing theories generally posit that the way in which information is presented, or the perspective taken in a message, influences a range of audience responses. As Entman (1993) states, a message frame will "promote a particular problem definition, causal interpretation, moral evaluation, and/or treatment recommendation...." (p. 52). As a result of the framing process, receivers notice, process, think about, and store information in a manner consistent with a particular message frame (Fiske & Taylor, 1991), which in turn may influence the information people use to form opinions (Price & Tewksbury, 1997). In essence, a frame is a perspective infused into a message that promotes the salience of selected pieces of information over others. When adopted by receivers, frames may influence individuals' views of problems and their necessary solutions.

Several prominent studies provide evidence supporting this claim in a variety of contexts, including how language choice influences risky decision-making (Kahneman & Tversky, 1984), how television news framing affects attributions of responsibility for both the causes of and the treatments for social problems (Iyengar, 1991), how political journalistic news norms help to define the ideas people express when talking about politics (Gamson, 1992), and how news coverage of political campaigns influences how the public thinks about political processes (Cappella & Jamieson, 1997). In sum, these research programs indicate that the way in which information is presented can influence how people understand, evaluate, and act on a problem or issue.

Regarding the cognitive processes through which framing effects occur, it is generally suggested that such effects are the result of information accessibility biases. According to Iyengar (1991), when fed a steady diet of one type of frame over another, individuals tend to recall and use the information consistent with the predominant frame when making a decision. Price and Tewksbury (1997) argue that such accessibility of applicable information from memory influences decision making in both the short and long term if those thoughts continue to be made accessible to the individual by repetitious exposure to certain frames over others. Cappella and Jamieson (1997) also argue that news frames stimulate access to certain information, beliefs, and/or inferences, making them increasingly accessible with repeated exposure. However, they further suggest that decision making is influenced by both memory-based and online processing rather than relying solely on memory-based influences.

There is great diversity in the rich extant framing literature in terms of conceptualization, operationalization, and context application, and the many calls for strong theory development to help make sense of this increasingly disparate area of influence have been generally unsuccessful. Still, there are helpful ways to view the framing literature that give it some clearer structure. In considering the various ways in which framing has been studied, Shah, McLeod, Gotlieb, and Lee (2009) identify two key dimensions—precision versus realism, and context-specific frames versus context-transcendent frames. Precision involves holding information content constant while manipulating only the way in which that information is presented, whereas realism allows for natural variation in messages (including their content) to allow for greater external validity. This is a critical distinction because framing effects based on precision can be argued to be solely a function of the *presentation* of the information, whereas framing based on realism, although perhaps more externally valid, conflates influence based on both content and style.

Regarding Shah et al.'s second dimension, context-specific research focuses on the frames that may exist within a certain topic that do not translate to other contexts or when applied to another context do not mean the same thing (e.g., an economic frame in health care is not the same as an economic frame in a political campaign), whereas context-transcendent views suggest that there are more generic forms of presentation that cut across contexts (strategy versus issue frames in politics or gain versus loss frames in health). These dimensions certainly highlight critical ways in which framing studies may vary, although the field still awaits more detailed theorizing building on these variations.

Given all media messages (and indeed all messages generally) involve selection and salience by virtue of their mere construction, framing is an inherent part of all persuasive messages. The question most central to this chapter, then, is what forms of media message construction result in what patterns of influence. As we look to the communication literature, framing is a central feature of research in both political and health communication. The political communication research tends to focus more on unintentional effects of the news media's presentation of issues, whereas health communication research considers more directly intentional efforts to influence audiences' attitudes and behaviors, so it is on the latter area that we will focus.

The bulk of research on framing, persuasion, and health is rooted primarily in prospect theory. Prospect theory is a particular brand of framing theory developed to explain choices involving risk in which people often prefer options incompatible with the most rational choice (Kahneman & Tversky, 1979, 1984; Tversky & Kahneman, 1981). More specifically, messages inviting risky decision making may present issues in terms of one of two basic frames: losses (e.g., disadvantages or detriments related to *not* engaging in an advocated behavior) or gains (e.g., benefits or advantages related to complying with an advocated behavior). In processing the framed options, message receivers subjectively evaluate them, assessing value based on whether they are expected to improve or impair the current situation. Importantly, this subjective perception is often at odds with the objective likelihood of experiencing an outcome.

Consequently, according to Tversky and Kahneman (1981), there are predictable shifts of preference depending on whether a problem is framed in terms of gains or losses. In general, people are more risk averse when faced with gain-framed messages.

That is, if a person sees the current situation as good or certain, she or he will hesitate to engage in a behavior perceived as potentially interfering with the current status of certainty. Conversely, people are predictably more risk-seeking when exposed to loss framed messages. That is, if a person perceives the present situation as costly, she or he will feel there is little to lose by engaging in a behavior that involves some risk.

Prospect theory asserts that generally speaking, loss frames are more effective at influencing behavior (Kahneman & Tversky, 1979). However, Rothman and Salovey (1997) note that when assessing the impact of frame type in the context of health messages, the type of behavior (e.g., prevention or detection) is relevant. More specifically, they argue that health prevention behaviors (e.g., exercise, teeth brushing, sunscreen use) are generally viewed as less risky compared with detection behaviors (e.g., cholesterol screening, dental visit, dermatological skin check) because by nature they provide more certain and desirable outcomes, helping to maintain current health and inhibit unwanted health problems. Thus, Rothman and Salovey argue that gain frames, which also focus on a behavior's health benefits, can be more effective than loss frames in the prevention behavior context, as evidenced by research promoting regular exercise (Robberson & Rogers, 1988), intentions and behaviors to wear sunscreen (Rothman, Salovey, Antone, Keough, & Martin, 1993; Block & Keller, 1995; Detweiler, Bedell, Salovey, Pronin, & Rothman, 1999), and obtaining a plaque-fighting mouthwash (Rothman, Martino, Bedell, Detweiler, & Salovey, 1999).

Conversely, because of the potential to be informed of an undesirable health state, detection behaviors are often considered risky and anxiety-evoking (Rothman & Salovey, 1997). Because loss frames generally lead to greater adherence in risky situations, loss-framed messages are thought to be more effective in promoting detection behaviors (Rothman et al., 1993; Banks et al., 1995), such as breast self-examinations (Meyerowitz & Chaiken, 1987); getting a mammogram (Banks et al., 1995); and dental exams (Rothman et al., 1999; see Rothman & Updegraff, 2011, for a current overview).

Although the relative advantages of the prevention-gain frame/detection-loss frame pairings are generally supported across individual studies, it is important to acknowledge critical potential moderators of these relationships. First, the predicted interaction is contingent on the targeted behaviors being perceived as relatively safe (prevention) versus relatively risky (detection). It is of course possible that objectively defined prevention or detection behaviors may be viewed as risky or safe, respectively, by specific audiences, thus disrupting the expected pattern of findings (Rothman & Updegraff, 2011). Second, a recent meta-analysis has called the strength of the detection-loss frame effect into question (O'Keefe & Jensen, 2009), suggesting the nature of the detection behavior itself (e.g., its ability to be cognitively or affectively engaging) may impact whether a particular frame offers persuasive advantage (see also Rothman & Updegraff, 2011). Third, personality traits or dispositions of the message receiver (e.g., promotion or prevention focus, approach or avoidance tendencies, regulatory focus) may influence the likelihood of framing effectiveness. For example, promotion-focused people, who are oriented toward growth and accomplishment (i.e., "wants"), may respond more favorably to gain-framed messages, whereas prevention-focused people, who are concerned with safety and security goals (i.e., "oughts"), may respond more favorably to a loss-framed message (Rothman, Wlaschin, Bartels, Latimer, & Salovey, 2008; Rothman & Updegraff, 2011). Further, additional audience factors, such as issue involvement, may influence frame effectiveness. Indeed, evidence suggests that issue involvement may lead to stronger framing effects (Maheswaran & Meyers-Levy, 1990; Rothman et al, 1993) perhaps because of closer information processing (Rothman & Salovey, 1997).

From a persuasion perspective, it is clear that the intentional framing of messages may have advantages to influencing attitudes, behavioral intentions, and behaviors regarding targeted health behaviors, and that a match between the audience's construal of the behavior and the message frame is critical to maximizing persuasive advantage. Understanding in more depth the factors relevant to such matching is obviously critical to harnessing framing for maximum benefit. Also greatly needed is a deeper understanding of the psychological process through which framing effects emerge (Rothman & Updegraff, 2011). Particularly overlooked, in our view, has been the role of emotion in these processes (Nabi, 2007). Apart from some general associations drawn between loss-framed messages/detection behaviors, gain-framed messages/prevention behaviors, and negative and positive feelings, respectively, there is little discussion of the role of emotion in framing effects. Deeper exploration into the ways in which specific emotions evoked within these contexts impact audience processing and decision making could be enlightening.

Also, with due respect to the extensive research on gain and loss frames in health messages, there are other forms of health message presentation that may be worth pursuing to better understand how message framing may influence health decision making. For example, as noted earlier, Nabi (2007) presents an emotions-as-frames model in which she argues that emotions themselves serve as frames to influence information accessibility and information seeking such that emotion-consistent behaviors result. Tests of these assumptions would help shed light on how different emotion frames, apart from or perhaps in conjunction with gain and loss frames, may influence health decision-making. Another context-transcendent frame set that might warrant greater attention is personal responsibility versus societal or environmental influence, in which the former frame may lead to more individual action, whereas the latter may lead to changes in public policy. Exploring the alternative ways in which health information may be presented, other than via gain versus loss, may allow for richer and more extensive applications of intentional message framing.

Finally we wish to make two additional observations. First, framing and health research tends to focus on how information is presented in text rather than how information might be presented visually or interactively. Research linking more innovative modes of information presentation to the framing literature may prove insightful. Second, there is little if any research or discussion on potential boomerang effects in the context of framing and health messages. Given the importance of understanding not simply when messages work, but also when they backfire, this line of inquiry, too, would be of great benefit, especially in light of the repeated exposure that is the goal of health campaigns.

Narrative Persuasion

Narrative persuasion offers a second common form of "subtle" influence. Although many definitions have been used, a *narrative* can be defined as a story with, "…an identifiable beginning, middle, and end that provides information about scene, characters, and conflict; raises unanswered questions or unresolved conflict; and provides resolution" (Hinyard & Kreuter, 2007, p. 778). A narrative structure can offer some advantages over more overt persuasive appeals for several reasons. First, narratives are able to attract attention in a competitive media environment. Indeed, scholars have noted the unique potential for entertainment media to reach audiences compared to traditional persuasive

messages or news media (Montgomery, 1990; Jin, 2006). Because entertainment narratives are appealing and engrossing, individuals are more likely to direct their attention to them, and by default, to the embedded educational message (Bandura, 2004). Second, stories featuring well-liked or attractive characters are well-suited for modeling behavior (e.g., Bandura, 1986). Third, narrative persuasion offers the unique potential to persuade without arousing traditional forms of resistance (e.g., reactance and counterarguing).

A growing body of research has examined how narrative media messages can influence viewers' attitudes and behaviors across a variety of health or social issues. We begin our discussion first by elaborating on the primary context of the study of persuasion and narrative—entertainment-education—before discussing the theoretical foundations of the persuasive influence of narrative.

ENTERTAINMENT-EDUCATION

One common application of narrative persuasion has been entertainment-education (EE). Generally speaking, EE refers to media programs that "entertain and educate, in order to increase audience members' knowledge about an educational issue, create favorable attitudes, and change overt behavior" (Singhal & Rogers, 1999, p. 9). Beginning with early programs developed in Mexico in the 1980s (Sabido, 1981), EE efforts have targeted a range of behaviors and topics, such as AIDS prevention, gender equity, condom use, sex education, and literacy (Sood, Menard, & Witte, 2004).

Generally speaking, evidence suggests that under the right circumstances, EE can be an effective form of persuasion (for review, see Singhal & Rogers, 2004). For example, one of the most successful documented EE efforts is "Soul City," an entertainment media campaign in South Africa that, among other elements, features a prime time television drama series that addresses various health-related topics each year, including HIV prevention and control (Singhal & Rogers, 2001). Using pre- and posttest panel surveys, evaluations have shown that broadcasting of this program associated with increases in knowledge of HIV transmission and prevention, positive attitudes toward condom use, and increases in prevention behaviors (Singhal & Rogers, 2001; Soul City Institute, 2005).

Although International EE interventions are typically developed with specific health or prosocial goals in mind, in the United States, educational storylines are typically embedded into otherwise purely entertainment programming (Singhal & Rogers, 1999; Greenberg, Salmon, Patel, Beck, & Cole, 2004). Sometimes these storylines appear through the work of advocacy groups (Greenberg et al., 2004), whereas in other cases they are developed solely by television writers (Singhal & Rogers, 2004). Research generally supports the effectiveness of this sort of EE program on audience awareness and knowledge of various health issues, such as condom efficacy (based on an episode of the situation comedy *Friends*) (Collins, Elliott, Berry, Kanouse, & Hunter, 2003), emergency contraception and human papillomavirus (based on a storyline from the prime time drama *ER*) (Brodie et al., 2001), and HIV and cancer plotlines in various entertainment television programs (Beck, 2004; Hether, Huang, Beck, Murphy, & Valente, 2008; Wilkin et al., 2007). There is also evidence that EE efforts can influence viewer attitudes toward stigmatized groups, such as individuals with HIV (O'Leary, Kennedy, Pappas-DeLuca, Nkete, Beck, & Galavotti, 2007; Lapinski & Nwulu, 2008) or mental illness (Ritterfeld & Jin, 2006). Moreover, EE may influence viewers' behavioral intentions. Specifically, viewers of television dramas featuring organ donation storylines were more likely to decide to donate if the drama explicitly encouraged it, particularly if viewers were emotionally involved in the narrative (Morgan, Movius, & Cody, 2009).

Exposure to an EE program can also prompt viewers to both seek out additional information about a topic, such as HIV (Kennedy, O'Leary, Beck, Pollard, & Simpson, 2004) or breast cancer screening (Wilkin et al., 2007), and inspire conversations about the topics embedded in the narrative (Valente, Kim, Lettenmaier, Glass, & Dibba, 1994; Papa et al., 2000; Sood, Shefner-Rogers, & Sengupta, 2006; Pappas-DeLuca et al., 2008). For example, a recent experiment showed that characters who model difficult conversations about safer sex can boost viewers' self-efficacy and encourage them to engage in similar conversations in their own lives (Moyer-Gusé, Chung, & Jain, 2011). Thus, extant research supports the influence of EE efforts on a range of persuasion-related variables, including knowledge, attitudes, behavioral intentions, information seeking, and conversation.

The narrative influence strategy typically used in EE programs is not without limitations. For example, because the underlying persuasive content in a narrative is less overt, viewers are free to actively construct its meaning. As a result, EE narratives can lead to misinterpretation among some viewers (Singhal & Rogers, 2001). Although evidence for EE effectiveness abounds, some studies have found that these narrative-based messages are effective at influencing only a subset of viewers and may lead to boomerang effects among others (e.g., Vidmar & Rokeach, 1974; Wilson et al., 1992; Moyer-Gusé & Nabi, 2011). Such findings highlight the need for greater understanding of the mechanisms by which narrative influence occurs.

THEORETICAL FOUNDATIONS OF NARRATIVE PERSUASION

One frequently cited explanation for the success of EE efforts is social cognitive theory (SCT) (Bandura, 1986). Social cognitive theory revolves primarily around the functions and processes of observational learning (Bandura, 1986, 2002b). That is, by observing others' behaviors, including those of media figures, one may develop rules to guide one's own subsequent actions. More specifically, Bandura (1986, 2002b) argues that observational learning is guided by four processes, which are moderated by observers' cognitive development and skills. First, *attention* to certain models and their behavior is affected by source and contextual features, like attractiveness, relevance, functional need, and affective valence. Second, *retention* processes focus on the ability to symbolically represent the behavior observed and its consequences, along with any rehearsal of that sequence. *Production* focuses on translating the symbolic representations into action, reproducing the behavior in seemingly appropriate contexts and correcting for any errors based on the feedback received. Finally, *motivational* processes influence which symbolically represented behaviors are enacted based on the nature or valence (positive or negative) of the reinforcement. Such reinforcement may come from the feedback generated by one's own behavior, the observed feedback given to others, or internal incentives (e.g., self-standards). As observational learning occurs via symbolic representations, the effects are believed to be potentially long-lasting.

Because of humans' capacity to think symbolically, mediated narratives are especially useful vehicles to achieve observational learning and increase self-efficacy to perform given behaviors (Bandura, 2001). Drawing from the above theoretical explication, SCT suggests that, in essence, for mediated content to positively affect audience members' behaviors, the audience must pay attention to attractive or similar models performing relevant behaviors. Models engaging in positive behaviors should be positively reinforced, whereas those engaging in negative behaviors should be negatively reinforced (Austin & Meili, 1994; Bandura, 2001). Thus, a character who is rewarded for his or her behavior serves to positively motivate and reinforce that behavior in the mind of the viewer, whereas behaviors for which characters are punished are negatively reinforced (Bandura, 2004). Bandura further argues that identification with a character (the process of temporarily taking on the role of that character) and perceived similarity may enhance this effect.

Beyond the potential for modeling, more recent theorizing in narrative persuasion has pointed to the ways in which narratives may reduce message resistance. First came the notion of *transportation,* or absorption into a story such that one loses track of the real world and experiences the unfolding events in the story (Gerrig, 1993; Green & Brock, 2000). Transportation is argued to minimize resistance to persuasion as the audience's focus on the plot reduces their motivation and/or ability to counterargue the message position. Building from this notion, Slater and Rouner (2002) proposed the extended elaboration likelihood model (E-ELM), which, although based on the ELM (described in a preceding section), was developed specifically to address how individuals process narrative messages. The E-ELM posits that, compared with more overt persuasive appeals, narrative messages foster greater absorption and identification with characters, both of which suppress counterarguing with the underlying persuasive subtext. This enhanced state of engagement is dependent upon the appeal of the storyline, the quality of production, and the "unobtrusiveness of persuasive subtext" (Slater & Rouner, 2002, p. 178). In this way, using a narrative structure may lead to effective persuasion by reducing viewers' motivation to generate counterarguments while viewing.

There is certainly evidence that transportation into mediated entertainment messages relates to story-consistent attitudes (e.g., Kennedy, Turf, Wilson-Genderson, Wells, Huang, & Beck, 2011; Murphy, Frank, Moran, & Patnoe-Woodley, 2011). And although some research supports the notion that the transportation-persuasion link is a function of reduced counterargument in the context of written narratives (Green & Brock, 2000), little is known about the relationship between absorption and counterarguing in the context of audiovisual media (Hinyard & Kreuter, 2007). Indeed, evidence on this point is mixed. Slater, Rouner, and Long (2006) found that watching a television drama about controversial issues (e.g., gay marriage, the death penalty) led to greater support for related public policies with very minimal counterarguing, whereas Moyer-Gusé and Nabi (2010) found transportation *positively* related to participants' self-reported counterarguing of a television drama regarding teen pregnancy. Thus, the effect of transportation on counterarguing is still somewhat of an open question.

Most recently, building on the strengths of both SCT and E-ELM, the entertainment overcoming resistance model (EORM) (Moyer-Gusé, 2008) focuses on how different features of media narratives (e.g., identification, parasocial interaction, perceived persuasive intent) can overcome a range of sources of persuasive resistance. For example, the EORM contends that narrative messages may reduce psychological reactance by diminishing viewers' perception that the message intends to persuade. Similarly, including characters with whom viewers have a parasocial relationship may make the underlying persuasive content feel less authoritative, thus also reducing reactance. Further, the EORM posits that a narrative message can increase perceptions of vulnerability to some threats via identification with characters, and thus motivate positive attitude and behavior change. Indeed, Moyer-Gusé and Nabi (2010) found evidence offering support for each of these claims, although the perceived vulnerability-identification association emerged only after some time had passed, which is consistent with other research on entertainment media and sleeper effects (e.g., Appel & Richter, 2007; Nabi, Moyer-Gusé, & Byrne, 2007; Moyer-Gusé et al., 2011). Further, evidence suggests that identification with main characters—another form of absorption into the narrative—reduced counterarguing with the underlying message (Moyer-Gusé & Nabi, 2010; Moyer-Gusé, Chung, & Jain, 2011). In sum, a few studies have tested portions of the EORM, finding support for several predictions of the model. By linking these message-based processes to various forms of resistance to persuasion, the EORM offers insight for message designers to reduce a range of barriers to persuasive success.

In sum, considering the unique ways in which narrative media messages can overcome various forms of resistance to persuasion appears to be a useful way to understand EE effects and perhaps persuasion effects more generally. Future research should continue to explore the mechanisms of narrative persuasion effectiveness. Specifically, given that most EE research has focused on dramatic narratives, the persuasive effects of other genres, such as comedy or mystery programming, should be considered.

Entertainment-education research could also benefit from a focus on identifying the right balance of entertainment and education content to maximize the effectiveness of EE messages. As noted, one limitation of EE is the potential for misinterpretation, in part stemming from the underlying persuasive message being too subtle or open to interpretation. One way this has been addressed in practice is by including an epilogue to underscore the intended message. However, little is known about how this strategy may alter EE effects. Indeed, several of the propositions of the EORM as well as the EELM depend on persuasive intent remaining in the background. Future research should examine the message features necessary to ensure that the underlying persuasive message is clear without coming across as didactic or interfering with the narrative experience.

Product Placement

Finally, we wish to address one more instance of a subtle form of persuasion in the media: product placement. Although definitions vary across the literature, product placement generally refers to the purposeful inclusion of a brand within some entertainment media content (Karrh, 1998; van Reijmersdal, Neijens, & Smit, 2009). Typically, this placement is bought or bartered by an advertiser to gain attention for a brand or to affect brand selection, and can be classified along three dimensions: visual, auditory, and plot connection (Russell, 1998). The visual dimension refers to the visual appearance of the brand on the screen (e.g., the number of times the product is shown, the relative size of the product on the screen, the positioning in the foreground or background). The auditory dimension addresses whether the brand is mentioned in dialog (e.g., how frequently the brand is named, emphasis placed on the brand itself, which character refers to the product). The third dimension, plot connection, involves how well-integrated the brand is into the message's storyline.

Although product placement has become increasingly popular as an advertising tactic, the research on its effectiveness is still rather diffuse and disconnected (e.g., Karrh, 1998; Balasubramanian, Karrh, & Patwardhan, 2006; van Reijmersdal et al., 2009). This discussion highlights the major trends in product placement research, focusing specifically on the dependent measures used to assess effectiveness, their interrelationships, and the psychological mechanisms used to explain them.

Early product placement research focused primarily on explicit memory of the placed brand as a measure of effectiveness (perhaps because of the centrality of ad recall in the advertising literature.) Explicit memory refers to what a viewer can consciously recall seeing (Law & Braun-LaTour, 2004), and research suggests that explicit memory is enhanced by the prominence of the product placement within the entertainment message (Gupta & Lord, 1998; Law & Braun, 2000; Yang & Roskos-Ewoldsen, 2007). For example, placements that are well integrated into the plot are more prominent and therefore more likely to be remembered than those that are tangential (Yang & Roskos-Ewoldsen, 2007). Similarly, placements are more memorable when a brand is depicted visually and verbally as opposed to just one or the other (Law & Braun, 2000). In these ways, more prominent placements are more likely to be explicitly remembered by audience members.

Although prominent placements are more likely to be recalled, importantly, this does not necessarily enhance brand choice. For example, Yang and Roskos-Ewoldsen (2007) in examining three levels of prominence (background, used by main character, connected to plot) found that although the more prominent placements were more readily recognized afterward, they had no effect on brand choice. In fact, explicit recall for the placement can actually lead to more negative attitudes toward the brand. Similarly, Law and Braun (2000) found that product placements that were depicted visually but not mentioned (i.e., less explicit), had a greater effect on brand choice than those that were depicted audio-visually or those that were mentioned verbally (i.e., more explicit), even though the visual-only placements were least likely to be explicitly recalled. That is, the least memorable placement was the one that most influenced brand preference.

Similar results have been found regarding connection to plot and placement within highly liked programs. Russell (2002) found that when a placement seemed out of place (such as a verbal reference to a product that is not well integrated into the plot), it was more likely to be recalled but less likely to enhance persuasion, perhaps because such placements are perceived by the audience as unnatural. Relatedly, Cowley and Barron (2008) found that viewers high, but not low, in program liking experienced less supportive attitudes in response to product placement within that program, arguably because fans are likely to pay more careful attention to the show, making them better able to explicitly recall the placement and be more conscious of the persuasive intent.

Taken together, these results show that more memorable placements do not necessarily translate into greater persuasion and indeed may interfere with persuasive effect. This apparent disjuncture may be explained based on the constructs of awareness of persuasive intent and cognitive resistance. More specifically, a prominent placement is more likely to activate viewers' cognitive defenses against persuasive messages. When a viewer notices a placement and elaborates on its persuasive intent, it may induce greater irritation and/or counterarguing, thus leading to greater resistance (e.g., Friestad & Wright, 1994). More prominent placements, because they are more likely to be noticed, can lead to this sort of elaboration and counterarguing. In other words, it is because the audience notices the placement that they are able to resist its influence. Conversely, if the audience is exposed to the product placement in more subtle ways (e.g., visual depiction only, brief screen time/mention, smooth integration into the plot), the product has been primed and thus made cognitively accessible to the viewer, but because of the limited awareness of the source of its activation, the viewer is less motivated and/or able to control its influence on their choices. Thus, by increasing the cognitive accessibility of a brand, more subtle product placements may increase the likelihood that it will be chosen. Indeed, research supports this notion that exposure to a placement increases brand accessibility (e.g., Yang, Roskos-Ewoldsen, Dinu, & Arpan, 2006; Yang & Roskos-Ewoldsen, 2007).

In essence, more prominent product placements increase the likelihood that an audience member will be aware of the persuasive intent and thus be more motivated and/or able to resist in terms of product choice. Conversely, less prominent placements, although less likely to be recalled, can lead to greater product selection because of cognitive priming and accessibility. Future research would certainly benefit from comparing the relative effectiveness of product placement relative to traditional advertising forms. In addition, understanding more clearly the conditions under which product placement influences attitudes and behaviors would be useful. Further, it would be helpful to consider more directly the way in which media features and processes influence product placement effectiveness. For example, does transportation encourage or impede a product's perceived prominence within a story and thus, in turn, influence the persuasive impact of the product placement? Additionally, some research has shown that when brands are used by liked characters, they are evaluated more favorably (d'Astous, & Chartier,

2000; Yang & Roskos-Ewoldsen, 2007). Given what is known about social cognitive theory, might liked characters' use of products increase audience liking for those products such that product prominence in the message might turn out to be a productive, rather than counterproductive, factor? Similarly, does liking a movie translate into liking products placed within them in ways that undermine the resistance associated with awareness of product placement? In sum, considering more directly the media effects variables relevant to the entertainment context together with the psychological process associated with product placement should allow both lines of research to move forward in meaningful ways.

Conclusion

Clearly a wide range of psychological perspectives have been applied to the context of media-based persuasion. Some of these perspectives (e.g., cognitive response models, expectancy value models, fear appeals) capture quite well the influence process associated with overt persuasive attempts in a very wide range of contexts, whereas others (e.g., framing, narrative, product placement) help capture the subtleties associated with persuasive messages conveyed in more specific media forms or contexts. And combined, both sets of literature make it quite clear that understanding what is necessary for successful persuasion requires understanding (and avoiding) the conditions of resistance to persuasion. Thus, future research will benefit from attention to the structure and design of messages that foster attention without simultaneously triggering psychological resistance. Closer consideration of issues related to emotional arousal, visual communication, transportation, and identification across these various contexts, we believe, will be critical to understanding this delicate balance. Especially given the extraordinary technological developments that are now influencing the creation, conveyance, and receipt of mediated persuasive messages, it is essential that scholars consider more fully the ways in which message construction interacts with psychological orientation to impact information processing and decision making. The marriage of psychological theory and media effects has been a fruitful one to this point, and their continued interrelationship will be critical to understanding more fully persuasion processes in the new media age.

Questions for Future Research

How will the assumptions of the ELM and other cognitive response models hold up in light of new forms of persuasive message design and delivery?

How does the construction of media-based persuasive messages designed to capture attention influence expectancy value–based calculations?

Under what conditions are positive emotional appeals effective and how do they compare with the effectiveness of negative emotional appeals?

What factors moderate the effectiveness of gain versus loss frames?

What entertainment message features link to what psychological states such that resistance to persuasion is minimized?

How does product placement effectiveness compare with the effectiveness of traditional forms of advertising?

References

Ajzen, I. (1985). From intentions to actions: A theory of planned behavior. In Kuhland, J., & Beckman, J., (Eds.), *Action-Control: From Cognitions to Behavior*. Heidelberg: Springer, pp. 11–39.

Ajzen, I., & Madden, T. (1986). Prediction of goal-directed behavior: Attitudes, intentions, and perceived behavioral control. *Journal of Experimental Social Psychology*, *22*, 453–474.

Appel, M., & Richter, T. (2007). Persuasive effects of fictional narratives increase over time. *Media Psychology*, *10*, 113–134.

Austin, E. W., & Meili, H. K. (1994). Effects of interpretations of televised alcohol portrayals on children's alcohol beliefs. *Journal of Broadcasting & Electronic Media*, *38*, 417–435.

Balasubramanian, S. K., Karrh, J. A., & Patwardhan, H. (2006). Audience response to product placement: An integrative framework and future research agenda. *Journal of Advertising*, *35*(3), 115–141.

Bandura, A. (1986). *Social Foundations of Thought and Action: A Social Cognitive Theory*. Englewood Cliffs, NJ: Prentice-Hall.

Bandura, A. (1997). *Self-Efficacy: The Exercise of Control*. New York: Freeman.

Bandura, A. (2001). Social cognitive theory of mass communication. *Media Psychology*, *3*, 265–299.

Bandura, A. (2002). Growing primacy of human agency in adaptation and change in the electronic era. *European Psychologist*, *7*, 1–16.

Bandura, A. (2002). Social cognitive theory of mass communication. In Bryant, J., & Zillmann, D. (Eds.), *Media Effects: Advances in Theory and Research*. Hillsdale, NJ: Lawrence Erlbaum Associates, pp. 121–154.

Bandura, A. (2004). Social cognitive theory for personal and social change by enabling media. In Singhal, A., Cody, M. J., Rogers, E. M., & Sabido, M. (Eds.), *Entertainment-Education and Social Change: History, Research, and Practice*. Hillsdale, NJ: Lawrence Erlbaum Associates, pp. 75–96.

Banks, S. M., Salovey, P., Greener, S., Rothman, A. J., Moyer, A., Beauvais, J., & Epel, E. (1995). The effects of message framing on mammography utilization. *Health Psychology*, *14*, 178–184.

Beck, V. (2004). Working with daytime and prime-time television shows in the United States to promote health. In Singhal, A., Cody, M. J., Rogers, E. M., & Sabido, M. (Eds.), *Entertainment-Education and Social Change: History, Research, and Practice*. Hillsdale, NJ: Lawrence Erlbaum Associates, pp. 207–224.

Block, L. G., & Keller, P. A. (1995). When to accentuate the negative: The effects of perceived efficacy and message framing on intentions to perform a health-related behavior. *Journal of Marketing Research*, *32*, 192–203.

Brehm, J. (1966). *A Theory of Psychological Reactance*. New York: Academic Press.

Brodie, M., Foehr, U., Rideout, V., Baer, N., Miller, C., Flournoy, R., & Altman, D. (2001). Communicating health information through the entertainment media: A study of the television drama ER lends support to the notion that Americans pick up information while being entertained. *Health Affairs*, *20*, 192–199.

Cappella, J. N., & Jamieson, K. H. (1997). *Spiral of cynicism: The Press and the Public Good*. New York: Oxford.

Chaiken, S. (1980). Heuristic versus systematic information processing and the use of source versus message cues in persuasion. *Journal of Personality and Social Psychology*, *39*, 752–766.

Chaiken, S. (1987). The Heuristic Model of Persuasion. In Zanna, M. P., Olson, J. M., & Herman, C. P. (Eds.), *Social influence: The Ontario Symposium*, vol. 5. Hillsdale, NJ: Lawrence Erlbaum Associates, pp. 3–39.

Chaiken, S., Liberman, A., & Eagly, A. (1989). Heuristic and systematic information processing within and beyond the persuasion context. In Uleman, J. S., & Bargh, J. A. (Eds.), *Unintended Thought*. New York: Guilford Press, pp. 212–252.

Cho, C.-H. (1999). How advertising works on the WWW: Modified elaboration likelihood model. *Journal of Current Issues & Research in Advertising*, *21*, 33–50.

Cohn, L. D., Macfarlane, S., Yañez, C., & Imai, W. K. (1995). Risk perception: differences between adolescents and adults. *Health Psychology*, *14*, 217–222

Collins, R. L., Elliott, M. N., Berry, S. H., Kanouse, E. E., & Hunter, S. B. (2003). Entertainment television as a healthy sex educator: The impact of condom efficacy information in an episode of Friends. *Pediatrics*, *112*, 1115–1121

Cowley, E., & Barron, C. (2008). When product placement goes wrong. *Journal of Advertising*, *37*(1), 89–98.

d'Astous, A., & Chartier, F. (2000). A study of factors affecting consumer evaluations and memory of product placements in movies. *Journal of Current Issues and Research in Advertising*, *22*, 31–40.

Detweiler, J. B., Bedell, B. T., Salovey, P., Pronin, E., & Rothman, A. J. (1999). Message framing and sunscreen use: Gain-framed messages motivate beach-goers. *Health Psychology*, *18*, 189–196.

Dillard, J., & Pfau, M. (2002). *Handbook of Persuasion: Developments in theory and practice*. Thousand Oaks, CA: Sage.

Eagly, A. H., & Chaiken, S. (1993). *The Psychology of Attitudes*. New York: Harcourt Brace.

Entman, R. M. (1993). Framing: Toward clarification of a fractured paradigm. *Journal of Communication*, *43*(4), 51–58.

Fishbein, M. (1979). A theory of reasoned action: Some applications and implications. *Nebraska Symposium on Motivation*, *27*, 65–116.

Fishbein, M., & Ajzen, I. (1975). *Belief, Attitude, Intention, and Behavior: An Introduction to Theory and Research.* Reading, MA: Addison-Wesley.

Fishbein, M., & Ajzen, I. (2010). *Predicting and Changing Behavior: The Reasoned Action Approach.* New York: Psychology Press.

Fiske, S. T., & Taylor, S. E. (1991). *Social Cognition,* 2nd ed. New York: McGraw-Hill.

Friestad, M., & Wright, P. (1994). The persuasion knowledge model: How people cope with persuasion attempts. *Journal of Consumer Research, 22,* 62–74.

Gamson, W. A. (1992). *Talking Politics.* New York: Cambridge University Press.

Gerrig, R. J. (1993). *Experiencing Narrative Worlds.* New Haven, CT: Yale University.

Green, M. C., & Brock, T. C. (2000). The role of transportation in the persuasiveness of public narratives. *Journal of Personality and Social Psychology, 79,* 701–721.

Greenberg, B. S., Salmon, C. T., Patel, D., Beck, V., & Cole, G. (2004). Evolution of an E-E research agenda. In Singhal, A., Cody, M. J., Rogers, E. M., & Sabido, M. (Eds.), *Entertainment-Education and Social Change: History, Research and Practice.* Hillsdale, NJ: Lawrence Erlbaum Associates, pp. 192–206.

Gupta, P. B., & Lord, K. R. (1998). Product placement in movies: The effect of prominence and mode on recall. *Journal of Current Issues and Research in Advertising, 20,* 47–59.

Hether, H. J., Huang, G. C., Beck, V., Murphy, S. T., & Valente, T. W. (2008). Entertainment-education in a media-saturated environment: Examining the impact of single and multiple exposures to breast cancer storylines on two popular medical dramas. *Journal of Health Communication, 13,* 808–823.

Hinyard, L. J., & Kreuter, M. W. (2007). Using narrative communication as a tool for health behavior change: A conceptual, theoretical, and empirical overview. *Health Education & Behavior, 34,* 777–792.

Holbert, R. L., Garrett, R. K., & Gleason, L. S. (2010). A new era of minimal effects? A response to Bennett and Iyengar. *Journal of Communication, 60,* 15–34.

Hovland, C. I., Janis, I. L., & Kelley, H. H. (1953). *Communication and Persuasion.* New Haven, CT: Yale University Press.

Iyengar, S. (1991). *Is Anyone Responsible? How Television Frames Political Issues.* Chicago: University of Chicago Press.

Jin, B. (2006). Viewing factors in public health entertainment-education programming. *Journal of the Northwest Communication Association, 35,* 79–94.

Kahneman, D., & Tversky, A. (1984). Choices, values, and frames. *American Psychologist, 39,* 341–350.

Kahneman, D., & Tversky, A. (1979). Prospect theory: An analysis of decision under risk. *Econometrica, 47,* 263–291.

Karrh, J. A. (1998). Brand placement: A review. *Journal of Current Issues and Research in Advertising, 20,* 31–49.

Kennedy, M. G., O'Leary, A., Beck, V., Pollard, W. E., & Simpson, P. (2004). Increases in calls to the CDC national STD and AIDS Hotline following AIDS-related episodes in a soap opera. *Journal of Communication, 54,* 287–301.

Kennedy, M. G., Turf, E. E., Wilson-Genderson, M., Wells, K., Huang, G. C., & Beck, V. (2011). Effects of a television drama about environmental exposure to toxic substances. *Public Health Reports, 126*(Suppl 1), 150–159.

Kim, M., & Hunter, J. (1993). Attitude-behavior relations: A meta-analysis of attitudinal relevance and topic. *Journal of Communication, 43,* 101–142.

Lapinski, M. K., & Nwulu, P. (2008). Can a short film impact HIV-related risk and stigma perceptions? Results from an experiment in Abuja, Nigeria. *Health Communication, 23,* 403–412.

Law, S., & Braun, K. A. (2000). I'll have what she's having: Gauging the impact of product placements on viewers. *Psychology and Marketing, 17,* 1059–1075.

Law, S., & Braun-LaTour, K. A. (2004). Product placements: How to measure their impact. In Shrum, L. J. (Ed.), *The Psychology of Entertainment Media: Blurring the Lines Between Entertainment and Persuasion.* Hillsdale, NJ: Lawrence Erlbaum Associates, pp. 63–78.

Leventhal, H. (1970). Findings and theory in the study of fear communications. In Berkowitz, L. (Ed.), *Advances in Experimental Social Psychology,* vol. 5. New York: Academic Press, pp. 119–186.

Lin, C.-L., Lee, S.-H., & Horng, D.-J. (2011). The effects of online reviews on purchasing intention: The moderating role of need for cognition. *Social Behavior and Personality, 39,* 71–82.

Madden, T., Ellen, P., & Ajzen, I. (1992). A comparison of the theory of planned behavior and the theory of reasoned action. *Personality and Social Psychology Bulletin, 18,* 3–9.

Maheswaran, D., & Meyers-Levy, J. (1990). The influence of message framing and issue involvement, *Journal of Marketing Research, 27,* 361–367.

Mongeau, P. (1998). Another look at fear-arousing persuasive appeals. In Allen, M., & Preiss, R. W. (Eds.), *Persuasion: Advances Through Meta-Analysis.* Cresskill, NJ: Hampton, pp. 53–68.

Montgomery, K. C. (1990). Promoting health through entertainment television. In Atkin, C., & Wallack (Eds.), *Mass Communication and Public Health: Complexities and Conflicts.* Newbury Park, CA: Sage, pp. 114–128.

Morgan, S. E., Movius, L., & Cody, M. J. (2009). The power of narratives: The effect of entertainment television organ donation storylines on the attitudes, knowledge, and behaviors of donors and nondonors. *Journal of Communication, 59,* 135–151.

Moyer-Gusé, E. (2008). Toward a theory of entertainment persuasion: Explaining the persuasive effects of entertainment-education messages. *Communication Theory, 18,* 407–425.

Moyer-Gusé, E., Chung, A. H., & Jain, P. (2011). Identification with characters and discussion of taboo topics after exposure to an entertainment narrative about sexual health. *Journal of Communication, 61,* 387–406.

Moyer-Gusé, E., & Nabi, R. L. (2011). Comparing the persuasive effects of entertainment-education and educational programming on risky sexual behavior. *Health Communication, 26,* 416–426.

Moyer-Gusé, E., & Nabi, R. L. (2010). Explaining the persuasive effects of entertainment education: An empirical comparison of three theories. *Human Communication Research, 36,* 25–51.

Murphy, S. T., Frank, L. B., Moran, M. B., & Patnoe-Woodley, P. (2011). Involved, transported, or emotional? Exploring the determinants of change in knowledge, attitudes, and behavior in entertainment-education. *Journal of Communication, 61,* 407–431.

Nabi, R., Moyer-Gusé, E., & Byrne, S. (2007). All joking aside: A serious investigation into the persuasive effect of funny social messages. *Communication Monographs, 74,* 29–54.

Nabi, R. L. (1999). A cognitive-functional model for the effects of discrete negative emotions on information processing, attitude change, and recall. *Communication Theory*, *9*, 292–320.

Nabi, R. L. (2002). Anger, fear, uncertainty, and attitudes: A test of the cognitive-functional model. *Communication Monographs*, *69*, 204–216.

Nabi, R. L. (2003). The framing effects of emotion: Can discrete emotions influence information recall and policy preference? *Communication Research*, *30*, 224–247.

Nabi, R. L. (2007). Emotion and persuasion: A social cognitive perspective. In Roskos-Ewoldsen, D. R., & Monahan, J. (Eds.), *Social Cognition and Communication: Theories and Methods*. Hillsdale, NJ: Lawrence Erlbaum Associates, pp. 377–398.

Nabi, R. L., Roskos-Ewoldsen, D., & Dillman-Carpentier, F. (2008). Subjective knowledge and fear appeal effectiveness: Implications for message design. *Health Communication*, *23*, 191–201.

O'Keefe, D. J., & Jensen, J. D. (2009). The relative persuasiveness of gain-framed and loss-framed messages for encouraging disease detection behaviors: A meta-analytic review. *Journal of Communication*, *59*, 296–316

O'Leary, A., Kennedy, M., Pappas-DeLuca, K. A., Nkete, M., Beck, V., & Galavotti, C. (2007). Association between exposure to an HIV story line in The Bold And The Beautiful and HIV-related stigma in Botswana. *AIDS Education Prevention*, *19*, 209–217.

Papa, M. J., Singhal, A., Law, S., Pant, S., Sood, S., Rogers, E. M., & Shefner-Rogers, C. L. (2000). Entertainment-education and social change: An analysis of parasocial interaction, social learning, collective efficacy, and paradoxical communication. *Journal of Communication*, *50*(4), 31–55.

Pappas-DeLuca, K. A., Kraft, J. M., Galavotti, C., Warner, L., Mooki, M., Hastings, P., Koppenhaver, T., Roels, T. H., & Kilmarx, P. H. (2008). Entertainment-education radio serial drama and outcomes related to HIV testing in Botswana. *AIDS Education and Prevention*, *20*, 486–503.

Perloff, R. M. (2010). *The Dynamics of Persuasion: Communication and Attitudes in the Twenty-First Century*, 4th ed. New York: Routledge.

Petty, R., & Cacioppo, J. (1986). The Elaboration Likelihood model of persuasion. In Berkowitz, L. (Ed.), *Advances in Experimental Social Psychology*, vol. 19. New York: Academic Press, pp. 123–205.

Petty, R., Cacioppo, J., Kasmer, J., & Haugtvedt, C. (1987). "Cognitive processing: Additional thoughts and a reply to Petty, Kasmer, Haugtvedt, and Cacioppo": A reply to Stiff and Boster. *Communication Monographs*, *54*(3), 257–263.

Petty, R., Kasmer, J., Haugtvedt, C., & Cacioppo, J. (1987). Source and message factors in persuasion. A reply to Stiff's critique of the Elaboration Likelihood Model. *Communication Monographs*, *54*(3), 233–249.

Petty, R. E., Brinol, P., & Tormala, Z. L. (2002). Thought confidence as a determinant of persuasion: The self-validation hypothesis. *Journal of Personality and Social Psychology*, *82*, 722–741.

Price, V., & Tewksbury, D. (1997). News values and public opinion: A theoretical account of media priming and framing. In Barnett, G., & Boster, F. (Eds.), *Progress in Communication Sciences*. Norwood, NJ: Ablex, pp. 173–212.

Ritterfeld, U., & Jin, S. -A. (2006). Addressing media stigma for people experiencing mental illness using an entertainment-education strategy. *Journal of Health Psychology*, *11*, 247–267.

Robberson, M. R., & Rogers, R. W. (1988). Beyond fear appeals: Negative and positive persuasive appeals to health and self-esteem. *Journal of Applied Social Psychology*, *18*, 277–287.

Rogers, R. W. (1975). A protection motivation theory of fear appeals and attitude change. *Journal of Psychology*, *91*, 93–114.

Rogers, R. W. (1983). Cognitive and physiological processes in fear appeals and attitude change: A revised theory of protection motivation. In Cacioppo, J. T., & Petty, R. E. (Eds.), *Social Psychophysiology*. New York: Guilford, pp. 153–176.

Rothman, A. J., Martino, S. C., Bedell, B. T., Detweiler, J. B., & Salovey, P. (1999). The systematic influence of gain- and loss-framed messages on interest in and use of different types of health behavior. *Personality and Social Psychology Bulletin*, *25*, 1355–1369.

Rothman, A. J., & Salovey, P. (1997). Shaping perceptions to motivate healthy behavior: The role of message framing. *Psychological Bulletin*, *121*, 3–19.

Rothman, A. J., Salovey, P., Antone, C., Keough, K., & Martin, C. D. (1993). The influence of message framing on intentions to perform health behaviors. *Journal of Experimental Social Psychology*, *29*, 408–433.

Rothman, A. J., & Updegraff, J. A. (2011). Specifying when and how gain- and loss-framed messages motivate healthy behavior: An integrated approach. In Keren, G. (Ed.), *Perspectives on Framing*. London: Psychology Press/Taylor & Francis, pp. 257–277.

Rothman, A. J., Wlaschin, J., Bartels, R. D., Latimer, A., & Salovey, P. (2008). How persons and situations regulate message framing effects: The study of health behavior. In Elliot, A. (Ed.), *Handbook of Approach and Avoidance Motivation*. Hillsdale, NJ: Lawrence Erlbaum Associates, pp. 475–486.

Russell, C. A. (1998). Toward a framework of product placement: Theoretical propositions. *Advances in Consumer Research*, *25*, 357–362.

Russell, C. A. (2002). Investigating the effectiveness of product placements in television shows: The role of modality and plot connection congruence on brand memory and attitude. *Journal of Consumer Research*, *29*, 306–318.

Sabido, M. (1981). *Towards the Social Use of Soap Operas*. Mexico City: Institute for Communication Research

San Jose-Cabezudo, R., Gutierrez-Arranz, A. M., & Gutierrez-Cillan, J. (2009). The combined influence of central and peripheral routes in the online persuasion process. *CyberPsychology & Behavior*, *12*, 299–309.

Shah, D. V., McLeod, D. M., Gotlieb, M. R., & Lee, N-J. (2009). Framing and agenda setting. In Nabi, R. L., & Oliver, M. B. (Eds.), *The SAGE Handbook of Media Processes and Effects*. Thousand Oaks, CA: Sage, pp. 83–98.

Sheppard, B., Hartwick, J., & Warshaw, P. (1988). The theory of reasoned action: A meta-analysis of past research with recommendations for modification and future research. *Journal of Consumer Research*, *15*, 325–343.

Singhal, A., & Rogers, E. M. (1999). *Entertainment-Education: A Communication Strategy for Social Change*. Thousand Oaks, CA: Sage.

Singhal, A., & Rogers, E. M. (2001). The entertainment-education strategy in communication campaigns. In Rice, R. E., & Atkin, C. K. (Eds.), *Public Communication Campaigns*, 3rd ed. Thousand Oaks, CA: Sage, pp. 343–356.

Singhal, A., & Rogers, E. M. (2004). The status of entertainment-education worldwide. In Singhal, A., Cody, M. J.,

Rogers, E. M., & Sabido, M. (Eds.), *Entertainment-Education and Social Change: History, Research, and Practice*. Hillsdale, NJ: Lawrence Erlbaum Associates, pp. 3–20.

Skalski, P., & Tamborini, R. (2007). The role of social presence in interactive agent-based persuasion. *Media Psychology, 10*, 385–413.

Slater, M. D., & Rouner, D. (2002). Entertainment-education and elaboration likelihood: Understanding the processing of narrative persuasion. *Communication Theory, 12*, 173–191.

Slater, M. D., Rouner, D., & Long, M. (2006). Television dramas and support for controversial public policies: Effects and mechanisms. *Journal of Communication, 56*, 235–252.

Smith, S. W., Lindsey, L. M., Kopfman, J. E., Yoo, J., & Morrison, K. (2008). Predictors of engaging in family discussion about organ donation and getting organ donor cards witnessed. *Health Communication, 23*, 142–152.

Sood, S., Menard, T., & Witte, K. (2004). The theory behind entertainment-education. In Singhal, A., Cody, M. J., Rogers, E. M., & Sabido, M. (Eds.), *Entertainment-Education and Social Change: History, Research, and Practice*. Hillsdale, NJ: Lawrence Erlbaum Associates, pp. 117–145.

Sood, S., Shefner-Rogers, L., & Sengupta, M. (2006). The impact of a mass media campaign on HIV/AIDS knowledge and behavior change in north India: Results from a longitudinal study. *Asian Journal of Communication, 16*, 231–250.

Soul City Institute. (2005). Health & development communication. Retrieved July 29, 2012 from http://www.soulcity.org.za/research/evaluations.

Stiff, J. B. (1986). Cognitive processing of persuasive message cues: A meta-analytic review of the effects of supporting information on attitudes. *Communication Monographs, 53*(1), 75–89.

Stiff, J. B., & Boster, F. J. (1987). Cognitive processing: Additional thoughts and a reply to Petty, Kasmer, Haugtvedt, and Cacioppo. *Communication Monographs, 54*, 250–256.

Triandis, H. (1977). *Interpersonal Behavior*. Monterey, CA: Brook/Cole.

Tversky, A., & Kahneman, D. (1981). The framing of decisions and the psychology of choice. *Science, 211*, 453–458.

Valente, T. W., Kim, Y. M., Lettenmaier, C., Glass, W., & Dibba, Y. (1994). Radio promotion of family planning in the Gambia. *International Family Planning Perspectives, 20*, 96–100.

van Reijmersdal, E. A., Neijens, P. C., & Smit, E. G. (2009). A new branch of advertising: Reviewing factors that influence reactions to product placement. *Journal of Advertising Research*, 429–449.

Vidmar, N., & Rokeach, M. (1974). Archie Bunker's bigotry: A study in selective perception and exposure. *Journal of Communication, 24*, 36–47.

Weinberger, M. G., & Gulas, C. S. (1992). The impact of humor in advertising: A review. *Journal of Advertising, 21*, 35–59.

Whittler, T. E., & Spira, J. S. (2002). Model's race: A peripheral cue in advertising messages? *Journal of Consumer Psychology, 12*, 291–301.

Wilkin, H. A., Valente, T. W., Murphy, S., Cody, M. J., Huang, G., & Beck, V. (2007). Does entertainment-education work with Latinos in the United States? Identification and the effects of a telenovela breast cancer storyline. *Journal of Health Communication, 12*, 455–469.

Wilson, B. J. (2007). Designing media messages about health and nutrition: What strategies are most effective? *Journal of Nutrition Education and Behavior, 39*(2 Suppl), S13-S19.

Wilson, B. J., Linz, D., Donnerstein, E., & Stipp, H. (1992). The impact of social issue television programming on attitudes toward rape. *Human Communication Research, 19*, 179–208.

Witte, K. (1992). Putting the fear back into fear appeals: The extended parallel process model. *Communication Monographs, 59*, 329–349.

Witte, K., & Allen, M. (2000). A meta-analysis of fear appeals: Implications for effective public health campaigns. *Health Education & Behavior, 27*, 591–615.

Yang, M., & Roskos- Ewoldsen, D. R. (2007). The effectiveness of brand placements in the movies: Levels of placements, explicit and implicit memory, and brand-choice behavior. *Journal of Communication, 57*, 469–489.

Yang, M., Roskos-Ewoldsen, D. R., Dinu, R., & Arpan, L. (2006). The effectiveness of "in-game" advertising: Comparing college students' explicit and implicit memory for brand names. *Journal of Advertising, 35*, 143–152.

Young, D. G. (2008). The privileged role of the late-night joke: Exploring humor's role in disrupting argument scrutiny, *Media Psychology, 11*, 119–142.

PART 4

Interactive and Emerging Technologies

Social Influence in Virtual Environments

Jim Blascovich *and* Cade McCall

Abstract

Four topics relevant to the operation of social influence in virtual media–based environments—particularly digital ones—are discussed: concepts, theory, the nature of social interaction, and new forms of social influence. The summary speculates on the future of virtual technology for scientific inquiry and applications regarding social influence processes.

Key Words: agency, communicative realism, consciousness, context, grounded versus virtual reality, immersion, response systems, self-relevance, virtual social influence

Introduction

In *Principles of Topological Psychology*, Kurt Lewin (1936) emphasized that understanding human social behavior necessitates weighty consideration of the environment in which it occurs. Gordon Allport's (1954) enduring definition of social psychology as the study of how the thoughts, feelings, and behaviors of individuals are influenced by the "actual, imagined, or implied presence of others" opened scholars' minds to the fact that social influence processes are not limited to the actual physical presence of others, but may instead be implicit or even fictional. Although neither of these scholars likely foresaw modern digital virtual media technology as the important arena for social interaction that it has become, both scholars specified essential requirements for understanding social influence within them. Regardless of their natures, physical or not, both person and environment must be taken into account.

In this chapter, four topics relevant to the operation of social influence in virtual media–based environments—particularly digital ones—are discussed: concepts, theory, the nature of social interaction, and new forms of social influence. The summary speculates on the future of virtual technology for scientific inquiry and applications regarding social influence processes.

Concepts

Today, the modifier *virtual* conjures visions of digital technology applied to whatever concept it modifies—specific worlds or environments, animated representations of artificial or human intelligence such as agents (i.e., digital algorithms generally represented as humans) and avatars, defined contexts such as games or social networks, and so on. However, the meaning of "virtual X"—that which is not real but displays the essential qualities of its modificand—is not limited to any particular technology. In fact, "virtual X" need not require any technology at all. That humans have virtual experiences endogenously via dreams and daydreams is indisputable. Most dream researchers report that people dream four to six times per night on average. Klinger (2009) has reported that individuals' minds wander an average of 2,000 times per day, occupying approximately 30% of their waking hours.

Additionally, over thousands of years, humans have continually developed and used ever more engaging or "immersive" media technologies to increase their ability to explore environments other than the physical ones within which they find themselves. Storytelling, painting, sculpture, theater, manuscripts, the printing press, photography, cinematography, radio and television, and, most recently, digital technologies all serve to facilitate psychological engagement in virtual environments.

That humans have evolved endogenous abilities to create and experience alternate or virtual realities and have invented ever more powerful media technologies to do so, strongly suggests that people are genetically predisposed, neurophysiologically wired, and motivated to frequent virtual environments. The functionality and adaptive significance of these developments is beyond the scope of this chapter, but has been argued elsewhere (Smallwood & Schooler, 2006). Blascovich and Bailenson (2011) argue that these developments suggest that terms like *virtual reality* or *virtual environment* are not tied to any particular technology (i.e., computer) or even any technology at all.

To answer the question, "What is virtual reality?" begs the more difficult question, "What is reality?" Like the question, "What is consciousness?" there is much disagreement among scholars over what reality is. Philosophers and perceptionists like Aldous Huxley and Roger Shepard argue that all perception is an illusion and there are many supporting arguments and relevant data.

Blascovich and Bailenson (2011) take a more pragmatic, relativistic approach, one they label *psychological relativity*. It is based on the assumption that nearly everyone appears to distinguish between what is real and what is not real based on their operational definition of the former. They argue that for most people, what is typically regarded as real is what is perceived as the physical or natural world and anything else, no matter how compelling, is virtual rather than real. According to this psychological relativity conception, the former is labeled *grounded reality* and the latter *virtual reality*, although it is not the case that the details of what constitutes physical or grounded reality are necessarily the same for all people. (Some people's grounded reality includes perceptions that are not shared by others and are sometimes regarded as hallucinations and even evidence of psychopathology.)

Theory

The emphasis in social psychology on the importance of the environment as well as the presence of implied or imaginary others precipitated by scholars such as Lewin and Allport during the mid-20th century faded somewhat in its last quarter. With some notable exceptions, a more individualistic cognitive framework became the zeitgeist (Fiske & Taylor, 1991). The field advanced remarkably in terms of theoretical models of social cognitive processes and especially the demonstration of the heavy influence of automatic, nondeliberative, or unconscious processes on social interaction and social influence (Wyer & Bargh, 1997).

Toward the end of the twentieth century, computer scientists (Lanier, 1992; Slater & Wilbur, 1997; Myers, Hudson, & Pausch, 1999), perceptionists (Loomis, Blascovich, & Beall, 1999), communication researchers (Biocca & Levy, 1995), and a few pioneering social psychologists (Blascovich et al., 2002) foresaw digital media technology opening new possibilities for social interaction and social influence and commenced related research and applications development. Most, lacking in-depth training in social psychology and/or technology, and even some with such training proceeded to build digital virtual worlds involving social intercourse and influence, arguably using their own intuitions to guide technological developments. The qualities of these intuitions were mixed at best with technology often aimed only toward producing high photographic realism and scholars developing and debating intuitions wrapped up in hypothetical constructs such as *presence* and *co-presence* seemingly endlessly.

Certainly, social interaction and social influence occur via human-to-human contact. Indeed, humans are most characteristically regarded as gregarious animals, and as a species have evolved substantial capacities and mechanisms for influencing and being influenced by others. These mechanisms operate both consciously or "deliberately" and unconsciously or "automatically," with the former category underlying reasoned actions and the latter underlying survival. It is safe to state that deliberate and automatic mechanisms influence one another albeit asymmetrically. Contrary to what humans might like to think, there is more "bottom-up" than "top-down" influence. Hence, *purely* cognitivistic (consciously reasoned) actions are less frequent than purely automatic (reflexive) ones.

Based on this reasoning, social psychologists, computer scientists, perceptionists, and other experts at the Research Center for Virtual Environments and Behavior at the University of California, Santa Barbara began discussions pertinent to a high-level structural model of social influence within digital immersive virtual environments to guide creation of human-centric virtual worlds and the understanding of social interaction and influence within it. It became known as The Threshold Model of Social Influence within Immersive Virtual Environments (TMSIVE) with initial instantiations published early in the new millennium (Blascovich et al., 2002) and a more fully developed model recently (Blascovich, in press).

The model does not so much address the questions of *if* or *why* social influence occurs in digital virtual environments as much as *how* it occurs. Humans are, after all, a gregarious species and have evolved endogenous mechanisms as well as exogenous technologies for virtual travel for purposes of social engagement. The TMSIVE, as of this writing, involves the confluence of three major and two minor determining dimensions or variables. The former include agency, communicative realism, and response system level; the latter, self-relevance and context.

Agency

Similar to those in natural or physical social worlds, agency in virtual worlds refers to users' theories of mind regarding other entities, such as human representations, within digital virtual environments. Hence, agency refers to the perceived mindfulness or sentience (e.g., attributions of consciousness, free will) of other representations. At the risk of oversimplification, agency attributions range from nonsentient (nonhuman, robotic) to sentient (human). By definition (Bailenson & Blascovich, 2005), a nonsentient representation is labeled an *agent,* whether human-looking or not, and a sentient representation is labeled an *avatar,* whether human-looking or not. Furthermore, in the five-factor TMSIVE model, *agent* and *avatar* represent endpoints on a bipolar continuum allowing the possibility of *cyborg* attributions (partly sentient and partly computer algorithm).

In digital immersive virtual environments, users make agency attributions via a priori and a posteriori information. A priori ones typically include user beliefs based on extra-environment information, whether provided before or during a digital virtual experience. A posteriori attributions are ones that users deduce from the behaviors of digital representations within the virtual world itself, consciously or unconsciously employing a sort of personal *Turing Test* process. In either case, users' agency attributions determine the qualitative aspects of their interactions with digital human–appearing representations in immersive virtual worlds.

Communicative Realism

Communicative realism in the TMSIVE is defined as the signal quality of communicative acts made or generated by agents and/or avatars in digital virtual environments in terms of the same communicative acts made by humans in grounded reality. Hence, communicative realism varies from high to low. Such realism is more important for digital representations that, although appearing human in terms of sound or visualization, are known by human interactants to be artificial or "agents," but typically only regarding their conscious or intentional acts. Indeed, it is quite likely that communicative realism whether by a known-to-be avatar or a known-to-be agent are equally influential on unconscious or automatic behaviors (Bailenson et al., 2003).

According to the TMSIVE, communicative realism as a latent variable is manifest by three types of communicative acts ordered hierarchically at two levels. The superordinate of the three is *movement realism,* which includes postures, proxemic behaviors such as interpersonal distance, facial expressions, gestures, gaze behaviors, and so on. Anthropometric realism (appearance and articulation of bodily joints) is subservient to movement realism because many human communicative movements cannot occur without the necessary body parts. For example, one's avatar or agent cannot wave the hand without a hand, wrist joint, arm, elbow, shoulder, and so on. Counterintuitively, perhaps, photographic realism is the least important and simply connotes personal identity, although the level of photographic realism necessary for such communication does not usually require high fidelity images. Considering the relationships among movement, anthropometric, and photographic realism necessary for communicative realism, movement realism can compensate for lower levels in the other two as cartoon animators have known for more than a century.

Response System Level

The third factor of the TMSIVE is response system level. Human actions and thoughts vary from automatic to deliberate. Furthermore, social influence can affect and be affected by uncontrolled, automatic actions and thoughts as well as controlled deliberate ones. We maintain that the former operate nearly identically in either grounded or virtual reality. For example, if a digital agent frowns, the user will mimic that facial expression (Bailenson & Yee, 2005; Stel et al., 2010). Similarly to what occurs in grounded reality, if a digital agent fires a gun, the user will exhibit a startle or defensive response.

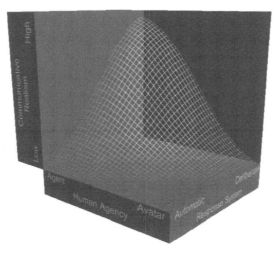

Figure 17.1 The Hypothesized Relationships Among Communicative Realism, Agency, and Response System Level in a Highly Self-Relevant Context.

Threshold of Social Influence

Figure 25.1 depicts the hypothesized relationships among communicative realism, agency, and response system level in a highly self-relevant (to the user) context. The three-dimensional surface depicted is the hypothesized threshold of social influence, which delineates the likely nonoccurrence (i.e., below) versus likely occurrence of social influence effects (e.g., conformity, facilitation, aggression) as a function of agency, communicative realism, and response system level. *Self-relevance* and *context,* the fourth and fifth factors in the model, interact to modulate the overall steepness of the threshold (see Blascovich, in press, for more details).

To illustrate hypotheses that can be drawn from the model, if agency is such that the human representation is believed to be an avatar (i.e., a representation of an actual human in real time), then neither communicative realism nor response system level play much of a role in terms of the occurrence of social influence effects. But, if agency is low such that the human representation is believed to be that of an agent (i.e., a representation of a computer algorithm), then social influence on conscious responses of users will be driven solely by communicative realism.

The Nature of Social Influence

In recent years, researchers in a variety of fields have used virtual environments to address basic social psychological questions, including questions regarding social influence. This corpus of research demonstrates that although digital simulations are unique to the modern world, we can use them to better understand humans as social animals and uncover some of the underlying mechanisms that drive social cognition and behavior.

Virtual environments have emerged as a methodological tool because they allow researchers to manipulate social variables and measure social responses in ways that would be difficult, if not impossible, in the physical world. In terms of environmental manipulations, researchers are able to put study participants in contexts that reach far beyond the walls of the laboratory. Studies can take place in subway car (Freeman et al., 2008), on a city street (Dotsch & Wigboldus, 2008; Gillath et al., 2008), or in the middle of a canyon (Kane et al., 2012), allowing researchers to examine cognitive and behavioral responses to the types of situations people might encounter in the "real" world. Furthermore, environmental manipulations can be particularly potent in triggering affective or motivational responses, tapping into basic, automatic responses to contextual variables. Virtual environments can produce threat by eliciting participants' fear of heights (Kane et al., 2012), or put participants at ease by placing them in a soothing environment (Hunter et al., 2004). As such, these new technologies afford researchers an increase in ecological validity without the sacrifice to experimental control associated with field research.

Virtual environments also allow researchers to manipulate the kinds of social contextual variables that affect social influence in a highly controlled fashion. Researchers can place participants in a dyad, a small group, or even a crowd. They can also manipulate the identity of the individuals with whom a participant interacts. So, for example, one can conduct a study on race by having one half of the participants interact with a white individual and the other half interact with a black individual while holding all other aspects of the interaction the same across conditions (McCall et al., 2009). Researchers can also manipulate the behavior of others within an interaction, algorithmically varying critical social cues such as eye gaze, proximity, mimicry, or facial expression. Again, these behavioral factors can be manipulated while holding all other features of the social interaction constant.

In addition to manipulations of social and environmental context, virtual environments afford a wide array of interactional tasks that would be difficult to create otherwise. Researchers can use an immersive first-person shooter game to look at aggression (McCall et al., 2009), or place participants in crowded bar to look at individual differences in interpersonal distancing (Pullen et al., 2006). In sum, virtual environments provide a highly controlled platform to manipulate where participants are, what they're doing, and with whom they're doing it.

Virtual environments also provide novel measures of behavior. One key source of data comes from the tracking technologies used to provide input into virtual environments. If a virtual world is navigable, then the virtual environment platform will necessarily have some way of tracking and rendering participants' viewpoints. If participants have a virtual body in the virtual environment, then the platform will use some form of tracking to control that body. Together these data offer a near-continuous record of participant behavior over the course of an interaction, including powerful measures of nonverbal behavior such as interpersonal distance and direct gaze (McCall et al., 2009). They also provide measures of attentional focus over the course of an interaction (McCall et al., 2010) and subtle changes in movement such as postural sway.

Of course traditional forms of social data (e.g., self-report, reaction times, content analyses) are also available in virtual environment research. More importantly, virtual environments allow social researchers use highly physically constraining measurement tools such as fMRI, EEG, or peripheral physiological measures without the usual constraints on their experience. Participants can have a face-to-face interaction while in an fMRI scanner (Wilms et al., 2010), engage in a violent game while attached to blood pressure and ECG sensors (Persky & Blascovich, 2007), or ride a roller coaster while EEG is being measured (Baumgartner et al., 2006).

Although virtual environments offer a methodological boon for researchers, the proposition that these synthetic environments can tell us something about the natural world prompts reasonable skepticism. Most obviously, how can we generalize about human psychology in the "real world" from data gathered in artificial environments? In fact, laboratory research on social behavior has always relied on simulation (Blascovich et al., 2002) and researchers have simulated a wide variety of contexts. They've staged accidents (Darley & Latané, 1968), placed participants in mock prisons (Haney, Banks, & Zimbardo, 1973), or had them go through imaginary job interviews (Word, Zanna, & Cooper, 1974). In the most common method along these lines, participants are merely asked to imagine vignettes (Robinson & Clore, 2001). Virtual environments are simply a new (and in some respects improved) tactic that make use of digital technology.

Another important point, addressed earlier in this chapter, is that a handful of factors help determine whether or not a virtual environment, or a virtual human inside that virtual environment, will elicit "real" social responses. As the threshold model of social influence suggests, the perceived agency of the virtual humans is critical. Participants will likely respond differently to an avatar than an agent. For one thing, the nature and range of intentions that participants project onto the virtual human will vary greatly depending on whether or not they think a human mind or an algorithm is driving behavior.

Communicative realism also affects participant responses in important ways. As the research on biological motion demonstrates (Johansson, 1973), naturalistic movement automatically triggers all kinds of social attributions (Dittrich et al., 1996). People are experts at using an assortment of different behaviors to make sense of social situations (eye gaze, facial expressions, gesture, vocal nonverbal). The degree to which a simulation exploits these channels undoubtedly alters the level of social influence of that virtual environment.

A perceiver's own motives further affect the degree he or she picks up on social cues and makes attributions to a virtual others' behavior. For instance, walking past an avatar during a task is likely to have less self-relevance to an individual than negotiating a financial exchange with that avatar. During a negotiation, the individual will make all kinds of inferences about the avatar's behavior and attend to whatever cues are available to maximize the likelihood of a positive outcome, whereas that amount and quality of processing is unnecessary when simply passing someone on the street.

Finally, the ability to generalize about social behavior from research conducted in virtual environments depends on the response system level of the specific social response in question and the way in which that response is assessed. On the one hand, if people consciously reflect about their experience in a virtual environment, their reflections may be influenced by the facts that the experience was a simulation and they were aware it was a simulation. If, however, responses are unobtrusively measured they will be less likely to be "tainted" by conscious reflection. Along these lines, subtle differences in nonverbal behavior have proved rich sources of data in a variety of paradigms (some of which are described in the following). Furthermore, any target behavior that is automatic or difficult to control is likely to reflect the same psychological processes, in or out of a simulation. As most anyone who has walked on the edge of a virtual precipice in a virtual world has observed, it is difficult to control the reflexive fear of falling despite the solid floor underneath one's feet.

Although all of these arguments suggest that virtual environments tell us something about human social influence, the best evidence for the parallels between virtual and physical world social responses is the body of social research using virtual environments produced in recent years. This work spans multiple disciplines and subject areas. More important, it tells us both about ways in which humans behave in virtual environments and ways in which they behave in general.

Proxemic behaviors, including interpersonal distance and orienting, provide powerful demonstrations of the parallels between virtual and physical social worlds. It goes without saying that walking around another person in the physical world is a distinctly different experience than walking around an inanimate object. We tend to leave a spatial buffer around ourselves and other people (Hall, 1959; Sommer, 1959) and the size of this buffer changes as a consequence of a variety of factors, including intimacy (Argyle & Dean, 1965) and liking (Mehrabian, 1969). Bailenson et al. (2001) explored related proxemic patterns in a virtual world. Ostensibly as part of a memory task, participants walked around a series of both agents and nonhumanoid objects. As one would predict from the literature on nonverbal behavior in the physical world, participants gave a wider berth to the agents and tended to get closer to the back than the front of them (Hayduk, 1983).

Furthermore, (female) participants responded to the gaze of the agents, walking further around agents who looked directly at them.

The fact that interpersonal distance functions much the same in virtual environments as in the physical world has yielded opportunities for investigations into nonverbal behavior in social interactions. Along these lines, virtual environments have proved fruitful in the study of the implicit expression of attitudes. Dotsch and Wigboldus (2008) placed Dutch participants at a virtual bus stop with an assortment of agents. They found that the participants kept a greater interpersonal distance from Moroccan-appearing agents compared with white-appearing avatars, and these differences were predicted by a virtual environment version of the Implicit Association Task (Greenwald et al., 1998; De Liver, Wigboldus, & van der Pligt, 2007). Furthermore, they demonstrated that the relationship between implicit prejudice and interpersonal distance was mediated by skin conductance responses to Moroccan agents.

Related research ties similarly subtle proxemic behaviors to overt patterns of aggression (McCall et al., 2009). In this study, participants first met black or white agents in a brief interaction. They then competed in a violent shooting game with those agents. Participants looked less at the faces and left more interpersonal distance between themselves and the agents when those agents were black. More importantly, these patterns in nonverbal behavior predicted levels of aggression toward the black agents during the shooting game. In terms of social behavior in virtual environments, these studies demonstrate that nonverbal patterns associated with prejudice can function in virtual environments just as they function in the physical world. In both studies, participants knew that they were interacting with virtual humans controlled by computers. Nevertheless, they showed patterns of avoidance associated with stigmatizing others in the physical world (Dasgupta, 2004). The sensitivity and continuous nature of these measures furthermore highlights the benefits of using virtual environments to study phenomena that are difficult to capture by traditional means (i.e., racial prejudice). Along those lines, neither Dotsch and Wigboldus (2008) nor McCall et al. (2009) found differences in explicit self-reports of prejudice. Instead, the effects emerged through unobtrusive tracking measures.

Proxemic behaviors in virtual environments have also proved beneficial in the study of social characteristics of clinical disorders. For example, one study (Kim et al., 2009) found that individuals with bipolar mania had larger interpersonal distances and more averted gaze than normal controls. Another (Park et al., 2009) found the same pattern with schizophrenic patients. These authors found that negative schizophrenic symptoms moderated the effects of emotions on proxemics. Whereas the interpersonal distance and gaze patterns displayed by normal controls were affected by the emotional displays of the agents (participants were relatively more avoidant of angry virtual environment versus happy faced agents), this pattern was not significant for patients. Along similar lines, other researchers (Pullen et al., 2006) have looked at the tendencies of patients with various prefrontal cortex lesions to move through (versus around) virtual others in a desktop virtual environment and at the tendencies of individuals in the autistic spectrum to "bump into" others in a virtual café (Parsons, Mitchell, & Leonard, 2004).

As these various studies demonstrate, gaze is as critical a cue in virtual worlds as it is in the physical world. Several researchers have taken advantage of this fact by using agents to study gaze perception. One methodological advantage in this domain is that researchers can parametrically vary the angle of gaze while measuring various responses. Gamer and Hecht (2007) used such a technique to assess perceptions of direction and gaze range. Their research suggests that a virtual head can produce the experience of "being looked at" and that the psychophysics of virtual gaze perception parallel those of physical gaze perception. Agent gaze has also been used to provide social stimulus within the confined physical environments necessary for brain imaging research. Several studies have employed agents to examine the neural and psychophysiological correlates of gaze perception during imaging or physiological measurement (Mojzisch et al., 2006; Wilms et al., 2010).

Recent research also suggests that individuals respond reflexively to agent gaze. In the physical world, when we see another person look in a given location, our attention is automatically drawn to that location. A recent study showed the same pattern in a virtual classroom (McCall et al., 2009b). Participants listened to a lecture with a group of agents. While the lecturer spoke, the agents occasionally oriented toward her. Despite the fact that those agents' behavior was irrelevant to the participants' task, they were more likely to attend to the speaker when the audience was also attending and to remember more of the speech if the audience spent more time oriented toward the speaker.

Another body of research has examined the phenomenon of mimicry in virtual environments. Bailenson and Yee (2005) found that an agent whose head rotations mimicked participants at a 4-second delay was more persuasive and was perceived as more positive by participants than an agent whose head rotations corresponded to the recorded movements of the experiment's previous participant. This finding parallels research in the physical world (Chartrand & Bargh, 1999). A virtual mimicker, however, is ideal because the mimicry itself can be determined algorithmically and performed consistently across interactions. Subsequent research in a similar virtual environment has demonstrated that socially anxious individuals are not as likely to be influenced by mimicked behavior as nonsocially anxious individuals (Vrijsen et al., 2010a). Conversely, individuals (at least nonsocially anxious individuals) will mimic an agent's head movements to some degree (Vrijsen et al., 2010b).

Although all of this research improves our understanding of nonverbal behavior, research also demonstrates the social effects of agent and avatar presence in a virtual environment. The power of avatar presence was leveraged in a study of social support in close relationships (Kane et al., 2012). In this study, participants completed the stressful task of walking along the edge of a cliff. The participant's close relationship partner was ostensibly placed in the world with the partner such that the participant could look across the ravine and see his or her partner. Participants were further led to believe the partner's nonverbal behavior in the virtual world was driven by his or her actual nonverbal behavior in another part of the lab. In reality, the researchers controlled the nonverbal of the partner's avatar, making some of the partners supportive (i.e., by attending the participant, cheering him or her on) and the others nonsupportive (i.e., by ignoring the partner). Participants with a supportive partner experienced less anxiety during the task and were less likely to avoid their partners in a subsequent interaction.

Perhaps it's not surprising that an avatar or his or her partner would influence people because the virtual human in that situation is simply a proxy for a living human. But what about agents, whose identity and behavior are entirely determined by the computer itself? Park and Catrambone (2007) addressed this question with a study on social facilitation, a phenomenon long studied in social psychology (Triplett, 1898; Zajonc, 1965). In this case, *social facilitation* refers to the fact that the mere presence of others can affect performance on tasks in which people tend to perform better on easy tasks and worse on more difficult tasks. Park and Catrambone found this same pattern of results when participants completed a set series of tasks in the presence of a lifelike agent.

Pertaub, Slater, and Barker (2002) also explored the facilitative virtual environment versus detrimental influence of agents. In their experiment, participants delivered a presentation to a virtual audience. In one condition the audience members yawned, fell asleep, slouched, or leaned backward, and avoided eye contact. In the positive condition, the audience nodded, smiled, leaned forward, and oriented themselves toward the participant. The data revealed that participants in the negative audience condition experienced significantly more anxiety about the speech. These results emerged despite the fact that participants knew that the virtual humans in the study were agents and not avatars.

People also appear to have some degree of empathy for agents. In one study demonstrating this effect (Gillath et al., 2008), participants walked along a virtual city street inhabited by a variety of agents. Intriguingly, high levels of dispositional compassion and empathic concern corresponded with attending to and approaching a beggar, but not a businessman, on the street. Personal distress, on the other hand, corresponded with staying further from the beggar. Nonverbal responses to agents are apparently influenced by attributions to their apparent needs.

Along these lines, in a virtual replication of the famous Milgram obedience demonstrations (Milgram, 1963), Slater et al instructed participants to repeatedly deliver a virtual electric shock to an agent whenever that agent failed to provide the correct response on a memory test. Despite the fact that the participants were fully aware that the agent was an agent and the events were imaginary, measures of psychological and physiological arousal were different for participants who saw and heard the agent virtual environment versus participants who only communicated with the agent through text. According to subjective accounts of the participants, they were in fact disturbed by the experience despite knowing that it was "not real." Further research has used the same paradigm to investigate the neural correlates of the distress experienced by participants in this paradigm (Cheetham et al., 2009).

The apparent power of agent presence has also been leveraged for research in the clinical domain. Freeman et al. (2008), for example, used a crowded virtual train to study paranoia in the general population. Traditionally, paranoia is difficult to assess with questionnaires or interviews because the veracity of suspicious attributions cannot be proved. With an experimental task, however, one can control the nature and threat of social targets, presenting participants with social interactions that others find neutral or positive. To this end, these researchers placed participants in a virtual subway and measured their attributions regarding agent behavior. Distinct portions of the study participants made paranoid attributions about the behavior of the avatars, and these attributions corresponded with persecutory thinking in everyday life.

Virtual Worlds and New Kinds of Social Processes

Virtual worlds don't just tell us something about the general nature of human social behavior; they also create new social phenomena. As the literature surveyed in the previous section illustrates, virtual environments are easily manipulated to elicit different social responses. Moreover, basic social phenomena (i.e., direct gaze, proximity) can be leveraged in novel ways to produce social influence.

This fact has been explored through what Bailenson et al. call transformed social interactions (TSIs) (Bailenson et al., 2004). In one demonstration of a TSI, there researchers manipulated the gaze behaviors of a presenter as he or she delivered a persuasive passage to two participants. The presenter's head orientation movements were virtually rendered either veridically, were reduced (such that the presenter gazed at his or her virtual computer 100% of the time), or were augmented (such that the presenter looked at each of the participants 100% of the time). The augmented gaze condition led to more agreement with the passage (although this effect was moderated by gender). What's novel about this setup is that the augmented gaze condition is physically impossible; in the physical world there is no way to deliver a speech to two people at one time and give each of them direct eye contact for the entire time. In a virtual environment, however, all it requires is a simple transformation of head angles. Similar nonverbal transformations using mimicry (Bailenson & Yee, 2005) or social orienting (McCall et al., 2009b) also illustrate ways in which basic social mechanisms can be leveraged to produce social influence.

The physical appearance of agents and avatars is also easily manipulated within digital environments in ways that have important implications for social influence. For example, Bailenson et al. (2006)

conducted a series of studies in which participants evaluated political candidates whose images were either morphed with images of the participants themselves or with images of other participants. Despite the fact that this manipulation was not consciously apparent to participants, political moderates and independents showed greater preference for the candidates that had been morphed with the self. Althouth self-preference effects are a well-explored phenomenon in psychology (James, 1890; Nuttin, 1987; Dijksterhuis, 2004), these findings demonstrate one powerful way in which they can be applied in a virtual environment.

Along similar lines, virtual environments provide new modes of self-perception. The Proteus Effect (Yee & Bailenson, 2007) refers to a phenomenon in which people conform to the behavior that they believe others would expect of their avatars. In one study on the Proteus Effect, participants who were assigned a more attractive avatar behaved more intimately with others in the virtual environment, disclosing more and reducing their interpersonal distance (Yee & Bailenson, 2007). In another experiment, participants assigned a taller avatar for a negotiation task behaved more confidently than participants who were assigned a shorter avatar (Yee & Bailenson, 2007). This effect was replicated in a subsequent study in which, interestingly, participants with the taller avatars were also more aggressive in a subsequent negotiation outside of the virtual world (Yee, Bailenson, & Ducheneaut, 2009).

Virtual environments also provide a novel application of social learning. Whereas traditionally social learning refers to the fact that humans can learn by simply observing others' behavior and the consequences of that behavior, virtual environments make it possible to observe yourself from an outsider's perspective. Fox and Bailenson (2009) explored this notion in a series of studies on exercise. In one study, participants whose avatars would appear to lose weight as a consequence of the participant's own exercise performed more exercise. In a subsequent study, participants who watched their avatar exercise were more likely to exercise over the next 24 hours. These and related studies (Fox & Bailenson, 2010) demonstrate that our virtual selves act not just as a symbolic extension of ourselves, but as an "inside route" to social influence.

These examples of transformed social interactions and manipulations of the virtual self scratch the surface of what's possible in virtual environments. More importantly for our purposes here, they illustrate that the social psychology of the post-digital world will need to explore the new ways in which we can experience ourselves and other people.

References

Allport, G. (1954). *The Nature of Prejudice*. Reading, MA: Addison-Wesley.

Argyle, M., & Dean, J. (1965). Eye-contact, distance and affiliation. Sociometry, 28, 289–304.

Bailenson, J., & Blascovich, J. (2005). Avatars. In Bainbridge, W. S., & Sims, W. (Eds.), *Berkshire Encyclopedia of Human-Computer Interaction*. Great Barrington, MA: Berkshire, pp. 64–68.

Bailenson, J. N., Beall, A. C., Loomis, J., Blascovich, J., & Turk, M. (2004a). Transformed social interaction: Decoupling representation from behavior and form in collaborative virtual environments. PRESENCE: Teleoperators and Virtual Environments, 13(4), 428–441.

Bailenson, J. N., Blascovich, J., Beall, A. C., & Loomis, J. M. (2001). Equilibrium revisited: Mutual gaze and personal space in virtual environments. PRESENCE: Teleoperators and Virtual Environments, 10, 583–598.

Bailenson, J. N., Blascovich, J., Beall, A. C., & Loomis, J. M. (2003). Interpersonal distance in immersive virtual environments. Personality and Social Psychology Bulletin, 29, 819–834.

Bailenson, J. N., Garland, P., Iyengar, S., & Yee, N. (2006). Transformed facial similarity as a political cue: A preliminary investigation. Political Psychology, 27, 373–386.

Bailenson, J. N., & Yee, N. (2005). Digital Chameleons: Automatic assimilation of nonverbal gestures in immersive virtual environments. Psychological Science, 16, 814–819.

Bargh, J. (1997). The automaticity of everyday life. In Wyer, R. (Ed.). *Advances in Social Cognition*, vol. 10,. London: Psychology Press, pp. 1–62.

Baumgartner, T., Valko, L., Esslen, M., & Jäncke, L. (2006). Neural correlate of Spatial Presence in an arousing and non-interactive virtual reality world—an EEG and Psychophysiology study. CyberPsychology & Behavior, 9(1), 30–45.

Biocca, F., & Levy, M. R. (1995). *Communication in the Age of Virtual Reality*. Hillsdale, NJ: Lawrence Erlbaum Associates.

Blascovich, J. (in press). Challenge, threat and social influence in digital immersive virtual environments. In J. Gratch & S. Marsella (Eds.). *Social emotions in nature and artifact: emotions in human and human-computer interaction*. Oxford: Oxford University Press.

Blascovich, J., & Bailenson, J. (2011). *Infinite Reality: Avatars, Eternal Life, New Worlds and the Dawn of the New Revolution*. New York: Harper-Collins Morrow.

Blascovich, J., Loomis, J., Beall, A., Swinth, K., Hoyt, C., & Bailenson, J. (2002). Immersive virtual environment technology as a research tool for social psychology. Psychological Inquiry, 13, 103–125.

Chartrand, T. L., & Bargh, J. A. (1999). The chameleon effect: The perception-behavior link and social interaction. Journal of Personality and Social Psychology, 76, 893–910.

Cheetham, M., Pedroni, A. F., Antley, A., Slater, M., & Jancke, L. (2009). Virtual Milgram: Empathic concern or personal distress? Evidence from functional MRI and dispositional measures. Frontiers in Human Neuroscience, 3(29).

Darley, J. M., & Latané, B. (1968). Bystander intervention in emergencies: Diffusion of responsibility. Journal of Personality and Social Psychology, 8, 377–383.

Dasgupta, N. (2004). Implicit ingroup favoritism, outgroup favoritism, and their behavioral manifestations. Social Justice Research, 17, 143–169.

De Liver, Y., Wigboldus, D., & van der Pligt, J. (2007). Positive and negative associations underlying ambivalent attitudes: Evidence from implicit measures. Journal of Experimental Social Psychology, *43*, 319–326.

Dijksterhuis, A. (2004). I like myself but I don't know why: Enhancing implicit self-esteem by subliminal evaluative conditioning. Journal of Personality and Social Psychology, *86*(2), 345–355.

Dittrich, W. H., Troscianko, T., Lea, S. E. G., & Morgan, D. (1996). Perception of emotion from dynamic point-light displays represented in dance. Perception *25*(6), 727–738.

Dotsch, R., & Wigboldus, D. H. J. (2008). Virtual prejudice. Journal of Experimental Social Psychology, *44*, 1194–1198.

Fiske, S., & Taylor, S. (1984). *Social Cognition*. Boston: McGraw-Hill.

Fiske, S. T., & Taylor, S. E. (1991). *Social Cognition*: New York: McGraw-Hill.

Fox, J., & Bailenson, J. N. (2009). Virtual self-modeling: The effects of vicarious reinforcement and identification on exercise behaviors. Media Psychology, *12*, 1–25.

Fox, J., & Bailenson, J. N. (2010). The use of doppelgängers to promote health behavior change.CyberTherapy & Rehabilitation, *3*(2), 16–17.

Freeman, D., Pugh, K., Antley, A., Slater, M., Bebbington, P., Gittins, M., et al. (2008). Virtual reality study of paranoid thinking in the general population. British Journal of Psychiatry, *192*(4), 258–263.

Gamer, M., & Hecht, H. (2007). Are you looking at me? Measuring the cone of gaze. Journal of Experimental Psychology, *33*, 705–715.

Gillath, O., McCall, C. A., Shaver, P., & Blascovich J. B. (2008). Reactions to a needy virtual person: Using an immersive virtual environment to measure prosocial tendencies. Media Psychology, *11*, 259–282.

Greenwald, A. G., McGhee, D. E., & Schwartz, J. K. L. (1998). Measuring individual differences in implicit cognition: The Implicit Association Test. Journal of Personality and Social Psychology, *74*, 1464–1480.

Hall, E. T. (1959). *The Silent Language*. Garden City, NY: Doubleday.

Haney, C., Banks, C., & Zimbardo, P. (1973). Interpersonal dynamics in a simulated prison. International Journal of Criminology and Penology, *1*, 69–97.

Hayduk, L. A. (1983). Personal space: Where we now stand. Psychological Bulletin, *2*, 293–335.

Hunter, H. G., Patterson, D. R., Magula, J., Carrougher, G. F., Zeltzer, K., Dagadakis, S., et al. (2011). Water-friendly virtual reality pain control during wound care. Journal of Clinical Psychology, *60*, 189–195.

James, W. (1890). *The Principles of Psychology*. New York: Holt.

Johansson, G. (1973). Visual perception of biological motion and a model of its analysis. Perception Psychophysics, *14*, 202–211.

Kane, H., McCall, C., Collins, N., & Blascovich, J. B. (2012). Mere presence is not enough: Responsive support in a virtual world. Journal of Experimental Social Psychology, *48*(1), 37–44.

Kim, E., Ku, J., Kim, J., Lee, H., Han, K., Kim, SI, et al. (2009). Nonverbal social behaviors of patients with bipolar mania during interactions with virtual humans. Journal of Nervous and Mental Disease, *197*(6), 412–418.

Klinger, E. (2009). Daydreaming and fantasizing: Thought flow and motivation. In Markman, K. D., Klein, W. M., & Suhr J.

A. (Eds.), *Handbook of Imagination and Mental Stimulation*. London: Taylor & Francis, pp. 225–240.

Lanier, J. (1992). An insider's view of the future of virtual reality. Journal of Communication, *42*, 150.

Lewin, K., Heider, F., Heider, G. M. (Trans.). (1936). *Principles of Topological Psychology*. New York: McGraw-Hill.

Loomis, J., Blascovich, J., & Beall, A. C. (1999). Immersive virtual environment technology as a basic tool in psychology. Behavior Research Methods, Instruments, & Computers, *31*, 557–564.

McCall, C., Blascovich, J., Young, A., & Persky, S. (2009). Using immersive virtual environments to measure proxemic behavior and to predict aggression. Social Influence, *4*, 138–154.

Mehrabian, A. (1969). Significance of posture and position in the communication of attitude and status relationships. Psychological Bulletin, *71*, 359–372.

Milgram, S. (1963). Behavioral study of obedience. Journal of Abnormal and Social Psychology, *67*, 371–378.

Mojzisch, A., Schilbach, L., Helmert, J. R., Pannasch, S., Velichkovsky, B. M., & Vogeley, K. (2006). The effects of self-involvement on attention, arousal, and facial expression during social interaction with virtual others: A psychophysiological study. Social Neuroscience, *1*, 184–195.

Myers, B., Hudson, S., & Pausch, R. (1999). Past, present and future of user interface software tools. *Institute for Software Research*. Retrieved July 13, 2012 from http://repository.cmu.edu/hcii/197/.

Nuttin, J. M. (1987). Affective consequences of mere ownership: The name–letter effect in twelve European languages. European Journal of Social Psychology, *17*, 381–402.

Park, S., & Catrambone, R. (2007). Social facilitation effects of virtual humans. Human Factors, *49*, 1054–1060.

Park, S. H., Ku, H., Kim, J., Jang, H. J., Kim, S. Y., Kim, S. H., et al. (2009). Increased personal space of patients with schizophrenia in a virtual social environment. Psychiatry Research, *169*, 197–202.

Parsons, S., Mitchell, P., & Leonard, A. (2004). The use and understanding of virtual environments by adolescents with autistic spectrum disorders. Journal of Autism and Developmental Disorders, *34*(4), 449–466.

Persky, S., & Blascovich, J. (2007). Immersive virtual environments virtual environmentrsus traditional platforms: Effects of violent and nonviolent video game play. Media Psychology, *10*, 135–156.

Pertaub, D. P., Slater, M., & Barker, C. (2002). An experiment on public speaking anxiety in response to three different types of virtual audience. Presence-Teleoperators and Virtual Environments, *11*(1), 68–78.

Pullen, E., Morris, R. G., Kerr, S., Bullock, P. R., & Selway, R. P. (2006). Exploration of social rule violation in patients with focal prefrontal neurosurgical lesions using a virtual reality simulation. International Journal on Disability and Human Development, *5*, 141–146.

Robinson, M. D., & Clore, G. L. (2001). Simulation, scenarios, and emotional appraisal: Testing the convergence of real and imagined reactions to emotional stimuli. Personality and Social Psychology Bulletin, *27*, 1520–1532.

Slater, M., & Wilbur, S. (1997). A framework for immersive virtual environments (five): Speculations on the role of presence in virtual environments. Presence Teleoperators and Virtual Environments, *6*, 603–616.

Smallwood, J., & Schooler, J. (2006). The restless mind. Psychological Bulletin, *132*, 936–958.

Sommer, R. (1959). Studies in personal space. Sociometry, *22*, 247–260.

Stel, M., Blascovich, J., McCall, C., Mastop, J., Van Baaren, R. B., & Vonk, R. (2010). Mimicking disliked others: Effects of a priori liking on the mimicry-liking link. European Journal of Social Psychology, *20*, 876–880.

Triplett, N. (1898). The dynamogenic factors in pacemaking and competition. American Journal of Psychology, *9*, 507–533

Vrijsen, J. N., Lange, W., Becker, E. S., & Rinck, M. (2010). Socially anxious individuals lack unintentional mimicry. Behaviour Research and Therapy, *48*(6), 561–564.

Vrijsen, J. N., Lange, W., Dotsch, R., & Wigboldus, D. H., & Rinck, M. (2010). How do socially anxious women evaluate mimicry? A virtual reality study. Cognition and Emotion, *24*(5), 840–847.

Wilms, M., Schilbach, L., Pfeiffer, U., Bente, G., Fink, G. R., & Kai, V. (2010). It's in your eyes—Using gaze-contingent stimuli to create truly interactive paradigms for social cognitive and affective neuroscience. Social Cognitive and Affective Neuroscience, *5*, 98–107.

Word, C. O., Zanna, M. P., & Cooper, J. (1974). The nonverbal mediation of self-fulfilling prophecies in interracial interaction. Journal of Experimental Social Psychology, *10*, 109–120.

Yee, N., & Bailenson, J. N. (2007). The Proteus Effect: Self transformations in virtual reality. Human Communication Research, *33*, 271–290.

Yee, N., Bailenson, J. N., & Ducheneaut, N. (2009). The Proteus Effect: Implications of transformed digital self-representation on online and offline behavior. Communication Research, *36*(2), 285–312.

Zajonc, R. B. (1965). Social facilitation. Science, *149*, 269–274.

Active Video Games: Impacts and Research

Barbara Chamberlin *and* Ann Maloney

Abstract

Exergames, or games that encourage physical activity, have several documented benefits for users, including increase of daily physical activity, and the potential for game players to reach moderate and even vigorous levels of activity. In addition to physiological impacts, exergames can affect social and psychosocial attributes, such as interest in exergaming, adherence, and motivation. Although research on this new field is in the early stages, this chapter summarizes research findings, giving particular attention to exergaming's potential in medical, school, and community programs. Based on that research and on their own experience in working with exergames users, the authors share recommendations on best uses of exergames, design guidelines for exergame developers, and areas for future research.

Key Words: active videogames, classroom, DDR, design, exergame, Kinect, Sony Playstation, Wii, xBox

Introduction

Video games and computer games often receive negative attention from educational and health advocates. Kinder critics have regarded them as useless toys or distractions, whereas harsher opponents hold them as "part of the problem," contributing to obesity, attention deficit disorder, violence, or sedentary behavior (Chan & Rabinowitz, 2006). Yet advocates of exergames, games that encourage physical activity by the game player, see their potential in combating or preventing obesity, increasing daily physical activity, and triggering a "gateway effect" in which those who are not normally active start with games and transition to other types of activity.

Research in emerging "serious games" highlights games' contributions to learning, behavior change, and awareness of social issues and world events. Game-playing surgeons increase their response time and dexterity when games rely on "twitch-speed" responses (Rosser et al., 2007). Students gain knowledge through game-based learning in math, social studies, science, and even food safety. Yet despite the evidence that computer and video games are engaging, interactive, and educational, critics—particularly those in obesity-prevention fields—continue to suggest time limits on *screen time* (Krebs & Jacobson, 2003), without differentiating between sedentary screen-time and active behaviors *encouraged by many video games.*

Exergames took off in popularity with the arcade game *DanceDanceRevolution* (*DDR*), introduced in 1998 (although several game companies had made inroads into active gaming starting in the early 1980s). In *DDR,* gamers dance on a pad so their feet work the controller, and points are awarded for dancing and increasing skill level. Innovation in products that combined exercise equipment and other nonstandard controllers with video game play continued. In 2003, Sony introduced the Eye Toy camera used with the PlayStation, which allowed game players to swing their arms and move their bodies so that the upper body and torso, instead of the traditional hand-held controller, controlled the game. Active video games did not enter the mainstream until Nintendo released the Wii in 2007. The Wii's handheld controllers included accelerometers, enabling the gamer to swing, turn, and jab, rather than depending on the button combinations of traditional controllers.

Within 2 years of the Wii's release, the game-playing and game-buying audience changed dramatically. In contrast with the usual model catering specifically to young men who regarded themselves as *gamers,* the Wii was marketed to and purchased by individuals of a wide variety of ages, and by both genders. Senior centers began hosting *Wii Bowling* teams. Online bloggers (often *DDR* expert gamers) and users of sites such as ddrfreak. com documented exergame-based weight loss programs, posting before and after photos demonstrating significant changes in body shape. Mothers' groups started exercise programs using the games, and the Wii was positioned near the checkout at Babies R Us. Titles targeting women, exercisers, children, dancers and families began appearing next to traditional titles, and in many cases outselling them. By 2008, the Wii outsold all the other major consoles combined: Among games, *Wii Play* topped the sales chart (McDougall & Duncan, 2008).

As anecdotal evidence of use continued to generate excitement—it seemed everyone had a brother, cousin, or mother-in-law who was playing and moving with the Wii—the health community remained tentative: *What evidence existed that these games were effective? In what ways are these games used? Despite the physical nature of the gameplay, do exergames enable activity over the threshold recommended for health (moderate to vigorous daily physical activity or MVPA)?*

Research on exergames began before the release of the Wii, and has been steadily increasing, with medical and academic journals now accepting research and papers on exergaming. The scope and breadth of measurement on active video games is expanding. Every major gaming console now has some kind of input device that facilitates full body movement of the game player to control game play. New plug-and-play technologies in the consumer market allow the game player (in many cases, children) to plug a toy or game directly into a television for full-body movement in games. Fitness centers and larger installations have an increasing selection of game-based activities for individual or group use.

Mobile devices enable a new breed of exergames, with accelerometers and pedometers measuring activity, while also providing incentive for tracking one's activity. Because of the increased availability and variety of exergames, they are used in homes, schools, after-school programs, fitness centers, and clinical settings. Clinicians may use them in physical therapy to supplement their traditional methods; pediatricians "prescribe" active game play as part of a strategy to get kids moving; physical education instructors and teachers in traditional classrooms use them to encourage physical activity throughout the day, or provide short bursts of activity between sedentary instruction. As use of active video games expands, so does related research. Measurement of physiological impacts (such as energy expenditure, changes in heart rate or oxygen consumption) is conducted with more rigor. A growing body of literature on psychosocial impacts, such as effect on self-esteem, self-efficacy, and influence on family and social networks, is entering journals, as is research on both adherence and motivation.

This chapter reviews the relevant evidence on physiologic, social, and long-term impacts of active video games. It shares examples of ways in which active videogames are being used, with recommendations on effective implementation. It concludes with design recommendations for development of active video games, and suggested areas for research.

Significance
Sedentary Activity and Increase of Obesity

Childhood obesity remains one of the most significant problems facing American youth. More than one-third of youth age 2 to 19 are considered overweight or obese with a body mass index (BMI) over the 85th percentile (Ogden, Carroll, & Flegal, 2008). Perhaps more important, the prevalence of obesity seems to increase among low-income youth. The Centers for Disease Control and Prevention (CDC) reports that one in seven low-income, preschool-aged children are considered clinically obese, with the highest rates occurring in minority groups, including American Indians and Hispanics (Freedman, 2011). Almost 21% of low-income, preschool-aged American Indian children and 18.5% Hispanic children are obese.

For some children, neighborhood crime or a lack of safety on walking routes, streets, or multiuse paths impede their access to traditional forms of exercise, such as walking or running. At the same time, exercise equipment or environments such as swimming pools, gymnasiums, or organized team activities may not be available in low-income areas, or may be prohibitively expensive (Gordon-Larsen, Nelson, Page, & Popkin, 2006).

Video Game Use and Impact

Games have tremendous potential to change both behavior and knowledge of children and their parents. Children are already gaming: 50% of children age 4 to 6 have played video games (Rideout, Vandewater, & Wartella, 2003); 71% of 5- to 6-year-olds know how to use a mouse (Vandewater et al., 2007). Children age 3 to 6 not only play a variety of video games, they also do so on different platforms: 20% of 0- to 2-year olds and 33% of 5- to 6-year-olds have access to a hand-held video game (Vandewater et al., 2007), whereas on a given day 27% of 5- to 6-year-olds are likely to have used a computer (for an average of 50 minutes). Children 11 to 14 years old on average play video games nearly 1.5 hours per day (Rideout, Foehr, & Roberts, 2010).

This group also spends a large amount of time playing with other electronic toys and learning systems (Lieberman, Fisk, & Biely, 2009). Children as young as two are capable of playing and enjoying video games: in 2011, 58% of games on iTunes App Store target preschoolers and toddlers (Shuler, 2012). Game-based learning for children could be leveraged as a convenient and effective way to disseminate knowledge and change behaviors that lead to obesity. Parents are gamers too: Almost 66% of parents or guardians play video games (Lenhart, Jones, & Macgill, 2008). Although younger adults (who represent 81% of all gamers) are more likely to play video games than older adults, almost 23% of adults 65 and older do game, and surprisingly, half of adult gamers are women (Lenhart et al., 2008).

There is understandable concern about excessive screen time for children, and the American Academy of Pediatrics recommends less than 2 hours per day and none before age 2 (Krebs & Jacobson, 2003). Yet, it is important to differentiate between *sedentary,* passive screen time (which may serve to draw users away from more active pursuits) and *active* screen time, in which the user expends energy or develops other aspects of fitness. Exergames show tremendous potential for creating positive changes in physiological measures in large populations. To date, they have been shown in defined populations to increase heart rate, and many games meet the threshold for maintaining

cardiovascular fitness. When placed in homes or accessible areas, exergames may increase the likelihood for exercise based on their entertainment value and activity level.

Research Implications

The study of active video games is relatively new and multidisciplinary. The entertainment industry creates experiences for amusement and ultimately looks to sales effectiveness as a metric of success. The medical field relies on studies of drug and device as evidence for treatments of health conditions. Scholars continue to show interest in the design of games to better encourage physical activity and other health behaviors. Game studies researchers look to the potential active games have to change behavior and study the roles incentives and social networks play in creating long-lasting change in game players. Most published research on exergames focuses on impacts to defined groups of individuals, such as 7- to 8-year-olds of normal body weight, or on obese teens. Emerging research is exploring additional physiological and psychosocial outcomes.

Exergaming as an emerging research field continues to define itself. In early 2011, a multidisciplinary group of scientists gathered at a conference focusing on the emerging field and sponsored by a new partnership between the American Heart Association (AHA) and Nintendo of America. The conference and its published proceedings, *The Power of Play: Innovations in Getting Active Summit,* served to query and legitimize this emerging field (Lieberman et al., 2011). Importantly, authors were asked to comment on the potential of active gaming as a gateway experience to motivate players to increase the frequency of physical activity as well as its duration and intensity. The AHA, Nintendo, research scientists and government agencies continue to devote resources to discovery in this emerging field, to devote resources to discovery in this emerging field, employing behavioral researchers to understand more about longer-term behavior changes that could be induced or maintained by exergames in many age groups.

Background
History of Active Games

In the 1980s, developers began integrating video game play with exercise or sport equipment, such as stationary bikes and simulated racquetball. HighCycle helped motivate or distract a cyclist using an online virtual landscape: If the user cycled fast enough, he or she could fly over the landscape.

In 1982, the Atari Puffer Project hooked up an exercise bike to the game system and used a handheld Gamepad, but this line ended when Atari entered bankruptcy. Hard-core cyclists tried out the motivational Computrainer, which measured physiological data such as power output and cadence. Computrainer is still available, and although it was developed for gaming platforms it is now also made for home computers. The game *VirtualRacquetball* used a hand-held controller, employing the position and orientation of an actual racquet, decades before the Wii-mote came into vogue. Some of the games combined telecommunications and allowed players to compete over phone lines, using head-mounted displays to enhance the experience. The interface developed for the Concept II (an ergometer for rowers) connected indoor rowing machines and measured traditional outputs like pace (strokes per minute) and work output (in units such as watts). The Concept II also connected to the Internet for indoor rowing communities in leagues, incorporating social networking concepts into the rowing competition.

By the 1990s, Life Fitness and Nintendo had entered into a partnership that created Exertainment System. FitLinxx, which provides feedback to gym users by quantifying work output from weight lifting, can be found today at health clubs. Systems such as these allow competition within gyms, because results (reps, days exercised) can easily be compared and posted by age or gender or time interval. More expensive and larger exergaming systems, like TectrixVR Bike by CyperGear INC and the VR Climber, provided more sophisticated interfaces for physical activity equipment, but were costly to install, expensive to repair, and intimidating for those unfamiliar with technology. Consequently only YMCAs and larger clubs could afford those exergames. Some facilities, such as the Xrtainment Zone, did invest in this kind of exergaming equipment to attract younger populations. Other exergames linked to existing exercise equipment, such as treadmills, elliptical machines, and stationary bicycles. These are useful to researchers when comparing game-enabled exercise with exercise on traditional equipment. But although exergaming development continued through the 1990s, it failed to gain the attention of a larger audience, and research into it was limited.

Everything changed with *DDR*, the most studied exergame in history. Originally introduced as a dancing game for game arcades, *DDR* displays a series of arrows presented in time with the music. Players dance on a large mat, with arrows indicating steps to the front, back, right, and left. General consumers were granted easier access in 1998, when Konami adapted the arcade game for the Playstation, allowing the game to be played at home on less expensive equipment. Investigators began measuring elevations in heart rates in people playing *DDR*, and looking at the implications of *DDR* use in homes, schools, or senior centers. Since the US release of *DDR,* seminal research on this classic game has demonstrated that *DDR* can demand energy expenditure at levels defined as moderate to vigorous physical activity (MVPA). Because more research has been conducted using this console-based game than any other, *DDR* is the early hero in this genre, and Lieberman (2006) has summarized its benefits.

By the time Bill Gates demonstrated the Exertris Interactive Gaming Bike in 2003, the Consumer Electronics Show had begun paying more focused attention to this genre. Since then, more cycling games had proliferated, such as a version for preschoolers by Fisher-Price called the Smart Cycle, in which toddlers cycle along with Dora the Explorer and other characters on screen. The PCGamerBike arrived in 2007, and just 2 years later, the Sony Eye Toy camera was the first to use a game player's arm and body motions to control game play. Others retrofit traditional video games to make them exergames, exemplified by Gamercize, which allows players to power their typical games (e.g., *Halo*) through a stepper or stationary bicycle while still holding a traditional hand controller.

Active Video Game Types

Commercially available gaming consoles (such as the Nintendo Wii, Sony PlayStation with Move Controllers, and Microsoft X-Box with Kinect controllers) are naturally the most accessible exergames for the majority of users. These consoles have evolved to use different input devices. Cameras used in EyeToy sense full body motion. The Nintendo Wiimote and Sony's Move sense swinging motion of the arms, spinning, and the force of the movements. Nintendo's Fit Balance Board senses distribution of body weight, enabling games that use tilting motions and can measure balance and encourage stepping. Newer body-sensing technologies, such as the infrared sensing in Microsoft's Kinect, respond to full body motion more accurately than cameras did, including movement toward and away from the camera. As game consoles mature, devices progress in using combinations of inputs to control the game.

Advocates believe exergames can engage players for longer periods of time than traditional physical exercises, keeping players motivated and leading to sustained effort. Some games may distract the player from recognizing physical exertion; other games encourage the player to monitor and control specific inputs. Newly emerging in active video game research is the use of physiological controls for the actual game play. For example, games can measure heartbeats and then use that information to control specific game attributes. *Health Defenders* allows the user to record heart rate data and relays it back to the player's mobile phone using Bluetooth protocols (Wylie & Coulton, 2008).

Mobile games and apps seem to hold the most potential in the new exergaming marketplace. Internal accelerometers found in iPhones and other smart phones have been used as pedometers in games. Cameras are now ubiquitous in mobile devices, and these can be used with a GPS in clever ways to document distances traveled or show how treasures have been found on a treasure hunt: This place-based relevance will likely be essential to new designs of exergames. Mobile platforms and the popularity of applications that can travel with the gamer will maximize convenience and lower costs of healthier game offerings.

Despite the immaturity and rapidly changing nature of this multidisciplinary new field, research indicates a real potential for energy expenditure and other important outcomes.

Implications for Use in the Medical Field

Health care professionals have come to expect rigorous research on interventions, and they have high expectations when it comes to the research into impacts of active video games. In addition to assessing energy expenditure, research may help identify types of users likely to benefit the most from a particular game. To accomplish this, it's important to know the specific ways in which games can lead to a healthier lifestyle. Certainly game manufacturers and designers do not wish to be subject to the Food and Drug Administration's complicated drug and device rules; however, if games can impact health in a significant ways, exergaming research must include typical outcome measures used in other therapies.

Providers may choose to "prescribe" a certain game and give users a recommendation of the strength or dose of this treatment. For example, in the popular *DDR* game, actual energy expenditure depends on the weight of the gamer, complexity of the footwork, meter of the song, and the total time spent playing. The "dose" a physician recommends may impact different patients in different ways. What do we know about active video games so far? Viewing exergames through this lens of medical treatment is a powerful way to review what the research reflects.

Who Should Deploy Exergaming?
A Case Study

Sue is a cheerful 16-year-old who lives with her intact family in a single-family home in a medium-sized Southern town. She loves Lady Gaga, and she's a good student, but a bit of a loner. She has struggled recently with her body image: She's been overweight most of her life, as have her siblings and parents. At her pediatrics appointment, she is surprised to learn she gained 15 pounds this year but did not grow at all in height. Her provider says that she has gone from being overweight to obese according to her BMI calculation. Before Sue's provider can decide whether to prescribe a Wii console to boost Sue's activity, she must consider several questions: What are the risks and benefits to this approach? What are the alternatives? What games are most appropriate for Sue, and which will yield greatest results? What evidence indicates it is an appropriate intervention? If Sue is to have success getting into better shape, gaming can't feel like a chore, and the game should not become boring after just a couple of weeks.

Sports medicine experts note that the frequency, intensity, and duration of the game play matters. Will she use more energy than her normal weight peers doing the same game? According to a study by Unnithan, oxygen use was significantly higher for overweight adolescents exergaming, compared with normal weight teens. According to a study by Unnithan, oxygen use was significantly higher for overweight adolescents exergaming, compared with normal weight teens (Unnithan, Houser, & Fernhall, 2006), not so according to Pate and team (R. Pate, 2008).

Sue is experiencing recent social avoidance and has low levels of physical activity, currently well below the recommended 60 minutes per day (US Department of Health and Human Services, 2008). With more homework in high school, Sue is busy with her classes, but is also on Facebook for long hours. Her family thinks she is online too much by herself in her room. Her family is not alone, because the latest report from the Pew Research Center (Rideout et al., 2010) shows the average youth Sue's age spends approximately 7.5 hours per day looking at a screen. Video games are fun, highly engaging, and rewarding, but Sue's parents worry that asking her to play more games is not the best way to increase her activity.

Even with anecdotal evidence posted on blogs, including many before/after pictures of youth who lost weight playing *DDR*, there is a fundamental question about how well this approach will work for someone new to *DDR*. Replicated research indicates that exergames can indeed increase physical activity, and we can likely conclude that Sue will be receptive to purchasing a home console game. Teens like it when health care workers endorse a product like a game instead of a pill. Online databases which share gaming research (www.healthgamesreserach.org) and web sites that offer game reviews and strategies for using exergames (www.exergamesunlocked.com) can be helpful.

As with any intervention to increase physical activity, it is unlikely that just the placement of equipment or exergames in the home would lead to increased physical activity. Sue will need motivation, help with goal setting, and possibly external incentives. What roles should her family, physician, school nurse, teachers, or personal coach play? Sue could be paired up with a peer for exergaming, but would this have a better result? This area has yet to be adequately studied. There are important questions. Should her family be strongly encouraged to play with her? Will exergame players like Sue enjoy some degree of mastery and have success leveling up in the game? Finally, could exergaming ward off feelings of discouragement about her chronic weight issues, whether or not it results in weight loss?

As research continues, attention is being paid to the effects of exergaming for different audiences, in different environments, and with different kinds of gameplay. It is early, but some findings are emerging.

Physiological Impacts

Much of the hope invested in exergaming lies in the possibility of it changing the physiology of the player, such as decreasing BMI, lowering blood pressure, or improving blood vessel function (i.e., flow-mediated dilation). The US Department of Health and Human Services recommends at least 30 minutes of MVPA for adults and at least 60 minutes for youth. However, most Americans fall short of these recommendations: Only 3% of youth meet MVPA goals (R. R. Pate et al., 2002).

To measure physiological impacts, most researchers evaluate caloric expenditure, resting heart rate, fitness, or oxygen consumption. However,

longer-term behavioral change is required to truly impact the physiology of an individual. To prove successful, the gamer must expend enough energy to meet MVPA and stay motivated enough to return to the activity regularly. Current research reflects both the physiological changes possible with exergames as well as the potential to change behaviors leading to a healthier lifestyle.

ENERGY EXPENDITURE

The fields of exercise science, public health, physiology, and human movement science have various approaches to measure energy expenditure. One approach is to study subjects in free-living conditions (in the real world) and use diaries or devices (such as accelerometers) to measure activity. Another approach is to study with more precision the activities in a laboratory setting, with more expensive equipment that can detect subtle changes in resting and active states. Strategies used also include taking a snapshot of all play on a certain playground at a certain time of day to see what percent of children are seated, talking, standing, or in active play. All of these approaches have been subject to comparisons and validation studies and encompass a very large literature. In addition, even the definition of what is sedentary is evolving (Pate, 2008).

When compared with traditional (nonactive) video games (like *Halo* or *Grand Theft Auto*), active video games burned more calories (Foley & Maddison, 2010). However, even sedentary game play can affect physiological measures: when boys age 7 to 10 years played a nonactive video game using traditional hand controllers, energy expenditure went up, as did heart rate, breathing rate, and oxygen consumed. Although 7- to 8-year-old children increased their weekly physical activity levels by 89 minutes per week for 12 weeks with *DDR*, they also reported a reduction in sedentary screen time, killing two birds with one stone (Maloney et al., 2008).

Research studies indicate exergames can increase energy expenditure from sedentary/light to moderate levels. Using accelerometers, devices strapped to the waists of subjects that measure activity (considered objective measurements), teams found positive effects on children's physical activity levels (Ni Mhurchu et al., 2008). Some of the activity exceeded the mark for "light to moderate" physical activities similar to walking, skipping, and jogging (Maddison et al., 2007). Some games, including *WiiFit,* can help players achieve intensity levels similar to those in unstructured free play.

Bauch, Beran, Cahanes, & Krug found that college-aged students who played *Wii Sports* expended energy at levels that could help meet physical activity guidelines (American Academy of Pediatrics Council on Sports Medicine and Fitness and Council on School Health, 2006). Playing *Wii Sports* bowling, tennis, and boxing involved significantly greater energy expenditure than sedentary games, but less than playing the real sport (Lee Graves, Stratton, Ridgers, & Cable, 2007). Of the *Wii Sports* collection of games, baseball and bowling were determined to be the most popular games for kids in a laboratory setting, and players of *Wii Sports* had measurable increases in energy expenditure, with the exception of those playing *Wii Golf* (B. Haddock, Siegel, & Wilkin, 2010a).

Players of DDR met American College of Sports Medicine (ACSM) heart rate intensity guidelines for developing and maintaining cardio-respiratory fitness, with no injuries during 201 hours of dance time (Tan, Aziz, Chua, & Teh, 2002). In a study of eight college females, energy expenditure was found to be the highest with *Wii Fit* games that involved more total body movement and used more muscle groups, as opposed to games that were lower intensity and involved mostly lower limb work (Worley, Rogers, & Kraemer, 2011).

Comparing Effectiveness

Exergames have been studied using head-to-head comparisons between two exergames or control groups. Some studies use a less active comparison, such comparing exergaming to just watching television or playing on a traditional stationary bike. For example, Kraft et al. measured heart rate and perceived exertion in college students (1) playing a video game with interactive bicycle, (2) playing *DDR*, and (3) using a traditional cycle while watching television. The game-enabled bike demanded more energy than *DDR*, which was also demanded more energy than the nongaming bike (Kraft, Russell, Bowman, Selsor, & Foster, 2011). Another team examined the differences in energy expenditure and enjoyment across four games, including shooter games, band simulation games, dance simulation games, and fitness games with a balance board (Lyons et al., 2011). Energy expenditure was assessed in 100 young adults age 18 to 35, and half of the sample were women. Results revealed that all games except shooter games significantly increased energy expenditure over resting energy expenditure. Fitness and dance games burned more calories than band simulation and shooter games. However, enjoyment

was higher in band simulation games than in other types. Lyons concluded that active video games can significantly increase energy expenditure, but some of these games were less enjoyable than some sedentary games. If better, more enjoyable active video games were created, this could further decrease sedentary behavior.

Biddis and Irwin (2010) reviewed 40 separate studies and summarized key findings, including that activities involving both upper and lower body movement yielded the greatest energy expenditure and reduced body fat and weight, but concluded that limited evidence supports exergame use to increase activity.

For exergames to meet with wider acceptance and perhaps even be reimbursed by insurance companies, more rigorous data will be required in larger populations to demonstrate effectiveness. Scholars have called for well-designed research with enough power to show changes in target populations, when compared with a control group over time. To date, most studies have been small-scale and short in duration (weeks).

FACTORS AFFECTING PHYSIOLOGICAL IMPACTS

How an exergame is played is important. If framed as a *friendly* competition, game play can increase intrinsic motivation and self-efficacy in already competitive individuals. However, it could also decrease engagement in individuals who are noncompetitive by nature (Song, Kim, Tenzek, & Lee, 2010). In overweight and obese teens, cooperative gameplay produced weight loss, promoted friendship quality, and improved self-efficacy—all of which increased motivation for sustained exergaming (Staiano, Abraham, & Calvert, 2010). Additionally, when competing against a peer, gamers tend to expend more energy (Staiano & Calvert, 2011). Other studies have shown that when engaged, youth obtain higher levels of energy output when distracted by social interactions and games. Studies are underway to determine the impact of family involvement on activity levels of obese and overweight children.

Studies have also demonstrated gender differences in energy expended during game play (L Graves, Stratton, Ridgers, & Cable, 2008; Sit, Lam, & McKenzie, 2010). Obviously, games offer different levels of game play, and therefore energy expenditure, so platform, game choice, and level selection can influence energy expenditure dramatically. This is not surprising, because one would also assume a wide variation in effort at the gym

Psychosocial Impacts

Active gaming may play a significant role in adherence, participation, and motivation. Subjects rank exergaming interventions positively in both several qualitative and quantitative studies. Haddock showed that for overweight or obese children, energy expenditure was significantly higher while riding the bike as it controlled the video game than while riding the bike alone, but that the children did not perceive a difference, meaning they did not realize they were working harder when they played the game than when they only rode the bike (B. L. Haddock, Siegel, & Wikin, 2009).

In a "free choice" environment, when given the opportunity to choose games that required high or low levels of exertion, game players did not avoid high-exertion games (B. Haddock, Siegel, & Wilkin, 2010b), indicating the potential for increased energy expenditure in more realistic, home-based use. Similarly, children have demonstrated preference for physically active video games over comparable sedentary versions of the same gameplay (Sit et al., 2010). Participants have ranked perceived exertion in exergames lower than in traditional activities (Wittman, 2010). The lower perceived exertion and the choice of the higher-energy games is encouraging, but more studies will be needed to confirm these early indications.

Research on avatars suggests that game players may project themselves onto a virtual avatar, or accept avatar characteristics after game play. Continuing research indicates great promise in influencing behavior with avatars, possibly most effective when avatars look like the gamer and lose or gain weight in accordance with the level of activity. The game player should also be able to design their own avatar, leading to greater self-efficacy and presence in the game (Lieberman, Peinado, Rodriguez, & Biely, 2011). From a child psychiatry perspective, projecting an ideal image of oneself is consistent with a child's natural imagination and fantasy, creating possibilities of identifying with another ego/persona.

HopeLab is embracing the potential of social gaming to increase physical activity via their online activity tracking and incentive program, *Zamzee*. Children wear the *Zamzee* meter, a three-axis accelerometer that records activity data, and then connect it to a computer to earn activity points and view their data. This both cognitively reinforces and incentivizes activity above a certain threshold that has been proved to affect health outcomes. Points earn users recognition and status within the system, via progress through various levels and leader boards and awarding of badges. Using their web sites, participants can receive additional incentives, such as virtual power-ups, and gift cards for $5 to $20. On average, users of the Zamzee and web site engaged in daily moderate to vigorous physical activity 59% more than users who wore a pedometer alone. Those receiving incentives saw the greatest increase in activity, and sustained that activity for 6 months (Omidyar, 2012). The role of extrinsic and intrinsic motivation resulting from (and encouraging) exergaming warrants additional study.

Psychiatric and Neurocognitive Benefits

Physical activity can improve depression symptoms, so it stands to reason that exergaming may be a mood lifter. One group used exergames for less severe cases (subsyndromal depression) and studied adults over a 12-week period, with follow-up at 20 to 24 weeks. Using *Wii Sports,* they structured their subjects' exergame play into three 35-minute sessions per week (Rosenberg et al., 2010). Eight-six percent of enrolled participants completed the 12-week intervention, yielding a significant improvement in depressive symptoms, mental health–related quality of life (QoL), and cognitive performance. There were no major adverse events, and improvement in depression symptoms was maintained at follow-up. This study will need to be replicated, but it is very encouraging as a treatment for mild mood disorders. A natural next project would be to study this in adolescents with depression and then move into prepubertal depression to look for effect sizes, comparing this with gold standard therapies.

Another study conducted in children examined the effects of exergaming on mood and short-term memory (STM), finding that children in an exergaming video game group increased their short-term memory compared with children with traditional video games, who experienced a decrease. Researchers have also seen a link between video game play and cognitive benefits in older adults. Various studies have shown benefits to older people of playing video games including improved reaction time, cognitive function, intelligence, coordination, attention span, and concentration (Torres, 2008). Brain fitness games are increasingly popular, and it is likely that future studies will employ exergames to improve mood or cognition. This will effectively merge the cognitive games and exergames research areas, which have traditionally been separated in journals and professional conference tracks.

Exergames for Specific Conditions

Some research highlights the use of video/virtual reality games' "distraction power" as part of pain management. Because pain control is critical in rehabilitation, video games also help the prognosis. Therapists currently use games and virtual reality for stroke rehabilitation (Saposnik et al., 2010), Parkinson's disease (Espay et al., 2010), management of pain, and more recently range of motion rehabilitation for burn patients. The Wii balance board's ability to measure balance makes it attractive for neurological rehabilitation and conditioning. Returning veterans from foreign wars are using games for distraction, pain control, rehabilitation, socialization, and reentry into family life.

For children with cerebral palsy, rehabilitation incorporating virtual reality video games may improve hand function and forearm bone health and improve brain activation patterns (Golomb et al., 2010). Positive results were also noted when using games as part of physical rehabilitation for teens (Widman, McDonald, & Abresch, 2006; Deutsch, Borbely, Filler, Huhn, & Guarrera-Bowlby, 2008).

Adverse Effects of Exergames

As with any new pastime, the increased popularity of exergaming raises concerns about its possible adverse effects. There is worry that children are becoming involved in screen time to the exclusion of creative play or time in natural environments (Louv, 2005; Anderson, Economos, & Must, 2008). There is also a concern about exergame injuries. Soon after the release of *DDR,* a report circulated on the Web about a youth in an arcade who experienced a cardiac event while playing. Fortunately, in such a public venue, this youth received first aid and CPR and did well (Thorsen, 2004). It seems inevitable that games that encourage vigorous physical activity will sometimes lead to sports-reported injuries. Research into exergames is taking this into account: One study documented 39 self-reported Wii-related injuries, finding 46% occurred during *Wii Sports Tennis* (Sparks, Chase, & Coughlin, 2009). As more youth participate in conventional sports such as soccer and hockey, incidents of head injury and concussion have been increasing. There is some concern that youth who have sustained a concussion need to rest their brains after injury. Some recommend that children recovering from an acute injury not engage in cognitively challenging games, so in some cases these may be restricted in inpatient pediatric units. It's also important to be aware that for people who suffer photically stimulated seizures, certain games may give rise to seizures. Other worries focus on the fear that youth will play games to the exclusion of other activities, social life, or family involvement, or that exergames may be dangerous to the population of those who overexercise as a result of distorted thinking, which is common in eating disorders. In these cases, attention should be focused on helping set limits on game play or physical activity.

Limitations of Existing Research

There are numerous limitations to the existing studies; many have been quite small, with convenience samples. There is also a lack of standardized testing in studies, so that it is difficult to compare findings or combine them in meta-analyses. As mentioned, the disjunct between the rapid pace of the gaming world and the slower pace of academic clinical trials creates ongoing challenges. Additionally, studies conducted by researchers hired by video game companies generally are under scrutiny because of concerns about conflict of interest. Because there is little funding set aside for exergaming studies, many good ideas for studies will not be pursued, especially since the significant downturn in spending on biomedical research, given the downturn of the economy and decreasing congressional funding.

Despite this, there is reason for optimism regarding the role of exergames in a healthy lifestyle. About 20 studies to date have produced encouraging results, building a foundation for the next generation of research publications. Ideally, future studies will offer high-quality controlled trials to establish effectiveness and sustainability of exergaming (Daley, 2009). With only one medication approved for pediatric obesity in the US, and with controversy surrounding bariatric surgery for youth, exergaming appears to be a less expensive and more benign way to help youth.

Uses of Exergames
CASE STUDY REVISITED

Given the status of existing research, it seems exergames have potential for impacting Sue's health and activity level given specific types of intervention. Her pediatrician has more evidence for exergaming efficacy when recommending games that encourage movement in both upper and lower limbs. Previous studies also suggest that giving Sue a choice of games may help, by encouraging her to experiment with several game types, giving her at least a week try to each. Variety in gaming is important: A library of games owned by the medical clinic would give Sue flexibility in checking out a new game each week, also providing weekly reminders to keep exergaming. When Sue comes to the clinic each week to trade in the old game for the new, a nurse visit for weight tracking could work very well and be a cost-effective way to track her progress at her medical home.

Sue's clinicians will be familiar with treatment guidelines and will encourage a comprehensive approach to her family. Knowing that exergames alone are not enough to motivate Sue, her pediatrician may wish to work through some additional incentives with Sue and her family. Using motivational interviewing and goal setting, her family can encourage her to make changes and increase her activity. One idea would be to use simple rewards if Sue tracks her progress and logs her daily activity. "Turn your TV off week" community events can support making healthy choices. Family dance nights in which the family exergames together could help her earn points to "buy" her favorite game from the pediatrician. Sue's pediatrician would find it beneficial to work with her family, possibly encouraging her family to create a social network for Sue. Sue's exergaming friends could be encouraged to come and play regularly with Sue, not emphasizing weight loss, but emphasizing daily physical activity. Sue's family should be given realistic expectations of exergaming: that they are a potentially powerful way to increase Sue's physical activity and displace sedentary screen time. By being more active, she may find relief from low mood and isolation, and stall or reverse her recent weight gain. Of course, exergames are not a cure, but they can be part of the solution along with nutritional counseling, better school policies around physical education, and supports from her community (like Safe Routes to School and safer trails in her neighborhood).

EXERGAMES: REAL-WORLD IMPLEMENTATION

Viewing exergames as a medical intervention is perhaps the most complex way of assessing the potential of exergames, but not the only possibility. Children and adolescents spend a large portion of their time in school; therefore, schools are in a favorable position to provide opportunities for students to be physically active (Russell R. Pate, Saunders, O'Neill, & Dowda, 2010). School-based physical activity doesn't only have to include physical education and recess; it can also include lessons in which students engage in active learning in the classroom. As exergames make their way into many school districts, they are becoming a popular mechanism for added physical activity throughout the day. Although in the early stages of research, exergame interventions have been shown to have positive implications on academic achievement, absenteeism, negative classroom behaviors, physical activity levels, and tardiness (Young, Marshak, Freier, & Medina, 2007; Shasek, 2009; Hellmich, 2010).

The console game market is often referred to as the "home market"—differentiating games played on television-connected consoles from arcade-style games found in businesses or public environments. Yet the use of console-based games, as well as other commercially available active games, has expanded beyond the living room. After-school leaders look to games as a way to engage youth in physical activity during their spare time at clubs and community centers. Senior living centers coordinate game-based bowling tournaments as a way to encourage socialization among their residents and connect them to an outside community. Public environments, from doctor's offices to laundromats and state fair displays, showcase exergames as a way to engage large groups of people in activity, model positive benefits of games, or eliminate boredom. Active games have been used to provide outlets for youth in the mental health system, who often move from foster to crisis homes, in and out of inpatient or crisis homes. Teachers and school administrators use games to provide "brain breaks," short bursts of physical activity before tests or during particularly sedentary classes, and as a carrot to get kids to arrive at school on time. Physical education instructors use active video games as one option for kids seeking to create a lifestyle that includes daily physical activity.

It is encouraging to see active video games embraced by a diverse collection of game players. New Mexico State University's Learning Games Lab spent 3 years investigating uses of active video games by granting games and equipment to schools, community centers, and programs. Researchers communicated regularly with recipients and documented what worked, what didn't, and how games could be used more effectively. Based on their work, they've drafted the following recommendations on using exergames in different environments.

EXERGAMES IN SCHOOLS

Many studies indicate that classroom-based physical activities have positive associations on academic behaviors, and academic achievement (Centers for Disease Control and Prevention, 2010). Several studies document an association between school-based physical activity, including physical education, and academic performance among school-age youth. Promoting physical fitness and increasing time in physical education can lead to improved grades and standardized test scores (Castelli, Hillman, Buck, & Erwin, 2007; Chomitz et al., 2009). A simple classroom-based physical activity program, integrated with the academic curriculum, can promote meaningful energy expenditure among school-aged children (Stewart, Dennison, Kohl III, & Doyle, 2004) and can also increase on-task behavior of all students (Mahar et al., 2006).

In an inner-city school, researchers from the Children's Digital Media Center included exergaming in an intervention with overweight students. Using the *Wii Fit* suite of games, they offered active games to an overweight and obese group of students in a "Wii Club" during after-school and lunch periods for 6 months. Data from this study showed that students who played cooperatively with a teammate lost more weight than those who continued in their normal daily routines. Playing competitively against peers, by contrast, did not result in weight loss. The exergames were also reasonably engaging to students. Fifty-four percent of the participants stayed in the Wii Club for the full time period, and 73% stayed much of the year.

Physical education teachers have had success using exergames as part of a larger physical education curriculum. In a small, early-college high school without a gym and with limited equipment, instructors used a Wii with more structured workout programs to encourage workouts with individualized focus. Numerous web sites show teachers how to set up exergames and how to align them with learning goals and state standards. Alternating traditional physical activity with days in the gym or cafeteria with exergames, instructors rotate students around several stations. Instructors also conduct large group activities, such as dance games, with one console and a classroom of students dancing together. By creating an exergame lab at an elementary school, one instructor sought to end food-based rewards at the school, and replaced

pizza parties with time "playing" in the lab. The lab also provides an opportunity for physical education during inclement weather, and models games that students can play at home to replace some of their traditional sedentary game play with active game play. Similarly, using exergames during parent nights, school fairs, and during parent–teacher conferences exposed families to the potential of games, providing opportunities for families to exercise together and think about ways to continue doing so in the home. During "Turn Your TV off Week," one educator in rural Maine gave away *DDR* sets and opened up the school for families to have contests in the gym for a week. The long Maine winter, with short daylight hours for outdoor play, yielded a high attendance rate. In a pilot study in middle schools in Maine, 60 youth were given access to a *DDR*-like game called *In the Groove*. During the 20 weeks, youth averaged 40 to 50 minutes in exergame play, logging about half of that time above MVPA thresholds (Maloney 2012).

In the classroom, teachers have had success using exergames for breaks throughout the day. In some elementary school classrooms, when the teacher found students' attention wavering, she used a Wii to get the class on their feet. In another, third grade students danced to a Wii-based song before spelling exams, boosting exam scores and students' self-confidence in testing. Several schools broadcast a dance game on the closed-circuit television screen first thing every morning and found increased attendance and decreased tardiness (documented late attendance). Teachers of students with behavior problems also used exergames as rewards for their students, giving students a goal to work toward, and giving them physical activity breaks to help their focus and concentration.

Considerations for School Implementation

Games appear to yield the most benefit as an additional tool for increasing physical activity as part of a physical education curriculum, and as an easy way to create short bursts of activity throughout the day. As with most community programs, exergames need an advocate and responsible caretaker in schools. When integrating exergames, it is recommended to give specific staff members ownership of the equipment, allowing them to have it at home for short periods of time to build familiarity. Train students and parent volunteers on how to set up the system, troubleshoot problems related to batteries or syncing peripherals, and help them learn which games work best with which audiences.

Some exergame advocates have had success in training student clubs, particularly at-risk kids, as game advocates, requiring that one of those student members be present whenever the equipment is used, and depending on their guidance for implementing it in use.

School administrators and staff often need reassurance that the gaming programs will be used appropriately. Sharing research and case studies of use in other schools is important in building buy-in. When using exergaming with young audiences, staff should be particularly careful to watch the language, song lyrics, and dance moves or clothing of on-screen characters. Well-meaning parents may misunderstand the use of active games in schools, if they hear students singing inappropriate song lyrics. It may help to educate family members before implementing exergames throughout the school day, communicating the benefits of active games and the ways in which they will be used.

EXERGAMES IN THE HOME

Anecdotally, home use of exergames has tremendous impact. Jennifer Mercurio, the "Losing Gamer," uses her online blog (LosingGamer.com) to chronicle her initially skeptical foray into exergaming through a 25-pound weight loss over a 6-month period. She devoted herself to using exergames daily for an hour, 5 days a week, and cycled through games, including dance games, action games, and games targeting weight loss with individualized workouts. Perhaps because she did not rely on only one game throughout her journey, she found enough diversity in the games to keep her engaged. Initially, she would allow the programs to design workouts for her. As her skills and fitness improved, she admits to feeling a bit limited—not in game play but in exercise. For her, the exergames served as a gateway to craving more rigorous physical activity. It is not uncommon for self-directed exercise initiatives to drop off after approximately 7 to 9 weeks. It is fair to expect exergames to do the same, so home users should understand this, and anticipate ways to help break through that dropoff period.

Home-based exergaming may be directed at physical activity for weight loss, or to increase other kinds of fitness, such as flexibility. However, it also has the potential for bringing families together to game. Adults, especially seniors, are better able to control active games, as they do not need the gaming dexterity required by handheld controllers. The playing field is leveled, in that players of all ages can compete equally in games. Young children are

better able to compete with older siblings, as well as with parents and grandparents. In a focus group conducted with both high and low users and in both parents and children in a *DDR* study, a key finding was enjoyment of the games after children went to bed. Worried about embarrassment, parents would play at night to get their exercise time after the children were tucked in. In fact, many parents went out to purchase pedometers to measure steps and keep up with their children in a pediatric *DDR* study in which only children were issued pedometers (Maloney, 2012). This signaled to researchers that parents wanted to measure their activity and try out the games, but may have felt self-conscious in doing so.

Importantly, home-based exergaming has the potential to transform sedentary screen time into active game time, however recent research indicates that simply granting access to exergames is likely not enough to change behavior. Baranowski et al. (2012) discovered that giving youth active video games in the home or other settings without supervision was not enough to increase physical activity. Youth in this study either did not play the active games at vigorous levels or did not get additional physical activity outside of exergame play to increase their daily physical activity. This indicates that providing additional motivation or incentives may be necessary in a home environment. In a free choice environment, youth—both boys and girls—have not shown preference toward exergames versus sedentary games. In fact, youth seem to alternate between the two options evenly; however, boys demonstrated more intensity in exergame play than girls (Lam, Sit, & McManus, 2011).

Exergames are often more easily made into multiplayer games, including more dancers, gamers, or movers who may not even need their own game controller. There are concerns that exergames take up living room space, but the space they occupy is far less than a treadmill or stationary bike in most cases (and dance mats or Wiimotes take up little space).

Considerations for Home Use

Families purchasing console games should commit to choosing active games as at least half their games purchases. Parents can facilitate active game play by playing with their families, rather than relying on children to automatically choose the active games. Certainly, gamers can "cheat" on active games, flicking the wrist to bowl while seated, rather than standing to cast a bowling ball. However, playing in groups with friends and as a social event can prevent this. Finally, when gaming at home, parents should reinforce the desired behavior by being involved, demonstrating activity when playing, and emphasizing the value of being active.

Because gamers naturally get tired of playing the same game repeatedly, and because different gamers like different types of games, home users should anticipate needing a variety of games, exchanging games with other players, or renting games to experiment with new titles. The mall and the Internet offer options for swapping out preowned games. Most importantly, home-based gamers must recognize the benefits that come from active gaming, and seek to change their behavior to increase activity. Although exergames can be just as engaging (and in some cases, more enjoyable) than sedentary video games, players may still need to schedule time to move, and must value the physical activity games can provide. Creating a family blog or journal noting exergame time may help, as may an incentive system, giving family members rewards for logging daily minutes.

EXERGAMES IN AFTER-SCHOOL AND COMMUNITY PROGRAMS

After-school programs and community programs have had success in using exergames to increase physical activity, but also to meet other goals. One program created an "Exergame Olympics" in which families competed to earn their community center a Wii. Programs have seen increased participation and attendance in optional programs by integrating exergames, and one program found a noted increase of participation by fathers in the program once exergames were introduced. Active games are frequently used as a center-based approach, in which individuals can cycle between activities and exergaming consoles, or as a break for physical activity in which an entire group exercises together, such as with dancing games.

During public events, exergaming stations gives community members access to games, as well as the opportunity to try out the games, and think about how they could integrate active games into their homes. Active games are appearing in physician's offices, as part of workplace fitness interventions, and at fairs and health expos. Most games work well when connected to a projector and displayed on a large screen. The bright graphics and music serve well in attracting an audience, particularly when an exergaming host can encourage onlookers to participate.

Considerations for After-School and Community Use

When using a system in public, such as at a fair, or in a waiting room or office, program leaders should expect to provide a host who can keep the equipment working, guide new users through menus, and encourage and facilitate game play by public members. Especially when using one system with a roomful of users, it is essential the host circulate through the users, offering encouragement, modeling big movements and active participation, and helping users realize the goal may not be a perfect score within the game, but the chance to move more.

New Mexico State University researchers have seen surprisingly little theft or equipment damage in the programs they supervise. However, they advise never leaving a system unattended. Several programs have had success with checkout systems, in which schools, leaders, or community organizers can borrow a console and set of games to use at monthly health events, fairs, and expos. It is common for adults in charge of programs with smaller budgets to worry that equipment will "walk off." Only 1 in 30 PlayStations disappeared in a home-based study, contrary to predictions. McDonalds and other larger corporations have devised stands and platforms so that exergames are secured for use in playgrounds and public areas, with great success. Laptop-based games can be easily secured with Kensington-style locks that run under $15 each.

As with school implementation, after-school programs need a champion of exergame use: someone who is familiar with the equipment and related technical issues and can assist in implementation. This kind of program oversight offers an excellent opportunity to involve youth in the process, giving them training and responsibility for taking exergaming out to other programs, such as game days in senior centers, fairs, and events. For those worried about the technology, an adult can almost always find a youngster who is tech savvy and able to connect the devices to screens and controllers.

When using exergames in public, remember that you may be placing the gamer in a fairly visible position, and be mindful of exergames that may display the gamer's weight or provide feedback to the gamer that could make him or her self-conscious. For example, the *Wii Fit* games allow users to weigh themselves and, if the user is overweight, the Wii avatar representing the player looks disappointed. Negative feedback, such as booing noises provided on some *DDR* games feel especially directed when an audience hears them, so look for options to disable negative feedback. As with gaming in schools, be aware of potentially offensive song lyrics, particularly in a public environment in which young children participate.

When using exergames with a crowd, do not expect the crowd to voluntarily participate. Use an exergaming host to dance, move, and game, gradually handing off control of the game to viewers, to encourage wider participation.

EXERGAMES WITH SPECIAL AUDIENCES

Programs for older audiences, such as those found in senior living apartments and community programs, were some of the first exergaming groups to receive national press coverage. Wii-based bowling leagues allow individuals to revisit their love of bowling, without the physically taxing aspects of traditional bowling. Such leagues also encourage socialization within apartments and senior groups and allow seniors to compete and socialize with other bowling teams. Other low-intensity exergames, such as golf or darts games, can also encourage mild physical activity and enable the same kind of game-based socialization found in bowling leagues.

Although little research has been published in using exergames with special needs populations, New Mexico State University researchers are finding success using games with children who have Down's syndrome, as well as with gamers with Asperger's syndrome and related disorders that can impact social functions. Exergames can provide physical activity and mild socialization for gamers who may not easily acclimate to traditional types of activity, and the individualization of the games equips a player to move at his or her own pace.

In many cases, exergames enable game play among broader audiences by providing a larger range of motions, not limiting video game play to those with dexterity in thumbs and fingers. Yet games that require full-body motion, such as Microsoft's X-Box Kinect, can provide additional barriers for those with limited movement ability.

Considerations for Use with Special Audiences

For seniors or users with visual impairment or restricted cognitive function, exergames are best viewed on large screens. Games with simple interfaces and large text work best. Games vary as to the degree of dexterity and gross motor skills needed, but those that mimic traditional real-world activities, such as bowling or dart throwing, may work best for populations who have played these activities.

When working with audiences with developmental delays or social disorders, restricting competition may make the experience less stressful and more enjoyable. Games that encourage collaboration or noncompetitive individual play help players work toward their own goals, without comparing themselves to a perceived norm.

Audiences have diverse needs. For therapists, teachers and program leaders, the best approach is a familiarity with existing games, and an awareness that people may have to chart their own individual paths as to what works best. The AbleGamers Foundation (ablegamers.org) works diligently to document games that enable play for people with disabilities, reviewing games and working with the game development industry to find ways to make games more accessible. In hospitals, it is important that the games be cleansed to decrease the possibility of disease transmission. Child Life professionals can be important brokers in pediatric units when they visit with children and encourage them to be "normal kids" while they are in the hospital—normal kids play exergames.

Design Considerations

As the exergames field matures, so too must the designs of active video games. Active video games are no longer used just in living rooms, but in schools, clinics, gyms, and community centers. Practitioners who use exergames in a wide variety of settings, and with a wide variety of audiences, have called for the analysis and improvement of exergame design, to enable use by diverse populations such as seniors, learners with special physical or physiological needs, children, and groups.

For example, dance games have been successful in increasing physical activity of school children, decreasing tardiness to class, and boosting test-taking skills; yet the seemingly inappropriate lyrics and suggestive dance moves could cause parents to disapprove of exergame interventions. Although not specifically designed for senior citizens, bowling games have found a tremendous audience, launching Wii bowling leagues nationally. Other games may have similar success with this audience, but small text or complex interfaces can be a deterrent because of vision problems typical in aging populations. Games can offer engaging physical activity for learners with social challenges, such as autism or Asperger's syndrome, but competition can sometimes feel extremely frustrating to these audiences. By enabling collaborative gameplay, in which players work together toward a goal, game developers can reach out to a wider range of gamers.

Game developers, researchers, and exergaming advocates have begun drafting design considerations to guide developers in making games more easily accessible to all populations, and more supportive of health-based goals. These include:

• Provide an easy, immediate start to the game. When users play in public or a group setting, it is frustrating to have to move through a series of menus, set up an avatar, or go through an assessment before getting into gameplay.
• Make text and buttons large, enabling use on older televisions and for populations with vision impairments.
• Provide enough feedback to guide the gamer in improvement, but be sensitive to displaying a user in a negative way that may make him or her self-conscious about weight or other negative physical attributes.
• Avoid risqué clothing, lyrics, and movements. If necessary, give the user the ability to filter them for younger audiences or public environments.
• When offering vigorous physical activity, consider allowing the user to customize needed behaviors, such as avoiding kneeling positions or rapid movements from seating to standing.
• Enable social networks, such as sharing scores and collaborating toward activity goals.
• Enable documentation and achievements across games, giving gamers the ability to work toward activity goals while still using a wide variety of activities.
• Provide suggested workouts, such as a 10-minute low-activity workout for warm-up, and a 20-minute aerobic game play. This would guide the player in setting his or her own activity regimen, and guide physicians who wish to prescribe specific types and durations of activity.

Aligning Activity Goals with Entertainment

Many exergames don't map directly to the fitness goals advocated by public health officials. Songs in *DDR* each last about a minute and a half, with these repeated in three cycles called stages, often amounting to a total of 5 minutes of play. Although this may be a good interval for enjoyment of the game, it is not an ideal amount of time for adults to partake in physical activity. Adults are advised to get bouts of 10 minutes of activity at a time, so a prompt in the game to play another stage may be advisable. On the positive side, *DDR* does have a workout mode that plays longer than 5 minutes, and it attempts to estimate caloric expenditure; however, its estimates

are based on certain assumptions and are considered inaccurate by exercise scientists.

If games are designed to give a certain period of entertainment, perhaps it is understandable that research shows that time spent playing *DDR* drifts downward over weeks to months (Maloney et al., 2008). To be fair, if research on exergaming is designed to look at only *DDR* play over several months, that particular study is probably expecting something that is not typical of gamers' use patterns. In sum, it may be expecting too much from *DDR* that steps and songs will be engaging for months to years, no matter how great it was at the beginning. The dance game *Dance Factory* attempted to get around this by allowing users to play their own CDs, with the game producing steps to go along, but this was largely a failure: Poor reviews revealed that *DDR* players were frustrated with the steps not falling on the dominant beat of the songs.

Creating sustainable behavior change with messages and published health campaigns is effective, but impacting social norms can be slow. If the field is to encourage exergames as part of a healthy lifestyle, then exergames need to have demonstrable, measurable, and lasting benefits over time in a target population. The field clearly needs longer-term studies, and researchers are now preparing to conduct such field trials (Maddison et al., 2009). Until this kind of data is in hand, there will be hesitation to bring exergames up to scale. It is also likely that insurance companies will demand a larger knowledge base before paying for exergames as treatments.

Conclusion

Realizing the promises of exergames will be challenging, but never before have so many societal forces aligned to focus on pediatric obesity. At this moment in history when technology is ubiquitous, individuals may be accepting and eager to play well-designed exergames and exchange some of their sedentary time for enjoyable, active time. Youth may be on their way to creating novel games, as seen in the *Ruckus Nation* competition from HopeLab, in which hundreds of entries were ranked in order of their promise to increase physical activity. Some of the winners in that contest had fascinating approaches to exergaming that have yet to be brought to market or to scale. Although research is still formative and hypothesis generating, we look forward to the next chapter of newer apps, hypothesis testing, and larger studies that establish the role of exergames in both prevention and treatment of health conditions.

Future Directions

How can exergames further enable and encourage physical activity? What attributes provide the most motivation to the player? How can the design of games facilitate participation and guide the player in setting and meeting physical activity goals? What kinds of games are most supportive? How can traditional gaming design constructs, such as narrative, challenge, and flow, be used to encourage physical activity by gamers?

What characteristics must an exergaming intervention include? In addition to simply placing an exergaming console in a home, classroom, or program, what actions lead to increases in physical activity? How can teachers, program leaders and physicians best support the active gamer?

In what ways can the medical community embrace and support active videogaming? What additional documentation, rigor, and research are needed for insurance companies and medical organizations to financially support and "prescribe" active game play? What "dosage" works best with what population?

What roles do social networks have in exergaming? How does the gamer's community, both face-to-face and in-game, influence his or her choices in exergaming? How can the gamer's network be used to make gameplay more enjoyable, and provide incentives for health-based gaming?

Acknowledgments

Special thanks for research and technical editing assistance from Michelle Garza, Rachel Gallagher, Amy Smith Muise, Liz Horton, and review by Emily Murphy. Research for this chapter was supported in part by National Research Initiative Grant #2008–55215–18837 from the USDA National Institute of Food and Agriculture.

References

Anderson, S. E., Economos, C. D., & Must, A. (2008). Active play and screen time in US children aged 4 to 11 years in relation to sociodemographic and weight status characteristics: a nationally representative cross-sectional analysis. *BMC Public Health, 8*(366). doi: 10.1186/1471–2458-8-366.

Baranowski, T., Abdelsamad, D., Baranowski, J., O'Connor, T. M., Thompson, D., Barnett, A.,...Chen, T. A. (2012). Impact of an active video game on healthy children's physical activity. *Pediatrics, 129*(3), e636–e642.

Biddiss, E., & Irwin, J. (2010). Active video games to promote physical activity in children and youth: A systematic review. [Review]. *Archives of Pediatrics and Adolescent Medicine, 164*(7), 664–672. doi: 10.1001/archpediatrics.2010.104

Castelli, D. M., Hillman, C. H., Buck, S. M., & Erwin, H. E. (2007). Physical fitness and academic achievement in third- and fifth-grade students. *Journal of Sport and Exercise Psychology, 29*(2), 239.

Centers for Disease Control and Prevention. (2010). *The association between school-based physical activity, including physical education, and academic performance.* Atlanta, GA.

Chan, P. A., & Rabinowitz, T. (2006). A cross-sectional analysis of video games and attention deficit hyperactivity disorder symptoms in adolescents. *Annals of General Psychiatry, 5*, 16. doi: 10.1186/1744–859X-5–16w.

Chomitz, V. R., Slining, M. M., McGowan, R. J., Mitchell, S. E., Dawson, G. F., & Hacker, K. A. (2009). Is there a relationship between physical fitness and academic achievement? Positive results from public school children in the northeastern United States. *Journal of School Health, 79*(1), 30–37. doi: 10.1111/j.1746–1561.2008.00371.x.

Daley, A. J. (2009). Can exergaming contribute to improving physical activity levels and health outcomes in children? *Pediatrics, 124*(2), 9. doi: 10.1542/peds.2008–2357.

Deutsch, J. E., Borbely, M., Filler, J., Huhn, K., & Guarrera-Bowlby, P. (2008). Use of a Low-Cost, Commercially Available Gaming Console (Wii) for Rehabilitation of an Adolescent With Cerebral Palsy. *Physical Therapy, 88*(10), 1196–1207. doi: 10.2522/ptj.20080062.

Espay, A. J., Baram, Y., Dwivedi, A. K., Shukla, R., Gartner, M., Gaines, L., et al. (2010). At-home training with closed-loop augmented-reality cueing device for improving gait in patients with Parkinson disease. *Journal of Rehabilitation Research and Development, 47*(6), 573–581. doi: 10.1682/jrrd.2009.10.0165.

Foley, L., & Maddison, R. (2010). Use of active video games to increase physical activity in children: a (virtual) reality? *Pediatric Exercise Science, 22*(1), 7–20.

Freedman, D. S. (2011). *Obesity—United States, 1988–2008.* Atlanta: Centers for Disease Control and Prevention Retrieved from http://www.cdc.gov/mmwr/preview/mmwrhtml/su6001a15.htm?s_cid=su6001a15_w.

Golomb, M. R., McDonald, B. C., Warden, S. J., Yonkman, J., Saykin, A. J., Shirley, B., et al. (2010). In-home virtual reality videogame telerehabilitation in adolescents with hemiplegic cerebral palsy. *Archives of Physical Medicine and Rehabilitation, 91*(1), 1–8.e1. doi: 10.1016/j.apmr.2009.08.153.

Gordon-Larsen, P., Nelson, M., Page, P., & Popkin, B. (2006). Inequality in the built environment underlies key health disparities in physical activity and obesity. *Pediatrics, 117*(2), 417–424. doi: 10.1542/peds.2005–0058.

Graves, L., Stratton, G., Ridgers, N., & Cable, N. (2008). Energy expenditure in adolescents playing new generation computer games. *British Medical Journal, 42*(7), 592.

Graves, L., Stratton, G., Ridgers, N. D., & Cable, N. T. (2007). Comparison of energy expenditure in adolescents when playing new generation and sedentary computer games: cross sectional study. *British Medical Journal, 335*(7633), 1282–1284. doi: 10.1136/bmj.39415.632951.80.

Haddock, B., Siegel, S., & Wilkin, L. (2010a). Children's choice of Wii Sports games and energy expenditure. *California Journal of Health Promotion, 8*(1), 32–39.

Haddock, B., Siegel, S., & Wilkin, L. (2010b). Energy expenditure of middle school children while playing Wii Sports games. *Californian Journal of Health Promotion, 8*(1), 32–39.

Haddock, B. L., Siegel, S. R., & Wikin, L. D. (2009). The addition of a video game to stationary cycling:

The impact on energy expenditure in overweight children. *Open Sports Science Journal, 2,* 42–46. doi: 10.2174/1875399x00902010042.

Hellmich, N. (October 11, 2010). Go to school and just dance—video games and other activities supplement gym class. *USA Today.* Retrieved from http://www.usatoday.com/printedition/life/20101011/justdance11_cv.art.htm.

Kraft, J. A., Russell, W. D., Bowman, T. A., Selsor, C. W., 3rd, & Foster, G. D. (2011). Heart rate and perceived exertion during self-selected intensities for exergaming compared to traditional exercise in college-age participants. *Journal of Strength & Conditioning Research.* doi: 10.1519/JSC.0b013e3181e06f13.

Krebs, N. F., & Jacobson, M. S. (2003). Prevention of pediatric overweight and obesity. *Pediatrics, 112*(2), 424.

Lam, J. W. K., Sit, C. H. P., & McManus, A. M. (2011). Play pattern of seated video game and active, exergame, alternatives. *Journal of Exercise Science & Fitness, 9*(1), 24–30.

Lenhart, A., Jones, S., & MacGill, A. (2008). Video games: Adults are players too. *Pew Internet & American Life Project.* Washington, DC: Pew Research Center.

Lieberman, D. A. (2006). *Dance Games and Other Exergames: What the Research Says.* Santa Barbara: University of California.

Lieberman, D. A., Chamberlin, B., Medina, E. Jr., Franklin, B. A., Sanner, B. M., Vafiadis, D. K., et al. (2011). The Power of Play: Innovations in Getting Active Summit 2011: A science panel proceedings report from the American Heart Association. *Circulation.* doi: 10.1161/CIR.0b013e318219661d.

Lieberman, D. A., Fisk, M. C., & Biely, E. (2009). Digital games for young children ages three to six: From research to design. *Computers in the Schools, 26*(4), 299–313. doi: 10.1080/07380560903360178.

Lieberman, D. A., Peinado, S., Rodriguez, K., & Biely, E. (2011). *The Psychology of Avatars: A Roundup of Research & Design Ideas.* Paper presented at the Games for Health, Boston.

Louv, R. (2005). *Last Child in the Woods.* Chapel Hill, NC: Algonquin Books.

Lyons, E. J., Tate, D. F., Ward, D. S., Bowling, J. M., Ribisl, K. M., & Kalyararaman, S. (2011). Energy expenditure and enjoyment during video game play: Differences by game type. *Medicine & Science in Sports & Exercise, 43*(10), 1987–1993. doi: 10.1249/MSS.0b013e318216ebf3.

Maddison, R., Foley, L., Mhurchu, C. N., Jull, A., Jiang, Y., Prapavessis, H., et al. (2009). Feasibility, design and conduct of a pragmatic randomized controlled trial to reduce overweight and obesity in children: The electronic games to aid motivation to exercise (eGAME) study. *BMC Public Health, 9,* 146. doi: 10.1186/1471–2458-9-146.

Maddison, R., Mhurchu, C. N., Jull, A., Jiang, Y., Prapavessis, H., & Rodgers, A. (2007). Energy expended playing video console games: an opportunity to increase children's physical activity? *Pediatric Exercise Science, 19*(3), 334–343.

Mahar, M., Murphy, S., Rowe, D., Golden, J., Shields, T., & Raedeke, T. (2006). Effects of a classroom-based program on physical activity and on-task behavior. *Medicine & Science in Sports & Exercise, 8.* doi: 10.1249/01.mss.0000235359.16685.a3.

Maloney, A., Bethea, T., Kelsey, K., Marks, J., Paez, S., Rosenberg, A., et al. (2008). A pilot of a video game (DDR) to promote physical activity and decrease sedentary screen time. *Obesity (Silver Spring), 16*(9), 2074–2080. doi: 10.1038/oby.2008.295.

Maloney, A. (2012). Can dance exergames boost physical activity as a school-based intervention? *Games for Health Journal.* (In Press).

McDougall, J., & Duncan, M. (2008). Children, video games and physical activity: An exploratory study. *International Journal on Disability and Human Development, 7*(1), 89. doi: 10.1515/IJDHD.2008.7.1.89.

Ni Mhurchu, C., Maddison, R., Jiang, Y., Jull, A., Prapavessis, H., & Rodgers, A. (2008). Couch potatoes to jumping beans: A pilot study of the effect of active video games on physical activity in children. *International Journal of Behavioral Nutrition and Physical Activity, 5,* 8. doi: 10.1186/1479–5868–5-8.

Ogden, C. L., Carroll, M. D., & Flegal, K. M. (2008). High body mass index for age among US children and adolescents, 2003–2006. *JAMA, 299*(20), 2401. doi: 10.1001/jama.299.20.2401.

Omidyar, P. (2012). *Zamzee Research Results.* Paper presented at the Obesity Society, San Antonio, TX. http://www.slideshare.net/hopelab/zamzee-research-results.

Pate, R. (2008). Physically active video gaming: An effective strategy for obesity prevention? *Archives of Pediatrics and Adolescent Medicine, 162*(9), 895. doi: 10.1001/archpedi.162.9.895.

Pate, R. R., Freedson, P. S., Sallis, J. F., Taylor, W. C., Sirard, J., Trost, S. G., et al. (2002). Compliance with physical activity guidelines: Prevalence in a population of children and youth. *Annals of Epidemiology, 12*(5), 305–308. doi: 10.1016/S1047–2797(01)00263–0.

Pate, R. R., Saunders, R. P., O' Neill, J. R., & Dowda, M. (2010). Overcoming barriers to physical activity: Helping youth be more active. *Health and Fitness Journal, 12*(1), 5.

Rideout, V. J., Foehr, U. G., & Roberts, D. F. (2010). *Generation M2: Media in the Lives of 8- to 18-Year-Olds.* Menlo Park, CA: Henry J. Kaiser Family Foundation.

Rideout, V. J., Vandewater, E. A., & Wartella, E. A. (2003). *Zero to Six: Electronic Media in the Lives of Infants, Toddlers and Preschoolers.* Menlo Park, CA: The Henry J. Kaiser Family Foundation.

Rosenberg, D., Depp, C. A., Vahia, I. V., Reichstadt, J., Palmer, B. W., Kerr, J., et al. (2010). Exergames for subsyndromal depression in older adults: A pilot study of a novel intervention. *American Journal of Geriatric Psychology, 18*(3), 221–226. doi: 10.1097/JGP.0b013e3181c534b5.

Rosser, J. C., Lynch, P. J., Cuddihy, L., Gentile, D. A., Klonsky, J., Merrell, R., et al. (2007). The impact of video games on training surgeons in the 21st century. *Archives of Surgery, 142*(2), 181–186.

Saposnik, G., Mamdani, M., Bayley, M., Thorpe, K. E., Hall, J., Cohen, L. G., et al. (2010). Effectiveness of virtual reality exercises in stroke rehabilitation (EVREST): Rationale, design, and protocol of a pilot randomized clinical trial assessing the Wii gaming system. *International Journal of Stroke, 5*(1), 47–51. doi: 10.1111/j.1747–4949.2009.00404.x.

Shasek, J. (2009). ExerLearning: movement, fitness, technology and learning. In Zemliansky, P., & Wilcox, D. (Eds.), *Design and Implementation of Educational Games.* Hershey, PA: Information Science Reference.

Shuler, C. (2012). *iLearn II: addendum, an analysis of the games category of the iTunes App Store.* New York: The Joan Ganz Cooney Center at Sesame Workshop.

Sit, C. H. P., Lam, J. W. K., & McKenzie, T. L. (2010). Children's use of electronic games: Choices of game mode and challenge levels. *International Journal of Pediatrics, 2010.*

Song, H., Kim, J., Tenzek, K. E., & Lee, K. M. (2010). *Intrinsic motivation in exergames: Competition, competitiveness, and the conditional indirect effect of presence.* Paper presented at the International Communication Association, Suntec City, Singapore. http://www.allacademic.com/meta/p405150_index.html.

Sparks, D., Chase, D., & Coughlin, L. (2009). Wii have a problem: A review of self-reported Wii related injuries. *Informatics in Primary Care, 17*(1), 55–57.

Staiano, A. E., Abraham, A., & Calvert, S. L. (May, 2010). *Improved Executive Functioning from Wii Active Exergame Play: A Study and Results.* Paper presented at the Games for Health Conference, Boston.

Staiano, A. E., & Calvert, S. L. (2011). Wii tennis play for low-income African American adolescents' energy expenditure. *Cyberpsychology: Journal of Psychosocial Research on Cyberspace, 5*(1).

Stewart, J. A., Dennison, D. A., Kohl III, H. W., & Doyle, J. A. (2004). Exercise level and energy expenditure in the TAKE 10! In Class Physical Activity Program. *Journal of School Health, 74*(10), 397–400.

Tan, B., Aziz, A. R., Chua, K., & Teh, K. C. (2002). Aerobic demands of the dance simulation game. *International Journal of Sports Medicine, 23*(2), 125–129. doi: 10.1055/s-2002–20132.

Thorsen, T. (2004). Teen has heart attack playing Dance Dance Revolution. Retrieved from GameSpot web site: http://www.gamespot.com/news/6101687/teen-has-heart-attack-playing-dance-dance-revolution.

Torres, A. (2008). *Cognitive effects of videogames on older people.* Paper presented at the ZON Digital Games 2008, Braga, Portugal. http://www.lasics.uminho.pt/ojs/index.php/zondgames08/index.

Unnithan, V. B., Houser, W., & Fernhall, B. (2006). Evaluation of the energy cost of playing a dance simulation video game in overweight and non-overweight children and adolescents. *International Journal of Sports Medicine, 27*(10), 804–809. doi: 10.1055/s-2005–872964.

US Department of Health and Human Services. (2008). *2008 physical activity guidelines for Americans: Be active, healthy and happy.* Washington, DC: US Department of Health and Human Services.

Vandewater, E. A., Rideout, V. J., Wartella, E. A., Huang, X., Lee, J., & Shim, M. (2007). Digital childhood: Electronic media and technology use among infants, toddlers, and preschoolers. *Pediatrics, 119*(e10006). doi: 10.1542/peds.2006–1804.

Widman, L. M., McDonald, C. M., & Abresch, R. T. (2006). Effectiveness of an upper extremity exercise device integrated with computer gaming for aerobic training in adolescents with spinal cord dysfunction. *Journal of Spinal Cord Medicine, 29*(4), 363–370.

Wittman, G. (2010). Video gaming increases physical activity. *Journal of Extension, 48*(2).

Worley, J., Rogers, S. N., & Kraemer, R. R. (2011). Metabolic responses to Wii Fit. *The Journal of Strength and Conditioning Research, 25*(3), 689–693.

Wylie, C. G., & Coulton, P. (2008). *Mobile exergaming.*

Young, T., Marshak, H. H., Freier, M. -C., & Medina, E. (2007). *"U Got 2 Move It" pilot study: Short-term impact of an after-school interactive video exertainment program for underserved children.* Dissertation. School of Public Health. Loma Linda University. Loma Linda, CA.

Serious Games: What Are They? What Do They Do? Why Should We Play Them?

Fran C. Blumberg, Debby E. Almonte, Jared S. Anthony, *and* Naoko Hashimoto

Abstract

Serious games are designed to entertain and educate players, and to promote behavioral change. This chapter reviews characterizations of serious games and the theoretical perspectives, most notably Social Cognitive Theory, that have been used to account for their effects, and game elements such as identity, immersion, and interactivity. It also surveys the diverse areas in which serious games have been used, such as health, education, civic engagement, and advertising. It concludes by identifying future directions for serious game design research and development that will promote transfer of skills and content from the game to the real world, including debriefing and explication of players' behaviors and cognitive skills while playing.

Key Words: challenge, debriefing, feedback, identity, immersion, interactivity, serious games, simulations

Introduction

The prominence of digital game play as a preferred activity among diverse age cohorts is evident from findings indicating that 67% of US households play computer and video games (Entertainment Software Association, 2010), 11- to 14-year-olds play video games for 90 minutes per day (Rideout, Foehr, & Roberts, 2010), and 33% of individuals age 2 and older had used an in-home digital game console in the last 4 months of 2006 (Nielsen Media Research, 2007). This widespread appeal has given rise to an expanding body of research attesting to the ramifications of computer and video game play for learning (see Gee, 2003; Squire, 2006) as related to, for example, academic achievement (Rosas et al., 2003; Satwicz & Stevens, 2008; Virvou & Katsionis, 2008 Papastergiou, 2009), cognitive skill enhancement (Greenfield et al., 1994; Sims & Mayer, 2002; Green & Bavelier, 2003, 2006, 2007; Boot, Kramer, Simons, Fabiani, & Gratton, 2008), and changes in attitude toward wide-ranging topics such as diet and

nutrition (Pempek & Calvert, 2009), product preference (Calvert, 2008; Mallinckrodt & Mizerski, 2007; Gross, 2010), and civic engagement (Bers, 2010; Ney & Jansz, 2010).

Governmental funding agencies and private foundations also have fueled extensive research and game development initiatives (such as *River City*, *QuestAtlantis*, *Whyville*, and *WolfQuest*[1]) to examine the academic ramifications of digital game play, particularly in the context of what have been referred to as *serious games*. These types of games, which are addressed in greater detail in this chapter, are generally designed to entertain and educate players, and promote behavioral change via the incorporation of prosocial messages (although our review of serious game types that follows also indicates the promulgation of what may be viewed as less prosocial messages, as in the case of advergames) embedded within game play (see Sherry et al., 2006). This goal was formally realized by the 2002 founding of the *Serious Game Initiative* by the Woodrow Wilson

International Center for Scholars to promote the development of games to advance policy decisions and leadership in the public sector (Woodrow Wilson International Center for Scholars, n.d.). The work of this high profile effort is furthered through its *Games for Change project* (www.gamesforchange.org), which emphasizes the development and support of games for social impact and *Games for Health project* (www.gamesforhealth.org), which emphasizes the use and development of technology to promote health and improve health care. Notably, the games that would emerge from these initiatives would be seen as sharing prosocial goals with games such as the unequivocally violent *World of Warcraft*, which has been cited for its opportunities to advance community building, citizenship, and peer mentoring (Curry, 2010; Dickey, 2011).

As part of the discussion that follows, we review what constitutes a serious game, which is not generally agreed on by scholars within the field. For example, some researchers argue (see Haring, Chakinska, & Ritterfeld, 2011) that what constitutes a serious game may only be evident via the resulting behavioral changes in the player; others argue that it is in the nature of the game itself (Crookall, 2010). Next, we describe the features or elements that typically comprise these games, and present some of the theoretical perspectives that have been used to frame these games, most notably, Social Cognitive Theory (Bandura, 1989; 2001). We also survey the diverse disciplines and areas in which serious games have been used, such as health, civic engagement, and very recently, advertising, as reflected by advergames. We conclude by identifying future directions and research questions that we see as salient for serious game design and development that will enable its players to transfer skills and content gained via the game context to the real world. In fact, how to effect transfer of skills across learning tasks and contexts has long concerned researchers and practitioners interested in learning (see Zimmerman, 2000; Barnett & Ceci, 2002) and remains a major challenge for those interested in promoting the instructional efficacy of serious games (see Hays, 2005; Mayo, 2011).

What Are Serious Games?

How best to characterize serious games remains elusive (see de Freitas, 2006). Bogost (2007) refers to serious games as persuasive in nature and viewed the serious game movement that was initiated in 2002 as directed toward building games that "support existing social cultural positions" (p. ix). According to Ben Sawyer (2006), cofounder of the Serious Games

Initiative, the "seriousness" of serious games is based in their purpose rather than the games themselves. Haring, Chakinsska, and Ritterfeld (2011) concur and acknowledge that off-the-shelf commercial games can be considered serious games if they impart important content to the player. In this context, "important" refers to content that serves to educate or train an individual to, for example, engage in scientific reasoning or work with others, as has been documented via the use of violent game titles such as *World of Warcraft* (see Dickey, 2011). Thus, these authors suggest that the appellation of *serious* to a game is less useful than adopting the nomenclature of *serious gaming* to refer to the processes and results accrued from having played a game (e.g., enhanced visual attention or knowledge about the Middle East conflict). Crookall (2010) further notes that the appellation of *serious* may serve a political function, whereby referring to game development as serious may provide a better platform from which to receive private and public funding. However, general agreement is found in the characterization of serious games as those that capitalize on computer technology and state-of-the-art video graphics for the purposes of instruction, training, or the prompting of attitude change among its players coupled with enjoyment (Zyda, 2005; Squire, 2006; DiPietro et al., 2007; Thompson et al., 2008; Crookall, 2010).

What game genres qualify as serious games also has garnered little consensus. For example, Annetta (2010) makes distinctions among serious games, serious educational games, simulations, and virtual worlds. In these characterizations, serious games are digital games designed to train its players on a particular skill with serious educational games (SEGs), including a further overlay of academic content. Simulations are seen as comparable to SEGs without the keeping of score or game economy. According to Hays (2005), simulations that include game features such as challenge and competition qualify as games. By extension, those simulation games that are designed to instruct and support specific learning goals may be considered serious games. Virtual worlds are further distinguished as three-dimensional environments in which social interaction figures more prominently than in the context of games or simulations.

Serious games have a long-standing tradition of use in the military to prepare soldiers for battle and instill requisite values and ethics. The first of these games was *Army Battle Zone*, developed by Atari in 1980. The edutainment genre that appeared a decade later was designed for a child audience and focused on the enhancement of reading, math, and science skills. Games within this genre yielded popular titles developed in 1996, such as *Where in the World Is Carmen Sandiego?* (Broderbund Software), *Oregon Trail* (Broderbund Software), and *Math Blaster* (Davidson & Associates). These games were initially praised for their ability to effectively and efficiently teach all levels of students with relatively simple graphics and easy to learn game play (Charsky, 2010). However, over time, edutainment games were viewed as limited by the software that was available at the time, as generally boring or "drill and kill" in nature, and as shallow in their learning goals (Van Eck, 2006; Charsky 2010). Second, from a business vantage point, edutainment games were not necessarily profitable (Mayo, 2011).

The serious games movement effectively took hold in 2002, largely fueled by the commercial success of *America's Army*, which had been intended for use as a recruitment tool for the US army. This game would later form the platform for future military training simulations and commercial titles available on game consoles (Jean, 2006). The Woodrow Wilson Center for International Scholars then funded the *Serious Games Initiative*, also in 2002, as noted, which was followed by the first *Serious Games Conference* in 2004.

Potentially, there is a relationship between the current movement in serious games and child and adolescent players for whom many of these games are targeted. This age group was seen more than 25 years ago as plagued by limited attention spans, as more visual in their learning styles, and as responsive to classroom learning that was perceived as entertaining (Affisco, 1994). Prensky (2001) later referred to youth as *digital natives*, fluent in the digital language of media, given their exposure to it from a young age. This presumed fluency may account for findings from recent national surveys attesting to the immersion of 8- to 18-year-olds in some form of media for, on average, 10 to 11 hours per day in 2010 (Rideout, Foehr, & Roberts, 2010) or more than half of their waking hours. In fact, this extensive use of media reflected an increase from rates reported among 8- to 18-year-olds in 2005 (Roberts, Foehr, & Rideout, 2005). Thus, this age group may be highly receptive to learning in the context of a serious game, particularly if based in current digital technology.

What Theoretical Perspectives Have Been Used to Frame Serious Games?

To date, three theoretical perspectives have been most frequently cited as providing a framework for serious game design: Social Cognitive Theory (Bandura, 1986), Self-Determination Theory (Deci & Ryan, 2000), and the Elaboration Likelihood Model (Petty & Cacioppo, 1986). Of the three, Social Cognitive Theory (SCT) has been most often referred to as a structure for game development and an account for behavioral change, primarily among serious games promoting health care knowledge (see Lieberman, 2001). This theory has a long-standing history in the study of media impact on behavior initiated with the famous "Bobo doll" study (Bandura, Ross, & Ross, 1961), which demonstrated the power of observational learning, or learning by watching others, on behavior change.

A construct that is based in SCT is self-efficacy, or one's perceptions of being able to accomplish a given task or enact a given behavior (see Bandura, 1989). This concept has figured prominently in the study of how serious games affect behavior (Klimmt & Hartmann, 2006). Self-efficacy is seen as enhanced through repeated game play and execution of behaviors needed to master a given game. The self-efficacy acquired in the game context is presumed to then transfer to real-life behaviors. A derivation of SCT is self-regulated learning theory, according to which individuals seek to manage their cognitions, behaviors, and learning in pursuit of a given goal (Zimmerman & Martinez-Pons, 1986; Zimmerman, 1990). Self-regulatory skills include goal setting, goal monitoring, and review of progress (Peng, 2008; Thompson et al., 2008), each of which has been seen as key to effective learning and behavior change in the context of serious games (Peng, 2008).

A second theory that has been linked to serious game development is Self-Determination Theory (SDT) as put forth by Deci and Ryan (2000). This theory provides a framework for the study of human motivation that defines the types and roles of intrinsic and extrinsic sources of motivation. According to SDT, individuals have innate tendencies toward psychological growth. Such tendencies can be facilitated or undermined by the social context via the satisfaction of three basic needs: competence, autonomy, and relatedness (Deci & Ryan, 2000). The need for competence refers to one's motivation to master the tasks and situations that are encountered and affect one's environment. The autonomy need refers to one's experience of volition or the desire to construe experience as one sees fit. The relatedness need pertains to the desire to be part of a group or culture; to feel wanted by others. Conditions that support the individuals' experience of autonomy, competence, and relatedness are argued to foster the most volition and qualitatively, the best levels of motivation and engagement for activities, including enhanced performance, persistence, and creativity. The degree to which any of these psychological needs is thwarted within a social context will result in a detrimental impact on wellness in that setting (Deci et al., 1994). Serious games using this theoretical perspective are structured to develop competence via task completion, provide choice to allow for player autonomy, and connect relevant goals to factors such as personal values that exist outside of the gaming environment (Ryan, Rigby, & Przybylski, 2006).

The Elaboration Likelihood Model (Petty & Cacioppo, 1986) also has been cited as a foundation for game development. According to this theory, there are two routes or ways through which attitudes are formed when encountering persuasive messages; the central and the peripheral processing routes. The central route to persuasion entails processing and analyzing of the argument posed by the message in a relatively deep fashion, such that the attitude change that occurs is stable and enduring. Factors that affect the likelihood that a message will be processed via the central route include the ability to critically evaluate the argument presented and the motivation to analyze this message. The peripheral route entails the processing of relatively superficial aspects of the message such as the attractiveness and credibility of the source of what may be seen as a less personally relevant message such that any induced attitude change is likely to be unstable and temporary (Petty & Cacioppo, 1986). Serious games developed along the guidelines of this theoretical approach use what has been referred to as *tailoring*, or the customizing of messages to the characteristics or culture of the player to increase the personal relevance and importance of a given game message, and then to enhance the likelihood that the message will be processed via the central processing route (Kroeze, Werkman, & Brug, 2006; Noar et al., 2007; Ritterfeld et al., 2009). Notably, the theories presented here have been used more often to inform game design than to account for behavioral change in the context of empirical studies.

What Are Elements That Comprise Serious Games?

Examination of the literature concerning serious game design and impact of game play on behavior and attitudes reveals a consistent emphasis on the interrelated elements of immersion, identity, interactivity, agency or control, challenge, narrative, and feedback (Hays, 2005; Thompson et al., 2008; Bryant & Fondren, 2009; Klimmt, 2009; Ritterfeld et al., 2009; Annetta, 2010; Charsky, 2010). This listing, rather than being definitive, is meant to reflect how serious game designers, and game designers in general, have structured game development (see Salen & Zimmerman, 2004), and how researchers have examined aspects of game play that contribute to engagement and learning (Lieberman, 2006; Annetta, 2010). The following surveys the research attesting to the efficacy of these features for attracting and maintaining players' interest in a game with the goal of fostering learning.

Immersion

The construct of immersion refers to players' sense of presence within the game. As with similar constructs, such as transportability (Green, Brock, & Kaufman, 2004; also see Chapter 24), one's perceived immersion within a game is linked to enjoyment of it (Wang, Shen, & Ritterfeld, 2009). According to Tamborini and Skalski (2006), presence can be characterized along three dimensions: spatial, social, and self. Spatial presence refers to players' sense of being physically embodied within the game environment. Social presence refers to the players' sense of interacting with virtual actors within the game, as if they were real. Self presence is related to the game element of identity and refers to the extent to which the persona or character that players adopt in a game is experienced as their actual self. Collectively, these dimensions provide a framework in which to examine how players become immersed in game play and their actions during the course of that play.

Other contributing factors to players' sense of presence are the differential perspectives they can assume during play (e.g., first person versus third person), the nature of the game as competitive or cooperative, the opportunity to co-play with others, and the sound effects and musical scores that accompany game play. Lim and Reeves (2010) recently examined the extent to which agency (e.g., choosing and creating one's avatar versus choosing a predesigned character or agent) and cooperative versus competitive play during a game influenced sense of presence among college students. Players using self-created avatars were more likely to report feeling "in," "present," and part of the game than those players using agents. Moreover, reported levels of presence were higher for those who played cooperatively as opposed to those who played competitively. This finding conforms to players' experience in other tasks that allow for cooperative play or co-creation of virtual worlds, as in *Second Life* (Kohler, Fueller, Stieger, & Matzler, 2010). Sound and music also have been linked to players' sense of immersion and enhanced learning. Richards et al. (2008) examined how music from within an immersive virtual world influenced college students' learning about the Macquarie Lighthouse. Students presented with music while learning remembered more facts than those students who received no music.

Although immersion is often seen as the hallmark of digital games, Kickmeier-Rust and Albert (2010) argue that this aspect is rarely captured in SEGs. These authors contend that immersion occurs when players experience a balance among the game challenges, their current ability to play the game, and their current knowledge about the game. These characteristics are also cited as aspects of the flow experience (see Sherry, 2004; Weber, Tamborini, Westcott-Baker, & Kantor, 2009), an experience induced by other elements we review. According to Kickmeier-Rust and Albert (2010), educational games that provide feedback about players' performance and tailor tasks or challenges to the player's current capabilities are most likely to facilitate immersion.

Identity

The identity element refers to the ability to enfranchise players into the game world environment. Researchers and game designers view this identification as desirable for its potential to engage players, thereby encouraging them to sustain game play. In the case of educational games, this identification is sought to promote attention to content to be learned (see Mayer & Johnson, 2010). One well-researched contributor to players' sense of linkage to the game is their ability to create an avatar (see Blascovich & Bailenson, 2011). Findings show that when players are able to create and personalize characters, they show greater arousal, as indicated by heart rate and skin conductance during game play (Lim & Reeves, 2010).

Often, avatar construction and identification are as central to the game as completing the goals or missions of the game. For example, Feldon and Kafai (2008) monitored student activity while playing *Whyville*, a science virtual world, over the course of 6 months. The authors found that students who played the game spent considerable time altering the appearance of their avatars. In fact, 33% of *Whyville* site hits were linked to virtual locations designated as places to buy and change avatar parts and accessories. Further, 54% of players reported using at least half of their *Whyville* salary to accessorize their avatars. Only 20% of the players perceived avatar appearance as peripheral to their game play.

In serious games used in educational settings, avatars may serve as a means to express aspects of the player (e.g., appearance, behavior) and as a means for learning. Falloon (2010) investigated the educational ramifications of using an avatar-based program, MARVIN, with a social studies and language theme among 11- to 13-year-old British students. According to student reports, the benefits of the program included the ability to create appropriate characters and settings for their class project, which they believed helped them better communicate their thoughts because their avatar presented the project. Moreover, students who were initially disengaged from classroom activities and projects reported greater engagement as a result of MARVIN implementation. Teachers also reported that using the avatar-based game as a part of their curriculum supported teamwork and collaboration, helped students create more cohesive class presentations, and improved their time management skills.

Interactivity

The interactivity element refers to the player's ability to initiate and receive feedback for actions during the game, whereby such actions influence the course of events that occur during the game (Renkl & Atkinson, 2007; Ritterfeld et al., 2009). The efficacy of this game feature for encouraging, sustaining, and managing game play has been well documented (see Grodal, 2000; Vorderer, 2000). In the context of serious games, the outcome of this communication between player and the game should foster players' learning (Moreno & Mayer, 2007). Players' ability to control and customize the pace, interface, level of challenge posed through the game, and receive immediate feedback (Prensky, 2001; DiPietro et al., 2007) serves to sustain their attention and engagement, and potentially enhance the likelihood that they will learn from it (Grodal, 2000; Sellers, 2006). In fact, according to Sherry (2004), the creation of this type of customized learning environment may lend itself to the player's attainment of flow or sense of pleasurable immersion with little conscious awareness of the apparent effort involved in playing.

The concept of multimodality is often confounded with that of interactivity (see Ritterfeld et al., 2009) and pertains to the presentation of game content knowledge through a combination of two or more sensory modalities. Ritterfeld et al. (2009) found support for multimodality as a vehicle for enhancing students' learning of science definitions in the context of a serious game independent of the impact of the game's interactivity.

Agency or Control

An element that is linked to that of interactivity is agency or control, which is facilitated in the current generation of digital games (see Spronck, Ponsen, Sprinkhuizen-Kuyper, & Postma, 2006; Wilson et al., 2006; Kickmeier-Rust & Albert, 2010) and has long been cited as a contributor to players' engagement in games (see Malone & Lepper, 1987). The ability to regulate aspects of game play, such as the use of the control mechanisms or changing the story line, is seen as a vital aspect of game play (Wood, Griffiths, Chappell, & Davies, 2004; Qin, Rau, & Salvendy, 2009) and has been found to contribute to player's enjoyment. For example, Zhu, Gedeon, and Taylor (2011) asked participants to play Foosball using both the joystick and camera control method (i.e., players' eye movement manipulated the Foosball players' movement). When using the camera, control method participants performed better (i.e., made more goals and kicks), suggesting that this technique required less cognitive resources than the manipulation of the joystick. Players also rated the use of the camera control method more positively, because of the greater perceived fluidity of play and control over game events. This finding did not conform to that of Klimmt, Hartmann, and Frey (2007). In their study, participants first played a standard version of a game. During a second session they either played the same version of the game, a version in which there was a delay in their actions being realized on screen (reflecting reduced interactivity), or a version in which the action in the game was far faster than in the standard version (reflecting reduced control). The authors found that players exposed to the standard game or the flawed control version did not report decreased enjoyment across the two game sessions. However, decreased enjoyment over play sessions was found for those players administered the flawed interactivity game version. The authors viewed this pattern as an indication that reduced control in a game may not necessarily decrease player enjoyment. One hypothesis they advanced is that the challenge posed by reduced control may create an enjoyable game experience for the player. This view finds support in that of Ang, Zaphiris, and Mahmood (2007), who contended that among expert players who are good at manipulating and adapting to obstacles in games, the loss of control may present a welcome challenge.

Challenge

The challenge element refers to the varying degrees of complexity that are possible within a game based on one's actions and are seen as contingent on the balance between the difficulty of the task and a player's ability or skill set (Salen & Zimmerman, 2004; Hsu, Wen, & Wu, 2007). According to Malone (1981), challenge is a major contributor to the intrinsic motivation inherent in digital games, and is seen as related to goals that players establish for their game play. The attainment of these goals, in turn, is linked to enhanced self-efficacy (see Malone & Lepper, 1987; Lieberman, 2006). That the challenge aspect of digital games is appealing also is found among diverse age groups. For example, in their focus group discussions among college students, Sherry et al. (2006) found that one of the major reasons the students played video games was for the opportunity to push or challenge themselves. Blumberg, Altschuler, and Almonte (2011) found comparable responses among their fourth to eighth grade focus group participants when asked what they liked about playing video games.

As with other game elements discussed in the preceding, the balance between the challenge posed by the game and the players' skills have ramifications for inducing flow (Sherry, 2004; Weber, Tamborini, Westcott-Baker, & Kantor, 2009). For example, Inal and Cagiltay (2007) found that challenge was crucial in inducing a flow state among 7- to 9-year-old children regardless of their game genre preference (e.g., action, adventure, puzzle). Nackle, Nackle, and Lindley (2009) found that young adults age 18 to 25 and late adults age 65 and older were more inclined to report feeling in flow when playing "Brain Training" games on Nintendo DS as opposed to on paper. Their reports of experiencing flow also were correlated with their sense of being challenged.

Narrative

The narrative is a compelling feature of diverse forms of entertainment media, including more antiquated forms such as radio and more current forms such as digital games, which is intended to foster a connection between the creator and the audience (Lee, Park, & Jin, 2006). Findings show that players of serious games see the narrative as a "hook" for game play. For example, Papastergiou (2009) found that adolescents' comments about improvements they would make to a serious computer science game they played in class pertained to embellishment of the plot.

The narrative aspect of a game facilitates co-constructed plans between player and the game and allows the player to experience diverse game threads rather than a single episodic sequence. As part of these threads, players can incorporate prior knowledge about the game environment and/or scenario with information provided within the game. Thus, the narrative may serve as a "sense making tool" that helps player attach personal relevance to the game story (Klimmt, 2009).

Narratives have been incorporated into SEGs that use story-based elements of game play (Mott et al., 2006; McNamara et al., 2009; Rowe et al., 2009) because they engage the player. Narratives have been used in well-regarded SEGs designed to promote science, such as *Quest Atlantis* (Barab et al., 2007) and *River City* (Ketelhut et al., 2007). At present, the body of research attesting to the durability of the learning acquired through games with compelling narratives on students' academic learning is limited.

Feedback

From a game design perspective, feedback helps to regulate the flow of game play (Salen & Zimmerman, 2004). From the player's vantage point, feedback provides information about the efficacy of game actions and helps to sustain interest in continuing game play (Liao, Chen, Cheng, Chen, & Chan, 2011). According to Kickmeier-Rust and Albert (2010), feedback is most effective, particularly in the context of educational games, when it is seamlessly integrated with game play and nondisruptive of that play. Lieberman (2006) views the feedback received within interactive games as helping to tailor the game experience to the player and as scaffolding the learning that occurs within it. Other researchers have likened feedback within interactive games to a pedagogical agent (see Gee, 2009; Gentile, 2011).

Players' reception to game feedback may depend on its packaging within the game environment, as evident in IBM's serious business game, *Innov8²*, which has incorporated real-time feedback game features (Sporer, 2010) that resemble social persuasion. *Innov8* is a simulation that involves investigating, discovering, and optimizing pain points in the business process (i.e., that point in time in which customers are eager to purchase a given product) in the business process of a simulated company. The game allows access to a business monitoring tool that leverages analysis technology to measure desired performance indicators, and a business modeling tool that enables simulating effects of key process

changes (e.g., hiring more employees) on process efficiency and efficacy within the game. Successful process improvement results in social feedback from other characters in the game that represent department managers typically present in real organizational settings. These features allow players to learn about their strengths and weaknesses, receive in-game performance evaluations, and test solutions and strategies during game play that are ultimately expected to enhance their business operations–specific self-efficacy and facilitate the transfer of game knowledge and skill to a real business setting (IBM, 2008; Conz, 2009).

In What Content Areas Are Serious Games Represented?

As noted, interest in serious game development has blossomed within the past decade and is represented across a diverse range of content areas. The following presents a sampling of areas in which serious games are used. Health care and education remain the areas in which serious games have increasingly featured and used (*Serious Games Initiative*, 2008). However, a broad trend of employing game mechanics to other "non-game environments" such as marketing, training, and social change also are evident. For example, Siemens' online video game *Plantville* simulates the experience of managing operations at a manufacturing facility (Bloomberg Businessweek, 2011). Such a trend is referred to as *gamification* in the business world, and business analysts at Burke (2011) suggest that by 2015 50% of companies that manage innovation and research will use gamification.

Advergames

A relatively new addition to the serious game taxonomy is the advergame. This form of advertising is characterized as free, branded entertainment featuring advertising messages, logos, and trade characters presented in an interactive game format designed to appeal to consumers of diverse ages (Mallinckrodt & Mizerski, 2007). In fact, advergames have been cited as a potent form of stealth advertising whereby the immersive aspect of the game may mask the persuasive intent of advertising messages (Montgomery & Chester, 2009; Gross, 2010). Using advergames to appeal and attract children and early adolescents has been seen as contentious given their oft cited inability to discern the persuasive goals of advertising messages (Gunter, Montgomery, 2001; Oates & Blades, 2005; Calvert, 2008). This issue was recently featured in on the front page of *The New York Times* (Richtel, 2011).

As with advertising in general, advergames are seen as serving several functions, including providing players with an enjoyable activity, promoting positive attitudes toward a given brand, allowing players to experiment and interact with the brand in the context of game play, and in some cases, educating players about the virtues of the product (Lee & Youn, 2008). The diversity of forms that advergames may take is evident in Lee and Youn's (2008) content analysis of the advergames that 100 leading US companies in 2004 had incorporated into their web sites. The authors found that 26 companies had used a total of 294 advergames. Among games in which both a brand name and a product were featured, more than half advertised food products. The games used most often reflected the game genres of arcade and puzzle games and often failed to focus prominently on the product as the centerpiece of the game (e.g., using a marble shooting game to advertise a cookie product). A relatively small percentage (16%) of the games sought to educate players about a given product's virtues or features; 59% offered players opportunities to "interact" with the brands.

Whether an advergame will impact players' recall of the product is affected by the extent to which the game is perceived as relevant to the brand or what Lee and Faber (2007) referred to as *game product congruity*. According to these authors, factors linked to congruity refer to the extent to which the product is perceived as the prominent feature of the game, as related to the theme of game, as appropriate for the goals of the game, and the extent to which the game advocates the lifestyle associated with the brand or product outside the game context. Surprisingly, Lee and Faber found that highly incongruent brands (e.g., pet food) placed within a race car game were better recalled than that of highly congruent brands (e.g., gasoline). Gross (2010) found that adult players preferred playing an incongruent advergame rather than a congruent game. However, those who played the highly congruent game showed greater recall of explicit information about the product name and the sponsoring company than those who played the less congruent game, as assessed via a recognition task. Similarly, those who played the highly congruent game showed greater implicit memory of brand attributes as assessed via a word fragment completion task.

A variant of an advergame, referred to as a *promogame*, was used by Burger King and featured the company's King mascot. Three promogames were built to be played on the Xbox platforms (see Kumar, 2008). Although these promogames were mostly

product incongruent, customers readily purchased the prerequisite Value Meal and spent an additional $3.99 for each game title, resulting in 3.2 million games sold, 40% increase in quarterly profit, and many millions of hours of brand exposure (Edery & Mollick, 2008).

Social Media and Marketing Games

Social media was originally built for use by Web-based and mobile technologies to turn communication into real-time interactive dialog. However, marketing professionals have realized its leveraging potential for helping companies achieve their business goals. Foursquare is a location-based social networking platform that allows users to alert their friends, in real-time, of their exact whereabouts using their mobile phone. The act of "checking in" to a specific location also results in incentives, which may vary from information about a demo or complimentary promotion at that location, user designation as Mayor of the location as the most frequent visitor, discount benefits as the Mayor, and badges that are earned from specific types of check-ins (Affect Strategies, 2010). In addition to displaying the user's number of mayorships and types of earned badges, a leader scoreboard can be viewed to compare performance against other friends and overall users, thereby creating a gaming experience that results in user engagement and business marketing and exposure.

Civic Engagement Games

Another area in which serious games are being targeted is that of civic engagement, which pertains to working individually or with others to promote acknowledgment of and action directed toward issues of public concern (Bers, 2010). Civic engagement, according to Bers (2010), can be further organized into four dimensions, each of which also can be seen as reflected in commercial titles such as *SimCity* and *World of Warcraft:* civic knowledge (content and processes warranted for informed citizenry); civic conversations (ability to engage in discourse with others about civic life from a moral vantage point); civic attitudes (ability to assume the perspectives of others and make informed decisions about civic issues); and civic behaviors (actions that further the social rights and well-being of others).

Interest in developing games to encourage this behavior has been attributed to findings demonstrating that among the adolescent demographic, instances of civic gaming experiences during commercial video game play (e.g., assisting others within a game, assuming responsibility for a game group or guild) are positively correlated with civic engagement behaviors offline such as donating to charity or staying abreast of political events, news, and controversies (Kahne, Middaugh, & Evans, 2008; Lenhart et al. 2008). Ferguson and Garza (2011) recently found evidence that adolescents who played more violent action games and had parents who were involved in their game play showed higher scores on a scale assessing civic attitudes and behaviors than peers who player fewer violent action games and experienced less parental involvement in that play. This finding provides an alternative perspective to the long-standing view that the playing of video games, particularly violent ones, is associated with aggressive affect and behavior (see Gentile et al., 2004; Bushman & Anderson, 2009).

Organizations such as Games for Change (G4C), founded in 2004, have played a key role in promoting interest in developing games that inspire social awareness and action among its players. Exemplars of the serious social change game oeuvre include *Peacemaker*[3] in which players are challenged to resolve the Middle East crisis by acting as the Prime Minister of Israel, the President of the Palestinian Authority, or the leader of another country. As part of the challenge, players must address concerns raised by all constituents in the conflict. Another high profile serious social game designed to be accessible to a preadolescent audience is *Ayiti: The cost of life*.[4] This game challenges its players to maintain the health, education, and survival of a small family living in rural Haiti. A more recent suite of serious games was launched in 2007 and introduced the iCivics project[5] as conceived by Justice Sandra Day O'Connor. These games were designed to provide elementary school-age players with exposure to the roles and responsibilities of different branches of government and potent political issues such as immigration.

Definitive statements attesting to the efficacy of serious game play for civic engagement real-world behavior remain elusive given the limited research available (Bers, 2010). In one of the few studies to examine the impact of playing one of four serious games with political content (*Airport Security*, *Darfur Is Dying*, *McDonald's Game*, or *September 12th*), Ney and Jansz (2010) found that players showed increased interest in learning about the content featured in the game and in sharing the content gained with others. Whether these self-reported interests on an online survey could eventuate in actual behavior is the critical issue for future investigations that should increase as the number of titles dedicated to civic engagement grows.

Industrial/Organizational

Game-based education and training for adult learners has a strong history in business and management science (Pasin & Giroux, 2011). In 2004, a survey of business school professors in North America found that more than 30% of 1,085 respondents had used business simulations (Faria & Wellington, 2004). In the last 10 years alone, new simulation games have been developed to teach marketing (Shapiro, 2003), financial management (Uhles, Weimer-Elder, & Lee, 2008), project management (Vanhoucke, Vereecke, & Gemmel, 2005), knowledge management (Leemkuil, de Jong, de Hoog, & Christoph, 2003; Chua, 2005), risk management (Barrese, Scordis, & Schelhorn, 2003), and microeconomics (Gold & Gold, 2010). Simulation games have been mostly characterized as a form of experiential learning because the process of knowledge creation relies on the transformation of self-experience (Haapasalo & Hyvonen, 2001; Battini et al., 2009).

According to Wolfe (1993) and Faria, Hutchinson, Wellington, and Gold (2009), management simulation games belong to one of three types: top management games (i.e., games including all aspects of an organization that typically involves strategic decisions), functional games (i.e., simulation games focusing on a specific area of business), and concept simulations (i.e., simulation games concentrating on a specific type of decision). For example, one well-known operations management game is the *Beer Game*, developed at the Sloan School of Management at the Massachusetts Institute of Technology (Goodwin & Franklin, 1994). This concept game helps learners experience and understand the bullwhip effect (Lee, Padmanabhan, & Whang, 1997), a particular situation that is created when several participants in the same supply chain attempt to anticipate the future demand of their immediate client. A more recent example is Siemens' online video game *Plantville*, which simulates the experience of managing operations at a manufacturing facility (*Bloomberg Businessweek*, 2011). In this game, the aim is to take three dilapidated factories and increase operational efficiency to meet customer orders. This situation requires hiring employees, redesigning layout, and buying and installing new Siemens equipment. The ultimate goal is to fuel equipment sales and help the Siemens employees learn more about the company's products.

Whether engaging in the simulation alone results in knowledge and skill transfer is questionable and is subject to efficacy evaluation. However, findings indicate that simulation games help students develop decision-making abilities for managing complex and dynamic situations (Machuca, 2000; Zantow et al., 2005; Pasin & Giroux, 2011).

Sustainability

Nissan Motor has very recently incorporated gamification within its new electric vehicle, the Nissan Leaf. When the car is driven in an ecologically efficient mode, messages on the dashboard alert the driver. An online portal connected to the car's dashboard also informs drivers know how well they are conserving energy, compared with other drivers in the region. The most efficient drivers are given virtual bronze, silver, gold, and platinum medals (*Bloomberg BusinessWeek*, 2011).

Education

Serious educational games represent a large share of serious game development. The design of these games has been approached from three different vantage points: (1) edutainment or games that tightly correspond to educational content; (2) preexisting commercial games that have been repurposed for education; and (3) games falling between the first two categories, with the goal of balancing fun and educational content (Moreno-Ger, Burgos, Martinez-Ortiz, Sierra, & Fernandez-Manjon, 2008).

Game titles under the edutainment category are primarily designed around educational content, with the inclusion of game-based features such as competition and fantasy. However, the design of games to specifically focus on educational content may detract from the entertainment value of the game (Kirriemuir & MacFarlane, 2004; Sims & MacFarlane, 2006; as cited in Moreno-Ger et al., 2008). Comparatively, preexisting commercial games designed for entertainment purposes and then repurposed for education (e.g., games in the *Civilization* series) (Squire & Barab, 2004) may fail to highlight the educational content and skills to be acquired. As noted informally and informally by many scholars (see Gee, 2003), the challenge is to balance the entertainment and educational aspects of games to create what Prensky (2001) referred to as "digital game-based learning."

Study findings on SEG efficacy have found evidence for increased students' engagement when working with content present via an educational game, as opposed to presentation via traditional teaching materials (Annetta, Minogue, Holmes, & Cheng, 2009; Papastergiou, 2009). However, compelling demonstrations of the success of SEGs are sparse. For example, Annetta et al. (2009) found that students who played an educational game did not demonstrate a greater understanding of genetics concepts presented in the game, despite being more engaged in the instruction. The authors noted a much-echoed need for further research to isolate and document the cognitive impact of game-based learning technology.

Health

As in the case of education, many serious games have been used to promote health improvement among patients and surgical training for health care professionals. For example, many games have been designed to increase patient treatment adherence and improve doctors' clinical skills. In fact, serious games have a relatively long-standing tradition in the health field, dating back to the 1980s, when commercial video games were used for therapeutic purposes, to later development of more customized games for health care intervention and improvement (Kato, 2010).

Serious games also have been developed for other treatment directives, such as delivering health-related information (e.g., *Bronkie the Bronchiasaurus*, Lieberman, 2001), modeling positive behaviors (e.g., *Re-Mission*, Kato et al., 2008), providing opportunities for players to vicariously practice positive health behaviors (e.g., *SpiroGame*, Vilozni, Barker, Jellouschek, Heimann, & Blau, 2001; *SnowWorld*, Hoffman et al., 2008), and physical therapy and rehabilitation following traumatic brain injury (e.g., Jannik, van der Wilden, Navis, Visser, Gussinklo, & Ijzerman, 2008). Serious games also have been shown to be effective replacements for costly forms of health care technology. For example, biofeedback is an intervention in which individuals learn how to change physiological activity for the purposes of improving health (Durand & Barlow, 2009). Expensive medical tools such as electroencephalographs and electrodermographs are typically used to measure physiological activity and provide feedback to the user to allow for change in cognition, emotions, and behavior, and to support desired physiological changes. Herndon, Decambre, and McKenna (2001) reported findings indicating how the playing of serious games could circumvent the need for this technology in the context of biofeedback training. One game was designed to train pelvic floor muscle groups involved in urinary continence among patients with pediatric voiding dysfunction (Herndon, Decambre, & McKenna, 2001). Specifically, accuracy of shooting a basketball through a hoop was related to the patient's ability to relax the pelvic floor muscles, whereby the shooting success rate communicated feedback to the patient about their abilities for pelvic floor muscle relaxation. Self-report and objective measures indicated significant improvements in symptoms and treatment compliance, and demonstrated significant outcomes among patients as young as 4 years old, a group previously assumed to be too young for biofeedback muscle training because of limited motivation and ability to cooperate (De Paepe et al., 2000).

Serious games also have been used to support mental health care treatment and have been linked to improved patient cooperation in the therapy process (Resnick, 1986), increased rapport between therapist and patients (Clarke & Schoech, 1994), and engagement among treatment-resistant children with conduct disorder who already had dropped out of therapy several times (Kokish, 1994). The first serious game supporting cognitive-behavioral therapy (*Treasure Hunt*, Brezinka, 2007) yielded positive therapist reports in the context of pilot studies, whereby child patients responded positively to the treatment, resulting in behaviors such as engaging in the game tasks independently. However, conclusions about the game's efficacy for treatment were limited.

A relatively new serious game genre is that of *exergames*, in which exercise and physical activity are requisite for game play. These games (e.g., *Dance Dance Revolution*, *Wii Fit*, *Dance Central*) have been linked to positive benefits with regard to caloric intake and energy expenditure (see Kato, 2010; Staiano & Calvert, 2011). For example, Graf et al. (2009) found that energy expenditure among preadolescents and adolescents during *Dance Dance Revolution* and *Wii Sport* game play was comparable to moderate-intensity walking. Exner et al. (2009) found weight loss among low-income black youth as a result of *Wii Sport* tennis play, particularly after play against peers as opposed to virtual characters. Staiano et al. (2011) also recently reported that cooperative play of *Wii Active* over an extended period of time yielded weight loss among overweight and obese youth relative to a control group.

Ultimately, relatively little empirical evidence has yet to appear in the scientific literature to support the efficacy of serious games for health on positive health outcomes (Kato, 2010). Accordingly, efforts have been made to address this gap. For example,

the *Games for Health project* lists more than 100 games, of which many require empirical efficacy studies across specific disease populations.

Medical Education

Correlational studies have established the relationship between commercial video game experience or skill and surgical skills (e.g., Grantcharov, Bardram, Funch-Jensen, & Rosenberg, 2003; Enochsson Isaksson, Tour, Kjellin, Hedman, et al., 2004; Shane, Pettitt, Morgenthal, & Smith, 2008). No findings demonstrating the causal relationship between playing of these games and surgical skill development, however, have been found (Kato, 2010). Further, development and evaluation of serious games for medical education are limited. An example of a serious game for medical education is the *Oncology* game (Fukuchi, Offutt, Sacks, & Mann, 2000), which was designed to help medical students gain knowledge of general principles in cancer care and teamwork skills. The goal of the game is to advance patients through surgery and radiation clinics to obtain the best treatment. Tasks within the game involve responding to general oncology questions to proceed through the game. Findings have shown significant knowledge gains about cancer care as a result of game play (Fukuchi et al., 2000).

Future Directions

Clearly, the reach of serious games continues to grow. However, questions remain about their efficacy as a vehicle for durable learning and how best to study that efficacy. One of the most consistent and pressing questions raised concerns whether serious game play promotes transfer of learning from the game to real-world settings. This question looms large in our review of the contexts and disciplines in which serious games have been designed to persuade (advergaming), train (medical education), and more generally disseminate content. A related question concerns how best to develop a research program to systematically examine transfer across game and more traditional learning contexts, particularly among learners at the elementary and secondary level, for which many serious games are being targeted. In fact, the need for this research agenda formed the basis for a National Science Foundation sponsored invitational conference, *Academic Lessons from Video Game Learning: Screen-to-Screen*, held October, 2010 at Fordham University and organized by the first author. Attendees representing a diverse range of expertise in media research and practice, cognitive and computer science, developmental psychology, educational technology and policy, and digital game and toy design largely agreed on the challenges involved in developing games to facilitate transfer of content and skills from the game to more traditional learning contexts. This challenge is fueled by the paucity of empirical research attesting to the educational efficacy of serious games in general, and with child and adolescent samples in particular. The group concurred that any research program developed to address this gap would require innovative techniques such as assessments embedded within the game, and more systematic consideration of those variables that might affect learning among players of different ages.

As part of the research that might emerge to study transfer of learning from the serious game to the real world, we see examination of debriefing as meriting greater consideration. This activity already has been linked to transfer of learning in the gaming and educational technology literature (de Freitas, 2006; Crookall, 2010). In his oft-cited report prepared for the Navy examining the efficacy of instructional games, Hays (2005) claimed that the educational value of games was questionable without deliberate efforts to scaffold learning outside the game environment: "Instructional games should be embedded in instructional programs that include debriefing and feedback so the learners understand what happened in the game and how these events support the instructional objectives" (p. 6).

Debriefing entails having players reflect on their game play experiences and the application of those experiences to real life. Doing so is seen as encouraging players to focus on what they have learned during the game and how that learning reflects the curriculum of the game. This function of debriefing may be likened to Moreno and Mayer's (2007) multimedia learning design principle of "reflection," whereby learners' reconsideration of correct responses during a learning event are seen as helping to promote deeper learning or effective integration and processing of the content to which they have been exposed.

Debriefing has been used effectively in serious games for business, often as postgame feedback provided by a supervisor. Researchers contend that after action review or the use of debriefing as an adjunct for serious business games allows instructors and students to critically evaluate their game play decisions and actions (Knerr et al., 2002; Raybourn, 2007). For example, playback of recorded game play or review of frequency statistics on actions taken performs important cognitive and metacognitive functions

that are imperative to solidifying the learning experience, incorporating feedback, and updating understanding that can be demonstrated in subsequent game play. We see examination of debriefing across a greater range of serious games and among a greater age range of players as a fruitful avenue for future study.

Another issue that warrants greater attention concerns the explication of what players do when playing games. At present, we know very little about what cognitive skills players use during game play, what types of behaviors that players enact during game play, and how they coordinate their behaviors and cognitions about game events. In fact, we know the least about these behaviors and skills as shown by child and adolescent players, for whom many serious games for education, health, and social change continue to be developed. Elucidating developmental differences in children's and adolescents' patterns of skill use during game play could ultimately inform effective educational game development (see Mayer & Johnson, 2010) that might be appreciated by its intended audience.

We have addressed this issue in our research program among children, adolescents, and adults (see Blumberg, Rosenthal, & Randall, 2008; Blumberg & Ismailer, 2009) by having our participants think aloud as they play an unfamiliar, commercial video game. The gathering of verbal protocols (see Chapter 8 for information about qualitative methodology in general) to illustrate individuals' problem-solving has a long-standing tradition in the study of expert versus novice differences in various domains (Ericsson & Simon, 1980). In our work, this research tactic has yielded a rich corpus of information about players' attention to game content, and their identification and selection of game strategies and goals in situ. Very briefly, among our adult participants we have found greater concern with the flow of game events while playing and greater consideration of insight and game strategies among those who play three or more times a week as opposed to those who play less. Among all participants, the proportion of comments referring to insight, strategies to master the game, and acknowledgment of impasses encountered significantly increased over the 20-minute play session. We saw this pattern of behavior as indicative of increasing engagement in the game, independent of players' liking of the game (which, on average, they did not). With our child and adolescent participants, we also found that predominant concerns pertained to the flow of game events. However, greater attention to insight and proximal goals while playing was demonstrated more among our late elementary school-age students than our early middle school-age students. Unlike our adult participants, comments reflective of insight gained while playing decreased over the course of game play. Collectively, these findings are among the first to provide an initial impression of how players of different ages negotiate their game play over the course of a play session. We see this information as contributing to informed decisions about how best to structure serious games to take advantage of different aged players' problem-solving approaches while playing.

As a final comment, we see the need for future serious game develop to be more enfranchising of expertise represented across a broad range of disciplines and practices and to be informed by research within and across these disciplines. A very prominent example of the virtues of a multidisciplinary approach to educational media development can be found in *Sesame Street*, arguably the most successful educational television program of all time. The success of this program continues to be based in a multidisciplinary design team, and an educational curriculum and delivery of that curriculum that is informed by empirical research (see Fisch & Bernstein, 2001). We see future serious game development also as benefiting from the inclusion of expertise represented by a diverse range of researchers and practitioners.

Clearly, serious games hold much promise for their ability to educate, train, and affect attitude change. Individuals of all ages embrace the playing of games and will undoubtedly continue to enjoy playing them. The challenge for the serious game field is to make compelling strides toward demonstrating that the playing of these games leaves durable memories in the minds of its players in addition to serving as a pleasurable way to pass time.

Acknowledgments

The authors wish to acknowledge the helpful comments and insight provided by the editor and John Randall in the preparation of this chapter.

Notes

1. Information about each of the games noted can be accessed as follows: *River City*—http://muve.gse.harvard.edu/rivercityproject; *QuestAtlantis*—http://atlantis.crlt.indiana.edu; *WolfQuest*—http://www.wolfquest.org, and *Whyville*—http://www.whyville.org.

2. Accessible via http://peacemakergame.com.

3. Accessible via http://ayiti.globalkids.org/game.

4. Accessible via http://www.icivics.org.

5. Accessible via http://www.ibm.com

References

Affect Strategies (2010). Five ways businesses can leverage Foursquare in marketing efforts, from Affect Strategies. Retrieved April 25, 2011 from http://www.affectstrategies.com/news/press-releases/five-ways-businesses-can-leverage-foursquare-marketing-efforts-affect-strategies.

Affisco, J. F. (1994) My experiences with simulation/gaming. *Simulation and Gaming*, 25,166–171.

Ang, C. S., Zaphiris, P., & Mahmood, S. (2007). A model of cognitive loads in massively multiplayer online role playing games. *Interacting with Computers*, 19, 167–179.

Annetta, L. A. (2010). The "I's" have it: A framework for serious educational game design. *Review of General Psychology*, 14, 105–112.

Annetta, L. A., Minogue, J., Holmes, S. Y., & Cheng, M. (2009). Investigating the impact of video games on high school students' engagement and learning about genetics. *Computers & Education*, 53, 74–85.

Bandura, A. (1989). Regulation of cognitive processes through perceived self-efficacy. *Developmental Psychology*, 25, 725–739

Bandura, A. (2001). Social cognitive theory: An agentic perspective. *Annual Review of Psychology*, 52, 1–26.

Bandura, A., Ross, D. & Ross, S. A. (1961).Transmission of aggression through imitation of aggressive models. *Journal of Abnormal and Social Psychology*, 63, 575–582.

Barab, S., Dodge, T., Tuzun, H., Job-Sluder, K., Jackson, C., Arici, A et al. (2007) The Quest Atlantis project: A socially-responsive play space for learning. In Shelton, B. E., & Wiley, D. (Eds.), *The Educational Design and Use of Simulation Computer Games*. Rotterdam: Sense Publishers, pp. 159–186.

Barnett, S. M., & Ceci, S. J. (2002). When and where do we apply what we learn? A taxonomy for far transfer. *Psychological Bulletin*, 128, 612–637.

Barrese, J., Scordis, N., & Schelhorn, C. (2003). Teaching introductory concepts of insurance company management: A simulation game. *Review of Business*, 24, 43–39.

Battini, B., Faccio, M., Persona, A., & Sgarbossa, F. (2009). Logistic Game: Learning by doing and knowledge-sharing. *Production Planning & Control*, 20(8), 724–736.

Bers, M. U. (2010). Let the games begin: Civic playing on high-tech consoles. *Review of General Psychology*, 14, 147–153.

Blascovich, J., & Bailenson, J. (2011). *Infinite Reality: Avatars, Eternal Life, New Worlds, and the Dawn of the Virtual Revolution*. New York: HarperCollins.

Bloomberg Businessweek (2011). The CEO guide to business gamification. Retrieved April 25, 2011 from http://www.businessweek.com/technology/special_reports/20110404ceo_guide_gamification.htm.

Blumberg, F. C., Altschuler, E. A., & Almonte, D. E. (March, 2011). Children's perceptions of learning in videogames and school. In Blumberg, F. C., & Fisch, S. M. (Co-chairs), *Children's Learning in Videogame and Academic Settings*. Symposium paper presented at Society for Research in Child Development Meeting, Montreal, CA.

Blumberg, F. C., & Ismailer, S. S. (2009). What do children learn from playing video games? In Ritterfeld, U., Cody, M., & Vorderer, P. (Eds.), *Serious Games: Mechanisms and Effects*. New York: Routledge Taylor & Francis, pp. 131–142.

Blumberg, F. C., Rosenthal, S. F., & Randall, J. D. (2008). Impasse-driven learning in the context of video games. *Computers in Human Behavior*, 24, 1530–1541.

Bogost, I. (2007). *Persuasive Games: The Expressive Power of Video Games*. Cambridge, MA: MIT Press.

Boot, W. R., Kramer, A. F., Simons, D. J., Fabiani, M., & Gratton, G. (2008). The effects of video game playing on attention, memory, and executive control. *Acta Psychologica*, *129*, 387–398.

Brezinka, V. (2007). Treasure Hunt—A psychotherapeutic game to support cognitive-behavioural treatment of children. *Verhaultenstherapie*, *17*, 191–194.

Bryant, J., & Fondren, W. (2009). Psychological and communicological theories of learning and emotion underlying serious games. In Ritterfeld, U., Cody, M., & Vorderer, P. (Eds.), *Serious Games: Mechanisms and Effects*. New York: Routledge Taylor & Francis, pp. 103–116.

Bushman, B. J., & Anderson, C. A. (2009). Comfortably numb: Desensitizing effects of violent media on helping others. *Psychological Science*, *20*, 273–277.

Burke, B. (2011). What's next: The gamification of everything. Retrieved April 25, 2011 from http://blogs.gartner.com/brian_burke/2011/01/27/whats-next-the-gamification-of-everything/.

Calvert, S. (2008). Children as consumers: Advertising and marketing. *The Future of Children*, *18*, 205–234.

Charsky, D. (2010). From edutainment to serious games: A change in the use of game characteristics. *Games and Culture*, *5*, 177–198.

Chua, A. Y. K. (2005). The design and implementation of a simulation game for teaching knowledge management. *Journal of the American Society for Information Science and Technology*, *56*, 1207–1216.

Clarke, B., & Schoech, D. (1994). A computer-assisted game for adolescents: Initial development and comments. *Computers in Human Services*, *11*, 121–140.

Conz, N. (2009). Farmers pilots use of IBM simulation game in call center training. Retrieved April 25, 2011 from http://www.insurancetech.com/management-strategies/showArticle.jhtml?articleID=217600673.

Crookall, D. (2010). Serious games, debriefing, and simulation/gaming as a discipline. *Simulation & Gaming*, *41*, 898–920.

Curry, K. (2010). Warcraft and civic education: MMORPGs as participatory cultures and how teachers can use them to improve civic education. *Social Studies*, *101*, 250–253.

de Freitas, S. (2006). Using games and simulations for supporting learning. *Learning, Media and Technology*, *31*, 343–358.

De Paepe, H., Renson, C., Van Laecke, E., Raes, A., van de Walle, J., & Hoebeke, P. (2000). Pelvic-floor therapy and toilet training in young children with dysfunctional voiding and obstipation. *British Journal of Urology International*, *85*, 889–893.

Deci, E. L., Eghrari, H., Patrick, B. C., & Leone, D. R. (1994). Facilitating internalization: The self-determination theory perspective. *Journal of Personality*, *62*, 119–142.

Deci, E. L., & Ryan, R. M. (2000). The "what" and "why" of goal pursuits: Human needs and the self-determination of behavior. *Psychological Inquiry*, *11*, 227–268.

Dickey, M. D. (2011). World of Warcraft and the impact of game culture and play in an undergraduate game design course. *Computers & Education*, *56*, 200–209.

DiPietro, M., Ferdig, R. E., Boyer, J., & Black, E. W. (2007). Towards a framework for understanding educational gaming. *Journal of Educational Multimedia and Hypermedia*, *16*, 225–248.

Duran, V. M., & Barlow, D. (2009). *Abornal psychology: An integrative approach*. Belmont, CA: Wadsworth Cengage Learning, p. 331.

Edery, D., & Mollick, E. (2008). *Changing the Game: How Video Games Are Transforming the Future of Business*. Upper Saddle River, NJ: FT Press.

Enochsson, L., Isaksson, B., Tour, R., Kjellin, A., Hedman, L., Wredmark, T., et al. (2004). Visuospatial skills and computer game experience influence the performance of virtual endoscopy. *Journal of Gastrointestinal Surgery*, *8*, 874–880.

Entertainment Software Association (2010). 2010 Essential Facts about the Computer and Video Game Industry. Retrieved July 17, 2010 from http://www.theesa.com/facts/pdfs/ESA_Essential_Facts_2010.pdf.

Ericsson, K. A., & Simon, H. A. (1980). Verbal reports as data. *Psychological Review*, *87*, 215–251.

Exner, A., Papatheodorou, G., Baker, C. M., Verdaguer, A., Hluchan, C. M., & Calvert, S. L. (April, 2009). *Solitary Versus Social Gross Motor Videogame Play: Energy Expenditure Among Low-Income African American Adolescents*. Poster presented at the biennial meeting of the Society for Research in Child Development, Denver, CO.

Falloon, G. (2010). Using avatars and virtual environments in learning: What do they have to offer? *British Journal of Educational Technology*, *41*, 108–122.

Faria, A. J., Hutchinson, D., Wellington, W. J., & Gold, S. (2009). Developments in business gaming: A review of the past 40 years. *Simulation & Gaming*, *40*, 464–487.

Faria, A. J., & Wellington, W. J. (2004). A survey of simulation game users, former-users, and never-users. *Simulation & Gaming*, *35*, 178–207.

Feldon, D. F., & Kafai, Y. B. (2008). Mixed methods for mixed reality: Understanding users' avatar activities in virtual worlds. *Educational Technology Research and Development*, *56*(5–6), 575–593.

Ferguson, C., & Garza, A. (2011). Call of (civic) duty: Action games and civic behavior in a large sample of youth. *Computers in Human Behavior*, *27*, 770–775.

Fisch, S. M., & Bernstein, L. (2001). Formative research revealed: Methodological and process issues in formative research. In Fisch, S. M., & Truglio, R. T. (Eds.) *"G" is for Growing: Thirty years of Research on Children and Sesame Street*. Hillsdale, NJ: Lawrence Erlbaum Associates, pp. 39–60.

Fukuchi, S., Offutt, L., Sacks, J., & Mann, B. (2000). Teaching a multidisciplinary approach to cancer treatment during surgical clerkship via an interactive board game. *The American Journal of Surgery*, *179*, 337–340.

Gee, J. P. (2003). *What Video Games Have to Teach Us About Learning and Literacy*. New York: Palgrave Macmillan.

Gee, J. P. (2009). Deep learning properties of good digital games. How far can they go? In Ritterfeld, U., Cody, M., & Vorderer, P. (Eds.), *Serious Games: Mechanisms and Effects*. New York: Routledge Taylor & Francis, pp. 67–82.

Gentile, D. A. (2011). The multiple dimensions of video game effects. *Child Development Perspectives*, *5*, 75–81.

Gentile, D. A., Lynch, P. J., Linder, J. R., & Walsh D. A. (2004). The effects of violent video game habits on adolescent hostility, aggressive behaviors, and school performance. *Journal of Adolescence*, *27*, 5–22.

Gold, H., & Gold, S. (2010). Beat the market: An interactive microeconomics simulation. *The Journal of Economic Education*, *41*, 216.

Goodwin, J. S., & Franklin, S. G. (1994). The beer distribution game: Using simulation to teach system. *The Journal of Management Development, 13*, 7–15.

Graf, D. L., Pratt, L. V., Hester, C. N., & Short, K. R. (2009). Playing active video games increases energy expenditure in children. *Pediatrics, 124*, 534–540.

Grantcharov, T., Bardram, L., Funch- Jensen, P., & Rosenberg, J. (2003). Impact of hand dominance, gender, and experience with computer games on performance in virtual reality laparoscopy. *Surgical Endoscopy, 17*, 1082–1085.

Green, C. S., & Bavelier, D. (2003). Action video game modifies visual selective attention. *Nature, 423*(6939), 534–538.

Green, C. S., & Bavelier, D. (2006). Effect of action video games on spatial distribution of visuospatial attention. *Journal of Experimental Psychology: Human Perception and Performance, 32*, 1465–1478.

Green, C. S., & Bavelier, D. (2007). Action video game experience alters the spatial resolution of attention. *Psychological Science, 18*, 88–94.

Green, M. C., Brock, T. C., & Kaufman, G. F. (2004). Understanding media enjoyment: The role of transportation into narrative worlds. *Communication Theory, 14*, 311–327.

Greenfield, P. M., Camaioni, L., Ercolani, P., Weiss, L., et al. (1994). Cognitive socialization by computer games in two cultures: Inductive discovery or mastery of an iconic code? *Journal of Applied Developmental Psychology, 15*, 59–85.

Grodal, T. (2000). Video games and the pleasures of control. In Zillman, D., & Vorderer, P. (Eds.), *Media Entertainment: The Psychology of Its Appeal*. Hillsdale, NJ: Lawrence Erlbaum Associates, pp. 197–214.

Gross, M. L. (2010). Advergames and the effects if game-product congruity. *Computers in Human Behavior, 26*, 1259–1265.

Gunter, B., Oates, C., & Blades, M. (2005). *Advertising to Children on TV. Content, Impact, and Regulation*. Hillsdale, NJ: Lawrence Erlbaum Associates.

Haapasalo, H., & Hyvonen, J. (2001). Simulating business and operations management—A learning environment for the electronics industry. *International Journal of Production Economics, 73*, 261–272.

Haring, P., Chakinska, D., & Ritterfeld, U. (2011). Understanding serious gaming. A psychological perspective. In Felicia, P. (Ed.), *Handbook of Research on Improving Learning and Motivation through Educational Games: Multidisciplinary Approaches*. Hershey, PA: IGI Global, pp. 29–50.

Hays, R. T. (2005). The effectiveness of instructional games: A literature review and discussion. Hays Technical Report 2005–2004 for the Naval Air Center Training Systems Division, Orlando, FL.

Herndon, C., Decambre, M., & McKenna, P. (2001). Interactive computer games for treatment of pelvic floor dysfunction. *The Journal of Urology, 166*, 1893–1898.

Hoffman, H. G., Patterson, D. R., Seibel, E., Soltani, M., Jewett-Leahy, L., & Sharar, S. R. (2008). Virtual reality pain control during burn wound debridement in the hydrotank. *Clinical Journal of Pain, 24*, 299–304.

Hsu, S. H., Wen, M. H., & Wu, M. C. (2007). Exploring design features for enhancing players' challenge in strategy games. *CyberPsychology & Behavior, 10*, 393–397.

Inal, Y., & Cagiltay, K. (2007). Flow experiences of children in an interactive social game environment. *British Journal of Educational Technology, 38*, 455–464.

Jannik, M. J., van der Wilden, G. J., Navis, D. W., Visser, G., Gussinklo, J., & Ijzerman, M. (2008). A low-cost video game applied for training of upper extremity function in children with cerebral palsy: A pilot study. *CyberPsychology & Behavior, 11*, 27–32.

Jean, G. (2006). *Game Branches Out Into Real Combat Training*. National Defense, February. Retrieved April 30, 2011 from http://www.nationaldefensemagazine.org/archive/2006/February/Pages/games_brance3042.aspx.

Kahne, J., Middaugh, E., & Evans, C. (2008). *The Civic Potential of Video Games*. Chicago: The John D. and Catherine T. MacArthur Foundation.

Kato, P. M. (2010). Video games in health care: Closing the gap. *Review of General Psychology, 14*, 113–121.

Kato, P. M., Cole, S. W., Bradlyn, A. S., & Pollock, B. (2008). A video game improves behavioral outcomes in adolescents and young adults with cancer: A randomized trial. *Pediatrics, 122*, e305–e317.

Ketelhut, D. J., Dede, C., Clarke, J., Nelson, B., &. Bowman, C. (2007). Studying situated learning in a multi-user virtual environment. In Baker, E., Dickieson, J., Wulfeck, W., & O'Neil, H. (Eds.), *Assessment of Problem Solving Using Simulations*. Hillsdale, NJ: Lawrence Erlbaum Associates, pp. 37–58.

Kickmeier-Rust, M. D., & Albert, D. (2010). Micro-adaptivity: Protecting immersion in didactically adaptive digital educational games. *Journal of Computer Assisted Learning, 26*, 95–105.

Kirriemuir, J., & McFarlane, A. (2004). Report 8: Literature review in games and learning. *Futurelab Series*. Retrieved July 22, 2011 from http://www.futurelab.org.uk/resources/documents/lit_reviews/Games_Review.pdf

Klimmt, C. (2009). Serious games and social change. Why they (should) work. In Ritterfeld, U., Cody, M., & Vorderer, P. (Eds.), *Serious Games: Mechanisms and Effects*. New York: Routledge Taylor & Francis, pp. 248–270.

Klimmt, C., & Hartmann, T. (2006). Effectance, self-efficacy, and the motivation to play video games. In Vorderer, P., & Bryant, J. (Eds.), *Playing Video Games: Motives, Responses, and Consequences*. Hillsdale, NJ: Lawrence Erlbaum Associates, pp. 143–177.

Klimmt, C., Hartmann, T., & Frey, A. (2007). Effectance and control as determinants of video game enjoyment. *CyberPsychology & Behavior, 10*, 845–847.

Kohler, T., Fueller, J., Stieger, D., & Matzler, K. (2010). Avatar-based innovation: Consequences of the virtual co-creation experience. *Computers in Human Behavior, 27*, 160–168.

Kokish, R. (1994). Experiences using a PC in play therapy with children. *Computers in Human Behavior, 11*, 141–150.

Knerr, B. W., Lampton, D. R., Martin, G. A., Washburn, D. A., & Cope, D. (2002). *Developing an After Action Review System for Virtual Dismounted Infantry Simulations*. I/ITSEC Conference, Orlando, FL.

Kroeze, W., Werkman, A., & Brug, J. (2006). A systematic review of randomized trials on the effectiveness of computer-tailored education on physical activity and dietary behaviors. *Annals of Behavioral Medicine, 31*, 205–223.

Kumar, M. (2008). ICE 08: Can Advergaming Spur Creativity? Gamasutra News, April 1, 2008. Retrieved July 20, 2012 from http://www.gamasutra.com/view/news/109019/ICE_08_Can_Advergaming_Spur_Creativity.php

Lee, M. & Faber, R. J. (2007). Effects of product placement in on-line games on brand memory. A perspective of the limited-capacity model of attention. *Journal of Advertising, 36*, 75–90.

Lee, K. M., Park, N., & Jin, S. (2006). Narrative and interactivity in computer games. In P. Vorderer & J. Bryant (Eds.), *Playing Video Games. Motives, Responses, and Consequences.* Hillsdale, NJ: Lawrence Erlbaum Associates, pp. 259–274.

Lee, H. L., Padmanabhan, V., & Whang, S. (1997). Information distortion in a supply chain: The bullwhip effect. *Management Science, 43*, 546–558.

Lee, M., & Youn, S. (2008). Leading national advertisers' use of advergames. *Journal of Current Issues and Research in Advertising, 30*, 1–13.

Leemkuil, H., de Jong, T., de Hoog, R., & Christoph, N. (2003). KM Quest: A collaborative internet-based simulation game. *Simulation & Gaming, 34*, 89–102.

Lenhart, A., Kahne, J., Middaugh, E., MacGill, A., Evans, C., & Vitak, J. (2008). *Teens, Video Games, and Civics.* Washington, DC: Pew Internet & American Life Project.

Liao, C. C., Chen, Z.-H., Cheng, H. N., Chen, F.-C., & Chan, T.-W. (2011). My-Mini-Pet: A handheld pet-nurturing game to engage students in arithmetic practices. *Journal of Computer Assisted Learning, 27*, 76–89.

Lieberman, D. A. (2001). Management of chronic pediatric diseases with interactive health games: Theory and research findings. *The Journal of Ambulatory Care Management, 24*, 26–38.

Lieberman, D. A. (2006). What can we learn from playing interactive games? In Vorderer, P., & Bryant, J. (Eds.), *Playing Video Games. Motives, Responses, and Consequences.* Hillsdale, NJ: Lawrence Erlbaum Associates, pp. 379–397.

Lim, S., & Reeves, B. (2010). Computer agents versus avatars: Responses to interactive game characters controlled by a computer or other player. *International Journal of Human-Computer Studies, 68*(1–2), 57–68.

Machuca, J. A. D. (2000). Transparent-box business simulators: An aid to manage the complexity of organizations. *Simulation & Gaming, 31*, 230–239.

Mallinckrodt, V., & Mizerski, D. (2007). The effects of playing an advergame on young children's perceptions, preferences, and requests. *Journal of Advertising, 36*, 87–100.

Malone, T. W. (1981). Toward a theory of intrinsically motivating instruction. *Cognitive Science, 4*, 333–369.

Malone, T. W., & Lepper, M. R. (1987). Making learning fun: A taxonomy of intrinsic motivations for learning. In Snow, R. E., & Farr, M. J. (Eds.), *Aptitude, Learning and Instruction: III. Conative and Affective Process Analyses.* Hillsdale, NJ: Lawrence Erlbaum Associates, pp. 223–253.

Mayer, R. E., & Johnson, C. I. (2010). Adding instructional features that promote learning in a game-like environment. *Journal of Educational Computing Research, 42*, 241–265.

Mayo, M. J. (2011). Bringing game-based learning to scale: The business challenges of serious games. *International Journal of Learning and Media, 2*, 81–100.

McNamara, S. D., Jackson, G. T., & Graesser, A. (2009). *Intelligent tutoring and Games (ITaG).* Workshop on Intelligent Educational Games. Brighton, UK. pp. 1–10.

Montgomery, K. C. (2001). Digital kids: The new online children's consumer culture. In Singer, D. G., & Singer, J. L. (Eds.), *Handbook of Children and the Media.* Thousand Oaks, CA: Sage, pp. 635–650.

Montgomery, K. C., & Chester, J. (2009). Interactive food and beverage marketing: Targeting adolescents in the digital age. *Journal of Adolescent Health, 45*, 18–29.

Moreno, R., & Mayer, R. E. (2007). Interactive multimodal learning environments. *Educational Psychology Review, 19*, 309–326.

Moreno-Ger, P., Burgos, D., Martinez-Ortiz, I., Sierra, J. L., & Fernandez-Manjon, B. (2008). Educational game design for online education. *Computers in Human Behavior, 24*, 2530–2540.

Mott, B., McQuiggan, S., Lee, S. Y., & Lester, J. (2006). Narrative-centered environments for guided discovery learning. In: *Workshop on Agent-Based Systems for Human Learning in conjunction with Fifth International Conference on Autonomous Agents and Multi-Agent Systems.* Hakodate, Japan, pp. 22–28.

Nackle, L. E., Nackle, A., & Lindley, C. A. (2009). Brain training for silver games: Effects of age and game form on effectiveness, efficiency, self-assessment, and gameplay experience. *CyberPsychology & Behavior, 12*, 493–499.

Ney, J. & Jansz, J. (2010). Political Internet games: Engaging an audience. *European Journal of Communication, 25*, 227–241.

Nielsen Media Research (2007). The State of the Console. Retrieved September 16, 2007 from http://www.nielsenmedia.com/nc/nmr_static/docs/Nielsen_Report_State_ Console_03507.pdf.

Noar, S. M., Benac, N. C., & Harris, S. M. (2007) Does tailoring matter? Meta-analytic review of tailored print health behavior change interventions. *Psychological Bulletin, 3*, 673–693

Papastergiou, M. (2009). Digital game-based learning in high school computer science education: Impact on educational effectiveness and student motivation. *Computers & Education, 52*, 1–12.

Pasin, F., & Giroux, H. (2011). The impact of a simulation game on operations management education. *Computers & Education, 57*, 1240–1254.

Pempek, T. A., & Calvert, S. L. (2009). Tipping the balance: Use of advergames to promote consumption of nutritious foods and beverages by low-income African American children. *Archives of Pediatrics & Adolescent Medicine, 163*, 633–637.

Peng, W. (May, 2008). *Mediated Enactive Experience: A Socio-Cognitive Approach to Analyze the Effects of Playing Serious Games.* Paper presented at the Annual Conference of the International Communication Association, Montreal, Canada.

Petty, R.E., & Cacioppo, J.T. (1986). The Elaboration Likelihood Model of Persuasion. In L. Berkowitz (Ed.), *Advances in Experimental Social Psychology* (Vol. 19). Orlando, Florida: Academic Press, Inc, pp. 124–206.

Prensky, M. (2001). Digital natives, digital immigrants. *On the Horizon, 9*, 1–6.

Qin, H., Rau, P. L., & Salvendy, G. (2009). Measuring player immersion in the computer game narrative. *International Journal of Human-Computer Interaction, 25*, 107–133.

Raybourn, E. M. (2007). Applying simulation experience design principles to creating serious games for adaptive thinking training. *Interacting with Computers, 19*, 206–214.

Renkl, A., & Atkinson, R. K. (2007). Interactive learning environments: Contemporary issues and trends. An Introduction to the special issue. *Educational Psychology Review, 19*, 235–238.

Resnick, H. (1986). Electronic technology and rehabilitation: A computerized simulation game for youthful offenders. *Simulation & Games, 17*, 460–466.

Richards, D., Fassbender, E., Bilgin, A., & Thompson, W. F. (2008). An investigation of the role of background music in

IVSs for learning. *Australian Journal of Research in Learning Technology, 16,* 231–244.

Richtel, M. (April 20, 2011). In online games, a path to young consumers. *The New York Times, A1,* A15.

Rideout, V., Foehr, U. G., & Roberts, D. F. (2010). *Generation M2: Media in the Lives of 8–18 Year-Olds.* Menlo Park, CA: Henry J. Kaiser Family Foundation.

Ritterfeld, U., Shen, C., Wang, H., Nocera, L., & Wong, W. L. (2009). Multimodality and interactivity: Connecting properties of serious games with educational outcomes. *Cyberpsychology & Behavior, 12,* 691–697.

Roberts, D. F., Foehr, U. G., & Rideout, V. J. (2005). *Generation M: Media in the Lives of 8–18 Year-Olds.* Menlo Park, CA: Kaiser Family Foundation.

Rosas, R., Nussbaum, M., Cumsille, P., Marianov, V., Correa, M., Flores, P., et al. (2003). Beyond Nintendo: Design and assessment of educational video games for first and second grade students. *Computers & Education, 40,* 71–94.

Rowe, P. J., Mott, B. W., McQuiggan, S. W., Robison, J. L., Lee, S., & Lester, C. J. (2009). *Crystal Island: A Narrative Centered Learning Environment for Eighth Grade Microbiology.* Workshop on Intelligent Educational Games. Brighton, UK, pp. 11–21.

Ryan, R. M., Rigby, C. S., & Przybylski, A. (2006). The motivational pull of video games: A self-determination theory approach. *Motivation & Emotion, 30,* 347–363.

Salen, K., & Zimmerman, E. (2004). *Rules of Play: Game Design Fundamentals.* Cambridge, MA: MIT Press.

Satwicz, T., & Stevens, R. (2008). Playing with representations: How do kids make use of quantitative representations in video games? *International Journal of Computers for Mathematical Learning, 13,* 179–206.

Sawyer, B. (2006). Serious games. Retrieved February 6, 2006 from http://www.seriousgames.org./index.html.

Sellers, M. (2006). Designing the experience of interactive play. In Vorderer, P., & Bryant, J. (Eds.), *Playing Computer Games: Motives, Responses, and Consequences.* Hillsdale, NJ: Lawrence Erlbaum Associates, pp. 9–22.

Serious Games Initiative. (2008). *Games for Health.* Retrieved April 25, 2011 from http://www.seriousgames.org/about2.html.

Shane, M., Pettitt, B., Morgenthal, C., & Smith, C. (2008). Should surgical novices trade their retractors for joysticks? Videogame experience decreases the time needed to acquire surgical skills. *Surgical Endoscopy, 22,* 1294–1297.

Shapiro, S. J. (2003). The marketplace game. *Academy of Marketing Science Journal, 31,* 92–96.

Sherry, J. L. (2004). Flow and media enjoyment. *Communication Theory, 14,* 328–347.

Sherry, J. L., Lucas, K., Greenberg, B. S., & Lachlan, K. (2006). Video game uses and gratifications as predictors of use and game preference. In Vorderer, P., & Bryant, J. (Eds.), *Playing Video Games: Motives, Responses, and Consequences.* Hillsdale, NJ: Lawrence Erlbaum Associates, pp. 259–274.

Sim, G., & MacFarlane, S., & Read, J. (2006). All work and no play: Measuring fun, usability, and learning in software for children. *Computers & Education, 46,* 235–248.

Sims, V. K., & Mayer, R. E. (2002). Domain specificity of spatial expertise: The case of video game players. *Applied Cognitive Psychology, 16,* 97–115.

Sporer, J. C. (2010). IBM's university programs. *Computer, 43,* 102–104.

Spronck, P., Ponsen, M., Sprinkhuizen-Kuyper, I., & Postma, E. (2006). Adaptive game AI with dynamic scripting. *Machine Learning, 63,* 217–248.

Squire, K. (2006). From content to context: Videogames as designed experience. *Educational Researcher, 35,* 19–29.

Squire, K., & Barab, S. A. (2004). Replaying history: Engaging urban underserved students in learning world history through computer simulation games. In Kafai, Y., Sandoval, B. W., Eneydy, N., Nixon, A., & Hernandez, F. (Eds.), *Proceedings of the Sixth International Conference of the Learning Sciences.* Hillsdale, NJ: Lawrence Erlbaum Associates.

Staiano, A. E., & Calvert, S. L. (2011). Exergames for physical education courses: Physical, social, and cognitive benefits. *Child Development Perspectives, 5,* 93–98.

Staiano, A. E., Terry, A., Watson, K., Scanlon, P., Abraham, A., & Calvert, S. L. (April, 2011). *Physical Activity Intervention for Weight Loss in Overweight and Obese Adolescents.* Poster presented at the biennial meeting of the Society for Research in Child Development, Montreal, Canada.

Tamborini, R., & Skalski, P. (2006). The role of presence in the experience of electronic games. In Vorderer, P., & Bryant, J. (Eds.), *Playing Video Games. Motives, Responses, and Consequences.* Hillsdale, NJ: Lawrence Erlbaum Associates, pp. 225–240.

Thompson, D., Baranowski, T., Buday, R., Baranowski, J., Thompson, V., Jago, R., et al. (2008). Serious video games for health: How behavioral science guided the development of a serious video game. *Simulation & Gaming, 41,* 587–605.

Uhles, N., Weimer-Elder, B., & Lee, J. G. (2008). Simulation game provides financial management training. *Healthcare Financial Management, 62,* 82–89.

Van Eck, R. (2006) Digital game-based learning: It's not just the digital natives who are restless. *EDUCAUSE Review,* March/April, 16–30.

Vanhoucke, M., Vereecke, A., & Gemmel, P. (2005). The project scheduling game (PSG): Simulating time/cost trade-offs in projects. *Project Management Journal, 51,* 51–59.

Virvou, M., & Katsionis, G. (2008). On the usability and likeability of virtual reality games for education: The case of VR-ENGAGE. *Computers & Education, 50,* 154–178.

Vizlioni, D., Barker, M., Jellouschek, H., Heimann, G., & Blau, H. (2001). An interactive computer-animated system (*SpiroGame*) facilitates spirometry in preschool children. *American Journal of Respiratory and Critical Care Medicine, 164,* 2200–2205.

Vorderer, P. (2000). Interactive entertainment and beyond. In Zillmann, D., & Vorderer, P. (Eds.), *Media Entertainment: The Psychology of Its Appeal.* Hillsdale, NJ: Lawrence Erlbaum Associates, pp. 21–36.

Wang, H., Shen, C., & Ritterfeld, U. (2009). Enjoyment of digital games. What makes them "seriously" fun? In Ritterfeld, U., Cody, M., & Vorderer, P. (Eds.), *Serious Games: Mechanisms and Effects.* New York: Routledge Taylor & Francis, pp. 24–47.

Weber, R., Tamborini, R., Westcott-Baker, A., & Kantor, B. (2009). Theorizing flow and media enjoyment as cognitive synchronization of attentional and reward networks. *Communication Theory, 19,* 397–422.

Wilson, A. J., Dehaene, S., Pinel, P., Revkin, S. K., Cohen, L., & Cohen, D. (2006). Principles underlying the design of "The Number Race," an adaptive computer game for remediation of dyscalculia. *Behavioral and Brain Functions (Online), 2*(19), Accessed July 5, 2011 from http://www.behavioral-andbrainfunctions.com/content/2/1/19.

Wolfe, J. (1993). A history of business teaching games in English-speaking and post-socialist countries. *Simulation & Gaming, 24,* 446–463.

Wood, R., Griffiths, M. D., Chappell, D., & Davies, M. (2004). The structural characteristics of video games: A psycho-structural analysis. *CyberPsychology & Behavior, 7,* 1–10.

Woodrow Wilson International Center for Scholars (n.d.). Taking games seriously. Retrieved April 18, 2011 from http://www.wilsoncenter.org/index.cfm?fuseaction=news.item&news_id=44559.

Zantow, K., Knowlton, D. S., & Sharp, D. C. (2005). More than fun and games: Reconsidering the virtues of strategic management simulations. *Academy of Management Learning & Education, 4,* 451–458.

Zhu, D., Gedeon, T., & Taylor, K. (2011). "Moving to the centre": A gaze-driven remote camera control for teleoperation. *Interacting with Computers, 23,* 85–95.

Zimmerman, B. J. (1990). Self-regulated learning and academic achievement: An overview. *Educational Psychologist, 25,* 3–17

Zimmerman, B. J., & Martinez-Pons, M. (1986). Development of a structured interview for assessing student use of self-regulated learning strategies. *American Educational Research Journal, 23,* 614–628.

Zimmerman, C. (2000). The development of scientific thinking skills in elementary and middle school. *Developmental Review, 27,* 172–223.

Zyda, M. (2005) From visual simulation to virtual reality to games. *Computer, 38,* 25–32.

Violent Video Games and Aggression

Barbara Krahé

Abstract

The potential impact of violent video games on increasing players' aggression is a highly controversial issue in public debate and has been examined thoroughly in the scholarly literature. This chapter reviews the current state of knowledge about the empirical evidence and theoretical explanations concerning the relationship between exposure to video game violence and aggressive affect, cognitions, and behavior. It starts by presenting results from content analyses on the extent to which violence features in video games before looking at usage intensity and the appeal of violent games. The main part of the chapter provides a review of meta-analytic, experimental, and longitudinal studies addressing the strength of the link between the use of violent video games and aggression, followed by a discussion of the psychological processes underlying short-term effects and long-term consequences of playing violent video games. The final section summarizes interventions directed at reducing the effects of media violence on aggression.

Key Words: aggression, general aggression model, media violence, longitudinal studies, violent video games

Introduction

Every time the public is shocked by an extreme act of seemingly senseless violence, such as a school shooting or a killing spree, commentators are quick to point to the perpetrators' preoccupation with violent media, particularly so called "shooter games," as a cause for their aggressive actions. When a 19-year-old student killed 15 people at his former school in Germany in 2002, the BBC report about the case was entitled "Playing the Game: Germany's Teenage Killer" and went on to say, "A particular favorite of the 19-year-old killer was the popular 'Counterstrike'—a game in which teams of terrorists battle against teams of police officers."[1] What seems like an obvious connection to some people is vigorously disputed by others, most notably in the gaming community and the video game industry. The academic debate about the effects of

exposure to violent video games is no less controversial, as reflected, for example, in the commentaries on Anderson et al.'s (2010) recent meta-analysis (Bushman, Rothstein, & Anderson, 2010; Ferguson & Kilburn, 2010; Huesmann, 2010).

This chapter discusses the current state of the evidence on the potential of violent video games for increasing players' aggression. It also presents theoretical accounts of the processes by which engaging in aggressive behavior in the virtual reality of video games might affect aggressive cognitions, feelings, and behavior in the real world. For the purpose of this discussion, violent video game play is defined as *any action by the player intended to cause harm to other human or human-like characters in the game,* whereby harm is typically inflicted in the form of physical violence. Much of the research and theorizing on violent contents across a range of media such as television, films, comic books, or music is relevant to the understanding of violent video game effects (see Anderson et al., 2003, for a review). In addition, a growing specialized literature examines the effects of specific features of video games, such as their interactive nature, on aggression-related outcome variables. To put these issues into context, we will first ask how much violence there is in contemporary video games, how widely violent games are used, particularly by children and adolescents, and what makes violent games so attractive.

How Much Violence Is There in Contemporary Video Games and Why Is It So Appealing?

Content analyses of video games show that violence features prominently in this type of media. More than 20 years ago, Braun and Giroux (1989) found a violence rate of 71% for a sample of 21 arcade games. Dietz (1998) analyzed 33 best-selling video games and found that about 79% contained some form of violence. Since then, hard- and software of game technology have improved dramatically; graphics and sound effects have become highly realistic (Dill, Gentile, Richter, & Dill, 2005), promoting players' arousal and sense of involvement (Ivory & Kalyanaraman, 2007). A content analysis of 396 video games rated T (for Teens) by Haninger and Thompson (2004) revealed that 94% contained violent content. An analysis of popular games in Germany also concluded that many games rated as suitable for children or adolescents contained substantial amounts of violence (Höynck, Mößle, Kleimann, Pfeiffer, & Rehbein, 2007). In addition to identifying high levels of violent content in contemporary video games, Smith, Lachlan, and Tamborini (2003) found that games directed at children often involve forms of violence that map on to everyday forms of aggression, such as slapping, boxing, or kicking.

Beyond counting the number of games containing violence, a qualitative analysis (see Chapter 7) of the way violence is presented is useful for understanding the underlying mechanism of media violence effects on aggression. For example, providing evidence that violence is frequently rewarded by positive consequences in media depictions suggests an explanation based on social learning principles. Addressing this task, Smith et al. (2004) conducted a contextual analysis of the use of guns in video games. They analyzed a sample of 10 hours of playing the 60 video games most popular in 1999 in which a total of 116 violent interactions involving the use of guns were identified. In 94% of all interactions, violence was justified by serving the protection of life, 27% of violent moves were followed by rewards, and not a single one was followed by punishment.

In contrast to films and TV programs, violent content in video games is not a fixed quantity but varies depending on the player's actions. As players differ in skill and motivation, there is both inter- and intra-individual variability in the virtual reality created in a game, resulting in different levels of violence encountered in the course of playing the same game (Weber, Behr, Tamborini, Ritterfeld, & Mathiak, 2009). Therefore, analyses identifying violent content on the basis of time sampling of playing periods, often by a small number of players, can only yield a broad picture of violence in different games. Weber et al. (2009) addressed this problem by examining violent content generated by 13 experienced gamers playing a prototypical first-person shooter game for a 50-minute period. Across all players, they found that violent actions accounted for 15% of all events and 7% of the total playing time. There were substantial individual differences between players, producing varying levels of exposure to violence within the game.

In addition to establishing how much violence there is in video games, assessing potentially negative effects of exposure to violent games needs to consider how much time users spend with these media contents. Surveys show that video games in general are highly popular across all age groups. Even in the age group of 65 and older, 23% report playing video games (Lenhart & Macgill, 2008), and among adolescents and young adults virtually everybody uses them. In a survey conducted in the United States in 2008, 97% of teenagers aged 12 to 17 reported playing video games, 31% reported playing every day. In terms of the preferred game content, about one-third of gaming teenagers reported that at least one of their three favorite games was rated Mature, with boys outnumbering girls by 3 to 1 in this group (Lenhart et al., 2008).

In a representative survey of adolescents aged 12 to 19 in Germany, only 20% reported not playing games at all, whereas 45% reported playing regularly, several times a week. Of those participants who were aware of existing age ratings for video games, 81% of boys (but only 36% of girls) said they had played games rated unsuitable for their age group, and 71% of boys (45% of girls) reported that violent games were used by many or most of their peers (Medienpädagogischer Forschungsverbund

Süd-West, 2010). In another representative survey in Germany carried out in 2005, 20% of 10-year-old boys reported that at the time of the survey they were playing at least one game with an age rating of 16 or 18, and one-third of boys aged 14 to 15 reported playing games rated 18+ or with no age rating at all on a regular basis (Höynck et al., 2007). These figures need to be seen in the context of binding legal regulations in Germany restricting access to these games for underage youths.

If violent video games are widely used among children and adolescents as well as adults, what makes them so attractive, particularly for male users? Compared with the large number of studies addressing the consequences of violent video game play, this question has received less attention in psychological research. The "uses and gratifications" approach stipulates that people select media contents that serve certain momentary or more stable needs (Rubin, 2009). Violent media contents may be selected to provide different gratifications, as discussed by Kirsh (2006): (1) *Vicarious aggression*, allowing users to disable their learned inhibitions against aggressive behavior and act out aggressive impulses that they cannot vent in real life without negative consequences; (2) *personal identity formation,* enabling them to experiment with different varieties of a masculine identity and elicit feelings such as fear, anger, or disgust in an intensity that they can control (Jansz, 2005); (3) *social identity formation* in the sense of gaining popularity among peers as a "tough guy" or someone with expert skills in a highly rated domain; (4) *defiance of restrictions* imposed by adults as a way of asserting independence, which explains the special appeal of games with higher age ratings, called the "forbidden fruit effect" (Bijvank, Konijn, Bushman, & Roelofsma, 2009); (5) *empowerment and social status* as a form of self-presentation, for example, appearing mature and brave through slaying others in a game and being able to handle blood and gore; and finally (6) *mood management,* for example, playing violent games to release anger after a frustration. Bushman and Whitacker (2010) found that angered participants were more attracted to violent games if they subscribed to the belief that violent video game play can purge angry feelings or after they were exposed to a newspaper article promoting this belief.

Finally, gender differences in attraction to violent video game content were found in line with traditional gender roles. Ashworth, Pyle, and Pancer (2010) showed that video games with a high potential for dominating the opponent were rated by men as more appealing than games affording less dominance, whereas potential for dominance decreased the attractiveness of a game for women. Gender was also found to moderate the appeal of another game feature, namely, whether engagement in violence was portrayed as justified (i.e., committed in the role of a police officer) or unjustified (committed in the role of a gangster). A study with college students in Taiwan found that when acting violently was unjustified, men enjoyed the game more, and identified more with their game character than did women, whereas no gender differences were found for violence that appeared justified (Lin, 2010).

However, the question remains to what extent violence as an isolated game feature accounts for the appeal of this type of media over and above the satisfaction of other needs, such as achieving a sense of competence and mastery. Across a series of correlational and experimental studies, Przybylski, Ryan, and Rigby (2009) found little evidence that including violence in video games increased their attractiveness. On the other hand, they established that individuals high on trait aggression were particularly attracted to games containing violence, supporting earlier results by Bushman (1995). Further supporting the idea of a match between players' dispositions and preference for violent game content, a study by Peng, Liu, and Mou (2008) showed that individuals high on trait physical aggression engaged in a more aggressive style of playing than did low scorers. In combination, these findings suggest that violent video games hold a special attraction for individuals with a high affinity for aggression. This begs the question of whether highly aggressive people are not only more drawn toward games with violent content, but also more strongly affected by the experience of playing violent games in terms of subsequent aggressive behavior. This question is addressed in a later section.

How Strong Is the Empirical Evidence on the Link Between Violent Video Game Play and Aggression?

The strength of the evidence in support of the claim that playing violent video games promotes aggressive cognitions, affect, and behavior is at the core of the controversy about the potentially harmful effects of this type of media. As will be shown, the issue here is not so much the actual magnitude of the effects but their evaluation in terms of relevance or practical significance, particularly in relation to other potential risk factors of aggression. This section reviews the evidence available so far regarding the effects of playing violent video games on aggression-related outcome variables. First, the latest meta-analyses are presented that integrate the published research on violent video games into a common statistical metric. This review is followed by the discussion of exemplary studies using experimental and longitudinal methods to address the question of the causal influence of violent video game use on aggression.

To examine the association between violent video game play and aggression, three main methodologies have been used. (1) *Cross-sectional studies* relate self-reports of violent video game use to aggressive cognitions, feelings, or behaviors. For example, Krahé and Möller (2004) asked eighth grade students to report on their use of video games that were rated for violent content by an independent group of media experts. The more violent video game play participants reported, the higher their acceptance of aggressive behavior as normative. Although correlational studies can detect a covariation between media violence usage and aggression, they cannot establish whether playing violent video games is a causal risk factor for aggression. (2) By contrast, *experimental studies* can test causal hypotheses about the short-term effects of media violence exposure by systematically varying the level of violence in media contents and assigning participants randomly to a violent game and a nonviolent game condition to observe differences in aggressive behavior. For example, Anderson, Gentile, and Buckley (2007, Study 1) asked children aged 9 to 12 to play either a violent or a nonviolent game for 20 minutes and then gave them the opportunity to deliver aversive noise blasts to an opponent. They found that children who had played the violent game administered significantly more high-intensity noise blasts to their opponent than did those in the nonviolent game condition. (3) Finally, *longitudinal studies* follow the same group of participants over two or more points in time to relate the use of violent video games at an earlier point in time to aggressive behavior observed later. This methodology enables researchers to test the hypothesis that differences in media violence usage precede differences in aggression (Anderson et al., 2007). By considering and controlling for other potential risk factors of aggression they can also gauge the long-term, cumulative effects of habitual exposure to media violence. A more detailed discussion of the experimental and longitudinal research literature on violent video games is discussed later in this section. First, however, we take a bird's eye view on the current state of the evidence by looking at findings from two recent meta-analyses integrating results from a large number of individual studies.

Evidence from Meta-analyses

The empirical literature on the effects of playing violent video games is growing at a fast pace. One way of keeping track with the messages that emerge from this prolific field of research regarding the risk of aggression is to consult meta-analytic reviews bringing together findings from a wide range of individual studies into overall measures of effect size. The first meta-analyses on media violence effects on aggression dealing exclusively with video games were published by Anderson and Bushman (2001) and Sherry (2001). Since then, several updated meta-analytic reviews have been presented, including evidence from *different methodologies* (correlational experimental, and longitudinal studies) and different *outcome variables* (aggressive cognitions, feelings, and behavior, physiological arousal, and prosocial behavior) across samples from *different countries* (Anderson, 2004; Anderson et al., 2010; Ferguson, 2007a,b). In addition, violent video game effects have been covered as part of broader meta-analyses of effects of violent content across different types of media (Ferguson & Kilburn, 2009). The most commonly used measure of effect size capturing the strength of the association is the correlation (r) between violent video game play and aggression-related outcome variables. In addition to meta-analyses based on quantitative measures of effect size, there are several qualitative reviews covering the extensive literature regarding the effects of violence in video games (e.g., Dill, & Dill, 1998; Bensley & Van Eenwyk, 2001; Gentile & Anderson, 2006; Barlett, Anderson, & Swing, 2009; Weber, Ritterfeld, & Kostygina, 2009).

Findings from the two most comprehensive meta-analyses by Ferguson (2007a) and Anderson et al., (2010) revealed similar effect sizes.[2] Ferguson (2007a) analyzed a total of 25 studies published between 1995 and 2005 with a total of just over 4,200 participants and calculated separate effect sizes for experimental and nonexperimental studies. The findings from his analysis are presented in Figure 20.1.

The effect sizes were larger in experimental than in nonexperimental studies across all outcome variables. When studies were coded for reliability of measurement, Ferguson found a negative correlation between reliability and effect sizes, leading him to conclude that the link between violent video game use and aggression-related outcomes may be inflated by methodological flaws.

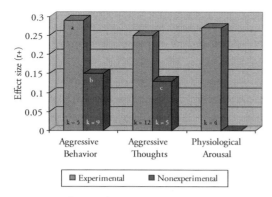

Figure 20.1 Effect Sizes from Experimental and Nonexperimental Studies for the Link Between Violent Video Game Play and Aggression-Related Outcomes.
Based on Ferguson, C. J. (2007a). Evidence for publication bias in video game violence effects literature: A meta-analytic review. *Aggression and Violent Behavior, 12,* 470–482.
Note. No effect sizes for physiological arousal were available from nonexperimental studies.
[a] corrected for publication bias: .15; [b] corrected for publication bias: .06; [c] corrected for publication bias: .11. Figures in the bars indicate *k* number of studies.

Anderson et al. (2010) included a much larger database of 136 studies, about one-third of which came from non-Western countries, most notably Japan. In total, the studies had more than 130,000 participants. To address the claim that effect sizes may be biased by poor methodology, their studies were categorized as to whether they met a set of best practice criteria (see Chapter 7), and effect sizes for the best practice studies were compared to the effect sizes obtained for the total set of studies. Figure 20.2 presents the effect sizes based on the sample of best practice studies.

Again, experimental studies produced higher effect sizes on all outcome variables than did nonexperimental studies. There was no significant difference in the effect sizes from Western and non-Western countries. A comparison of the effect sizes from the best practice studies with those computed for the total set of studies showed that with the exception of aggressive affect, effect sizes were higher in the best practice studies than in the full sample. Thus, there is no support in this large database for the claim that the effect of violent video game on aggression is inflated because of inadequate methodologies.

Although the sample of studies included by Anderson et al. (2010) was more than five times higher than the Ferguson (2007a) sample and covered a wide international literature, the magnitude of the effects found in the two meta-analyses are highly similar. The correlations are in the region of .15 to .25, with stronger effect sizes for experimental studies using laboratory measures of aggressive behavior. Following Cohen (1988), *r* values in the region of ±.10 are considered small, in the region of *r* = ±.30 medium, and in the region of ±.50 and above large effects. Thus, the effect sizes shown in the two meta-analyses fall into the small to medium range. This does not mean, however, that they are without practical significance, as claimed by some critics (e.g., Ferguson & Kilburn, 2010). Rosenthal (1990)

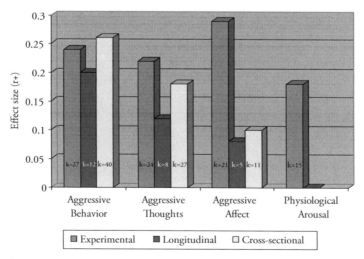

Figure 20.2 Effect Sizes from Experimental, Longitudinal, and Cross-Sectional Studies for the Link Between Violent Video Game Play and Aggression-Related Outcomes
Based on Anderson, C. A., Ihori, N., Bushman, B. J., Rothstein, H. R., Shibuya, A., Swing, E. L., Sakamoto, A., & Saleem, M. (2010). Violent video game effects on aggression, empathy, and prosocial behavior in Eastern and Western countries: A meta-analytic review. *Psychological Bulletin, 136,* 151–173.
Note. No effect sizes for physiological arousal were available from nonexperimental studies. Figures in the bars indicate *k* number of studies.

demonstrated that a correlation of $r = .20$ between media violence and aggression shifts the odds of someone with high media violence usage showing high levels of aggressive behavior from 50%:50% to 60%:40%. This means that of 100 high users of media violence, 60% will fall into the high aggression group, compared with 40% of low media violence users. Considering how widely violent media are available and used around the world, this difference of 20% translates into a large number of individuals who may become more aggressive as a result of exposure to violent media stimuli. Therefore, if only one in a hundred thousand players were inspired by a violent game to commit a violent act, the consequences of several million people playing that game would be alarming (Sparks & Sparks, 2002). The effect sizes established in empirical studies provide a basis for gauging the probability that aggressive behavior will be increased in the global community of players as a result of exposure to violent video games.

Experimental Studies

A large number of experimental studies examined the hypothesis that playing violent video games leads to short-term increases in aggressive behavior. In this section, evidence is reviewed on the impact of violent video game on aggressive *behavior* as the critical outcome variable. Studies examining violent video game effects on aggressive affect and cognitions or addressing the role of specific game features are discussed later in the chapter.

A common laboratory measure of aggressive behavior is the so-called "noise blast paradigm," a competitive reaction time task in which players deliver aversive noise blasts to an alleged opponent every time they are faster than the opponent in pressing a button (Bartholow & Anderson, 2002). Several studies have demonstrated that more aversive noise blasts were delivered after playing a violent compared with a nonviolent video game (e.g., Bartholow & Anderson, 2002; Anderson & Murphy, 2003; Anderson, Carnagey, Flanagan, Benjamin, Eubanks, & Valentine, 2004, Exp. 3; Sestir & Bartholow, 2010; see, however, Ferguson & Rueda, 2010, for a disconfirming result). Using behavioral observation in a free-play situation as a more realistic measure, Irwin and Gross (1995) found that boys who had played a violent game showed more physical aggression toward objects and more verbal aggression toward objects as well as a same-age confederate than those who had played the nonviolent game. In terms of the duration of short-term effects, Barlett, Branch, Rodeheffer, and

Harris (2009) found differences between players of violent versus nonviolent games in the amount of aversively hot sauce administered to another person, as measure of aggressive behavior, up to 10 minutes after the end of the game-playing session.

Anderson and Carnagey (2009) pitted violent content against competitiveness by comparing two competitive sports simulation games, one nonviolent and one with excessive violence. Participants playing the violent sports game delivered more high-intensity noise blasts to an opponent (indicating aggressive behavior) than those in the nonviolent game condition. Because both games were equally competitive, this difference points to the unique effect of violent content on aggression.

Longitudinal Studies

Longitudinal studies enable researchers to examine the cumulative effects of habitual use of violent media over time and to test two alternative causal explanations of the relationship between media violence and aggression: (1) that exposure to violent media makes users more aggressive ("socialization" hypothesis), or (2) that more aggressive individuals are more strongly attracted by violent media ("selection" hypothesis). Just a few years ago, Anderson et al. (2007, p. 33) stated that "to date there are no major longitudinal studies that specifically focus on violent video game effects." This statement is no longer true, as there are now several such studies with children and adolescents in the international research literature. Anderson et al. (2007, Study 3) followed 430 students in third to fifth grade over a period of 5 months and found that violent video game use at Time 1 remained a unique predictor of verbal and physical aggression at Time 2, even after controlling for a number of additional variables, such as sex, race, parental involvement, and hostile attributional style (i.e., the dispositional tendency to attribute hostile intentions to others). In addition to demonstrating an aggression-enhancing effect of video game violence, Anderson et al. (2007) established a link—albeit weaker—between violent game play and a decrease in *prosocial behavior* over time. The association remained significant after controlling for several covariates but disappeared when Time 1 prosocial behavior was included in the analysis.

A Japanese study by Shibuya, Sakamoto, Ihori, and Yukawa (2008) studied 591 fifth graders twice within a 1-year interval. They found a significant link between Time 1 violence in participants' favorite video games and Time 2 hostility in boys, but no link with anger or aggressive behavior. However,

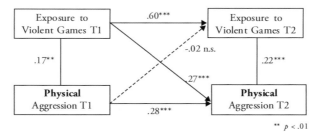

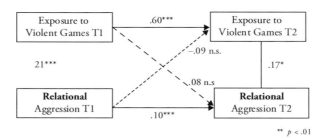

Figure 20.3 Links Between Video Game Use and Physical as Well as Relational Aggression in Adolescents Over 30 Months
Reprinted with permission from Möller, I., & Krahé, B. (2009). Exposure to violent video games and aggression in German adolescents: A longitudinal analysis. *Aggressive Behavior, 35,* 75–89.

a content analysis showed significant links with Time 2 aggressive behavior for games that included an attractive perpetrator and presented violence as justified. For girls, no significant links emerged between violent video game use and later aggressive affect or behavior. A German study with third and fourth graders showed a similar gender difference (von Salisch, Kristen, & Oppl, 2007). Over a 1-year period, they found a significant path of ß = .07 from using first-person shooters to overt aggression in boys, but not in girls. Among the boys, the reverse path, from Time 1 aggression to Time 2 use of first-person shooters was substantially higher in this sample (ß = .22), supporting the "selection" hypothesis that more aggressive individuals selectively prefer violent media content.

For adolescents, two short-term longitudinal studies from Japan with participants aged 12 to 18 found bivariate correlations of .23 and .34, respectively, between Time 1 violent video game playing and Time 2 physical aggression assessed four months later (Anderson et al., 2008). A German study with 12- to 14-year-olds found that Time 1 violent video game use was significantly linked to aggression (ß = .18) and delinquency (ß = .29) at Time 2 2 years later, controlling for other potential risk factors, such as poor school climate and parents' use of physical violence (Hopf, Huber, & Weiß, 2008). A

further study with German adolescents by Möller and Krahé (2009) covered a period of 30 months and considered both physical and relational aggression. The path models linking violent video game use to physical as well as relational aggression are shown in Figure 20.3.

Controlling for Time 1 physical aggression, a significant path was found from violent video game use to physical aggression 30 months later. This finding supports the "socialization" hypothesis of violent video game effects. There was no support for the "selection" hypothesis, as aggression at Time 1 was unrelated to violent video game use at Time 2. There was also no evidence of a crossover effect from video game violence that is typically physical in nature on relational aggression, i.e., behavior aimed at damaging the target person's social relationships (Crick & Grotpeter, 1995).

Similar findings are reported from a study with Dutch adolescents by Lemmens, Valkenburg, and Peter (2011) covering a period of 6 months. The cross-lagged path from violent video game use at Time 1 to self-reported aggression at Time 2 was significant, whereas the path from Time 1 aggression to Time 2 violent video game use was not. Although girls used violent games much less than did boys, the paths from violent video game use to aggression did not differ significantly between the gender groups.

Finally, a recent study by Ferguson (2011) followed 302 adolescents over a 1-year period and found a significant bivariate correlation between Time 1 reports of violent video game use and Time 2 bullying behavior. However, violent video game use did not explain unique variance over and above other risk factors, such as antisocial personality and depressive symptoms, nor did it predict other measures of aggressive behavior. It should be noted that this study differed from previous research in the measurement of violent video game use by relying on ratings by the Entertainment Software Ratings Board (ESRB) as an estimate of video game violence exposure. There is some indication that these ratings provide more lenient assessments of the amount of violence compared, for example, to ratings by parents (Walsh & Gentile, 2001) or experienced gamers (e.g., Haninger & Thompson, 2004), which may have resulted in an underestimation of the level of violence contained in participants' video game diet (see also Höynck et al., 2007, for a similar finding regarding age ratings in Germany).

In addition to longitudinal studies focussing specifically on video games, there is further evidence from studies using broader measures of media violence exposure including television and movies instead or alongside of violent video games. This research, spanning developmental periods from preschool age (Ostrov, Gentile, & Crick, 2006; Christakis & Zimmerman, 2007) to adolescence (Slater, Henry, Swaim, & Anderson, 2003; Krahé & Möller, 2010), also identified habitual media violence use as a significant predictor of aggression over time. Extending the time frame into adulthood, Huesmann, Moise-Titus, Podolski, and Eron (2003) found that television violence viewing at age 10 predicted aggression measured 15 years later, controlling for a number of other risk factors of aggression. No evidence was found for the reverse pathway, representing the selection hypothesis, from early aggression to subsequent television violence viewing.

Overall, there is clear support for the idea that using violent media socializes users into aggression. At the same time, there is also support for the idea that highly aggressive individuals selectively prefer violent media (Anderson et al., 2003). There is no inherent contradiction between the two processes because it is possible that they are mutually reinforcing. Indeed, the "downward spiral" model by Slater et al. (2003) proposes that even though more aggressive individuals may show a preference for violent media, the more intense use of these

media may reinforce their aggressive tendencies. In their 2-year study in which adolescents were measured at four points in time, they found that trait aggression was linked to greater use of violent media cross-sectionally, and that the use of violent media predicted aggressiveness both cross-sectionally and prospectively. This finding showed that as predicted by the selection hypothesis, more aggressive individuals were more attracted to violent media at Time 1, and higher levels of violent media use were linked to higher aggression at the subsequent points in time, as predicted by the socialization hypothesis.

Taken together, the experimental and longitudinal evidence discussed in this section further illustrates the link apparent in the meta-analytic reviews between violent video game play and aggression and is consistent with research looking at violent content in other media. Both experiments and longitudinal studies support the assumption of a causal effect of violent video games on aggression. However, as noted by Huesmann (2010), this is not to say that violent media usage "determines" aggressive behavior. Not every heavy user of violent games will display detectable signs of aggression, just as not every drunken driver will cause a fatal accident, but the risk of aggression is increased among the high usage group. Media violence may reinforce the effects of other risk factors, not least exposure to violence in the real world (Browne & Hamilton-Giachritsis, 2005). At the same time, there may be differences in the aggression-enhancing effects of media violence use depending on characteristics of the media stimuli, such as the presentation of violence as justified or unjustified or the interactive versus noninteractive role assigned to users. We will examine potential moderators of the media violence-aggression link in the next section.

How Does Playing Violent Video Games Increase Aggression?

Theoretical explanations of the underlying process that lead from violent video game play as an input variable to aggressive behavior as an outcome distinguish between short-term effects of a single playing episode and long-term effects of habitual use of violent video games over extended periods of time. The main mechanisms identified in the literature as accounting for the impact of violent media on aggression are listed in Table 20.1.

In large part, the underlying psychological processes are assumed to be the same for video games as for other violent media stimuli, such as movies and television programs, so that we can draw on a

Table 20.1 Processes Underlying the Effects of Media Violence Exposure on Aggression

Short-Term Processes	Long-Term Processes
• Physiological arousal	• Observational learning
• Anger affect	• Development of aggressive scripts
• Activation of aggressive cognitions	• Disinhibition
• Imitation	• Desensitization

large body of literature pertaining to violent content across different types of media. In addition, it will be asked how certain features of violent video games, most notably their interactive nature, give rise to processes that are specific to this type of media.

Processes Underlying Short-Term Effects

Short-term exposure to violent media affects aggressive behavior through three main processes: (1) the elicitation of arousal and aggressive affect, (2) the activation of aggressive cognitions, and (3) the instigation of imitational learning. These processes are illustrated by representative examples from the experimental research literature.

1. Exposure to violent media stimuli leads to an *increase in physiological arousal as well as affective arousal* in the form of state anger and hostility. As shown in Figures 20.1 and 20.2, the meta-analyses by Anderson et al. (2010) and Ferguson (2007a) found evidence that violent video game use increases physiological arousal, with effect sizes of $r = .18$ and $r = .27$, respectively. This increased arousal may facilitate aggression by enhancing the person's activity level and strengthen dominant responses. For example, a person confronted with a provocation is more likely to respond aggressively if he or she is already in a state of increased arousal, as suggested by Zillmann's (1979) "excitation transfer model." This model suggests that arousal by a media stimulus may be erroneously attributed to the arousal caused by a provocation and mislabeled as anger if the person is no longer aware of the source of the initial arousal, thus reinforcing an aggressive response to the provocation (Zillmann & Bryant, 1974).

Whereas physiological indicators, such as heart rate or skin conductance, provide a quantitative index of arousal, *affective arousal* reflects the subjective perception of the quality of arousal. Several studies demonstrated that exposure to violent media stimuli elicit feelings of state anger and hostility that trigger subsequent aggressive behavior. Bushman and Huesmann (2006) found an effect size of $r = .27$ for the link between media violence and angry affect across different types of methods and media genres, Anderson et al. (2010) reported an effect

size of $r = .29$ from experimental studies of video game violence.

2. At the cognitive level, violent media stimuli activate *aggressive thoughts, feelings, and self-concepts.* Watching media depictions of aggressive interactions increases the ease with which users can access their own aggressive thoughts and feelings. The underlying mechanism is a process of *priming* whereby a particular external stimulus, such as an aggressive act, directs the individual's attention to the congruent mental constructs, such as aggressive cognitions, thus lowering the threshold for using them to interpret social information. Asking subjects to list their thoughts following exposure to a violent or nonviolent videotape, Bushman (1998) found that respondents who had watched a violent videotape produced more aggressive associations to homonyms with both an aggressive and a nonaggressive meaning (such as box, punch). They were also faster in identifying letter strings making up aggressive words than were respondents shown a nonviolent videotape (see also Bushman & Anderson, 2002). Bösche (2010) replicated faster recognition times for aggression-related words after playing a violent compared with a nonviolent video game. In addition, he also found faster accessibility of positively valenced words in the violent game condition, which is an indication that violent entertainment is connected with positive associations. Demonstrating an effect on attitudes, Lee, Peng, and Klein (2010) showed that participants who had played a violent game for 2 hours were more lenient in their judgments of criminal behavior than those who had played a nonviolent game.

Furthermore, there is evidence that even brief periods of media violence use may activate aggression-related aspects of players' self-concept. Playing a violent video game for 10 or 20 minutes increased the speed with which aggression-related words were associated with the self in an Implicit Association Test (IAT) compared with a nonviolent control condition, eliciting a process of learning aggressive self-views (Uhlmann & Swanson, 2004; Bluemke et al., 2010). No parallel effects were found on explicit self-report measures of aggression, suggesting that the effects of violent media cues operated at the automatic level. The link between violent media use and the self was underlined further in a study by Fischer, Kastenmüller, and Greitemeyer (2010). Their participants played either a violent (boxing) game or a nonviolent (bowling) game. In each condition, half of the participants could personalize their game character by modeling its physical appearance after themselves. The other half played the respective game with a nonpersonalized character. Participants playing the personalized violent game subsequently administered more hot sauce to another person as a measure of aggressive behavior than those playing the nonpersonalized violent game, and both groups acted more aggressively than the players of the nonviolent game in either the personalized or nonpersonalized condition. The effects were mediated by self-activation (feeling strong, active, and motivated) that was higher in the personalized than in the nonpersonalized violent game conditions.

However, it seems that aggressive media contents not only serve as primes for aggressive cognitions, but the priming of aggressive thoughts then leads to a preference for violent media contents. Langley, O'Neal, Craig, and Yost (1992) first activated aggressive cognitions by asking participants to compose short stories using words from a list of aggressive (versus nonaggressive) terms. Then, they were given the choice of different film clips described as varying in aggressive content. Participants who had written aggression-related stories in the priming task expressed a greater preference for violent film clips than those who had written a story based on the neutral words. These findings tie in with longitudinal evidence based on the "downward spiral" discussed earlier in that media violence promotes aggressive cognitions just as aggressive cognitions feed into preferences for violent media.

3. A further process explaining short-term effects of exposure to violent video games is *imitational learning*. Exposure to aggression may instigate social learning processes that result in the acquisition of new behaviors. As revealed in the content analyses mentioned earlier, much of the aggression in violent video games is rewarded or at least goes unpunished. Moreover, it is often shown by attractive characters with whom viewers identify. As social learning theory suggests, learning through modeling is particularly likely under these circumstances (Bandura, 1983). The most obvious way in which aggression portrayed in the media is incorporated in the recipients' behavioral repertoire is reflected in copycat aggression. Studies conducted as early as the 1960s showed that children imitate the behaviors observed by attractive role models (Bandura et al., 1963).

In a study by Schutte, Malouff, Post-Gorden, and Rodasta (1988), children were randomly assigned to playing either a violent (karate) video game or a nonviolent (jungle swing) game. In a subsequent free play period, children in the nonviolent group played more with the jungle swing than those in the violent group, whereas children in the violent group showed more aggressive behavior, such as hitting an inflatable doll or hitting another child.

MODERATORS OF SHORT-TERM EFFECTS

The principles discussed so far identified psychological processes affecting users of violent media stimuli in terms of their readiness to engage in aggression. However, it is likely that not all users are affected by violent media stimuli to the same extent and that differences in the way violence is presented also moderates the effects. This section discusses evidence on individual differences and media-specific characteristics as moderators of the short-term effects of media violence on aggression.

THE MODERATING ROLE OF INDIVIDUAL DIFFERENCES

Several studies have shown that individuals differ in their aggressive responses to media violence depending on trait aggression and trait hostility. Anderson and Carnagey (2009) showed that playing a violent video game increased the accessibility of aggressive cognitions compared with a nonviolent control group only among participants high on trait aggression (see Giumetti & Markey, 2007 for similar results). However, in a study by Anderson (1997), playing a violent game increased hostile affect only among participants low on trait hostility. An explanation for the latter finding may be that for individuals high on trait hostility, hostile feelings are chronically accessible, so that the effect of the violent game as a short-term aggressive prime had no additional effect on them. By contrast, people not habitually hostile were induced by the prime to activate aggression-related affective states.

Bushman (1995, Study 3) explored the impact of a violent versus nonviolent film on unprovoked and provoked aggressive behavior by respondents differing in trait aggressiveness. On the measure of unprovoked aggression, both aggressive and nonaggressive participants acted more aggressively than respondents exposed to a nonviolent film. Following prior provocation, however, the aggression-enhancing effect of the violent film was significantly more pronounced for the aggressive than for the nonaggressive respondents.

The impact of short-term exposure to media violence is also affected by users' past experience with violent media contents. For example, Bartholow, Sestir, and Davis (2005) showed that after playing a violent video game for 20 minutes, high habitual users of violent video games were more aggressive on a competitive reaction task than low habitual users. High users also scored lower on empathy and higher on trait hostility than low users, and these differences partly explained the differences in aggressive behavior (see also Anderson & Dill, 2000).

Concerning the role of gender, evidence was presented at the beginning of this chapter that boys are far more attracted to violent video games than are girls. Whether they are differentially affected when exposed to the same level of violent content has not been established conclusively in the literature. The meta-analysis by Anderson et al. did not yield a significant gender difference in the experimental studies, indicating that both gender groups are equally affected by violent video games. Studies with all-female samples also revealed effects of violent media stimuli on aggression in women. Anderson and Murphy (2003) found higher levels of aggression after playing a violent as compared with a nonviolent video game, and Fischer and Greitemeyer (2006) showed that women who had listened to men-hating lyrics acted more aggressively toward a male target person than women exposed to neutral lyrics. However, other studies found no effects of playing a violent versus a nonviolent game on women (Bartholow & Anderson, 2002; Deselms & Altman, 2003; Polman, Orobio de Castro, & van Aken, 2008). Given that violent game characters are typically male, women cannot identify with aggressive media models in the same way as men, which may account at least partly for their lower preference for this type of media and, possibly, lower levels of aggression following exposure to violent contents (see, however, Jansz & Martis, 2007, for an increasing presence of female game characters in dominant roles). This line of reasoning is supported by the finding that women playing a violent game with a female avatar showed more aggressive thoughts in a word completion task than women playing the same game with a male avatar (Eastin, 2006).

THE MODERATING ROLE OF GAME FEATURES

The different ways in which violence is presented also affect the strength of the link between violent video game use and aggression (see Barlett et al., 2009, for a review). Carnagey and Anderson (2005) conducted three studies in which they explored the importance of reward and punishment of violent action in a video game on subsequent aggressive cognitions, affect, and behavior. All participants played a racing game, Carmaggedon 2, but they were randomly assigned to three different conditions: (1) a condition in which killing race opponents and pedestrians was rewarded by extra points, (2) a condition in which killing race opponents and pedestrians was punished by taking points away, and (3) a nonviolent condition in which killing pedestrians or competitors was not possible. Blood pressure and pulse were recorded as measures of arousal to make sure that the three versions did not differ in terms of their arousal quality. State hostility after the 20-minute playing period was measured as an index of aggressive affect (Exp. 1). A word completion test presenting words that could be completed to yield either an aggressive or a nonaggressive meaning was used as a measure of aggressive cognition (Exp. 2), and administering aversive noise blasts to an opponent in a competitive reaction time task was chosen as a measure of aggressive behavior (Exp. 3). The results are displayed in Figure 20.4.

For aggressive affect, the findings reveal that both groups engaging in violent actions while playing the video game experienced higher levels of state hostility than the group that could not engage in violent actions. For aggressive cognition and aggressive behavior, participants in the reward group scored significantly higher than those in the punishment and the nonviolent control groups. The latter two groups did not differ significantly on either cognitions or behavior.

Barlett, Harris, and Bruey (2008) varied the amount of blood visible during the playing of a violent game and found significantly higher arousal, state hostility, and number of aggressive words in a word completion task in the condition in which large amounts of blood were displayed. Similarly, Barlett, Harris, and Baldassaro (2007) found that playing a violent video game with a controller in the shape of a realistic gun lead to a higher increase in arousal from baseline than playing with a standard controller.

Regarding differences between noninteractive exposure to media violent as opposed to active involvement, Polman et al. (2008) compared children actively playing a violent or nonviolent video game with a group of children who passively observed the same actions shown on a television screen. This ensured that both groups received exactly the same input but differed in terms of active involvement. The results showed that boys in the violent-active condition were more aggressive than boys in the

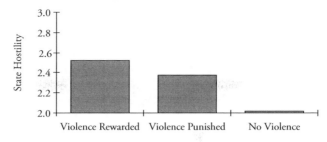

(i) Aggressive affect (State hostility)

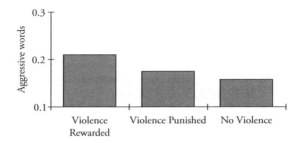

(ii) Aggressive cognition (Proportion of aggressive word completions)

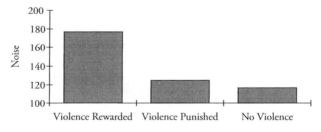

(iii) Aggressive behavior (Duration x intensity of noise blasts)

Figure 20.4 Effects of Reward and Punishment of Violence in Video Games
Adapted from Carnagey, N. L., & Anderson, C. A. (2005). The effects of reward and punishment in violent video games on aggressive affect, cognition, and behavior. *Psychological Science, 16,* 882–889, Table 2.

passive-violent condition. However, they were not more aggressive than boys in the active-nonviolent condition, and no effects of involvement or violence level of the game were found for girls.

Finally, both similarity to and wishful identification with violent game characters were found to increase the effects of violent game playing on aggression. A recent study by Williams (2011) examined the effect of physical likeness between players and their game characters on players' physical state anger after playing a violent or a nonviolent game. Participants were either instructed to create an avatar that resembled them in various physical features, such as skin color, height, build, hair style, or they were given an avatar dissimilar to their own appearance. As expected, a main effect for violence level was found, in terms of higher state

anger after playing the violent as compared with the nonviolent game. More importantly, a significant interaction was found between violence level of the game and physical resemblance of the main character: Participants who had played the violent game with an avatar resembling them were significantly angrier than those playing the violent game with a dissimilar avatar or those who had played a nonviolent game with either a similar or dissimilar avatar. Using wishful identification with the main character as a quasi-experimental variable, Konijn, Bijvank, and Bushman (2007) found higher levels of aggression after playing a violent game in boys the more they wanted to be like the main character, whereas wishful identification with the main character of the nonviolent games was unrelated to aggressive behavior.

Processes Explaining Cumulative Effects of Habitual Use of Violent Games

To explain the impact of habitual exposure to media violence on aggressive behavior, several interlocking processes have been proposed (see Huesmann & Kirwil, 2007, for a summary). The most widely studied mechanisms are *observational learning, disinhibition,* and *desensitization.* None of these mechanisms is specific to violent media contents; they pertain to the long-term effects of exposure to violence in real life as well as in the virtual reality of the media.

Observational learning plays a key role in the adoption of aggression as part of the individual's behavioral repertoire. Just as real-life models are imitated, particularly if their aggressive behavior is followed by positive consequences, as shown by Bandura, Ross, and Ross (1961, 1963), media models are a powerful source of learning by observation. Violent media characters are typically presented as strong, powerful, and acting in pursuit of a good cause, making them appealing models to imitate. Huesmann et al. (2003) found positive correlations between childhood identification with same-sex aggressive media characters and aggression measured 15 years later in both men and women. Moreover, children who perceived television violence as "real" were significantly more aggressive as young adults. The longitudinal study with Japanese children by Shibuya et al. (2008) showed that playing video games in which violence was committed by an attractive as opposed to a less attractive perpetrator predicted higher levels of hostility and aggression 12 months later.

Observational learning is not limited to the imitation of specific acts of aggression, it also involves the acquisition of more general aggressive knowledge structures or *aggressive scripts.* Habitual exposure to violent media promotes the learning, rehearsal, and reinforcement of pro-aggression beliefs and attitudes, hostile perceptions, and expectations as well as the acquisition of aggressive behavioral scripts (Huesmann, 1998). The more individuals use violent media, the more they encounter stimuli relevant to their aggressive scripts. Over time, the frequent activation of aggressive scripts will make them more easily accessible, thus increasing the likelihood that they will be used to interpret incoming stimuli. Children are particularly susceptible to this effect because their aggressive scripts are still more malleable than those of adults (Huesmann, 1998). In a study of third to fifth graders, Gentile and Gentile (2008) showed that playing multiple violent video games predicted a higher tendency to attribute hostile intent to others 5 months later, which in turn was linked to higher physical aggression. Habitual violent video game play was also associated with higher trait hostility in an adolescent sample studied by Gentile, Lynch, Linder, and Walsh (2004), which was associated with more frequent involvement in physical fights and arguments with teachers. These links support the role of violent media usage in promoting hostile schemata that lower the threshold for aggressive behavior.

The second process by which the habitual use of violent media impacts aggressive behavior is *disinhibition.* Exposure to violent media contents may weaken the viewers' inhibitions against aggression by making aggression appear as a common and accepted feature of social interactions. The fact that many violent acts are presented as justified and do not show the suffering of victims undermines the perception of violence as antisocial and harmful. As noted by Huesmann (1998), such normative beliefs are an integral part of aggressive scripts and are used to decide which behavioral options will be activated in a given situation. In line with this proposition, Huesmann and Kirwil (2007) reported longitudinal evidence that normative beliefs about aggression in adulthood were predicted by childhood preferences for violent media contents and that the normative acceptance of aggression partly mediated the link between childhood exposure to media violence and adult aggressive behavior. Presenting aggression as justified was correlated with higher hostility and aggression assessed a year later in the Japanese study by Shibuya et al. (2008). Möller and Krahé (2009) found that the more adolescents played violent video games, the more accepting they were of physical aggression in interpersonal conflict situations assessed 30 months later. Acceptance of aggression as normative was significantly associated with both physical aggression and hostile attributional style. Further support for the disinhibiting effect of violent video game play comes from a study by Hummer et al. (2010), who studied brain activity indicating inhibition of unwanted and inappropriate responses. Using functional magnetic resonance imaging (fMRI) technology, they found that immediately after playing a violent game, participants showed reduced brain activity required to suppress unwanted responses compared with a comparison group who had played a nonviolent game, identifying a neurobiological basis for the disinhibiting effects of exposure to media violence.

The third process through which habitual exposure to violent media stimuli has a long-term effect on aggression is *desensitization*. In general terms, desensitization refers to the gradual reduction in responsiveness to an arousal-eliciting stimulus as a function of repeated exposure. In the context of media violence, desensitization more specifically describes a process "by which initial arousal responses to violent stimuli are reduced, thereby changing an individual's 'present internal state'" (Carnagey, Anderson, & Bushman, 2007, p. 491). In particular, desensitization to violent media stimuli is thought to reduce anxious arousal. Fear is a spontaneous and probably innate response of humans in reaction to violence. As with other emotional responses, repeated exposure to media violence can *decrease* negative affect because violent stimuli lose their capacity to elicit strong emotions the more often the stimulus is presented (Anderson & Dill, 2000).

Several studies have shown that in the long run, habitual exposure to media violence may reduce anxious arousal in response to depictions of violence. Research has found that the more time individuals spent watching violent media depictions, the less emotionally responsive they became to violent stimuli (e.g., Averill, Malstrom, Koriat, & Lazarus, 1972) and the less sympathy they showed for victims of violence in the real world (e.g., Mullin & Linz, 1995). In a series of studies with children aged 5 to 12, Funk et al. demonstrated that habitual usage of violent video games was associated with reduced empathy with others in need of help (Funk, Buchman, Jenks, & Bechtoldt, 2003; Funk, Baldacci, Pasold, & Baumgardner, 2004).

Bartholow, Bushman, and Sestir (2006) used event-related brain potential data (ERPs) to compare responses by violent and nonviolent video game users to violent stimuli and relate them to subsequent aggressive responses in a laboratory task. They found that the more violent games participants played habitually, the less brain activity they showed in response to violent pictures and the more aggressively they behaved by administering aversive noise blasts to an opponent. No effect of habitual exposure to media violence was found for ERP responses to nonviolent negative stimuli (such as pictures of accident victims or disfigured babies), indicating that desensitization was specific to the violent content of the media diet. In a later study, Engelhardt, Bartholow, Kerr, and Bushman (2011) established that reduced ERP mediated the link between high use of violent video games and aggressive behavior.

Using skin conductance levels as a measure of arousal during exposure to a violent film clip, Krahé,

Möller, Huesmann, Kirwil, Felber, and Berger (2012) found that the more participants were used to violent media, the less physiological arousal they showed while watching graphic scenes of violence and the more pleasant arousal they reported to have experienced. Higher pleasant arousal was associated with faster recognition of aggression-related words. Participants in this study were also exposed to sad and funny film clips, for which no association with habitual media violence was found, further demonstrating that the effects were specific to violent media contents.

MODERATORS OF LONG-TERM EFFECTS

The current literature provides little information about moderators of long-term effects of media violence use because most studies that included further variables potentially related to aggression, such as trait aggression, school performance, socioeconomic status, age, or gender, controlled for them in the statistical analyses rather than considering them in interaction with violent media use (e.g., Huesmann et al., 2003; Anderson et al., 2007, 2008; Christakis, & Zimmerman, 2007; Ferguson, 2011). Anderson et al. (2010) did not find significant differences as a function of age and gender in their meta-analysis of longitudinal studies and concluded that the effects of playing violent video games over time apply to large proportions of the population at least through college age. Regarding trait aggression as a moderator, Krahé and Möller (2010) found an interaction between Time 1 physical aggression and media violence exposure on Time 2 aggression. Violent media use predicted an increase in aggression only among those participants who scored low on physical trait aggression at Time 1, whereas media violence use did not predict a further increase in aggression among the high trait aggression group.

This section addressed the question how exposure to media aggression increases viewers' aggressive response tendencies in the short term and over time. Anderson and Bushman (2001) have presented a model of the effects of violent video game play based on the General Aggression Model (GAM) that shows how cognitive and affective processes triggered by violent video games contribute to an increase in aggressive personality. The model is presented in Figure 20.5.

Short-term effects, such as activation of aggressive cognitions and instigation of anger affect, may become chronic with regular exposure and exert a long-term effect on aggressive behavior by giving rise to perceptual schemata and aggressive expectation

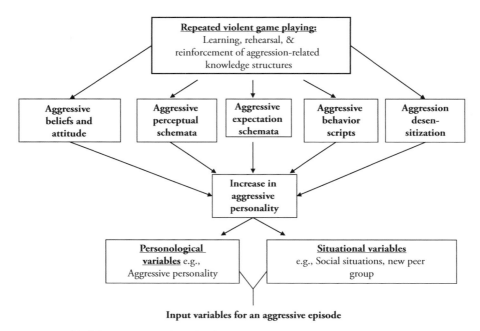

Figure 20.5 Process Model of the Long-Term Effects of Video Game Violence
Reprinted with permission from Anderson, C. A., & Bushman, B. J. (2001). Effects of violent video games on aggressive behavior, aggressive cognition, aggressive affect, physiological arousal, and prosocial behavior: A meta-analytic review of the scientific literature. *Psychological Science, 12,* 353–359, p. 355.

schemata. Aggressive perceptual schemata describe the tendency to perceive the behavior of others as guided by aggressive intentions, aggressive expectation schemata lead people to overestimate the likelihood that others will show aggressive behavior.

How Can the Effects of Violent Video Game Play on Aggression be Mitigated or Prevented?

The research reviewed so far has demonstrated significant effects of playing violent video games on aggressive feelings, thoughts, and behaviors. What, then, can be done to prevent or mitigate these effects? Theoretical models that explain the long-term effects of exposure as a result of observational learning, aggressive scripts, disinhibition, and desensitization suggest that interventions should start at an early age when aggressive scripts are not yet consolidated and therefore more open to change.

Compared with the large number of studies linking media violence use to aggression, the current body of knowledge about effective intervention strategies is limited, and the majority of available studies focused only on short-term changes in experimental settings (see Anderson et al., 2003; Cantor & Wilson, 2003 for reviews). Typically, interventions designed to mitigate the aggression-enhancing effects of media violence exposure focus on one or

both of two target variables: *restricted consuming* and *critical consuming*. Restricted consuming refers to an overall reduction of media exposure and the substitution of violent with nonviolent media content. Critical consuming refers to the promotion of an understanding of how media violence influences users and of the mechanisms by which violence is presented as acceptable, successful, and detached from negative consequences. Critical consuming is therefore directed at increasing an important aspect of media literacy, namely, "the ability to analyze and evaluate media" (Kirsh, 2010, p. 241).

Focusing on restricted overall consuming only, Robinson, Wilde, Navracruz, Haydel, and Varady (2001) demonstrated the efficacy of an intervention with third and fourth graders over a period of 6 months. The intervention included a 10-day complete turnoff of television, videos, and video games, followed by a prescribed budget of no more than 7 hours of screen time per week. Participants in the intervention group showed not only a reduction of media use compared with the control group, but also a significant decrease in peer-rated aggression and observed verbal aggression from baseline to posttest. However, the intervention and control groups did not differ in terms of a decrease in parent ratings of aggression from baseline to posttest.

Byrne (2009), on the other hand, focused exclusively on the aspect of critical consuming. She compared two intervention conditions with a control group in a sample of fourth and fifth graders. In the "basic condition," students received a lesson on media violence effects in terms of an *evaluative mediation*, for example, watching violent clips and critically evaluating the aggressive characters. In the "activity condition," participants were given the same instruction but were additionally required to write a paragraph about what they had learned and were videotaped reading it aloud. No difference was found between the activity and the control conditions immediate postintervention and at the 6-month follow-up, whereas the basic condition showed a significant *increase* in the willingness to use aggression, indicating a boomerang effect.

Using a combined approach of reducing media violence usage *and* promoting critical consuming, Rosenkoetter, Rosenkoetter, Ozretich, and Acock (2004) conducted an extensive intervention over a 12-month period with children in first through third grade. It was designed to reduce the amount of violent television viewing and lower the level of identification with violent television characters. The intervention produced different effects for boys and girls. Girls in the intervention group scored higher on knowledge about television violence effects and lower on television violence viewing as well as identification with violent television characters. The effect of the intervention on reducing peer-nominated aggression was significant only for boys. In a subsequent study with children in first to fourth grade, Rosenkoetter, Rosenkoetter, and Acock (2009) implemented a similar program over a 7-month period with an immediate postintervention measurement and an 8-month follow-up. Participants in the intervention group reported watching less violent television and expressed more critical attitudes about media violence than those in the control group, both immediately postintervention and 8 months later. The short-term effect of reduced identification with violent characters was no longer present at the follow-up. No effect of the intervention on peer-rated aggression was found, neither immediately postintervention nor at the 8-month follow-up.

In a recent study by Möller, Krahé, Busching, and Krause (2012), a sample of 683 seventh and eighth graders in Germany were assigned to two conditions: a 5-week intervention and a no-intervention control group. Measures of exposure to media violence and aggressive behavior were obtained about 3 months before the intervention (Time 1) and about 7 months postintervention (Time 2). The intervention group showed a significantly larger decrease in the use of violent media from Time 1 to Time 2 than the control group. Participants in the intervention group also scored significantly lower on self-reported aggressive behavior (physical aggression and relational aggression) at Time 2 than those in the control group, but the effect was limited to those with high levels of initial aggression. Further analyses revealed that the effect of the intervention on aggressive behavior was mediated by an intervention-induced decrease in the normative acceptance of aggression.

A second approach to prevention involves the limitation of access to violent media contents for children and adolescents. Various age classification systems have been developed to identify media with violent content and designate them as suitable or unsuitable for certain age groups (see Bushman & Cantor, 2003, for a summary of the most commonly rating systems in the United States, the British Board of Film Classification [BBFC] for movie ratings in the United Kingdom, http://www.bbfc.co.uk/, or the Pan European Game Information system [PEGI], http://www.pegi.info/en/). Ratings either employ content labels or age labels, and a meta-analysis of parent polls by Bushman and Cantor (2003) showed that parents overwhelmingly preferred content-based ratings. Empirical analyses have revealed several problems with rating systems (see Gentile & Anderson, 2006, for a summary). First, parents are not familiar or do not use the ratings in regulating their children's media diet (Gentile, 2010). Second, media rated as suitable for children and adolescents often contain substantial levels of violence, and there appears to be a trend over time toward greater tolerance for violent content in media accessible to a younger audience. A historical analysis of movies rated between 1950 and 2006 conducted by Nalkur, Jamieson, and Romer (2010) found a steady increase in violent content in films rated PG-13 (containing material that may be inappropriate for children under 13). Third, ratings are often not matched by consumer perceptions of the same titles, especially for cartoon and fantasy games and for media containing some level of violence, which undermines their perceived validity (Funk, Flores, Buchman, & Germann, 1999; Walsh & Gentile, 2001). Finally, and probably most difficult to amend, warning labels have been found to enhance the appeal of violent media to those whom they should protect. Demonstrating the "forbidden fruit" effect, Bijvank et al. (2009) asked children and adolescents to evaluate the attractiveness of video games that came with different age recommendations or violent content indicators taken from the PEGI system. In line with their predictions, the authors found that adding an age label to a video game made it more attractive to children under the indicated age, and that adding a warning label about violent content equally increased the attractiveness of the game, particularly for boys. Brehm's (1966) psychological reactance theory provides a theoretical explanation of the forbidden fruit effect. He stipulates that having the freedom of choice is a basic need in humans and that reactance arises as an unpleasant emotional state in response to restrictions of that sense of freedom. Increasing the perceived attractiveness of the denied option is seen as a strategic option enabling individuals to alleviate the feeling of reactance by restoring freedom at the psychological level. These findings raise questions about the effectiveness of rating systems and highlight the challenges involved in shielding children and adolescents from violent media content.

Conclusions

Evidence from a large body of research has shown that playing violent video games affects players' readiness to engage in aggressive behavior. There is a consensus in the field that playing violent video games is only one of many risk factors for aggression, and the effects are of small to moderate magnitude. This is not to say, however, that they should be dismissed as irrelevant, as claimed by some critics. Sales figure and user surveys across the world demonstrate that violent video games are highly popular and widely used forms of entertainment, especially in childhood and adolescence. Therefore, even small effect sizes translate into substantial differences in aggressive behavior that may be attributed to the influence of video game violence.

Playing violent video games may affect aggressive behavior through different mechanisms. Immediate effects on aggressive behavior were shown to be mediated by an increase in physiological arousal and aggressive affect, the priming of aggressive thoughts, and the instigation of imitational learning of aggressive acts that were observed or actively carried out in the virtual reality. Habitual violent video game play provides opportunities for sustained observational learning that promotes the development of knowledge structures, such as hostile expectations and attributional styles, and the formation of aggressive scripts. Through the portrayal of violence as normal

and appropriate, media violence strengthens the normative acceptance of aggression that disinhibits aggressive behavior. Finally, repeated exposure to violent media cues leads to reduced physiological and affective arousal by violent media stimuli that is related to a decrease in emotional responsiveness to real-life violence and suffering.

Compared with the wealth of studies investigating the link between video game violence and aggression, research on effective interventions to prevent or mitigate the aggression-enhancing effects of violent media use is only beginning to emerge. In addition to reducing exposure, approaches that promote a critical attitude toward media violence and an understanding of the psychological processes triggered by violent media stimuli have been found to have some success, but more research is needed to develop intervention strategies that take different user characteristics and different types of media into account.

Future Directions

Despite the progress achieved in more than 25 years of research on violent video games, and in research on media violence effects more generally, a number of questions remain unresolved. There are three key questions that should be addressed in future research.

1. What are the long-term effects of habitual use of violent video games that starts in childhood? At present, there are no longitudinal studies on violent video game use beyond adolescence, so it is unclear how the continuous engagement in virtual violence affects aggression in adulthood. In addition, most of the available evidence from longitudinal research is limited to two points in time. However, for a conclusive test of the variables mediating the link between violent video game use and aggression over time, more than two measurement points are required so that the mediators can be assessed as temporal precursors of aggression.

2. Are all heavy users of violent video games equally susceptible to long-term effects on aggression? Whereas several moderators of short-term effects have been identified, longitudinal studies have typically treated additional risk factors for aggression as covariates rather than examining their interaction with violent video game use. For example, it could be the case that violent video game use by individuals low on initial trait aggression does little to increase their aggression, whereas highly aggressive individuals show a further increase if they are heavy users of violent video games. Alternatively, given that high trait aggression tends to persist over time,

it is conceivable that highly aggressive users would remain highly aggressive even if they abstained from playing violent video games, whereas initially less aggressive individuals would be more affected. The findings by Krahé and Möller (2010) provide some support for the latter hypothesis, but further studies are required to clarify the role of trait aggression as a moderator of long-term violent video game effects.

3. A final question refers to the role of gender in the susceptibility to violent video game effects. Is gender simply a marker of differences in usage intensity, with violent games having more appeal for male users, or are there gender-specific effects? For example, it could be the case that female users are more likely to show an increase in relational as compared to physical aggression as a result of violent video game use, given that there is some indication that this is the preferred mode of expression of aggression for females (e.g., Smith, Rose, & Schwartz-Mette, 2010). Studies showing stronger effects of playing violent games that afford a high identification with the aggressor point in this direction.

Notes

1. http://news.bbc.co.uk/2/hi/europe/1959632.stm.

2. The analysis by Anderson et al. (2010) includes the studies covered in earlier meta-analyses from the same research group (Anderson & Bushman, 2001; Anderson, 2004), and the analysis by Ferguson (2007a) includes the studies covered by Ferguson (2007b).

References

Anderson, C. A. (1997). Effects of violent movies and trait aggressiveness on hostile feelings and aggressive thoughts. *Aggressive Behavior, 23,* 161–178.

Anderson, C. A. (2004). An update on the effects of playing violent video games. *Journal of Adolescence, 27,* 113–122.

Anderson, C. A., Berkowitz, L., Donnerstein, E., Huesmann, L. R., Johnson, J. D., Linz, D., et al. (2003). The influence of media violence on youth. *Psychological Science in the Public Interest, 4,* 81–110.

Anderson, C. A. & Bushman, B. J. (2001). Effects of violent video games on aggressive behavior, aggressive cognition, aggressive affect, physiological arousal, and prosocial behavior: A meta-analytic review of the scientific literature. *Psychological Science, 12,* 353–359.

Anderson, C. A., & Carnagey, N. L. (2009). Causal effects of violent sports video games on aggression: Is it competitiveness or violent content? *Journal of Experimental Social Psychology, 45,* 731–739.

Anderson, C. A., Carnagey, N. L., Flanagan, M., Benjamin, A. J., Eubanks, J., & Valentine, J. C. (2004). Violent video games: Specific effects of violent content on aggressive thoughts and behavior. *Advances in Experimental Social Psychology, 36,* 199–249.

Anderson, C. A., & Dill, K. E. (2000). Video games and aggressive thoughts, feelings, and behavior in the laboratory and in life. *Journal of Personality and Social Psychology, 78,* 772–790.

Anderson, C. A., Gentile, D. A., & Buckley, K. E. (2007). *Violent Video Game Effects on Children and Adolescents: Theory, Research, and Public Policy.* New York: Oxford University Press.

Anderson, C. A., Ihori, N., Bushman, B. J., Rothstein, H. R., Shibuya, A., Swing, E. L., et al. (2010). Violent video game effects on aggression, empathy, and prosocial behavior in Eastern and Western countries: A meta-analytic review. *Psychological Bulletin, 136,* 151–173.

Anderson, C. A., & Murphy, C. R. (2003). Violent video games and aggressive behavior in young women. *Aggressive Behavior, 29,* 423–429.

Anderson, C. A., Sakamoto, A., Gentile, D. A., Ihori, N., Shibuya, A., Yukawa, S., et al. (2008). Longitudinal effects of violent video games aggression in Japan and the United States. *Pediatrics, 122,* 1067–1072.

Ashworth, L., Pyle, M., & Pancer, E. (2010). The role of dominance in the appeal of violent media depictions. *Journal of Advertising, 39,* 121–134.

Averill, J. R., Malstrom, E. J., Koriat, A., & Lazarus, R. S. (1972). Habituation to complex emotional stimuli. *Journal of Abnormal Psychology, 80,* 20–28.

Bandura, A. (1983). Psychological mechanisms of aggression. In Geen, R. G., & Donnerstein, E. I. (Eds.), *Aggression: Theoretical and Empirical Reviews*, vol. 1. New York: Academic Press, pp. 1–40.

Bandura, A., Ross, D., & Ross, S. A. (1961). Transmission of aggression through imitation of aggressive models. *Journal of Abnormal and Social Psychology, 63,* 575–582.

Bandura, A., Ross, D., & Ross, S. A. (1963). Vicarious reinforcement and imitative learning. *Journal of Abnormal and Social Psychology, 67,* 601–607.

Barlett, C. P., Anderson, C. A., & Swing, E. L. (2009). Video game effects—Confirmed, suspected, and speculative. *Simulation & Gaming, 40,* 377–403.

Barlett, C., Branch, O., Rodeheffer, C., & Harris, R. (2009). How long do the short-term violent video game effects last? *Aggressive Behavior, 35,* 225–236.

Barlett, C. P., Harris, R. J., & Baldassaro, R. (2007). Longer you play, the more hostile you feel: Examination of first person shooter video games and aggression during video game play. *Aggressive Behavior, 33,* 486–497.

Barlett, C. P., Harris, R. J., & Bruey, C. (2008). The effect of the amount of blood in a violent video game on aggression, hostility, and arousal. *Journal of Experimental Social Psychology, 44,* 539–546.

Bartholow, B. D., & Anderson, C. A. (2002). Effects of violent video games on aggressive behavior: Potential sex differences. *Journal of Experimental Social Psychology, 38,* 283–290.

Bartholow, B. D., Bushman, B. J., & Sestir, M. R. (2006). Chronic violent video game exposure and desensitization to violence: Behavioral and event-related brain potential data. *Journal of Experimental Social Psychology, 42,* 532–539.

Bartholow, B. D., Sestir, M. A., & Davis, E. B. (2005). Correlates and consequences of exposure to video game violence: Hostile personality, empathy, and aggressive behavior. *Personality and Social Psychology Bulletin, 31,* 1573–1586.

Bensley, L., & Van Eenwyk, J. (2001). Video games and real-life aggression: A review of the literature. *Journal of Adolescent Health, 29,* 244–257.

Bijvank, M. N., Konijn, E. A., Bushman, B. J., & Roelofsma, P. H. M. P. (2009). Age and violent-content labels make video games forbidden fruits for youth. *Pediatrics, 123,* 870–876.

Bluemke, M., Friedrich, G., & Zumbach, J. (2010). The influence of violent and nonviolent computer games on implicit measures of aggressiveness. *Aggressive Behavior, 36,* 1–13.

Bösche, W. (2010). Violent content enhances video game performance. *Journal of Media Psychology, 21,* 145–150.

Braun, C. M., & Giroux, J. (1989). Arcade video games: Proxemic, cognitive and content analyses. *Journal of Leisure Research, 21,* 92–105.

Brehm, J. (1966). *A Theory of Psychological Reactance.* Oxford, UK: Academic Press.

Browne, K. D., & Hamilton-Giachritsis, C. (2005).The influence of violent media on children and adolescents: A public health approach. *The Lancet, 365,* 702–710.

Bushman, B. J. (1995). Moderating role of trait aggressiveness in the effects of violent media on aggression. *Journal of Personality and Social Psychology, 69,* 950–960.

Bushman, B. J. (1998). Priming effects of media violence on the accessibility of aggressive constructs in memory. *Personality and Social Psychology Bulletin, 24,* 537–545.

Bushman, B. J., & Anderson, C. A. (2002). Violent video games and hostile expectations: A test of the General Aggression Model. *Personality and Social Psychology Bulletin, 28,* 1679–1686.

Bushman, B. J., & Cantor, J. (2003). Media ratings for violence and sex. *American Psychologist, 58,* 130–141.

Bushman, B. J., & Huesmann, L. R. (2006). Short-term and long-term effects of violent media on aggression in children and adults. *Archives of Pediatrics and Adolescent Medicine, 160,* 348–352.

Bushman, B. J., Rothstein, H. R., & Anderson, C. A. (2010). Much ado about something: Violent video game effects and a school of red herring: Reply to Ferguson and Kilburn (2010). *Psychological Bulletin, 136,* 182–187

Bushman, B. J., & Whitacker, J. L. (2010). Like a magnet: Catharsis beliefs attract angry people to violent video games. *Psychological Science, 21,* 790–792.

Byrne, S. (2009). Media literacy interventions: What makes them boom or boomerang? *Communication Education, 58,* 1–14.

Cantor, J. & Wilson, B. J. (2003). Media and violence: Intervention strategies for reducing aggression. *Media Psychology, 5,* 363–403.

Carnagey, N. L., & Anderson, C. A. (2005). The effects of reward and punishment in violent video games on aggressive affect, cognition, and behavior. *Psychological Science, 16,* 882–889.

Carnagey, N. L., Anderson, C. A., & Bushman, B. J. (2007). The effect of video game violence on physiological desensitization to real-life violence. *Journal of Experimental Social Psychology, 43,* 489–496.

Cohen, J. (1988). *Statistical Power Analysis for the Behavioral Sciences,* 2nd ed. New York: Academic Press.

Christakis, D. A., & Zimmerman, F. J. (2007). Violent television viewing during preschool is associated with antisocial behavior during school age. *Pediatrics, 120,* 993–999.

Crick, N., & Grotpeter, J. K. (1995). Relational aggression, gender, and social-psychological adjustment. *Child Development, 66,* 710–722.

Deselms, J. L., & Altman, J. D. (2003). Immediate and prolonged effects of videogame violence. *Journal of Applied Social Psychology, 33,* 1553–1563.

Dietz, T. L. (1998). An examination of violence and gender role portrayals in video games: Implications for gender socialization and aggressive behavior. *Sex Roles, 38,* 425–442.

Dill, K. E., & Dill, J. C. (1998). Video game violence: A review of the empirical literature. *Aggression and Violent Behavior, 3,* 407–428.

Dill, K. E., Gentile, D. A., Richter, W. A., & Dill, J. C. (2005). Violence, sex, race, and age in popular video games: A content analysis. In Cole, E., & Daniel, J. H. (Eds.), *Featuring Females: Feminist Analyses of Media.* Washington, DC: American Psychological Association, pp. 115–130.

Eastin, M. R. (2006). Video game violence and the female game player: Self-and Opponent gender effects on presence and aggressive thoughts. *Human Communication Research, 32,* 351–372.

Engelhardt, C. R., Bartholow, B. D., Kerr, G. T., & Bushman, B. J. (2011). Thus is your brain on violent video games: Neural desensitization to violence predicts increased aggression following violent video game exposure. *Journal of Experimental Social Psychology, 47,* 1033–1036.

Ferguson, C. J. (2007a). Evidence for publication bias in video game violence effects literature: A meta-analytic review. *Aggression and Violent Behavior, 12,* 470–482.

Ferguson, C. J. (2007b). The good, the bad and the ugly: A meta-analytic review of positive and negative effects of violent video games. *Psychiatric Quarterly, 78,* 309–316.

Ferguson, C. J. (2011). Video games and youth violence: A prospective analysis in adolescents. *Journal of Youth and Adolescence, 40,* 377–391.

Ferguson. C. J., & J. Kilburn. (2009). The public health risks of media violence: A meta-analytic review. *Journal of Pediatrics, 154,* 759–763.

Ferguson, C. J., & Kilburn, J. (2010). Much ado about nothing: The misestimation and overinterpretation of violent video game effects in Eastern and Western nations: Comment on Anderson et al. (2010). *Psychological Bulletin, 136,* 174–178.

Ferguson, C. J., & Rueda, S. M. (2010). The Hitman study: Violent video game exposure effects on aggressive behavior, hostile feelings, and depression. *European Psychologist, 15,* 99–108.

Fischer, P., & Greitemeyer, T. (2006). Music and aggression: The impact of sexual-aggressive song lyrics on aggression-related thoughts, emotions, and behavior towards the same and the opposite sex. *Personality and Social Psychology Bulletin, 32,* 1165–1176.

Fischer, P., Kastenmüller, A., & Greitemeyer, T. (2010). Media violence and the self: The impact of personalized gaming characters in aggressive video games on aggressive behavior. *Journal of Experimental Social Psychology, 46,* 192–195.

Funk, J. B., Baldacci, H. B., Pasold, T., & Baumgardner, J. (2004). Violence exposure in real-life, video games, television, movies, and the internet: Is there desensitization? *Journal of Adolescence, 27,* 23–39.

Funk, J. B., Buchman, D. D., Jenks, J., & Bechtoldt, H. (2003). Playing violent video games, desensitization, and moral evaluation in children. *Applied Developmental Psychology, 24,* 413–436.

Funk, J. B., Flores, G., Buchman, D., & Germann, J. N. (1999). Rating electronic games: Violence is in the eye of the beholder. *Youth and Society, 30,* 283–312.

Gentile, D. A. (2010). Are motion picture ratings reliable and valid? *Journal of Adolescent Health, 47,* 423–424.

Gentile, D. A., & Anderson, C. A. 2006). Violent video games: The effects on youth, and public policy implications. In Dowd, N., & Singer, D. G. (Eds.), *Handbook of Children, Culture and Violence.* Thousand Oaks, CA: Sage, pp. 225–246.

Gentile, D. A., & Gentile, J. R. (2008). Violent video games as exemplary teachers: A conceptual analysis. *Journal of Youth and Adolescence, 37,* 127–141.

Gentile, D. A., Lynch, P. J., Linder, J. L., & Walsh, D. A. (2004). The effects of violent video game habits on adolescent hostility, aggressive behaviors, and school performance. *Journal of Adolescence, 27,* 5–22.

Giumetti, G. W., & Markey, P. M. (2007). Violent video games and anger as predictors of aggression. *Journal of Research in Personality, 41,* 1234–1243.

Haninger, K., & Thompson, K. M. (2004), Content and ratings of teen-rated video games. *Journal of the American Medical Association, 291,* 856–865.

Höynck, T., Mößle, T., Kleimann, M., Pfeiffer, C. & Rehbein, F. (2007). *Jugendmedienschutz bei gewalthaltigen Computerspielen: Eine Analyse der USK-Alterseinstufungen.* [Youth media protection with regard to violent computer games: An analysis of the USK age ratings]. KFN-Forschungsbericht; Nr. 101. Hannover: Kriminologisches Forschungsinstitut Niedersachsen.

Hopf, W., Huber, G., & Weiß, R. (2008). Media violence and youth violence: A 2-year longitudinal study. *Journal of Media Psychology, 20,* 79–96.

Huesmann, L. R. (1998). The role of information processing and cognitive schema in the acquisition and maintenance of habitual aggressive behavior. In Geen, R. G., & Donnerstein, E. (Eds.), *Human Aggression: Theories, Research and Implications for Social Policy.* San Diego: Academic Press, pp. 73–109.

Huesmann, L. R. (2010). Nailing the coffin shut on doubts that violent video games stimulate aggression: Comment on Anderson et al. (2010). *Psychological Bulletin, 136,* 179–181.

Huesmann, R. L., & Kirwil, L. (2007). Why observing violence increases the risk of violent behavior by the observer. In Flannery, D. J., Vazsonyi, A. T., & Waldman, I. (Eds.), *The Cambridge Handbook of Violent Behavior and Aggression.* Cambridge, UK: Cambridge University Press, pp. 545–570.

Huesmann, L. R., Moise-Titus, J., Podolski, C. L., & Eron, L. (2003). Longitudinal relations between children's exposure to TV violence and their aggressive and violent behavior in young adulthood. *Developmental Psychology, 39,* 201–229.

Hummer, T. A., Wang, Y., Mosier, K. M., Kalnin, A. J., Dunn, D. W., & Mathews, V. P (2010). Short-term violent video game play by adolescents alters prefrontal activity during cognitive inhibition. *Media Psychology, 13,* 136–154

Irwin, A. R., & Gross, A. M. (1995). Cognitive tempo, violent video games, and aggressive behavior in young boys. *Journal of Family Violence, 10,* 337–350.

Ivory, J. D., & Kalyanaraman, S. (2007). The effects of technological advancement and violent content in video games on players' feelings of presence, involvement, physiological arousal, and aggression. *Journal of Communication, 57,* 532–555.

Jansz, J. (2005). The emotional appeal of violent video games for adolescent males. *Communication Theory, 15,* 219–241.

Jansz, J., & Martis, R. G. (2007). The lara phenomenon: Powerful female characters in video games. *Sex Roles, 56,* 141–148.

Kirsh, S. J. (2006). *Children, Adolescents, and Media Violence.* Thousand Oaks, CA: Sage.

Kirsh, S. J. (2010). *Media and Youth: A Developmental Perspective.* Oxford, UK: Wiley.

Konijn, E. A., Nije Bijvank, M., & Bushman, B. J. (2007). I wish I were a warrior: The role of wishful identification in the effects of violent video games on aggression in adolescent boys. *Developmental Psychology, 43,* 1038–1044.

Krahé, B., & Möller, I. (2004). Playing violent electronic games, hostile attributional style, and aggression-related norms in German adolescents. *Journal of Adolescence, 27,* 53–69.

Krahé, B., & Möller, I. (2010). Longitudinal effects of media violence on aggression and empathy among German adolescents. *Journal of Applied Developmental Psychology, 31,* 401–409.

Krahé, B., Möller, I., Huesmann, L. R., Kirwil, L., Felber, J., & Berger, A. (2011). Desensitization to media violence: Links with habitual media violence exposure, aggressive cognitions and aggressive behavior. *Journal of Personality and Social Psychology, 100,* 630–646.

Langley, T., O'Neal, E. C., Craig, K. M., & Yost, E. A. (1992). Aggression-consistent, -inconsistent, and -irrelevant priming effects on selective exposure to media violence. *Aggressive Behavior, 18,* 349–356.

Lee, K. M., Peng, W., & Klein, J. (2010). Will the experience of playing a violent role in a video game influence people's judgments of violent crimes? *Computers in Human Behavior, 26,* 1019–1023.

Lemmens, J. S., Valkenburg, P. M., & Peter, J. (2011).The effects of pathological gaming on aggressive behavior. *Journal of Youth and Adolescence, 40,* 38–47.

Lenhart, A., Kahne, J., Middaugh, E., Macgill, A. R., Evans, C., & Vitak, J. (2008). *Teens, Video Games, and Civics. Pew Internet and American Life Project.* Retrieved May 8, 2011 from http://pewinternet.org/~/media//Files/Reports/2008/PIP_Teens_Games_and_Civics_Report_FINAL.pdf.pdf.

Lenhart, A., & Macgill, A. R. (2008). *Over half of American Adults Play Video Games, and Four Out of Five Young Adults Play.* Pew Internet and American Life Project. Available online from: http://www.pewinternet.org/~/media//Files/Reports/2008/PIP_Adult_gaming_memo.pdf.pdf

Lin, S.-F. (2010). Gender differences and the effects of contextual features on game enjoyment and responses. *Cyberpsychology, Behavior, and Social Networking, 13,* 533–537.

Medienpädagogischer Forschungsverbund Süd-West (Ed.) (2010). JIM-Studie 2010. Retrieved May 8, 2011 from http://www.mpfs.de/fileadmin/JIM-pdf10/JIM2010.pdf.

Möller, I., & Krahé, B. (2009). Exposure to violent video games and aggression in German adolescents: A longitudinal analysis. *Aggressive Behavior, 35,* 75–89.

Möller, I., Krahé, B., Busching, R., & Krause, C. (2012). Efficacy of an intervention to reduce the use of media violence and aggression: An experimental evaluation with adolescents in Germany. *Journal of Youth and Adolescence, 41,* 105–120.

Mullin, C. R., & Linz, D. (1995). Desensitization and resensitization to violence against women: Effects of exposure to sexually violent films on judgments of domestic violence victims. *Journal of Personality and Social Psychology, 69,* 449–459.

Nalkur, P. G., Jamieson, P. E., & Romer, D. (2010). The effectiveness of the Motion Picture Association of America's rating system in screening explicit violence and sex in top-ranked movies from 1950 to 2006. *Journal of Adolescent Health, 47,* 440–447.

Ostrov, J., Gentile, D. A., Crick, N. R. (2006). Media exposure, aggression and prosocial behavior during early childhood: A longitudinal study. *Social Development, 15,* 612–627.

Peng, W., Liu, M., & Mou, Y. (2008). Do aggressive people play violent computer games in a more aggressive way? Individual difference and idiosyncratic game play experience. *CyberPsychology & Behavior, 11,* 157–161.

Polman, H., Orobio de Castro, B., & van Aken, M. (2008). Experimental study of the differential effects of playing versus watching violent video games on children's aggressive behavior. *Aggressive Behavior, 34,* 256–264.

Przybylski, A. K., Ryan, R. M., & Rigby, C. S. (2009). The motivating role of violence in video games. *Personality and Social Psychology Bulletin, 35,* 243–259.

Robinson, T. N., Wilde, M. L., Navracruz, L. C., Haydel, K. F., & Varady, A. (2001). Effects of reducing children's television and video game use on aggressive behavior: A randomized controlled trial. *Archives of Pediatric Adolescent Medicine, 155,* 17–23.

Rosenkoetter, L. I., Rosenkoetter, S. E., & Acock, A. C. (2009). Television violence: An intervention to reduce its impact on children. *Journal of Applied Developmental Psychology, 30,* 381–397.

Rosenkoetter, L. I., Rosenkoetter, S. E., Ozretich, R. A., & Acock, A. C. (2004). Mitigating the harmful effects of television violence. *Journal of Applied Developmental Psychology, 25,* 25–47.

Rosenthal, R. R. (1990). Media violence, antisocial behavior, and the social consequences of small effects. In Surette, R. (Ed.), *The Media and Criminal Justice Policy: Recent Research and Social Effects.* Springfield, IL: Charles C Thomas, pp. 53–61.

Rubin, A. M. (2009). Uses and gratifications: An evolving perspective of media effects. In Nabi, R., & Oliver, M. B. (Eds.), *The Sage Handbook of Media Processes and Effects.* Los Angeles: Sage, pp. 147–159.

Schutte, N. S., Malouff, J. M., Post-Gorden, J. C., & Rodasta, A. L. (1988). Effects of playing videogames on children's aggressive and other behaviors. *Journal of Applied Social Psychology, 18,* 454–460.

Sestir, M. A., & Bartholow, B. D. (2010). Violent and nonviolent video games produce opposing effects on aggressive and prosocial outcomes. *Journal of Experimental Social Psychology, 46,* 934–942.

Sherry, J. L. (2001). The effects of violent video games on aggression. A meta-analysis. *Human Communication Research, 27,* 409–431.

Shibuya, A., Sakamoto, A., Ihori, N., & Yukawa, S. (2008). The effects of the presence and contexts of video game violence on children: A longitudinal study in Japan. *Simulation & Gaming, 39,* 528–539.

Slater, M. D., Henry, K. L., Swaim, R. C., & Anderson, L. L. (2003). Violent media content and aggressiveness in adolescents: A downward spiral model. *Communication Research, 30,* 713–736.

Smith, R. L., Rose, A. J., & Schwartz-Mette, R. A. (2010). Relational and overt aggression in childhood and adolescence: Clarifying mean-level gender differences and associations with peer acceptance. *Social Development, 19,* 243–269.

Smith, S. L., Lachlan, K., Pieper, K. M., Boyson, A. R., Wilson, B. J., Tamborini, R., et al. (2004). Brandishing guns in American media: Two studies examining how often and in what context firearms appear on television and in popular video games. *Journal of Broadcasting & Electronic Media, 48,* 584–606.

Smith, S. L., Lachlan, K., & Tamborini, R. (2003). Popular video games: Quantifying the presentation of violence and its context. *Journal of Broadcasting & Electronic Media, 47,* 58–76.

Sparks, G. G., & Sparks, C. W. (2002). Effects of media violence. In Bryant, J., & Zillmann, D. (Eds.), *Media Effects: Advances in Theory and Research,* 2nd ed. Hillsdale, NJ: Lawrence Erlbaum Associates, pp. 269–285.

Uhlmann, E., & Swanson, J. (2004). Exposure to violent video games increases automatic aggressiveness. *Journal of Adolescence, 27,* 41–52.

von Salisch, M., Kristen, A., & Oppl, C. (2007). *Computerspiele mit und ohne Gewalt.* [Computer games with and without violence]. Stuttgart: Kohlhammer.

Walsh, D. A., & Gentile, D. A. (2001). A validity test of movie, television, and video-game ratings. *Pediatrics, 107,* 1302–1308.

Weber, R., Behr, K.-M., Tamborini, R., Ritterfeld, U., & Mathiak, K. (2009). What do we really know about first-person shooter games? An event-related, high resolution content analysis. *Journal of Computer-Mediated Communication, 14,* 1016–1037.

Weber, R., Ritterfeld, U., & Kostygina, A. (2009). Aggression and violence as effects of playing violent video games. In Vorderer, P., & Bryant, J. (Eds.), *Playing Video Games.* London: Routledge, pp. 347–361.

Williams, K. D. (2011). The effects of homophily, identification, and violent video games on players. *Mass Communication and Society, 14,* 3–24.

Zillmann, D. (1979). *Hostility and Aggression.* Hillsdale, NJ: Lawrence Erlbaum Associates.

Zillmann, D., & Bryant, J. (1974). Effect of residual excitation on the emotional response to provocation and delayed aggressive behavior. *Journal of Personality and Social Psychology, 30,* 782–791.

Children, Adolescents, and the Internet: Are There Risks Online?

Ed Donnerstein

Abstract

Media psychologists have studied the impacts of media portrayals for decades. This body of research is rich in both theory and data. Although we know a great deal about traditional media like television, the platforms and devices available to children and adolescents to view and interact with today are far beyond those we studied only a few years ago (see Chapter 2). The media landscape is rapidly changing, and this chapter looks at some of the effects of the Internet and these newer technologies on risk-related behaviors for these audiences. The effects of exposure to violence, sex, food marketing, and the concerns of cyberbullying and sexual exploitation are examined within the context of children and adolescents' increasing move away from traditional media platforms. This is emerging and ongoing research and offers both theoretical and empirical opportunities for the future of media psychology.

Key Words: advergames and internet marketing, cyberbullying, Internet and media violence, new media use, social networking sites

Introduction

There is rarely a week that goes by without some news story on the negative impacts of new technologies and the Internet. I can think back to the story of the college student who committed suicide after his classmates recorded his sexual activities and placed them on the Internet (http://www.reuters.com/article/2011/04/20/us-rutgers-suicide-indictment-idUSTRE73J4NR20110420). These acts, whether to intentionally harm or as a "prank" even prompted the White House to convene in 2011 a summit on the increasing use of cyberbullying. We are also constantly reminded of the perils of sexting, and the ramifications such actions can have for criminal behaviors such as the distribution of child pornography. Or what about the recent findings (Pew, 2010) that 80% of teens with cell phones actually have them in bed, costing hours of needed sleep.

The preceding are just passing examples of how the growing use of technologies by children and adolescents are changing the landscape for what we might consider to be risk factors from media exposure. Over the past decade the American Academy of Pediatrics (2011) has released a series of important policy statements on the effects of media exposure on children and adolescent health. These include (1) media violence, (2) advertising, (3) music videos, (4) sexuality, and (5) overall violence prevention (http://aappolicy.aappublications.org). All of these statements make it quite clear that the mass media can act as a significant risk factor in the health and behavior of many adolescents and children. There are many chapters in this book that discuss this research, and for decades this inquiry into the negative impact of mass media on youth has been a primary issue for media psychologists. The question raised in this chapter, however, is slightly different. In thinking about all the research on mass media effects, the question to be looked at in the pages that follow is, "What is the role of new technology in these issues?"

If we go back to the emerging years of research on media effects, we can certainly see that much has changed. Think about the 1960s, when there was a proliferation of research on media violence. It might be hard to believe, but there were only four major media platforms to consider…movies, print, radio, and television. Even television was restricted to very few channels. In studying the same issue today the platforms in which media can be "viewed" are immense and continually changing. In looking at today's media platforms, Gutnick et al. (2011) note the following: movies, print, radio, television, cable television, home video game consoles, portable music players, DVDs, home computers, portable hand-held video game systems, the Internet, cell phones, MP3 players, DVRs, electronic interactive toys, Internet-connected smart phones, and tablet computers. Furthermore, those few television stations of the 1960s are now in the thousands. Does this change the impact? In some ways the answer is yes. This chapter takes a look at this potential and important change.

Is Anyone Online and Using These Technologies?

The first question we can ask is if these new media platforms are being used by today's youth. The answer is a definite affirmative. In their ongoing analysis of teen Internet use, the Pew Foundation (2009) notes that in the last decade online use has gone from 70% to 95%, home broadband from 8% to 73%, and cell phone use from 30% to 75% among teens (with 83% among 17-year-olds). Wireless connectivity, making the use of these new technologies easier and faster, has also shown substantial increases during this time. In its most recent study of media use, the Kaiser Foundation (2010) found that Internet use among 8- to 18-year-olds has gone from 47% to 84% in the past decade, with more than one-third having such access in their bedrooms. The Kaiser study also indicated that the amount of time viewing TV content had increased over the last decade, but this increase is accounted for primarily by the viewing of such programming over the Internet and mobile devices. Adolescents now spend more than 10 hours a day with some form of media. Perhaps as interesting is the Pew finding (Pew, 2011) that teens actually spend more time contacting their friends via texting (54%) than face-to-face (33%). We should note that these types of findings are not just part of the culture of American youth, but are quite similar in other countries such as England, France, Italy, and most of the European Union (e.g., Livingstone & Haddon, 2009).

Unlike traditional media such as television, the Internet and new technologies (e.g., mobile devices) give children and adolescents access to just about any form of content they can find (e.g., Livingstone & Haddon, 2009). From the perspective of a child or adolescent it does not take much effort to have access to any form of violence, advertising, or sexual behavior, which we can consider risky with regard to health (Donnerstein, 2009, 2011, 2012; Strasburger, Jordan, & Donnerstein, 2010). Furthermore, this can be done in the privacy of their own room with little supervision from their parents.

Might these newer technologies have differing effects than traditional media? Malamuth, Linz, and Yao (2005) have provided a perspective on Internet violence, but I believe their theoretical perspective applies just as equally to all forms of harmful materials. According to these authors, the Internet provides motivational, disinhibitory, and opportunity aspects that make it somewhat different than traditional media in terms of its potential risky impact.

In terms of motivation, the Internet is ubiquitous in that it is always on and can be accessed easily, thus leading to high levels of exposure. In the world of new technology there is no "family-viewing hour." There is little parental supervision and media use today is basically 24/7. Because online activities are often more interactive and engaging, they have the ability for increased learning, both of positive and negatives attitudes and behaviors. The disinhibitory aspect implies that the content is often unregulated, which is quite true given its global reach. Studies suggest that extreme forms of violent or sexual content are more prevalent on the Internet than in other popular media (e.g., Strasburger et al., 2010). Participation is private and anonymous, which allows for the searching of materials a child or adolescent would normally not do with traditional media. There is the suggestion that finding such materials on blogs and chat rooms could increase social support for these images and messages (e.g., sites for bulimia, hate groups). Finally, online media exposure is much more difficult for parents to monitor than media exposure in traditional venues. Opportunity aspects play a more important role in the area of cyberbullying or child sexual exploitation, issues we discuss later. Potential victims are readily available, and the identity of the aggressor is often unknown.

In thinking about the Internet and new media technologies, a number of concerns that are examined in this chapter put youth at risk. These include:

a. Access to traditional media violence (both television/film and video games)
b. Cyberbullying
c. Sexual exploitation, particularly of children
d. Exposure to explicit sexual materials both intentional and accidental
e.Access to unhealthy food marketing

The Internet as a Medium for Media Violence

The Internet, and all the platforms and devices in which it can be accessed, allows the individual to view traditional television/film and video games through live streaming or downloads. For the child or adolescent, access to what might be considered restricted materials (adult rated) is much easier via both legal and "illegal" outlets. A number of chapters in this book examine the effects of media violence both in traditional television/film and also video games. There is no question but that newer technologies have not only expanded the realm of materials, but also sources for viewing (e.g., Donnerstein, 2011). As Malamuth et al. (2005) note, the motivation and disinhibitions once relegated to traditional media have been substantially changed. As the Kaiser survey found (Kaiser, 2010), television content is now part of a multitude of mobile devices, and more readily available. There are a number of theoretical reasons to expect even stronger effects from violence exposure with new technologies. The ability for interaction, rehearsal, repetitiveness, privacy, and other mechanisms all suggest that effects discussed by other scholars in this book would be enhanced.

The Internet and its varying web sites offer another dimension. Web sites offer not only the prospect of viewing more severe violence (e.g., real decapitations and executions), but also access to hate and terrorist groups. Some online archives provide instructions for making bombs or other weapons. Since the events of September 11, 2001, terrorist groups have made extensive use of the Internet to recruit and spread propaganda. The proliferation of hate speech and hate groups has also become easily accessible on the Web. A report by the Simon Wiesenthal Center (2009) indicates that in the past decade there has been a tenfold increase of Internet-based hate groups who make extensive use of social networking sites for recruitment. In an extensive survey of European countries, the EU Kids Online project (Livingstone & Haddon, 2009) found that seeing graphic violent or hateful content was experienced by approximately one-third of teenagers, making it one the higher risk concerns.

Recent research suggests that the types of materials found exclusively on the Internet may have a relationship to aggressive behavior. In a national survey of youth, Ybarra, West, Markow, Leaf, Hamburger, & Boxer (2008) found an association between the viewing of Internet violence and self-reported seriously aggressive behavior. Although exposure to violence in the media overall was related to aggressive behavior, youth who reported that many or all of the web sites they visited depicted real people fighting, shooting, or killing, were five times more likely to report engaging in seriously violent behavior. These types of sites seemed to be "unique" to the Internet and included (1) hate sites; (2) web sites showing pictures of dead people or people dying, or a "snuff" site; (3) web sites showing satanic rituals, (4) web sites showing pictures of war, death, or "terrorism"; or (5) web sites showing cartoons, such as stick people or animals, being beaten up, hurt, or killed. The authors suggest that the interactive environment of the Internet and the depiction of real people engaged in violence many explain the stronger association with reported seriously violent behavior.

Finally, not only can adolescents view violence on the Internet, but they can also create and upload violent materials. The viewer is no longer a passive participant, but now becomes the creator of violent images. Furthermore, they have the ability to place that material across the globe instantaneously. Finally, web sites and in particular social networking sites, blogs, chat rooms, and e-mail allow not only for the creation of aggression, but also the ability to actually aggress against another, in what has been termed *cyberbullying*. We now discuss this important issue.

Cyberbullying

One of the issues over the years that has become of paramount concern is the use of the Internet in terms of aggressing or harassing others. This behavior is referred to as *cyberbullying*, which is an umbrella term related to constructs such as online bullying, electronic aggression, and Internet harassment (Tokunaga, 2010). Cyberbullying involves behaviors such as:

1. Sending unsolicited and/or threatening e-mail
2. Spreading rumors

3. Making inflammatory comments about that than in public discussion areas

4. Impersonating the victim online by sending messages that cause others to respond negatively to this individual

5. Harassing the victim during a live chat or leaving abusive messages on web pages about the victim

Surveys in the United States, Europe, and Australia have indicated that somewhere between 15% and 35% of teens report being bullied online. More interesting is the finding that between 10% and 20% actually admit to bullying others. There are very little gender differences. Girls are just as likely involved in cyberbullying behaviors as boys (e.g., Donnerstein, 2011). We should note that school is still by far the most common place youth report being bullied.

The effects of being a victim of cyberbullying are often the same as children who are bullied in person, which includes such things as a drop in grades, lower self-esteem, or depression. Recent research (Wang, Nansel, & Iannotti, 2010) suggests that the effects of depression in adolescents might even be stronger from cyberbullying. There are a number of reasons why the impact of cyberbullying might be "harsher" to its victims. First, the place the child considers to be the most secure, his or her home and even bedroom, has now become a place where he or she can be a victim. Second, because of the anonymity of the aggressor and the inability to see the victim's reactions, effects can be perceived as more severe. Third, effects can be "forever" in cyberspace. Postings on blogs, web sites, or chat rooms are difficult to remove, and they maintain and prolong the consequences. Finally, for some individuals it may seem totally inescapable because being online for many children and adolescents is the place these individuals socialize and interact with friends. Therefore, it often becomes very difficult to get away from potential online bullying (National Crime Prevention Council, 2009).

Tokunaga (2010) has offered a number of suggestions as to why individuals might engage in cyberbullying compared with traditional forms of bullying:

1. Anonymity is offered through electronic media. The importance of disinhibition plays a significant role in many forms of aggression.

2. It is an opportunistic offense, because the resulting harm can occur without any actual physical interaction. It can take place any time of day or night from any location.

3. There is a lack of supervision or observance by others for the most part, and can require little if any planning.

4. Because of the high anonymity, the threat of being caught has been reduced. Furthermore, there is accessibility; victims can be reached through a number of electronic devices, such as cell phones, e-mail, and instant messaging around the clock and around the globe.

In early 2011 the president of the United States held a White House summit to look at ways to mitigate bullying, with a particular focus on the Internet. This increasing emphasis on a significant social issue should help both focus and facilitate needed research into the causes and prevention in this emerging area among media psychologists.

We should also be cognizant of the use of forms of cyberbullying in dating abuse. The sending of nude photos, deleting friends from Facebook accounts, or using smartphone cameras to harass, are all forms of cyberbullying and within the context of a relationship, dating violence. This is an important social issue. The Liz Claiborne company in conjunction with educational groups has put together an excellent curriculum and overview of this issue (loveisnotabuse.com), which reviews the literature as well as solutions.

Sexual Exploitation

The sending of sexual information over e-mail or postings on bulletin boards by those targeting children has been a continuing social issue. Only recently, Facebook pulled pages from some of its sites linked to pro-pedophilia advocacy groups. As researchers have noted (Mitchell, Finkelhor, Jones, & Wolak, 2010), children are more accessible to offenders through social networking sites, e-mail, and texting because it is anonymous behavior and normally outside the supervision of parents. Children may also find the privacy and anonymity of this type of communication much more conducive for them to have discussions of intimate relationships than to meet in a face-to-face situation. For the potential offender there is certainly easier access to web sites and other Internet groups that encourage and legitimize these types of behavior with children and adolescents.

A comprehensive series of studies on these issues has come from the Crimes Against Children Research Center at the University of New Hampshire. These studies (see Wolak, Finkelhor, Mitchell, & Ybarra, 2008) involved a random national sample of 1,500 children age 10 to 17 interviewed in 2,000 and then an additional sample of 1,500 interviewed in 2005 on youths' experiences with the Internet. The major findings from this study were:

1. There was a 9% increase over the 5-year period (25%–34% of respondents) in exposure to unwanted sexual materials. It is interesting to note that this increase occurred in spite of the fact that more families were using Internet filtering software (>50%) during this period.

2. Fifteen percent of all of the youth reported an unwanted sexual solicitation online in the previous year, with 4% reporting an incident on a social networking site specifically. Perhaps more important, about 4% of these were considered "aggressive" in that the solicitor attempted to contact the user offline. These are the episodes most likely to result in actual victimizations.

3. Additionally, in this study 4% of those surveyed were asked for nude or sexually explicit pictures of themselves.

4. Four percent said they were upset or distressed as a result of these online solicitations.

Although these may be relatively small percentages, these are large-scale national surveys, so the number of youth impacted is actually quite substantial. In discussing and considering the role of the Internet, particularly social networking sites, Mitchell et al. (2010) see these sites as being particularly amenable for sexual exploitation for a number of reasons:

1. It is a safer and easier platform to initiate sexual relationships.

2. One can gather and access information about the victim.

3. It is possible to quickly disseminate information or pictures about the victim.

4. The potential victim feels "safer," and anonymity might facilitate more open sexual disclosure.

Viewing of Sexual Materials

Teens have always searched for sexual materials. The effects of exposure to sexual media are significant and have been reviewed elsewhere (i.e., Wright, Malamuth, & Donnerstein, 2012). Newer technologies, we all agree, make this process easier, faster, and more far-reaching. For example, Salazar, Fleischauer, Bernhardt, and DiClemente (2009) found that 17% of web sites visited by teens were X-rated (sexually explicit) and at least 6% contained

sexual violence. Other studies have shown unwanted and accidental exposure between 50% and 65% for teens (Wolak, Mitchell, & Finkelhor, 2007; Braun-Courville & Rojas, 2009).

There are recent studies that are suggestive of an association between Internet exposure and sexual attitudes and behaviors. Two large-scale, longitudinal surveys of youth conducted in the Netherlands (Peter & Valkenburg, 2008, 2009) found that more frequent "intentional" exposure to sexually explicit Internet material was associated with greater sexual uncertainty and more positive attitudes toward uncommitted sexual exploration (i.e., sexual relations with casual partners/friends or with sexual partners in one-night stands). Additionally, adolescents' exposure to Internet sex predicted stronger beliefs that women are sex objects. In another study, Braun-Courville and Rojas (2009) looked at the sexual behaviors of adolescents in a cross-sectional design in New York. More than 50% of the participants had visited sexually explicit web sites. Analyses revealed that adolescents exposed to these types of sites were more likely to have (1) multiple lifetime sexual partners, (2) had more than one sexual partner in the last 3 months, (3) used alcohol or other substances during their last sexual encounter, and (4) engaged in anal sex. Furthermore, adolescents who visit these sites displayed higher sexual permissiveness scores compared with those who had never been exposed. Finally, a study by Lo and Wei (2005) found that exposure to Internet pornography had a stronger effect on sexual attitudes than exposure to such content in traditional media (e.g., magazines).

At present we do not know the full extent of the influence of the Internet on sexual attitudes and behaviors. However, as Brown and L'Engle (2009) note, "By the end of middle school many teens have seen sexually explicit content not only on the Internet but in more traditional forms of media as well. Such exposure is related to early adolescents' developing sense of gender roles, sexual relationships, and sexual behavior, including perpetration of sexual harassment" (p. 148). As children and adolescents move further away from traditional media to newer technologies it will become increasingly important for researchers to explore the extent and nature of online sexual influence. The ability to have more frequent and explicit exposure (including sexual violence) is now part of the domain of every adolescent who has access to the Internet, and we know that represents the vast majority of youth.

Internet Advertising to Children

For decades there has been a focus on the marketing of unhealthy food products to children. There has always been the understanding that children are a "special" audience who do not have the cognitive abilities to process commercial intent or fully comprehend the differences between an advertisement and a television program. For these and other reasons, there are fairly strict regulations on advertising directly aimed at the child audience. Consequently, traditional media such as television in the United States and in other countries have fairly strict regulations regarding both the amount and the type of advertising that can be directed to children. The Internet, however, can often move away from these regulations. Although there is a recent proposal from the Federal Trade Commission for some regulation guidelines in this area, the adoption by the food industry is voluntary (http://www.ftc.gov/opa/2011/04/foodmarket.shtm).

As an example, the Institute of Medicine of the National Academy of Science recently published a series of studies looking at childhood obesity as a major health issue (i.e., Kunkel & Castonguay, 2011). One concern was food marketing to children, and the proliferation of advertisements that primarily market unhealthy food choices. The research was quite clear on the negative impacts of unhealthy foods being marketed to children in terms of increased obesity and other health-related issues. Although guidelines could be created for traditional media advertising, such as television, the types of ads considered problematic have now crossed over to the Internet.

For example, the Kaiser Foundation (2006) found that more than 85% of companies that advertise to children on television were also providing children with similar forms of advertising on the Internet. In fact the majority of these companies have web sites specifically created for children. In a recent content analysis of these types of sites, Cai and Zhao (2010), found that:

1. 87% of children's most popular web sites include some form of advertising
2. 75% of these web sites offer children the ability to download logos, screensavers, or even wallpapers they could use for their computers
3. 75% of the sites have what are now called *advergames,* in which companies product or brand characters are featured in an online interactive game format

Advergames have been described as web sites that engage children in interesting activities while immersing them in a product-related environment. They also begin to blur the boundaries between commercial and noncommercial content, something that is regulated in traditional media venues (e.g., Kunkel & Castonguay, 2012). Figures 19.1 and 19.2 give an idea of the types of advergames to which children are exposed online. It is interesting to note in Figure 19.2 that for the child to play the game online, he or she needs to purchase the actual product (e.g., a sugary cereal) to participate.

In a recent review of children and advertising that looked at both the effects and policy regulations within the mass media, Kunkel and Castonguay (2011) noted the following with respect to the Internet:

1. The type of food ads that are most heavily advertised on television are also strongly featured online.
2. The pattern of marketing of unhealthy foods to children seen on television are now being replicated on the Internet.
3. A child's ability to discriminate a commercial from other material on the Internet seems to be much more difficult than it is for the child to do this on traditional media, such as television.

Conclusion

In this book there are a number of chapters that examine the "harmful" impacts of exposure to the mass media, particularly with regard to children and adolescents. Unlike more traditional media such as television, in which we have an abundance of research conducted over the decades, there is general agreement that considerably more research is needed with regard to the Internet in its role as a technology for the learning, social, and cognitive development of children and adolescents. We need to expand our understanding of these new technologies as even more youth come online and the technology itself changes. After all, 5 years ago we would have hardly discussed the impacts of social networking sites or smartphones.

This chapter was not intended to review media effects such as violence, video games, or children's advertising. This is well covered in other chapters. Rather, the intent was to expand the discussion to newer technologies, in particular the Internet, so that we can begin to examine the varying media youth have at their disposal for being exposed to what we consider risk-related content.

As I have suggested elsewhere (Donnerstein, 2011), the issue of Internet effects is at a place that

Figure 21.1 Example of a Food-Related Web Site.
From Donnerstein, E. (2009). The role of the internet. In Strasburger, V., Wilson, B., & Jordan, A. (Eds.), Children, Adolescents and the Media, 2nd ed. Thousand Oaks, CA: Sage, pp. 471–498.

video game violence was a decade ago. There are a good deal of speculation and theoretical assumptions to assume that the Internet will be a substantial factor in the development of children's attitudes and behaviors in areas that we might consider risky. Video game research was fortunate to have solid empirical and theory-driven research (e.g., Anderson, Gentile & Buckley, 2007; Anderson et al., 2010) to establish

Figure 21.2 Example of an Advergame on the Same Web Site.
From Donnerstein, E. (2009). The role of the internet. In Strasburger, V., Wilson, B., & Jordan, A. (Eds.), *Children, Adolescents and the Media,* 2nd ed. Thousand Oaks, CA: Sage, pp. 471–498.

our knowledge base of effects in this area. We are beginning to see this within the realm of research on the Internet and new technologies.

In thinking about the future of this inquiry, a number of scholars have pointed to research areas that need specific consideration (i.e., Livingstone & Haddon, 2009; McDonald et al., 2009). Some of these recommendations are as follows:

1. Longitudinal research to examine the causal relationships between online participation and engaging in risk related behaviors like aggression and sexual behaviors
2. The major risk factors (i.e., individual, environmental, social) that are related to a child or adolescent "acting" on this Internet exposure
3. Given the increasing use of the Internet by younger children (<12), there is a need for specific research on this population. In particular there is a strong need for research for those less than 6 years of age, who have less capacity to "cope" with riskier online content.
4. Research on expanding platforms such as mobile phones and virtual game environments as well as peer-to-peer exchanges. We are now beginning to see expanding research on social networking sites.
5. Increased research on public health issues such as self-harm, suicide, drugs, and addiction

A recent special issue of the *Journal of Adolescent Health* was devoted to the emerging issue of electronic media and adolescent aggression (Ferdon & Hertz, 2007). In one article, Huesmann (2007) comments on the emergence of newer technologies and notes the decades of research and theory on traditional media. He notes that this extensive research and theory development provided the media psychology research community with significant insights into the role new technology might play in the development of child and adolescent behaviors. In many ways, "The technology conduit may be changing, but the influential processes (e.g., priming, activation and desensitization) may be the same" (Ferdon & Hertz, 2007).

References

American Academy of Pediatrics (2011). *AA Policy.* Retrieved July 13, 2012 from http://aappolicy.aappublications.org/

Anderson, C. A., Gentile, D. A., & Buckley, K. E. (2007). *Violent Video Game Effects on Children and Adolescents.* New York: Oxford University Press.

Anderson, C. A., Shibuya, A, Ihori, N, Swing, E. L., Bushman, B. J. Sakamoto, A., et al. (2010). *Violent video game effects on aggression, empathy, and prosocial behavior in eastern and western countries: A meta-analytic review. Psychological Bulletin, 136*(2), 151–173.

Braun-Courville, D., & Rojas, M (2009). *Exposure to sexually explicit web sites and adolescent sexual attitudes and behaviors. Journal of Adolescent Health, 45,* 156–162.

Brown, J. D., & L'Engle, K. L. (2009). *X-rated: Sexual attitudes and behaviors associated with U.S. early adolescents' exposure to sexually explicit media. Communication Research, 36,* 129–135.

Cai, X., & Zhao, X. (2010). *Click here, kids! Online advertising practices on popular children's websites. Journal of Children and Media, 4,* 134–154.

Donnerstein E. (2009). The role of the internet. In Strasburger, V., Wilson, B., & Jordan, A. *Children, Adolescents and the Media,* 2nd ed. Thousand Oaks, CA: Sage, pp. 471–498.

Donnerstein, E. (2011). The media and aggression: From TV to the Internet. In Forgas, J., Kruglanski, A., & Williams, K. (Eds). *The Psychology of Social Conflict and Aggression.* New York: Psychology Press, pp. 267–284.

Donnerstein, E. (2012). The Internet as "fast and furious" content. In Warburton, W., & Braunstein, D. (Eds). *Growing Up Fast and Furious.* Sydney: The Federation Press.

Federal Trade Commission (2011). *Interagency Working Group Seeks Input on Proposed Voluntary Principles for Marketing Food to Children.* Retrieved July 13, 2012 from http://www.ftc.gov/opa/2011/04/foodmarket.shtm

Ferdon, C. D., & Hertz, M. F. (2007). *Electronic media, violence, and adolescents: An emerging public health problem. Journal of Adolescent Health, 41,* S1–S5.

Gutnick, A., Robb, M., Takeuchi. L., & Kotler, J. (2011). *Always Connected: The New Digital Media Habits of Young Children.* New York: Joan Ganz Cooney Center.

Huesmann, R. L. (2007). *The impact of electronic media violence: Scientific theory and research. Journal of Adolescent Health, 41,* S6–S13.

Kaiser Family Foundation. (2006). *It's Child's Play: Advergames and the Online Marketing of Food to Children.* Menlo Park, CA: Kaiser.

Kaiser Family Foundation (2010). *Generation M2: Media in the Lives of 8- to 18-Year-Olds.* Menlo Park, CA: Kaiser.

Kunkel, D., & Castonguay, J. (2012). Children and television advertising: content, comprehension, and consequences. In Singer, D., & Singer, J. (Eds). *Handbook of Children and the Media.* Thousand Oaks, CA: Sage.

Livingstone, S., & Haddon, L. (2009). *EU Kids Online: F inal Report.* LSE, London: EU Kids Online. Retrieved July 13, 2012 from http://www2.lse.ac.uk/media@lse/research/EUKidsOnline/EU%20Kids%20Online%20reports.aspx

Lo, V., & Wei, R. (2005). *Exposure to Internet pornography and Taiwanese adolescents' sexual attitudes and behavior. Journal of Broadcasting & Electronic Media, 49,* 221–237.

Malamuth, N., Linz, D., & Yao, M. Z. (2005). The Internet and aggression: Motivation, disinhibitory and opportunity aspects. In Amichai-Hamburger, Y. (Ed.), *The Social Net: Human Behavior in Cyberspace.* New York: Oxford University Press, pp. 163–191.

McDonald, H. S., Horstmann Strom, K. J., & Pope, M. W. (2009). *The Impact of the Internet on Deviant Behavior and Deviant Communities.* Durham, NC: Duke University, The Institute for Homeland Security Solutions. Retrieved July 13, 2012 from www.ihssnc.org

Mitchell, K., Finkelhor, D., Jones, L., & Wolak, J. (2010). *Use of social networking sites in online sex crimes against minors: An examination of national incidence and means of utilization. Journal of Adolescent Health, 47,* 183–190.

National Crime Prevention Council (2009). Retrieved July 13, 2012 from http://www.ncpc.org/

Peter, J., & Valkenburg, P. M. (2008). *Adolescents' exposure to sexually explicit Internet material, sexual uncertainty, and attitudes toward uncommitted sexual exploration: Is there a link?* Communication Research, 35, 579–602.

Peter, J., & Valkenburg, P. M. (2009). *Adolescents' exposure to sexually explicit internet material and notions of women as sex objects: Assessing causality and underlying processes. Journal of Communication, 59, 407–433.

Pew Foundation (2009). *The Pew Internet & American Life Project.* Philadelphia: The Pew Charitable Trusts.

Pew Foundation (2011). *The Pew Internet & American Life Project.* Philadelphia: The Pew Charitable Trusts.

Salazar, L., Fleischauer, P. J., Bernhardt, J. M., & DiClemente, R. (2009). Sexually explicit content viewed by teens on the Internet. In Jordan, A., Kunkel, D., Manganello, J., and Fishbein, M. (Eds.), *Media Messages and Public Health: A Decision Approach to Content Analysis* . New York: Routledge, pp. 116–136.

Simon Wiesenthal Center. (2009). www.wiesenthal.com.

Strasburger, V. C., Jordan, A. B., & Donnerstein, E. (2010). *Health effects of media on children and adolescents. Pediatrics, 125, 756–767.

Tokunaga, R. (2010). *Following you home from school: A critical review and synthesis of research on cyberbullying victimization. Computers in Human Behavior, 26, 277–287.

Wang, J., Nansel, T., & Iannotti, R. (2010). *Cyber and traditional bullying: Differential association with depression. Journal of Adolescent Health, 48*(4), 415–417.

Wolak, J., Mitchell K. J., & Finkelhor, D. (2007). *Unwanted and wanted exposure to online pornography in a national sample of youth internet. Pediatrics, 119, 247–257.

Wolak, J., Finkelhor, D., Mitchell, K. J., & Ybarra, M. L. (2008). *Online "predators" and their victims: myths, realities, and implications for prevention and treatment. American Psychologist, 63, 111–128.

Wright, P., Malamuth, N. & Donnerstein, E. (2012). Research on sex in the media: What do we know about effects on children and adolescents. In Singer, D., & Singer, J. (Eds). *Handbook of Children and the Media.* Thousand Oaks, CA: Sage.

Ybarra, M. L., West, M. D., Markow, D., Leaf, P. J., Hamburger, M., & Boxer, P. (2008). *Linkages between Internet and other media violence with seriously violent behavior by youth. Pediatrics, 122, 929–937.

Pathological Technology Addictions: What Is Scientifically Known and What Remains to Be Learned

Douglas A. Gentile, Sarah M. Coyne, *and* Francesco Bricolo

Abstract

Several case studies, research studies, and anecdotal reports suggest that there is a subset of people for whom computer, Internet, and video games have several of the symptoms of a dysfunctional compulsive disorder, often referred to in the popular press as an *addiction*. Although several scientific studies have measured various facets of this issue, there has been no common framework within which to view these studies. This chapter examines the international literature, and finds that there is robust construct validity (via convergent validity and comorbidity) for pathological technology use, regardless of how individual researchers have defined or measured it. Most measurement approaches demonstrate high reliability. Most studies show broad patterns of construct validity similar to other "addictions." Pathological use also shows some evidence of predictive validity. Questions concerning definitional issues are raised, and a common set of diagnostic criteria are proposed. Several questions remain to be studied, including the prevalence of pathological technology use, its etiology, its course, and the best way to diagnose and treat it. Nonetheless, it is clear that some people are already suffering from problems associated with pathological use, and the psychiatric and psychological communities would benefit from a common framework within which to approach and study it.

Key Words: addiction, computer, impulse control disorders, Internet, video games

Introduction

Over fifteen years have passed since the brief but important debate over the "Internet and the future of psychiatry" (Huang & Alessi, 1996; Stein, 1997). That debate focused on a lack of research on potentially problematic uses of computers and the Internet. However, since then there have been several reports of psychopathological symptoms correlated with the use of digital technology, including Internet, computer, video game, and cell phone "addiction" (Yoo et al., 2004; Choo et al., 2010). Most of the early reports of technology addiction were case studies, but researchers have recently begun demonstrating the psychometric properties of tests for diagnosing pathological computer-related behaviors, and have begun testing the construct validity of pathological technology use. However, for this work to advance,

a common framework is needed. The purpose of this chapter is to review the international literature within such a common framework and describe what is known at this time as well as what remains to be studied.

Many people speak colloquially about the Internet or video games being "addicting." This seems intuitively understandable, as many of us have felt compelled to send one more e-mail or play just one more game of *Solitaire* before bed. However, it is critical that we not mistake this phenomenological feeling for a clinically significant issue. As yet, there is no diagnosis for technology addiction. Furthermore, there is still considerable debate about how to define addictions in general (Shaffer, Hall, & Vander Bilt, 2000; Shaffer & Kidman, 2003; Shaffer, LaPlante, LaBrie, Kidman, Donato, & Stanton, 2004). This debate is made more complex by virtue of the fact that the conceptual framework within which diagnoses are made is constantly changing. The purpose of this chapter is not to resolve that debate, but to summarize what is and is not known about the reliability and validity of problematic uses of technology.

Technology use can cause changes in users' thoughts, feelings, and behaviors, and as technologies change their effects can change (Kipnis, 1997). Also, new technologies often engender worries about problems associated with them (West, 1988). It is necessary to maintain an open mind about these claims, but to require scientific evidence before accepting them. Because this is a young research area, it is has been argued that researchers should take a holistic approach in this stage of the research (Galimberti, 1999; Tisserand, 2000). We do not consider digital technologies to be "bad." They are tools, and are used in a positive and healthy manner by most people. However, some people may misuse these tools. Just as washing oneself is a positive and healthy behavior, if one cannot control the impulse to wash and this disrupts other healthy functioning, it is a problem that requires treatment. Our interest is not to condemn digital technologies, but to promote the healthy use of them.

Our current conceptual framework includes two primary facets. First, if pathological technology use exists, it should demonstrate similar morphological characteristics to other behavioral "addictions," such as pathological gambling. Second, we argue that different computer-based technologies evidence similar disorders. Therefore, we will use the term *pathological technology use* (PTU) to include use of computers, Internet, cell phones and video games, because each of them requires a computer processor (even a hand-held video game, such as *a Nintendo DS* or *PSP*). Furthermore, as will be shown, the pattern of diagnosable symptoms and outcomes appears similar regardless of the particular technology or platform used.

Early Anecdotal Evidence and Case Studies

Early reports provided anecdotal evidence of video games being "addicting." For example, two counselors reported in 1983 about a student seeking help with an addiction to *Pac-Man*.

> Symptoms of video game addiction proved similar to other addictions: compulsive behavioral involvement, lack of interest in other activities, association mainly with other addicts, and, in this particular instance, failing grades due to diminished school

activity.... After an episode of overindulgence, the student reported feelings of guilt, anger, and helplessness in controlling his actions. When he tried to stop, he developed physical as well as mental symptoms; he broke out in a sweat and got the "shakes." (Soper & Miller, 1983, p. 40)

Keepers (1990) reported a case study of a 12-year-old boy who had stolen money from both parents, a sister, a brother, other adults, and had even stolen and cashed forged checks of up to $100 to support his *Ms. Pac-Man* habit. He regularly skipped school to play video games, and consequently, his grades dropped from As and Bs to Ds and Fs. He had ended standing friendships and replaced them with other friends whose primary interests were video gaming. He reported attaining an "intensely pleasurable, concentrated state" while playing, during which he was unaware of the passage of time or his surroundings (p. 49). During the early phases of his treatment in a residential home, he routinely obsessed about video games, although there were none present in the treatment facility. During treatment, it became clear to the clinicians that the video game playing was in part an escape response to marital and family conflicts in his family.

In a national phone and Web-based survey of 596 Internet users, 100% of "dependent" respondents reported academic, relationship, financial, and occupational problems because of their Internet use (Young, 1997). Students were reported to have difficulty being alert in class, studying, and completing assignments, resulting in poor grades for many, and academic probation and even expulsion for some. Nonstudents reported damage to their relationships, including one mother forgetting "such things as to pick up her children after school, to make them dinner, and to put them to bed" because of obsessive Internet use. Dependent respondents reported significant financial and work problems. They also reported becoming angry and resentful when others tried to reduce their computer use, and lying about their use, which over time hurt the quality of their relationships as trust was eroded.

Griffiths (2000) provided five case studies of adolescents and adults showing multiple problems with video game, computer, and Internet abuse. For example, Gary, a 15-year-old, reported averaging at least 3 to 4 hours a day on the computer, with more on weekends and holidays, resulting in his school work suffering. He viewed the computer as his "friend," and showed a lack of confidence when dealing with peers, resulting in greater withdrawal from them and increased depression. As his computing increased, he became less willing to participate in household chores and provoked confrontational situations with his family.

Surveys of the massively multiplayer online role-playing game *EverQuest* players show a high incidence of players saying they feel like they are addicted. For example, in a survey of 2,328 *EverQuest* players, 35% say they "definitely" consider themselves addicted to it, and 27% say they "probably" are addicted (Yee, 2001, 2002). In addition, 77% say they sacrifice other activities in their lives to be able to play the game, including sleep, work, school, and time with friends and family (Griffiths, Davies, & Chappell, 2004a). One man, age 28, stated:

> I am addicted to EQ and I hate it and myself for it. When I play I sit down and play for a minimum of 12 hours at a time, and I inevitably feel guilty about it, thinking there are a large number of things I should be doing instead, like reading or furthering my education or pursuing my career. But I can't seem to help myself; it draws me in every time. I have been out of work now for over a month and now find myself in a stressful, depressed state that is only quelled when I am playing EQ, because it's easy to forget about real world troubles and problems, but the problem is when you get back to the real world, problems and troubles have become bigger, and it's a bad, bad cycle. I've tried quitting seriously on several occasions, but I was shocked to find each time that the experience reminds of what I've heard quitting heroin is like. There are serious withdrawal pangs, anxiety, and a feeling of being lost and not quite knowing what next to do with yourself. (Yee, 2001, p. 67)

Finally, several news reports document excessive computer and video game use, with extreme results. For example, a 21-year-old American man who played *EverQuest* for 12 hours a day apparently had psychotic episodes after prolonged play and ultimately committed suicide (Miller, 2002). Two South Korean men died after excessive play, one playing for 50 hours straight (Reuters News Service, 2005b) and one for 86 hours straight (Associated Press, 2002). These and other tragedies have caused several countries to consider various measures designed to curb people's amount of online gaming (Reuters News Service, 2005a).

These types of reports confirmed that some users of computer and game technologies exhibit symptoms that are almost identical to the symptoms of substance and behavioral addictions. A substantial and growing body of research has attempted to define the problem with some success, although the approach has largely been piecemeal.

Definitional Issues

There is a debate over whether using the term *addiction* is reasonable when discussing computer or video game behavior (Blaszczynski, 2008; Turner, 2008; Wood, 2008; Byun et al., 2009; Griffiths, 2009). The term is not well-defined as used in the popular media and vernacular speech. This potential confusion has been mirrored in academic publications. For example, in one study of "cyber-game addiction," the authors state that they use the terms *habit* and *addiction* as interchangable synonyms (Chou & Ting, 2003). They discuss consumption behaviors as "rational addictions," in which people anticipate the outcomes of their behaviors (based on past experiences) and choose to form habits and addictions to maximize the positive outcomes they desire. The authors do note that there is an irrational aspect to habits and addictions, and provide data to support that point. Yet, the blurring of a line between habits and addictions seems unnecessary and unwise.

The line has been blurred further by discussions of "positive addictions" (Glasser, 1976; Shapira et al., 2003). Positive addictions have been defined as habitual behaviors that are considered good for the individual, rather than destructive. Some have gone so far as to suggest that perhaps addiction is a meaningless term, other than to serve pejorative aims. "The idea that people can generate their own internal addictive pharmacology can be applied to all sorts of behaviors other than gambling and drug-taking, including such valued activities as playing the violin, walking to the North Pole, or becoming a Member of Parliament" (Davies, 1992, p. 73). It seems to us that for the term *addiction* to have any meaning, it must refer to something clinically significant. This brings up a second problem with using *addiction* to refer to technology use.

Addiction, as often used in the psychological literature, refers to a physiological dependence on a chemical substance. But this too is nonspecific. The *Diagnostic and Statistical Manual of Mental Disorders,* 4th Revision (DSM-IV) currently recognizes both substance addictions and what we might consider behavioral addictions, such as compulsive gambling (American Psychiatric Association, 1994). However, the DSM-IV does not use the term *addiction* to describe either the pathological use of substances or compulsive gambling or other so-called addictive behaviors (although it appears that the upcoming

DSM-V will: http://www.dsm5.org/proposedrevision/pages/substanceuseandaddictivedisorders.aspx). Instead, the DSM-IV uses the terms *dependence, abuse, intoxication,* and *withdrawal* for substances and *pathological* gambling for gambling disorders.

Even if an addiction is behavioral rather than substance based, it is likely that physiology is still involved. The brain produces its own opiates, endorphins, in response to high arousal. In response to winning at a slot machine, a person is likely to release endorphins and feel a consequent rush of good feelings. Over time, tolerance may develop, and it may take a larger "win" to get the same effect. One study showed that problem gamblers have higher increases in dopamine levels while playing blackjack than nonproblem gamblers (Meyer et al., 2004). Endogenous dopamine release in the brain has also been shown to occur during video game play, and this release is positively correlated with performance (Koepp et al., 1998).

In defining technology addiction, the critical dimension that divides pathological from nonpathological feelings and behaviors is whether they are dysfunctional. In fact, clinicians often use this criterion of dysfunction to categorize other behaviors as pathological or not. In the case of video games, for example, playing is not initially pathological, but becomes pathological for some when the activity becomes dysfunctional, harming the individual's social, occupational, family, school, and psychological functioning. It is for this reason that we are not currently including television in our definition of technology addiction—we do not believe there are sufficient data yet to demonstrate dysfunction because of television use (whereas there are a lot of data with computers and video games). In fact, the seminal article on television addiction is titled, "Television Addiction Is No Mere Metaphor" (Kubey & Csikszentmihalyi, 2002). Unfortunately, there are very little data to support this view at this point in time, although we recognize that future studies may change this.

Critical Features of Addictions

Several validated approaches to defining addictions exist. Brown, for example, summarized six core facets for the presence of addiction (1991). These are:

1. *Salience:* The activity dominates the person's life, either cognitively or behaviorally.
2. *Euphoria/relief:* The activity provides a "high."
3. *Tolerance:* Greater activity is needed to achieve the same "high."

4. *Withdrawal symptoms:* The person experiences unpleasant physical effects or negative emotions when unable to engage in the activity.
5. *Conflict:* The activity leads to conflict with others, work, or the self.
6. *Relapse and reinstatement:* The activity is continued despite attempts to abstain from it.

The DSM-IV sets out 10 criteria that are indicative of pathological gambling (American Psychiatric Association, 1994). Together they comprise a biosocial-psychological perspective on addiction by including symptoms at several levels of analysis. They include:

1. Is cognitively preoccupied with gambling (cognitive salience)
2. Needs to gamble with increasing amounts of money to achieve the desired excitement (tolerance)
3. Feels restless or irritable when attempting to cut down or stop (withdrawal symptoms)
4. Gambles as a way of escaping from problems or relieving a dysphoric mood (euphoria or mood modification)
5. After losing money, often returns to get even (behavioral salience)
6. Lies to family members or others about the extent of gambling (conflict: antisocial behavior that damages relationships)
7. Commits illegal acts to finance gambling (conflict: antisocial behavior)
8. Has jeopardized or lost a significant job, relationship, or educational or career opportunity because of gambling (conflict: damage to other important areas of life)
9. Has repeated unsuccessful efforts to control, cut back, or stop gambling (relapse and reinstatement)
10. Relies on others to provide money to relieve desperate financial situations (conflict: damage to relationships/codependency)

Using this scheme, people are classified as pathological gamblers if they exhibit at least five of the ten symptoms. This approach seems appropriate. Although pathological gamblers as a group show these symptoms, any individual is only likely to present a subset of them, and each individual may present a different subset.

Defining Technology Addictions

Most researchers attempting to define pathological technology use have modified the DSM criteria

(APA, 1994) or Brown's (1991) definitions. In general, although some researchers have added or subtracted individual elements, most researchers have adapted the DSM compulsive gambling criteria in defining computer addiction, video game addiction, and Internet addiction.

We suggest the term *pathological technology use* (PTU) based on the principle that the technologies are not in themselves "bad" or "good" in the way that some substances are in themselves physically harmful. Instead, the problem is attributed to the use.

If these criteria for definition are adopted, then one additional issue may be resolved. If PTU is a unique problem, then it would fit most clearly under the current DSM-IV Axis I category "impulse-control disorders not elsewhere classified." Understanding such a disorder as an impulse control disorder may be beneficial for understanding the nature of the problem, and suggests potential avenues for treatment, although there is little research yet either to confirm or disconfirm this hypothesis (Gentile et al., 2011). Nonetheless, considering whether PTU fits better as an impulse-control disorder or an addictive disorder similar to substance disorders may be a false dichotomy. Perhaps it would be best simply to note that pathology is defined by the compromising of multiple areas of life (e.g., family, health, work). The DSM currently is based on a descriptive framework, addictions are broader than substance-related disorders, and the science of addiction is still evolving (NIDA, 2010).

Regardless of how one settles on definitions, it is important to determine whether there is sufficient evidence that PTU satisfies several basic criteria. Four issues relevant to this question have been addressed in the scientific literature: the reliability, construct, predictive validity, and comorbidity of pathological technology use. It is important to demonstrate each of these before concluding that pathological technology use is potentially clinically significant.

Research on the Reliability of Measurement

Researchers have measured pathological technology use in several ways, and most have shown sufficient reliability. Most studies have used scales based on the DSM-III-R or DSM IV pathological gambling criteria (Fisher, 1994; Griffiths & Dancaster, 1995; Phillips, Rolls, Rouse, & Griffiths, 1995; Griffiths & Hunt 1995, 1998; Griffiths, 1997; Salguero & Moran, 2002; Tejeiro Salguero, Bersabé Morán, 2002; Chou & Ting, 2003; Chiu, Lee, & Huang, 2004; Nichols & Nicki, 2004; Johansson & Götestam, 2004a; Grüsser, Thalemann, Albrecht, & Thalemann, 2005; Charlton & Danforth, 2007; Gentile, 2009; Meerkerk, Van Den Eijnden, Vermulst, & Garretsen, 2009; Choo, Gentile, Sim, Li, Khoo, & Liau, 2010). Most show reliability of α = .70 or higher. For example, Lemmens, Valkenburg, and Peter (2009) created a 21-item scale, and then a shortened seven-item scale that measured the seven underlying criteria described by Brown (1991). They used structural equation modeling and found that a second-order factor model (using the seven criteria) fit the data best. Furthermore, both scales showed high reliabilities (α = .81 to .94).

Several other studies have used or adapted Young's 20-item scale on Internet addiction (also based on Brown's 1991 criteria, on which respondents provide answers on a five-point Likert scale [rarely to always], yielding a continuous total score ranging from 20 to 100) (Young, 1998). Although one study of 535 Korean elementary school children reports a high reliability (α = .92) (Yoo et al., 2004), a second conducted a factor analysis of the data from 86 adults and found that the 20 items cluster into six distinct factors (Widyanto & McMurran, 2004).

Although most studies have defined technology addictions by basing them on DSM or Brown's criteria, other approaches exist in the literature. LaRose, Mastro, and Eastin (2001) used only four items to measure perceived Internet addiction (e.g., I use the Internet so much it interferes with other activities). These four items did not correspond clearly with DSM criteria, and were scored on a seven-point Likert scale (verbally anchored from strongly agree to strongly disagree) rather than on the presence of symptoms. The approach taken by the DSM is to note the presence or absence of particular symptoms, although in clinical practice, clinicians tend to pay attention to the severity of symptoms rather than solely their presence. Nonetheless, the reliability reported was acceptable (α = .77). Other researchers have also set their own criteria for Internet or gaming addiction with acceptable reliability (Ng & Wiemer-Hastings, 2005; Wan & Chiou, 2006). Finally, some researchers have teamed with companies such as Nielsen to measure actual computer and online behavior, rather than self-reports of behaviors, demonstrating that this may be a valuable (although expensive) approach (Bricolo, Gentile, Smelser, & Serpelloni, 2007). It should be noted, however, that this approach only allows for measuring online activities, and does not provide evidence of how those activities may disrupt other areas of life.

Despite the methodological differences in construct measurement and the wide differences in populations (both in terms of age and culture), almost all the preceding studies displayed high reliability and unidimensionality of the "addiction" construct. The strongest results appear to be displayed by those studies using a checklist approach based on DSM criteria (including Brown's summary of DSM criteria). Nonetheless, the fact that the construct is robust across measurement approaches and participants is good evidence that there is a reliable construct worth measuring.

Research on Construct Validity: Convergent Validity

If pathological technology use is a valid construct, it should show construct validity in several salient domains, such as showing convergent validity with several other indicators. For example, the DSM diagnostic criteria focus on aspects of tolerance, withdrawal, damage to ability to function in social and occupational lives, and so on, but one symptom that is not asked is how *much* one uses a substance or gambles. This is appropriate, because regular or even heavy use is not a necessary indicator of addiction (McMurran, 1994). However, if pathological tech users did *not* spend more time with technology than nonaddicted users, it would be evidence for a lack of validity in the construct. Several behaviors can be hypothesized to co-occur with pathological use that show (or fail to show) convergent validity. These include, but are not limited to large amounts of time spent with them, an awareness of feeling "addicted," attempts to control the amount of use, use as a way to control stress, and having more emotional reactivity to technology. Gentile (2009) described several potential variables that could demonstrate the construct validity of pathological game use, and we expand on them here. As is shown in Table 22.1, there is robust convergent validity between measures of pathological use, regardless of the method of measurement or the particular medium studied (i.e., computer, video games, Internet). As would be predicted, pathological users spend more time with their medium, they are more heavily engaged with it (they know more about it, they use it more extensively), they show some evidence of tolerance (at least with regard to violent content), they use it as a stress-coping tool, and they and others are likely to feel concerned about their own use.

Research on Construct Validity: Comorbidity

Another domain in which pathological technology use should show construct validity is correlations with other problems or risk factors. If PTU is similar to other addictions, then "addicted" individuals should show patterns of correlations and comorbidity similar to other addictions. These include but are not limited to higher incidence of depression, likelihood of attention deficit disorders, trait hostility, antisocial behaviors, aggressive behaviors, poorer school performance, being male (e.g., nearly two-thirds of individuals with pathological gambling are male), lower parent education, lower self-esteem, and higher substance use (APA, 1994).

As is shown in Table 21.2, there is fairly robust convergent validity with pathological use, regardless of the method of measurement or the particular medium studied (i.e., computer, video games, Internet). As predicted, pathological users show patterns of correlations and comorbidity similar to those found in other addictions. Some researchers have measured other clinical disorders and have found that pathological technology users often show comorbidity with psychiatric disorders (Black, Belsare, & Schlosser, 1990; Shapira, Goldsmith, Keck, Khosla, & McElroy, 2000). Shapira et al. (2003) summarized those studies and noted that the most typical comorbid or primary disorders were mood disorders, substance use disorders, anxiety disorders, impulse control disorders, and personality disorders. Other studies have found that pathological use is also comorbid with ADHD and anxiety/depression (Gentile, 2009; Gentile et al., 2011).

Several personality factors are correlated with pathological use, most notably higher trait hostility/animosity (see Table 21.2). Other studies reveal relations with other personality traits, such as being high on neuroticism, psychoticism, sensation seeking, and impulsivity, while being low on agreeableness, extraversion, and emotional stability. Surprisingly, although Type A personality is typically correlated with addictions, Griffiths and Dancaster (1995) did not find a statistically significant difference between college students who were or were not "addicted" to video games. However, they reported that twice as many Type A as Type B respondents reported being "addicted" to video games at some point in their lives. It should be noted that their sample was very small (*n* = 24), resulting in low statistical power.

Several studies find that pathological technology users show higher rates of aggressive and antisocial behaviors, a pattern found in other addictions (see

Table 22.1 Measures of Convergent Validity with Pathological Technology Use by Study.

Frequency of Use/Play

Study	Frequency of Use/Play Variable
Charlton and Danforth (2007)	*Amount of MMPORG play*
Chou and Ting (2003) Ferraro et al. (2007)	Amount of MMORPG play Duration of Internet usage
Fisher (1994)	Frequency and duration of arcade VG play
Gentile (2009)	Frequency of VG play, Number of years of VG play
Griffiths and Hunt (1998) Grüsser et al.(2007)	Amount and frequency of VG play Frequency of VG play
Johansson and Göttestam (2004a,b) Ko et al. (2007)	Amount and frequency of Internet use and VG play Frequency of Internet use
LaRose et al. (2001) Porter et al. (2010)	Frequency of Internet use Frequency of VG play
Tejeiro Salguero et al. (2002)	Frequency and duration of VG play
Widyanto and McMurran (2004)	Amount of Internet use (various types)
Yoo et al. (2004)	Amount of Internet use
Young (1997)	Weekly amount of Internet use

Engagement with Computers/Video Games

Study	Engagement Variable
Fisher (1994)	Amount of money spent on arcade VG play
Gentile (2009)	Has VG system in bedroom
Griffiths and Hunt (1998) Grüsser et al. (2005)	Earlier initiation of VG play, high emotions (both positive and negative) surrounding play Use of computers for games
Johansson and Göttestam (2004a) Johansson and Göttestam (2004b)	Uses Internet for multiple functions Types of video games played
LaRose et al. (2001)	Perceived Internet self-efficacy
Morahan-Martin and Schumacher (2000)	Frequency of visiting game sites
Porter et al. (2010)	Use of online role-playing games
Yoo et al. (2004)	Uses Internet to play games

Other Markers of Technology Use

Study	Other Variable
Fisher (1994)	Worried they play VGs "too much" Borrow money to play arcade VGs
Gentile (2009)	*Report feeling "addicted" to games, have friends who are "addicted" to games, skip chores and homework to play games*
Griffiths and Hunt (1998)	Play VGs because there is "nothing else to do"
Grüsser et al. (2005)	Use games as a stress coping strategy
Grüsser et al. (2007)	High craving to play
Tejeiro Salguero et al. (2002)	Think they play VGs too much Think they have a problem with their VG playing

This table is not meant to be exhaustive of studies of pathological technology use, but rather illustrative.

Table 22.2 Measures of Comorbidity with Pathological Technology Use (by Study).

Other Disorders

Black, Belsare, and Schlosser (1990)	Substance use, mood disorders, anxiety disorders, psychotic disorders Impulsive control disorders (compulsive buying, pathological gambling, pyromania, compulsive sexual behavior, kleptomania) Personality disorders (borderline, narcissistic, antisocial, etc.)
Choo et al. (2010)	Impulsivity
Feng, Yan, and Guo (2003)	Depression, anxiety
	ADHD, depression, anxiety
Gentile (2009)	Diagnosed attention deficit disorder
Gentile et al. (2011)	Depression, anxiety, social phobia, ADHD symptoms
Jenaro et al. (2007)	Anxiety
Ko et al. (2009)	Depression, ADHD
Mythily et al. (2008)	Depression
Peng and Liu (2010)	Depression
Shapira et al. (2000)	Mood disorders, substance use disorders, anxiety disorders, impulse control, and personality disorders
Tejeiro Salguero and Bersabé Morán (2002)	Dependence disorders
Wood et al. (2004)	Pathological gambling
Yoo et al. (2004)	ADHD, anxiety, and depression

Personality Factors

Charlton and Danforth (2010)	Low emotional stability, agreeableness, and extraversion
Chen, Tu, and Wang (2008)	High neuroticism
Chiu et al. (2004)	High sensation seeking, boredom inclination, and trait animosity
Choo et al. (2010)	Hostility
Feng, Yan, and Guo (2003)	High on psychoticism and trait lying
Gentile et al. (2011)	High on impulsivity, low on empathy and emotion regulation
Griffiths and Dancaster (1995)	More likely to be Type A
Ko et al. (2007)	High excitability, low self-esteem, high hostility
Mehroof and Griffiths (2009)	High on neuroticism, sensation seeking, trait and state anxiety
Montag et al. (2010)	Low on self directedness
Nichols and Nicki (2004)	More boredom prone
Yee (2002)	Low self-esteem
Yoo et al. (2004)	More withdrawn and more internalizing problems

Table 22.2 (Continued)

Aggression and Antisocial Behaviors	
Feng, Yan, and Guo (2003)	Delinquent and externalizing problems
Gentile et al. (2011)	Greater violent game exposure, higher normative beliefs about aggression, hostile attribution bias, aggressive fantasies, physically aggressive behavior, relationally aggressive behavior, and victimization
Griffiths and Hunt (1998)	Report higher aggressive feelings after playing video games
Mehroof and Griffiths (2009)	Aggression
Yoo et al. (2004)	Aggression, delinquent and externalizing problems
Social/Relationship Behaviors	
Choo et al. (2010)	Low on social competence and social functioning, higher fights with parents
Ferraro et al. (2007) Feng, Yan, and Guo (2003)	Compromised quality of life More social problems
Gentile et al. (2011)	High on social phobia, low on social competence, poorer parent–child relationship
Ko et al. (2007)	High on social phobia
Liu and Kuo (2007)	High on social anxiety
Morahan-Martin and Schumacher (2000)	High on loneliness
Mythily et al. (2008)	Low on friendships
Nichols and Nicki (2004)	High on social loneliness, family loneliness, and emotional loneliness
Odaci and Kalkan (2010)	High on loneliness, communication anxiety, and dating anxiety
Peng and Liu (2010)	High on shyness
Porter et al. (2010)	Find it easier to meet people online, fewer real-life friends
Yoo et al. (2004)	High on social problems
Young (1997)	High on relationship problems
Academic Problems	
Chiu et al. (2004)	Poor academic performance
Choo et al. (2010)	Poor academic performance
Gentile et al. (2011)	Poor academic performance
Mythily et al. (2008)	Poor academic performance
Rehbein et al. (2010)	Poor academic performance High on truancy
Young (1997)	Poor academic performance

(continued)

Table 22.2 (Continued)

Family Problems	
Chiu et al. (2004)	Poor family functioning
Feng, Yan, and Guo (2003)	Low family intimacy and family expressiveness High family conflict
Gentile (2009)	Poor parent–child relationships
Ko et al. (2007)	Poor family functioning
Liu and Kuo (2007)	Poor parent–child relationships
Mythily et al. (2008)	Low parental monitoring
Yen et al. (2007)	High parent–adolescent conflict Lower family functioning Positive attitude to adolescent substance use

Other Problems or Risk Factors	
Chuang (2006)	More seizures
Jenaro et al. (2007)	More insomnia
Lam et al. (2009)	More alcohol use and stressful events
Peng and Liu (2010)	More rumination and other maladaptive thinking
Porter et al. (2010)	Excessive caffeine consumption
Rehbein et al. (2010)	More suicidal thoughts Lower sleep time
Young (1997)	Increased financial problems Poorer occupational functioning Increased physical problems

This table is not meant to be exhaustive of studies of pathological technology use, but rather illustrative.

Table 21.2). Studies also find problems in social or relational contexts, including higher levels of loneliness and problems in social competence and functioning. Other studies have found that pathological users also report feeling anxiety in dating situations (Odaci & Kalkan, 2010). Pathological users also report poorer family relationships (see Table 21.2). A number of studies now show that such individuals report lower levels of intimacy, worse parent–child relationships, and poorer family functioning. Interestingly, one study (Mythily et al., 2008) found that lower levels of parental monitoring were present for pathological users, showing a relationship between parenting behaviors and levels of pathological use of technology. Conversely, one other study showed that good parent–child communication could help prevent pathological use of the Internet (Van den Eijnden et al., 2010). Similar to other addictions, it may be that pathological technology use may be displacing time with friends, family, or romantic partners. Accordingly, such individuals may not spend the time necessary to build good social relationships or develop appropriate social skills. Problems may also occur if pathological users are lying to or stealing from these individuals. Furthermore, although it is not represented in Table 21.2, almost every study finds that males are more likely than females to show pathological use (again, similar to other addictions). Finally, most studies that have looked at potential outcomes of pathological use have found significant problems, such as poorer school performance, insomnia, suicidal thoughts, financial problems, and more relationship problems. It should be noted that in our review, despite many benefits of the Internet and video games in general, we did not find one study showing any positive aspect of *pathological* use of computer or video games.

It should be noted that almost all of these studies are correlational, and it is possible that these problems preceded the pathological use or are both caused by a third factor. At a broader level of analysis, the presence of comorbid pathologies is not, by itself, strong evidence that pathological technology use is a unique taxon. It may be that the behavioral phenotypical expressions of pathological use are a manifestation of one of these other underlying disorders (Shaffer et al., 2004), or one disorder leads to another as a complication, or they arise because of common antecedents (Shaffer, 2004). Further research is needed to provide evidence to help interpret comorbidity in this domain (but see the following for the existing evidence). At this time, however, it seems reasonable to view the pattern of correlations and comorbidity (in conjunction with other evidence of reliability and validity) as similar to the patterns shown in other addictions.

Research on Construct Validity: Predictive Validity

The studies of pathological technology use provide evidence for construct validity (see Tables 21.1 and 21.2). However, much remains to be studied. If PTU is similar to other addictions, then it should predict poorer outcomes for pathological users and might predict comorbid mental health problems. At the time of this writing, only two longitudinal studies have been published. One focused on 881 Chinese adolescents between 13 and 16, using Young's 20-item Internet addiction scale (Lam & Peng, 2010). Adolescents were surveyed twice 9 months apart. Pathological Internet use predicted increased risk of depression (but not general anxiety) 9 months later, after controlling for several potential confounding factors (e.g., sex, age, family dissatisfaction, illness).

A larger study of 3,034 Singaporean children and adolescents followed across 2 years gave some of the first clear evidence of whether variables such as depression and poor school performance are predictors of or predicted by pathological video gaming (Gentile et al., 2011). Because of their large sample size, they were able to classify gamers into four types: those who never were pathological across the 2 years, those who became pathological gamers, those who were pathological at the start but stopped being pathological, and those who were and stayed pathological gamers. Similar to the study by Lam and Peng, depression became worse if youth became

pathological gamers. Furthermore, anxiety, social phobia, and school performance also became worse after becoming a pathological gamer. Additionally, if children stopped being pathological gamers, their depression, anxiety, social phobia, and school performance all improved. This pattern suggests that these are likely to be outcomes of pathological technology use rather than predictors of it. At a minimum, it suggests that these issues are truly comorbid, such that they can influence each other.

Conclusion and Implications

Four questions have been addressed in the literature. The first question is whether tests for pathological use are reliable. Although researchers have defined and measured the disorder in many different ways, almost all have been reliable. In general, those that conform more closely to the DSM-IV pathological gambling criteria appear to be the most reliable.

The second question is whether the construct of pathological technology use shows construct validity. Researchers have provided evidence for construct validity in two ways: convergent validity and comorbidity. Again, although researchers have defined the problem differently, there is robust evidence that pathological use shows high convergent validity with other theoretically relevant variables.

The third question is whether construct validity is shown in patterns of correlations and comorbidity similar to those shown in other addictions. Again there is robust evidence in support of this hypothesis.

The fourth question is whether pathological technology use shows predictive validity. Although there are only two studies published to date, they both demonstrate that PTU predicts poorer outcomes in the long run.

Therefore, we conclude that there is sufficient evidence at the present time to warrant concern and to consider the implications for (1) developing standardized diagnostic criteria defining PTU; (2) measuring the prevalence of PTU; and (3) defining the etiology, course, and treatment of PTU. Although research in each of these areas is still immature, some preliminary conclusions can be drawn.

Diagnostic Criteria

Although researchers have used several different approaches to measuring pathological technology use, there are many similarities. Our position is that there is a need for specific diagnostic criteria for clinical use and to direct future research efforts. Based on the available data, we therefore propose the following diagnostic criteria for pathological technology use for adults. We argue that it is fair to consider PTU as akin to pathological gambling, which is classified in the DSM-IV as an impulse control disorder. We do not believe that technologies are similar to substances in that they are "addictive." Instead, the core issue is that use becomes pathological as the person becomes less able to control the impulses to use technologies, which is what causes damage to social, occupational, and other functioning. At the time of this writing, the DSM-V is under development and it appears that a new categorization will be created titled "addiction and related disorders," which will include both substance addictions and pathological gambling. The American Psychiatric Association considered it for inclusion in the DSM-V, but decided there was not sufficient research yet (APA, 2010).

The criteria that follow focus on damage to social, family, occupational, school, and psychological functioning, similar to how other disorders are diagnosed, including pathological gambling. We propose, therefore, the following criteria for clinical use with adult populations.

1. Persistent and recurrent maladaptive use of computers, video games, the Internet, or other digital technologies, as indicated by at least half of the following:

   a. Is preoccupied with computer use (e.g., preoccupied with reliving past experiences, planning the next opportunity to use/play, or thinking of ways to get more time/money with which to use/play more)

   b. Needs to spend more time and/or money on computers/video games/Internet access in order to achieve the desired excitement

   c. Has repeated unsuccessful efforts to control, cut back, or stop using/playing

   d. Is restless or irritable when attempting to cut down or stop using/playing

   e. Lies to family members, therapist, or others to conceal the extent of involvement with technologies/Internet

   f. Has committed illegal/unsocial acts such as theft from family, friends, or elsewhere to get more video games or more access to computers/Internet

   g. Has jeopardized or lost a significant relationship, job, or educational or career opportunity because of technology/Internet use

   h. Relies on others to provide money to relieve a desperate financial situation caused by excessive money spent on computer/Internet/video game fees.

   i. Uses computers/video games/Internet as a way of escaping from problems or of relieving a dysphoric mood (e.g., feelings of helplessness, guilt, anxiety, depression)

2. The excessive technology/Internet is not better accounted for by a manic episode, and is not better accounted for by other Axis I disorders.

Although these criteria are based very directly on pathological gambling, it is our current thinking that 11 may not be a particularly good symptom. Using media as a coping method is highly normative in a way that gambling is not. Therefore, although we currently use an item based on this, we are starting to seriously question its value, and have some studies underway to attempt to test our measurement approach further. (At the time of this writing, our preliminary data suggest that it may be better not including it, but instead to include an item on skipping meals, bathing, or the toilet.)

There are several potential additional symptoms that do not appear to be good diagnostic criteria. For example, some researchers have suggested that there is a time distortion effect of gambling on video game lottery terminals (Diskin & Hodgins, 1999). That is, pathological gamblers tend to lose a sense of the time spent when gambling. Chou and Ting (2003) directly measured this with video games, asking whether players played longer than they intended to. In our experience, this is such a typical experience for video game players and computer users that it would not discriminate pathological users from healthy users. Indeed, in an experimental study with college students, Wood and Griffiths (2007) found that time loss was not necessarily a precipitating or facilitating factor related to video game addiction. It may be that there are distinct differences in the frequency or extent of such experiences for pathological users, but further study is required to determine if there is a difference that is diagnostically valid. Charlton (2002) surveyed 404 undergraduates on several facets of computer use, including 10 items he created based on Brown's six facets of addiction. He factor analyzed 47 variables, finding three factors. The first factor he defined as computer "engagement," a nonpathological interest in and frequent use of computers. The second factor was an "addiction" factor, and the third was "comfort" factor (how comfortable participants were using computers). Of particular interest was the fact that three of the addiction items measuring salience, euphoria, and tolerance loaded more heavily on the engagement factor than on the addiction factor (although they also loaded on the addiction factor). His interpretation was that these features may either not be discriminatory for pathological use, or that perhaps they indicate early symptoms in the etiology of pathological use. Although more research is necessary to test both of these hypotheses, we believe that his approach to measurement of these issues may not be sufficient. For example, his items were worded gently rather than strictly. "I tend to want to spend increasing amounts of time using computers" rather than "I need to spend more and more time and/or money on computers in order to achieve the desired excitement," and "I rarely think about computing when I am not using a computer" compared with "Over time, I have become more preoccupied with computing, studying computing, or planning the next opportunity to use a computer." He also measured his items on a five-point Likert scale (strongly agree to strongly disagree), rather than the dichotomous yes/no approach suggested by DSM symptom checklists. Furthermore, "euphoria," or positive feelings associated with the behavior (measured by Charlton as "I often experience a buzz of excitement while computing") are not used by the DSM-IV for either pathological gambling or substance related disorders. It is likely that there are positive feelings about *any* repeated behavior, making this facet unlikely to be discriminatory for clinical use. In defining pathological use of technology, it will be critical to discriminate between high engagement that is pathological and that which is nonpathological (Brockmyer, Fox, Curtiss, McBroom, Burkhart, & Pidruzny, 2009; see also Chapter 11).

It is likely that these methodological issues account for some of the overlap Charlton found between "engaged" participants and "addicted" participants. Therefore, we present potential survey items in Appendix A. Future should address both content and wording of these items. We recommend setting a time boundary on any definition of PTU, because this is how many other DSM diagnoses are made (e.g., substance disorders, depression), and suggest using 1 year because this is the amount of time used with regard to substance addictions. Setting time periods in clinical diagnoses are important both by evincing stability of the disorder over time, as well as by being able to recognize when problematic behaviors have ceased. It is important to note that these items are not intended to be used to make self-diagnoses, but to help define the issue for future studies.

Another question that requires further study is whether it is more appropriate to define pathological technology use as a continuous or discontinuous variable. There are two facets to this issue. The first is whether to measure in a dichotomous (e.g., yes, no), trichotomous (e.g., yes, no, sometimes), or continuous fashion (e.g., strongly agree, agree, neither agree nor disagree, disagree, strongly disagree). At the very least, this issue is critical for identifying prevalence rates. Gentile (2009) tested the difference between considering "sometimes" as equivalent to a yes or a no, or leaving it as midway between yes and no with a large national sample. Considering sometimes as equivalent to yes yielded good reliability, and also the highest prevalence ($\alpha = .77$; 19.8% prevalence). Considering sometimes as equivalent to no yielded slightly poorer reliability and the most conservative prevalence ($\alpha = .74$; 7.9%). Considering sometimes as halfway between yes and no yielded the highest reliability and a prevalence that is close to the conservative approach ($\alpha = .78$; 8.5%).

The second facet is whether pathological use itself is better defined as a dichotomous state (a patient either has or does not have the disorder), or as a place on a continuum (a patient shows fewer or more symptoms, suggesting extent of disorder). Both of these approaches have been used by different researchers with success, and there is not clear evidence of one approach being better. The DSM-IV tends to approach disorders as dichotomous states, although clinicians in clinical practice tend to view patients on continua.

Our preliminary recommendation is that perhaps three groups should be defined based on the number of symptoms they present: a pathological group (at least 5 symptoms based on the 10 items in Appendix A), an at-risk group (at least three symptoms), and a normal group (less than three symptoms). This approach has been used successfully by other researchers (Yoo et al., 2004; Johansson & Götestam, 2004b), although it remains to be tested with the items presented here in Appendix A. It is important to note that by making this recommendation, we do not mean to imply that this categorical approach is necessarily the best way to define PTU. We recommend it simply because it has the most empirical evidence at this time. Furthermore, although the DSM tends to use a symptom-counting approach to diagnosis, in practice, clinicians tend to evaluate problems based on relative severity. Some people with only one symptom may still suffer severe consequences, whereas others with several may not. Therefore, these definitions should be considered and revised in relation to the broader psychological and psychiatric debate regarding the merits of defining psychopathologies in categorical, dimensional, or multi-axial terms (Shaffer, 2004).

Studies of clinical use of these criteria are needed, particularly to determine whether the criteria are appropriate for both adult and child populations. Some behaviors are normal in childhood and pathological in adulthood (e.g., antisocial personality disorders and borderline personality disorders are not diagnosable in childhood). It may be that the criteria should be different for different ages, but we will not know that until more data are collected.

There is one final issue regarding the definition of pathological technology use. We are recommending that pathological use of computers, video games, the Internet, online games, and so on be considered different manifestations of the same underlying disorder. This is similar to the approach taken by the DSM-IV with gambling addiction. In a review of gambling addiction, Dowling, Smith, and Thomas (2005) found that not all types of gambling addiction were the same. "The weight of recent research evidence [indicates] that different gambling activities are heterogeneous in nature and that gamblers and problem gamblers engaging in these various gambling activities comprise heterogeneous populations" (p. 36). That is, a person who has a problem gambling on horses doesn't also usually have a problem gambling on slot machines, and vice versa. Thus, although video games are not identical to the Internet, the data reviewed here suggest that pathological use of each appears to show the same types of symptoms. Until further research is conducted clearly demonstrating that these different technology activities discriminate wholly separate taxons, it is more parsimonious to consider them to be the same type of disorder.

Some researchers of Internet addiction have suggested that there are several distinct types of Internet addiction, including addiction to online sex and addiction to online gambling (Putnam & Maheu, 2000; Davis, 2001; Demmel, 2002; Griffiths, 2003). It is our opinion that these issues are not the same as pathological technology use, and would be better defined as other types of impulse control disorders, as the underlying disorder is about sex or gambling and the Internet is simply the delivery mechanism used. Treating a pathological gambler's *computer use* is unlikely to resolve the underlying problem.

Prevalence

Assuming that PTU is a valid construct, it is important to examine prevalence rates, etiology, the course of the illness, and treatment. Pathological technology use has now been identified as existing in a host of different countries all over the world, including Singapore (Choo et al., 2010), China (Deng & Zhu, 2006; Zhang, Amos, & McDowell, 2008; Lawrence, Peng, Mai, & Jing, 2009), the Netherlands (Lemmens et al., 2009; van Rooij et al., 2010), Norway (Johansson & Gotestam, 2004a,b), Taiwan (Ko et al., 2007), Turkey (Odaci & Kalkan, 2010), the United States (Gentile, 2009), the United Kingdom (Griffiths & Hunt, 1998; Mehroof & Griffiths, 2009), Spain (Tejeiro Salguero & Bersabé Morán, 2002), South Korea (Yoo et al., 2004), Tunisia (Halayem et al., 2010), and others. Studies have provided different estimates of the prevalence of pathological technology use, ranging between 1% and 20%, although they seem to be converging on a number between 7% and 12% of technology users. Recent prevalence estimates include 8.5% (Gentile, 2009) and 8.1% (Morahan-Martin & Schumacher, 2000) in the United States, 8.7% in Singapore (Choo et al., 2010), 10.3% (Peng & Li, 2009) and 10.8% (Lam et al., 2009) in China, 8.0% in Australia (Porter, Starcevic, Berle, & Fenech, 2010), 11.9% in Germany (Grüsser, Thalemann, & Griffiths, 2007), and 7.5% in Taiwan (Ko et al., 2007). These studies have not used a common methodology or definition, however, so each estimate of prevalence should be considered to be preliminary. Nonetheless, it is striking that even with such different populations and methods the prevalence is fairly similar across studies.

Etiology

The etiology of pathological technology use is largely unknown. Some authors have speculated about pieces of a possible etiology. LaRose et al. (2001) described a social–cognitive approach to understanding Internet usage. Within that context, Internet usage can be predicted from expected positive outcomes, expected negative outcomes, perceived self-efficacy, and self-regulatory mechanisms; pathological use would be caused by deficient self-regulation and perhaps distortions of expectations.

The framework for addiction etiology proposed by the National Institute of Drug Abuse describes the balance between risk and protective factors. The essential feature of this model is that the "weights" of risk and protective factors are always changing during life, and the "vulnerability" profile is defined within a particular window of time. Following this model, there is a need to measure the balance between risk and protective factors (Pickens & Svikis, 1989; Serpelloni, 2006). Yet, it is unclear at this time what those factors may be. For example, one case study of a 43-year-old Internet "addicted" homemaker demonstrated that a "nontechnologically oriented" woman without a history of psychiatric or drug abuse problems, used the Internet so much that resulted in significant impairment to her family life (Young, 1996).

Certainly, we've discussed a number of factors related to pathological use, such as having other psychological disorders (e.g., ADHD, depression, or anxiety), having a certain personality showing higher levels of impulsivity, neuroticism, and psychoticism, showing more aggression and hostility, and showing problems in family, school, and relationships (see Table 21.2). For example, Yoo et al. (2004) suggest that ADHD may be a necessary factor, or at least is a risk factor, for developing pathological Internet use because the Internet fits the cognitive style of the condition, and may compensate for poor social skills, interpersonal difficulties, and the lack of pleasure in other daily activities. This demonstrates a potential problem that currently exists with definitions and interpretation—in this example, it is unclear whether PTU and ADHD would be independent but comorbid, or whether one is a risk or predictive factor for the other.

Griffiths has discussed the differences between structural and situational variables that affect gambling addiction, and how the structural characteristics of video game/Internet technology may work to enhance the addictiveness (Griffiths, 2003; Griffiths & Wood, 2000). For example, immediate feedback, continuous play, and accessibility are all made easier through computer technology. It is possible that these situational and structural characteristics will need to be accounted for when measuring the etiology of pathological technology use, as different types of activities vary widely in them. However, as Griffiths notes, although there is evidence that both gambling and the Internet can be addictive, there is no evidence (to date) that Internet gambling is "doubly addictive" (Griffiths, 2003, p. 562).

Some researchers have suggested that the amount of time spent with games or technology is a risk factor for pathological use (Johansson & Götestam, 2004a,b). As noted, how much one uses alcohol or gambles is not one of the symptoms used to diagnose those addictions. Indeed, Gentile (2009) provided evidence that amount of video gaming was not sufficient on its own to diagnose pathological gaming. Nonetheless, in a later longitudinal study (Gentile et al., 2011), a high amount of gaming (greatly above the average) was one predictor of who became a pathological gamer. Therefore, although amount of use is probably neither a necessary or sufficient cause, it does seem to act as a risk factor.

In the longitudinal study of 3,034 youth, several other factors also predicted who became pathological gamers across the 2 years (Gentile et al., 2011). These included high impulsivity, low social competence, and poorer emotion regulation. In a longitudinal latent growth curve model, impulsivity, social competence, and amount of video game play predicted the number of pathological symptoms reported both initially (intercept) and changes (slope) in them, which in turn predicted depression, anxiety, social phobias, and school performance 2 years later (Fig. 21.1).

Other risk factors for the etiology of pathological technology use have included the positive emotional experience of "flow" (Chou & Ting, 2003) (the experience of time distortion and feeling of being *in* the game), having prior underlying disorders (Young, 1996), being a new user (Young, 1997; Widyanto & McMurran, 2004), or the "intense" connection possible between human and machine because the machine does not have a self-organizing function (Wassenaar, Van Doorn, & Dierssen, 1998).

Although more research is clearly needed to test these variables and potential models, the proposed DSM-style diagnostic criteria bring with them certain assumptions. The theoretical model underlying most DSM diagnoses is that there is a biological basis in part for most disorders (although this is no longer a requisite component for diagnoses of impulse control disorders or substance use disorders). There is limited evidence that high video game users may have different patterns of brain activation than lower users (Kronenberger et al., 2005; Hoeft et al., 2008). The evidence is net yet sufficient to make a statement about whether there is a biological underpinning to PTU. For most people, computer and video game use is part of a healthy lifestyle. However, some people develop a misuse of it that impairs their functioning. Therefore, we have described the problem on the basis of behavior alone, although future studies may document biological risk factors.

Course

Once one becomes a pathological technology user, it is important to know how long one stays pathological. To our knowledge, only three studies have examined the course of pathological technology use. A number of studies by Ko et al. (2007, 2009) have found that about 50% of adolescents in Taiwan who were classified as pathological users of the Internet showed signs of being "addicted" 1 and 2 years later. High hostility, depression, and ADHD, among other variables predicted stability of addiction. In the study

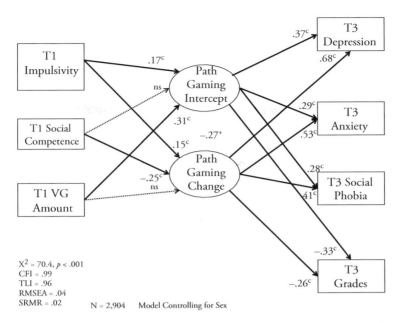

Figure 22.1 Predictors (Time 1) and outcomes (Time 3) of pathological gaming symptoms across two years. Adapted from Gentile, D. A., Choo, H., Liau, A. K., Sim, T., Li, D., Fung, D., et al. (2011). Pathological video game use among youths: A two-year longitudinal study. *Pediatrics, 127,* e319–e329.

of more than 3,000 Singaporean children, 84% of the children who would be classified as pathological gamers at Time 1 remained pathological gamers 2 years later, leading the authors to report "pathological gaming is not just a 'phase' that children go through" (Gentile et al., 2011, p. 325). Furthermore, a small group (1.3%) of children who did not show signs of pathological gaming did so 2 years later. As noted earlier, these individuals ended up with higher levels of depression, anxiety, and social phobias at the end of the study. Combined, these studies show that pathological computer/gaming use is relatively stable over time and that pathological use can predict several factors previously thought to be just "symptoms" of use (e.g., depression, anxiety, social phobias). Although none of these studies have gone beyond 2 years, it should be noted that staying at a pathological level for 2 years is not a minor issue. By definition, these youth are damaging their family, social, academic, and occupational lives, and this damage could have serious long-term consequences. Future research should examine pathological technology use over a longer period of time to assess the course and outcomes of such use from childhood to adulthood.

Treatment

A number of studies exist on the treatment of pathological technology use (see Griffiths & Meredith,

2009, for a review). Two case reports suggest that it is treatable. For one 12-year-old boy, residential treatment with family therapy over 6 months was reported to be successful (Keepers, 1990). For another 18-year-old college student, a cognitive-behavioral approach combining relaxation training, in vivo exposure, and response prevention was reported to have demonstrated a 90% reduction in video game playing (Kuczmierczyk, Walley, & Calhoun, 1987). Other studies have shown limited success in treating pathological use of video game or the Internet. For example, Shek, Tang, and Lo (2009) report that their indigenous multilevel counseling program for Chinese adolescents showed promise in reducing Internet "addiction" over the course of treatment. Kim (2008) found that a course of reality therapy group sessions reduced Internet addiction levels and increased self-esteem in South Korean college students. Programs using cognitive behavioral therapy have also seen some success in decreasing Internet addiction in adolescents, while increasing time management skills (Du, Jiang, & Vance, 2010). Finally, one study showed that 6 weeks of bupropion sustained release treatment decreased the "craving" for video game play (Han, Hwang, & Renshaw, 2010). Combined, these studies show some promise that pathological technology use can be treatable. However, in each of the preceding studies, the sample sizes were relatively low (around 11 to 35 participants) and the course was not followed longer than a few weeks of treatment. Accordingly, there is great need for future research to continue to assess treatment of pathological technology use.

Currently there is concern in clinical practice because there have not been well-defined criteria to diagnosis pathological technology use, and no evidence-based therapies have yet been established and widely accepted by clinicians (Griffiths & Meredith, 2009). Therefore, it is important to create quality assessment tools, with a clinical focus on whether the problematic behaviors compromise work or family life, and whether patients present a diagnosable psychiatric disease in the present or the past.

Although there is not evidence about the stages of change and treatment (Connors, Donovan, & Di Clemente, 2001) in people with PTU, the psychological and psychiatric communities need to consider the questions raised here for at least three reasons. First, clearly some people are already suffering from problems associated with PTU. Without consensus in the field, many go untreated with consequent disruptions to their jobs, relationships, finances, and mental health. Second, with each year, higher percentages of children and adults gain access to digital technologies, and children are beginning to use computers and to play video games at younger ages. Therefore, more people have greater opportunities to interact with computers, the Internet, and video games, which may result in higher numbers of people experiencing problems. Finally, as the technologies improve, they will become more interactive and more pervasive. Indeed, the next generation of technologies is already being created, called *pervasive games,* stressing the pervasive and ubiquitous nature of these games. Pervasive games are no longer confined to the virtual domain of the computer, but integrate the physical and social aspects of the real world (Magerkurth, Cheok, Mandryk, & Nilsen, 2005, p. 2). These features may increase the likelihood of pathological use. Therefore, additional scientific research that will allow us to properly define, diagnose, and treat pathological technology use is greatly needed. Nonetheless, the existing evidence on pathological use of the Internet, computer, and video games is strong enough to warrant concern and serious attention.

Acknowledgments

The authors wish to thank David Shaffer for his thoughtful detailed comments on an earlier draft, and Ryan Tapscott for his help with preparing the manuscript. Correspondence concerning this manuscript should be addressed to Douglas A. Gentile, Iowa State University, Department of Psychology, W112 Lagomarcino Hall, Ames, IA 50011–3180. Phone: 515–294–1472; Fax: 515–294–6424; E-mail: dgentile@iastate.edu.

Appendix A
Suggested Pathological Technology Use Questionnaire Items for Adults (Recommended Scale: Yes/No/Sometimes)

1. During the past year, have you become more preoccupied with playing video games, studying video game playing, or planning the next opportunity to play? (Y/N/S)

2. In the past year, have you needed to spend more and more time and/or money on video games to achieve the desired excitement? (Y/N/S)

3. In the past year, have you ever felt you could not stop playing video games? (Y/N/S)

4. In the past year, have you become restless or irritable when attempting to cut down or stop playing video games? (Y/N/S)

5. In the past year, have you ever lied to family or friends about how much you play video games? (Y/N/S)

6. In the past year, have you ever committed illegal/unsocial acts such as theft from family, friends, or elsewhere to get video games? (Y/N/S)

7. (For students) In the past year, have you ever done poorly on a school assignment or test because you spent too much time playing video games? (For nonstudents) In the past year, has your work ever suffered (e.g., postponing things, missing deadlines, being too tired to function well, etc.) because you spent too much time playing video games? (Y/N/S)

8. In the past year, have you ever needed friends or family to help you financially because you spent too much money on video game equipment, software, or game/Internet fees? (Y/N/S)

9. In the past year, have you damaged or lost a significant relationship with someone because of your video gaming? (Y/N/S)

10. In the past year, have you played video games as a way of escaping from problems or bad feelings? (Y/N/S)

Notes: We are currently unclear about the value of item 10, as it is highly normative. We include it here because it is typically used, but our current research suggests it may be better to replace it. These items are shown for measuring pathological video game use, but could be modified to ask about computer use and Internet use if one wanted to measure those specifically.

Scoring: We currently recommend scoring a "yes" response as 1, a "no" as 0, and a "sometimes" as 0.5. Items are summed, with higher scores indicating a greater number of pathological symptoms. In keeping with DSM-style criteria, a respondent could be considered pathological if they score equal to or higher than half of the number of items given, but see our recommendations for scoring three groups (pathological, at risk, and normal).

References

American Psychiatric Association (1994). *Diagnostic and Statistical Manual of Mental Disorders*, 4th ed. Washington, DC: Author.

American Psychiatric Association (2010). *APA announces draft diagnostic criteria for DSM-5.* Retrieved May 4, 2011 from http://www.Dsm5.Org/newsroom/documents/diag%20 %20criteria%20general%20final%202.05.pdf.

Associated Press (2002). *Man dies after playing computer games non-stop.* Retrieved November 27, 2005 from http://www.smh.com.au/articles/2002/10/10/1034061260831.html.

Black, D. W., Belsare, G., & Schlosser, S. (1990). *Clinical features, psychiatric comorbidity, and health-related quality of life in persons reporting compulsive computer use behavior. Journal of Clinical Psychiatry, 60,* 839–844.

Blaszczynski, A. (2008). *Commentary: A response to "problems with the concept of video game 'addiction': Some case study examples." International Journal of Mental Health and Addiction, 6,* 179–181.

Bricolo, F., Gentile, D. A., Smelser, R. L., & Serpelloni, G. (2007). *Use of the computer and Internet among Italian families: First national study. Cyberpsychology & Behavior, 10,* 789–797.

Brockmeyer, J. F., Fox, C. M., Curtiss, K. A., McBroom, E., Burkart, K.M., & Pidruzny, J. N. (2009). *The development of the Game Engagement Questionnaire: A measure of engagement in video game-playing. Journal of Experimental Social Psychology, 45,* 624–634.

Brown, R. I. F. (1991). Gaming, gambling and other addictive play. In Kerr, J. H ., & Apter, M. J. (Eds.), *Adult Place: A Reversal Theory Approach.* Amsterdam: Swets & Zeitlinger, pp. 101–118.

Byun, S., Ruffini, C., Mills, J. E., Douglas, A. C., Niang, M., Stepchenkova, S., et al. (2009). *Internet Addiction: Metasynthesis of 1996–2006 quantitative research. CyberPsychology & Behavior, 12,* 203–207.

Charlton, J. P. (2002). *A factor-analytic investigation of computer 'addiction' and engagement. British Journal of Psychology, 93*(Part 3), 329–344.

Charlton, J. P., & Danforth, I. D. W. (2007). *Distinguishing addiction and high engagement in the context of online game playing. Computers in Human Behavior, 23,* 1531–1548.

Charlton, J. P., & Danforth, I. D. W. (2010). *Validating the distinction between computer addiction and engagement: Online game playing and personality. Behaviour and Information Technology, 29,* 601–613.

Chen L. S., Tu, H. H., & Wang E. S. (2008). *Personality traits and life satisfaction among online game players. CyberPsychology & Behavior, 11,* 145–149.

Chiu, S. I., Lee, J. Z., & Huang, D. H. (2004). *Video game addiction in children and teenagers in Taiwan. CyberPsychology & Behavior, 7,* 571–581.

Choo, H., Gentile, D. A., Sim, T., Li, D., Khoo, A., & Liau, A. K. (2010). *Pathological video-gaming among Singaporean youth. Annals Academy of Medicine, 39,* 822–829.

Chou, T. J., & Ting, C. C. (2003). *The role of flow experience in cyber-game addiction. CyberPsychology & Behavior, 6,* 663–675.

Chuang, Y. (2006). *Massively multiplayer online role-playing game-induced seizures: A neglected health problem in internet addiction. Cyberpsychology and Behavior, 9,* 451–456.

Connors, G. J., Donovan, D. M., & Di Clemente, C. C. (2001). *Substance Abuse Treatment and Stages of Change.* New York: The Guilford Press.

Davies, J. B. (1992). *The Myth of Addiction.* Chur, Switzerland: Harwood Academic Publishers.

Davis, R. A. (2001). *A cognitive-behavioral model of pathological internet use. Computers in Human Behavior, 17,* 187–195.

Demmel, R. (2002). *Internet addiction: Ein literaturüberblick. Sucht: Zeitschrift für Wissenschaft und Praxis, 48,* 29–46.

Deng, P., & Zhu, Z. (2006). *PS-DA model of game addiction: Theoretical hypothesis and case analysis. Edutainment, 2006,* 444–452.

Diskin, K. M., & Hodgins, D. C. (1999). *Narrowing of attention and dissociation in pathological video lottery gamblers. Journal of Gambling Studies, 15,* 17–28.

Dowling, N., Smith, D., & Thomas, T. (2005). *Electronic gaming machines: Are they the 'crack-cocaine' of gambling? Addiction, 100,* 33–45.

Du, Y., Jiang, W., & Vance, A. (2010). *Longer term effect of randomized, controlled group cognitive behavioural therapy for internet addiction in adolescent students in Shanghai. Australian and New Zealand Journal of Psychiatry, 44,* 129–134.

Feng, Y., Yan, X., & Guo, X. (2003). *Behavior problem and family environment of children with video games dependence. Chinese Mental Health Journal, 17*(6), 367–368.

Ferraro, G., Caci, B., D'Amico, A., & Di Blasi, M. (2007). *Internet addiction disorder: An Italian study. Cyberpsychology and Behavior, 10,* 170–175.

Fisher, S. (1994). *Identifying video game addiction in children and adolescents. Addictive Behaviors, 19,* 545–553.

Galimberti, U. (1999). *Psiche e Tecne: L'uomo Nell'età Della Tecnica.* Milan: Feltrinelli.

Gentile, D. A. (2009). *Pathological video game use among youth 8 to 18: A national study. Psychological Science, 20,* 594–602.

Gentile, D. A., Choo, H., Liau, A. K., Sim, T., Li, D., Fung, D., et al. (2011). *Pathological video game use among youths: A two-year longitudinal study. Pediatrics, 127,* e319–e329.

Glasser, W. (1976). *Positive Addiction.* New York: Harper & Row.

Griffiths, M. (2000). *Does internet and computer "addiction" exist? Some case study evidence. CyberPsychology & Behavior, 3,* 211–218.

Griffiths, M. (2003). *Internet gambling: Issues, concerns, and recommendations. CyberPsychology & Behavior, 6,* 557–568.

Griffiths, M., & Wood, R. T. A. (2000). *Risk factors in adolescence: The case of gambling, video game playing, and the internet. Journal of Gambling Studies, 16,* 199–225.

Griffiths, M. D. (1997). *Computer game playing in early adolescence. Youth & Society, 29,* 223–238.

Griffiths, M. D., & Dancaster, I. (1995). *The effect of type A personality on physiological arousal while playing computer games. Addictive Behaviors, 20,* 543–548.

Griffiths, M. D., Davies, M. N., & Chappell, D. (2004a). *Demographic factors and playing variables in online computer gaming. CyberPsychology & Behavior, 7,* 479–487.

Griffiths, M. D., Davies, M. N., & Chappell, D. (2004b) *Online computer gaming: A comparison of adolescent and adult gamers. Journal of Adolescence, 27,* 87–96.

Griffiths, M. D., & Hunt, N. (1995). *Computer game playing in adolescence: Prevalence and demographic indicators. Journal of Community and Applied Social Psychology, 5,* 189–194.

Griffiths, M. D., & Hunt, N. (1998). *Dependence on computer games by adolescents. Psychological Reports, 82,* 475–480.

Griffiths, M. D., & Meredith, A. (2009). *Videogame addiction and its treatment. Journal of Contemporary Psychotherapy, 39,* 247–253.

Grüsser, S. M. Thalemann, R., Albrecht, U., & Thalemann, C. N. (2005). *Exzessive computernutzung im Kindesalter—Ergebnisse einer psychometrischem Erhebung. Wiener Klinische Wochenschrift, 117,* 188–195.

Grüsser, S. M., Thalemann, R., & Griffiths M. D. (2007). *Excessive computer game playing: Evidence for addiction and aggression? Cyberpsychology & Behavior, 10,* 290–292.

Halayem, S., Nouira, O., Bourgou, S., Bouden, A., Othman, S., & Halayem, M. (2010). *Le Telephone Portable: Une nouvelle addiction chez les adolescents. La Tunisie Medicale, 88,* 593–596.

Han, D. H., Hwang, J. W., & Renshaw, P. F. (2010). *Bupropion sustained release treatment decreases craving for video games and cue-induced brain activity in patients with internet video game addiction. Experimental and Clinical Psychopharmacology, 18,* 297–304.

Hoeft, F., Watson, C. L., Kesler, S. R., Bettinger, K. E., & Reiss, A. L. (2008). *Gender differences in the mesocorticolimbic system during computer game-play. Journal of Psychiatric Research, 42,* 253–258.

Huang, M. P., & Alessi, N. E. (1996). *The internet and the future of psychiatry. American Journal of Psychiatry, 153,* 861–869.

Jenaro, C., Flores, N., Gomez-Vela, M., Gonzalez-Gil, F., & Caballo, C. (2007). *Problematic internet and cell-phone use: psychological, behavioral, and health correlates. Addiction, Research, and Theory, 15,* 309–320.

Johansson, A., & Götestam, K. G. (2004a). *Internet addiction: Characteristics of a questionnaire and prevalence in Norwegian youth. Scandinavian Journal of Psychology, 45,* 223–229.

Johansson, A., & Götestam, K. G. (2004b). *Problems with computer games with monetary reward: Similarity to pathological gambling. Psychological Reports, 95,* 641–650.

Keeper, G. A. (1990). *Pathological preoccupation with video games. Journal of the American Academy of Child and Adolescent Psychiatry, 29,* 49–50.

Kim, J. (2008). *The effect of a R/T group counselling program on the internet addiction level and self-esteem of internet addiction university students. International Journal of Reality Therapy, XXVII,* 4–12.

Kipnis, D. (1997). *Ghosts, taxonomies, and social psychology. American Psychologist, 52,* 205–211.

Ko, C., Yen, J., Chen, C., Yeh, Y., & Yen, C. (2009). *Predictive values of psychiatric symptoms for internet addiction in adolescents: A two year prospective study. Archives of Pediatrics & Adolescent Medicine, 163,* 937–943.

Ko, C., Yen, J., Yen, C., Lin, H., & Yang, M. (2007). *Factors predictive for incidence and remission of internet addiction in young adolescents: A prospective study. Cyberpsychology &Behavior, 10,* 543–551.

Koepp, M. J., Gunn, R. N., Lawrence, A. D., Cunningham, V. J., Dagher, A., Jones, T., et al. (1998). *Evidence for striatal dopamine release during a video game. Nature, 393,* 266–268.

Kronenberger, W.O., Mathews, V. P., Dunn, D. W., Wang, Y., Wood, E. A., Giauque, A. L., et al. (2005). *Media violence exposure and executive functioning in aggressive and control adolescents. Journal of Clinical Psychology, 61,* 715–737.

Kubey, R., & Csikszentmihalyi, M. (2002). *Television addiction is no mere metaphor. Scientific American, 286,* 74–80.

Kuczmierczyk, A. R., Walley, P. B., & Calhoun, K. W. (1987). *Relaxation training, in vivo exposure and response-prevention in the treatment of compulsive video-game playing. Scandinavian Journal of Behavior Therapy, 16,* 185–190.

Lam, L. T., Peng, Z., Mai, J., & Jing, J. (2009). *Factors associated with internet addiction among adolescents. Cyberpsychology &Behavior, 12,* 551–555.

Lam, L. T., & Peng, Z. W. (2010). *Effect of pathological use of the internet on adolescent mental health: A prospective study. Archives of Pediatrics & Adolescent Medicine, 164*(10), 901–906. doi: 10.1001/archpediatrics.2010.159

LaRose, R., Mastro, D., & Eastin, M. S. (2001). *Understanding internet usage: A social-cognitive approach to uses and gratifications. Social Science Computer Review, 19,* 395–413.

Lemmens, J. S., Valkenburg, P. M., & Peter, J. (2009). *Development and validation of a game addiction scale for adolescents. Media Psychology, 12,* 77–95.

Liu, C., & Kuo, F. (2007). *A study of internet addiction through the lens of the interpersonal theory. CyberPsychology & Behavior, 10,* 799–804.

Magerkurth, C., Cheok, A. D., Mandryk, R. L., & Nilsen, T. (2005). *Pervasive games: Bringing computer entertainment back to the real world. ACM Computers in Entertainment, 3,* 1–19.

McMurran, M. (1994). *The Psychology of Addiction.* London: Taylor & Francis.

Meerkerk, G. J., Van den Eijnden, R. J. J. M., Vermulst, A. A., & Garretsen, H. F. L. (2009). *The compulsive internet use scale (CIUS): Some psychometric properties. CyberPsychology & Behavior, 12,* 1–6.

Mehroof, M., & Griffiths, M. D. (2010). *Online gaming addiction: The role of sensation seeking, self-control, neuroticism, aggression, state anxiety, and trait anxiety. Cyberpsychology, Behavior, and Social Networking, 13,* 33–316.

Meyer, G., Schwertfeger, J., Exton, M. S., Jansen, O. E., Knapp, W., Stadler, M. A., et al. (2004). *Neuroendocrine response to casino gambling in problem gamblers. Psychoneuroendocrinology, 29*(10), 1272–1280.

Miller, S. A. (2002). *Death of a game addict. Milwaukee Journal Sentinel.* Retrieved April 2, 2002 from http://www.jsonline.com/news/State/mar02/31536.asp.

Montag, C., Jurkiewicz, M., & Reuter, M. (2010). *Low self-directedness is a better predictor for problematic internet use than high neuroticism. Computers in Human Behavior, 26,* 1531–1535.

Morahan-Martin, J., & Scumacher, P. (2000). *Incidence and correlates of pathological Internet use among college students. Computers in Human Behavior, 16,* 13–29.

Mythily, S., Qiu, S., & Winlow, M. (2008). *Prevalence and correlates of excessive internet use among youth in Singapore. Annals, Academy of Medicine, Singapore, 37,* 9–14

National Institute on Drug Addiction (2010). *The Science of Addiction.* Washington, DC: NIDA. Retrieved July 30, 2012 from http://www.nida.nih.gov/scienceofaddiction/.

Nichols, L. A., & Nicki, R. (2004). *Development of a psychometrically sound Internet addiction scale: A preliminary step. Psychology of Addictive Behaviors, 18,* 381–384.

Odaci, H., & Kalkan, M. (2010). *Problematic Internet use, loneliness and dating anxiety among young adult university students. Computers & Education, 55,* 1091–1097.

Peng, L. H., & Li, X. A. (2009). *Survey of Chinese college students addicted to video games. China Education Innovation Herald, 28,* 111–112.

Peng, W., & Liu, M. (2010). *Online gaming dependency: A preliminary study in China. CyberPsychology & Behavior, 13,* 329–333.

Phillips, C. A., Rolls, S., Rouse, A., & Griffiths, M. (1995). *Home video game playing in schoolchildren: A study of incidence and patterns of play. Journal of Adolescence, 18,* 687–691.

Pickens, R. W., & Svikis, D. S. (1989). *Biological Vulnerability to Drug Abuse* Rockville, MD: Department of Health of Human Services (NIDA Research Monograph, Number 89).

Pomerleau, O. F., Fertig, J., Baker, L., & Cooney, N. (1983). *Reactivity to alcohol cues in alcoholics and non-alcoholics: Implications for a stimulus control analysis of drinking. Addictive Behaviors, 8,* 1–10.

Porter, G., Starcevic, V., Berle, D., & Fenech, P. (2010). *Recognizing problem video game use. Australian and New Zealand Journal of Psychiatry, 44,* 120–128.

Putnam, D. F., & Maheu, M. M. (2000). *Online sexual addiction and compulsivity: Integrating web resources and behavioral telehealth in treatment. Sexual Addiction & Compulsivity, 7,* 91–112.

Rehbein, F., Kleimann, M., & Moßle, T. (2010). *Prevalence and risk factors of video game dependency in adolescence: Results of a German national study. CyberPsychology & Behavior, 13,* 162–168.

Reuters News Service (2005a). Asia tackles online game addiction. Retrieved November 27, 2005 from http://www.msnbc.msn.com/id/9340038/.

Reuters News Service (2005b). South Korean man dies after 50 hours of computer games. Retrieved November 26, 2005 from http://www.msnbc.msn.com/id/8888579/.

Salguero, R. A. T., & Moran, R. M. B. (2002). *Measuring problem video game playing in adolescents. Addiction, 97,* 1601–1606.

Serpelloni, G., & Gerra, G. (2002) Vulnerabilità all'addiction. Accessed: July 30, 2012 at http://veneto.dronet.org/biblioteca/vis_vul.php

Shaffer, D. (2004). Concepts of diagnostic classification. In Wiener, J. M., & Dulcan, M. I. (Eds.), *The American Psychiatric Publishing Textbook of Child and Adolescent Psychiatry.* Washington, DC: American Psychiatric Press, pp. 77–85.

Shaffer, H. J., Hall, M. N., & Vander Bilt, J. (2000). *"Computer addiction": A critical consideration. American Journal of Orthopsychiatry, 70,* 162–168.

Shaffer, H. J., & Kidman, R. (2003). *Shifting perspectives on gambling and addiction. Journal of Gambling Studies, 19,* 1–6.

Shaffer, H. J., LaPlante, D. A., LaBrie, R. A., Kidman, R. C., Donato, A. N., & Stanton, M. V. (2004). *Toward a syndrome model of addiction: Multiple expressions, common etiology. Harvard Review of Psychiatry, 12,* 367–374.

Shapira, N. A., Goldsmith, T. D., Keck, P. E., Khosla, U. M., & McElroy, S. L. (2000) *Psychiatric features of individuals with problematic internet use. Journal of Affective Disorders, 57,* 267–272.

Shapira, N. A., Lessig, M. C., Goldsmith, T. D., Szabo, S. T., Lazoritz, M., Gold, M. S., et al. (2003). *Problematic internet use: Proposed classification and diagnostic criteria. Depression and Anxiety, 17,* 207–216.

Shek, D. T. L., Tang, V. M. Y., & Lo, C. Y. (2009). *Evaluation of an internet addiction treatment program for Chinese adolescents in Hong Kong. Adolescence, 44,* 359–373.

Soper, W. B., & Miller, M. J. (1983). *Junk-time junkies: An emerging addiction among students. The School Counselor, 31,* 40–43.

Stein, D. J. (1997). *Internet addiction, internet psychotherapy. American Journal of Psychiatry, 154,* 890.

Tejeiro Salguero, R. A., & Bersabé Morán, R. M. (2002). *Measuring problem video game playing in adolescents. Addiction, 97,* 1601–1606.

Tisserand, I. N. (2000). *New risks of addiction for new populations: the example of hackers. Annales de Medecine Interne, 151*(Suppl), B49–52.

Turner, N. E. (2008). *A comment on "problems with the concept of video game 'addiction': Some case study examples." International Journal of Mental Health and Addiction, 6,* 186–190.

Van den Eijnden, R. J. J. M., Spijkerman, R., Vermulst, A. A., Van Rooij, T. J., & Engels, R. C. M. E. (2010). *Compulsive internet use among adolescents: Bidirectional parent-child relationships. Journal of Abnormal Child Psychology, 38,* 77–89.

Van Rooij, A. J., Schoenmakers, T. M., Vermulst, A. A., Van den Eijnden, R. J. J. M., & van de Mheen, D. (2010). *Online video game addiction: identification of addicted adolescent gamers. Addiction, 106,* 205–212.

Wassenaar, J. S., Van Doorn, A. B. D., & Dierssen, A. H. J. (1998). *The human-computer interface: Autonomy and addiction—a neuro-cognitive study. CyberPsychology & Behavior, 1,* 353–360.

West, M. I. (1988). *Children, Culture, & Controversy.* Hamden, CT: Archon Books.

Widyanto, L., & McMurran, M. (2004). *The psychometric properties of the internet addiction test. CyberPsychology & Behavior, 7,* 443–450.

Wood, R. T. A. (2008). *Problems with the concept of video game "addiction": Some case study examples. International Journal of Mental Health and Addiction, 6,* 169–178.

Wood, R. T. A., & Griffiths, M. D. (2007). *Time loss whilst playing video games: Is there a relationship to addictive behaviours. International Journal of Mental Health and Addiction, 5,* 141–149.

Wood, R. T. A., Gupta, R., Derevensky, J. L., & Griffiths, M. (2004). *Video game playing and gambling in adolescents: Common risk factors. Journal of Child & Adolescent Substance Abuse, 14,* 77–100.

Yee, N. (2001). *The Norrathian Scrolls: A Study of EverQuest* (Version 2.5). Retrieved November 28, 2005, from http://www.nickyee.com/eqt.

Yee, N. (2002). *Ariadne: Understanding MMORPG Addiction.* Retreived November 28, 2005, from http://www.nickyee.com/hub/addiction/home.html.

Yen, J., Yen, C., Chen, C., Chen, S., & Ko, C. (2007). *Family factors of internet addiction and substance use experience in Taiwanese adolescents. Cyberpsychology and Behavior, 10,* 323–329.

Young, K. S. (1996) *Psychology of computer use: XL. Addictive use of the internet: A case that breaks the stereotype. Psychological Reports, 79,* 899–902.

Young, K. S. (1997). *Internet addiction: The emergence of a new clinical disorder. CyberPsychology & Behavior, 1,* 237–244.

Young, K. S. (1998). *Caught in the Net.* New York: Wiley.

Yoo, H. J., Cho S. C., Ha, J., Yune, S. K., Kim, S. J., Hwang, J., et al. (2004). *Attention deficit hyperactivity symptoms and internet addiction. Psychiatry and Clinical Neurosciences, 58,* 487–494.

Zhang, L., Amos, L., & McDowell, W. C. (2008). *A comparative study of Internet addiction between the United States and China. CyberPsychology & Behavior, 11,* 727–729.

Video Games and Attention

Robert West *and* Kira Bailey

Abstract

The widespread consumption of video games has led social commentators and scientists to question the effects of this medium on the human experience. Within the social and cognitive sciences, investigators have devoted considerable energy to characterizing the effects of video game experience on cognitive and social information processing and behavior (Anderson et al., 2010; Green, Li, & Bavelier, 2010). This chapter considers the emerging literature demonstrating a relationship between video game experience and clinical attention deficits, and provides an integrative review of the literature related to the association between video game experience and attention within three domains (visuospatial processing, executive function, and emotion). This literature reveals that video game experience can both enhance and disrupt various aspects of attention related to these aspects of mental life. Building on existing evidence, future research should seek to identify the boundary conditions under which effects of video game experience are observed and determine the effects of this medium on attention in natural settings.

Key Words: attention deficits, emotion, executive function, visuospatial processing

Introduction

The widespread use of console and computer-based video games has generated intense interest in the effects of this medium on cognitive and social information processing in recent years. Recent data suggest that 67% of American households own at least one video game console, and the average video gamer spends 8 hours a week playing (Entertainment Software Association, 2011). Given these statistics, it seems clear that experience with video games has the potential to shape the mental life of a wide range of the population. Additionally, the continued development of games that target specific audiences (e.g., Brain Age for senior adults) means that the positive and negative effects of video games may be expressed over most of the lifespan in the near future. Complimenting other chapters in this volume, the current chapter provides an integrative review of the

effects of video games on various aspects of attention as related to clinical attention deficits, visuospatial processing, executive function or cognitive control, and emotion. As the reader will discover from examining the literature described herein, video game experience is associated with changes in performance across a broad spectrum of tasks that in some instances represent enhancements in the efficiency of information processing (Dye, Green, & Bavelier, 2009a) and in other instances represent disruptions of optimal functioning (Gentile, 2009; Bailey, West, & Anderson, 2010a). This evidence converges with the emerging sentiment that the effects of video games on cognition and emotion can be best understood through the application of a multidimensional approach that transcends the simplistic interpretation of the effects of this medium as good or bad (Gentile, 2011).

Before reviewing the literature examining the effects of video games on attention, we provide some general introductory information designed to facilitate navigation by the reader through the literature considered in the chapter. For most of the studies reviewed in the following pages, one of two methodological approaches has been employed to examine the association between video games and attention (i.e., individual difference and training or priming studies). The individual difference approach capitalized on natural variation in video game experience in the population and typically contrasts video game players (Players)—individuals who play video games on a daily or weekly basis—with non-video players (Non-players)—individuals who do not play video games or those who play video games infrequently. The individual difference approach is limited in that Players are self-selected, making causal inference related to differences in performance between Players and Non-players difficult. Training studies are often used to demonstrate a causal link between video games and information processing. In these studies, Non-players are "trained" to play either a targeted or control video game for some varying number of hours (e.g., 10–50) and tested before and after training on tasks relevant to the question under investigation. The presence of a training group by occasion interaction (i.e., demonstrating a significant [or greater] effect of training in the targeted group relative to the control group) is taken as evidence for a causal effect of video games. Much of this literature, particularly within the context of visuospatial processing, has focused on action video games wherein the player navigates through a virtual environment and is often tasked with destroying enemies. Common features of action video games include transient events and quickly moving objects, a "high degree of perceptual, cognitive, and motor load," "unpredictability," "an emphasis on peripheral processing" (Green, Li, & Bavelier, 2010), and violence or aggression (Anderson et al., 2010). Additionally, a small number of studies have examined the effects of real-time strategy games on attention and executive function (e.g., Basak et al., 2008; Boot et al., 2008).

Video Games and Attention Deficits

Video game usage has become a ubiquitous aspect of American society. Approximately 23% of 8- to 18-year-olds reported playing video games at least once a day in 2009 (Gentile, 2009). Recent work has revealed that between 8% and 9% of children and adolescent Players meet criteria for pathological video game use (Gentile, 2009; Gentile et al., 2011). Pathological gamers play video games more frequently and for longer periods of time, skip other activities (e.g., homework, chores) to play video games, and report using video games to escape their problems more often in comparison with their peers. Several negative outcomes are associated with pathological video game play, such as increased aggression, poor performance in school, and the development of depression and anxiety (Gentile et al., 2011). The relationship between pathological video game use and disorders of attention has been a topic of much speculation, but a relatively small body of literature has examined this association. However, the data from these studies are converging on the conclusion that pathological video game play (i.e., video game addiction) and attention deficit hyperactivity disorder (ADHD) are closely related (Bioulac, Arfi, & Bouvard, 2008; Gentile, 2009; Gentile et al., 2011).

In the last decade, the United States has seen an increase in the number of children age 4 to 17 who are diagnosed with ADHD. From 2003 to 2007, 9.5% of school-age children were diagnosed with ADHD, reflecting a 22% increase in the number of cases from previous years (Centers for Disease Control, 2010). The symptoms of ADHD can be broadly divided into inattentiveness, hyperactivity, and impulsivity (National Institute of Health, 2010). Although children and adolescents with ADHD frequently find it difficult to perform tasks that require sustained attention, they spend many hours watching television, surfing the Internet, and playing video games (Weiss & Weiss, 2002; Yoo et al., 2004). Studies have shown that ADHD is associated with an increased likelihood of developing substance abuse during adolescence (Biederman et al., 1998; Wilens, Biederman, & Mick, 1998; Tapert al., 2002). This finding, coupled with the increased number of hours spent on the Internet and playing video games, may be cause for concern. For example, Internet addiction in 10- to 12-year-olds is associated with a greater number of ADHD symptoms related to impulsivity and inattentiveness, and children diagnosed with ADHD are more likely to possess symptoms of Internet addiction (Yoo et al., 2004). These investigators suggested several reasons for the relationship between ADHD and Internet addiction, such as the lack of inhibitory control, need for immediate rewards, and poor social skills resulting from ADHD. The study also reported that children with ADHD spend more time playing games than other activities online, a finding that provides a link between Internet addiction and pathological video game use.

A few studies have explored the relationship between the amount of time spent playing video games and the number of ADHD symptoms. In a sample of ninth and tenth graders, Chan and Rabinowitz (2006) found that playing console or Internet video games for more than an hour a day was positively correlated with scores on the inattention and ADHD subscales of the Connor's Parent Rating scale. Similarly, in a sample of 6- to 16-year-olds, 34% of children diagnosed with ADHD endorsed five or more statements on a Problem Video Game Playing survey modeled after the DSM-IV criteria for pathological gambling and substance abuse (Bioulac et al., 2008). These children had more severe symptoms of ADHD compared with children with the disorder who did not score more than four on the Problem Video Game Playing survey. None of the control children endorsed more than four of the statements. Although there were no differences in the number of hours ADHD and control children spent playing video games, parent reports revealed that hyperactive children were less likely to stop playing on their own and they responded to requests to stop playing with more negative behavior (e.g., arguing, whining, crying) than the control children. These findings suggest that for some children, ADHD may be associated with an increase in the likelihood of pathological video game use.

Two recent studies provide evidence for an association between pathological video game use and ADHD symptoms (Gentile, 2009; Gentile et al., 2011). Gentile developed an 11-item pathological video game use scale adapted from the DSM-IV criteria for pathological gambling. Endorsing one to four of the items was considered within the normal range, whereas endorsing five or more was taken to reflect the presence of pathological gaming. In a large sample of 8- to 18-year-olds, 8.5% of participants met criteria for pathological video game use (Gentile, 2009). Pathological gamers were twice as likely to be diagnosed with an attention deficit disorder. Similar results have been reported in a longitudinal study of children and adolescents from Singapore, where approximately 9% met criteria for pathological video game use (Gentile et al., 2011). Children who started out as pathological video game users and remained that way for the duration of the study reported more symptoms of ADHD than their peers who never met criteria for pathological video game use. The longitudinal design of the study allowed the researchers to investigate risk

factors and outcomes of pathological video game use. Impulsivity represented one risk factor for pathological video game use at the beginning of the study and predicted increases in pathological video gaming use over time. Pathological game use also predicted greater impulsivity (Gentile et al., 2011), suggesting that there may be a reciprocal relationship between these variables. Specifically, based on these data it appears that disruptions of impulse control and attention may increase the likelihood of pathological video game use, and that pathological gaming may also exacerbate the symptoms of ADHD.

Given the prevalence of pathological video game use and ADHD, it is critical that we gain an understanding of how these conditions interact. Before future research can shed light on the matter, a standardized measure of pathological video game use should be developed. Although all of the measures to date have been based on well-established criteria for pathological gambling, differences in the scales may be problematic for cross-study comparisons (Bioulac et al., 2008; Gentile, 2009; Gentile et al., 2011). These measures have also been created under the assumption that pathological video game use is highly similar to pathological gambling, based in part on research showing that video game play activates the mesocorticolimbic system, an area involved in reward circuitry (Hoeft et al., 2008). Further research will be necessary to confirm similarities between pathological gambling and gaming.

There are several interesting questions that future research could address. The biggest question is whether the relationship between ADHD and pathological video game use is causal, and if so, which is the cause and which the effect? There is already some evidence that impulsivity, one of the main symptom categories for ADHD, is a risk factor for developing pathological video game use (Gentile et al., 2011). Bioulac et al. (2008) have also suggested that a subset of ADHD children with the most severe symptoms may be particularly susceptible to pathological video game use. These findings are suggestive of a causal link between ADHD and pathological video game use, but are not conclusive. In addition to whether or not the relationship is causal, it will also be important to know whether or not video game use exacerbates symptoms of ADHD. One study demonstrated that experience with action video games was negatively correlated with the engagement of proactive cognitive control in a sample of college students (Bailey et al., 2010a), suggesting that action video game use could increase problems with inattention and impulsivity. In contrast, training on a real-time strategy video game was shown to improve cognitive control in older adults (Basak et al., 2008). It seems possible, and even likely, that different types of video games may have different effects on attention (Gentile, 2011; see also chapter 16), with action-based video games exacerbating attention disorders and slower-moving strategy-based games possibly leading to improvements in cognitive control. Understanding the differential effects that video game genres have on attention may prove to be as important as defining the relationship between ADHD and pathological video game use.

Visuospatial Processing

A significant body of research has examined the association between action video game experience and visuospatial processing (Dye et al., 2009a; Green et al., 2010). These studies have incorporated both individual difference and training methods, demonstrating robust associations between action video game experience and chronic exposure to action video games that can be induced in Non-players with 10 to 50 hours of training (Green & Bavelier, 2003; Li et al., 2009), and are durable for at least 5 months (Feng, Spence, & Pratt, 2007). Research in this area of inquiry can be broadly divided into five related domains examined in the current review of the literature (i.e., visual acuity, spatial selective attention, attention orienting, visual enumeration, and temporal processing).

Visual Acuity

The effects of action video game experience on fundamental aspects of visual acuity have been examined in three studies. Li et al. (2009) considered the relationship between action video game experience and contrast sensitivity—a primary determinant of visual acuity—in a series of experiments incorporating individual difference and training methods (Figure 23.1E). This study revealed that contrast sensitivity was enhanced in Players relative to Non-players between 3 and 12 cycles per degree, and that this effect was induced in Non-players with 50 hours of training on two action video games. The effect of training represented a dramatic 43% to 58% improvement in contrast sensitivity. Converging with these data, Li et al. also found that the integration time (i.e., the presentation duration required to detect a difference between two stimuli) required for contrast detection was significantly lower in Players than

in Non-players, and that this effect could also be induced with 50 hours of training. The association between action video game experience and visual acuity has also been examined in the visual crowding paradigm (Green & Bavelier, 2007). In this task individuals judge the orientation of a T (up/down) surround by two flanking Ts and the distance between stimuli varies over trials (Figure 23.1D). Experiment 1 of this study examined the association between individual differences in action video game experience and crowding, and Experiment 2 examined the effect of 30 hours of training on an action or non-action video game. In both experiments, the size of the crowding zone was smaller for Players than for Non-players or those trained on the non-action video game. Also, in Experiment 1 individual differences in video game experience were associated with variation in visual threshold, with Players having lower thresholds than Non-players. Interestingly, this effect did not interact with eccentricity (i.e., the distance from fixation) indicating that the effects of video game experience were relatively constant across the visual field and were similar within and outside of the region of space most often used during video game play (Green & Bavelier, 2007). These findings are important because they reveal a far transfer effect (i.e., transfer across very different tasks) of action video games on low-level visual processing, and such demonstrations are relatively few in the intervention literature (Li et al., 2009).

The association between action video game experience and the temporal resolution of vision has been examined in a study using the simultaneity judgment and temporal order tasks (Donohue, Woldorff, & Mitroff, 2010). In this study the point of subjective simultaneity (i.e., the point at which individuals cannot discriminate between the nonoverlapping onset of two visual objects) in the simultaneity judgment task was lower for Players than for Non-players, and did not differ from zero for the Players. The data for the temporal-order judgment task revealed a similar pattern of results, although the association between action video game experience and the temporal resolution of visual and auditory processing was less robust for this task. Together, the results of these studies demonstrate that action video game experience is associated with enhancements of the spatial and temporal resolution of visual acuity, that these effects are similar across the visual field, and that these effects can be induced with 30 to 50 hours of video game experience.

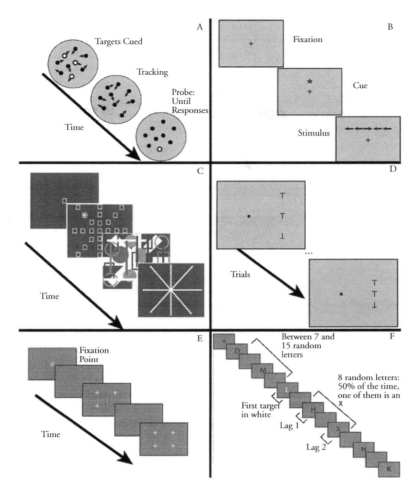

Figure 23.1 Examples of Stimulus Displays for Six Task Used to Examine the Association Between Action Video Game Experience on Spatial and Temporal Aspects of Visuospatial Processing That Reveal an Advantage of Players Over Non-Players. **A.** Multiple-object tracking task wherein individuals track the location of randomly moving targets over time. **B.** Attention networks task that measures alerting, orienting, and conflict monitoring attention systems. **C.** Useful Field of View task that measures visual selective attention or speed of processing. **D.** Visual crowding task, (*E*) contrast detection task that measure contrast sensitivity or visual acuity, and (*F*) attentional blink task to measure the temporal allocation of visual attention.

Adapted from Green, C. S., Li, R., & Bavelier, D. (2010). Perceptual learning during action video game playing. Topics in Cognitive Science, 2, 202–216.

Attention Orienting

The association between action video game experience and the exogenous orienting or capture of attention has been examined by a number of investigators. Two studies have used variations of the Posner cueing task (Posner, 1980) to examine this relationship (Castel, Pratt, & Drummond, 2005; Dye, Green, & Bavelier, 2009b). Castel et al. used a target detection task to measure attentional orienting and inhibition of return. These investigators observed the typical cue validity by stimulus onset asynchrony interaction in the response time data, providing evidence for attentional orienting and

inhibition of return. This effect did not interact with individual differences in video game experience, leading to the conclusion that action video game experience does not influence attentional processes associated with the orienting of attention (Castel et al., 2005). Dye et al. examined the association between action video game experience and attentional orienting in the attention networks task (Fan et al., 2002) in 7- to 22-year-olds (Figure 23.1B). In this study, the attentional orienting effect was greater for Players than for Non-players, indicating that there may be an association between action video game experience and attentional orienting.

The association between action video game experience and attentional orienting has also been explored in studies examining attentional capture (i.e., the slowing of response time or reduction in accuracy that occurs when salient distractors occur in the environment (West et al., 2008; Chisholm et al., 2010). West et al. examined the association between individual differences in action video game experience and performance on a visual point of subjective simultaneity task with an attentional orienting cue, and in a motion detection task. Both of these tasks revealed significant differences in performance between Players and Non-players. The point of subjective simultaneity was longer for Players than for Non-players, reflecting stronger capture of attention by the cue in the Players. Additionally, the Players were better able to detect the change in motion in the motion detection task than were the Non-players. These findings lead to the suggestion that exogenous attentional orienting is enhanced in Players relative to Non-players.

Chisholm et al. (2010) used an attention capture task that required individuals to indicate the orientation of a bar that appeared inside a shape singleton and ignore a color singleton that appeared on some trials. These investigators found that attentional capture in response time was significantly reduced in Players (M = 93 ms) relative to Non-players (M = 162 ms). This effect was interpreted as resulting from an increase in the efficiency with which Players could redirect attention from the distractor to the target following the capture of attention (Chisholm et al., 2010). Based on the results of these studies it appears that action video game experience may be associated with alterations in the exogenous and possibly endogenous orienting of attention, and this effect can both facilitate and disrupt the efficiency of information processing. However, the mixed results observed across studies indicate that additional research may be warranted to ascertain the extent of the effect of video game experience on the exogenous and endogenous orienting of attention.

Visual Enumeration

The visual enumeration task has been used to study the association between action video game experience and the number of items that can be attended in a briefly flashed display (Green & Bavelier, 2003, 2006). In this task, individuals view a varying number of simple geometric objects (e.g., circles or squares) and judge the number of objects presented in the display (Trick & Pylyshyn, 1993).

The typical behavioral finding is that response time and accuracy are relatively constant for displays with one to four items and then increases (for response time) or decreases (for accuracy) for displays containing five to twelve objects. The number of items that can be processed in parallel (i.e., with 0 or minimal display size × response time or accuracy slope) is described as the subitizing range, and performance for larger display sizes is often described as the counting range (Trick & Pylyshyn, 1993).

Green and Bavelier (2003, 2006) have reported effects of action video game experience for both the subitizing and counting portions of the display size function. For response accuracy, the subitizing range is about two items greater for Players (M = 5.0) than for Non-players (M = 3.0). This association appears to be similar in magnitude across the visual field, and is observed when individuals respond via manual or vocal output. Additionally, an effect of action video games can be induced in Non-players with as little as 10 hours of video game training (Green & Bavelier, 2003), and the size of the training effect can be similar to that related to individual differences (Green & Bavelier, 2006). Response time is similar for Players and Non-players for display sizes of one to five or six items, and is then slower for Players relative to Non-players (Green & Bavelier, 2006). The slower response times for Players may seem surprising given the finding that response time is typically faster for Players than Non-players (Dye et al., 2009a). However, for this particular task the increase in response time may result from an enhancement of the fidelity of the visual representation once the display is terminated, that facilitates counting or estimation processes and bolsters accuracy for larger displays (Green & Bavelier, 2006). The effects of action video games on response time appear to require more extended experience than the effects on accuracy, as these effects are not observed with 10 hours of training. The effect of training may be somewhat specific to action video games, as 21 hours of training on a real-time strategy game did not have an effect on visual enumeration (Basak et al., 2008). Additionally, the generalizability of the effect of action video game experience on visual enumeration should be examined in future research, as at least one study (Boot et al., 2008) failed to replicate the individual difference and training effects observed by Green and Bavelier.

Spatial Selective Attention

The association between action video game experience and spatial selective visual attention has been examined in studies using the Useful Field of View (Figure 23.1C), visual search (Castel et al., 2005), and perceptual load tasks. In the Useful Field of View task individuals are required to identify the location of a peripheral target that may or may not be presented with a set of distractors. Across trials the target is presented 10, 20, or 30 degrees from fixation. Three studies have reported a significant association between action video game experience and performance on the Useful Field of View task (Green & Bavelier, 2003, 2006; Feng et al., 2007), with Players performing better than Non-players. Green and Bavelier (2006) demonstrated that the advantage of Players over Non-players on the Useful Field of View task was observed regardless of whether the target is presented in isolation or with distractors, and regardless of whether or not individuals perform a secondary task that requires the discrimination of a stimulus presented at fixation. Furthermore, these investigators observed that the advantage of Players over Non-players was somewhat diminished when the target was presented 30 degrees from fixation and distractors were present (Green & Bavelier, 2006), leading to the suggestion that this task condition may approach some capacity limit of Players. Feng et al. (2007) replicated the findings of Green and Bavelier related to individual differences in action video game experience. These investigators also observed that individual differences in video game experience may attenuate sex-related differences in performance on the Useful Field of View task.

The causal effect of action video game experience on the Useful Field of View task has been examined in three training studies. Green and Bavelier (2003) reported that only 10 hours of video game training resulted in improvements in performance on the Useful Field of View task that were somewhat less dramatic than the effect associated with individual differences in action video game experience. These investigators replicated this effect in a study using 30 hours of training, in which again the effect of training appeared to be somewhat weaker than the association between individual differences in action video game experience and performance on the Useful Field of View task (Green & Bavelier, 2006). Feng et al. (2007) also found that 10 hours of video game training led to significant improvements in performance of the Useful Field of View task, and that training reduced sex-related differences in performance on the Useful Field of View task. Additionally, these investigators found that the size of the effect of training was similar to

that observed for individual differences and that the effect was maintained for up to 5 months after training. Similar to data from the individual difference studies, the effect of training on the Useful Field of View task appears to be relatively constant across the visual field demonstrating that the effect of action video games on selective visual attention extends beyond the region of the visual field that is most commonly used during video game play (Green & Bavelier, 2006). The effect of video game training in the Useful Field of View task appears to be somewhat specific to action video games as Basak et al. (2008) failed to find an effect of training on a real-time strategy game on task performance. There may also be some variation in the optimal parameters for training with action video games as Boot et al. (2008) failed to observe a significant effect of action video game training on the Useful Field of View task.

The perceptual load task has been used to examine the association between action video game experience and the processing of visual distractors or task irrelevant information (Green & Bavelier, 2003, 2006). In this task, the influence of distractors is measured by examining the size of the target-distractor compatibility effect. The typical finding is that the size of this effect is reduced as perceptual load increases. Consistent with the typical finding, the size of the compatibility effect is reduced as perceptual load increases in Non-players. In contrast, in Players the size of the compatibility effect appears to be insensitive to perceptual load across the range of conditions that have been examined in the extant literature. These data demonstrate that there may be costs associated with the enhancement of the spatial selective attention observed in Players relative to Non-players, and are consistent with other evidence indicating that action video game experience is not always associated with improvements in the "control" of visual attention (West et al., 2008).

Temporal Processing in Vision

The attentional blink paradigm has been used to examine the association between video game experience and the temporal limits of visual attention (Figure 23.1F) (Green & Bavelier, 2003). In this task individuals are required to detect a briefly presented target stimulus embedded in a stream of task-irrelevant stimuli. The typical finding is that the occurrence of a target early in the series disrupts the detection of a second target in the series (i.e., the attentional blink) and this effect is greatest when the second target occurs within two or three items of the first. Green and Bavelier reported that the magnitude of the attentional blink was attenuated in Players relative to Non-players for lags of one to five items, and that a similar effect was induced with 10 hours of action video game training for lags of four or five items. Based on these data, Green and Bavelier argued that the temporal allocation of attention is enhanced with action video game experience (Chisholm et al., 2010). Boot et al. (2008) failed to replicate the association between action video game experience related to individual differences or training with an action video game, leading to the suggestion that further research is likely needed to identify the boundary conditions of this association.

As an interim summary, video game experience is associated with enhancements of visuospatial processing across a wide range of tasks measuring aspects of visual acuity, exogenous and endogenous orienting of visual attention, and visual search. The ubiquitous nature of this effect leads one to wonder whether the effects of video games on visuospatial processing could result from the modification of a fundamental mechanism that transcends the information processing demands of the particular paradigm. The nature of one possible mechanism is considered later in the chapter in the section examining The Basis of Action Video Game Effects.

Executive Function

Executive functions represent those cognitive processes that serve to facilitate flexible, adaptive, or goal-directed behavior in the individual (Stuss et al., 1994; Miyake et al., 2000; Miller & Cohen, 2001). Across different theoretical and methodological approaches, similar concepts have been studied as executive or frontal lobe functions, and cognitive control. Although these three constructs are not synonyms, it is beyond the scope of the current chapter to examine their similarities and differences. However, excellent theoretical and empirical work addressing this intersection is found in a variety of sources (Miyake et al., 2000; Miller & Cohen, 2001). The following sections examine the relationship between video game experience and executive functions revealed in studies using individual difference, priming, and training studies.

Task Switching

The relationship between video game experience and the ability to fluently switch between two or more tasks has been examined in a number of studies using the task switching paradigm (Boot et al.,

2008; Karle, Watter, & Shedden, 2010; Strobach, Frensch, & Schubert, 2010). In these studies individuals perform two or more simple tasks (e.g., indicating whether a digit is odd or even, or less than or greater than 5) in a block of trials. The relevant task is defined by a cue that is presented before the onset of the target stimulus; the cue may or may not remain present after the onset of the target stimulus. The primary dependent variable in these studies has been "switch costs" for response time. Switch costs represent the difference in response time between trials in which the individual switches from one task to another relative to trials in which the same task is performed on consecutive trials (Logan & Bundesen, 2003; Monsell, 2003).

The most consistent finding in studies of the association between action video game experience and task switching is that switch costs are reduced in Players relative to Non-players (Boot et al., 2008; Karle et al., 2010; Strobach et al., 2010). A significant association between individual differences in video game experience and task switch costs has been reported by three independent groups of investigators using different task cues and stimuli indicating that the effect as related to chronic video game experience is relatively robust. Additionally, two studies have reported that the benefit of video game experience on task switching costs may be realized with 15 to 21 hours of training in Non-players (Basak et al., 2008; Strobach et al., 2010). In contrast to the two studies demonstrating reductions in task switching costs with video game training, Boot et al. failed to find an effect of training on an action video game or a real-time strategy game on task switch costs with 21 hours of training. The primary difference between the studies of Boot et al. and Basak et al. appears to be related to the research participants, who represented younger or older adults, respectively.

One study has sought to examine the locus of the effect of video game experience on task switch costs (Karle et al., 2010). In this study the investigators argued that video game experience may serve to facilitate the development of stimulus-response mappings and that this in turn leads to the reduction in task switch costs. This account is consistent with the idea that video game experience may enhance information integration in Players that benefits performance in a wide range of tasks (Green, Pouget, & Bavelier, 2010). Karle et al. tested this idea in two experiments. In Experiment 1, Players and Non-players performed a task switching paradigm in which one task was mapped to the left hand and the other task was mapped to the right hand. The investigators argued that this paradigm would maximize stimulus-response mappings while at the same time minimizing stimulus-response and proactive interference. In Experiment 2, Players and Non-players performed a task switching paradigm in which one hand was used to perform three different tasks. The investigators argued that this paradigm would maximize stimulus-response and proactive interference. In Experiment 1, task switch costs were reduced in Players relative to Non-players. In contrast, this difference was eliminated in Experiment 2. These findings converge with those of Boot et al. and Basak et al. in which the two tasks were also mapped to different hands, and may indicate that the benefit of video game experience on task switching is limited to instances in which interference between stimulus-response mapping is minimized.

Stroop and Flanker Tasks

The association between video game experience and selective attention and cognitive control has been examined in studies incorporating the flanker task (Eriksen & Schultz, 1979) and the Stroop task (Stroop, 1935; MacLeod, 1991). In these tasks, individuals must selectively attend to one attribute of a stimulus while ignoring or inhibiting a response to another attribute of a stimulus. For instance, in the color-word Stroop task individuals are asked to name or identify the color of a stimulus (e.g., RED presented in blue) while ignoring the meaning of the word. In the flanker task, individuals are required to identify the direction of a central stimulus while ignoring distractors presented in the periphery. There is a prepotent tendency to process the words or flanking letters that leads to interference (i.e., an increase in errors or slowing of response time) when the two dimensions of the stimuli are incongruent. Evidence from studies using behavioral (Kronenberger et al., 2005), functional neuroimaging (Mathews et al., 2005), and electrophysiological (Bailey et al., 2010a) methods reveals that there are reliable correlations between video game experience and specific processes underpinning cognitive control in these tasks.

Evidence from three behavioral studies demonstrates that the interference or compatibility effect can be greater for Players than for Non-players. In a study using a card-based neuropsychological version of the color-word Stroop task, Kronenberger et al. (2005) found a moderate correlation ($r = -.33$) between the Stroop effect and exposure to violent video games and television. Consistent with this finding, Dye et al. (2009b) found that the flanker

interference effect was greater for Players than for Non-players who were 7 to 22 years of age. Swing (2008) replicated the correlation between flanker interference and video game experience in a sample of college students, and extended this finding by examining the effect of video game genre. In this sample, experience with first person shooter video games ($r = .16$) and real-time strategy games ($r = .20$), games was associated with greater flanker interference. In contrast, experience with third-person shooter games was not significantly correlated with flanker interference ($r = .04$). These findings may indicate that it is not video game experience per se that influences selective attention, but rather specific characteristics that are differentially embodied in various game genres (Gentile, 2011).

The reason for the association between video game experience and interference is not well understood. Dye et al. (2009b) suggested that the greater flanker effect in Players might result from these individuals having greater visual attentional resources than Non-players, leading to greater processing of the distractors in this task. This account might also explain the correlation between the Stroop effect and video game experience observed by Kronenberger et al. (2005) using the card version of the Stroop task in which multiple color-words are presented in close proximity to the currently relevant color-word. Also consistent with this idea, the magnitude of the Stroop effect is similar for Players and Non-players in the single trial version of the Stroop task in which a single stimulus is presented in the display for each trial (Bailey, 2009; Wang et al., 2009; Bailey et al., 2010a).

Two studies have examined the relationship between video game experience and neural recruitment during performance of the counting Stroop task using functional magnetic resonance imaging (fMRI). Mathews et al. (2005) examined the association between individual differences in media violence exposure and neural recruitment during performance of the counting Stroop task wherein individuals are required to indicate the number of digits presented in a display and the number and identity of the digits can be congruent (e.g., 22) or incongruent (e.g., 222). Those individuals with low levels of media violence exposure demonstrated a typical pattern of greater activation within the anterior cingulate cortex (ACC) and the left inferior frontal gyrus for incongruent trials relative to neutral trials. In contrast, individuals with high levels of media violence exposure failed to demonstrate significant activation within the ACC for incongruent trials relative to congruent trials. Wang et al. (2009) extended these findings in a study examining neural recruitment during performance of the counting Stroop task after individuals had played either a violent video game or a nonviolent video game. In this study, the nonviolent video game group demonstrated greater recruitment in left dorsolateral prefrontal cortex (DLPFC), right pre-motor cortex, pre-supplementary motor area, and the right inferior parietal lobe for incongruent relative to congruent stimuli. Additionally, a functional connectivity analysis revealed greater connectivity between the dorsal ACC and left DLPFC in nonviolent players relative to violent players during performance of the Stroop task (Wang et al., 2009). These data demonstrate a causal effect of video game experience on functional recruitment and connectivity related to cognitive control after only 30 minutes of game play.

Complimenting work using fMRI, two studies have used event-related brain potentials (ERPs) to examine the association between individual differences in action video game experience and the neural correlates of cognitive control in the Stroop task (Bailey, 2009; Bailey et al., 2010a). Bailey et al. tested Players and Non-players on the Stroop task and varied the response-to-stimulus interval (i.e., 500 or 2,000 ms) between blocks. The magnitude

of the interference effect for response time was similar for low Players and high Players in the task. In contrast, the conflict adaptation effect reflecting tuning of cognitive control across trials was sensitive to gaming status. Specifically, there was no effect of gaming status on the conflict adaptation effect with a 500-ms RSI and the effect was significant in the Non-players, but not the Players, with a 2,000 ms RSI (Figure 23.2). The ERP data revealed two interesting effects. First, the amplitude of the medial frontal negativity—related to conflict detection (Liotti et al., 2000; West et al., 2005)—was attenuated in Players relative to the Non-players. Second, the amplitude of a left frontal slow wave was similar for Players and Non-players between 500 and 1,000 ms after stimulus onset, and was attenuated in the Players but not the Non-players between 1,000 and 2,000 ms after stimulus onset. Based on these findings, Bailey et al. argued that Players may not be able to endogenously maintain cognitive control when the task context is not intrinsically engaging (i.e., in the 2,000-ms RSI condition).

Working Memory

The N-back (Kirchner, 1958), visual short-term memory (VSTM) (Vogel & Machizawa, 2004), and operation span (Turner & Engle, 1989) tasks have

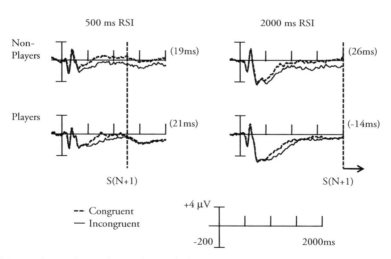

Figure 23.2 Grand-Averaged ERPs for a Left Lateral Frontal Electrode (F5) Demonstrating the Association Between Action Video Game Experience Proactive Cognitive Control in the Stroop Task

Notice that the slow wave differentiating congruent and incongruent stimuli and the conflict adaptation effect for response time is insensitive to RSI in the low Players and attenuated or eliminated in the high Players in the 2,000-ms RSI condition. For the ERPs the tall bar represents stimulus onset, the short bars represent 500-ms increments, and the dashed vertical lines represent the approximate timing of stimulus onset for the next trials. Note that stimulus onset for the next trial in the 2,000-ms RSI condition would extend beyond the end of the epoch represented by the horizontal arrow.

Adapted from

Bailey, K. M., West, R., & Anderson, C. A. (2010a). A negative association between video game experience and proactive cognitive control. Psychophysiology, 47, 34–42.

been used to examine the association between working memory and video game experience. Two studies failed to find a significant relationship between performance on the operation span task and individual differences in video game experience or training on a first-person shooter or real-time strategy game (Basak et al., 2008; Boot et al., 2008). The evidence from the N-back task is somewhat mixed. Boot et al. (2008) failed to find a correlation between individual differences in video game experience and performance on the N-back task or an effect of video game training on performance of the N-back task. In contrast, Basak et al. (2008) did find a reduction in focus switch costs in response time for older adults that were trained on a real-time strategy game. Bailey (2009) examined the association between individual differences in video game experience and the neural correlates of working memory maintenance in the N-back task. In this study, slow wave activity elicited during the response-to-stimulus interval that distinguished between low and high working memory load conditions was attenuated in Players relative to Non-players. Additionally, Bailey et al. (2010b) demonstrated that this effect could be induced with as little as 10 hours of training on the action video game Unreal Tournament. As is the case with the N-back task, studies using the VSTM task have revealed mixed results. Basak et al. (2008) found that training on a real-time strategy game lead to an enhancement of visual short-term memory capacity. Consistent with this finding, Boot et al. (2008) found that the capacity of visual short-term memory was greater for Players than Non-players. These researchers were not able to induce this effect with 21 hours of training on a first-person shooter or real-time strategy game in younger adults. The results of these studies indicate that there may be an effect of video game experience on working memory. However, it appears that further work is necessary to identify the conditions under which this association is observed.

As an interim summary, the effects of video games on various executive functions appear to be more diverse than the effects on visuospatial processing with video game experience being associated with enhancements of some abilities (e.g., flexibly switching between task sets when interference is minimal), little effect on other abilities (e.g., conflict resolution or response selection when interference is present), and decrements in still other abilities (e.g., adaptive processing over time). This latter effect is interesting given the emerging association between video games and clinical disorders of attention that are associated with increased distractibility and a decrease in the ability to persist in goal-directed behavior over time.

Emotion

Exposure to video game violence has been linked to increases in aggression, decreases in prosocial behavior, and desensitization to violence (see Anderson et al., 2010 for a review). An emerging literature demonstrates that action video game experience also influences the allocation of attention to positive and negative affect (Bartholow, Bushman & Sestir, 2006; Kirsh, Mounts, & Olczak, 2006; Kirsh & Mounts, 2007; Bailey, West, & Anderson, 2011). The association between action video game experience and emotion has been examined in the domains of face processing and affective picture processing.

Kirsh et al. (2006; Kirsh & Mounts, 2007) have demonstrated that attention to positive and negative affect related to facial expression can be altered by experience with violent media, including action video games. These studies examined the happy-face advantage (i.e., the finding that people are typically faster to respond to happy than angry facial expressions) (Billings, Harrison, & Alden, 1993; Leppanen, Tenhunen, & Heitanen, 2003) in a change detection task. Kirsh et al. (2006) had participants press a key when they noticed that a neutral face had morphed into a happy or angry face (Kirsh et al., 2006). Individuals low in media violence exposure were faster to identify a neutral face morphing into a happy face than a neutral face morphing into an angry face, demonstrating the happy-face advantage. In contrast, individuals high in media violence exposure were faster to identify a neutral face morphing into an angry face than a neutral face morphing into a happy face. Kirsh and Mounts (2007) extended this finding in a study in which participants played a violent (action) or nonviolent video game for 15 minutes before completing the face-morphing task. Individuals who played a violent video game were slower to identify neutral faces morphing to happy than individuals who had played a nonviolent video game.

The association between action video game experience and the processing of positive emotion in facial expression was replicated in a training study using the emotion search task in combination with ERPs (Figure 23.3) (Bailey & West, 2011). In this study, participants viewed an array of schematic faces and indicated whether or not a happy or threatening face appeared in the array. For individuals in a

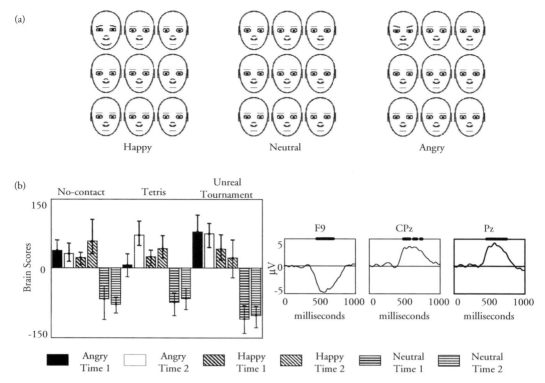

Figure 23.3 A. Example of displays for targets (i.e., happy and angry) and non-targets (i.e., neutral) in the emotion search task. **B.** Results of a Partial Least Squares analysis for the ERP data for the emotion search task. The left panel depicts the strength of the contrast between conditions (i.e., a video game group × stimulus type × occasion interaction) and the errors bars represent the 95% confidence interval. Notice that the brain score for Happy faces in the post-test does not differ from zero for the Unreal Tournament players. The right panel demonstrates the time course of this effect at posterior (CPz and Pz) and left lateral frontal electrodes, and reveals that the effect represents a modulation of the P3 component.

no-contact control group or those who played Tetris for 10 hours, the P3 component distinguished targets (i.e., happy or threatening faces) from non-targets at the pre- and post-test. In contrast, for participants who played Unreal Tournament for 10 hours the amplitude of the P3 was attenuated for happy faces in the post-test relative to the pre-test, and action video game experience did not appear to influence the orienting of attention to threatening faces in these individuals. These data, together with those reported by Kirsh et al. (2006; Kirsh & Mounts, 2007), indicate that both chronic and acute action video game experience may disrupt the allocation of attention to positive affect conveyed by facial expression.

Action video game experience is also associated with alterations in the allocation of attention to negative and violent stimuli during affective picture processing. Bartholow et al. (2006) used ERPs to examine the neural basis of reduced attention to violent stimuli associated with individual differences in chronic exposure to action video games.

In this study, individuals viewed neutral, negative violent (e.g., a man holding a knife to a woman's throat), and negative nonviolent (e.g., decaying dog corpse) pictures while ERPs were recorded. The investigators were particularly interested in the association between action video game experience and the amplitude of the P3 component elicited by violent and negative nonviolent pictures. The amplitude of the P3 was attenuated for violent pictures in violent Players relative to nonviolent Players. In contrast, the amplitude of the P3 for nonviolent negative pictures was similar for these individuals. These findings may indicate that action video game experience is associated with a reduction in the likelihood that attention would be oriented to violent pictures. Bailey et al. (2011) replicated and extended the findings of Bartholow et al. (2006) in two experiments. In Experiment 1, the magnitude of the negativity bias for the P3 or late posterior positivity was attenuated in Players relative to Non-players for violent pictures, but not negative pictures, when individuals rated the colorfulness of the pictures. In contrast, in Experiment 2 the association between the negativity bias and action video game experience was eliminated or reversed when individuals rated how threatening the pictures were. These findings indicate that the association between the allocation of attention to violent stimuli and action video game experience is modulated by the goals of the individual or the degree to which the detection of threat is relevant to task performance.

When the divergent findings from the face processing and affective picture processing literature are considered together, it appears that exposure to video game violence has different effects on attention to affect expressed in the face (Kirsh & Mounts, 2007; Bailey & West, 2011) and affect associated with interactions between individuals portrayed in scenes (Bartholow et al., 2006; Bailey et al., 2011). Although this seems unintuitive at first, it may reflect the specific tasks that individuals are expected to perform in an action video game. Attending to positive facial expressions would not benefit survival in a video game that requires the player to locate and destroy enemy targets, whereas attending to angry or threatening faces could be beneficial. Frequent exposure to video game violence may decrease attention to positive affect displayed in the face in favor of sensitizing the individual to negative facial expressions that are more task-relevant (e.g., identifying an enemy). Attention to violent interactions between other people may be lessened due to the individual's frequent violent interactions within the video games, while leaving their attention to positive social interactions between others unaffected. The finding that orienting attention to the level of threat portrayed in pictures enhanced the response to violent pictures in the Players further supports the idea that action video games train individuals to attend to violent stimuli when sensitivity to these stimuli facilitates survival (Bailey et al., 2011).

The Basis of Action Video Game Effects

The evidence reviewed in the previous sections demonstrates that action video game experience can affect performance on a wide range of cognitive and affective information processing tasks. Furthermore, the findings of these studies demonstrate that the effects of action video games range from low level aspects of vision related to acuity (i.e., contrast sensitivity) to higher levels of information processing related to cognitive control and evaluative judgments related to emotion. Given the wide range of effects that are associated with action video game experience, one might wonder whether there is a common underlying mechanism that could drive all of these effects? Two recent papers have sought to identify common mechanisms that could account for the effects of action video games (Dye et al., 2009a; Green et al., 2010).

Dye et al. (2009a) took a meta-analytic approach to identifying a common mechanism that accounts for the faster response time that is often observed in Players relative to Non-players. In this paper the authors used a Brinley plot (Brinley, 1965) analysis to examine the response time advantage of Players relative to Non-players on a range of choice response tasks (e.g., spatial cueing, inhibition of return, attention networks task, visual search, N-back) in which average response time varied between roughly 200 and 2,000 ms. As is commonly observed in the literature using the Brinley plot method, there was a highly significant correlation between average response time for Players and Non-players across the tasks (R^2 = .98) and the slope of the regression line predicting RT for Players from RT for Non-players was less than 1. This finding indicates that Players are consistently faster than Non-players across a wide range of tasks and baseline response times. Dye et al. also extended the Brinley analysis to examine the effects of video game training. In this analysis, the correlation between pre-test and post-test performance was very high for those individuals trained on action or control video games, and the effect of training on response time was greater for the action gamers than for the control gamers. Based upon these results the authors argued that action video game experience may enhance speed of processing that in turn facilitates performance across a range of tasks.

The generalizability of the effect of action video game experience on speed of processing could have important implications within the context of developmental psychology in which increases and then decreases in speed of processing across the lifespan are thought to account for developmental differences across a wide range of tasks (Kail & Salthouse, 1994; Salthouse, 1996). Additionally, speed of processing training in older adults is known to positively impact real-world behaviors associated with driving (i.e., leading to a reduction in at fault crash frequency) (Ball et al., 2002; Roenker et al., 2003) and activities of daily living (Willis et al., 2006). Therefore, as suggested by Dye et al. (2009a), "action video game training may therefore prove to be a helpful training regimen for providing a marked increase in speed of processing" (p. 325) that positively affects the lives of individuals.

Based on the success of Dye et al. (2009a) in identifying a general speed of processing factor that may provide a common mechanism for the effects of action video game experience on cognition, we attempted to replicate the results of these investigators with the data from three experiments from our laboratory in which individuals completed a range of tasks measuring visuospatial processing, cognitive control, and affective information processing (Bailey, 2009; Bailey et al., 2010a, 2011). The Brinley plot representing data for 66 experimental conditions, including seven different tasks and 67 Players and 67 Non-players is portrayed in Figure 23.4. In this analysis, there is a strong linear relationship between response time for Non-players

and Players (R^2 = .95) as expected based on the results of Dye et al. However, in our analysis the slope was greater than 1 (b = 1.054), indicating that Non-players tended to be faster than Players, representing the opposite of what Dye et al. found.

To identify the reason for the difference between our findings and those of Dye et al. (2009a), we examined Figure 23.4 for systematic variation from the best fitting regression line. One interesting pattern is that response time for affective picture processing appears to be consistently slower for Players than for Non-players (i.e., the open circles in Figure 23.4). To determine whether the association between affective picture processing and action video game experience might account for differences

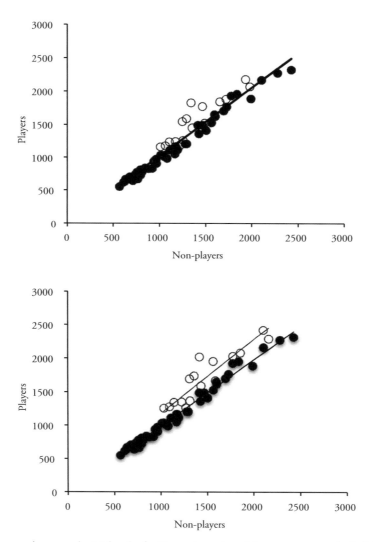

Figure 23.4 The upper panel portrays the Brinley plot for 66 experimental conditions across seven tasks, including 67 action Players and 67 low or Non-players from our laboratory. The lower panel portrays the Brinley plot for these data with separate intercepts and slopes for affective picture processing and the more cognitive measures from these studies.

between the two datasets, we performed a second analysis testing the effect of emotion and the emotion by video game experience interaction. Adding emotion (ΔR^2 = .024, F(1,63) = 51.85, p < .001) and the interaction (ΔR^2 =.004, F(1,62) = 10.77, p < .01) resulted in significant improvements in the fit of the model to the data (R^2 = .98). These results indicate that there are differences in both the intercept and slope for affective picture processing and the other tasks that are generally more cognitive in nature. In the final model the regression weight for action video game experience was not different from one (b = .991), failing to replicate the findings of Dye et al., even after controlling for the influence of affective picture processing. The results of the analyses of our data lead to two conclusions: (1) There may be a distinct association between action video game experience and affective picture processing, and (2) the speed of processing advantage of Players relative to Non-players may be constrained to certain types of tasks or task conditions, rather than representing a general characteristic of information processing.

Green et al. (2010) provide an alternative to the speed of processing account of the widespread advantage of Players over Non-players in choice response time tasks. These investigators argue that increases in "the strength of the connections between the neural layer providing the momentary evidence and the layer integrating the evidence over time, captures improvements in action-gamers behavior" that serves to improve probabilistic inference (p. 1573). Across a series of experiments, Green et al. demonstrate that a faster integration rate leads to a decrease in decision boundary and has no effect on non-decision processes for both visual and auditory tasks. The generalization of the effect to an auditory task represents an important finding as it demonstrates that the effect of action video games extends beyond the sensory modality most relevant for game experience. This finding is also consistent with the wide range of tasks that are sensitive to the effects of action video game experience and may account for some data that seem inconsistent with the speed of processing account. As an example, in the visual enumeration task action video game experience is associated with both greater accuracy and slower response time when there are seven or more elements in the display (Green & Bavelier, 2006). This slowing of response time for Players relative the Non-players is clearly inconsistent with the speed of processing account. However, if stronger connections between visual areas can support the formation of a more durable representation of the briefly flashed display, this could allow Players more time to "count" or otherwise estimate the number of items in the display. The slowing of response time for Players in the visual enumeration task could then be interpreted as resulting from an overall increase in the amount of information that is available for the slow (controlled) decision process with larger displays. It is not immediately clear how the dynamic improvement of connection strength within neural circuits would account for the slowing of reaction times seen with action video game experience during affective picture processing, although this could represent one interesting line of future research.

Conclusion

This chapter has reviewed the literature relevant to the effects of video games on attention as related to visuospatial processing, cognitive control, and emotion, in addition to emerging evidence demonstrating an association between pathological video game use and attention deficits. Evidence from these studies demonstrates that video game experience affects performance on a wide variety of tasks that range from low-level aspects of visual acuity, to the temporal and spatial allocation of visual attention, to the goal-directed control of information processing and emotion. Training studies reveal that the effects of video game experience can emerge with as little as 10 hours of training (Green & Bavelier, 2003; Feng et al., 2007), and may persist for several months. It appears that video game experience sometimes benefits task performance and sometimes disrupts task performance in each of the domains that were considered. This evidence leads to the conclusion that there may be little value in making sweeping generalizations regarding the positive or negative effects of video games on attention, cognition, and emotion (Gentile, 2011). Instead it appears that, as is the case for most complex domains of human experience, a full understanding of the effects of video games on attention will require a nuanced scientific approach that capitalizes on diverse methodologies, including behavioral and neuroscientific approaches that incorporate individual difference, training, and longitudinal studies. Some progress has been made in identifying a core neurocognitive mechanism (i.e., efficient information integration) that may account for the effects of video game experience related to visual processing (Green et al., 2010). Future research will provide insight into whether this, or other core mechanisms account for the effects of video game experience across the cognitive and social information processing systems.

Future Directions

(1) What is the nature of the effect of video game experience on attention in various domains? Individual differences studies have focused almost exclusively on Players versus Non-players using a binary contrast to capture the effect of video game experience. This makes it impossible to determine whether the effect of video game experience is continuous or linear, or whether the effect is more discrete, reflecting a breakpoint associated with some critical level of experience. Based on two datasets from our laboratory it appears that there may be both linear and non-linear effects of action video game experience. For instance, in the Stroop task the association between action video game experience and the conflict adaptation effect is significant for low or Non-players ($M = 30$ ms), and absent in mid-Players ($M = 2$ ms) and high-Players ($M = 10$ ms). This finding leads to the suggestion that even moderate levels of chronic action video game experience may disrupt proactive cognitive control. In contrast, differences in affective picture processing between negative and violent stimuli appear to reflect a more linear decrease in neural activity from Non-players to Mid- and High-players (Bailey et al., 2011).

(2) Are there different effects of various game genres on attention? Most of the individual difference and training studies reviewed in this chapter examined the effects of action video games. However, there is some evidence that real-time strategy games (Basak et al., 2008) or music games (e.g., Rock Band) (Bailey, 2009) may have different effects on attention than action video games.

(3) To what degree do the effects of video game experience on attention extend to cognition in the real world? All of the literature considered in this review examines performance on highly controlled laboratory tasks; however, we know that training effects on tasks that are sensitive to action video game experience (e.g., Useful Field of View) predicts practical outcomes related to driving and other activities of daily living in older adults (Ball et al., 2002). Also, the association between video game experience and attention deficits clearly extends to ecologically based outcomes.

(4) To what degree do the effects of video game experience across domains overlap in the same individuals? Most of the extant literature has reasonably tended to focus on a single domain (i.e., visuospatial processing, executive function, emotion) making it difficult to examine benefits and costs of video game experience in the same individuals (for exceptions, see Basak et al., 2008; Boot et al., 2008). In a recent study using ERPs, our laboratory has demonstrated desensitization to positive facial expression and enhanced visual processing resulting from 10 hours of training on an action video game in the same individuals (Bailey & West, 2011). These findings reveal the importance of considering multiple domains and possibly levels of analysis within a given study.

(5) Are there tasks that could be standardized to serve as behavioral or biomarkers of the effects of video game experience on attention, cognition, and emotion? As seen in the literature reviewed in this chapter, there appears to be significant variability in the robustness of the effect of video game experience in any given task or paradigm. As an example, several studies have demonstrated the sensitivity of the Useful Field of View task to video game experience (Green & Bavelier, 2003, 2006; Feng et al., 2007), although others have failed to replicate this effect (Boot et al., 2008). A robust task or set of tasks that could serve as a baseline across studies will likely facilitate our understanding of the complex relationship between video games and laboratory and ecological measures of attention.

References

Anderson, C. A., Shibuya, A., Ihori, N., Swing, E. L., Bushman, B. J., Sakamoto, A., et al. (2010). Violent video game effects on aggression, empathy, and prosocial behavior in Eastern and Western countries. *Psychological Bulletin, 136*, 151–173.

Bailey, K. (2009). *Individual differences in video game experience: cognitive control, affective processing, and visuospatial processing.* Unpublished master's thesis, Iowa State University, Ames, IA.

Bailey, K., & West, R. (2011). *The effects of action video games on visual and social information processing.* Manuscript submitted for publication.

Bailey, K. M., West, R., & Anderson, C. A. (2010a). A negative association between video game experience and proactive cognitive control. *Psychophysiology, 47*, 34–42.

Bailey, K., West, R., & Anderson, C. A. (2010b, May). *You are what you play: Video game experience and cognitive control.* Paper presented at the 82nd annual meeting of Midwestern Psychological Association, Chicago, IL.

Bailey, K., West, R., & Anderson, C. A. (2011). The association between chronic exposure to video game violence and affective picture processing: An ERP study. *Cognitive, Affective, & Behavioral Neuroscience, 11*, 259–276.

Ball, K., Berch, D. B., Helmers, K. F., Jobe, J. B., Leveck, M. D., Marsiske, M., et al. (2002). Effects of cognitive training interventions with older adults. *The Journal of the American Medical Association, 288*, 2271–2281.

Bartholow, B. D., Bushman, B. J., & Sestir, M. A. (2006). Chronic violent video game exposure and desensitization to violence: Behavioral and event-related brain potential data. *Journal of Experimental Social Psychology, 42*, 532–539.

Basak, C., Boot, W. R., Voss, M. W., & Kramer, A. F. (2008). Can training in a real-time strategy video game attenuate cognitive decline in older adults? *Psychology and Aging, 23*, 765–777.

Biederman, J., Wilens, T. E., Mick, E., Faraone, S. V., & Spencer, T. (1998). Does attention-deficit hyperactivity disorder impact the developmental course of drug and alcohol abuse and dependence? *Biological Psychiatry, 44*, 269–273.

Billings, L. S., Harrison, D. W ., & Alden, J. D . (1993). Age differences among women in the functional asymmetry for bias in facial affect perception. *Bulletin of the Psychonomic Society, 31*, 317–320.

Bioulac, S., Arfi, L., & Bouvard, M. P. (2008). Attention deficit/hyperactivity disorder and video games: A comparative study of hyperactive and control children. *European Psychiatry, 23*, 134–141.

Blumberg, F. C., Almonte, D. E., Anthony, J. S., & Hashimoto, N. (2012). Serious games: What are they? What do they do? Why should we play them? In Dill, K. (Ed.), *The Oxford Handbook of Media Psychology*. New York: Oxford University Press.

Boot, W. R., Kramer, A. F., Simons, D. J., Fabiani, M., & Gratton, G. (2008). The effects of video game playing on attention, memory, and executive control. *Acta Psychologica, 129*, 387–398.

Brinley, J. F. (1965). Cognitive sets, speed and accuracy of performance in the elderly. In: Welford, A. T., & Birren, J. E. (Eds.), *Behavior, Aging, and the Nervous System*. Springfield, IL: Charles C Thomas, pp. 114–149.

Castel, A. D., Pratt, J., & Drummond, E. (2005). The effects of action video game experience on the time course of inhibition of return and the efficiency of visual search. *Acta Psychologica, 119*, 217–230.

Centers for Disease Control (2010). Rates of parent-reported ADHD increasing. Retrieved April 15, 2011 from http://www.cdc.gov/Features/dsADHD/.

Chan, P. A., & Rabinowitz, T. (2006). A cross-sectional analysis of video games and attention deficit hyperactivity disorder symptoms in adolescents. *Annals of General Psychiatry, 5*, 16.

Chisholm, J. D., Hickey, C., Theeuwes, J., & Kingstone, A. (2010). Reduced attentional capture in action video game players. *Attention, Perception, & Psychophysics, 72*, 667–671.

Donohue, S. E., Woldorff, M. G., & Mitroff, S. R. (2010). Video game players show more precise multisensory temporal processing abilities. *Attention, Perception, and Psychophysics, 72*, 1120–1129.

Dye, M. W. G., Green, C. S., & Bavelier, D. (2009a). Increasing speed of processing with action video games. *Current Directions in Psychological Science, 18*, 321–326.

Dye, M. W. G., Green, C. S., & Bavelier, D. (2009b). The development of attention skills in action video game players. *Neuropsychologia, 47*, 1780–1789.

Entertainment Software Association. (2011). Industry facts. Retrieved April 12, 2011 from http://www.theesa.com/facts/index.asp.

Eriksen, C. W., & Schultz, D. W. (1979). Information processing in visual search: A continuous flow conception and experimental results. *Perception & Psychophysics, 25*, 249–263.

Fan, J., McCandliss, B. D., Sommer, T., Raz, A., & Posner, M. I. (2002). Testing the efficiency and independence of attentional networks. *Journal of Cognitive Neuroscience, 14*, 340–347.

Feng, J., Spence, I., & Pratt, J. (2007). Playing an action video game reduces gender differences in spatial cognition. *Psychological Science, 18*, 850–855.

Gentile, D. A. (2009). Pathological video-game use among youth ages 8 to 18. *Psychological Science, 20*, 594–602.

Gentile, D. A. (2011). The multiple dimensions of video game effects. *Child Development Perspectives, 5*, 75–81.

Gentile, D. A., Choo, H., Liau, A., Sim, T., Li, D., Fung, D., et al . (2011). Pathological video game use among youths: A two-year longitudinal study. *Pediatrics, 127*, e319–e329.

Green, C. S., & Bavelier, D. (2003). Action video game modifies visual selective attention. *Nature, 423*, 534–537.

Green, C. S., & Bavelier, D. (2006). Enumeration versus multiple object tracking: The case of action video game players. *Cognition, 101*, 217–245.

Green, C. S., & Bavelier, D. (2007). Action-video-game experience alters the spatial resolution of vision. *Psychological Science, 18*, 88–94.

Green, C. S., Li, R., & Bavelier, D. (2010). Perceptual learning during action video game playing. *Topics in Cognitive Science, 2*, 202–216.

Green, C. S., Pouget, A., & Bavelier, D. (2010). Improved probabilistic inference as a general learning mechanism with action video games. *Current Biology, 20*, 1573–1579.

Hoeft, F., Watson, C. L., Kesler, S. R., Bettinger, K. E., & Reiss, A. L. (2008). Gender differences in the mesocorticolimbic system during computer game-play. *Journal of Psychiatric Research, 42*, 253–258.

Kail, R., & Salthouse, T. A . (1994). Processing speed as a mental capacity. *Acta Psychologica, 86*, 199–225.

Karle, J. W., Watter, S., & Shedden, J. M. (2010). Task switching in video game players: Benefits of selective attention but not resistance to proactive interference. *Acta Psychologica, 134*, 70–78.

Kirchner, W. K. (1958). Age differences in short-term retention of rapidly changing information. *Journal of Experimental Psychology, 55*, 352–358.

Kirsh, S. J., & Mounts, J. R. W. (2007). Violent video game play impacts facial emotion recognition. *Aggressive Behavior, 33*, 353–358.

Kirsh, S. J., Mounts, J. R. W., & Olczak, P. V. (2006). Violent media consumption and the recognition of dynamic facial expressions. *Journal of Interpersonal Violence, 21*, 571–584.

Kronenberger, W. G., Matthews, V. P., Dunn, D. W., Wang, Y., Wood, E. A., Giauque, A. L., et al. (2005). Media violence exposure and executive functioning in aggressive and control adolescents. *Journal of Clinical Psychology, 61*, 725–737.

Leppanen, J., Tenhunen, M., & Hietanen, J. (2003). Faster choice-reaction times to positive than to negative facial expressions. *Journal of Psychophysiology, 17*, 113–123.

Li, R., Polat, U., Makous, W., & Bavelier, D. (2009). Enhancing the contrast sensitivity function through action video game training. *Nature Neuroscience, 12*, 549–551.

Liotti, M., Woldorff, M. G., Perez, R., & Mayberg, H. S. (2000). An ERP study of the temporal course of the Stroop color-word interference effect. *Neuropsychologia, 38*, 701–711.

Logan, G. D., & Bundesen, C. (2003). Clever homunculus: Is there an endogenous act of control in the explicit task-cueing procedure? *Journal of Experimental Psychology: Learning, Memory, and Cognition, 29*, 575–599.

MacLeod, C. M. (1991). Half a century of research on the Stroop effect: An integrative review. *Psychological Bulletin, 109*, 163–203.

Mathews, V. P., Kronenberger, W. G., Wang, Y., Lurito, J. T., Lowe, M. J., & Dunn, D. W. (2005). Media violence exposure and frontal lobe activation measured by functional magnetic resonance imaging in aggressive and nonaggressive adolescents. *Journal of Computer Assisted Tomography, 29*, 287–292.

Miller, E. K., & Cohen, J. D. (2001). An integrative theory of prefrontal cortex function. *Annual Review of Neuroscience, 24*, 167–202.

Miyake, A., Friedman, N. P., Emerson, M. J., Witzki, A. H., Howerter, A., & Wager, T. D. (2000). The unity and diversity of executive functions and their contributions to complex "Frontal Lobe" tasks: A latent variable analysis. *Cognitive Psychology, 41*, 49–100.

Monsell, S. (2003). Task switching. *Trends in Cognitive Sciences, 7*, 134–140.

National Institute of Health (2010). Attention deficit hyperactivity disorder (ADHD). Retrieved April 10, 2011 from http://www.nimh.nih.gov/health/publications/attention-deficit-hyperactivity-disorder/complete-index.shtml.

Posner, M. I. (1980). Orienting of attention. *The Quarterly Journal of Experimental Psychology, 32*, 3–25.

Roenker, D. L., Cissell, G. M., Ball, K. K., Wadley, V. G., & Edwards, J. D. (2003). Speed-of-processing and driving simulator training results in improved driving performance. *Human Factors, 45*, 218–233.

Salthouse, T. (1996). The processing-speed theory of adult differences in cognition. *Psychological Review, 103*, 403–428.

Strobach, T., Frensch, P. A., & Schubert, T. (2010, November). *Effects of video game practice on executive control skills: Evidence from dual-task and task-switching tests.* Paper presented at the 51st annual meeting of Psychonomic Society, St. Louis, MO.

Stroop, J. R. (1935). Studies of interference in serial verbal reactions. *Journal of Experimental Psychology, 18*, 643–662.

Stuss, D. T., Shallice, T., Alexander, M. P., & Picton, T. W. (1994). A multidisciplinary approach to anterior attentional functions. *Annals of the New York Academy of Sciences, 769*, 191–211.

Swing, E. L. (2008). *Attention abilities, media exposure, school performance, personality, and aggression.* Unpublished master's thesis, Iowa State University, Ames, IA.

Tapert, S. F., Baratta, M. V., Abrantes, A. M., & Brown, S. A. (2002). Attention dysfunction predicts substance involvement in community youths. *Journal of the American Academy of Child & Adolescent Psychiatry, 41*, 680–686.

Trick, L. M., & Pylyshyn, Z. W. (1993). What enumeration studies can show us about spatial attention: Evidence for limited capacity preattentive processing. *Journal of Experimental Psychology: Human Perception and Performance, 19*, 331–351.

Turner, M. L., & Engle, R. W. (1989). Is working memory capacity task dependent? *Journal of Memory and Language, 28*, 127–154.

Vogel, E. K., & Machizawa, M. G. (2004). Neural activity predicts individual differences in visual working memory capacity. *Nature, 428*, 748–751.

Wang, Y., Mathews, V. P., Kalnin, A. J., Mosier, K. M., Dunn, D. W., Saykin, A. J., et al. (2009). Short term exposure to a violent video game induces changes in frontolimbic circuitry in adolescents. *Brain Imaging and Behavior, 3*, 38–50.

Weiss, M., & Weiss, G. (2002). Attention deficit hyperactivity disorder. In: Lewis M (ed). *Child and Adolescent Psychiatry: A Comprehensive Textbook.* Philadelphia: Lippincott Williams & Wilkins, 647–650.

West, R., Jakubek, K., Wymbs, N., Perry, M., & Moore, K. (2005). Neural correlates of conflict processing. *Experimental Brain Research, 167*, 38–48.

West, G. L., Stevens, S. A., Pun, C., & Pratt, J. (2008). Visuospatial experience modulates attentional capture: Evidence from action video game players. *Journal of Vision, 8*, 1–9.

Wilens, T. E., Biederman, J., & Mick, E. (1998). Does ADHD affect the course of substance abuse? Findings from a sample of adults with and without ADHD. *American Journal on Addictions, 7*, 156–163.

Willis, S. L., Tennstedt, S. L., Marsiske, M., Ball, K., Elias, J., Koepke, K. M., et al. (2006). Long-term effects of cognitive training on everyday functional outcomes in older adults. *The Journal of the American Medical Association, 296*, 2805–2814.

Yoo, H. J., Cho, S. C., Ha, J., Yune, S. K., Kim, S. J., Hwang, J., et al. (2004). Attention deficit hyperactivity symptoms and Internet addiction. *Psychiatry and Clinical Neurosciences, 58*, 487–494.

PART 5

Meta Issues in Media Psychology

A General Framework for Media Psychology Scholarship

W. James Potter

Abstract

This chapter presents a critical analysis of many of the assumptions and practices that characterize the media effects literature. The thesis argued here is that a Generating-Findings perspective has been useful in producing this literature, but that this perspective has outlived its usefulness. It is time to shift into a new perspective now that the media effects literature has grown so large and fragmented and now that the distribution technologies as well as the culture itself has changed so much over the past few decades. The suggested newer perspective on media research and scholarship—called the Mapping-Phenomenon perspective—builds off the strengths in the existing literature while moving beyond its limitations. This new perspective requires a clear conceptualization of "mass" media along with its four major components of industries, audiences, messages, and effects.

Key Words: categorical thinking, conceptualizations, critical analysis, exposure states, lineation theory, mass media, media effects, new media environment, research assumptions, theory-driven research, unresolved debates

Introduction

The literature about the mass media phenomenon has grown very large and has recently been estimated to be about 10,000 published studies (Potter & Riddle, 2006). This literature has also grown highly complex with many different topics, subtopics, and sub-subtopics, each with its own set of scholars, questions, methods, and findings. Given the complexity, each scholar is forced to focus on an increasingly smaller sliver of the overall phenomenon when designing yet another research study. And given the growth in the complexity and size of the literature, it has been several decades since scholars could adequately review the full literature in an article-length treatment (McLeod & Reeves, 1980; Roberts & Maccoby, 1985) and now it is very challenging for scholars to review a subarea of the literature in a chapter (Bryant & Zillmann, 2002; Nabi & Oliver, 2009).

The growing size and complexity along with the narrowing of reviews have resulted in a fragmentation of the media literature. This fragmentation makes it more difficult each year for scholars to keep up with the big picture. This fragmentation also makes it significantly more difficult each year to convey to the general public the full power of explanation produced by all this research. And it makes it much more difficult to convey to each new generation of students a big picture appreciation of the mass media. As the literature continues to grow, these problems become even more pressing.

The thesis of this chapter is that it is time for media scholars to examine many of the assumptions and practices that have gotten us to this point and to make some changes so as to meet the evolving challenges of our scholarly field. We have produced an amazingly diverse and rich literature from our scholarly activity that has now extended over nine decades (Lowery & DeFleur, 1988), but now the literature has grown so large and complex, the challenge of examining our phenomenon of interest has shifted. The phenomenon of the mass media itself has changed with the digitization of information, the proliferation of platforms, many of which offer interactive capabilities, the conglomeratization of ownership, and the subsequent changes in marketing strategies. We cannot continue to use some of the practices, methods, and ways of thinking about the media in the same way and expect to generate the same payoffs as we have in the past. Our challenge is different.

My approach in this chapter is first to outline the assortment of practices and approaches that have gotten us to this point. I call this the Generating-Findings perspective. Then I will show how our challenge has been changing over time and present a series of arguments about how our past practices can be altered and augmented to meet the new challenges. I call this set of new thinking and practices the Mapping-Phenomenon perspective.

This argument for a shift from Generating-Findings to a Mapping-Phenomenon perspective begins with a critical analysis of the media literature. By "critical analysis" I do not mean that I am arguing that the scientific approach generally or the psychological approach particularly are bankrupt and that they have produced nothing but false or sterile findings. To the contrary, these approaches have produced a great wealth of insight about the media phenomenon. By *critical analysis* I mean to focus attention on the flaws in the way we are constructing understanding about our phenomenon, rather than reviewing the great mass of individual findings in the research, which is the purpose of a number of the other chapters in this volume. Therefore, I make a series of arguments about where our conceptualizations and methods are breaking down, and then make recommendations for how we can generate more useful research studies that better reveal the evolving nature of our changing phenomenon. To address this task, the chapter has five major sections to lay out the main points of Lineation Theory. In the first section, I will focus attention on the full phenomenon of the mass media and argue for the importance of ideas from its four component facets to work together in producing more powerful explanation of the media. Then each of the other four sections focuses on the four facets of media organizations, audiences, messages, and effects.

The Mass Media Phenomenon

The argument that we need to evolve out of a Generating-Findings perspective and into a Mapping-Phenomenon perspective requires a contrasting of these two perspectives, which I will present first in this section. Then I will take the initial step in illuminating recommendations to bring about the Mapping-Phenomenon perspective by arguing for a re-conceptualization of the idea of "mass" media.

Generating-Findings Perspective on the Mass Media

There are five salient factors that characterize the Generating-Findings perspective. These factors are engaging in wide ranging debates that have been left unresolved, the dominance of inductive processes, a small proportion of theory-generated research, little programmatic research, and emphasizing empiricism over synthesis. This literature, of course, contains many studies that do not exhibit all five of these characteristics and even some that do not exhibit any of them; however, when taken as a whole, the overall mass media literature can accurately be characterized by these five factors.

UNRESOLVED DEBATES

Media scholars, like communication scholars more generally, have engaged in many debates over the years as they struggle to define their focal phenomenon as well as their role as scholars. The most prevalent of these have concerned debates about paradigms, which have illuminated disagreements about the nature of the communication phenomenon and the best way to study it. These paradigm debates have been featured prominently in three major publications: the 1983 *Journal of Communication* Ferment in the Field issue; *Rethinking Communication* (Dervin et al., 1989); and the 1993 Ferment in the Field II. In the first volume of *Rethinking Communication,* the editors point out that the many contributors to the debate "have charted some radically different paths to scholarship. The diversity is so great, the positions sometimes so intense, the commitments to in opposition that it might be easy to conclude that the field is quickly moving toward a state of incompatibilities" (Dervin et al., 1989, p. 9). These forums were very successful in demonstrating many issues in the paradigm debates. However, with no synthesis or summary chapters to any of these volumes, they left readers in the midst of controversies.

There has also been considerable debate about how the field's important terms should be conceptualized, particularly mass media (Lowery & DeFleur, 1988; Thompson, 1995; Webster & Phalen, 1997; McQuail, 2005) and media effects (Fortuno, 2005). Also there is a fundamental disagreement about the nature of media audience; that is, whether it is active or passive (Himmelweit, Oppenheim, & Vince, 1958; Schramm, Lyle, & Parker, 1961; Biocca, 1988; Eastman, 1998; Power, Kubey, & Kiousis, 2002). Another debate is concerned with the issue of whether meaning resides in the media text or the mind of the audience members. Experimental psychologists place the locus of meaning in the texts they select for their treatments. In contrast, critical and cultural scholars argue that meaning resides in the audience (Hall, 1980; Newcomb, 1984; Radway, 1984; Allen, 1987).

The positive effect of these debates has been to raise awareness about as many parts of the mass media phenomenon as well as approaches to research. And it remains a welcoming field for scholars from almost any background and training. However, the unresolved nature of these debates has fostered the continuation of exploratory research, which continues to fragment the scholarly field into subsections defined by different methods or different conceptualizations for important constructs.

RELIANCE ON INDUCTION

Most of the research in the Generating-Findings phase has been inductive in nature. That is, individual research studies have typically been motivated by research questions rather than by an a priori reasoned system of explanation. Researchers have collected data, and then looked for patterns in those data. When they found a pattern—such as a statistically significant treatment difference across means or a relatively strong degree of association among variables—they reported their findings as a suggestive answer to their research question. Answers are "suggestive," because the inductive method requires continual replication of studies to build up greater evidence of a pattern until readers of the literature can have greater confidence that the pattern is a robust one that is worthy of their attention, rather than an anomaly of a particular measurement device, sample, or treatment (Popper, 1959).

With the inductive approach, all questions, methods, and assumptions are equal as far as their potential for leading scholars to interesting insights about their phenomenon of interest. All kinds of constructs with all kinds of definitions were tried, many of which were imported from other fields (Reeves & Borgman, 1983; Rice, Borgman, & Reeves, 1988). All kinds of pairs of constructs were tested to see what was related to what. This brainstorming activity was necessary to "feel our way in the dark" and find out where were the boundaries and contours of the phenomenon.

THEORY-DRIVEN RESEARCH

A key characteristic of Generating-Findings research is a lack of theory in guiding the design of studies in a majority of the literature, and many scholars see this as a problem (Shoemaker & Reese, 1990; So & Chan, 1991; Stevenson, 1992). It is understandable that the research in new scholarly fields is question driven, because few theories exist, but this is no longer the case with mass media research. However, about two-thirds of the empirical research continues to largely ignore the many existing theories. For example, in an analysis of published literature on mass communication from 1965 to 1989 in eight competitive peer-reviewed journals, Potter, Cooper, and Dupagne (1993) found that only 8.1% of 1,326 articles were guided by a theory and provided a test of that theory; another 19.5% were tests of hypotheses, but these hypotheses were not derived from a theory. A similar pattern was found in an analysis of studies published in *Journalism & Mass Communication Quarterly,* when Riffe and Freitag (1997) reported that only 27.6% of the studies used an explicit theoretical framework and another 45.7% were guided by hypotheses or research questions but no explicit theory. They found no change in these percentages over the 25-year period they examined from 1971 to 1995. Similar findings were reported by Kamhawi and Weaver (2003) who examined all articles published in 10 communication journals from 1980 to 1999 and found that only 30.5% specifically mentioned a theory. Likewise, Potter and Riddle (2007) analyzed mass media effects articles published in 16 journals from 1993 to 2005 and found that only 35.0% of coded articles featured a theory.

It is ironic that with so little theory-driven research, we still have a very large number of theories in the mass media literature. In their analysis, Potter and Riddle (2007) found fewer than 300 articles (out of 936 articles they examined) featured a theory, yet there were 144 theories in those articles. But only 12 of these theories were mentioned in five or more studies; the remaining 132 theories were spread out over 168 articles. This indicates a pattern of thin theory development; that is, there are few theories that are introduced in a theory piece, and then show up in multiple tests where they are shaped and refined. The same pattern was found by Kamhawi and Weaver (2003), who reported that only three theories were mentioned in as many as 10% of their analyzed articles. These patterns led Kamhawi and Weaver (2003) to argue that:

> theoretical development is probably the main consideration in evaluating the disciplinary status of the field. As our field grows in scope and complexity, the pressure for theoretical integration increases. It seems that scholars in the field should be developing and testing theories to explain the process and effects of mass communication. (p. 20)

LITTLE PROGRAMMATIC RESEARCH

In *Milestones in Mass Communication Research,* Lowery and DeFleur (1988) argue that the "study of mass communication has been particularly unsystematic." They elaborate this point by saying that scholars "almost never coordinated their efforts or built upon the results of previous research." They said many of the questions guiding the research "were not theoretically significant" (p. 3). This condition persists today. Scholars who publish many studies typically undertake a study or two on one topic, and then move on to another topic, publish a few studies on that topic, and then move on to another topic. Relatively few scholars identify themselves with a particular theory or programmatic line of research and conduct more than a handful of studies that substantially build on one another.

LITTLE SYNTHESIS

There are few published efforts at synthesizing parts of this very large literature. In our recent content analysis of the mass media effects literature (Potter & Riddle, 2006), we found only 47 articles out of the 936 we examined that could remotely be regarded as synthesis pieces. Most of these (*n* = 36) were stand-alone narrative reviews, many of which were fairly descriptive and did not ascend to the standard of synthesis. The other 11 published articles were meta-analyses, which provide the beginning steps of synthesis but often do not complete the synthesis task. By synthesis, I mean that the literature on a topic is critically analyzed to reject faulty findings and bring forth credible findings into a second stage, where those credible findings are organized into groups, and the groups of findings calibrated by importance. Thus, the value

of critical reviews of the literature that ascend to synthesis is to present the most valid findings from empirical studies on a topic and present those findings as an organized set to reveal not just the content, but also the structure of knowledge generated thus far on that topic.

Our past practices have been necessary to explore the boundaries of the phenomenon; try out the usefulness of different approaches; try on different definitions to see which ones fit our conceptualizations the best; and play around with various collections of variables to find out what is related to what. This Generating-Findings activity is an essential initial step in building a scholarly field. However, we have now produced a large number of ideas and findings, and unless we engage in a considerable amount of critical analysis and synthesis, we are left in a condition in which the findings from each individual published study are regarded as equally valid and equally important. Because humans cannot absorb the detail in the findings from 10,000 (or more) individual studies, it is impossible to grasp the big picture of media scholarship. In response to this condition, media scholars default to setting their focus on a selection of ever-smaller topic areas so they can achieve a sense of staying up to date on a research literature. But this default serves to move the field toward fragmentation and into increasingly isolated pockets of scholars rather than using the findings to build larger arcs of knowledge (McQuail, 1989; Jensen & Rosengren, 1990; Berger, 1991; Hardt, 1992; Pietila, 1994; Power, Kubey, & Kiousis, 2002).

It is important to shift out of the Generating-Findings perspective. By using the verb *shift,* I am calling for an evolution of practices and thought, rather than a revolution, in which we throw everything out and try to start over. Instead, we need to use the ideas and findings we have generated in the Generating-Findings phase by foregrounding the ideas we have found to be most useful while backgrounding others. There are many examples of scholars who have been operating from much more of a Mapping-Phenomenon perspective for years; however, these scholars are a small minority. The dominant perspective has been Generating-Findings.

The Mapping-Phenomenon Perspective

This section highlights five major characteristics of the Mapping-Phenomenon perspective. These include shaping our findings into knowledge; focusing on depth over breadth; convergence over divergence; getting past categorical thinking; and focusing on the big picture.

SHAPING FINDINGS INTO KNOWLEDGE

The primary scholarly work in a Mapping-Phenomenon perspective is the working with existing ideas and findings to organize them in extend their power of capturing the essence of our phenomenon. It requires the calibration of existing concepts so as to focus attention most strongly on the most important ones. It requires the analysis of existing definitions for key terms, weeding out the less useful definitions, and further explicating the more useful ones. It requires the critical assessment of existing theories, deducing strong tests from their key propositions, and then using the results of those empirical tests to pare away faulty predictions, and extending the theory's predictive power by synthesizing additional propositions. It requires the backgrounding of methods as tools that are useful only in so far as they can access various parts of our phenomenon of interest.

DEPTH OVER BREADTH

In shifting into the Mapping-Phenomenon phase, we need to focus our attention on the most important topic areas and marshal our limited resources to make progress in increasing the power of our explanations. We need to focus our attention on the more promising among the many theories that have been suggested and conduct much more programmatic research to develop those systems of explanation. A positive outcome of a higher proportion of programmatic research will be a much more systematic testing of the utility of various definitions, assumptions, and procedures then the moving toward a convergence to the most useful of them. The Generating-Findings phase has produced the raw materials (ideas, definitions, assumptions, and empirical findings) from which to build a scholarly field. In the Mapping-Phenomenon phase, we can build that field. But we need a design; that is, we need to agree on what we are about and how we can most usefully examine our phenomenon. This requires cooperation and convergence.

GETTING PAST CATEGORICAL THINKING

The diversity of world views, scholarly traditions, methods, and conceptualization of key ideas has been a strength—not a weakness—in the development of the field *up to this point*. The phenomenon of the mass media is complex, and the examination of that complex phenomenon benefits

from thinking from many different perspectives. However, the problem with the debates is not the diversity of thinking, but the compartmentalization of that thinking. Although the debates have offered the potential to expand the thinking of individual scholars, the debate format is limiting because of its polarizing effects. Debates tend to either turn off readers who then fail to take the opportunity to learn, or the debates persuade readers to side with one position and thereby demonize what they are told is the polar opposite positions. If we are to take advantage of the full range of great ideas, we need to respect and understand all those ideas, and then see if we can unify ourselves through a synthesis of the best ideas. In short we need to get beyond the debates that foster categorical thinking.

Rather than participate in the debate about whether the audience is active or passive, it would be far better to work for a synthesis (Livingstone, 1990; Webster & Phalen, 1994; Power, Kubey, & Kiousis, 2002). For example, Livingstone (1990) writes about the danger of taking either side in this debate when she says, "If we see the media or life events as all-powerful creators of meaning, we neglect the role of audiences: if we see people as all-powerful creators of meaning, we neglect the structure of that which people interpret" (p. 23). There are times when audience members are active and other times when they are passive. The key to advancing our understanding of audiences is to get beyond the debate about which of these positions is more descriptive of the audiences and instead to focus our resources on finding out why the audience is passive at certain times and active at other times.

FOCUS ON THE BIG PICTURE

Perhaps the most important characteristic of the Mapping-Phenomenon perspective is the focus on the big picture; that is, the nature of the mass media as our phenomenon of interest. Thus, we need more thinking at the broadest level. We need more macro-level theorizing.

I am not arguing that individual empirical studies are also not important. On the contrary, individual studies are essential. But when scholars design their individual studies and get down in the micro details of their one topic, their decisions will be much better if they keep in mind how their study fits into the map of the overall phenomenon. By carefully positioning their study in the design stage of the research, they can more clearly direct their eventual findings to the part of the overall Mapping-Phenomenon system in which those findings will have the most impact. Without such positioning in the design, the findings can easily get lost in the clutter of a fragmented literature. This is why programmatic research is so important: Each new study is clearly positioned along a developing path. This is why theory testing is so important: Each test is clearly positioned as making a contribution in shaping a particular part of an identifiable system of explanation. This is why critical reviews of the literature are so important: They provide a map of a particular topic area. And at the most macro level, this is why a general framework is so important: It can provide the global map of the phenomenon. I will suggest how to get started on this enormous task in the remainder of this chapter as I lay out some ideas for each of the four major facets of the overall media phenomenon.

Media Organization Facet

With the rise of the new media environment over the past several decades, we need to rethink what qualifies an organization to be regarded as a "mass" medium. A common—and relatively simple—way of defining the mass media has been to list the major media of information dissemination. As each new medium came along, it was easy to add it to the list, which grew from books, magazines, and newspapers to include film, recordings, radio, broadcast television, and cable television. However, in the past three decades, with the rise of personal computers and the digitization of information, the boundaries that made each medium distinct have become significantly blurred. Now that it is no longer useful to define mass media simply by listing certain technological channels, scholars need to focus attention on the particular characteristics of communication technologies so as to provide a useful definition of "mass" media.

What are the key characteristics of a technology that would make a channel of communication qualify as a "mass" medium? The answer to this question lies in how the technology makes it possible to disseminate information quickly to a relatively large number of people. Each new mass medium started with a technological development that made it possible for senders of messages to reach a wider audience and do so more quickly than was previously possible (Innis, 1951; McLuhan, 1964; Noll, 2007). The earliest of these technological innovations was the printing press in the 15th century, which greatly expanded the reach of the printed word. Then with the rise of newspapers and magazines, information was made available to people beyond elites to a more general population and they were able to send out new information weekly and even daily.

At the turn of the 20th century, the new media of recordings and film continued to make all kinds of messages available even faster and to a wider range of people—even those who could not read. With the introduction of radio, and then television, information access was no longer a problem: Messages of all kinds were made available to everyone in the general population. With the rise of personal computers in the 1980s followed by other new communication technologies, anyone in the general population could access any kind of information at any time.

New Media Environment

We now find ourselves in a media environment unlike any we have ever before experienced. The newest technological developments of personal computers, the Internet (with wi-fi and broadband fiberoptic connections), cell phones, and other hand-held portable devices for connecting to messages and other people have not just changed society but have changed the older, more traditional media themselves. For more how the Internet and especially the Web have evolved, see Chapter 2.

This new media environment is characterized by four inter-related features of technological convergence, interactivity, information saturation, and a shift in marketing.

TECHNOLOGICAL CONVERGENCE

Media convergence is the movement away from distinct media channels toward a common platform in which all kinds of messages are shared (Jenkins, 2006; Nayar, 2010). The common platform thus allows for the user to access words, pictures, video, and audio, as well as send their own text and voice messages. Nayar (2010) argues that all media are now crossover media, which means that they all adapt and borrow from each other. "Movies merge into computer games, and computer games generate fan sites, movie plots, and toys; advertisers use computer gameworlds...A cell phone serves as an email device...as a camera, a movie-making device, a conferencing facility, and a personal diary" (p. 2). Not only are the media reconfigured, but society is also reconfigured where "computer-mediated communication becomes the dominant form of social interaction" (p. 3). This convergence has been made possible through a process of what Bolter and Grusin (2000) call *remediation,* in which all media engage in a complex and ongoing process in which the tactics, styles, and content of other media are mimicked, and then critiqued and extended.

This convergence is also a product of the conglomeration of media ownership. Jenkins (2003) explains, "Technological convergence is attractive to media industries because it opens multiple entry points into the consumption process and at the same time, enables consumers to more quickly locate new manifestations of a popular narrative" (p. 284). Thus, companies who own many platforms of communication can achieve economies of scale by amortizing the cost of producing a message across many different outlets; that is, once they have paid to have a message produced, they can send it out through the newspapers, magazines, cable channels, and Internet sites they own or control.

INTERACTIVITY

With the introduction of personal computers and the innovation to network them, people began to use the mass media in interactive ways so they could connect to other people with similar interests and thus create their own content. More than two decades ago, Rice (1984a) recognized the profound change that computers represented to media communication because of their ability to allow audience members to interact. Thus, the distinction between sender and receiver has broken down within the mass communication experience.

The technological potential for interaction has attracted an increasing demand for platforms in which people can share their expertise (e.g., Wikipedia), share personal observations (blogs and Twitter), share all aspects of their personal lives (Facebook), or create a new personal life (dating sites, Second Life). More and more people are using communication media platforms to participate in all kinds of activities, such as gaming, relationship building, and public activism. Now there are communication networks growing up on just about every possible human interest, and people use this interactive technology to network with others who share their interests.

INFORMATION SATURATION

This potential for all kinds of interactions along with the digitization of information and increasingly high speed access has touched off an explosion of information creation. Rice (1984b) pointed out that by the early 1980s, "approximately half of the U.S. gross national product is devoted to the creation, handling, and distribution of information" (p. 23). Since that time, even newer information

technologies have been added, and the amount of information created and disseminated each year has grown exponentially. It was estimated that in 2007 there were more than 281 exabytes of information produced in that 1 year alone (Infoniac.com, March 13, 2008). That is 28-million bytes produced in that 1 year for each byte of information stored in the entire Library of Congress. Much of this information is recorded and transmitted by the mass media. Throughout the world, radio stations send out 65.5 million hours of original programming each year, and television adds another 48 million hours. In the United States alone, there are now more than 400,000 book titles published annually (Potter, 2010). The amount of information available has fundamentally changed the audience experience with the media. No longer is there a problem with information access; the problem is now how to adapt to a flood of messages aggressively competing for our attention.

To deal with all these exposure opportunities, audiences have been spending more time with the mass media (Angwin, 2009), especially the younger generation (Kaiser Family Foundation, 2005). People now spend more than 70% of their day on average with the media, and much of this is multitasking in which multiple media are accessed at the same time (Ransford, 2005).

Given all the choices and the multitasking during exposures, the audience media experience has changed over time. When the number of choices is large, humans typically make quick intuitive decisions based on prior conditioning rather than informed choice, which requires more effort (Schwartz, 2004; Wright, 2007). This is clearly the case in the new media environment in which there are an overwhelming number of choices every minute of every day. Therefore, people rely largely on automatic routines that have been conditioned by the mass media over the years (Potter, 2009).

SHIFT IN MARKETING

The amount of information available has fundamentally changed how media companies market their messages. To survive in the new media environment with so many message alternatives constantly competing for audience members' attention, all mass media—the newer technologies as well as the more traditional older media—have been developing a particular marketing strategy. This strategy begins with identifying needs in some segment of the general population, and then working to attract the attention of the people in that niche segment

(Hirsch, 1981; Arens, Weigold, & Arens, 2009). The strategy then directs the mass media business to create or stimulate content that can attract members of that niche audience to their particular platform where they can charge those people an access fee (subscription to a newspaper, magazine, web site, Internet game, etc.), a usage fee (downloading music, video, texting, etc.), and also charge advertisers an access fee to their constructed audiences. The media businesses must also condition their audience members for repeat exposures so as to amortize the high cost of attracting those people over many repeat exposures and thus make the enterprise economically viable. The mass media businesses now not only offer their own constructed messages, but they also offer users the ability to create and share their own messages.

New Conceptualization of "Mass" Media

Given the salient features of the new media environment, we need a definition of "mass" media that focuses on their special characteristics of technological channels, senders, and audiences. It should include the newer media as well as the more traditional media. Such a definition is as follows. The "mass" media employ technological devices of message dissemination that can reach audiences within a relatively short time, even simultaneously, make messages public (available to anyone), and extend the availability of messages in time and space. Channels are not defined ostensively, because although the ostensive form of definition has been useful in the past, it has lost its usefulness with the blurring of distinctions across channels.

With "mass" media, the sender of messages must have an awareness of specific niche audiences and actively promote itself so as to attract as many audience members of that niche as possible, and then condition audience members for habitual repeated exposures. Given the nature of the sender along with the technological characteristics specified in the previous paragraph, we can reason that a person who sets up a Facebook page and creates messages to attract a certain niche audience may be very successful in attracting and conditioning visitors for repeat exposures, but it is Facebook and not the page designer who is the mass medium because it is the organization of Facebook that has created the technological and marketing platform that makes the pages possible. In this case, the sender of personal messages through his or her Facebook account is actually working for Facebook without pay by creating—along with hundreds of millions of other Facebook users—the content.

With the "mass" media, the audience must be composed of people who are: (1) widely dispersed geographically; that is, not all in one place; (2) aware of the public character of what they are seeing or hearing; and (3) encountering messages in a variety of exposure states but most often in a state of automaticity. Audience members are both receivers and senders of messages.

Mass communication is defined as the process of using the mass media to disseminate messages; that is, it is the process of designing, manufacturing, and marketing messages to specific niche audiences in a manner to maximize exposures within those niches and conditioning niche audience members for habitual repeat exposures to subsequent messages. This definition has important implications for all four facets of the mass media phenomenon. The mass media organizations are businesses that have clear economic goals. If they also have social, aesthetic, or cultural goals, those are secondary to their economic goals. To meet these goals on a regular basis they have developed specific strategies to identify potential niche audiences, attract audience members to their messages so as to construct those audiences, and then condition those audiences for habitual exposures so that they can maintain a stable business model of charging for exposures and renting those audiences out to advertisers.

This definition of the mass media also has implications for the idea of audiences that must be regarded as composed of individuals who have been identified as having particular interests and then having been successfully attracted by certain messages in a highly competitive environment for attention. Audience members also have had a significant history of conditioning with certain types of messages and not others. Researchers who gather information from audience members need to take this history into consideration as an essential context when designing their particular studies.

Too often when psychological researchers approach the mass media and examine their effects, they assume that the media organizations should have a high level of social responsibility and criticize the media when they do not act that way. However, we must realize that the media regard themselves primarily as economic entities rather than social entities; therefore, their fundamental goal is to maximize their value to their owners. Most mass media organizations in the world, and especially in Western countries, are owned by people and organizations who buy shares in the company (Owers, Carveth, & Alexander, 1998).

Even when mass media organizations are publically held corporations focused on seeking financial resources, they can also become concerned with achieving other goals besides purely financial ones. For example, media organizations often pursue the goal of gaining prestige and exercising influence or power in society (Tunstall, 1971). McQuail (2005) adds that some media companies are run for "idealistic" social or cultural purposes, such as trying educate the public. This means that the value of a media organization to its owners is sometimes measured in nonfinancial terms, such as the prestige or satisfaction of owning a media business (Bates, 1998) or the influence that some media business is able to exert as an authority (Padioleau, 1985). Doyle (2002) points out that "Most countries have a state-owned broadcasting entity which takes the form of a public corporation and which is dedicated to 'public service' television and radio broadcasting" and "their primary goal is to provide a universally available public broadcasting service rather than to make a profit" (p. 5).

Media Audience Facet

Although the Generating-Findings perspective has produced many research findings, we must be careful to evaluate those findings for validity. With audience research, there is reason to believe that many of those findings—especially with amount of exposure and motives—may be faulty because they rely on self-reports. Self-reports have always been a suspect measure, but this is especially the case in media studies, in which audiences are overwhelmed with choices, so their filtering and exposure decisions are typically so mundane that they are accomplished in an automatic fashion with very little cognitive effort. As a result, there is little memory from which to recall exposure decisions, particular motives, or specific gratifications.

In shifting toward a Mapping-Phenomenon perceptive, we need to think more carefully about the experiences an audience member encounters when exposed to mass media messages. In the new media environment of information saturation, overwhelming choice, and the media aggressively competing for their time and attention, audience members have many different kinds of exposure experiences. To organize the kinds of experiences that would help scholars design research studies, I propose a Media Exposure Experience Matrix that is constructed of two dimensions I believe are the two most important constructs of audiences—exposure states and information processing tasks.

Exposure States

If we are to map the audience facet of the mass media phenomenon, we need to elaborate attention more carefully so we can increase the validity of findings about audience experiences during exposures. There are four qualitatively different exposure states: automatic, attentional, transported, and self-reflexive. The exposure experience is very different across these four states for audience members. Until researchers can acknowledge these differences and build sensitivity to these differences into their designs and measures, much of the findings of those studies will continue to be faulty. What audience members remember from each of these states and what they are able to tell researchers about their experiences greatly vary across these four states. Let's now examine each of these four states.

THE AUTOMATIC STATE

In the automatic state, people are in environments in which they are exposed to media messages but they are not aware of those messages; that is, their minds are on automatic pilot, screening out all the messages from conscious exposure. There is no conscious goal or strategy for seeking out messages; however, screening out of messages still takes place. This screening out continues automatically with no effort until some element in a message breaks through people's default screen and captures their attention.

In the automatic processing state, message elements are physically perceived but processed automatically in an unconscious manner. This exposure state resides above the threshold of human sense perception but below the threshold of conscious awareness. The person is in a perceptual flow that continues until an interruption stops the exposure or "bumps" the person's perceptual processing into a different state of exposure or until the media message moves outside of a person's physical or perceptual ability to be exposed to it.

In the automatic state, people can look active to outside observers, but they are not thinking about what they are doing. People in the automatic state can be flipping through the pages of a magazine or clicking through the channels on a television. Although there is evidence of behavior, this does not necessarily mean that people's minds are engaged and they are "making" decisions. Rather, the decisions are happening to them automatically.

Exposure to much of the media, especially radio and television, is in the automatic state. People often have no conscious awareness of the exposure when it is taking place, nor do they have a recollection of the details in the experience later. Therefore, what happens in this exposure state cannot be measured on self-report questionnaires, such as viewing diaries.

This is one of the most overlooked conditions in all of media scholarship. For example, Thompson (1995) said that one of the shortcomings of mass media research has been the neglect of describing the mundane character of how people encounter media messages in their everyday life. He says that "the reception of media products is a routine, practical activity which individuals carry out as an integral part of their everyday lives. If we wish to understand the nature of reception, and then we must develop an approach which is sensitive to the routine and practical aspects of receptive activity" (p. 38). He continues, "The reception of media products should be seen, furthermore, as a routine activity, in the sense that it is an integral part of the regularized activities that constitute everyday life" (p. 39).

THE ATTENTIONAL STATE

Attentional exposure refers to people being aware of the messages and actively interacting with the elements in the messages. This does not mean they must have a high level of concentration, although that is possible. The key is conscious awareness of the messages during exposures.

Within the attentional state there is a range of attention depending on how much of a person's mental resources one devotes to the exposure. The rheostat metaphor works in this exposure state. At minimum, the person must be aware of the message and consciously track it, but there is a fair degree of elasticity in the degree of concentration, which can range from partial to quite extensive processing depending on the number of elements handled and the depth of analysis employed.

THE TRANSPORTED STATE

When people are in the attentional state but then are pulled into the message so strongly that they lose awareness of being apart from the message, they cross over into the transported state. In the transported state, audience members lose their sense of separateness from the message; that is, they are swept away with the message, enter the world of the message, and lose track of their own social world surroundings. For example, watching a movie in a theater, people can get so caught up in the action so that they feel they are involved with action. They experience the same intense emotions as do the characters. They lose the sense that they are in a theater. They lose track of real time and—in its place—experience the narrative's time. Their concentration level is so high that they lose touch with their real-world environment.

The transported state is similar to the idea of flow as expressed by Csikszentmihalyi (1988), who defines *flow* as a state of high concentration and internally generated pleasure. Most of the time, people are producing something during flow, such as an artist working on a painting, but there are other times when people are engaging in flow activities such as sports and games to avoid boredom. There is a distortion of time. Hours can pass like minutes and conversely, a few seconds can seem to last a long time. Also, the person temporarily loses the awareness of self that in normal life often intrudes in consciousness and causes psychic energy to be diverted from what needs to be done. According to Csikszentmihalyi, there are two key requirements for flow. First, there needs to be a challenge in a task so that it absorbs people; that is, it challenges their level of skill. Thus, tic tac toe is a game of low complexity and has a low challenge; therefore, it is not likely to lead to flow, whereas chess is very complex and involving; therefore, it is much more likely to lead to flow. Second, there needs to be a set of rules known to the person. Ambiguous situations do not offer the potential for flow. The rules direct attention on the task and provide guideposts for satisfaction.

The transported state is similar but not identical to flow as expressed by Csikszentmihalyi. It is similar in the sense that people are swept away by the experience and lose track of time as well as their real-world surroundings. It is different in the sense that the transported state is triggered and maintained by media messages that intensely resonate with the audience member, whereas flow is triggered and heightened by a challenge that slightly exceeds the person's skill level. In the transported state, people project themselves deeply into the media story; in flow, people project themselves into a challenge, and as they work hard they are continually monitoring their progress in meeting that challenge.

The transported state is also similar to what various scholars have referred to as *presence*. However, presence has been used in a variety of ways. For example, Lombard and Ditton (1997) analyzed the literature and found that the term was used in six different ways, including: social richness (the extent to which a medium is perceived as sociable, warm, sensitive, personal, or intimate when it is used to interact with other people); realism (the degree to which a medium can produce seemingly accurate representations of objects, events, and people); transportation (which includes three distinct types of transportation: "You are there," in which the user is transported to another place; "It is here," in which another place and the objects within it are transported to the user; and "We are together," in which two or more communicators are transported together to a place that they share); immersion (the senses are immersed in the virtual world); social actor within medium (parasocial interactions with characters in the medium); and medium as social actor (the medium itself—like a computer—is regarded as being alive and having a personality). Lee (2004) has also attempted an explication of presence that she concludes is "a psychological state in which virtual objects are experienced as actual objects in either sensory or nonsensory ways" (p. 27).

Other scholars have used the term *transportation* in a different way than that used here. For example, Green, Garst, and Brock (2004) say a "transported individual is cognitively and emotionally involved in the story and may experience vivid mental images tied to the story's plot" (p. 168). They say that transportation may aid in suspension of disbelief, which reduces a person's motivation to counterargue the issues raised in the story. I argue that suspension of disbelief is a process that is required for the transportation state to be entered and maintained. To illustrate, a producer of a media message will meet audience members in their real-world experience in terms of settings, plots, and characters. Then gradually, step by step, pull the audience away from their world and transport them into another experience by making the settings more attractive, glamorous, and intriguing; making the plot more vibrant, faster, and intense; and making the characters bigger than life. Audience members must accept each step away from their mundane everyday real-world existence by willingly accepting each sweetened setting, plot point, and character alteration until they are transported into an experience.

The transported state is not conceptualized here as a neighborhood within the attentional state; that is, it is not simply the high end of the attentional state. Instead, the transported state is qualitatively different than the attentional state. Although attention is very high in the transported state, the attention is also very narrow; that is, people have tunnel vision and focus on the media message in a way that eliminates the barrier between them and the message. People are swept away and "enter" the message. In this sense, it is the opposite of the automatic state in which people stay grounded in their social world and are unaware of the media messages in their perceptual environment. In the transported exposure state, people enter the media message and lose track of their social world.

THE SELF-REFLEXIVE STATE

In the self-reflexive state, people are hyperaware of the message *and of their processing of the message*. It is as if they are sitting on their own shoulder and monitoring their own reactions as they experience the message.

In the self-reflexive state, people are not only consciously aware of the elements in the message, but they are aware of their processing of those elements; that is, they experience their own processing. This represents the fullest degree of awareness; that is, people are aware of the media message, their own social world, and their position in the social world while they process the media message. In the self-reflexive exposure state, the viewer exercises the greatest control over perceptions by reflecting on questions such as, "Why am I exposing myself to this message?" "What am I getting out of this exposure and why?" and, "Why am I making these interpretations of meaning?" Not only is there analysis, but there is also meta-analysis. Although the self-reflexive and transported states might appear similar in that they are characterized by high involvement by audience members, the two exposure states are very different. In the transported state, people are highly involved emotionally and they lose themselves in the action. In contrast, the self-reflexive state is characterized by people being highly involved cognitively while very much aware of themselves as they analytically process the exposure messages.

Information-Processing Tasks

Audiences engage in a great many tasks when processing information from the media. To help organize all these many tasks, three categories of filtering messages, meaning matching, and meaning construction (Fig. 23.1) are offered here. Audience members are constantly confronted with exposure choices, so an essential ongoing exposure task is filtering. When information is encountered during any exposure, audiences must continually assess meaning either through meaning matching or meaning construction.

Filtering Message

Task: To make decisions about which messages to filter out (ignore) and which to filter in (pay attention to)

Goal: To attend to only those messages that have the highest utility and avoid all others

Focus: Messages in the environment

Type of Problem: Frequently partially specified because the criterion of utility is constantly changing

Meaning matching

Task: To use basic competencies to recognize symbols and locate definitions for each

Goal: To access previously learned meanings efficiently

Focus: Referents in messages

Type of Problem: Frequently fully specified

Meaning Construction

Task: To use skills in order to move beyond meaning matching and construct meaning for one's self in order to get more personal value out of a message

Goal: To interpret messages from more than one perspective as a means of identifying the range of meaning options, then choose one or synthesize across several

Focus: One's own knowledge structures

Type of Problem: Almost always partially specified

Figure 24.1 Summary of Three Tasks of Information Processing.

The important questions governing the filtering task are, "How can we make good decisions about filtering messages in a way that on the one hand helps us take advantage of the positive effects, and on the other hand protects us from the negative effects of being overwhelmed or from having our minds shaped by forces outside our control?" And furthermore, "How can we achieve this in a relatively efficient manner?"

Once we have filtered-in messages, we need to determine their meaning. The meaning assessment task is composed of two separate processes of meaning matching and meaning construction. This distinction is based partially on the idea of closed codes and open codes, as expressed by Hall (1980), who pointed out that designers of messages have a choice of using closed or open codes when encoding meaning in their messages. This encoding can be done in a denotative fashion in which "the televisual sign is fixed by certain, very complex (but limited or 'closed') codes" as well as in a connotative fashion that "is more open, subject to more active transformations" (p. 134). As for the decoding of the meaning by individuals, Hall says that messages are open to more than one meaning; that is, the codes in media messages are polysemic. However, he does not believe the codes are "pluralistic." For a code to be pluralistic, all readings must be given equal status. Hall says there is one dominant reading of a code; this is usually the reading that is preferred by the encoder of the message. Oppositional and negotiated readings are also possible. An oppositional reading is one in contrast to the dominant one, and a negotiated reading is one that is created when a reader constructs a new interpretation somewhere between the writer's intention and the reader's natural position. Hall (1980) says that when audiences decode messages, they need to know the codes or meaning system. People in a given culture share the same meanings for particular codes. Thus, communicators use the codes to design messages, and receivers use the codes to decode them.

In this general framework, I build off of Hall's initial ideas and elaborate them in the distinction between the information processing tasks of meaning matching and meaning construction. With meaning matching, meaning is assumed to reside outside the person in an authority, such as a teacher, an expert, a dictionary, a text book, or the like. The task for the person is to find those meanings and memorize them. Thus, parents and educational institutions are primarily responsible for housing the authoritative information and passing it on to the next generation. The media are also a major source of information, and for many people the media have attained the status of an authoritative source, so people accept the meanings presented there. Thus, the meaning-matching task involves working with closed codes.

Although meaning matching is essentially a task composed of fully specified problems, meaning construction, in contrast, is composed of partially specified problems, and this makes it a much more challenging task, because it requires reasoning, and reasoning is a process that requires some insight (Evans, 1999). Some steps in the process of meaning construction may deal with closed codes, but there is more to it. Because the process is only partially specified, accessing one's memory for denoted meanings will not completely meet the challenge posed by meaning construction tasks.

Meaning construction is a process wherein people transform messages they take in and create meaning for themselves. There are many meanings that can be constructed from any media message, and furthermore there are many ways to go about constructing that meaning. Thus, people cannot learn a complete set of rules to accomplish this; instead, they need to be guided by their own information goals and use well-developed skills to creatively construct a path to reach their goals.

The two processes of meaning matching and meaning construction are not discrete; they are intertwined. To construct meaning, a person has to first recognize key elements in media messages and understand the sense in which those elements are being used in the message. Thus, the meaning matching process is more fundamental, because the product of the meaning-matching process then is imported into the meaning-construction process.

Recall from an earlier section that there has been a considerable debate among communication scholars regarding the degree to which meaning resides in the message. The question is, "Do people learn denoted meanings for symbols (Ellis, 1995; Thompson, 1995), or do people construct their own meanings during media exposures (e.g., see Barthes, 1967; Deetz, 1973; Foucault, 1984; Bochner, 1985; Shotter & Gergen, 1994)." This debate in essence is how much of communication is meaning matching and how much is meaning construction. This, of course, is a useless debate because audiences are constantly engaged in both meaning matching and meaning construction.

The Media Exposure Experience Matrix

The Media Exposure Experience Matrix crosses exposure states with information processing tasks (Fig. 23.2). It reminds us to consider that there are qualitatively different experiences that have been amalgamated under the term *exposure*, and that to understand how people process information from the media we need to deal with the exposure states separately. Thus, this set of four exposure states helps us get past the debate over whether the audience is active or passive. People are often active, but they are also often passive. This set of exposure states provides a way of understanding the experience of being passive (in the automatic state that occurs most of the time) and the different experiences of being active (attentional, transported, and self-reflexive).

If we are to do a better job of mapping the audience facet of the mass media phenomenon, we need to be more careful in considering what our research participants can tell us about the experience of their media exposures. It is likely that the validity of the data generated by the typically used measures of time spent with various media will be much higher from attentional and especially self-reflexive exposures than with automatic and transported exposures. If we do not make this distinction in our measurement designs, then we will continue to average valid responses with wild guesses and this will trap us in a Generating-Findings perspective.

The matrix does not rely on motives. Of course motives can be plugged into certain cells of this

Media Exposure Model

Exposure States	Information Processing Tasks		
	Filtering	Meaning Matching	Meaning Construction
Automatic	Screening	Highly Automatic	Highly Automatic
Attentional	Searching	Automatic	Typical Construction
Transported	Swept	Personal & Highly Automatic	Highly Emotional Construction
Self-Reflexive	Deep Analysis	Sorting Through Learned Meanings	Highly Personalized Construction

Figure 24.2 Media Exposure Model.

matrix to help explain exposures, but researchers are cautioned to consider the degree to which their participants are aware of their motives. Also, researchers need to consider the level of generality of the motives.

The purpose of this matrix is to highlight the importance of the interaction of exposure states with information-processing tasks. It is hoped that this matrix will enhance researchers' ability to explain what happens during exposures. To illustrate this point, note how one published research study could have expanded its explanatory power by using the Media Exposure Experience Matrix. Pool, Koolstra, and van der Voort (2003) conducted an experiment to find out if background use of media influenced adolescents' performance on homework. They found that music in the background left homework performance unaffected. Also, there was no indication that background media influenced the amount of time spent to complete homework assignments. However, watching soap operas during homework reduced student performance. These are interesting results, but they appear equivocal. Also, they do not explain why exposure to one type of media message could reduce homework performance, whereas another form of message would leave it unaffected. In their results, the focus is on type of message or

medium. However, if we used the Media Exposure Experience Matrix, we would shift the focus of explanation to the experience of the audience member during the exposure, and this could help explain the pattern of results. It is likely that background music was experienced by most students in the automatic exposure state where they did not need to expend any mental energy, saving their full cognitive capacity for their homework. In contrast, it is likely that many, but not all, students watching soap operas were in a transported exposure state, thus having no cognitive resources left over for studying during that time. Furthermore, it is likely that students who were in a transported exposure state in both soap operas and music had the lowest performance on homework. Therefore, exposure state would seem to be a much better predictor of audience cognitive allocations than would genre of media message.

The power of the Media Exposure Experience Matrix is that it allows for rational, conscious models of information selection and processing but does not require them. For example, there are many rational models in which audience members make a series of decisions consciously taking into consideration their motives and gratifications (Rosengren, 1974; Palmgreen & Rayburn, 1985), reality of messages and consequences of exposure (Comstock et al., 1978), how news is processed (Graber, 1984), or consistency considerations (Donohew & Tipton, 1973). For example, Donohew and Tipton (1973) created a model to explain information seeking, avoiding, and processing. This model includes five decision points of consistency of message, whether to reject it or not, what action to take if one does not reject it, closure, and whether sources are broad or narrow. Each of these is a cognitive decision that requires some evaluation and thought. I am not arguing against the usefulness of such rational models; however, I am arguing that there are a variety of exposure states and that rational models are not likely to be able to explain what occurs in either the automatic or transported states.

Media Messages Facet

The key construct in moving thinking about the message facet out of the Generating-Findings perspective to a Mapping-Phenomenon perspective is the *narrative line*. The narrative line is the formulaic structure that message producers use to construct their messages in an efficient manner; it is also what audiences use so as to follow the progression of ideas in messages and thus trigger meaning matching as well as guide meaning construction.

For Producers of Media Messages

People who construct messages are confronted with a very large number of decision points, and at each decision point, many options are usually available. When a person selects a particular option at a decision point, the person goes off on that option's path and soon arrives at another decision point with its own set of options. To continue in the process of message design, the person must select one of the options at that decision point, and then move down that option's path to the next decision point. The process of designing a message can be regarded as navigating through the maze of options.

The training of producers of media messages is focused on their learning a complex structure of decision making. Producers need to envision the sequence of decisions they must make in the design of their messages and the options available to them at each decision point. And even more important, producers must learn how other producers—especially the most successful ones—typically navigate through all these decision points. They learn this by analyzing the messages of other producers; that is, the paths that other producers take through this decision maze. Those paths are the narrative lines of those messages.

To simplify and routinize this process of producing media messages, particular formulas have evolved. Some of these formulas are very general and apply to all kinds of media messages. For example, whether a message is designed to be entertainment, an advertisement, or news/information, it typically must have a hook (to attract attention and set up expectations for what will be presented in the message), a story line (in which there is a logical progression from one event or idea to the next), and a satisfying resolution (the cognitive or emotional payoff sufficient to reward the audience member for the time and effort spent on processing the message). Within each of these three mega-genres (entertainment, advertising, and news/information), there are subgenres that are often keyed to a medium (e.g., the television situation comedy, the romance novel, the action/adventure film).

Success as a producer of media message, therefore, is keyed to two things. First, the degree of success is tied to the extent to which a producer has a complete picture of the options maze, at least for his or her genre and subgenre neighborhood. Producers who understand the implications of each decision and where it takes them are in more control of the design process and are more likely to create the messages they envision. Second, the degree of success is tied to the extent to which a person has an understanding of how successful producers have made their decisions; that is, an understanding of message formulas and conventions.

For Audiences of Media Messages

The narrative line is also important to audiences. Audience members learn to spot particular message elements to signal to them how to go about understanding a media message. The more salient and recognizable story elements are to audience members at the very beginning of a message, the easier it will be for audiences to process those messages; that is, to locate the appropriate algorithm and use an algorithm that offers a great deal of familiar guidance to the processing of the unfolding message. When this occurs well, the audience members can accomplish message processing with very low psychic costs. In contrast, when people encounter a message type for which they have no existing algorithm or when the algorithm they use to process the message has a lot of gaps, people experience a high psychic cost; in this case they will typically terminate the exposure unless the message delivers a high degree of benefits, thus making the high cost worthwhile.

Typically audience members focus on the *what* of messages and are unconcerned about the *why* and *how* producers made their decisions. Keeping the focus solely on the *what* makes message processing much more efficient for audience members and allows them to process the messages in the state of automaticity. However, at times people want to conduct more analysis to try to understand more about why they liked it so much or hated something about it. For example, people who go to a 2-hour film in an art theater might spend several hours thinking about the director's work and building a context for the film, and then during the film they might be very active in analyzing the elements on the screen, and after the film continue to construct a more elaborate understanding of the narrative line through conversations with other film buffs. Audience members then can use the narrative line automatically to match meaning or more analytically to construct meaning. This is what many scholars mean by media literacy (Christ & Potter, 1998).

Critique of Message Research

Now that I have laid out a general framework line of thinking on mass media content which I call Lineation Theory, it is time to raise the question, "Given the current literature, how well have we been mapping the phenomenon of mass media content?" My answer to this question is that the literature on media content is far less developed than the literatures on the other three mass media facets. This literature is the most scattered and exhibits the least conceptual leverage; that is, it is the most exploratory, question-driven, and descriptive. Therefore, the biggest challenge in evolving from a Generating-Findings to a Mapping-Phenomenon perspective lies with altering our approach to designing research that examines the message facet of the mass media.

This section presents a general broad-stroke critique of the literature on mass media content. The critique of the media message literature is composed of five areas: lack of overviews, breadth of content covered, methods used, manifest/latent content, and leveraging findings.

LACK OF OVERVIEWS

If we are to evolve from a Generating-Findings to a Mapping-Phenomenon perspective, we need to assess where we are as a scholarly field in terms of understanding the general patterns of content that appear across all forms of the mass media. First, we need to know how large this literature on

media content has grown and what topic areas are the most prevalent. Second, we need a topic-by-topic critical analysis to inventory the content patterns from the findings of all the individual studies. Once we have constructed this map of our literature, we will have the basis for identifying the crucial gaps in our understanding about our phenomenon, and this will help us most efficiently orient toward where we need to concentrate our content scholarship so as to construct a map of our phenomenon. This is the beginning point. Unfortunately, there are currently no general overviews, nor are there many reviews by medium or topic to help us begin this task.

Over the years of reading scholarly communication journals, I have noticed many published content analyses of various media messages, especially of violence, risky behaviors (e.g., drinking, smoking, drug use), demographics of characters, and types of news topics covered. However, there are very few general overviews of these studies, so it is difficult to know the size of this content analysis literature. One example of a content analysis of the published literature is a study by Riffe and Freitag (1997), who conducted an analysis of 25 years of published content analyses in *Journalism & Mass Communication Quarterly* and reported finding 486 content analysis studies in that one journal alone. This article is valuable in telling us how many content analysis studies were published in this one journal over 25 years, but there are no studies that give us a larger picture of the size of the literature over all communication journals or a longer span of years. Furthermore, there are few relatively broad reviews of content analysis literature to synthesize what is known about topic areas.

The coverage of mass media messages is limited to certain media. The coverage of messages in television and film has been more extensive than the coverage of messages on radio, recordings, or books. Magazine messages have received some attention, but those content analyses have focused primarily on ads. The Internet is starting to attract attention of media scholars.

The media message analysis literature appears to be concentrated in a few media and a few topic areas, such as minorities in mass media content (Greenberg, Mastro, & Brand, 2002) or violence in the media (Potter, 1999). For example, Shoemaker and Reese (1996) synthesized the content analysis literature into several general conclusions about media content and reported that television content (both news and entertainment) contains a high level of violence that is consistent over time; in media content, women and the aged appear less often than men and younger adults; and in general, portrayals in media reflect the power relations of the common society. Thus there are three areas that have been well examined in the mass media, at least on television. They are violence; the demographics of age, gender, and ethnicity; and the power relations among people or characters belonging to the different demographic groups.

The strength of this concentration is that there is a high degree of triangulation on those areas that are covered. These areas have a collection of different scholars using different samples, coders, and often codes to arrive at very similar findings. Thus, on these few topics there is high convergence and therefore a high degree of confidence in the findings. However, the downside of this concentration of resources is that there are large areas of media content that are virtually unexamined as of yet.

It is understandable why the literature of mass media content is fragmentary. There are so many topics of interest compared with the number of mass media scholars that there are not enough resources to cover all topics. This is characteristic of the young nature of the field and is not meant to be a criticism of past research efforts. The task of covering the entire spectrum of mass media messages is enormous; we need to start somewhere. But as the field matures, we need to shift our resources around to achieve a more balanced coverage of all areas across the range of content. It is an irony that many mass media scholars are motivated to conduct their content analyses because of a perceived imbalance in news coverage topics or types of people; then when they document these imbalances in their research findings, they strongly criticize the mass media for not being more balanced and presenting a wider range of coverage of topics and people to more accurately reflect the world they are covering. Yet by so doing, media scholars are creating a literature that is even more out of balance with the phenomenon they are trying to cover.

METHOD

Scholars who study mass media content either use a quantitative methodology of content analysis or a qualitative methodology, such as textual analysis. As for quantitative content analysis, the key to reaping its benefits lies in following the scientific rules well. The two problem areas are sampling and testing the consistency of coding decisions. As for sampling, the challenge is in constructing a sampling frame that represents the population. If this cannot be achieved well, random sampling from a flawed sampling frame will not allow the analyst to generalize to the population. Also, analysts must test for coding reliability, and this is not always reported. Furthermore, when it is reported, many of the tests do not correct for chance agreement, so the reliability figures are artificially high, leading readers to believe that the coders were more consistent in their decisions than was the actual case.

The social science literature built from content analyses does very little in the way of inferring patterns. Much of this literature is composed of studies that simply count the occurrence of particular elements, such as demographic characteristics or acts of violence. Some studies make comparisons of counts across content groupings, such as medium (comparing counts from television with those from newspapers), vehicles (comparing counts from *The New York Times* with those from the *Washington Post*), content provider (ABC, CBS, Fox, and NBC), or genre (counts from comedy shows with those from dramatic programs). These comparisons qualify as patterns, but this is a relatively weak form of patterning. A stronger form of patterning is looking for regularities among elements within messages. Some of this was done in the analyses presented by the National Television Violence Study (1997), in which analysts looked for the co-occurrence of lack of harm to victims, lack of remorse from perpetrators, and lack of graphicness in the depiction of the violent act. The co-occurrence of these elements was an indication of the violence being sanitized. Coders did not code for degree of sanitization; instead, the analysts inferred a pattern of sanitized violence from several elements of content that were coded. There are not many examples of patterning in the social science content analysis literature; however, over time more content analysts are building this feature into their designs.

A nonquantitative literature has been generated by scholars taking a more humanistic approach, such as using textual analysis, semiotics/semiology, genre analysis, discourse analysis, dialogic analysis, Marxist analysis, feminist analysis, psychoanalytical analysis, postmodern analysis, and myth analysis. The intention of scholars using these methods is not to count the prevalence of elements in mass media content. Instead, these scholars are much more interested in identifying patterns qualitatively and explaining those patterns by linking them to something outside the content itself. The number of qualitative content studies published is much smaller than the number of quantitative content studies. For much more detail on the value of the qualitative approach, please see Chapter 8 on qualitative research and media psychology.

MANIFEST AND LATENT CONTENT

Often, analysts design studies that require the coding of latent content rather than manifest content. This creates more of a challenge to achieve coder consistency. To help the coders, analysts will develop a codebook with many rules and guidelines then subject coders to many detailed training sessions. Throughout this procedure, analysts will pilot test on coder consistency. When coder consistency is too low, analysts will add more rules and guidelines to the codebook as well as continue with coder training. Usually this procedure will result in improvements in coder consistency until the reliability figures ascend to an acceptable level.

This procedure of adding coding rules and retraining coders, however, typically leads coders away from their natural meanings for media messages. The further away they are moved from their everyday meanings, the less their coding will resemble the way typical people understand the media messages. For example, this has been a problem in media violence content analyses. In content analyses of violence, social scientists typically focus on acts that are intended to harm victims physically; these acts still get counted even when they are nongraphic, humorous, or fantasy. Whereas the general public defines acts of violence primarily in terms of actions that tend to offend them; that is, are high in graphicness, reality, and seriousness (see Potter, 2003 for a more complete discussion of this point).

LEVERAGING FINDINGS

In his classic 1969 methods book, *Content Analysis for the Social Sciences and Humanities,* Holsti said that content analysis is a method for "making inferences by objectively and systematically identifying specified characteristics of messages" (p. 14). Holsti argued that once the coding is finished and quantitatively analyzed, the researcher makes inferences about the results—either inferences about the causes of the communications analyzed or the effects of those messages. This idea has been supported by other scholars in their subsequent writings about the method of content analysis (Stempel, 1981; Riffe, Lacy, & Fico, 1998; Neuendorf, 2001).

A fair number of content analysts have attempted such linkages in their discussion sections. However, these linkages are usually to negative effects or practices. To illustrate, the mass media theories most often used for this purpose are cultivation, social learning theory, and agenda setting. With cultivation, content analysts expressly look for content patterns in the media world that different from content patterns in the social world. Thus, the focus of these content analyses is to find patterns of deviation that will lead the population to false beliefs about the social world. Social learning theory is a popular theory used in content analyses of violence and sexual occurrences. Analysts document risky patterns in the content portrayals, and then use social learning theory to argue that these risky portrayals will lead audiences to learn faulty social information. And tests of agenda setting rely on content analyses of newscasts to identify the media agenda for news, and then argue that the media present a narrow agenda rather than a more complete range of news stories.

Furthermore, when content analysts do not relate their inferred patterns to particular media theories, they still frequently relate them to a criticism of the media. Popular topics among researchers using scientifically based content analyses include violence, sexual portrayals, "bad" language, and misleading images of society (body images, health behaviors, degree of affluence, family interaction patterns, and bias in news stories). Of course, these are all relevant topics for content analyses. However, we need more of a balance that reveals patterns of messages that do not necessarily have a negative influence.

The past research on messages is limited to either a content analysis of largely manifest message elements or a more in-depth qualitative analysis of one particular message (television show, television series, etc.). The problem is that we have not put the two together to develop rich descriptions of narrative formulas. We need to dig deeper into the way media organizations tell us stories as well as how we tell our own stories using the various forms of the interactive media. For a fascinating exploration of this topic, see Chapter 2.

Media Effects Facet

The literature examining the effects facet of the mass media phenomenon is very large. The studies in this literature have followed a strategy that has focused on dealing with individuals in groups and looking for differences across groups. Although this strategy has been valuable in the past to generate many suggestive findings about effects, I argue that the challenge of studying media effects has changed and we now must focus more on individuals as units of analysis if we are to provide more direct tests of mass media influence.

In this section, I begin with a critique of what I call the Groups-Differences strategy that has been so dominant in media effects research up to this point. This critique is then used as a foundation for a reconceptualization of media influence leading to media effects.

Critique of the Groups-Differences Strategy for Designing Media Effects Studies

By a Groups-Differences strategy, is meant that the media effects literature is focused less on effects directly and more on differences in means across groups, hence the name Groups-Differences. To explain what is meant by this research strategy and why it is limited, let's begin with the idea of "comparison." Essentially, all research designs require comparison. A research design could compare values on a variable with some standard; a design could compare the change in values on a variable over time; or a design could compare means of variables across groups. With media effects studies, the scores on effects measures are never compared with some standard (such as a threshold for an effect), and they are rarely compared with previous measures on the same research participants over time to develop an historical pattern. Instead, the typical mass media effects design compares effects measures aggregated as means across groups, where groups are either determined by an experimental treatment or some characteristic of the research participants, such as gender, age, and so on.

With the Groups-Differences strategy, the procedure is as follows. An "effects" measure is taken from all participants, means are computed for each group, and then those means are compared across groups. With experiments, groups are determined a priori as treatments, and participants are randomly assigned to the groups. If there are relatively large differences in means across groups, the researchers conclude that differences were generated by the differential treatments—usually a media message. With surveys, participants are grouped in the data analysis according to characteristics such as age, gender, amount of media use, and so on. If there are relatively large differences in means across these attribute groups, the researchers conclude that

differences are attributable to the grouping variables, hence the name Groups-Differences for this strategy.

This Groups-Differences strategy to research design produces results that are only *suggestive* of effects, not a direct test of effects. To illustrate this point, consider a simple example of two-group experiment in which 40 participants are assigned to a treatment group and 40 to a control group. Let's say the effects measure is taken on a 10-point scale. We find that the mean of both groups is 5.0 on the effects measure, so we conclude that the treatment had no effect. However, what if we found a pattern in which all 40 participants in the control group scored 4, 5, and 6 to average the 5.0 group mean, but that in the treatment group 20 participants scored a 2 and the other 20 participants scored an 8, which would still compute to a group mean of 5.0. With this data pattern, we can see the two groups are not the same in their effects patterns, although the group means are identical. Perhaps the treatment stimulated half the participants to greatly increase the effect scores while at the same time stimulating the other half to greatly decrease their effect scores. However, without a test retest to document change, we cannot know if the split in treatment group outcomes was owing to the treatment itself, faulty assignment of participants to treatments, or an interesting interaction between the effect measure and some unmeasured characteristic in the participants. And more important, the design of comparing group means not only gives us no way of examining the differing reaction patterns, but it also masks the pattern itself by comparing only means across the two groups.

The Groups-Differences strategy for designing effects studies focuses our attention on questions such as, "In which group was there a greater mean on a particular effects measure?" "Were the differences in group means large enough for us to conclude that such a difference could not have occurred by chance alone?" and "What is the degree of relationship between the distributions of two scores?" Almost every study in the published literature can provide clear answers to these Groups-Differences questions, but those answers tell us nothing about how any one participant was affected, and they tell us very little about what the effect experience was.

The popularity of the Groups-Differences strategy can be attributed to its ability to provide a way around the category-continuum problem and the effect-criterion problem. Rather than solve either of these problems, the Groups-Differences strategy avoids them by shifting the focus to group averages and comparing those averages across groups. Thus, this strategy has provided great utility to researchers who are more anxious to generate some empirical findings than to work out some difficult conceptual issues first. Thus the Groups-Differences strategy contributes much more to the Generating-Findings perspective than to the Mapping-Phenomenon perspective.

CATEGORY-CONTINUUM PROBLEM

One problem for researchers in documenting whether media effects occur or not is that most effects are not categorical. There are, of course, some effects that are truly categorical; that is, there is either clear evidence that some people experience an effect, whereas other people clearly do not. For example, with a learning effect, either a person has learned a particular fact from exposure to a particular media message and can recall that fact or cannot. Another example is an attitudinal effect in which a person has either changed his or her opinion about something or he or she has not. With truly categorical effects, it is a simple matter to identify who exhibits an effect and who does not.

Mass media effects researchers, however, rarely examine effects in such a categorical manner, because there are few naturally occurring categorical effects. Furthermore, many natural categorical effects are far more interesting to study when they are transformed into continua. To illustrate, let's say we show 12 children a violent cartoon then put them in a room with a variety of toys (guns, knives, swords, building blocks, clay, crayons, etc.). We observe that five of those children choose to play with the violent toys, while the remaining seven children ignore the violent toys. In this case, we can clearly regard the five children who play with the violent toys as exhibiting an aggression effect and the other seven children as not exhibiting such an effect. This example makes it appear that aggressive play is a categorical variable; however, this is rarely the case in research studies. Typically, there are many behaviors exhibited that make it impractical to maintain the categorical nature of this variable. For example, what if some children play with the violent toys for five seconds, whereas other children play with the violent toys for 10 minutes, should all these children be regarded as being in the same category of aggression? With most effects measures, researchers use continuous measures, and this opens the door for the next problem.

EFFECT-CRITERION PROBLEM

This is the challenge of determining what should be regarded as threshold for evidence of an effect. Because social scientists typically use continuous measures for media-influenced effects, they end up with a distribution of effects scores and must decide at what point on the distribution they should establish a threshold, such that participants with higher scores are regarded as exhibiting the effect, whereas participants with lower scores are regarded as not exhibiting the effect. To illustrate, let's say we conduct an experiment to test an aggressive effect from exposure to media messages, so we show our participants one of several movies (high violence, low violence, no violence), then give them the chance to deliver shocks to an opponent in a game they play after the exposure. What if an experimental participant delivers only one shock; is that enough to conclude that she was behaving aggressively? What if there are participants who deliver 15, 40, and 100 shocks? We cannot select a point along the distribution of effect measures in a nonarbitrary manner and use it as a threshold, such that all scores on one side of that threshold represent participants who experienced the effect, whereas the scores on the other side of the threshold represent participants who did not experience the effect.

Social scientists have taken a shortcut around this effects criterion problem by using a combination of two techniques. One technique is to divide research participants into groups so that the degree of evidence of an effect can be compared across groups. The second technique is to rely on statistical significance for differences. This is the Groups-Differences strategy. Although this Groups-Differences strategy helps researchers get around the threshold problem, this practice fundamentally alters the research question. That is, researchers are no longer posing questions such as, "Is there an effect?" "How many people experienced an effect?" or even, "Did *more people* in one treatment experience an effect compared with the number of people experiencing the effect in another treatment?" Instead, the question we really answer is, "Are the differences across group means on a continuous measure of an effect large enough for us to conclude those differences could not have occurred by chance alone?"

Experiments by their very nature always set up group comparisons. Surveys also rely on group comparisons in which group means are compared across respondent groups as constructed typically by their demographics, psychological characteristics, or media exposure patterns. With survey methods, researchers typically use continuous variables, but then correlate scores across pairs of distributions rather than means across groups. But my point still holds. Survey researchers avoid the problem of identifying who in their samples experienced effects and instead report correlation coefficients that are interpreted in the context of probability; that is, the magnitude of the coefficients are compared with probability tables to determine if they could have occurred by chance alone.

With qualitative methods, researchers observe people in interactions with the media and each other, and then offer conclusions about whether certain people are affected by particular media experiences (see Chapter 8 for more detail on this point). To support their conclusions they offer rich descriptions of patterns of behavior and patterns of thinking. This leaves the reader of this scholarship questioning whether other people exhibiting slightly different patterns of behavior would also have impressed the qualitative scholar enough to conclude that those people were also experiencing a media effect. The qualitative scholar writes about an X-ness that can be interpreted as evidence of a media effect. But the reader is left wondering about the perimeters of X-ness; that is, how far can people deviate from those patterns of behaving as described by the qualitative scholar before losing the essence of X-ness? In short, what is the threshold of the effect?

The Groups-Differences strategy has generated a very large literature. This literature has high value in suggesting where there *may be* effects, but it cannot be used to make direct and defensible claims about whether there *are* effects or not. Please do not take my claim out of context; I am not arguing that the media exert no influence, nor am I arguing that the mass media exert no influences that lead to effects. My argument here is that mass media researchers have not been generating the kind of evidence needed to support directly their claims for media effects when they fall prey to the limitations imposed by the Groups-Differences strategy. We need to reconceptualize what we mean by media influence and media effect.

Reconceptualizing Mass Media Influence

To move beyond the limitation imposed by the Groups-Differences strategy for designing effects studies, we need to focus on using the individual as not just the unit of measurement but also the unit of analysis. Thus the key comparison shifts from group means to changes in an individual's effect measure over time. When we shift the research design to looking for patterns of effect score changes over time, we can more directly assess mass media influence. With this shift in research design, we can conceptualize the media as exerting four different patterns: gradual long-term change, gradual long-term nonchange (reinforcement), immediate shift, and short-term fluctuation change (Fig. 23.3). Let's examine each of these four patterns in some detail.

With a long-term change type of effect, the messages from the mass media gradually alter a person's baseline. Figure 23.3A illustrates this pattern. The line in the figure represents a person's baseline on a particular effect. Over time, there is a slow gradual upward slope that indicates an increasing degree of the effect. An example of this is a cultivation effect in which over time a person is more likely to believe the world is a mean and violent place. In contrast with a long-term reinforcement type of effect, the media influence serves to maintain the status quo with the particular effect (see Fig. 23.3B). There is no slope to the baseline—it is flat. An example of this occurs when a person continually exposes herself to the same political point of view in magazines, newspapers, television, and the Internet. Her or his political attitude experiences greater and greater reinforcement; that is, it becomes more and more fixed and hence much more difficult to change.

With an immediate shift type of effect, the media influence serves to alter something in a person during an exposure or shortly after a particular exposure and that alteration lasts for a very long time (see Fig. 23.3C). That alteration may be relatively minor. However, there are times when the degree of change might be relatively dramatic. An example of a dramatic immediate change effect might be when a young person watches a movie about an attractive person in a particular career—say a heart surgeon—and the person decides she or he wants to be a heart surgeon, talks about this career choice continually, and alters her or his study habits to earn the grades necessary to go to college and medical school.

With a short-term fluctuation change type of effect, the media trigger a fluctuation off the baseline during or shortly after the exposure. The change is short-lived and the person returns to the baseline level quickly (see Fig. 23.3D). This is a fairly prevalent finding in a lot of studies of public information/attitude campaigns. Researchers find a spike up in knowledge, attitude change, or behavioral intention as a result of exposure to some media material, but this change is not observed in subsequent measurement periods beyond a few days after the exposure.

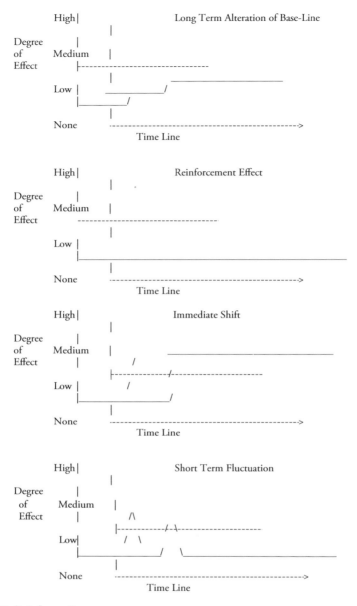

Figure 24.3 Types of Media Influence Patterns.

Baselines differ in terms of slope and elasticity. Slope refers to angle (an upward slope indicates a generally increasing level of an effect, whereas a downward slope indicates a generally decreasing level of an effect) and degree (a sharp angle reflects a relatively large degree of change in effects level, whereas a flat slope reflects a continuing level in the baseline). Elasticity reflects how entrenched the baseline is. Over time a baseline that has been reinforced continually by the same kind of media messages with become highly entrenched, making it less and less likely that there will be fluctuations off the baseline, and when there are fluctuations, those fluctuations are smaller and smaller over time.

The baseline is the best estimate of a person's degree of effect at any given time. It is formed over the long term by the constant interaction of three types of factors: psychological traits of the person, sociological experiences of the person, and media exposure patterns. This is likely to be the most important aspect of media effects.

Fluctuations have three characteristics: duration, magnitude, and direction. The *duration* refers to how long the fluctuation lasts before returning to the baseline. *Magnitude* refers to how far the fluctuation deviates from the baseline. And *direction* refers to whether the fluctuation moves upward (thus representing an increases the level) or downward (thus representing a decrease in the level).

Notice the dotted line in all four graphs in Figure 23.3. These dotted lines represent the manifestation level. In Figure 23.3A, notice that the baseline stays below the manifestation level. This indicates that the degree of the effect has not reached a level at which there are spontaneous observables. By this I mean that the research participants exhibit something that clearly indicates a change that can be attributed to media influence. In two of the other three graphics, there are examples of the baseline breaking above the manifestation level; with those three patterns we have clear manifestations of a media influenced effect.

Should we limit our conceptualization of media effects to only those effects in which manifestations occur? I would answer no; we should also be sensitive to what occurs below the manifestation level. Returning to Figure 23.3A, notice that the baseline has a positive slope, which indicates a gradual long-term change. The line does not move above the manifestation level, but something is happening that indicates media influence. For example, let's say a young girl exposes herself to lots of print messages on a particular topic. Over time these exposures gradually increase her reading skills and increase her interest in that topic as her knowledge base grows. Her baseline moves close to the manifestation level. Then one day she picks up an article on the topic, and begins telling all her friends about what she has just learned. (This activity takes place above the manifestation level because it is spontaneous and easy to observe her knowledge, attitudes, and emotions as she exhibits them to her friends.) However, is it accurate to conclude that this manifestation was caused by the one exposure to the article alone? No, of course not. We must account for the long-term media influence that allowed her to practice her reading skills and grow her interest in this topic. The magnitude of the manifestation level is a combination of the initial level on the baseline and the magnitude of the fluctuation itself. Contrast this with a young boy who did not have this pattern of practicing his reading skills or growing his interest on this topic; his baseline would be far below the manifestation level. If he were to read the same article, he is not likely to manifest the same indicators as did the girl; however, the boy could still have been influenced by his exposure to the article (change in level), although he did not manifest that effect.

Limiting the conceptualization of mass media effects to manifestations greatly reduces our understanding of the phenomenon. We need to make a distinction between manifest and process effects. It is likely that most of mass media influence is in the form of process effects rather than manifest effects. If we do not pay attention to process effects, we will greatly limit our ability to understand media influence. Process effects are more difficult to measure and make strong cases for their validity than are manifest effects. This challenge parallels the challenge of social scientists who wanted to break through the limits imposed by behaviorism; it was much more difficult to measure attitudes, cognitive states, and other internal hypothetical constructs and make strong cases for their validity compared with behaviors. We are indeed fortunate that social scientists continually rise to this challenge. It is time to rise to the challenge of more clearly documenting process effects in addition to manifest effects.

With this conceptualization of media influence, the mass media are regarded as exerting an ongoing influence. Their influence is not limited to certain kinds of messages; instead, their influence is constant and continuing. Some of this influence is direct; that is, it occurs with exposure to media messages. This media influence also occurs indirectly as people encounter other people and institutions that have themselves been influenced by the media and pass that influence along in conversations and in institutional practices. Also, media influence is indirect when people think about media messages and continue to process that information and make meaning from it long after a media exposure is over.

The media exert their influence in a constellation of other factors of influence. Some of these factors have to do with the person who is being exposed to the messages—factors such as traits, states, habits, memories, and goals. Some of these factors have to do with the situation—such as whether a person is being exposed alone or with others who talk about the exposure, societal supports, and sanctions. Also, the media are not monolithic; that is, there are many different types of media factors. Some of these factors are medium characteristics, some are genre characteristics (news messages have different characteristics than entertainment or advertising messages), and some are characteristics about the message itself (e.g., characters, plots, production elements).

To illustrate these patterns, let's consider a disinhibition effect, which is a lowering of people's inhibitions that prevent them from behaving aggressively. Let's say Leo is a 12-year-old boy who has been raised to be highly aggressive and has low trait empathy, whereas Julie is a 35-year-old mother who was raised by the golden rule and has high trait empathy. Leo's disinhibition effect baseline is likely to be higher than Julie's. Let's say that Leo is continually exposed to many media messages of violence (in movies, television shows, and video games) where the consequences to the victims are sanitized, whereas Julie avoids all such messages. Adding these elements to the prediction, we can say that there will be a relatively large difference between the levels of Leo's and Julie's disinhibition baselines. This example is supported by research. Haridakis (2002) found that aggression (physical, verbal, anger, and hostility) were all predicted by trait variables such as gender, disinhibition, locus of control, and long-term experience variables such as experience with crime and television viewing. Furthermore over time, Leo's baseline is likely to have an upward slope, whereas Julie's is likely to have a downward slope.

Now let's say that Leo and Julie watch a Dirty Harry movie in which a great deal of violence is perpetrated by a rouge police officer who is glamorized, humorous, and successful in his use of violence. Perhaps Leo is highly attracted and entertained by Harry; he strongly identifies with Harry and wants to be like him. Leo is likely to show a sharp fluctuation increasing his level on a disinhibition effect. In contrast, Julie is horrified by Harry and finds his actions reprehensible and insulting to her. Julie is likely to show a sharp fluctuation decreasing her level on a disinhibition effect. Although the media message presented is the same for both Leo and Julie, the experience for each is very different because of what the two people bring to the exposure situation. This history is captured in their baseline.

Let's say that Julie watches a lot of crime drama in which criminals' violent acts are always punished and the suffering of victims is continually shown (such as the *Law & Order* television series). This is likely to condition Julie's disinhibition baseline at a low level and keep it there. If she were to see a violent portrayal in which the perpetrator was glamorized and the violence were sanitized, she would likely not experience much of a fluctuation effect, because her baseline has been so strongly reinforced. A reinforcement pattern is one in which the position of the baseline is entrenched;

that is, the baseline continues at its current level, and its elasticity is reduced, rendering fluctuations more rare. If the elasticity of the baseline is narrow, and then the long-term stable factors (traits and typical story formula) are dominant; but if the elasticity is wide, and then the immediate factors (dispositions and idiosyncratic factors in the portrayals) are dominant. Reinforcement narrows the elasticity.

Given the analysis of mass media influence in the preceding, I propose the following formal definition of mass media effect. A mass media effect takes place when one of four patterns occur and the shape of that pattern can be attributed to mass media influence. The four patterns are (1) gradual alteration of the baseline, (2) reinforcement of the baseline, (3) sudden alteration of the baseline, and (4) sudden fluctuation from the baseline with a return to the baseline. Notice that this definition has two necessary conditions. One of these necessary conditions is that the set of four patterns is necessary; that is, there must be one of four patterns, but any one of these four patterns would satisfy this necessary condition. The second necessary condition is that the pattern must be attributable to mass media influence. Implied in this general definition are other elements of defining mass media effects; however, those other elements are not used as inclusion rules because those elements are too broad. To illustrate, one of these elements is timing. Implied in this definition is that a mass media effect can occur immediately or take a long time to occur, so timing is too broad to be used as an inclusion rule. However, timing is still an important characteristic that can be used to organize different kinds of mass media effects once they have been included by the formal definition.

Conclusion

It is important that we alter our thinking and methods to move to more direct assessments of the essential nature of each of the four component facets of the mass media phenomenon. This is a significant challenge. Once we address that challenge, we need to also consider all four facets simultaneously when designing any study. None of the facets exists separately from the others; they are all part of the same thing, like the facets of a diamond are all the diamond. When we design any study to examine the phenomenon of mass media, we need focus on one facet, but also consider the knowledge from the other three facets as essential contexts in that design.

References

Allen, R. C. (Ed.) (1987). *Channels of Discourse*. London: Allen and Unwin.

Angwin, J. (2009). *Stealing MySpace: The Battle to Control the Most Popular Website in America*. New York: Random House.

Arens, W. F., Weigold, M. F., & Arens, C. (2009). *Contemporary Advertising*, 12th ed. New York: McGraw-Hill.

Barthes, R. (1967). *Elements of Semiology*. London: Cape.

Berger, C. R. (1991). Communication theories and other curios. *Communication Monographs, 58,* 101–113.

Biocca, F. A. (1988). Opposing conceptions of the audience. In Anderson, J. A. (Ed.), *Communication Yearbook,* 11th ed. Newbury Park, CA: Sage, pp. 51–80.

Bochner, A. P. (1985). Perspectives on inquiry: Representation, conversation, and reflection. In Knapp, M. L., & Miller, G. R. (Eds.), *Handbook of Interpersonal Communication*. Newbury Park, CA: Sage, pp. 27–58.

Bolter, J. D., & Grusin, R. (2000). *Remediation: Understanding New Media*. Cambridge, MA: MIT Press.

Christ, W. G., & Potter, W. J. (1998). Media literacy, media education, and the academy. *Journal of Communication, 48,* 5–15.

Csikszentmihalyi, M. (1988). The flow experience and its significance for human psychology. In Csikszentmihalyi, M., & Csikszentmihalyi, I. S. (Eds.), *Optimal Experience: Psychological Studies of Flow in Consciousness*. New York: Cambridge University Press, pp. 15–35.

Comstock, G., Chaffee, S. Katzman, N., McCombs, M., & Roberts, D. (1978). *Television and Human Behavior*. New York: Columbia University Press.

Deetz, S. (1973). Words without things: Toward a social phenomenology of language. *Quarterly Journal of Speech, 59,* 40–51.

Dervin, B., Grossberg, L., O'Keefe, B. J., & Wartella, E. (Eds.). (1989). *Rethinking Communication*. Newbury Park, CA: Sage.

Donohew, L., & Tipton, L. (1973). A conceptual model of information seeking, avoiding, and processing. In Clark, P. (Ed.), *New Models for Mass Communication Research*. Beverly Hills, CA: Sage, pp. 243–268.

Doyle, G. (2002). *Understanding Media Economics*. London: Sage.

Eastman, S. T. (1998). Programming theory under strain: The active industry and the active audience. In Roloff, M. E., & Pauson, G. D. (Eds.), *Communication Yearbook,* vol. 11. Thousand Oaks, CA: Sage, pp. 323–377.

Ellis, D. G. (1995). Fixing communicative meaning: A coherentist theory. *Communication Research, 22,* 515–544.

Evans, J. (1999). Cultures of the visual. In Evans, J., & Hall, S. (Eds.). *Visual Culture: A Reader*. London: Sage, pp. 11–19.

Fortunato, J. A. (2005). *Making Media Content: The Influence Of Constituency Groups On Mass Media*. Hillsdale, NJ: Lawrence Erlbaum Associates.

Foucault, M. (1984). *The Foucault Reader* (Rabinow, P., Ed.). New York: Pantheon.

Graber, D. (1984). *Processing the News*. New York: Longman.

Green, M. C., Garst, J., & Brock, T. C. (2004). The power of fiction: Determinants and boundaries. In Shrum, L. J. (Ed.). *The Psychology of Entertainment Media: Blurring the Lines Between Entertainment and Persuasion*. Hillsdale, NJ: Lawrence Erlbaum Associates, pp. 161–176.

Greenberg, B. S., Mastro, D., & Brand, J. E. (2002). Minorities and the mass media: Television into the 21st century. In Bryant, J., & Zillmann, D. (Eds.). *Media Effects: Advances in Theory and Research,* 2nd ed. Hillsdale, NJ: Lawrence Erlbaum Associates, pp. 333–352.

Grossberg, L., Wartella, E., & Whitney, D. C. (1998). *Mediamaking: Mass Media in a Popular Culture*. Thousand Oaks, CA: Sage.

Hall, S. (1980). Encoding and decoding in the television discourse. In Hall, S., Hobson, D., Lowe, A., & Willis, P. (Eds.), *Culture, Media, Language*. London: Hutchinson.

Hardt, H. (1992). *Critical Communication Studies: Communication, History and Theory in America*. New York: Routledge.

Himmelweit, H. T., Oppenheim, A. N., & Vince, P. (1958). *Television and the Child*. London: Oxford University Press.

Hirsch, P. M. (1981). Institutional function of elite and mass media. In Katz, E., & Szecsko, T. (Eds.), *Mass Media and Social Change*. London: Sage, pp. 187–200.

Holsti, O. R. (1969). *Content Analysis for the Social Science and Humanities*. Reading, MA: Addison-Wesley.

Infoniac.com (March 13, 2008). The amount of digital information reached 281 exabytes (281 billion gigabytes). Retrieved September 11, 2009 from http://www.infoniac.com/hi–tech/amount–digital–information–reached–281–exabytes.html.

Innis, H. A. (1951). *The Bias of Communication*. Toronto: University of Toronto Press.

Jenkins, H. (2003). Quentin Tarantino's Star Wars? Digital cinema, media convergence, and participatory culture. In Thorburn, D., & Jenkins, H. (Eds.). *Rethinking Media Change: The Aesthetics of Transition*. Cambridge, MA: MIT Press, pp. 281–312.

Jenkins, H. (2006). *Convergence Culture: Where Old and New Media Collide*. New York: New York University Press.

Jensen, K. B., & Rosengren, K. E. (1990). Five traditions in search of the audience. *European Journal of Communication, 5(2/3),* 207–238.

Kaiser Family Foundation (March, 2005). Key Findings from New Research on Children's Media Use. Retrieved August 23, 2009 from http://www.kaisernetwork.org/health_cast/hcast_index.cfm?display=detail&hc=1377.

Kamhawi, R., & Weaver, D. (2003). Mass communication research trends from 1980 to 1999. *Journalism & Mass Communication Quarterly, 80,* 7–27.

Lee, K. M. (2004). Presence, explicated. *Communication Theory, 14,* 27–50.

Livingstone, S. M. (1990). *Making Sense of Television: The Psychology of Audience Interpretation*. New York: Pergamon Press.

Lombard, M., & Ditton, R. (1997). At the heart of it all: The concept of presence. *Journal of Computer Mediated Communication, 3(2).* Retrieved March 23, 2007 from http://jcmc.indiana.edu/vol3/issue2/lombard.html.

Lowery, S. A., & DeFleur, M. L. (1988). *Milestones in Mass Communication Research,* 2nd ed. White Plains, NY: Longman.

McLuhan, M. (1964). *Understanding Media: The Extensions of Man*. New York: New American Library.

McQuail, D. (1989). Communication research: Past, present and future. In Ferguson, M. (Ed.), *Public Communication: The New Imperatives*. London: Sage, pp. 135–151.

McQuail, D. (2005). *McQuail's Mass Communication Theory,* 5th ed. London: Sage.

National Television Violence Study (NTVS). (1997). *Scientific Report*. Thousand Oaks, CA: Sage.

Nayar, P. K. (Ed.) (2010). *The New Media and Cybercultures Anthology*. Malden, MA: Wiley-Blackwell.

Neuendorf, K. A. (2001). *Content Analysis Guidebook*. Thousand Oaks, CA: Sage.

Newcomb, H. (1984). On the dialogic aspects of mass communication. *Critical Studies in Mass Communication, 1,* 34–50.

Noll, A. M. (2007). *The Evolution of Media*. New York: Rowman & Littlefield.

Owers, J., Carveth, R. Alexander, A. (1998). An introduction to media economics theory and practice. In Alexander, A., Owers, J., & Carveth, R. (Eds.), *Media Economics: Theory and Practice,* 2nd ed. Hillsdale, NJ: Lawrence Erlbaum Associates, pp. 1–43.

Padioleau, J. (1985). *Le Monde et le Washington Post*. Paris: PUF.

Palmgreen, P., & Rayburn, J. D. (1985). An expectancy-value approach to media gratifications. In Rosengren, K. E. (Ed.) *Media Gratification Research*. Beverly Hills, CA: Sage, pp. 61–72.

Pietila, V. (1994). Perspectives on our past: Charting the histories of mass communication studies. *Critical Studies in Mass Communication, 11,* 346–361.

Pool, M. M., Koolstra, C. M., & van der Voort, T. H. A. (2003). The impact of background radio and television on high school students' homework performance. *Journal of Communication, 53,* 74–87.

Potter, W. J. (1999). *On Media Violence*. Thousand Oaks, CA: Sage.

Potter, W. J. (2009). *Arguing for a General Framework for Mass Media Scholarship*. Thousand Oaks, CA: Sage.

Potter, W. J. (2010). *Media Literacy,* 5th ed. Thousand Oaks, CA: Sage.

Potter, W. J., Cooper, R., & Dupagne, M. (1993). The three paradigms of mass media research in mainstream journals. *Communication Theory, 3,* 317–335.

Potter, W. J., & Riddle, K. (November, 2006). *A Content Analysis of the Mass Media Effects Literature*. Paper presented at the annual convention of the National Communication Association, San Antonio, TX.

Potter, W. J., & Riddle K. (2007). Profile of mass media effects research in scholarly journals. *Journalism & Mass of Communication Quarterly, 84,* 90–104.

Popper, K. R. (1959). *The logic of scientific discovery*. New York: Harper & Row.

Power, P., Kubey, R., & Kiousis, S. (2002). Audience activity and passivity. In Gudykunst, W. B. (Ed.), *Communication Yearbook 26*. Hillsdale, NJ: Lawrence Erlbaum Associates, pp. 116–159.

Radway, D. J. (1984). *Reading the Romance*. Chapel Hill, NC: University of North Carolina Press.

Ransford, M. (September 23, 2005). Average person spends more time using media than anything else. *Ball State University News Center*. Retrieved October 30, 2006 from www.bsu.edu/up/article/0,1370,32363–2914–36658,00.html.

Reeves, B., & Borgman, C. L. (1983). A bibliometric evaluation of core journals in communication research. *Human Communication Research, 10,* 119–136.

Rice, R. E. (1984a). Development of new media research. In Rice, R. E. et al. (Eds.), *The New Media: Communication, Research, and Technology*. Beverly Hills, CA: Sage, pp. 15–31.

Rice, R. E. (1984b). New media technology: Growth and integration. In Rice, R. E. et al. (Eds.), *The New Media: Communication, Research, and Technology*. Beverly Hills, CA: Sage, pp. 33–54.

Rice, R. E., Borgman, C. L., & Reeves, B. (1988). Citation networks of communication journals, 1977–1985: Cliques and positions, citations made and citations received. *Human Communication Research, 15,* 256–283.

Riffe, D., & Freitag, A. (1997). A content analysis of content analyses: Twenty-five years of *Journalism Quarterly. Journalism & Mass Communication Quarterly, 74,* 873–882.

Riffe, D., Lacy, S., & Fico, F. G. (1998). *Analyzing Media Messages: Using Quantitative Content Analysis in Research*. Hillsdale, NJ: Lawrence Erlbaum Associates.

Rosengren, K. E. (1974). Uses and gratifications: A paradigm outlined. In Blumler, J. G., & Katz, E. (Eds.), *The Uses of Mass Communications: Current Perspectives of Gratifications Research*. Beverly Hills, CA: Sage, pp. 269–286.

Schramm, W., Lyle, J., & Parker E. B. (Eds.) (1961). *Television in the Lives of Our Children*. Stanford, CA: Stanford University Press.

Schwartz, B. (2004). *The Paradox of Choice: Why More Is Less*. New York: HarperCollins.

Shoemaker, P. J., & Reese, S. D. (1990). Exposure to what? Integrating media content and effects studies. *Journalism Quarterly, 67,* 649–652.

Shoemaker, P. J., & Reese, S. D. (1996). *Mediating the Message: Theories of Influences on Mass Media Content,* 2nd ed. White Plains, NY: Longman.

Shotter J., & Gergen, K. J. (1994). Social construction: Knowledge, self, others, and continuing the conversation. In Deetz, S. (Ed.), *Communication Yearbook,* vol. 17. Thousand Oaks, CA: Sage, pp. 3–33.

So, C., & Chan, J. (1991). *Evaluating and Conceptualizing the Field of Mass Communication: A Survey of the Core Scholars*. Paper presented at the Annual Meeting of the AEJMC, Boston.

Stempel, G. H. III. (1981). Content analysis. In Stempel, G. H. III, & Westley, B. H. (Eds.) *Research Methods in Mass Communication*. Englewood Cliffs, NJ: Prentice-Hall, pp. 119–131.

Stevenson, R. L. (1992). Defining international communication as a field. *Journalism Quarterly, 69,* 543–553.

Thompson, J. B. (1995). *The Media and Modernity: A Social Theory of the Media*. Stanford, CA: Stanford University Press.

Tunstall, J. (1971). *Journalists at Work*. London: Constable.

Webster, J. G., & Phalen, P. F. (1994). Victim, consumer, or commodity? Audience models in communication policy. In Ettema, J., & Whitney, D. C. (Eds.), *Audiencemaking: How Media Create the Audience*. Thousand Oaks, CA: Sage, pp. 19–37.

Webster, J. G., & Phalen, P. F. (1997). *The Mass Audience: Rediscovering the Dominant Model*. Hillsdale, NJ: Lawrence Erlbaum Associates.

Wright, A. (2007). *Glut: Mastering Information through the Ages*. Washington, DC: Joseph Henry Press.

Engaging with Stories and Characters: Learning, Persuasion, and Transportation into Narrative Worlds

Melanie C. Green *and* Karen E. Dill

Abstract

Although individuals often believe they are immune to media influence, a substantial body of research suggests that media presentations, including fictional narratives, can influence individuals' attitudes and beliefs. The current chapter explores reasons why individuals fail to recognize media effects in their own lives, and explains the mechanisms by which media influence occurs. We highlight the operation of unconscious processes that can account for both pervasive media effects and a lack of awareness of these effects. We also focus specifically on transportation, the experience of cognitive and emotional immersion into a story. Transported readers experience emotions in response to a story, form connections with characters, and are more cognitively open to story claims.

Key Words: characters, emotions, narrative transportation, persuasion, stories, fiction.

Introduction

The general public spends most of their free time engaged with media, much of which is fictional media. Factual information is presumed to accurately represent real-world events and knowledge, whereas fictional information has uncertain accuracy—an author may include veridical information, but may also invent settings, characters, or ideas. Because of the uncertain truth status of fiction, individuals often assume that they will not or should not be influenced by fiction. Indeed, it is a widespread belief that when one reaches the age that one can differentiate between fact and fiction in the media, one is no longer subject to learning or persuasion through fictional media (Dill, 2009).

Although one's understanding and perception of mediated images and narratives does change with the developmental cycle (Cantor, 1998b), adults are by no means immune to learning and persuasion through fictional media. For example, research has demonstrated that adults' knowledge about the American legal and criminal systems comes more from learning through fictional media than through nonfiction or direct experience, even though the same adults would not understand or believe that this was the case (Haney & Manzolatti, 1980; Glasser, 1988).

Learning from fiction, just as learning from nonfiction, can have either positive or negative effects. Although the potential harm from fictional works often receives more attention (as when protestors boycott films or attempt to have certain books removed from school reading lists or library shelves; e.g., Del Fattore, 2002), fictional works can also have personal and societal benefits. Perhaps the best example of the positive influence of fiction comes from entertainment education (see Slater, 2002 and Singhal et al., 2003 for reviews). Social and health messages embedded in television programs, telenovelas (soap operas), and comic books have helped encourage behaviors ranging from vocational training to family planning in developing nations, and have increased awareness of issues such as drunk driving and cancer screening in the United States.

Perception of Persuasion by the Audience

Although there is clear and growing evidence of the effects of fictional communications on individuals' beliefs and behaviors, laypeople often do not have an accurate understanding of these effects (Reeves & Nass, 2012). The third person effect (TPE) (Davison, 1983, 1996) predicts that individuals will tend to believe that others are more persuasible by media content than they are, and that consumers will change their behavior based on their beliefs about media persuasion (e.g., sexual risk taking, body image, and attitudes towards censorship) (Golan & Day, 2008). Ego enhancement and optimism have been posited as possible causes of the TPE (Davison, 1996; Golan & Day, 2008). That is, individuals are motivated to believe they are less persuasible so as to maintain a positive view of themselves.

Consistent with this motivational explanation, additional research has specified that a reverse TPE occurs for positive media content. In other words, we believe we are more easily influenced by positive media messages and others are more easily influenced by negative media messages (Douglas, Sutton, & Stathi, 2010). This is similar to the actor–observer bias in the literature on the correspondence bias (Gilbert, Pelham, & Krull, 1988; Gilbert & Malone, 1995), which posits that we attribute negative behaviors to the person when making attributions about another person, but to the situation when making attributions about the self. Similarly, we attribute positive behaviors to our own dispositions when making self attributions. The latter is analogous to the reverse TPE.

When we show this pattern of attributional biases, we are protecting or enhancing the ego. So it follows—and has been demonstrated—that we are less likely to attribute persuasibility to those who are more similar to us or to our in-group than to those who are different from us or more socially distant (Scharrer, 2002; Scharrer & Leone, 2006).

In Reeves and Nass's (1996) *The Media Equation: How People Treat Computers Television, and New Media Like Real People and Places*, the authors define the media equation as the idea that media equal real life. In other words, people "respond socially and naturally to media even though they believe it is not reasonable to do so" (p.8) and these responses take place outside of conscious awareness. This is because it is adaptive for our brains to perceive and react to people; our brains were not made to differentiate between a person in the media (or even a computer voice or smartphone assistant like Siri) and a real live person (see also Dill, 2009).

Consciousness and Our Understanding of Media

Part of our lack of awareness of how media teach and influence us reflects a larger misunderstanding of how the mind works. To fully elaborate on how our minds process media, we must first acknowledge that the mind is not a unitary entity. In everyday life we equate consciousness with mind. From that erroneous assumption comes the notion that if we "know the difference between fantasy and reality," then we cannot be influenced by fantasy (Dill, 2009).

The Adaptive Unconscious

In *Strangers to Ourselves,* Wilson (2002) argues that consciousness is not the tip of our mental iceberg; it is more like a single snowball on top of the tip of the iceberg. In a watershed article, Nisbett and Wilson (1977) suggested that many times we do not have direct access to our higher-order cognitions. For example, when given a hint, people can solve a problem more quickly and accurately than people who were not given a hint, but they generally do not report knowing that the hint helped them solve the problem. Likewise, many lower-order cognitive processes happen outside awareness as well (Wilson, 2002). Wilson argues that mental processes such as elements of decision making happen outside of our conscious awareness because the mind is adaptive and functions to help us make sense of a complex world in a way that is quick and efficient and does not overtax conscious processing.

> People possess a powerful, sophisticated, adaptive unconscious that is crucial for survival in the world. Because this unconscious operates so efficiently out of view, however, and is largely inaccessible, there is a price to pay in self-knowledge. There is a great deal about ourselves that we cannot know directly, even with the most painstaking introspection. (Wilson, 2002, Preface, para 2, Kindle edition)

Wilson's theory of the adaptive unconscious is not the Freudian psychodynamic view, but rather the notion that the unconscious mind evolved before the conscious mind and its functions include "sizing up the world, warning people of danger, setting goals, and initiating action" (Wilson, 2002, para 3, Kindle edition). This is essentially a functionalist psychology that postulates the mind as an adaptive system operating largely behind the scenes. One side effect of this state of affairs is a disconnect between what we know, feel, and act on and what we *think consciously* that we know, feel, and act on. The connection to media is clear: Our mind processes much of what we take in via the media outside of our awareness, leaving our conscious processing of media influence fraught with misunderstanding.

Mechanisms of Persuasion Through Fiction

Although individuals frequently fail to recognize the power of media influence, studies indicate that fictional narratives can often be just as powerful as factual ones in changing beliefs (Green et al., 2006). For example, Strange and Leung (1999) showed that a narrative about a teenage school dropout could change readers' beliefs about the causes of students dropping out of high school, regardless of whether those narratives were described as news articles or fictional stories. Green and Brock (2000) showed changes in both specific and general beliefs related to a story about an attack on a young child at a shopping mall; these changes occurred even when the narrative was clearly described as fiction. Slater (1990) examined attitudes toward social groups in particular, and found that fiction was especially effective for changing attitudes about unfamiliar social groups. Television narratives involving controversial contemporary issues such as the death penalty have been shown to reduce resistance to attitude change that stems from prior liberal/conservative ideology (Slater, Rouner, & Long, 2006).

Much of the research on fiction focuses on the effects of fictional narratives on attitudes or worldviews, but Marsh, Meade, and Roediger (2003) have shown that individuals also learn "false facts" from fiction. That is, individuals use even misinformation that appears in stories when they answer general knowledge questions. For example, if a person read a story in which a character says that Saturn is the largest planet, he is more likely to give that answer later (rather than the correct answer, Jupiter). This is a robust effect: Reading a story a second time only makes this effect stronger, and warnings about possible errors do not eliminate it (Marsh & Fazio, 2006).

Psychological research has focused not only on establishing the effects of fiction on real-world beliefs and attitudes, but also on the mechanisms by which this impact occurs (e.g., Green & Brock, 2000; Slater & Rouner, 2002). Cognitive psychology approaches have focused on the way information is represented in memory. Even though individuals often remember that they read a particular piece of information as part of a story, the fictional information also appears to be quickly integrated with

related knowledge in individuals' memory. People believe they knew the fictional information all along (even when their "knowledge" is misinformation provided by the experimental narratives) (Marsh et al., 2003). Fictional information becomes accessible in mind, and creates new memory connections between concepts. In sleeper effects, discussed in more detail later in this chapter, the source of the media misinformation becomes disconnected from the content. In essence, we integrate the information or misinformation into our mental storehouse of information without consciousness of where and how we acquired the information and therefore without critical analysis of the source. In this state of unconscious acceptance of fictional information, media storytelling becomes an effective mode of persuasion.

Transportation into Narrative Worlds

In addition to studies of memory, research has focused on how the nature of individuals' experience with a media presentation can determine its effect. Specifically, one important mechanism of narrative influence is transportation, the feeling of being "lost in a book" (Gerrig, 1993; Green & Brock, 2000). Transportation is a melding of concentration, affective engagement, and mental imagery, all focused on the events of the narrative (Green & Brock, 2000). Transported readers may lose track of time, fail to notice events going on around them, and experience vivid mental images of settings and characters. Although transportation research has largely focused on written narratives, the transported state also applies to experiences with other forms of media (e.g., Green et al., 2008). The sense of immersion in a story has been described by communication researchers with different terms, including involvement, engagement, and presence, but we focus on transportation in the current chapter.

Transportation can be measured with a self-report questionnaire (Green & Brock, 2000). The scale contains 11 general items that could apply to any story, and additional items asking about vivid mental images of main story characters. Example transportation scale items include, "I was emotionally involved in the narrative while reading it" and, "I could picture myself in the scene of the events described in the narrative." The items tap the cognitive, emotional, and mental imagery components of transportation. Participants answer each item on a scale of 1 (not at all) to 7 (very much). The scale has shown good internal consistency, as well as discriminant and convergent validity.

TRANSPORTATION, LITERATURE, AND THE BRAIN

In *Literature and the Brain,* Holland (2009a) provides an in-depth analysis of the interplay between the conscious and unconscious mind and how we make sense of the narratives and images we encounter in the media. When we are "lost in" or "carried away" by a work of media (also called rapt, entranced, or transported), we enter what Csikszentmihalyi (1998) called a state of *flow.* It is of no small interest to note that flow has been linked to human happiness (Csikszentmihalyi, 1998). When we find flow, we find engagement with life. And so with media, we seek the flow state offered by mediated images and stories (see also Chapter 2). From this perspective, the four aspects of this transported state include the: (1) lost sense of bodily awareness, (2) lost awareness of environment, (3) suspension of reality testing, and (4) experience of real emotions in relation to the characters and story (Holland, 2009a).

WHERE IS A STORY?

The first two factors relate to the "where" of our experience with media. Although the perception happens in the brain, and the images and story are on a screen or page, neither of these is where we locate them. Rather, we experience characters and stories as "out there." We process this "where" information through a dorsal stream that runs through the dome of the skull into the parietal lobe and to the motor strips of the frontal lobes of the brain. This neural pathway is quick and therefore cruder and serves to help us know where and how to act in relation to what we perceive (Holland, 2009a). In other words, this "where–how" perception is adaptive and happens outside of consciousness. When the media content reaches our conscious awareness, it has already been processed for us and we already have associated affect, which in part ranks the importance of the information for our survival and success as organisms.

TRANSPORTATION AND ATTITUDE/BELIEF CHANGE

One of the most important consequences of experiencing stories in this immersive way is that individuals can adopt new beliefs or attitudes about the real world based on what they learned from the story. In general, factors that increase the likelihood of becoming transported should also increase the likelihood of story-consistent attitude or belief change.

Transportation may aid in belief change in several ways. First, transportation reduces counterarguing about the issues raised in the story. Next, transportation may affect beliefs by making narrative events seem more like personal experience. If a reader or viewer feels as if she has been part of narrative events, the lessons implied by those events may seem more powerful (Green, 2004). Transportation creates vivid mental images that may serve as especially powerful persuasive arguments. Finally, attachment to characters may play a critical role in narrative-based belief change. If a viewer likes or identifies with a character (see Bandura, 1986; Singhal et al., 2003), statements made by the character or implications of events experienced by that character may carry special weight.

REDUCTION IN COUNTERARGUING

As noted, one consequence of narrative transportation is reduced scrutiny and counterarguing. This reduced critical response may be in part because the persuasive implications of narratives are often implied or subtle, especially relative to straightforward rhetorical appeals. Individuals transported into a compelling narrative world also may not have the cognitive resources to counterargue story implications, because their mental energy is devoted to imagining or engaging with the narrative. In addition, transportation is a pleasurable state (Green, Brock, & Kaufman, 2004), and transported individuals are typically not motivated to interrupt this experience to critique the story, argue against the implications of the story, or question the real-world validity of the story (Green & Brock, 2000; Escalas, 2004). Even after reading or viewing is completed, individuals do not generally take the time or effort to think back over the story and correct their attitudes for any possible influence from it, especially because they likely do not think they will be influenced by entertainment. Indeed, Marsh and Fazio (2006) demonstrated that individuals do not appear to monitor fiction for incorrect information, even in the face of explicit warnings about misinformation.

Holland (2009a) refers to this aspect of transportation as suspension of reality testing (his third aspect of transportation), and proposes that the cause of this suspension of reality testing is the fact that we know we cannot change the story or images. In other words, because we know we cannot influence the media content, we turn off our reality testing mechanism. Interestingly, this suspension of reality testing leads to our acceptance of ideas and information in the fictional story. Holland (2009b) also proposes that while immersed in a narrative, we do not doubt impossible or improbable media content such as the existence of Spiderman or his habit of traveling via spiderweb (Holland, 2009b). It is important to understand that we may doubt them cognitively or rationally, but unconsciously we do not doubt them. This is likely to be one reason for sleeper effects that have been demonstrated to occur after exposure to false content embedded in narrative fiction. For example, fictional stories with accurate and inaccurate health information embedded in them were both persuasive to readers: Those who read the story with the accurate information believed that information just as those who read the story with the inaccurate information believed the inaccurate information (Appel & Richter, 2007). In short, our suspension of reality testing transfers to ideas embedded in a fictional narrative. And, definitional of a sleeper effect, after the source of our learning is forgotten, we are still convinced by what we learned.

And there is convincing evidence that goes on beyond learning specific facts. The nonconscious mind processes affective and emotional content (Wilson, 2002; Holland, 2007, 2009a). In its role of maximizing our adaptive fitness, the nonconscious brain processes quickly and thus often "thinks" in stereotypes (Wilson, 2002). This relates to the work of Gilbert and others (Gilbert et al., 1988; Gilbert & Malone, 1995; Chartrand & Bargh, 1999) on automatic versus effortful processing. Because stereotypical thinking happens first and at a nonconscious level, we are largely unaware we are doing it. It is only with effortful processing that we can adjust our original (stereotypical) categorizations.

One of the strongest claims about the power of automatic processing comes from work by Gilbert et al. (Gilbert, 1991; Gilbert, Tafarodi, & Malone, 1993), who suggested that "you can't not believe everything you read." That is, these authors suggested that the process of understanding information requires believing it, even if only very briefly. This position has been widely accepted in social psychology, and helps provide a theoretical underpinning for some fiction media effects.

Recent studies by Hasson, Simmons, and Todorov (2005) and Richter, Schroeder, and Wohrmann (2009) have shown important limitations on the "comprehension = belief" effect. Specifically, these studies suggest the existence of an epistemic monitoring process that is able to efficiently validate incoming information if individuals have accessible and relevant background knowledge related to the new information. That is, if individuals have expertise or experiences with a given area, they do not necessarily instantly believe false information in that domain. However, Richter et al. (2009) explicitly

note that transportation into narrative worlds is "a special case of an epistemic mindset that prevents individuals from epistemic monitoring" (p. 552). That is, even though individuals may, under some circumstances, be able to easily identify false information, they may not be motivated to do so if they are transported into a narrative world. Furthermore, even if individuals are motivated to correct story-based information, they may not be easily able to do so (Green & Donahue, 2011).

PERCEIVED REALISM

The question of reality testing becomes more complex when extended to narrative rather than isolated pieces of information. Holland (2009a) suggests that we suspend our reality testing in the face of media narratives, but other researchers have noted that media reality judgments have multiple aspects. For example, Hall (2003) proposes six dimensions: plausibility, typicality, factuality, emotional involvement, narrative consistency, and perceptual persuasiveness. Individuals may know that a narrative did not actually happen, and thus may judge it as less factual, but at the same time the characters and situations may ring true to them, and thus the narrative is judged to be highly plausible. Indeed, plausibility and typicality appear to be more important than strict factuality in individuals' perceptions of the realism of a media narrative (Shapiro & Chock, 2003; Green & Garst, 2008).

Busselle and Bilandzic (2008) proposed that readers are attempting to construct mental models while reading, and transportation occurs when the model construction process proceeds smoothly. Violations of narrative coherence disrupt the process of simulating the narrative world, and thus reduce engagement and persuasive power. In this view, readers and viewers simply accept the story world unless something happens to make them question the realism of the story (e.g., a character acting in an unpredictable or inconsistent way). This perspective is consistent with other approaches that suggest that the default approach is to accept or believe information in media presentations, and that constructing disbelief is an effortful process (Prentice, Gerrig, & Bailis, 1997; Gerrig & Rapp, 2004). Because of this psychological tendency to be accepting of fictional content, media presentations can have subtle and unrecognized effects on viewers' beliefs.

PARTICIPATORY RESPONSES

Even though readers cannot actually participate in the action of a story, research has indicated that readers often react as if they were part of story events. In some sense, the story becomes real for participants. Gerrig (e.g., Polichak & Gerrig, 2002) refers to these reactions as "participatory responses" or "p-responses." These p-responses can range from relatively automatic and reflexive "as if" responses, in which individuals respond as they would to a real situation (for example, wanting to yell, "Run!" when danger is threatening a sympathetic character) to relatively more complex responses such as problem solving (attempting to gain information from the narrative to predict outcomes) or replotting responses (mentally undoing earlier narrative events to try to change the outcome). The kinds of participatory responses that readers have to a narrative can affect their emotional responses, their memory for narrative events, and their real-world judgments.

NEUROSCIENCE OF NARRATIVE RESPONSE

Recent work in neuroscience is identifying some of the brain structures that may contribute to our powerful responses to narratives. Research on mirror neurons shows evidence that when we watch someone act or feel, what we watch is mirrored in our brain (Hurley, 2004; Rizzolatti & Destro, 2007). For example, the same neurons that would fire if we were to strike out at someone fire when we see a character in a movie strike out. The difference is that when viewing media characters act, we inhibit our own impulse to act—in this case, the instigation to aggress. The function of mirror neurons is the ability to empathize with or imitate what we see others doing around us. Of course, empathy and imitation evolved to function in a system of face-to-face contact rather than in the circumstance of viewing fictional media. Therefore, when a system that was meant to operate in face-to-face situations is applied to mediated social situations, errors can and do occur.

Beyond mirror neurons, which may have more limited applicability to some forms of narrative such as text, researchers have shown that brain areas used in theory of mind (understanding the perspectives of others) overlap with those used in story comprehension (Mar, 2011). Research on the neuroscience of narrative is in its early stages, but provides exciting possibilities for understanding the links between story engagement and other forms of mental processing, such as empathizing with real others, imagining possible future situations, and other imaginative mental activities.

MENTAL IMAGERY

The transportation-imagery model (Green & Brock, 2002) highlights the role of visual imagery in transportation-based belief change. According to this model, images take on meaning from their role in a story; the image of a single shoe lying in a roadway takes on new meaning if a story tells how the owner of the shoe was killed by a drunk driver. The transportation experience links the vivid images with beliefs implied by the story. This linkage may be one basis for the power of narrative-based persuasion. It may be difficult for verbal or statistical arguments to overcome the power of a mental image (Dill & Burgess, in press). Even though a person may know rationally that swimming in the ocean is quite safe, he may not be able to shake the mental picture of a shark attack (similar to the availability heuristic) (Tversky & Kahneman, 1974). Additionally, over time, recalling the image may re-evoke the plot or other central aspects of the original communication, thus reinforcing the story-relevant beliefs. The transportation-imagery perspective implies that individuals' imagery ability and situations that allow for the formation of rich mental images (e.g., descriptive language, ample time for reading) increase the persuasive power of a story.

Although most research on the transportation-imagery link has focused on the role of mental images created in the minds of readers, some recent advertising work has explored the ability of a single image to create a story, and to invite readers into an experience of transportation by constructing their own story around an evocative picture. Specifically, Phillips and McQuarrie (2010) identified a subset of high fashion ads that present bizarre or disturbing images, such as a woman crawling across a roof with a tiger behind her. They label these types of images *grotesque,* and propose that part of their effectiveness lies in their transporting nature. Phillips and McQuarrie note that only a subset of fashion magazine readers will engage with these kinds of ads, but present evidence that the ads are effective at creating interest and brand connection among that subset of the audience. The idea that even single images can create transporting stories is an exciting area for future research, with applications that likely extend beyond the fashion industry and these specific grotesque advertisements.

CONNECTIONS WITH CHARACTERS

The connections that individuals form with narrative characters can also be an important source of narrative influence. Individuals may have a variety of responses to narrative characters, ranging from liking to identification to parasocial relationships (Moyer-Gusé, 2008). Transported readers often show high levels of identification with protagonists, but these concepts are conceptually separate; *transportation* refers to general immersion into the story world, whereas *identification* means adopting the goals and perspective of a specific character (Moyer-Gusé & Nabi, 2010; Sestir & Green, 2010; Tal-Or & Cohen, 2010). Konijn (Chapter 11) notes the confusion in the study of identification with characters, suggesting that identification has been blurred with other factors such as character liking and emotional connectedness with characters.

Much of the research on entertainment–education has given special focus to the role of characters, drawing on social cognitive theory (Bandura, 2001). Social cognitive theory states that we can learn vicariously by seeing the experiences of other people and the way in which other people's decisions or behaviors are rewarded and punished. Entertainment–education typically provides characters who can serve as positive, negative, or transitional models. Positive models engage in the desired behavior (e.g., family planning, literacy training, use of a designated driver while drinking) and gain benefits as a result; negative characters fail to take the recommended actions and experience bad outcomes. Transitional characters may be resistant to the recommendations at first, but then are converted and triumph through choosing the right path. When individuals identify with these characters, they are motivated to make changes in their own attitudes and behaviors (Singhal et al., 2003).

Identification effects also extend to implicit or unconscious attitudes. Identifying with a smoking character in a movie, for instance, increased viewers' associations of themselves with smoking and, for smokers, increased smoking intentions (Dal Cin et al., 2007). These effects emerged even though smoking was incidental to the plot of the movie.

Much of the research on character identification has focused on main characters or those who are sympathetic in some way. However, evil characters can also prompt strong reactions and emotions. Hoorn & Konijn (2003) have proposed the "perceiving and experiencing fictional characters" theory, which adds consideration of the ethics and aesthetics of characters. This theory explores the interplay of involvement with and distance from characters, providing a more complex view of responses to fictional characters.

Character Idealization and Imaginative Insertion

Greenwood (2007) discussed the differences among character identification (perceived similarity with the character), character idealization (wanting to be like the character), and imaginative insertion (the idea that when we watch a story, we imagine being in the character's place). She studied the relationships between identification and idealization and aggression in 85 female undergraduates and found that behavioral idealization (wanting to do what the character does) and not identification was related to aggressive feelings and aggressive behaviors. For instance, college women who watched Buffy the Vampire Slayer (the favorite female action hero of this sample) and who wished they could do the things Buffy did in the show, were more aggressive than those who thought differently about the character and the story. This research demonstrates how audience variables play a role in processing of media narratives, as discussed by Isbouts and Ohler (see Chapter 2) and Potter (see Chapter 24).

Transportation Likelihood

Not all narratives or all situations create transportation. Rather, aspects of the individual, the narrative, and the situation can all influence the extent of immersion into a story. Primary influences on transportation include story quality, individual differences in "transportability," the match between reader knowledge and story content, and reader goals. Stories that are well-written and are higher in perceived realism are more transporting (see Kreuter et al., 2007 for a discussion of elements of quality narratives). Stories that match a reader's prior knowledge are more transporting, but individuals can become transported even without this prior familiarity (Green, 2004; Mazzocco, Green, & Brock, 2007). Readers who have a goal of immersion or entertainment are more likely to be transported than individuals who have a more surface-level focus (for example, proofreading; Green & Brock, 2000).

Video games offer a particularly engaging narrative fictional world in which learning takes place as part of the mechanics of the game itself in addition to incidental content learning (Gentile & Gentile, 2008). Furthermore, game engagement is hypothesized to correlate positively with game effects (Brockmyer et al., 2009). Brockmyer et al. (2009) developed the Game Engagement Questionnaire to measure game involvement, which they related to other concepts such as immersion, presence, flow, and absorption. To test the measure's relationship to behavior, the authors devised a situation in which participants were given the chance to get engaged in video game play, and then were interrupted by a voice asking them if they had lost their keys. Results indicated that those with higher GEQ scores were less likely to respond to the question, and were slower to respond than those with lower GEQ scores. This lack of behavioral responsiveness to a social cue indicated greater transportation into the world of the video game.

INDIVIDUAL DIFFERENCES

Stories may not affect all individuals equally. The transportation-imagery model proposes that individuals who have greater mental imagery ability and higher empathy may be more likely to be transported into narratives (Green & Brock, 2002). Furthermore, some people have a dispositional tendency to become easily immersed in stories, whereas others are less likely to do so. This individual difference has been termed *transportability* (Green, 1996; Dal Cin, Zanna, & Fong, 2004; Bilandzic & Busselle, 2008).

Mazzocco et al. compared rhetorical (non-narrative) and narrative persuasive messages on the topics of affirmative action and tolerance for homosexuality (Mazzocco et al., 2011). Results indicated that narratives were more effective at producing attitude change, but only for participants who had rated themselves as highly transportable. Interestingly, for those who reported having difficulty being transported into stories, narratives actually led to less story-consistent attitude change than non-narratives. Consistent with hypotheses, the effectiveness of narratives for highly transported participants was mediated by emotional responses to the story as opposed to rational or cognitive responses.

However, transportability may not always be necessary. In these studies, the situational likelihood of becoming transported was probably relatively low: participants were completing the study as part of a course requirement, and the stories themselves were relatively brief. With more elaborate stories or freely chosen narratives, transportation (and belief change) may be likely to occur even for individuals who are not predisposed to become transported into stories generally.

Persistence of Narrative-Based Attitude and Belief Change

To the extent that narrative persuasion successfully impacts the emotional bases of attitudes, and also to the extent that narratives provide vivid, readily recallable argument representations, we might expect narrative persuasion to yield strong and persistent attitudes. Attitudes that have both cognitive and emotional foundations tend to persist more

over time (Rosselli, Skelly, & Mackie, 1995), and stories with stronger emotional content are more likely to be remembered and repeated (Heath, Bell, & Sternberg 2001). Furthermore, to the extent that individuals form emotional connections with the characters in a narrative, they may be more likely to think about these characters in the future. This connection may also serve to keep the narrative alive in readers' minds and thus reinforce its messages. If Wilson (2002) is right, they may do this also at a nonconscious level and would not be cognitively aware of why they acted on their persuasion because the persuasion was nonconscious.

Real Emotions for Fictional Media

According to Holland (2009a), the fourth aspect of media transportation is the experience of real emotions while consuming fictional media. Why do we cry at sad movies? Is there an adaptive advantage for responding with real emotions to fictional media? There might be when we consider that one motive for media consumption is similar to the motive for playing a game—it affords us the chance to practice or play with meaningful content without the risk that accompanies that content in real life. We may take pleasure from watching a film or story resolve itself in the way that offers us the most gratification personally. As Konijn (see Chapter 11) notes, the research indicates that the more emotional a viewer of media is, the more persuasible he or she is to the content being viewed. When a viewer feels a story is real emotionally, he or she believes it and is influenced by it more readily (see also Chapter 16).

Theorists argue about whether our emotional reaction to characters and events comes from empathy in the sense of a vicarious feeling or in the sense that one projects oneself into the story (Holland, 2009a). Whichever mechanism applies to a given situation, the important result is that we "begin to believe, to feel as real, the imaginary worlds" of media (Holland, 2009a, p. 58). Note that there is an important nuance here: We react with emotional realism, we think about the characters and stories as if they were true, but consciously, after a certain age, we can label them as fiction. But the fact remains that the conscious labeling of fantasy and reality does not preclude persuasion via media (Dill, 2009).

CHILDREN'S REAL FEAR INDUCED BY FICTIONAL MEDIA

Adults can consciously label what is impossible or possible, likely or unlikely to happen outside of a story. But a deeper and more realistic analysis of the fantasy–reality distinction belies its apparent simplicity. We can see how blurry the fantasy–reality boundary is if we examine how children understand these differences.

Children exposed to fictional stories involving realistic threats such as fire and drowning experienced more negative emotions like fear and worry than did children in control groups who watched benign scenes involving fire or water (Cantor & Omdahl, 1991; Cantor, 1998a). Furthermore, watching fear-inducing fictional media transferred into children's understanding and expectations for their own lives. First, watching a fear-inducing film about fires or floods caused children to increase their estimates of the likelihood that these events would happen to them personally. And when asked about their liking for various activities in what was purportedly an unrelated study, the children who had seen a fictional drama about house fires were less interested in building a fire than controls. Likewise, children who had seen a fictional drama about floods reported liking water-related activities like canoeing less than those who hadn't seen the flood film (Cantor & Omdahl, 1991).

These types of effects extend from childhood into adulthood as well. For instance, Harrison and Cantor (1999) asked college students to recall their experiences with frightening media. More than 90% of participants (whose average age was 20.5) reported a media-induced fright experience and 50% of these said the film had changed their attitudes or behaviors. For example, they developed a fear of blood or avoided situations such as they had seen in the film.

These examples of children and young adults changing their attitudes and behaviors based on experience with fictional media illustrate how fantasy becomes reality. In other words, viewing a fictional story, which the participants could have identified as "just a story" or "not real," had real effects on their lives. They were now afraid of or avoided in their actual lives the types of experiences they had seen in the film. If you erase the concept of fictional media and understand the participants' experiences as such, you see that their reactions were adaptive. In other words, if you saw someone die by drowning in real life, avoiding the water would be adaptive. Because our brains were not constructed to differentiate between fictional observing stories in the media and observing real-life events (Reeves & Nass, 1996; Dill, 2009), it makes perfect sense that we would apply lessons from fictional media lessons to real life. Furthermore, if Wilson's adaptive

unconscious is in operation, these may largely be nonconscious choices and outside of our ability to fully access their operation.

Other Effects of Fiction
ATTRIBUTION THEORY AND MEDIA PSYCHOLOGY

We mentioned that "reading is believing" in an earlier section. This is also true for reading a person, such as when we make stereotype-consistent judgments when we see a person, whether face to face or via media. According to the model of Gilbert et al. of correspondence bias, the attribution process has three stages: categorization, characterization, and correction. Categorization means identifying the behavior, and characterization involves making a personality attribution for the behavior. Correction, which may or may not come, involves factoring in situational constraints and adjusting for them in terms of causation of behavior (Gilbert & Malone, 1995).

Implicit in the categorization process is accepting what one sees as true. Therefore, for the purposes of media psychology, we should note that to understand what we see in the media, we must first accept it as true. Only after believing it can we adjust our original understanding. Therefore, the first step in digesting media messages is believing them. The connection of this theory to an understanding of how media messages persuade is then clear. Rather than suspending our disbelief, we first believe. This is not a conscious decision to believe, but a nonconscious, effortless process. Correcting our first belief is an effortful process, and one that may never happen (Gilbert et al., 1988; Gilbert & Malone, 1995). This line of reasoning fits closely with research on stereotypes in the media. Even if we say we are not influenced by stereotypical content in the media, we actually are processing this content nonconsciously and are not likely to be aware of the influence of stereotypical content (Devine, 1989, 2001; Wilson, 2002; Brenick et al., 2007).

SOCIAL ABILITY

Mar et al. (2006) have found that lifetime exposure to fiction is a positive predictor of measures of social ability, such as perceiving the mental states of others. Nonfiction reading (e.g., philosophy, business, self-help) did not provide these benefits. These authors suggest that understanding characters in a fictional world provides parallels to understanding real interaction partners. In fact, social learning may well be a motive for some media users.

Just as fiction creates openness to new beliefs and attitudes about the world, it may also help expand the self, or allow people to explore new possible selves (Green, 2005). In one study, under conditions of high identification, participants temporarily displayed increased activation of trait characteristics displayed by a character in a film clip within their self-concept (Sestir & Green, 2010).

Perhaps nowhere is the self/media character boundary more permeable than between a person and his or her avatar. Working in Stanford University's Immersive Virtual Environment Technology (IVET) lab, Fox and Bailenson (2009) created avatars that sported 3D digital images of their participants' faces. These researchers demonstrated that participants who saw their digital doppelganger exercise were more likely to subsequently exercise themselves. They framed their results in terms of character identification.

In another study in the IVET lab, Fox, Bailenson, and Binney demonstrated that presence, or "the user's feelings that the virtual environment is real and that the user's sensations and actions are a response to the virtual world" differentially affected the imitative behavior of men and women (2009, p. 294). Specifically, highly present men who watched their avatar eat candy were more likely to imitate the witnessed behavior than less present men, whereas low present women were more likely to imitate the same behavior than highly present women. The authors explained the sex differences in terms of differing social norms for eating high-calorie food for men and women.

Other research has documented shifts in personality, particularly in response to literary texts (Djikic et al., 2009), and in deepening self-understanding (Kuiken, Miall, & Sikora, 2004). In these studies, individuals did not necessarily change to match themselves to a story character, but rather, engaging with a literary text appeared to provide an opportunity for individuals to think about themselves differently or become open to some form of change.

Media Literacy: Can Conscious Understanding Influence the Unconscious?

If it is true that changes in attitudes and behaviors happen outside of conscious awareness, can media literacy training change our responses to fictional media? Nairn and Fine (2008) note that ethical decisions are made about advertising to children based on the age at which children can cognitively understand that advertisements are trying to sell them

something. Based on Piaget's stages of development, this is thought to be around 7 to 11 years of age. However, Nairn and Fine reviewed research on recent models of attitude change that propose two different types of attitudes—explicit and implicit (Nosek, Banaji, & Greenwald, 2002; Amodio & Devine, 2006; Payne, Burkley, & Stokes, 2008). These are roughly equivalent to what Wilson (2002) calls conscious and nonconscious. Individuals are aware of their explicit attitudes, and are generally able to report them easily when asked. Implicit attitudes, on the other hand, are unconscious associations that are formed and sometimes activated automatically, without intention or awareness.

Nairn and Fine argue that cognitive awareness of selling intent is not enough to guarantee the ability to resist implicit attitude change attempts. "Substantial evidence now shows that judgments and behaviors, including those relating to consumption, can be strongly influenced by implicitly acquired affective associations, rather than via consciously mediated persuasive information" (Nairn & Fine, 2008, p. 447). Persuasion by implicit means can be "… controlled only with difficulty by conscious, effortful cognitive activity" (Nairn & Fine, 2008, p. 460). Analogous to the awareness of selling intent, awareness of fictional/fantasy status is unlikely to be sufficient to allow individuals to resist implicit attitude change.

Conclusion

Although many people dismiss fictional media as mere entertainment, the research reviewed here indicates that individuals' attitudes, beliefs, and behaviors can be influenced by media presentations for better or for worse. This influence may be explicit, but it can also be automatic and unconscious, and therefore less likely to be recognized and more difficult to defend against. Stories may be especially likely to create these changes when individuals are transported into them. Indeed, this transportation experience is often sought out as a benefit of a good story. People want movies and television shows to take them to a different world, to remove them from mundane reality or from the limits of their own personal experience. "Traveling" to these new worlds created by authors and producers can be exhilarating and informative, but may also have unintended consequences. Just like real-world travelers, media users should exercise caution and awareness to help insure that their journeys into narrative worlds leave them with worthwhile rather than harmful souvenirs.

References

Amodio, D. M., & Devine, P. G. (2006). Stereotyping and evaluation in implicit race bias: Evidence for independent constructs and unique effects on behavior. *Journal of Personality & Social Psychology, 91*(4), 652–661.

Appel, M., & Richter, T. (2007). Persuasive effects of fictional narratives increase over time. *Media Psychology, 10*(1), 113–134.

Bandura, A. (1986). *Social foundations of thought and action: A social cognitive theory.* Englewood Cliffs, NJ: Prentice-Hall.

Bandura, A. (2001). Social cognitive theory: An agentic perspective. *Annual Review of Psychology, 52,* 1–25.

Bilandzic, H., & Busselle, R. W. (2008). Transportation and transportability in the cultivation of genre-consistent attitudes and estimates. *Journal of Communication, 58*(3), 508–529. doi:10.1111/j.1460–2466.2008.00397.x.

Brenick, A., Henning, A., Killen, M., O'Connor, A., & Collins, M. (2007). Social evaluations of stereotypic images in videogames: Unfair, legitimate, or "just entertainment"? *Youth & Society, 38*(4), 395–419.

Brockmyer, J. H., Fox, C. M., Curtiss, K. A., McBroom, E., Burkhart, K. M., & Pidruzny, J. N. (2009). The development of the Game Engagement Questionnaire: A measure of engagement in video game-playing. *Journal of Experimental Social Psychology, 45,* 624–634.

Busselle, R., & Bilandzic, H. (2008). Fictionality and perceived realism in experiencing stories: A model of narrative comprehension and engagement. *Communication Theory, 18,* 255–280.

Cantor, J. (1998a). "But it's only make-believe" Fantasy, fiction and fear. *"Mommy, I'm Scared" How TV and Movies Frighten Children and What We Can Do To Protect Them.* San Diego: Harcourt Brace, pp. 89–110.

Cantor, J. (1998b). *"Mommy, I'm Scared"; How TV and Movies Frighten Children and What We Can Do To Protect Them.* San Diego: Harcourt Brace.

Cantor, J., & Omdahl, B. (1991). Effects of fictional media depictions of realistic threats on children's emotional responses, expectations, worries, and liking for related activities. *Communication Monographs, 58,* 384–401.

Chartrand, T. L., & Bargh, J. A. (1999). The chameleon effect: The perception-behavior link and social interaction. *Journal of Personality and Social Psychology, 76*(6), 893–910.

Csikszentmihalyi, M. (1998). *Finding Flow: The Psychology of Engagement with Everyday Life.* New York: Basic Books.

Dal Cin, S., Gibson, B., Zanna, M. P., Shumate, R., & Fong, G. T. (2007). Smoking in movies, implicit associations of smoking with the self, and intentions to smoke. *Psychological Science, 18,* 559–563.

Dal Cin, S., Zanna, M. P., & Fong, G. T. (2004). Narrative persuasion and overcoming resistance. In Knowles, E. S., & Linn, J. (Eds.), *Resistance and Persuasion.* Hillsdale, NJ: Lawrence Erlbaum Associates, pp. 175–191.

Davison, W. P. (1983). The third-person effect in communication. *Public Opinion Quarterly, 47,* 1.

Davison, W. P. (1996). The third person effect revisited. *International Journal of Public Opinion Research, 8*(2), 113–119.

DelFattore, J. (2002). Controversial narratives in the schools: Content, values, and conflicting viewpoints. In Green, M. C., Strange, J. J., & Brock, T. C. (Eds.), *Narrative Impact: Social and Cognitive Foundations.* Hillsdale, NJ: Lawrence Erlbaum Associates, pp. 131–156.

Devine, P. G. (1989). Stereotyping and prejudice: Their automatic and controlled components. *Journal of Personality & Social Psychology, 56,* 5–18.

Devine, P. G. (2001). Implicit prejudice and stereotyping: How automatic are they? introduction to the special section. *Journal of Personality & Social Psychology, 81*(5), 757–759.

Dill, K. E. (2009). *How Fantasy Becomes Reality: Seeing Through Media Influence.* New York: Oxford University Press.

Dill, K. E., & Burgess, M. C. R. (in press). Seeing is believing: Towards a theory of media imagery and social learning (MISL). In Shrum, L. J. (Ed.), *The Psychology of Entertainment Media: Blurring the Lines Between Entertainment and Persuasion,* 2nd ed. New York: Routledge.

Djikic, M., Oatley, K., Zoeterman, S., & Peterson, J. (2009). On being moved by art: How reading fiction transforms the self. *Creativity Research Journal, 21*(1), 24–29.

Douglas, K. M., Sutton, R. M., & Stathi, S. (2010). Why I am less persuaded than you: People's intuitive understanding of the psychology of persuasion. *Social Influence, 5,* 133–148.

Escalas, J. E. (2004). Imagine yourself in the product: Mental simulation, narrative transportation, and persuasion. *Journal of Advertising, 33*(2), 37–48.

Fox, J., & Bailenson, J. N. (2009). Virtual self-modeling: The effects of vicarious reinforcement and identification on exercise behaviors. *Media Psychology, 12,* 1–25.

Fox, J., Bailenson, J., & Binney, J. (2009). Virtual experiences, physical behaviors: The effect of presence on imitation of an eating avatar. *Teleoperators & Virtual Environments, 18,* 294–303.

Gentile, D. A., & Gentile, J. R. (2008). Video games as exemplary teachers: A conceptual analysis. *Journal of Youth and Adolescence, 37,* 127–141.

Gerrig, R. J. (1993). *Experiencing Narrative Worlds: On the Psychological Activities of Reading.* New Haven, CT: Yale University Press.

Gerrig, R. J., & Rapp, D. N. (2004). Psychological processes underlying literary impact. *Poetics Today, 25,* 266–281.

Gilbert, D. T. (1991). How mental systems believe. *American Psychologist, 46*(2), 107–119. doi:10.1037/0003–066X.46.2.107.

Gilbert, D. T., & Malone, P. S. (1995). The correspondence bias. *Psychological Bulletin, 117,* 21–38.

Gilbert, D. T., Pelham, B. W., & Krull, D. S. (1988). On cognitive busyness: When person perceivers meet persons perceived. *Journal of Personality and Social Psychology, 54,* 733–740.

Gilbert, D. T., Taforadi, R. W., & Malone, P. S. (1993). You can't not believe everything you read. *Journal of Personality and Social Psychology, 65,* 221–233.

Glasser, I. (1988). Television and the construction of reality. *Applied Social Psychology Annual, 8,* 44–51.

Golan, G. J., & Day, A. G. (2008). The first-person effect and its behavioral consequences: A new trend in the twenty-five year history of third-person effect research. *The New York Times, 11,* 539–556.

Green, M. C. (1996). *Mechanisms of narrative-based belief change.* Unpublished masters thesis, Ohio State University.

Green, M. C. (2004). Transportation into narrative worlds: The role of prior knowledge and perceived realism. *Discourse Processes, 38,* 247–266.

Green, M. C. (2005). Transportation into narrative worlds: Implications for the self. In Tesser, A., Stapel, D. A., & Wood, J. W. (Eds.), *On Building, Defending and Regulating* the Self: A Psychological Perspective. New York: Psychology Press, pp. 53–75.

Green, M. C., & Brock, T. C. (2000). The role of transportation in the persuasiveness of public narratives. *Journal of Personality and Social Psychology, 79,* 701–721.

Green, M. C., & Brock, T. C. (2002). In the mind's eye: Transportation-imagery model of narrative persuasion. In Green, M. C., Strange, J. J., & Brock, T. C. (Eds.), *Narrative Impact: Social and Cognitive Foundations.* Hillsdale, NJ: Lawrence Erlbaum Associates, pp. 315–341.

Green, M. C., Brock, T. C., & Kaufman, G. F. (2004). Understanding media enjoyment: The role of transportation into narrative worlds. *Communication Theory, 14,* 311–327.

Green, M. C., & Donahue, J. K. (2011). Persistence of attitude change in the face of deception: The effect of factual stories revealed to be false. *Media Psychology, 10*(1), 64–90.

Green, M. C., & Garst, J. (2008). The power of fiction: Exploring boundaries. In van Peer, W., & Auracher, J. (Eds.), *New Beginnings in Literary Studies.* Newcastle, UK: Cambridge Scholars Press, pp. 185–196.

Green, M. C., Garst, J., Brock, T. C., & Chung, S. (2006). Fact versus fiction labeling: Persuasion parity despite heightened scrutiny of fact. *Media Psychology, 8*(3), 267–285.

Green, M. C., Kass, S., Carrey, J., Feeney, R., Herzig, B., & Sabini, J. (2008). Transportation across media: Print versus film comparisons. *Media Psychology, 11*(4), 512–539.

Greenwood, D. N. (2007). Are female action heroes risky role models? Character identification, idealization and viewer aggression. *Sex Roles, 57,* 725–732.

Hall, A. (2003). Reading realism: Audiences' evaluations of the reality of media texts. *Journal of Communication, 53*(4), 624–641. doi:10.1111/j.1460–2466.2003.tb02914.x

Haney, C., & Manzolatti, J. (1980). Television criminology: Network illusions of criminal justice realities. In Aronson, E. (Ed.), *Readings on the Social Animal.* San Francisco: Freeman.

Harrison, K., & Cantor, J. (1999). Tales from the screen: Enduring fright reactions to scary media. *Media Psychology, 1,* 97.

Hasson, U., Simmons, J. P., & Todorov, A. (2005). Believe it or not: On the possibility of suspending belief. *Psychological Science, 16,* 566–571.

Heath, C., Bell, C., & Sternberg, E. (2001). Emotional selection in memes: The case of urban legends. *Journal of Personality and Social Psychology, 81,* 1028–1041.

Holland, N. (2007). *Literature and Happiness.* Gainesville, FL: PSYART Foundation.

Holland, N. N. (2009a). *Literature and the Brain.* Gainesville, FL: PSYART Foundation.

Holland, N. N. (June 2, 2009b). Why don't we doubt Spiderman's existence (1)? Retrieved from http://www.psychologytoday.com/blog/is-your-brain-culture/200907/why-dont-we-doubt-spider-mans-existence-1.

Hoorn, J. F., & Konijn, E. A. (2003). Perceiving and experiencing fictional characters: An integrative account. *Japanese Psychological Research, 45,* 250–268.

Hurley, S. (2004). Imitation, media violence and freedom of speech. *Philosophical Studies, 117,* 165–218.

Konijn, E. (2012). The role of emotion in media use and effects. In Dill, K. E. (Ed.), *The Oxford Handbook of Media Psychology.* New York: Oxford University Press.

Kreuter, M. W., Green, M. C., Cappella, J. N., Slater, M. D., Wise, M. E., Storey, D., et al. (2007). Narrative communication in cancer prevention and control: A framework to guide research and application. *Annals of Behavioral Medicine, 33*(3), 221–235.

Kuiken, D., Miall, D. S., & Sikora, S. (2004). Forms of self-implication in literary reading. *Poetics Today, 25,* 171–203.

Mar, R. A. (2011). The neural bases of social cognition and story comprehension. *Annual Review of Psychology, 62,* 103–134.

Mar, R. A., Oatley, K., Hirsh, J., de la Paz, J., & Peterson, J. B. (2006). Bookworms versus nerds: Exposure to fiction versus non-fiction, divergent associations with social ability, and the simulation of fictional social worlds. *Journal of Research in Personality, 40*(5), 694–712.

Marsh, E. J., & Fazio, L. K. (2006). Learning errors from fiction: Difficulties in reducing reliance on fictional stories. *Memory and Cognition, 34,* 1140–1149.

Marsh, E. J., Meade, M. L., & Roediger, H. L. (2003). Learning facts from fiction. *Journal of Memory and Language, 49*(4), 519–536.

Mazzocco, P., Green, M. C., & Brock, T. C. (2007). The effects of a prior storybank on the processing of a related persuasive communication. *Media Psychology, 10*(1), 64–90.

Mazzocco, P. M., Green, M. C., Sasota, J. A, & Jones, N. W. (2011). This story is not for everyone: Transportability and narrative persuasion. *Social Psychology and Personality Science, 1,* 361–368.

Moyer-Gusé, E. (2008). Toward a theory of entertainment persuasion: Explaining the persuasive effects of entertainment-education messages. *Communication Theory, 18*(3), 407–425. doi:10.1111/j.1468–2885.2008.00328.x.

Moyer-Gusé, E., & Nabi, R. L. (2010). Explaining the effects of narrative in an entertainment television program: Overcoming resistance to persuasion. *Human Communication Research, 36*(1), 26–52. doi:10.1111/j.1468–2958.2009.01367.x.

Nabi, R. (2012). Media and persuasion. In Dill, K. E. (Ed.), *The Oxford Handbook of Media Psychology.* New York: Oxford.

Nairn, A., & Fine, C. (2008). Who's messing with my mind? The implications of dual-process models for the ethics of advertising to children. *International Journal of Advertising, 27*(3), 447–470.

Nisbett, R. E., & Wilson, T. D. (1977). Telling more than we can know: Verbal reports on mental processes. *Psychological Review, 84*(3), 231–259.

Nosek, B. A., Banaji, M. R., & Greenwald, A. G. (2002). Harvesting implicit attitudes and beliefs from a demonstration website. *Group Dynamics: Theory, Research, and Practice, 6*(1), 101–115.

Payne, B. K., Burkley, M. A., & Stokes, M. B. (2008). Why do implicit and explicit attitude tests diverge? The role of structural fit. *Journal of Personality and Social Psychology, 94*(1), 16–31. doi: 10.1037/0022–3514.94.1.16.

Phillips, B., & McQuarrie, E. (2010). Narratives and persuasion in fashion advertising. *Journal of Consumer Research, 37,* 368–392.

Polichak, J. W., & Gerrig, R. J. (2002). Get up and Win! In M. C. Green, J. J. Strange, & T. C. Brock (Eds.), *Narrative impact: Social and cognitive foundations.* Mahwah, NJ: Lawrence Erlbaum Associates, pp. 71–97.

Prentice, D. A., Gerrig, R. J., & Bailis, D. S. (1997). What readers bring to the processing of fictional texts. *Psychonomic Bulletin & Review, 4,* 416–420.

Reeves, B., & Nass, C. I. (1996). *The Media Equation: How People Treat Computers, Television, and New Media Like Real People and Places.* New York: Cambridge University Press.

Richter, T., Schroeder, S., & Wohrmann, B. (2009). You don't have to believe everything you read: Background knowledge permits fast and efficient validation of information. *Journal of Personality and Social Psychology, 96*(3), 538–558.

Rizzolatti, G., & Destro, M. F. (2007). Understanding actions and the intentions of others: The basic neural mechanism. *European Review, 15*(2), 209–222.

Rosselli, F., Skelly, J. J., & Mackie, D. M. (1995). Processing rational and emotional messages: The cognitive and affective mediation of persuasion. *Journal of Experimental Social Psychology, 31*, 163–190.

Scharrer, E. (2002). Third-person perception and television violence: The role of out-group stereotyping in perceptions of susceptibility to effects. *Communication Research, 29*(6), 681.

Scharrer, E., & Leone, R. (2006). I know you are but what am i? Young people's perceptions of varying types of video game influence. *Mass Communication & Society, 9*(3), 261–286.

Sestir, M., & Green, M. C. (2010). You are who you watch: Identification and transportation effects on temporary self-concept. *Social Influence, 5*(4), 272–288.

Shapiro, M. A., & Chock, T. (2003). Psychological processes in perceiving reality. *Media Psychology, 5*(2), 163–198. doi:10.1207/S1532785XMEP0502_3

Singhal, A., Cody, M. J., Rogers, E. M., & Sabido, M. (Eds.) (2003). *Entertainment-Education and Social Change: History, Research, and Practice*. Hillsdale, NJ: Lawrence Erlbaum Associates.

Slater, M. D. (1990). Processing social information in messages: Social group familiarity, fiction versus nonfiction, and subsequent beliefs. *Communication Research, 17*, 327–343.

Slater, M. D. (2002). Entertainment education and the persuasive impact of narratives. In Green, M.C., Strange, J. J., & Brock, T. C. (Eds.), *Narrative Impact: Social and Cognitive Foundations*. Hillsdale, NJ: Lawrence Erlbaum Associates, pp. 157–181.

Slater, M. D., & Rouner, D. (2002). Entertainment-education and elaboration likelihood: Understanding the processing of narrative persuasion. *Communication Theory, 12*(2), 173–191.

Slater, M., Rouner, D., & Long, M. (2006). Television dramas and support for controversial public policies: Effects and mechanisms. *Journal of Communication, 56*, 235–252.

Strange, J. J., & Leung, C. C. (1999). How anecdotal accounts in news and in fiction can influence judgments of a social problem's urgency, causes, and cures. *Personality and Social Psychology Bulletin, 25*, 436–449.

Tal-Or, N., & Cohen, J. (2010). Understanding audience involvement: Conceptualizing and manipulating identification and transportation. *Poetics, 38*, 402–418.

Tversky, A., & Kahneman, D. (1974). Judgment under uncertainty: Heuristics and biases. *Science, 185*, 1124–1131.

Wilson, T. D. (2002). *Strangers to Ourselves: Discovering the Adaptive Unconscious*. Cambridge, MA: Harvard University Press.

The Political Narrative of Children's Media Research

Jeff J. McIntyre

Abstract

This narrative recounts the strategy and struggle of children's media advocates who have engaged the media industry over proposed federal policy. Beginning with the issues surrounding scientific research, this chapter recounts the difficulties in translating research for policymakers and the media. This, in turn, can lead to political fights over interpretation of scientific terms and data—which sets the foundation for debates over funding and the use of the scientific research in the political arena. The political strategy of media industry and children's media advocates is examined in a case study of the effort around the Federal Communications rulemaking on *Children's Television Obligations of Digital Television Broadcasters*.

Key Words: Children's Media Policy Coalition, Children's Television Act, Disney, Federal Communications Commission, Federal Trade Commission, public interest obligations, Viacom

Introduction

Over the course of my career working on children's media issues, there has been one consistent theme in the larger political narrative of kids and media. The children's media industry is a bully. If, as Marshall McLuhan once posited, the medium is the message, then we as child advocates, researchers, and public health officials must understand the political medium that informs the policies, debates, and regulations that impact children's media.

These behind-the-scenes political machinations often stand in stark contrast to the kid-friendly, family-friendly image that all children's media companies portray. Although the smiling faces of our favorite cartoons, child stars, and children's media role models entertain and teach our children, the children's media industry is often busy attempting to influence the White House, Congress, a range of federal agencies, and the state and federal legal system. Simply put, the industry representatives

will do anything and everything to do the minimal amount of work to get Congress off their backs and diminish potential industry regulations.

Children are a complicated political entity with little tangible political power—they don't vote or make donations. Yet, children can be very influential politically—often serving as the poster child for a given issue (e.g., health care, gun safety). Children have become pawns in larger presidential campaigns. All politicians position themselves to be portrayed as a friend of children. And, after the enactment of the Children's Television Act (CTA) in 1990, children would become the prominent population protected by congressional statute at the Federal Communications Commission.

This chapter relates a specific behind-the-scenes experience with the larger media industry on a niche political issue—the transition of public interest obligations for children from analog to digital broadcasting. Although this narrative dives deep into the workings of policy wonks, industry representatives, and lobbyists, it stands as a good case study of the fight that children's advocates have repeatedly faced in Washington when attempting to work with politicians and the media industry. Unfortunately, the best of intentions have often been met with suspicions, roadblocks, legal loopholes, and stalemates. The lesson to be gained is that—much like children themselves—the children's media advocates are largely powerless in the face of the larger, well-funded global media industry. It has only been when we have found a point of leverage—a "hammer" (to use one of former Senate Commerce Committee member Senator Fritz Hollings' favorite terms) that the greatest actions have happened on a federal level for children's media.

Individuals often cite their own experience as parents as a foundation for expertise in child development and children's policy. I, however, am a believer in research being our base of knowledge for the proper grounding of policy proposals and decisions. As a representative of children and a representative of the research on children, it is my job to translate research into policy (and policy needs into research priorities).

The research on children's media is vast and encompasses many disciplines. For instance, the three main reports on media violence done by the Surgeon General, the National Institutes of Health, and the National Cable Television Association have bibliographies of hundreds of studies. This large amount of data presents a difficult proposition for policymakers. With so many issues competing for their attention, federal representatives rarely have time for more than a few sentences to understand an issue. Casually referred to as an "elevator speech," it is my job to distill the hundreds of studies on children and media into a simpler form, more easily understood by the layperson. Usually, for our purposes, those laypersons are members of Congress or federal agencies.

As child advocates, we summarize large methodological tracts and bodies of research to elucidate the finer points of child development and experience to our audience. For Members of Congress, this means that everything has to be boiled down to one page because, frankly, there is neither the time nor the attention span to review anything more than that.

Consider reducing a given study to three to five talking points while staying true to its intent. Then do that with an entire body of research, without the usual social science qualifiers that many researchers are so eager to include. Politicians and the public, unfamiliar with the nuances of the scientific method, will interpret the qualifier as uncertainty. That perception, in turn, can undercut any conclusions derived from the research.

When we speak to the media about research in a political context, this distillation is increased by a factor of 10 because the press only wants a sound bite. If the issue is controversial, even further simplicity is necessary and must be presented in a compelling, novel, and insightful manner, usually in less than 10 words.

In the case of most children's media research, advocates are not just talking to the media; we are talking to the media about the media in the media. How is this accomplished without coming across as simpletons, such as the South Park character that cautions children, "Drugs are bad … mmmkay?" as his main health message. Surely, as the research demonstrates, there is more to providing for a healthy media environment for our children than "Just Say No."

Fortunately, the areas of concern in children's media are so broad and the risk factors so plentiful that the national media and the public consciousness have already engaged the issue for their own purposes and understanding. With media platforms becoming more mobile, media usage has become omnipresent, whereas the risks have become more normalized.

The normalization of risk does not diminish the impact of that risk, but it can diminish the precautions against that risk. "I grew up with Wile E. Coyote dropping anvils on people and I'm not a serial killer" our opponents will say. We, as advocates and researchers, must then educate and push for changes to decrease the risk of harm—usually against the argument of "everybody does it."

In considering the impact of violence in the media on children, I have often been asked, "Why talk about media violence when there's domestic violence, child abuse, handgun proliferation, substance abuse, and so on?" Well, the answer, from the child advocate's viewpoint, is that we do talk about those things. Child advocates and the public health trade associations have a rich history of advocacy in those areas. Supporting that history is a body of research on those topics and many more related to violence prevention. It is a sneaky question aimed at getting us to prioritize risk and separate the media impact from other risk factors. The media and the media industry look for their easily digestible version and, by implication, a quick fix. Unfortunately, there is no quick fix to the majority of issues facing our children today. As pediatricians and child psychologists know, individuals vary. Children's behavior is a complex recipe, but with many common elements.

There is, however, an inability to predict when a national conversation will bring a given issue into the public consciousness and political spotlight. It is important to recognize that we are not the only ones interpreting this research. It is common for everyone with a vested interest in the issue to consider it—and to clarify it with a varying degree of skill or agenda. For those who are successful in simplifying their research message, the resolution is often referred to as "common sense." We need to be wary of the use of that phrase. Calling a position out and labeling it as common sense usually means it is not. Still, major campaigns are waged and vast amounts of money are spent to convince the public that a given position is really "sensible"—often on both sides of the issue. Nowhere is this more evident than in issues related to the most familiar of populations and platforms—children and the media.

In "common sense" terms, the psychological research on violence in the media states that kids learn from what they are exposed to, including violence in the media. The countering argument on the other hand, and in equally "common sense" terms, states that television and movies do not cause violence.

Because both of these points seem obvious, as advocates we must simplify our decades of research on media violence and personalize it so that it resonates with the media and the public and simultaneously fends off the media industry attempts to marginalize and redefine our data. One of the most common industry tactics is to put words in advocates' mouths, for example, "Television *causes* violence/obesity/sexual behavior" and then use those words against us. By defining the terms of the conversation and then defeating the argument we are told we are making—the media companies seek to characterize our proposals and research as threatening, anti–free speech, and harmful to the parental right to make decisions for their own children without government interference. This adept sleight of hand by industry representatives does a disservice to American families and is at best a naïve interpretation of research and free speech.

The House Committee on Juvenile Delinquency held the very first congressional hearings on media violence in the 1950s. Television represented a dramatic change in American culture. With the prevalence of televisions came fear, suspicion, and speculation on what this technological encroachment into American homes would bring. In hindsight, we see the contribution television made to the cultural shift that occurred in the 1960s, the 1970s, and beyond.

Many of the fears brought by television were unfounded—for example, that the Beatles haircuts would create teen sexual behavior (just like Elvis' gyrating hips). This echoed earlier cultural fears that had been waged against comic books—specifically that reading Batman would "turn kids homosexual" (Wertham, 1954). These same cultural wars would be fought over Ozzy Osbourne and Judas Priest's influence, the role of Janet Jackson's "wardrobe malfunction" and the cry over the violence in *Gremlins* and *Indiana Jones* that led to the creation of a PG-13 rating for films.

Throughout the course of the knee-jerk reactions of both critics and industry, basic questions remained. Was the media an influence in children's lives? Child development experts agreed that children learned from their environments, but to what degree and how did the learning take place? And, was influence dependant on how much time children spent immersed in a media environment?

By the end of the 1990s there had been three major meta-analyses completed on the topic of children and violence in the media.

- The Surgeon General's Report (1972)
- The National Institutes of Mental Health report for the National Institute of Health (1982)
- The National Television Violence Study (1997)

Each of these studies represented a vast collection of public health research on the exposure to violence in the media on children. Using the same guidelines and methodologies as found in elsewhere in the surgeon general's office and the National Institutes of Health, there were broad conclusions arrived at and substantiated by all three studies. Later summarized by the Joint Statement on the Impact of Entertainment Violence (Academy of Pediatrics, 2000), those are:

- Children who see a lot of violence are more likely to view violence as an effective way of settling conflicts. Children exposed to violence are more likely to assume that acts of violence are acceptable behavior.
- Viewing violence can lead to emotional desensitization toward violence in real life. It can decrease the likelihood that one will take action on behalf of a victim when violence occurs.

- Entertainment violence feeds a perception that the world is a violent and mean place. Viewing violence increases fear of becoming a victim of violence, with a resultant increase in self-protective behaviors and a mistrust of others.
- Viewing violence may lead to real-life violence. Children exposed to violent programming at a young age have a higher tendency for violent and aggressive behavior later in life than children who are not so exposed.

Of course, the industry disputed these claims. Using arguments recycled from the earlier industry battles against tobacco regulation, the response to the research fell into the same tired clichés.

- TV doesn't cause violence.
- I watched it and I'm okay.
- The study is biased, poorly done, or political.
- The solution is too expensive and will cost the industry too much money.
- It doesn't matter because it's free speech anyway.

In dealing with issues of media and public health, there's a helpful process that can be followed if there is to be action taken. The following questions may be beneficial in addressing these issues:

1. Is there a problem? (e.g., media violence influences kids)
2. Is there research that demonstrates a relationship? (e.g., meta-analysis)
3. Is there a solution? (e.g., V-chip)
4. Is that solution constitutional? (Central Hudson test)

Generally, the arguments against those concerned about media violence fall into one of those four categories—and not necessarily in that order. (There is one other argument—that any solution is too expensive and will cost the industry money.)

Rarely will the researcher's specific issue of study be the focus of the industry response. Instead, the focus tends to rely on one of four industry reactions:

1. Children do not learn from watching media, especially media violence.
2. The research is poorly done, agenda-driven, out of touch, political, etc.
3. It's solely the parent's responsibility.
4. Any offered solutions are unconstitutional.

In the years following the Columbine shootings and the shootings in Paducah, Springfield, and other places in the late 1990s, news coverage of media violence escalated at an exponential rate. Children's media experts were quoted everywhere from *The New York Times,* CNN, and TV Asahi in Japan to Inside Edition and the *National Enquirer.* One statistic cited from the American Psychological Association's (APA) Task Force on Children and Television, that children will witness 8,000 murders and 100,000 acts of violence before they leave elementary school (Huston et al., 1992), may well be the most quoted statistic in the history of that Association.

As an advocate and as APA's point person on this issue at the time, I am very pleased with the success of this message. It was short, simple to understand, emphasized the young age of viewers of media violence, and gave the public something tangible they could witness when they saw a child watch an act of violence or murder on television. Children's media advocates were able to effectively use the media to promote a message about violence prevention that has shaped a national debate about the welfare of our children. The vast array of research on children in the media served as a foundation for the national conversation on media, kids, and violence throughout the course of that public examination.

The research promoted the message which, in return, promoted the research to policymakers. For example, when the Federal Trade Commission (FTC) released its report in 2000 on the Marketing of Violence to Children (FTC, 2000), the bibliography reflected the studies of numerous children's media researchers. As a result, when I testified before the Senate Commerce Committee on that FTC report, Senators McCain and Hollings were able to address the effects of violent content in media being marketed to children by Hollywood on a scientific basis and not one dictated by the unpredictable arguments of an industry seeking to defend itself by any means necessary.

Those who have heard the industry representatives speak understand that they are experts at personalizing issues. Media representatives often speak in broad but personal themes about artistic freedom, first amendment rights, and American values. One does not have to go very far in the creative community to find criticisms, especially from an artistic point of view. However, for the studios, the issue is not about art but for concern about the product and the profit.

As the debate has continued, the media industry has attempted to challenge the foundation of research in much the same way the tobacco industry challenged health-based research in the 1970s and 1980s and the gun industry challenged gun violence research in the 1980s and 1990s.

These are the arguments that the media industry attempts to define and make for advocates:

- Cause-and-effect versus correlation
- Industry reps insist that researchers are saying "causal" about effects when correlative risk factors are the subject. This immediately backs the researcher into a defensive position.
- Prevalence of risk factors
- How many studies make a difference?

That last argument heard often in response to a claim by children's media advocates that there are thousands of studies documenting the relationship between exposure to media violence and heightened levels of aggression in kids. The industry's response is that there are not thousands of studies, but only hundreds.

So, how many studies would it take? Probably thousands and thousands, ongoing each year, corresponding to each variation or development in the market, to address the impossible standard of determining causation (instead of harm reduction). Obviously this cannot be done. And if there were thousands of studies, they would think of another argument because it would fit the purposes of obfuscation, deflection, and persuasion. This inability to communicate the message of harm reduction against the media industry's insistence that the research demands causation has been a significant stumbling block for advocates to overcome. Sex does not cause AIDS. Guns do not cause violence. Alcohol does not cause automobile accidents. Yet there are steps we can reduce to reduce the risks and harm to individuals in this area.

Fortunately, it is not up to the industry to set the standards. Rather, it is the purview of the community of scientists to develop and adhere to the standards of research within their given discipline. These are the same standards of research that have been also adhered to in numerous other areas: studies on diabetes, evaluations on poverty, obesity, HIV risk factors, and violence prevention. By focusing on the scientific method and process, the individual researcher will open himself or herself (and perhaps his or her given discipline) to attack. However, in doing so, it changes the terms of the debate from the researcher's defensive posture to a more aggressive position of defending science—an important priority in all scientific fields.

The more this research has been challenged in the press, the more the media industry has moved itself into a corner. Generally speaking, the Western press and, by default, the general public does not pay much attention to in-depth debates on methodological considerations on the latest scientific meta-analysis. In the case of media violence, by the time the media industry representatives attempted to micromanage individual studies, more research was being released. These studies, resting on the previous decade's findings of a relationship between media violence and aggression, were even more conclusive:

- Ninety-eight percent of all households have a television (Rideout, Roberts, & Foehr, 2005).
- Sixteen percent of kids between 8 and 18 spend 10½ hours a day immersed in media (Rideout, Roberts, & Foehr, 2005).
- Out of 500 members of a test audience held by Sony for the slasher film, *I Still Know What You Did Last Summer,* 100 audience members were between the ages of 9 and 11 (Federal Trade Commission, 2000).

In the larger political debate, the press loved this. It made the point and it made great headlines. It gave us, as representatives of children, a foothold to talk about the effects of exposure of unhealthy media and the prevalence of media and marketing in kids' lives. Because of the existence of quality research done by researchers with an eye toward public consumption and policy, children's media advocates in Washington, DC have been able to campaign more effectively for change and promote research consistent with children's best interests as determined by the public health community.

We have learned strategic lessons from the history of advocacy against tobacco and other larger global industries. As a threatened industry becomes desperate and reactionary, there is a predictable hierarchy of industry action that Corporate Accountability International (2010) defined after their experience working to address unhealthy food marketing to children by restricting the use of toys in Happy Meals in California.

The typical industry pattern for defense engagement is:

- Rewriting the policy
- Scare tactics and threats
- Industry lobbying
- Frame the supporters of the ordinance as big government (e.g., nanny state)

- Ask for an exemption
- The voluntary approach (e.g., industry self-regulation as a good actor)
- Damage control (in California Happy Meal example)

Elements of these steps are presented in the case study on public interest obligations for children's digital media that follows. I would also add an eighth step, pursued by the video game industry in response to laws restricting violent video game access by minors. The video game industry won all legal challenges to overturn the law, and then began to sue individual, cash-strapped states for damages for daring to pass a law that tried to protect children.[1] As a scare tactic for states considering addressing this issue, it was a very persuasive deterrent. Fortunately, in children's media, as in tobacco, good research stands on its own, especially when the research has occurred over a period of three decades and thousands or "just" hundreds of studies.

The politics of video game violence illustrates the complexity of dealing with the issue of media influence on children. While at the American Psychological Association, I helped organize a symposium of top researchers doing work on children and the media environment. These sorts of gatherings are common in scientific trade associations—the top people in the field are brought in to discuss, collaborate, brainstorm, and provide leadership to the Association on a given issue. We organized 12 to 15 of the top researchers in the field, combining traditional media (e.g., television) researchers with several up and coming academics that were beginning to look at the new interactive media.

This new interactive media was rudimentary by today's definitions. Growth was being propelled by the increasing mass market popularity of Sony PlayStations and Nintendo Game Boys. The first generation of several violent video games—*Doom, Postal, Grand Theft Auto*—were causing concern among conservative parents' groups, and politicians were responding with furrowed brows and the threat of congressional hearings.

Keeping up with the latest in technology became a slippery slope for public researchers. Industry demanded that unless the research spoke to the latest platform it was not relevant. Given the demands of grant timelines, proposal writing, peer review, and the publication cycle—industry's assertion that research must be both immediate and relevant to the technology du jour while longitudinal and demonstrating causality spoke to their attempt to deconstruct scientific research as irrelevant to their topic. Indeed, based on these requirements, science would not be able to speak to any matter, much less an issue with policy implications.

With the zeitgeist of the recent debate over television violence that resulted in the passage of the V-chip requirement in the 1996 Telecommunications Act, video games and interactive media were the issue with policy implications.

Psychologists, pediatricians, child development experts, and researchers wanted to explore how learning occurred in these environments. Although traditional child development demonstrates how children can learn by doing, interactive environments presented a different set of questions for researchers. When playing a video game, children are immersed in real-time decision making. Players use the same behaviors present in tangible games—goal-oriented behavior dictated by rule-driven parameters. However, the virtual world allowed for a new set of circumstances and consequences to be explored. Weapons could be gained easily. You could earn "health." Rewards were often given for maiming or killing others in the game—whether opponents or not. And, the reboot/start over function often allowed players to learn a given level by "dying" several times so as to figure out the levels. Indeed, hitting Save at the appropriate time in a game allows the player to focus on the specific level without having to process through the entire game repeatedly.

These were important issues for child development researchers. How did children learn in virtual environments? How were rewards and punishments processed? Were children under the age of 7 to 8 (who cannot discern persuasive intent because of their developmental level) more vulnerable to learning negative social behavior?

In our discussion in the APA researcher meeting, it became apparent that these were difficult questions in which no substantial public research had been completed. There were years, and even decades, of research on the effects of watching television on children. But when moved to the interactive virtual realm and targeted to children—basic questions about how children learn were still outstanding.

As part of these researcher symposia, APA brought in a variety of federal officials to speak on emerging priorities and give an insider view to the various parts of the federal process. Congressional staffers, Agency officials, legal counsel, and the APA's government relations staff presented on a variety of topics.

As a priority, most researchers are concerned about funding.

- How do I get my grant proposal considered?
- What are the best agency departments to house my grant?
- What are the agency priorities that I can reflect in my proposal?

This convening proved to be particularly helpful. When one high-ranking agency official finished his talk, he ended by stating that he was grateful to be presenting at the APA—at which his agency had long supported behavioral research.

As we went around the room, each of the researchers then disputed his or her claim of funding. No one had received funding from his or her agency in the area of interactive media. Several researchers had been turned down repeatedly. This caused great consternation among the federal agency officials because they were confident they had funded a wide array of research in this area. Upon further round table conversation, the dilemma was defined.

Scientific research is divided into two types—basic and applied. Basic research is usually driven by a scientist's curiosity or interest in a question pertaining to the fundamentals of an essential concept; for example, "How do children learn?" One of the main goals of this type of research is to expand knowledge, not to invent or create something new.

Applied research is designed to explore functional problems; for example, curing a disease or building a better light bulb. Most researchers believe that basic research creates the foundation for the applied science that follows. The basic work must be established before the next step in research can explore the wider applications.

In our discussion, we discovered that the common element to the rejected grant proposals was the repeated use of the term "video game" when referring to the medium the researchers were interested in exploring. Because video games are a very specific media platform, available in limited supply and applicable to a certain percentage of the population, federal funding agencies considered this applied research that was not very competitive against the other pressing needs for relevant research. Why should federal funding go to exploring games when there were so many other pressing needs? "Games" equals "play," and "play" is not a priority for federal officials making tough decisions.

We knew the researchers were after something different. In the same way the military had use interactivity for safe combat training and the aviation

industry had used flight simulators for safer, realistic flight training—the scientists in the room wanted to explore how a child's basic learning could take place in an interactive environment. It was not the video game, per se, they were interested in. Instead, it was an interest in how learning takes place in an interactive environment, regardless of whether it was a specific video game. Do virtual environments result in virtual learning? Or, as the military and aviation industries displayed—could there be real world learning from virtual environments? And, when mixed with the wide breadth of issues in the variety of developmental levels of children—how did learning for children take place? This was not, as the original federal funders assumed, about building a better video game. This was as fundamental as anything Piaget had researched—and with technology growth and market proliferation increasing at an exponential rate—these were important, basic questions that need a public base of research for our public officials to consider as these technologies become more prominent in our world.

In the end, a new consortium for research in this area was funded. The Children's Digital Media Center (CDMC) was created to gain a greater understanding of how interactive digital media experiences affect children's long-term social adjustment, academic achievement, and personal identity. Specific objectives of the CDMC included:

- Monitoring and synthesizing emerging research trends in the area of children and interactive digital media
- Carrying out a program of collaborative research on interactive digital media and its effects on children
- Encouraging broader understanding of digital media through comparative communication analysis, particularly comparisons with other electronic media
- Promoting more effective application of research by developing collaborative projects with industry and policy communities
- Disseminating knowledge about children and digital media through conventional and online publication, workshops, and conference presentations

The CDMC is located at Georgetown University, the University of California Riverside, the University of Massachusetts, the University of Texas at Austin, the University of Pennsylvania, Cornell University, and Northwestern University, and has been funded in large part by two 5-year grants from the National

Science Foundation, totaling $9.95 million Children's Digital Media Center (2012).

The fight over public interest obligations for children's digital media best exemplifies the behind-the-scenes political struggles children's advocates have waged against larger industry forces in Washington. David versus Goliath is not an apt analogy for the work children's media experts have encountered against larger media conglomerates. David versus 10 Goliaths (and their lawyers) is much closer.

After the long, complicated work involved in the negotiation of the television ratings system and the fight for quality educational programming rules at the Federal Communications Commission in the 1990s, the leaders of the Children's Media Policy Coalition were concerned about always being on the defensive regarding children's media. So much of the process seemed to be about protecting children from harmful influences, from restricting media, advertising, violence, sexual media, and so on. What about a more positive direction?

With the tide on technology and interactive media gaining momentum each day, the Coalition agreed that now was the correct time to try to change the conversation. Instead of always waging against media, couldn't we—at this technological and media intersection—try to offer something positive, something that would help frame the kids media environment in a healthy way? Why not, using the prevention-based models favored by pubic health experts, help create a healthy media environment for kids, instead of just trying to postpone or prevent the tide of unhealthy media?

The media platforms were growing and changing so rapidly that we thought the time was right to influence the direction of children's media. Instead of the constantly defensive mindset, why not try to put policies in place that help steer a more positive direction for children's media? With the upcoming digital transition, we set our sights on the most obvious of policy targets—transferring the broadcast public interest obligations for children to digital. We aimed to supplement the rules set forth under the Children's Television Act that required broadcast companies to meet public interest obligations to receive broadcast licenses. Broadcasters can comply by showing a minimum of 3 hours of educational and informational children's programming per week. Children's media advocates originally sought a requirement of 5 hours of educational programming between Monday and Friday. Under industry pressure, the FCC softened the requirements to

3 hours per 7 day week (FCC, 1979). The act also limits the amount of advertising that can be shown during children's programming.

One of the goals of the Children's Media Policy Coalition has been to ensure that digital broadcasters meet their public interest obligations to children by providing children with educational programming. As the technology and platforms evolved, it was important that the Children's Television Act be updated for the digital age before the digital transition occurred.

Over the next several years, our coalition of child advocates, public health groups, and education organizations conferred with experts in the field, held meetings to put our notes and thoughts together, and made countless visits to the eighth floor of the Federal Communications Commission, where the offices of all the FCC Commissioners are centrally located. In 2000, the FCC opened the period for comments on the obligation of digital broadcasters to provide educational and informational programming for children and the requirement that digital broadcasters limit the amount of advertising in children's programs.

By the end of the process, new rules were established by the FCC that translated the old analog public interest obligations to the digital signal. When the transition from analog broadcast to digital finally occurred, the public interest obligations would be in place. Even more encouraging, the Commission passed the new order by a 5–0, bipartisan vote. Although most of the children's media issues had been supported by both political parties, it was especially heartening to get such overwhelming bipartisan support from an FCC that had been contentious in the early battles over broadband and media ownership. Former Chairman Powell lists this as his top accomplishment for the public interest while chairman (FCC, 2005).

After the 5–0 vote, a colleague and I stood in the hallway corridor of the FCC. "Did we just do that? Does it seem strange that no one seemed to notice?" Indeed, after the tribulations of the television ratings negotiations—during which we were stalked outside our offices by the press and caught between two presidential contenders hoping to maximize on the issue—this seemed anticlimactic.

This did not last long.

Soon we were to discover that various parts of the media industry had filed petitions to reconsider at the FCC over the 5–0 public interest vote. Petitions for reconsideration are filed by the entities that disagree with the Commission's Report &

Order on a given issue. It is a common administrative tool used to continue the fight over continued concerns found in opposition to the FCC's position. Even so, we found the petitions filed against the *Children's Television Obligations* of *Digital Television Broadcasters* ruling in response to a 5–0 bipartisan vote to be surprising (FCC, 2000).

There are many layers to passing laws. Once Congress passes a law, politicians often claim victory and the public attention span moves to the next topic. For most issues, the passing of the law is just the first step. Budgets are an area in which power to implement a law can be given or taken away. But in this instance of children's media issues, much power rests in rulemakings of the Federal Communications Commission. It is the behind the scenes rulemaking proceedings, the timing of notices, and the negotiations that occur among government, industry, and public interest groups that often determine whether a given law will have substance or not.

In anticipation of the January 1, 2006 deadline for implementation, we contacted the staff at the FCC in January 2005 to find out what next step was in response to the industry petitions. We were told that the Commission directed the industry to work it out with the Children's Media Policy Coalition organizations, come back to the FCC for approval, and the Commission would go forward with the industry/advocate agreed-on order.

Traditionally, the three big for-profit media industry players in children's media are Viacom (Nickelodeon), Disney, and Turner Networks (The Cartoon Channel). There are other significant players like Sesame Workshop (which does not accept advertising and often sets a great example), advertisers, and smaller networks (e.g., Fox, Ion, Discovery). Because Viacom, Disney, and Turner had led the petitions for reconsideration and were the players with the most sway in the industry, the Children's Media Policy Coalition leadership made calls to the Washington representatives of those companies in January 2005 to begin conversations to craft a deal on the public interest obligations order.

There was no response. Weeks went by as my colleagues and I made several repeat attempts to begin the conversation over changes to the FCC order. Privately, there were several places we thought the FCC had overreached in their order, places where we thought we could easily barter so as to get a quick resolution to the process. Still, there was no response to our calls to several of the industry representatives for several months.

In the Children's Media Policy Coalition there are a core of a few groups that worked the kid's media issues as a priority—Children Now, the American Psychological Association, and the American Academy of Pediatrics. Our three organizations would reach out to other groups in the Coalition that had identified children's media as a priority but could not dedicate as much time because of other policy challenges in their organization (e.g., health care, education issues, budget reauthorization). Other organizations who would still consider the children's media issues important would join the effort as we were able to provide leadership and direction. As is the case with most Washington political coalitions, organizations differed in their involvement on a given Coalition issue based on their stance. For instance, the National Education Association might be very concerned and involved on issues around educational programming—but not as involved on issues of food marketing.

After several months had passed without word from the industry on negotiating changes to the FCC Report and Order, we began to receive emails from various Coalition partners describing attempts by media industry representatives to set up meetings with the heads of their organizations. Prominent public health organizations, education associations, and child advocacy groups were calling and e-mailing to say that industry had reached out to them about the FCC Order. Meanwhile, the three lead organizations (Children Now, APA, and AAP)—with whom the FCC had specifically directed the industry to speak—were still being ignored in their attempts to craft a resolution with industry. Something was amiss.

Several of these organizations, like the American Psychiatric Association, had not been a part of the Children Media Policy Coalitions immediate efforts for years. Our partnership with the American Psychiatric Association had stalled several years earlier during the implementation of the FCC rulemaking over the 1996 Telecommunications Act. With health care reform and other pressing issues to manage, they had given their resources other priorities. We had maintained a friendly, professional relationship and they had continued to support occasional Coalition sign-on letters. However, it had been several years since we had last heard from them.

Other organizations represented that same level of semi-involvement with the CMPC. As we determined, the industry representatives seemed to be circumventing the Children's Media Policy

Coalition Leadership by contacting other members of the Coalition in an attempt to peel them off the Coalition approach. The industry appeared to be using a political strategy of divide and conquer. That is, a strategy that breaks up existing power structures and prevents smaller power groups from linking up. Individually, the children's media advocates had little power. Organized and focused, however, the Coalition was able to create leverage opportunities via Capitol Hill and the federal agencies to better advocate for quality children's media. If the industry representatives were successful with one of the larger organizations, like the American Medical Association or the National PTA, then our ability to coalesce groups around a common negotiation stance would be dramatically compromised. With a major public health or education organization giving the industry needed political cover, there was no guarantee that the Congress or the FCC would not rule favorably for the industry for political expedience. It would be a political low-hanging fruit that would allow the Commission to avoid a fight, declare victory, and move on to other pressing issues.

Although most of the organizations had promptly contacted us to find out more about the unsolicited contact, one major association engaged the industry representatives more fully. With new staff, the organization was not as familiar with the history of children's media issues and seemed eager to craft a partnership that would be impressive to their board and constituency. Fortunately, our coalition partners were able to intervene after several weeks of calls to that organization's leadership, their board of directors, and meetings with their local Washington representatives to find out what was going on.

As the months progressed toward the FCC's implementation deadline, the Coalition was able to hold the line in our effort to communicate with the industry over the FCC's rulemaking. What had begun as a good-natured attempt to orchestrate a common agreement to move forward on an order all parties could agree on turned into a complex series of political machinations aimed at defending children's interests against a determined industry was actively seeking to exploit legal loopholes and gain political victory.

This was the face of the children's media industry—aggressive, determined, and with enough resources to flex every legal option to circumvent the FCC and child advocates in pursuit of unrestricted access to children. Although this is often the norm for inside the beltway politics, it was disappointing to see good faith efforts rewarded in this way. Still, we were to be introduced to another side of the children's media industry we had not yet seen—the bully.

As the deadline for implementation crept closer, the Coalition realized we were in a position of great power. Do nothing, refuse to meet in the same manner as the industry had refused to meet with us-and the FCC Order would go into effect without compromise. We had no reason to converse with the industry except to expedite the process. We stopped our attempts to contact the industry.

Then, the children's media industry bully introduced itself. Congressional staff had alerted us that two of the major children's media companies—Viacom (representing its Nickelodeon subsidiary) and the Walt Disney Company—intended to file lawsuits seeking an injunction citing the overreach of the FCC. The Children's Media Policy Coalition leadership had yet to have our calls returned by the industry representatives when we received news of the oncoming lawsuits. Why enter into a good faith negotiation, even when prompted by federal regulators, when there were resources to exploit legal options available? In this way, these companies held themselves above the federal agencies, the political due process, and the public health community. By asserting the legal right to challenge over a negotiated settlement, the priorities of these companies came into sharp focus. They would do the minimum amount necessary to get Congress and federal regulators off their backs. By entering into a conversation with children's advocates, those advocates would then be in a position of negotiating power that the industry would not want to cede. By filing suit in a particular circuit, Viacom and Disney would be able to pick a circuit court more favorable to their perspective. It was a compliment of sorts—the US legal system would be easier to manipulate than we would be.

That was a problem. For all the political networking we had accomplished in Congress and in the federal agencies, the federal courts were a new arena. As the filings would be industry versus the FCC, we were excluded from the potential proceeding. Filing amicus briefs was always an option, but in a circuit court that is historically sympathetic to industry concerns, that represented a weak move against formidable force. If the Children's Media Policy Coalition were to be relevant, we had to move. We filed a lawsuit against the FCC.

This was no easy maneuver. After several meetings, the Children's Media Policy Coalition determined that the suit was the best way to go. If one of our organizations could file suit in a more favorable court circuit before Viacom or Disney dropped their suit, there was a good chance their suits would be deferred to our circuit court and the industry advantage of a favorable court would evaporate. After much conversation within our coalition, the United Church of Christ's Office of Communications stepped up. With the help of the Coalition's legal counsel, UCC filed a suit against the FCC saying that the agency's Report and Order did not go far enough in protecting children's interests—in direct opposition to the oncoming industry lawsuits that said the FCC went too far (Boliek, 2005).

We were successful in beating the industry suits to the punch by just a few days. Viacom and Disney filed their lawsuits shortly after—and the next step in the industry strategy began to appear. Disney hired former Clinton administration Solicitor General and heavyweight appellate litigator Seth Waxman to advise the company on the new FCC rules (Mohammed, 2005). Our collection of nonprofit, grassroots, and membership organizations were facing several well-funded, heavily resourced companies determined to get their way.

In October of 2005, with less than 3 months before the implementation of the Federal Communications Commissions Report and Order, we received word that the circuit courts where Viacom and Disney had filed their suits—had transferred their cases to the circuit court where the United Church of Christ had filed their suit. The tide shifted—we got home court advantage.

Suddenly, we heard from the industry and they wanted to talk to craft a settlement agreeable to all parties. With the implementation deadline weeks away, they were eager to put all interested parties into the same room to negotiate a deal.

The talks represented an eclectic range of organizations and vocations. We blended advocates, public health officials, and academics with industry lawyers, lobbyists, programming officials, and corporate partners—occasionally packing more than 30 people into a room. To Disney's credit, they flew their interactive experts in from Burbank to consult on the technical aspects of the talks. They were a definite asset to the discussions and a benefit to have in the room.

Because these negotiations occurred behind closed doors and were off-limits to the press, I feel compelled to keep the specifics of our conversations confidential. There's an old saying that making laws is much like making sausage—everyone wants to enjoy the benefits but no one wants to know about the process. Although the issues discussed were contentious, both industry and advocates were affable and results-oriented in the discussion. Although often epitomizing the worst of inside the beltway politics, our negotiations also symbolized the best when industry and advocates came together after several meetings to present the Federal Communications Commission with a negotiated settlement on public interest protections for children in the digital media environment.

Under the negotiated agreement, the majority of the original Federal Communications Commission Report and Order was left intact. The industry and child advocate parties recommended clarifications for rules on host selling, Web crawl, promotions, preemption, and multicasting within the original report and order. The FCC approved (FCC, 2004).

Conclusion

Experience has shown that industry and child advocates often approach the same issue with very different perspectives, agendas, and resources. Although child advocates push for a public health perspective grounded on the foundation of harm reduction and prevention, media industry representatives stand on the law. If there is no legal compulsion or threat of legal action, it is very difficult to achieve substantial industry action. Although shaming tactics and boycotts have certain effectiveness, they are best applied to individual instances (e.g., advertisers on specific television shows) rather than against larger industry practices. For children's media advocates to be truly powerful, we must facilitate valid research, represent it truthfully, and organize together.

Questions and Future Directions

- What areas of research are needed in children's media to empower policymakers to make the best decisions about interactive platforms?
- What mechanisms can help better link organizations and nontraditional partners concerned about children's media?
- Can industry lawsuits aimed at seeking punitive damages for the introduction of media regulations have a potential effect on academic freedom?

Notes

1. Video Software Dealers Association, and Entertainment Software Association, Plaintiffs, v. Arnold Schwarzenegger, in his official capacity as Governor of the State of California; Bill

Lockyer, in his official capacity as Attorney General of the State of California; George Kennedy, in his official capacity as Santa Clara County District Attorney; Richard Doyle, in his official capacity as City Attorney for the City of San Jose; and Ann Miller Ravel, in her official capacity as County Counsel for the County of Santa Clara, Defendants. United States District Court for the Northern District of California, San Jose Division, August 2007.

References

Academy of Pediatrics (2000). *Joint statement on the Impact of Entertainment Violence on Children.* Retrieved from http://www.aap.org/advocacy/releases/jstmtevc.htm.

Boliek, B. (2005). *Viacom, UCC Dispute FCC Kid Regs.* Billboard Law Newsletter. Retrieved from http://www.allbusiness.com.

Children's Digital Media Center (2012). *About CDMC.* Washington, DC: Georgetown University. Retrieved from http://cdmc.georgetown.edu/about.cfm.

Corporate Accountability International (2010). *SF Passes Healthy Meal Law Removing Toys from Unhealthy Meals.* Boston: Corporate Accountability International.

Federal Communications Commission (2000). Notice of Proposed Rulemaking, Children's Television Obligations of Digital Television Broadcasters, Docket 00–167, FCC 00–344.

Federal Communications Commission (2004). *FCC Adopts Children's Programming Obligations for Digital Television Broadcasters.* Press Release.

Federal Communications Commission (2005). *Policy Highlights of Michael K. Powell's FCC Tenure.* Retrieved from http://hraunfoss.fcc.gov/edocs_public/attachmatch/DOC-256206A2.pdf.

Federal Trade Commission (2000). *Marketing Violent Entertainment to Children: A Review of Self-Regulation and Industry Practices in the Motion Picture, Music Recording & Electronic Game Industries.* Washington, DC: Federal Trade Commission.

Federal Trade Commission (2000). *Marketing Violent Entertainment to Children: A Review of Self-Regulation and Industry Practices in the Motion Picture, Music Recording & Electronic Game Industries.* Washington, DC: Federal Trade Commission.

Huston, A. C., Donnerstein, E., Fairchild, H., Feshbach, N. D., Katz, P. A., Murray, J. P., et al. (1992). *Big World, Small Screen: The Role of Television in American Society.* Lincoln: University of Nebraska Press.

Mohammed, A. (2005). Kids' television rules face challenge: Viacom, Disney oppose the FCC's new guidelines. *Washington Post,* October 6.

National Institute of Mental Health (1982). *Television and Behavior: Ten Years of Scientific Progress and Implications for the Eighties,* vol. 1. Washington, DC: U.S. Government Printing Office.

National Television Violence Study (1996). Studio City, CA: Mediascope.

Notice of Proposed Rulemaking, Children's Television Programming and Advertising Practices (1979). Docket No. 19142, FCC 2d-138.

Rideout, V., Roberts, D. F., & Foehr, U. G. (2005). *Generation M: Media in the Lives of 8–18 Year Olds.* Washington, DC: Kaiser Family Foundation

Surgeon General's Scientific Advisory Committee on Television and Social Behavior. (1972). *Television and Growing Up: The Impact of Televised Violence.* Washington, DC: U.S. Government Printing Office.

Wertham, F. (1954). *Seduction of the Innocent.* New York: Rinehart and Company.

Media Psychophysiology: The Brain and Beyond

Bruce D. Bartholow *and* Paul Bolls

Abstract

This chapter provides an overview of the effects of consuming media content spanning entertainment, news, and advertising—content that is increasingly delivered over a wide range of technological platforms (e.g., computers, televisions, smart phones)—on the psychophysiological responses of media audiences, focusing in particular on how media content affects neural responses and the ways in which those neural responses act as biological mechanisms of psychological and behavioral responses. The chapter highlights the psychophysiological approach to studying how individuals interact with media, and provides a theoretically and methodologically rich environment for advancing the scientific study of how all forms of mediated experience influence thoughts, feelings, and actions. The chapter focuses in particular on how the media psychophysiology approach has been applied to understanding media violence and persuasion, underscoring the ways in which this approach has provided a way to address questions of long-standing interest to scholars in the field.

Key Words: brain, cognition, emotion, event-related potentials, heart rate, media violence, persuasion, psychophysiology, skin conductance

Introduction

The study of media effects—that is, how consumption of media influences psychological and behavioral responses among consumers—has a long history within the fields of psychology and communication (Bryant & Thompson, 2002). Although numerous theoretical approaches have been developed over the years, the current chapter focuses primarily on recent advances encapsulated within Lang's (2009) conceptualization of media use as consisting of a temporally dynamic interaction between the human mind and media content, defined broadly as mediated sensory information that varies in motivational significance across exposure. This conceptualization of media use moves the study of media effects forward by shifting the focus from static media effects to mental processes, embodied in neural activity, that underlie the effects of media content on individuals and provides

a general framework for studying media use that can accommodate current as well as future forms of media (Lang, 2009; Lang & Ewoldsen, 2010). The psychophysiological approach is central to this theoretical perspective of media use and uniquely enables researchers to observe the activity of the mind—embodied in the brain—across time during media use, providing critical data for the development of new explanations of media effects (Bolls, Wise, & Bradley, 2012; Potter & Bolls, 2012).

Before discussing the psychophysiological study of media effects, however, it is important to first consider why scholars of human experience, even those unconcerned with media effects per se, should care about the study of media effects on brain and behavior. The simplest reason, in a nutshell, is that media use occurs on a scale that is nearly too massive to comprehend. According to the Advertising Age

Data Center (www.adage.com/datacenter/), the top five media companies in the United States alone now earn more than $100 billion in combined annual net revenue. US media industry revenue has averaged about a 5% annual increase through the first decade of the 21st century—a decade that included several years of economic recession. Given that media industry revenue is completely dependent on audience behavior, these figures point to a huge and steadily increasing appetite for media content among the American public. This media blitzkrieg phenomenon is a relatively recent development in human history. The advent of the printing press in the 15th century represented one of the first opportunities for mediated communication on a relatively large scale (Fang, 2008). But it wasn't until the 20th century that truly massive numbers of people began to be exposed to media on a regular basis.

The story of television provides the most poignant example. First introduced in the mass market at the end of World War II, television exploded onto the American cultural landscape incredibly rapidly. By 1955, two-thirds of all homes in the United States contained a television set; by 1960, the figure was 93%. By the middle of the 1960s, television had become a part of the daily lives of virtually all Americans (Nielsen Media Research, 1998). With each annual increase in global population comes a corresponding increase in the numbers of homes containing at least one television. For example, the Nielsen Corporation reports that the number of "TV Homes" increased in virtually every one of the top 150 television markets in the United States between 2010 and 2011.

The rise in media availability has led to a culture in which media consumption is now the great American pastime. For example, the Bureau of Labor Statistics reports that in 2010 watching television accounted for around half of all time spent on leisure activities among people ages 15 and up (2011), amounting to just under 3 hours per day, every day. The next most reported category of leisure activities, "socializing and communicating," accounted for less than one-third that much time. These television use figures are likely underestimates, given that they rely on self-report. Nielsen Corporation data indicate that the average American actually watches more than 4 hours of television per day, or around 28 hours per week. At this rate, an American who lives to the age of 65 will have spent nearly 9 years of his or her life watching television. When considering that the majority of Americans also consume multiple other forms of media in addition to television, it is not

an exaggeration to suggest that media consumption is the single activity that most Americans engage in most, perhaps second only to sleeping. Thus, any scholar or policymaker who believes that exposure to environmental stimuli has an important influence on behavior should be keenly interested in the study of media effects.

The scientific study of how media exposure affects media users is nearly as old as mass media itself. The first major scientific effort to study media effects occurred in the early 1930s. This effort, known as The Payne Fund Studies, consisted of a series of eight published volumes reporting the results of experiments specifically designed to test the effects of motion pictures on the attitudes and behaviors of youth (Wartella & Reeves, 1985). The popularization of different forms of mass media throughout the 20th century—film, radio, television—led to substantial concern over possible negative effects of media on individuals and society. It was during this time that specific areas of inquiry into the effects of media emerged, such as the study of the role of media in opinion change (Hovland, Janis, & Kelly, 1953) and the relationship between violent media content and aggression (Bandura, Ross, & Ross, 1963).

Early pioneers in the field used mainly self-report measures (i.e., questionnaires) to investigate how people evaluate, understand, and respond to media content. For example, Gerbner et al. made extensive use of self-report questionnaires in their effort to understand the effects of frequent viewing of violent television programs on peoples' values and perceptions of society (Gerbner & Gross, 1976). Experiments performed by early pioneers interested in the effects of persuasive and propaganda techniques in mass media relied on self-report measures of attitude change to provide evidence of effects (Lasswell, 1927/1971; Hovland, 1951). A few of the early studies attempted to directly observe behavior, as was done in Albert Bandura's experiment on media violence in which researchers observed children's play behavior after exposure to a violent film (Bandura, Ross, & Ross, 1963). An emphasis on the measurement of self-reported perceptions and observation of behavior—as illustrated by this brief review of landmark studies—was appropriate for early research on media effects that was focused on documenting relationships between media exposure and attitudinal or behavioral outcomes.

Still, measuring bodily responses as a way to gain insight into the influence of media on individuals was a small, easy to overlook, part of the very earliest formal research on media effects. One experiment that was part of the previously mentioned Payne Fund Studies included the measurement of skin resistance and pulse rate as indices of emotional reactions to a popular film, *The Feast of Ishtar* (Dysinger & Ruckmick, 1933). This experiment was one of the earliest to illustrate the importance of understanding characteristics of both media content and the individuals who mentally process media. Yet, unfortunately the methodological insight and important conclusions resulting from this experiment were mostly ignored because of the emerging dominance of the behaviorist paradigm in psychology. Researchers working under a behaviorist paradigm in the early 20th century considered mental processes as something that could not possibly be validly measured, and moreover viewed mental processes as unnecessary to the development of psychological theories (Smith, 1996). That is, even though most scholars in the field understood that the brain must play a vital role in determining psychological and behavioral responses, they nevertheless treated the mind like a kind of "black box" whose mysteries were best left unexamined (Geiger & Newhagen, 1993).

The dominance of the behaviorist paradigm in psychology led media scholars to focus exclusively on attempting to demonstrate linkages between characteristics of media content and supposed effects of media exposure in a simple stimulus–response manner (Paisley, 1984). A stimulus–response approach to understanding media effects can be seen in early theorizing about communication, including content transmitted through media channels (Potter & Bolls, 2012). Lasswell's (1927/1971) classic definition of communication, "Who Says What to Whom in What Channel With What Effect," defined the proper focus for researchers working at this time. Shannon and Weaver (1949) elaborated on Lasswell's definition with their model of communication as a phenomenon involving a sender, message, channel, and receiver. These two early theoretical publications about the nature of communication limited the conceptualization of media effects to linkages between the stimulus (sender/message) and observable responses (the effect). Mental processes were not believed to be explicitly observable. Thus, the mind and brain, along with insights to be gained from their study, remained hidden, and researchers viewed media effects from a stimulus–response perspective. This approach to understanding media effects is illustrated in Figure 27.1.

This view began to change with the advent of the so-called cognitive revolution in experimental psychology, in which the strict behaviorist approach was replaced with an information-processing approach (Lachman, Lachman, & Butterfield, 1979). The cognitive revolution, along with formal development of the psychophysiological approach, have been credited with changing the paradigm for media effects research by enabling researchers to explore mental processes that intervene in determining media effects (Lang, Potter, & Bolls, 2009). These developments essentially shifted the paradigm from

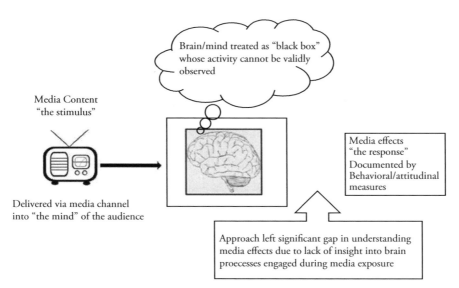

Figure 27.1 Model depicting the stimulus-response approach to media effects research that treated brain activity as scientifically unobservable and therefore was only able to document the occurrence of effects or responses to media content without insight into how the brain processes media content.

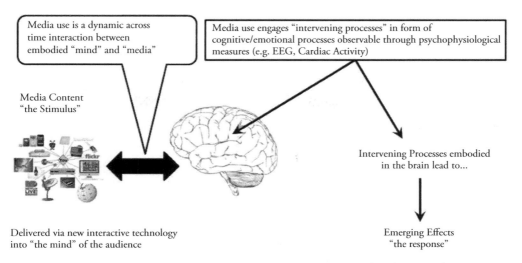

Figure 27.2 Model Depicting the Stimulus-Intervening Processes-Response Approach to Media Effects Research.
This approach uses psychophysiological measures to observe brain activity that act as intervening processes between exposure to media content and observable media effects.

one focused on stimulus–response relationships to one that investigates media effects as occurring in a more complex stimulus-intervening processes–response fashion (Potter & Bolls, 2012). Figure 27.2 illustrates this more complex and theoretically rich way of conceptualizing media effects.

The importance of bursting open the black box and investigating mental processes instantiated in brain activity evoked by media exposure was noted by the communication scholar Wilbur Schramm, who commented, "Most of the communication process is in the 'black box' of the central nervous system, the contents of which we understand only vaguely" (Schramm, 1971, pp. 24). It was during this stage of media effects research that researchers began to use various behavioral measures not only to gauge overt reactions to media, but also as indices of presumed, underlying cognitive operations carried out during media exposure. For example, media scholars interested in observing variation in levels of attention engaged during media exposure turned to secondary task reaction time—a measure that had gained traction in cognitive psychology—as well as time spent looking at the screen (Anderson & Burns, 1991; Basil, 1994).

In recent years, the cognitive revolution has been supplanted by another shift in focus, which we might call the "cognitive neuroscience revolution" (Sherry, 2004; Weber, Sherry, & Mathiak, 2009). This new age of media research is characterized by scholars from both media studies and psychology using various psychophysiological measures to understand not only the information processing operations engaged by media content, but also the neural underpinnings of those operations and the bodily responses they instantiate. The value of this new approach was recognized in the introduction to a special issue of the journal *Media Psychology* dedicated to the use of brain imaging in media effects research, in which it was claimed that the opportunity to observe brain activity during exposure to media content promises the potential to discover biological explanations for previously observed media effects (Anderson et al., 2006). Most broadly, cognitive neuroscience is the study of the biologic substrates of complex cognition, with a particular emphasis on the neural structures and processes that give rise to mental processes (Gazzaniga, Ivry, & Mangun, 2002). The cognitive neuroscience approach to understanding media effects is grounded in a theoretical orientation that assumes that integrating responses to media derived from cognitive, neural, and peripheral physiological levels provides a more comprehensive understanding of responses to media than can be achieved by investigating any one or two of these levels alone (Ochsner & Lieberman, 2001). The focus of this chapter is primarily on the influence of this new theoretical and methodological approach on the study of media effects.

Theoretical Approaches to Media and the Brain

Media studies and psychology are two distinct disciplines that make unique contributions to research on how the brain processes media. Broadly, psychological scientists engage in the study of behavior, including how environmental influences and individual differences contribute to the various ways in which the brain causes behavior. In particular, social psychologists are primarily concerned with the influence of situational and environmental factors on behavior. Scholars working in media studies are primarily interested in providing insight into a wide range of mental processes engaged by media use occurring not only within traditional media—such as television and radio—but also newer, interactive digital forms of media. In this way, social psychology and media studies share a common orientation toward understanding how exposure to salient stimuli in the environment—media content, in this case—causes changes in behavior, via their effects on internal states, such as cognitions and emotions (Carnagey & Anderson, 2003). The increasing convergence between the general theoretical approach in social psychology with the specific focus on the cognitive and emotional processes engaged by media, and the larger, cross-disciplinary focus on grounding psychological and behavioral processes in brain function has led to the emergence of a new area of scholarship aptly called media psychology research (Potter & Bolls, 2012).

Media psychology research is distinct from the two disciplines that form its foundation in its entire focus on understanding—to paraphrase a famous anti-drug slogan—the brain "on" media. Psychological experiments on media effects often involve exposing participants to some form of media, and media studies includes psychology as part of its epistemological foundation. Separately, however, these two disciplines lack critical conceptual and operational components required for truly advancing knowledge of the brain "on" media. Psychological experiments that feature the effects of some form of mediated stimuli on brain and/or behavior can advance understanding of how those stimuli are processed at a basic level, but without consideration of current trends in the media industry (e.g., how various media are typically presented) and how individuals actually consume media, this research lacks the level of ecological validity necessary to truly understand the typical media consumption experience and its neural correlates. Similarly, experiments conducted in media studies must be grounded in the most current knowledge of brain structure and function so as to avoid producing very shallow, limited understanding of the influence of media on individuals and the internal (i.e., brain-based) processes that are affected by media exposure.

The specific approach to media psychology research covered in this chapter continues to advance knowledge of brain processes underlying effects of media use by uniting scientists under a common research paradigm. This paradigm combines conceptual understanding of the nature of the human brain and current knowledge of media effects and industry practices with the methodological expertise required to measure nervous system activity engaged during media use. Potter and Bolls (2012) termed this paradigm *media psychophysiology*.

Psychophysiology has emerged as a distinct paradigm within psychology with its own assumptions about the human mind and a distinct collection of measures for studying it (Cacioppo, Tassinary, & Berntson, 2007). In the broadest terms, psychophysiology is the study of the physiological and biological bases of psychological processes (Stern, Ray, & Quigley, 2001; Andreassi, 2007). Media psychophysiology extends the psychophysiological paradigm to studying how the brain processes media content. This chapter provides an overview of media psychophysiology as a paradigm for studying brain processes associated with the effects of media content and reviews relevant research by scholars working in this area. The chapter closes with considerations for future media psychophysiology research in light of continuing advancements in knowledge and measurement of brain processes as well as a constantly changing media industry and environment.

Media Psychophysiology: Studying the Brain "On" Media

At its core, media psychophysiology is concerned with development of theories—and formulating testable hypotheses based on those theories—concerning both the effects of media on psychological and behavioral responses and the functional organization of central and peripheral nervous system responses more generally. In that respect, media psychophysiology is much more than simply a collection of measures of physiological responses engaged during media use. Researchers working during the 1970s who produced the first sustained effort to apply physiological measures to the study of media effects made the mistake of viewing physiological measures as a tool for demonstrating stimulus–response linkages between characteristics of media content and physiological changes, rather than as indices of psychological processes instantiated in nervous system activity (Lang, Potter, Bolls, 2009; Potter & Bolls, 2012). This group of researchers—primarily led by Dolf Zillmann—searched for physiological effects of media content, primarily erotica or violence, on a range of peripheral nervous system measures, including blood pressure, skin temperature, and heart rate as a way of observing the effect of media content on emotional arousal (Zillmann & Bryant, 1974; Zillmann, Hoyt, & Day, 1974; Zillmann, Mody, & Cantor, 1974; Cantor, Zillmann, & Einsiedel, 1978; Donnerstein & Barrett, 1978). Their work produced several interesting results concerning the effects of sexual and violent content, but psychophysiological data obtained in their experiments often failed to support predicted effects of media content on physiological responses. Looking back on these studies through the lens of the psychophysiological paradigm, we now know that their conceptualization of arousal as a unitary concept under which physiological systems should be expected to uniformly increase or decrease, along with their view of physiological measures as simply a collection of measures of physiological responses to media content, was misguided. By focusing on trying to record physiological responses as supposed effects of media exposure, researchers overlooked complexities in the mind–body–environment relationship and how physiological activity reflects psychological processes targeted at helping individuals adapt and respond to their environment. In other words, they lacked a strong research paradigm capable of providing a more accurate conceptualization of physiological measures as indicators of mental processes evoked by media use.

Media psychophysiology has emerged as a distinct paradigm for applying psychophysiological measures to the study of brain processes evoked by media use that ultimately produce the effects of media content on behavior. This approach contains a clear set of theoretical assumptions about the brain—including appropriate methods for determining the psychological meaning of brain activity—and media use. These theoretical assumptions provide a foundation for formulating testable hypotheses about how individuals process media content as well as possible effects that might emerge from media exposure. This paradigm also provides methodological guidelines that aid researchers in validly collecting and analyzing the range of psychophysiological data that can be observed during media use. We offer this paradigm and its more recent focus on directly observing brain activity through central nervous system measures—combined with peripheral nervous system measures—as the research approach most likely to produce practically valuable insight into media effects. Thus, we turn now to a brief discussion of theoretical assumptions that make media psychophysiology a distinct research paradigm.

Media psychophysiology shares with the more general psychophysiological paradigm core theoretical assumptions about the nature of the mind/brain and the manner in which physiological activity reflects underlying psychological processes. These assumptions have been discussed in detail elsewhere (Cacioppo, Tassinary, & Berntson, 2007; Potter & Bolls, 2012). Thus, we provide a brief overview of just a few of the more fundamental assumptions here.

The Brain Is Embodied

This assumption provides a starting point for how to conceptualize the brain and the entire range of mental experience. Here, mental experience is conceptualized as embodied in the brain—an organ that is connected to all the other organs through a system of afferent and efferent neurological, chemical, and muscular connections. This assumption is best summed up by the statement, "Cognition depends on the kinds of experiences that come from having a body with particular perceptual and motor capacities that are inseparably linked and that together form the matrix within which reasoning, memory, emotion, language, and all other aspects of life are meshed" (Thelan Schöner, Scheier, & Smith et al., 2001, p. 1).

Cognitive/Emotional Processes Can Be Inferred from Bodily Reactions

This assumption is the crux of the entire psychophysiological approach. The psychophysiological enterprise focuses on establishing relationships between physiological response patterns and psychological constructs (Cacioppo, Tassinary, & Berntson, 2007). Because of the assumption that mental experience is embodied in the brain and the brain is connected to the rest of the body through the nervous system, these response patterns can span multiple physiological systems across the peripheral and central branches of the nervous system. The ultimate goal is to identify valid and reliable physiological indices of psychological constructs involved in information processing (Cacioppo, Tassinary, & Berntson, 2007). A focus on physiological response patterns as indicators of psychological processes engaged when an individual interacts in a complex social environment rather than simply responses to environmental stimuli—such as media content—is what truly separates media psychophysiology as a strong research paradigm from simply a collection of measures of physiological responses.

The Work of the Brain Happens over Time

The assumption that cognitive operations embodied in the brain unfold over time was recognized as a fundamental theoretical principle of the information processing approach that took hold during the cognitive revolution (Lachman, Lachman, & Butterfield, 1979). This assumption is carried over to the psychophysiological approach and provides part of the foundation for mapping physiological response patterns to specific psychological processes as well as the analysis of data obtained from psychophysiological measures. That is, the cognitive and affective states that people experience (e.g., as the result of external and internal stimulus events) lead to changes that occur over the course of milliseconds or seconds, and the impacts of these changes on biological and physiological systems increase and decrease along with the vagaries of cognitive and affective experience (Lang, Potter, & Bolls, 2009). Suffice it to say that temporal characteristics of both psychological processes and psychophysiological measures should guide the valid operational application of specific measures in experiments as well as the interpretation of the observed physiological activity evoked during media use.

Psychophysiological Measures Are Monstrosities

This fact was recognized early on in the development of the psychophysiological approach (Gardiner, Metcalf, & Beebe-Center, 1937/1970). It emphasizes that relationships between physiological response patterns and psychological constructs are correlational, not causal. The correlational nature of psychophysiological measures emerges from homeodynamic relationships between different physiological systems in the human organism as well as between the organism and the myriad of possible influences on physiological activity contained in the environment. Berntson and Cacioppo (2007) proposed homeodynamic regulation as an alternative to homeostasis as a way of describing regulatory mechanisms at work in helping an organism adapt and respond to environmental stimuli. Homeodynamic regulatory processes are dynamic in the sense that they do not reflect simple, rigid feedback mechanisms but are complex, with lags, limits, and feed-forward components whose functioning can vary across time as an organism proceeds through the environment. The implication of this assumption is that researchers must recognize that psychophysiological measures are under the influence of multiple, dynamic inputs whose influence on physiological activity can change

according to characteristics of the environment as well as the individual. Researchers need to exercise a high degree of control over experimental design and procedures to use psychophysiological measures to investigate psychological processes associated with media use and possible media effects.

In addition to sharing the core paradigmatic assumptions contained in the general psychophysiological approach, the media psychophysiology paradigm includes a unique way of conceptualizing media content and use. There have been two broad historical perspectives in media effects research for conceptualizing media use. The hypodermic needle model was one of the earliest theoretical perspectives in media effects research and conceptualized media use as a predominantly passive activity in which exposure to media content in essence injects the effects of media into individuals (Wartella & Reeves, 1985). As researchers discovered that media effects are more complicated and nuanced than that, they moved to a conceptualization of media use as a more active phenomenon in which audience members purposefully select media content based on motivations and gratifications sought from media—an approach that became known as uses and gratifications theory (Rubin, 2009). Neither of these theoretical perspectives on media use can be explicated at a detailed enough level to take into account the nature of foundational neural processes, developed over the course of evolution to aid individuals in successfully adapting to a complex environment, that dynamically unfold across time during media selection and exposure. More recent media psychology research is beginning to identify specific ways that basic motivational processes emerging from neural activity grounded in evolutionarily old brain systems significantly influence not only the way media content is mentally processed but even the specific kinds of media content individuals are drawn to seek out (Potter et al., 2006; Lee & Lang, 2009; Leshner, Bolls, & Wise, 2011; Potter, Lee, & Rubenking, 2011; Wang, Lang, & Busemeyer, 2011). A new theoretical perspective for conceptualizing media content and media use—generally referred to as *motivated mediated message processing*—has emerged from this line of reasoning (Lang & Yegiyan, 2009). Motivated mediated message processing offers an explication of media content and use in a way that is consistent with the psychophysiological approach and provides a foundation for research focused on analyzing media effects as a phenomenon spanning cognitive/emotional, neural, and peripheral physiological levels (Lang, 2009; Potter & Bolls, 2012).

Under the umbrella of the media psychophysiology paradigm, the motivated mediated message processing perspective provides a unique and useful conceptualization of both media content and media use to complement the theoretical assumptions and methodologies associated with the psychophysiological approach. This approach focuses on how media content affects neural responses and the ways in which those neural responses act as biological mechanisms of psychological and behavioral outcomes. Although not formally recognized as a unifying paradigm for all such research, experiments in this area clearly reflect the theoretical assumptions and methodologies identified here as the media psychophysiology paradigm. We hope that, in addition to being a useful review of recent research, this chapter supports more unified theoretical thinking among interdisciplinary researchers. We now turn to reviewing recent media psychophysiology research that is indeed revealing, in new ways, the brain "on" media.

Before doing so, however, we wish to offer two important caveats concerning this chapter. First, although numerous studies using peripheral psychophysiological measures (predominantly heart rate, skin conductance, and facial EMG) have appeared in the media psychophysiology literature since the late 1980s, several thorough reviews of this research have appeared in recent years (Ravaja, 2004; Lang, Potter, & Bolls, 2009; Potter & Bolls, 2012). Thus, the specific focus of this chapter is on reviewing research in which measures of central nervous system activity have dominated, especially electroencephalography (EEG), event-related brain potentials (ERPs), and functional magnetic resonance imaging (fMRI). Second, the current review is limited to media effects research on violence and persuasive messages encompassing public health campaigns and advertising. We do not pretend to cover all media domains in this chapter.

The Psychophysiology of Media Violence
Violence in Media

Although violence in entertainment is as old as civilization itself (think the Roman Coliseum), it was not until the advent of motion pictures and radio in the early 20th century, followed by television by the middle of that century, that the masses were exposed to entertainment media—and hence media violence—on a regular basis. Media violence has been defined as "any overt depiction of a credible threat of physical force or the actual use of such force intended to physically harm an animate being or group of beings" (National Television Violence Study, 1998, p. 41). Violence in the media might not be of great concern were there not so much of it. One of the first motion pictures to see wide distribution, *The Great Train Robbery* (Edison & Porter, 1903), depicted a gang of bandits robbing a passenger train and the posse of concerned citizens dispatched to hunt them down. The film is very short, containing only 14 scenes and lasting only 12 minutes, but involves a striking amount of violence: of the 14 scenes, fully half depict threats of violence or actual physical assaults (e.g., the telegraph operator is bound at gunpoint; several fights occur aboard the moving train; a passenger attempts to make an escape but is instantly shot down). Films such as this one set the stage for violence as a central theme in the movies, a trend still evident today. Increasingly, films rated as appropriate for younger viewers contain graphic depictions of violence. As reported by Nalkur et al. (2010), since the advent of the film ratings system in 1968, "explicit violence in R-rated films increased, while films that would previously have been rated R were increasingly assigned to PG-13" (p. 440).

Television, too, has consistently been a venue for depictions of violence, both dramatized and real. Although often excluded from major content analyses of televised violence, television news programs feature some of the heaviest doses of violence in the media (van der Molen, 2004). For example, local news broadcasts often are found to overemphasize violent crime and sensational presentations of violence (Chavez & Dorfman, 1996; Dorfman et al., 1997; Romer, Jamieson, & Aday, 2003), and violent world events constitute the most frequently covered topics on national network newscasts (Johnson, 1996; Lowry, Nio, & Leitner, 2003). This same trend is reflected in "reality-based" television programs (e.g., *COPS*, *America's Most Wanted*), which give the impression that violence and murder are commonplace. According to one study (Oliver, 1994), although murder accounts for only 0.2% of the crimes reported by the FBI, fully 50% of the crimes shown on programs like these are murders. This overemphasis on televised violence has a major impact on public perceptions of the dangerousness of society, leading people to believe that violent crime rates are much higher than they actually are (see Bushman & Anderson, 2001; Lowry et al., 2003).

The newest forms of media, video games and the Internet, are continuing this long-established trend for violence as a content staple. An overwhelming majority of children age 8 to 18 play video games daily or weekly; approximately 60% of all children are playing a video game at any given time of day or night (Kaiser Family Foundation, 2010). As with other forms of media, many of the most popular video games contain explicitly violent themes. For example, sales data from 2010 and 2011 indicate that half of the 10 best-selling games in each year contained explicitly violent themes.

Scientists have many reasons for being interested in understanding effects of media violence. Perhaps chief among these is that research consistently has shown that exposure to environmental cues associated with violence is a reliable predictor of increased aggression (Bandura, Ross, & Ross, 1961; Berkowitz & LePage, 1967; Berkowitz, 1989; Anderson, Benjamin, & Bartholow, 1998; Bartholow et al., 2005). Thus, it follows that media depictions of violence could facilitate aggressive responses (Carnagey & Anderson, 2003). The next section first considers psychophysiological studies aimed at understanding potential effects of media violence on processes relevant for aggression, and then turns to other recent work investigating media violence effects on cognitive and affective information processing more generally.

Psychophysiological Studies of Media Violence Effects

As noted, early psychophysiological research on media violence was focused on attempting to understand effects of media violence on "arousal" (Zillmann & Bryant, 1974; Zillmann et al., 1974a,b; Cantor et al., 1978; Donnerstein & Barrett, 1978). In large part such studies were designed to test aspects of various arousal theories of aggression, which posit that exposure to "exciting" media content (e.g., violence, sex) increases arousal, and that this arousal takes time to dissipate. If provoked while in such an aroused state, an individual is likely to misattribute the source of the arousal to the provocation, prompting a retaliatory response (Zillmann, 1983). Unfortunately, the results of such studies were rarely straightforward, owing largely to the fact that, as later theorists described in detail (Cacioppo & Tassinary, 1990), arousal is not a single or simple construct, and there is rarely—if ever—a one-to-one relationship between the psychological construct of arousal and physiological responses thought to represent it. Therefore, contemporary research has turned away from this early focus on a potential causal role of media violence on simple arousal, and focuses instead on understanding the ways in which psychophysiological measures can contribute to building and testing broad theories of media violence

effects (Carnagey & Anderson, 2003; Carnagey, Anderson, & Bartholow, 2007).

One such theory that has received considerable attention in the media violence literature is desensitization (see Brockmyer, this volume), an idea that—somewhat ironically, given earlier research on arousal theory—posits a role for *reduced* arousal following media violence exposure as a causal factor in aggression-related responses. Research has shown that exposure to media violence initially produces fear, disgust, and other avoidance-related motivational states (Cantor, 1998). According to desensitization theory, repeated exposure to violence, whether in the media or in life, results in habituation of the initially negative cognitive, emotional, and physiological responses people experience when they see blood and gore (Rule & Ferguson, 1986; Funk et al., 2004), which in theory can produce more calloused attitudes toward violence and, ultimately, increased aggression. Numerous studies have provided evidence for the basic premise that media violence can produce desensitization to violence, in that individuals exposed to violent media content are less physiologically aroused by subsequent depictions of actual violence (Lazarus et al., 1962; Cline, Croft, & Courrier, 1973; Thomas et al., 1977; Thomas, 1982; Linz, Donnerstein, & Adams, 1989; Carnagey, Anderson, & Bushman, 2007), and are less empathic toward the pain and suffering of others (Bushman & Anderson, 2009) than are participants initially exposed to nonviolent media.

However, it was not until relatively recently that researchers directly addressed the question of whether desensitization as a result of media violence exposure could be a pathway to increased aggressiveness. In an initial study, Bartholow, Bushman, and Sestir (2006) recorded ERPs—electrical activity in the brain elicited by stimulus and response events, corresponding to various information-processing operations (Fabiani, Gratton, & Federmeier, 2007)—from a group of participants varying in their history of video game violence exposure (VVE) while they viewed a series of evaluatively neutral (e.g., a towel lying on a table), violent (e.g., a main holding a gun in another man's mouth), and negative but nonviolent (e.g., a rotting dog corpse) images. The amplitude of the P300 component of the ERP elicited by emotionally evocative images has been linked to the extent to which the contents of the images activates relevant underlying motivational propensities (e.g., to approach or avoid) (Nieuwenhuis, Aston-Jones, & Cohen, 2005). Thus, and based on the idea that repeated exposure to violent video games would lead to desensitization to depictions of real violence, Bartholow et al. hypothesized that high-VVE participants would show reduced P300 responses to violent images than would their low-VVE peers. Consistent with this prediction, the P300 response elicited by violent pictures was significantly smaller among high-VVE participants than low-VVE participants, but responses to negative nonviolent images did not differ between the groups (Fig. 27.3). These findings suggest that violence-related images elicit less avoidance/withdrawal motivation among high-VVE individuals, consistent with the tenets of desensitization theory (Bailey, West, & Anderson, 2011).

In the second half of the study, participants completed a competitive game in which they were given the chance to deliver blasts of noxious noise to an ostensible opponent. The intensity of noise blasts set by participants constitutes an often-used and externally valid laboratory measure of aggression (Carlson, Marcus-Newhall, & Miller, 1989; Bushman, 1995; Anderson & Bushman, 1997; Giancola & Chermack, 1998; Anderson, Lindsay, & Bushman, 1999; Bartholow & Anderson, 2002). Bartholow et al. (2006) found that participants high in VVE generally set louder noise blasts for

their ostensible opponents than did low-VVE participants. Moreover, and consistent with the desensitization hypothesis, there was a strong, negative correlation between the levels of noise punishment participants set for their opponents and the size of their brain responses to violent images measured in the first part of the study. That is, participants with smaller P300 responses to violence—a hypothesized neural indication of desensitization—tended to blast their opponents with louder noise during the reaction-time task.

Although Bartholow et al.'s (2006) findings were generally consistent with desensitization theory, that study suffered from a major limitation because it was correlational in nature—participants were preselected on the basis of their self-reported history of video game violence exposure, rather than being randomly assigned to violent or nonviolent game exposure conditions (see also Bailey et al., 2011). Thus, it could be that their media violence history did not cause them to become desensitized, but that individuals with small brain responses to violence (caused by unknown factors) simply tend to play a lot of violent video games. To address this limitation, Engelhardt, Bartholow, Kerr, and Bushman (2011) recruited

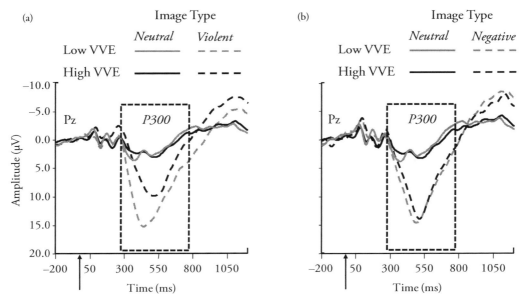

Figure 27.3 A. Related brain potentials waveforms recorded from a midline parietal scalp location (electrode Pz) elicited by images of real violence (*dashed lines*) and evaluatively neutral images (*solid lines*) among participants high and low in previous video game violence exposure (VVE). The vertical arrow at time zero on the time line indicates picture onset. The P300 is the large, positive dip in the waveform peaking around 450 ms following picture onset. Low-VVE participants showed a larger P300 response to violent images than did high-VVE participants. **B.** Related brain potentials waveforms recorded from electrode Pz by images depicting very negative (but not violent) scenes. VVE level had no effect on the amplitude of the P300 elicited by negative, nonviolent images.

Adapted from Bartholow, B. D., Bushman, B. J., & Sestir, M. A. (2006). Chronic violent video game exposure and desensitization: Behavioral and event-related brain potential data. *Journal of Experimental Social Psychology, 42,* 532–539.

male and female participants varying in VVE and randomly assigned them to play either a violent or nonviolent video game in the lab for 25 minutes before completing the picture-viewing and aggression tasks used in Bartholow et al. (2006). Figure 27.4 shows the ERP data from that study. Inspection of Figure 27.4 indicates that, consistent with what Bartholow et al. (2006) found, high-VVE individuals showed smaller P300 responses to violence compared with their low-VVE peers. However, of greater interest is that, among low-VVE participants, those who had just played a violent video game in the lab showed smaller P300 responses to violence than did their counterparts who had just played a nonviolent game. This finding indicates that a brief exposure to video game violence caused acute desensitization to violence, which cannot be attributed to preexisting differences in neural responses. Also of interest is the finding that high-VVE participants showed reduced P300 amplitude to violence regardless of the game played in the lab, suggesting that these individuals had already been desensitized and another brief exposure to video game violence did not further desensitize them (i.e., a floor effect). Finally, Engelhardt et al. found that among those low in VVE, the size of the P300 elicited by violent pictures significantly mediated the effect of the video game exposure

manipulation (violent or nonviolent) on aggressive behavior during the reaction-time task (intensity and duration of noise blasts). These data are the first to show that acute desensitization to violence can be a mechanism through which aggression can increase following exposure to video game violence.

A complimentary approach used in recent research aimed at understanding how media violence exposure could affect aggression has been to investigate the neural structures and circuits that are engaged when playing violent compared to nonviolent video games. One of the first such studies (of which we are aware) was conducted by Weber, Ritterfeld, and Mathiak (2006), who used fMRI to investigate neural structures that increase and decrease in activation during violent video game play. These authors recorded fMRI while participants played a violent video game, and afterward coded each game scene in terms of its content. Of interest, Weber et al. found a negative linear relationship between the potential for violence in a scene and the blood oxygen level dependent (BOLD) signal change in both the rostral anterior cingulate cortex (rACC) and the amygdala, structures implicated in affect/emotion-related processing. Similarly, Kelly, Grinband, and Hirsch (2007) found that repeated exposure to violent movie clips, but not to equally arousing nonviolent movie clips

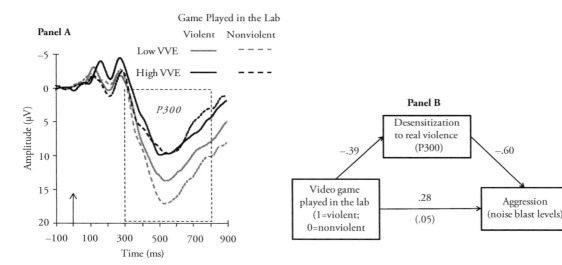

Figure 27.4 A. Related brain potentials waveforms recorded from a midline parietal scalp location (electrode Pz) elicited by images of real violence as a function of type of video game played in the lab and previous video game violence exposure. The vertical arrow at time zero on the time line indicates picture onset. The P300 is the large, positive dip in the waveform peaking around 500 ms following picture onset. **B.** Schematic showing the mediating effect of desensitization to real-life violence (P300) on the increase in aggression that occurs after playing a violent relative to a nonviolent video game. The standardized coefficient in parentheses is the effect of game condition on aggression when P300 amplitudes are included in the regression model. The bootstrapping method (Shrout & Bolger, 2002) indicated a significant indirect effect, i.e., the effect of game condition on aggression via P300 amplitude.

Adapted from Engelhardt, C. R., Bartholow, B. D., Kerr, G. T. & Bushman, B. J. (2011). This is your brain on violent video games: Neural desensitization to violence predicts increased aggression following violent video game exposure. *Journal of Experimental Social Psychology, 47*, 1033–1036.

(e.g., fearful scenes), led to diminished response in a network of neural areas, such as right-lateral orbito-frontal cortex and amygdala, which has been associated with decreased control over reactive aggression (Goyer et al., 1994; Raine et al., 1998). Kelly et al. also reported a significant association between the magnitude of this diminished neural response to violence and scores on a self-reported reactive aggression scale (Bartholow et al., 2006; Engelhardt et al., 2011). Although far from definitive, these findings suggest that violent media exposure could produce acute (or chronic) desensitization to violence by reducing the extent to which the emotional impact of violence is elaborated in the brain, which could weaken control over impulsive aggressive responses.

In addition to contributing to theories underlying effects of media violence exposure on aggressive behavior, researchers have used the media psychophysiology approach to better understand how exposure to media violence might influence a broad array of cognitive and affective processes. One such approach reflects what is known as skills transfer. The possibility that skills acquired during training in computer-based tasks or games could transfer to untrained behaviors has intrigued researchers for years (Fabiani et al., 1989; Frederickson & White, 1989; Gopher, Weil, & Bareket, 1994). Recently, Green et al. have reported findings suggesting that long-term experience with so-called "action" video games, most of which contain violent themes, might lead to enhancement in certain cognitive skills, particularly those related to the scope of attention (Green & Bavelier, 2003, 2006, 2007; Dye, Green, & Bavelier, 2009a,b), and that some such effects can occur after relatively short-term training (e.g., 30 hours over the course of 1 month) (Green & Bavelier, 2007). For example, Green and Bavelier (2003) reported that, in comparison to nongamers, self-reported action video game players showed a broader scope of visual selective attention on a range of tasks (see also Dye et al., 2009b).

Although such effects have been lauded as demonstrating the benefits of extended exposure to violent video games (as a counterpoint to the oft-cited harmful effects of such exposure) (Anderson et al., 2010), an expanded scope of visual attention can be detrimental in some contexts. For example, if the goal of a particular task involves controlling attention so as to avoid the influence of peripheral distracters, then an expanded scope of visual attention can actually impede task performance. For example, in the flanker task (Eriksen & Eriksen, 1974; Eriksen & Schultz, 1979), widely used to assess attention and executive control, participants' goal is to categorize a centrally presented target stimulus flanked by to-be-ignored distracter stimuli (i.e., the flankers). The measure of primary interest is generally the flanker compatibility effect in reaction time, representing the extent to which participants can ignore the flankers and focus their attention on the target. The results of a number of previous studies (Green & Bavelier, 2003; Dye et al., 2009b) show that action game players experience larger flanker compatibility effects than do nongamers, indicating that gamers have greater difficulty controlling attention in the presence of visual distracters (but see Green & Bavelier, 2007, for an alternative interpretation). Such a result is unsurprising given the demands of many action/violent games to direct attention broadly, but could indicate difficulties in the development and maintenance of self-regulatory cognitive control abilities, a core feature of which is the control of attention (Friedman & Miyake, 2004; Miyake & Friedman, 2012).

Indeed, West et al. have conducted a series of studies showing that extended exposure to violent video games is associated with some specific deficits in cognitive control processes relying on control of attention. For example, Bailey, West, and Anderson (2010) used behavioral and ERP measures to investigate the influence of violent game exposure on proactive and reactive cognitive control. As described by those authors (and others; see Braver, Gray, & Burgess, 2007), "proactive control represents a future-oriented form of control that serves to optimize task preparation; reactive control represents a just-in-time form of control that serves to resolve conflict within a trial" (Bailey et al., 2010, p. 1005). Bailey et al. found that both behavioral and neural indices of proactive control were attenuated in participants with considerable violent game experience relative to those with little such experience. Specifically, the amplitude of frontal negativities in the ERP measured on high-conflict trials (i.e., those requiring cognitive control) was smaller among high-VVE compared with low-VVE participants, complimenting a reduced ability among high-VVE participants to adapt to conflict on a trial-to-trial basis as revealed in patterns of behavioral responses. In contrast, measures of reactive control did not differ for high- and low-VVE participants. Taken together, these findings suggest that video game experience may selectively interfere with proactive cognitive control processes that help to maintain goal-directed, self-regulatory cognition and action.

Another approach to studying video game effects on cognition involves measuring cognitive performance and its neural correlates, immediately following an acute exposure to one type of game or another. For example, Wang et al. (2009) had groups of adolescents (*n* = 22 each) play a violent (first-person shooter) or nonviolent (car racing) video game for 30 minutes before completing a counting Stroop and an emotional Stroop task, during which their brain activity was assessed using fMRI. In contrast with the nonviolent game group, participants who had played the violent game showed less activation in areas of dorsolateral prefrontal cortex (DLPFC), areas typically associated with cognitive control during performance of cognitively demanding tasks such as the Stroop (MacDonald et al., 2000; Kerns et al., 2004). Moreover, participants exposed to the violent game showed weaker functional coupling between left DLPFC and dorsal ACC, also suggesting less efficient engagement of a network of areas important for cognitive control (Botvinick et al., 2001; Kerns et al., 2004).

Other, suggestive evidence of cognitive control difficulties following acute violent game exposure has come from recent studies by Engelhardt and Bartholow (2011, 2012). For example, Engelhardt and Bartholow (2011) had participants play a violent or nonviolent video game (or no game) before completing a flanker task. Results indicated that participants who had played a violent game for 30 minutes made more errors identifying targets on incompatible flanker trials (i.e., those requiring attention control) than did participants who hadn't played a video game before the flanker task. In contrast, accuracy was not significantly affected by exposure to a nonviolent game. In a follow-up experiment, Engelhardt and Bartholow (2012) again randomly assigned participants to play either a violent or nonviolent video game, after which participants completed a different cognitive control task, the spatial Stroop task (Lu & Proctor, 1995), which requires participants to respond to targets on the basis of their physical orientation while ignoring their spatial location. Consistent with Bailey et al.'s (2010) findings among high- relative to low-VVE participants, Engelhardt and Bartholow (2012) found that the amplitude of the medial frontal negativity (i.e., the N2 component) in the ERP elicited on high-conflict trials was attenuated following violent relative to nonviolent game exposure. Interestingly, trait physical aggressiveness (Buss & Perry, 1992) differentially moderated the N2 and frontal slow wave components following violent and nonviolent game play. Specifically, whereas N2 amplitude increased (i.e., increased conflict) as a function of increasing levels of trait aggression following violent game play, N2 amplitude and trait aggression were uncorrelated following nonviolent game play. Conversely, frontal slow wave amplitude (implementation of proactive control) increased along with increasing levels of trait aggression following nonviolent game play, but was unaffected by trait aggression following violent game play. Although very preliminary, this pattern of results suggests that interaction with violent and nonviolent media differentially affects reactive and proactive cognitive control functions for individuals high versus low in trait aggressiveness. More research is needed to determine what, if any, implications such findings have for understanding the influence of video game violence on aggression (see also Bailey et al., 2010).

Summary

Although the literature on the psychophysiology of media violence remains quite small, recent work paints something of a mixed picture in terms of potentially beneficial and harmful effects of exposure. Some studies indicate that repeatedly playing violent "action" video games can lead to increases in the scope of visual attention (Green & Bavelier, 2003, 2007; Dye et al., 2009a) and decreases in overall response speed (Dye et al., 2009b). However, such findings should be interpreted with caution, especially given evidence that these effects can actually be detrimental to performance in contexts in which controlling and focusing attention are important (Dye et al., 2009b; Wang et al., 2009; Bailey et al., 2010; Engelhardt & Bartholow, 2011, 2012). Moreover, recent ERP and fMRI evidence suggests that both acute and repeated exposure to violent video games is associated with decreases in activation of neural circuits underlying some forms of cognitive control (Wang et al., 2009; Bailey et al., 2010; Engelhardt & Bartholow, 2012). Future work should be directed at not only continuing to document such effects and their limitations, but to better understand the mechanisms by which playing violent video games influences neurocognitive processes underlying cognitive control, as well as the implications of such effects for regulating social behaviors, such as aggression.

The Psychophysiology of Persuasion

Some of the earliest research on media effects investigated persuasive effects of media content. This area of research has grown significantly since the early work of Hovland (1951) and Lasswell

(1927), coinciding with the exponential growth of media content aimed at persuading target audiences. Leading advertisers, such as AT&T and American Express, now spend more than $1 billion annually on this practice (see www.adage.com/datacenter/). At an estimated $2.6 billion, the 2012 election in the United States is predicted to shatter previous records for spending on political advertising (see www.adage.com). Arguably, advertising is the most pervasive form of media content, as savvy advertisers have moved beyond traditional ad placements (e.g., commercial breaks in television and radio programming) to placing their messages into entertainment content and social media channels, as well as attempting to push messages virally over the Internet (Sissors & Baron, 2010). Current advertising practice views any screen, mobile or traditional, as a potentially valuable communication channel through which persuasive media content can be delivered.

The effects of persuasive media content have implications not only for every business engaged in marketing products through advertising, but also for politicians seeking personal advancement and non-profit organizations dedicated to achieving social change. This clearly means that research on the effects of persuasive messages can have important implications for economic activity, public health, and the shape of the democratic political process. Research in this area has been applied to both promoting the interests of organizations engaged in persuasive media campaigns as well as at making individuals more resistant to and critical of persuasive media messages (Perloff, 2008).

Before reviewing some of the recent experiments investigating how the brain processes persuasive media content, it is important to note an interesting recent development that makes this a unique area of media effects research. Although research on the effects of other forms of media content primarily has been confined to the academic community, both academics and media industry professionals are extensively engaged in conducting research on the effects of persuasive media content. Proprietary research firms as well as research departments housed in advertising agencies began to expand over the last half of the 20th century and continue to conduct extensive research directed at making clients' advertisements more persuasive. One of the first applications of psychophysiological measures in the study of persuasive media content was conducted by Herbert Krugman, director of public opinion research at General Electric. Krugman used EEG in an attempt to identify brain activity reflective of increased attention paid to advertisements (Krugman, 1971). More recently, one proprietary research company, Sands Research (www.sandsresearch.com), has begun an annual practice of publicizing their research on Super Bowl advertisements in which they use EEG and other psychophysiological and self-report measures to identify the most effective Super Bowl advertisement of the year. Although psychophysiological measures have historically been part of the toolbox that advertising industry researchers use in conducting their work, a renewed interest in EEG and the more recent application fMRI in advertising research has led to the development of a specialized area termed neuromarketing (Du Plessis, 2011). Several published articles have critiqued the value, validity, and ethical implications of neuromarketing research (Kenning, 2008; Marci, 2008; Nairn & Fine, 2008). Further, because of the fact that the majority of neuromarketing research is proprietary and therefore not subject to a peer review process (or even accessible to anyone except paying clients), we cannot say whether or not researchers conducting this work are following the media psychophysiology research paradigm presented in this chapter. This aside, neuromarketing represents an interesting, explicit attempt to conduct research on brain mechanisms underlying the effects of persuasive media content. Readers interested in learning more about neuromarketing can find numerous relevant advertising industry web sites and blogs, neuromarketing company web pages, and recent books discussing the implications of neuroscience for advertising, such as *The Branded Mind* (Du Plessis, 2011). We now turn to a brief review of the peer reviewed published research adopting a psychophysiological approach to studying how the brain processes persuasive media content.

Research using psychophysiological measures to study how the brain processes persuasive media content has a history that mirrors the more general history of psychophysiology and media effects research. A number of early experiments produced promising results in terms of the ability to index mental processes that might underlie persuasion. For instance, Krugman's (1971) work identified specific patterns in the EEG signal recorded from frontal cortex that were significantly associated with attending to and remembering commercials. Other researchers used skin conductance recorded during exposure to advertisements in an attempt to predict product purchase intentions (Hopkins & Fletcher, 1994). These early efforts were primarily directed at attempting to establish psychophysiological measures as effective tools for applied advertising copy testing, in the tradition of the stimulus–response paradigm referred to earlier in this chapter, rather than generating deep insight into brain processes engaged during exposure to persuasive media messages. The shift toward research with the latter goal occurred in the 1980s, with researchers who adopted the stronger psychophysiological theoretical approach previously reviewed.

A pioneering experiment in that vein was conducted by Reeves et al. (1985), who used EEG to study the interaction between features of television advertisements and attention. In one experiment, they identified alpha blocking, a decrease in activity in the alpha frequency band of the EEG signal, recorded from frontal cortical regions, as a physiological indicator of increases in orienting attention to scene changes occurring in a television advertisement. This experiment involved exposing participants to nine advertisements placed in televised sitcoms that were spread across three commercial breaks. The EEG signal was averaged over each half-second over the course of each advertisement. This experiment was one of the first in media psychophysiology to use such a fine-grained, intra-stimulus data analysis, matching each half-second of recorded data to specific features occurring within the advertisements. This analysis yielded the first significant theoretical insight into the degree to which attention quickly reacts to rapidly occurring and changing content within television advertisements. Thus, early on, researchers working under a media psychophysiology paradigm realized the value of using psychophysiological measures to not only index brain processes unfolding over the entire course of a segment of media content, but also to examine momentary yet potentially critical processes evoked at specific time points within a message. Subsequent work using measures of cardiac activity replicated the result that scene changes within television advertisements automatically orient attention toward the advertisement (Lang, 1990). Taken together, these two early experiments offer insight into both central and peripheral nervous system activity underlying processes related to attention during exposure to advertisements.

A large number of psychophysiological studies have used peripheral nervous system measures to index brain processes theorized to unfold during exposure to persuasive media content. Specifically, heart rate has been used primarily as an indicator of cognitive resources allocated to encoding information from the message, skin conductance has been used to index arousal, facial EMG has been used to index the valence of emotional responses, and more recently, the startle eye blink response has been used to index the extent to which media content is perceived to be aversive (Potter & Bolls, 2012). Experiments in this area have primarily focused on investigating how advertising content affects motivational and emotional responses. For instance, in a recent experiment Leshner et al. exposed participants to antitobacco advertisements varying in the extent to which they featured disgust-eliciting visual images (Leshner, Bolls, & Wise, 2011). This study revealed specific patterns of cardiac acceleration and an associated decrease in corrugator facial muscle activity (reflecting expression of negative affect), which researchers interpreted as reflecting defensive withdrawal of attention from the message, gradually resulting in a decrease in the intensity of negative emotional responding. In a recent study of political advertising (Bradley, Angelini, & Lee, 2007), the startle eye blink response was recorded along with skin conductance during exposure to negative and positive political advertisements. The results of this experiment revealed that while negatively toned ads evoke intense levels of aversive motivational responses, they are better remembered than positive ads. Potter et al. (2006) recorded corrugator EMG activity as an indicator of negative emotional responding during exposure to advertisements embedded in different types of entertainment programs. Their findings revealed that the content in which commercials are embedded significantly impacts the intensity of emotional responding they elicit.

Although experiments conducted with peripheral measures clearly do not shed light on the anatomical makeup and specific functioning of neural networks involved in how the brain processes persuasive media content, this brief review clearly indicates that such studies have produced valuable insight into general cognitive and emotional processes embodied in the brain that unfold across time while individuals are exposed to persuasive content. Peripheral nervous system measures have historically been the most accessible for researchers wishing to conduct research on the psychophysiology of persuasive media content, and therefore such studies represent the majority of efforts to produce knowledge of persuasive media effects. This historical trend is changing, however, as more researchers embrace a neuroscience perspective under the media psychophysiology paradigm and central nervous system measures that directly index brain processes become more accessible to media effects researchers.

A majority of research on persuasive media content conducted under this newer neuroscience perspective has relied on EEG to directly index brain activity theorized to be important to understanding how individuals process persuasive media messages. A strong argument for the validity of the EEG in advertising research, particularly when used in combination with other psychophysiological measures, was recently made by Ohme Matukin, and Pacula-Lesniak (2011). Their work integrating EEG and eye tracking provided evidence concerning the ability to detect frontal neural activity reflecting positive and negative emotional responding that is sensitive to the focus of visual attention directed to specific elements of interactive advertisements. This line of research is typical of one area of focus in neuroscience-based research on persuasive media content, in that the primary objective is to illustrate that central nervous system measures like EEG are sensitive to very specific variations in advertisement content. Along this line, Ohme et al. provided further evidence of the effectiveness of EEG in this context by applying it to identifying which of three Sony television ads were most effective at eliciting activity in frontal cortex that could be tied to favorable reactions to ads (Ohme et al., 2010). This study relied on a theoretical model positing that left hemisphere dominance reflects brain processes underlying a favorable shift in attitudes toward an advertised brand (Silberstein & Nield, 2008), a specific application of a more general theory proposing that left-frontal EEG asymmetry reflects favorable, approach-motivated responses to stimuli (Harmon-Jones, 2003; Harmon-Jones & Harmon-Jones, 2011). Advertising researchers have also turned to ERP components of the EEG signal in developing insight into brain activity underlying effective advertising. The P3a event-related potential was recently used to indicate the degree to which brand logos presented in interactive advertising evoke an automatic increase in attention (Treleaven-Hassard et al., 2010). Research designed to identify specific patterns of brain activity underlying mental processes leading to persuasion during advertising exposure is clearly going to be a growing part of advertising research (Perrachione & Perrachione, 2008).

One of the more theoretically interesting lines of research in the psychophysiology of persuasion focuses on discovering the neural networks that are active during exposure to media content. For instance, Morris et al. (2009) used fMRI to observe activity in emotional networks in the brain during exposure to television advertisements. These authors found that variation in bilateral activation in the inferior frontal gyri and middle temporal gyri represented the valence dimension (pleasantness–unpleasantness) of emotional experience, while activity in the right superior temporal gyrus and right middle frontal gyrus distinguished feelings associated with the arousal or intensity of emotional experience elicited by advertisements. Other experimental work has focused on investigating brain activity reflective of increasing or decreasing support for a political candidate. For example, Kato et al. (2009) used fMRI to scan brain regions during exposure to political advertising and then correlated the observed hemodynamic activity with self-reported increase or decrease in support for the political candidate portrayed. The results indicated that increased activation in the medial prefrontal cortex correlated with increased support for a candidate while increased activation in the dorsolateral prefrontal cortex correlated with decreased support. In an interesting cross-cultural experiment, Faulk et al. (2009) explored neural mechanisms underlying the subjective experience of being persuaded. Their experiment included both an American and a Korean sample exposed to both text- and video-based advertisements. They identified a consistent neural network across cultures and stimuli in which increased activity in the dorsal medial prefrontal cortex, posterior superior temporal sulcus, temporal pole, and ventral lateral prefrontal cortex correlated with self-reports of feeling persuaded.

Although intriguing, such work is best considered preliminary to more theoretically informed investigations of the cognitive neuroscience of persuasive media, given that identifying neural regions that appear active during certain kinds of persuasive appeals and (in some cases) how this activity correlates with self-reported phenomenological experience does not necessarily translate into discovery of the neural basis of persuasion or advertising effectiveness. For example, what does it mean, in terms of understanding the psychological phenomenon of persuasion, that activity in dorsomedial prefrontal cortex, post superior temporal sulcus, temporal pole, and ventrolateral prefrontal cortex correlates with self-reported persuasion? Still, such work suggests avenues for future research in which the specific features of media appeals that best lead to attitude change can be linked to specific neural structures underlying basic neurocognitive and affective processes, which in turn can be linked with behavior.

There is a small but growing body of research utilizing EEG and fMRI to specifically explore brain activity evoked by specific features of persuasive media content. One general feature of advertising that has been investigated is whether the advertisement primarily uses a logical or emotional appeal. For example, Cook et al. (2011) recorded EEG while participants were exposed to print advertisements that varied according to using a logical or emotion-based strategy to persuade. Distinct patterns of brain activity were found for these two different kinds of advertisements, with ads presenting a logical argument evoking greater activity in orbitofrontal, anterior cingulate, and hippocampal regions compared with ads focusing on emotion. Brain activity evoked specifically in response to the presence of experts in advertisements also has been investigated. Klucharev, Smidts, and Fernandez (2008) found that effects of celebrities in ads appear to influence memory through variation in activity in the medial temporal lobe. In an experiment investigating antidrug abuse public health messages, Langleben et al. (2009) used fMRI to scan participants' brain activity during exposure to televised antidrug messages varying in message sensation value. Whereas messages coded as high on sensation value evoked greater activation primarily in the occipital cortex, messages coded as low in sensation value evoked greater prefrontal and temporal activation, a pattern also associated with messages being better recognized. This pattern of findings suggests that prefrontal and temporal activation underlies increased message recognition, and that low sensation value messages may be more effective than high sensation value messages.

Summary

Research conducted under the psychophysiological paradigm has provided tremendous insight into brain mechanisms underlying the processing of persuasive media content, in part because brain networks associated with very important subprocesses involved in persuasion have been identified. Consideration of the studies reviewed above suggests several conclusions. First, increased left frontal cortical activity is particularly involved in attitude change during exposure to persuasive messages, a finding consistent with theory linking relative left-frontal cortical activation to approach motivation (Harmon-Jones, 2003; Harmon-Jones & Harmon-Jones, 2011). Second, brain areas like the hippocampus and temporal lobes that are generally viewed to be part of the brain's memory network also are at work in forming memory representations of advertisements. Third, the available evidence suggests that processing persuasive media content involves extensive brain networks that underlie cognitive and emotional responses. This is not surprising given the complexity of media content in general and advertisements in particular. That being said, it does appear particularly promising that very specific features of advertisements evoke distinguishable patterns of brain activity (Klucharev et al., 2008; Langleben et al. 2009; Cook et al., 2011). Future research in this area is bound to provide valuable insight into the psychophysiology of persuasion as well as implications for advertising in society. The advertising industry is jumping at neuroscience as a way to probe inside the mind of the consumer, with the ultimate goal of increasing industry profits. A more socially sustainable outcome of such work could be advancing research that examines how public health messages intended to persuade people to make healthier decisions are processed, as well as studies targeted toward understanding brain activity underlying potentially harmful effects of advertising.

Conclusions and Future Directions

Relative to its predecessors, the field of media psychophysiology is still very young. Still, a few tentative conclusions can be drawn on the basis of extant evidence. First, augmenting traditional behavioral and self-report measures with measures of neural responses to media holds significant promise to advance understanding of how people perceive and are influenced by media. However, researchers need to beware of the potential pitfalls of this exciting new approach, such as the use of psychophysiological measures (especially neural measures) as an end unto themselves. For example, simply demonstrating that exposure to a certain category of media content produces activation in a given collection of neural structures provides very little in the way of advancing understanding of media effects or how media affects behavioral outcomes that we ultimately wish to explain. After all, we as psychological and media scientists have known for a long time that cognition, emotion, and behavior all stem from the brain. At a very basic level, psychophysiological measures suffer from the same limitations as any other measures in terms of requiring validation as indices of particular psychological processes of interest. Thus, researchers interested in using a media psychophysiological approach need to use their extant knowledge of experimental design and behavioral science to ground their investigations. As Cacioppo et al. aptly summarized the issue some years ago, "just because you're imaging the brain doesn't mean you can stop using your head" (Cacioppo et al., 2003, p. 650).

Second, just as Lewin (1935) advised decades ago when attempting to account for behavior, it is becoming increasingly clear that researchers need to focus on both elements of the classic Person × Situation formula when attempting to understand media effects. That is, although some broad generalities certainly exist, not all individuals will process or respond to media content in the same ways. Rather than treating this variability simply as noise in the data, researchers should endeavor to identify stable individual difference factors that can reliably predict how various media will differentially affect neurophysiological and behavioral outcomes.

The future of media psychophysiology is intimately bound up with the ever-changing landscape of media vehicles and trends in media usage. Given the increasing influence of social media (e.g., Facebook, Twitter) on the lives of many people, media psychophysiology scholars will need to devote more attention to studying these forms of media and how they might differ from more traditional forms. Similarly, with the explosion in the use of small, portable media vehicles (e.g., smart phones), media can now be literally anywhere and everywhere a person finds themselves. This near-constant exposure to media has important and as-yet ill-understood implications for a vast array of social phenomena, including not only persuasion but basic dynamics of interpersonal interaction and cognition. Finally, the field will also change according to trends in psychophysiological measurement and meaning. What should never change, however, is the understanding that a solid scientific foundation, based in conceptual and theoretical models that are just as sophisticated and cutting-edge as the technologies used to study them, is required to adequately investigate the complex brain–behavior relationships that media psychophysiologists seek to understand.

Acknowledgments

Preparation of this chapter was supported by grant P60 AA011998 from the National Institute on Alcohol Abuse and Alcoholism and grant BCS 0847872 from the National Science Foundation, and by a Reynolds Journalism Institute Fellowship.

Direct correspondence to Bruce D. Bartholow, Department of Psychological Sciences, 210 McAlester Hall, University of Missouri, Columbia, MO 65211. E-mail: BartholowB@missouri.edu.

References

Anderson, C. A., Benjamin, A. J. Jr., & Bartholow, B. D. (1998). Does the gun pull the trigger? Automatic priming effects of weapon pictures and weapon names. *Psychological Science, 9*, 308–314.

Anderson, C. A., & Bushman, B. J. (1997). External validity of "trivial" experiments: The case of laboratory aggression. *Review of General Psychology, 1*, 19–41.

Anderson, C. A., Lindsay, J. J., & Bushman, B. J. (1999). Research in the psychological laboratory: truth or triviality? *Current Directions in Psychological Science, 8*, 3–9.

Anderson, C. A., Shibuya, A., Ihori, N., Swing, E. L., Bushman, B.J., Sakamoto, A., Rothstein, H.R., & Saleem, M. (2010). Violent video game effects on aggression, empathy, and prosocial behavior in Eastern and Western countries. *Psychological Bulletin, 136*, 151–173.

Anderson, D. R., Bryant, J., Murray, J. P., Rich, M., Rivkin, M. J., & Zillmann, D. (2006). Brain imaging-an introduction to a new approach to studying media processes and effects. *Media Psychology, 8*, 1–6.

Anderson, D. R., & Burns, J. (1991). Paying attention to television. In Bryant, J., & Zillmann, D. (Eds.), *Responding to the Screen: Reception and Reaction Processes*. Hillsdale, NJ: Lawrence Erlbaum Associates, pp. 3–26.

Andreassi, J. L. (2007). *Psychophysiology: Human Behavior & Physiological Response*, 5th ed. Hillsdale, NJ: Lawrence Erlbaum Associates.

Bailey, K., West, R., & Anderson, C. A. (2010). A negative association between video game experience and proactive cognitive control. *Psychophysiology, 47*, 34–42.

Bailey, K. , West, R., & Anderson, C. A. (2011). The association between chronic exposure to video game violence and affective picture processing: An ERP study. *Cognitive, Affective, & Behavioral Neuroscience, 11*, 259–276.

Bandura, A., Ross, D., & Ross, S. A. (1961). Transmission of aggression through imitation of aggressive models. *Journal of Abnormal and Social Psychology, 63*, 575–582.

Bandura, A., Ross, D., & Ross, S. A. (1963). Imitation of film-mediated aggressive models. *The Journal of Abnormal and Social Psychology, 66*, 3–11.

Bartholow, B. D., & Anderson, C. A. (2002). Examining the effects of violent video games on aggressive behavior: potential sex differences. *Journal of Experimental Social Psychology, 38*, 283–290.

Bartholow, B. D., Anderson, C. A., Carnagey, N. L., & Benjamin, A. J. Jr. (2005). Interactive effects of life experience and situational cues on aggression: The weapons priming effect in hunters and nonhunters. *Journal of Experimental Social Psychology, 41*, 48–60.

Bartholow, B. D., Bushman, B. J., & Sestir, M. A. (2006). Chronic violent video game exposure and desensitization: Behavioral and event-related brain potential data. *Journal of Experimental Social Psychology, 42*, 532–539.

Basil, M. D. (1994). Secondary reaction-time measures. In Lang, A. (Ed.), *Measuring psychological responses to media*. Hillsdale, NJ: Lawrence Erlbaum Associates, pp. 85–98.

Berkowitz, L. (1989). The frustration-aggression hypothesis: Examination and reformulation. *Psychological Bulletin, 106*, 59–73.

Berkowitz, L., & LePage, A. (1967). Weapons as aggression-eliciting stimuli. *Journal of Personality and Social Psychology, 7*, 202–207.

Berntson, G. G., & Cacioppo, J. T. (2007). Integrative physiology: Homeostasis, allostasis, and the orchestration of systemic physiology. In Cacioppo, J. T., Tassinary, L. G., &

Berntson, G. G. (Eds.), *Handbook of Psychophysiology*, 3rd ed. New York: Cambridge University Press, pp. 433–452.

Bolls, P. D., Wise, K., & Bradley, S. D. (2012). Embodied motivated cognition: A theoretical framework for studying dynamic mental processes underlying advertising exposure. In Rodgers, S., & Thorson, E. (Eds.), *Advertising Theory*. New York: Routledge, pp. 105–119.

Botvinick, M. M., Braver, T. S., Carter, C. S., Barch, D. M., & Cohen, J. D. (2001). Conflict monitoring and cognitive control. *Psychological Review*, 108, 624–652.

Bradley, S. D., Angelini, J. R., & Lee, S. (2007). Psychophysiological and memory effects of negative political ads. *Journal of Advertising*, 36, 115–127.

Braver, T. S., Gray, J. R., Burgess, G. C. (2007). Explaining the many varieties of working memory variation: Dual mechanisms of cognitive control. In Conway, A., Jarrold, C., Kane, M., Miyake, A., & Towse, J. (Eds.), *Variation in Working Memory*. Oxford, UK: Oxford University Press, pp. 76–106.

Bryant, J., & Thompson, S. (2002). *Fundamentals of Media Effects*, 1st ed. New York: McGraw-Hill.

Bushman, B. J. (1995). Moderating role of trait aggressiveness in the effects of violent media on aggression. *Journal of Personality and Social Psychology*, 69, 950–960.

Bushman, B. J., & Anderson, C. A. (2001). Media violence and the American public: Scientific facts versus media misinformation. *American Psychologist*, 56, 477–489.

Bushman, B. J., & Anderson, C. A. (2009). Comfortably numb: Desensitizing effects of violent media on helping others. *Psychological Science*, 20, 273–277.

Buss, A. H., & Perry, M. P. (1992). The aggression questionnaire. *Journal of Personality and Social Psychology*, 63, 452–459.

Bureau of Labor Statistics (2011). *American time use survey summary*. Retrieved from the Bureau of Labor Statistics website: http://www.bls.gov/news.release/atus.t11.htm

Cacioppo, J. T., Berntson, G. G., Lorig, T. S., Norris, C. J., Rickett, E., & Nusbaum, H. (2003). Just because you're imaging the brain doesn't mean you can stop using your head: A primer and set of first principles. *Journal of Personality and Social Psychology*, 85, 650–661.

Cacioppo, J. T., Tassinary, L. G., & Berntson, G. G. (2007). Psychophysiological science: Interdisciplinary approaches to classic questions about the mind. In Cacioppo, J. T., Tassinary, L. G., & Berntson, G. G. (Eds.), *Handbook of Psychophysiology*, 3rd ed. New York: Cambridge University Press, pp. 1–18.

Cantor, J. (1998). *"Mommy, I'm Scared:" How TV and Movies Frighten Children and What We Can Do to Protect Them*. San Diego: Harvest/Harcourt.

Cantor, J. R., Zillmann, D., & Einsiedel, E. F. (1978). Female responses to provocation after exposure to aggressive Andy Roddick films. *Communication Research*, 5, 395–412.

Carnagey, N.L., & Anderson, C.A. (2003). Theory in the study of media violence: The General Aggression Model. In Gentile, D. (Ed.), *Media Violence and Children*. Westport, CT: Praeger, pp. 87–106.

Carnagey, N. L., Anderson, C. A., & Bartholow, B. D. (2007). Media violence and social neuroscience: New questions, new opportunities. *Current Directions in Psychological Science, 16*, 178–182.

Carnagey, N. L., Anderson, C.A., & Bushman, B. J. (2007). The effect of video game violence on physiological desensitization to real-life violence. *Journal of Experimental Social Psychology*, 43, 489–496.

Chavez, V., & Dorfman, L. (1996). Spanish language television news portrayals of youth and violence in California. *International Quarterly of Community Health Education, 16*, 121–138.

Cline, V. B., Croft, R. G., & Courrier, S. (1973). Desensitization of children to television violence. *Journal of Personality and Social Psychology*, 27, 360–365.

Cook, I. A., Warren, C., Pajot, S. K., Schairer, D., & Leuchter, A. F. (2011). Regional brain activation with advertising images. *Journal of Neuroscience, Psychology, and Economics, 4*, 147–160.

Donnerstein, E., & Barrett, G. (1978). Effects of erotic stimuli on male aggression toward females. *Journal of Personality and Social Psychology*, 36, 180–188.

Dorfman, L., Woodruff, K., Chavez, V., & Wallack, L. (1997). Youth and violence on local television news in California. *American Journal of Public Health*, 87, 1311–1316.

Du Plessis, E. (2011). *The branded mind*. Philadelphia: Kogan Page Limited.

Dye, M. W. G., Green, C. S., & Bavelier, D. (2009a). The development of attention skills in action video game players. *Neuropsychologia*, 47, 1780–1789.

Dye, M. W. G., Green, C. S., & Bavelier, D. (2009b). Increasing speed of processing with action video games. *Current Directions in Psychological Science*, 18, 321–326.

Dysinger, W. S., & Ruckmick, C. A. (1933). *The Emotional Responses of Children to the Motion Picture Situation*. New York: Macmillan.

Edison, T. A. (Producer), & Porter, E. S. (Writer/Director). (1903). *The Great Train Robbery* [Motion picture]. United States: Edison Manufacturing.

Engelhardt, C. E., & Bartholow, B. D. (2011). *Effects of Violent and Nonviolent Video Games on Interference Control*. Unpublished Manuscript, University of Missouri.

Engelhardt, C. E., & Bartholow, B. D. (2012). *Acute Video Game Effects on Neurophysiological Indices of Cognitive Control*. Manuscript in preparation.

Engelhardt, C. R., Bartholow, B. D., Kerr, G. T. & Bushman, B. J. (2011). This is your brain on violent video games: Neural desensitization to violence predicts increased aggression following violent video game exposure. *Journal of Experimental Social Psychology*, 47, 1033–1036.

Eriksen, B. A., & Eriksen, C. W. (1974). Effects of noise letters on the identification of target letters in a non-search task. *Perception and Psychophysics, 16*, 143–149.

Eriksen, C. W., & Schultz, D. W. (1979). Information processing in visual search: A continuous flow conception and experimental results. *Perception & Psychophysics, 25*, 249–263.

Fabiani, M., Buckley, J., Gratton, G., Coles, M. G. H., Donchin, E., & Logie, R. (1989). The training of complex task performance. *Acta Psychologica*, 71, 259–299.

Fabiani, M., Gratton, G., & Federmeier, K. (2007). Event related brain potentials. In J. T. Cacioppo, L. G. Tassinary, & G. G. Berntson (Eds.), *Handbook of psychophysiology* (3rd ed.). New York: Cambridge University Press, pp. 85–119.

Fang, I. (2008). *Alphabet to internet: mediated communication in our lives*. St. Paul, MN: Rada Press.

Faulk, E. B., Rameson, L., Berkman, E. T., Liao, B., Kang, Y., Inagaki, T. K., & Lieberman, M. D. (2009). The neural correlates of persuasion: A common network across cultures and media. *Journal of Cognitive Neuroscience, 22*, 2447–2459.

Frederickson, J. R., & White, B. Y. (1989). An approach to training based on principled task decomposition. *Acta Psychologica, 71,* 89–146.

Friedman, N. P., & Miyake, A. (2004). The relations among inhibition and interference cognitive functions: A latent variable analysis. *Journal of Experimental Psychology: General, 133,* 101–135.

Funk, J. B., Bechtoldt-Baldacci, H., Pasold, T., & Baumgartner, J. (2004). Violence exposure in real-life, video games, television, movies, and the internet: Is there desensitization? *Journal of Adolescence, 27,* 23–39.

Gardiner, H. M., Metcalf, R. C., & Beebe-Center, J. G. (1937/1970). *Feeling and Emotion.* Westport, CT: Greenwood Press.

Gazzaniga, M. S., Ivry, R. B. & Mangun, G. R. (2002). *Cognitive Neuroscience: The Biology of the Mind,* 2nd ed. New York: Norton.

Geiger, S., & Newhagen, J. (1993). Revealing the black box: Information processing and media effects. *Journal of Communication, 43,* 43–50.

Gerbner, G., & Gross, L. (1976). Living with television: The violence profile. *Journal of Communication, 26,* 172–199.

Giancola, P. R., & Chermack, S. T. (1998). Construct validity of laboratory aggression paradigms: A response to Tedeschi and Quigley (1996). *Aggression and Violent Behavior, 3,* 237–253.

Gopher, D., Weil, M., & Bareket, T. (1994). Transfer of skill from a computer game trainer to flight. *Human Factors, 36,* 387–405.

Goyer, P. F., Andreason, P. J., Semple, W. E., Clayton, A. H., King, A. C., et al. (1994). Positron-emission tomography and personality disorders. *Neuropsychopharmacology, 10,* 21–28.

Green, C. S., & Bavelier, D. (2003). Action video game modifies visual selective attention. *Nature, 423,* 534–537.

Green, C. S. & Bavelier, D. (2006). Effect of action video games on the spatial distribution of visuospatial attention. *Journal of Experimental Psychology: Human Perception and Performance, 32,* 1465–1478.

Green, C. S., & Bavelier, D. (2007). Action-video-game experience alters the spatial resolution of vision. *Psychological Science, 18,* 88–94.

Harmon-Jones, E. (2003). Clarifying the emotive functions of asymmetrical frontal cortical activity. *Psychophysiology, 40,* 838–848.

Harmon-Jones, E., & Harmon-Jones, C. (2011). Social neuroscience of asymmetrical frontal cortical activity: Considering anger and approach motivation. In A. Todorov, S. Fiske, & D. Prentice (Eds.), *Social Neuroscience: Toward Understanding the Underpinnings of the Social Mind.* New York: Oxford University Press, pp. 173–187.

Hopkins, R., & Fletcher, J. E. (1994). Electrodermal measurement: Particularly effective for forecasting message influence on sales appeal. In Lang, A. (Ed.), *Measuring Psychological Responses to Media.* Hillsdale, NJ: Lawrence Erlbaum Associates, pp. 113–132.

Hovland, C. I. (1951). Changes in attitude through communication. *The Journal of Abnormal and Social Psychology, 46,* 424–437.

Hovland, C. I., Janis, I. L., & Kelly, H. H. (1953). *Communication and Persuasion.* New Haven, CT: Yale University Press.

Johnson, R. N. (1996). Bad news revisited: The portrayal of violence, conflict, and suffering on television news. *Journal of Peace Psychology, 2,* 201–216.

Kato, J., Ide, H., Kabashima, I., Kadota, H., Takano, K., & Kansaku, K. (2009). Neural correlates of attitude change following positive and negative advertisements. *Frontiers in Behavioral Neuroscience, 3,* 1–13.

Kelly, C. R., Grinband, J., & Hirsch, J. (2007). Repeated exposure to media violence is associated with diminished response in an inhibitory frontolimbic network. *PLoS One, 12,* 1–8.

Kenning, P. H. (2008). What advertisers can do and cannot do with neuroscience. *International Journal of Advertising, 27*(3), 472–473.

Kerns, J. G., Cohen, J. D., MacDonald, A. W. 3rd, Cho, R. Y., Stenger, V. A., & Carter, C. S. (2004). Anterior cingulate conflict monitoring and adjustments in control. *Science, 303,* 1023–1026.

Klucharev, V., Smidts, A., & Fernandez, G. (2008). Brain mechanisms of persuasion: how expert power modulates memory and attitudes. *Social Cognitive & Affective Neuroscience, 3,* 353–366.

Krugman, H. E. (1971). Brainwave measures of media involvement. *Journal of Advertising Research, 11,* 3–9.

Lachman, R., Lachman, J. L., & Butterfield, E. C. (1979). *Cognitive Psychology and Information Processing: An Introduction.* Hillsdale, NJ: Lawrence Erlbaum Associates.

Lang, A. (1990). Involuntary attention and physiological arousal evoked by structural features and emotional content in TV commercials. *Communication Research, 17,* 275–299.

Lang, A. (2009). The limited capacity model of motivated mediated message processing. In Nabi, R. L., & Oliver, M. B. (Eds.), *The Sage Handbook of Media Processes and Effects.* Thousand Oaks, CA: Sage, pp. 193–204.

Lang, A., & Ewoldsen, D. (2010). Beyond effects: Conceptualizing communication as dynamic, complex, nonlinear, and fundamental. In Allen, S. (Ed.), *Rethinking Communication: Keywords in Communication Research.* Cresskill, NJ: Hampton Press, pp. 111–122.

Lang, A., Potter, R. F., & Bolls, P. D. (2009). Where psychophysiology meets the media: Taking the effects out of media research. In Bryant, J., & Oliver, M. B. (Eds.), *Media Effects: Advances in Theory and Research,* 3rd ed. New York: Routledge, pp. 185–206.

Lang, A., & Yegiyan, N. S. (2009). Motivated mediated message processing: How media elicit motivation that influences how media are processed. In Beatty, M. J., McCroskey, J. C., & Floyd, K. (Eds.), *Biological Dimensions of Communication: Perspectives, Methods, and Research.* Cresskill, NJ: Hampton Press, pp. 135–158.

Langleben, D. D., Loughead, J. W., Ruparel, K., Hakun, J. G., Busch-Winokur, S., Holloway, M. B., et al. (2009). Reduced prefrontal and temporal processing and recall of "high sensation" value ads. *NeuroImage, 46,* 219–225.

Lasswell, H. D. (1927/1971). *Propaganda Technique in World War I.* Cambridge, MA: MIT Press.

Lazarus, R. S., Speisman, M., MordkoV, A. M., & Davison, L. A. (1962). A laboratory study of psychological stress produced by a motion picture film. *Psychological Monographs: General and Applied, 34* Whole No. 553.

Lee, S., & Lang, A. (2009). Discrete emotion and motivation: Relative activation in the appetitive and aversive motivational systems as a function of anger, sadness, fear, and joy during televised information campaigns. *Media Psychology, 12,* 148–170.

Leshner, G., Bolls, P., & Wise, K. (2011). Motivated processing of fear appeal and disgust images in televised anti-tobacco ads. *Journal of Media Psychology: Theories, Methods, and Applications, 23,* 77–89.

Lewin, K. (1935). *A dynamic Theory of Personality, Selected Papers.* New York: McGraw-Hill.

Linz, D., Donnerstein, E., & Adams, S. M. (1989). Physiological desensitization and judgments about female victims of violence. *Human Communication Research, 15,* 509–522.

Lowry, D. T., Nio, J. T. C, & Leitner, D. W. (2003). Setting the public fear agenda: Longitudinal analysis of network TV crime reporting, public perceptions of crime, and FBI crime statistics. *Journal of Communication, 53,* 61–73.

Lu, C. H., & Proctor, R.W. (1995). The influence of irrelevant location information on performance: a review of the Simon and spatial Stroop effects. *Psychonomic Bulletin and Review, 2,* 174–207.

MacDonald, A. W. 3rd, Cohen, J. D., Stenger, V. A., & Carter, C. S. (2000). Dissociating the role of the dorsolateral prefrontal and anterior cingulate cortex in cognitive control. *Science, 288,* 1835–1838.

Marci, C. D. (2008). Minding the gap: the evolving relationships between affective neuroscience and advertising research. *International Journal of Advertising, 27,* 473–475.

Miyake, A., & Friedman, N. P. (2012). The nature and organization of individual differences in executive functions: Four general conclusions. *Current Directions in Psychological Science, 21,* 8–14.

Morris, J. D., Klahr, N. J., Shen, F., Villegas, J., Wright, P., He, G., et al. (2009). Mapping a multidimensional emotion in response to television commercials. *Human Brain Mapping, 30,* 79–76.

Nairn, A., & Fine, C. (2008). Who's messing with my mind? *International Journal of Advertising, 27,* 447–470.

Nalkur, P.G., Jamieson, P.E., & Romer, D. (2010). The effectiveness of the motion picture association of America's rating system in screening explicit violence and sex in top-ranked movies from 1950 to 2006. *Journal of Adolescent Health, 47,* 440–447.

National Television Violence Study (1998). *National Television Violence Study,* vol 3. Thousand Oaks, CA: Sage.

Nielsen Media Research. (1998). *Galaxy explorer.* New York: Author.

Nieuwenhuis, S., Aston-Jones, G., & Cohen, J.D. (2005). Decision making, the P3, and the locus coeruleus-norepinephrine system. *Psychological Bulletin, 131,* 510–532.

Ochsner, K. N., & Lieberman, M. D. (2001). The emergence of social cognitive neuroscience. *American Psychologist, 56,* 717–734.

Ohme, R., Matukin, M., & Pacula-Lesniak, B. (2011). Biometric measures for interactive advertising research. *Journal of Interactive Advertising, 11,* 60–72.

Ohme, R., Reykowska, D., Wiener, D., & Choromanska, A. (2010). Application of frontal EEG assymmetry to advertising research. *Journal of Economic Psychology, 31,* 75–793.

Oliver, M. B. (1994). Portrayals of crime, race, and aggression in "reality based" police shows: A content analysis. *Journal of Broadcasting and Electronic Media, 38,* 179–192.

Paisley, W. (1984). Communication in the communication sciences. In Dervin, B., & Voight, M. (Eds.), *Progress in Communication Sciences.* Norwood, NJ: Ablex, pp. 2–42.

Perloff, R. M. (2008). *The Dynamics of Persuasion: Communication and Attitudes in the 21st Century.* New York: Lawrence Erlbaum Associates.

Perrachione, T. K., & Perrachione, J. R. (2008). Brains and brands: Developing mutually informative research in neuroscience and marketing. *Journal of Consumer Behavior, 7,* 303–318.

Potter, R. F., & Bolls, P. D. (2012). *Psychophysiological Measurement and Meaning: Cognitive and Emotional Processing of Media.* New York: Routledge.

Potter, R. F., LaTour, M. S., Braun-LaTour, K. A., & Reichert, T. (2006). The impact of program context on motivational system activation and subsequent effects on processing a fear appeal. *Journal of Advertising, 35,* 67–80.

Potter, R. F., Lee, S., & Rubenking, B. E. (2011). Correlating a motivation-activation measure with media preference. *Journal of Broadcasting & Electronic Media, 55,* 400–418.

Raine, A., Meloy, J. R., Bihrle, S., Stoddard, J., LaCasse, L., et al. (1998) Reduced prefrontal and increased subcortical brain functioning assessed using positron emission tomography in predatory and affective murderers. *Behavioral Science and Law, 16,* 319–332.

Ravaja, N. (2004). Contributions of psychophysiology to media research: Review and recommendations. *Media Psychology, 6,* 193–235.

Reeves, B., Thorsen, E., Rothschild, M., McDonald, D., Hirsch, J., & Goldstein, R. (1985). Attention to television: Intrastimulus effects of movement and scene changes on health of variation over time. *International Journal of Neuroscience, 27,* 241–255.

Romer, D., Jamieson, K. H., & Aday, S. (2003). Television news and the cultivation of fear of crime. *Journal of Communication, 53,* 88–104.

Rubin, A. M. (2009). Uses and gratification: An evolving perspective of media effects. In Nabi, R. L., & Oliver, M. B. (Eds.), *The Sage Handbook of Media Processes and Effects.* Thousand Oaks, CA: Sage, pp. 147–160.

Rule, B. K., & Ferguson, T. J. (1986). The effects of media violence on attitudes, emotions, and cognitions. *Journal of Social Issues, 42,* 29–50.

Schramm, W. (1971). The nature of communication between humans. In Schramm, W., & Roberts, D. F. (Eds.), *The Process and Effects of Mass Communications.* Urbana, IL: University of Illinois Press, pp. 1–53.

Shannon, C. E., & Weaver, W. (1949). *The Mathematical Theory of Communication.* Urbana, IL: University of Illinois Press.

Sherry, J. L. (2004). Media effects theory into the nature/nurture debate: A historical overview and directions for future research. *Media Psychology, 6,* 83–109.

Silberstein, R. B., & Nield, G. E. (2008). Brain activity correlates of consumer brands choice shift associated with television advertising. *International Journal of Advertising, 27,* 359–380.

Sissors, J. Z., & Baron, R. B. (2010). *Advertising Media Planning.* New York: McGraw-Hill.

Smith, L. D. (1996). *B. F. Skinner and Behaviorism in American Culture.* Bethlehem, PA: Lehigh University Press.

Stern, R. M., Ray, W. J., & Quigley, K. S. (2001). *Psychophysiological Recording,* 2nd ed. New York: Oxford University Press.

Thelen, E., Schöner, G., Scheier, C., & Smith, L. B. (2001). The dynamics of embodiment: A field theory of infant perseverative reaching. *Behavioral and Brain Sciences, 24,* 1–34.

Thomas, M. H. (1982). Physiological arousal, exposure to a relatively lengthy aggressive film, and aggressive behavior. *Journal of Research in Personality, 16,* 72–81.

Thomas, M. H., Horton, R. W., Lippincott, E. C., & Drabman, R. S. (1977). Desensitization to portrayals of real life aggression as a function of television violence. *Journal of Personality and Social Psychology, 35*, 450–458.

Treleaven-Hassard, S., Gold, J., Bellman, S., Schweda, A., Ciorciari, J., Critchley, C., et al. (2010). Using the p3a to gauge automatic attention to interactive television advertising. *Journal of Economic Psychology, 31*, 777–784.

van der Molen, W. (2004). Violence and suffering in television news: toward a broader conception of harmful television content for children. *Pediatrics, 113*, 1771–1775.

Wang, Y., Mathews, V. P., Kalnin, A. J., Mosier, K. M., Dunn, D. W., Saykin, A. J., et al. (2009). Short term exposure to a violent video game induces changes in frontolimbic circuitry in adolescents. *Brain Imaging and Behavior, 3*, 38–50.

Wang, Z., Lang, A., & Busemeyer, J. R. (2011). Motivational processing and choice behavior during television viewing: An integrative dynamic approach. *Journal of Communication, 61*, 71–93.

Wartella, E., & Reeves, B. (1985). Historical trends in research on children and the media, 1900–1960. *Journal of Communication, 35*, 118–133.

Weber, R., Ritterfield, U., & Mathiak, K. (2006). Does playing violent video games induce aggression? Empirical evidence of a magnetic functional resonance imaging study. *Media Psychology, 8*, 39–60.

Weber, R., Sherry, J., & Mathiak, K. (2009). The neurophysiological perspective in mass communication research: Theoretical rationale, methods and applications. In M. J. Beatty, J. C. McCroskey, & K. Floyd (Eds.), *Biological dimensions of communication: Perspectives, methods, and research.* Creskill, NJ: Hampton Press, pp. 43–74.

Zillmann, D. (1983). Transfer of excitation in emotional behavior. In Cacioppo, J. T., & Petty, R. E. (Eds.), *Social Psychophysiology: A Sourcebook.* New York: Guilford Press, pp. 215–240.

Zillmann, D., & Bryant, J. (1974). Effect of residual excitation on the emotional response to provocation and delayed aggressive behavior. *Journal of Personality and Social Psychology, 30*, 782–791.

Zillmann, D., Hoyt, J. L., & Day, K. D. (1974a). Strength and duration of the affect of aggressive, violent, and erotic communications on subsequent aggressive behavior. *Communication Research, 1*, 286–306.

Zillmann, D., Mody, B., & Cantor, J. R. (1974b). Empathetic perception of emotional displays in films as a function of hedonic and excitatory state prior to exposure. *Journal of Research in Personality, 8*, 335–349.

The Japanese Approach to Research on the Psychological Effects of Media Use

Akira Sakamoto

Abstract

The main objective of this chapter is to illustrate Japanese trends in the study of the psychological effects of media exposure, particularly electronic media. The chapter describes: (1) the history of media tool dissemination in Japan and its current state; (2) the current state and background of Japanese studies on psychological effects of use of media, and characteristics of such studies in comparison with American studies; and (3) five types of actual or potential contributions of Japanese studies to global study trends. These five types were cross-cultural generalization of research findings, expansion of study areas, deepening of understanding of preceding study findings, execution of studies unique to Japan, and execution of social experiments using the process of media tool dissemination. After these descriptions, the chapter states a brief conclusion, and finally discusses the future direction of Japanese studies.

Key Words: information literacy, Internet, interpersonal relationships, Japanese study, mobile phone, prosocial behavior, psychological health, television, video game, violence

Introduction

The psychological effects of media use such as television programs, video games, and the Internet have been studied around the world, and American research has been most influential. A good number of studies have been conducted in Japan, too. However, most of their findings have been published in Japanese; thus; the study trends are not well known outside Japan. Therefore, the main objective of this chapter is to describe the Japanese trends of research on the psychological effects of media use, particularly electronic media.

This chapter outlines the history and current state of media tool dissemination in Japan; (2) describes the current state, background, and characteristics of studies on psychological effects of use of media; and introduces actual or potential contributions of Japanese studies to the development of international studies. After these descriptions, the chapter states a

belief conclusion, and finally argues the desired future of Japanese studies. So far, some papers have been published to introduce international readers to Japanese research on the psychological effects of playing video games or media effects on violence (Kodaira, 1998; A. Sakamoto, 2000, 2005). This chapter provides a more comprehensive view of Japanese media effects research. This means that this chapter covers not only the effects of video games, but also television, the Internet, and other media tools, as well as their effects on violence and other psychological elements.

The History and Current State of Media Tool Dissemination in Japan

To help readers understand media effects research in Japan, this section briefly introduces the history and current state of dissemination of major media tools in Japan. The media tools include television, video games, the Internet, and mobile phones.

In Japan, television broadcasting started in 1953, and most families had a black-and-white television by the mid-1960s. However, this was replaced by color television by the mid-1970s. The amount of viewing decreased around 1980 but it recovered in the mid-1980s. Today, television is the most familiar media tool among Japanese families (Kodaira, 2008).

Video games experienced an explosive growth in popularity among Japanese families after Nintendo released a game console named *Family Computer* in 1983. After selling many pieces of hardware and software in 1992, Nintendo's profit finally surpassed the profit of Toyota Motor Corporation, which is one of the leading Japanese automobile companies. The profit level has fluctuated since then, but video games have attained firm popularity among Japanese children (A. Sakamoto, 2004).

In the early 1980s, online services started to provide e-mail and bulletin board systems (BBS), and in the mid-1980s, the number of users dramatically increased. In the early 1990s, users switched from these online services to the Internet, and the number of Internet users started to increase. In the mid-1990s, Internet users outnumbered the users of these online services; and finally, in the late 1990s, the number of Internet users who viewed or posted messages to web sites dramatically increased (Kawaura, 2009).

Meanwhile, mobile phone services started in 1987 and mobile phone owners started to increase at the beginning of the 1990s. In 1997, mobile phone–based e-mail services started, and in 1999 users were able to use the Internet on their mobile phone. Because Japanese mobile phone service providers did not implement short message service (SMS), text-based communication could not be established between phones of different carriers. This resulted in Internet-based e-mail exchange among mobile phone users. In Japan, many people, including children, own a mobile phone. They use their mobile phone to connect to the Internet, and not only engage in e-mail–based communication, but also view web sites, post messages, or create web sites (Matsuda, 2008).

Television, video games, the Internet, and mobile phones spread as described in the preceding, and Table 28.1 shows how each of them is used recently. Nakano and Watanabe (2007) created the table by analyzing the data from *the Time Use in the IT Age* survey. It was conducted in 2006 by the NHK Broadcasting Culture Research Institute, with 3,826 respondents between age 10 and 69.

The table suggests that on Sundays, the respondents watched television for at least 3½ hours, rarely played a video game, and increased the amount of time using personal computers (PCs), the Internet, or mobile phones from 2001 to 2006.

Table 28.2 is the result of a survey by the Cabinet Office of Japan (2007), including data on how children use their time. The participating children used (watched) television more than any other media tools. On average, elementary school children 10 years old or older watched television for 2 hours 40 minutes and senior high school students watched television for approximately 3 hours on a weekday. Meanwhile, elementary school children used the Internet on their mobile phone for approximately 7 minutes a day on a weekday, whereas senior high school students spent for approximately 1 hour and 40 minutes, showing a great age difference. Male respondents played more video games than their female counterparts, and female respondents used the Internet on their mobile phone more than their male counterparts. Female senior high school students used the Internet on their mobile phone for almost 2 hours a day.

An Overview of Japanese Media Effects Research

As described in the previous section, many Japanese individuals use media tools on a regular basis. In addition, Japan is a country that has produced many influential media technologies, and the possible psychological effects of media use attracted Japanese researchers' attention and motivated them to study this issue. This section introduces the current state, background, and characteristics of such studies in Japan.

Current State of Research

In Japan, many psychologists are interested in the influence of media on individuals; therefore, there is a large amount of literature. For example, academic books written in Japanese with such titles as *Introduction to Media Psychology* (T. Sakamoto, 2002), *Media and Human Development* (A. Sakamoto, 2003), *Children and New Media* (Kitada & Otawa, 2007), *Television and Development of Children* (Muto, 1987), *Video Games and the Minds of Children* (A. Sakamoto, 2004), and *Frontiers in Internet Psychology* (Kawaura, Morio, & Miura, 2009) have been published. They introduce both international and Japanese studies, and a variety of analysis is conducted and arguments are made based on such information.

Table 28.1 Percentage of Media Tool Users and Average Amount of Time of Use on Sundays

	Media Tool Users (%)[*]		Amount of Use of Time (hours: minutes)	
	2006	2001	2006	2001
Television	89	91	3:33	3:52
Radio	11	12	0:17	0:15
Print[†]	45	49	0:34	0:33
CD, MD, and audiotape	15	14	0:16	0:17
Videos	14	12	0:16	0:13
Video game	8	9	0:09	0:10
Viewing a web site[‡]	20	9	0:15	0:06
E-mail exchange	37	22	0:25	0:13
Internet[§]	44	26	0:40	0:19
PC[¶]	23	15	0:27	0:16
Mobile phone[#]	48	34	0:35	0:20

[*]"Percentage of media tool users" means the percentage of individuals who used a media tool for more than 15 minutes.
[†]"Print" includes newspaper, magazine, comic, book, and so on.
[‡]"Viewing a web site" and "E-mail exchange" can be either via a PC or a mobile phone.
[§]The value is the sum of values for "Viewing a web site" and "E-mail exchange."
[¶]The value is the sum of values for PC-based "Viewing a web site," "E-mail exchange," and "Other."
[#]The value is the sum of values for mobile phone-based "Viewing a web site," "E-mail exchange," and "Other."
This table was based on the study by Nakano, S., & Watanabe, Y. (2007). *Kyuuzou suru intahnetto riyou no jittai: IT jidai no seikatsu jikan chousa 2006 kara* [The rapid increase of Internet use: From the 2006 time use survey in the IT age]. *The NHK Monthly Report on Broadcast Research, 57*(4), 20–39. (Originally in Japanese)

Table 28.2 Average Amount of Time of Media Tool Use on a Weekday by Elementary, Junior High, and Senior High School Students (Hours: Minutes)

	Total	Male	Female
Elementary School			
Watching television	2:40	2:44	2:38
Playing a video game	1:02	1:19	0:44
Using the Internet on a mobile phone	0.07	0:02	0:11
Using the Internet on a PC	0:17	0:17	0:17
n	319	145	174
Junior High School			
Watching television	2:45	2:48	2:42
Playing a video game	0:50	1:09	0:31
Using the Internet on a mobile phone	0:49	0:14	0:55
Using the Internet on a PC	0:34	0:33	0:34
n	451	233	218

(continued)

Table 28.2 (Continued)

	Total	Male	Female
Senior High School			
Watching television	2:56	2:58	2:54
Playing a video game	0:46	1:06	0:26
Using the Internet on a mobile phone	1:44	1:28	2:00
Using the Internet on a PC	0:43	0:39	0:48
N	396	197	199

The table is based on The Cabinet Office of Japan (2007). *A Report from the 5th Survey of Attitudes to Information Society and Young People in It.* Retrieved May 1, 2011 from http://www8.cao.go.jp/youth/kenkyu/jouhou5/index.html. (Originally in Japanese).

In addition, there are currently no Japanese journals specializing in media effects research to introduce related papers, but they are introduced in a wide variety of journals published by academic societies that may cover such topics. For example, there are psychological academic societies such as the Japanese Psychological Association, the Japanese Society of Social Psychology, the Japan Society of Developmental Psychology, the Japanese Association of Applied Psychology, and the Japan Society of Personality Psychology; and sociology-related academic societies such as the Japan Society for Studies in Journalism and Mass Communication and the Japan Society for Socio-Information Studies. These sociology-related journals introduce research papers that deal with sociological aspects of psychological effects of use of media. Furthermore, there are the Japan Association of Simulation and Gaming and the Digital Games Research Association Japan, and these academic societies often publish papers that discuss psychological effects of video games on individuals. There are also education technology–related societies such as the Japan Society for Educational Technology, the Japanese Society for Information and Systems in Education, the Japan Association for Educational Media Study, and the Japan Society of Educational Information. These societies publish a large number of study papers that assess the effectiveness of the educational use of computers and the Internet.

Usually, these societies not only publish journals introducing peer-reviewed papers, but also hold an annual conference, and many researchers make presentations on their studies at the conference. At a conference held by an academic society having a few thousands members, such as the Japanese Psychological Association, the Japanese

Society of Social Psychology, the Japan Society of Developmental Psychology, and the Japan Society for Educational Technology, it seems there are more than a few presentations about the psychological effects of media use every year. In Japan, not only peer-reviewed papers in academic journals, but also papers presented at academic society conferences are widely distributed because the proceedings of presented papers are usually created at Japanese academic society conferences, making individual papers easily accessed or cited; and as a result, researchers put much effort into creating papers to be presented at conferences. For media effects research, Japanese researchers are able to easily refer to a large number of presented papers to collect information on Japanese studies (although they are in general not peer-reviewed and therefore the quality of some may be questionable).

This chapter does not provide the specific number of media effect studies conducted in Japan because it is difficult to define the extent that they cover. However, the following case example should serve as a guide. Anderson et al. (2010) conducted meta-analysis using results of studies on the effects of violent video games on individuals' aggressive behavior, aggressive cognition, aggressive affect, prosocial behavior, empathy, and physiological arousal. They collected data from Western studies, mainly from the United States, and Eastern studies such as Japanese studies, and integrated them. Anderson et al. first evaluated the methodological appropriateness of each study. Then, in their analysis, they used only the effects observed in the subject studies whose methods met a certain standard, and whose data on the impact of extraneous variables, such as sex, should be controlled could be removed. As a result, they collected 144 valid effects from the

Western studies and 64 from the Eastern studies, accounting for one-third of the total. The number of individuals studied was 20,598 in the Western studies, whereas it was 32,436 in the Eastern studies, accounting for more than half of the total. Most of the Eastern studies came from Japan, indicating that the number of studies conducted in Japan was not far behind that of the Western countries.

Besides studies on video games, in Japan, a large number of media effect research studies are conducted covering television, the Internet, and mobile phones. It appears that the effects of Internet and mobile phone use are much more frequently studied than those of video games.

Research Background

The current research state as described seems to be formed from multiple backgrounds. Among them, the two described in the following seem to be the most influential.

First is support from the government and commercial industry for studies on effective use of media tools. Media tools may be useful in many fields if used tactfully; therefore, their development has been highly anticipated. Development of media tools would increase the value of the media industry itself. Thus, the government and commercial industry have been supporting development and research of media tools that people could effectively use. Such support in fact has promoted research activities, serving as one of the major contributing factors for stable implementation of a large amount of research. One of the major study fields is television, computer, and Internet use in education and at school (Shirai & Sakamoto, 1987; A. Sakamoto et al., 2002; Shimizu et al., 2008). This is a frequently studied subject in educational technology research, and it has been supported by the government, broadcasting industry, computer industry, and educational industry, which wish to promote the use of these media tools. This has led to a large number of research projects. Another example is frequently implemented advertisement research that aims to create high-quality advertisements. This type of research has been supported by the advertisement industry. They support journals that introduce advertisement research papers. They also provide grants for advertisement research projects.

The second background is the concern about possible harmful effects of use of media. As with the United States, there have been concerns about the harmful effects of television since the time Japanese people started to watch it. To respond to these concerns, studies on the effects of television were conducted from time to time from the 1950s to the present. It seems that attention to the harmful effects on academic skills, daily time usage, or delinquency was great in the past, but recently public concerns about the effects of violence have become greater, and researchers have been actively studying this issue since some heinous crimes occurred.

One of the well-known heinous crimes is the case that occurred in Kobe in 1997. A second-year male junior high school student murdered a fifth grade boy, decapitated him, and placed the head in front of the boy's school in the early morning. A person who happened to walk in front of the school saw the body part, and it quickly developed into huge news. The criminal sent a letter to the mass media claiming responsibility. He provided reasons for committing the crime by describing a fantastic world that could be found in a cartoon or video game, and the media claimed that his crime may have been inspired by cartoons or video games.

Another example is the case that occurred in Nagasaki in 2004. A sixth grade girl cut her female classmate in the neck using a box cutter in the classroom, and the classmate bled to death. How she murdered her classmate strikingly resembled a scene of a drama she had watched the previous day; therefore, some claimed that the television program influenced her. However, the influence of the Internet was much more strongly noted than that of the television program. The attacker and the victim had argued on the Internet before the murder; also, in Internet-based group novel writing, popular among children, the attacker was writing a novel about children killing each other.

These cases intensified concerns about the harmful effects of media use on violence or criminal activities. Accordingly, concerns about the harmful effects on social and academic skills seemed to be exacerbated. As a result, the necessity of studying these effects was emphasized, and some researchers voluntarily started research projects. The public also indicated their willingness to support such research; for instance, government agencies and public benefit corporations conducted or outsourced studies on the harmful effects of media use to teams of researchers. Organizations in the media industry also began to study this topic. The increased necessity for research seems to have facilitated approval of researchers' applications for research funding and promoted research activities.

Although the interest in the harmful effects of media use and related studies increased, it seems that some were concerned that focusing only on such interest might result in biased treatment of media, possibly resulting in excessive media control; therefore, there was a growing consensus that it was necessary to understand the positive effects of media use. In fact, researchers have recently begun paying attention to studies suggesting that use of media tools may contribute to prosocial behavior (Ihori et al., 2008) or high cognitive skills (Kamakura, Tomiyasu, & Baba, 2009; Omi, Hattori, & Sakamoto, 2009).

Research Characteristics: Comparison with American Studies

As described, it seems that the state of current Japanese research has been formed by the two backgrounds and others. In this section, Japanese studies are compared with American counterparts to discuss the characteristics of Japanese studies in terms of research areas, methodology, and theories.

Japanese psychology in general is strongly influenced by American psychology, and the influence is particularly strong in social psychology. An American book such as *Advances in Experimental Social Psychology* is often used as a textbook in social psychology courses at Japanese graduate schools. Research on the psychological effects of media use is mostly conducted by social psychologists, and they plan their own study by referring to the research area and topic as well as American methodologies. For this reason, it seems that Japanese studies highly resemble American studies. They are also based on American theories, such as the general aggression model (Anderson & Bushman, 2002), the rich get richer theory (Kraut et al., 2002), and the social compensation theory (McKenna & Bargh, 1998), and there are hardly any theories that fit Japanese culture. Additionally, there are no strong attempts to develop theories unique to Japan.

However, research areas seem to have some differences between the United States and Japan, although they share similarities. For example, American researchers frequently study the harmful effects of media use on obesity or drug use. However, this topic does not attract much attention in Japan. This may reflect the fact that Japan has fewer obese individuals and less serious drug issues than the United States.

Studies of violence are often conducted in Japan, but they attract less attention than in the United States. This may be because Japan has fewer violent crimes, and as described earlier, the public has not paid much attention to media-caused violence.

Recently, the effects of video game or Internet use on violence started to attract attention, and researchers started to study this subject. Still, because research projects were not actively implemented in the past, there is little accumulation of study data with regard to television and violence.

On the other hand, it may be that the effects of media use on interpersonal relationships attract more attention in Japan than in the United States. Japanese people are strongly interested in maintaining good interpersonal relationships. The Youth Affairs Administration of the Management and Coordination Agency (1995) conducted a study with Japanese, American, and Korean parents to find personality traits that they wished for their children. The most frequently provided answers by Japanese parents were "concern for others (61.9%)" and "follow rules and do not bother others (44.8%)," whereas American parents tended to answer "sense of responsibility (49.8%)" and "fairness and justice (32.0%)." Taking into account such cultural backgrounds, the possibility that use of media affects or weakens interpersonal relationships would attract attention in Japan.

Strong interest in mobile phone–related studies is another characteristic of Japanese studies (Ito, Okabe, & Matsuda, 2005; Akasaka & Sakamoto, 2011). Japanese users generally use their mobile phones not only to make calls, but also to use the Internet. Therefore, mobile phones have become an important communication tool. Also, the use of mobile phones has also widely spread among children. These factors seem to have greatly motivated researchers to study the effect of use of mobile phones.

Although there are some differences between the United States and Japan in areas studied, it seems they are not found in media effects research. Only a few studies have actually compared results of studies between the two countries (Anderson et al., 2008; Gentile et al., 2009), but these studies indicated that media effects would be consistent across the countries. Also, Japanese researchers often replicate results of studies conducted in the United States, and Japanese researchers appear to have little doubt that research studies can be generalized across the two cultures and countries.

As mentioned, there are only a few studies that compare the size of media effects (Anderson et al., 2008; Gentile et al., 2009). However, there are studies that compare how media tools are used, and many of them suggest that they are in fact different. For example, young American people use their mobile phone to talk to their family, whereas young Japanese people use their mobile phone to be away from their family and keep in touch with their friends at night (Ishii, 2006). Meanwhile, Keaten, Kelly, Pribyl, and Sakamoto (2009) suggested that the Japanese often use e-mail, whereas Americans prefer face-to-face communication when they deal with difficult personal situations. They argued that the Japanese are afraid of being judged by others and therefore tend to use e-mail to avoid that emotional impact. On the other hand, there was a study suggesting that American undergraduate students tended to contact their professor by e-mail, whereas their Japanese counterparts make a phone call or try to establish face-to-face communication (Richardson & Smith, 2007). Richardson and Smith explained this result, saying that paying respect to elders is important for Japanese people, and e-mail would not let them do so properly. There are also other findings, for example, American undergraduate students tend to use their mobile phone to make calls, whereas Japanese counterparts use their mobile phone to send and receive e-mail; and American and Japanese students have different tolerance levels for talking on mobile phones in public, which varies depending on the situations (Baron & af Segerstad, 2010).

The (Potential) Contribution of Japanese Media Effects Research

As outlined in the previous section, Japanese studies are less known overseas. Therefore, they have so far had a limited influence on global study trends. However, Japanese studies have been showing five trends that are expected to have a substantial contribution to the development of global study trends in the future provided that their international presence increases. This section introduces these five trends using major examples.

Cross-Cultural Generalization

Implementation of media effects research is said to be "unevenly distributed in the world" (von Feilitzen, 1998, p. 47), and has been centered in the United States. Although media effects research findings accumulate in the United States, the extent of the cross-cultural generalizability of these findings may be questionable.

Japanese researchers often plan their studies with reference to previous American studies; for this reason, the same or similar inter-variable relationships as the previous studies tend to be examined. These studies can be assumed to explore the possibility of cross-cultural generalization of research findings. In

fact, Japanese researchers often replicate the findings of previous American studies.

For example, Hashimoto, Tsuji, Ishii, Kim, and Kimura (2004) replicated the research finding that "the rich get richer" suggested by Kraut et al. (2002). Kraut et al. (1999) first conducted a longitudinal survey in the United States and concluded that the use of the Internet caused low-quality communication, resulting in deterioration of users' psychological health. Based on this study they produced the "Internet paradox" theory. Kraut et al. (2002) later conducted two longitudinal surveys. In their report, they made changes to the "Internet paradox" theory and produced the "rich get richer" theory. Hashimoto et al. (2004) conducted a similar longitudinal survey to replicate the "rich get richer" phenomenon in Japan.

Another example is the study conducted by Iwao (2000) that replicated the result of content analysis carried out by Gerbner and Gross (1976). Gerbner and Gross analyzed violence portrayed in television drama programs broadcast from 1967 through 1975 and indicated that 79.8% of programs showed violence, and that violent behavior was observed 7.4 times per hour. Based on their methodology, Iwao (2000) analyzed Japanese television drama programs broadcasted from 1977 through 1994 and indicated that approximately 80% of programs showed violence, and that violent behavior was observed 8.1 times per hour. Therefore, the result of the study on Japanese television drama programs was similar to the study result produced by Gerbner and Gross (1976).

Such study results provide information on the generalizability and robustness of research findings that are mainly established in the United States and have implications for study trends not only in Japan but around the world. To support this statement, there are a few studies that gained recognition by using Japanese study results to examine cross-cultural generalizability of preceding research findings.

One of the examples is the meta-analysis by Anderson et al. (2010) introduced earlier. To examine the effects of violent video games on aggression, they compared Western studies, mainly conducted in the United States, and Eastern studies, including many Japanese studies. Their study did not indicate much difference, suggesting that the effects of violent video games on aggression could be robust and generalized cross-culturally. There is also a study by Anderson et al. (2008) in which they analyzed the data of American and Japanese longitudinal surveys on the effects of violent video games on aggression. They found that violent video games influenced aggression in both countries, suggesting the cross-cultural generalizability of research findings. Furthermore, Gentile et al. (2009) reported results of the experiment conducted in the United States, the correlation study conducted in Singapore, and the longitudinal survey in Japan that examined the effects of prosocial video games on prosocial behavior. Then they pointed out that the positive effects of prosocial video games could be generalized across not only methodologies, but also cultures.

Expansion of Study Areas

Japanese studies not only replicate previous American studies, as mentioned, but also apply their methodologies to expand areas of study. For example, after Gerbner and Gross (1976) conducted their study, four university research groups conducted the National Television Violence Study (NTVS) from 1994 through 1997 (Federman, 1996, 1997, 1998), which is another famous content analysis of violence shown in television programs. The analysis indicated that 57% of fiction programs showed violence, there was no punishment of assailants in 73% of violent scenes, the pain of victims caused by violence was not shown in 58% of violent scenes, and only 4% of programs showing violence had an antiviolence message.

Based on this study, the Japanese Television Violence Study (JTVS) was conducted in Japan (A. Sakamoto, 2007). A research group mainly consisting of members from Ochanomizu University conducted this study. Using the NTVS coding system, they coded 543 Japanese fiction programs broadcasted from 2003 through 2006. One of the researchers went to the United States and received training from the NTVS members. The study showed that 54% of fiction programs showed violence, there was no punishment of assailants in 81% of violent scenes, the pain of victims caused by violence was not shown in 40% of violent scenes, and only 4% of programs showing violence had an antiviolence message. The overall result was similar to that of the NTVS.

In the JTVS, not only were the findings of the NTVS replicated, but the scope of analysis was also expanded. For instance, the NTVS was designed primarily for analysis of violence shown in fiction programs, but in the JTVS, researchers modified the NTVS coding system such that prosocial behavior could be analyzed. Then, together with violence, prosocial behavior shown in programs was

analyzed. As one of the findings, Sado, Sakamoto, and Suzuki (2004) reported that, although 68.6% of television programs broadcast in 2003 showed violence, 45.3% showed prosocial behavior. In particular, the discrepancy was significant in animation programs; 83.3% showed violence, whereas only 33.3% showed prosocial behavior.

In addition to fiction programs, news programs and commercials were also analyzed in the JTVS. Horiuchi et al. (2009) showed that 44.7% of news programs showed violence, more often than other genres of programs (17.9%). Meanwhile, Tajima et al. (2007) analyzed 7,599 commercials broadcasted from 2005 through 2007 on television and concluded that the percentage of commercials that showed violence was quite low (4.75%) and almost all of these commercials advertised movies or animation programs and were broadcast late at night or in the morning.

Furthermore, the JTVS members employed the NTVS coding system to analyze violence shown in video games and compared the coding results with those of violence shown on television (A. Sakamoto et al., 2008). The study indicated that more often in video games than television violence was intense, violence was much more often rewarded and less frequently punished, and violence resulted in only minor injury. The study at the same time suggested that violence was depicted more realistically in television programs than in video games.[1]

Deepening of Understanding

Some Japanese studies have been conducted to promote better understanding of international research findings. One of the examples is Japanese research examining the effects of Internet use on psychological health. This was examined in a number of studies around the world after Kraut et al. (1999) conducted their Internet paradox study. However, these studies were often one-shot surveys. One-shot surveys generally discover correlations only, and longitudinal surveys are required to understand the causality between Internet use and psychological health (Finkel, 1995).[2]

A study by Takahira (2009) presented a comprehensive view of these longitudinal surveys. Including a study by Kraut et al. (1999) and two studies by Kraut et al. (2002), Takahira collected a total of 12 longitudinal surveys. Other than the studies by Kraut et al., four studies out of nine were written in English; two studies from the United States (Jackson et al., 2006; Bessière et al., 2008), one from the Netherlands (Van den Eijnden et al.,

2008), and one from Sweden (Thomee et al., 2007). The other five studies were conducted in Japan (Hashimoto et al., 2004; Ando et al., 2004, 2005; Shimura, 2005; Takahira, Ando, & Sakamoto, 2008). Different papers introduced different results. Some claimed that use of the Internet harmed psychological health, causing depression, loneliness, or stress, and some claimed it improved psychological health.

Takahira then created a list of these studies and organized the results, referring to the theories produced, such as the Internet paradox theory by Kraut et al. (1999), the rich get richer theory by Kraut et al. (2002), and the social compensation theory by McKenna and Bargh (1998). For example, Takahira argued that: (1) Use of the Internet harmed individuals' psychological health when it was used for communication purposes such as e-mail exchange, chat, or posting messages to BBS, instead of to acquire information. (2) The level of harm increased when individuals tried to form a new interpersonal relationship using the Internet. (3) When individuals used the Internet to maintain face-to-face interpersonal relationships, psychological health improved for those having more social resources than those having less. (4) When individuals used the Internet to form a new interpersonal relationship, psychological health improved for individuals having less social resources than those having more. The term *social resources* refers to abundant social support or a high level of extroversion.

In making this argument, Takahira referred not only to the studies introduced in the six English papers from the United States, the Netherlands, and Sweden, but also to the five Japanese studies. The use of such international resources reinforced Takahira's argument. As suggested in this example, Japanese researchers have produced a number of empirical studies that could help our understanding of international research findings, and at the same time, have conducted analysis to promote such understanding based on these studies.

Unique Studies

Within the Japanese study trends, some studies show development that appears quite unique, such as the strong interest in and study of mobile phone use. In general, Japanese mobile phone users not only exchange e-mail, but also view web sites, post messages, or create web sites. Also, the use of mobile phones has spread widely among children. Almost all Japanese senior high school students own one (The Cabinet Office of Japan, 2007).

Probably because of these facts, Japanese researchers show strong interest in mobile phones. For example, the issue of whether the Internet is used with mobile phones or PCs has been attracting attention. Kobayashi (2010) studied this issue. He conducted a longitudinal survey and as a result suggested that PC-based Internet use promoted interactions with others and improved social tolerance in users. *Social tolerance* refers to a tendency to accept different feelings or opinions and is an important factor of democracy. He also studied the effects of Internet use on mobile phones. The result suggested that, unlike PC-based Internet use, mobile phone–based Internet use only promoted repetitive communication with others sharing common traits, and lowered social tolerance, leading to formation of a norm to exclude others with different traits. Kobayashi argued that because messages are short in mobile phone–based Internet use, a sender and a receiver must share a common background to establish communication, and this promotes communication with others with common traits.

Another theme that is attracting much attention and being studied frequently in Japan is how the use of mobile phones influences interpersonal relationships. Use of a mobile phone started to spread widely in the mid-1990s. As its use spread, more individuals relied on it, giving an impression that it hampered face-to-face, direct communication. For this reason, there was public concern that the use of a mobile phone may weaken interpersonal relationships. This is similar to the concern discussed in the Internet paradox theory developed by Kraut et al. (1999).

The weakened relations theory, however, has often been rejected based on results of studies conducted in the late 1990s and later with children and undergraduate students (Hashimoto, 1998). Around 2000, the fragmented or selective relations theory was developed to replace the weakened relations theory (Tsuji, 1999; Matsuda, 2000).[3] The fragmented or selective relations mean that individuals have partners specific to each area of activity and always select the partners they interact with depending on the area. For example, individuals may interact with their work partners only in work-related activities, or they may interact with people they met through a hobby only in hobby-related activities. In such cases, the relationship is tight and intense only within the area of a particular activity. Researchers showed that this was the type of interpersonal relationship that use of mobile phones promoted, and argued that the reason why the weakened relations theory was considered plausible was that researchers noted that users did not share many areas with one partner, and for the overall trend, individuals interacted with others sufficiently through mobile phones. Also, in line with this, there is an argument that such partiality and selectivity of interpersonal relationships has caused the mobile phone dependency prominently observed in children (Suzuki & Tsuji, 2005). Recently, there seems to be a growing argument that mobile phone–based interpersonal relationships are holistic instead of partial or selective, and the use of mobile phones has made interactions with each person more intense than before (Nakamura, 2003; Akasaka & Sakamoto, 2008).

Although the studies introduced in the preceding overlap some parts of the Internet paradox research, it seems that Japanese studies on mobile phones are still different, and are characterized by attention to the entirety of mobile phone use, including the use of non-Internet functions such as the telephone, instead of mere Internet use; and focus on the concept of fragmented or selective relations in theoretical discussion. Overseas literature is not cited much in these studies. Also, most of these studies are reported in Japanese and seem to be hardly heard outside of Japan.

Social Experiments

Generally speaking, comparison of changes observed in an area before and after media tool dissemination (treatment condition), and changes of the same period observed in an area in which the use of subject media tools already spread or has not spread (control condition) allows a quasi-experiment for examining the effects of use of media. One of the well-known examples of such a quasi-experiment is the one conducted by Harrison and Williams (1986). They measured creativity, spatial perception ability, and the vocabulary of children at two different time points in an area with no television broadcasting (No-Tel condition), an area with only one channel available (Uni-Tel condition), and an area in which all channels were available (Multi-Tel condition). Between the two time points, television broadcasting started in the No-Tel area. Analysis of obtained data revealed that although creativity of children under the No-Tel condition was higher than children under other conditions at the first measurement, such difference was no longer observed at the second measurement. Therefore, they suggested that viewing television may reduce creativity.

This type of social experiment is quite meaningful because it does not involve artificial or unrealistic elements that are seen in a laboratory experiment, and at the same time causality can be estimated to a certain degree.[4] It should be noted, however, such an experiment can be carried out only during media tool dissemination, meaning there is only one opportunity per area. If the global study trends are influenced by studies from only a small number of countries, social experiment results also have a limited influence on global study trends. Implementation of social experiments in many countries and regions, and delivery of research findings to researchers across the world, will be quite meaningful.

Japanese researchers have also conducted social experiments using the process of media tool dissemination. In 1999, high-speed Internet was introduced to three junior high schools (treatment condition) and was not introduced to two schools (control condition) in Ogaki, a city located near Nagoya. Around the time of introduction of the Internet to these schools, Naito et al. (2003) conducted a quasi-experiment to examine whether or not use of high-speed Internet improved students' ability to practically use information. The phrase *ability to practically use information* is used in the field of Japanese education and basically means the same as *information literacy*. All the subject schools were located in similar environments, and Naito et al. compared changes in students' ability to practically use information between the two conditions. The result indicated that the junior high school students who used high-speed Internet improved their skill to collect information, which was regarded as a part of the ability to practically use information. In this quasi-experiment, students' ability to practically use information was measured twice before and once after the introduction of the Internet. The two measurements before the introduction allowed control of changes in the baseline between the conditions (Shadish, Cook, & Campbell, 2002).

Another example is the study by Kashibuchi et al. (2003). In this study, they examined how the use of high-speed Internet influenced junior high school students' understanding of Internet safety and etiquette. Kashibuchi et al. conducted a study with students who went to a junior high school with or without high-speed Internet and measured their level of understanding of Internet safety and etiquette three times as with Naito et al. (2003). When they compared students' level of understanding before and after the introduction of high-speed

Internet, they found that the changes observed in students going to the school with high-speed Internet were the same as those observed in students going to the school without high-speed Internet. Kashibuchi et al. therefore argued that, when children used the Internet, mere use thereof would not improve their understanding of Internet safety and etiquette, and proper education aiming to improve it should be implemented.

As described, Japanese researchers have already conducted and will continue to conduct social experiments using the process of media tool dissemination, and Japanese studies should serve as a means to deliver findings of social experiments to researchers across the world.

Conclusion

This chapter first outlined the history and current state of media tool dissemination in Japan, and subsequently overviewed the current state, background, and characteristics of Japanese research on the psychological effects of media use. In this overview, some situations related to Japanese research were described, for example: (1) Many studies on psychological effects of media use have been conducted in Japan, and a fair amount of literature on this issue can be found. (2) It seems that support from the government and the commercial industry for studies on effective use of media tools and concerns about possible harmful effects of media use can regarded as important backgrounds that have affected the Japanese study trends. (3) Because Japanese studies have been greatly affected by American studies, methodologies and theories found in Japanese studies are very similar to those of American studies, but as to research areas that have attracted attention from researchers, there seems to be little difference between the two countries. (4) Finally, there are few research results suggesting that the strength of media effects is different between the two countries.

The paper also argued that a fair number of Japanese studies have the potential to contribute to the development of global study trends, although their actual influence on the trends has so far been limited probably because they are not well known internationally. For example, Japanese researchers often replicate, expand, or attempt to better understand international research findings that come from the United States or other countries. In Japan, there are also areas of study that may be unique to Japan or social experiments that are conducted using the process of media tool dissemination. It seems that each of these experiences and findings can actually be useful for international researchers.

Thus, this chapter has introduced a variety of issues of Japanese research on the psychological effects of media use. If this chapter has some effect, however small, to enhance understanding of and interests in Japanese studies from international researchers, and promotes better communication between international and Japanese researchers, the author will be very flattered.

Future Directions

In the last part of this chapter, the author argued three issues that Japanese research on the psychological effects of media use should cope with in the future.

First, both the quantity and quality of Japanese studies should be much enhanced. As described, many studies in this area have already been conducted in Japan. However, in observing the excellent work of overseas researchers, it is felt there is much room for improving Japanese research activities. In coping with the Japanese media problems to be solved, it is necessary to refer to the findings of Japanese as well as overseas studies, because such problems are often related to situations peculiar to Japan. For example, mobile phones are important in Japan, but the findings of overseas research cannot be much referred to because the dissemination and functions of mobile phones are different between Japan and other countries. Therefore, it is necessary that Japanese studies provide problem solving findings. It is greatly expected that the number of researchers engaging in these research activities will increase, and additionally, each researcher will continue to try to improve the quality of research with learning from excellent international studies.

The second issue is contribution to establishment of generalized cross-cultural theories. Cultural differences, such as those between the United States and Japan, can function as important variables that moderate inter-variable relationships, including the effects of media use. Examining such moderating effects, explaining process-generating effects, and establishing comprehensive cross-cultural theories are required. In current media effects research, however, these are rare; there are only a few studies in which cultures are compared and the moderating effects of cultural variables are examined, and theoretical discussions have not been developed yet. Therefore, cultural variables should be more greatly incorporated into media effects research in the future. Implementation of studies in this area has so far been greatly centered on the United States, and it seems this has prevented the examination of cultural variables. The author believes that studies in Japan and other countries should be promoted because they will provide findings from non-American perspectives, leading to more interest in cultural variables from international researchers, including Americans.

The last issue is the sharing of information with countries outside of Japan. As described, studies that may elaborate on international research findings have been conducted in Japan but they are not well known overseas and have not exerted their potential.

One of the most significant reasons why Japanese studies are less well known overseas is that the majority of them are published in Japanese. English is not the native language of the Japanese people and is quite different from Japanese. It is a great handicap for Japanese people to write papers in English. Accordingly, producing high-quality papers is a difficult task (Takano & Noda, 1993). However, for Japanese researchers, sharing research findings with international researchers should not only increase the value of their studies, but also contribute to the development and increase the value of international studies. For this reason, Japanese researchers should strive harder to publish and deliver their research findings to international researchers in English.[5]

To English-speaking researchers as well, distribution of research findings presented by non-English speakers would be meaningful for the development of research in which English-speaking researchers are involved. Therefore, the author believes it will be rewarding for English-speaking researchers to consider taking the action necessary to realize greater distribution of papers written by non–English-speaking researchers. To achieve the common goal, which is to find the truth about effects of use of media, it seems necessary to explore ways for researchers around the world to work together.

Notes

1. Polkinghorne (see Chapter 8) stated that qualitative research was not still popular in psychology, and argued the significance of content analysis research based on the qualitative approach. Recently, the significance of the qualitative approach has been understood in Japanese psychology, and the Japanese Association of Qualitative Psychology was established in 2004. The association holds annual meetings and publishes a journal for qualitative psychology. However, like the United States, the qualitative approach has not generally been influential in Japanese psychology yet. Actually, Japanese content analysis research based on the qualitative approach is often found in the field of sociology, but psychological research is usually based on the quantitative approach, as is found in Iwao (2000) and A. Sakamoto (2007).

2. Prot and Anderson (see Chapter 7) explained the methodological characteristics of one-shot surveys and longitudinal surveys in detail, although they used the terms "cross-sectional correlational studies" and "longitudinal studies" when referring to those research designs, respectively.

3. The phrase "fragmented or selective relations" is not usually used in Japan. This was used here because some researchers use "fragmented" (Tsuji, 1999), whereas others use "selective" (Matsuda, 2000) to express such interpersonal relations.

4. Prot and Anderson (see Chapter 7) explained the methodologies of experimental, cross-sectional correlational, and longitudinal studies in detail, and did not include the issues of quasi-experiments there. Quasi-experiments are similar to the longitudinal studies they addressed in that researchers can avoid some weaknesses of laboratory experiments and estimate causality to some extent by using those research designs. However, there are also differences between them in that the longitudinal studies do not have experimental manipulations, whereas the quasi-experiments do have them, although they are not quite complete. It seems that the longitudinal studies have difficulty in detecting the effects of media use on psychological variables in such cases as (1) when there are only small differences in the amount of media use measured in the first time period between participants, or (2) when the psychological variables cannot be changed because they have already been much affected by media use before the first time period of measurement. In such cases, the strengths of quasi-experiments could be larger.

5. Karen Dill, the editor of this book, suggested that researchers might engage in more translations, especially the use of automatic translation systems, to transmit their research findings to international researchers. At present, the Japan Society of Educational Technology has two journals in Japanese and English, and often makes the authors who published a paper in the Japanese journal translate it to English so as to publish in the English journal. There are already such activities in Japan, but they have not become popular yet, probably because the cost of work on translated papers is very large for both Japanese researchers and academic societies. The use of automatic translation systems seems to be useful in that it can decrease the load and costs. However, Japanese and English are very different languages, and the quality of automatic translations is not excellent yet. Therefore, it seems unclear whether international researchers will refer to awkward translated papers that have not been published in respected journals. In spite of such difficulties, since there is a possibility that the use of automatic translation systems will improve the Japanese situation, it would be meaningful to look for ways to actualize it.

References

Akasaka, R., & Sakamoto, A. (2008). The effect of mobile phone use on children's friendships: The examination of causality based on a panel study. *Japanese Journal of Personality, 16,* 363–377. (Originally in Japanese)

Akasaka, R., & Sakamoto, A. (2011). *Keitai to pahsonariti* [Mobile phones and personality]. In Sakamoto, A. (Ed.), *Media and Personality.* Kyoto, Japan: Nakanishiya Shuppan, pp. 103–144. (Originally in Japanese)

Anderson, C. A., & Bushman, B. J. (2002). Human aggression. *Annual Review of Psychology, 53,* 27–51.

Anderson, C. A., Sakamoto, A., Gentile, D. A., Ihori, N., Shibuya, A., Yukawa, S., et al. (2008). Longitudinal effects of violent video games on aggression in Japan and the United States. *Pediatrics, 122,* e1067–e1072.

Anderson, C. A., Shibuya, A., Ihori, N., Swing, E. L., Sakamoto, A., Rothstein, H. R., et al. (2010). Violent video game effects on aggression, empathy, and prosocial behavior in Eastern and Western countries: A meta-analytic review. *Psychological Bulletin*, *136*, 151–173.

Ando, R., Sakamoto, A., Suzuki, K., Kobayashi, K., Kashibuchi, M., & Kimura, F. (2004). Effects of the Internet use on life satisfaction and social efficacy: A panel study of male students in a vocational college of information technology. *Japanese Journal of Personality*, *13*, 21–33. (Originally in Japanese)

Ando, R., Takahira, M., & Sakamoto, A. (2005). Effects of Internet use on junior high school students' loneliness and social support. *Japanese Journal of Personality*, *14*, 69–79. (Originally in Japanese)

Baron, N. S., & af Segerstad, Y. H. (2010). Cross-cultural patterns in mobile-phone use: Public space and reachability in Sweden, the USA, and Japan. *New Media & Society*, *12*, 13–34.

Bessière, K., Kiesler, S., Kraut, R., & Boneva, B. (2008). Effects of internet use and social resources on changes in depression. *Information, Communication & Society*, *11*, 47–70.

Federman, J. (Ed.) (1996). *National Television Violence Study I*. Thousand Oaks, CA: Sage.

Federman, J. (Ed.) (1997). *National Television Violence Study II*. Thousand Oaks, CA: Sage.

Federman, J. (Ed.) (1998). *National Television Violence Study III*. Thousand Oaks, CA: Sage.

Finkel, S. (1995). *Causal Analysis with Panel Data*. Thousand Oaks, CA: Sage.

Gentile, D. A., Anderson, C. A., Yukawa, S., Ihori, N., Saleem, M., Ming, L. K., et al. (2009). The effects of prosocial video games on prosocial behaviors: International evidence from correlational, longitudinal, and experimental studies. *Personality and Social Psychology Bulletin*, *35*, 752–763.

Gerbner, G., & Gross, L. (1976). Living with television: The violence profile. *Journal of Communication, 26*, 173–200.

Harrison, L. F., & Williams, T. M. (1986). TV and cognitive development. In Williams, T. M. (Ed.), *The Impact of TV: A Natural Experiment in Three Communities*. Orlando, FL: Academic Press, pp. 87–142.

Hashimoto, Y. (1998). *Pahsonaru media to komyunikeisyon koudou* [Personal media and communication behavior]. In Takeuchi, I., Kojima, K., & Hashimoto, Y. (Eds.), *Media Communication Theory*. Tokyo: Hokuju Shuppan, pp. 326–346. (Originally in Japanese)

Hashimoto, Y., Tsuji, D., Ishii, K., Kim, S., & Kimura, T. (2004). Analyzing the effect of internet use by panel survey. *The Research Bulletin of the Institute of Socio-Information and Communication Studies, the University of Tokyo*, *21*, 305–454. (Originally in Japanese)

Horiuchi, Y., Sado, M., Suzuki, K., Hasegawa, M., Sakamoto, A., Isshiki, N., et al. (2009). Content analysis of violence appearing in Japanese news programs: Its characteristic features compared to the real world and other TV genres. *Japanese Journal of Applied Psychology*, *34*(Suppl), 15–20.

Ihori, N., Sakamoto, A., Shibuya, A., & Yukawa, S. (2008). Effects of video games on aggressive as well as positive social behavior of children: A panel study with elementary school students. *Journal of Digital Games Research*, *2*, 35–44. (Originally in Japanese)

Ishii, K. (2006). Implications of mobility: The uses of personal communication media in everyday life. *Journal of Communication*, *56*, 346–365.

Ito, M., Okabe, D., & Matsuda, M. (Eds.) (2005). *Personal, Portable, Pedestrian: Mobile Phones in Japanese Life*. Cambridge, MA: MIT Press.

Iwao, S. (2000). *Terebi dorama no messeiji: Syakaishinrigaku teki bunseki* [Messages from television dramas: Social psychological analysis]. Tokyo: Keiso Shobo. (Originally in Japanese)

Jackson, L. A., von Eye, A., Biocca, F. A., Barbatsis, G., Zhao, Y., & Fitzgerald, H. E. (2006). Children's home internet use: Antecedents and psychological, social, and academic consequences. In Kraut, R., Brynin, M., & Kiesler, S. (Eds.), *Computers, Phones, and the Internet: Domesticating Information Technology*. New York: Oxford University Press, pp. 145–167.

Kamakura, T., Tomiyasu, S., & Baba, A. (2009). The educational effects of the history classes using MMORPG: Report of the experiment in a technical high school. *Journal of Digital Games Research*, *3*, 1–12. (Originally in Japanese)

Kashibuchi, M., Sakamoto, A., Kobayashi, K., Ando, R., Kimura, F., Adachi, N., et al. (2003). The effects of Internet in school on students' readiness for informationized society: A quasi-experimental study of secondary school students. *Japan Journal of Educational Technology*, *26*, 377–383. (Originally in Japanese)

Kawaura, Y. (2009). *Nihon no intahnetto shinrigaku no kenkyuushi: Pasokon tsuushin kara intahnetto made* [The history of internet psychology in Japan: From online computer services to the Internet]. In Kawaura, Y., Morio, H., & Miura, A. (Eds.), *Frontiers in Internet Psychology: Individual, Group, and Society*. Tokyo: Seishin Shobo, pp. 5–15. (Originally in Japanese)

Kawaura, Y., Morio, H., & Miura, A. (Eds.) (2009). *Intahnetto shinrigaku no hurontia: Kojin, syuudan, syakai* [Frontiers in Internet psychology: Individual, group, and society]. Tokyo: Seishin Shobo. (Originally in Japanese)

Keaten, K., Kelly, L., Pribyl, C., & Sakamoto, M. (2009). Fear and competence in Japan and the U.S.: Fear of negative evaluation, affect for communication channels, channel competence, and use of computer mediated communication. *Journal of Intercultural Communication Research*, *38*, 23–39.

Kitada, A., & Otawa, N. (Eds.) (2007). *Kodomo to nyuumedia* [Children and new media]. Tokyo: Nihontosho Center. (Originally in Japanese)

Kobayashi, T. (2010). *Kan'youna syakai wo sasaeru jouhou tsuushin gijutsu: Yuruyakani tsunagariau netto jidai no syakaishinri* [Information communication technology to support a tolerant society: Social psychology in the era of the loosely connected net]. Tokyo: Taga Shuppan. (Originally in Japanese)

Kodaira, S. I. (1998). A review of the research on media violence in Japan. In Carlsson, U. & von Feilitzen, C. (Eds.), *Children and Media Violence*. Goteborg, Sweden: The UNESCO International Clearinghouse on Children and Violence on the Screen, pp. 81–105.

Kodaira, S. I. (2008). *Eizou media no tenkai: Terebi no toujou soshite mirai* [The development of image media: The emergence of television and the future]. In Hashimoto, Y. (Ed.), *Media Communication Science*. Tokyo: Taishukan Shoten, pp. 29–49. (Originally in Japanese)

Kraut, R., Kiesler, S., Boneva, B., Cummings, J., Helgeson, V., & Crawford, A. (2002). Internet paradox revisited. *Journal of Social Issues*, *58*, 49–74.

Kraut, R., Lundmark, V., Patterson, M., Kiesler, S., Mukopadhyay, T., & Scherlis, W. (1999). Internet paradox: A social technology that reduces social involvement and psychological well-being? *American Psychologist*, *53*, 1017–1031.

McKenna, K. Y. A., & Bargh, J. A. (1998). Coming out in the age of the Internet: Identity demarginalization through virtual group participation. *Journal of Personality and Social Psychology, 75*, 681–694.

Matsuda, M. (2000). Friendship of young people and their usage of mobile phones: From the view of "superficial relation" to "selective relation." *Journal of Socio-information Studies, 4*, 111–122. (Originally in Japanese)

Matsuda, M. (2008). *Denwa no hatten: Keitai bunka no tenkai* [The development of telephones: The spread of mobile phone culture]. In Hashimoto, Y. (Ed.), *Media Communication Science*. Tokyo: Taishukan Shoten, pp. 11–28. (Originally in Japanese)

Muto, T. (Ed.) (1987). *Terebi to kodomo no hattatsu* [Television and development of children]. Tokyo: University of Tokyo Press. (Originally in Japanese)

Naito, M., Sakamoto, A., Mouri, M., Kimura, F., Kashibuchi, M., Kobayashi, K., et al. (2003). The effect of the Internet in schools on children's ability of practical use of information: A quasi-experimental study of secondary school students. *Educational Technology Research, 26*, 11–20.

Nakamura, I. (2003). Loneliness and the uses of the short message service (SMS). *Matsuyama University Review, 14*, 85–99. (Originally in Japanese)

Nakano, S., & Watanabe, Y. (2007). *Kyuuzou suru intahnetto riyou no jittai: IT jidai no seikatsu jikan chousa 2006 kara* [The rapid increase of Internet use: From the 2006 time use survey in the IT age]. *The NHK Monthly Report on Broadcast Research, 57*(4), 20–39. (Originally in Japanese)

Omi, R., Hattori, H., & Sakamoto, A. (2009). TV viewing and children's cognitive skills. *Media Asia, 37*, 42–53.

Richardson, R., & Smith, S. (2007). The influence of high/low-context culture and power distance on choice of communication media: Students' media choice to communicate with professors in Japan and America. *International Journal of Intercultural Relations, 31*, 479–501.

Sado, M., Sakamoto, A., & Suzuki, K. (2004). Content analysis of prosocial and antisocial behavior in Japanese TV programs. *Japan Journal of Educational Technology, 28*(Suppl), 77–80. (Originally in Japanese)

Sakamoto, A. (2000). Video games and violence: Controversy and research in Japan. In von Feilitzen, C., & Carlsson, U. (Eds.), *Children in the New Media Landscape: Games, Pornography, Perceptions*. Goteborg, Sweden: The UNESCO International Clearinghouse on Children and Violence on the Screen, pp. 61–77.

Sakamoto, A. (Ed.) (2003). *Media to ningen no hattatsu: Terebi, Terebigeimu, Intahnetto, soshite robotto* [Media and human development: Psychological effects of television, video games, the Internet, and Robots]. Tokyo: Gakubunsha. (Originally in Japanese)

Sakamoto, A. (2004). *Terebigeimu to kodomo no kokoro: Kodomotachi ha kyoubouka shiteikunoka?* [Video games and the minds of children: Are they becoming violent?]. Tokyo: Metamor Publishing. (Originally in Japanese)

Sakamoto, A. (2005). Video games and the psychological development of Japanese children. In Shwalb, I. D. W., Nakazawa, J., & Shwalb, B. J. (Eds.), *Advances in Applied Developmental Psychology: Theory, Practice, and Research from Japan*. Greenwich, CT: Information Age Publishing, pp. 3–21.

Sakamoto, A. (Ed.) (2007). *Terebi bangumi no bouryoku byousya ni taisuru hyouka shisutemu no kouchiku: Naiyoubunseki to juudanteki chousa ni motozuite* [Establishment of a system to assess violence shown in television programs: Based on content analysis and longitudinal studies] (Report on the 2003–2006 Study Funded by the Grants-in-Aid for Scientific Research A from the Japan Society for Promotion of Science). Tokyo: Department of Psychology, Ochanomizu University. (Originally in Japanese)

Sakamoto, A., Isogai, N., Kimura, F., Tsukamoto, K., Kasuga, T., & Sakamoto, T. (2002). Using the Internet as the sociality trainer of shy people: An experiment of female university students. *Educational Technology Research, 25*, 1–7.

Sakamoto, A., Minamisawa, U., Horiuchi, Y., Shibuya, A., Suzuki, K., Sado, M., et al. (July, 2008). The amount and characteristics of violence scenes in Japanese television and video games. In Anderson, C., & Sakamoto, A. (Chairs), *Media Violence: Racism, Sexism, and Aggression*. Symposium talk presented at the 18th World Meeting of International Society for Research on Aggression, Budapest, Hungary.

Sakamoto, T. (Ed.) (2002). *Media shinrigaku nyuumon* [Introduction to media psychology]. Tokyo: Gakubunsha. (Originally in Japanese)

Shadish, W. R., Cook, T. D., & Campbell, D. T. (2002). *Experimental and Quasi-Experimental Designs for Generalized Causal Inference*. Boston: Houghton Mifflin.

Shimizu, Y., Yamamoto, T., Horita, T., Koizumi, R., & Yokoyama, T. (2008). The comprehensive analysis results for advancement of student's academic achievement in classes by use of ICT. *Japan Journal of Educational Technology, 32*, 293–303. (Originally in Japanese)

Shimura, M. (2005). *Intahnetto no komunikeisyon riyou ga kojin ni motarasu kiketsu* [Effect of Internet communication on individuals]. In Ikeda, K. (Ed.), *Internet community and daily living*. Tokyo: Seishin Shobo, pp. 112–131. (Originally in Japanese)

Shirai, T., & Sakamoto, T. (Eds.) (1987). *Terebi ha youji ni nani ga dekiruka: Atarashii youjibangumi no kaihatu* [What can television do for young children? The development of new television programs for young children]. Tokyo: The Japan Association for Educational Broadcasting. (Originally in Japanese)

Suzuki, K. & Tsuji, D. (2005). *Keitai wa "han shakaiteki sonzai" ka?: Danpenka suru kankeisei* [Is the mobile phone an "anti-social device"? Fragmented interpersonal relations]. *Quarterly InterCommunication, 55*, 64–69. (Originally in Japanese)

Tajima, S., Suzuki, K., Sado, M., Hasegawa, M., Horiuchi, Y., Sakamoto, A., et al. (July, 2007). *Content analysis of violent images in Japanese TV commercials*. Paper presented at the 7th Biennial Conference of Asian Association of Social Psychology, Kota Kinabalu, Malaysia.

Takahira, M. (2009). *Intahnetto riyou to seishinteki kenkou* [Use of the Internet and psychological health]. In Kawaura, Y., Morio, H., & Miura, A. (Eds.), *Frontiers in Internet Psychology: Individual, Group, and Society*. Tokyo: Seishin Shobo, pp. 20–58. (Originally in Japanese)

Takahira, M., Ando, R., & Sakamoto, A. (2008). Effect of Internet use on depression, loneliness, aggression, and preference for Internet communication: A panel study with 10- to 12-year-old children in Japan. *International Journal of Web Based Communities, 4*, 302–318.

Takano, Y., & Noda, A. (1993). A temporary decline of thinking ability during foreign language processing. *Journal of Cross-Cultural Psychology, 24*, 445–462.

The Cabinet Office of Japan (2007). *A Report from the 5th Survey of Attitudes to Information Society and Young People in It*. Retrieved May 1, 2011 from http://www8.cao.go.jp/youth/kenkyu/jouhou5/index.html. (Originally in Japanese)

Thomee, S., Eklof, M., Gustaffson, E., Nilsson, R., & Hagberg, M. (2007). Prevalence of perceived stress, symptoms of depression and sleep disturbances in relation to information and communication technology use among young adults. *Computers in Human Behavior, 23*, 1300–1321.

Tsuji, D. (1999). *Wakamono no komyunikeisyon no hen'you to atarashii media* [Changes in communication among young people and new media tools]. In Hashimoto, Y., & Funatsu, M. (Eds.), *Children and Young People, and Communication*. Tokyo: Hokuju Shuppan, pp. 11–27. (Originally in Japanese)

Van den Eijnden, R. J. J. M., Meerkerk, G. J., Vermulst, A. A., Sijkerman, R., & Engels, R. C. M. E. (2008). Online communication, compulsive Internet use, and psychosocial well-being among adolescents: A longitudinal study. *Developmental Psychology, 44*, 655–665.

von Feilitzen, C. (1998). Introduction. In Carlsson, U., & von Feilitzen, C. (Eds.), *Children and Media Violence*. Goteborg, Sweden: The UNESCO International Clearinghouse on Children and Violence on the Screen, pp. 45–54.

Youth Affairs Administration of the Management and Coordination Agency (1995). *Kodomo to kazoku ni kansuru kokusai hikaku chousa no gaiyou* [An overview of international comparison of children and families]. Retrieved May 1, 2011 from http://www8.cao.go.jp/youth/kenkyu/kodomo/kodomo.htm. (Originally in Japanese)

PART 6

Conclusions and Future Directions

Media Content Analysis: Qualitative Methods

Michael R. Neal

Abstract

Although qualitative methods traditionally suffer from concerns about reliability, validity, and researcher bias (see Chapter 8), new computer-assisted methods can assist in addressing these issues. Intelligent software, integrated with mixed methods and visualizations can be a valuable tool for media psychology researchers. Techniques for automated text coding assistance, concept, theme, and data relationship extraction with advanced text analytics capabilities provide the ability for researchers to examine large volumes of poor quality data, such as those found in social media studies.

The current chapter examines quantitative, qualitative, and text analytics methods within the context of a qualitative media content analysis. For media researchers, an example within the chapter provides insight into many of the challenges of extracting meaning from text. As an exemplar of integrated methods, this chapter extends the exploration of a definition for media psychology from the Introduction of this handbook to derive a definition of media psychology from the actual content of the *Handbook*.

Key Words: automated analysis, content analysis, media psychology, qualitative methodology, quantitative methodology, sampling bias, social media, text analytics, text corpus, visual display

Content Analysis of the *Oxford Handbook of Media Psychology*

The proliferation of electronic data via social media, traditional media on the Internet, and digital translations of audio and video content provides a rich and vast source of data for analysis by social scientists. Although the availability of usable data has increased significantly, the ability to analyze that very data is challenged due to traditional manual analysis methods with significantly increased data volumes. For example, manual coding and analysis of hundreds of thousands of Twitter messages is impractical for many research projects. Therefore, many traditional methods require a sampling strategy to reduce data sizes to a manageable collection. Unbiased sampling strategies for data collection and reduction are often difficult to create for these data,

and time to publish results is often shorter because of the timeliness and relevance of those data. New methods for content analysis are needed to meet these demands for emerging media psychology research. One approach is a content analysis that incorporates elements of grounded theory, intelligent and (at least partially) automated computer software, and generous use of visualization techniques to assist researchers with new and integrated analysis methods.

Early practitioners of media studies conducted content analyses on printed books, and these systematic analyses of texts were performed several times by religious scholars prior to 1900 (Krippendorff, 2004). Early media content analyses included propaganda studies from World War II, notably those by Harold Lasswell (Neuendorf, 2002). In 1954,

James Flanagan provided a formal method for analysis called critical incident technique (CIT), which provided specific procedures for psychological research (Wertz et al., 2011). The General Inquirer Project at Harvard in the 1960s was created to analyze written messages (Neuendorf, 2002). More broadly, the field of qualitative research and the use of that term expanded greatly in the late 1980s and 1990s (Wertz et al., 2011). Today, qualitative research and content analysis techniques continue to evolve as a mainstream science, which strives to adapt to changing data and research needs (Wertz, et al., 2011).

In the 21st century, content and data for media psychologists are found in a range of sources from historical records and massive media collections, including newspapers, magazines, websites, blogs, text messages, tweets, Facebook pages, and emails. Audio content, such as radio programs, interview transcripts, and conversations, can be transcribed into text. Likewise, video, such as television, movies, news footage, and YouTube videos, can also be transcribed or computer translated into text. Finally, images can be described with added text and metadata (additional or ancillary information about the data) encoded with demographics and other descriptive data. All of these sources may be combined or examined individually as part of a study. This extensive proliferation of traditional, electronic, and social media data is leading to strong interest in content analyses, more powerful software tools, and integrated methods.

With more tools and formal methods available to media psychology researchers, high quality analysis for a wide range of media is possible and can further advance this emerging field. There are many potential methods that are software assisted and augmented by visualization, and several of these techniques are discussed later in this chapter when meaning making is covered. One such analysis will be performed on this handbook as both an exemplar and a meaning extraction exercise. This will assist creating a definition of media psychology derived from this first edition of the *Oxford Handbook of Media Psychology*.

Media Content Analysis Methods

Traditionally, content analysis is divided into quantitative (counting) and qualitative (meaning) methods, which are used separately or together (i.e., mixed methods) to interpret data. Quantitative measurements are generally straightforward and noncontroversial because they primarily involve counting words or concepts. Concepts are symbols, often textual, that represent categories or actual objects in the world (Lakoff, 1987). Qualitative analyses, however, can be controversial and subject to criticism, replicability, and doubt because these analyses are not reduced to mathematical equations with accepted defined use-case scenarios. There are many qualitative methods for interpreting text, and researcher skill, experience, bias, and process affect the outcomes. In media content analyses, these issues also exist, as well as how to handle large amounts of data.

Media qualitative analysis, especially a content analysis, has the central problem of how to reduce the complete text corpus (i.e., text collection) to smaller sets of text and concepts (Weber, 1990). This reduction is often the first step in a meaning-making exercise where extraction of key elements is performed based on the researcher's knowledge and method. These key elements are expressed as concepts. These concepts then become their own unit of meaning (Popping, 2000).

Important aspects of content analysis include sampling, units of measure, coding, validity, and reliability, which can alleviate concerns over repeatability and bias. An overview of both quantitative and qualitative methods for content analyses is explored within the framework of media-specific analyses. Note this chapter is concerned with content analyses of text data or data converted to text. For an examination of multimedia analysis techniques see Ali, Lee, and Smeaton (2011).

Quantitative Analysis

Quantitative analysis is concerned primarily with counting and statistics. There are several aspects of measuring in content analysis. One is to focus on the concepts themselves. To begin a quantitative analysis, because of the volume of some data collections, the researcher should be cognizant of preferred parameters of concept extraction. Carley (1993) provided guidance for researchers for approximate quantitative ranges for a desired number of concepts by proposing that 100 to 500 concepts provides sufficient generalization for a proper analysis, whereas fewer than 25 concepts hides meaning. The number of concepts generated can typically be configured in a software program.

Once the general parameters of extraction are determined, the measurements should be designed. Numeric measurements often include word, or concept, frequencies. The existence of a word (i.e., frequency >0) may itself indicate meaning, or the number of times a word or concept appears and where it appears may indicate a different or expanded meaning. Words can be combined into more general concepts and concepts into themes to provide associations. One method of determining associations is the proximity between concepts as calculated by the distance between them, which indicates if the words "co-occur." Co-occurrence frequencies of words and concepts can be used to determine relationships and assist with meaning extraction by providing the researcher an indication of the concepts that are discussed together most often.

To extract meaning, the researcher must make observations or establish a method for analysis. For example, the top ten concepts might be meaningful. The co-occurring words to specific concepts will also show relationships, especially if emotive words are used (i.e., potential sentiment indicators). The frequencies themselves and relative counts are indications of strength, or coverage, across the text collection. Substantial drop-offs in frequencies or other statistics may also serve to group similarities of concepts or relationships of concepts. Prior to completing the study design, it is incumbent on the researcher to explore all quantitative measures available though software tools and manual processes.

While quantitative measures can provide insight, it is important to also analyze the text in its own context to retain meaning (Miles & Huberman, 1994). Numbers often have a meaning specific in the context, and this should be part of the analysis. For example, one method of analysis is to create a category and assign word frequencies for words found in each category. For a study examining the number of violent incidents against women in a television drama series, example categories might be threatening language, demeaning statements, and actual violent acts. The strength of representations of the frequencies in these categories provides a measure of meaning (Weber, 1990). In addition to meaning extraction itself, differences in frequency counts of words and concepts can also be used for comparative analysis of texts or sub-collections of texts (Carley, 1993). Thus, meaning can be inferred from purely numerical analysis, but the context and richness found in textual data augment meaning with examples and details.

Qualitative Analysis

Qualitative research in media psychology focuses less on numeric data measurements and more on the meaning embedded in the data. The field of qualitative analysis has evolved over the previous decades with many distinct types of analyses. Qualitative data are unique and can offer insights into information because the data can preserve chronology, consequences of specific events, and often detailed explanations (Miles & Huberman, 1994). The analyses of these data in the social sciences are broad-based and can also provide insight into experiences, emotions, and cultural phenomena (Strauss & Corbin, 1998). Due to the varied nature of the data, wide-ranging researcher questions, and methods for examining these data, many methods have evolved with different approaches and techniques.

The research question itself guides the selection of the specific qualitative method by a set of characteristics (Richards & Morse, 2007). Whichever method is selected, however, the primary difficulty with analyzing any text collection is often the determination of meaning. Different analysts can and often do read the same text and extract different meanings. The researcher makes a determination of both what he or she sees in the data as well as how to describe it, and the process of interpretation is left to the researcher. In a purely traditional qualitative examination, it is solely researcher interpretation that makes meaning.

The phrase "interpretation of meaning" does not imply that no formal methods exist for this process. In fact, there is a strong historical basis for qualitative research as a science (see Packer, 2011). Many well-established qualitative analysis methods have been developed which inform media studies. In particular, Wertz et al. (2011) provided a case study for five qualitative analysis techniques: phenomenological psychology, grounded theory, discourse analysis, narrative analysis, and intuitive inquiry. Wertz and colleagues provided a running conversation among the five authors and experts in their respective fields analyzing the same data. This insightful book also provides an exemplar of how different approaches may be valid and answer similar or diverse research questions across a single data collection. Frost et al. (2010) described the project Pluralism in Qualitative Research (PQR) undertaken to explore integration of several methods. This project examined approaches and methods of several research assistants in analyzing data with four qualitative methods to better understand processes and nuances of differing methods. These efforts show that integration and use of multiple qualitative methods in a single study warrants attention. As Wertz et al. noted, qualitative traditions share roots and historically inform each other. Therefore, even if quantitative measurements and computer-assisted software are only part of the process, media psychology researchers should consider these traditional approaches for their analyses as well.

One qualitative methodology, which supports the discovery of concepts, themes, and relationships in the data, is grounded theory. Traditional grounded theory described by Glaser and Strauss (1967) leads to the discovery of theory and uncovers unknown qualities about the data. In media studies, a well-defined question at the inception of a study is not always the case. The more open the question, the more discovery is done and, typically, the more objective the analysis. Because data drive the results, grounded theory is often considered to be the best method to reduce researcher bias in qualitative analyses. The codes in grounded theory assist the researcher in segmenting, classifying, and dividing the data according to conceptual meaning (Wertz et al., 2011). This approach alone may or may not provide an answer to a specific research question or thoroughly illuminate a collection of media Therefore, researchers can and often should combine methodologies by adding additional forms of qualitative research to their overall process. For example, a combination of grounded theory and content analysis can be an excellent approach (Bernard & Ryan, 1998).

As previously observed, a central fundamental component of grounded theory or any of these formalized qualitative methods is the question of how to derive meaning from texts. If a researcher is examining a manageable collection of short texts and is an expert in his or her field, a particular method such as those listed by Wertz et al. (2011) is appropriate. However, if the number of texts is large or a simple content analysis is desired at the start of a project, either for meaning making, data reduction, or as a navigation and search aid, there are more technical approaches to be examined. These include several specific techniques informed by text analytics such as content extraction, semiotic analysis, semantic network, and part of speech analysis.

While grounded theory describes an approach for making meaning, there are many techniques to perform this task. First, computer assisted or automated text analysis performs the function of bringing organization and structure to naturally unstructured text collections (Popping, 2000). Next, data must be synthesized into output a researcher can analyze, make inferences from, and explore the underlying data in order to extract meaning.

Text coding is the process of examining text in a specific, measurable unit and extracting relevant data. Researchers look for words, phrases, and word sense from defined measurements of units of text (i.e., words, sentences, paragraphs, tweets). Coding is accomplished by progressively identifying and integrating categories to compose meaning (Willig, 2008). There are three general methods of coding: (1) manual: by person(s) coding from codebooks, instructional guides, or intuition; (2) computer-assisted: beginning with coding then often some automation for remaining documents; and (3) computer generated: by statistical algorithms or network analysis informed by text analytics techniques.

There are several computer-assisted techniques for data reduction and meaning making from large text collections. Hopkins and King (2010) provided a method analyzing multiple document sets and determining estimates of coverage for researcher input categories of interest. They provided document generalizations appropriate for many social science content analyses. Smith and Humphreys (2006) provided a system that performs statistical analysis over an entire collection, generates a coding dictionary from that specific corpus, and identifies concepts, themes, and co-occurrence frequencies. This system has a basis in grounded theory and implementation with quantitative foundations, and it is the theory underlying the product Leximancer used in the analysis later in this chapter.

Semiotic analysis is an approach for meaning assignment. Since a text collection is a series of text components used to convey a message, the meaning found in these texts can be discerned by using linguistic techniques of analysis (Berger, 2005). The search for signs in the text produces meaning points from that text. Another approach for content analysis is semantic network analysis (Van Atteveldt, 2008). Text content is represented as a network of objects. In another approach, Tauszik and Pennebaker (2010) examined part of speech analysis in text analytics. They contended that nouns, regular verbs, and adjective/adverbs represent content words, while parts of speech such as pronouns, prepositions, articles, and conjunctions (e.g., *it*, *and*, *the*) comprise style words. They observed that these style words are how people communicate, and content words contain what is being communicated. In another method, Bernard and Ryan (1998) offered that text analysis has become a method to create and extract an entire model, or schema, from the data, especially for discourse analysis. Schema mapping is a well-known technique from psychology (see Lakoff, 1987).

In summary, there are many approaches in qualitative analysis of which content analysis is one. A content analysis is best when both quantitative and qualitative approaches are combined (Weber, 1990). This has been traditionally called mixed methods. With large and varied text collections found in media and social media, mixed methods may not be limited to quantitative versus qualitative, but may be an integration of multiple qualitative methods as a sequential process. Additional qualitative methods such as those demonstrated by Wertz et al. (2011) can be explored by following those concept links deep into the actual text to ensure context and associated meaning derivable by a specific technique, such as narrative analysis.

Issues in Content Analysis

No matter which content analysis approach is taken, from a manual analysis by an acknowledged expert to a fully automated, computer-driven statistical analysis of a text, there are several issues researchers must address. The primary concerns are sampling strategies and study reliability. These issues address researcher bias, which must be limited to ensure meaningful and worthy results. Reliability is critical in a qualitative study, so that results can be reproduced and understood by other researchers conducting similar and derivative studies.

Sampling is a method to take subsets of documents to study. Especially when manual coding is to be performed or research-intensive interpretation is required for the entire text collection, sampling is a practical and required method to enable a project to be considered and then completed. In theory, it simply requires two major activities: identify the complete text collection and identify units of analysis within these texts (Bernard & Ryan, 1998). In practice, sampling can be used to reduce voluminous data to a manageable amount of data. However, an artificial sampling plan to reduce data or to allow a particular analysis method may create an element of bias before the text is analyzed. It is also possible that data may be inadvertently omitted. With increasingly large media collections and research questions examining specific issues or subtleties, researchers should evaluate other options to avoid sampling simply to reduce analysis time.

Sample collections require a definition of data resolution. This decision is important for a study because it impacts both the data collected and the analysis segment size. For example, a media psychologist might study treatment of race in television comedies. A sample and resolution might be specified as follows: television comedies, 1/2 hour, and Wednesday nights between 8:00 pm and 11:00 pm. For a microblogging social media communication such as Twitter, samples might range from tweets from a single user or a collection of tweets on a specific topic during a specific time period. Content analysts must determine these units to measure. Importantly, these units of measure can significantly impact relationships of words and coding because frequencies of occurrence and concept discovery are restricted to occur within these units. Researchers must be cognizant of the sampling strategy chosen and the data generated from that strategy.

Finally, reliability and repeatability must be examined, especially if automated tools and large text collections are used. One measure of accuracy is tied to statistical norms, and accuracy is the strongest form of reliability (Weber, 1990). Thus, a computer program, which uses proven methods and is repeatable, is a good tool to aid in a valid content analysis. By following a formal methodology, utilizing computer tools, and employing visual aids for both analysis and communication, media psychologists can limit these issues for their content analyses.

Making Meaning from Text

Whatever tools a researcher uses to assist in qualitative research, he or she must understand the basic theory for text reduction and concept extraction if it will be part of his or her research process. To understand how a software tool examines and processes text, an example text segment from this handbook will be examined and manually processed. This example of coding is one of the critical stages for a content analysis and meaning making. This paragraph is from Rutledge (Chapter 3, this volume):

> The ubiquity of technology is driving home the point that human experience is not separable from technology and vice versa. While emerging technologies and new models of communication add to the complexity of study, the integration of media into daily life highlights the importance of the human experience and systems of relationships as the focal point of study. It is here where media psychology brings a different perspective than other fields of study. It has the breadth of theory and tools to examine the behavior and interactions of individuals, groups, and organizations. It is not constrained by the type of technology, but understands the mediation that technology affords.

It can, therefore, apply the lens of psychology to any form of human experience mediated by technology. (p. 56)

A human coder would easily ignore the many words that do not add to meaning, such as articles and prepositions. The pronoun *it* would be consciously replaced with actual nouns and those concepts carried forward. To examine how meaning might be made of this paragraph and data reduced to a few concepts, the paragraph will be examined in one potential scenario.

First, the resolution needs to be set for coding. For this example, the resolution is a sentence. Words are examined selected based on their importance. In a statistics-based program, several processing iterations are made to identify significant occurrences of words and create a coding dictionary. Since this example is only a single paragraph, it will be assumed that the full text collection was examined to generate the coding dictionary from all text. The paragraph is repeated with underline, bold, and italics denoting identified concepts and their counts shown afterwards.

> The ubiquity of *technology* is driving home the point that human experience is not separable from *technology* and vice versa. While emerging *technologies* and new models of communication add to the complexity of study, the integration of ***media*** into daily life highlights the importance of the human experience and systems of relationships as the focal point of study. It is here where ***media*** **psychology** brings a different perspective than other fields of study. It has the breadth of theory and tools to examine the behavior and interactions of individuals, groups, and organizations. It is not constrained by the type of *technology*, but understands the mediation that *technology* affords. It can, therefore, apply the lens of **psychology** to any form of human experience mediated by *technology*.
> Concepts: *technology* (6), ***media*** (2), **psychology** (2)

In this paragraph, the concepts *technology*, *media*, and *psychology* all appear. Although *study*, *human*, *experience*, and *point* also have frequency counts greater than 1, an arbitrary assumption has been made that those concepts are less frequent elsewhere in the text. Thus, this text contains these three concepts of interest: *technology*, *media*, and *psychology*. There is an implied relationship because of their co-occurrence. A qualitative analysis other than content analysis would likely yield more results such as the context of the discussion connecting

technology and how media psychology fits into that context. For the content analysis, this segment would be a prism into the entire text as part of the overall text reduction to meaningful concepts. It is imperative, however, that the researcher can query or visually navigate to this specific text to retrieve original context when desired.

This type of analysis performed over a large text collection sentence by sentence demonstrates how it is possible to derive concepts and relationships. In many studies using qualitative analysis, computer programs traditionally perform mundane tasks for researchers, such as the elimination of uninteresting words like prepositions and articles. These are generally called stop words (e.g., *the, and, of, for*). Options are usually available to select stemming for frequency counts, which combines words with plural and singular forms (e.g., *technology = technologies*). Researchers may also need to combine synonyms from these extraction lists to provide more accurate total counts. Finally, compound words (e.g., "media psychologist") are important to identify and separate from individual counts where they are independent entities. Careful attention to these options, often subtle in text collections, will assist in accuracy and consistency of the results. Whatever approach is used, it is imperative that researchers understand the strengths and weaknesses of their approach and all tools used.

Automated and Intelligent Software Tools

A content analysis can be done without a computer. Although, at a minimum, a computer usually serves as a document file folder, backup mechanism, and a search tool for and within documents. As software continues to become more sophisticated, there will be a trend towards intelligent software integrated into multiple analysis methods that can enable studies not previously possible.

There are several areas where computer technology can expand to assist in automating and assisting in content analysis. For software to act with intelligence, it must be able to responsibly and consistently replace tasks that a human can provide at least as well. In one scenario, Van Atteveldt (2008) proposed three main areas for continued intelligent tool development: (1) expand concept abstraction beyond just counting word frequency counts, (2) extract relationships and their associated structures, and (3) develop algorithms where computers can do extractions. There are a number of software solutions available with varied capabilities that continually evolve. The availability and capability of these tools is not the scope of this chapter, and the reader is directed to evaluate the current capabilities of tools and products.

A primary capability of these software programs is to perform or assist with coding for later retrieval, comparison, and reporting. Coding is one of the critical aspects of qualitative research, and software can significantly enhance this capability with tools for organization, automated tagging, and document manipulation. Another key capability is search and retrieve, which is tied directly to coding and tagging source text segments and words and phrases of interest. For example, one traditional technique that researchers use is to manually code text on a line-by-line method, assigning an action to each line (Wertz et al., 2011). This time-consuming process allows for interpretation by the researcher as each line is manually coded, as in the earlier example of the Rutledge paragraph. However, manually coding tens of thousands of documents is not practical for most studies even if multiple human coders are employed (which then introduces coding inconsistencies known as interrater reliability).

Unfortunately, a simple computer analysis line by line can also be problematic. For example, the term *North Carolina* is a compound concept of the words *North* and *Carolina*. A software tool which looks strictly at word frequency counting will determine that *North Carolina*, *South Carolina*, and *Dr. Carolina Smith* yields three counts of the concept *Carolina*. A human coder recognizes these differences immediately and codes these as three distinct concepts. Therefore, computer-based tools must use algorithms to intelligently handle cases such as these.

Another issue for coding is the need for a coding dictionary. A predefined thesaurus applied prior to coding can miss concepts contained in the actual text, and a thesaurus constructed from a sample of the texts can miss data in the complete texts (Carley, 1993). Therefore, a tool that generates a corpus-specific (i.e., from the text collection itself) coding dictionary from analysis of the text in that particular collection will be most effective. If a coding dictionary is input, then it must be specific to the domain of the text collection at a minimum.

Automated and computer-assisted coding approaches, although occasionally creating issues, must be used in many media analyses wherein volumes are significant and manual coding can become time and cost prohibitive. For example, one recent study of public sentiment in Twitter used 1 billion tweets as its study data (O'Connor,

Balasubramanyan, Routledge, & Smith, 2010). As more media psychologists endeavor to examine these large text collections, intelligent and at least partially automated tools will become a staple of the researcher process. Fortunately, a large amount of data lends itself to a statistics-based approach for data reduction and meaning extraction.

As software capability evolves to support more complexity and linguistic nuances, the promise is that approaches can be developed, refined, and customized to support multiple methods of qualitative analysis. Strides have been made for content analysis and extraction of meaning quantitatively and qualitatively with concept and theme identification and relationship inferences. However, truly intelligent software will be enabling in many ways by allowing integration of modes of multimedia, the fast and inexpensive processing of voluminous data, and the reproducibility and understanding of language required for many qualitative analyses. Visualizations and smart querying will also be a component of these new software programs. The ultimate solution may be a hybrid system in which automation provides insights and meaning indicators, but the researcher remains in the process to interpret and guide the software.

Leximancer Text Analytics Software

The software tool used in the content analysis of this handbook is a statistics-based software tool called Leximancer. Leximancer uses machine learning and is language, vernacular, and syntax agnostic. Leximancer performs automatic coding of concepts from the text. This is appropriate for a content analysis because the methods that employ both quantitative and qualitative methods achieve the best results (Weber, 1990). While Leximancer automatically creates its own coding dictionary, it also has the capability to input a researcher's own concept seeds for forcing a focus on specific concepts found in the text collection. It has a feature to input a predefined sentiment list to assist in extracting sentiment (positive and negative emotive words) associated with concepts. This reduces researcher bias in the initial steps of a content analysis, because Leximancer serves as a discovery agent for the text collection. The concepts generated from the text compose themes for further explorations.

One advantage to a statistically based tool such as Leximancer is its ability to simulate human concept extraction. For example, a literal examination of text would miss a concept in a text block if that exact text did not appear. By using an approach that identifies surrounding, co-occurring words, the existence of those words can be used to indicate occurrence of the concept. This has a significant benefit in that the actual word does not need to be present for the concept to be found in the text. Evidence words in the form of a thesaurus provide statistical evidence that clusters of words all relate to one or more concepts. This mimics the role of a researcher, who understands that context and related words indicate a concept occurrence. Finally, it is important to observe that, in this type of thematic analysis, the relationship is discovered by software, but the nature of the relationships is the domain of the researcher (Popping, 2000).

Visual Analysis and Display

Visual data display for analysis is an important tool for a researcher. Visual displays can be used to provide insight into a text collection, as an aid in navigation into the text collection, and to convey results and meaning. Historically, imagery has served a role to provide abstraction of complexity and amplification of relevance in the study of meaning (Barry, 1997). In text analytics, visualization has often been used for quantitative data wherein numerical relationships are represented by a variety of techniques. Traditional charts include bar graphs showing word frequencies. However, visualization techniques in many fields have expanded beyond a simple display of facts to an effort to convey ideas (Yau, 2011).

There are two equally important reasons for using visual data mapping, or an art-informed inquiry. First, the researcher may derive new meaning and discover new insights, and secondly, share these insights in an easily understandable manner for readers and other researchers (Butler-Kisbe & Poldma, 2010). The selection of visualization metaphors is also important, and researchers should consider both existing and meaningful representations.

Concept Maps

One method of visual representation of a text collection is a concept map. At its core, written communication represented by a text collection is composed of words. Novak and Cañas (2006) stated that the roughly 460,000 words in the English language are mostly concept labels and can be further combined into other representations. Text collections for studies naturally contain a subset of this number, and further reductions are used as previously discussed to reduce the concepts, or word representations, to a smaller number. A concept map

then takes these remaining high value concepts and creates a visual representation in circles or boxes of the concept labels (see Figure 29.2 as an example).

Performing a content analysis is, in many ways, a data reduction exercise. The text is reduced and collated into themes, concepts, and thesauri describing evidence why these reductions were made. In data visualization, a technique called multidimensional scaling (MDS) serves the same function by clustering similar data into smaller collections, or groups for display (Yau, 2011). For text visualization, positioning of data on a coordinate system where similar text items cluster together form a meaningful visualization. These displays can be further heat-mapped to illustrate other dimensions of the concepts (i.e., hot or frequent topics are color coded to hot colors such as red and yellow, whereas low-occurring counts are cold colors such as blue). The purpose of these techniques is to view similar concepts from the data and visually allow for pattern searching and identification of outliers (Yau, 2011).

In Figure 29.1, the concepts from the previous analysis of the paragraph by Rutledge (this volume) are displayed. This diagram was created in a simple drawing program, but it conveys considerable information.

For example, the size of the circles adjacent to the concept labels can be used to denote relative frequency counts. Relationships can be displayed by connecting lines, and proximity of concepts can represent general proximity in the text. Concept maps allow the researcher to create and study the visual representation and relationships while taking a break from detailed textual examination (Butler-Kisbe & Poldma, 2010). Finally, encircling

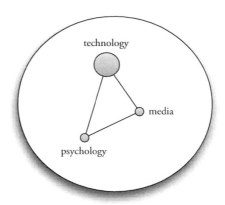

Figure 29.1 Theme Circle, Concept Labels, and Connections from Rutledge Paragraph.

concepts in proximity to each other in order to illustrate general topics found in the text can create a theme. For the Rutledge paragraph example, recall *technology* was the most frequent concept whereas *media* and *psychology* appeared in close proximity. All these concepts appeared together, which potentially represents a theme from the data. This example is intentionally small for illustration purposes, but the power of this type of visual display is readily observed when a large text collection such as the *Handbook* is represented with a dozen theme circles and their related concepts as shown in Figure 29.2. When these representations are combined into a concept map representing an entire text collection, the researcher can quickly affirm the content or learn new concepts and themes shown in this map.

Concept maps can be used in a systematic way for analysis. For example, ideas can be initially formed, emergent concepts explored, and representations created. Concept maps are particularly useful in initial stages of analysis when ideas are fuzzy and not yet organized (Butler-Kisbe & Poldma, 2010). Concept maps also provide a powerful psychological function in qualitative analysis. Butler-Kisbe and Poldma further elaborated:

> Concept maps allow the researcher to step outside the constraints of linear thinking and to engage in, and encourage the messy and nonlinear work of, the brain, and in so doing, tease out ideas and connections in the data that might otherwise remain implicit. It is when these implicit thoughts become apparent that the analysis can be pushed to a deeper level. (p. 11)

The reinforcing use of imagery can confirm data or guide a researcher to more areas of the analysis. For example, in early analysis of draft chapters, the concept *dill* was an outlier not shown with other themes. This is an interesting result because Dr. Karen Dill is the editor of the *Handbook*, and her name appears often throughout this text in that capacity. Because the software counted each time her name appeared on editorial notes, her name was an artifact from metadata to the chapters. This example represents an instance when the appearance of a term can be misleading, and it also shows the power of a visual outlier when examining a large set of data.

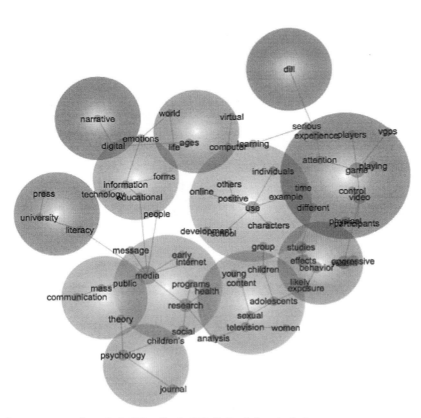

Figure 29.2 Early Concept Map from *Oxford Handbook of Media Psychology* Analysis.

Future Media Psychology Studies

Media psychology researchers face many of the same challenges as qualitative researchers in the social sciences. In particular, validity of research must continue to be addressed. With the ever-increasing volumes of data and the availability of computer tools, researchers now must address validity in the form of reproducibility and stability as well as communication of complexities in their methods and tools. Procedures and documentation methods must be standardized to help address these issues and provide confidence in evolving research methods.

In an example of the current state of research reporting on qualitative studies, Bluhm, Harman, Lee, and Mitchell (2010) examined management sciences articles to summarize methods and approaches from the previous 10 years of journal articles in Europe and North America. Because of the lack of standard reporting parameters and inconsistency of data reported, Bluhm et al. did not examine techniques used in the analyses, but they discussed only what was reported. They found that 45% of the articles they reviewed had poor and incomplete descriptions of both analysis techniques and data collection methods.

The combination of computer assisted and automated text processing software tools with enhanced visualization provides further challenges for reporting study parameters. Table 29.1 is provided as an exemplar for the type of data that should be added in a summary table for media psychology qualitative research. Collection of this data will allow communication of methods as well as repeatability of results by other researchers using the same or similar tools and techniques. The study parameters for content analysis of this handbook will be summarized in this format in the Discussion section of this chapter.

The initial table rows are informational. They are included in the use case wherein multiple studies are compiled for reference. The analysis method includes the general method or techniques used in the study. For instance, Content Analysis and Semiotic Analysis are examples. The Data Collection Method is short descriptive text describing how the data were collected. The Data Summary provides quantitative measures of the data. The Software Tools row includes all tools used and their respective version numbers. The Software Configuration section is critically important for reliability by reproducibility. If another researcher uses the same data and applies the same software configurations with the same software tool, the results should be replicated. This is the qualitative researchers' incarnation of quantitative researchers' use of a tool such as SPSS for consistent and acceptable statistical analyses.

Note, there are no results per se of the actual study. The reporting of results is left to the definition of the particular discipline (e.g., specific journal policies). However, it is not necessarily the purview of a journal or style guide to explain what needs to be disclosed for transparency, trustworthiness, and peer evaluation.

Table 29.2 contains a fictitious study with values inserted to demonstrate how a study's parameters and data can be standardized. The use of methods distilled to short descriptions and tools, data collec-

Table 29.1 Example Template to Disclose Pertinent Details in Media Psychology Research Projects.

Study Name	
Researchers: names	**Date: study date**
Study Question	
Analysis Method(s)	Examples include quantitative methods such as content analysis, discourse analysis, narrative analysis. Examples also include text analytics techniques such as statistical analysis, part of speech analysis, semiotic analysis.
Data Collection Method	Description on how the data was collected and any media considerations (e.g., translated from Spanish from audio to text by human transcribers)
Data Summary	Quantitative overview
Software Tools	List of all software tools used
Software Configuration	List of all changes made to default configurations and features enabled

Table 29.2 Summary of Fictitious Study on Twitter Commentary for a Political Study

Fictitious Study to Demonstrate Template	
Researchers: Neal, M., Pase, S.	Date: April 2012

Does Twitter Discussion From the January/February 2012 Republican Nomination Process Include Stereotypical Election Terminology?

Analysis Method(s)	Content Analysis into major themes Narrative Analysis of those themes
Data Collection Method	Purchase of keywords *Republican Democratic Primary* from GNIP Inc.'s Twitter Full Pipe. No sampling. All data collected was used.
Data Summary	$N = 1.35$ billion tweets; demographic data retained; user names removed
Software Tools	MyText Analytics Software 3.1, MySQL Database 2011
Analysis Tool Method	MyText Analytics Software uses word frequencies and network analysis to extract themes.
Software Configuration	MyText Analytics Software configurations: 1. Data resolution set to 1 sentence to treat tweets as a sentence. 2. Stemming ON so singular and plural words are combined. 3. Network Threshold setting to .45 on final run to remove visual noise from the display and only show top 25% of themes.

tion, and parameters provide a solid foundation for understanding what was done in the media study.

The data contained in this summary table provide a quick summary of the methods, software, configuration, and data collection. They address many of the concerns of Bluhm et al. (2010) on reporting and also address the issue of reproducibility for computer tools as their usage becomes more prevalent in media psychology research.

Content Analysis of This Handbook

The opening chapter of this volume provided several definitions of media psychology and the results from a survey of the *Oxford Handbook of Media Psychology* authors. Several succinct definitions emerged. Now that the *Handbook* has been completed, there is a further approach for defining this emerging field that can provide a more detailed yet expansive view of media psychology, at least in the context of the content submitted to this handbook. A content analysis was performed on the Table of Contents and on the actual book chapter text to determine the nature of the content written by the *Handbook* authors.

One could claim that a review of the table of contents for a book is at least a cursory content analysis. However, the title of a chapter is necessarily limited in scope compared with the content of the chapter itself, and the chapter content may

show emphasis and connections not revealed by a simple title. Furthermore, the editor drafted initial titles and the authors interpreted the editor's general content area themselves. Finally, a content analysis across all chapters helped determine dominant global themes, which may have existed embedded in chapters regardless of the theme of the chapter. Examples include elucidations of media psychology theory and methods, as well as themes (e.g., children and the media) and contextual factors (e.g., areas of controversy) and ideas (e.g., negative effects) that transcend specific content domains. Relationships are also important between concepts in different chapters and concepts within chapters. An examination of all themes and concepts and their relationships will best provide a survey of media psychology as found in this handbook.

Methodology

Two analyses will be performed on the *Oxford Handbook of Media Psychology*. First, a manual content analysis will be conducted on the Table of Contents. Then a computer-assisted content analysis will be done for each of the content chapters of the *Handbook*. The results of these two analyses will be compared, and a definition of media psychology will be produced.

The examination of the text of the Table of Contents will be a simple word frequency count of the titles with inconsequential parts of speech removed. This word count approach will use the repeated words for each chapter title to provide an indication of the aggregated summary of the *Handbook* contents in the succinct style of the short text descriptions.

The second analysis will be for chapters of the *Handbook* that are content chapters. Thus, the introduction and concluding chapters will be excluded. The content analysis of chapter text will be conducted using two distinct methods. First, a grounded theory approach will be used in which the concepts are identified and summarized according to themes. Evidence words in the form of a thesaurus of related words will be found automatically for each concept. This is done using a statistics-based approach in the software tool Leximancer to assist in an unbiased examination of raw text data. Concepts from the *Handbook* will be identified over several passes of the data, with configurations adjusted for data characteristics and data anomalies. Second, concepts related to media, psychology, and media psychology will be interpreted to understand the other topics that are explicitly tied to those concepts and to produce a definition of media psychology.

The Leximancer text analytics software program Version 4.0 (www.Leximancer.com) will perform coding and automated concept extraction for the *Handbook*. A coding dictionary will be generated automatically from the actual book text and successive iterations of coding, to generate themes, concepts, and a thesaurus of evidence words for those concepts. Quantitative data will be created, and the concept map is used to navigate to specific data excerpts for detailed examination of the source text. Frequency counts and concepts will be examined for the concepts *media*, *psychology*, and the compound *media-psychology*. Related concepts are first identified to what concepts appear together, or co-occur, in the text. This provides insight into proximity of concepts and when particular themes are discussed.

Sampling for the study was straightforward. All text from chapters was included with the exception of the introduction and concluding chapters. The nature of these chapters, focusing on describing and summarizing the *Handbook*, might arguably skew the results.

The source chapter files were Microsoft Word format except the *Video Games and Attention* chapter (Chapter 22, this volume), which was in Portable Data format (PDF). All changes and edits were accepted and saved. This removed metadata such

as the anomaly of the editor's name (i.e., *dill* concept discussion from earlier as its own concept). The References were left in to participate in the analysis. Tables, appendices, and figures were included, although no text extraction or augmentation was performed on embedded images.

As with any content analysis, the method must address the issues of reliability and validity. Reliability refers to stability and reproducibility. Both stability and reproducibility are achieved by use of a computer-driven tool whereby there are no issues with interrater reliability. Additionally, a measure of accuracy is tied to statistical norms, and accuracy is the strongest form of reliability (Weber, 1990). Thus, the use of a statistic-based software tool such as Leximancer aids in reliability through accuracy. Another aspect of reproducibility is manifested in procedures and process decisions researchers make. For example, when using a tool to assist in text analytics, software configurations can alter results as well as editing of the source text. Editing source text can be problematic as it introduces version control issues for the data. For large data collections, this may impact reproducibility. Therefore, no modification should be made to the original source data. Also important is a careful documentation of software configurations to allow reproducibility. Explanation of the reason for configurations is included as an aid in understanding.

Results

The first analysis is of the Table of Contents for the *Oxford Handbook of Media Psychology*. The Table of Contents contains chapter names for all 29 chapters, which are divided into six parts. Parts One and Six are administrative in nature, as they contain the introduction and conclusion. Therefore, content found in them for this study would be redundant to the chapters and Parts with content. Table 29.3 shows the Part titles with a description of the content for that Part.

The Part descriptions serve more as an organizing function than as a potential description of media psychology. Therefore, only the actual chapter titles were expanded into text paragraphs sans punctuation. Table 29.3 aggregates the text for each chapter title organized by Part. For the analysis, all of this text was combined into a single text extract for the word frequency counts.

Word frequencies were used as an indication of strength and order of importance. A free tool was used to count the frequencies (http://writewords. org.uk/word_count.asp). The words *and, the, in,*

Table 29.3 List of Chapter Titles Organized into Parts for the Oxford Handbook of Media Psychology.

Part: Title	Merged Chapter Titles
Two: History and Methods	storytelling and media narrative models from Aristotle to augmented reality is there a need for a distinct field of media psychology media psychology and its history inside media psychology the story of an emerging discipline as told by a leading journal media literacy history progress and future hopes research methods design and statistics in media psychology qualitative research and media psychology
Three: Issues and Media Types	children's media use a positive psychology approach media violence desensitization and psychological engagement why is it hard to believe that media violence causes aggression representation of gender in the media video game violence serious games what are they what do they do why should we play them race ethnicity and the media sexual media practice how adolescents select engage with and are affected by sexual media the psychology underlying media-based persuasion
Four: Interactive and Emerging Technologies	children adolescents and the internet are there risks online the role of emotion in media use and effects pathological technology addictions what is scientifically known and what remains to be learned video games and attention
Part Five: Meta Issues in Media Psychology	a general framework for media psychology scholarship media psychophysiology the brain and beyond engaging with stories and characters learning persuasion and transportation into narrative worlds the political narrative of children's media research Japanese approach to research on psychological effects of use of media

to, of, use, a, for, we, its, and *from* were excluded as inconsequential. These are typically listed in a stop list for computer programs to ignore and include parts of speech such as articles, prepositions, pronouns, and non-descriptive verbs. An analysis of the Merged Chapter Titles column then provided an indication of the concepts discussed by the chapter titles. Table 29.4 shows the results of the word frequency counts with a relative percentage to the most frequent word, *media*.

The Relevance Percentage column shows how each topic compares with *media* at 100% relevant as the most frequent word. For example, for *psychology*, 11/20 is 55%. This indicates that the word *psychology* appears slightly more than half as often as *media* (i.e., 55%). While not meant to be precise, this measure provides an initial overview of relative occurrences of terms. For example, the terms *media* and *psychology* appear substantially more often than the other terms. *Media* appears in 19 titles, *psychology* or a derivative in 11 titles, and both *media* and *psychology* in 10 titles. Six titles contained neither word.

Although this example is meant to be simple, several issues in analyzing text are illustrated. For example, a researcher has to decide which words are to be ignored. Although prepositions and articles make

Table 29.4 Meaningful Word Frequency Counts Greater than 1 from Chapter Titles.

Concept	Count	Relevance Percentage
media	20	100
psychology*	11	55
research	4	20
children	3	15
narrative	3	15
violence	3	15
adolescents	2	10
approach	2	10
effects	2	10
games	2	10
history	2	10
persuasion	2	10
sexual	2	10
video	2	10

Note: *The terms psychology, psychological, and psychophysiology were combined for this count.

sense, words like *approaches* and *effects* are a researcher's decision. When a large amount of text is analyzed, the inclusion, exclusion, or combination of terms and concepts can have meaningful effects. In this example, including the term *psychophysiology* moved the *psychology* root term to above 50%. Stemming (i.e., including plurals and extended words as roots) also affects counts and relationship analysis.

This type of manual examination can easily be done on a small text collection such as a table of contents. From this technique, a definition of media psychology is composed of the following concepts or topics: *research, children, narrative, violence, adolescents, approach, effects, games, history, persuasion, sexual,* and *video.* These are the results of the content analysis. Now the researcher's interpretation is required as to the meaning of these concepts. Several indicate content, such as *media* and *games,* whereas others indicate activity, such as *research* and *approach.* The Discussion section will provide the final analysis, as it is an interpretation of these results.

Oxford Handbook Entire Text Analysis

The next analysis was the chapter text of the *Oxford Handbook of Media Psychology.* Again, the Introduction and concluding chapters were omitted. A first run was performed with all default settings to provide an overview of the data and identify any issues or modifications required in settings.

The quantitative measurements for the *Handbook* were as follows: 25 book chapters with one chapter in each file. There were 1,271 pages in APA format, double-spaced with a mean 50.84 pages per chapter. The text was comprised of 23,833 sentences. A thesaurus of evidence words was generated with a total of 1,409 words.

The initial run produced a thematic summary, which serves as an indicator of the overall concepts grouped by themes. The themes are ranked for importance by summing the co-occurrence counts for all of the concepts within each theme. The logic is that more important concepts tend to be connected (i.e., co-occur) with other concepts on the map. The summary of ordered theme occurrences is shown in Figure 29.3.

These theme connectivity scores are ranked relative to one another by dividing each by the highest score. The themes chart indicates that *video, media,* and *db-id* (an anomaly discussed below) are dominant concepts in the *Handbook.* Although the themes are grouped using a mathematical threshold, the researcher can adjust them for reclustering. The results presented use the default setting in

Leximancer, which provides a generalized coverage analysis, and it is used here to provide an overall picture of the data.

This initial analysis by Leximancer identified concepts and reported their counts. Concepts are not simply word counts. A coding dictionary is developed automatically during the analysis, which evolves into a thesaurus, or list of evidence words, for each concept. This dictionary identifies word clusters and extracts concepts from the word occurrences. For example, if the thesaurus for *media* included *psychology, game,* and *research,* and those words occurred together without the explicit word *media,* Leximancer would still count an occurrence of the *media* concept. This is a powerful technique that mimics the interpretation capabilities of a manual coder. As noted earlier, the dynamically created thesaurus contained 1,409 word entries used for coded concepts specific to the *Handbook* content. The top concepts from the initial run are listed in Table 29.5.

This list is where researchers can look to quickly obtain a view of the initial text analysis. For example, the concepts *violence* and *violent* will be merged to provide a single concept on the topic of violence. Other potential anomalies can be identified at this point. Quick queries of the underlying data provide an indication of the actual text and provide a sense of confidence in the researcher.

This first run discussion would typically not be represented in a study. These results are included here as an example of the process a researcher using automated tools typically performs. For example, the theme *db-id* is an anomaly of the use of Microsoft Word as a data storage mechanism. The top five thesaurus terms for this concept in the *db-id* theme are *titlesecondary-title, secondary-title, app, db-idm,* and *contributorstitlesttle.* These are all terms associated with the computer program Endnote and its internal codes. Data anomalies are easily recognized by human coders but can be problematic for computer-assisted techniques. This is why a general query capability should be a feature of any tool to facilitate investigation of actual text segments coded.

There are two methods to deal with this anomaly. One is to change the storage mechanism to portable document format (PDF). The second option is to adjust configuration of the software tool. In this case, it is preferable to save the file as PDF to better emulate the state of the final chapter data for the *Handbook.* The use of draft chapters in Word proved a poor choice due to the inconsistent use and

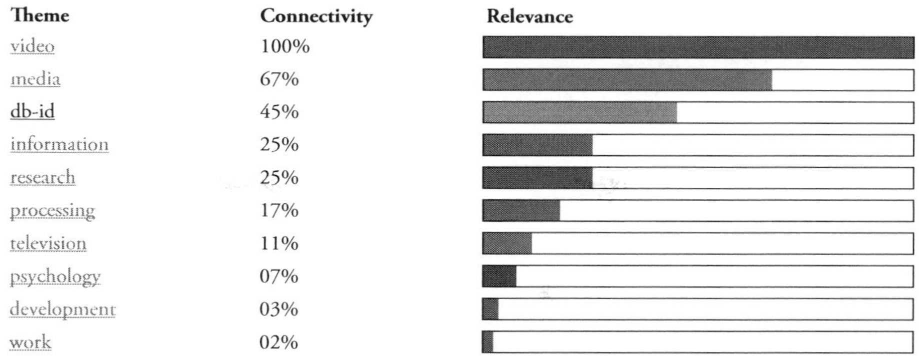

Theme	Connectivity	Relevance
video	100%	
media	67%	
db-id	45%	
information	25%	
research	25%	
processing	17%	
television	11%	
psychology	07%	
development	03%	
work	02%	

Figure 29.3 Ordered List of Themes, Their Connectivity, and Relevance from the Initial Run.

processing of metadata. The reason this issue was disclosed here is to highlight potential problems with the use of computer tools even though the tool was not incorrect, given the data. It was the data that were not correct. Although working through these issues is not difficult with software configuration, a better approach was to save the chapter drafts into PDF. This removed all the metadata and ensured consistent representations of the text (i.e., all chapters in the same format). The second run was performed and the anomalies were no longer present.

This detail is exposed to the reader to illustrate the need to both understand potential data anomalies and the capabilities of the chosen software tool to deal with those anomalies. All details concerning data preparation and software configuration must be provided in the study with justifications. It is important in media research, just as in traditional

Table 29.5 Top 10 Concepts Identified in Initial Run.

Concept	Count	Relevance Percentage
media	2,550	100
video	1,577	62
game	1,305	51
research	1,028	40
effects	908	36
violence	729	29
violent	669	26
studies	614	24
use	613	24
content	574	23

qualitative research, to document decisions and provide reasoning and justification, so readers of the research can understand decision points during the analysis.

Once the data were prepared, configuration of Leximancer needed to be performed. First, word variants were enabled to merge stems. The compound concept *video* AND *game* was created because video game is a prevalent topic in the *Handbook*. The compound concept *media* AND *psychology* was also created to determine relationships this combination would have. The concepts *violent* and *violence* were merged to indicate one singular concept. The final configuration included the addition of *et* and *al* to the stop word list to exclude APA citation repetition as a concept. The words *thus* and *use* were also added to the stop list because they surfaced as a concept due to the large use of the term by several writers and the interpretation of the researcher as inconsequential words.

Leximancer was then rerun for the final time. The resulting Theme Summary is shown in Figure 29.4.

The themes, which are based on dominant concepts found, changed in several ways. The anomalies from Endnote citation insertions are gone. Video remained the top theme and six of the original themes are present in the final run (i.e., video, research, media, television, information, and development). These themes are indicators of underlying clusters of concepts, so a more detailed analysis is required to extract sufficient meaning.

The final concept map is shown in Figure 29.5. The Media theme is near the center bottom of the diagram. Spacing is indicative of relationships. This visualization is an excellent tool to explore the general content of the data as well as relationships and connections.

Theme	Connectivity	Relevance
video	100%	
effects	72%	
research	51%	
media	47%	
time	36%	
television	32%	
information	17%	
development	08%	
communication	08%	
literacy	04%	

Figure 29.4 Ordered List of Themes, Their Connectivity, and Relevance from the Final Run.

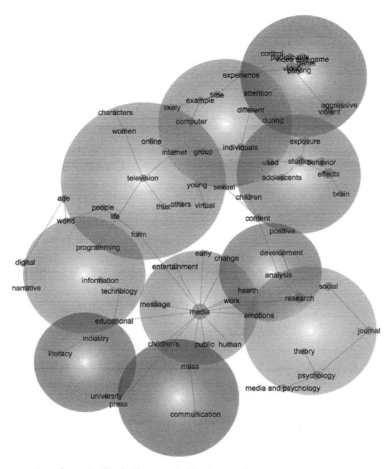

Figure 29.5 Final Concept Map from Handbook Chapters Final Leximancer Run.

This visualization of the data in the concept map is not used for formal interpretation of the data, but it is used more for orientation and general verification by this researcher. In Leximancer, mouse clicking on the interactive concept map is also a way to navigate and query the data and relationships.

In order to make meaning, the concepts and their relationships are used as the foundation of the content analysis. The top concept frequency counts are shown in Table 29.6.

These 15 concepts represent the top concepts by relative frequency. All represent a minimum of a

Table 29.6 Concepts Identified in Final Run with Relevance Over 20%.

Concept	Count	Relevance Percentage
media	3,428	100
research	1,637	48
video	1,582	46
game	1,532	45
effects	1,451	42
video game	1,447	42
violent	1,397	41
studies	1,298	38
psychology	1,238	36
social	915	27
behavior	912	27
aggressive	868	25
journal	831	24
television	743	22
experience	702	20

Table 29.7 Top Related Concepts to the Concept *Media.*

Concept	Count	Likelihood (%)
media psychology	641	100
literacy	198	99
mass	246	98
children's	192	87
digital	171	82
industry	109	74
age	160	72
entertainment	132	65
educational	202	64
content	396	63

20% relevance threshold to the top concept *media*. That is, all of these concepts represent a relative proportion of representation when *media* is 100%. This measure provides an indication of relevant occurrence of each concept. This gives a statistical indication of the coverage of these topics by all authors in the *Handbook*. For example, *video* and *game* are each individual concepts and the compound *video* AND *game* all have similar frequency counts. One interesting observation is that m*edia* dominates substantially as a concept with a count nearly two times as much as the next concept *research*.

Another indicator of the topic coverage is the relationship of concepts to each other. The concepts most related to the concept *media* are shown for illustrative purposes in Table 29.7. The Likelihood percentage is the likelihood that when a related concept (e.g., *literacy*) appears in a text segment, the concept *media* appears there as well.

Thus, of all comments about *entertainment*, 65% of them mention *media*. This Likelihood score is derived from the count 132 divided into the total frequency count for the concept *entertainment*, which was 204 (132/204 = .65). The second

concept is *literacy*, which is part of a compound of media literacy. The researcher must consider if the concept *literacy* as well as *mass*, the next concept in the list, should be modified in reporting, as is done here to illustrate a single concept of a type of media. In many ways, this step is an exercise to determine what the concepts actually represent. These results provide an illustrative example for the need, even in a grounded theory technique, for researcher to interpret the results of automated software-driven content discovery. Query features in software are essential here to allow a researcher access to the source text segments.

The next concept to be further investigated is *psychology*. The top related concepts are shown in Table 29.8.

The Likelihood score is important in this summary as well. For example, of all text segments containing *journal*, 41% of them mention *psychology* as well. An exploration of the actual text reveals that psychology journals are a topic of conversation. The next concepts of *social, human,* and *development* are more traditionally associated with psychology terms. Note the Likelihood score indicates the strength of the relationship relative to other co-occurring concepts. It does not indicate the meaning of the relationship, and that task is the responsibility of the researcher and should be in the Discussion section of a research paper.

Finally, a further exploration involved the examination of the compound concept *media-psychology*. This was manually added to the coding dictionary.

Table 29.8 Top Related Concepts to the Concept *Psychology.*

Concept	Count	Likelihood (%)
media and psychology	641	100
journal	341	41
social	359	39
human	63	26
development	64	22
theory	82	21
university	37	19
work	48	19
media	641	19
research	299	18
communication	89	18
positive	57	17
technology	50	17

Table 29.9 Top Related Concepts to Concept *Media-Psychology.*

Concept	Count	Likelihood (%)
psychology	641	52
media	641	19
human	36	15
research	236	14
entertainment	28	14
technology	39	13
work	31	12
theory	41	10
early	17	10
communication	50	10
development	29	10
brain	23	10
journal	80	10
social	88	10

It is often valuable to create a compound concept and investigate concepts related to it. For a study of the *Oxford Handbook of Media Psychology*, the compound concept *media-psychology* was created to examine the related, co-occurring concepts, and the results are shown in Table 29.9.

As one would expect, the concepts *psychology* and *media* were the most related concepts. However, *psychology*, with a 52% Likelihood score (i.e., probability that *media-psychology* is mentioned given *psychology*) differs significantly from *media* with a Likelihood score of 19% (i.e., probability that *media-psychology* given *media*). The large difference in these two scores indicates that *media* appears with many more and diverse concepts than does *psychology*. The next most related concepts starting at *human* at 15% down to *social* at 10% represent the remaining most related concepts. After these concepts, the remaining related concepts had a likelihood of less than 10%; that is, less than a 10% chance they were found in close proximity to *media-psychology* and were not retained for the study. Table 29.10 shows the top concept counts for a comparison.

The overlap with *psychology* shows that media psychology is more closely tied to *psychology* than *media*. The bolded concepts show this overlap. Interestingly, in these top concept counts, *media*

Table 29.10 Top Related Concepts to the Media-Psychology, Psychology, and Media Concepts.

Media Psychology	Psychology	Media
psychology	media and psychology	media psychology
media	**Journal**	literacy
human	**Social**	mass
research	**Human**	children's
entertainment	**Development**	digital
technology	**Theory**	industry
work	University	*entertainment*
theory	**Work**	educational
early	**Media**	content
communication	**Research**	*brain*
development	**Communication**	*early*
brain	Positive	sexual
journal	**Technology**	exposure
social	Life	public

Note: Bolded text represents concepts shared between *Media Psychology* and *Psychology*. Italic text denotes shared concepts between *Media Psychology* and *Media*.

does not overlap at all with *psychology*. The overlap of *psychology* to *media-psychology* is 11 of 15 concepts, or 73.3 %. The representation of *media* in *media-psychology* is 3 per 15 concepts or 33%. This means that when media and psychology appear together in text, there is a greater than 2 to 1 probability that a *psychology* concept is being discussed rather than a *media* concept.

A final note from the results section is to include a table summarizing all pertinent information for the study. As discussed previously, reliability and reproducibility are issues with media qualitative analysis. Table 29.11 is an implementation of Table 29.2, which is an exemplar for transparency and information summary and disclosure. Table 29.11 provides this summary to enable readers and researchers to understand the general parameters of the study and specific software tools used and their configurations. This should increase transparency and bring some standardized view to information disclosure to enable reproducibility.

Discussion

The Table of Contents review calculated word frequencies of the titles to indicate what authors believed their content would cover. Words were eliminated that provided no addition to meaning, such as articles and prepositions. The result of this analysis was that *media* is the dominant term mentioned 20 times with *psychology* second at 11 mentions. The terms *media* and *psychology* appear substantially more often than the other terms in the title as well. *Media* appears in 19 titles, *psychology* or a derivative in 11 titles, and both *media* and *psychology* in 10 titles. Six titles contained neither word. From this data, a definition of media psychology is composed of the following concepts, or topics: *research, children, narrative, violence, adolescents, approach, effects, games, history, persuasion, sexual,* and *video*. *Media* dominates the discussion as evidenced by its nearly two times representations in both number of words (20) and number of titles (19) over *psychology*, mentioned 11 times across 11 titles. The remaining terms contain three action words in *research, effects,* and *approaches*, suggesting that research, study of effects, and approaches are considered. The remaining words indicate the subtopics to *media psychology*. Thus, a succinct definition from the Table of Contents is that media psychology is dominated by media topics and addresses research, effects, and approaches on the topics of *children, narrative, violence, adolescents, effects, games, history, persuasion, sexual,* and *video*.

Table 29.11 Summary of Study Parameters including Data Collection and Software Configuration.

Content Analysis of the Oxford Handbook of Medial Psychology	
Researcher: Neal, M.	Date: April 2012
What is the definition of media psychology as expressed in the content of the *Oxford Handbook of Medial Psychology*	
Analysis Method(s)	Content Analysis into major themes and concepts.
Data Collection Method	Provided chapter final drafts by the editor of the *Handbook*.
Data Summary	25 book chapters with one chapter in each file, PDF format 1,271 pages in APA format, double-spaced 23,833 sentences
Software Tools	Leximancer Text Analytics Software
Analysis Tool Method	Leximancer Text Analytics Software uses machine learning and statistical methods to extract themes, concepts, and relationships (by co-occurrence).
Software Configuration	Leximancer Software configurations: 1. Word variants were enabled to merge stems. 2. Compound concepts created: 　a. *video* AND *game* 　b. *media* AND *psychology* 3. The concepts *violent* and *violence* were merged to indicate one singular concept. 4. Added to the stop list (ignored words): 　a. *et* and *al* to exclude APA citation concept 　b. *thus* and *use* as inconsequential

Whereas the Table of Contents analysis indicates what the editor and chapter authors believe the contents to represent, a more detailed analysis explored the entire text of the *Handbook*. The themes discovered and concept map generated by Leximancer were used as navigation aids to explore text excerpts and the concepts discovered. It is these concepts and their relationships defined by co-occurrence that provide insight into the contents.

Two approaches were taken to examine the data. First, the major concepts were examined by frequency of occurrence. The fact that a concept appears more than others is an indicator of strength of coverage. From this analysis, the concept *media* at 3,428 occurrences was found to have more than twice the frequency count of the next most discussed concept of *research* at 1,637 occurrences. The frequencies are roughly divided into two bands after *media*, which include *research, video, game, effects, video game, violent, studies,* and *psychology*. This tier represents from 36% to 48% relative percentage. *Video* (1,582), *game* (1,532), and the compound concept *video-game* (1,447) represent nearly identical frequencies, which indicate that they rarely occur in separate contexts. The third tier contains *social, behavior, aggressive, journal, television,* and *experience* and represents from 20% to 27% relevance percentage. These banded counts provided a summary of the topics and amount of coverage the topics generated throughout the *Handbook*.

The second approach examined the relationship of concepts to the key concepts of *media-psychology, media,* and *psychology*. This added depth to the analysis by examining specific relationships. These relationships showed that *media* was most related and occurred in the chapters with *literacy, mass* (media), *children's,* and *digital*, all with more than 80% Likelihood that they occurred with *media. Psychology,* individually, was related to *journals, social* (psychology), *developmental* (psychology), *theory, university, media, communication, research, technology,* and *public*. Interestingly, *journal*, the most prevalent concept apart from *media*, was only a 41% Likelihood indicating that it occurred less than one half the time with *psychology*. One interpretation of these much lower counts is that psychology was a more independent concept and did not have strong relationships to many other concepts in this data. The only concepts with a greater than 20% Likelihood score for *psychology* were *journal, social, human, development,* and *theory*. Finally, when *media* and *psychology* were combined and related concepts examined, *psychology* exceeded

52% Likelihood score, indicating that slightly over one half of the time, *psychology* appeared with *media psychology*. Conversely, *media*, the next most related topic, occurred only 19% of the time with *media psychology*.

The two approaches of examining concept frequencies and concept relationships provide the first step in the content analysis, as the data gathered to this point is mostly quantitative in nature and an excellent indicator of the concepts and their relationships in the *Handbook*. For interpretation, much as in the Table of Contents review, the meaning of the dominant concepts' frequency and ratios and relationships need to be examined in context of the research question, which is to define media psychology. The strength of concept coverage indicates a dominance of media discussion with *mass* media, *digital* media, and media *literacy* as subtopics. The final cluster of frequency bands represents more psychology-related concepts of *social, behavior, aggressive,* and *experience. Television* is media related and *journal* discusses publication in general. One of the more indicative findings is the top related concept comparison shown in Table 29.10. The overlap of *psychology* shows that *media psychology* is 73% and more closely tied to *psychology* than *media*. Interestingly, in these top concept counts, *media* does not overlap at all with *psychology*. The representation of *media* in *media-psychology* is only 33%. This means that when *media* and *psychology* appear together in text, there is a greater than 2 to 1 probability that a *psychology* concept is being discussed rather than a *media* concept.

This detailed analysis of the *Handbook* chapters leads to the following observations of the content of the *Handbook*. The concept *media*, by a large margin, dominates media psychology. *Media* has many closely related topics including mass media and media literary and examines research and effects with adolescents and children. *Psychology* is less dominant and is much more closely related to the concept *media psychology. Media* is more connected to and interwoven with the rest of the text than *psychology*. Therefore, a definition that emerges from this content analysis is that media psychology is the study and research of effects and media literacy on children and adolescents with a focus on media, including topics of aggression, social psychology, and experiences.

Conclusions

The purpose of this chapter was twofold. First, a media content analysis approach with automated software tools was described. This included the growing interest in visual data mapping, the trend towards intelligent software integrated into methods that permits research not previously possible, and the automated analysis of large datasets in a way that addresses some of the concerns of qualitative research. Issues facing media psychology researchers were discussed, including the need to thoroughly document software choices, configurations, and iterations to aid in reproducibility and communication of study results. An example template was provided to illustrate the details computer-assisted analyses for media studies should include.

The second purpose of this chapter was to determine what the authors of this handbook discussed in their individual chapters and derive a map of the discipline through an analysis of the concepts most often used in the book itself. Two approaches were taken to extract a definition of media psychology from the *Oxford Handbook of Media Psychology*. First, the Table of Contents was reviewed to determine what the editor and chapter authors intended their content to cover. Second, the actual chapter contents were analyzed to determine what the authors of the *Handbook* actually discussed. The assistance of statistical algorithms in Leximancer, visualization for initial understanding, explorations, and further inquiry assisted in a deeper understanding and ease of use in further examination of actual text excerpts as evidence of the concept compositions.

Through these two analyses, a detailed examination of media psychology was conducted. The concepts found from the Table of Contents showed that media psychology is dominated by media topics and addresses research, effects, and approaches on the topics of children, narrative, violence, adolescents, effects, games, history, persuasion, sexual, and video. Finally, the definition that emerged from the chapters' content analysis was that media psychology is the study and research of effects and media literacy on children and adolescents with a focus on media, including the topics of aggression, social psychology, and experience.

References

Ali, N. M., Lee, H., & Smeaton, A. F. (2011). Use of content analysis tools for visual interaction design. In Zaman, H. B., Robinson, P., Petrou, M., Olivier, P., & Shih, T. K. (Eds.), *Proceedings of the Second International Conference on Visual Informatics: Sustaining Research and Innovations—Volume Part II (IVIC'11)*. Berlin: Springer-Verlag, pp. 74–84.

Barry, A. M. S. (1997). *Visual Intelligence: Perception, Image, and Manipulation in Visual Communication*. Albany: State University of New York Press.

Berger, A. A. (2005). *Media Analysis Techniques*. Thousand Oaks, CA: Sage Publications.

Bernard, H. R., & Ryan, G. W. (1998). Text analysis: Qualitative and Quantitative Methods. In Bernard, H. R. (Ed.), *Handbook of Methods in Cultural Anthropology*. Lanham, MD: Altamira Press, 595–646.

Bluhm, D. J., Harman, W., Lee, T. W., & Mitchell, T. R. (2010). Qualitative research in management: A decade of progress. *Journal of Management Studies*, 48(8), 1866–1891.

Butler-Kisber, L., & Poldma, T. (2010). The power of visual approaches in qualitative inquiry: The use of collage making and concept mapping in experiential research. *Journal of Research Practice*, 6(2), Article M18.

Carley, K. (1993). Coding choices for textual analysis: A comparison of content analysis and map analysis. *Sociological Methodology*, 23, 75–126.

Frost, N., Nolas, S. M., Brooks-Gordon, B., Esin, G., Holt, A., Mehdizadeh L., & Shinebourne, P. (2010). Pluralism in qualitative research: The impact of different researchers and qualitative approaches on the analysis of qualitative data. *Qualitative Research*, 10 (4), 441–460.

Glaser, B. G., & Strauss, A. L. (1967). *The discovery of grounded theory: Strategies for qualitative research*. New York: Aldine.

Hopkins, D., & King, G. (2010). A method of automated nonparametric content analysis for social science. *American Journal of Political Science*, 54(1), 229–247.

Kazdin, A. E. (2002). *Research Design in Clinical Psychology*, 4th ed. Needham Heights, MA: Allyn and Bacon.

Krippendorff, K. (2004). *Content Analysis: An Introduction to Its Methodology*, 2nd ed. Thousand Oaks, CA: Sage Publications.

Lakoff, G. (1987). *Fire, Woman, and Other Dangerous Things: What Categories Reveal about the Mind*. Chicago: The University of Chicago Press.

Miles, M. B., & Huberman, A. M. (1994). *Qualitative data analysis*. Thousand Oaks, CA: Sage Publications.

Neuendorf, K. A. (2002). *The Content Analysis Guidebook*. Thousand Oaks, CA: Sage Publications.

Novak J. D., & Cañas A. J. (2006). *The theory underlying concept maps and how to construct them (Technical Report No. IHMC CmapTools 2006–01)*. Pensacola, FL: Institute for Human and Machine Cognition.

O'Connor, B., Balasubramanyan, R., Routledge, B. R., & Smith, N. A. (2010). From tweets to polls: Linking text sentiment to public opinion time series. *Tepper School of Business*. Paper 559. Retrieved from http://repository.cmu.edu/tepper/559

Packer, M. J. (2011). *The Science of Qualitative Research*. Cambridge: Cambridge University Press.

Polkinghorne, D. E. (this volume). Qualitative research and media psychology. In Dill K. E. (Ed.), *Oxford Handbook of Media Psychology*. New York: Oxford University Press.

Popping, R. (2000). *Computer-Assisted Text Analysis*. Thousand Oaks, CA: SAGE Publications.

Richards, L., & Morse, J. M. (2007). *User's Guide to Qualitative Methods*, 2nd ed. Thousand Oaks, CA: Sage Publications.

Rutledge, P. (this volume). Is there a need for a distinct field of media psychology? In Dill, K. E. (Ed.), *Oxford Handbook of Media Psychology*. New York: Oxford University Press.

Smith, A. E., & Humphreys, M. S. (2006). Evaluation of unsupervised semantic mapping of natural language with Leximancer concept mapping. *Behavior Research Methods*, 38, 262–279.

Strauss, A., & Corbin, J. (1998). *Basics of Qualitative Research: Techniques and Procedures for Developing Grounded Theory.* London: Sage Publications.

Tausczik, Y. R., & Pennebaker, J. W. (2010). The psychological meaning of words: LIWC and computerized text analysis methods. *Journal of Language and Social Psychology, 29*, 24–54.

Weber, R. P. (1990). *Basic Content Analysis.* Beverly Hills, CA: Sage Publications.

Wertz, F. J., Charmaz, K., McMullen, L., Josselson, R., Anderson, R., & McSpadden, E. (2011). *Five Ways of Doing Qualitative Analysis: Phenomenological Psychology, Grounded Theory, Discourse Analysis, Narrative Research, and Intuitive Inquiry.* New York: Guilford Press.

Willig, C. (2008). *Introducing Qualitative Research in Psychology: Adventures in Theory and Method,* 2nd ed. Philadelphia: Open University Press.

Van Atteveldt, W. (2008). *Semantic Network Analysis: Techniques for Extracting, Representing, and Querying Media Content.* Charleston, SC: BookSurge Publishers.

Yau, N. (2011). *Visualize This: The FlowingData guide to Design, Visualization, and Statistics.* Indianapolis, IN: Wiley Publishing.

Media Psychology: Past, Present, and Future

Karen E. Dill

Media use and its role in our lives is growing and changing. As these changes unfold, the discipline of media psychology has emerged to investigate and better understand the interaction between humans and media.

Worldwide, nearly 7 trillion text messages were sent in 2010. China and India have, by far, the most mobile device users, accounting for almost a third of the world market. Although the United States is a distant third in the percentage of mobile device users, 88% of American adults own a mobile device—and they are more likely to own a mobile device than any other digital device such as a computer or tablet (MobiThinking, 2012). Texting is on the increase and talking on the phone is on the decrease. Among US teens, texting is by far the most common daily communication activity (69% of teens text daily), followed by cell phone calls (35%) and in person socializing outside of school (29%) (Lenhart, 2012).

Social networking via media is a relatively new phenomenon, but one that has embedded itself in social life around the globe. Sixty-six percent of American Internet users access social media online. The average American Facebook user born in Generation X has 197 Facebook friends, and the average Millennial has 318 (MobiThinking, 2012; Ranie, 2012). Facebook reported that 425 million people used its mobile app monthly in 2011. Today, the average Facebook user spends 405 minutes on Facebook online monthly (Osborne, 2012).

Though new media use captures our attention and imagination, some traditional media use is also growing. Television viewing continues to rise, with Americans and Australians, for example, reporting increases in traditional television viewing and also increased viewing through online streaming and DVR use as well as increased media multitasking.

According to Nielsen (NielsenWire, 2011) the average American spends 20% of his or her day watching television.

Why Media Psychology? Why Now?

The sheer amount of current media use, the evolving media landscape and its importance to our daily lives all clearly suggest the need for us to understand our relationship with media both as creators and consumers (Bartholow & Bolls, Chapter 27). As Bartholow and Bolls (Chapter 27) put it: "media use occurs on a scale that is nearly too massive to comprehend." The way we send and receive information of many kinds is shifting and we want to know what implications this has for us as users and creators. For example, there is a shift from reading news via print media to both reading and writing content online and on smartphones. These changes from print to digital and from passive to active users and cocreators (Chapter 2) excite public curiosity. Our discipline of media psychology is the field that is best poised to answer questions scholars, consumers, educators, health care providers, journalists, politicians, and the general public need to know about the evolving role of media in our modern lives.

To help us understand media psychology, this volume (see, e.g., Bartholow & Bolls, Tuma, and Brown Rutledge; Chapters 3, 4, and 27) offers a history and some preliminary definitions of the discipline. These chapters explore the essential ideas and approaches of the field and what it offers. For example, Tuma (Chapter 4) asserts that media psychology has its roots in disciplines like media studies, and social and perceptual psychology, and argues that the deeper and foundational roots of media psychology are to be found in past research on the psychology of the image, culture, aesthetics and of what she calls the "mediation of reality through our senses" (Tuma, Chapter 4).

Brown Rutledge (Chapter 3) explains that media psychology emerged from foundational disciplines such as sociology, media studies, and communications, but that the discipline is unique in that "the focus of inquiry [shifts] from media-centric to human-centric." Rather than focusing on specific media tools (e.g., what's the role of Facebook in human social interactions?) she focuses attention on the "space between" humans and technology, thus making the discipline of human factors highly relevant to media psychology. Rutledge also notes that definitions of media psychology have proved elusive in the past.

Bartholow and Bolls (Chapter 27) also trace the history and melding of media studies and psychology, especially social psychology. They note that "Psychological experiments on media effects often involve exposing participants to some form of media, and media studies includes psychology as part of its epistemological foundation. Separately, however, these two disciplines lack critical conceptual and operational components required for truly advancing knowledge of the brain 'on' media" (Bartholow & Bolls, Chapter 27). All of these are arguments that a variety of related fields came together and formed something novel to address the fact that the human mind that we study is now very often the mind "on media" and that media psychology therefore is crucial to our understanding of human psychology.

Taken together, the chapters in this *Handbook* argue that there is something important about our new and emergent field of media psychology that its constituent fields lack. I think we can yet improve upon the discipline as we know it if we also heed our authors' advice on how to create this more perfect union of the discipline of media psychology. Specifically, the authors tell us collectively that there are specific ways we can enrich our methodologies, our theoretical foundations, and the way we tell others outside our discipline about our work and how it applies to the hopes and concerns many of us have for the fast changing role of media in everyday life. I will elaborate on these ideas later in this chapter.

As discussed in Chapter 1 of this volume, there are current working definitions of media psychology. As noted, one working definition that received informal support among authors of the *Handbook* follows: **Media psychology is the scientific study of human behavior, thoughts, and feelings experienced in the context of media use and creation** (Dill, Chapter 1). Brown Rutledge (Chapter 3) offers this definition: **Media psychology uses the lens of psychology to study and understand the complex relationship between humans and the evolving digital environment**. Neal (Chapter 29) uses cutting-edge semantic analysis software to derive a map of the discipline through the words of the authors of the *Handbook*. His research uncovered subject themes including children and adolescents; content themes including violence, sex, video games, persuasion and narrative; and research themes including effects, approaches, journals, and research.

For a new discipline like the field of media psychology, solidifying a definition for the discipline is important. The pages of this volume help us do just that. For instance, I find Bartholow and Boll's definition of media psychophysiology very apt and also more generally applicable as a definition of media psychology. I'll paraphrase it here as follows: **media psychology is the study of the brain "on" media**. Or as they may prefer, media psychology is the study of the embodied brain "on" media.

The False Dichotomy: Media as All Bad or All Good

One important issue to understand as the field of media psychology grows and evolves is the context in which those changes are taking place. An important facet of that context is the tendency for reductionist and dichotomous thinking about media. Specifically, media psychology research—and the public, journalistic, and governmental understanding of it—has tended to view media and its effects as either bad or good, harmful or beneficial. Sex and violence in the media are among the most commonly-researched media effects (see Derwin & Demerode, Chapter 5, for a discussion). Debates about sex and violence in the media (see Huesmann, DuBow, & Yang, Chapter 9; McIntyre, Chapter 26; Potter, Chapter 24; Prot & Anderson, Chapter 7; Shafer, Bobkowski & Brown, Chapter 13), for instance, tend to be seen as disagreements between media detractors and media enthusiasts—lovers and haters of media themselves, rather than as fair-minded analyses of research data. We might call this the **Love/Hate Media Debate**. This is, of course, a false dichotomy because media are neither all inherently harmful nor inherently beneficial but generate nuanced, varied, and changing effects and influences to individuals and cultures.

For example, in 2012, a group of experts (Pew, 2012) predicted that youth who grow up with today's Internet will likely both benefit and suffer because of it. This is an example of the benefit/harm perspective of media experts that is not inappropriate in substance, but that leads to misunderstandings in practice. It's not difficult to see why media psychology and the public understanding of it have taken on this benefit/harm framework. Psychologists and other professionals tend to take a child protective stance, thus seeking to identify and prevent harm. As Arke notes, when Clinton administration cabinet officials met and addressed the issue of media violence and American children, they concluded, "that the media is so much a part of daily life that few people are aware of the impact of media, whether it be positive or negative" (Arke, Chapter 6).

Concern for negative media effects is reasonable. Given the natural interest in raising healthy children, it's understandable that media psychologists have focused on harmful effects in the hope of helping people avoid them. In addition to media violence effects (see, e.g., example Brockmyer, Chapter 12; Krahe, Chapter 20), other topics of concern covered in this volume include technology addiction (Gentile et al.), sexual content (Shafer et al., Chapter 13), racial and sex role stereotyping (Behm-Morawitz & Ortiz, Chapter 14; Scharrer, Chapter 15), media-related attention deficits (West & Bailey, Chapter 23), and issues of newer technology and children such as sexting and cyberbullying (Donnerstein, Chapter 21).

Enthusiasm for and interest in all that technology offers society are equally understandable. For example, Rutledge notes (Chapter 3), "The proliferation of media, and particularly social technologies, has created growing interest across society in understanding how technologies fit into individual life and society as a whole." She cites civic engagement and social support as benefits of media in everyday life. Gregory (Chapter 10) cautions that in terms of media effects, "The sky is not falling," and calls for a positive psychology perspective on children's media use that emphasizes prosocial and other positive outcomes. Similarly, Blumberg et al. (Chapter 19) explain how and why the growing genre of serious games have positive effects, persuading and educating players in areas ranging from health and education to civic engagement. Blumberg et al. address how the use of avatars can provide rich experiences and alter our sense of self for the better. Blascovich and McCall explain how new virtual environments provide a context for experiencing and studying social interactions and influence. Chamberlin and

Maloney (Chapter 18) concur with Blumberg et al. and with Blascovich and McCall about the potential positive use of video game avatars. They also explain how exergames, a popular genre of video games, have not only physical benefits, but also psychological and social ones.

Headlines probably sell more magazines and newspapers when they purport to share information that the public needs to know, including risks and benefits of media. It is true that positive and negative effects of media use are supported by research. However, I argue that media psychology and public discussion of it should actively avoid reinforcing a false dichotomy of media as either all good or all bad, because this stance is reductionist and therefore limiting. It also tends to send the message that media psychologists are biased and fight among themselves. A critical thinking approach to media psychology is key...that is, an approach that recognizes one's own biases, but also fairly weighs evidence and does not frame research by personal perspectives but by scientific principles (see also Huesmann et al., Chapter 9). Avoiding the substance and the appearance of this bias in the field can be difficult and fraught with pitfalls (see, for example, Huesmann et al., Chapter 9; McIntyre, Chapter 26; Prot & Anderson, Chapter 7), especially if industry has a vested interest in a benefits approach to the media that profit them.

I want to stress once again that studying harmful and beneficial media effects are not bankrupt perspectives, but have value. In fact, from an evolutionary psychology perspective, it is understandable that we would focus on identifying risks (Wilson, 2002) and factors that would help us survive and thrive. But there is a danger associated with approaching research from a wrongheaded stance that assumes that all or most media are either inherently harmful or beneficial. It is this biased polarization that set the stage for Huesmann et al. (Chapter 9) to explain why people do not want to believe that media violence causes aggression, despite research evidence that would have been more than ample to convince an audience in a domain that did not impinge upon their feelings of self-worth. One reason why a chapter like the one by Huesmann and colleagues is so important is that when we understand better how and why people react the way they do to media psychology research findings, we can take a respectful and informed approach to how we communicate that work to the public.

Moving forward, our approach to media psychology should include identifying and avoiding bias, but also not allowing bias to undermine the most reasonable interpretations of quality research. One way to address this issue is to endeavor to do research that is rich and contextual and that shows multiple media facets rather than focusing on a single facet. Another is to use a broad range of approaches in one's programmatic line of research, being especially careful to avoid the reductionist version of the **Love/Hate Media Debate**. Furthermore, as a scientific community we must not tolerate any *ad hominem* arguments. These and other signs that criticism has moved out of the realm of science and into the domain of bias should be considered seriously. This would include reviews and other public communications that make inappropriate, nonscientific criticisms or *ad hominem* attacks.

Communicating about Communication

Media psychologists should emphasize effective communication about our work to the public and other stakeholders in our graduate training programs. As we have seen (for example, McIntyre, Chapter 26) when we try to ensure that public policy is informed by research, business interests can stand in the way of the public good. And because businesses have resources academics do not generally have, skillful arguments can be made which obfuscate important research in media psychology.

Additionally, the fact that media psychology is a vibrant field with broad interest to the public, businesses, journalists, and lawmakers likely has multiple feedback effects on the field. For instance, the aforementioned stakeholders are not scientists and may tend to ask for oversimplifications of media psychology research. Stakeholders may, in fact, discourage nuance in reporting our findings and encourage the **Love/Hate Media Debate**. After all, stakeholders are busy and may focus rather simplistically on benefit and harm because, from an evolutionary psychology perspective, they most urgently need to know what relates to their ability to survive and thrive. In terms of communicating research findings, questions scientists field may therefore tend toward sound bites that oversimplify and exacerbate the **Love/Hate Media Debate**. And as Potter (Chapter 24) posits, debates such as the media violence debate have a tendency to turn off an audience because those who already disagree with one side of the debate will not engage with that argument.

Furthermore, we know from the chapter by Huesmann et al. (Chapter 9) that there are a number of reasons why a variety of stakeholders may reject our research findings. This problem is complex and

will call for complex solutions. For now, the important thing is to begin to recognize the issue and formulate ways of addressing it (see, e.g., Dill, 2009, Chapter 9). One of those solutions is to explicitly include graduate coursework that addresses how to communicate one's research work to a variety of stakeholders. McIntyre's chapter notes a number of pitfalls to communicating media psychology research to legislators, journalists, and the public. I provide below a set of basic assumptions and ideas for addressing our issues with communicating media psychology research and application. This is meant as a starting point and a basis for future collaboration on these issues.

Effective Communication about Media Psychology Research and Application: Tools and Assumptions

1. Effective communication begins with an understanding of the audience receiving the message. It is important to address how to communicate basic scientific principles in a way the audience understands. For example, considering how a variety of audiences understand cause and effect and how they understand a variety of research evidence types is important to ensure audience understanding.

2. Using communications and psychology literature and work of related fields to understand how to make compelling and concise arguments and how to respond to a variety of arguments and criticisms.

3. Understanding how to make arguments in a variety of time frames and settings.

4. Using a variety of media platforms and applications to communicate media psychology content.

5. Roleplaying common situations in which media psychologists are asked to discuss their work, such as radio talk shows, television interviews, and e-mails and phone calls from journalists of a variety of types.

Considerations for an Interdisciplinary and International Field

We will continue to define and refine the field of media psychology. As we do, one of the issues will be that the people who do media psychology come from a variety of fields. Several authors in this volume have mentioned by name a variety of fields that contribute research on topics in media psychology. The interdisciplinary nature of the field presents both challenges and opportunities to our growing body of knowledge and to how the field will advance. One aspect of a truly interdisciplinary field is that the individual disciplines bring with them preferences for both methods and theories. Sometimes these preferences lean toward being biases. They can also lead to favoritism to the researchers' personal history and training. Derwin and DeMerode (Chapter 5) elaborate on these issues, which include barriers and biases at the journal, departmental, and conference levels.

In addition to being an Interdisciplinary field, media psychology is also an international field. I've endeavored here to include media psychologists from around the world, although the emphasis was on researchers from the United States. The United States is still arguably the epicenter for the discipline of psychology (Schultz & Schultz, 2011), having many training programs, journals, and psychological associations that are internationally recognized as important. However, like the interdisciplinary nature of the field, the variety of geographic and cultural venues that produce media psychology research strengthens the field. Sakamoto (Chapter 28) explains, for example, the relationship between media psychology research in the United States and Japan and also the specific Japanese approach to media psychology. Sakamoto (personal communication, 2011) also suggests that a lack of sufficient translations (for example, from Japanese to English) is still a barrier to disseminating research findings in the field. I therefore suggest that one important part of strengthening the international aspects of media psychology is to work, whenever and however possible, toward creating more translations of media psychology work. Greater support for translations is available today than ever before, including some automated translation aids.

The Future of Theory and Method in Media Psychology
Extending and Complicating Theoretical Approaches

The **Love/Hate Media Debate** may come in part from Potter's (Chapter 24) point that we have been lost in generating discreet findings rather than taking a more theoretical approach to the field. Similarly, Prot and Anderson (Chapter 7) warn against our doing research in a conceptual vacuum, ignoring what is broadly known about psychological processes.

In this *Handbook*, a number of authors address broad theoretical issues. For example, Nabi and Moyer-Gusé (Chapter 16) explore underlying theory and frameworks of media persuasion. Konijn (Chapter 11) explores the role of emotion in media use and creation, while also juxtaposing emotional and cognitive experiences of media. Green and Dill (Chapter 25) examine media influence via transportation into narrative worlds and consider why the audience may not comprehend that they have been changed by their interactions with media. Similarly, as noted previously, Huesmann, Dubow, and Yang (Chapter 9) explain why it is hard for people to believe that media violence exposure causes increased aggression.

Bartholow and Bolls build on Lang's view of media as a dynamic interaction between mind and medium, tracing an area ripe with theoretical and methodological advances. This psychophysiological approach "moves the study of media effects to mental processes, embodied in neural activity, that underlie the effects of media content on individuals and provides a general framework for studying media that can accommodate current as well as future forms of media" (p. 2). Multiple chapters in this volume concur that it is the theory and underlying constructs that matter rather than the particular tools themselves, which will come and go (see, e.g., Bartholow & Bolls, Chapter 27; Nabi & Moyer-Gusé, Chapter 16; Brown Rutledge, Chapter 3).

In working toward a greater understanding of broad theoretical concerns like the emotional and cognitive processing of media and media persuasion, it is time to complicate arguments about the role of the audience as well. If we've tended to polarize around the notion that media are all good or bad, we've also polarized around the audience as savvy thinkers versus automatons. Such arguments belie the true nuance, richness, and variability of audience experience.

An increased emphasis on theory might well encourage stakeholders and scientists both to think more in terms of the underlying psychological mechanisms rather than discreet findings and reductionist views of media as primarily good or bad. For example, understanding how using social networking sites or avatars contributes to the construction of self is a more nuanced approach to media psychology than beginning with the notion that using social networking sites or avatars is inherently either largely harmful or beneficial.

At the same time as we are careful to avoid thinking that the tool is more important than the psychology behind its use, we should understand that the evolution of media themselves may offer us both new facets of media psychology to study and new tools with which to study them. We've already seen Bartholow and Bolls explain how evolving psychophysiology equipment and methods help us answer important theoretical questions. Neal also demonstrates how the latest software tools can help us answer questions about textual data that were difficult or impossible to answer without automation. The media we study and the tools we study them with will continue to change rapidly (Isbouts & Ohler, Chapter 2) and media psychologists will need to keep pace thoughtfully with these changes.

Media Psychology Methods

In these pages, you will find the perspectives of some of the finest minds in media psychology research methods that exist anywhere in the world. I have every confidence that the methods content of this book will be highly read and cited and will become very useful tools for training graduate students in media psychology. In reading the methods content of this *Handbook*, students, mentors, and other interested parties can take stock of what is and what could be ahead on the methodological landscape of our field.

Across the history of psychology, we have witnessed a variety of trends in methodology and design. I read the following from the first published book called *Media Psychology* (originally published in 2003) with great interest:

"There was no single text that covered all the material to which I wished to introduce students...Most relevant texts were aimed at media and communications students, and assumed a lot of background knowledge about media history that psychology undergraduates rarely possess. Others failed to go beyond the basic "effects" paradigm, or were largely concerned with cognitive processing of media rather than placing them in a social and cultural context. Others, typically those in the European media studies tradition, erred in the opposite direction, blandly dismissing psychology as at best a relic of behaviorism, at worst as fascist propaganda!" (Giles, 2010, p. ix).

In the 2010 edition, reworked and retitled as the *Psychology of the Media*, Giles writes: "Media scholars are hostile toward effects research because they see it as removing all context from media, reducing them to mere stimuli...This rift in understanding stems as much as anything from the different perspectives of psychologists and media scholars. A psychologist is primarily interested in understanding why human beings behave as they do, and media constitute just one of several influences that contribute to the overall picture. A media scholar, however, is primarily interested in media and their products as cultural objects, so chopping them into 10-minute clips of violence...makes little sense. It turns cultural material into meaningless chunks of information" (Giles, 2010, p. 16).

From the standpoint of an American psychologist, the first time I discovered this perspective was a watershed moment for me. As someone who had taught introductory psychology courses for years, I knew well that the very essence of our research methods approach was to emphasize the hierarchical goals of psychological research as being: to describe, predict, explain, and control human behavior, thoughts, and feelings. Anyone may open the methods section of a typical introductory psychology textbook and find this content. And of course, what "explain" means to a psychologist is experimental work, or what Giles had referred to as the "effects tradition." So a major goal of the American approach to psychology is this "effects tradition." By some transitive property then, Giles appeared to be saying that there are a lot of folks who question the entire American approach to psychology, and maybe even psychology itself. Questioning the appropriateness of methods tends to make a field stronger than if scholars used a method unreflectively. However, I advocate employing a variety of methodologies that have real strengths rather than rejecting any of them utterly.

I relate my experience here because it represents the point of view of an American social psychologist (now beginning to call herself a media psychologist) during the early years of this new thing we were calling media psychology. Across the history of psychology, we have seen different movements appear and evolve. At this time in the history of media psychology there are disciplinary, subdisciplinary and geographic boundaries in media psychology. These approaches are especially relevant to methods, though they have broader implications. One question we can all consider is whether and how these various approaches might coalesce over time. Will they remain distinct or will they intertwine and evolve together?

I would be remiss if I did not point out that many outside of psychology who study media do effects research. There are volumes published by communications researchers devoted to effects research. Also, examining the *Handbook* authors' definitions of media psychology, and the research approaches used in this *Handbook*, you will see that effects research is strongly represented.

I agree that the themes Giles identifies here are reflective of some of the current perspectives of our field. In fact, a variation of this argument takes place in the pages of the *Handbook* as a variety of views are proposed and discussed. These are fundamental questions: How can we best study what's important about media psychology? What are some assumptions and approaches that have validity? In what ways can our approaches be clarified, improved, and extended? I believe there is room for a variety of methodologies and approaches to media psychology to be embraced and respected for what they offer us in terms of knowledge and insight.

This *Handbook* contains descriptions of the most popular approach to media psychology research (see, e.g., Huesmann, Dubow, & Yang, Chapter 9; Potter, Chapter 24; Prot & Anderson, Chapter 7), the quantitative methods approach favored in the United States. As noted, the United States is still arguably the geographical and philosophical home of modern psychology (Schultz & Schultz, 2011) and also influences media psychology research in other countries such as Japan (Sakamoto, Chapter 28).

This *Handbook* also presents compelling arguments about how those methods should be augmented and extended. Potter (Chapter 24) argues that traditional experiments (what he calls "Groups-Differences" studies) should evolve to include research that specifically tracks how the individual changes from baseline over time. Prot and Anderson explain the value of using multiple methods in multiple settings in order to triangulate via multiple operationalism to support or elaborate a conceptual relationship.

Qualitative research addresses how we make meaning from media (Polkinghorne, Chapter 8). If we fail to focus on this issue of meaning making, we miss a tremendous opportunity to understand the human experience with media more deeply than ever before. Increasing our output of excellent qualitative research is an important goal for the future of media psychology and a key way we will contribute a growing body of knowledge that is of broad interest and significance.

Because qualitative research is valued more in other fields outside of psychology (see Polkinghorne, Chapter 8), conducting more high quality qualitative research will both strengthen the research methods commonly used in psychology and take

advantage of the interdisciplinary nature of our field. Hybrids tend to be stronger than nonhybrids and this applies to fields as well as to organisms. Rather than rejecting theories and methods that are nontraditional in our individual fields (which can occur via journal editors and reviewers, hiring committees, and publishing houses, for example), true multiple operationalism should embrace high quality research from a variety of theoretical and methodological traditions. We are in a particularly good place to make this happen as we move forward together to shape the field of media psychology.

Applying Lewin's Person × Situation Perspective

Brown Rutledge argues that media psychology shifts the focus from the medium to the human. Meanwhile, Potter argues that we not debate the primacy of the medium or the audience, but study both. Polkinghorne (Chapter 8) explains that qualitative research is used to study both the experience (of using and creating media) by the human being and the content of the media itself. In this way, we can learn more about the intensive experiences of the audiences and creators of media.

Bartholow and Bolls (Chapter 27) suggest balancing the study of mind and content. They suggest using Lewin's classic social psychological approach of viewing the person in the situation as the unit of analysis. They remind us that situations and responses are dynamic. For instance, a person playing a video game is the correct tableau for a media psychologist, understanding that the action and reactions are dynamic. As William James said, "you can't step into the same river twice;" and the mind on media is ever changing like a river. I would also add another classic social psychological perspective to this viewpoint, namely that the subject matter we are studying is the human perception of the content rather than any attempt to objectify the content itself.

So, in our field some favor audience-centered and some favor media-centered approaches. And some favor experimental approaches, whereas others feel they isolate content from its important context. One way to address both of these issues is to move more deeply into a truly interdisciplinary approach to media psychology...one that, as Bartholow and Bolls say, balances mind with content and sees them both as rich and dynamic. This would entail a broader unit of analysis and richer methodologies that borrow from and respect all the disciplines that form our foundation as a field. Embracing multiple operationalism, including methods from all our constituent disciplines, and holding in mind both content and context, are important ways of addressing these issues.

The study of narrative—including narrative effects and qualitative studies of those effects—also moves beyond simply studying the person or the medium as relatively static and isolated. In this next section, I continue to emphasize the importance of studying the person in the situation, or the mind on media, using engagement with narrative as one instantiation of this perspective.

Engagement with Narrative and Character

"In the history of human experience, one of our most pervasive and enduring reference points is our need for story. Stories help us to understand ourselves in terms of who we are, what we need, and why we behave the way we do" (Isbouts & Ohler, p. 2).

> ... people are genetically predisposed, neurophysiologically wired, and motivated to frequent virtual environments ... Story telling, painting, sculpture, theater, manuscripts, the printing press, photography, cinematography, radio and television, and, most recently, digital technologies all serve to facilitate psychological engagement in virtual environments. (Blascovich & McCall, p. 3)

> Narratives have the ability to activate human faculties—such as feeling, empathy and affinity—that remain mostly dormant with intellectual rhetoric and learning. Stories can impart not only information but also meaning ... Stories, in sum, are quite simply the literary vehicle of our thoughts. (Isbouts & Ohler, p. 5)

Recall that in the *Psychology of the Media*, Giles relates that media effects research is viewed as bankrupt by some because, "It turns cultural material into meaningless chunks of information" (2010, p. 16). And indeed, as someone who values and conducts experiments, one of my misgivings about them is just this: that isolating media content tends to decontextualize it and sidestep the richness of the experience of the person's interaction with the medium. As Prot and Anderson (Chapter 7) rightly relate, every methodology has strengths and weaknesses. The strengths of experimentation are widely recognized. But it is only through multiple operationalism that we can gain the clearest, richest, and most nuanced picture of the phenomena we seek to understand.

Summary and Conclusions

I believe that the future of media psychology should respect and support multiple operationalism, including methodologies that are more popular outside the discipline in which we earned our doctoral degrees. As a social psychologist trained in a strong effects tradition, I will step outside of that training and suggest that we need to embrace a richer and more contextualized approach to media psychology research that includes both a view of the dynamic person in the dynamic situation and the increased use of qualitative methods.

One aspect of this approach will be to pay careful attention to elaborating on our human attraction to and engagement with narrative and characters. Humans are compelled by story. It is no accident that most of the time when we have a choice, we choose to engage with story, whether it be via television, Facebook, a video game, or a song. We need to understand this engagement with story better than we do now and also understand our psychological connection to the characters and figures in those stories.

So it is vital that as we move forward we learn more about engagement with narrative and meaning making via media. The word "narrative" was one of the words that the content analysis of the *Handbook* (Neal, Chapter 29) revealed was used most often by the *Handbook* authors. Leximancer is a fine-grained tool and the Leximancer results were not simple word counts, but contextual interpretations of words, adjusting for factors such as word frequency in the English language. The presence of the concept of "narrative" as a key term in this *Handbook* is promising and I believe, is the harbinger of things to come in media psychology.

Focusing on our engagement with story and our ability to make meaning from story has implications for methodology, data analysis, and for the framing of research studies and the questions we ask. As communications and psychology researchers (and those from related fields) come together, we must eschew taking solely a person approach or solely a media approach, but form a more perfect union which integrates and goes beyond those viewpoints. The future of media psychology must address the dynamic human mind "on" media, which are themselves dynamic and multifaceted. It also must build on the assumption that the content of our field is the perception of the user in the context of the fluid mediated situation.

Moving forward, there are some clear directions we can take to improve our basic and applied scientific contributions to academia and for our stakeholders (who include the business community, lawmakers, journalists, educators, and the public—notably parents).

I'd like to thank all of the authors of the chapters in this *Handbook*. Your research and the compelling way you communicated key insights have made this *Handbook* a great resource for other media psychologists and for our students. I am grateful for your contributions and look forward to what I know will be a fascinating future for our discipline.

Future Directions for the Field of Media Psychology

What follows is a list of some of the items I've emphasized throughout this chapter, for easy reference. To review, I believe media psychologists should:

1. Emphasize the development of theory in media psychology and use theory as a foundation for programmatic research.

2. Focus more on the big picture issues such as narrative, transportation, persuasion, emotional engagement and the social psychology of media, particularly with regard to new media (for example, self concept as related to mediated projections of self like avatars and social networking site content and audience as content creators).

3. Expand and develop qualitative research methods and tools; provide editorial and reviewer support for publishing high quality qualitative media psychology research. Refine current experimental approaches to study how media use and creation changes individuals.

4. Avoid simplistic arguments that present media audiences as uniformly weak or strong, easily persuasible or uniformly savvy. Instead study audience factors in deeper, more nuanced ways (for instance, elaborate on audience transportation, and cognitive and emotional aspects of persuasion and attention) and complicate our view of the audience.

5. Openly address and challenge the **Love/ Hate Media Debate**...or the notion that media are all good or all bad. As researchers, avoid the tendency to take either extreme position or to make *ad hominem* attacks on researchers perceived as advocating the "other side."

6. Develop training for media psychologists to communicate our work to stakeholders that takes into account the interested audience, and the debates and controversies in which our research is disseminated.

7. Break down barriers between the disciplines that do media psychology research and application. For instance, support interdisciplinary programs, journals, and faculty hires. Within that approach, support a wide array of quality research perspectives that allow critical analysis and not simply tradition to influence scholarship in our field.

8. Continue to grow international collaborations and approaches to media psychology. This includes seeking to translate work not originally published in English. Lack of adequate translation hampered the understanding of Wilhelm Wundt's work for generations (Schultz & Schultz, 2011). This should be much less of an issue in the modern era in which translations are more easily accessible. At the same time, we should not underestimate the influence of inadequate translation on scholars' ability to contribute to the field.

Acknowledgment

Karen E. Dill, School of Psychology, Fielding Graduate University.

Thanks to Jim Potter for comments on an earlier draft of this chapter. Correspondence concerning this chapter should be addressed to Karen E. Dill, School of Psychology, Fielding Graduate University, 2112 Santa Barbara St., Santa Barbara, CA, 93105. E-mail: kdill@fielding.edu

References

Bartholow, B. D., & Bolls, P. (2013). Media Psychophysiology: The brain and beyond. In Dill, K. E. (Ed.), *The Oxford Handbook of Media Psychology*. New York: Oxford University Press.

Brockmyer, J. F. (2013). Media violence, desensitization, and psychological engagement. In Dill, K. E. (Ed.), *Oxford Handbook of Media Psychology*. New York: Oxford Universitiy Press.

Dill, K. E. (2009). *How Fantasy Becomes Reality: Seeing Through Media Influence*. New York: Oxford University Press.

Giles, D. (2010). *Psychology of the Media*. New York: Palgrave Macmillan.

Huesmann, L. R., Dubow, E. F., & Yang, G. (2013). Why is it hard to believe that media violence causes aggression? In Dill, K. E. (Ed.), *The Oxford Handbook of Media Psychology*. New York: Oxford University Press.

Isbouts, J.-P., & Ohler, J. (2013). Storytelling and media: Narrative models from aristotle to augmented reality. In Dill, K. E. (Ed.), *The Oxford Handbook of Media Psychology*. New York: Oxford University Press.

Krahe, B. (2013). Video game violence. In Dill, K. E. (Ed.), *The Oxford Handbook of Media Psychology*. New York: Oxford University Press.

Lenhart, A. (2012). *Teens, Smartphones & Texting*. Washington, DC: Pew Internet and American Life project.

McIntyre, J. (2013). The political narrative of children's media research. In Dill, K. E. (Ed.), *Oxford Handbook of Media Psychology*. New York: Oxford.

MobiThinking . (2012). Retrieved February 22, 2012, from *Global Mobile Statistics 2012*. http://www.mobithinking.com/mobile-marketing-tools/latest-mobile-stats-mobilemessaging

Nabi, R. L., & Moyer-Gusé, E. (2013). The psychology underlying media-based persuasion. In Dill, K. E. (Ed.), *The Oxford Handbook of Media Psychology*. New York: Oxford Universitiy Press.

NielsenWire . (2011). Cross Platform Report: Americans watching more TV, mobile and web video.

Osborne, C. (February 28, 2012). Retrieved from *How long do we spend on social media sites?* http://www.zdnet.com/blog/igeneration/how-long-do-we-spend-on-social-media-sites-infographic/15415

Potter, W. J. (2013). A general framework for media psychology scholarship. In Dill, K. E. (Ed.), *Oxford Handbook of Media Psychology*. New York: Oxford University Press.

Prot, S., & Anderson, C. A . (2013). Research methods, design, and statistics in media psychology. In K. E. Dill (Ed.), *Oxford Handbook of Media Psychology*. New York: Oxford University Press.

Ranie, L. (2012). *The Emerging Information Landscape: The 8 Realities of the "New Normal."* Washington, DC: Pew Internet and American Life Project.

Rutledge, P. (2013). Is there a need for a distinct field of media psychology? In Dill, K. E. (Ed.), *The Oxford Handbook of Media Psychology*. New York: Oxford University Press.

Sakamoto, A. (2013). Japanese approach to research on psychological effects of use of media. In Dill, K. E. (Ed.), *The Oxford Handbook of Media Psychology*. New York: Oxford University Press.

Schultz, D. P., & Schultz, S. E. (2011). *A History of Modern Psychology*. New York: Wadsworth.

Wilson, T. J. (2002). *Strangers to Ourselves: Discovering the Adaptive Unconscious*. Cambridge, MA: Harvard University Press.

INDEX

M

Mack, Arien, 63
MacKay, N. J., 235
Madonna, 234
magnitude, 445
Mahmood, S., 339
Mahood, C., 276
Malamuth, N., 374, 375
Maldonado, H., 46
malicious pleasure, 193
Malmstrom, E. J., 215
Malone, T. W., 339
Maloney, A., 537
Malouff, J. M., 361
manifest content, 440
Manjoo, Farhad, 72
Mann, C., 138
many-to-many world, 45
Mapping-Phenomenon perspective, 426–28
Mar, R. A., 457
Marathon 2, 128
Marathon Man, 196
MARC. *See* Media Action Research Center
Mares, M. L., 203, 235
Markow, D., 375
Marsella, S., 200
Marsh, E. J., 451, 452
Martens, H., 101
Martino, S., 236
Martins, N., 269
MARVIN, 338
Masaccio, 13, 14*f*
masculinity, 277
Maslow, Abraham, 142
mass communication, 76, 242
mass customization, 35
massively multiplayer online role-playing game (MMORPG), 125
mass media
  defining, 57n8
  effect-criterion problem and, 442–43
  effects facet in, 440–41
  exposure states of, 431–32
  influence pattern types in, 444*f*
  literature, 425–26
  message research of, 438
  new conceptualization of, 430–31
  participatory media shift from, 33
  printing press introducing, 45
  reconceptualizing influence of, 443–46
  research methods of, 439–40
  technology characteristics of, 428
  during World War II, 44
Massoni, K., 273
Mastro, D. E., 269, 386
Math Blaster, 336
Mathiak, K., 484
Matthews, V. P., 216
Maxwell, S., 81
Mayer, R. E., 345
Mazzocco, P. M., 456
McCall, C., 310, 537
McGee, I., 279
McIntyre, J., 538
Mckee, K. A., 273
McKenna, K. Y. A., 504
McKenna, P., 343
McLeod, D. M., 291

McLuhan, Eric, 29*f*
McLuhan, Marshall, 3, 29, 29*f*, 33, 36, 40n21, 462
McLuhan lens, 29
McMahon, B., 102, 104
McQuarrie, E., 454
Mead, G. H., 143
Meade, M. L., 451
meaning, 155n5
meaning construction, 435
meaning-making process, 154, 517
meaning matching, 435
media. *See also* children's media; interactive media; mass media
  adolescence processing messages of, 232
  adolescent exposure to, 226
  Asian's representation in, 254–55
  biases built in to, 29
  body dissatisfaction from, 229
  cause-effect relations and socialization of, 159
  children influenced by, 467–72
  children's long-term impact of, 181–82
  defining, 49–50
  digital, 243
  domestic roles in, 277–78
  effects research of, 273–74, 477*f*
  emotional involvement in, 190–94
  empathy in users of, 189
  engagement with, 245n1
  gender-related attitudes and behavior influenced by, 274–76
  healthier storytelling with, 182–83
  High School student use of, 498*t*–499*t*
  human brain influenced by, 474–77
  information from, 187
  Internet changing landscape of, 26
  Internet communications as, 3
  involvement in, 231–32
  Japan and, 497–500, 498*t*
  legacy, 3
  love/hate debate on, 536–38
  Middle Easterners representation in, 255
  modern use of, 3
  multiple platform communications in, 52
  Native American representation in, 255
  participatory, 32*f*
  persuasion, 487
  physical appearance in, 276–77
  prejudicial attitudes and beliefs from, 256–58
  prosocial, 180
  psychology history and, 536
  race/ethnicity relations improved through, 262
  race/ethnicity represented in, 252–53, 255–56
  sad, 201
  school-aged children's instructions on, 105–6
  sexual behavior and, 223
  sexual health promoted by, 242
  sexual scripts in, 229–30
  social, 3, 27, 46–47, 341, 535
  U.S. consumption of, 475
  violence justified in, 213
  women underrepresented in, 268–69
Media Action Research Center (MARC), 97

media education, 96–98, 100, 101–2, 104
media effects, 50–51, 126, 127, 129–30, 540
The Media Equation: How People Treat Computers, Television, and New Media Like Real People and Places (Reeves And Nass), 450
media exposure
  of adolescence, 226
  of children, 178–79
  cumulative influence of, 112
  flow experiences from, 177, 219
  on Internet, 374–75
  self-esteem influence of, 260–61
  violence in, 539
Media Exposure Experience Matrix, 431, 435–37, 436*f*
media imagery and social learning (MISL), 259
media literacy, 32–33
  advocacy needed for, 106–7
  children's importance of, 182
  delivery method of, 101–2
  education of, 245
  graduate program in, 105
  NAMLE and, 100
  school curriculum and, 98
  U.S. approach to, 96, 98–101
  violent video clips and, 103
media literacy education (MLE), 241
media messages
  about gender, 267–68
  adolescence processing, 232
  attentional state of, 432
  human brain processing, 196, 203
  narratives of, 437–38
  vividness of, 258
Media Practice Model (MPM), 224–25
media psychology
  challenges in, 56
  communicating effectively about, 538
  defining, 5, 5*t*, 8, 44, 536
  doctoral program in, 49
  future studies in, 522–23
  Google Trends search for, 49*f*
  as hybrid discipline, 4
  love/hate debate about, 538
  multidisciplinary platform of, 43–44
  positive psychology role in, 55–56
  psychology and communications in, 6
  qualitative research used in, 138
  research in, 137, 186–87, 478, 522*t*
  systems thinking in, 51
  theoretical approaches and methods in, 539–41
Media Psychology (Giles), 4, 540–42
media psychophysiology, 478–83
mediasts, 31
mediated experience, 50
mediated society influencing, 194
mediated space, 66
mediation, 245n2
mediator variable, 123*f*
media violence, 7, 109
  adolescence influenced by, 225
  aggressive behavior link with, 168–69
  American Psychology Association and, 160
  Anderson, C. A., studies of, 128–29, 168
  arousal influenced by, 482

20113020R00329

Made in the USA
Middletown, DE
14 May 2015